101
Tiny House Designs

The Ultimate Collection of Tiny House Design

By Michael Janzen

© 2017 Michael Janzen
All rights reserved.
ISBN-13: 978-1978499751
ISBN-10: 1978499752

For Julia, Katie, and Reagan

Preface

Since 2007 I've been obsessed with tiny house design. I've always been a bit biased toward minimalist and efficient design, but in 2007 I discovered the tiny house movement and was hooked.

Fast forward to 2017 and some things still remain the same about the tiny house movement. The main core values are still there. When you choose less over more, you're choosing to rebalance your life in a direction that provides more freedom and happiness. This process requires choosing to let go of all but the most important things in your life; and our homes tend to be one of those important things.

When you apply this practice to a home the things that can ususally go are rarely used possessions, rooms you rarely use, the time it takes to maintain it, and all the associated costs. What stays is pride in ownership, comfort, family, friends, fun, and security.

A home that is right-sized provides a balance between all things and that's what makes a home truly valuable, regardless of the market price.

I've designed many tiny houses over the past 10 years, and I have to admit, it can still be a challenge to visualize the right size home without drawing a lot of pictures. I think this is true for many people.

I drew this collection of 101 tiny house designs to help people find their right-sized home. Inside you'll find 101 design concepts from 12 to 32 feet long. You'll see a variety of styles, layouts, themes, and common patterns. Throughout the book, I'll point out any notable details and features.

You'll also see families of designs that share similar traits but are different sizes. This should help show how function changes as size increases.

Designing a tiny house is a balancing act, especially for the smallest homes. For example, a large kitchen or bathroom can eat up space that could have otherwise been used for seating, dining, or sleeping. So each layout is the result of a series of choices and compromises.

If you're designing your own home while browsing the designs here, I suggest making a list - or even sketches - of the features that are most important to you. For example, if you know that you want a big kitchen with full-size appliances, draw it first so you know what kind of space it requires. Then arrange everything else around these core elements.

As you turn the pages you'll also notice some common elements in the drawings, like chairs, tables, cabinets, toilets, sinks, showers, ladders, stairs, windows, and doors. I decided early on that I'd use common elements between the designs to make it easier to compare them without causing confusion by introducing an infinite array of differently sized furnishings.

Most everything is drawn on a 2-foot grid. For example, the 'comfy chair' is 2' x 2', as are most of the cabinets and appliance. Most of the showers and tubs are at least 32" in both directions. The windows are typically sized on even 1-foot increments. The French doors are all 5-feet wide and 82" tall. The single exterior entry doors are 32" wide and 82" tall. All interior doors are pocket doors and most are exactly 2-feet wide.

You may also notice that I've used only two roof pitches, 10/12 (40°) and 3/12 (14°). The steeper 10/12 pitch looks great for traditional gable roofs. The shallower 3/12 pitch allows the use of a wider selection of roofing materials than a shallower pitch. Roofing manufactures specify the minimum pitch for their products. You are more likely to find roofing choices that require slopes no shallower than a 3/12 pitch. So as a practical solution, I tend to avoid roofs flatter than 3/12.

All the houses are 8' 6" wide and under 13' 6" tall. These are the most common highway limits for trailers.

It's also worth mentioning my somewhat odd way of describing which walls are the front and back walls of a tiny house. I always refer to the front wall as the wall on the back of the trailer. So when facing the back of the trailer, the right and left walls are literally the walls to your right and left. The back wall is the one over the trailer tongue, even when the front door is there. I chose to do this years ago to help communicate consistently.

This is a book of ideas and illustrations for tiny house dreamers. I hope you enjoy this peek into a tiny house designer's mind & sketchbook. I had a ton of fun drawing it and hope you find inspiration here too!

Contents

12-Foot Tiny House Designs - 1

14-Foot Tiny House Designs - 51

16-Foot Tiny House Designs - 93

18-Foot Tiny House Designs - 143

20-Foot Tiny House Designs - 185

22-Foot Tiny House Designs - 235

24-Foot Tiny House Designs - 273

28-Foot Tiny House Designs - 323

32-Foot Tiny House Designs - 373

12-Foot Tiny House Designs

#1

Tiny House #1 - Overview

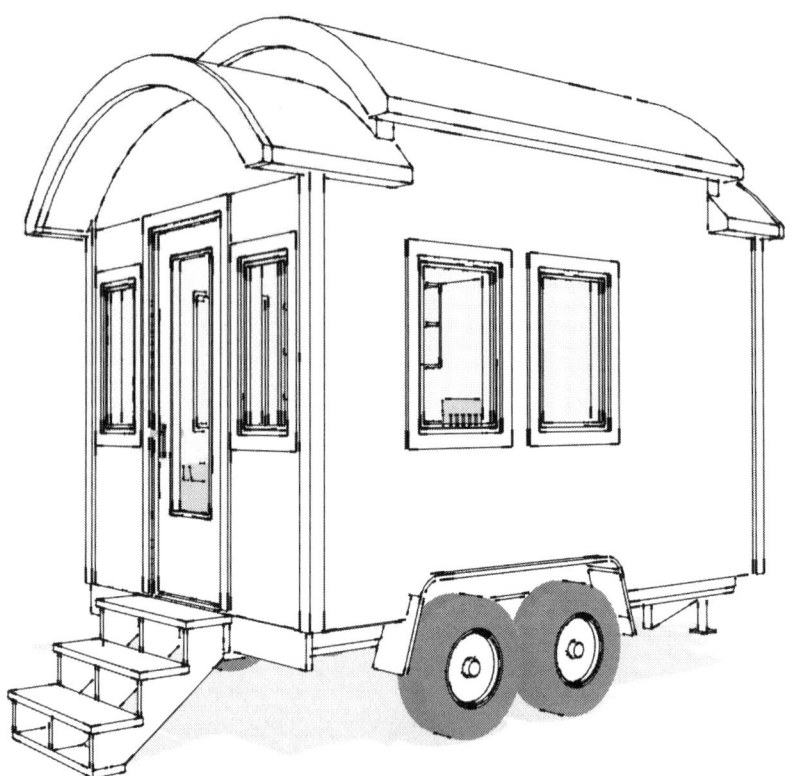

Front Right

Summary:

There have been many smaller tiny houses, but 8 x 12 feet seems like the best place to start for this book. When the tiny house movement was new, this small size was actually common.

The curved Vardo inspired roof sets this tiny house design apart from most tiny houses. It's a little harder to build, but has a captivating personality. Inside are all the essentials: kitchen, bathroom, storage, sleeping loft, desk & chair, and seating for guests.

Features:

12-Foot Tiny House on Wheels
Curved Vardo Roof
Standard Bathroom (32" shower, toilet, wall mounted sink)
Tiny Kitchen
Small Loft for a Queen Bed
Utility Cabinet over Trailer Tongue

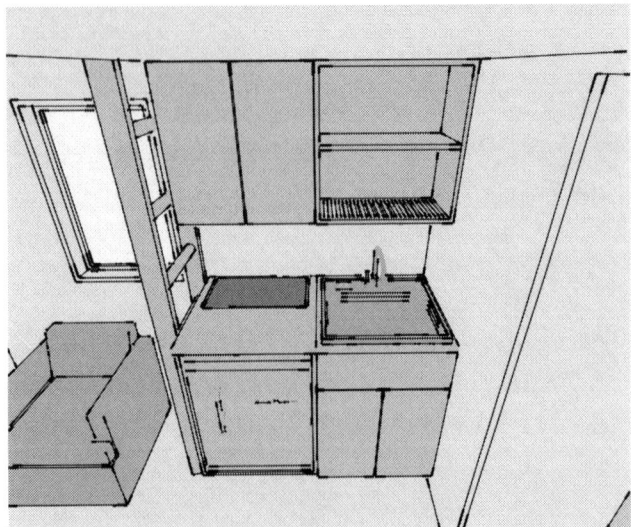

Kitchen

View from Loft

2

Tiny House #1 - Floor Plan & Exterior

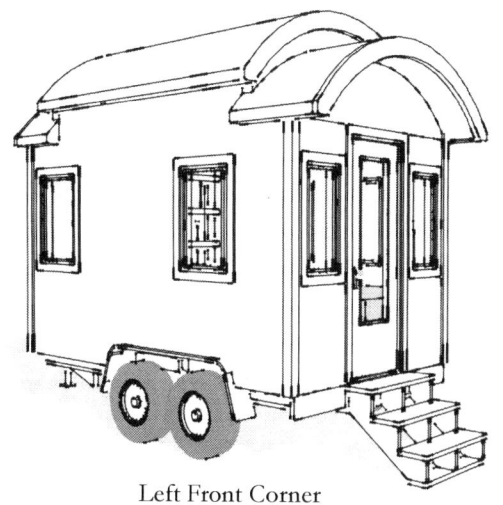
Left Front Corner

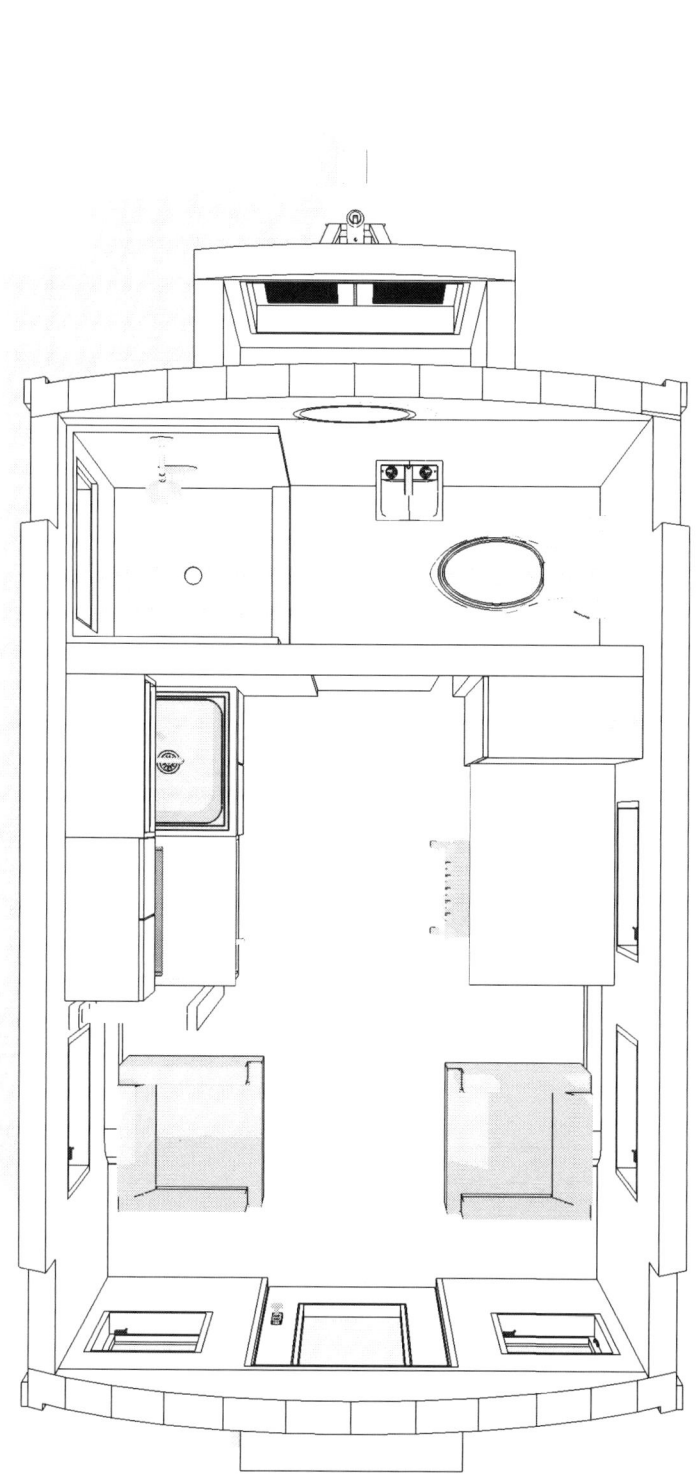
Floor Plan

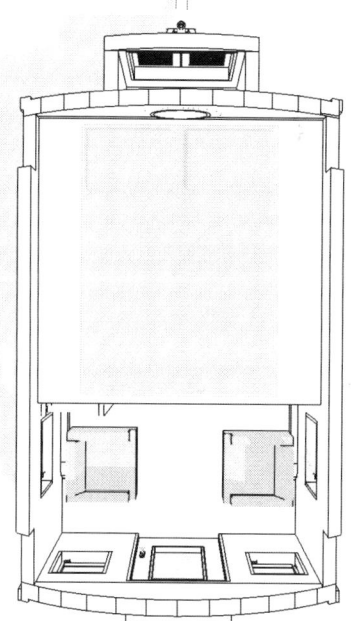
Floor Plan - Loft

Back Left Corner

Tiny House #1 - Interior Views

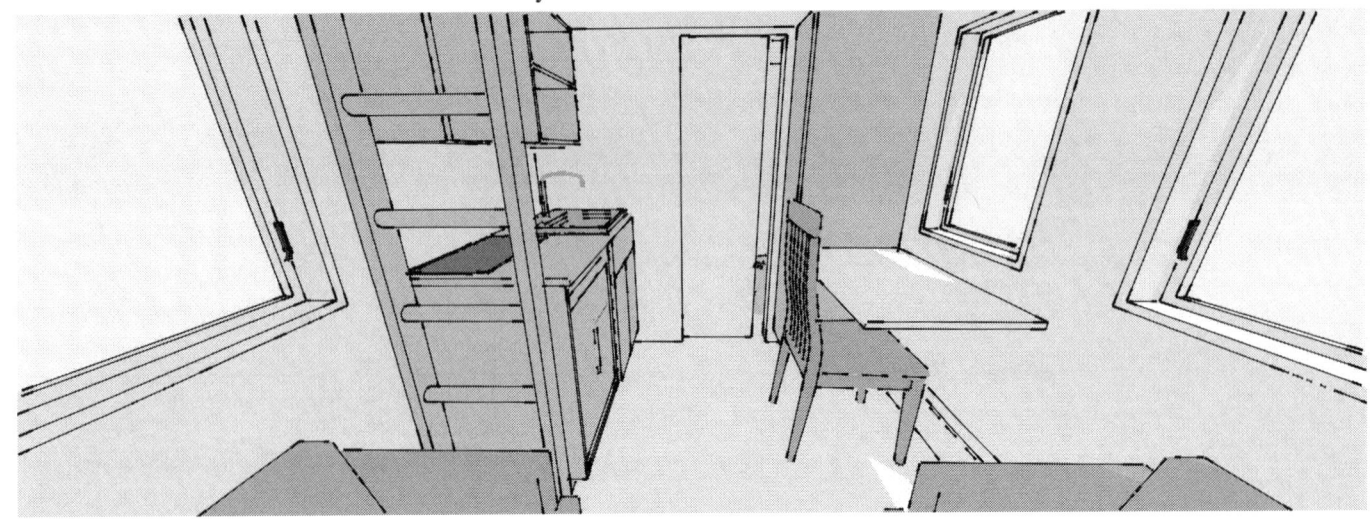

Interior from Front Door

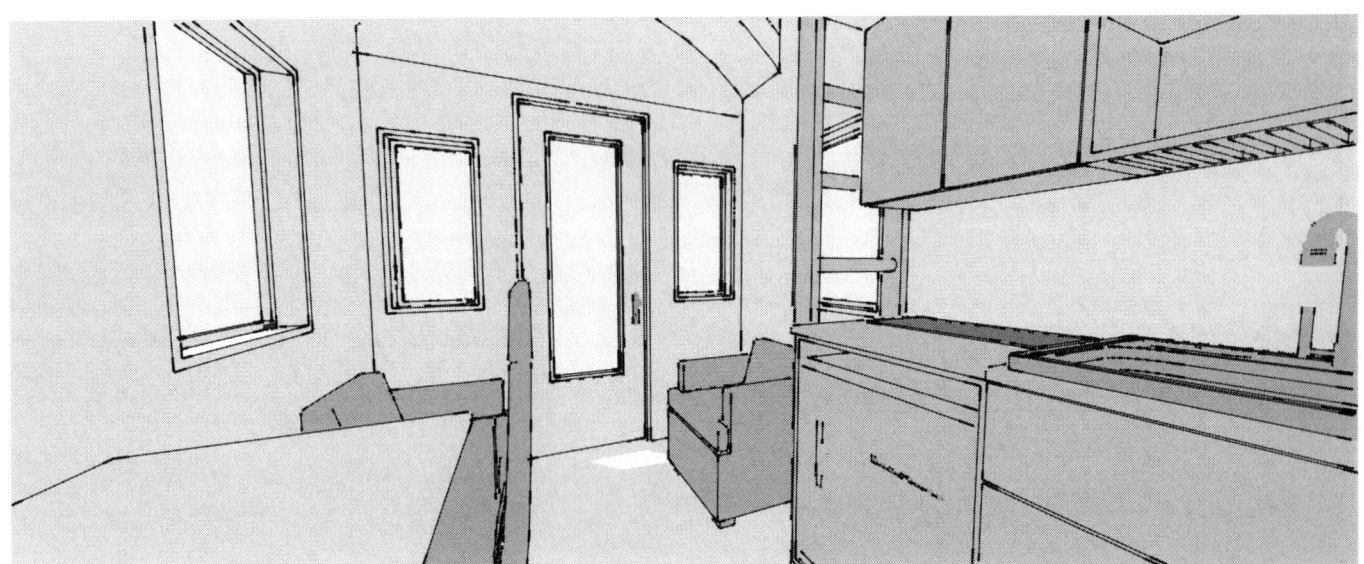

Interior from Bathroom

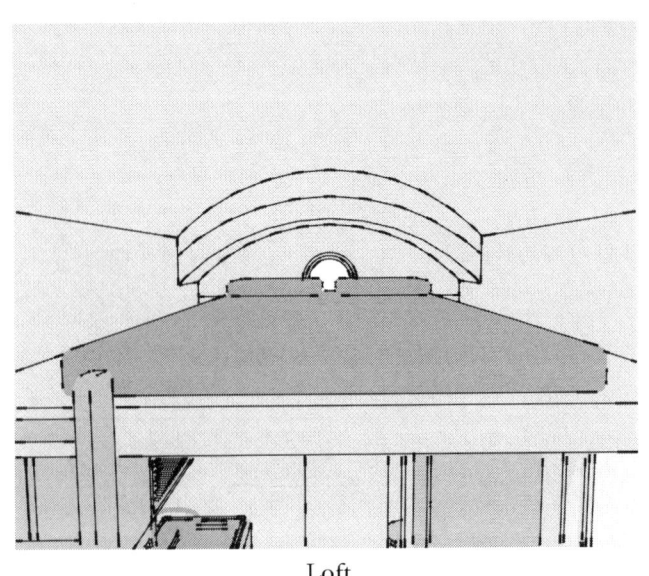

Loft

Bathroom

Tiny House #1 - Elevations

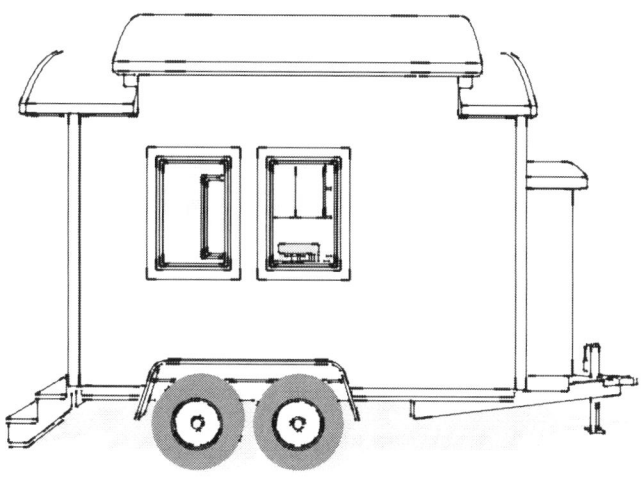

Right

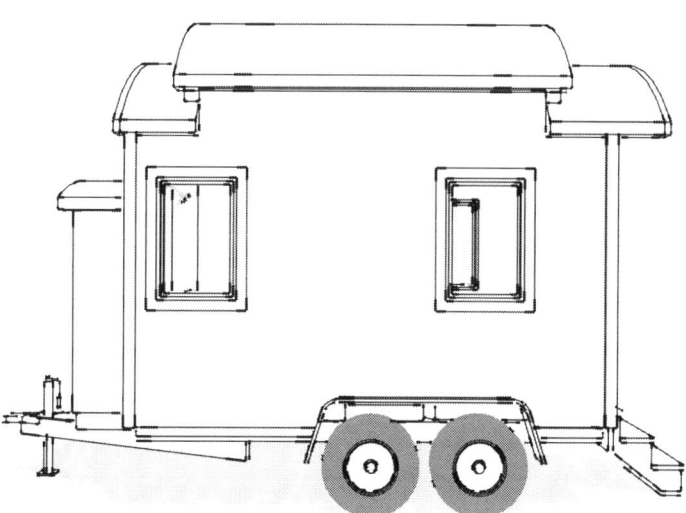

Left

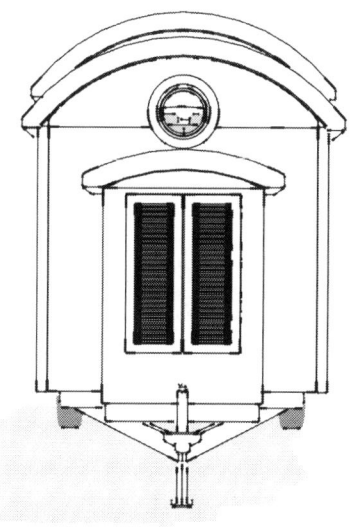

Back

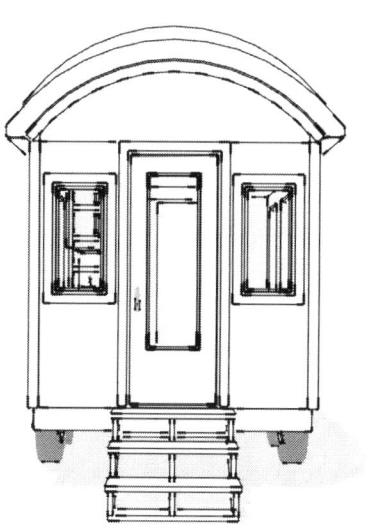

Front

#2

Tiny House #2 - Overview

Front Right

Summary:

A classic tiny house with a 10/12 gable pitched roof, small gable dormers, and a French door entry. Inside is a bathroom with a bay window, 32-inch square shower, toilet, and generous vanity. The kitchen has the basics: a sink, small refrigerator, small cooktop, and storage. Also on the lower level is space for two small chairs. The loft has room for a queen bed and is accessed by a movable ladder.

Features:

12-Foot Tiny House on Wheels
Gable Roof with Gable Dormers
Bathroom with Bay Window
Small Loft
Small Kitchen

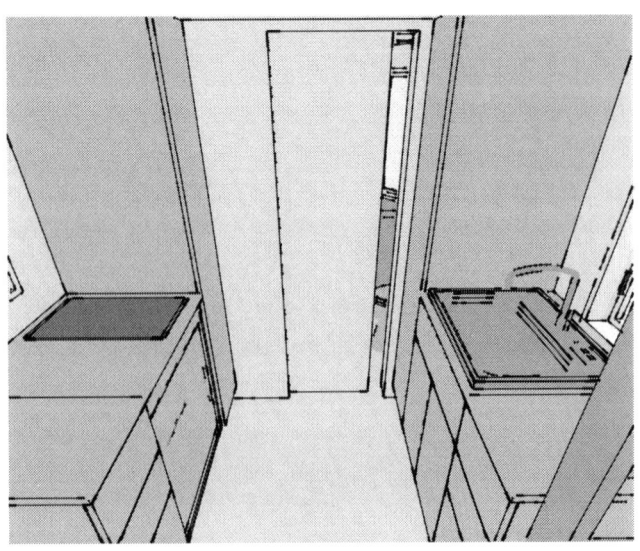

Kitchen

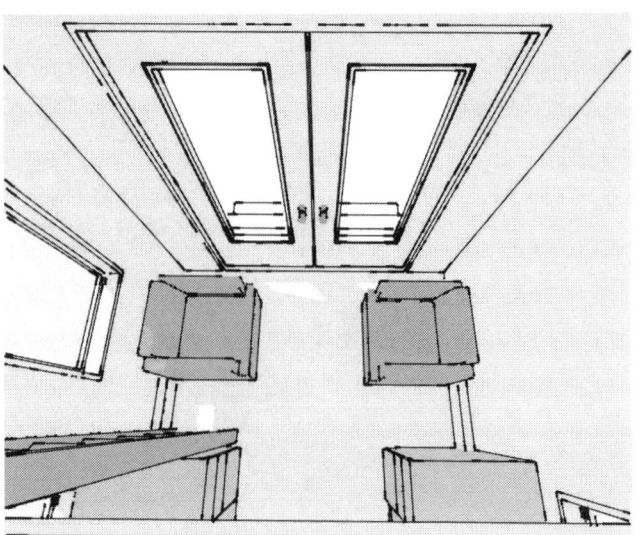

View from Loft

Tiny House #2 - Floor Plan & Exterior

Left Front Corner

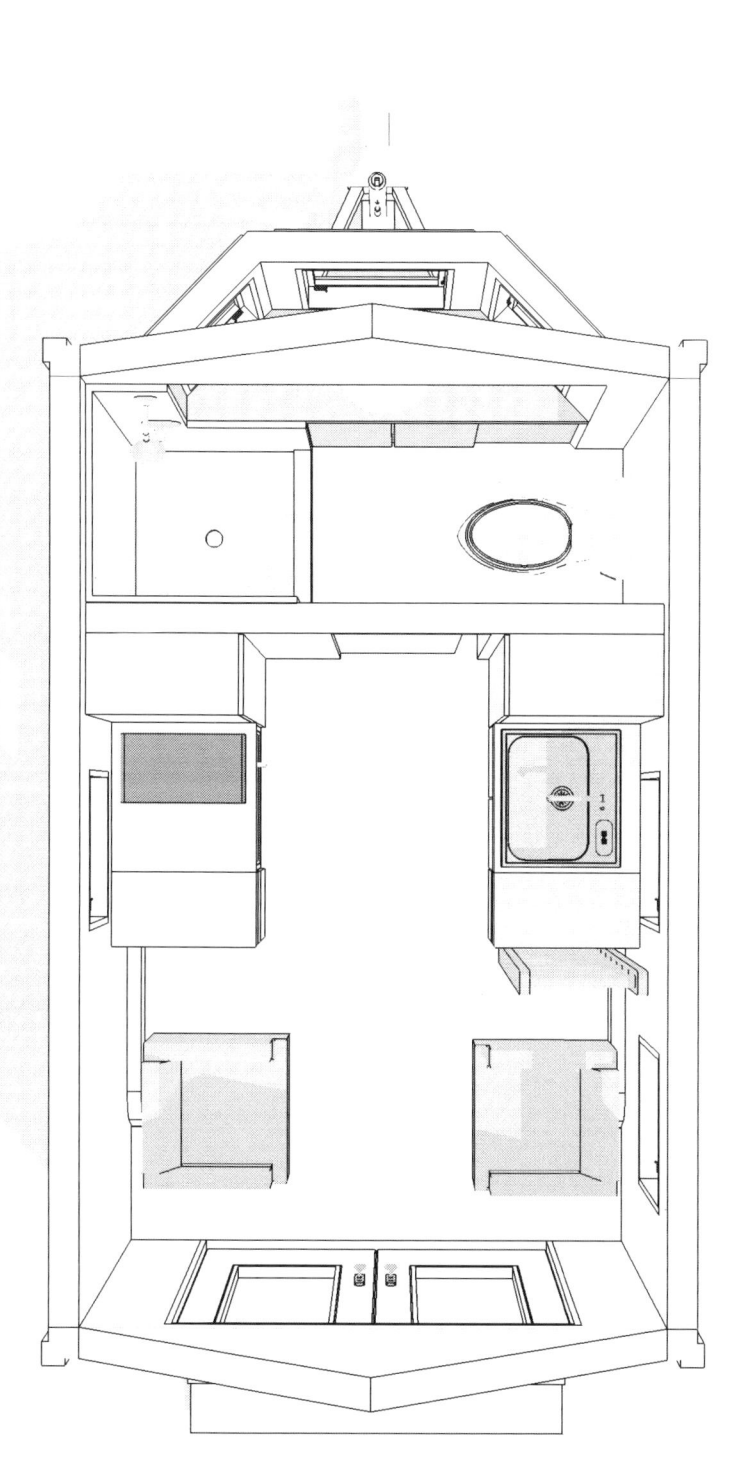
Floor Plan

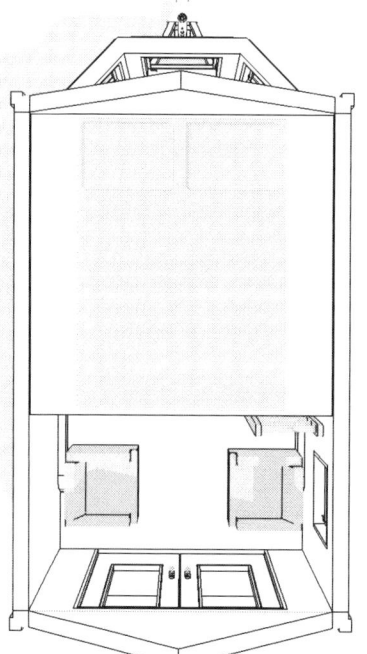
Floor Plan - Loft

Back Left Corner

Tiny House #2 - Interior Views

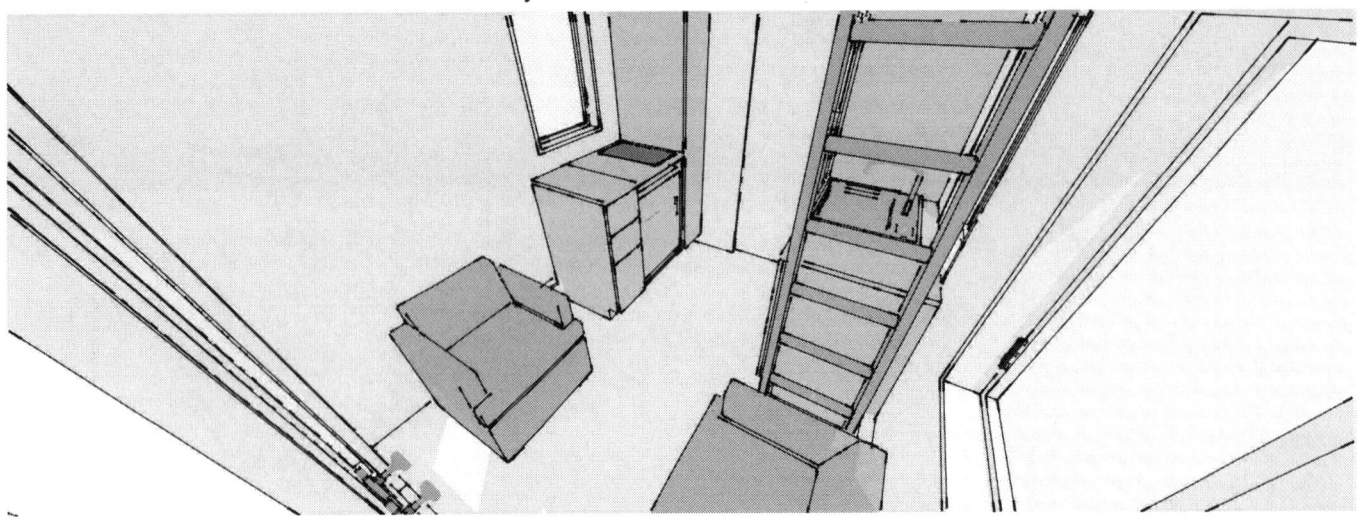

Interior from Entry

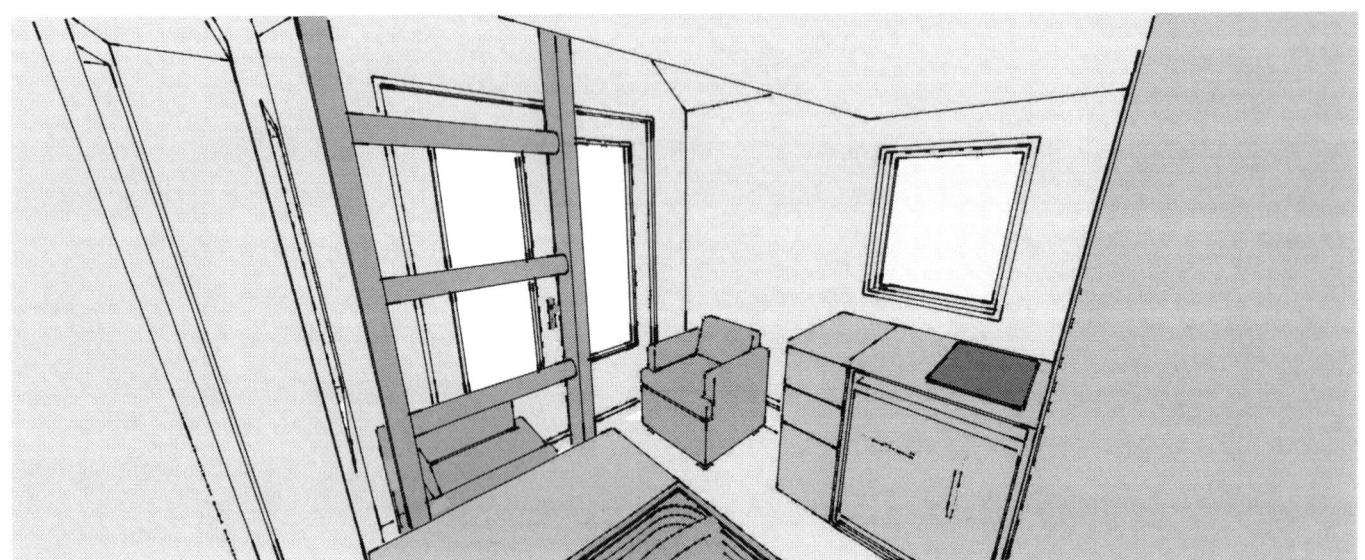

Interior from Kitchen

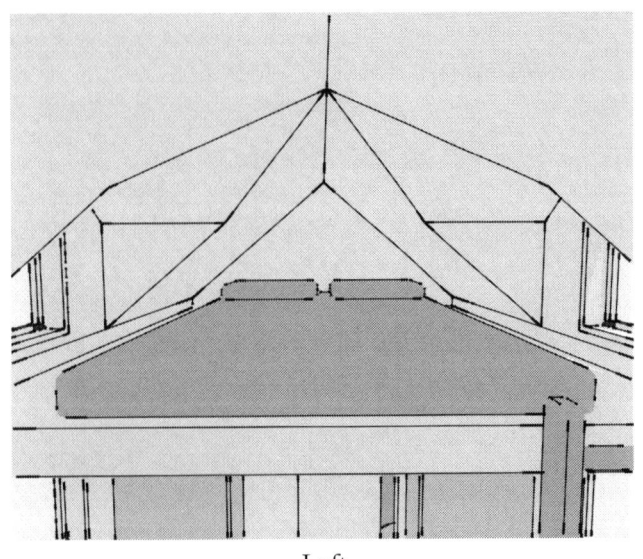

Loft 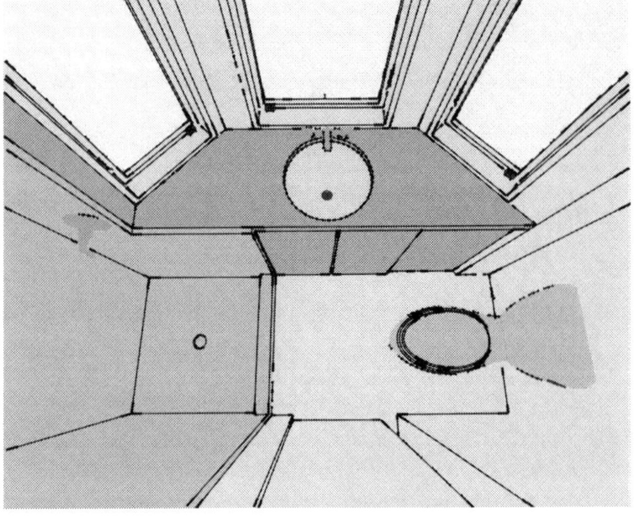   Bathroom

Tiny House #2 - Elevations

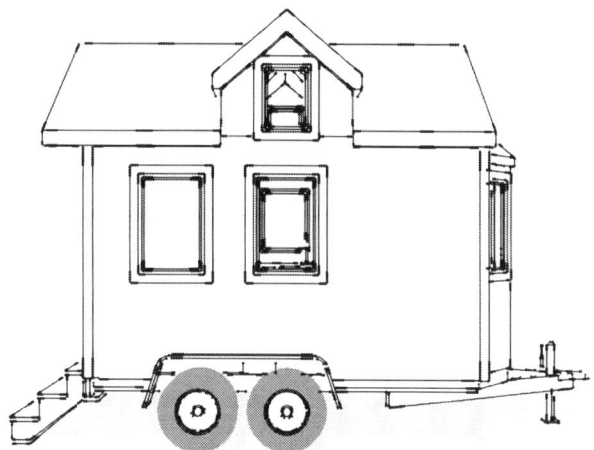

Right

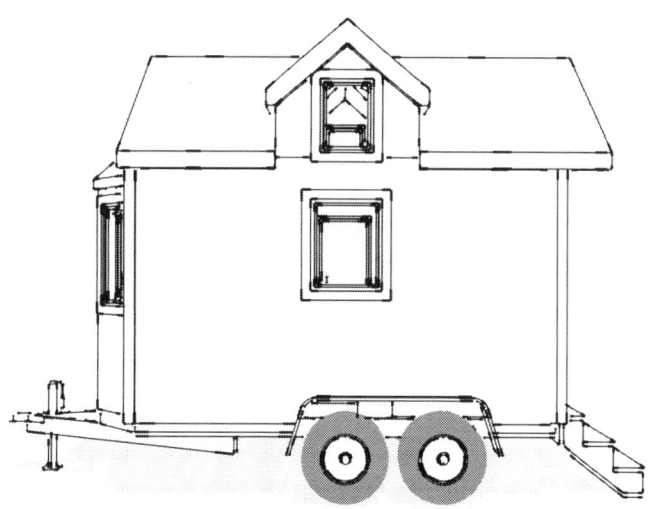

Left

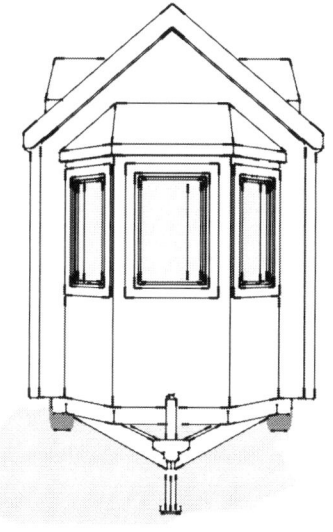

Back

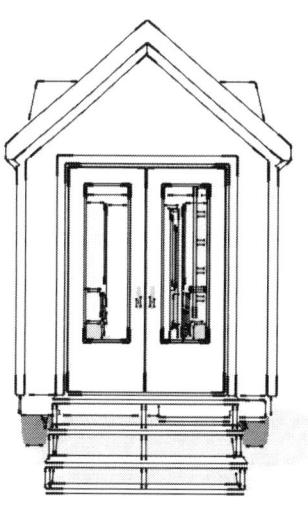

Front

#3

#3 - Overview

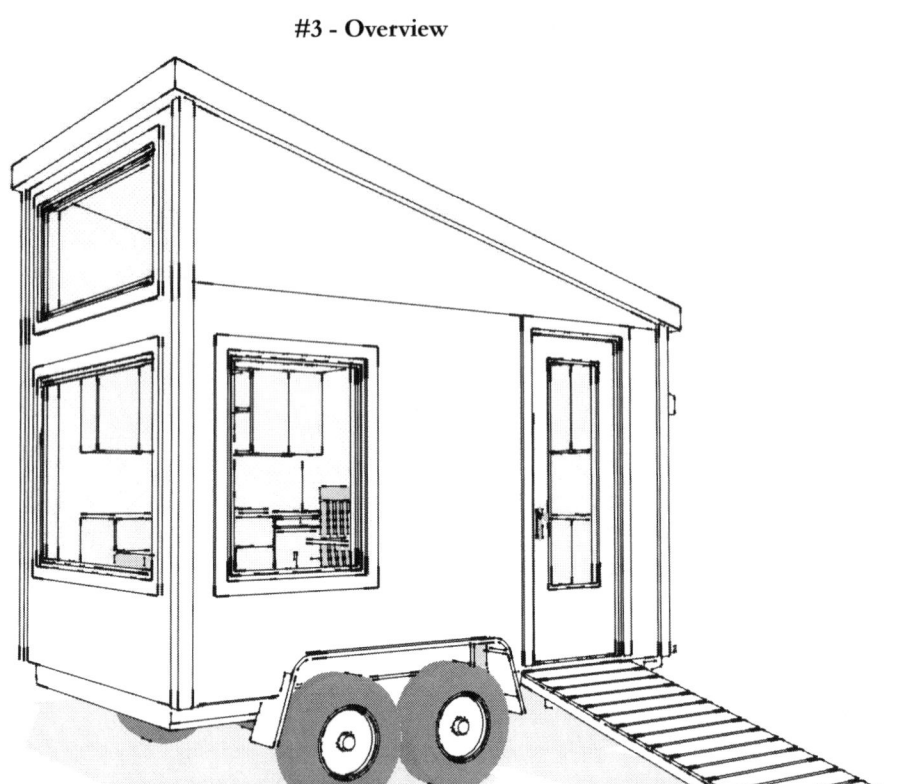

Front Right

Summary:

The wedge shape of this tiny house would make it more aerodynamic than most tiny homes. A fold-up ramp on the side would provide easy access. Inside you'll find a tiny wet bathroom with shower, toilet, and tiny wall mounted sink. The kitchen has the basics: a sink with drain rack cabinet above, small refrigerator, small cooktop, and storage. Also on the lower level is space for two small comfy chairs and a desk. The loft has room for a queen bed and is accessed by a fixed vertical ladder just inside the entry.

Features:

12-Foot Tiny House on Wheels
Shed Roof
Tiny Wet Bathroom
Small Loft
Large Windows
Side Entry with Ramp
Utility Cabinet over Trailer Tongue

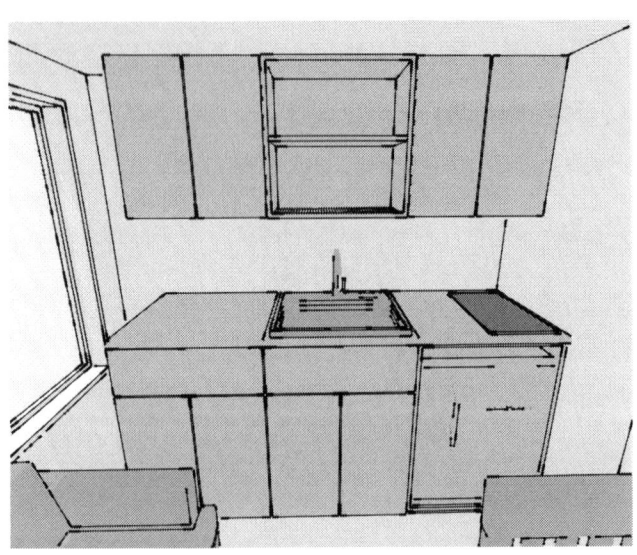

Kitchen

View from Loft

Tiny House #3 - Floor Plan & Exterior

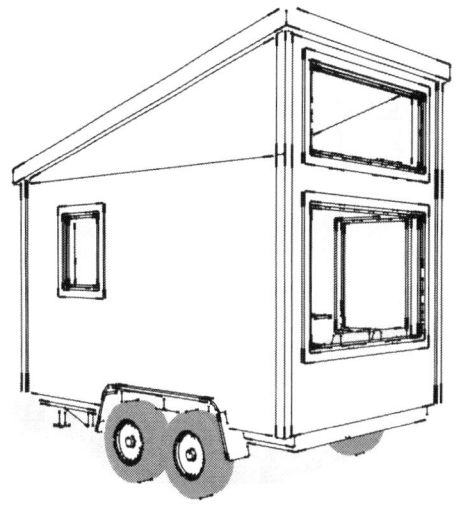

Left Front Corner

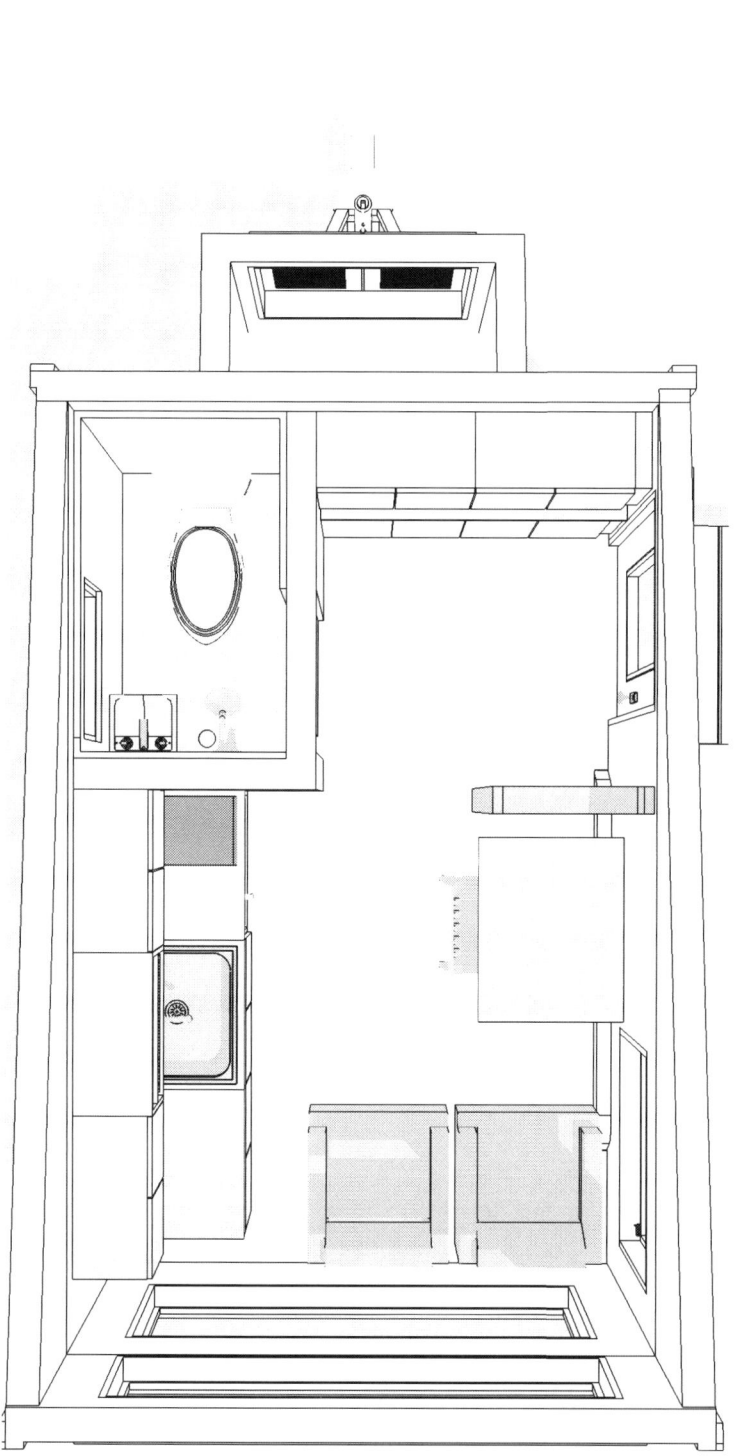

Floor Plan

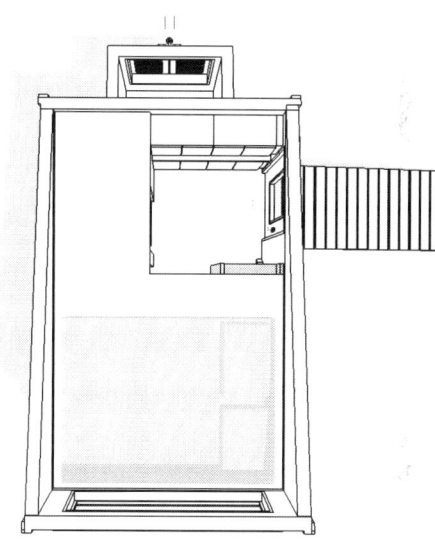

Floor Plan - Loft

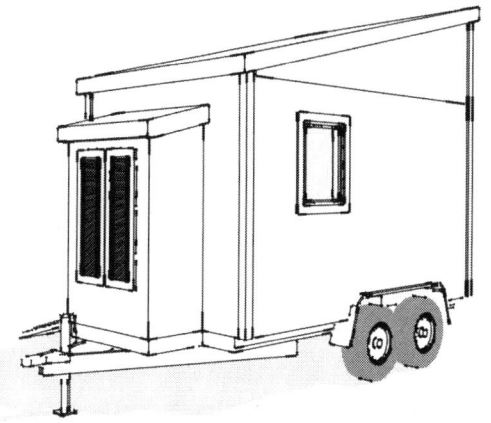

Back Left Corner

Tiny House #3 - Interior Views

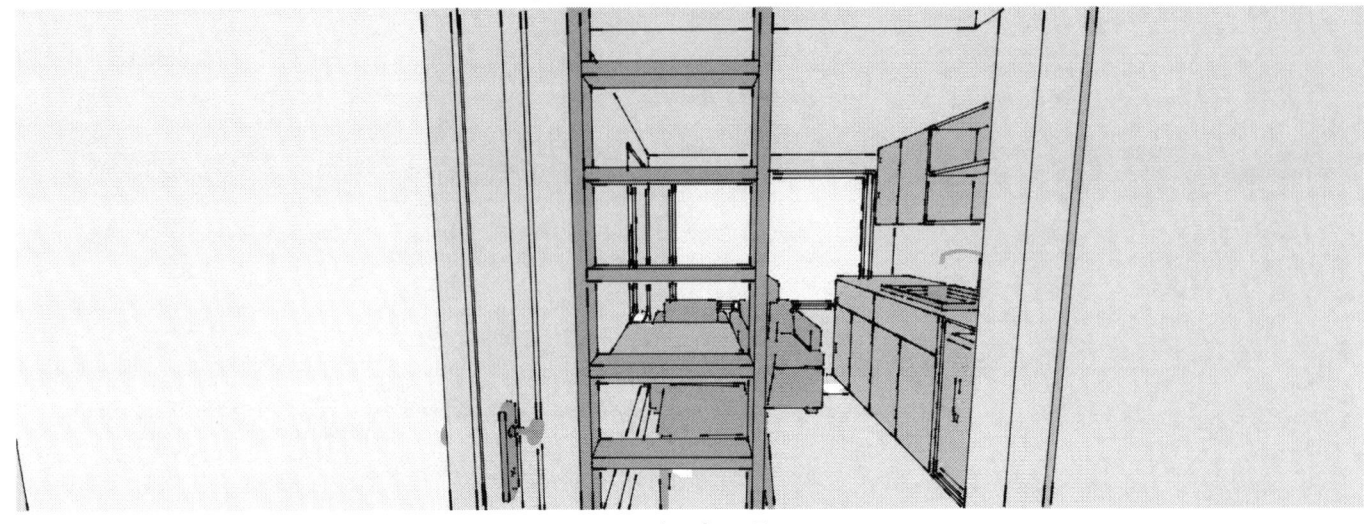

Interior from Entry

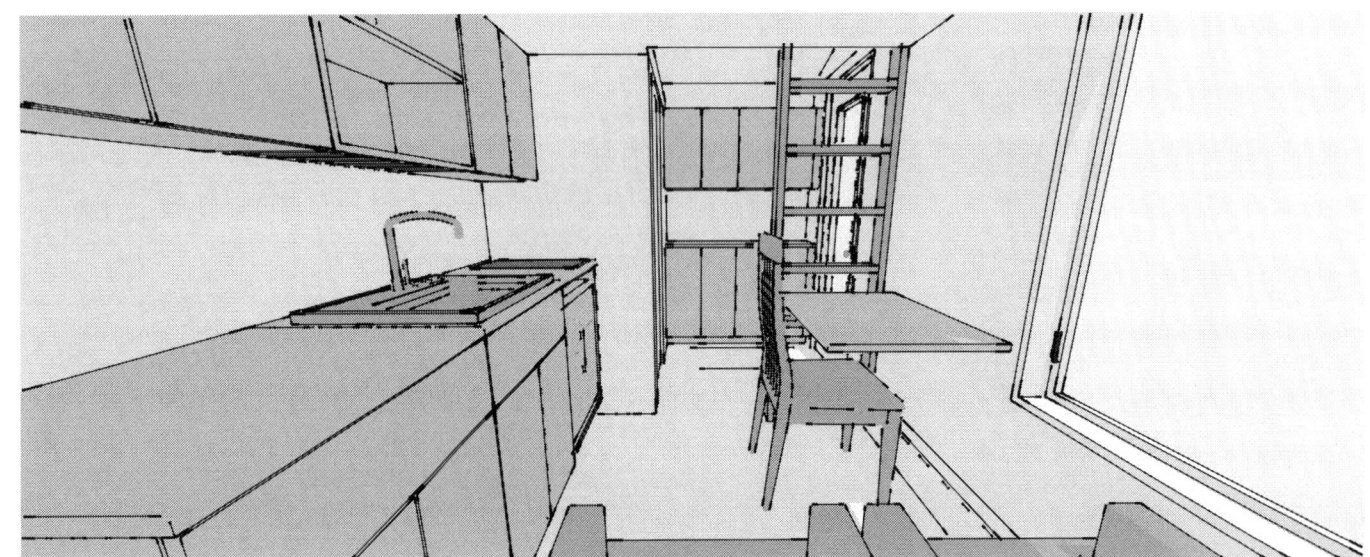

Interior from Kitchen

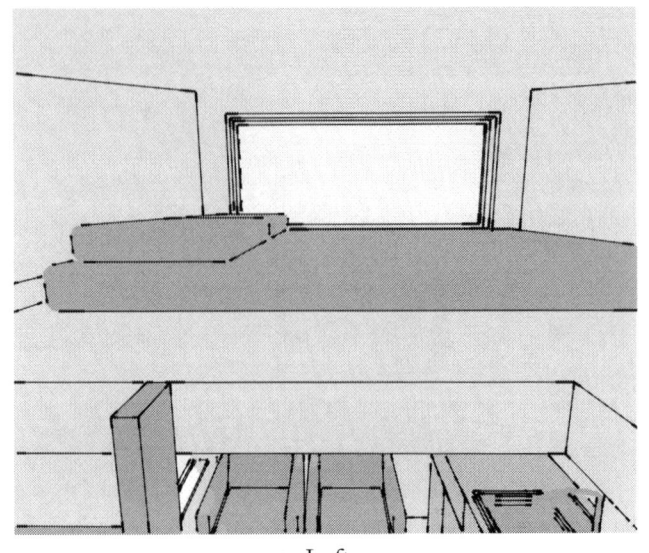

Loft

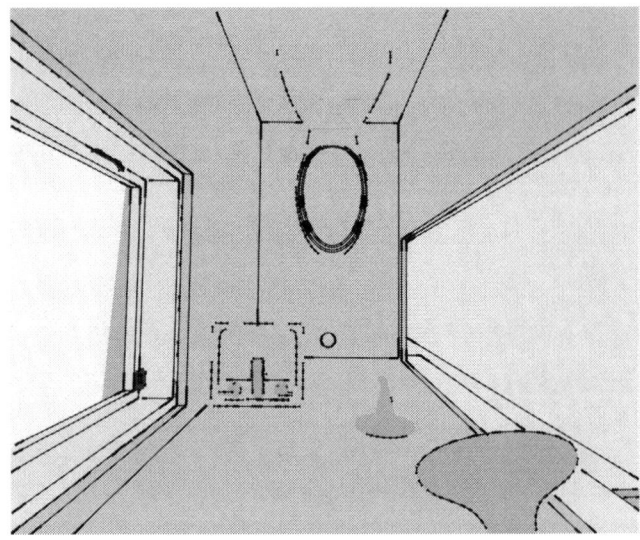

Bathroom

Tiny House #3 - Elevations

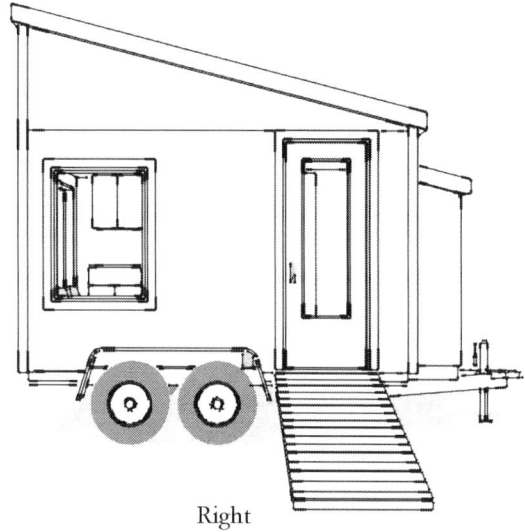

Right

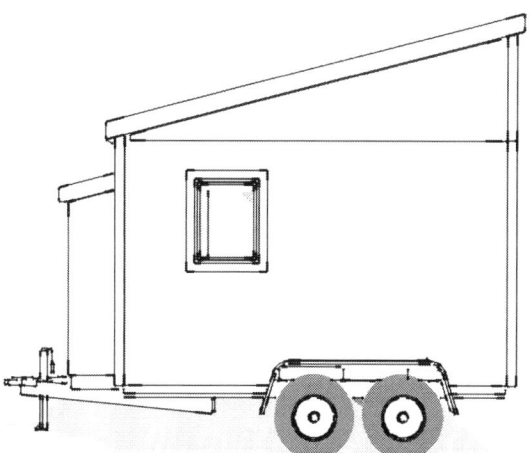

Left

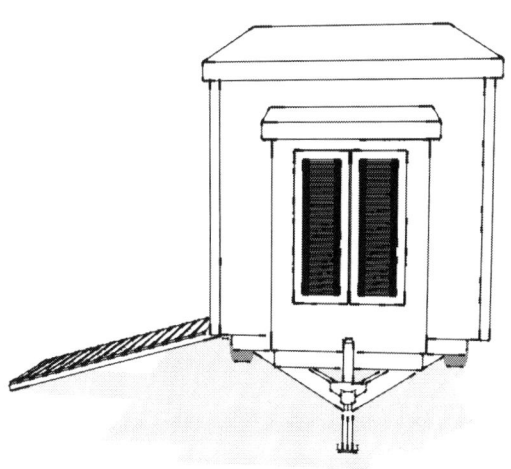

Back

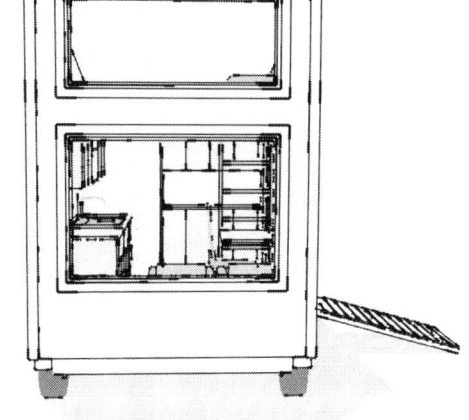

Front

#4

Tiny House #4 - Overview

Front Right

Summary:

A 10/12 cross gable roof with large windows and a side entry. A fold-up ramp would provide easy access. Inside is a tiny wet bathroom with shower, toilet, and tiny wall mounted sink. The kitchen extends over the trailer tongue and has the basics: a sink, small refrigerator, small cooktop, and storage. Also on the lower level is space for a small chair, love seat, and a desk. The loft has room for a queen bed and is accessed by wall mounted ladder rungs.

Features:

12-Foot Tiny House on Wheels
10/12 Cross Gable Roof
Tiny Wet Bathroom
Small Loft
Large Windows
Side Entry with Ramp
Extended Kitchen Space over Trailer Tongue

Kitchen

View from Loft

Tiny House #4 - Floor Plan & Exterior

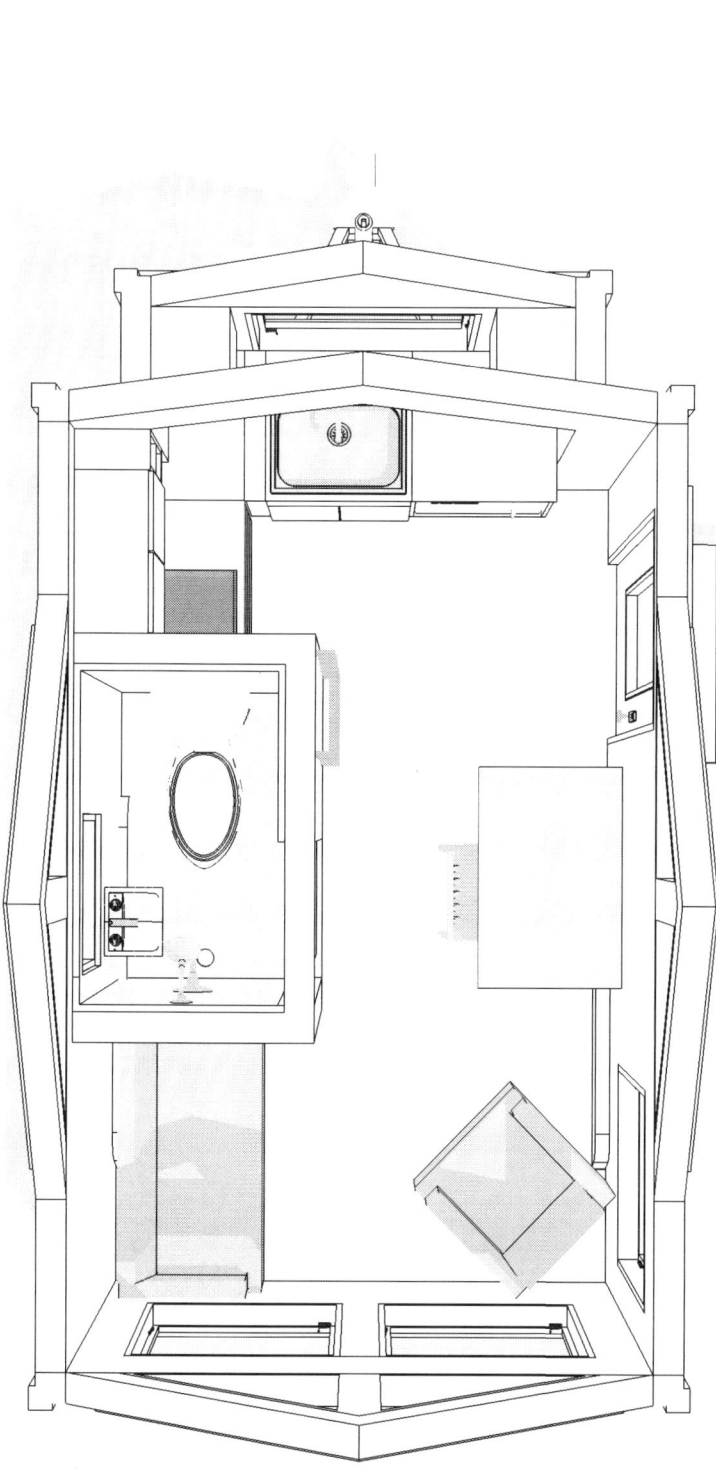

Floor Plan

Left Front Corner

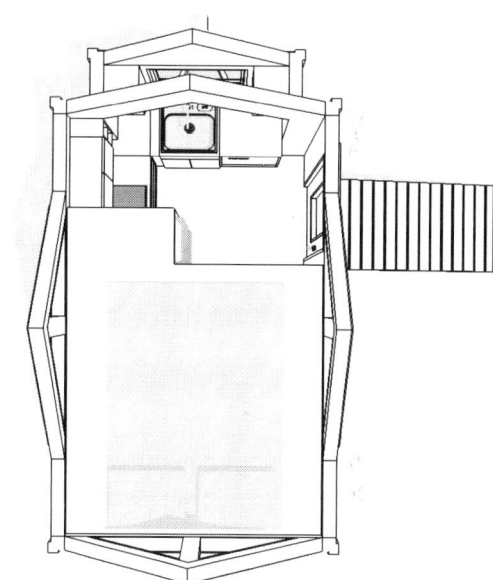

Floor Plan - Loft

Back Left Corner

Tiny House #4 - Interior Views

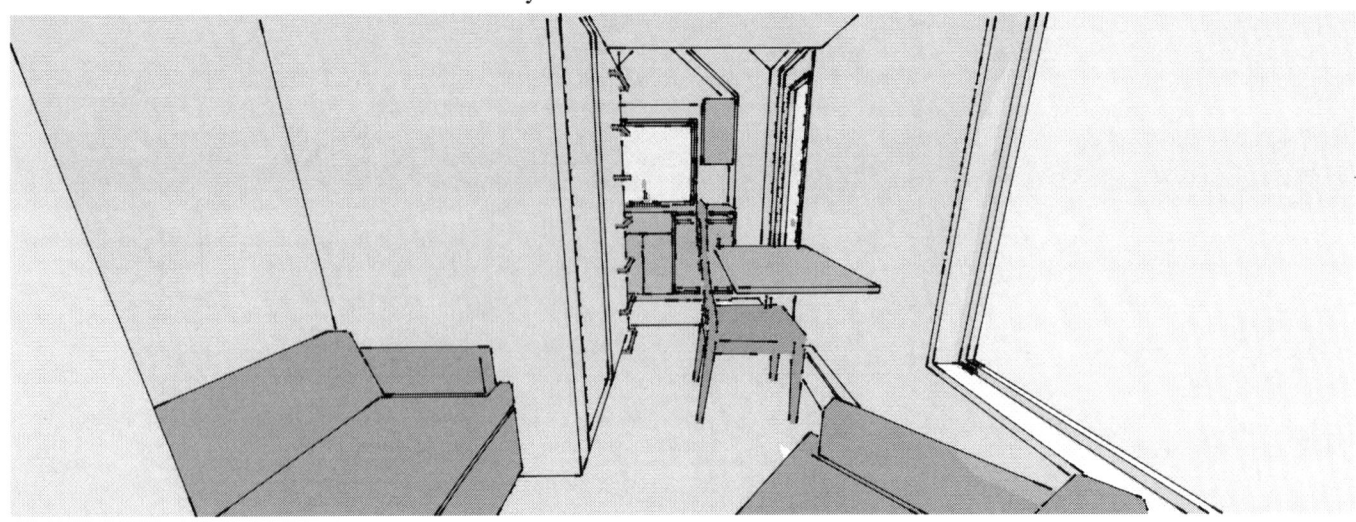

Interior from Living Room

Interior from Kitchen

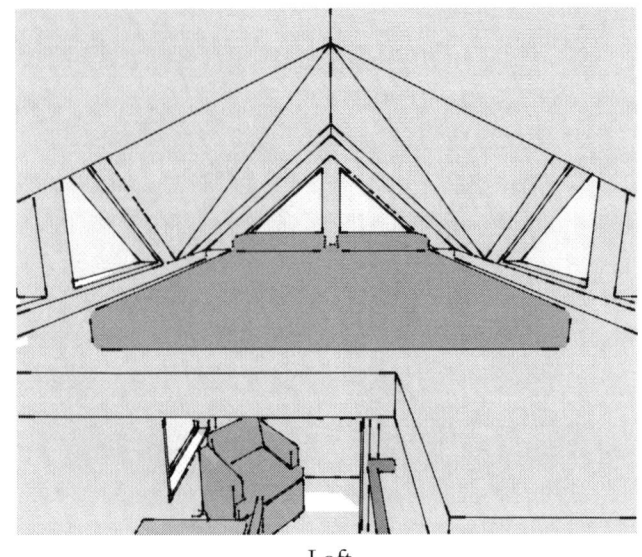

Loft

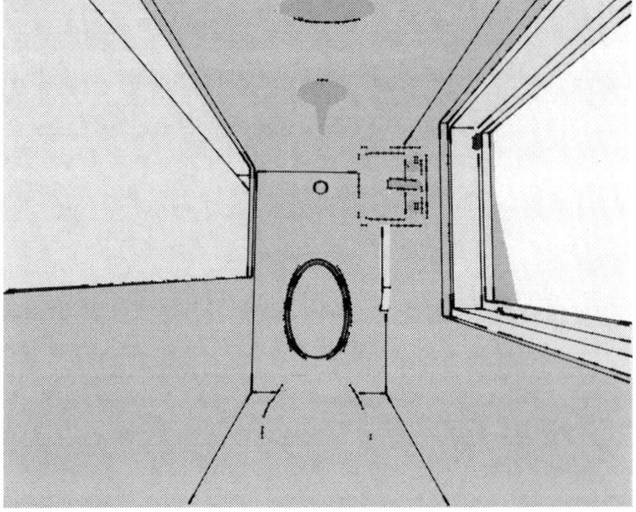

Bathroom

Tiny House #4 - Elevations

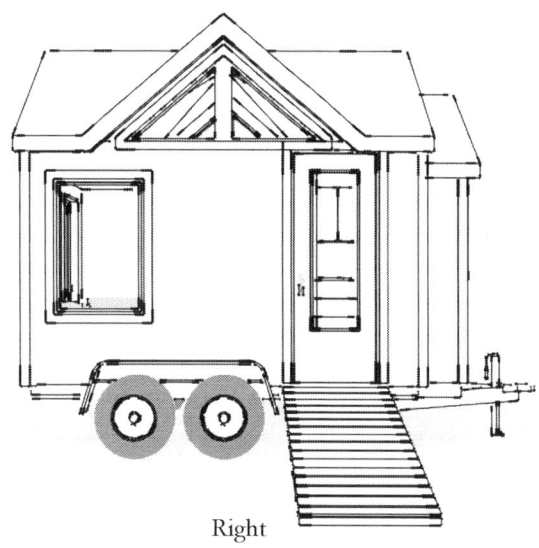

Right

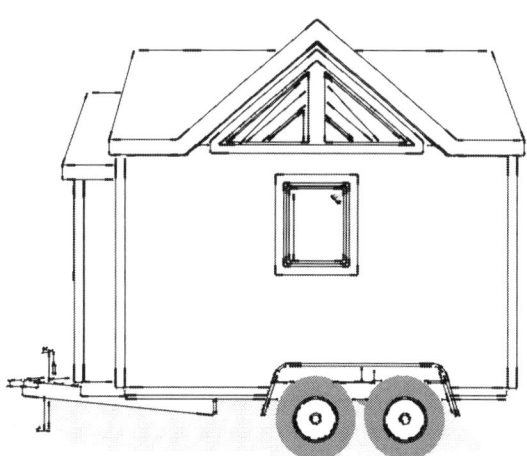

Left

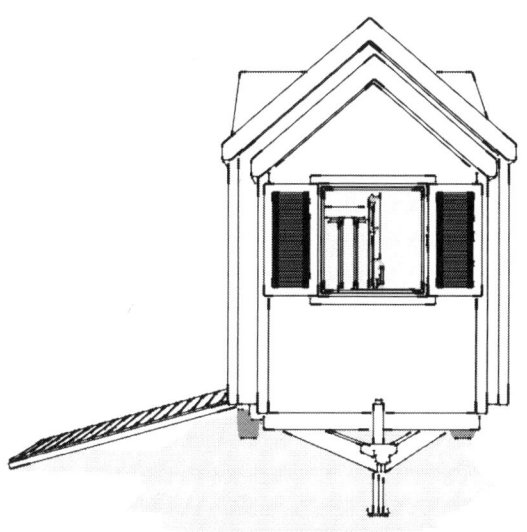

Back

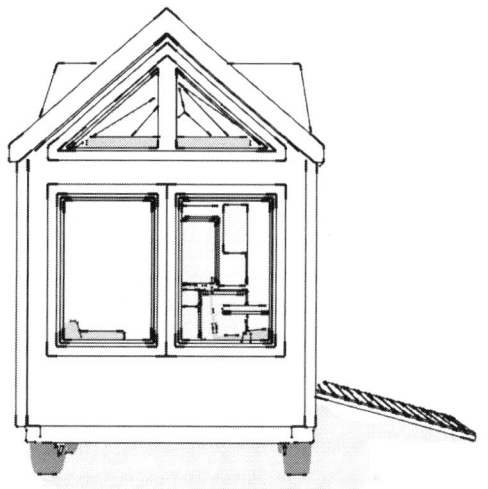

Front

#5

Tiny House #5 - Overview

Front Right

Summary:

This tiny house has a 10/12 gable roof with large 3/12 shed dormers. The entry is over the trailer tongue and has fold-up steps. Just inside the entry is a small wet bathroom with shower, toilet, and tiny wall mounted sink. The kitchen has the basics: a sink, small refrigerator, small cooktop, and storage. Also on the lower level is space for a small chair and table. The loft has space for a queen bed and is accessed by wall mounted ladder rungs just inside the entry.

Features:

12-Foot Tiny House on Wheels
10/12 Gable Roof
3/12 Shed Dormers
Small Wet Bathroom
Small Loft
Trailer Tongue Entry
Fold-up Steps

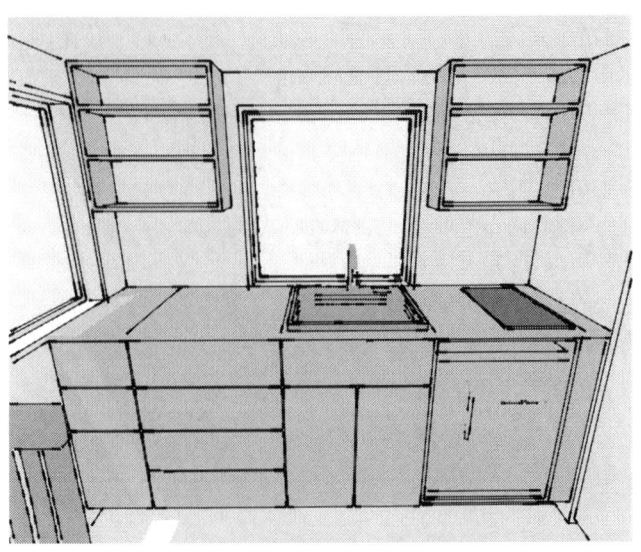

Kitchen

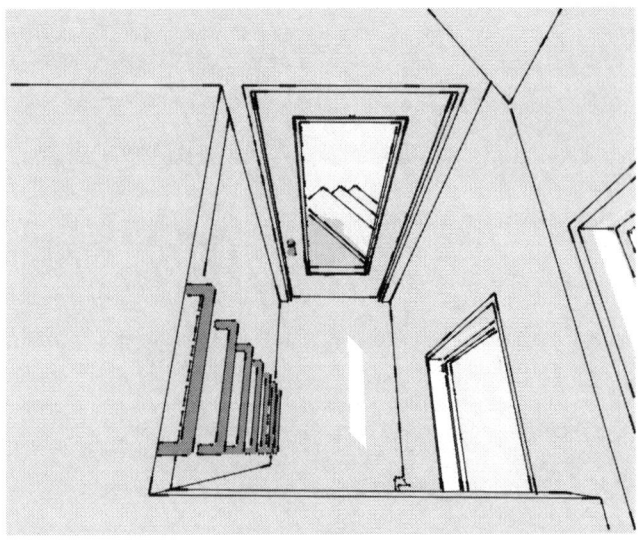

View from Loft

Tiny House #5 - Floor Plan & Exterior

Left Front Corner

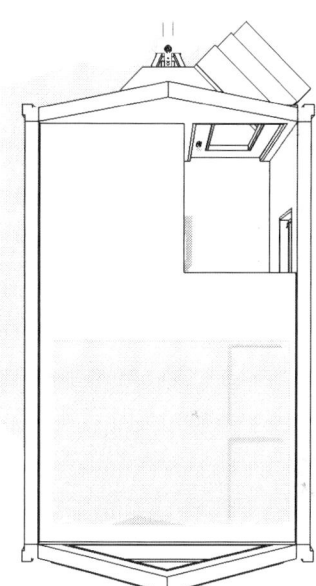
Floor Plan - Loft

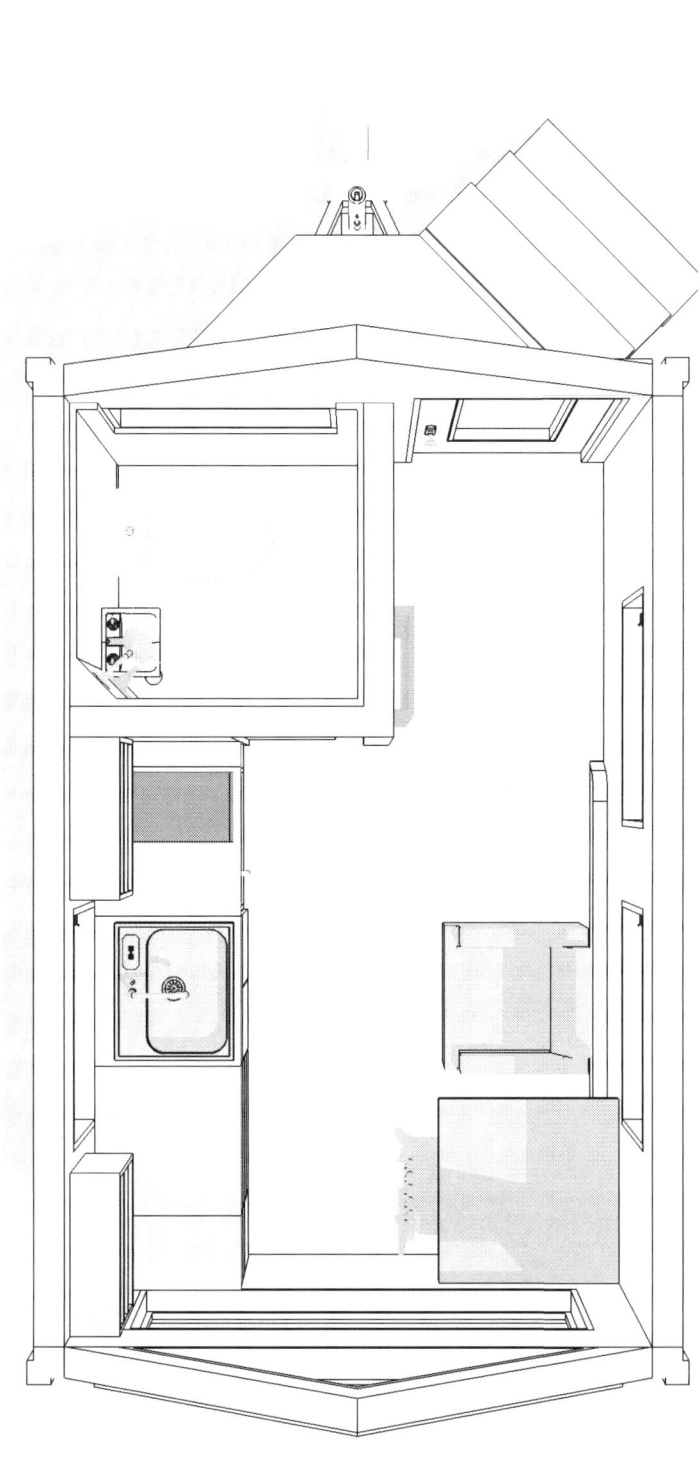
Floor Plan

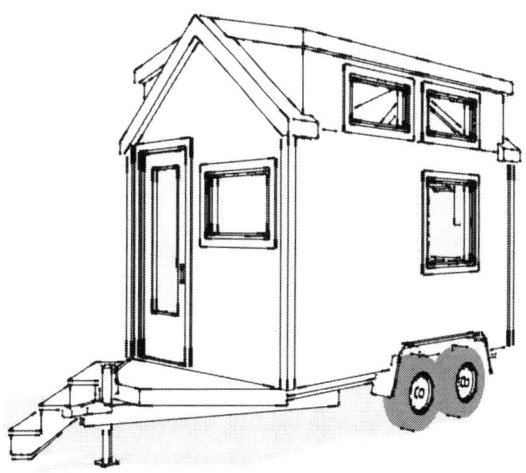
Back Left Corner

Tiny House #5 - Interior Views

Interior from Entry

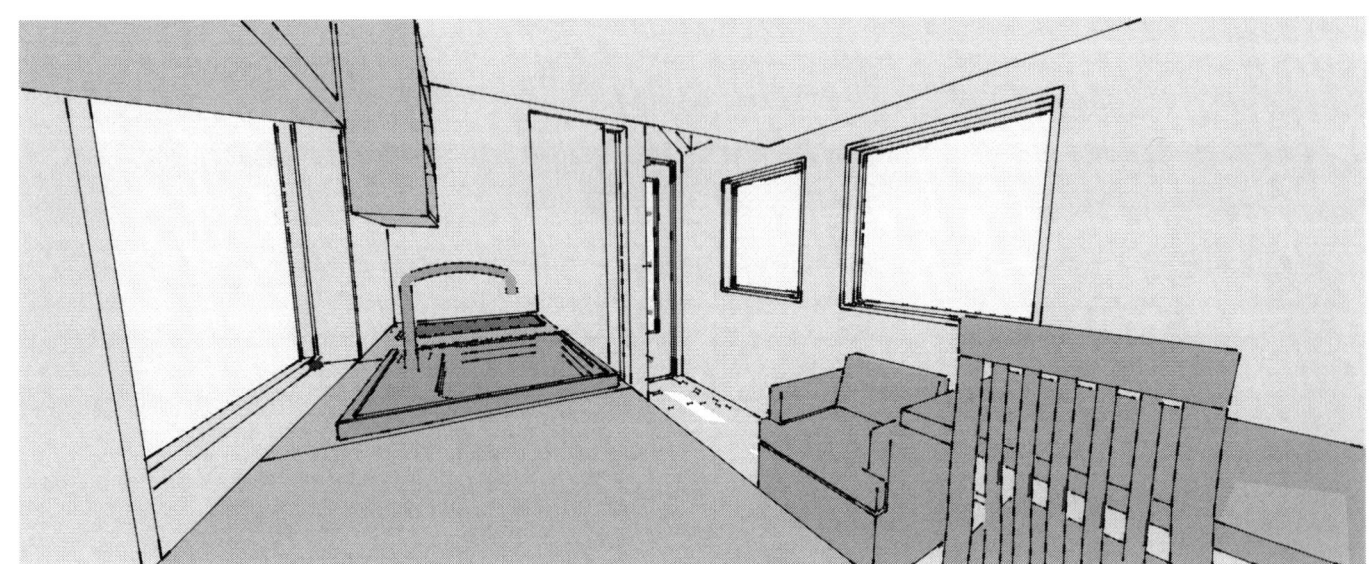

Interior from Kitchen

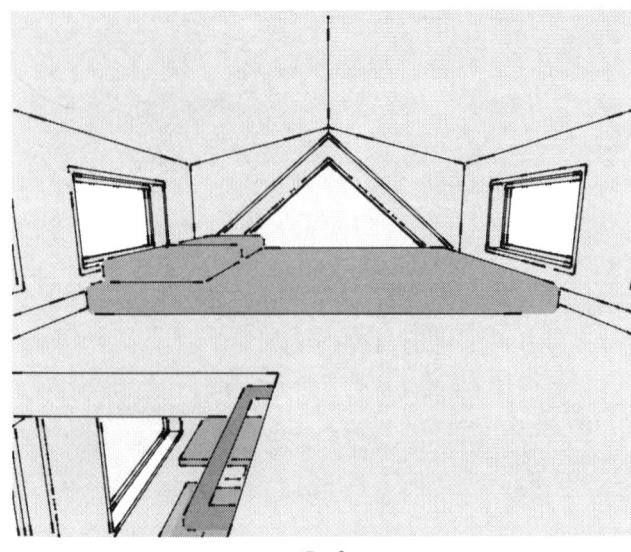

Loft

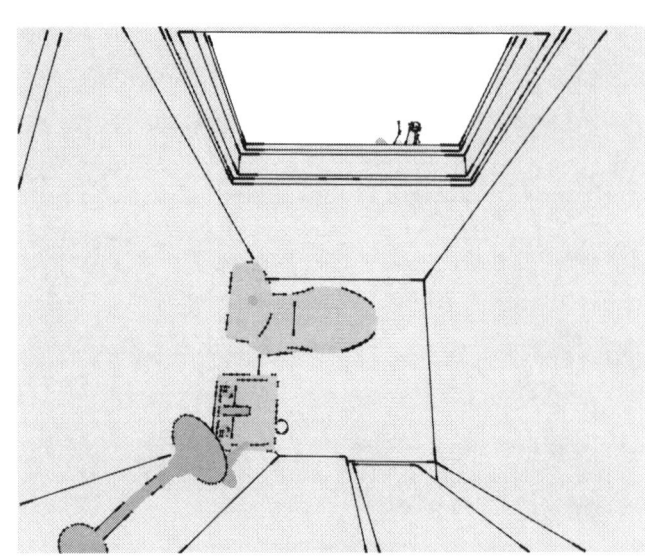

Bathroom

Tiny House #5 - Elevations

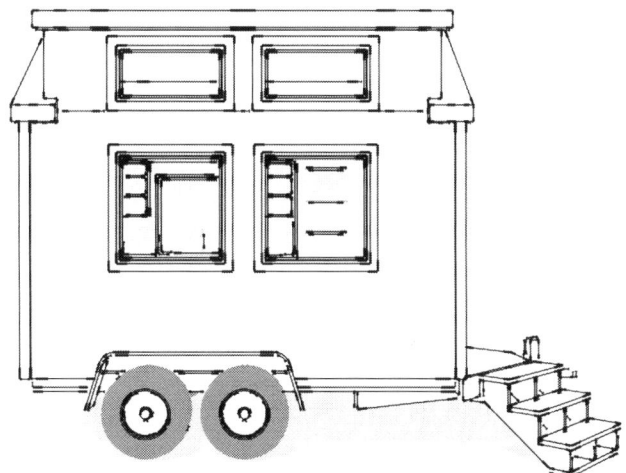

Right

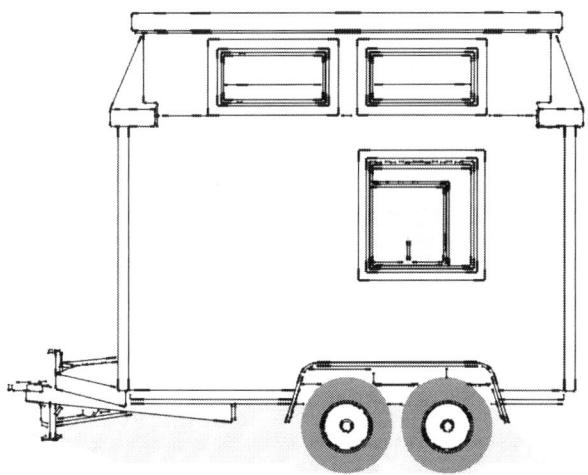

Left

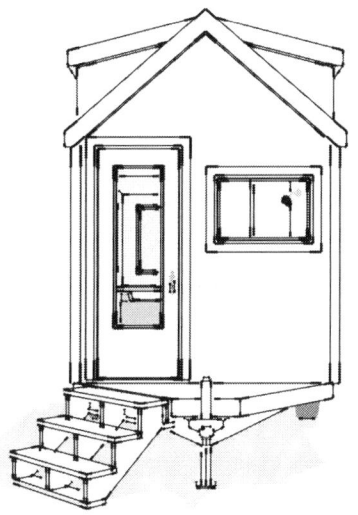

Back

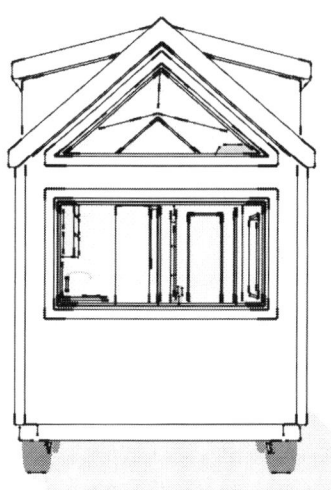

Front

#6

Tiny House #6 - Overview

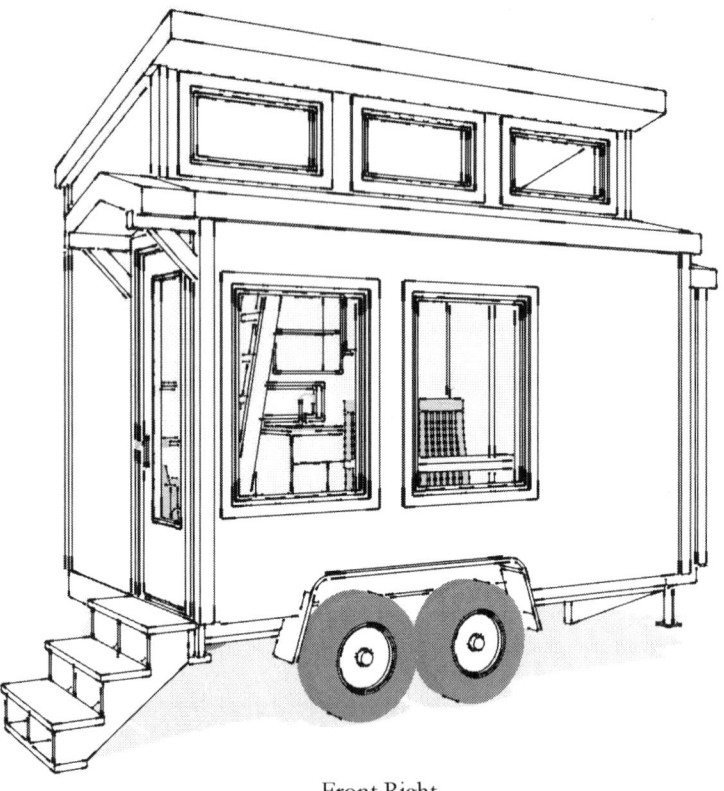

Front Right

Summary:

A 3/12 shed roof with plenty of windows. The front corner entry has fold-up steps. Inside is a small bathroom with shower, toilet, and generous vanity located in a bump-out extension over the trailer tongue. The tiny kitchen has a sink with a cabinet drain rack, small refrigerator, small cooktop, microwave, and storage. There's also space for a small chair and ottoman as well as and a table/desk. The loft has room for a queen bed which is accessed by a fixed ladder. The window over trailer tongue is shown with shutters that would help prevent damage from rocks & debris while on the road.

Features:

12-Foot Tiny House on Wheels
3/12 Shed Roof with Clerestory
Small Bathroom with Large Vanity
Small Loft
Fold-up Steps

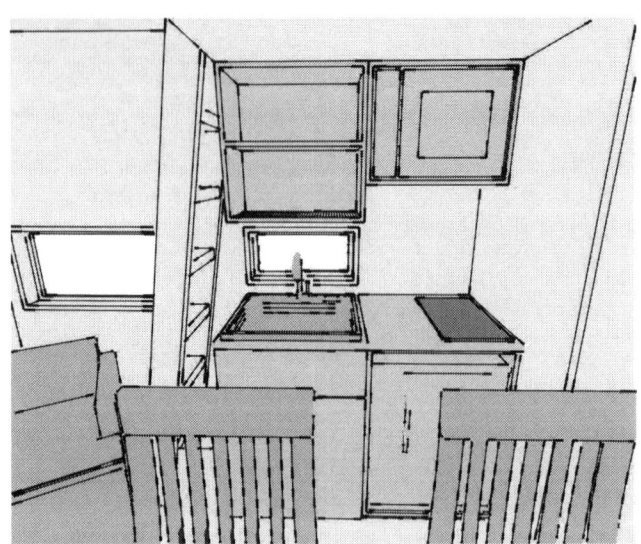

Kitchen

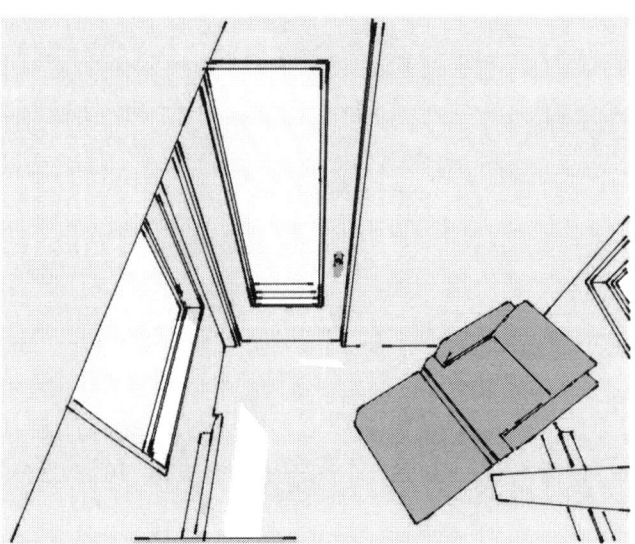

View from Loft

Tiny House #6 - Floor Plan & Exterior

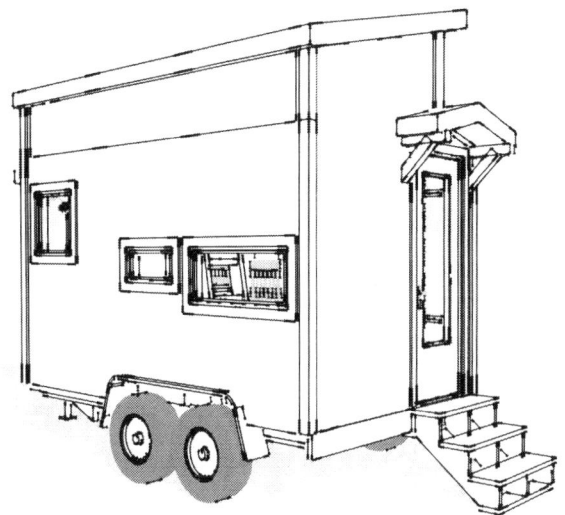
Left Front Corner

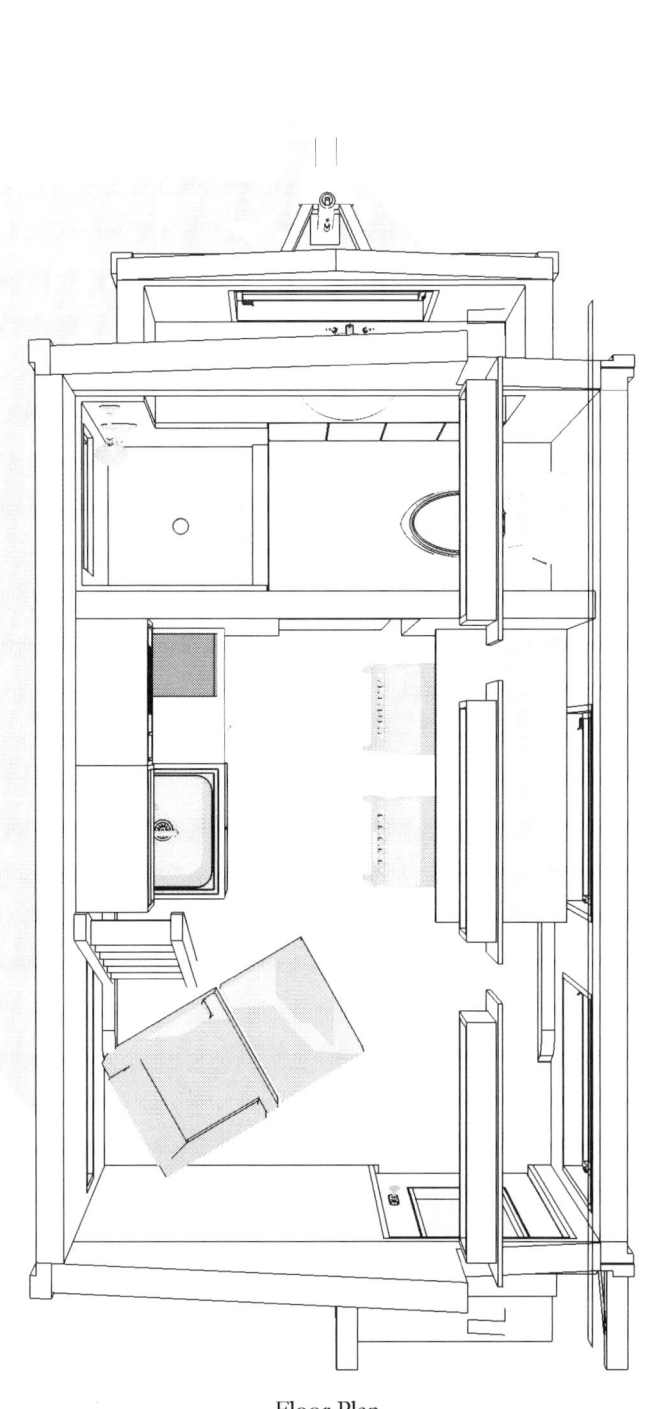
Floor Plan

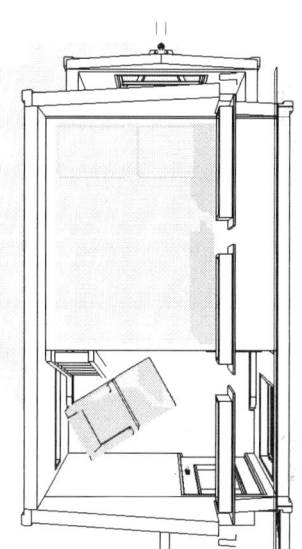
Floor Plan - Loft

Back Left Corner

Tiny House #6 - Interior Views

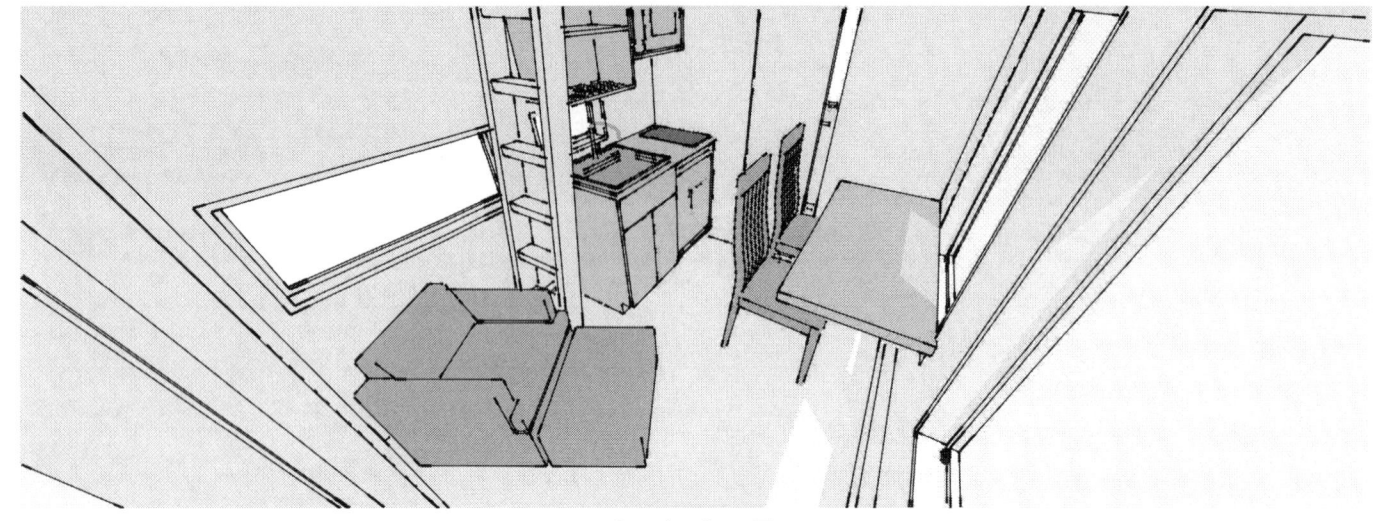

Interior from Entry

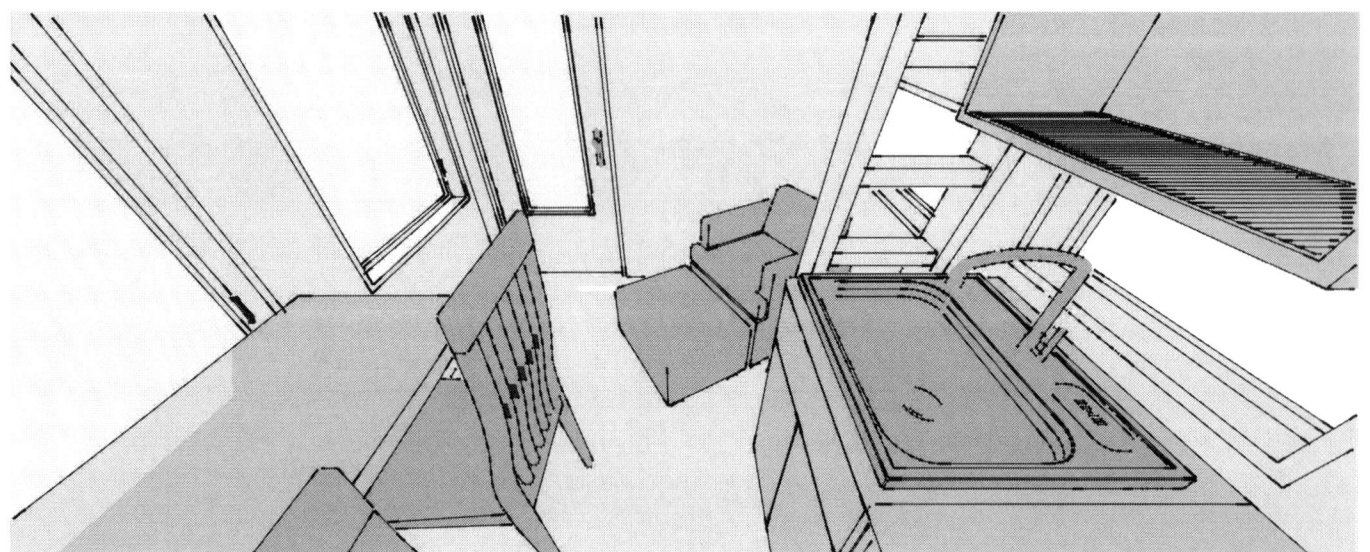

Interior from Kitchen

Loft

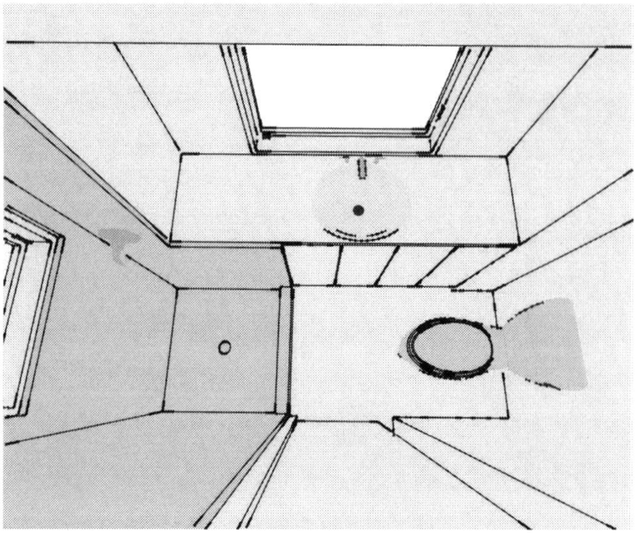

Bathroom

Tiny House #6 - Elevations

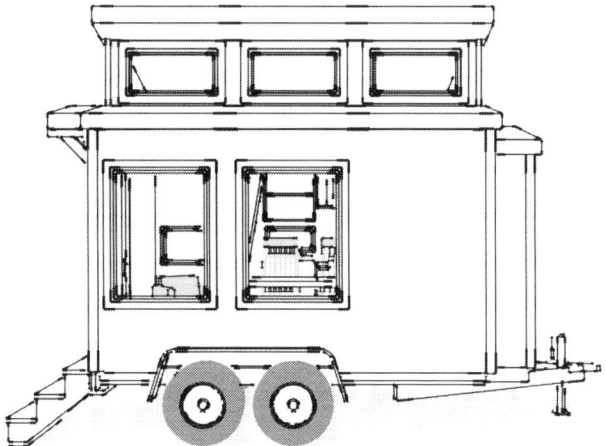

Right

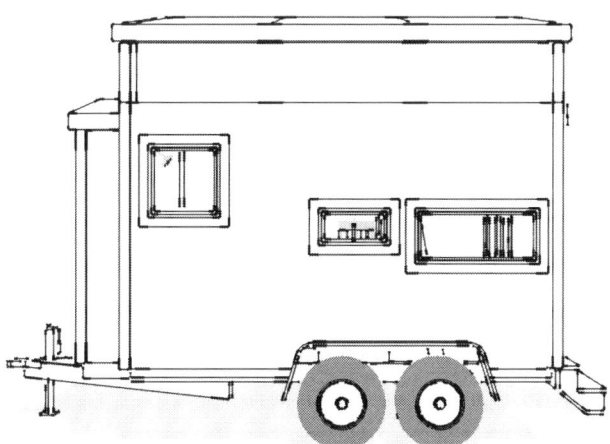

Left

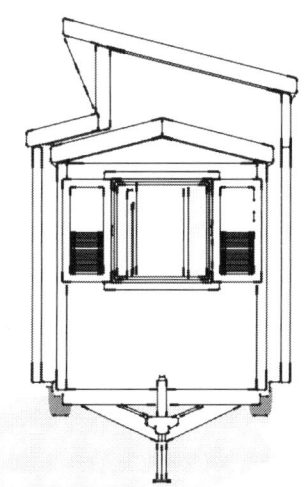

Back

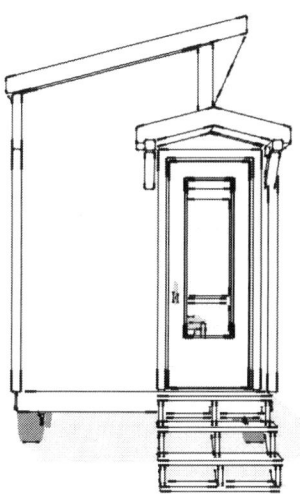

Front

#7

Tiny House #7 - Overview

Front Right

Summary:

Here's a gambrel roofed tiny house with plenty of windows. The front corner entry has fold-up steps. Inside is a wet bathroom with shower, toilet, and small wall mounted sink. The tiny kitchen has a sink with a cabinet drain rack, small refrigerator, small cooktop, microwave. The house also has a long and shallow set of cabinets along the right wall below the windows... so there is quite a bit of storage. On the back wall is a desk that fits neatly in a bay window. The loft is small but thanks to the gambrel roof it has ample headroom.

Features:

12-Foot Tiny House on Wheels
Gambrel Roof
Bay Window with Desk
Wet Bathroom
Small Loft
Fold-up Steps

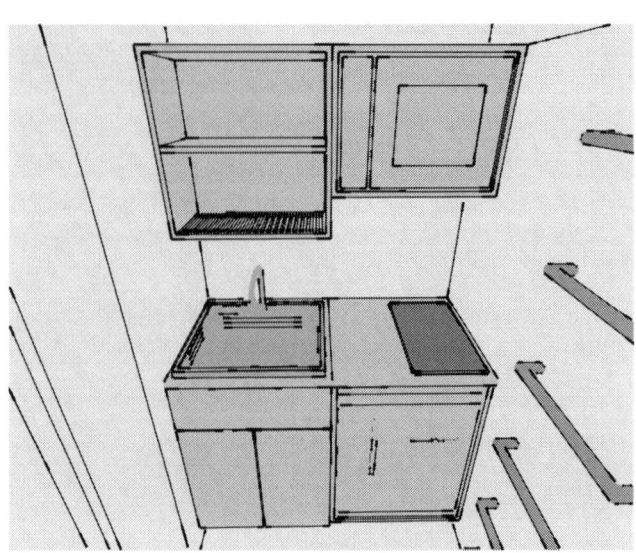

Kitchen

View from Loft

Tiny House #7 - Floor Plan & Exterior

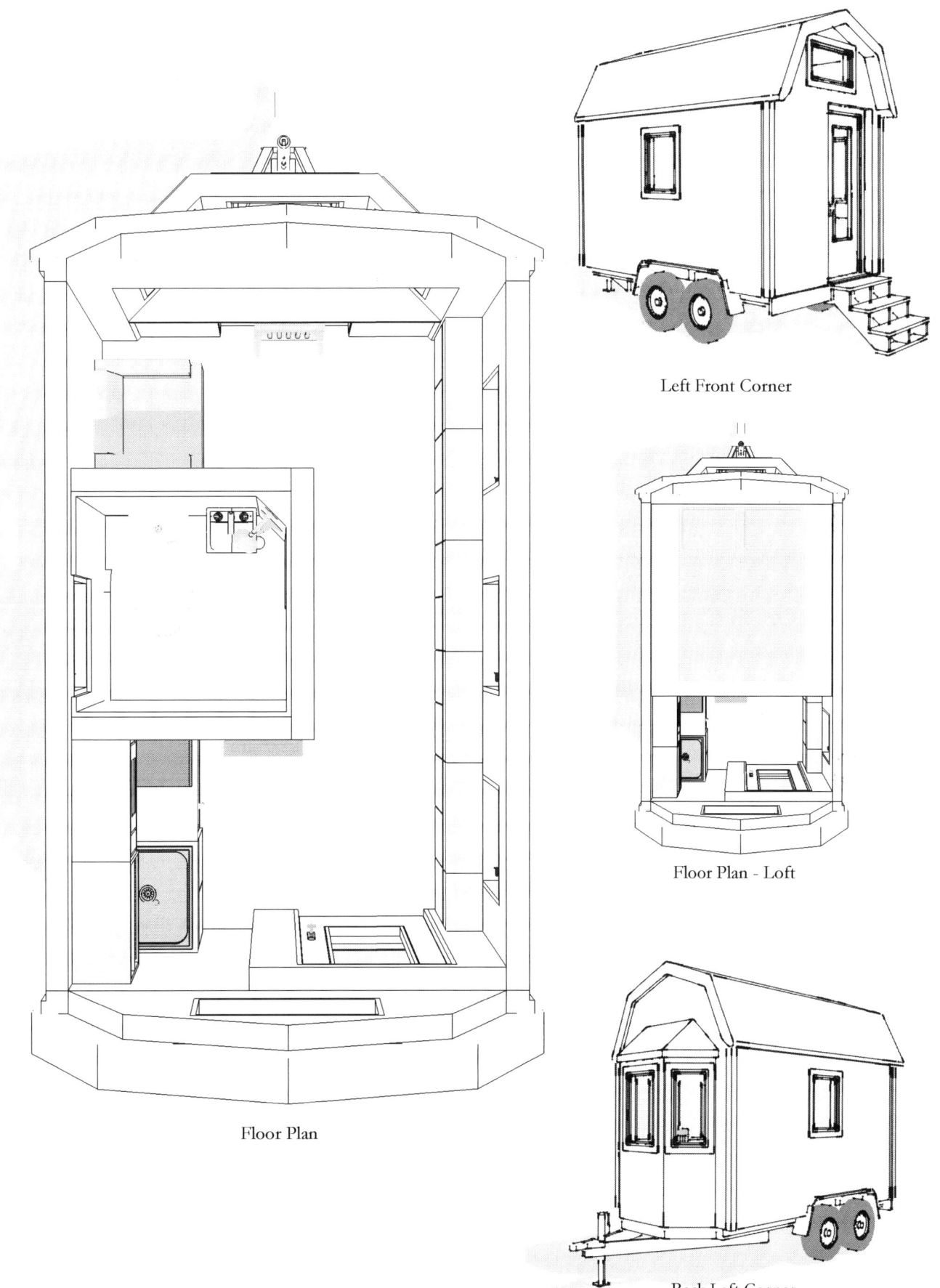

Left Front Corner

Floor Plan - Loft

Floor Plan

Back Left Corner

Tiny House #7 - Interior Views

Interior from Entry

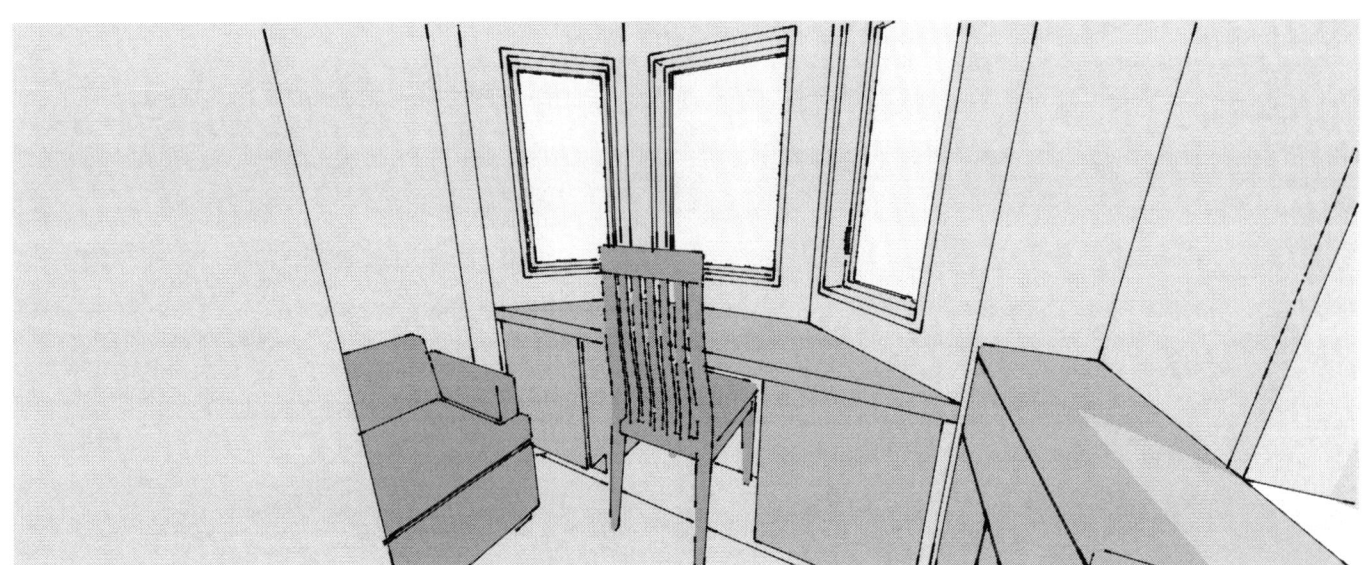

Interior - Desk in Bay Window

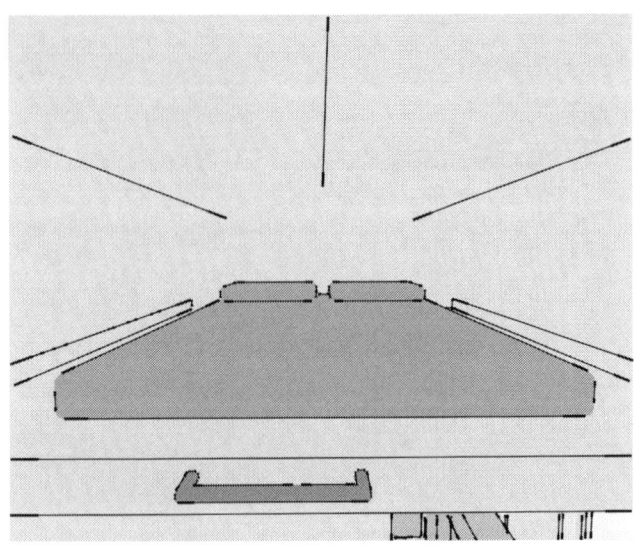

Loft

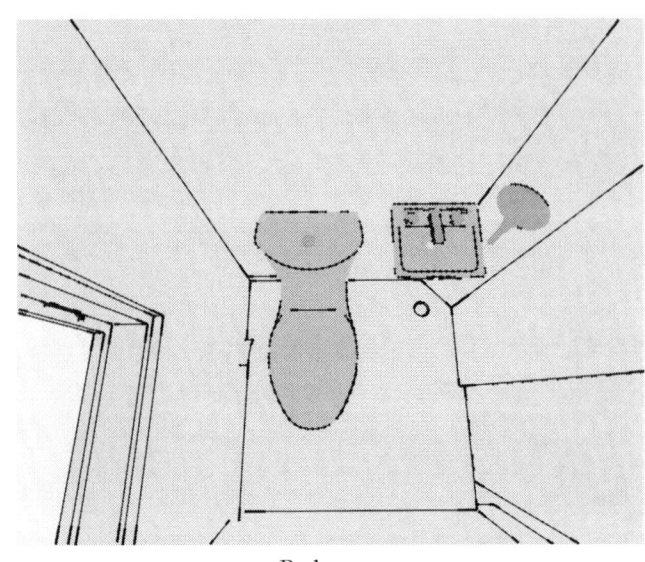

Bathroom

Tiny House #7 - Elevations

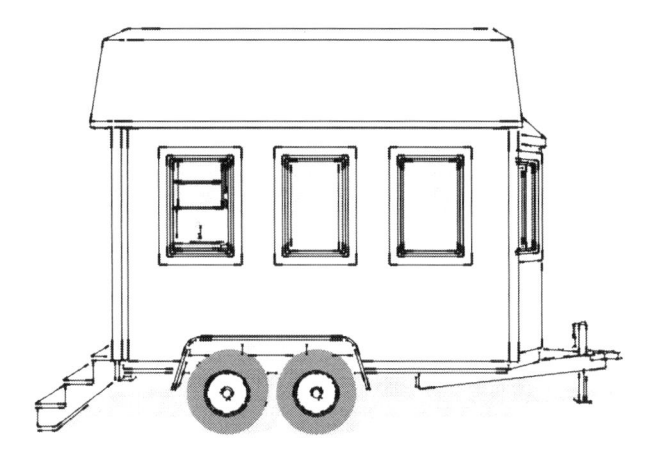

Right

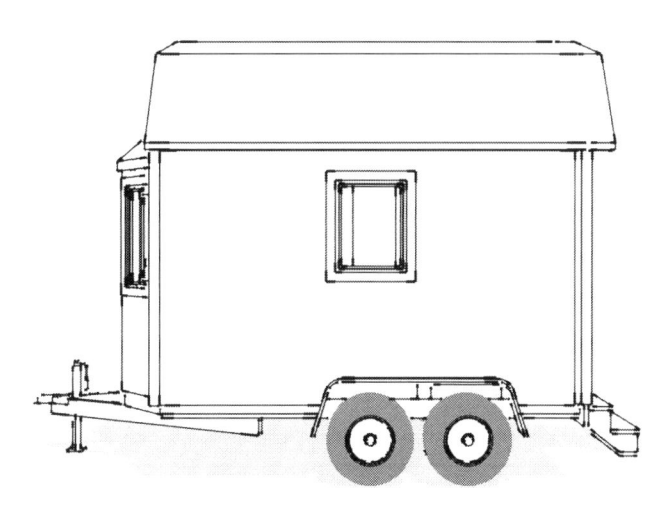

Left

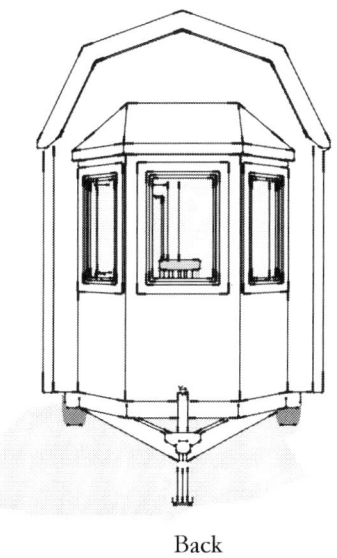

Back

Front

29

#8

Tiny House #8 - Overview

Front Right

Summary:

This house has a 10/12 Dutch gable roof with gable dormers. The front entry has fold-up steps. Inside the house is a small bathroom with shower, toilet, and wall mounted tiny sink. A bathroom cabinet extends into a portion of the bay window extension over the trailer tongue. The tiny kitchen also extends into another portion of the same bay window. The kitchen has a sink, small refrigerator, small cooktop, and storage. There's also space for two small chairs and a desk in the front of the house. The loft has space for a queen bed under the dormers. The loft is accessed by a movable ladder.

Features:

12-Foot Tiny House on Wheels
10/12 Dutch Gable Roof with Gable Dormers
Kitchen Extended in Bump-out over Trailer Tongue
Small Bathroom
Small Loft
Fold-up Steps

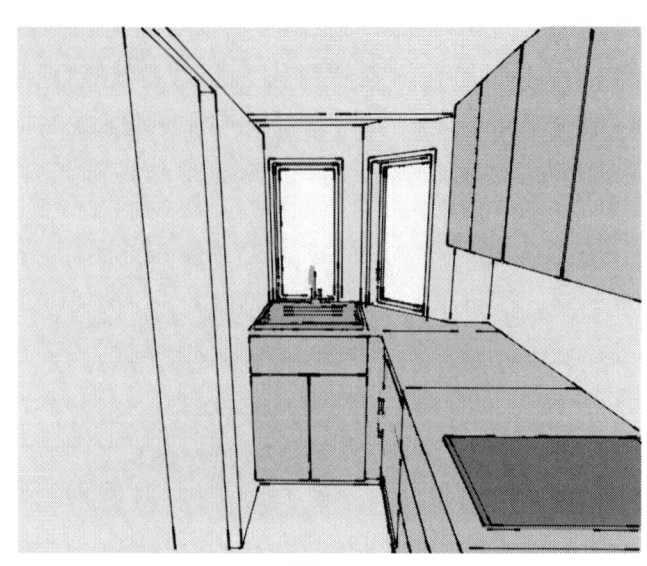

Kitchen

View from Loft

Tiny House #8 - Floor Plan & Exterior

Left Front Corner

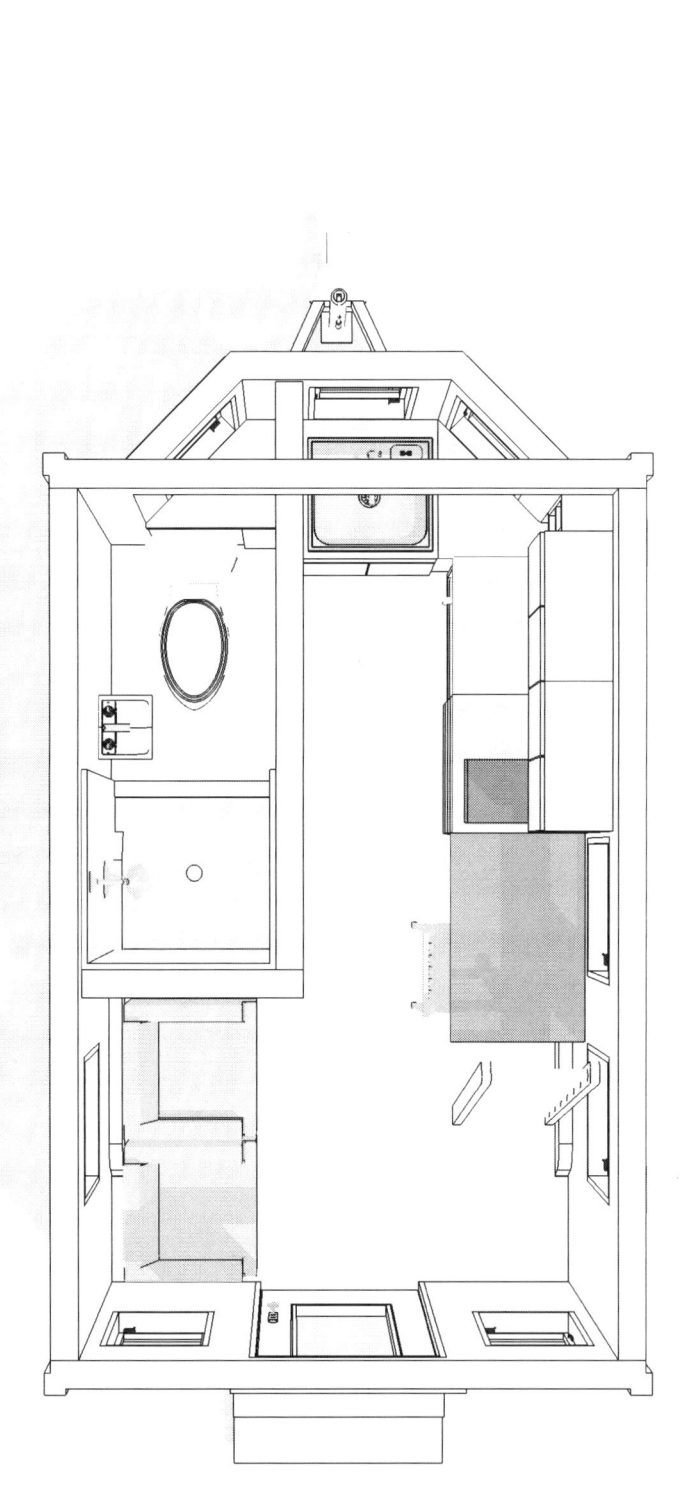

Floor Plan - Loft

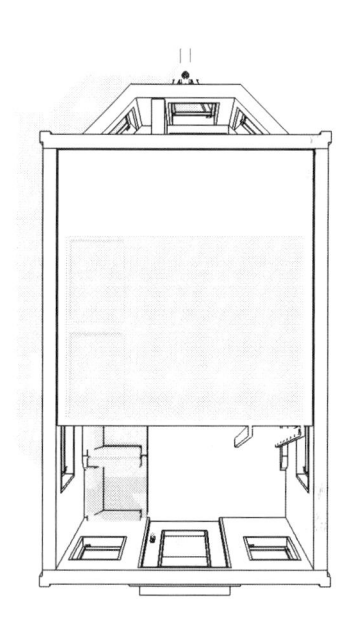

Floor Plan

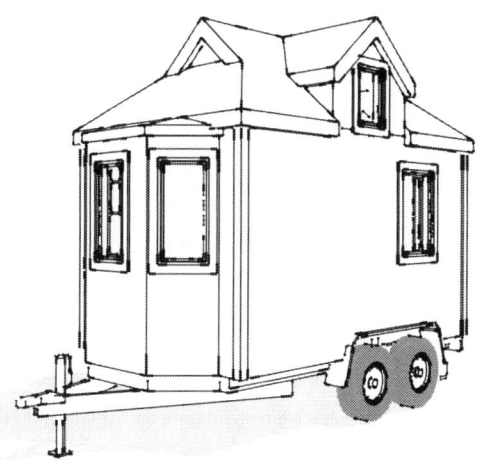

Back Left Corner

Tiny House #8 - Interior Views

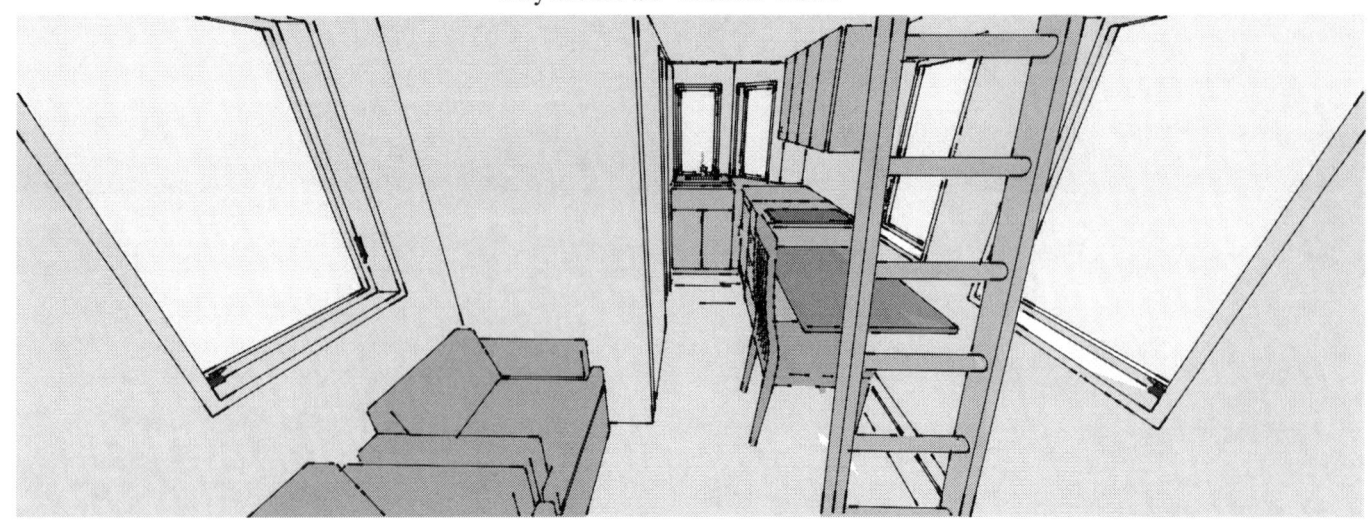

Interior from Entry

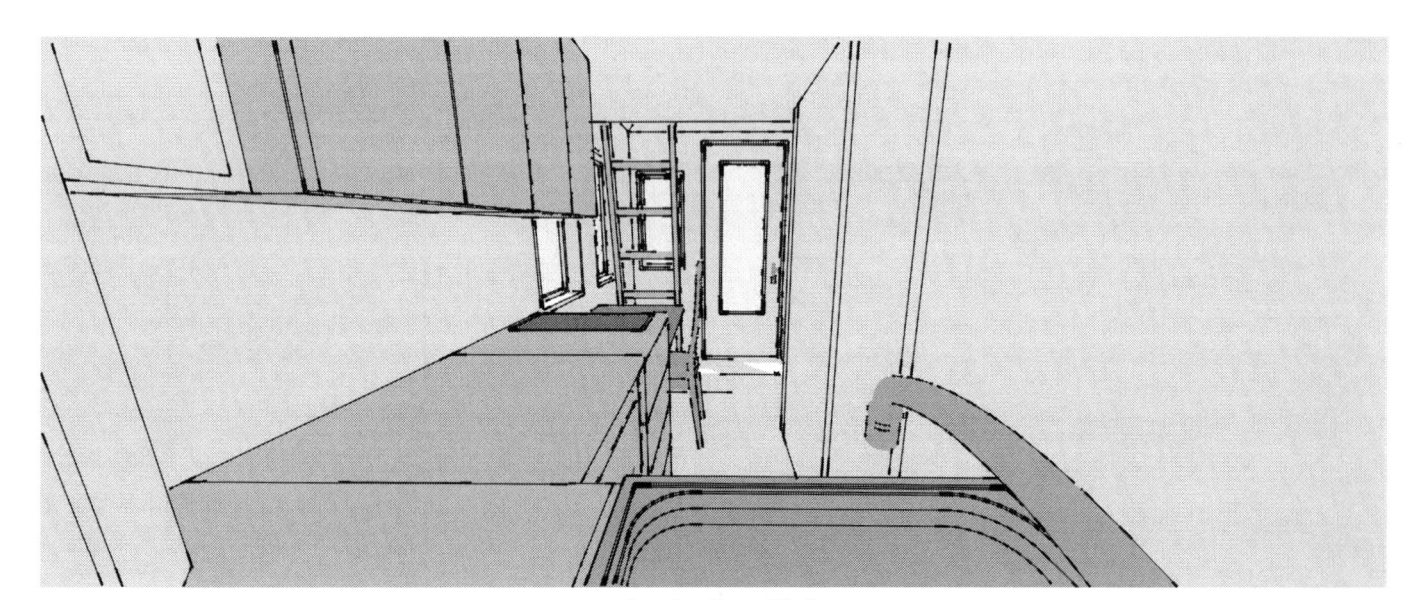

Interior from Kitchen

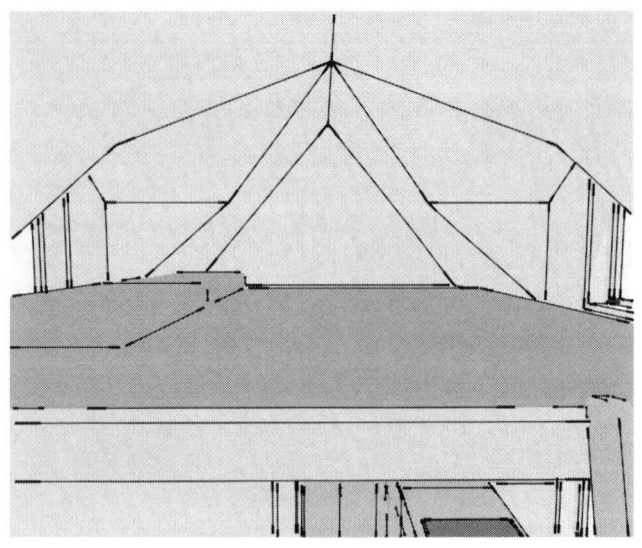

Loft

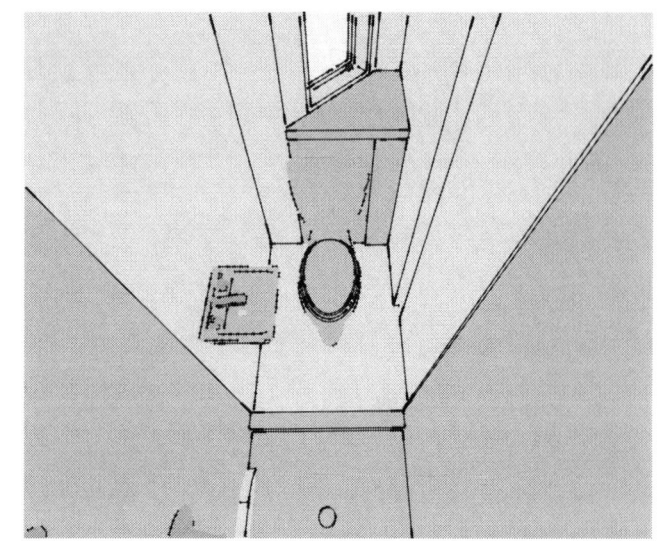

Bathroom

Tiny House #8 - Elevations

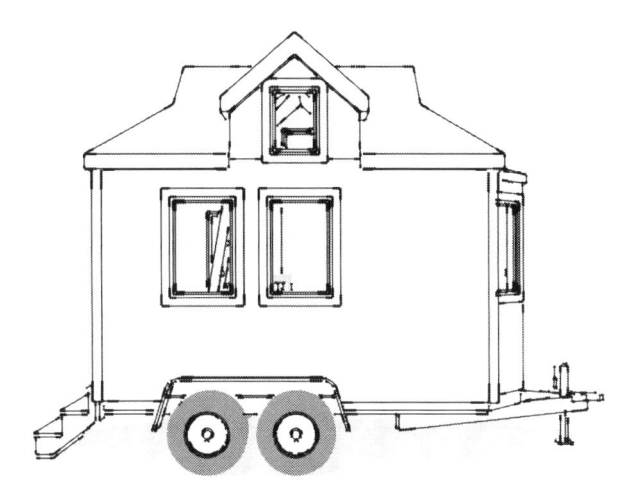

Right

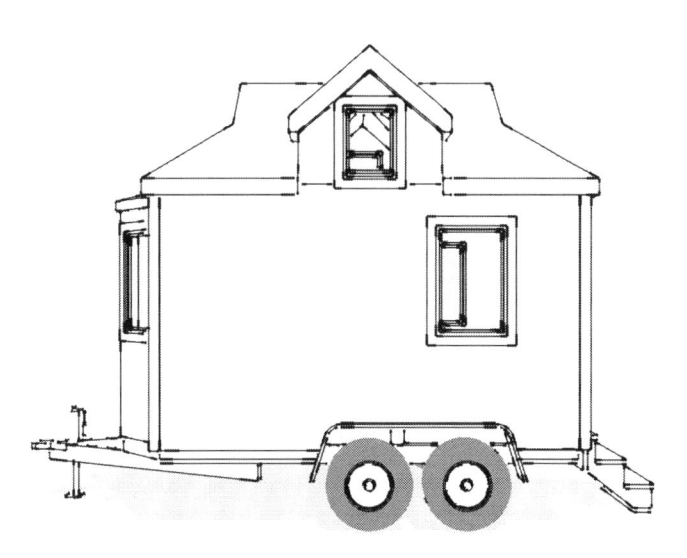

Left

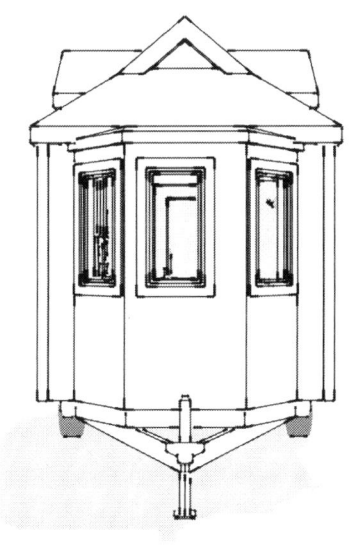

Back

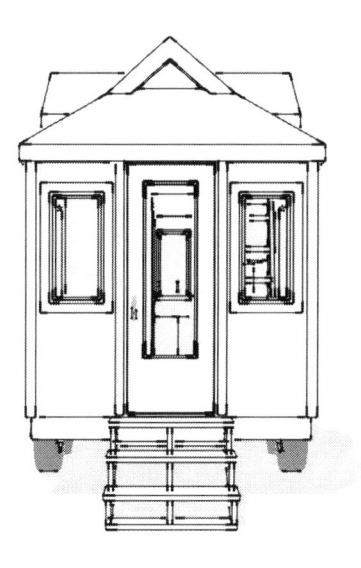

Front

9   Tiny House 9 - Overview

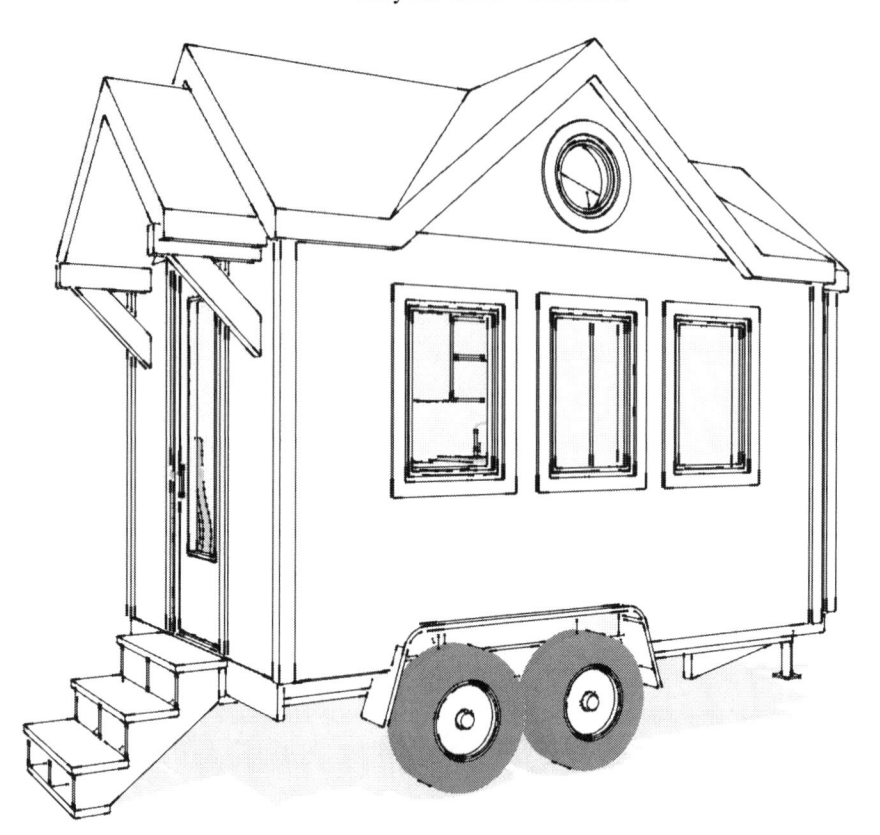

Front Right

Summary:

This tiny house has a complicated roof. It started as a cross gable with a hip roof over the back but it also has a gable roof extension over the entry and rear extension. Inside it has a bathroom with a shower, toilet, and vanity in the bump-out. The tiny kitchen has a sink with a cabinet drain rack, small refrigerator, small cooktop, and storage. There's also space for two small chairs in the front of the house and a table. The loft has room for a queen bed under the cross gable. The loft is accessed by a movable ladder.

Features:

12-Foot Tiny House on Wheels
10/12 Cross Gable Roof combined with a Hip Roof
Bump-out over Trailer Tongue to Extend Bathroom
Small Loft
Fold-up Steps

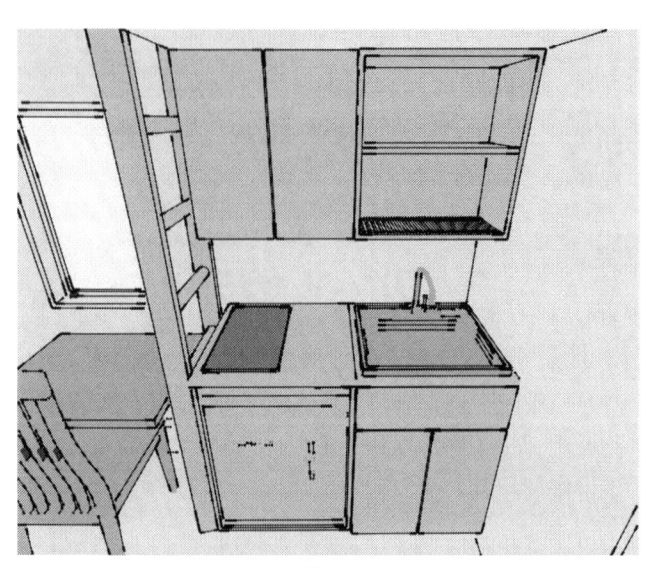

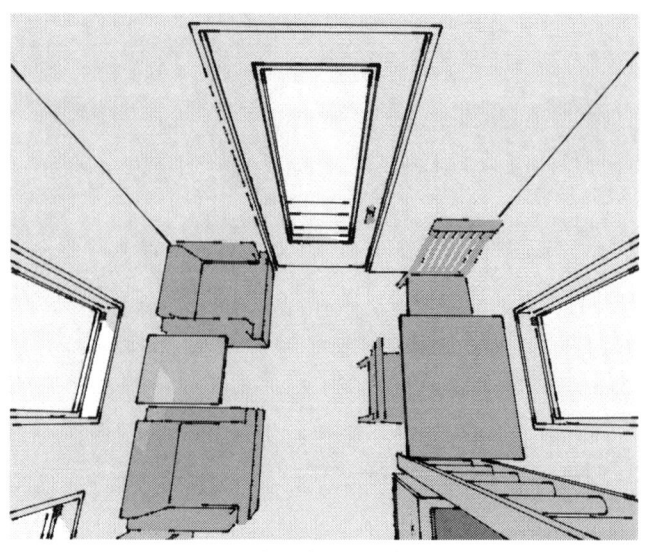

Kitchen   View from Loft

Tiny House 9 - Floor Plan & Exterior

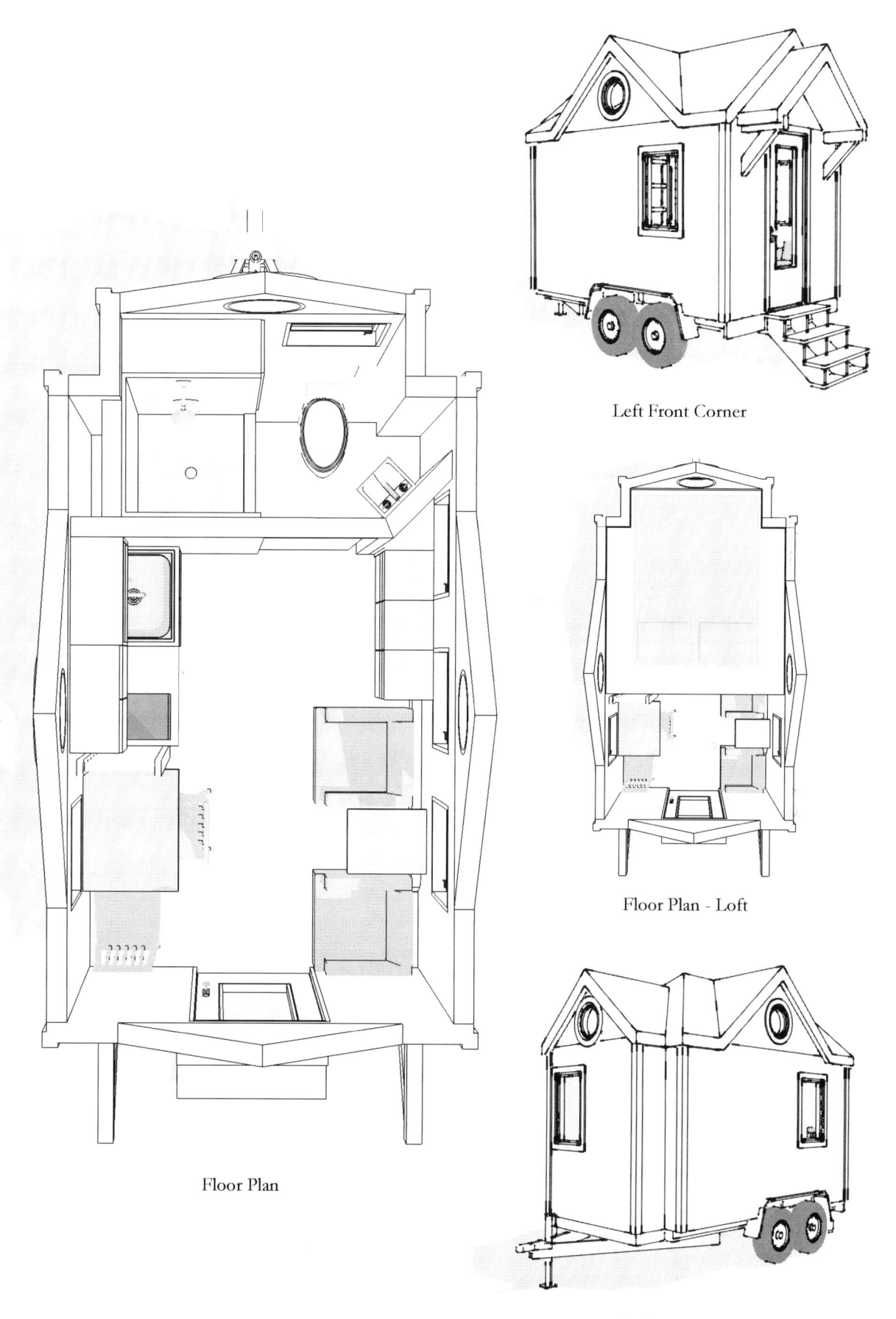

Left Front Corner

Floor Plan - Loft

Floor Plan

Back Left Corner

Tiny House 9 - Interior Views

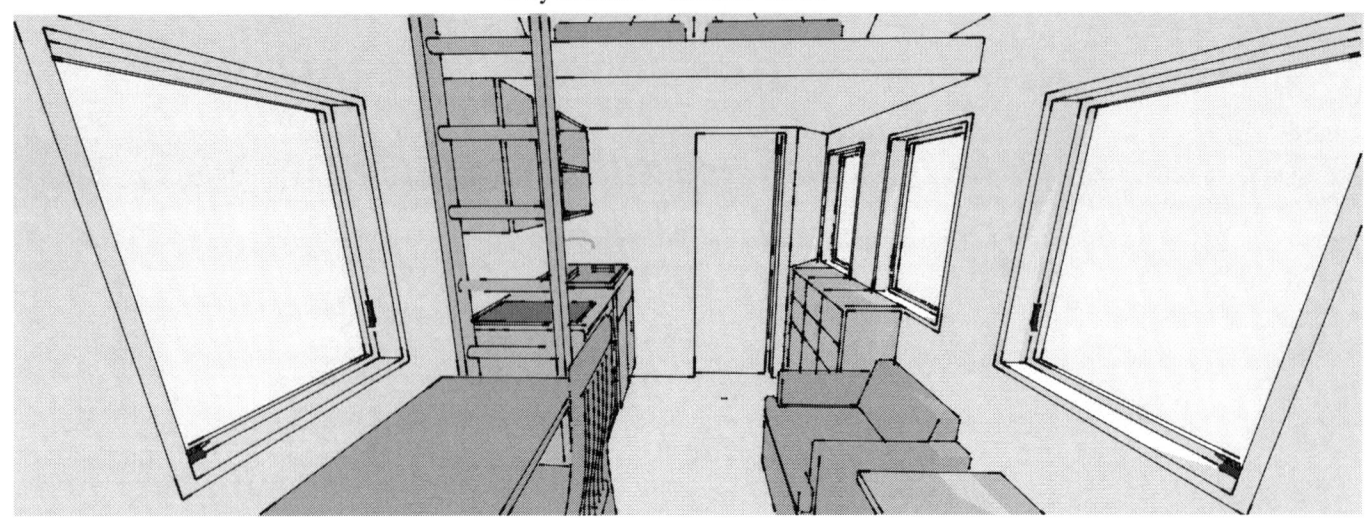

Interior from Entry

Interior from Kitchen

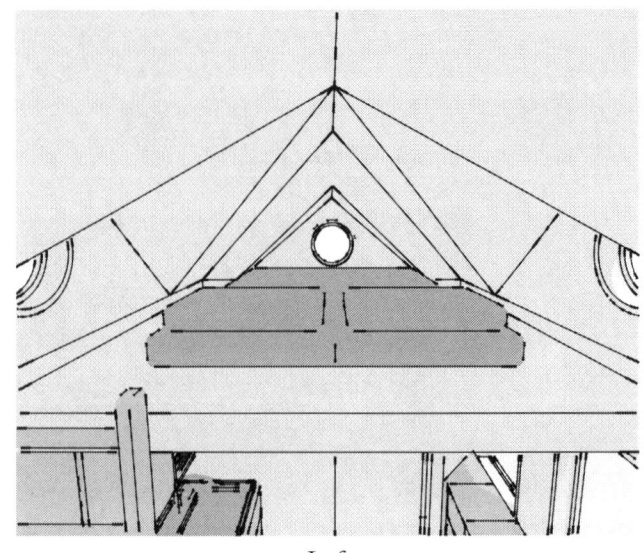

Loft

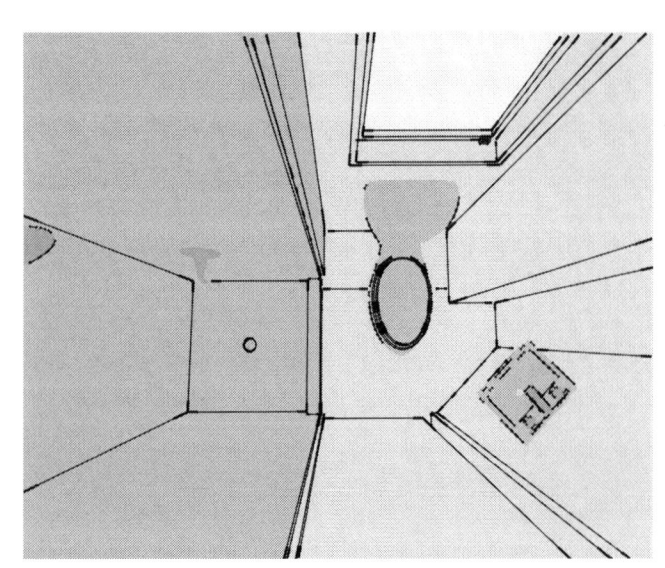

Bathroom

36

Tiny House 9 - Elevations

Right

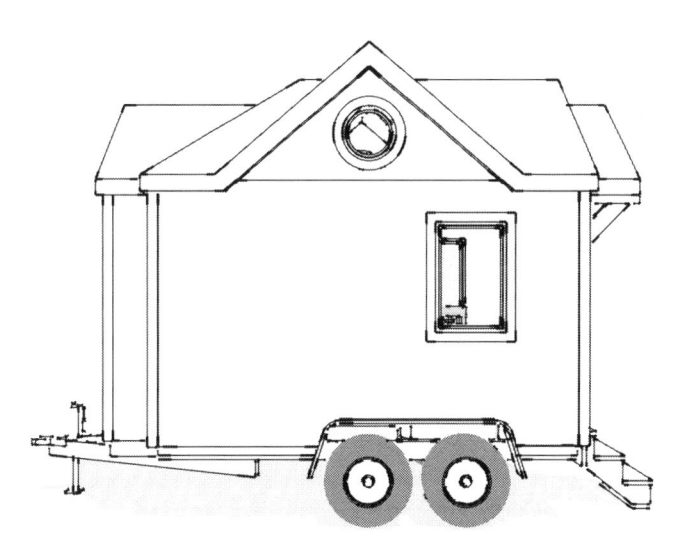

Left

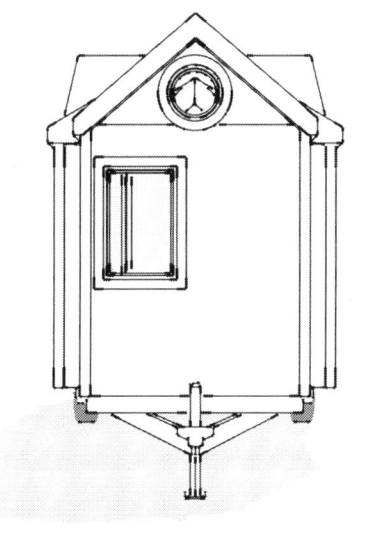

Back

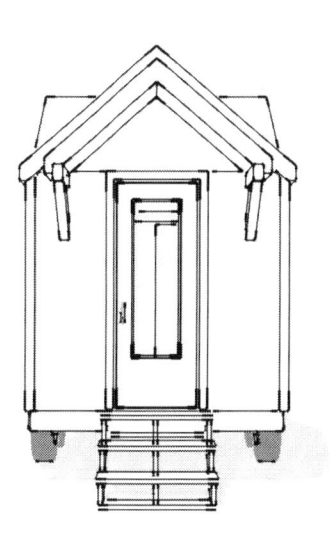

Front

#10

Tiny House #10 - Overview

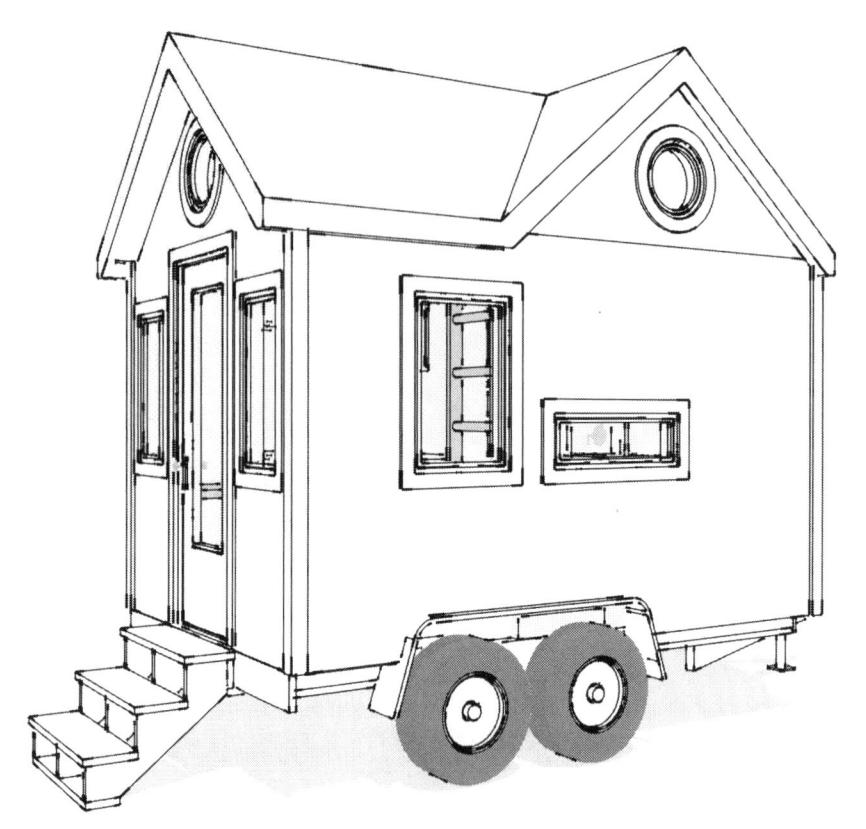

Front Right

Summary:

This one has a 10/12 cross gable roof with an aerodynamic profile on the trailer tongue side. The front entry has fold-up steps. Inside the house is a standard bathroom with a shower, toilet, and wall mounted tiny sink. The kitchen has a sink with cabinet drain rack above, small refrigerator, small cooktop, microwave, and storage. There's also a desk and chair in the front of the house. The loft has space for a queen bed under the cross gable. The loft is accessed by a movable ladder.

Features:

12-Foot Tiny House on Wheels
10/12 Cross Gable
Standard Bathroom
Small Loft
Fold-up Steps

Kitchen

View from Loft

Tiny House #10 - Floor Plan & Exterior

Left Front Corner

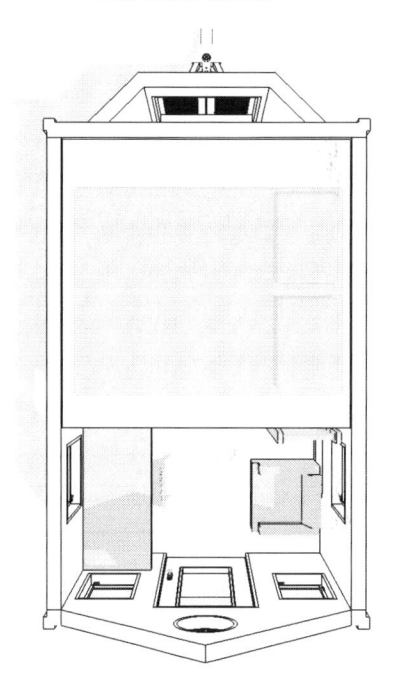

Floor Plan - Loft

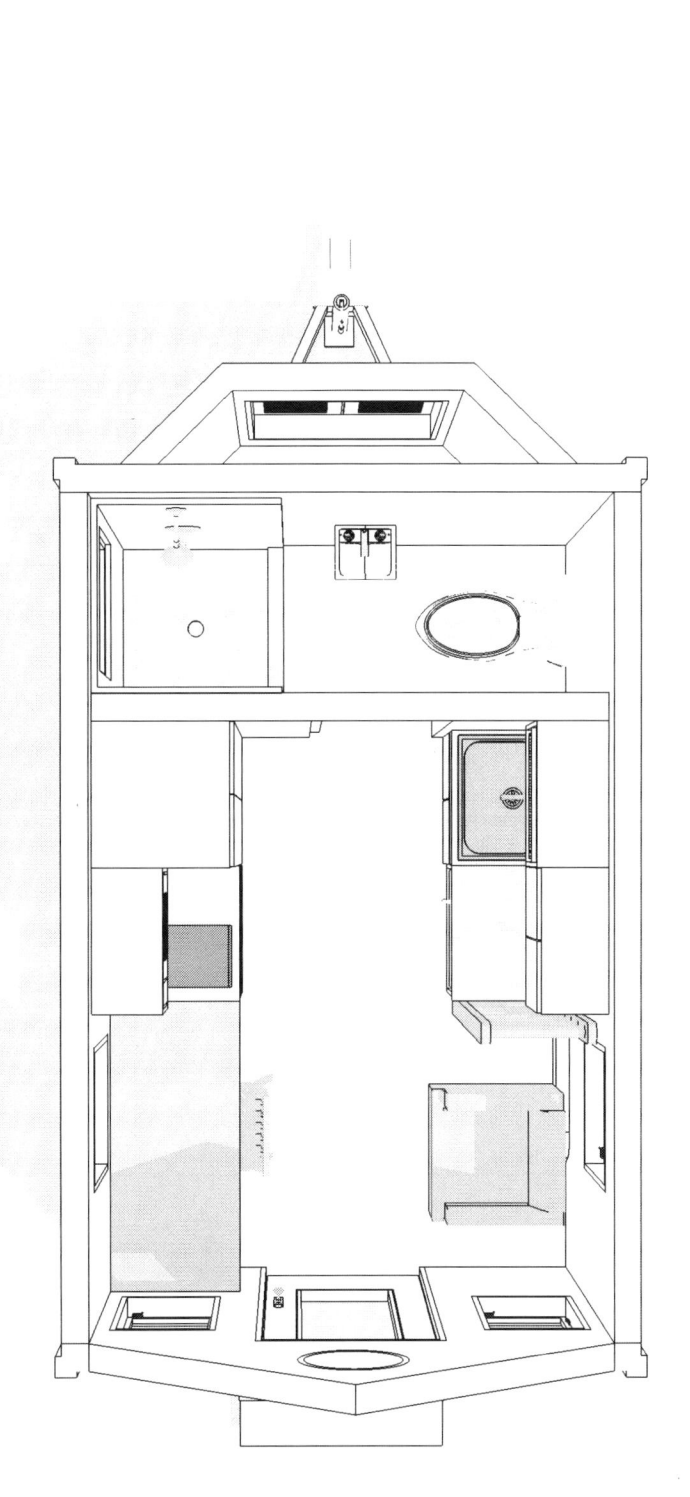

Floor Plan

Back Left Corner

Tiny House #10 - Interior Views

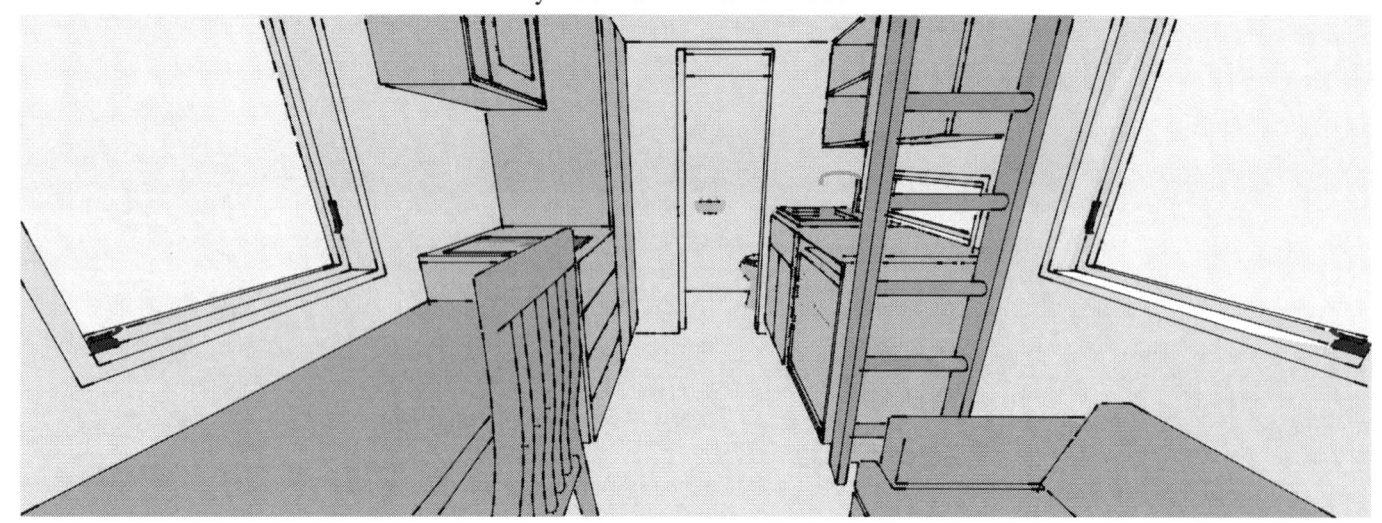

Interior from Entry

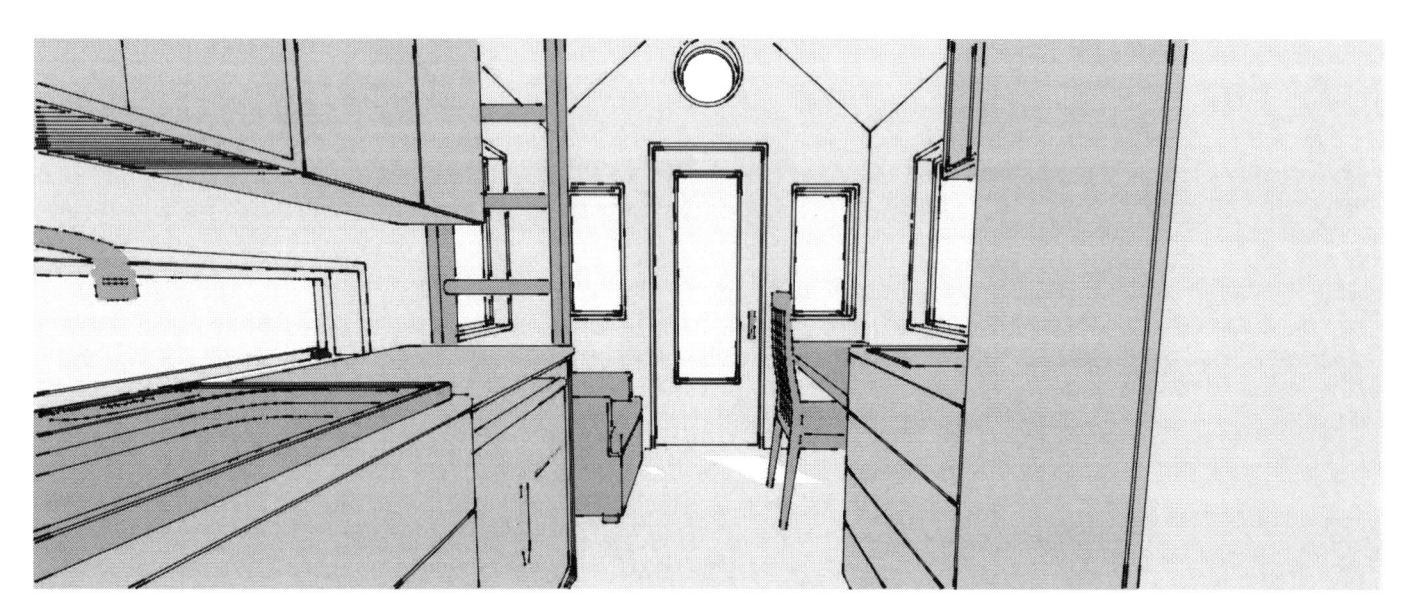

Interior from Kitchen

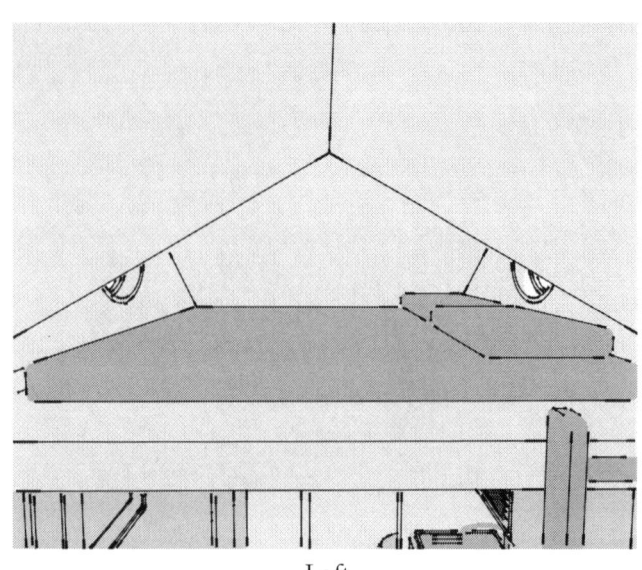

Loft

Bathroom

Tiny House #10 - Elevations

Right

Left

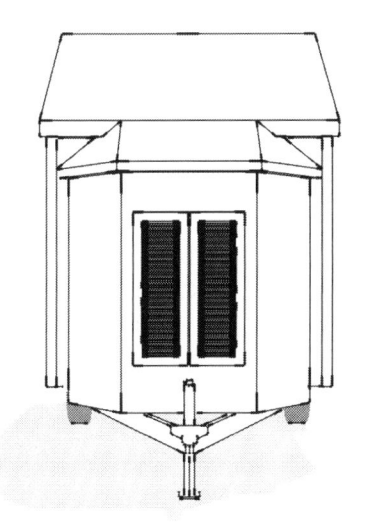

Back

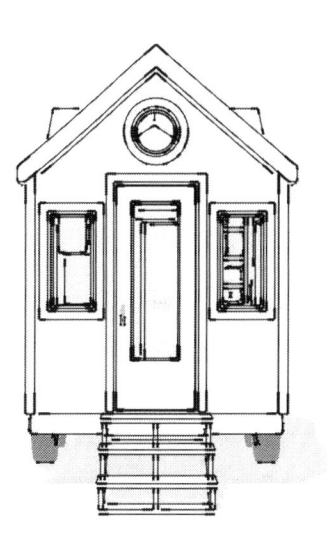

Front

41

#11

Tiny House #11 - Overview

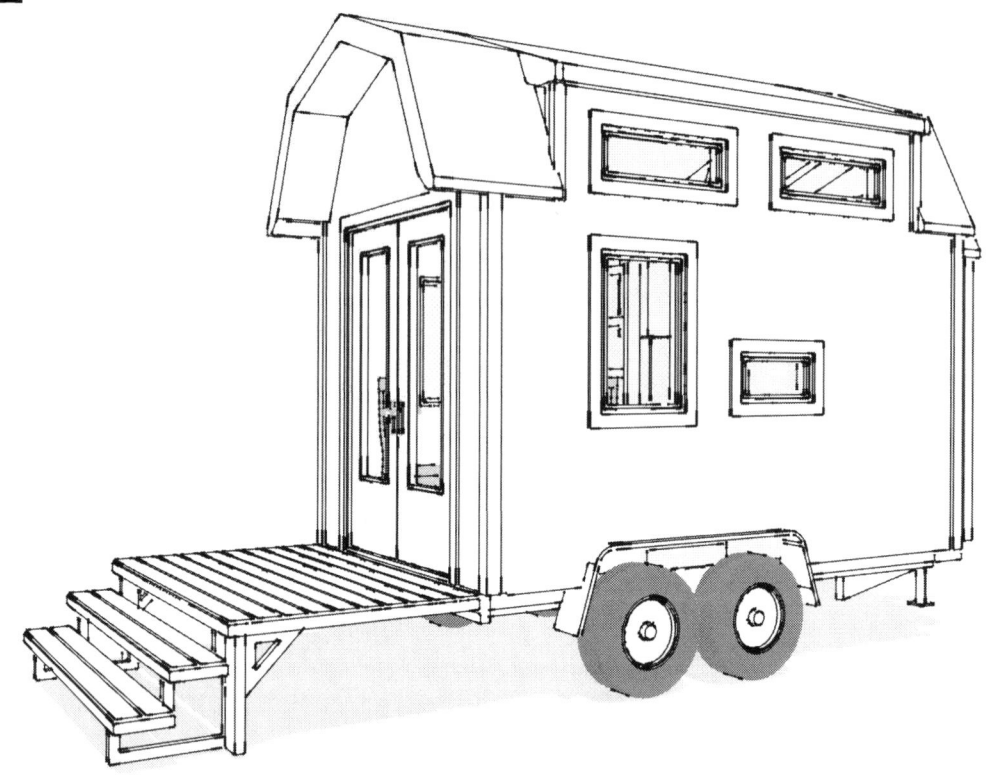

Front Right

Summary:

This tiny house has a gambrel roof with shed dormers that create a loft with an open feel. The front entry has french doors and a fold-up deck with steps. Inside the house is a generous bathroom with a narrow soaking tub/shower, toilet, and vanity. The tiny kitchen has a sink with cabinet drain rack above, small refrigerator, small cooktop, and storage. There's also a table for two and room for a small comfy chair. The loft has room for a queen bed and is accessed by a movable ladder.

Features:

12-Foot Tiny House on Wheels
Gambrel Roof with Shed Dormers
Generous Bathroom with Narrow
   Soaking Tub
Spacious Loft
Fold-up Deck and Steps

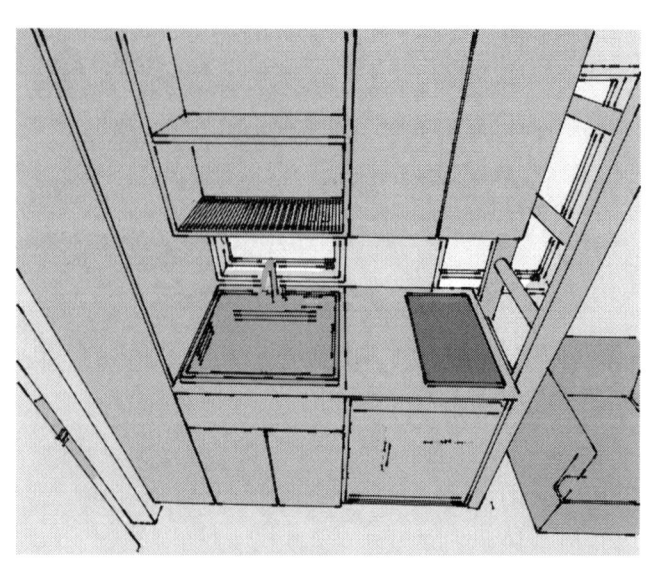

Kitchen

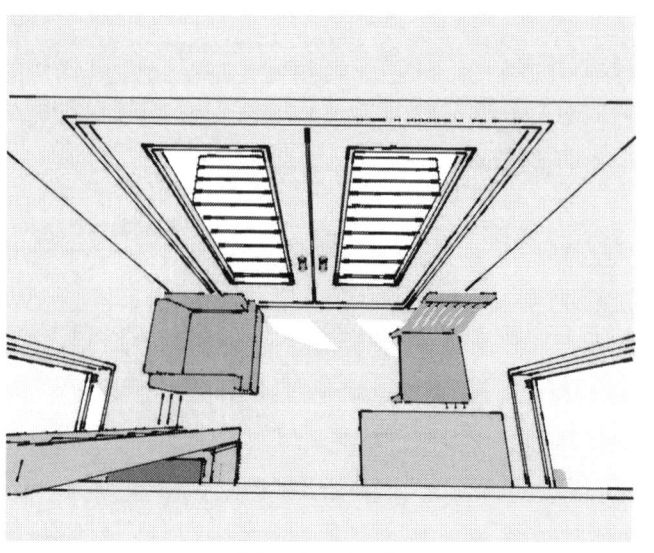

View from Loft

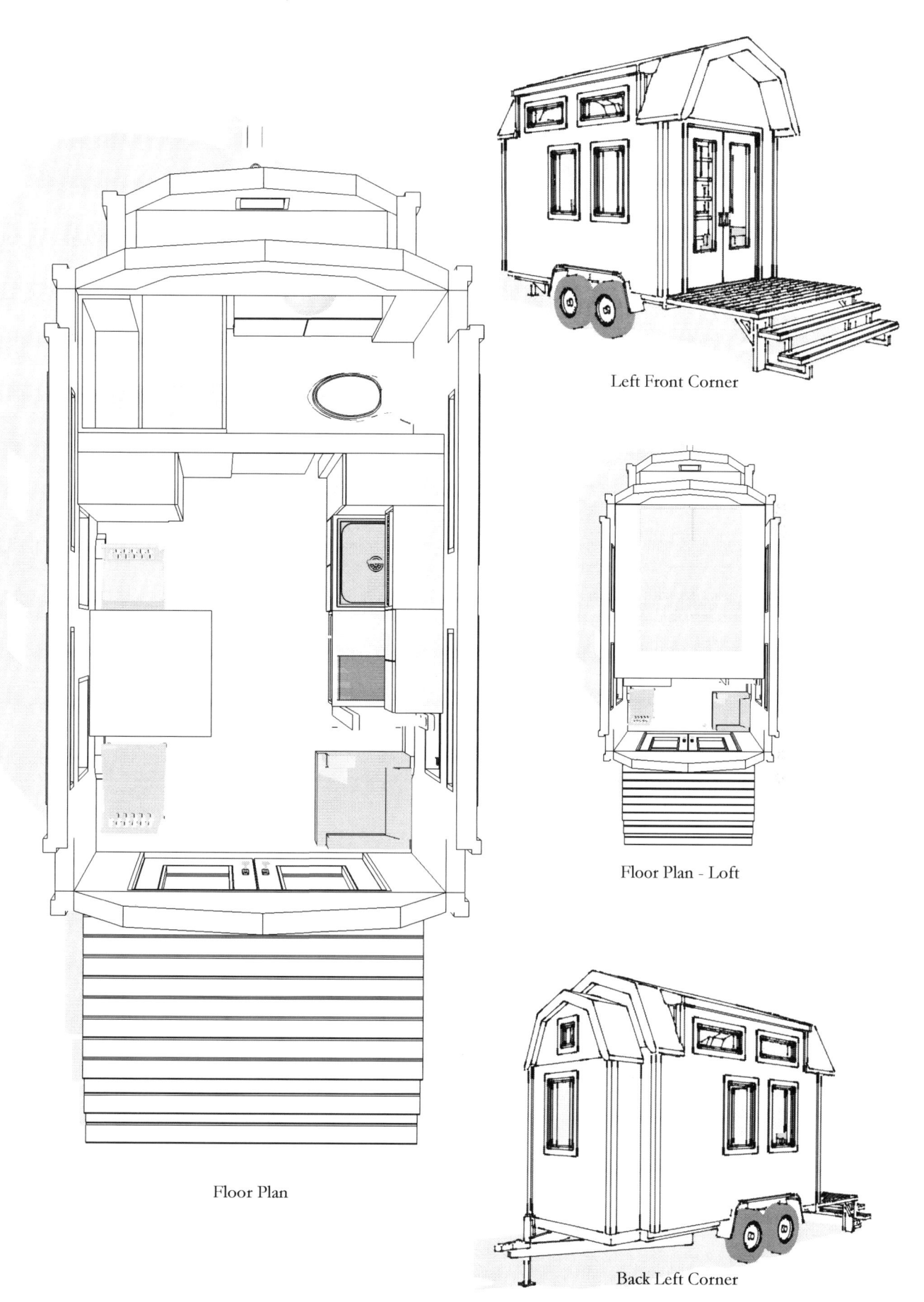

Tiny House #11 - Floor Plan & Exterior

Left Front Corner

Floor Plan - Loft

Floor Plan

Back Left Corner

Tiny House #11 - Interior Views

Interior from Front

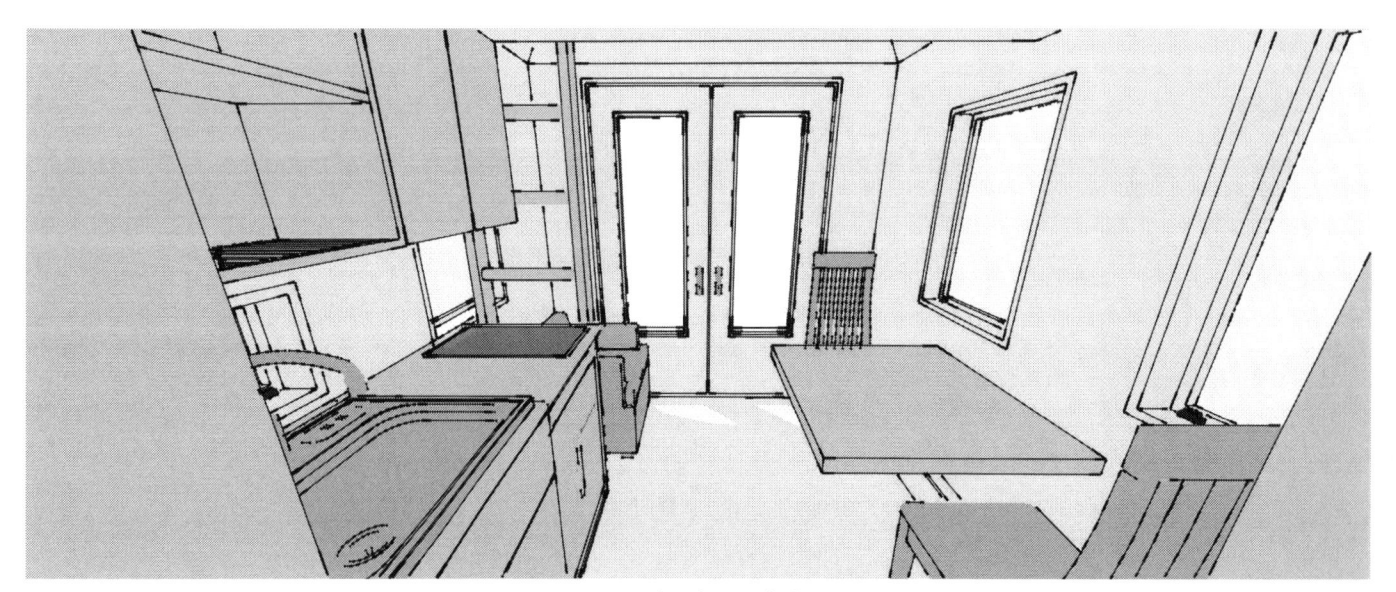

Interior from Kitchen

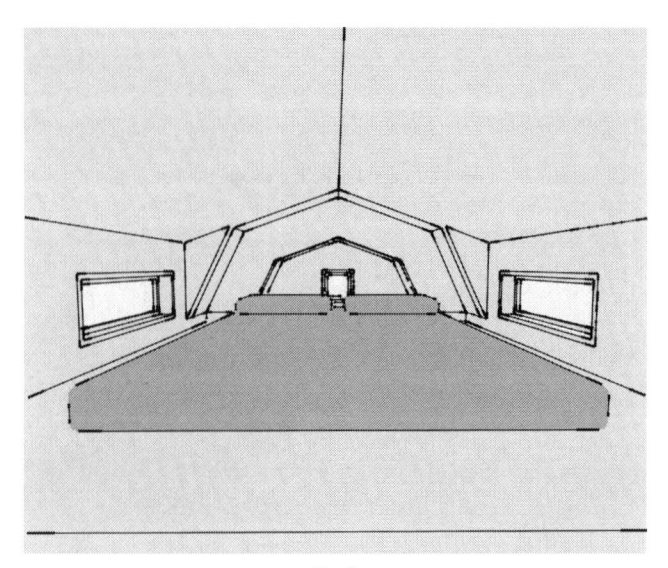

Loft

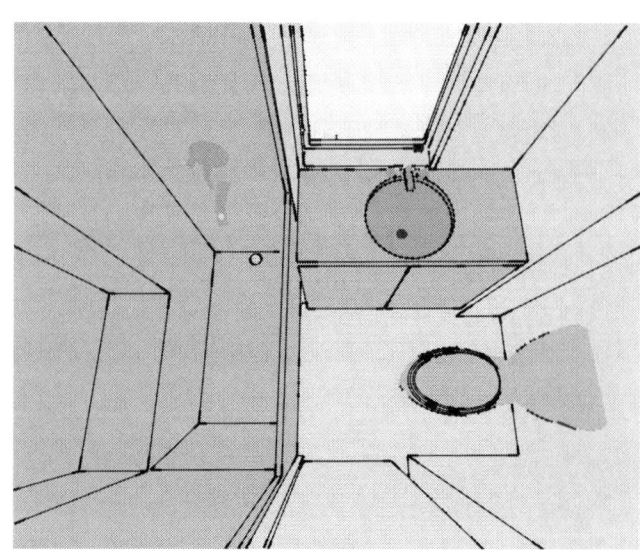

Bathroom

Tiny House #11 - Elevations

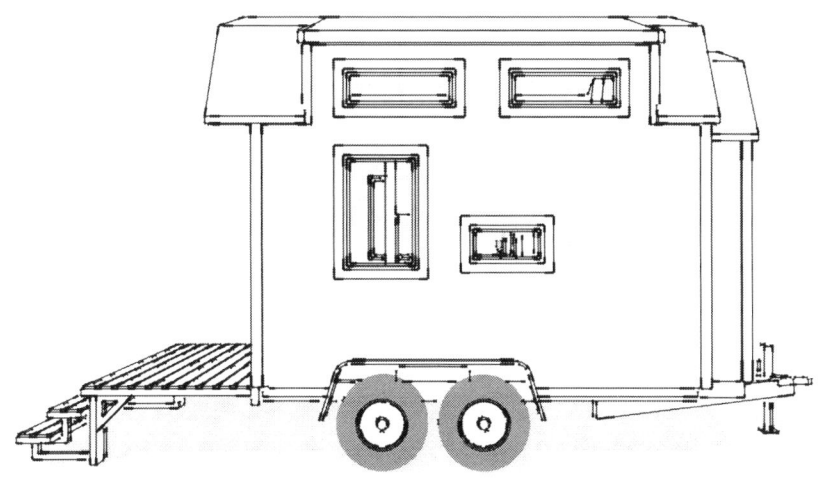

Right

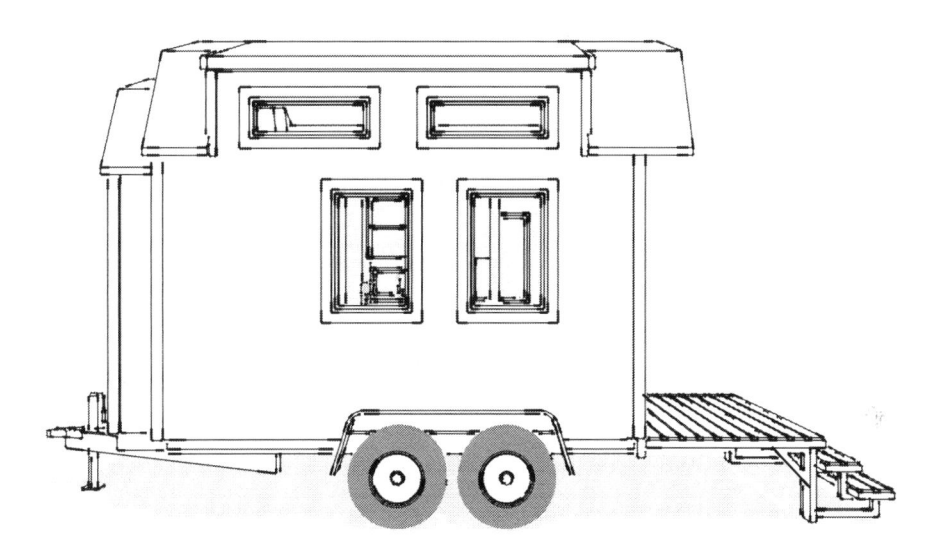

Left

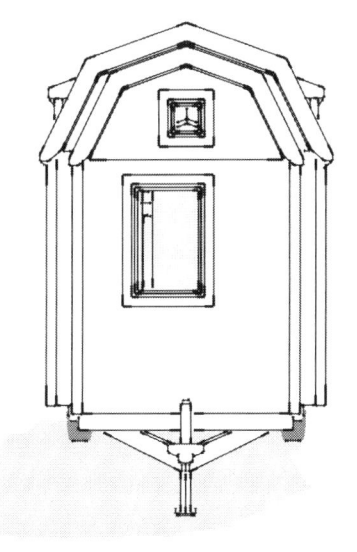

Back

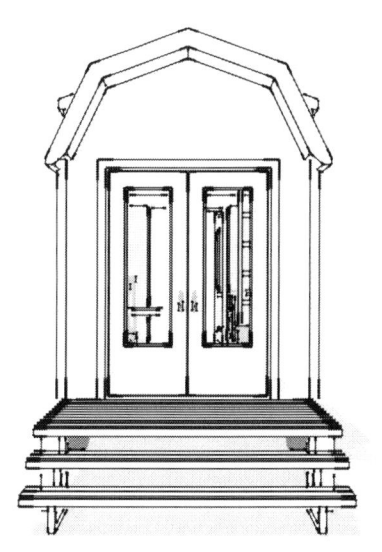

Front

#12

Tiny House #12 - Overview

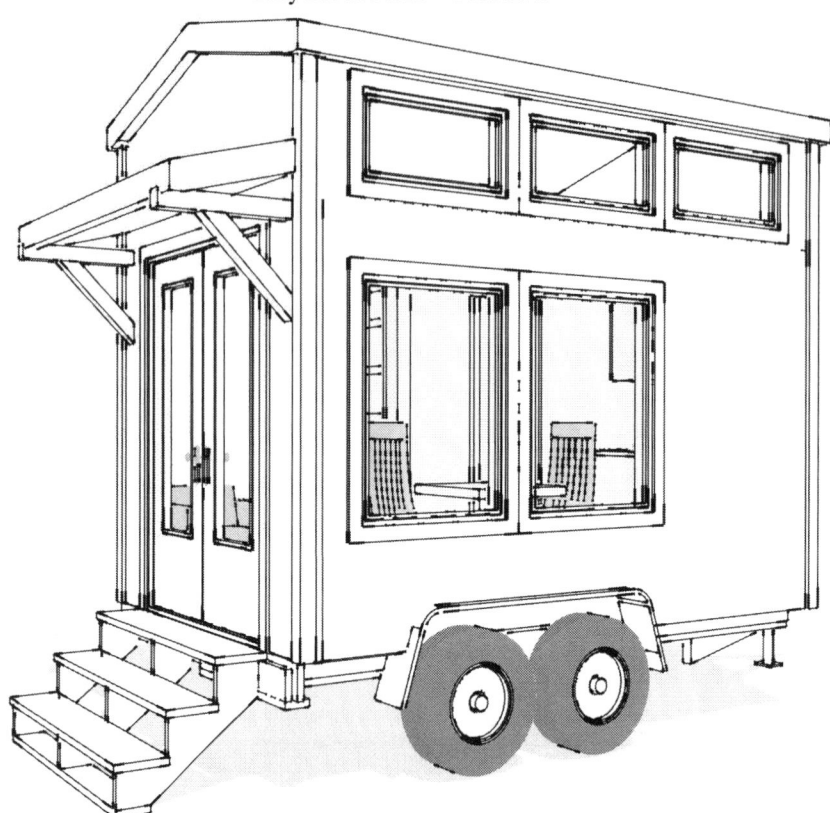

Front Right

Summary:

The 3/12 gable roof on this tiny house allows the walls to be very tall and create a very open loft. The front entry has french doors and a fold-up steps. Inside the house is a small bathroom with 32-inch shower, toilet, and wall mounted sink. The kitchen has ample counter space, a sink in the bay window extension over the trailer tongue, a small refrigerator, small cooktop, and ample storage. There's a table for two and two comfy chairs. The loft has space for a queen bed and is accessed by a movable ladder.

Features:

12-Foot Tiny House on Wheels
Tall 3/12 Gable Roof
Small Bathroom
Kitchen Extends into Bay Window
Spacious Loft
French Doors
Fold-up Steps

Kitchen

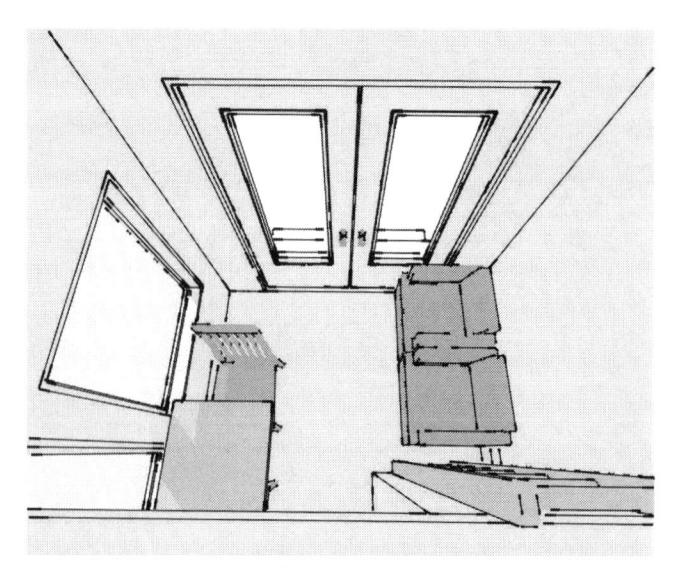

View from Loft

Tiny House #12 - Floor Plan & Exterior

Left Front Corner

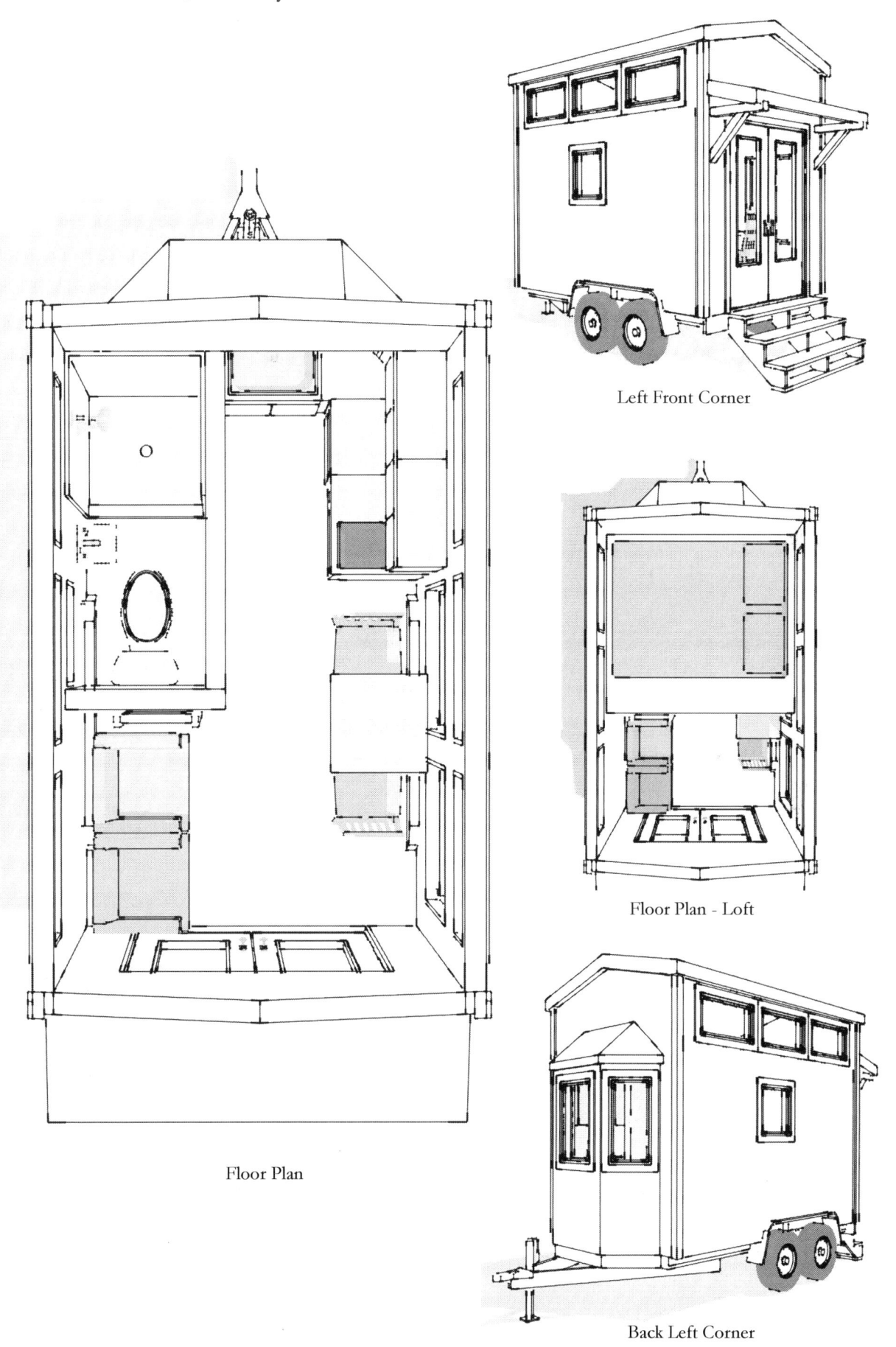

Floor Plan - Loft

Floor Plan

Back Left Corner

47

Tiny House #12 - Interior Views

Interior from Entry

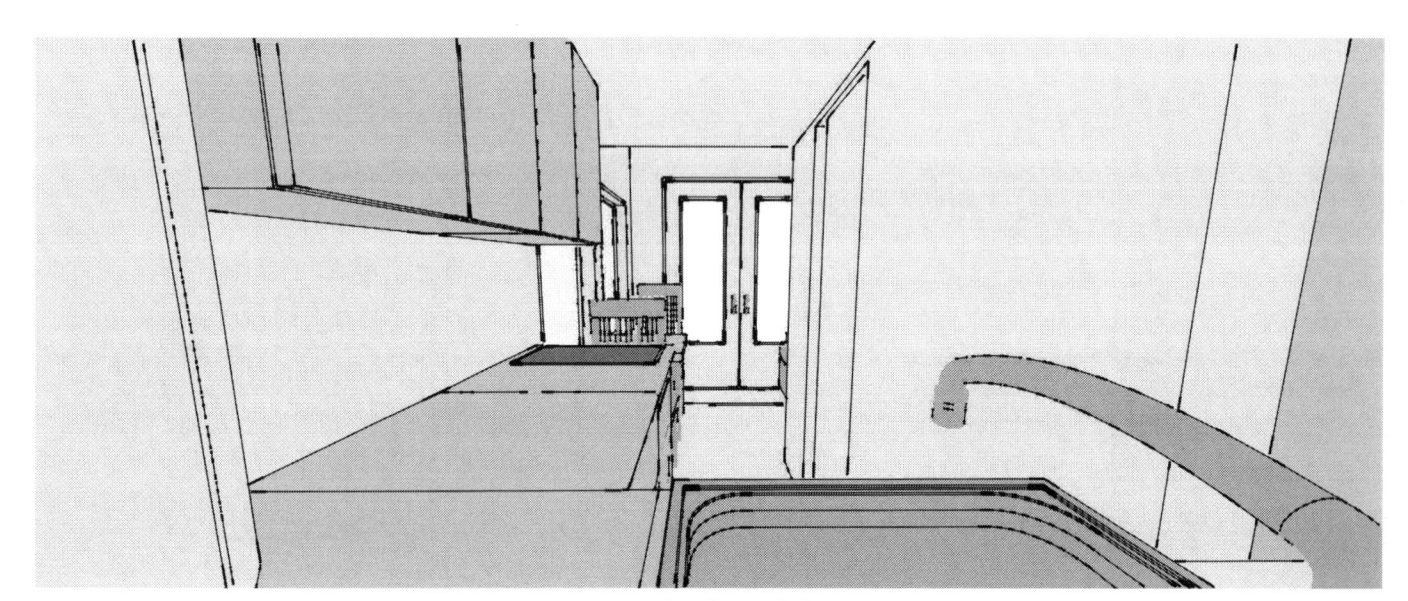

Interior from Kitchen

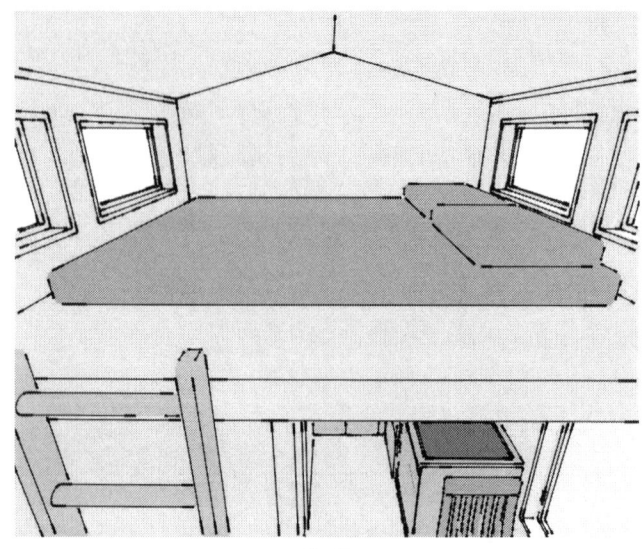

Loft

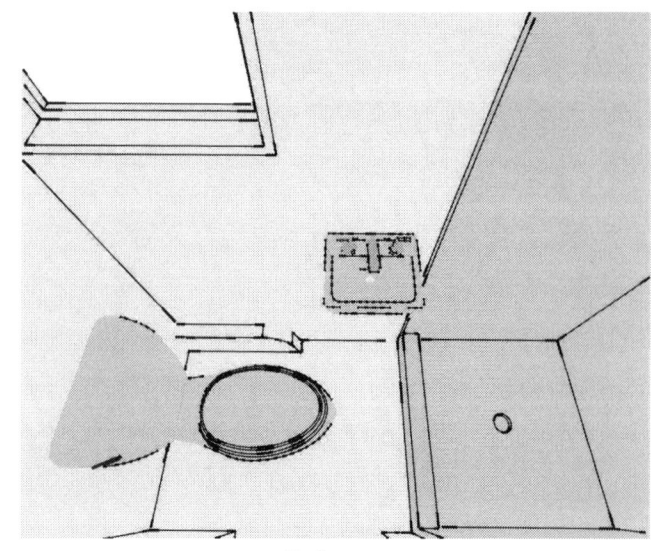

Bathroom

Tiny House #12 - Elevations

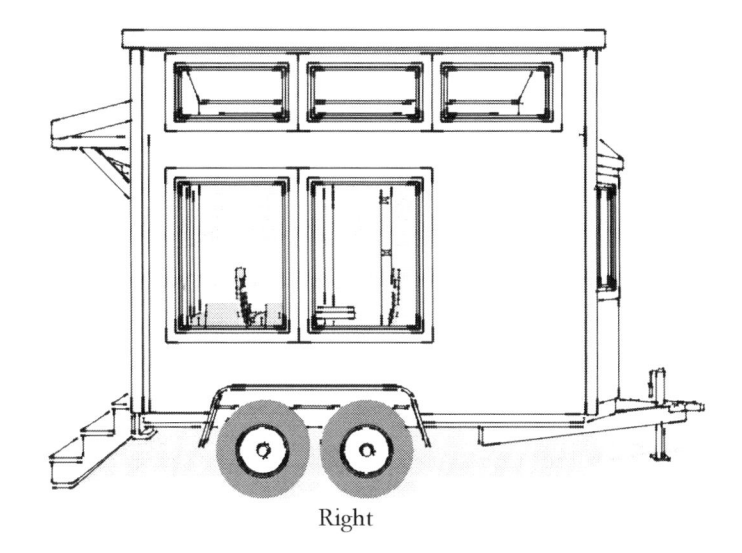

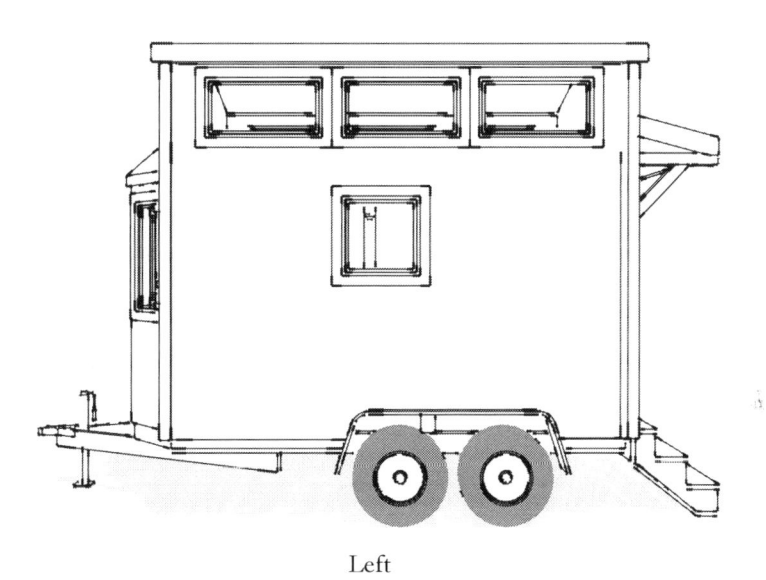

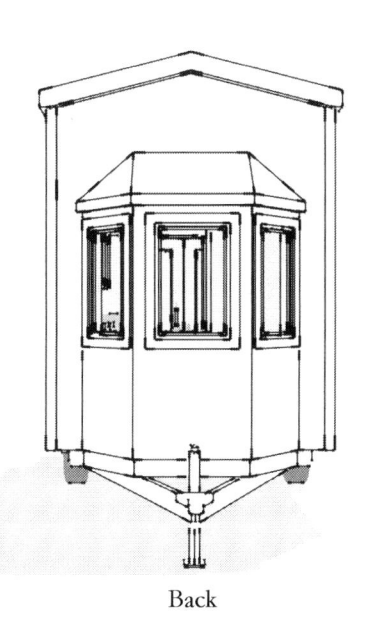

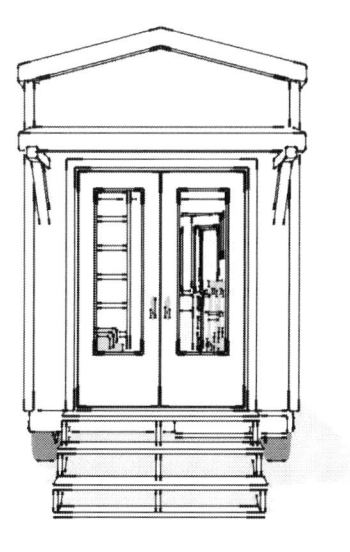

Right

Left

Back

Front

14-Foot Tiny House Designs

#13

Tiny House #13 - Overview

Front Right

Summary:

This tiny house has a 3/12 shed roof that provides the foundation for a contemporary design. The diagonal bump-out on the back adds space inside and helps build on that contemporary design appearance. Just inside the entry is a tiny kitchen with just the essentials: a sink, small refrigerator, and stovetop. The standard bathroom has a shower, toilet, and wall mounted sink. There's plenty of room for four comfy chairs in the living room. The loft has space for a queen bed and is accessed by a ladder rungs attached to the wall. Over the trailer tongue, next to the kitchen and bathroom, is a tiny mechanical closet for utility items.

Features:

14-Foot Tiny House on Wheels
3/12 Shed Roof
Standard Bathroom
Tiny Kitchen
Side Entry with Fold-up Ramp
Extensions on Front and Back

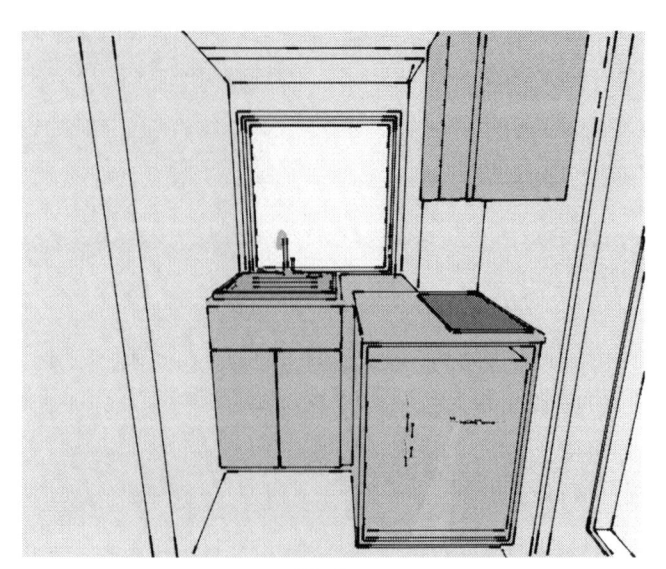

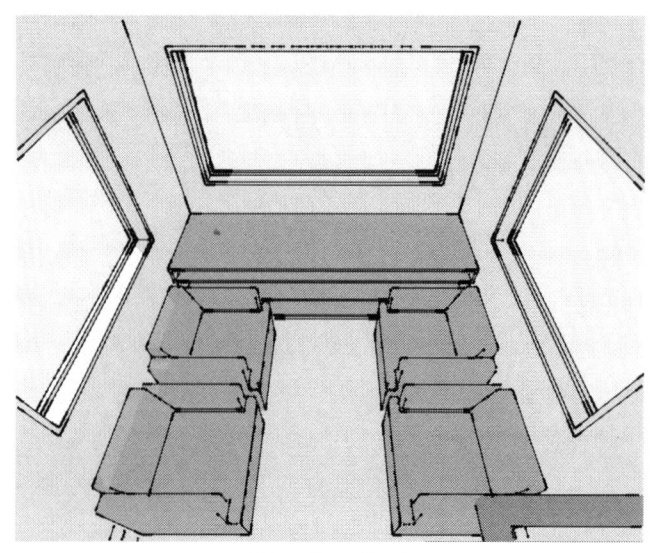

Kitchen

View from Loft

Tiny House #13 - Floor Plan & Exterior

Left Front Corner

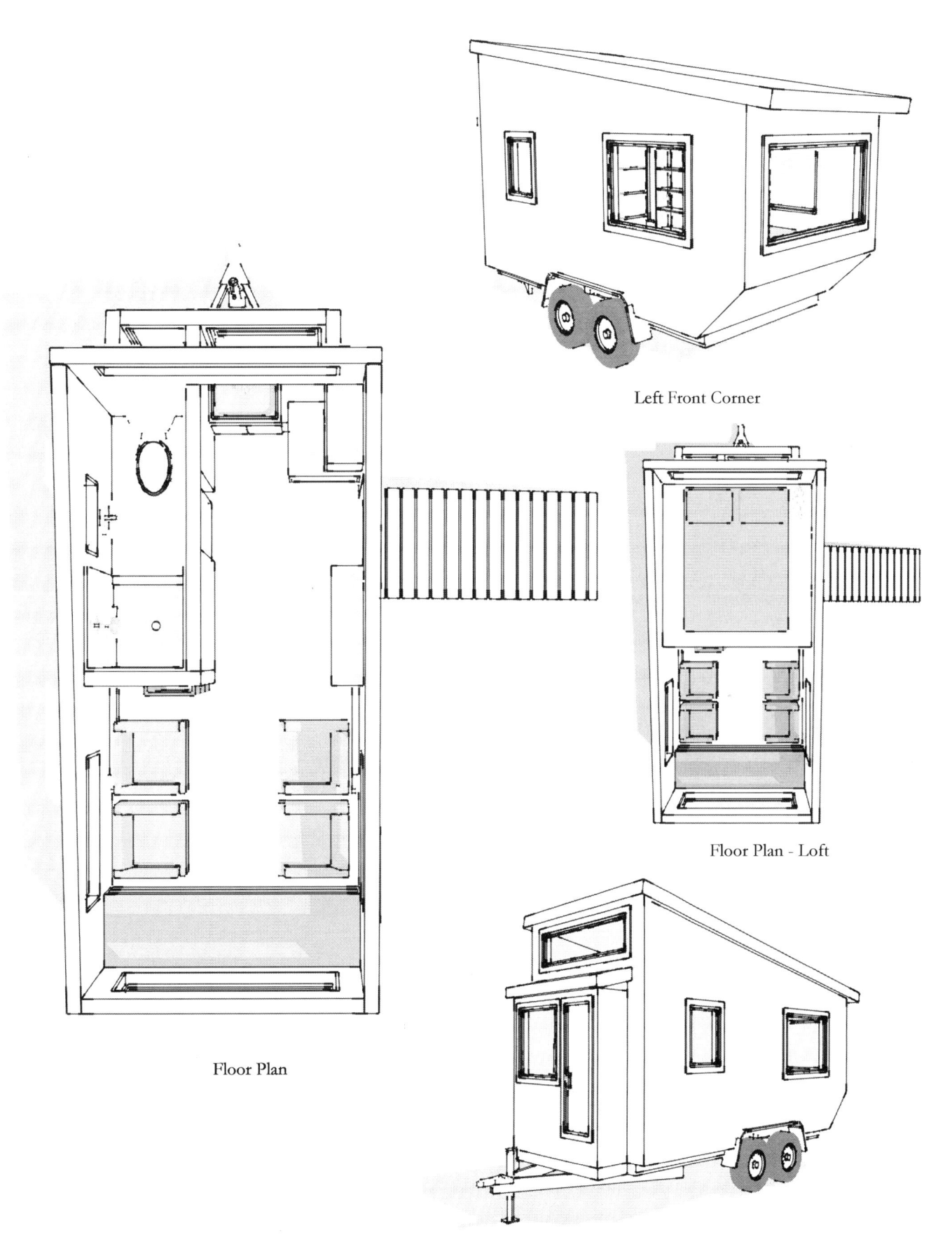

Floor Plan - Loft

Floor Plan

Back Left Corner

53

Tiny House #13 - Interior Views

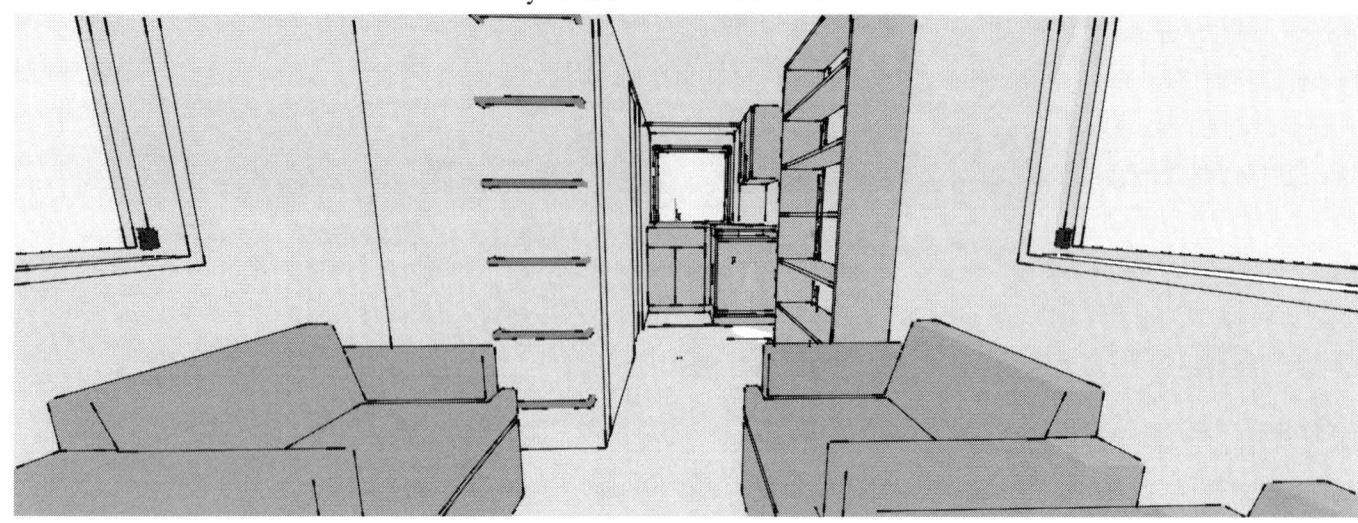

Interior from Living Room

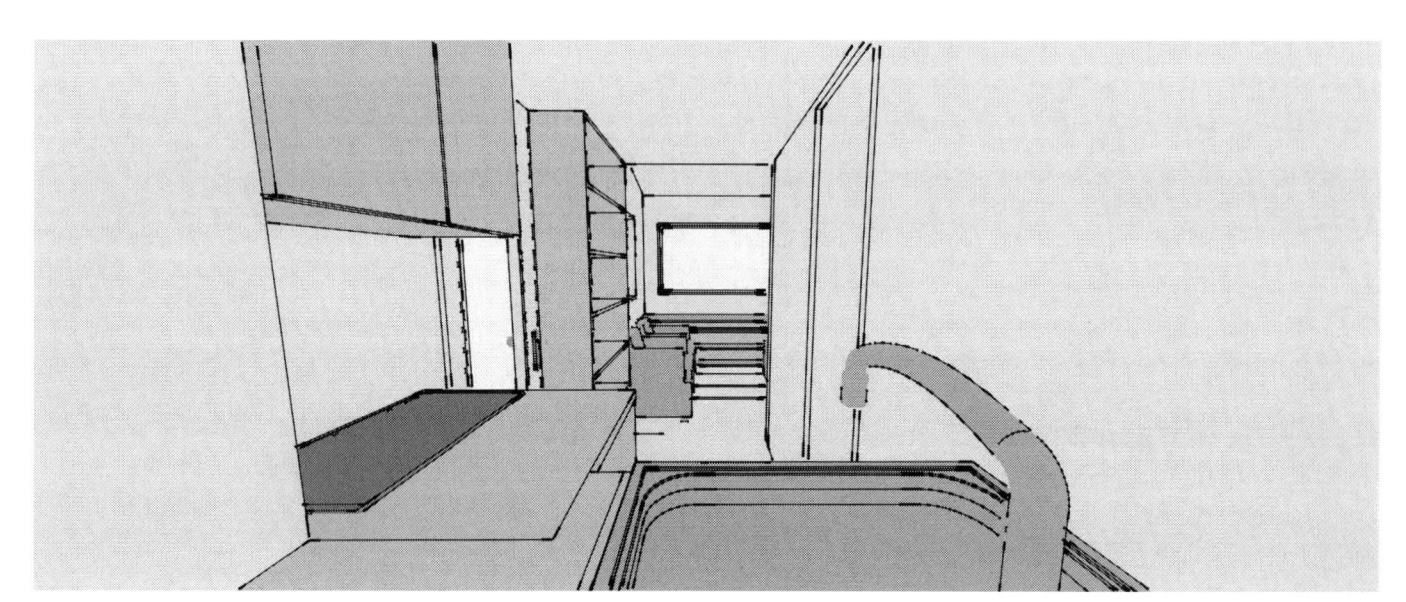

Interior from Kitchen

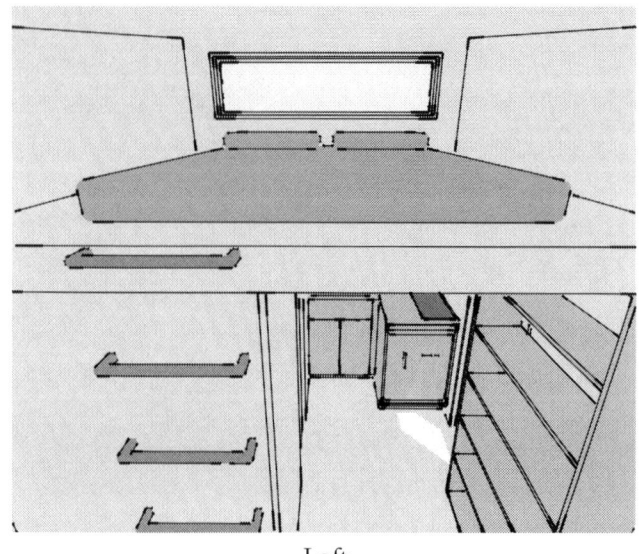

Loft

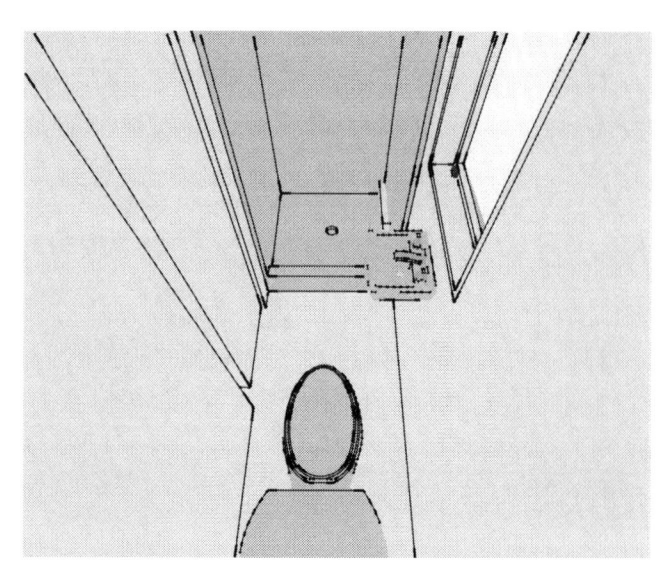

Bathroom

54

Tiny House #13 - Elevations

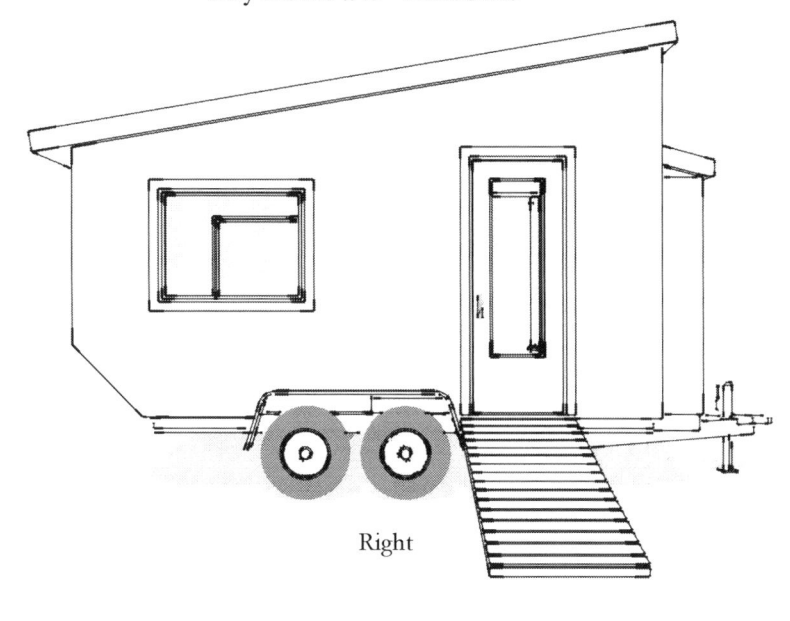

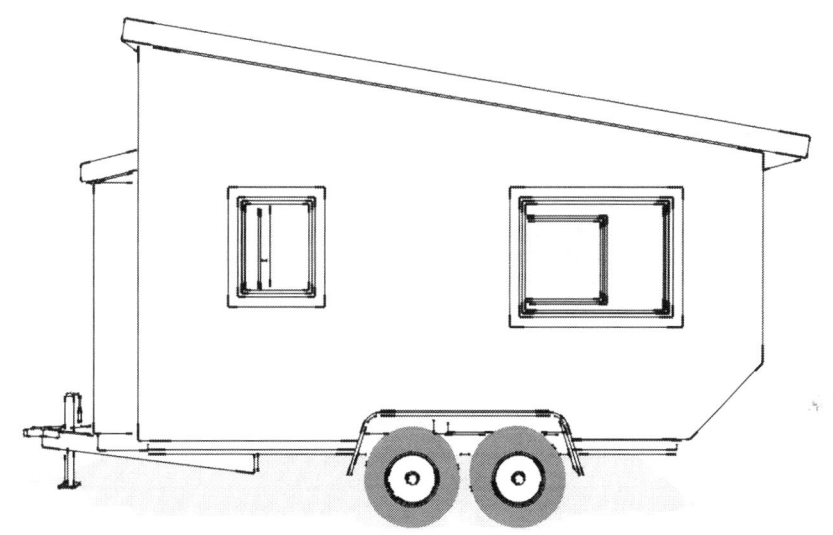

Right

Left

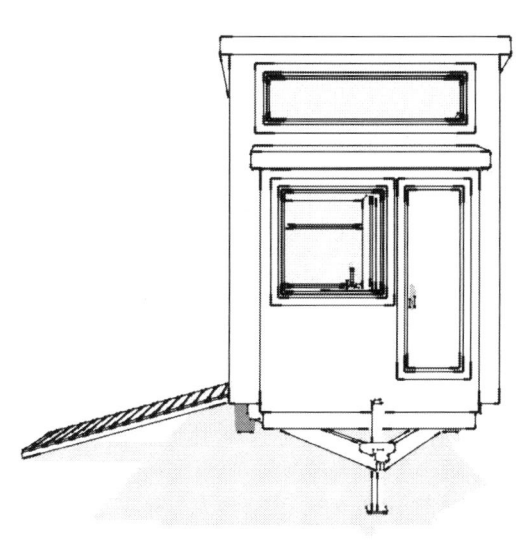

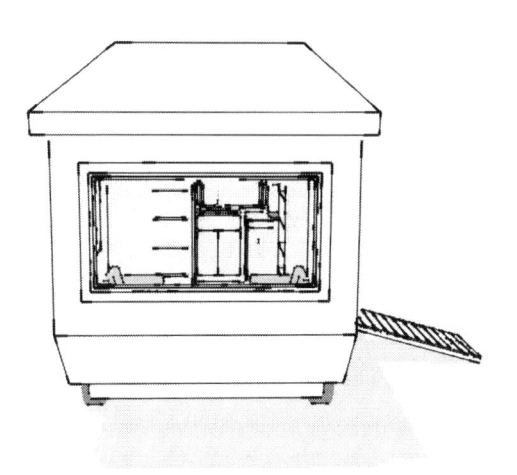

Back

Front

#14

Tiny House #14 - Overview

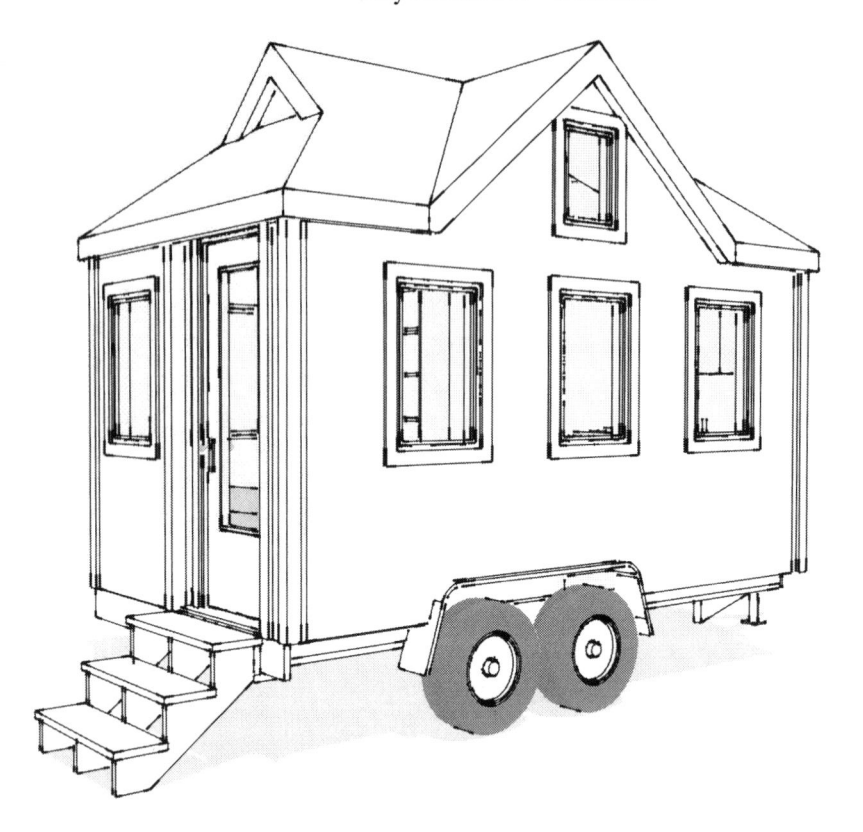

Front Right

Summary:

The cross gable roof with dutch gables over the front and back give this design a cozy cottage feel. The front entry has fold-up steps that lead into a small living room with two comfy chairs. The kitchen has a good amount of counter space and room for the essentials: a sink, small refrigerator, and stovetop. The small bathroom has a shower, toilet, and wall mounted sink. The loft has space for a queen bed and is accessed by a movable ladder. Over the trailer tongue is a mechanical closet for utility items that has an aerodynamic profile.

Features:

14-Foot Tiny House on Wheels
10/12 Dutch Cross Gable
Small Bathroom
Ample Kitchen
Front Entry with Fold-up Steps
Trailer Tongue Extension with Utility Closet

Kitchen

View from Loft

Tiny House #14 - Floor Plan & Exterior

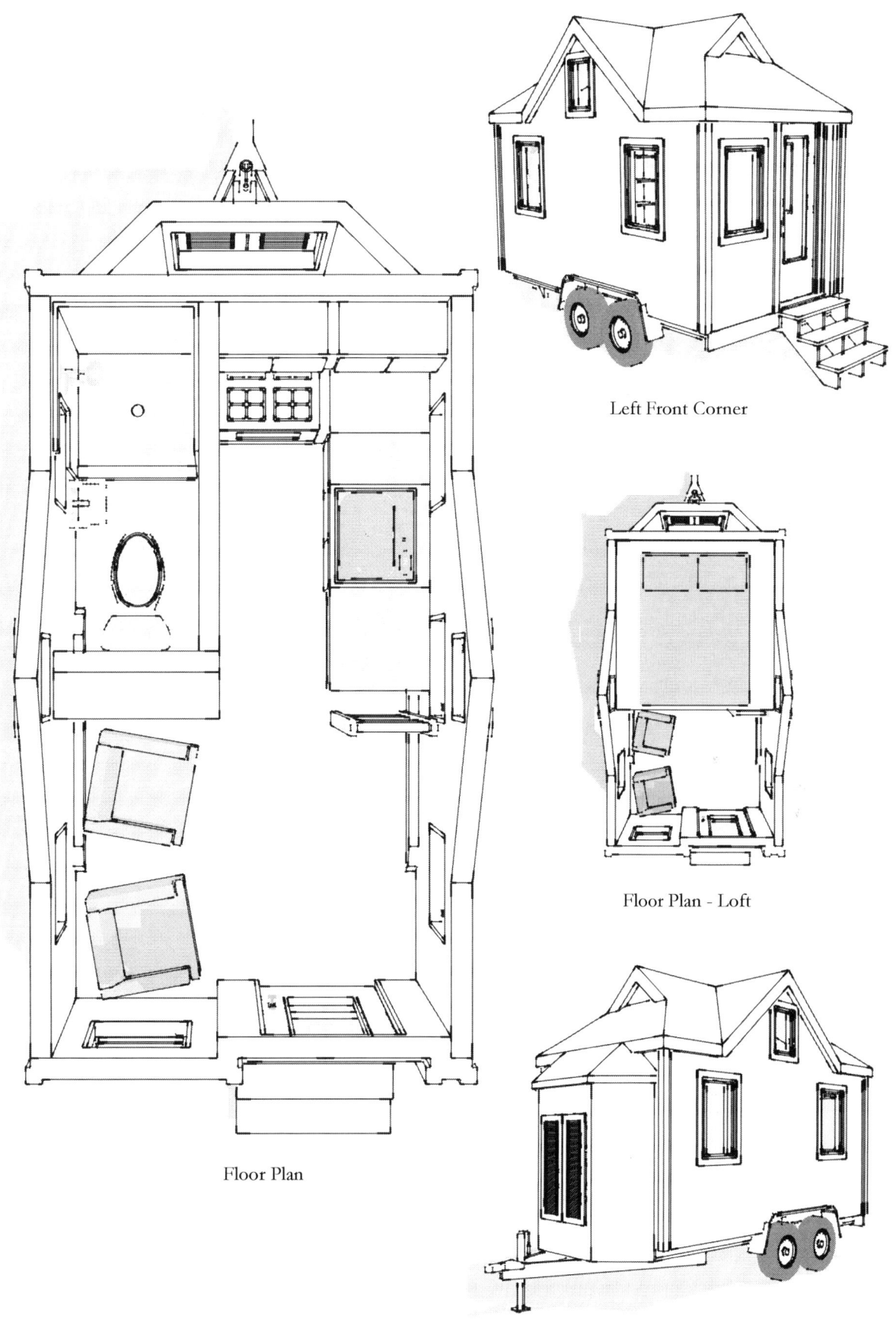

Left Front Corner

Floor Plan - Loft

Floor Plan

Back Left Corner

57

Tiny House #14 - Interior Views

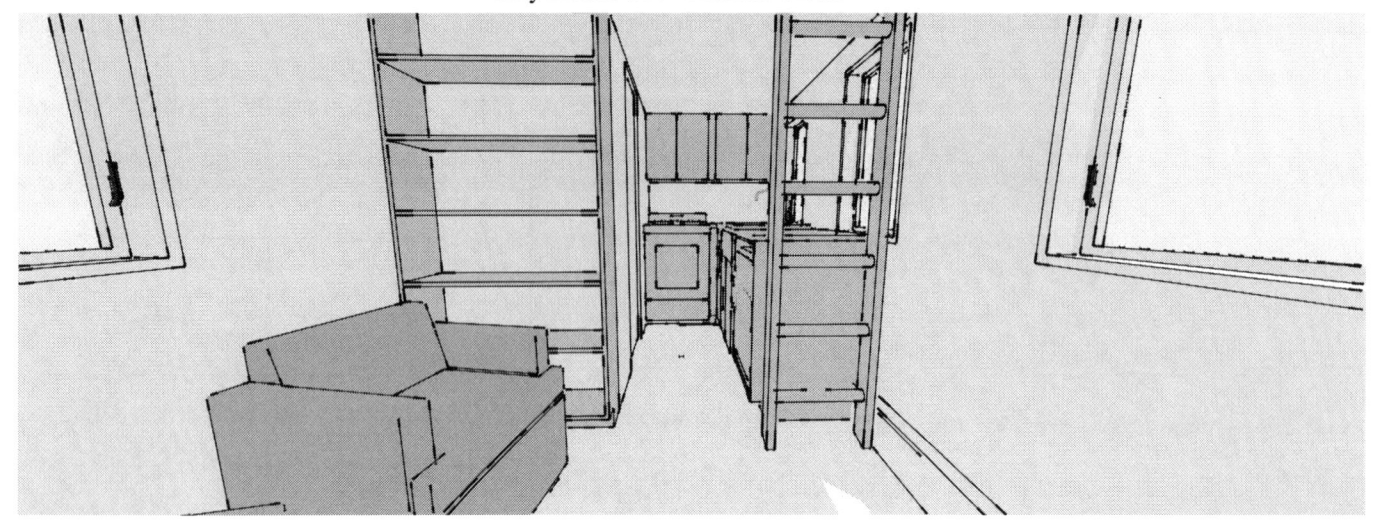

Interior from Entry

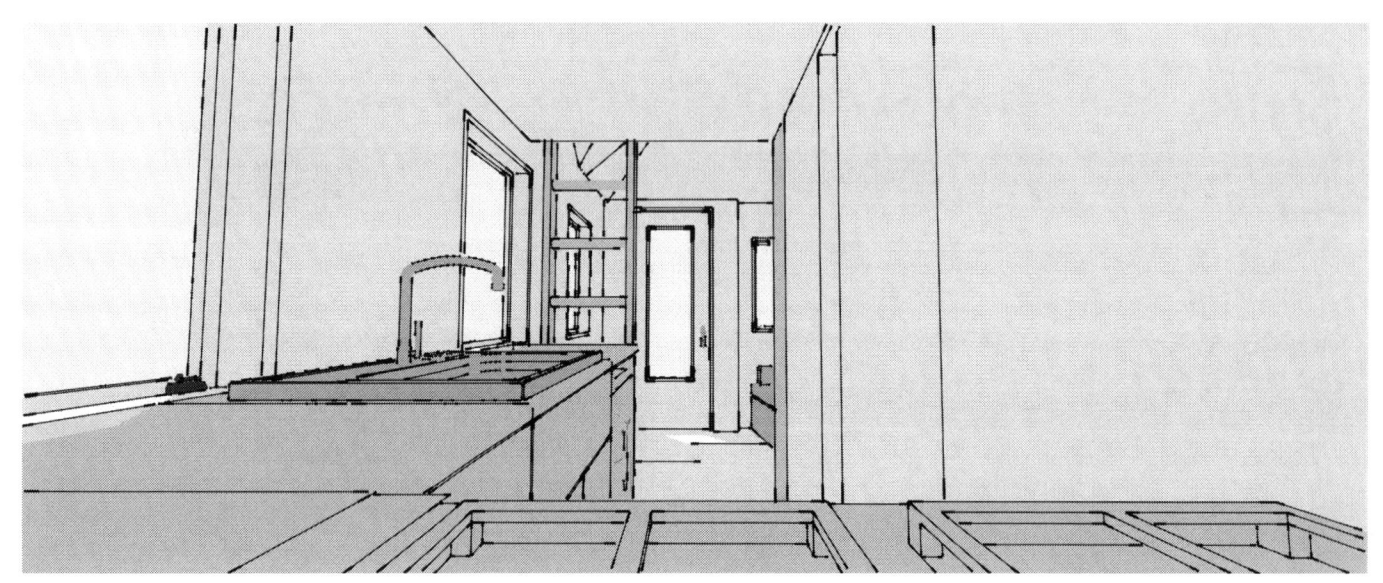

Interior from Kitchen

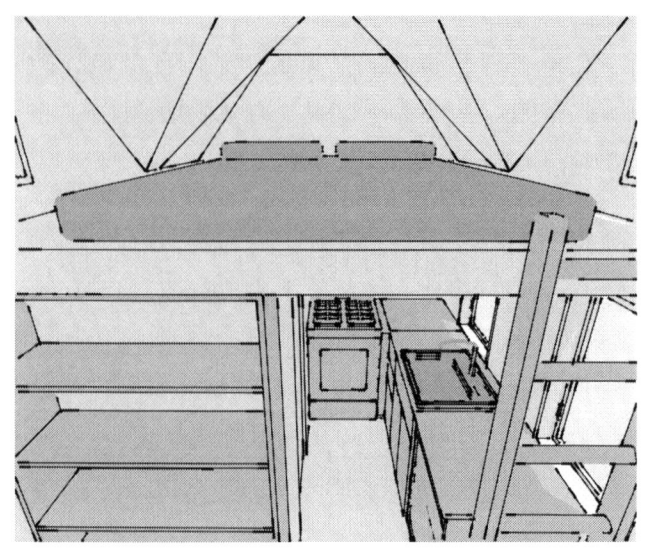

Loft

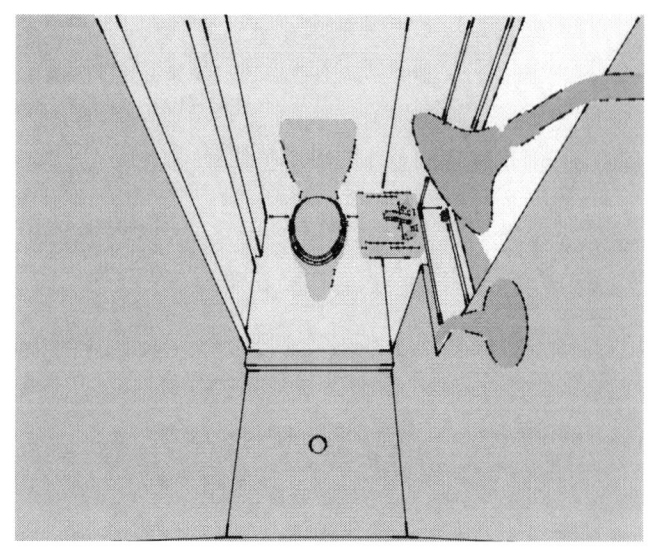

Bathroom

Tiny House #14 - Elevations

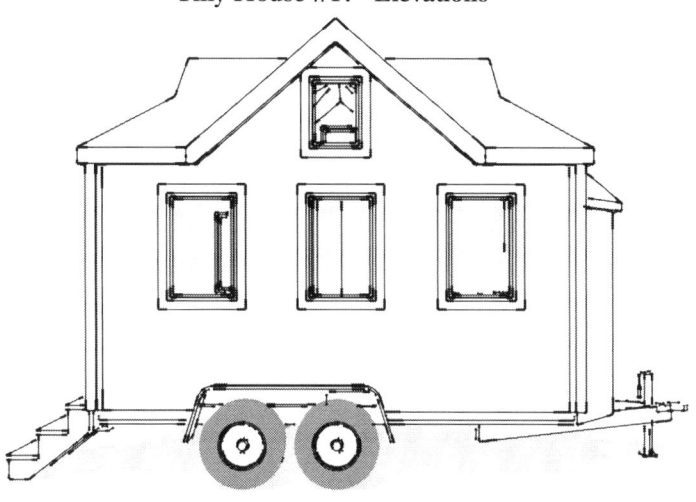

Right

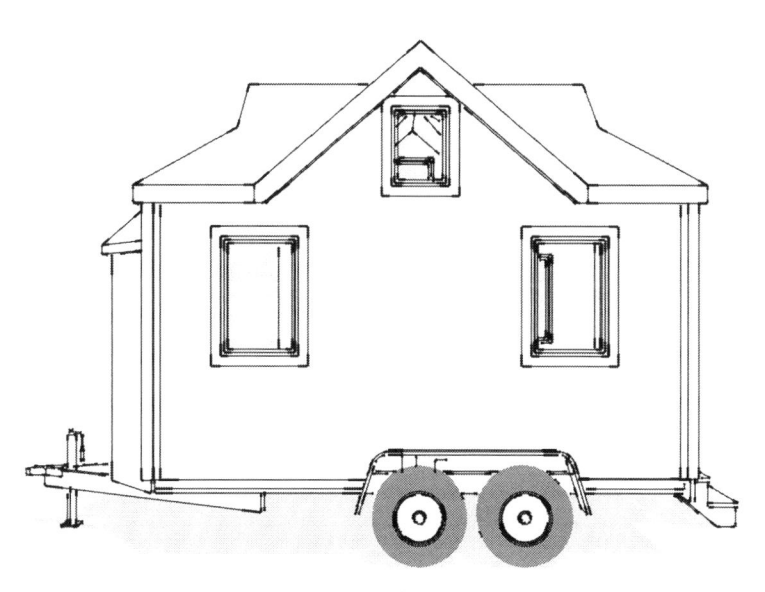

Left

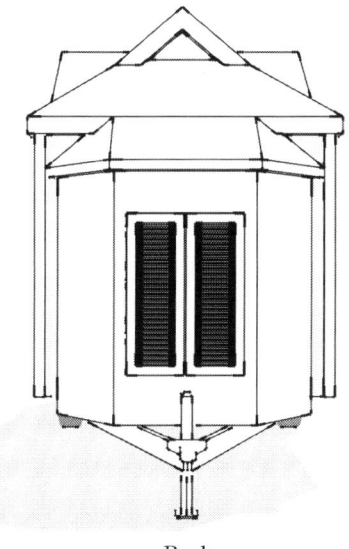

Back

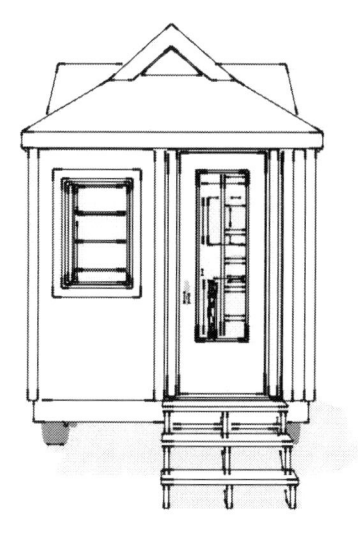

Front

59

#15

Tiny House #15 - Overview

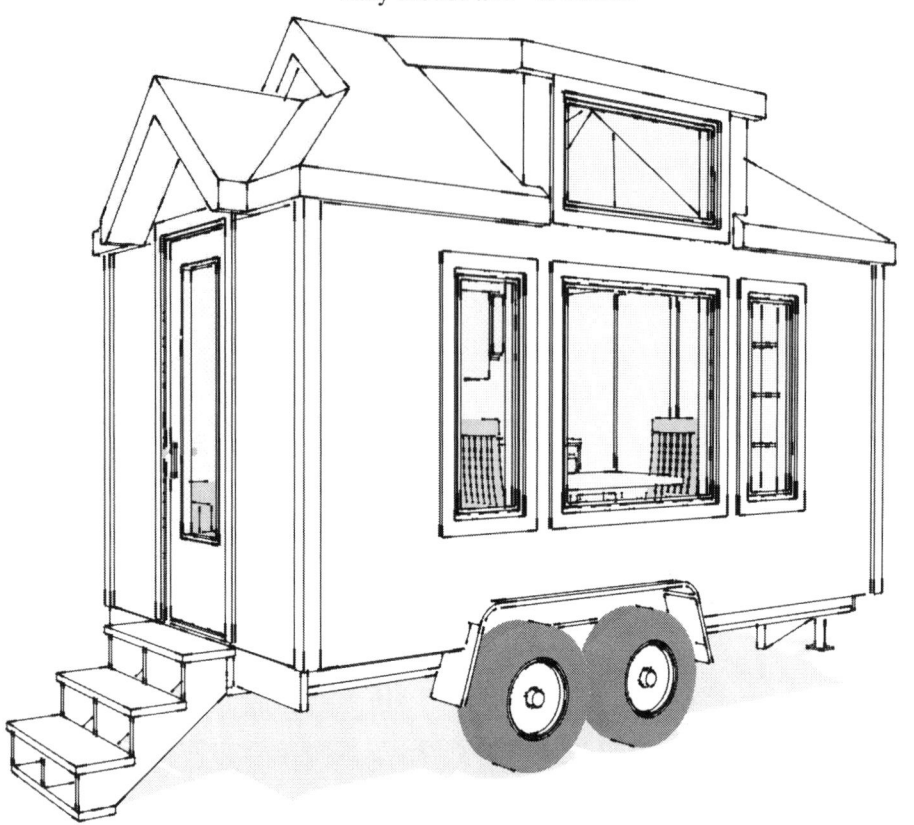

Front Right

Summary:

This house is similar to #14 with some notable differences. It has a 10/12 Dutch gable roof with shed dormers and a gable roof extension over the centered front door. The kitchen has a sink with cabinet drying rack above, a small refrigerator, stovetop, and microwave. The small bathroom has a shower, toilet, wall mounted sink, and a small cabinet behind the toilet. The loft has space for a queen bed and is accessed by ladder rungs attached to a floor-to-ceiling cabinet. Over the trailer tongue is a mechanical closet for utility items. The trailer tongue side of the house has an aerodynamic profile.

Features:

14-Foot Tiny House on Wheels
10/12 Dutch Gable with Shed Dormers
Small Bathroom
Small Kitchen
Front Entry with Fold-up Steps
Trailer Tongue Extension with Utility Closet

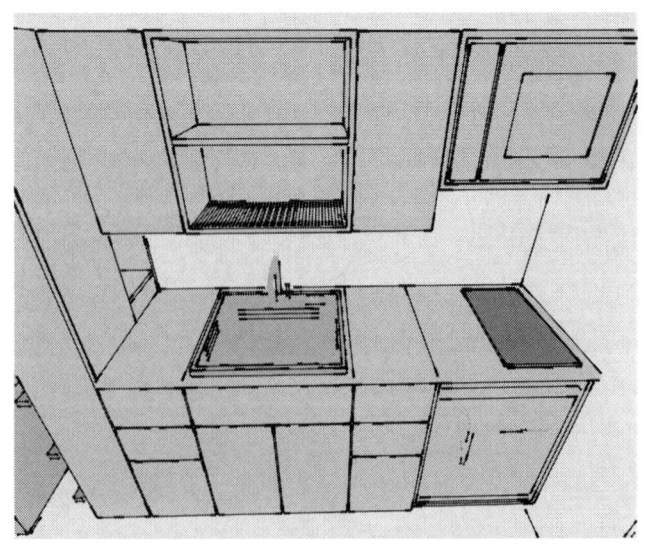

Kitchen

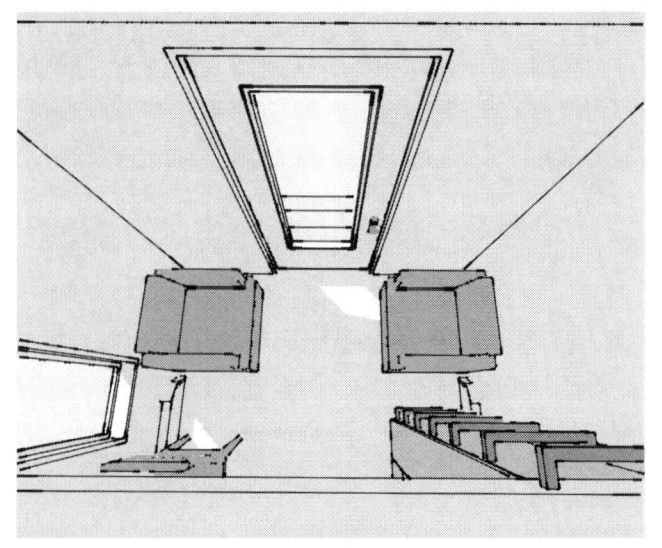

View from Loft

Tiny House #15 - Floor Plan & Exterior

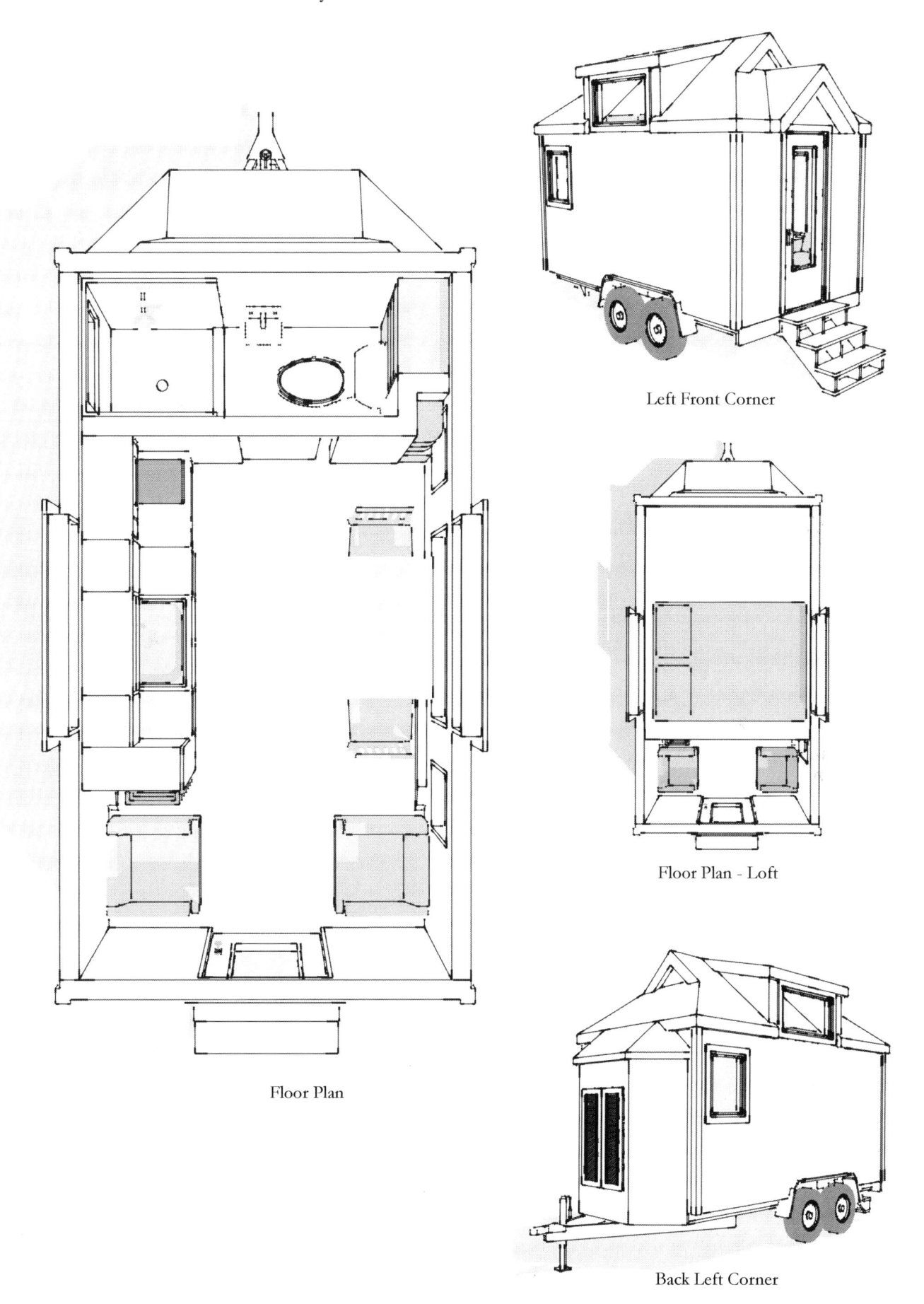

Floor Plan

Left Front Corner

Floor Plan - Loft

Back Left Corner

61

Tiny House #15 - Interior Views

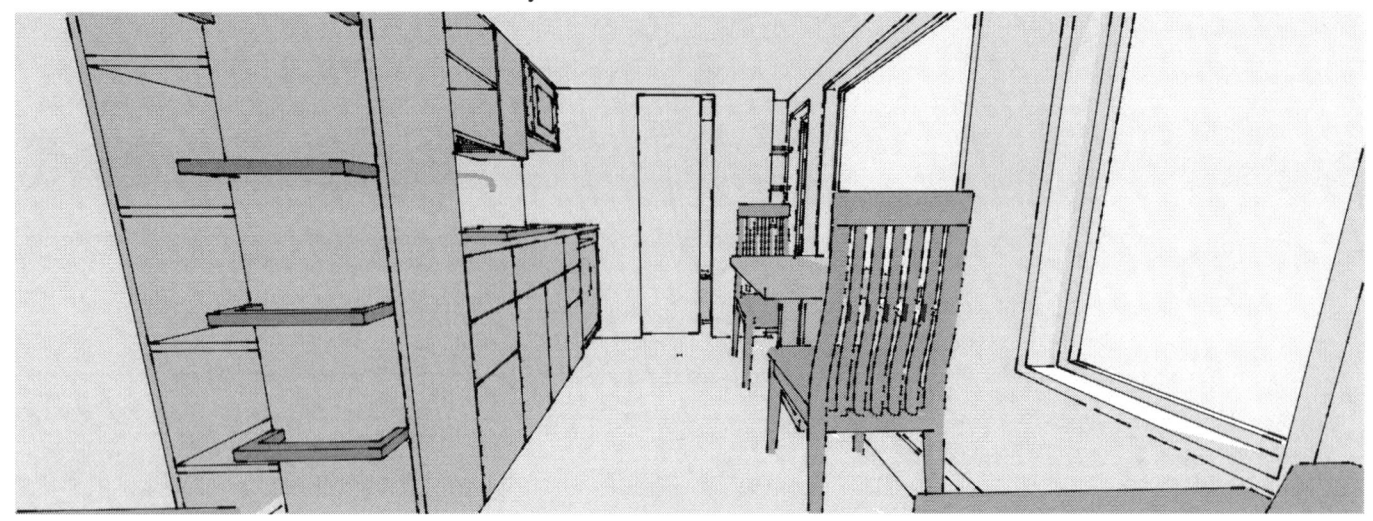

Interior from Entry

Interior from Kitchen

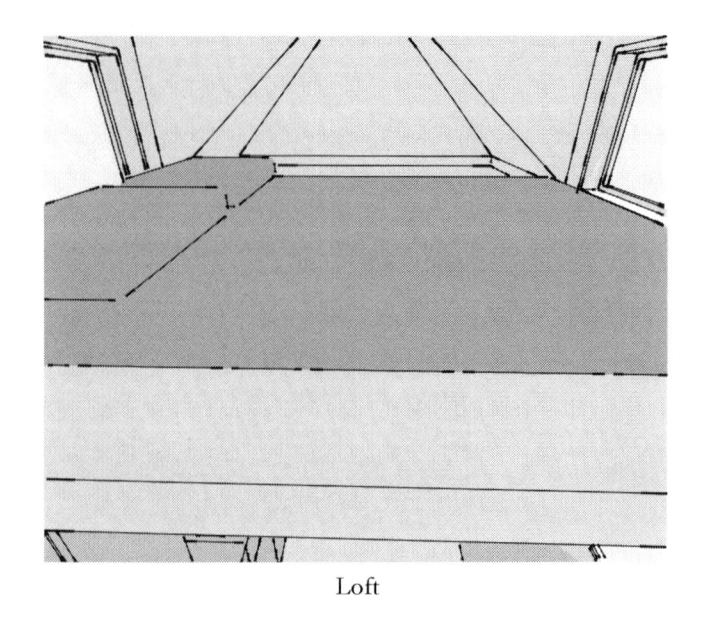

Loft

Bathroom

Tiny House #15 - Elevations

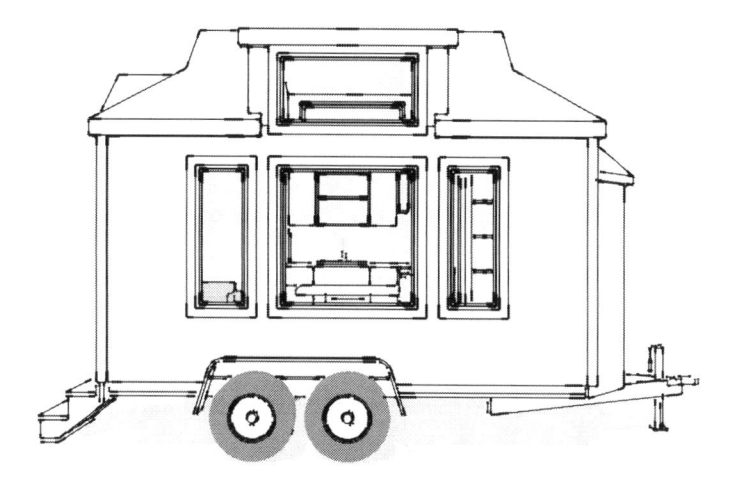

Right

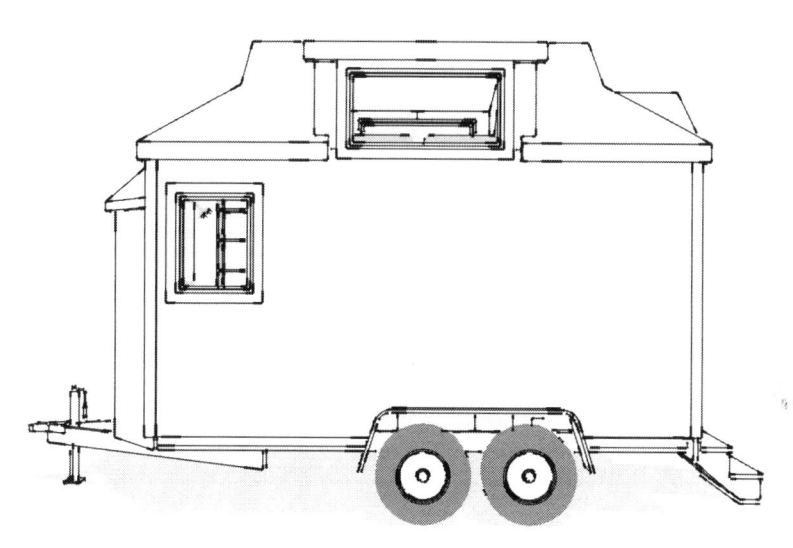

Left

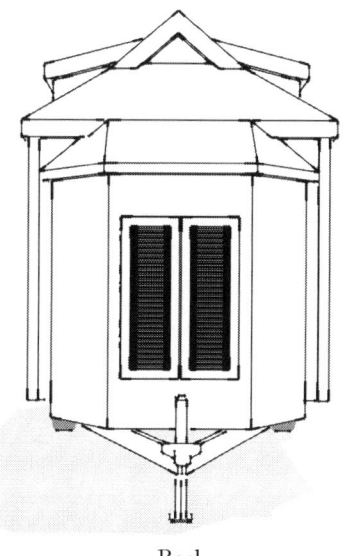

Back

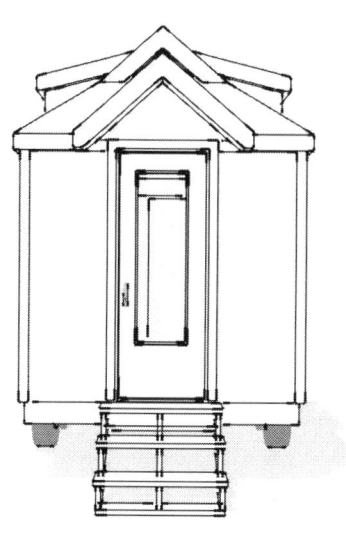

Front

63

#16

Tiny House #16 - Overview

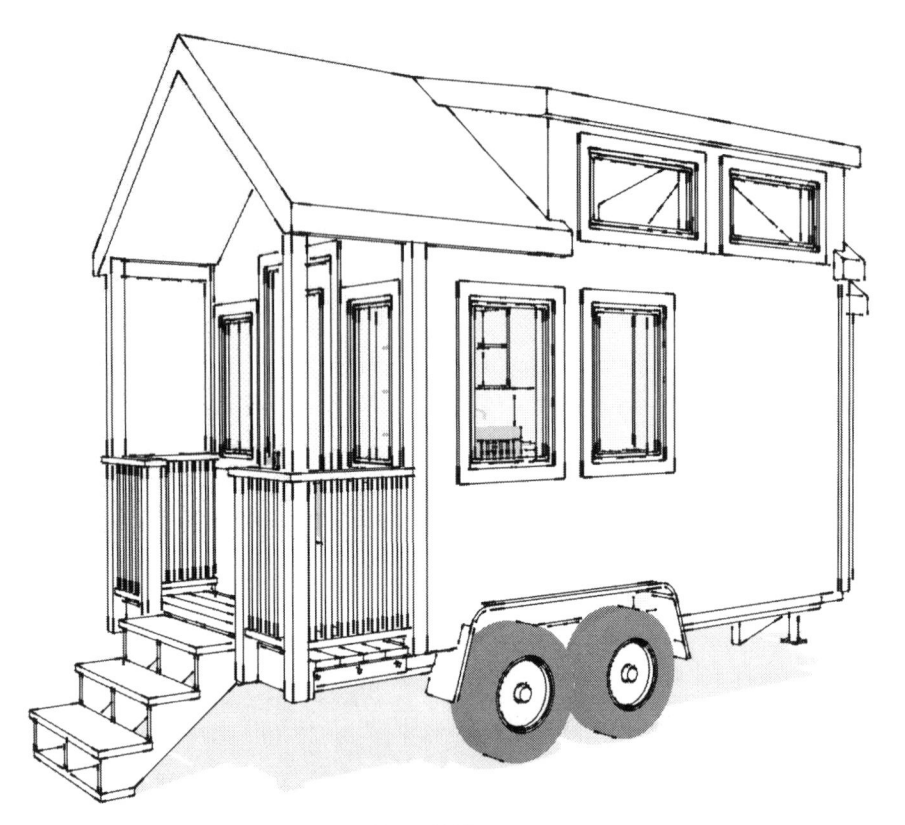

Front Right

Summary:

This house has a 10/12 gable roof with 3/12 shed dormers, plus a 2-foot deep porch with fold-up steps. The kitchen has a sink with cabinet drying rack above, a small refrigerator, and stovetop. The bathroom extends over the trailer tongue and has a 32-inch shower, toilet, wall mounted sink, and plenty of storage. The loft has space for a queen bed and is accessed by ladder rungs attached to an interior wall. The shed dormers over the loft provide plenty of headroom.

Features:

14-Foot Tiny House on Wheels
10/12 Gable with Shed Dormers
Bathroom Extended over Trailer
   Tongue
Small Kitchen
Front Entry with Porch and
   Fold-up Steps

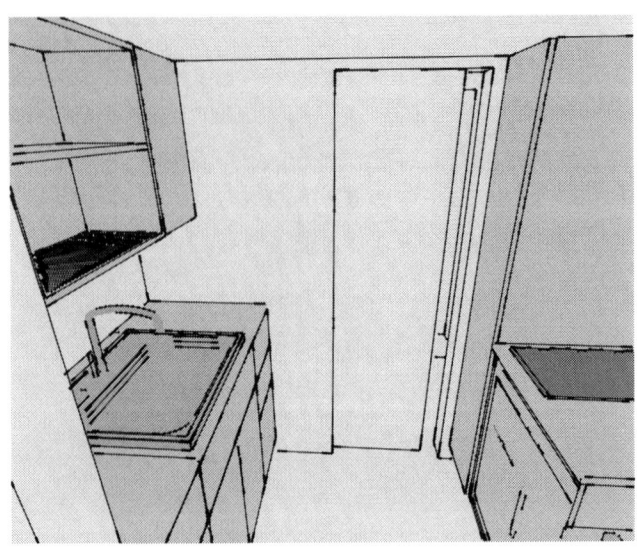

Kitchen

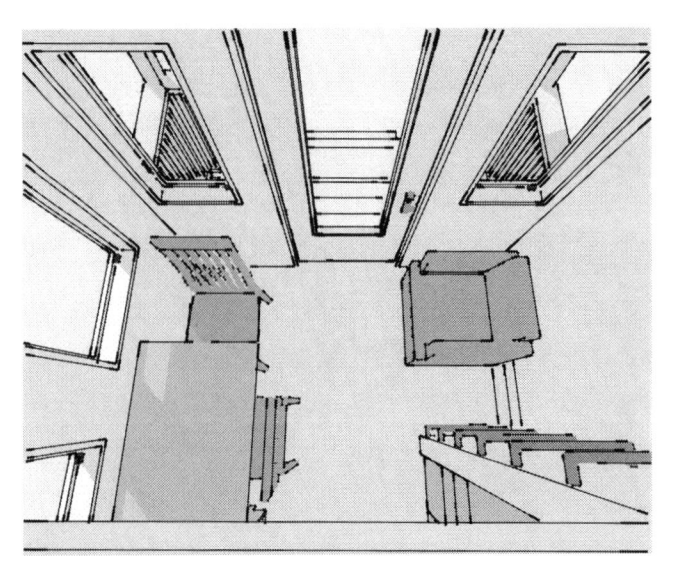

View from Loft

Tiny House #16 - Floor Plan & Exterior

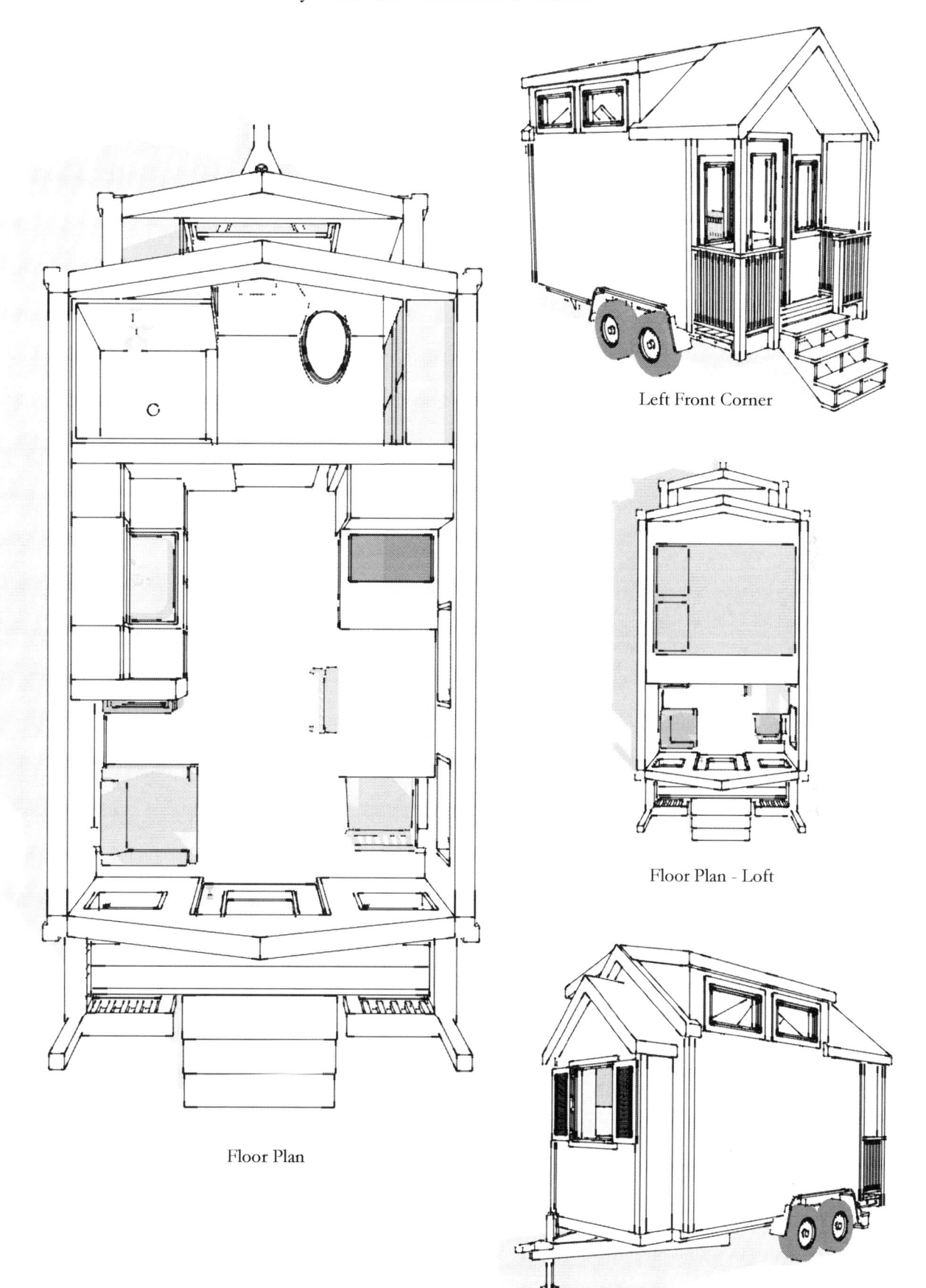

Left Front Corner

Floor Plan - Loft

Floor Plan

Back Left Corner

Tiny House #16 - Interior Views

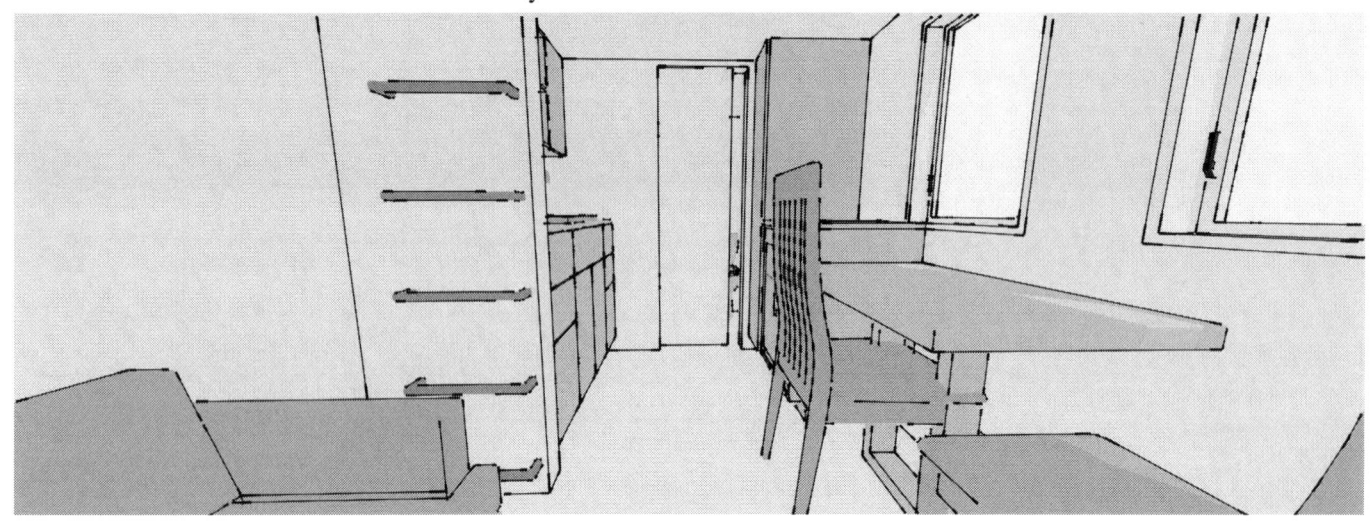

Interior from Entry

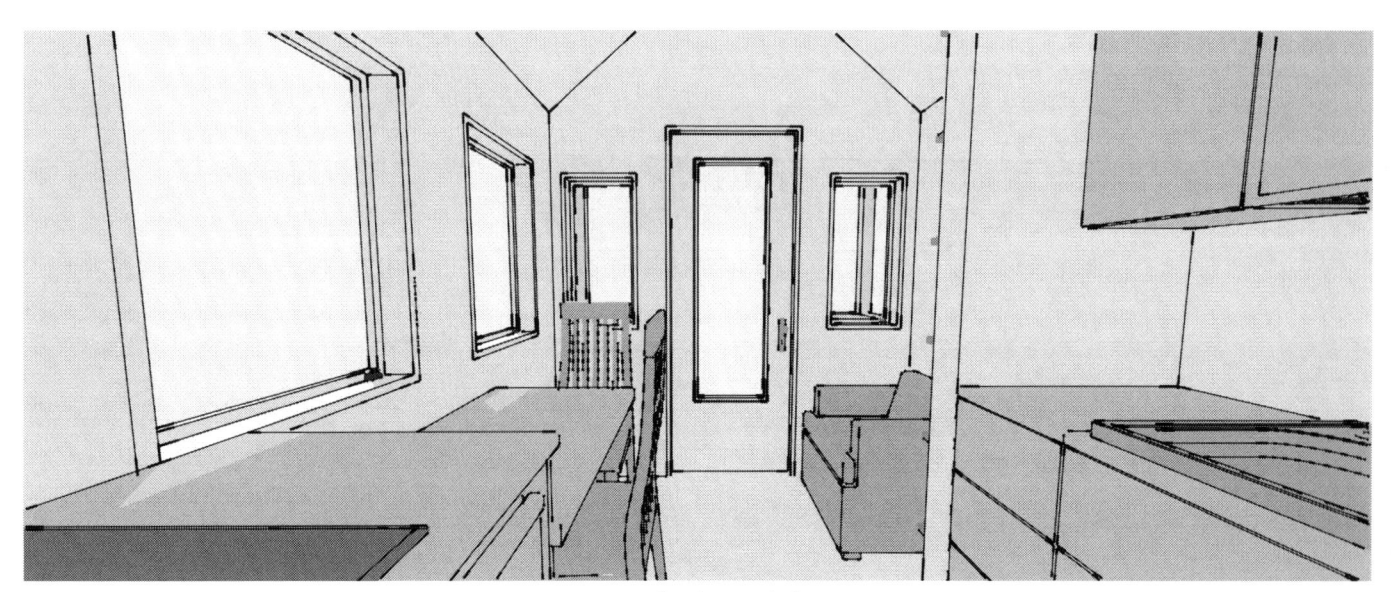

Interior from Kitchen

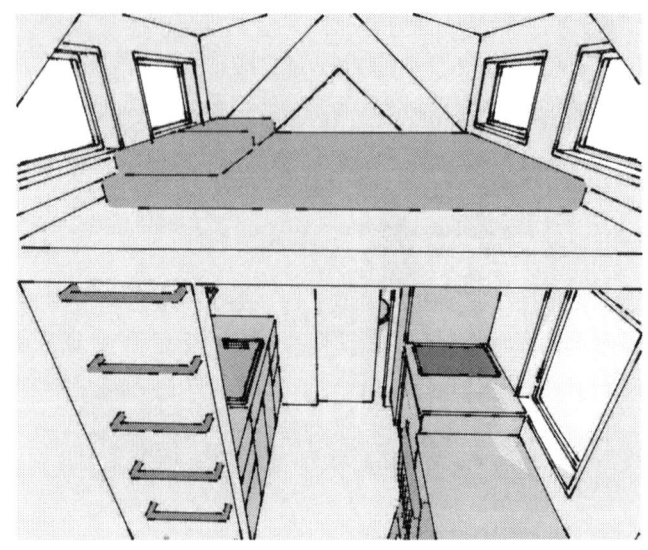

Loft

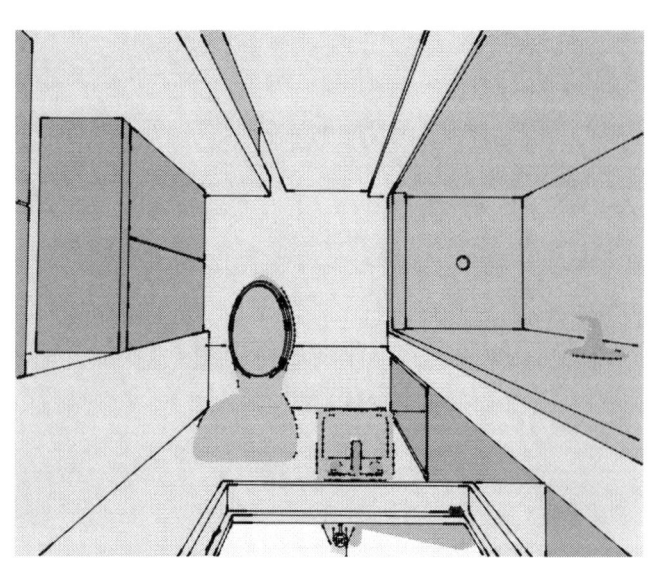

Bathroom

Tiny House #16 - Elevations

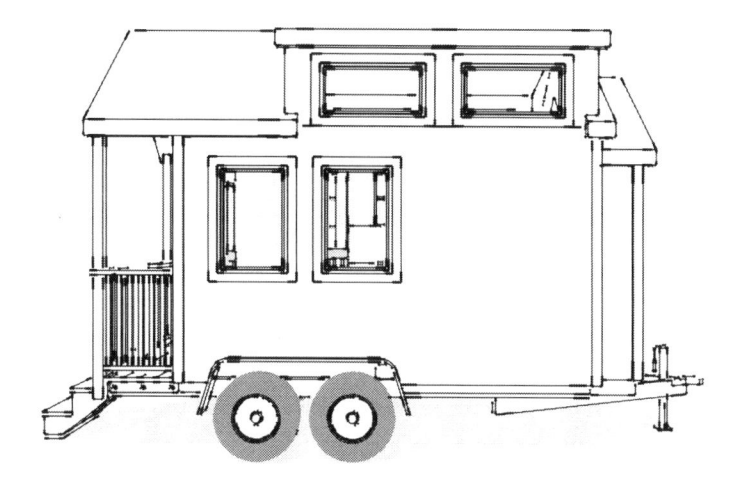

Right

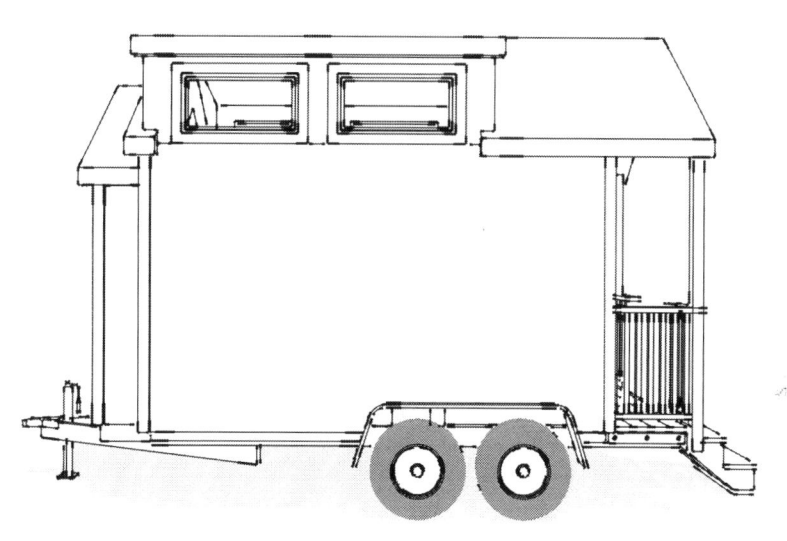

Left

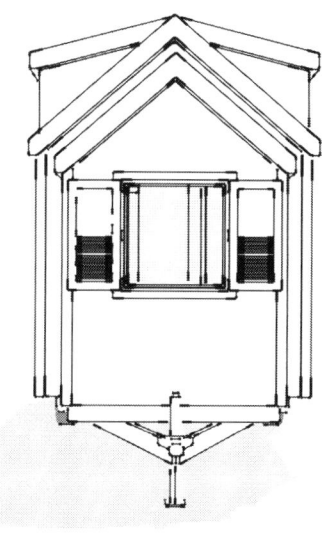

Back

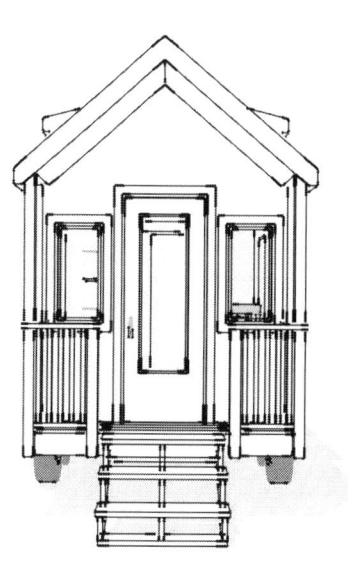

Front

#17

Tiny House #17 - Overview

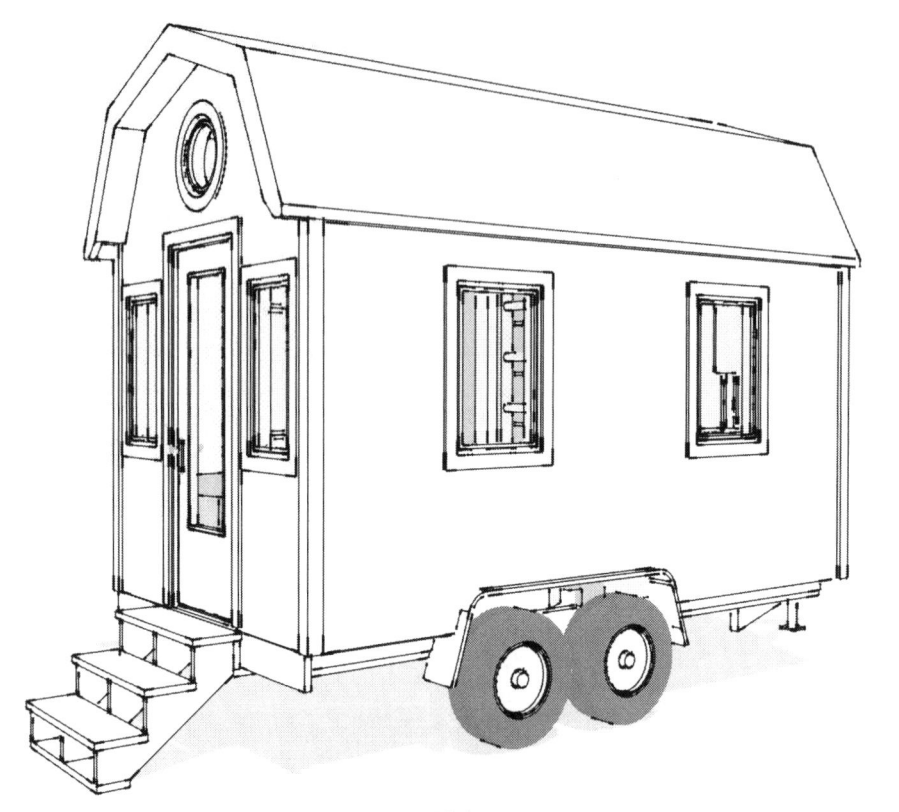

Front Right

Summary:

The barn-like gambrel roof provides a lot of headroom in the loft. The kitchen and bathroom extend over the trailer tongue in a bay window. The kitchen has the essentials: a sink, small refrigerator, stovetop, and plenty of cabinets. The bathroom has a shower, toilet, wall mounted sink, and small cabinet behind the toilet. The loft has space for a queen bed and is accessed by a movable ladder.

Features:

14-Foot Tiny House on Wheels
Gambrel Roof
Small Kitchen with Ample Counters
Front Entry with Fold-up Steps
Bay Window Extension over Trailer
 Tongue Extends Bathroom and
 Kitchen

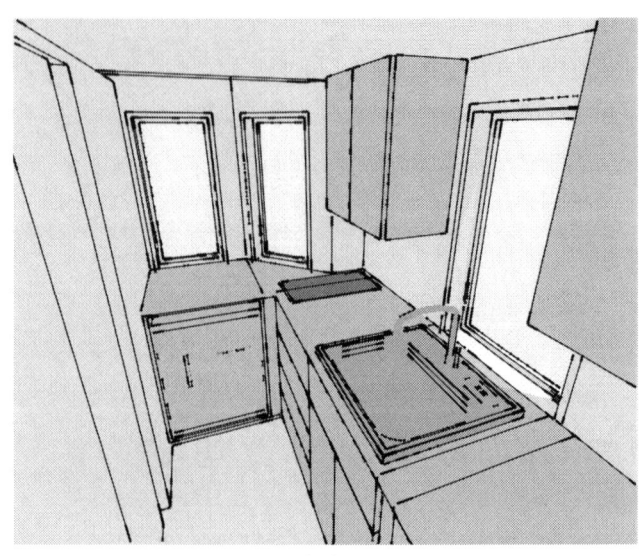

Kitchen

View from Loft

Tiny House #17 - Floor Plan & Exterior

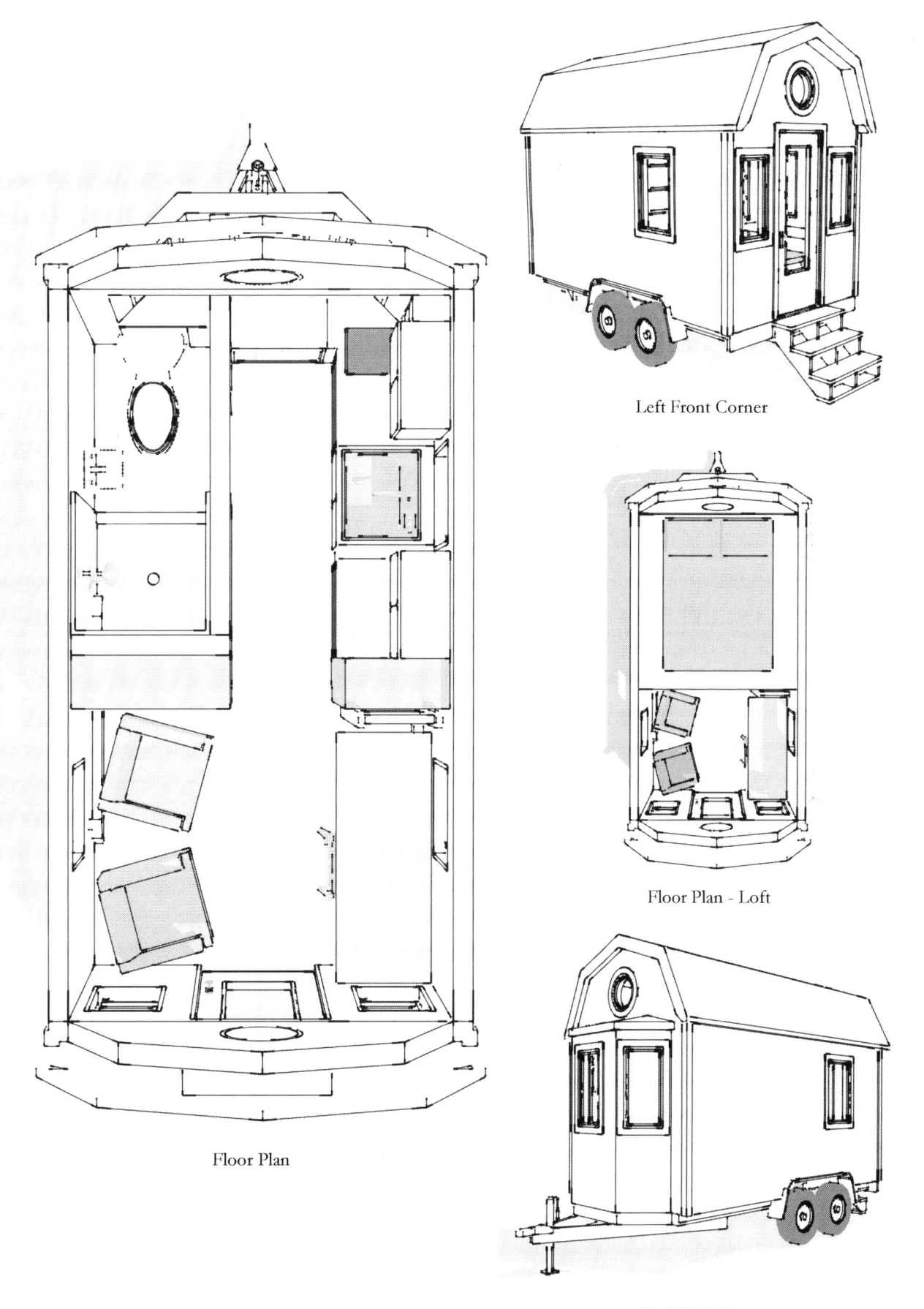

Left Front Corner

Floor Plan - Loft

Floor Plan

Back Left Corner

Tiny House #17 - Interior Views

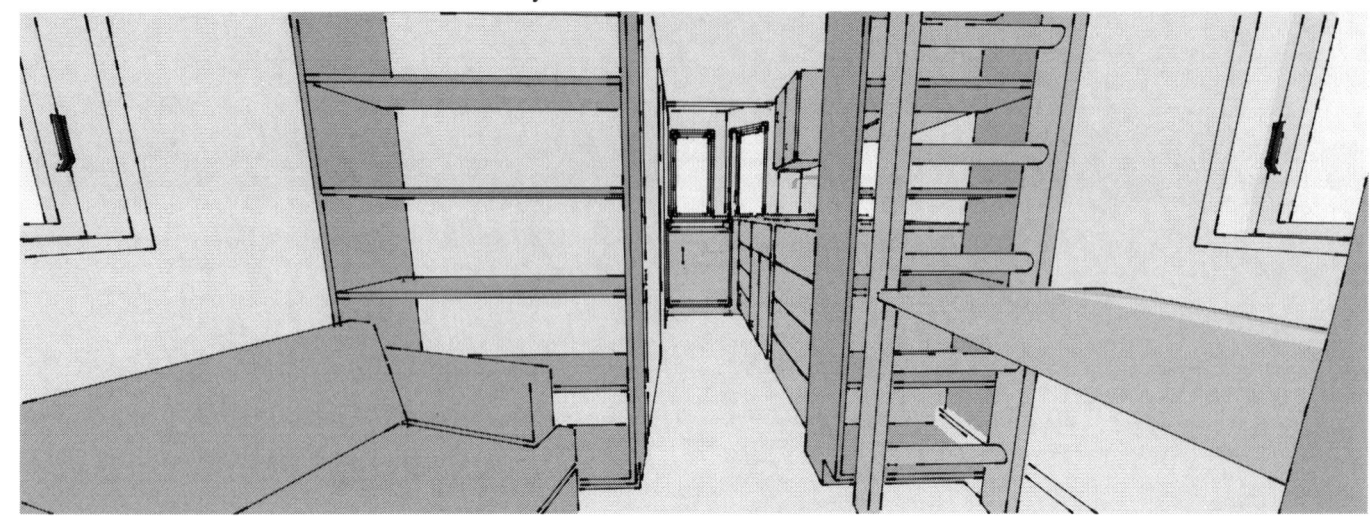

Interior from Entry

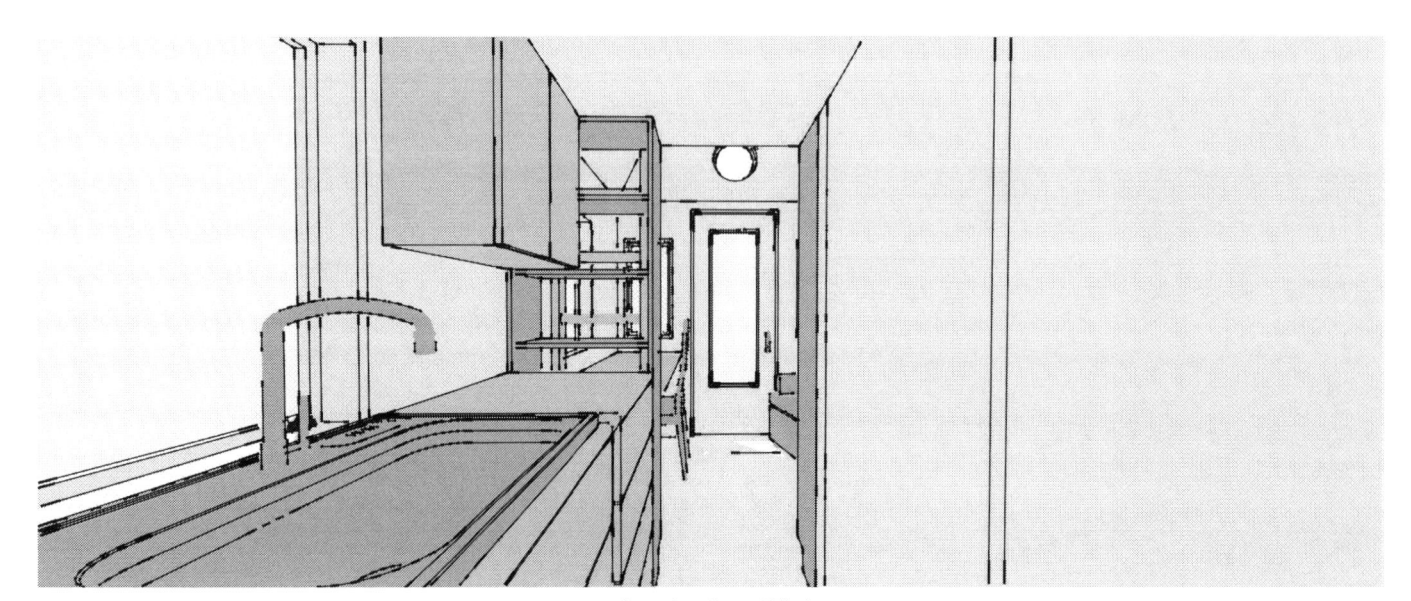

Interior from Kitchen

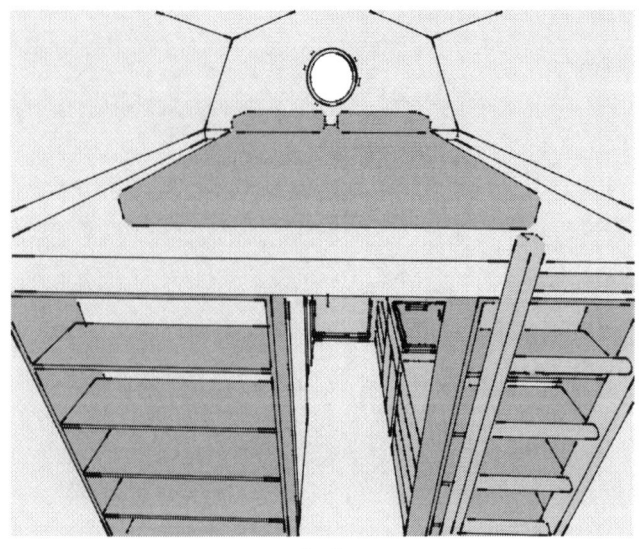

Loft

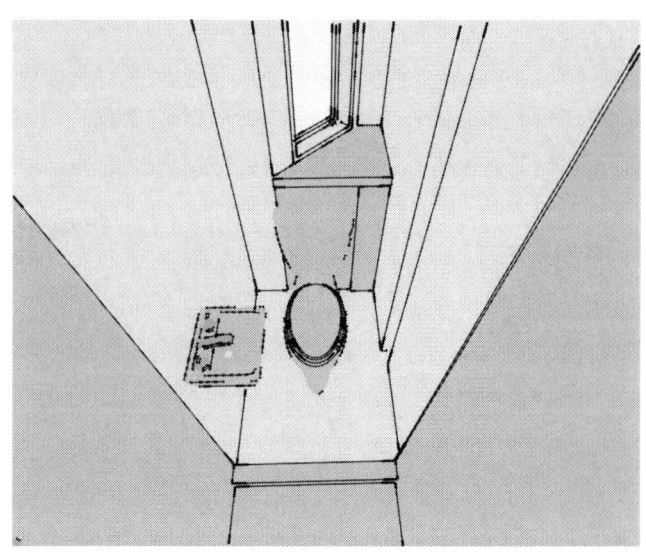

Bathroom

Tiny House #17 - Elevations

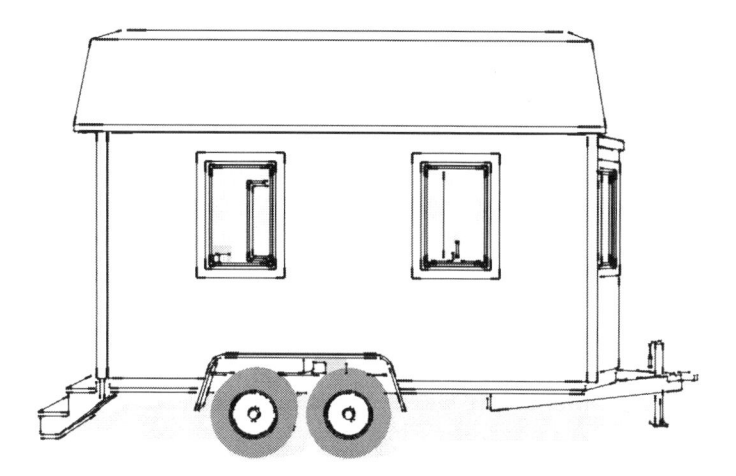

Right

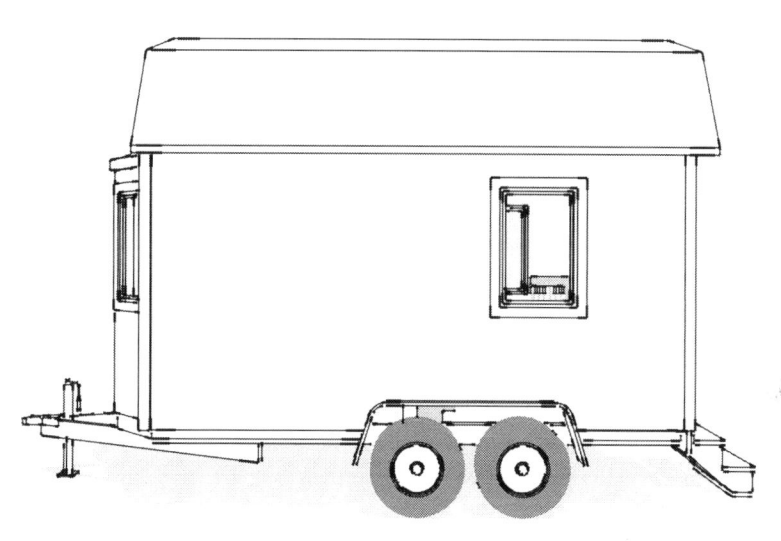

Left

Back

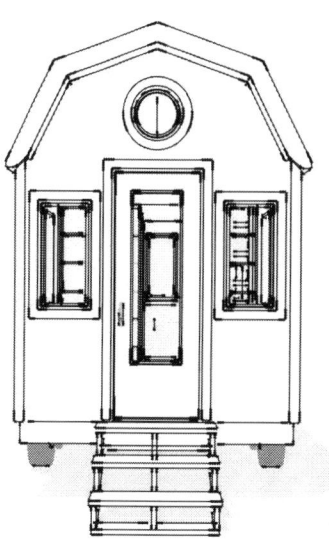

Front

#18

Tiny House #18 - Overview

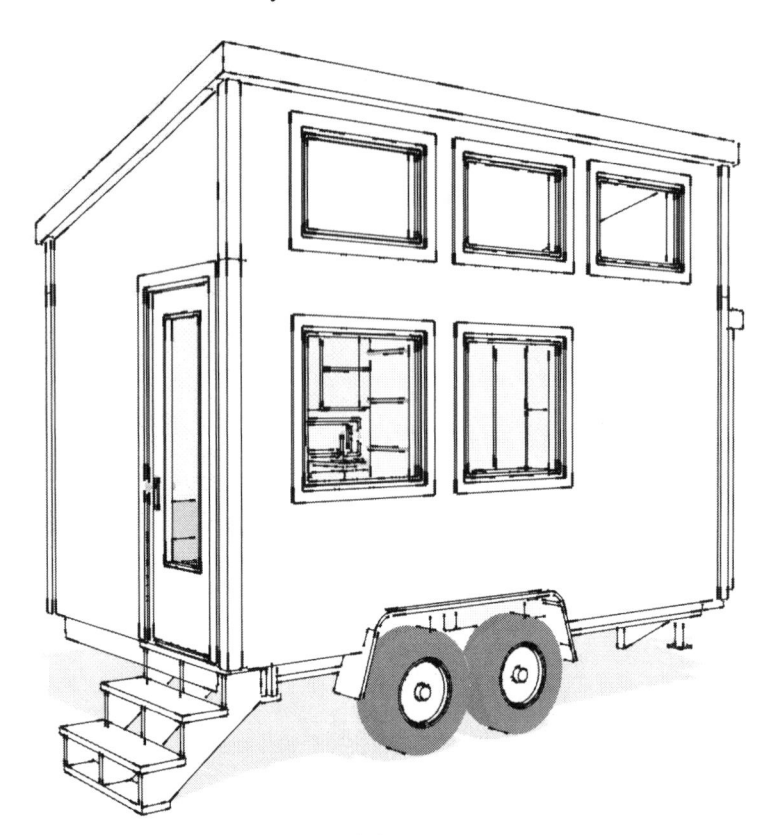

Front Right

Summary:

This tiny house has a 3/12 shed roof, plenty of headroom in the loft and space for a queen bed. The kitchen has the essentials: a sink with cabinet drying rack above, a small refrigerator, stovetop, and plenty of cabinets. The bathroom has a shower, toilet, and wall mounted sink. The loft is accessed by ladder rungs attached to an interior wall. Over the trailer tongue is a mechanical utility closet.

Features:

14-Foot Tiny House on Wheels
Shed Roof
Standard Bathroom
Small Kitchen with Ample Counters and Storage
Front Entry with Fold-up Steps
Mechanical Utility Closet Extension over Trailer Tongue

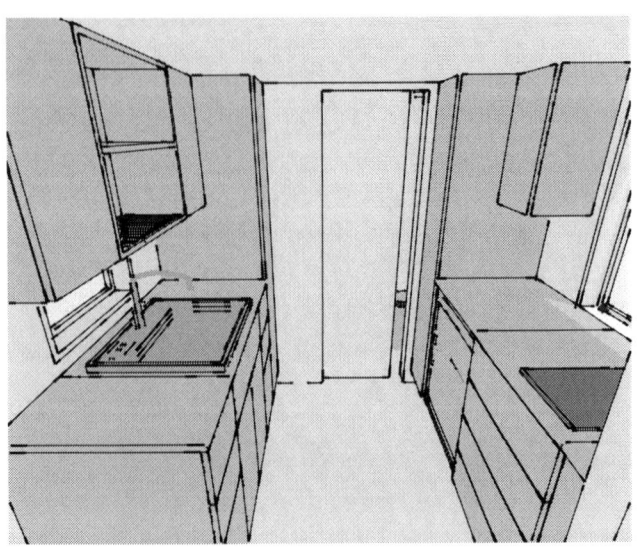

Kitchen

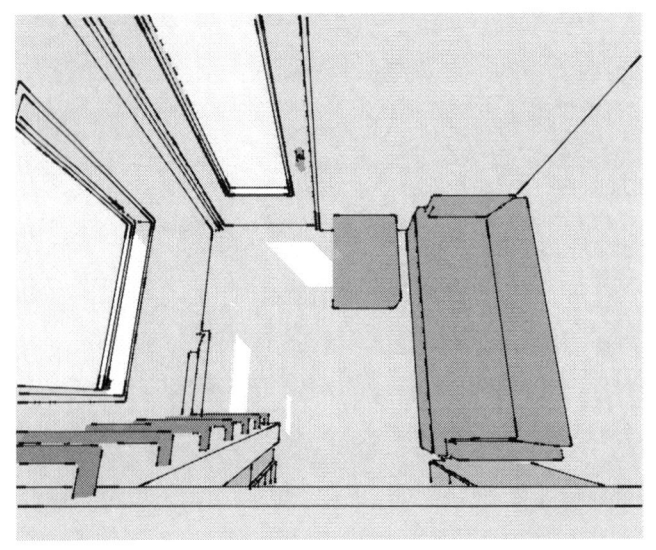

View from Loft

Tiny House #18 - Floor Plan & Exterior

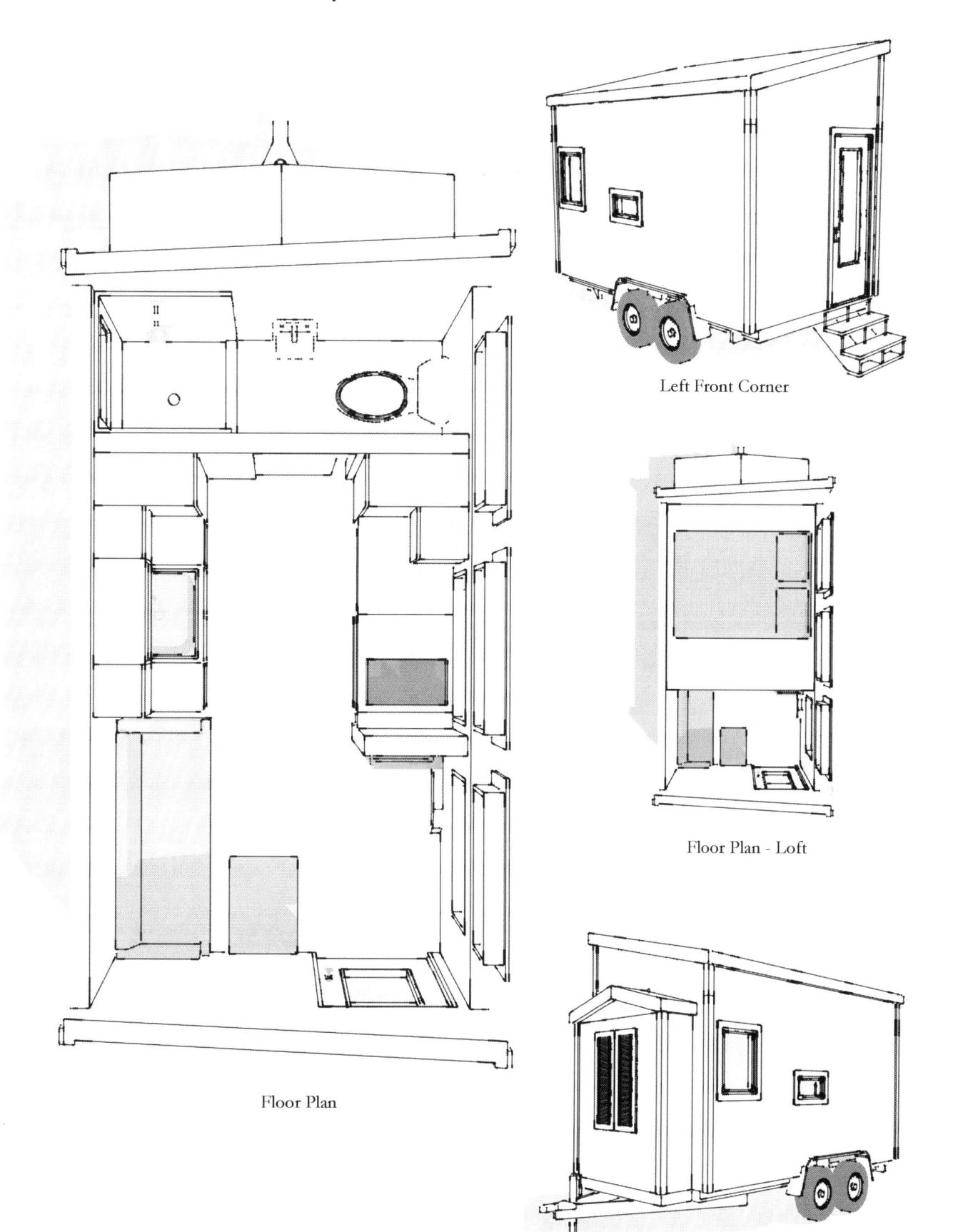

Left Front Corner

Floor Plan - Loft

Floor Plan

Back Left Corner

Tiny House #18 - Interior Views

Interior from Entry

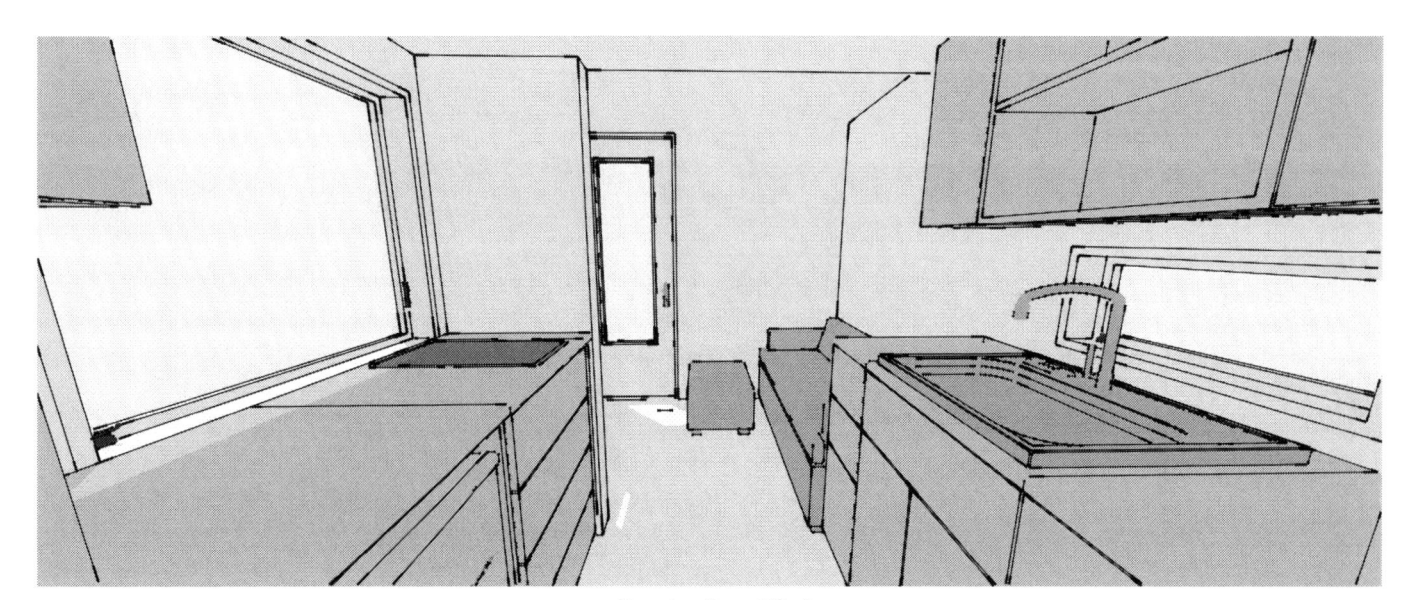

Interior from Kitchen

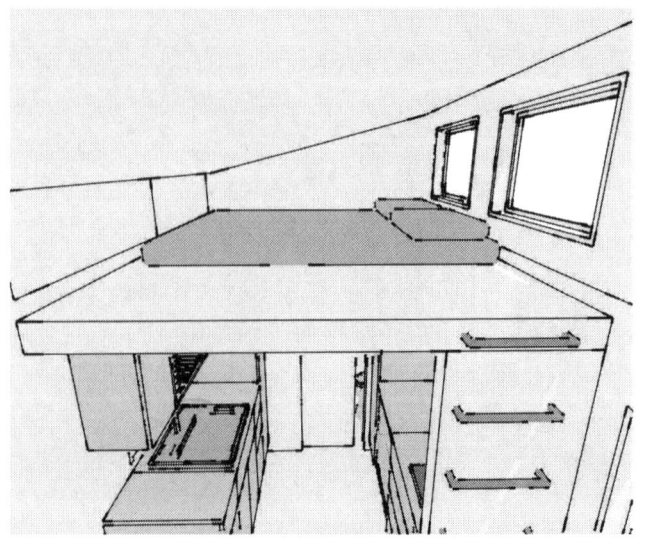

Loft

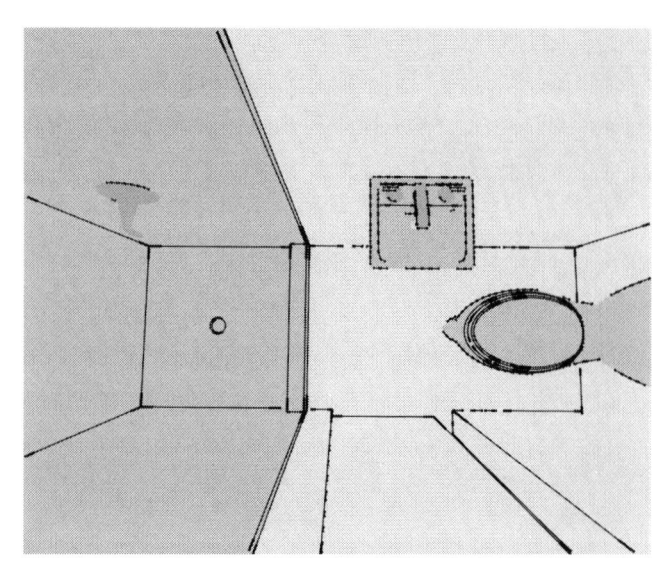

Bathroom

Tiny House #18 - Elevations

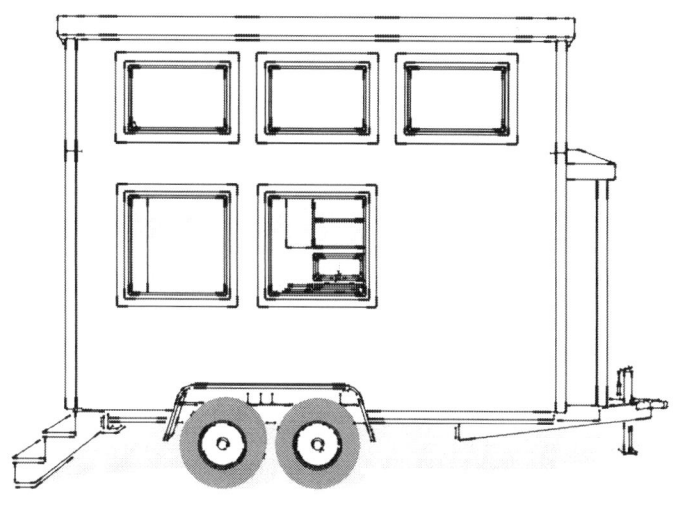

Right

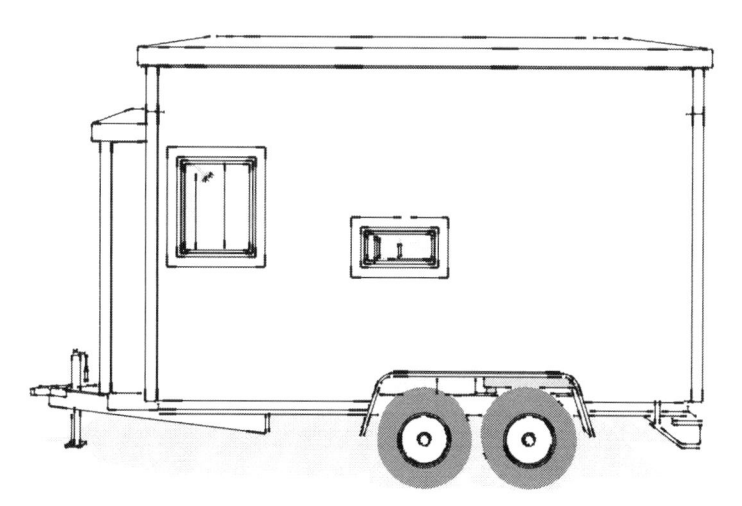

Left

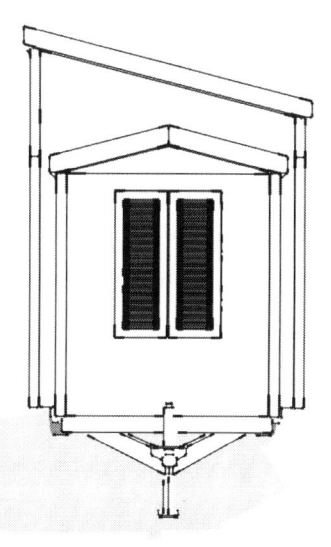

Back

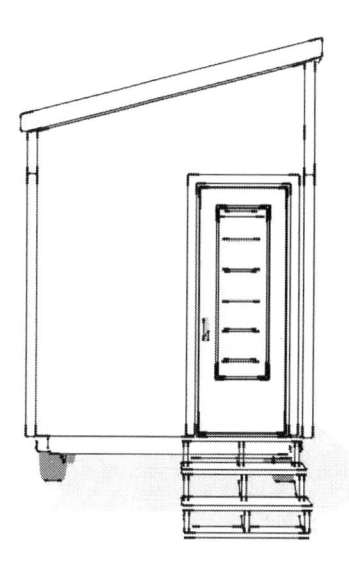

Front

#19

Tiny House #19 - Overview

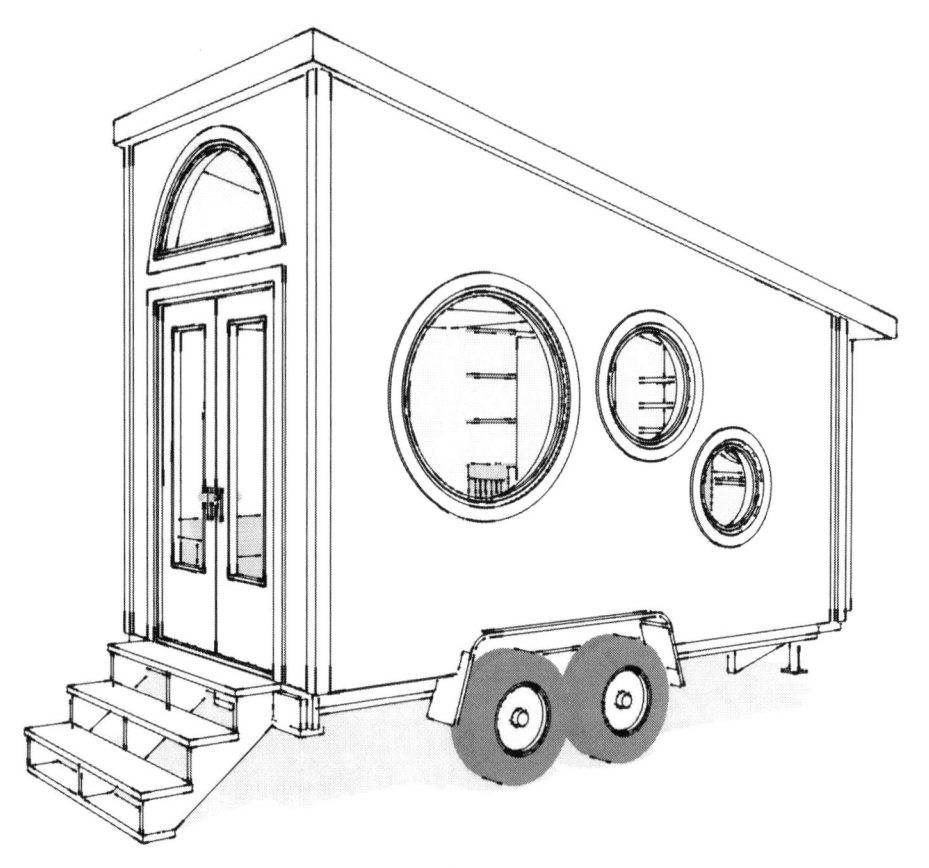

Front Right

Summary:

Round windows aren't common or inexpensive and require a certain aesthetic taste… but they sure make this tiny house design look like one groovy pad. The 3/12 shed roof provides plenty of headroom in the loft and space for a queen bed. The kitchen has the essentials: a sink with cabinet drying rack above, a small refrigerator, stovetop, microwave, shelves that compliment the round window, and plenty of counter space. The bathroom has a 32-inch shower, toilet, and wall mounted sink. The loft is accessed by ladder rungs attached to an interior wall.

Features:

14-Foot Tiny House on Wheels
Shed Roof
Small Bathroom
Small Kitchen Extends over Trailer Tongue
French Door Entry with Fold-up Steps
Groovy Round Windows

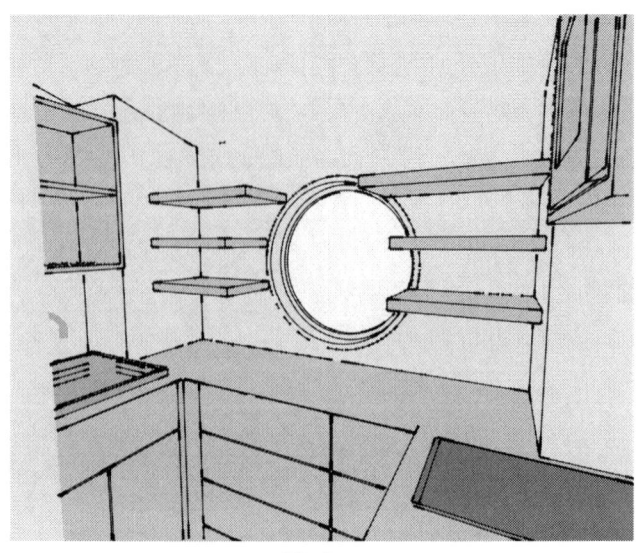

Kitchen

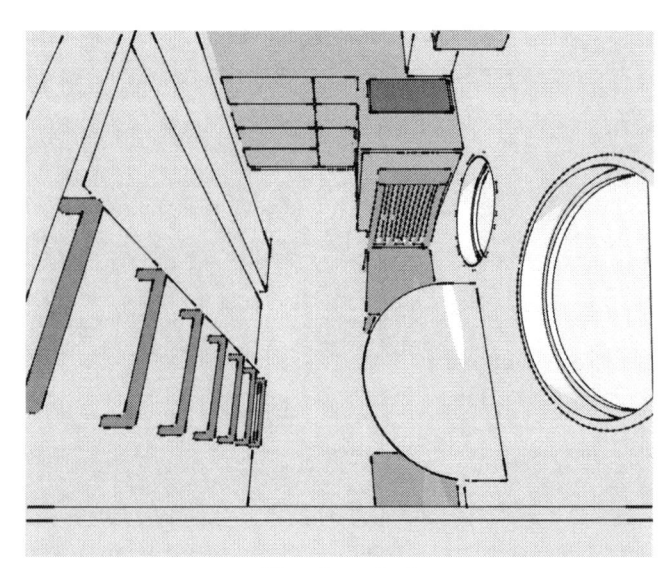

View from Loft

Tiny House #19 - Floor Plan & Exterior

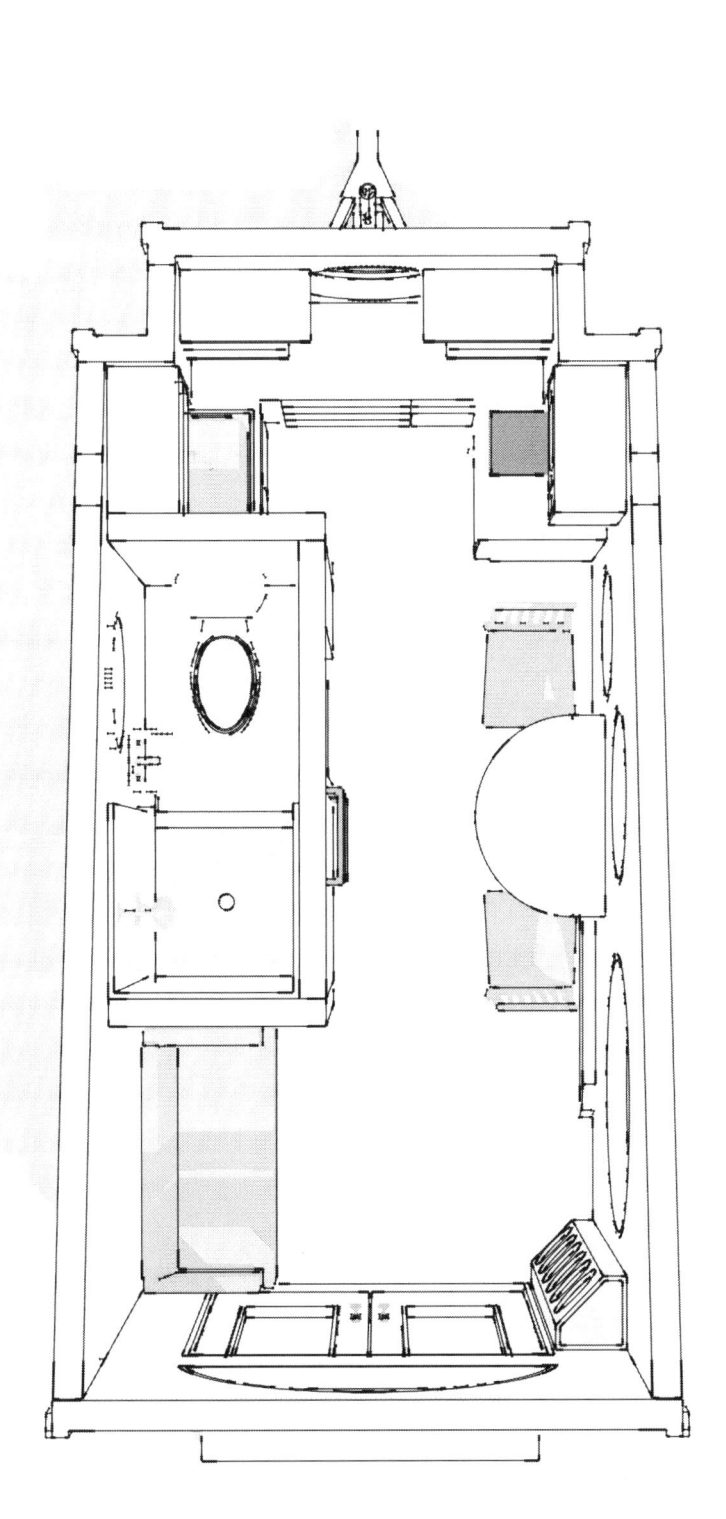

Floor Plan

Left Front Corner

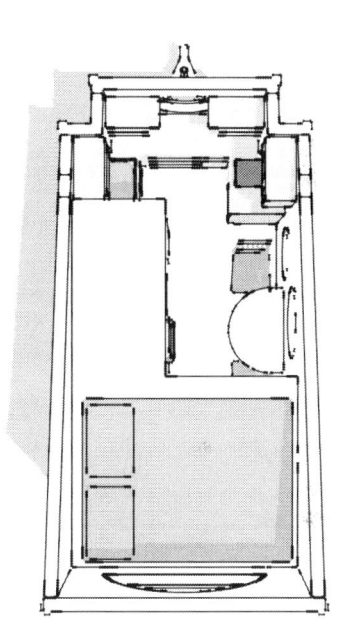

Floor Plan - Loft

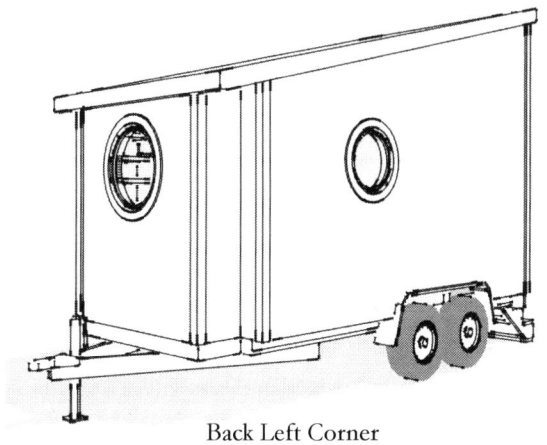

Back Left Corner

Tiny House #19 - Interior Views

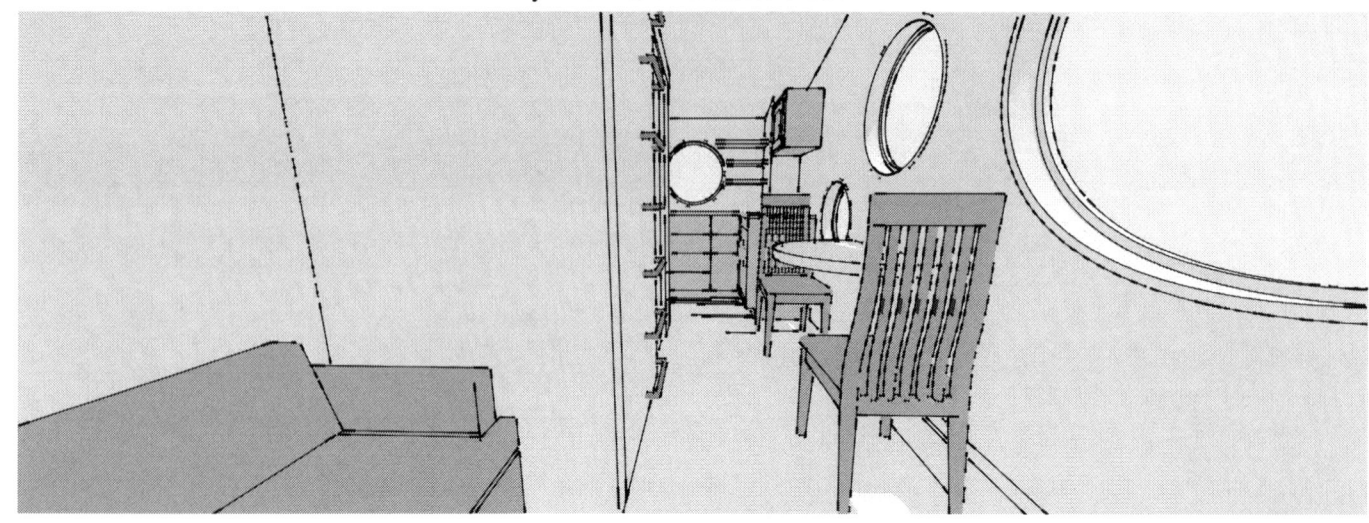

Interior from Entry

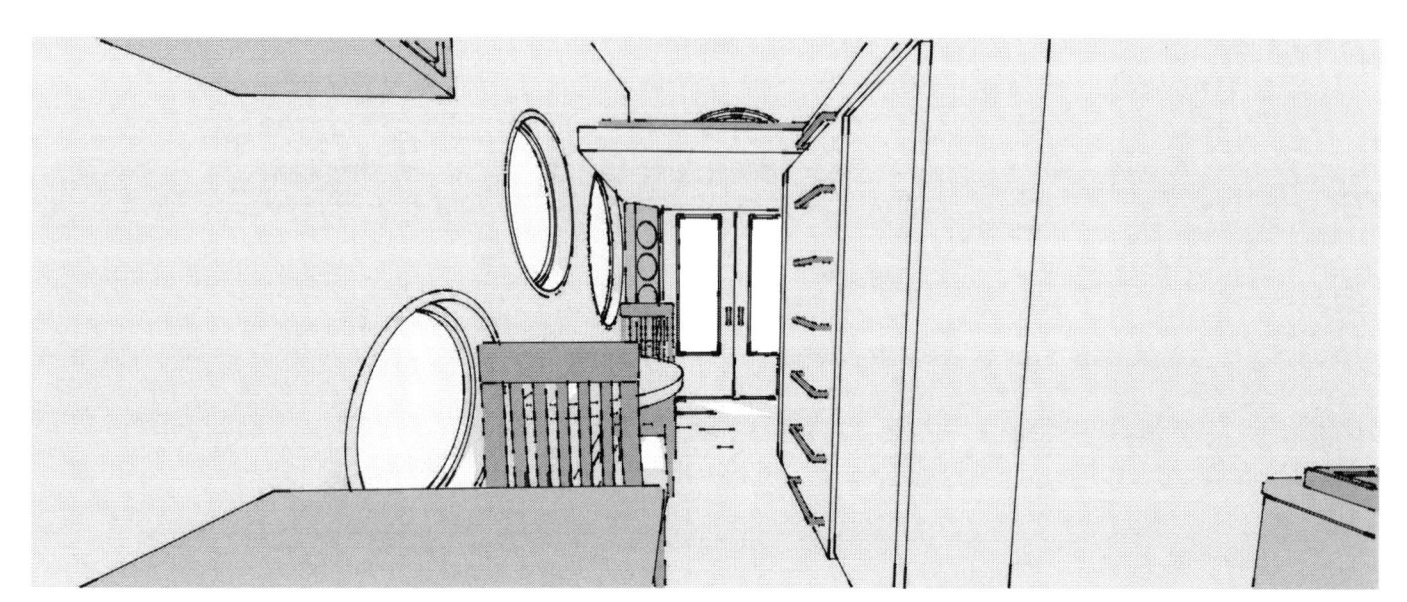

Interior from Kitchen

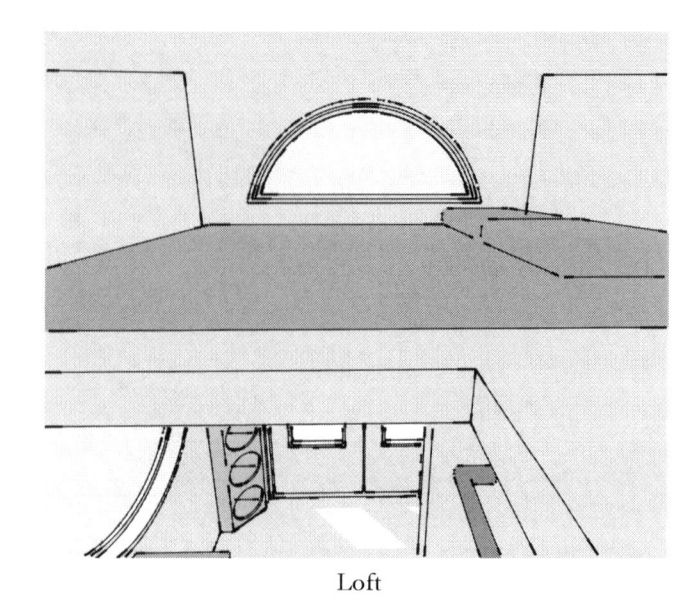

Loft

Bathroom

78

Tiny House #19 - Elevations

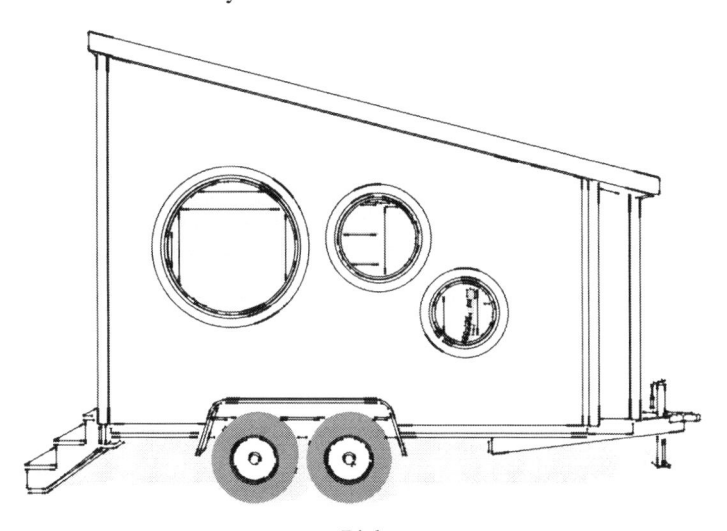

Right

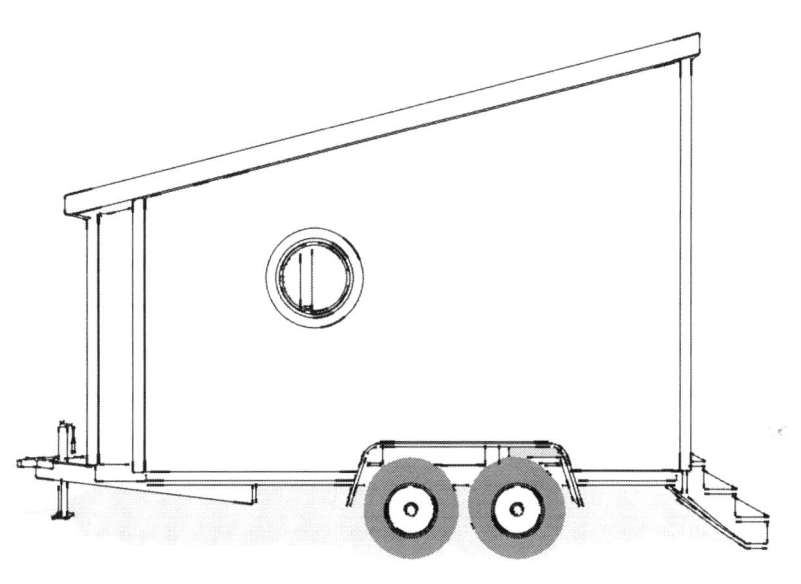

Left

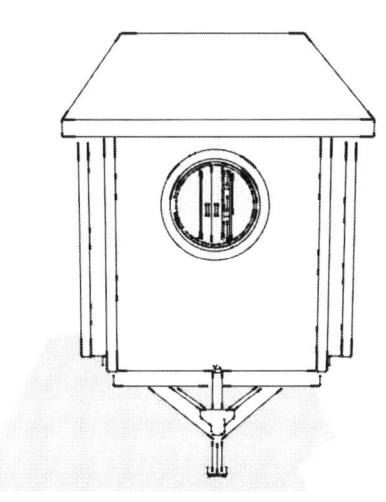

Back

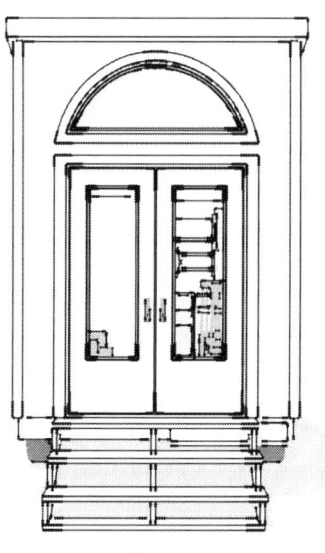

Front

#20

Tiny House #20 - Overview

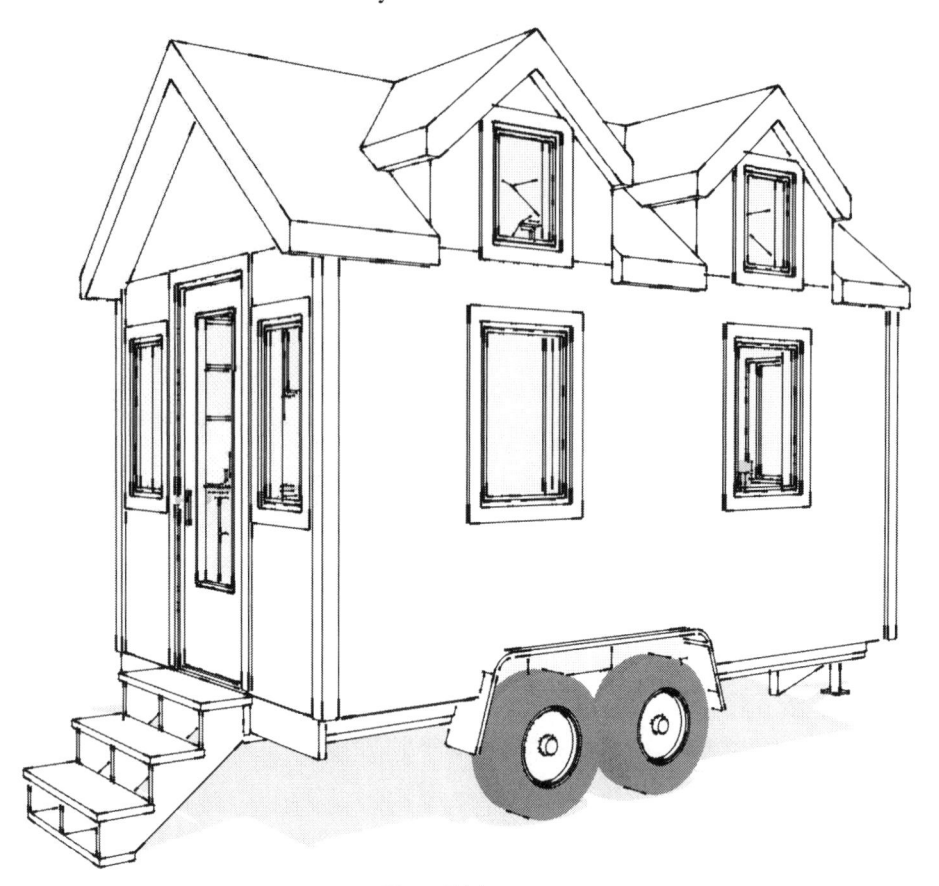

Front Right

Summary:

The 10/12 gable roof with gable dormers makes this one cute little tiny house. The kitchen has the essentials: a sink with cabinet drying rack above, a small refrigerator, stovetop, and microwave. The wet bathroom has a shower, toilet, and wall mounted sink. The loft is accessed by ladder rungs attached to an interior wall. The gable dormers don't add a lot of headroom, but they will add to a cozy cottage feel in the loft. A desk fits neatly into a bay window that extends over the trailer tongue.

Features:

14-Foot Tiny House on Wheels
Gable Roof with Gable Dormers
Desk in Bay Window Extension
Wet Bathroom
Small Kitchen
Entry with Fold-up Steps
Ample Storage

Kitchen

View from Loft

Tiny House #20 - Floor Plan & Exterior

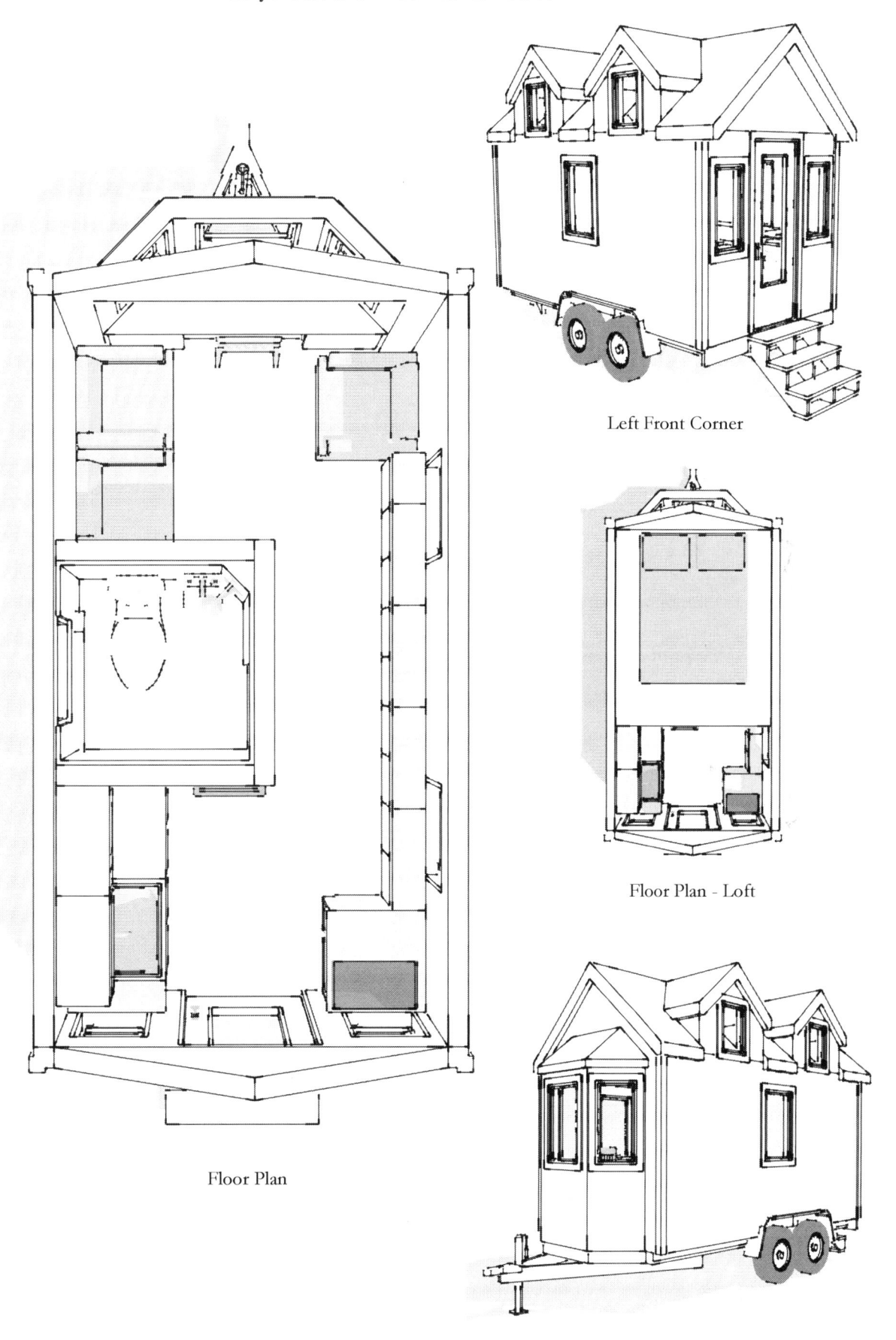

Floor Plan

Left Front Corner

Floor Plan - Loft

Back Left Corner

81

Tiny House #20 - Interior Views

Interior from Hall

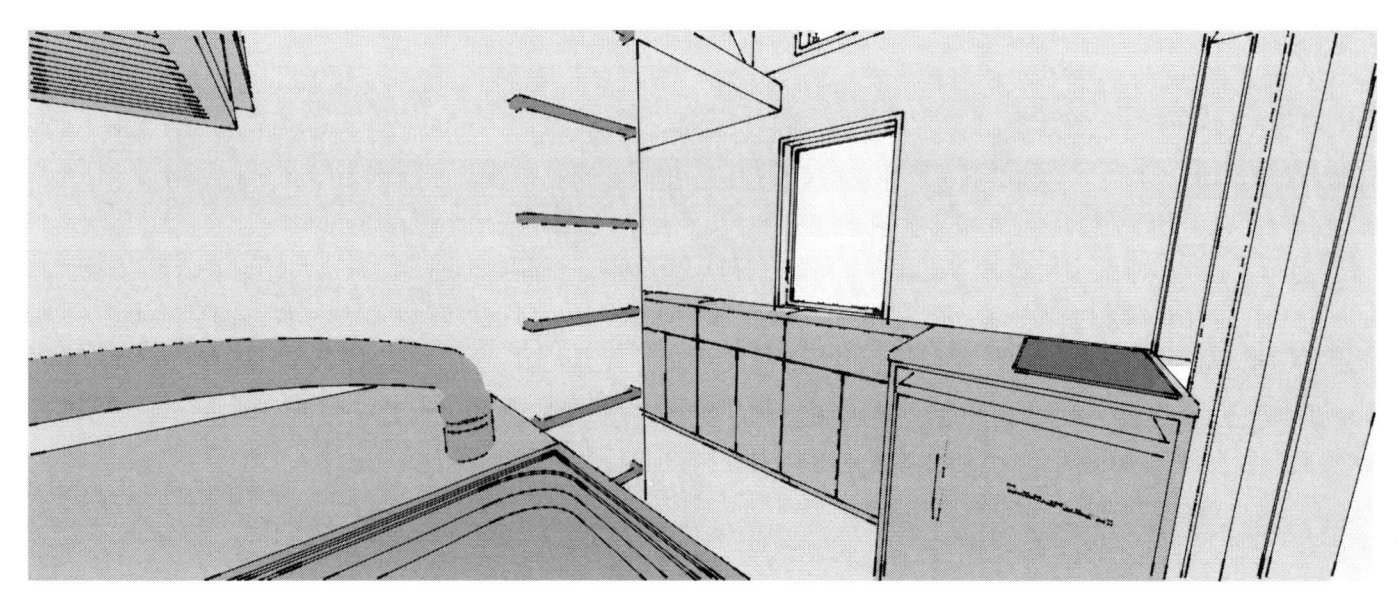

Interior from Kitchen

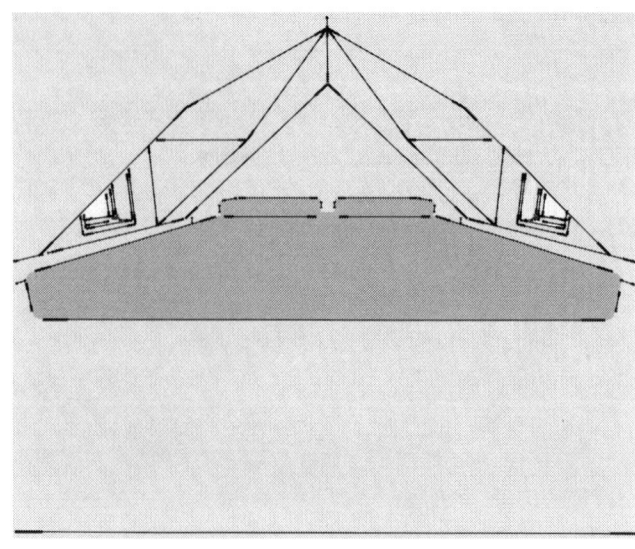

Loft

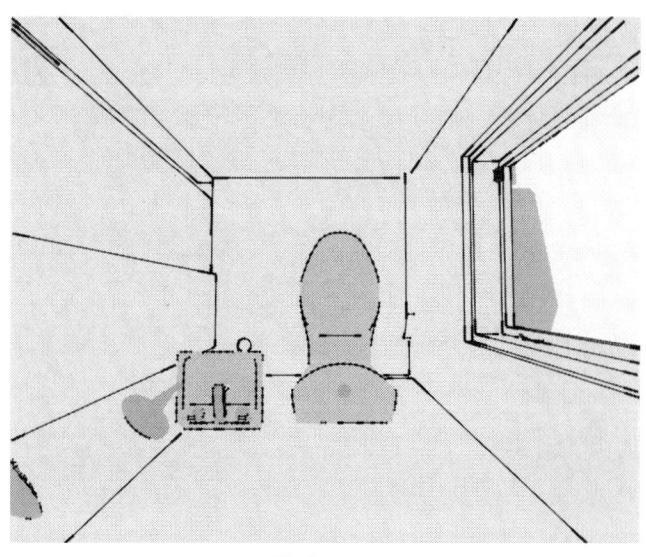

Bathroom

Tiny House #20 - Elevations

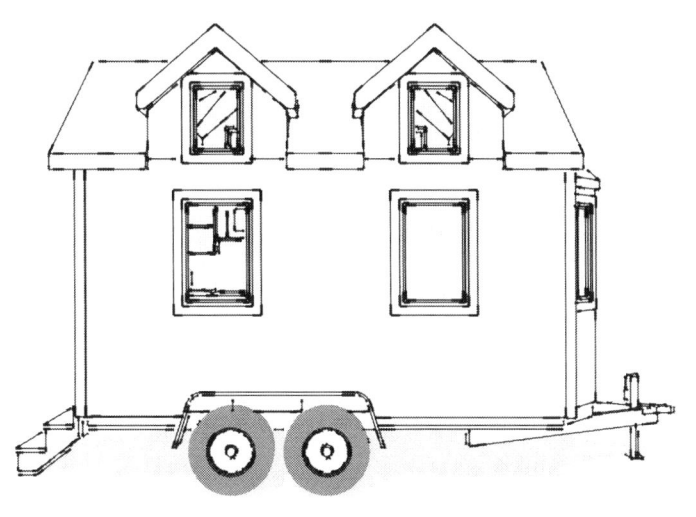

Right

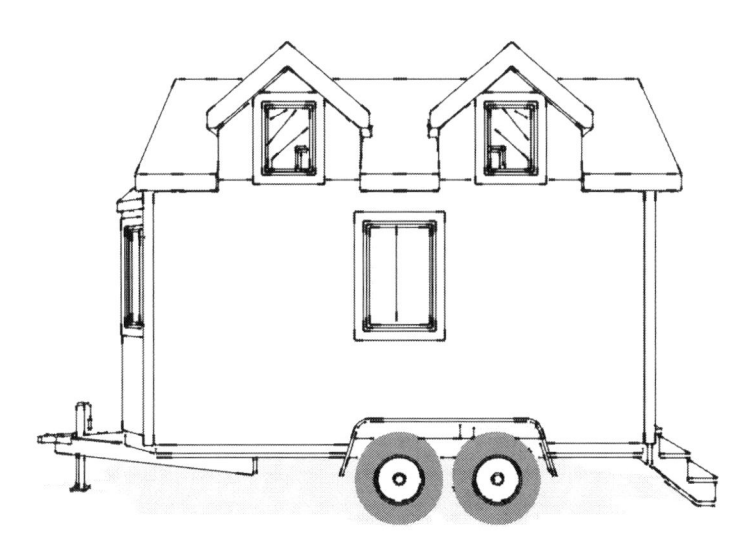

Left

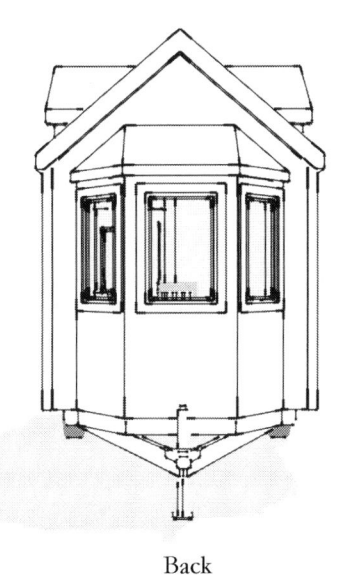

Back

Front

#21

Tiny House #21 - Overview

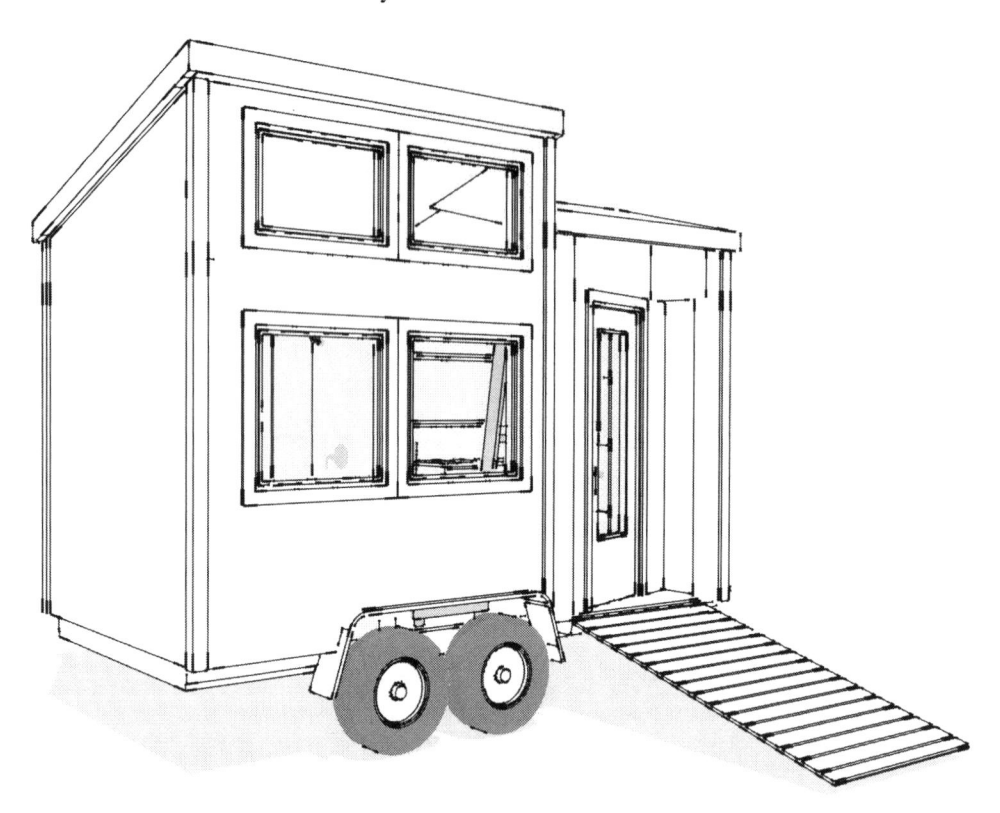

Front Right

Summary:

This tiny house has a combination of a 3/12 shed roof over the loft and living room and a 3/12 gable roof over the kitchen. It also has a diagonal side entry which guides those entering the house toward the living room. The kitchen is just inside the entry and has the essentials: a sink, small refrigerator, and stovetop. Large windows give the kitchen a great view. A floor to ceiling kitchen cabinet makes up for the lack of overhead cabinets. The bathroom has a soaking tub/shower, toilet, and wall mounted sink. The loft is accessed by a fixed ladder attached to an exterior wall.

Features:

14-Foot Tiny House on Wheels
Combination Shed and Gable Roof
Diagonal Side Entry with Fold-up
  Ramp
Bathroom with Soaking Tub/Shower
Small Kitchen

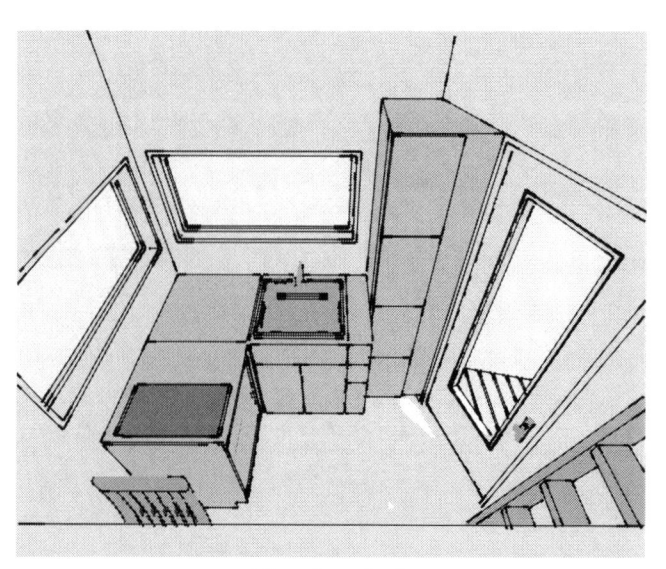

Kitchen

View from Loft

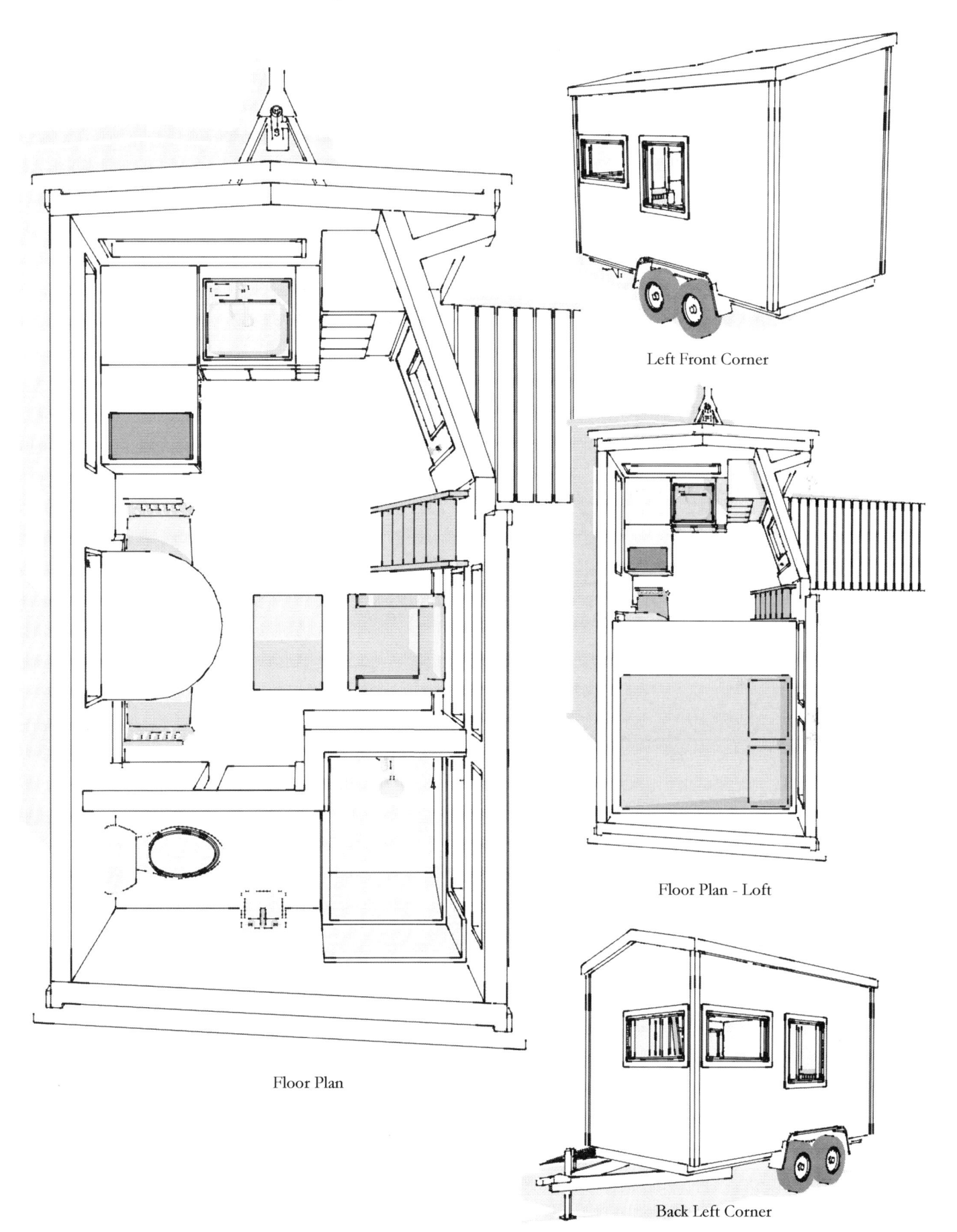

Tiny House #21 - Floor Plan & Exterior

Left Front Corner

Floor Plan - Loft

Floor Plan

Back Left Corner

Tiny House #21 - Interior Views

Interior

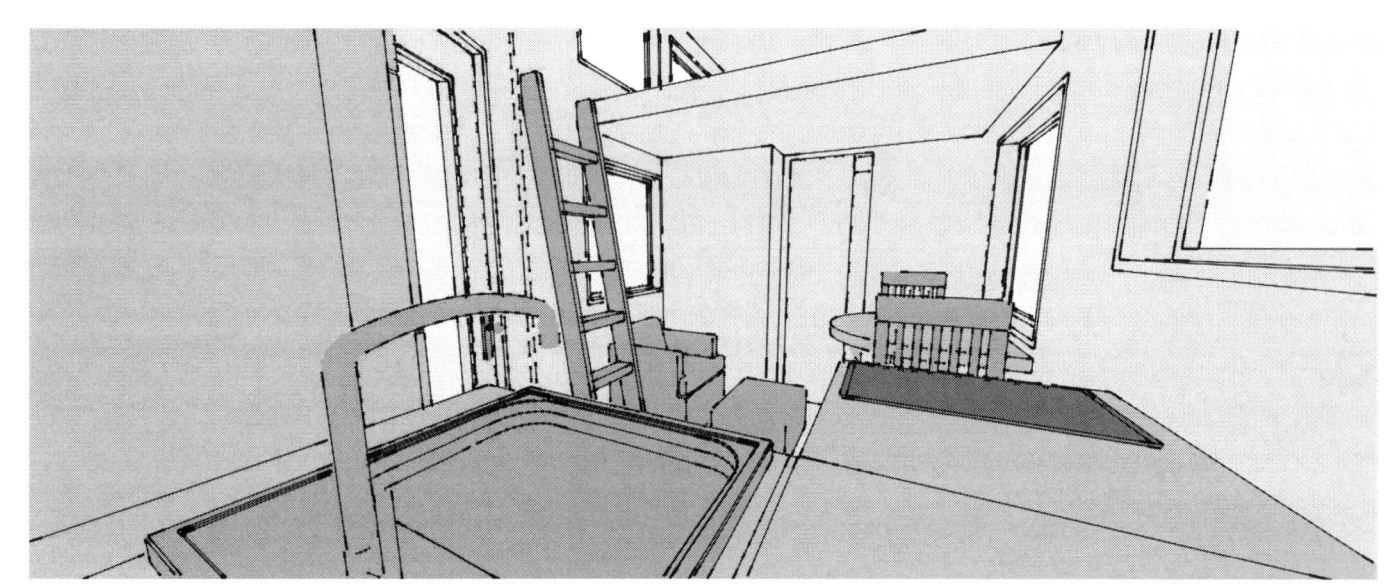

Interior from Kitchen

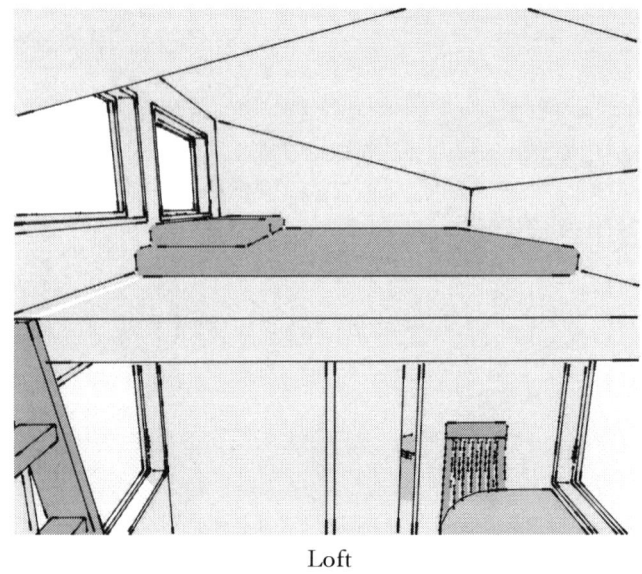

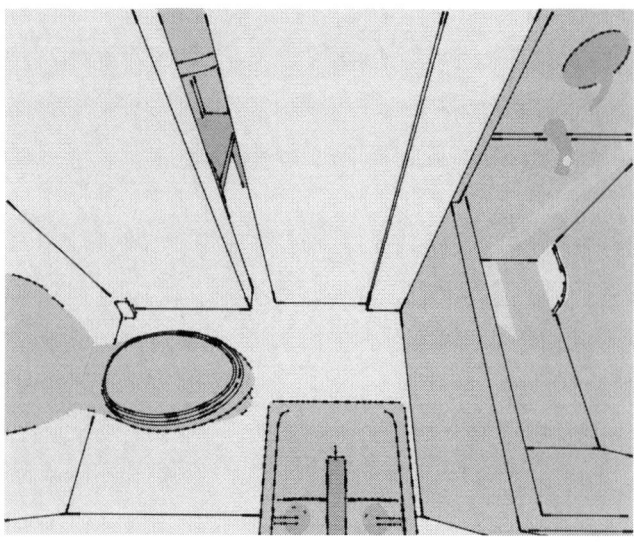

Loft

Bathroom

Tiny House #21 - Elevations

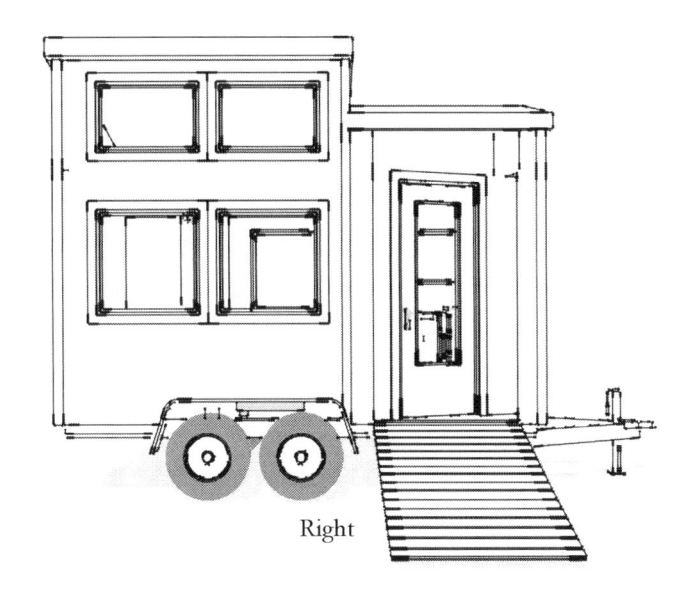

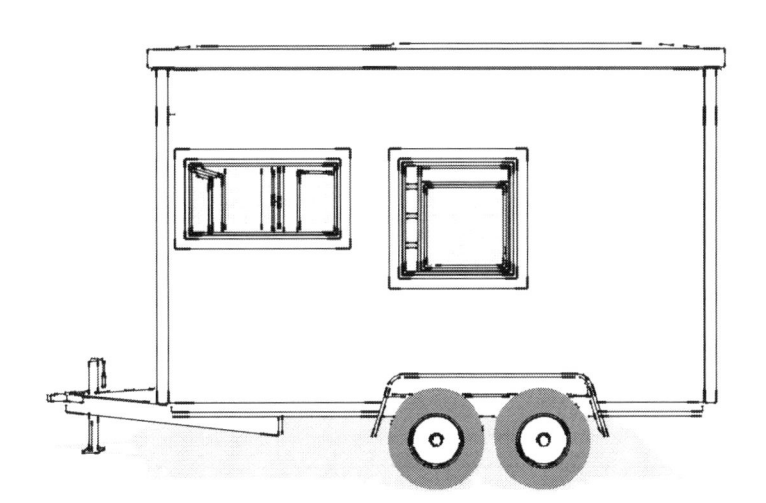

Right

Left

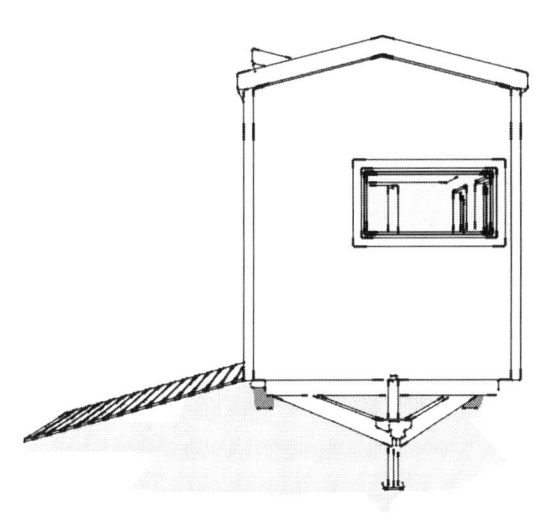

Back

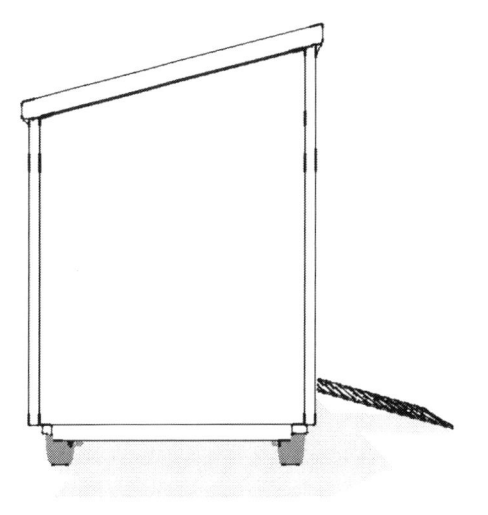

Front

#22

Tiny House #22 - Overview

Front Right

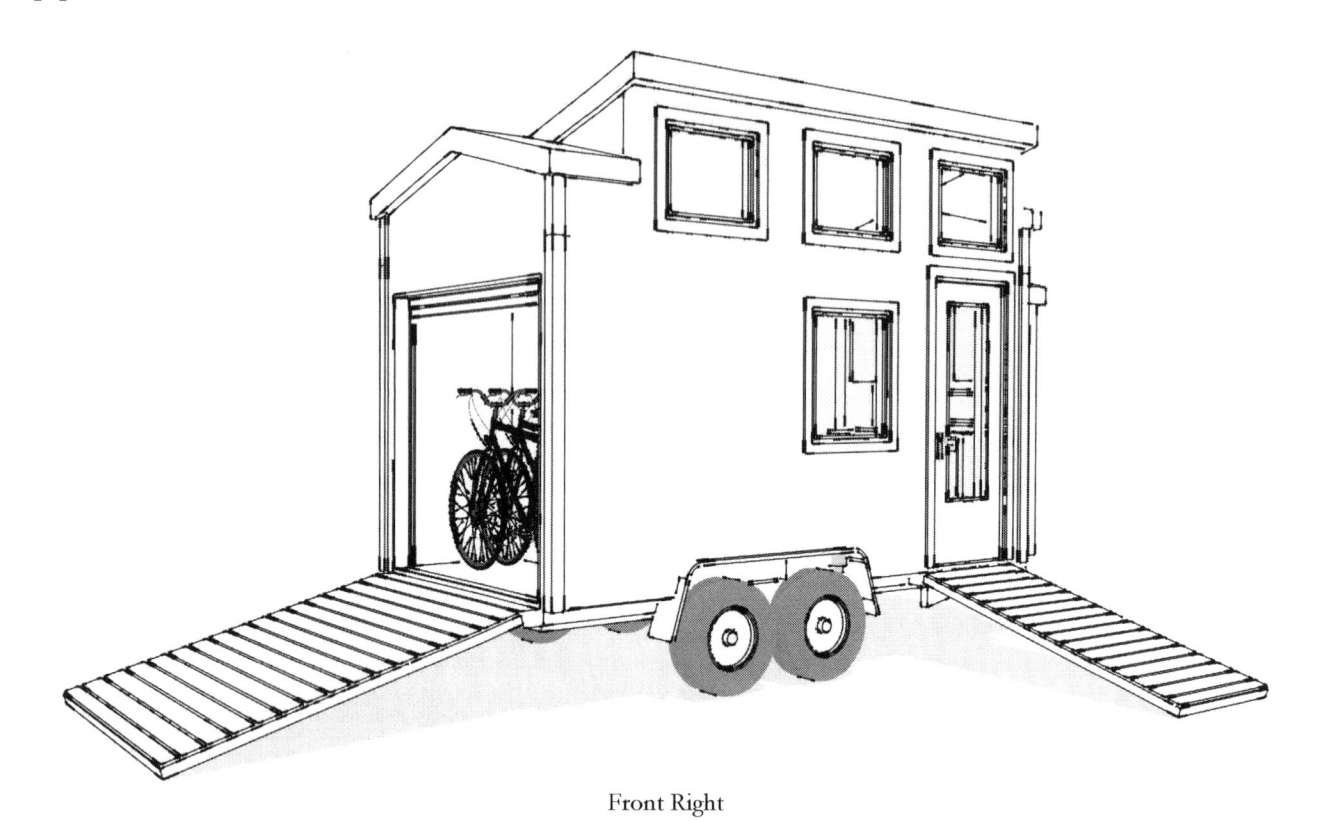

Summary:

This tiny house has a tiny garage that's just big enough for a couple of bikes or your favorite sports equipment. To access the garage there's a fold-down ramp, roll-up door, and interior door from the bathroom. The roof has a combination of a 3/12 shed roof and a 3/12 gable roof. The side entry opens onto a small kitchen that's built over a trailer tongue extension. The living room has room for a couple of comfy chairs and a shared ottoman. The kitchen has just the essentials: a sink with drying rack cabinet, small refrigerator, and stovetop. The loft is accessed by ladder rungs permanently attached to an exterior wall.

Features:

14-Foot Tiny House on Wheels
Combination Shed and Gable Roof
Garage for Sports Equipment
Bathroom with Garage Entry
Small Kitchen
Side Entry with Fold-up Ramp

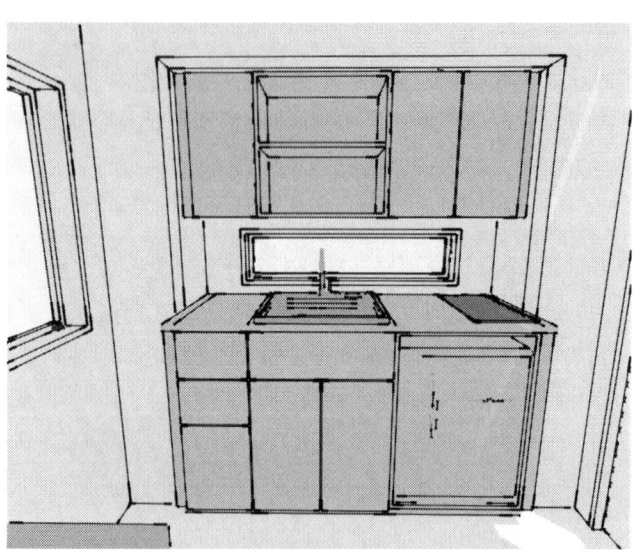

Kitchen

View from Loft

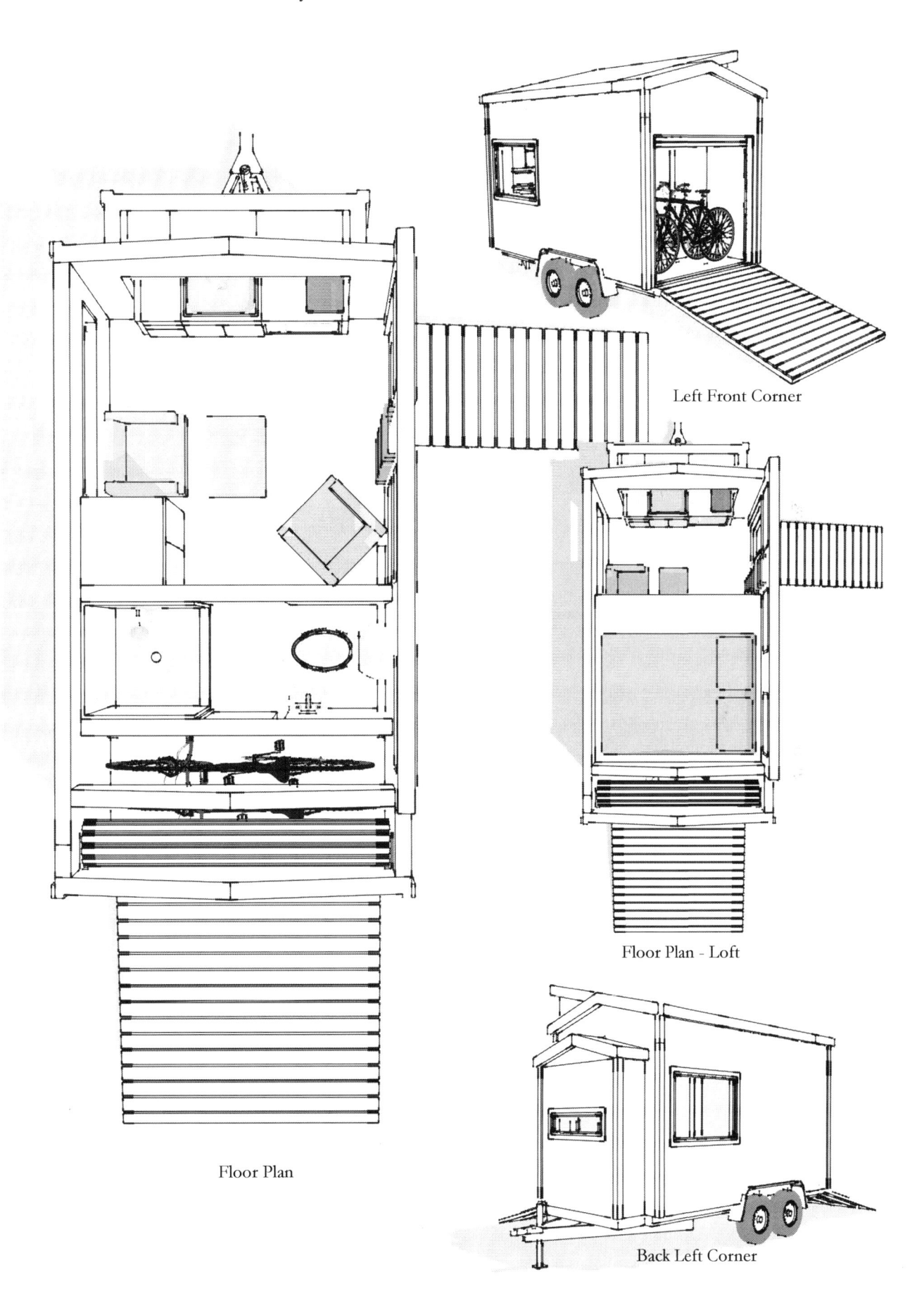

Tiny House #22 - Floor Plan & Exterior

Left Front Corner

Floor Plan - Loft

Floor Plan

Back Left Corner

Tiny House #22 - Interior Views

Interior from Bathroom

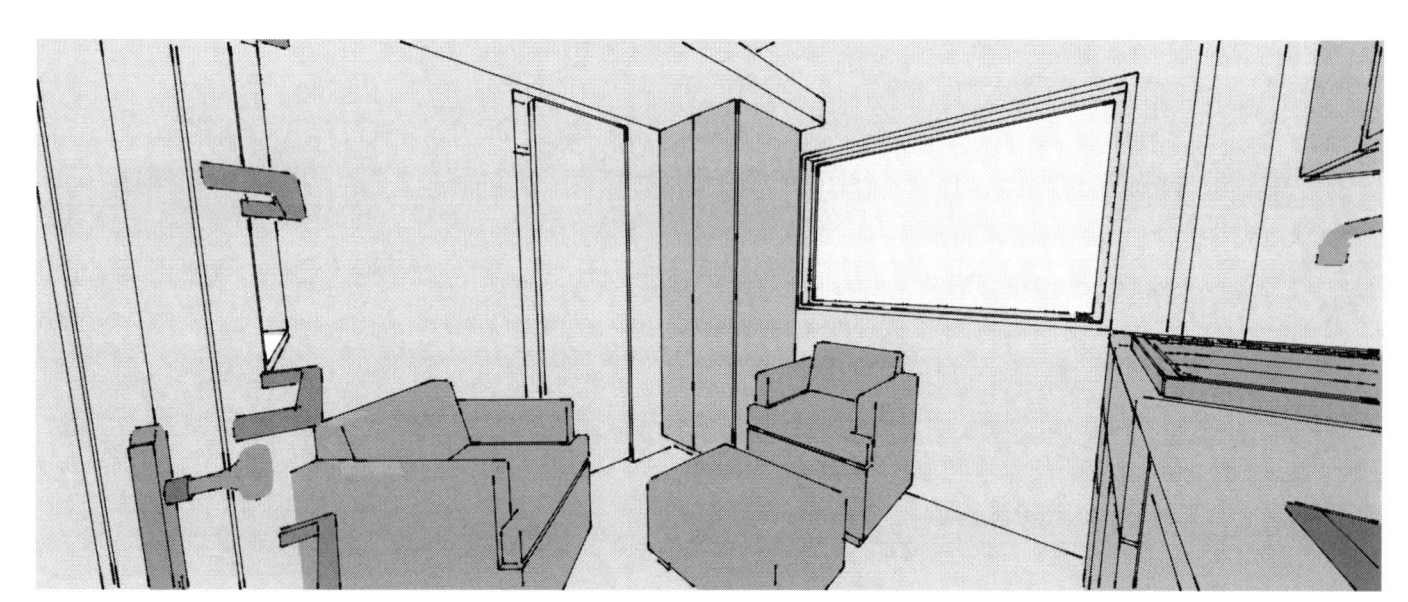

Interior from Entry

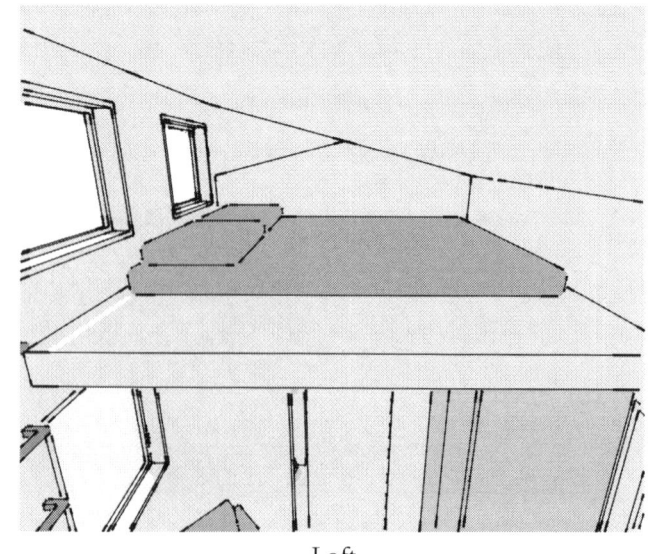

Loft

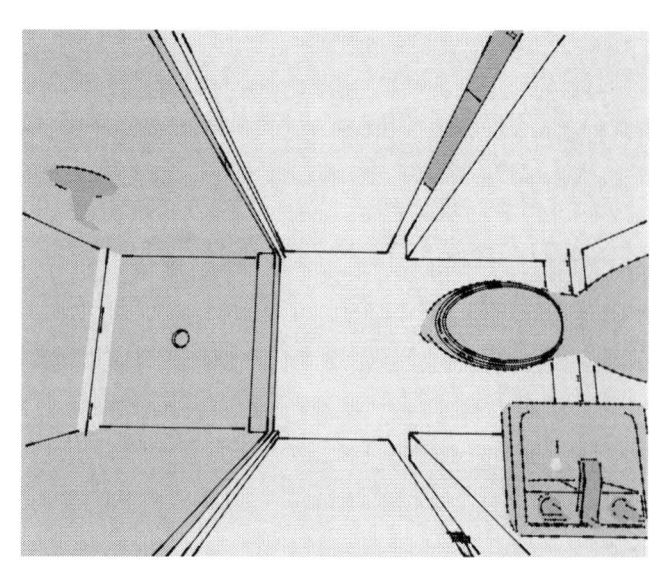

Bathroom

Tiny House #22 - Elevations

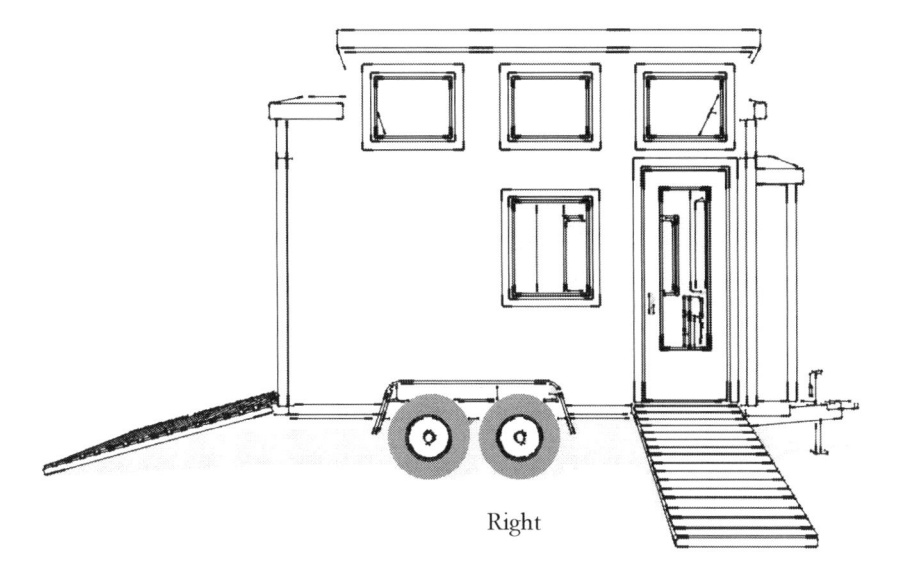

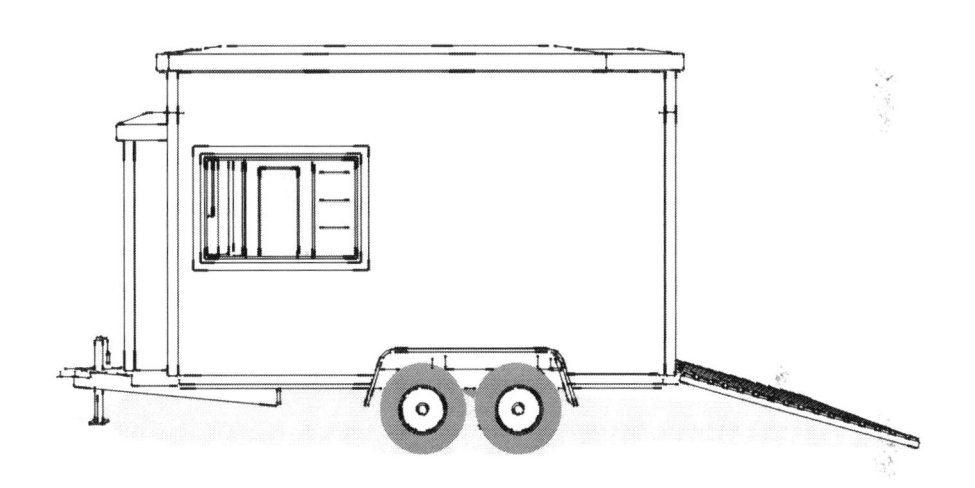

Right

Left

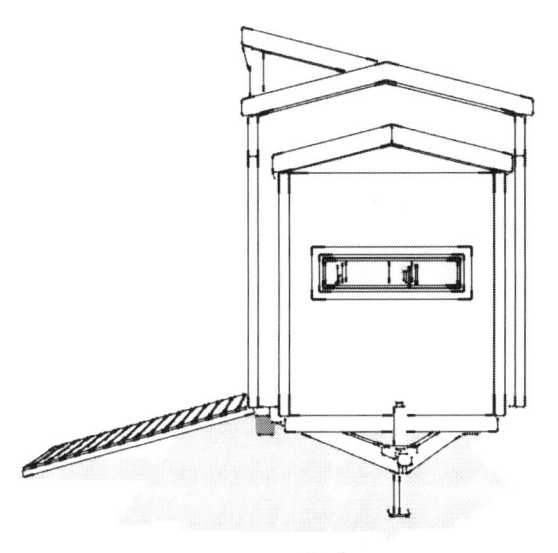

Back

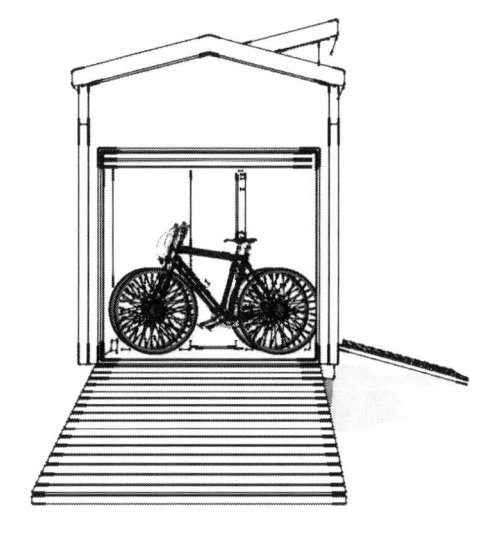

Front

16-Foot Tiny House Designs

#23

Tiny House #23 - Overview

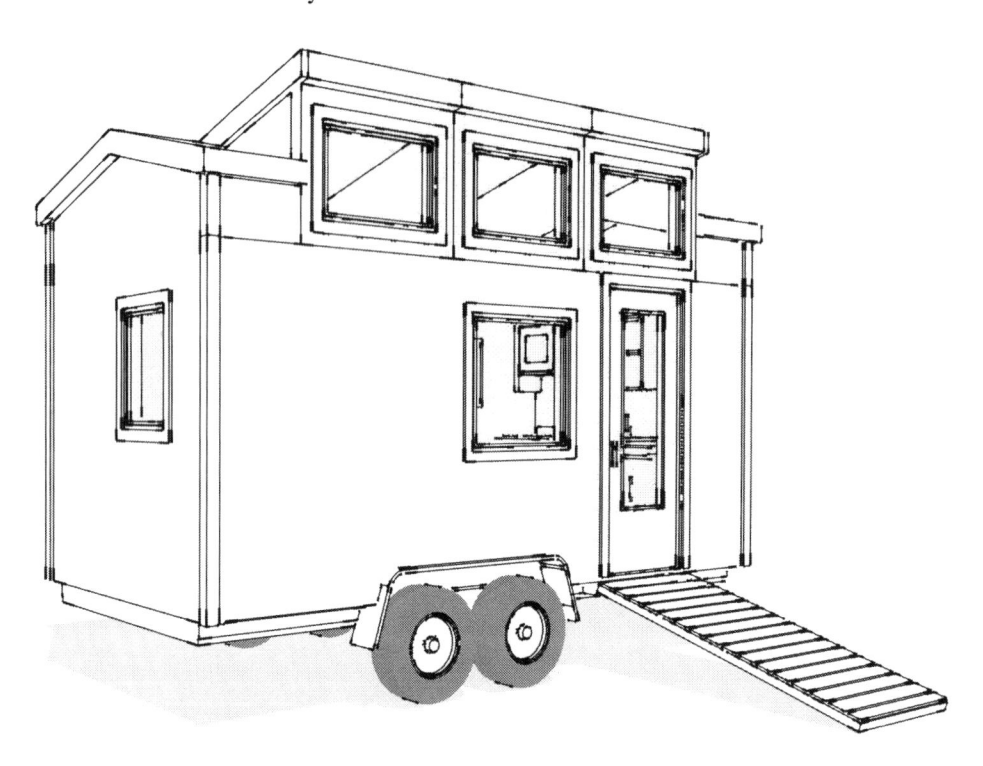

Front Right

Summary:

This tiny house also has a combination of a 3/12 shed roof and a 3/12 gable roof. The side entry opens to the kitchen and living room. The kitchen has a sink with drying rack cabinet, small refrigerator, range, and microwave. The living room has room for a couple of comfy chairs. Stairs lead to the loft. Below the stairs is storage and a desk. The bathroom has a 32-inch shower, toilet, and wall mounted sink.

Features:

16-Foot Tiny House on Wheels
Combination Shed and Gable Roof
Standard Bathroom
Kitchen includes Range
Side Entry with Fold-up Ramp
Stairs

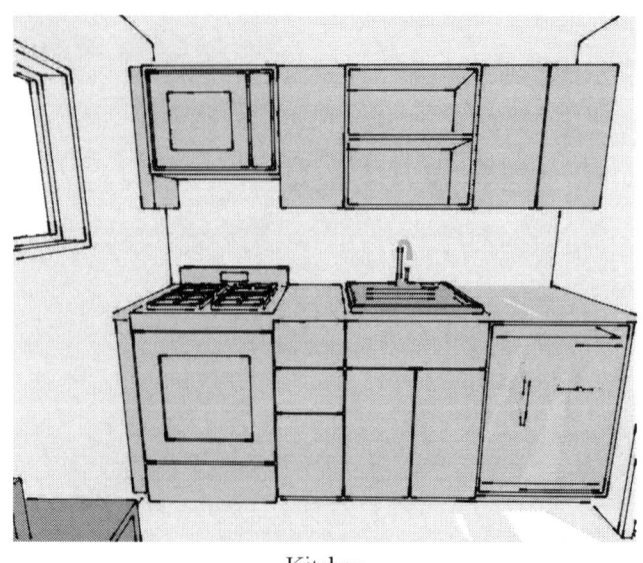

Kitchen

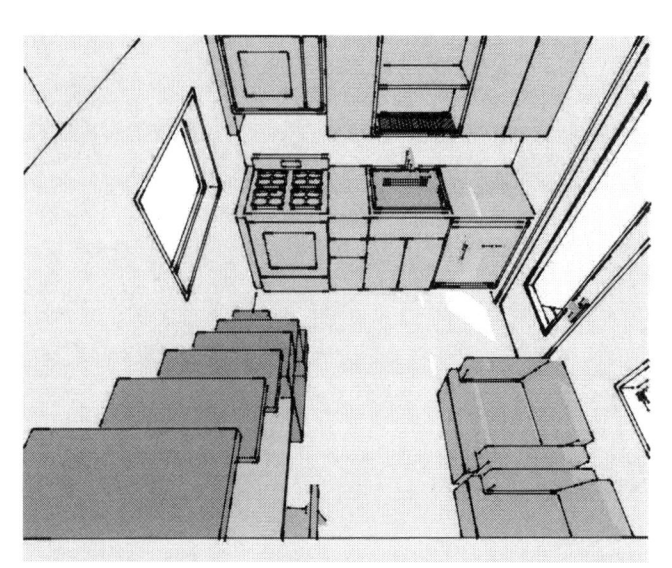

View from Loft

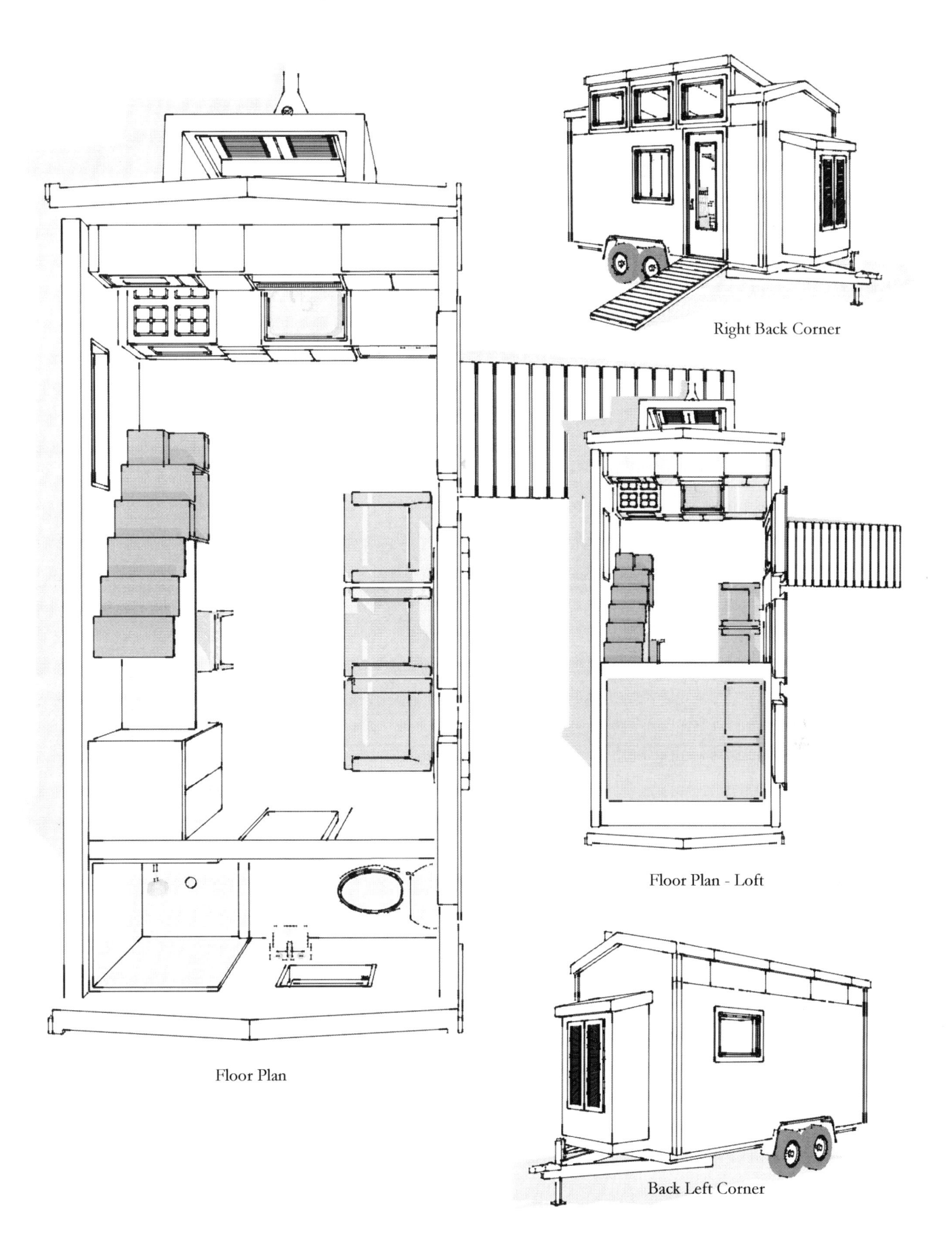

Tiny House #23 - Floor Plan & Exterior

Right Back Corner

Floor Plan - Loft

Floor Plan

Back Left Corner

Tiny House #23 - Interior Views

Interior from Bathroom

Interior from Entry

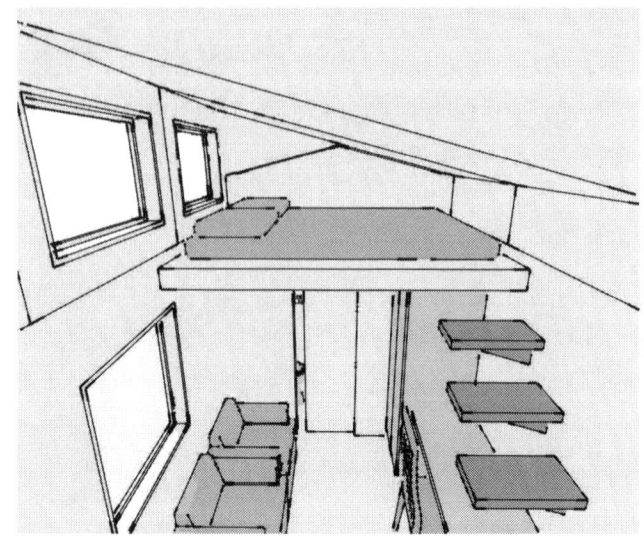

Loft

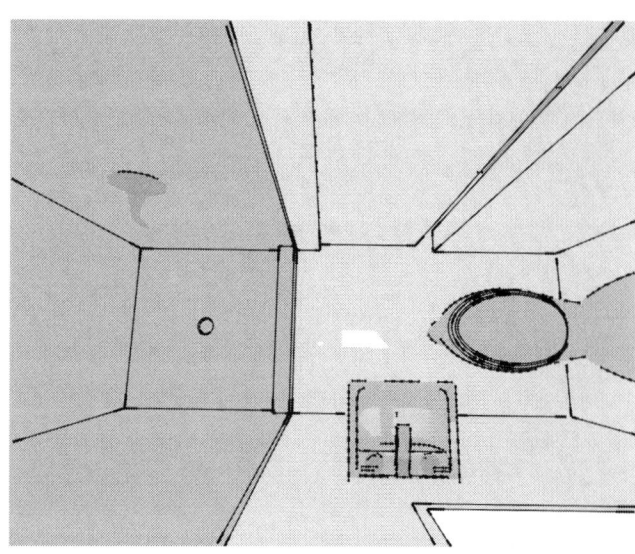

Bathroom

Tiny House #23 - Elevations

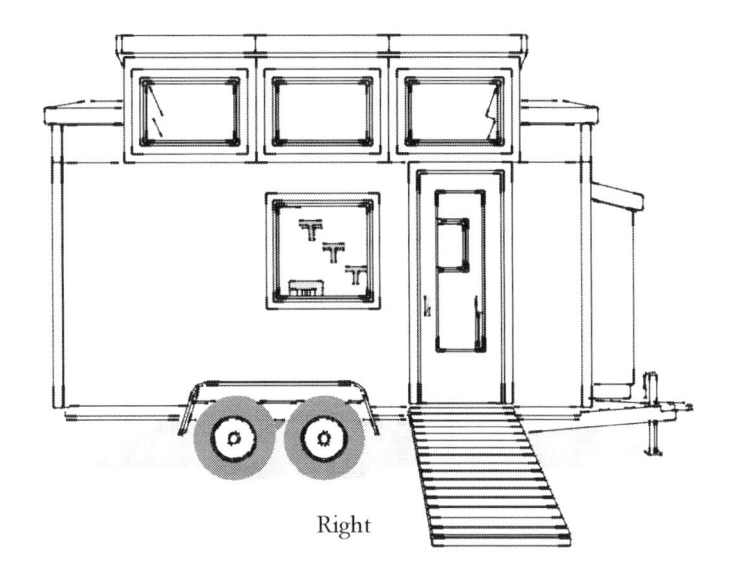

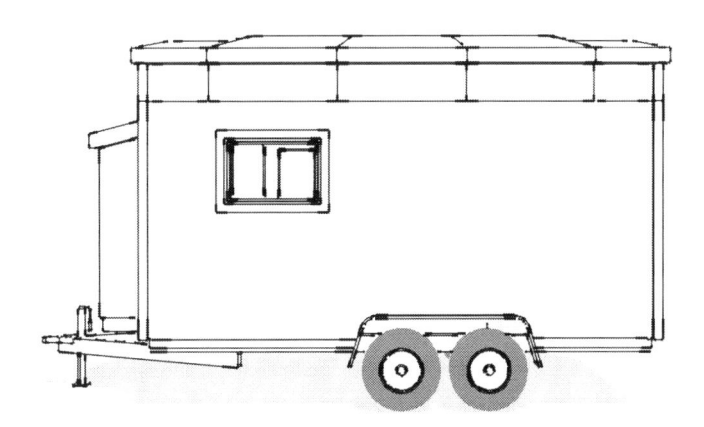

Right

Left

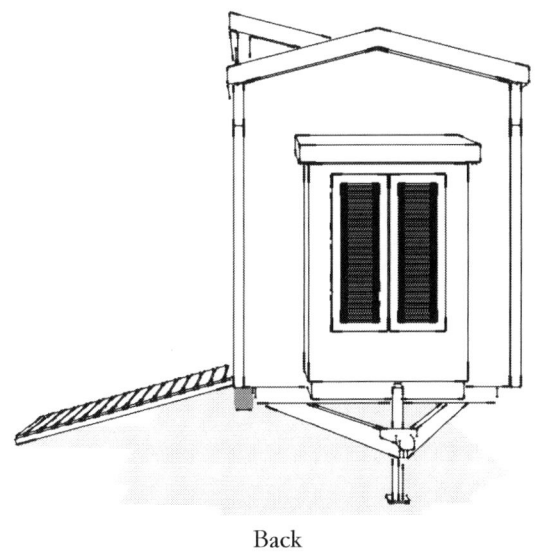

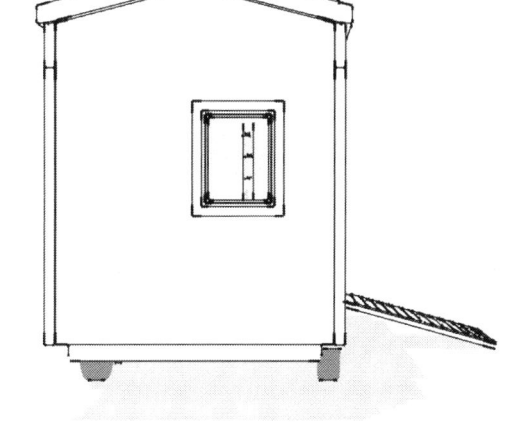

Back

Front

#24

Tiny House #24 - Overview

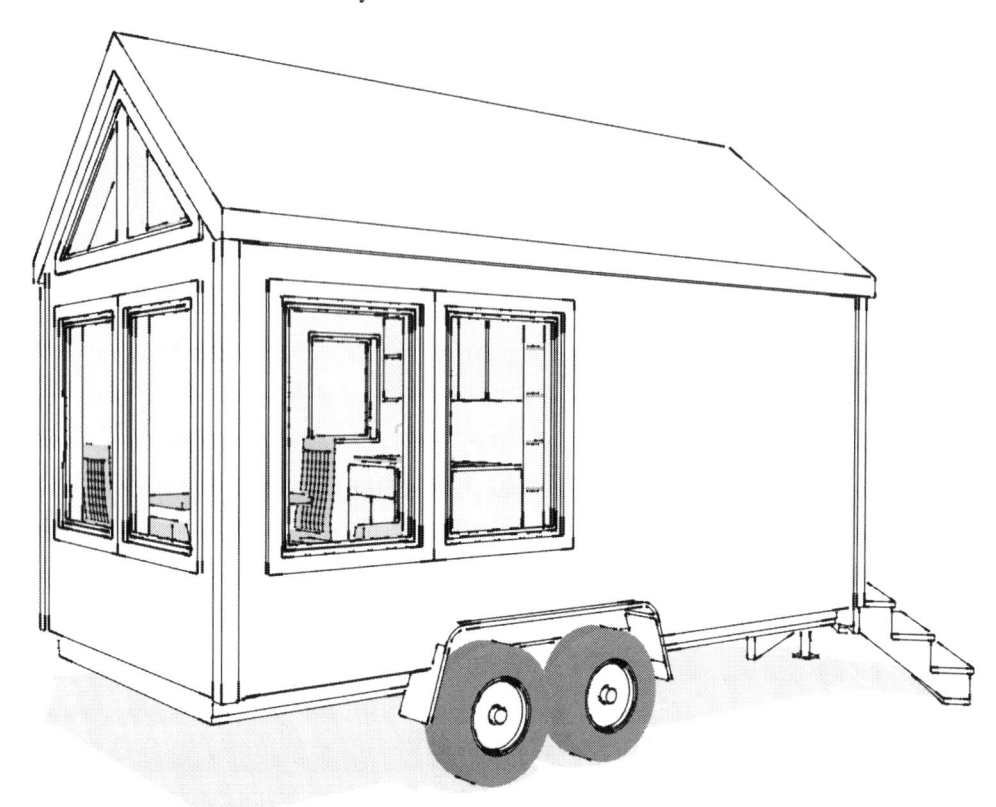

Front Right

Summary:

This tiny house has a simple 10/12 gable roof. The trailer tongue side entry leads to a short hallway. Inside the bathroom is a soaking tub/shower, toilet, and wall mounted sink. The tiny kitchen has the essentials: a sink with drying rack cabinet, stovetop, and small refrigerator. There's also room for a couple of comfy chairs and a table. Ladder rungs permanently attached to the wall lead to a large loft with extra space for storage or an additional twin mattress. Headroom in the loft is somewhat limited due to the simple gable roof.

Features:

16-Foot Tiny House on Wheels
Gable Roof
Trailer Tongue Side Entry with Fold-up Steps
Bathroom with Soaking Tub/Shower
Tiny Kitchen
Large Windows

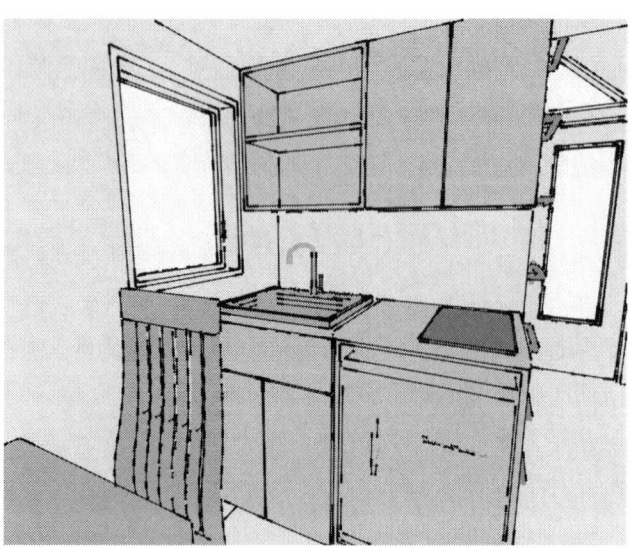

Kitchen

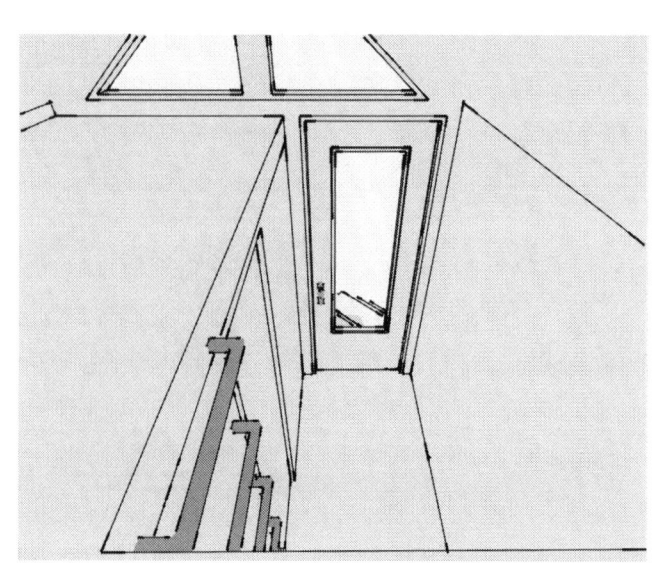

View from Loft

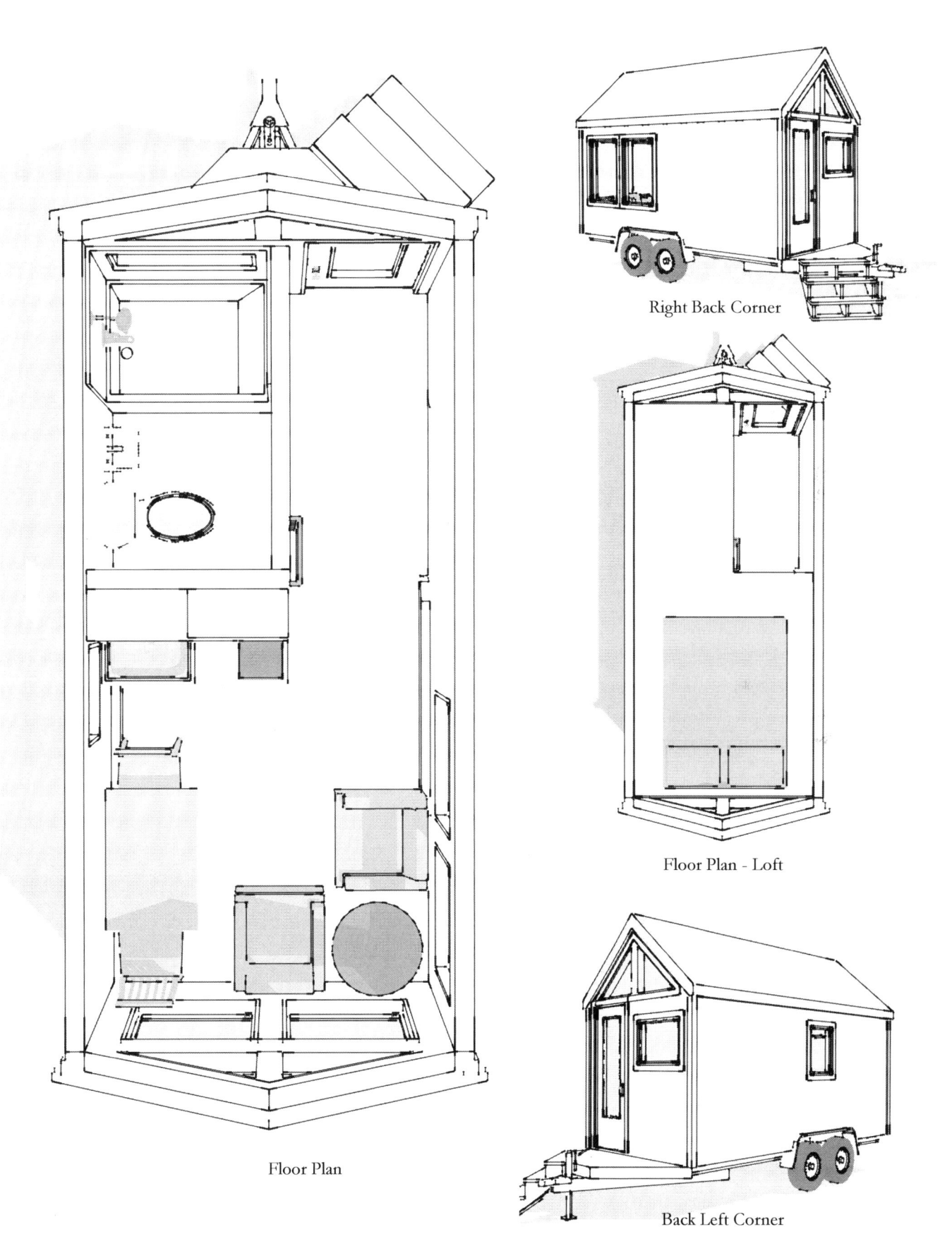

Tiny House #24 - Floor Plan & Exterior

Floor Plan

Right Back Corner

Floor Plan - Loft

Back Left Corner

99

Tiny House #24 - Interior Views

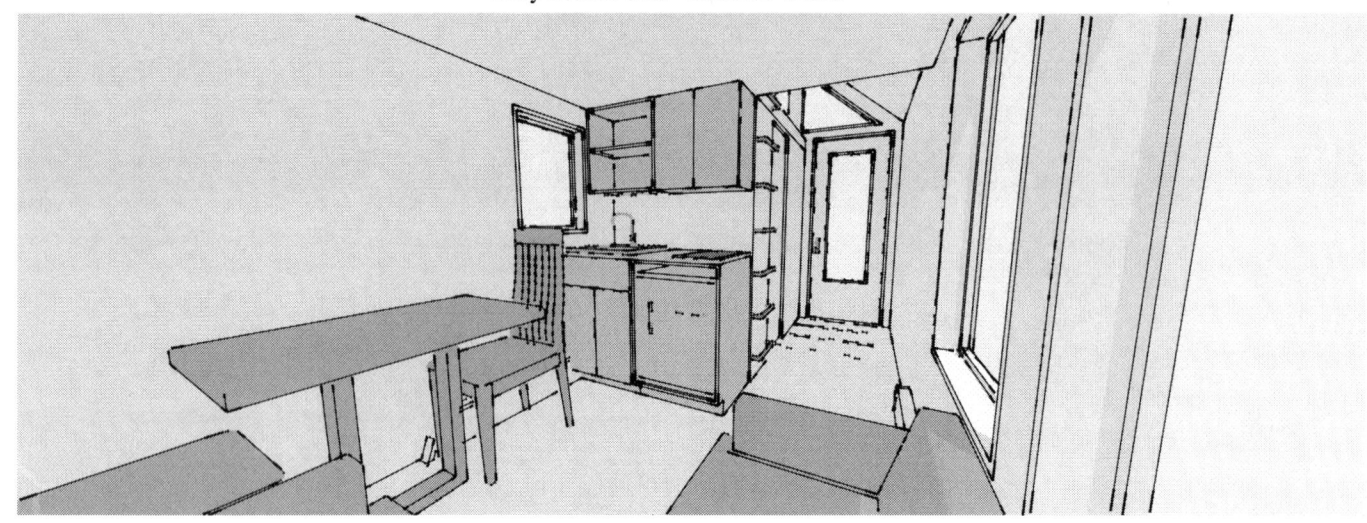

Interior from Bathroom

Interior from Entry

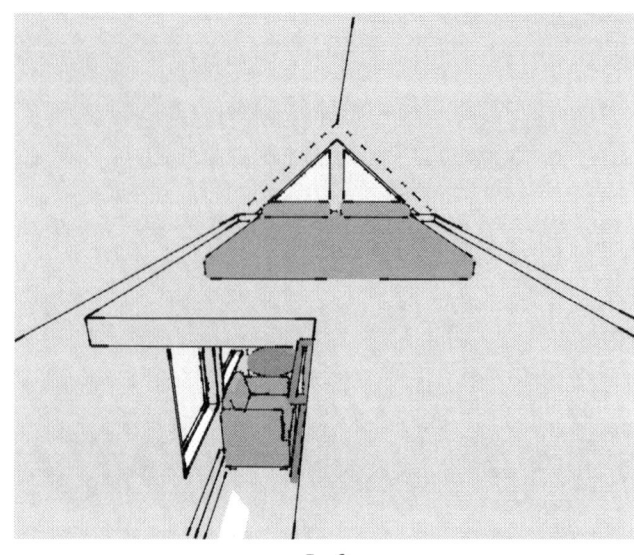

Loft

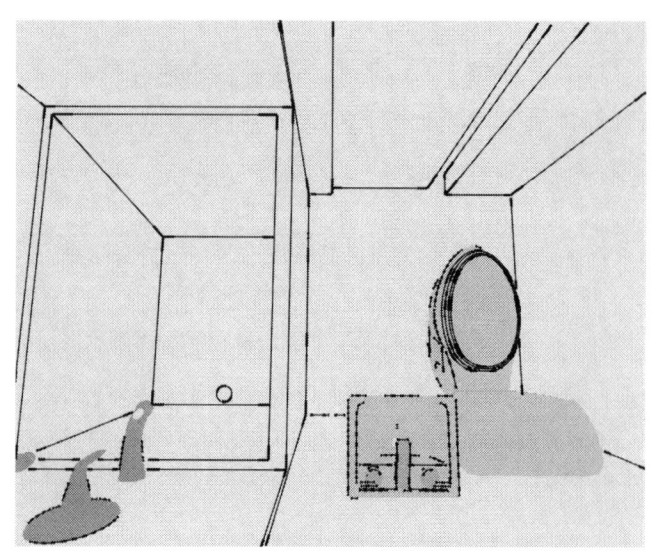

Bathroom

Tiny House #24 - Elevations

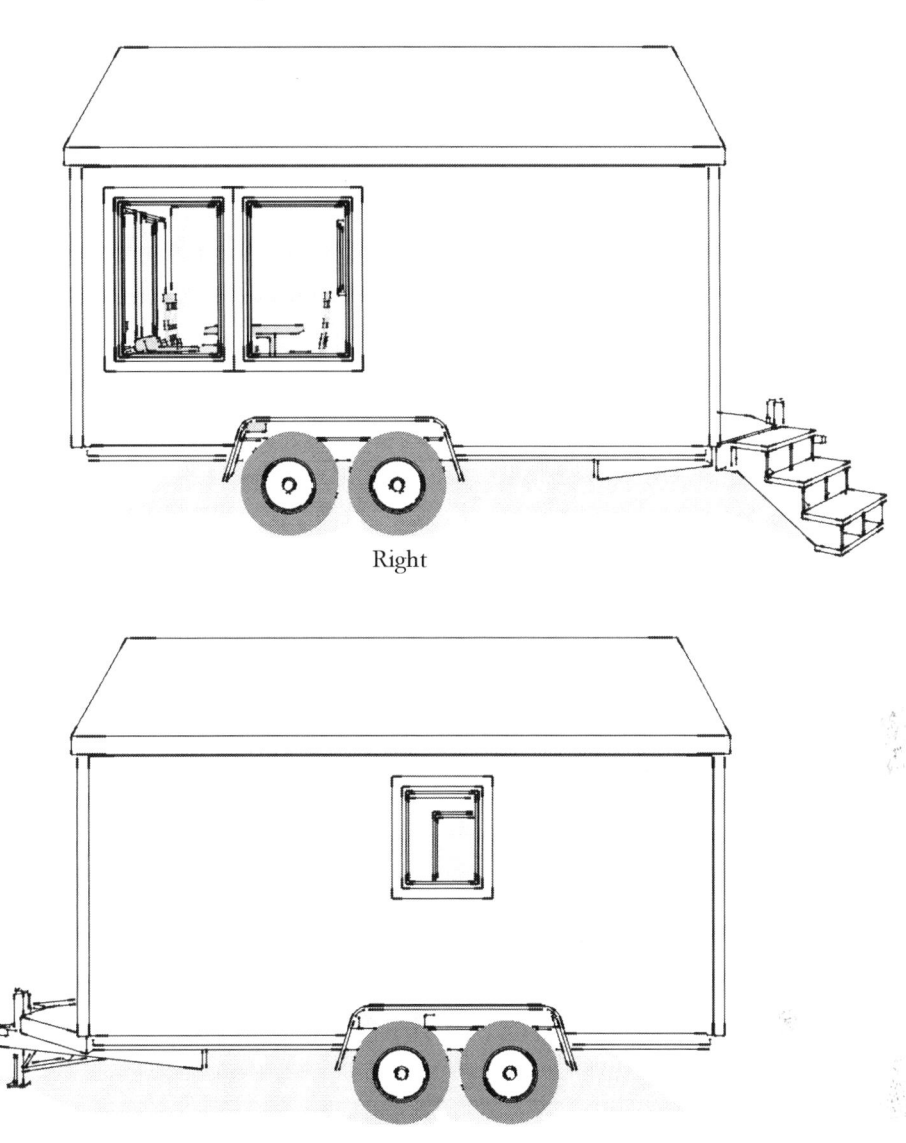

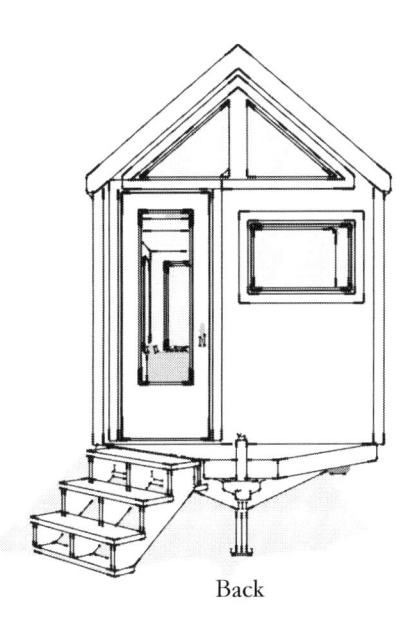

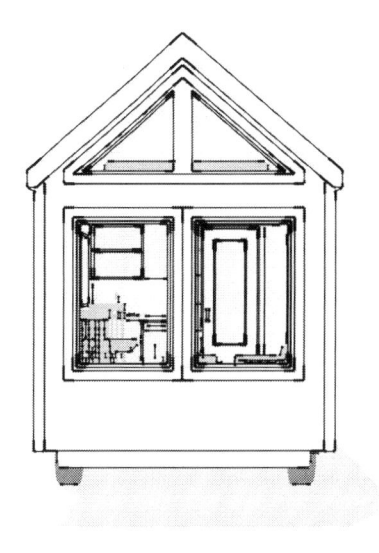

Right

Left

Back

Front

#25

Tiny House #25 - Overview

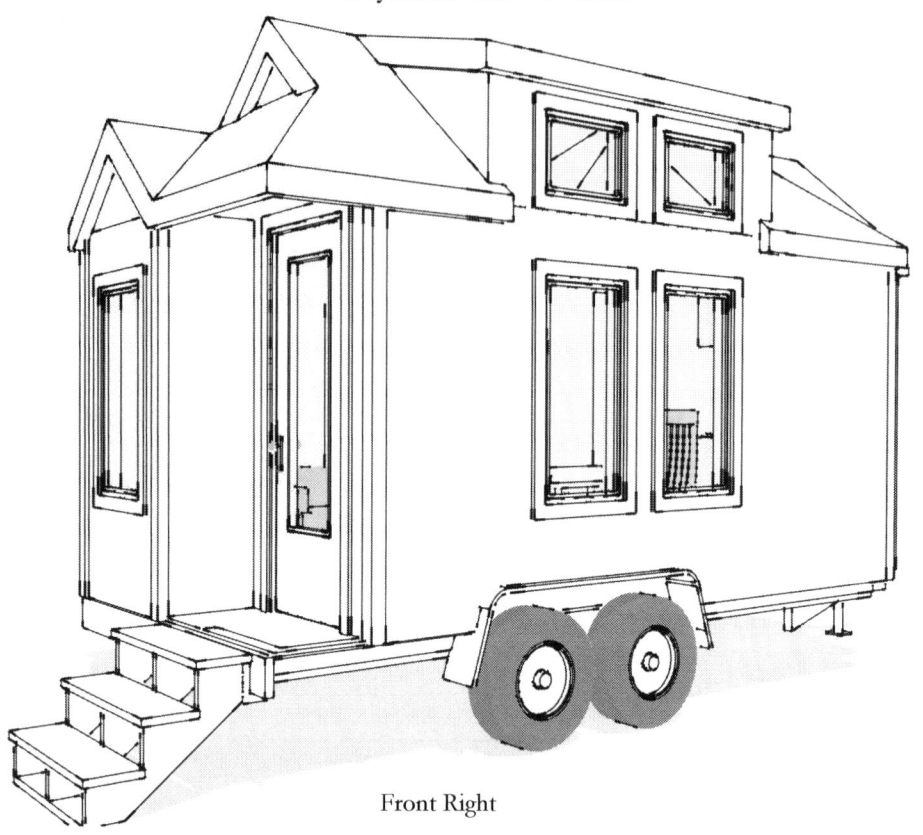

Front Right

Summary:

This tiny house has one of the complicated roofs that's hard to build but super cute. Just inside the entry are two comfy chairs, a table, and alternating step stairs that lead to the loft. The loft has space for a queen size bed. The kitchen has a sink, range, small refrigerator, and microwave. Over the trailer tongue is a bump-out that extends both the kitchen and bathroom. The standard bathroom has a 32-inch shower, toilet, wall mounted sink, and storage cabinet.

Features:

16-Foot Tiny House on Wheels
Dutch Gable Front, Hip Roof Back, with Shed Dormers
Kitchen and Bathroom Extend into Bump-out Extension over Trailer Tongue
Standard Bathroom
Kitchen that includes a Range
Steep Alternating Step Stairs to Loft

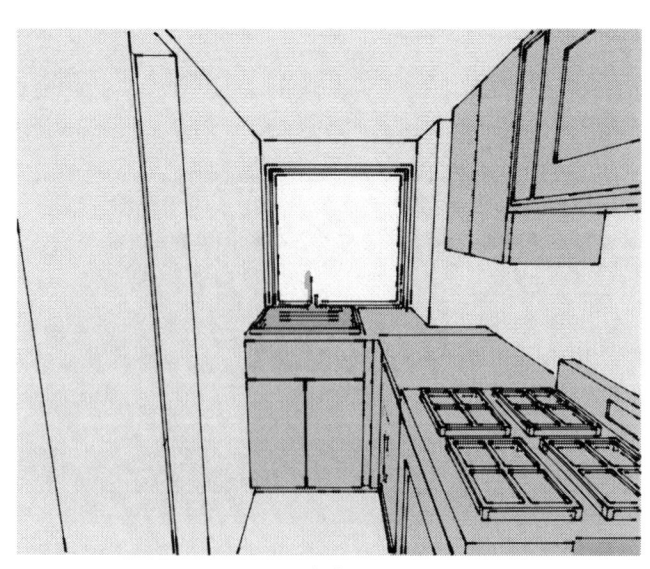

Kitchen

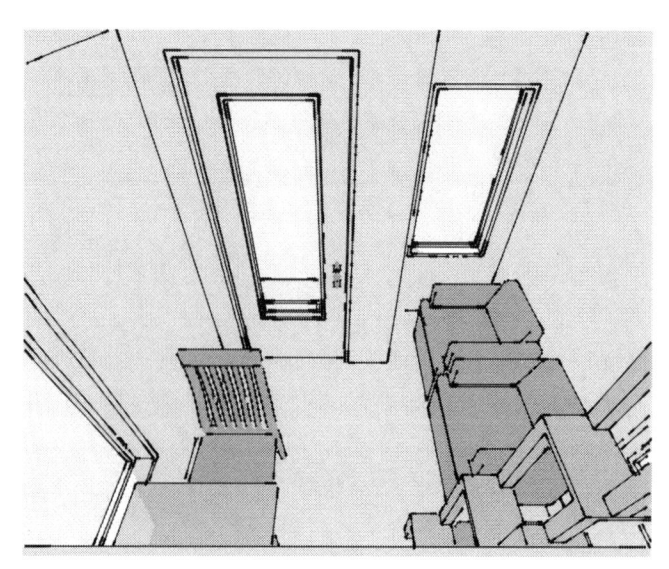

View from Loft

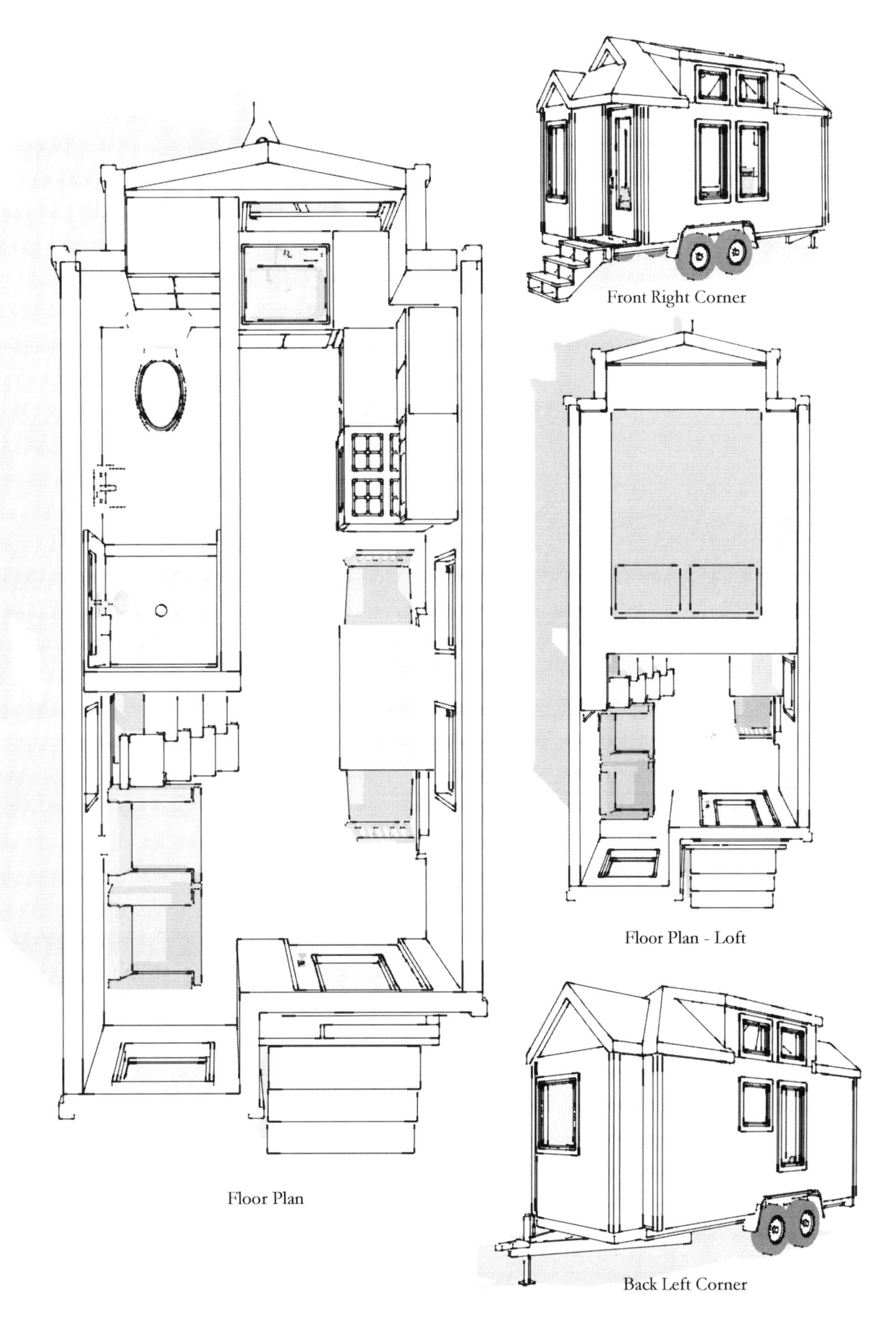

Tiny House #25 - Floor Plan & Exterior

Front Right Corner

Floor Plan - Loft

Floor Plan

Back Left Corner

Tiny House #25 - Interior Views

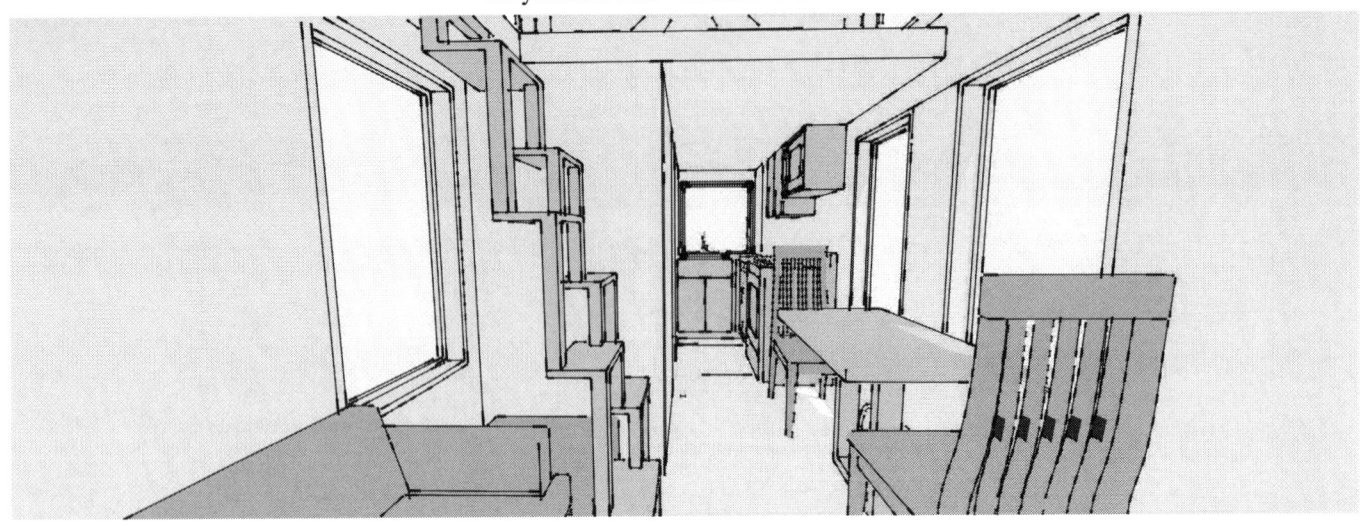

Interior from Entry

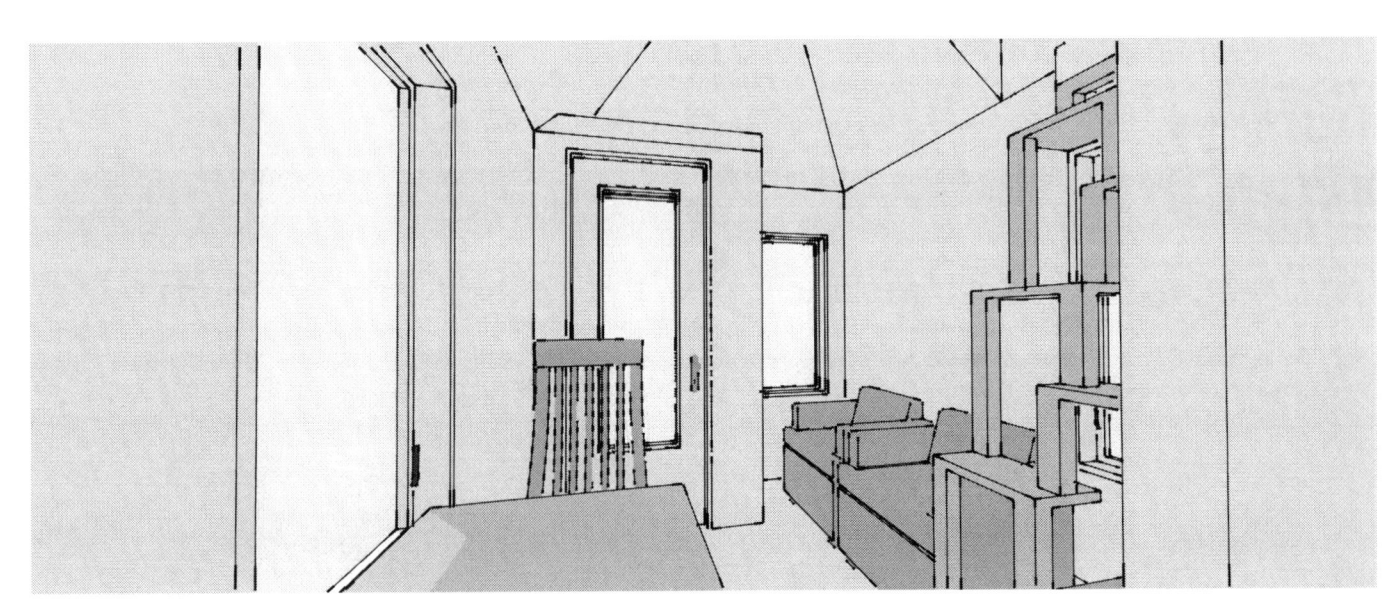

Interior from Kitchen

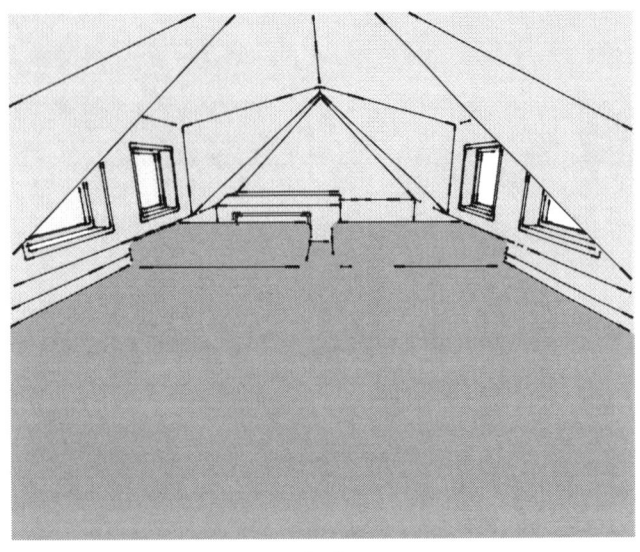

Loft

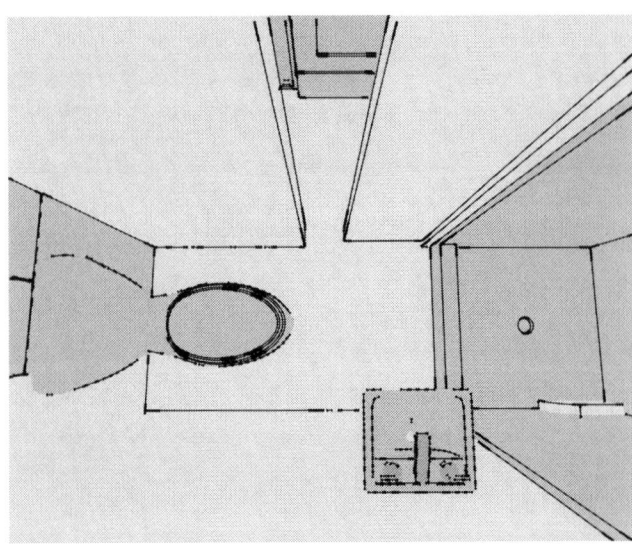

Bathroom

Tiny House #25 - Elevations

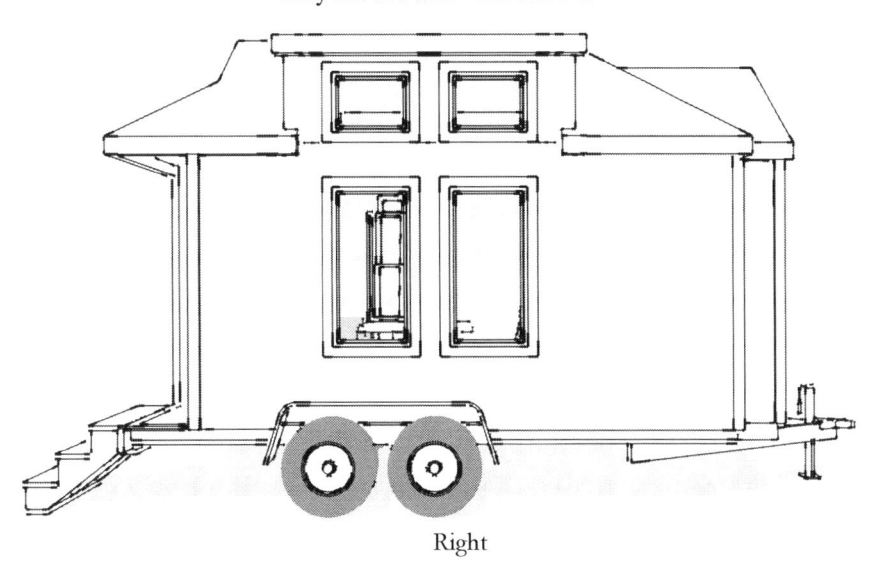

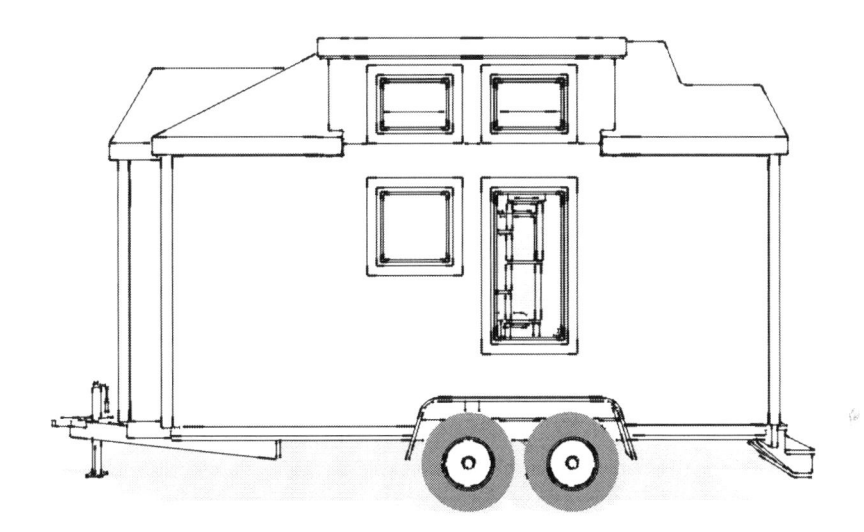

Right

Left

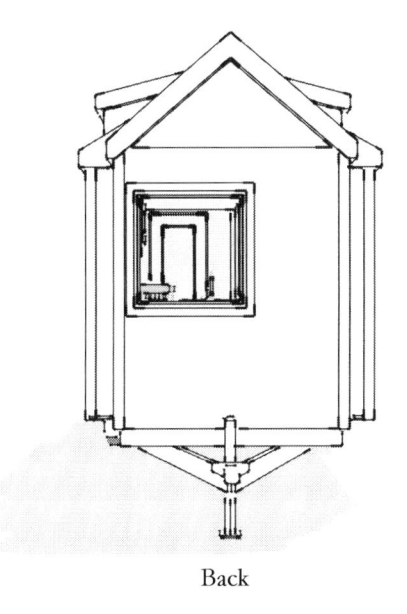

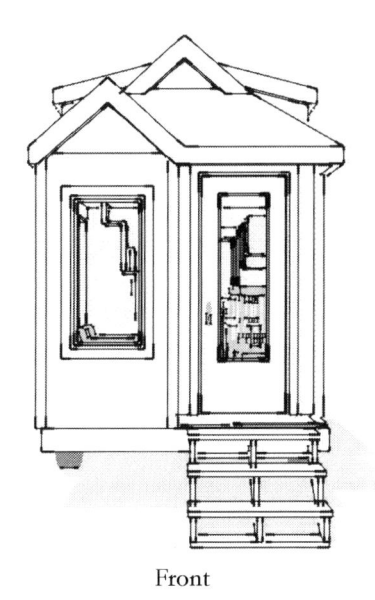

Back

Front

105

#26

Tiny House #26 - Overview

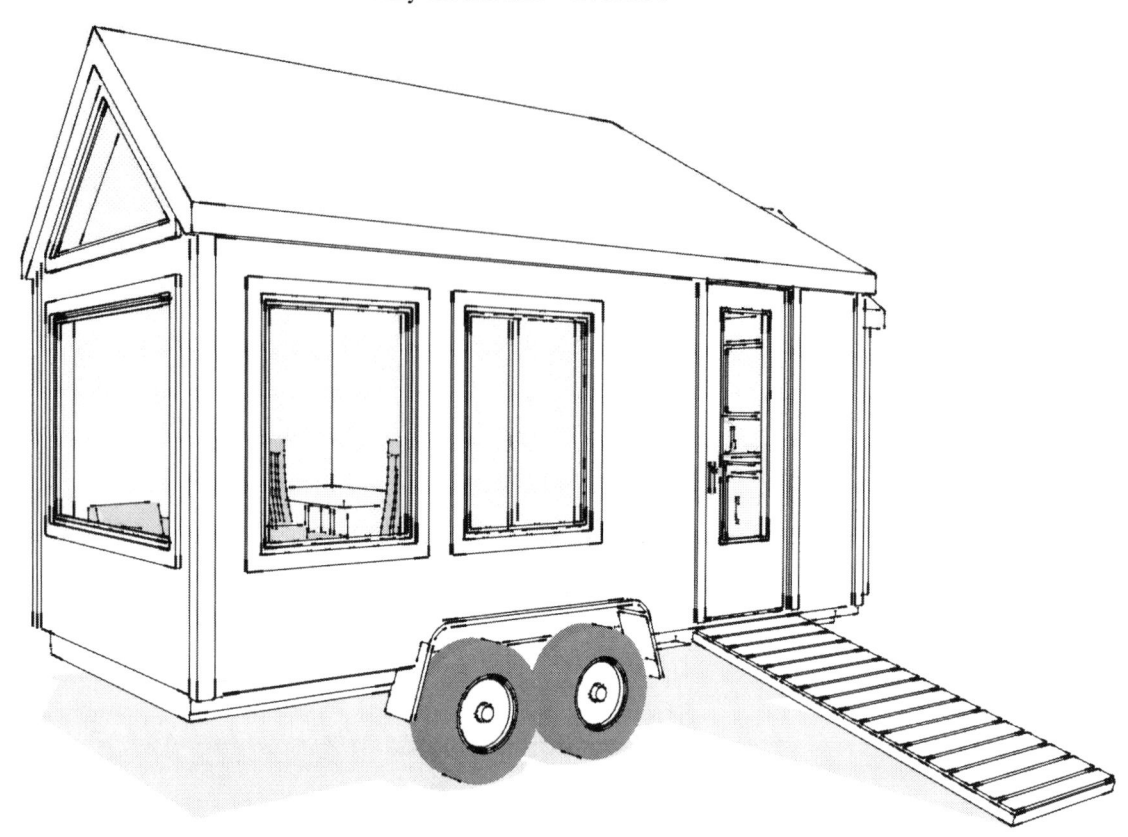

Front Right

Summary:

Tiny house #26 has a simple 10/12 gable roof that ends in a hip on the trailer tongue side - adding to aerodynamics. Just inside the side entry is the kitchen and loft ladder. The loft has space for a queen size bed. Over the trailer tongue is a gable roofed extension that extends the kitchen. The kitchen has plenty of storage, a sink, stovetop, and small refrigerator. The bathroom has a soaking tub/shower, toilet, wall and mounted sink. The living room has two small comfy chairs and a table for two.

Features:

16-Foot Tiny House on Wheels
Gable Roof with Hip
Kitchen Extends over Trailer Tongue
Side Entry with Ramp
Bathroom with Soaking Tub

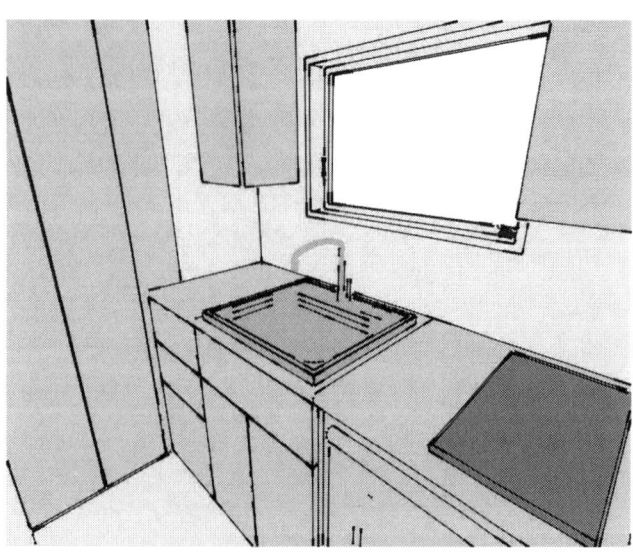

Kitchen

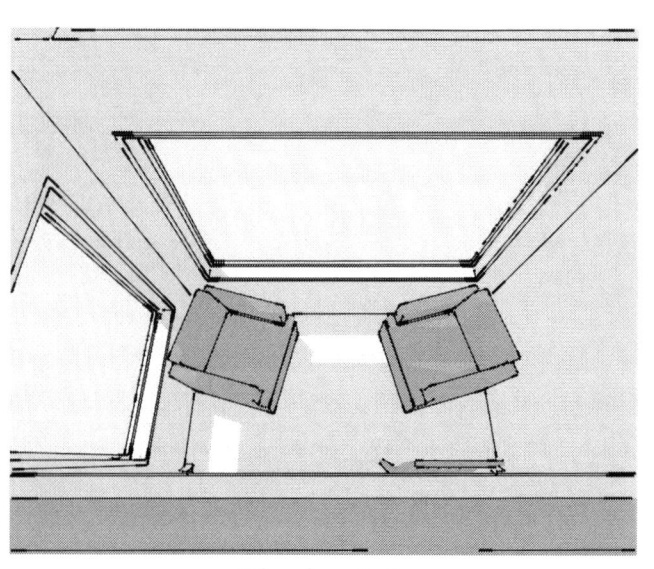

View from Loft

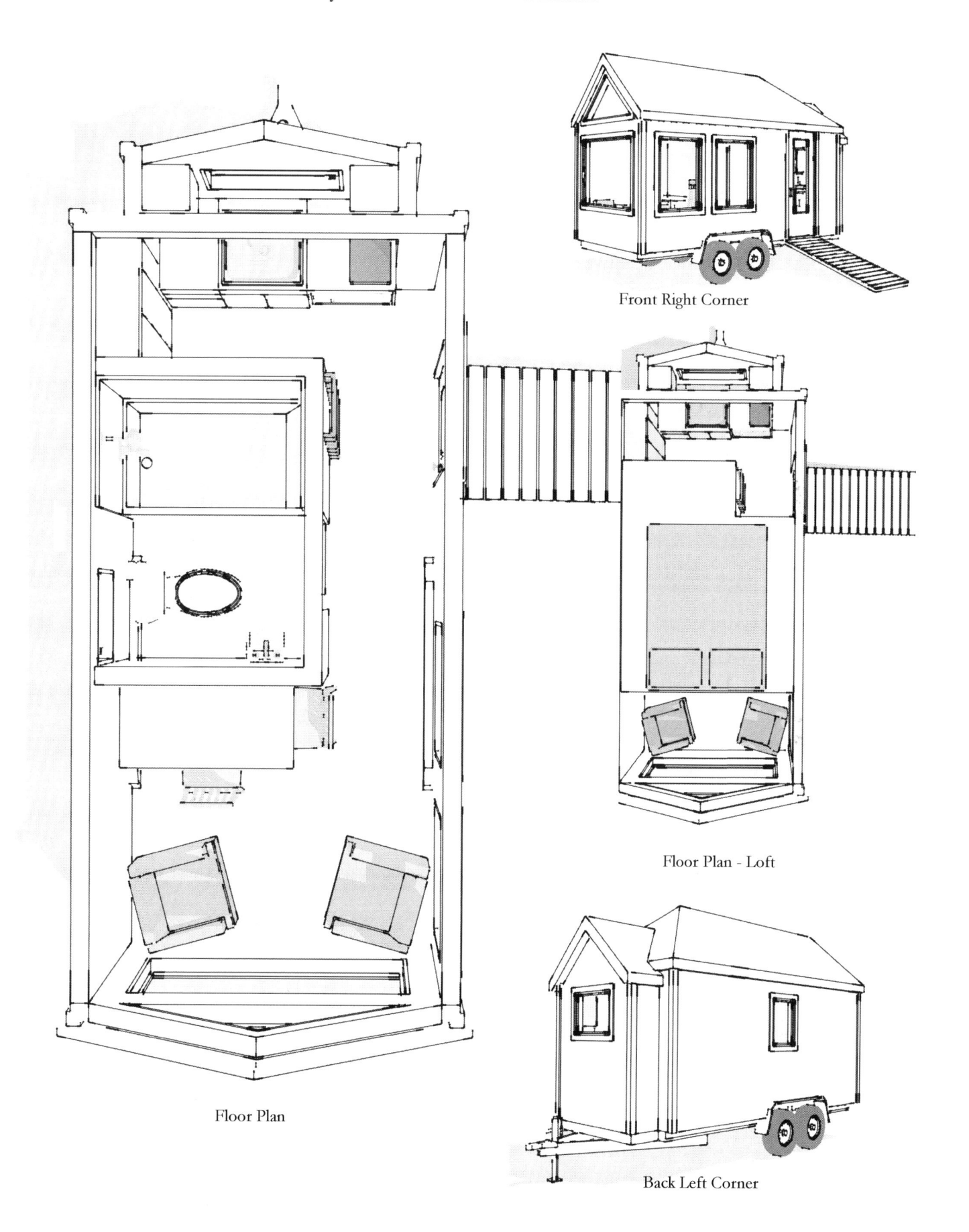

Tiny House #26 - Floor Plan & Exterior

Front Right Corner

Floor Plan - Loft

Floor Plan

Back Left Corner

107

Tiny House #26 - Interior Views

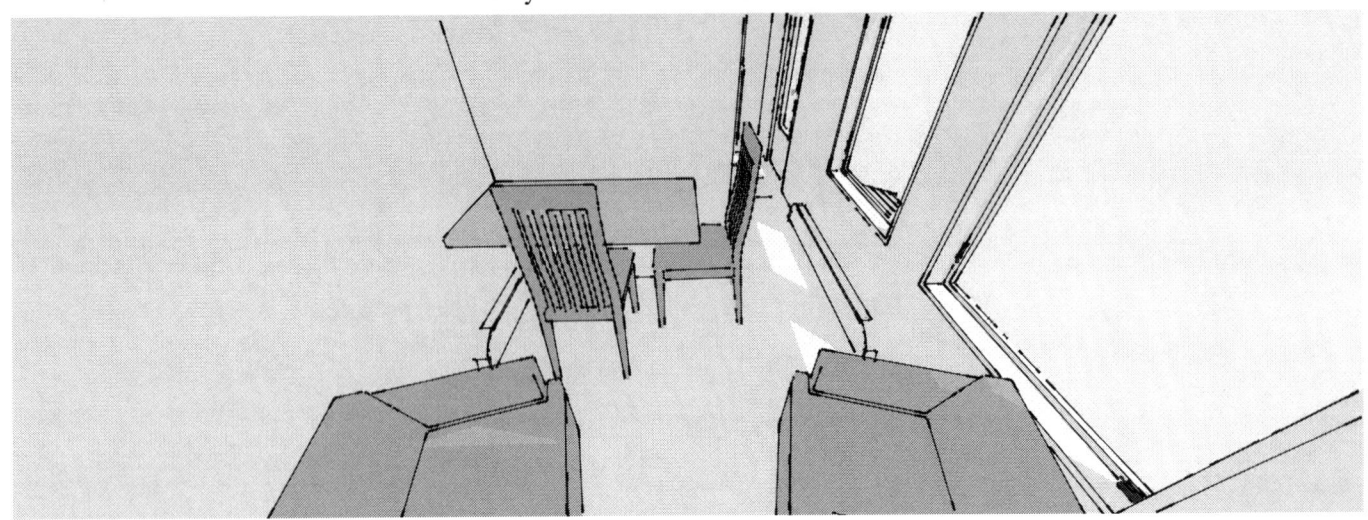

Interior from Living Room

Interior from Kitchen

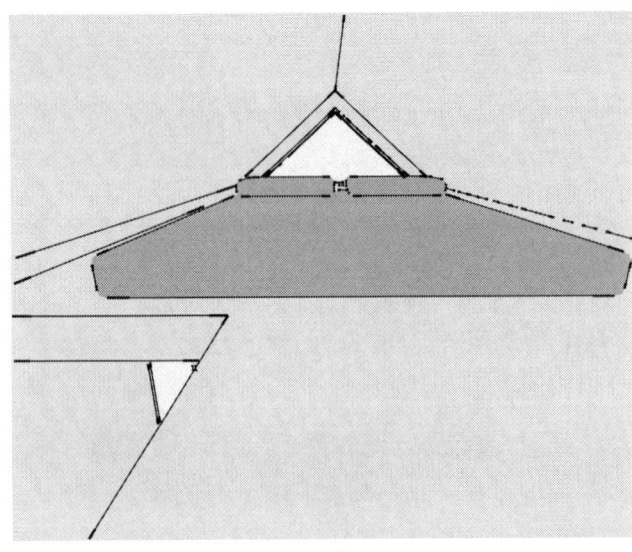

Loft

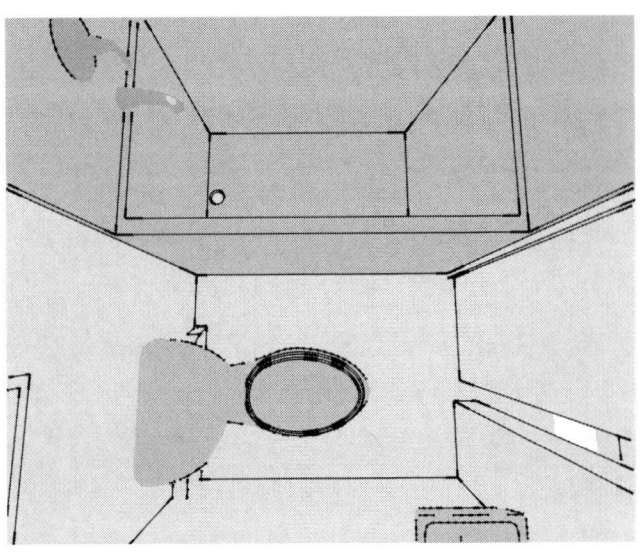

Bathroom

Tiny House #26 - Elevations

Right

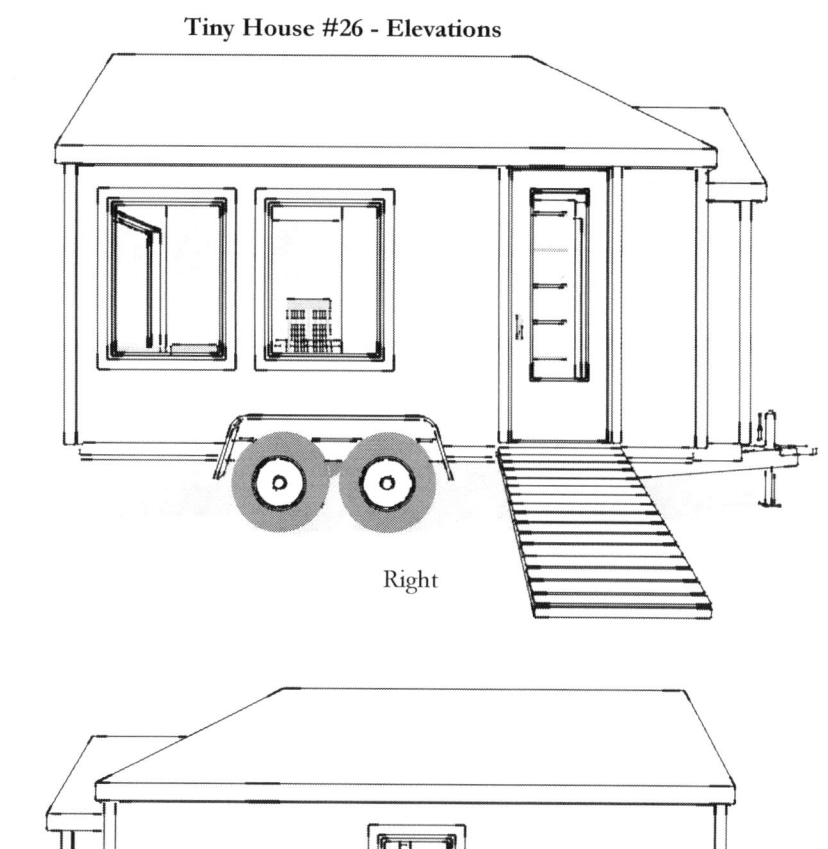

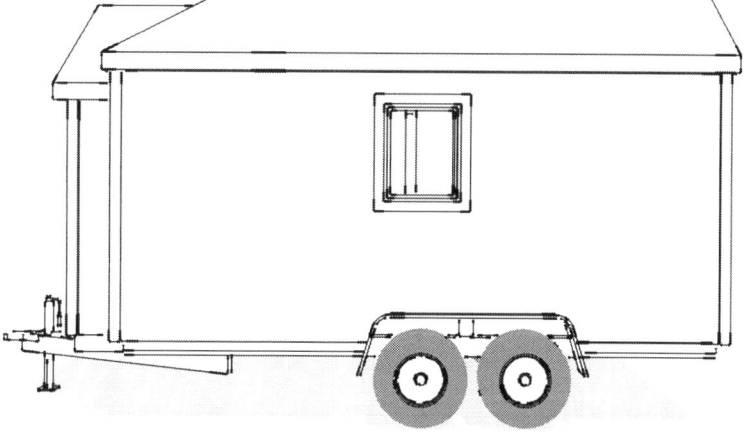

Left

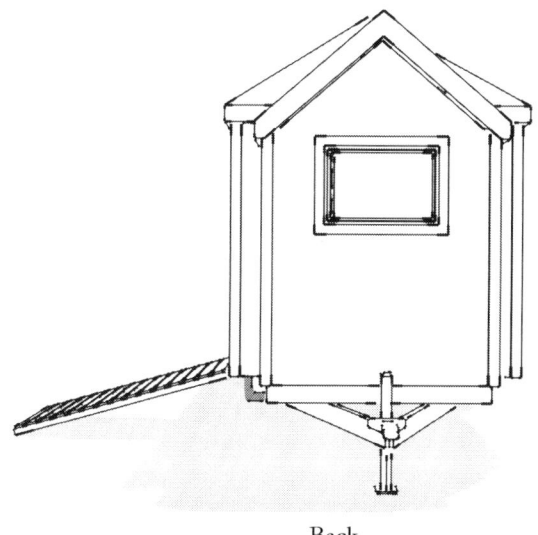

Back

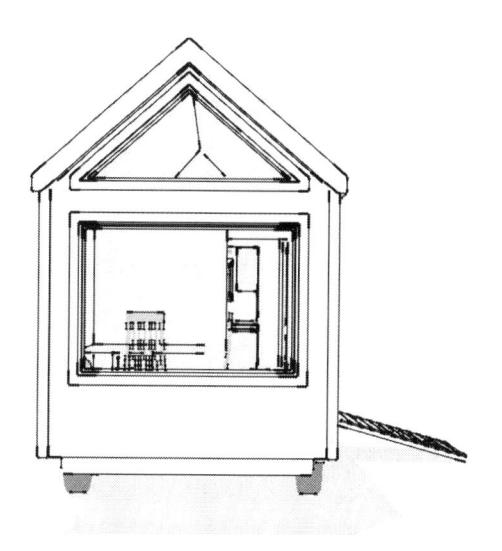

Front

109

#27

Tiny House #27 - Overview

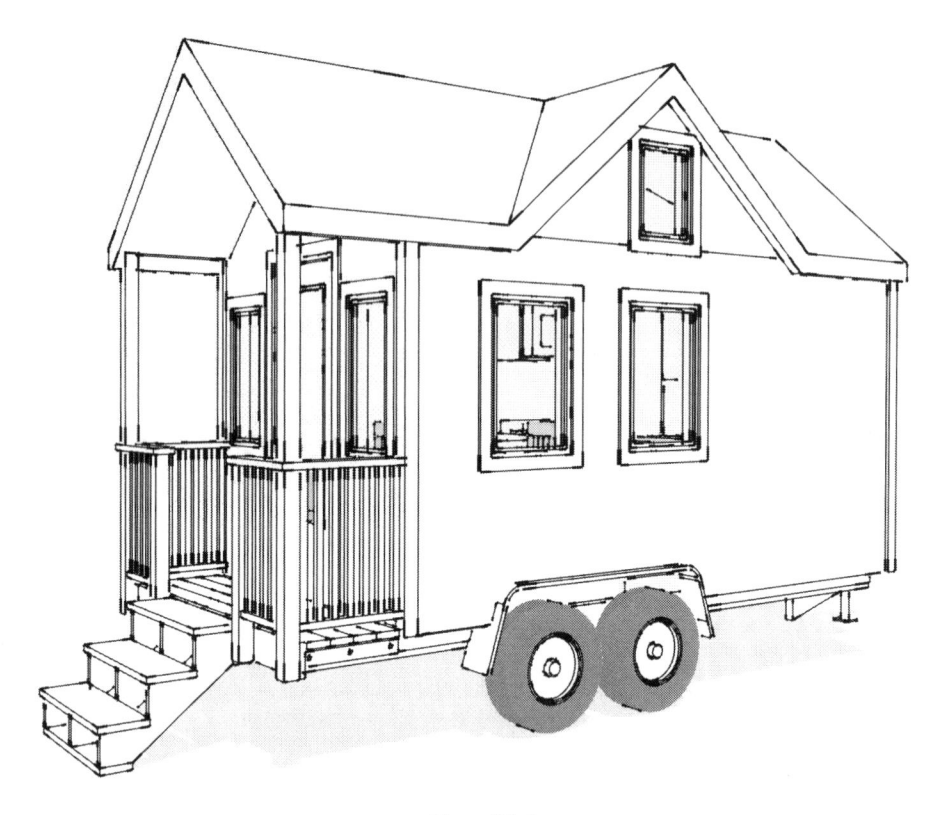

Front Right

Summary:

This tiny house design has a 10/12 cross gable roof and 2-foot deep porch. Just inside the entry are two comfy chairs and a table for two. The kitchen has plenty of storage, a sink with a cabinet drain rack above, range, microwave, and small refrigerator. The standard bathroom has a 32-inch shower, toilet and wall mounted sink. The loft has space for a queen size bed and is accessed by a movable ladder. Over the trailer tongue is a mechanical storage closet.

Features:

16-Foot Tiny House on Wheels
Cross Gable Roof
Front Porch
Utility Closet over Trailer Tongue
Standard Bathroom
Kitchen that includes a Range

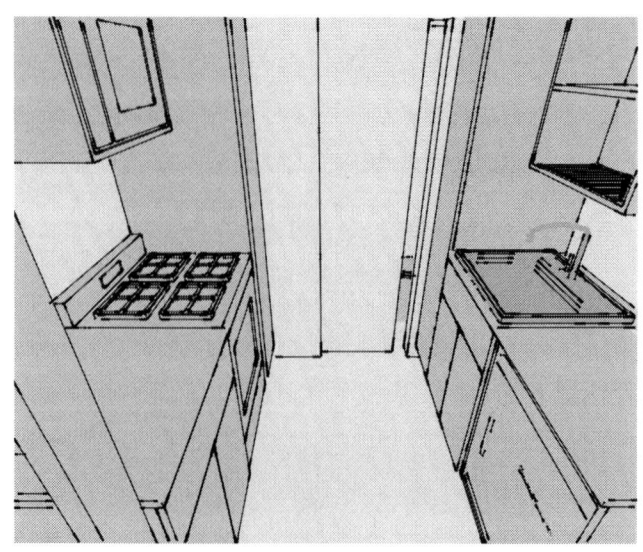

Kitchen

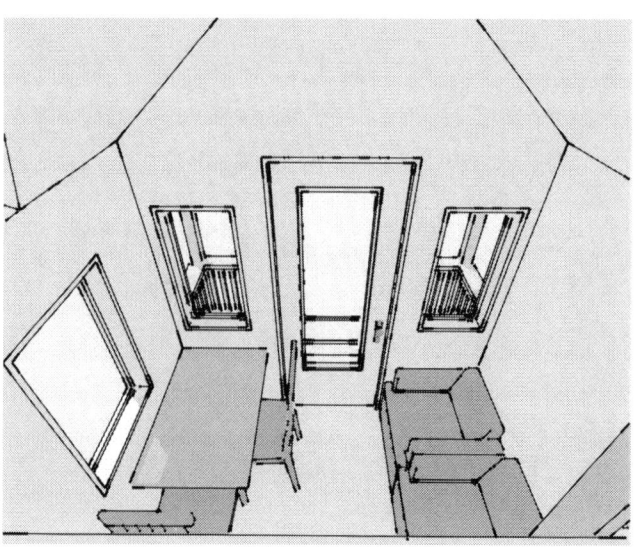

View from Loft

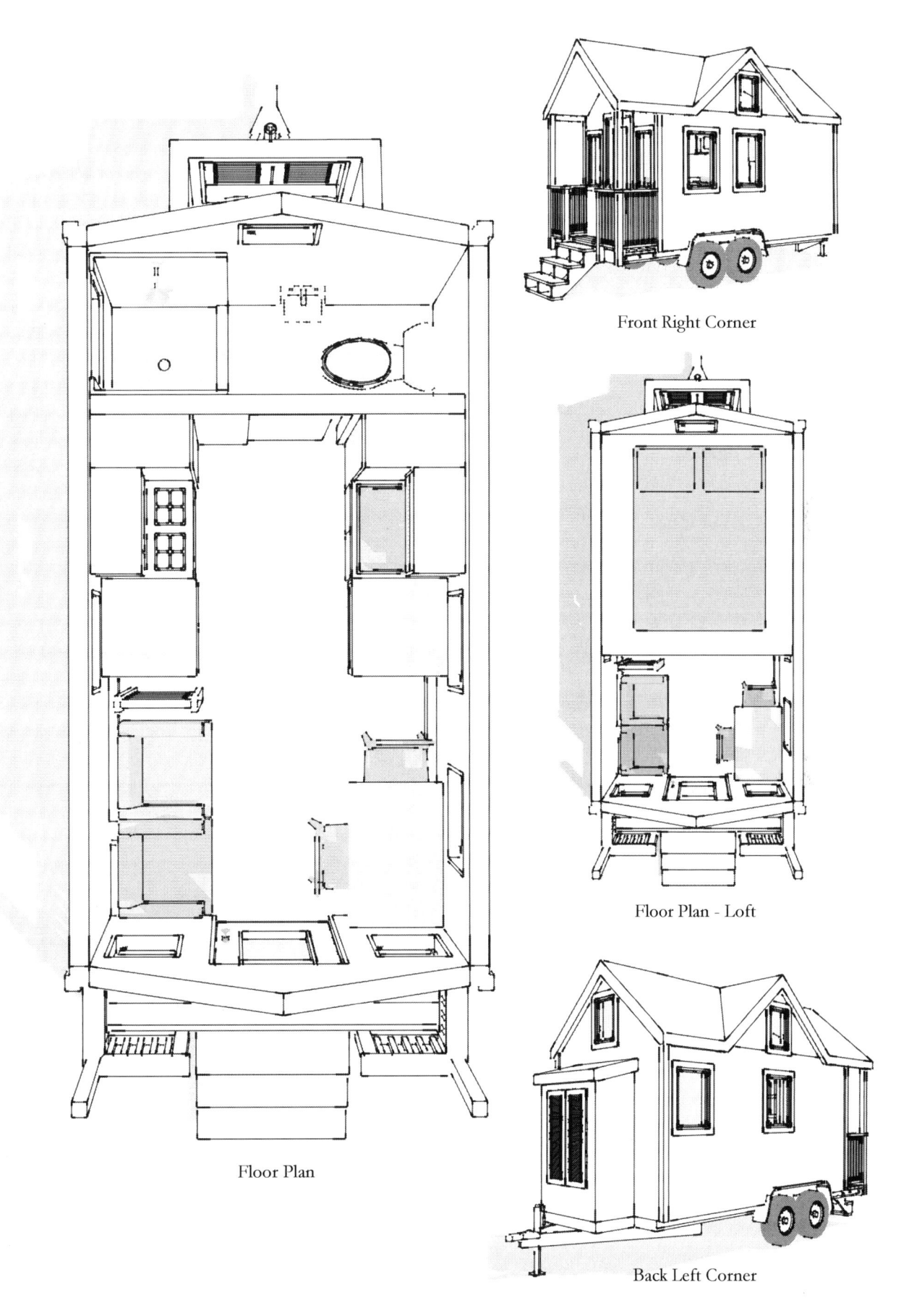

Tiny House #27 - Floor Plan & Exterior

Front Right Corner

Floor Plan - Loft

Floor Plan

Back Left Corner

Tiny House #27 - Interior Views

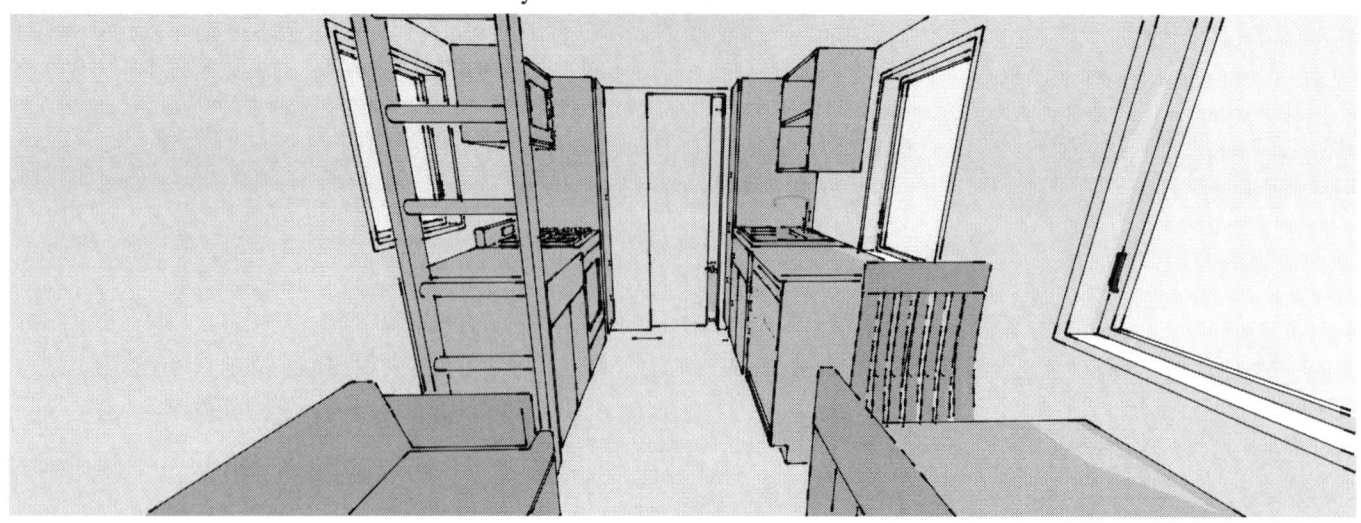

Interior from Entry

Interior from Kitchen

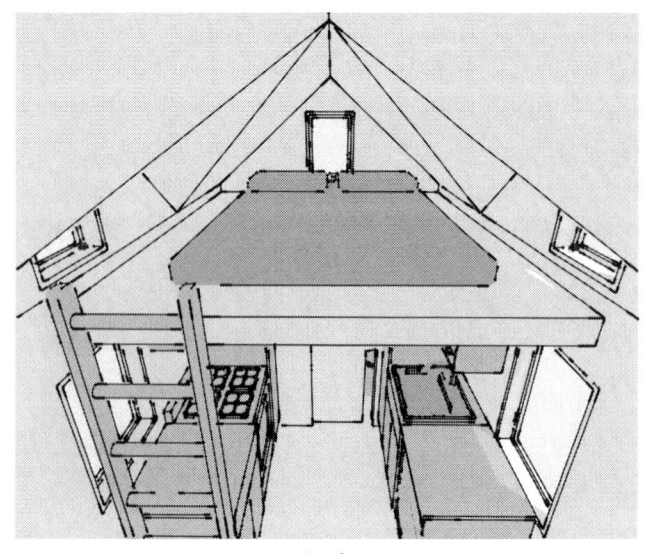

Loft

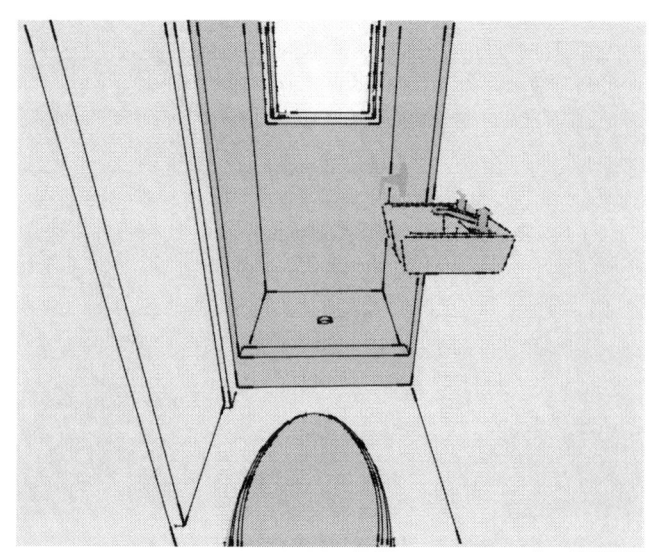

Bathroom

112

Tiny House #27 - Elevations

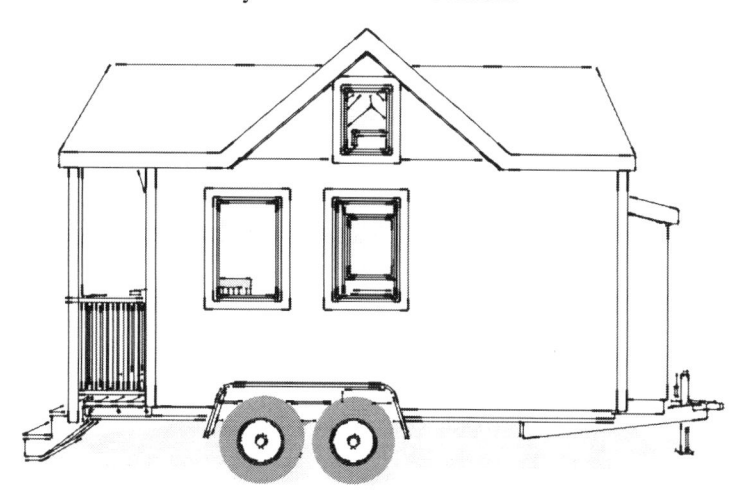

Right

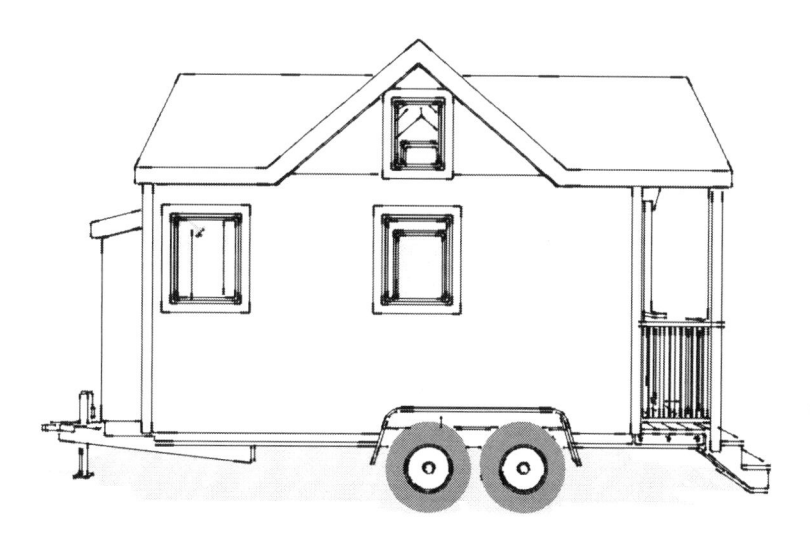

Left

Back

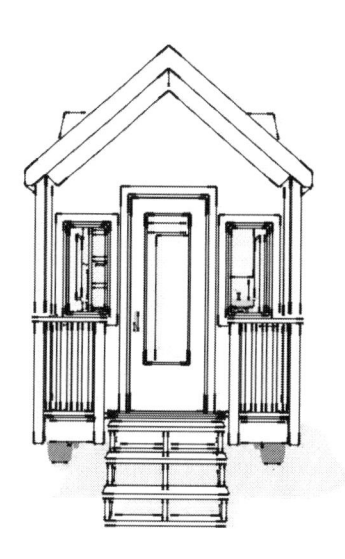

Front

113

#28

Tiny House #28 - Overview

Front Right

Summary:

This tiny house design has a 10/12 double cross gable roof and an aerodynamic profile on the trailer tongue side. Inside the entry are two comfy chairs and a table for two. The kitchen has plenty of storage, a sink, stovetop, and small refrigerator. The standard bathroom has a 32-inch shower, toilet and wall mounted sink. The loft has space for a queen size bed and is accessed by ladder rungs permanently attached to an interior wall. Over the trailer tongue is a mechanical storage closet.

Features:

16-Foot Tiny House on Wheels
Double Cross Gable Roof
Standard Bathroom
Tiny Kitchen
Ample Storage
Mechanical Closet over Trailer Tongue

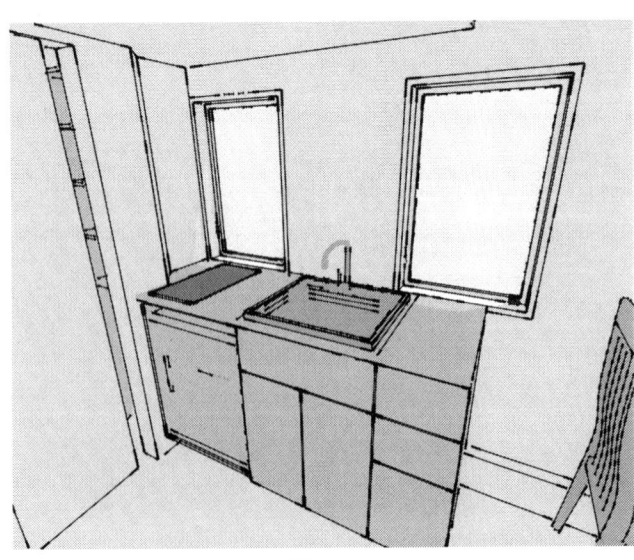

Kitchen

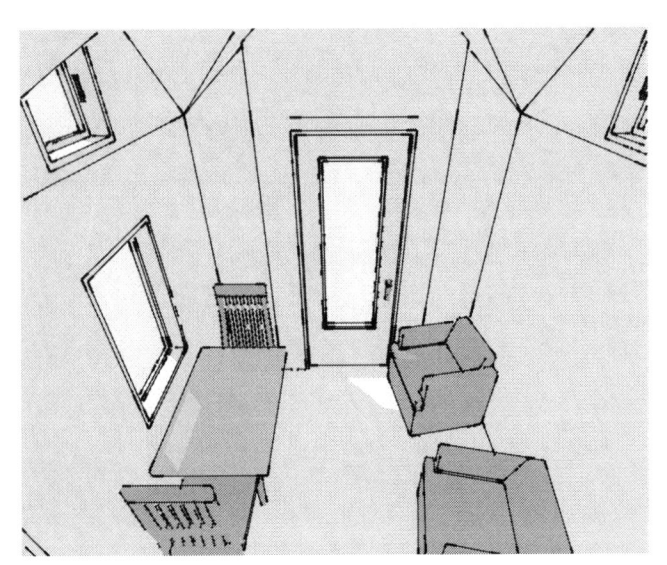

View from Loft

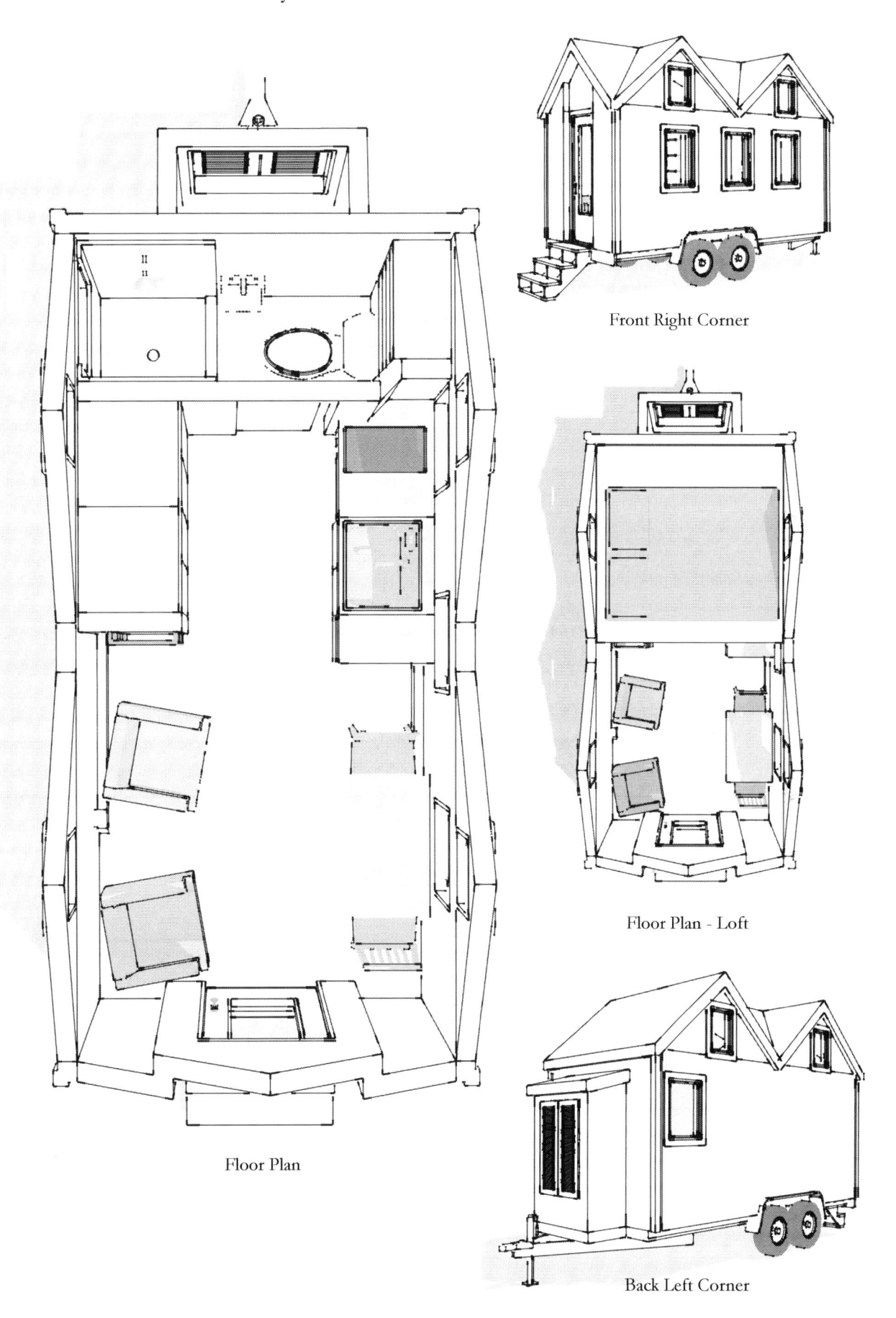

Tiny House #28 - Floor Plan & Exterior

Front Right Corner

Floor Plan - Loft

Floor Plan

Back Left Corner

115

Tiny House #28 - Interior Views

Interior from Entry

Interior from Kitchen

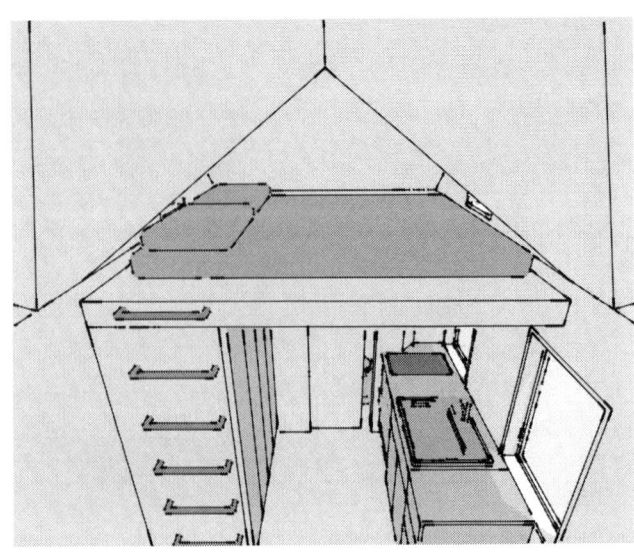

Loft

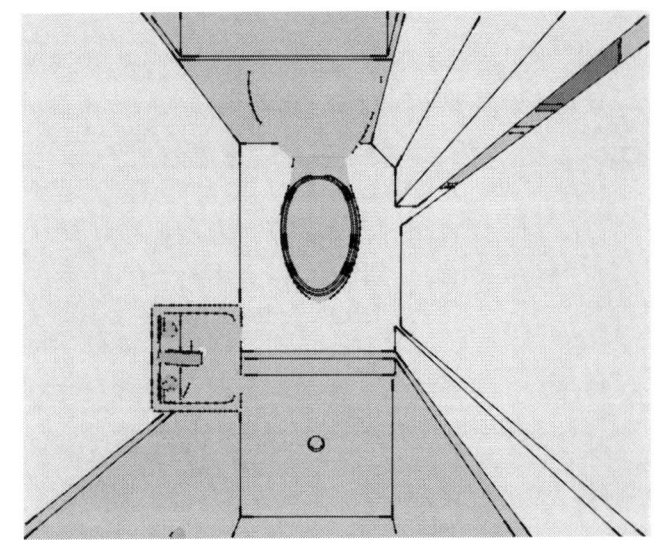

Bathroom

116

Tiny House #28 - Elevations

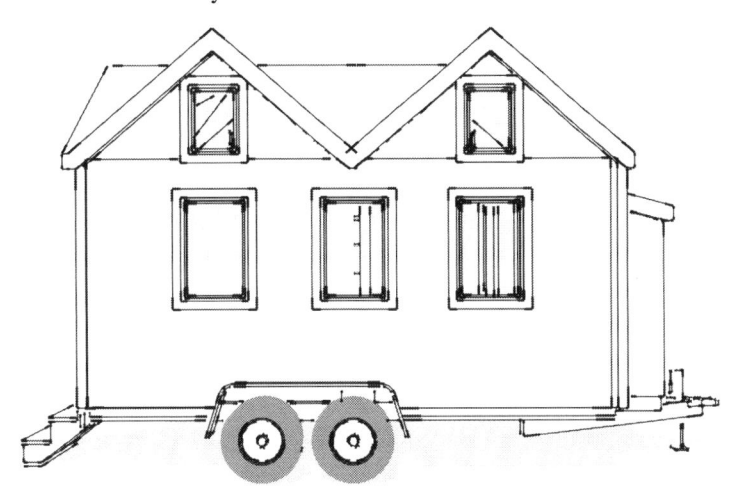

Right

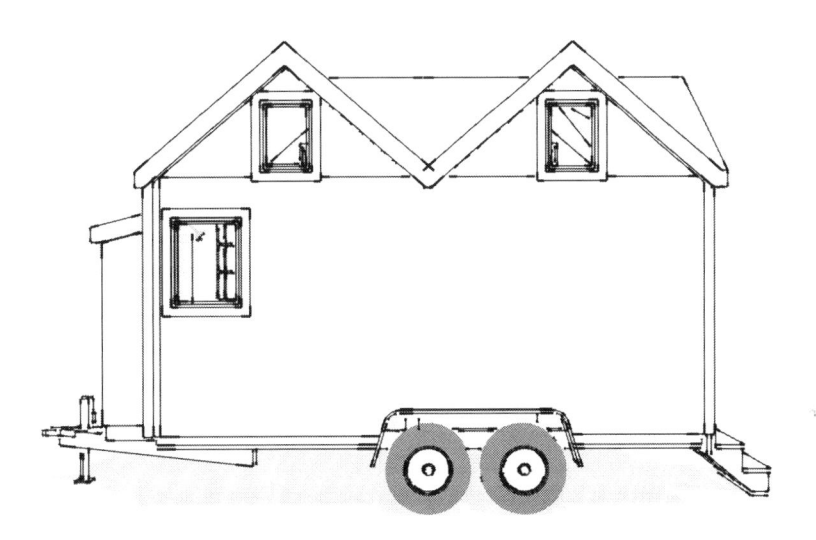

Left

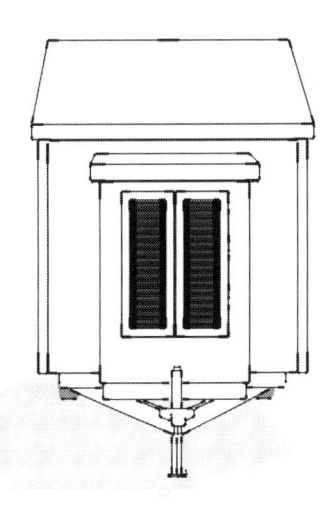

Back

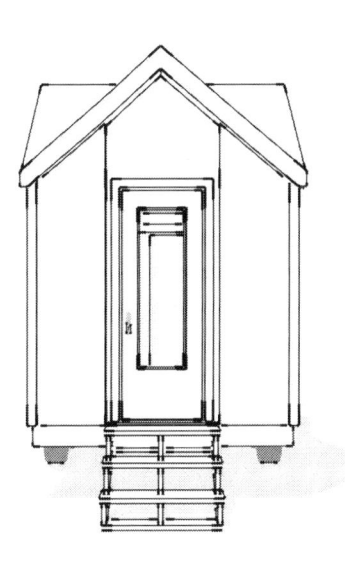

Front

117

#29

Tiny House #29 - Overview

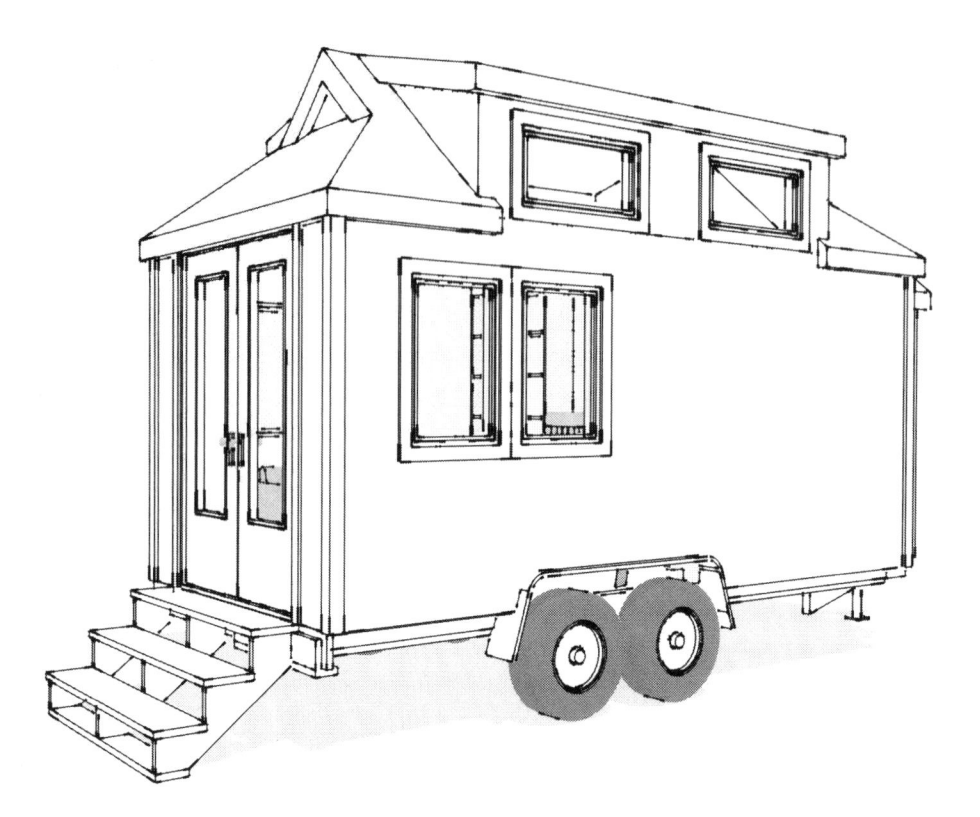

Front Right

Summary:

This tiny house design has a 10/12 dutch gable roof with 3/12 shed dormers that increase headroom in the loft. Inside you'll find two comfy chairs separated by a coffee table and a table for two or three. The small kitchen has plenty of storage and the essentials: a sink, stovetop, and small refrigerator. The small bathroom has a 32-inch shower, toilet, wall mounted sink, and storage cabinet. The loft has space for a queen size bed and is accessed by a movable ladder. The kitchen and bathroom are extended by a bump-out over the trailer tongue.

Features:

16-Foot Tiny House on Wheels
Dutch Gable with Shed Dormers
Small Bathroom
Kitchen with Ample Storage
French Doors with Fold-up Steps

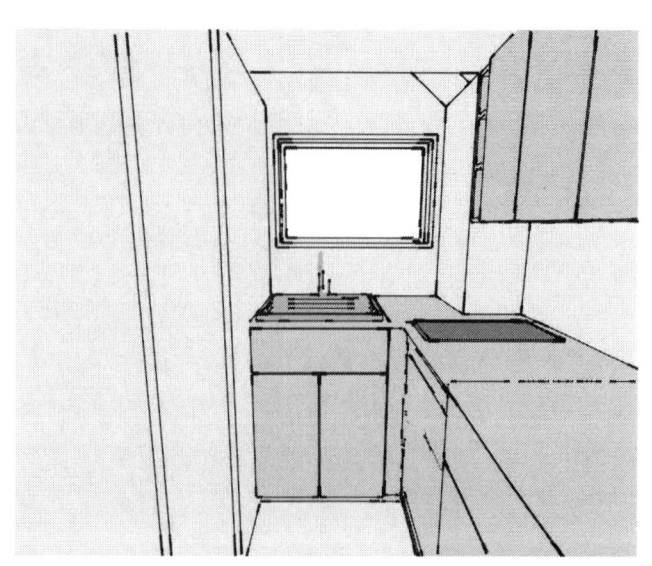

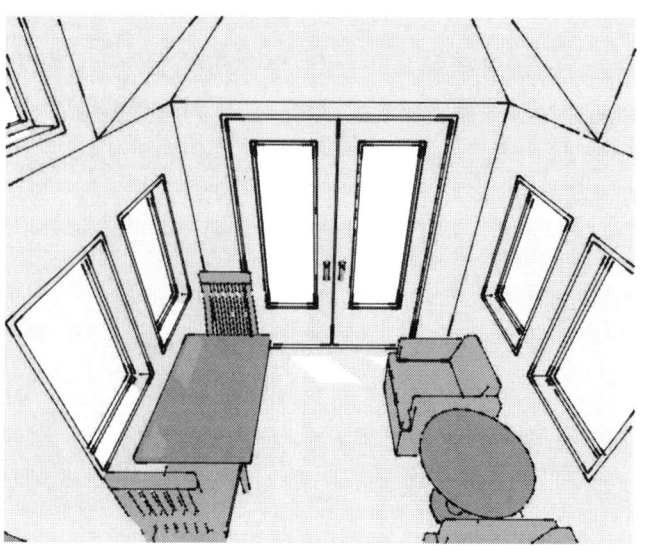

Kitchen

View from Loft

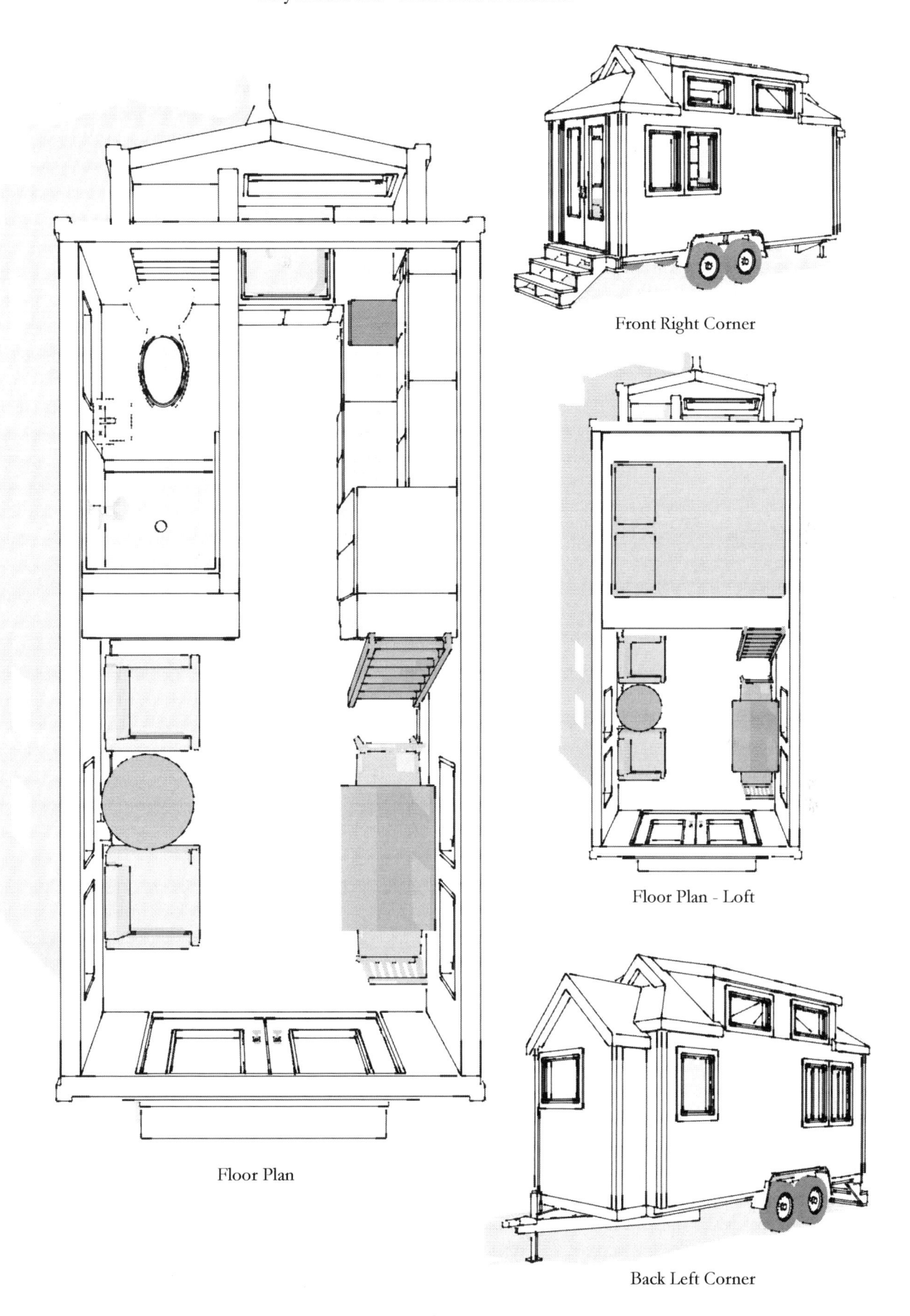

Tiny House #29 - Floor Plan & Exterior

Front Right Corner

Floor Plan - Loft

Floor Plan

Back Left Corner

Tiny House #29 - Interior Views

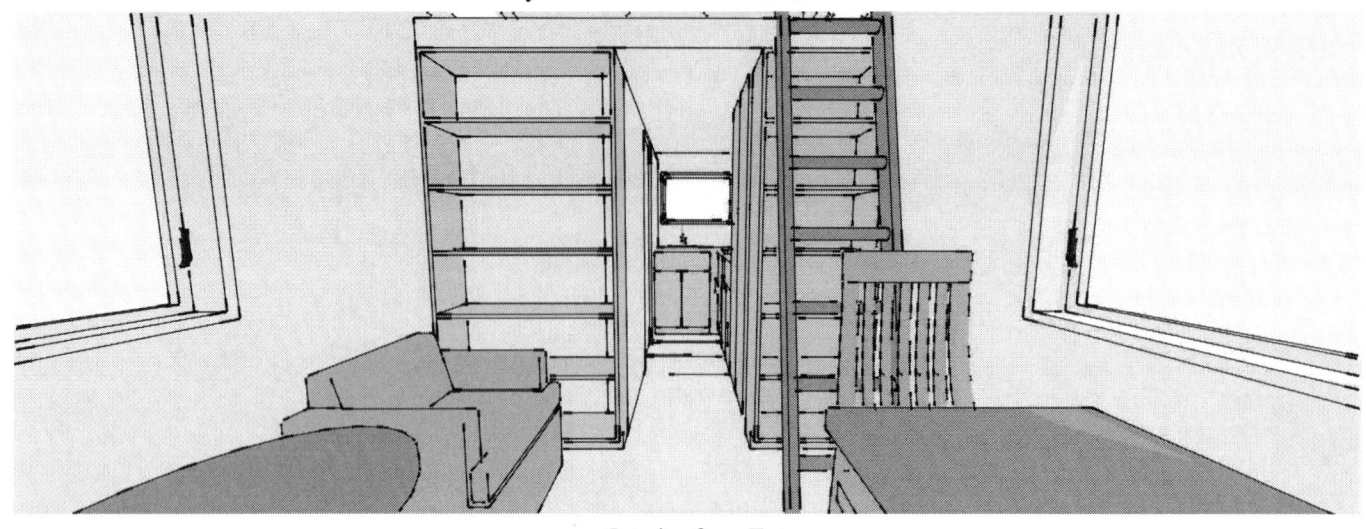

Interior from Entry

Interior from Kitchen

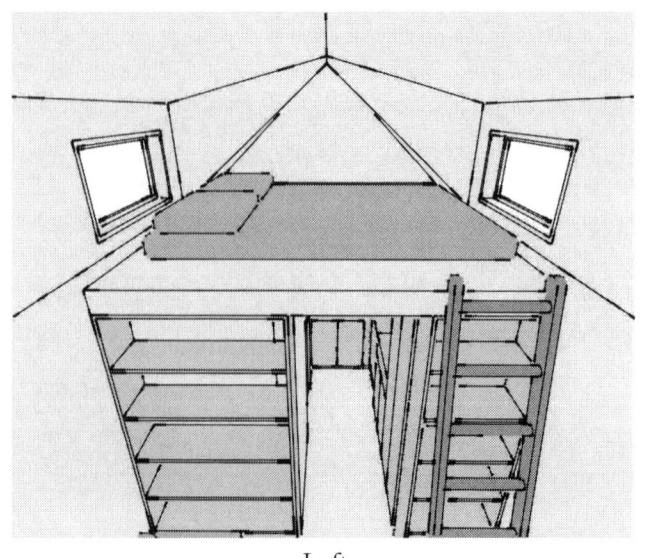

Loft

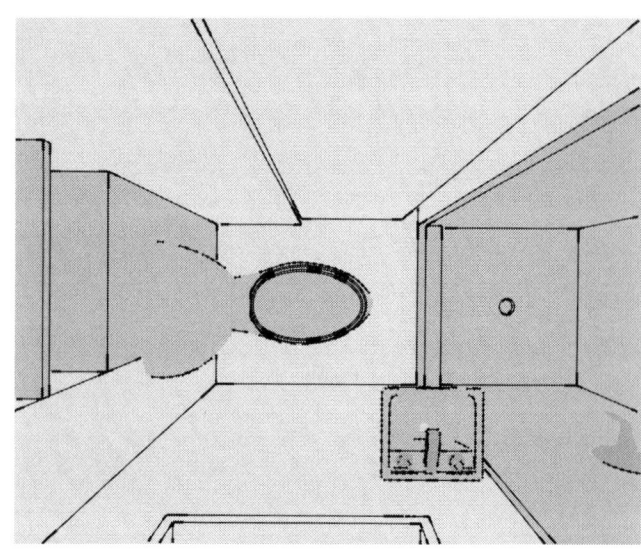

Bathroom

Tiny House #29 - Elevations

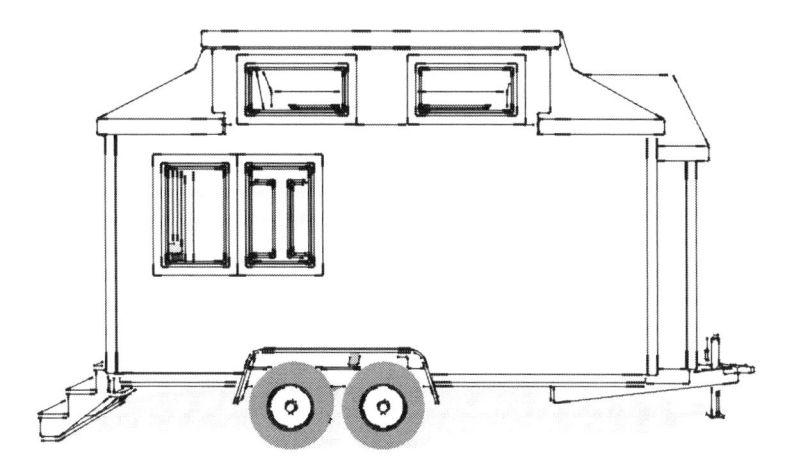

Right

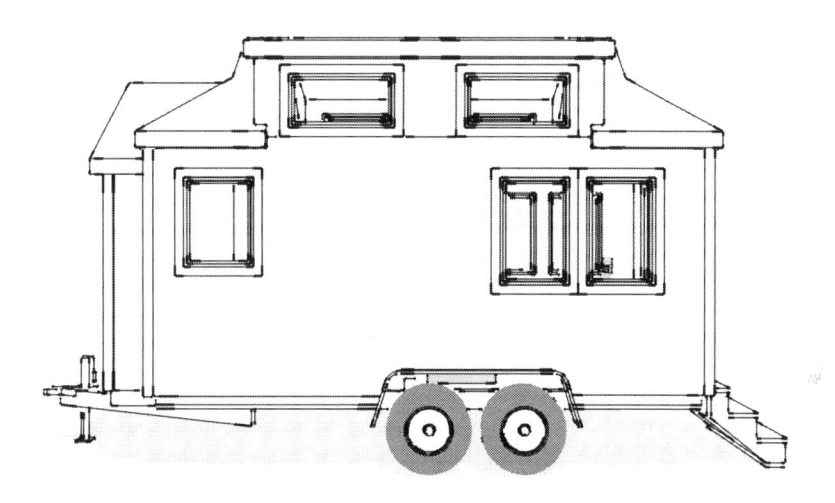

Left

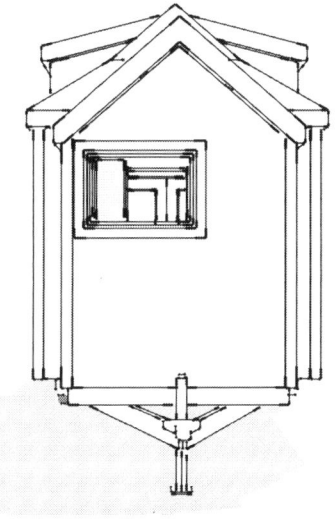

Back

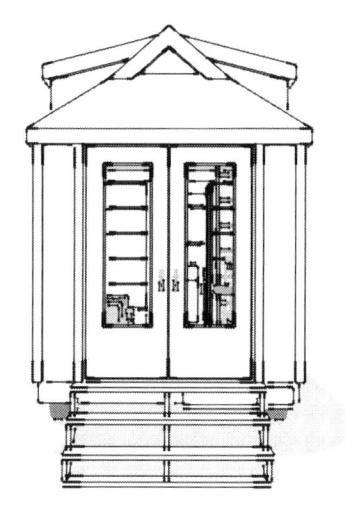

Front

#30

Tiny House #30 - Overview

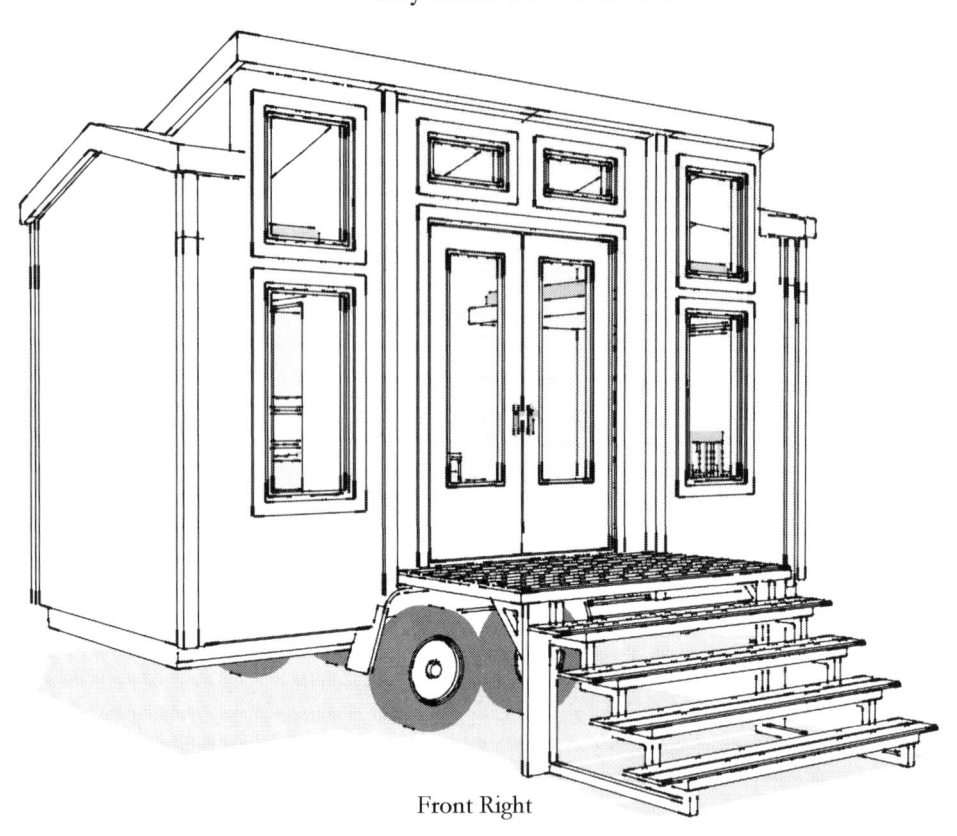

Front Right

Summary:

Typically a tiny house entry is not located over the trailer fenders. But sometimes, with the proper deck and/or steps it makes an impressive statement. This tiny house design has a 3/12 gable roof on the ends and a 3/12 shed roof in the center. Upon entering you take two steps down to a simple kitchen with a small refrigerator, sink with cabinet drain rack above, and stovetop. To the right of the kitchen is a table for two and two comfy chairs. The bathroom is to the left of the entry and has a slightly larger 42"x32" shower, toilet, and wall mounted sink. The two lofts - each with a twin bed - are accessed by wall mounted ladder rungs.

Features:

16-Foot Tiny House on Wheels
Combination Shed and Gable Roof
Bathroom with Larger Shower
Simple Kitchen
French Doors with Fold-up Deck and Steps
Entry over Trailer Fenders

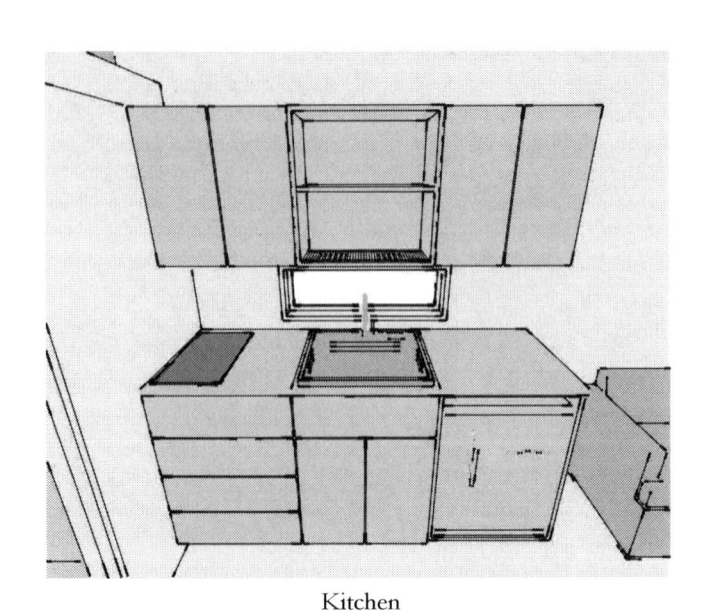

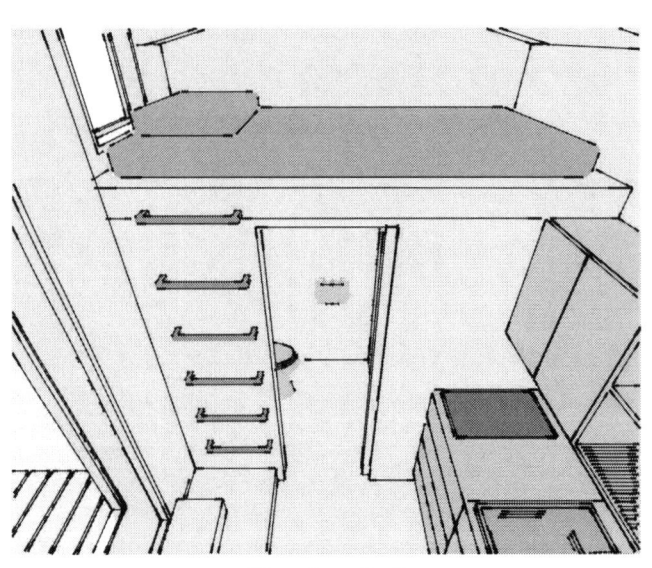

Kitchen

View from Loft

Tiny House #30 - Floor Plan & Exterior

Front Right Corner

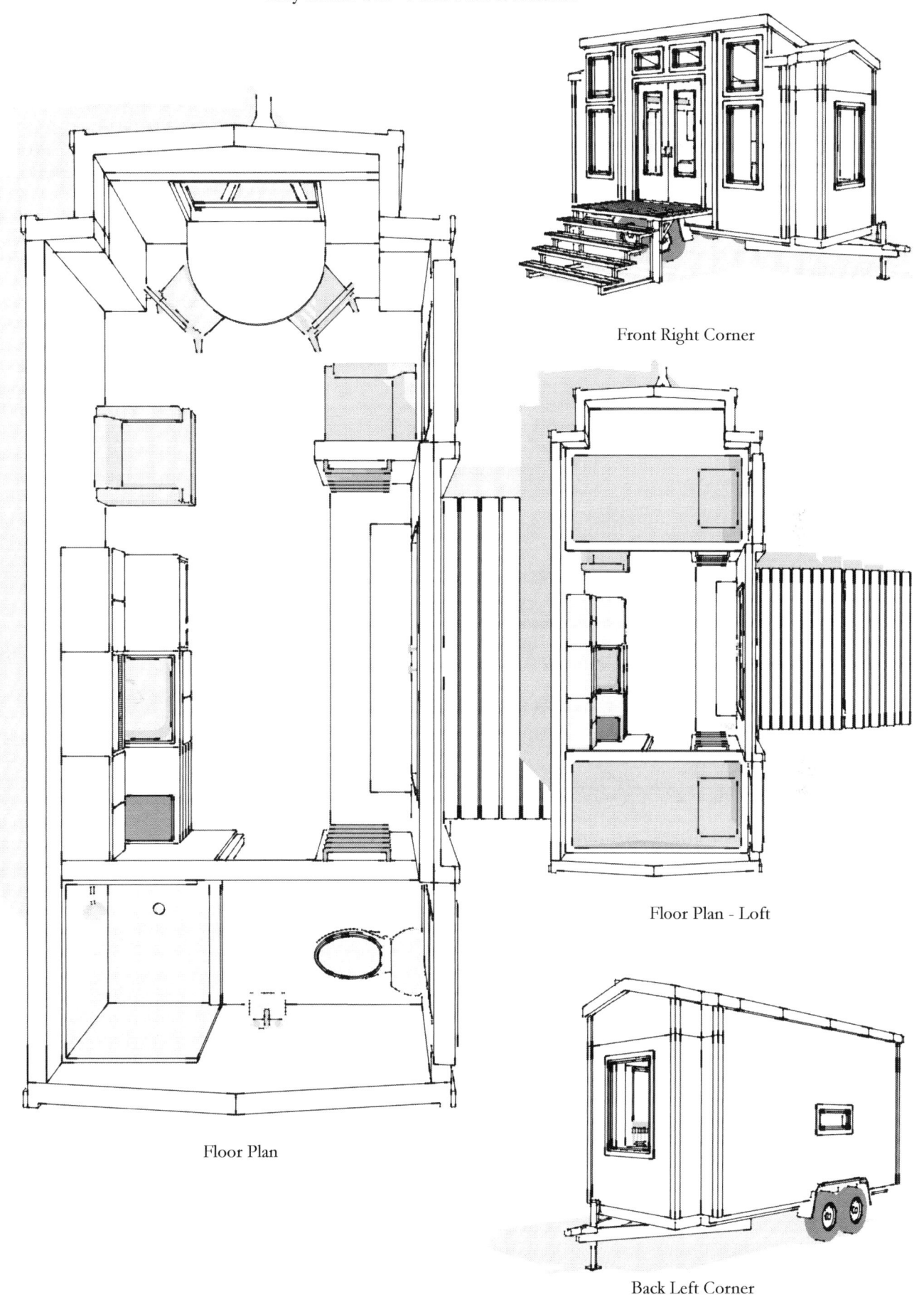

Floor Plan - Loft

Floor Plan

Back Left Corner

Tiny House #30 - Interior Views

Interior from Entry

Interior from Kitchen

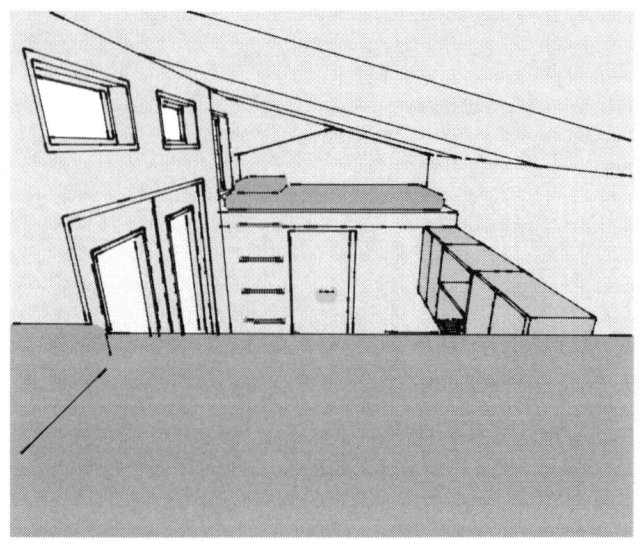

Loft

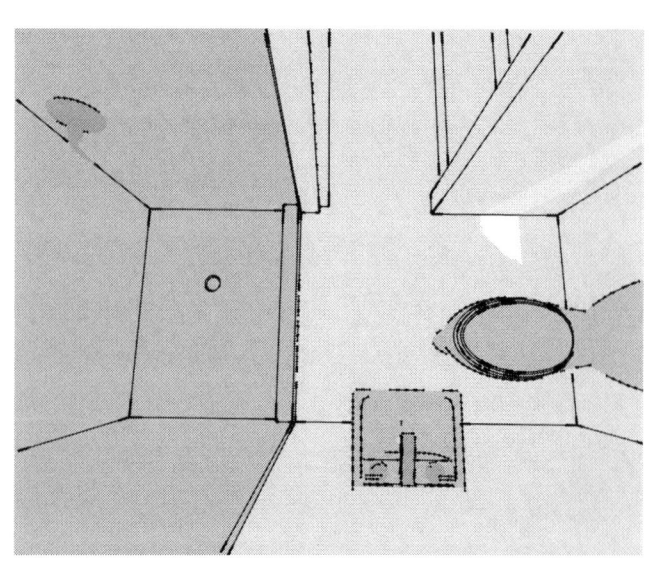

Bathroom

Tiny House #30 - Elevations

Right

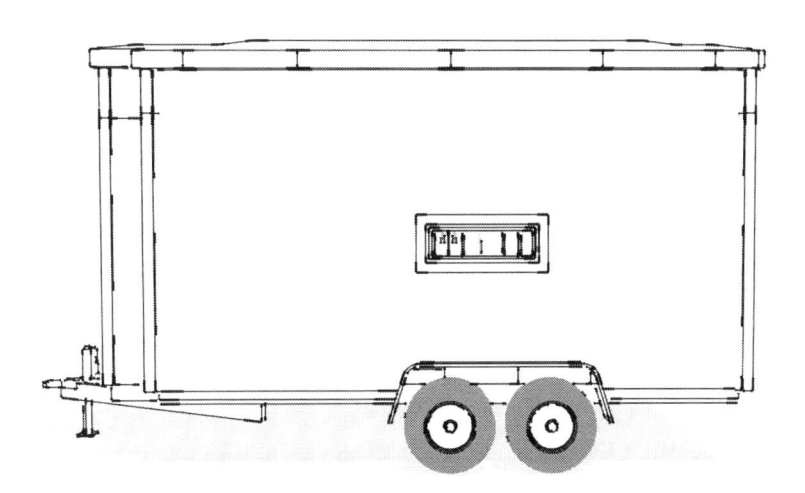

Left

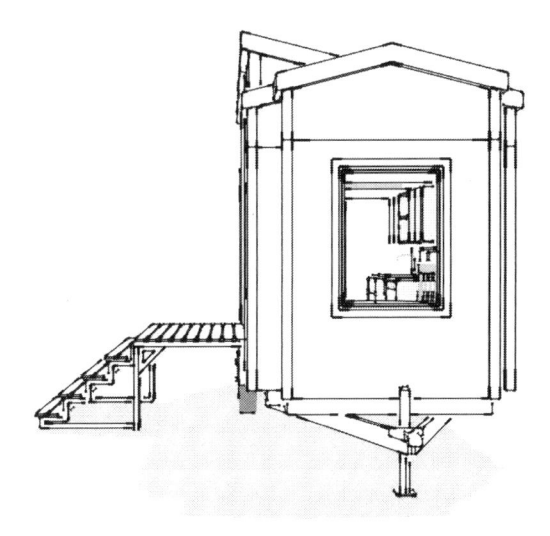

Back

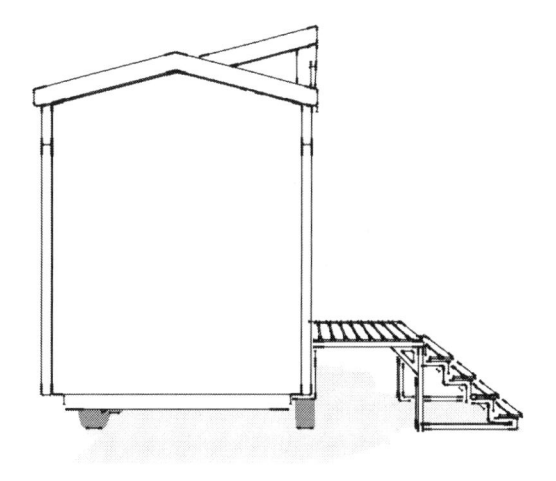

Front

#31

Tiny House #31 - Overview

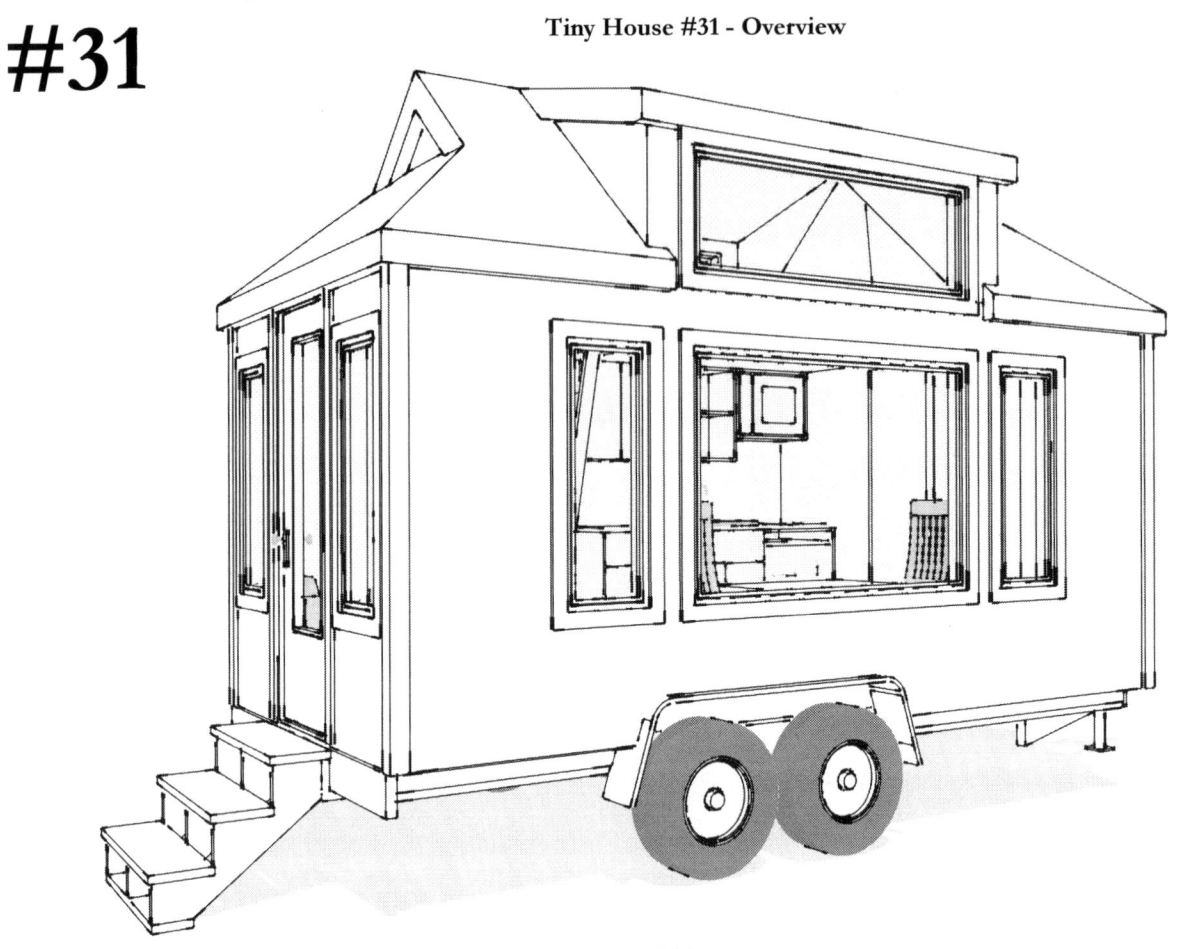

Front Right

Summary:

This tiny house has a 10/12 dutch gable roof, 3/12 shed dormers, and large windows. Inside is an open room with two comfy chairs, each with their own ottoman, a table for two, and a simple kitchen. The kitchen has a small refrigerator, sink with cabinet drain rack above, and stovetop. The standard bathroom has a 32-inch shower, toilet, and wall mounted sink. The loft has space for a queen bed and is accessed by a movable ladder.

Features:

16-Foot Tiny House on Wheels
Dutch Gable with Shed Dormers
Standard Bathroom
Simple Kitchen
Entry with Fold-up Steps
Large Windows

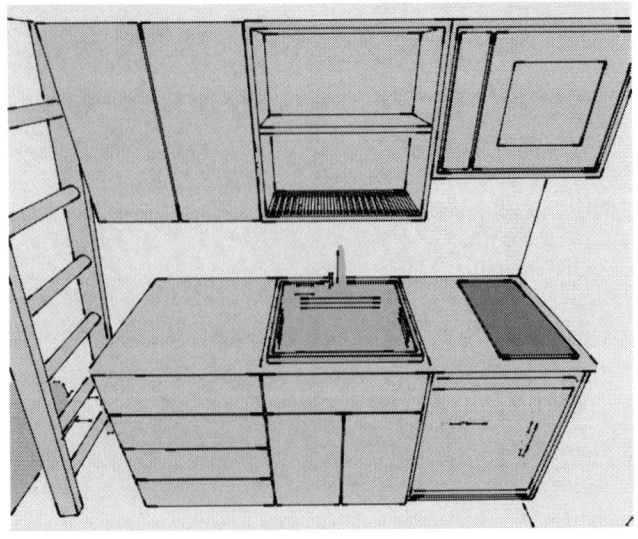

Kitchen

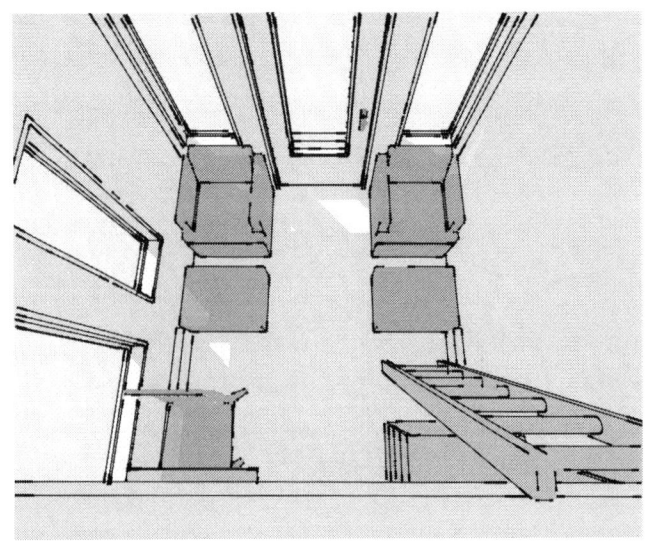

View from Loft

Tiny House #31 - Floor Plan & Exterior

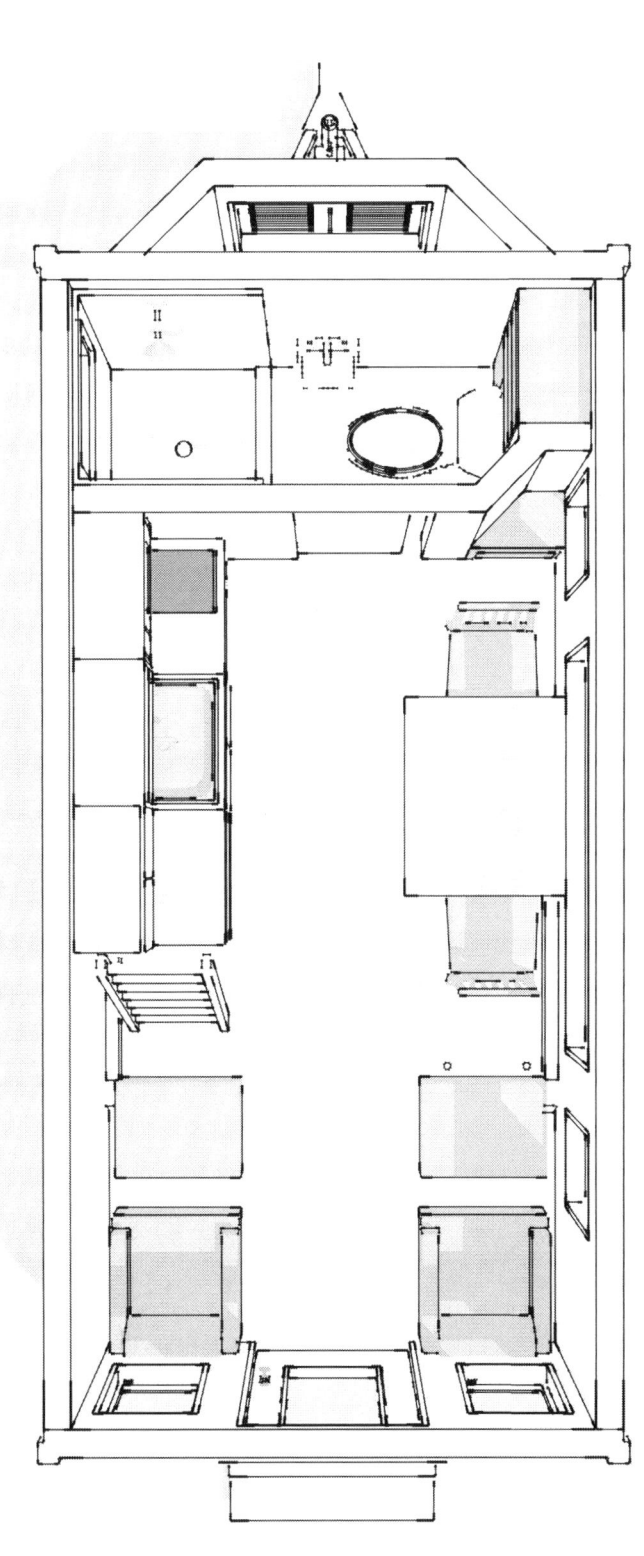

Front Right Corner

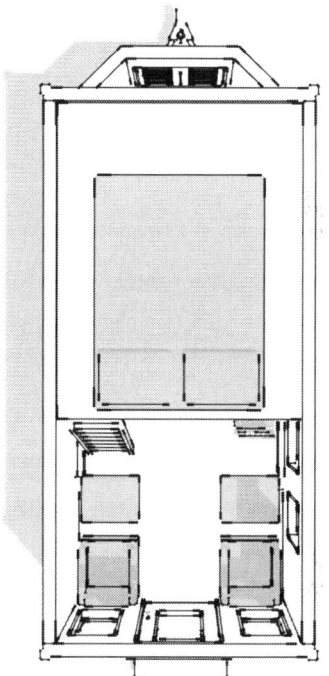

Floor Plan - Loft

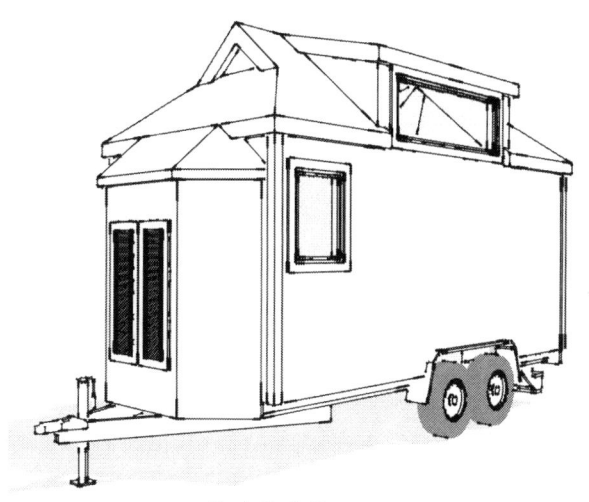

Floor Plan

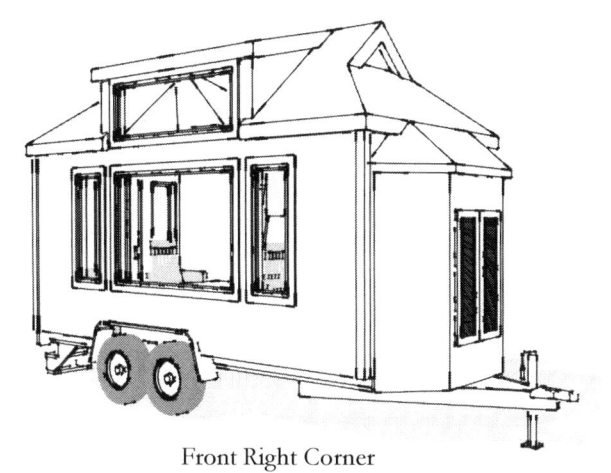

Back Left Corner

Tiny House #31 - Interior Views

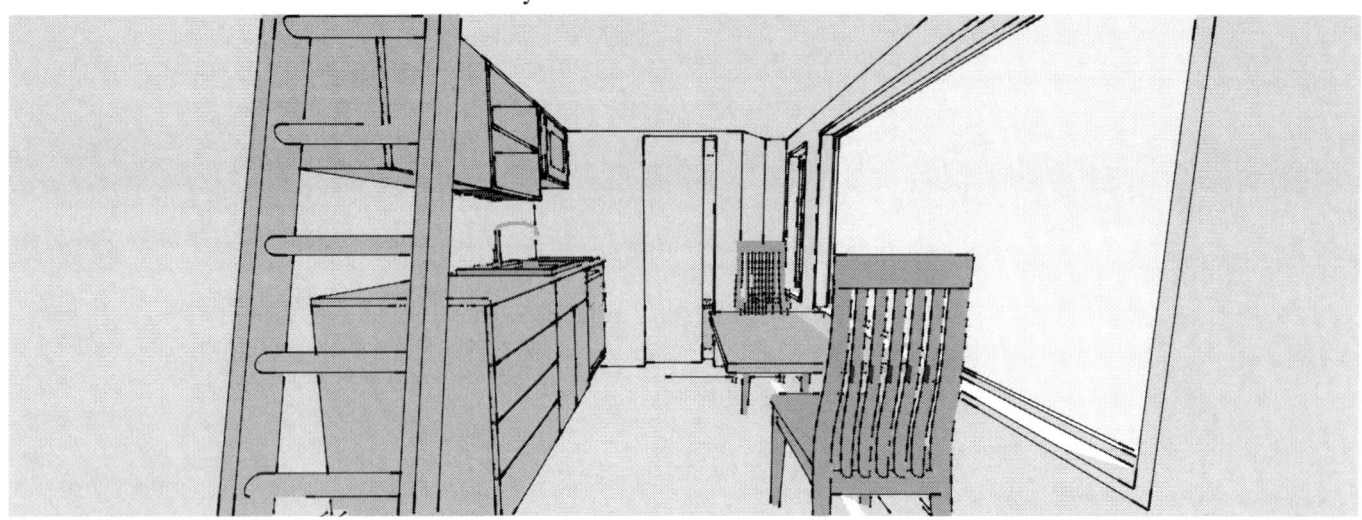

Interior from Entry

Interior from Kitchen

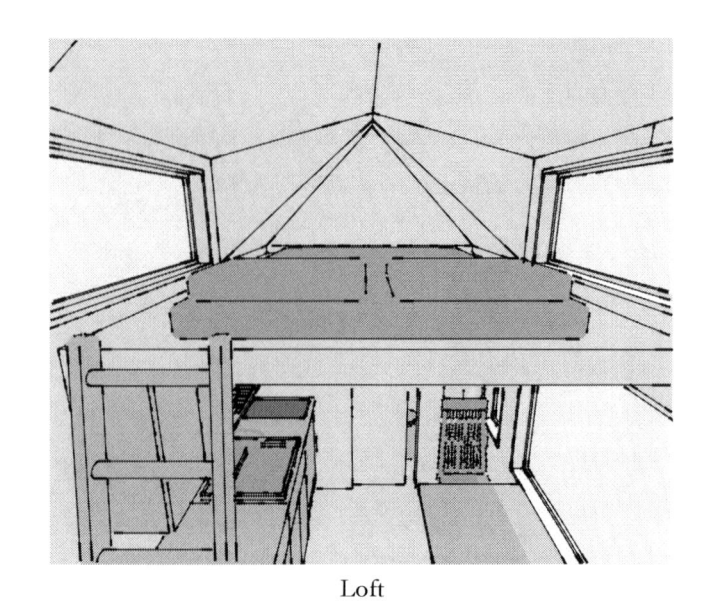

Loft

Bathroom

Tiny House #31 - Elevations

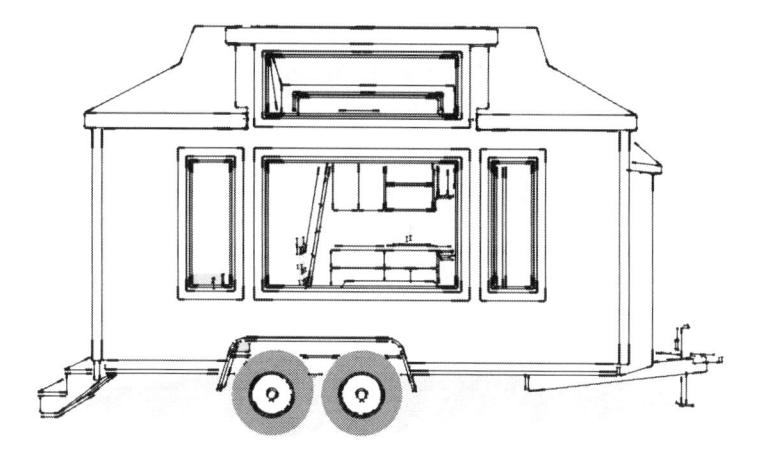

Right

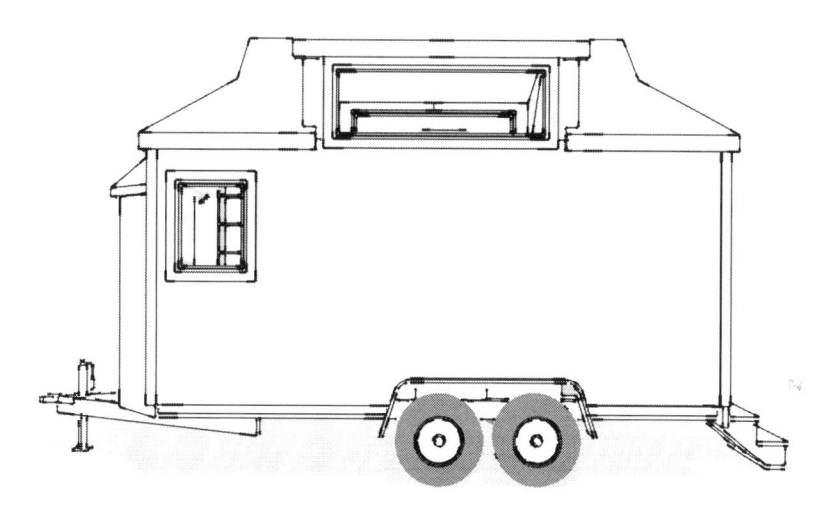

Left

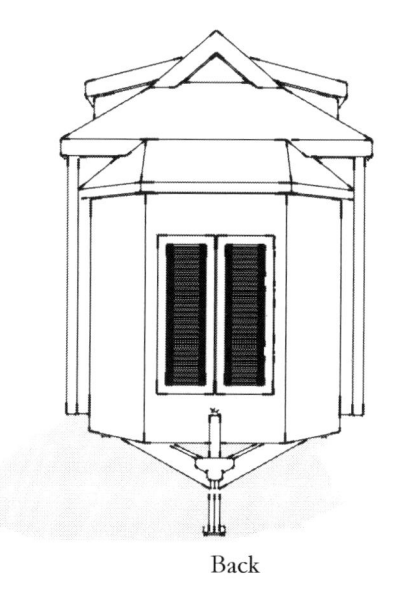

Back

Front

129

#32

Tiny House #32 - Overview

Front Right

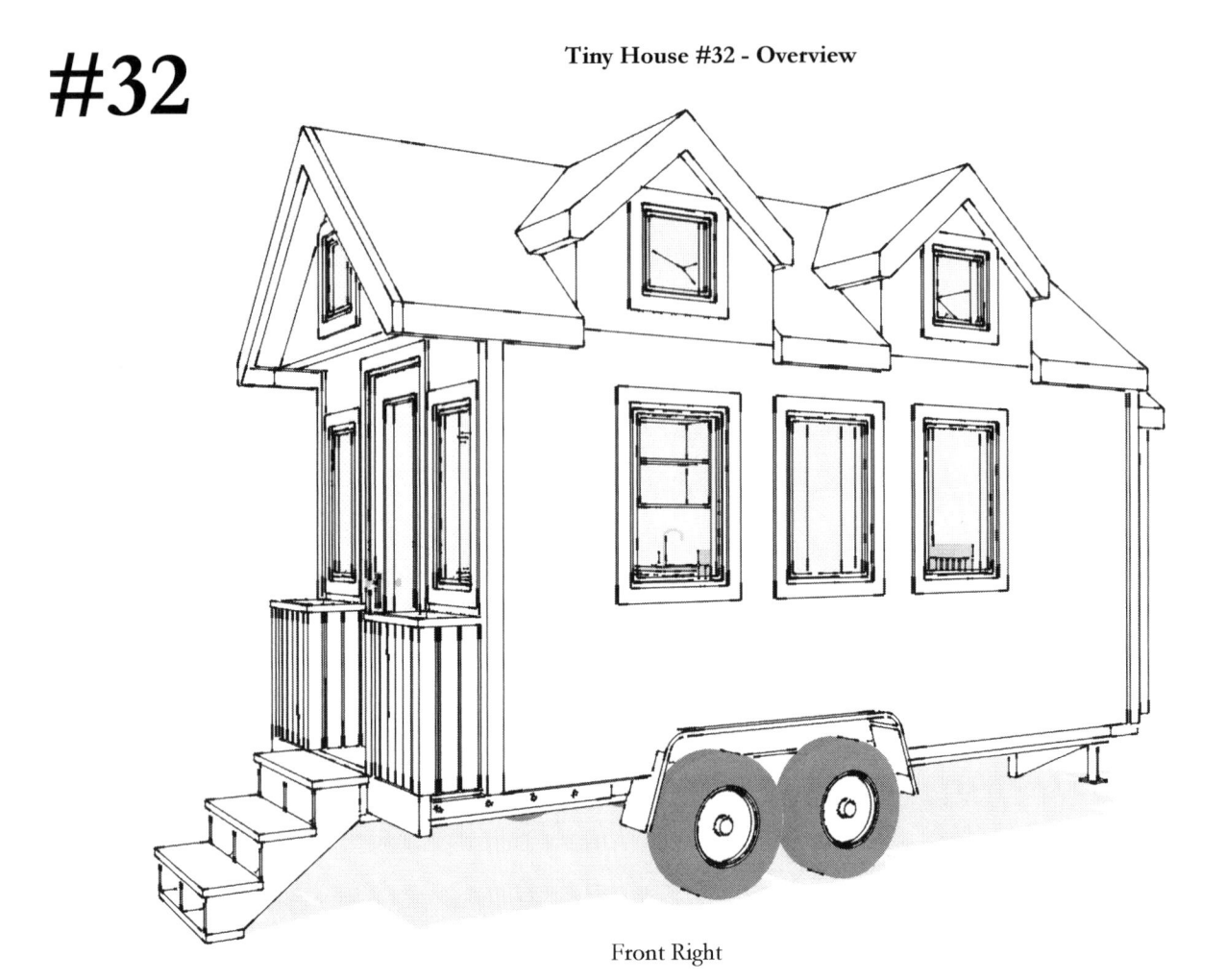

Summary:

What a classic cutie! This tiny house has a 10/12 gable roof with gable dormers and an inset front wall with flower planters flanking the front door. Inside are two comfy chairs and a table for two. The simple kitchen has plenty of storage, a small refrigerator, sink with cabinet drain rack above, and stovetop. The bathroom is extended over the trailer tongue and has a 32-inch shower, toilet, vanity, and storage. The loft has space for a queen bed and is accessed by a movable ladder.

Features:

16-Foot Tiny House on Wheels
Gable with Shed Dormers
Standard Bathroom
Simple Kitchen
Entry with Fold-up Steps
Flower Planters

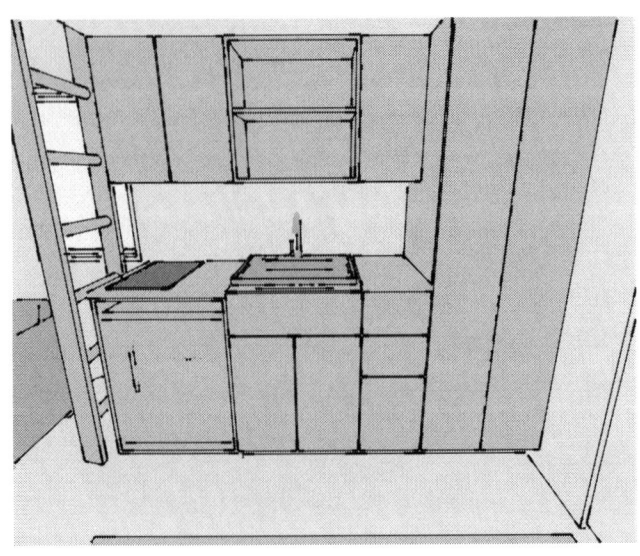

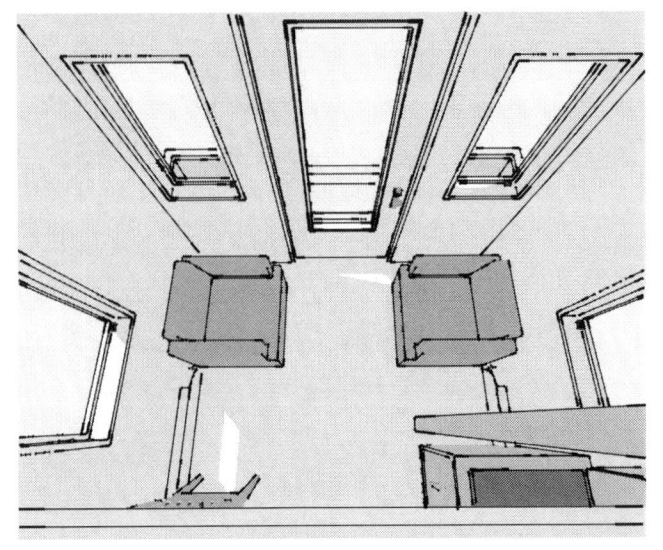

Kitchen

View from Loft

Tiny House #32 - Floor Plan & Exterior

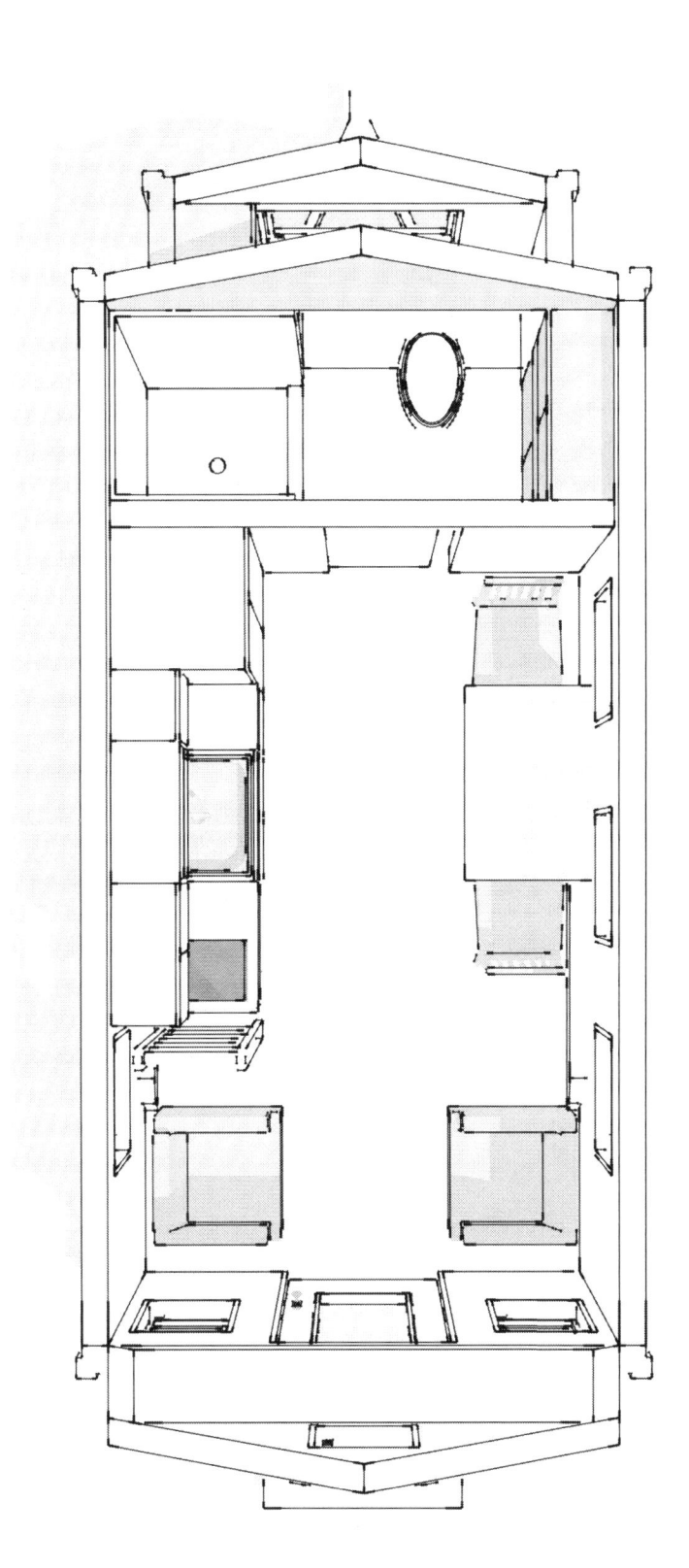

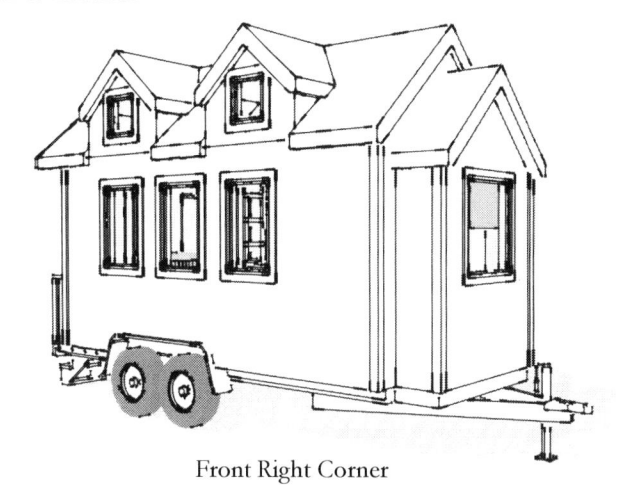

Front Right Corner

Floor Plan

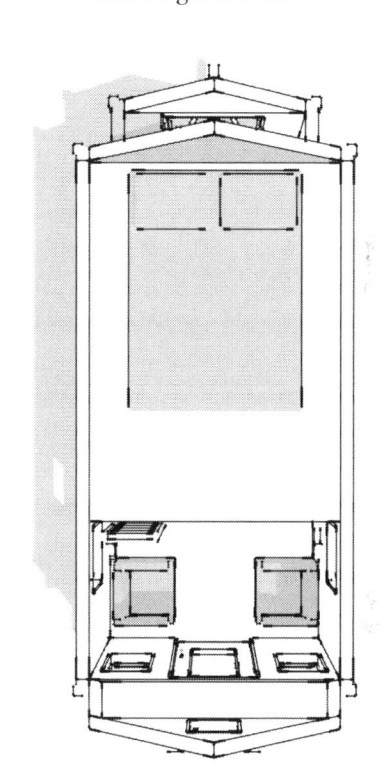

Floor Plan - Loft

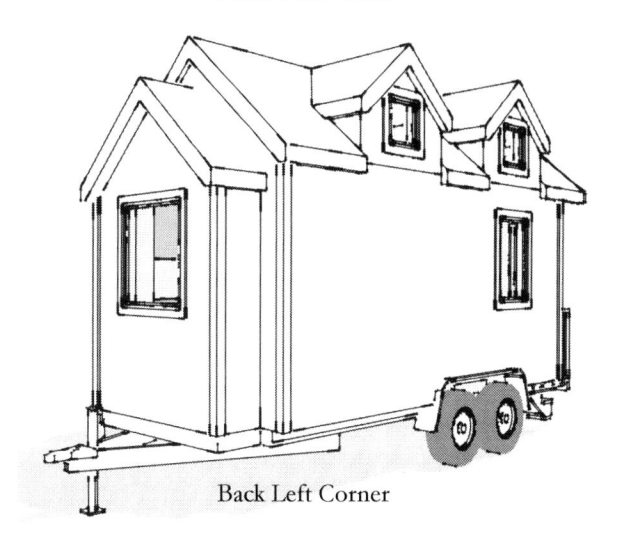

Back Left Corner

Tiny House #32 - Interior Views

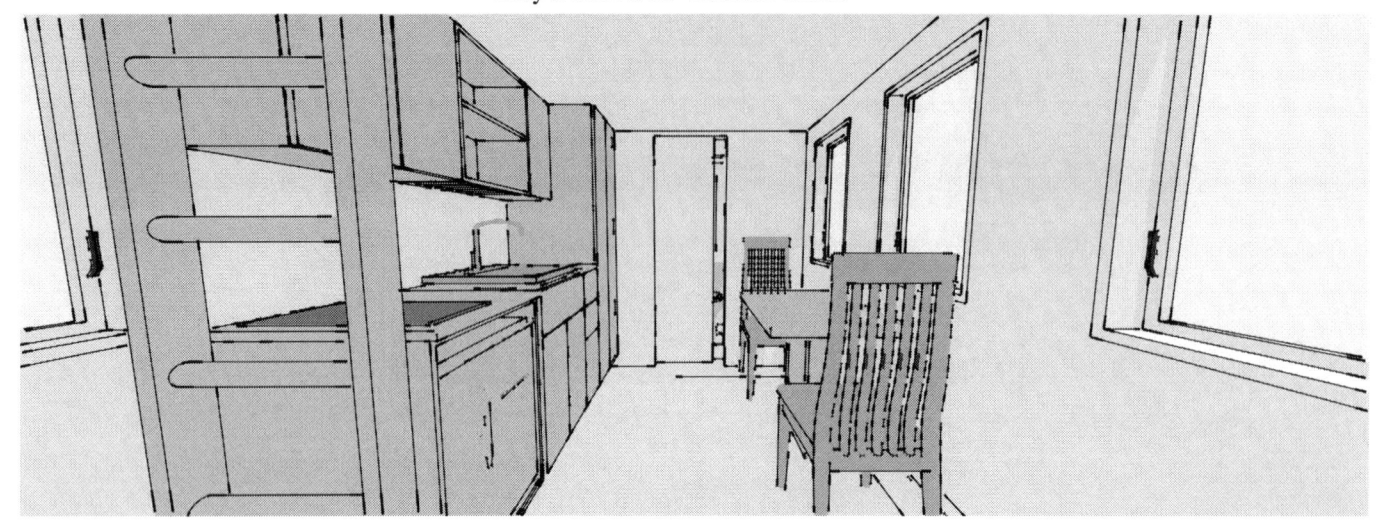

Interior from Entry

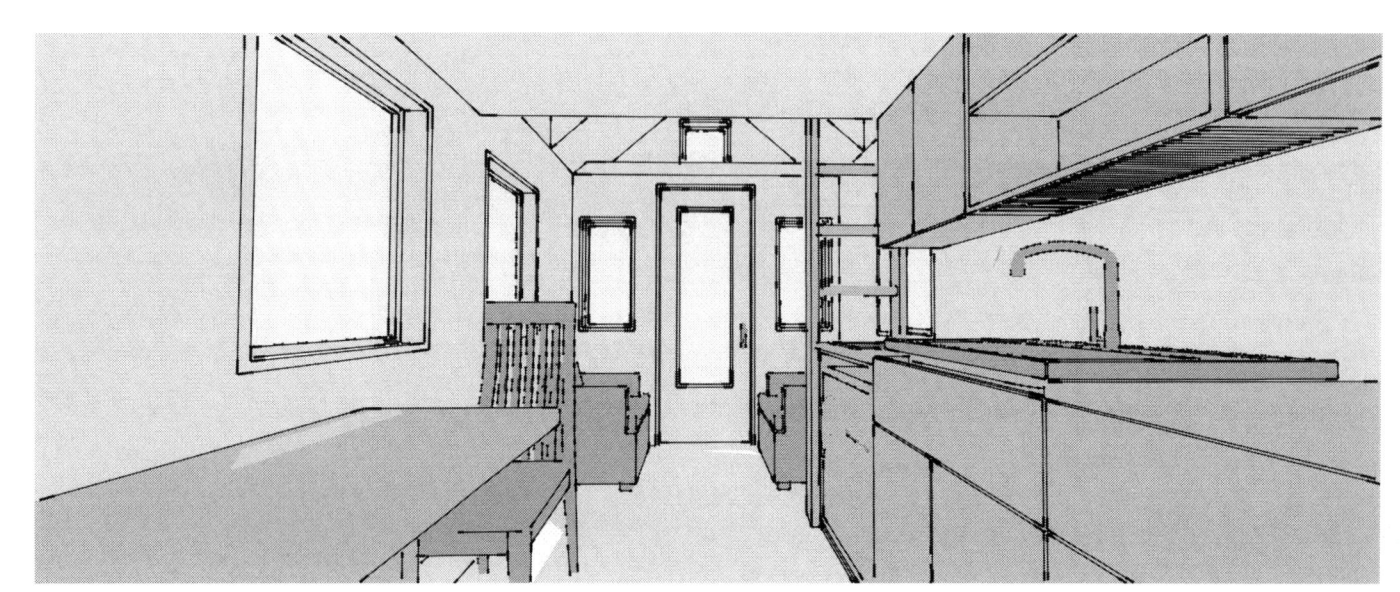

Interior from Kitchen

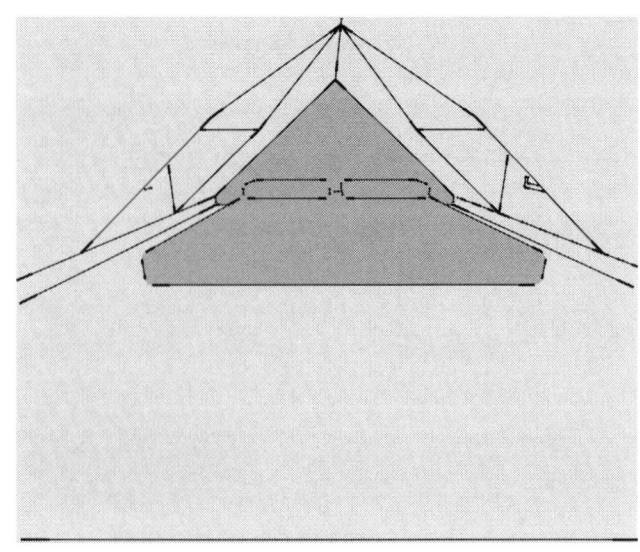

Loft

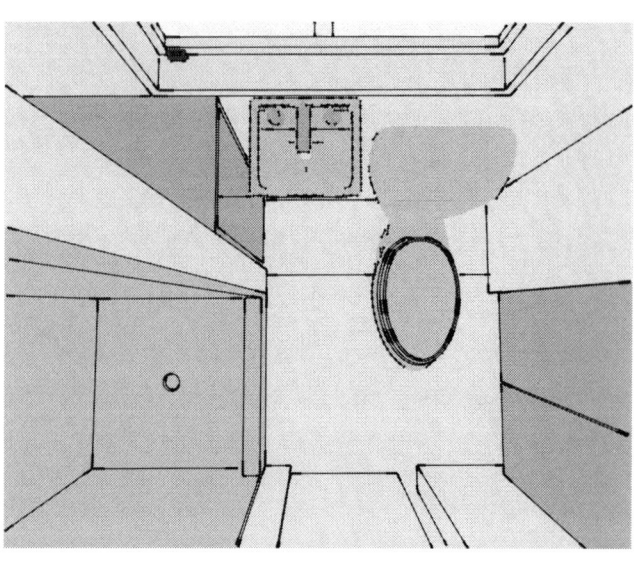

Bathroom

Tiny House #32 - Elevations

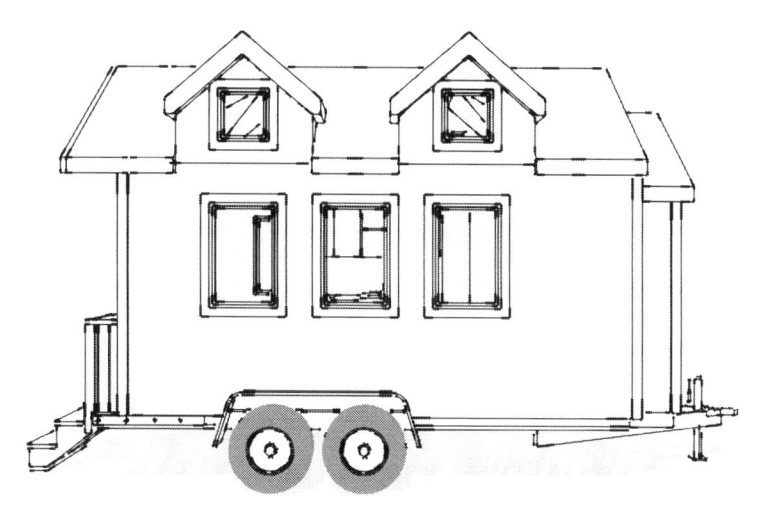

Right

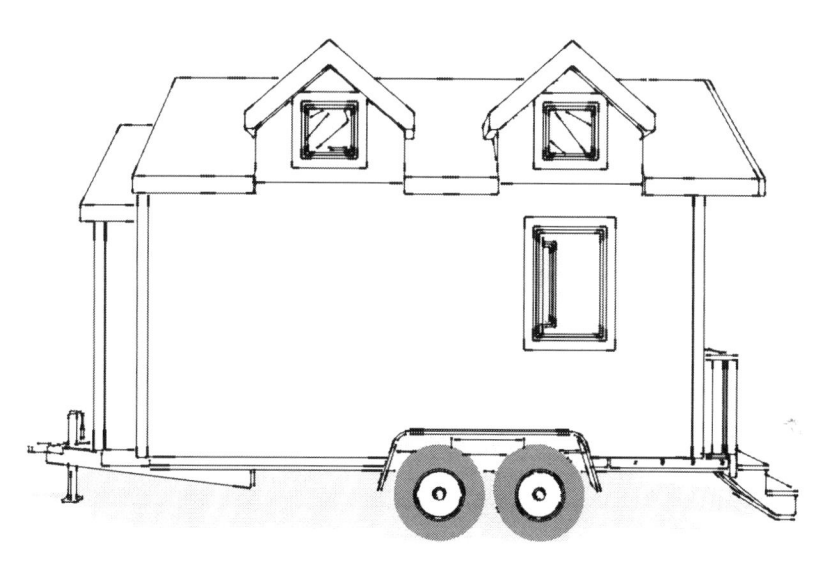

Left

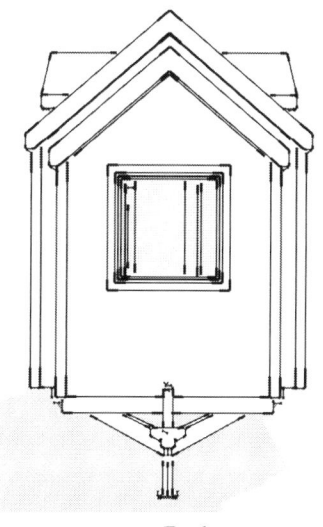

Back

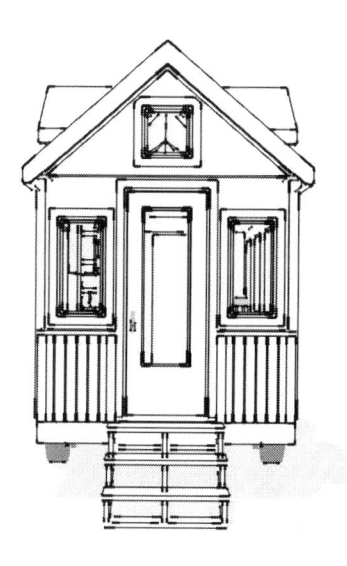

Front

133

#33

Tiny House #33 - Overview

Front Right

Summary:

This tiny house has a 3/12 shed roof with a slightly sloped front wall for a more aerodynamic profile. Inside the entry is a tiny kitchen which has a small refrigerator, sink with cabinet drain rack above, and stovetop. The bathroom is next to the kitchen and has a 32-inch shower, toilet, wall mounted sink, and storage. The loft has space for a queen bed and is accessed by ladder rungs attached to an interior wall. The living room has a table for two, a sofa, and a comfy chair.

Features:

16-Foot Tiny House on Wheels
Shed Roof
Standard Bathroom
Tiny Kitchen
Side Entry with Fold-up Steps
Large Windows
Sloped Wall Trailer Tongue Side

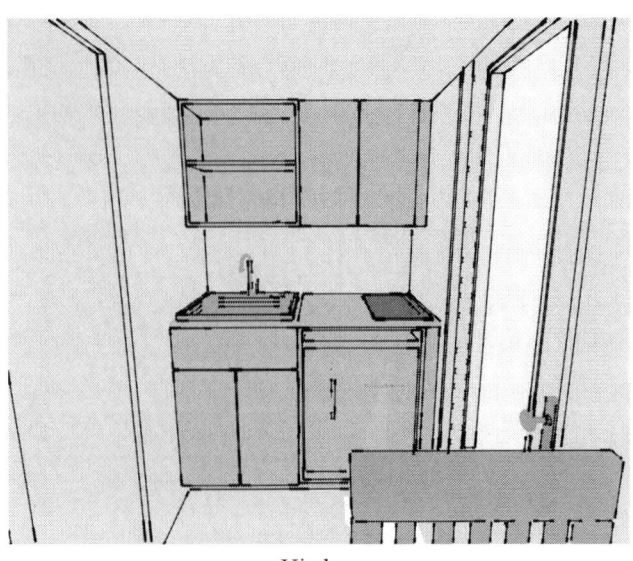

Kitchen

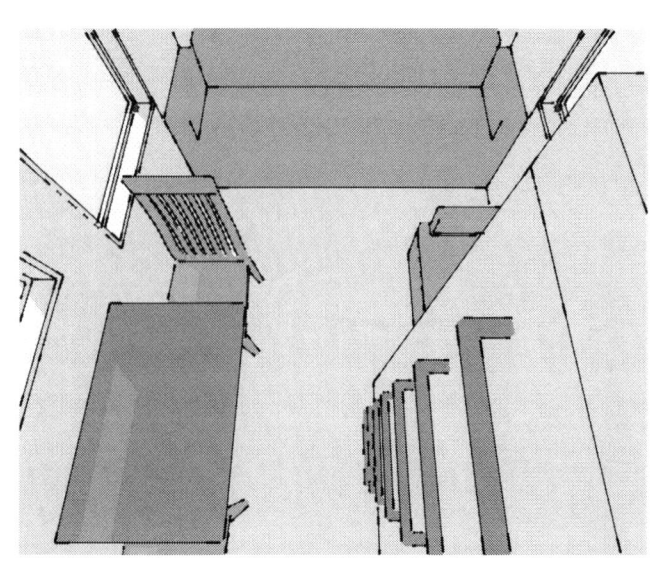

View from Loft

Tiny House #33 - Floor Plan & Exterior

Front Right Corner

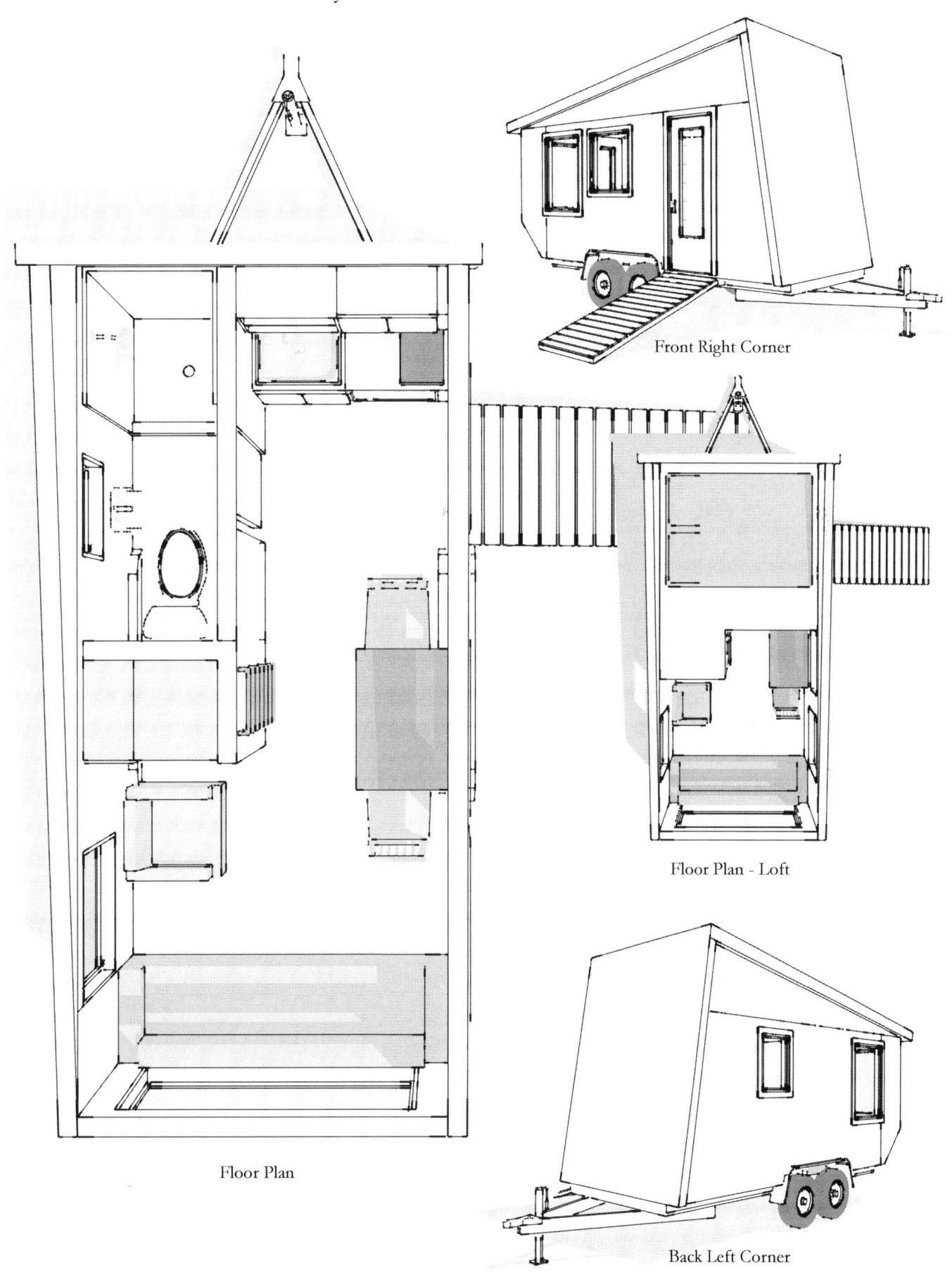

Floor Plan - Loft

Floor Plan

Back Left Corner

Tiny House #33 - Interior Views

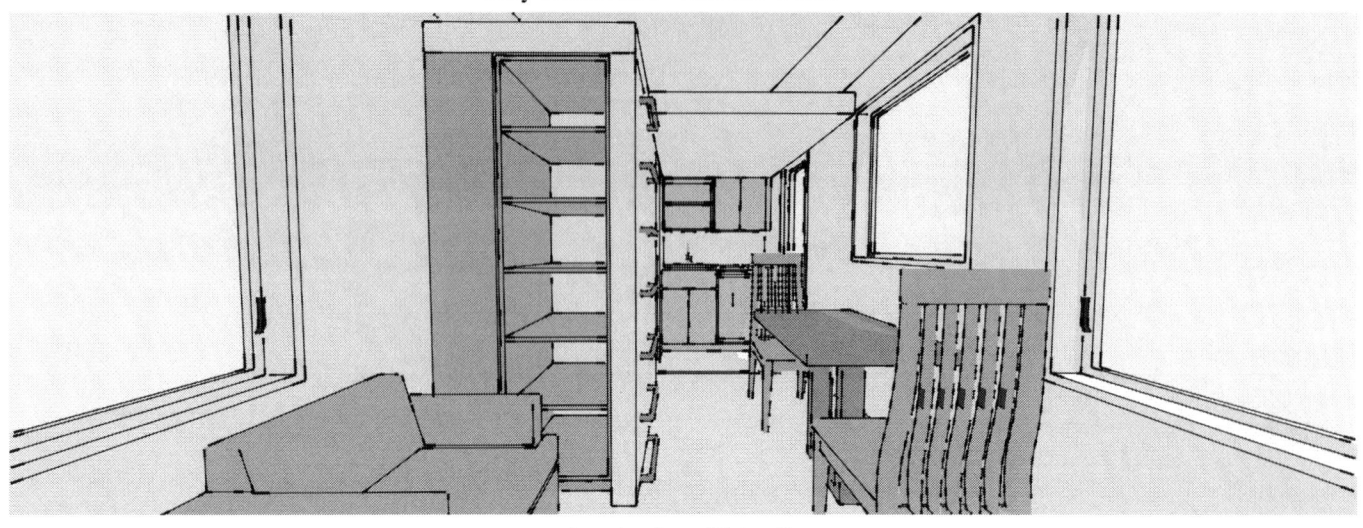

Interior from Living Room

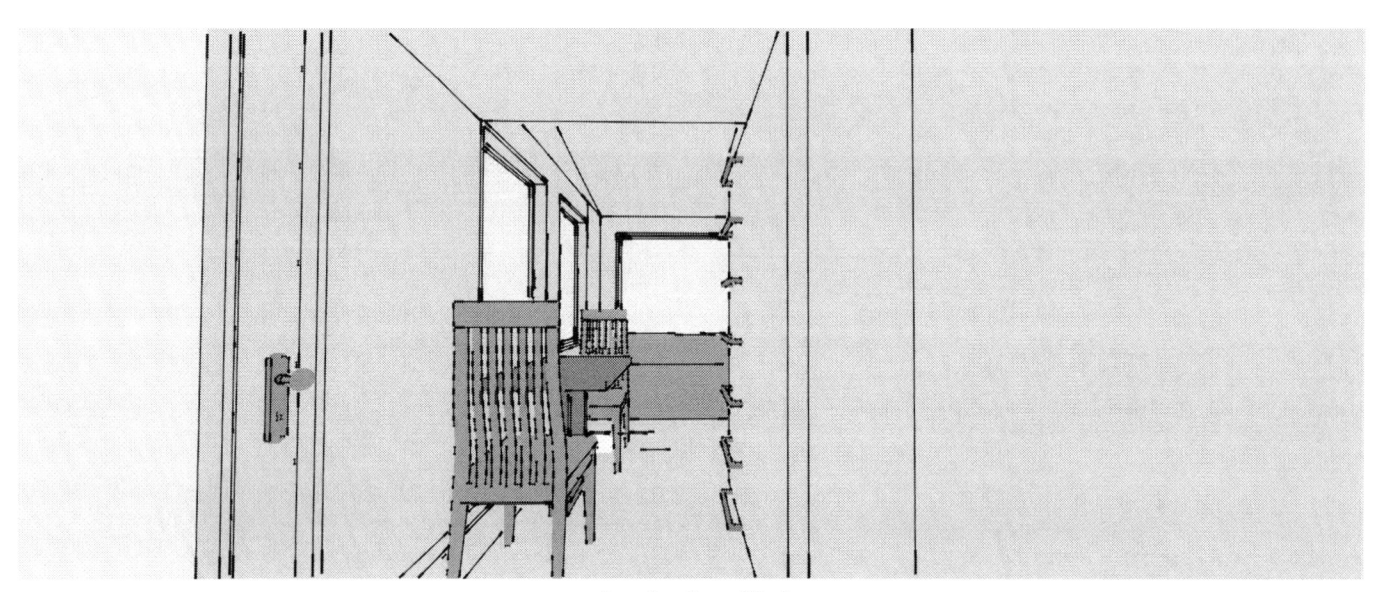

Interior from Kitchen

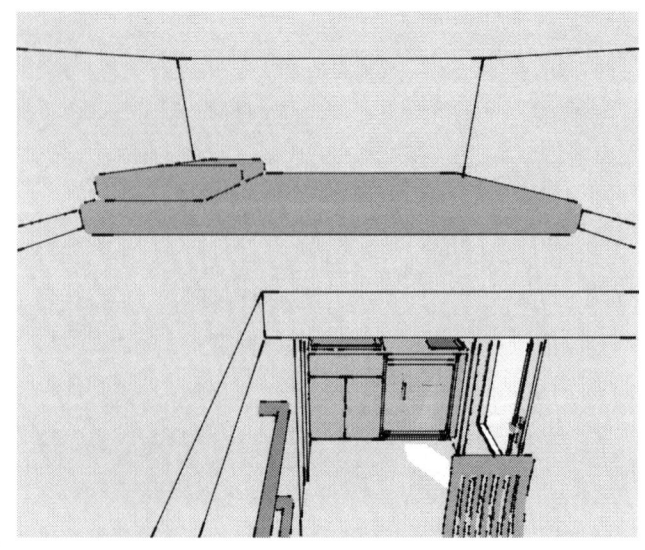

Loft

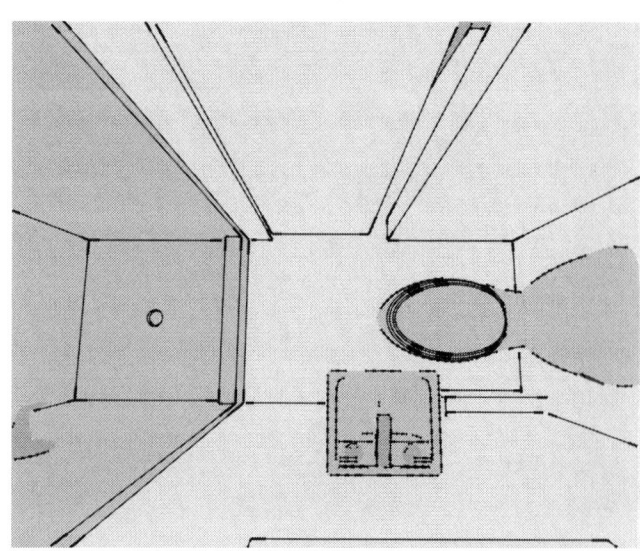

Bathroom

Tiny House #33 - Elevations

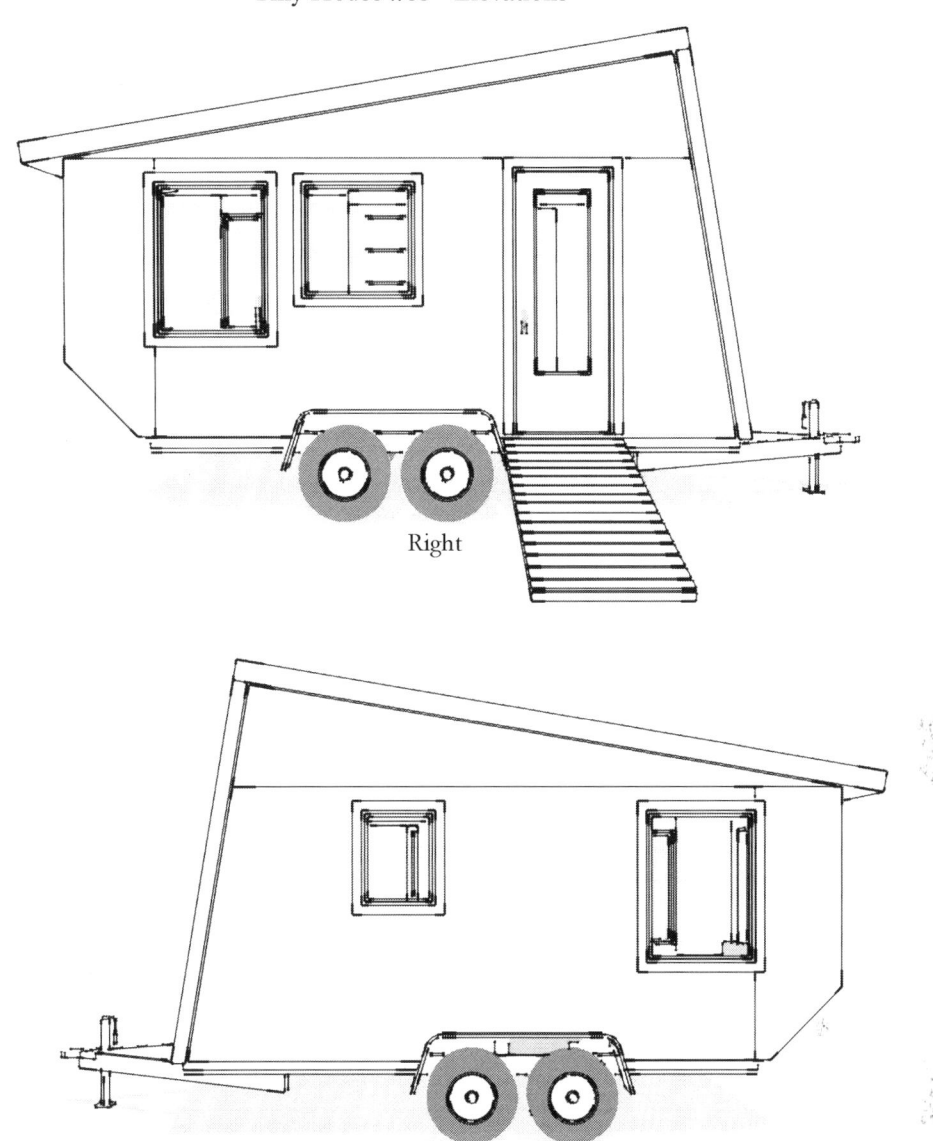

Right

Left

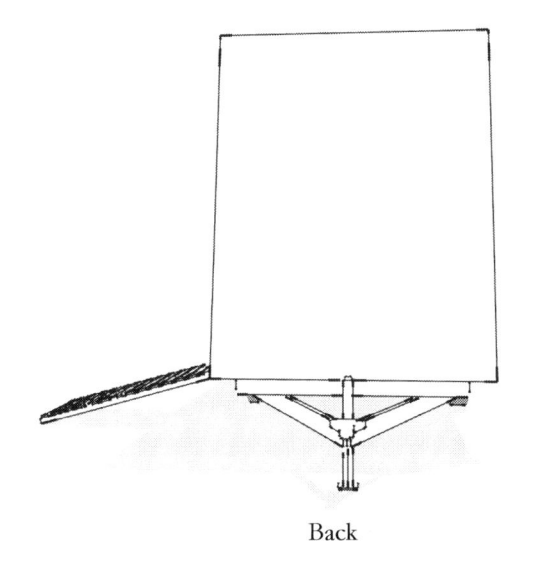

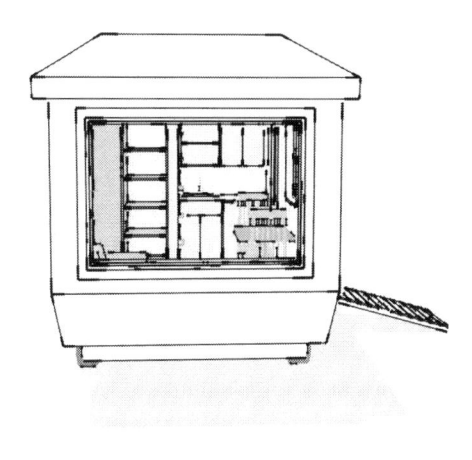

Back

Front

137

#34

Tiny House #34 - Overview

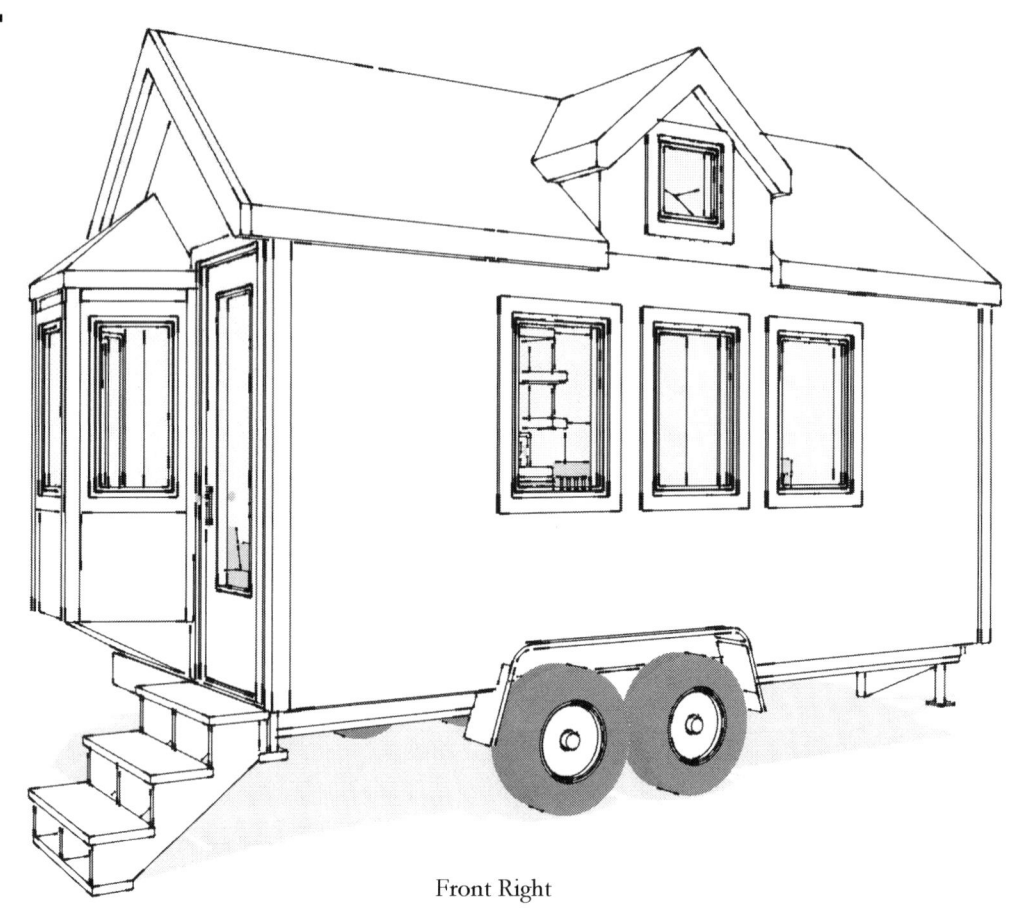

Front Right

Summary:

This tiny house has a 10/12 gable roof and bay windows in the front and back. The tiny kitchen has a small refrigerator, sink with cabinet drain rack above, stovetop, and plenty of storage. The bathroom extends in a bay window over the trailer tongue and has a 32-inch shower, toilet, and vanity. The loft has space for a queen bed and is accessed by a spiral staircase. The living room has a table for two and two comfy chairs.

Features:

16-Foot Tiny House on Wheels
Gable Roof with Gable Dormers
Bathroom in Bay Window Extension
Small Kitchen
Entry with Fold-up Steps
Bay Window in Front
Spiral Stairs to Loft

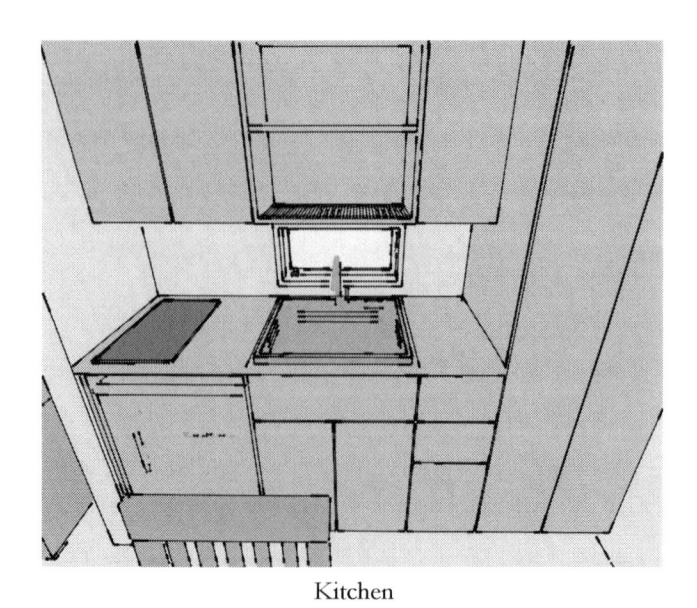

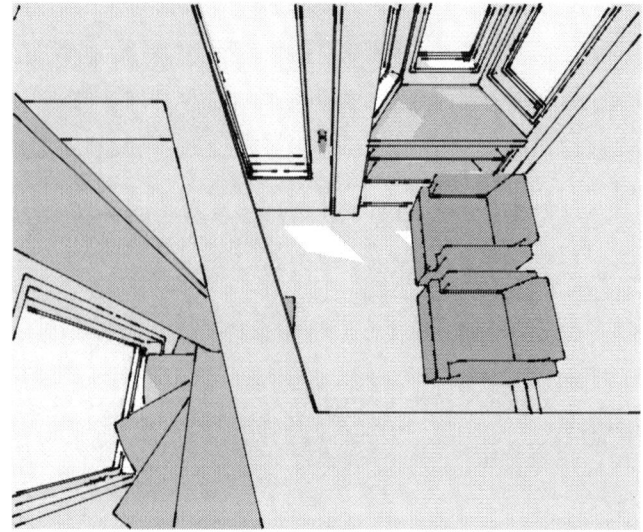

Kitchen

View from Loft

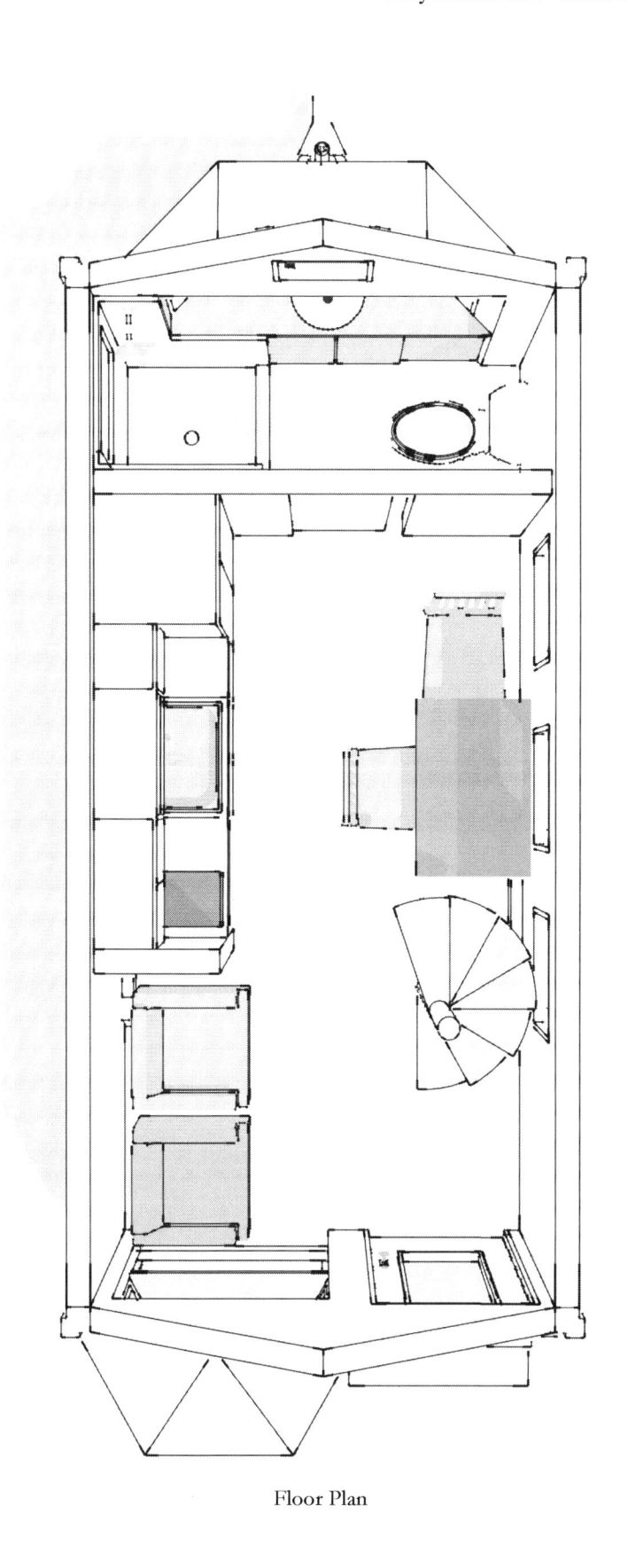

Tiny House #34 - Floor Plan & Exterior

Front Right Corner

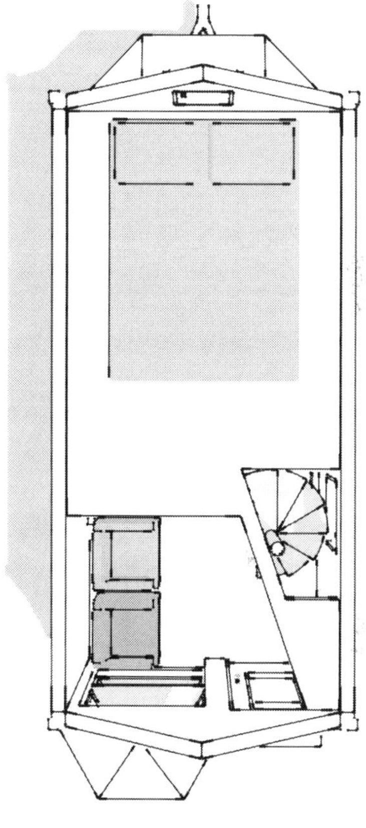

Floor Plan - Loft

Floor Plan

Back Left Corner

Tiny House #34 - Interior Views

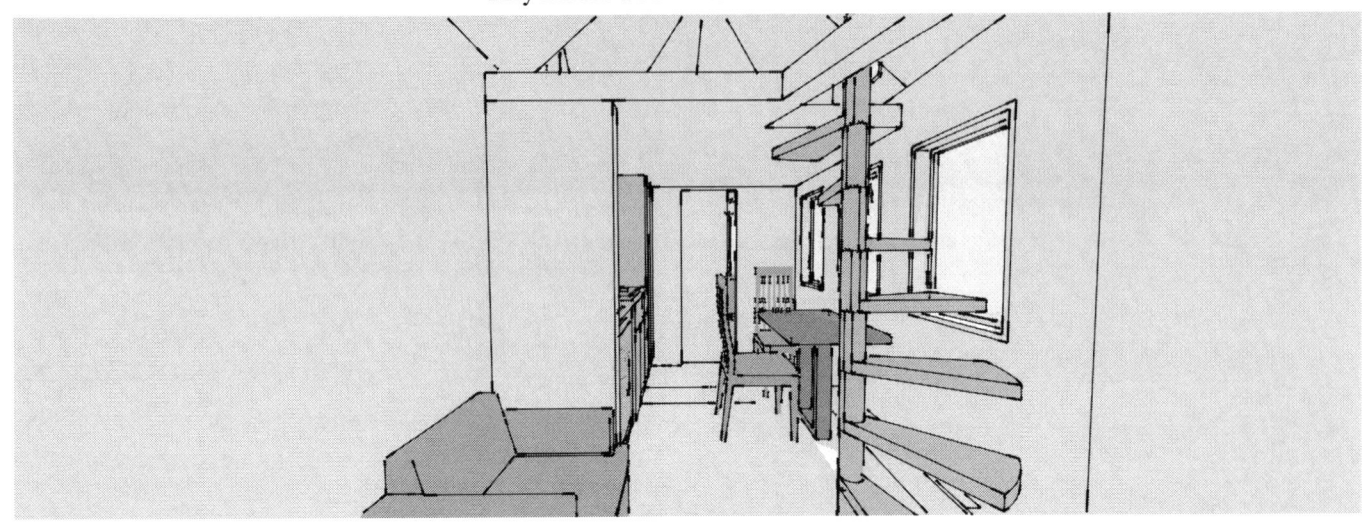

Interior from Entry

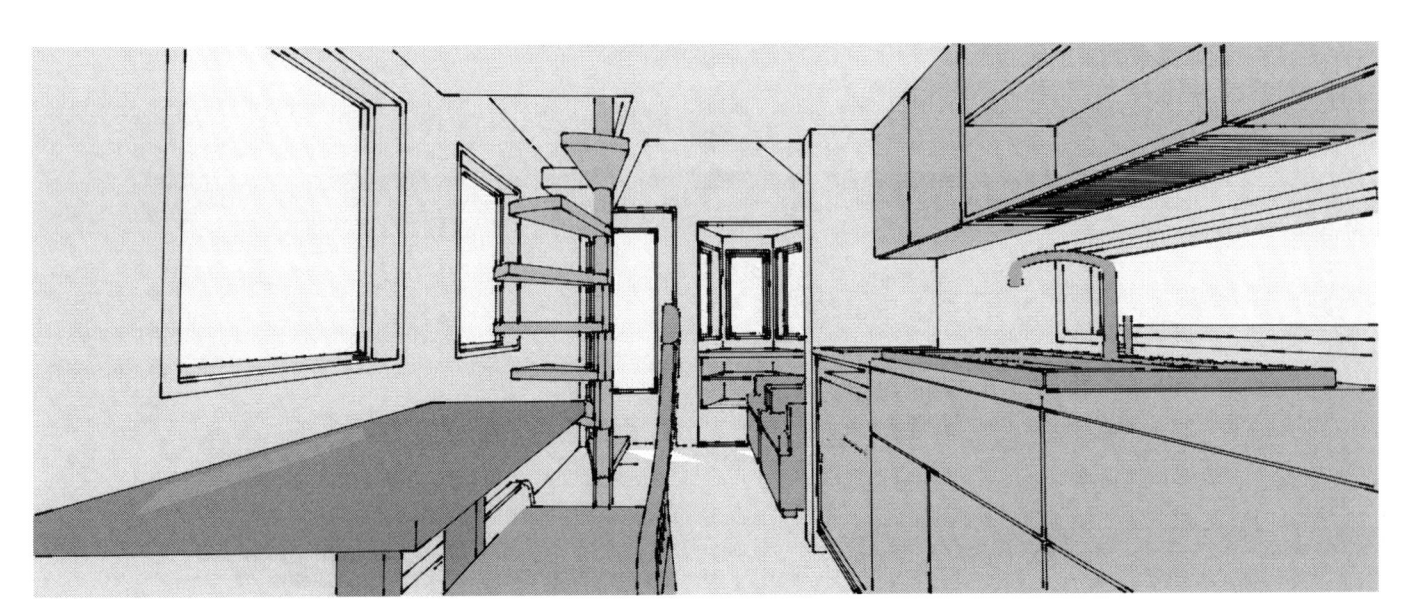

Interior from Kitchen

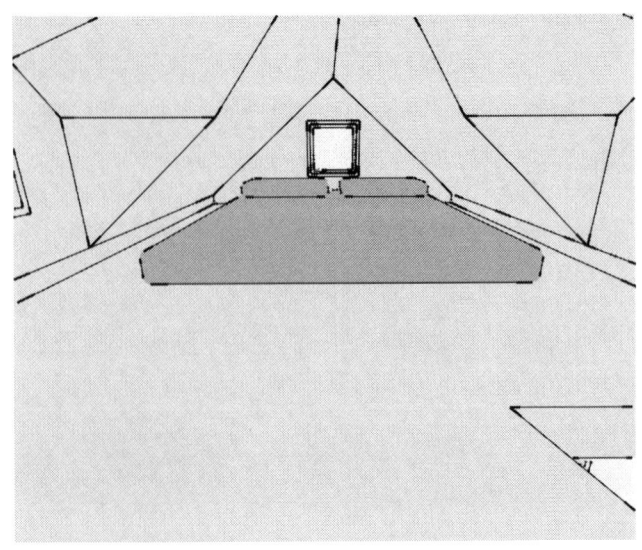

Loft

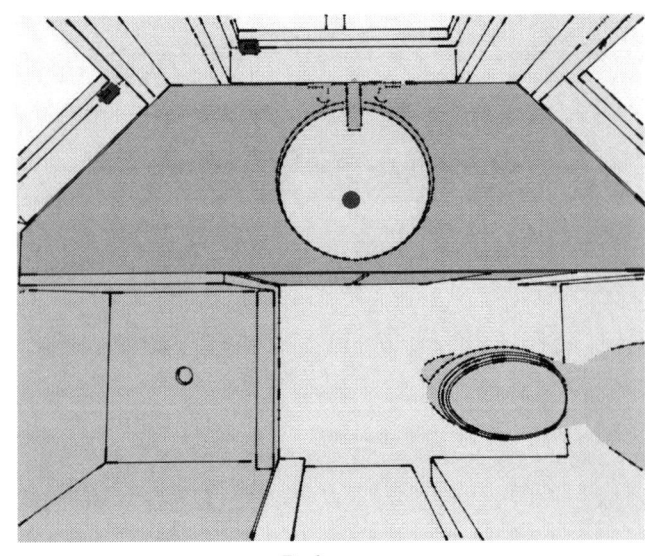

Bathroom

Tiny House #34 - Elevations

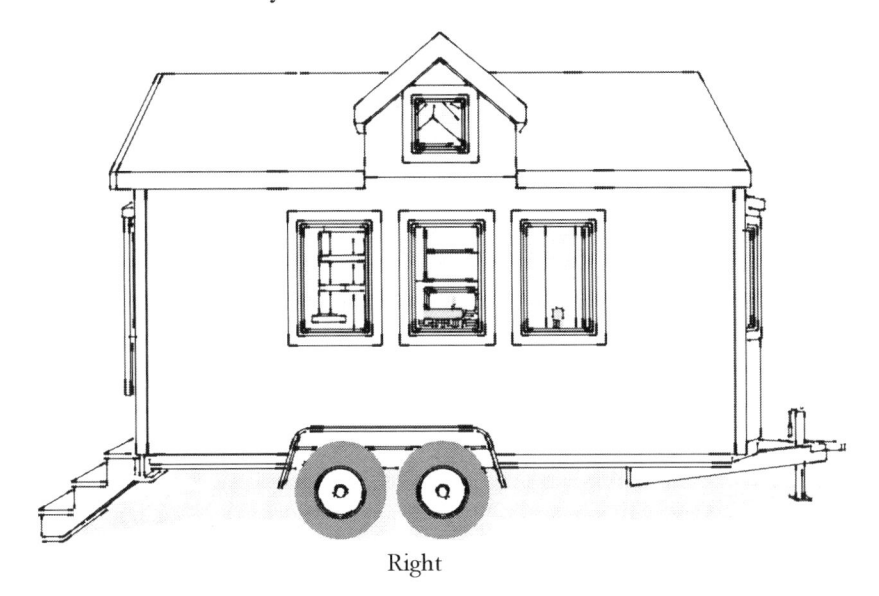

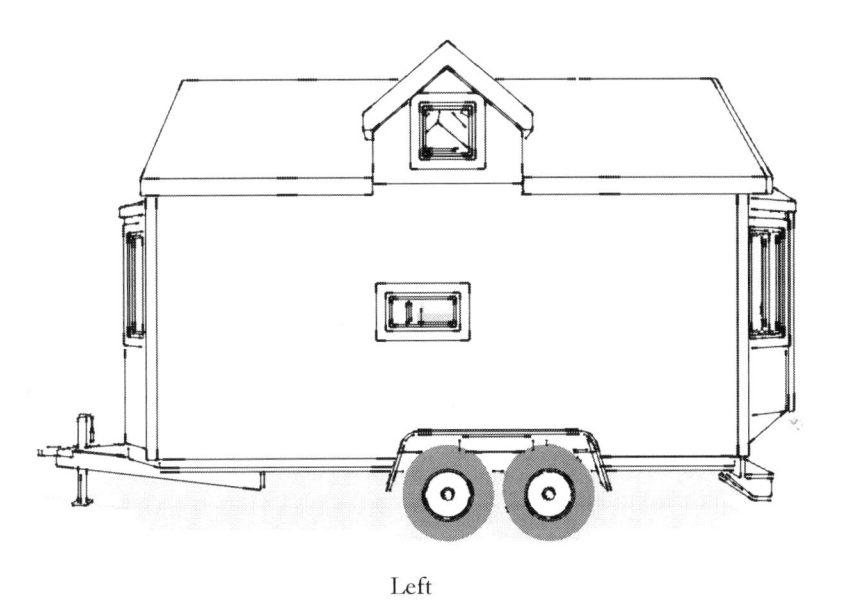

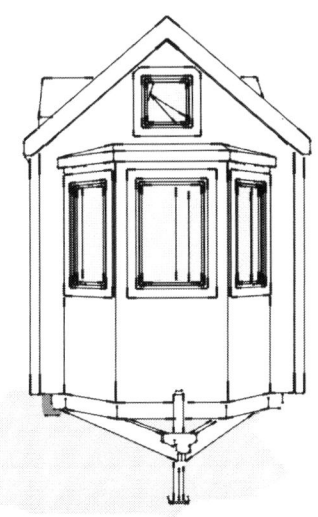

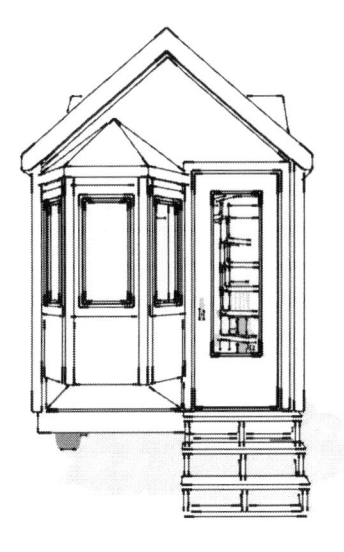

Right

Left

Back

Front

18-Foot Tiny House Designs

#35

Tiny House #35 - Overview

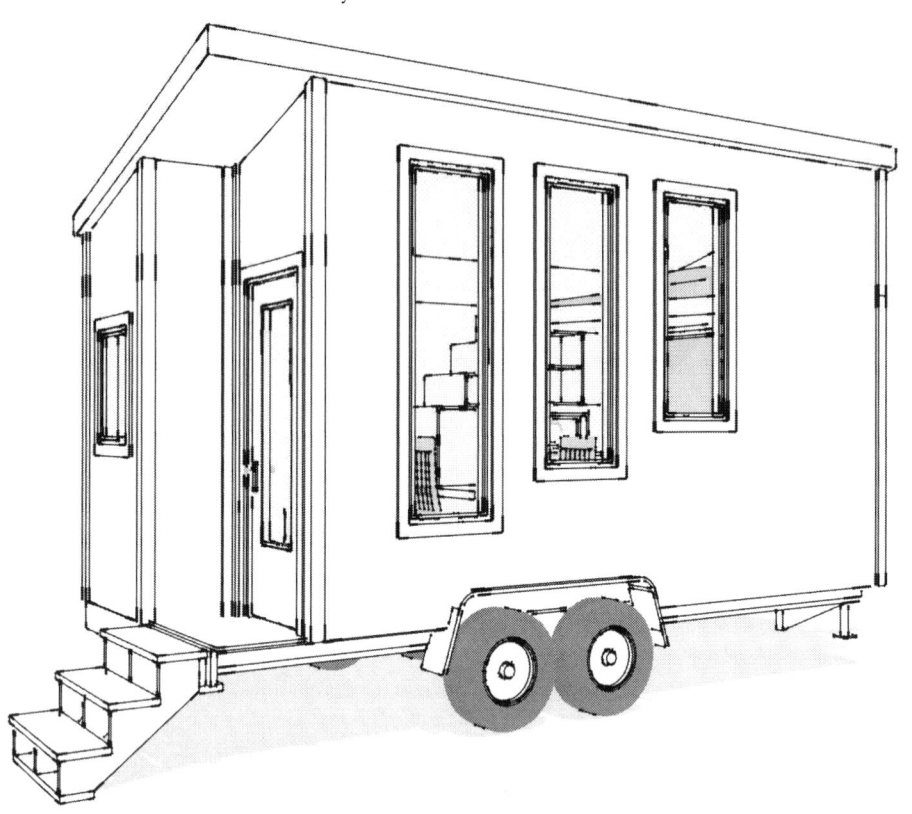

Front Right

Summary:

This tiny house has a 3/12 shed roof and large windows that follow the rise of the stairs inside. The kitchen has a full size refrigerator, sink with cabinet drain rack above, and stovetop. The bathroom has a 32-inch shower, toilet, and wall mounted sink. The loft has space for a queen bed. Inside the front door is a table for two and a chair and ottoman. The stairs provide a lot of storage and display opportunities. Handrail not shown but recommended.

Features:

18-Foot Tiny House on Wheels
Shed Roof
Standard Bathroom
Small Kitchen
Inset Entry with Fold-up Steps
Storage Stairs to Loft

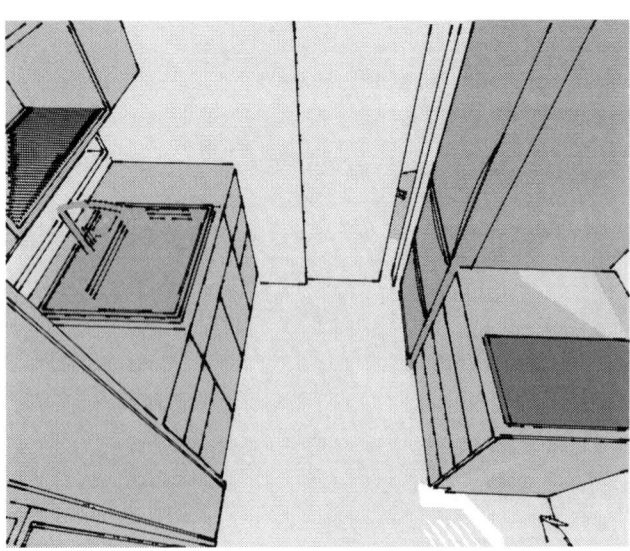

Kitchen

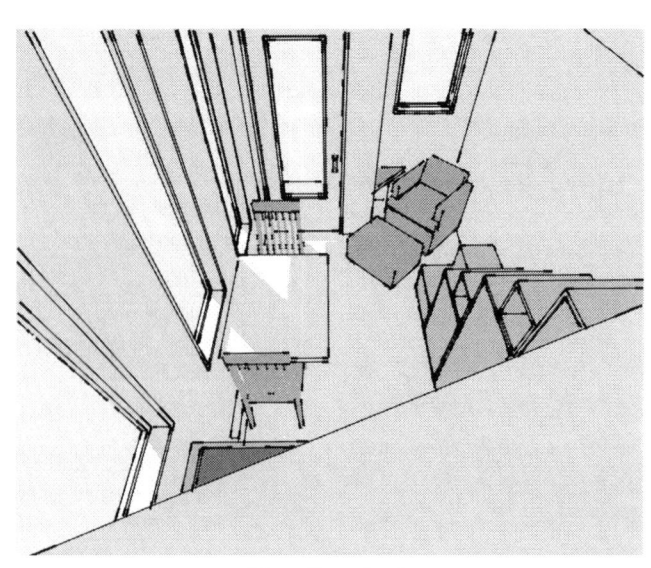

View from Loft

Tiny House #35 - Floor Plan & Exterior

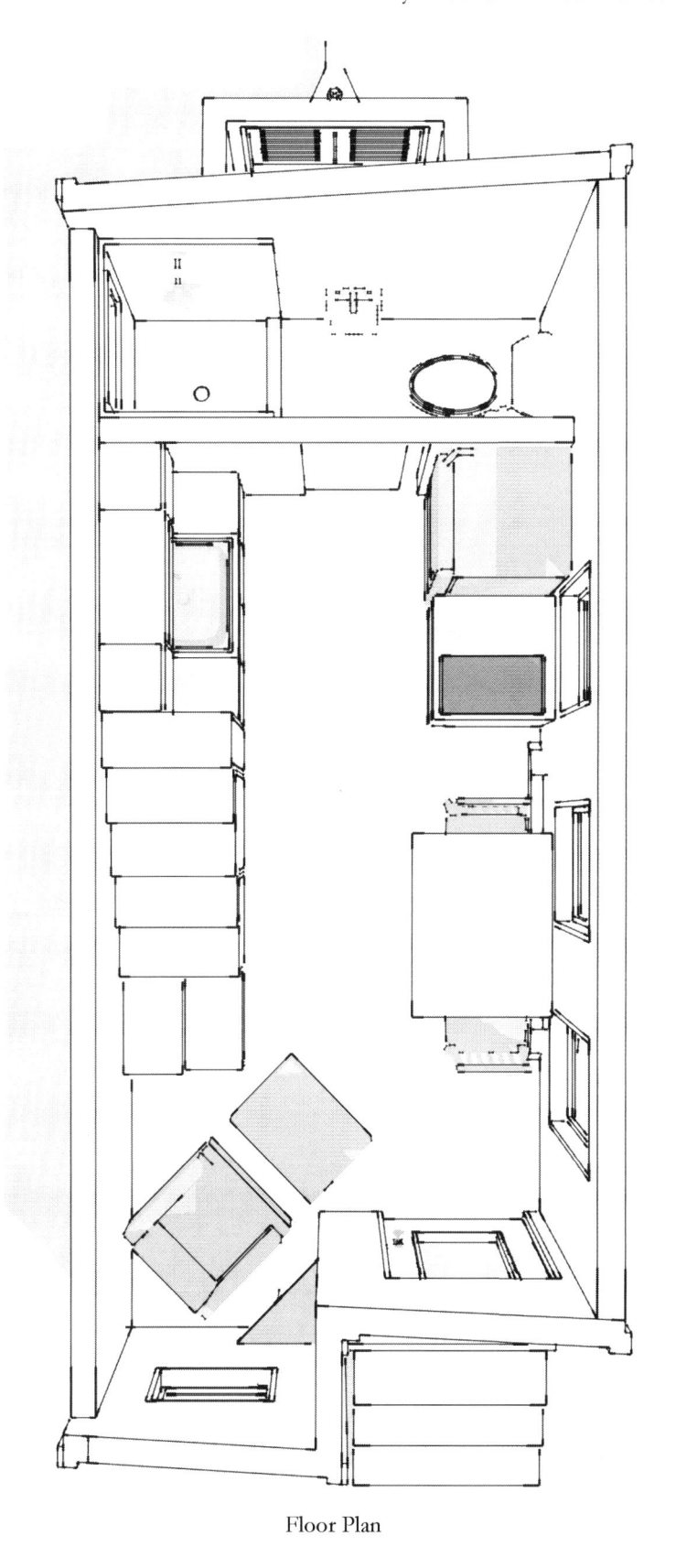

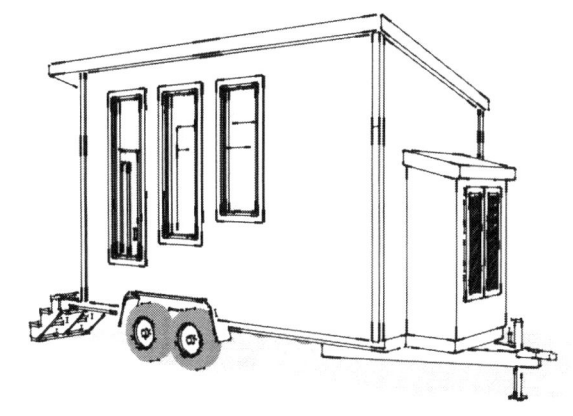

Front Right Corner

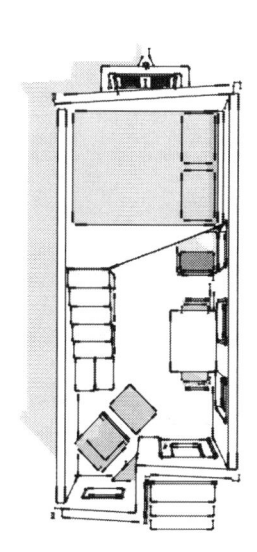

Floor Plan - Loft

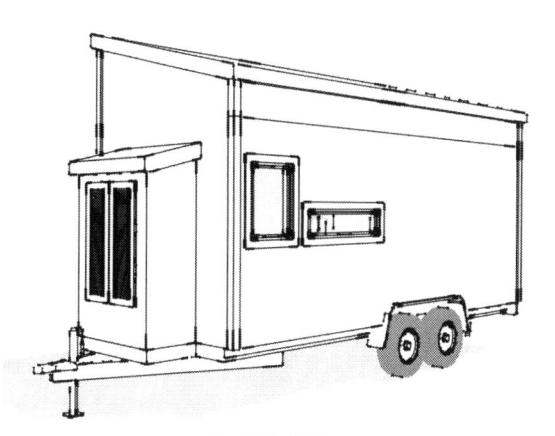

Floor Plan

Back Left Front

145

Tiny House #35 - Interior Views

Interior from Entry

Interior from Kitchen

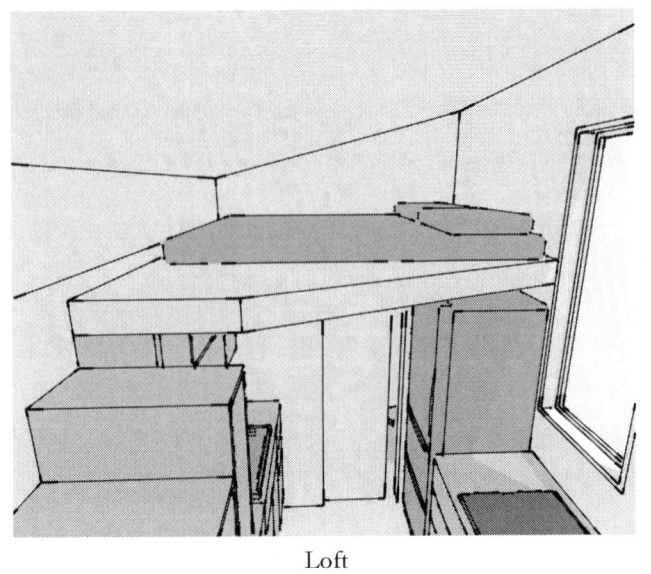

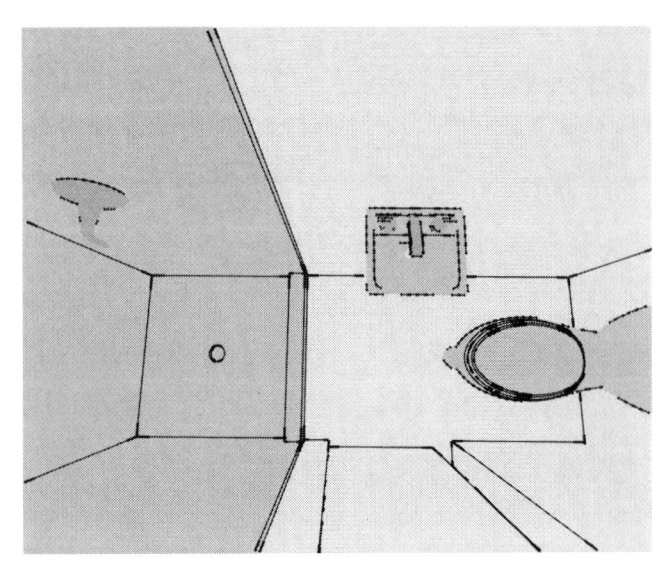

Loft

Bathroom

146

Tiny House #35 - Elevations

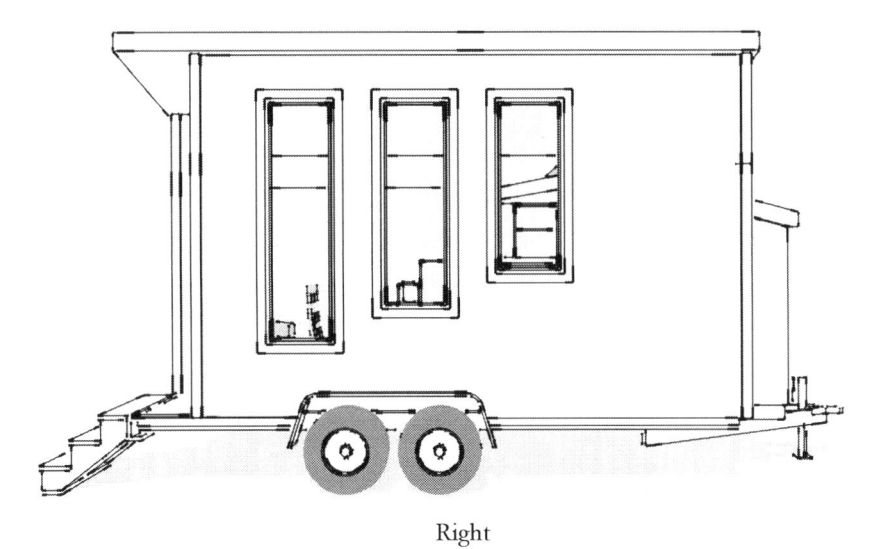

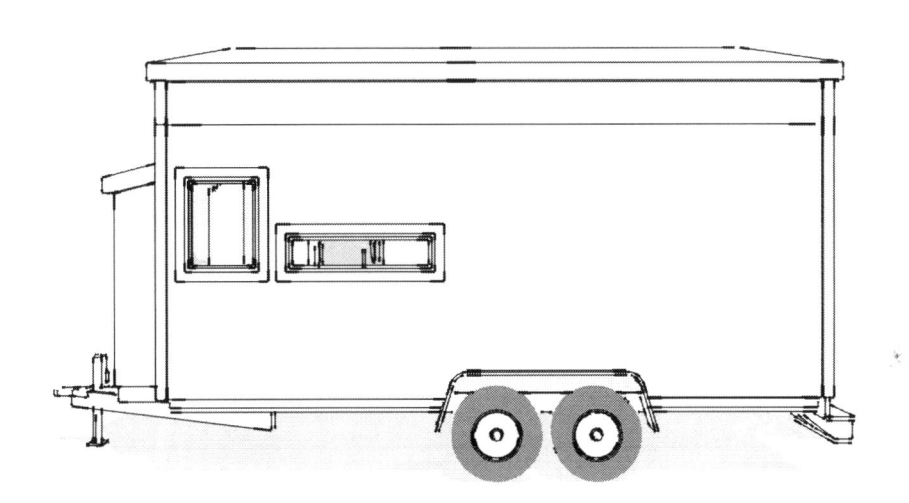

Right

Left

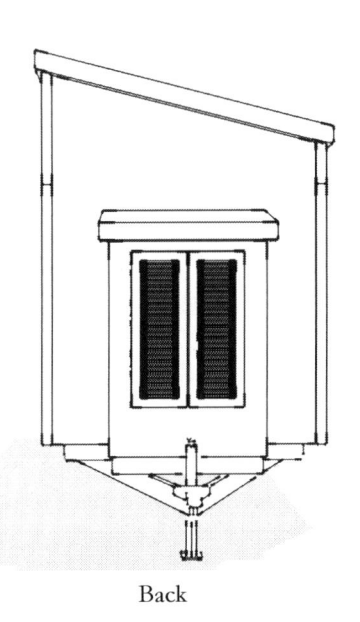

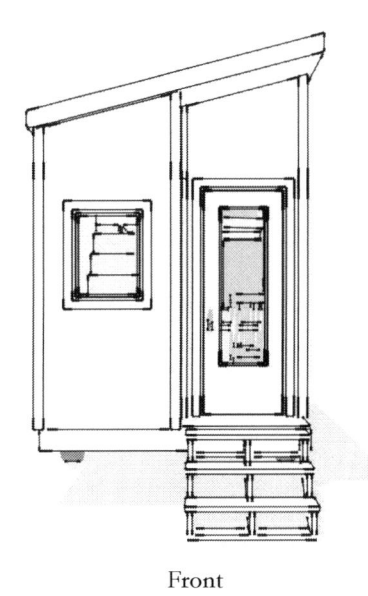

Back

Front

#36

Tiny House #36 - Overview

Front Right

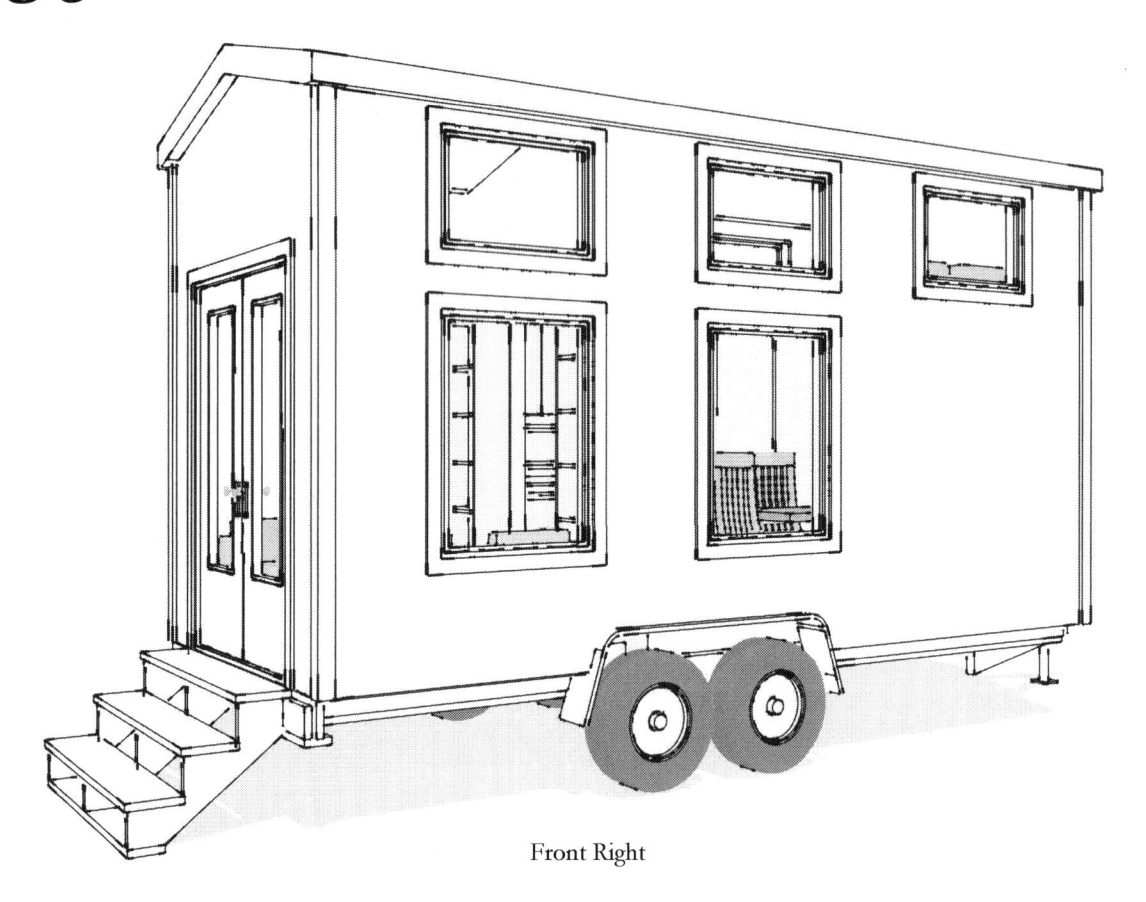

Summary:

This tall tiny house has a 3/12 gable roof and large windows. The kitchen has a small refrigerator, sink with cabinet drain rack above, and stovetop. The bathroom has a large bay window, a soaking tub, toilet, and vanity. The loft has space for a queen bed and is accessed by wall mounted ladder rungs. Inside the front door are three comfy chairs. In the kitchen there's a table for two.

Features:

18-Foot Tiny House on Wheels
Tall 3/12 Gable Roof
Bathroom with Soaking Tub, Vanity, and Bay Window
Small Kitchen
French Door Entry with Fold-up Steps
Separate Rooms

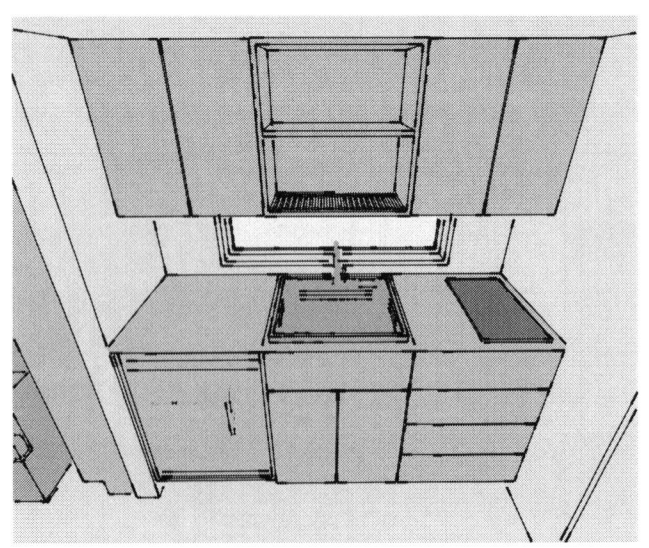

Kitchen

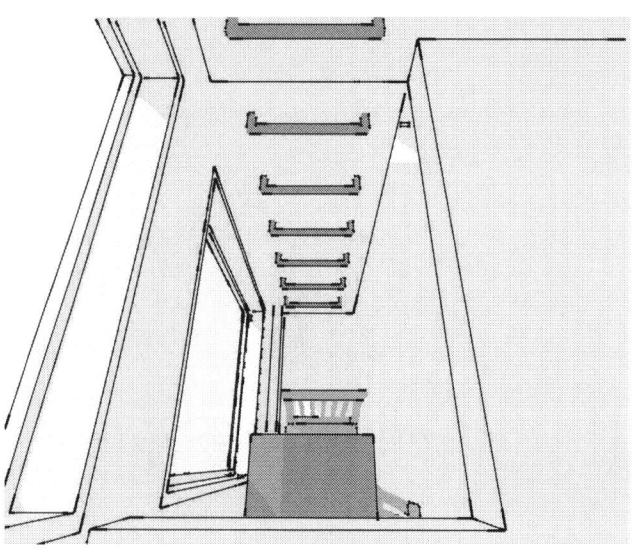

View from Loft

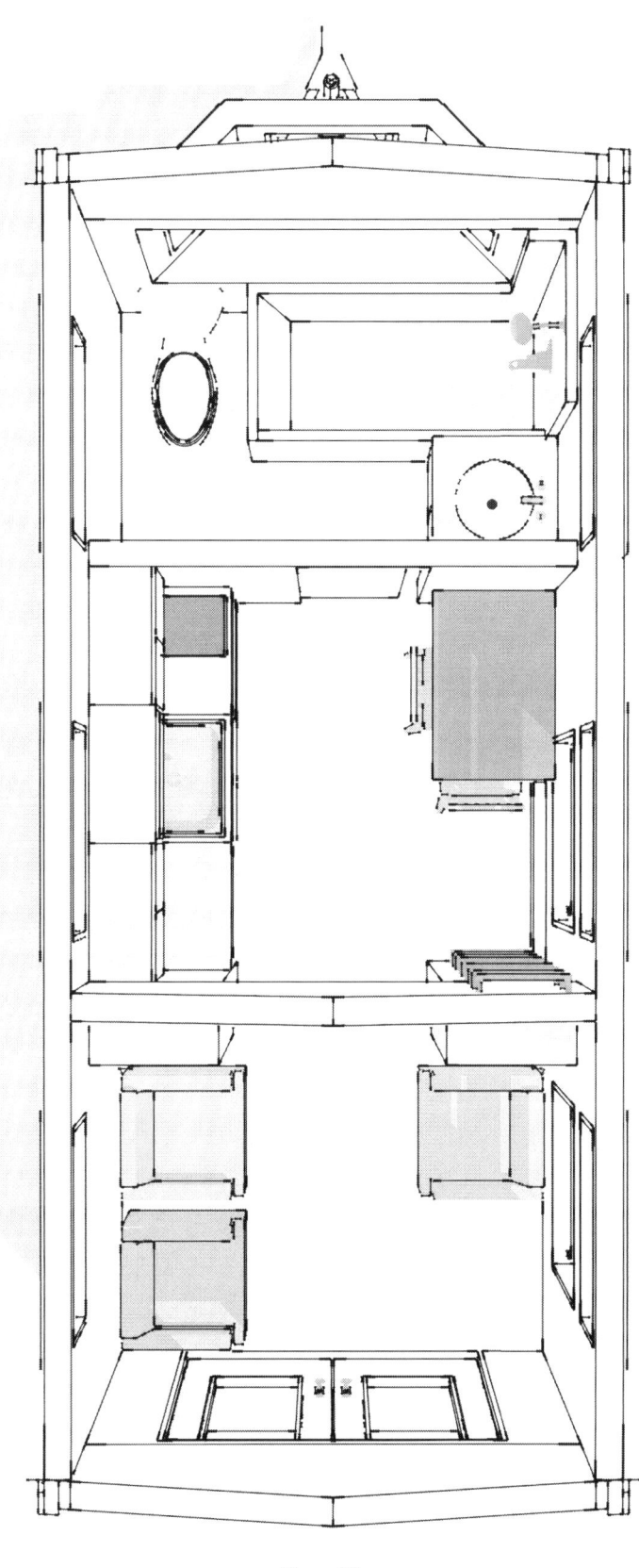

Tiny House #36 - Floor Plan & Exterior

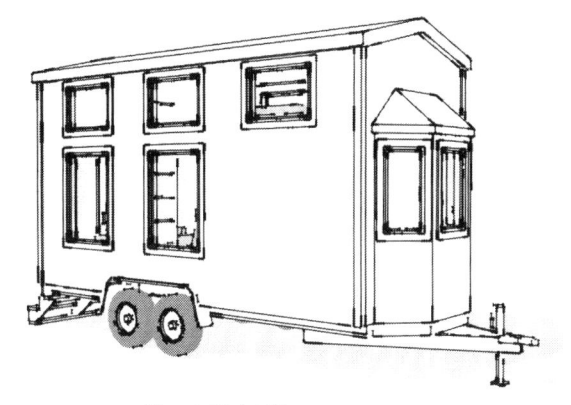

Front Right Corner

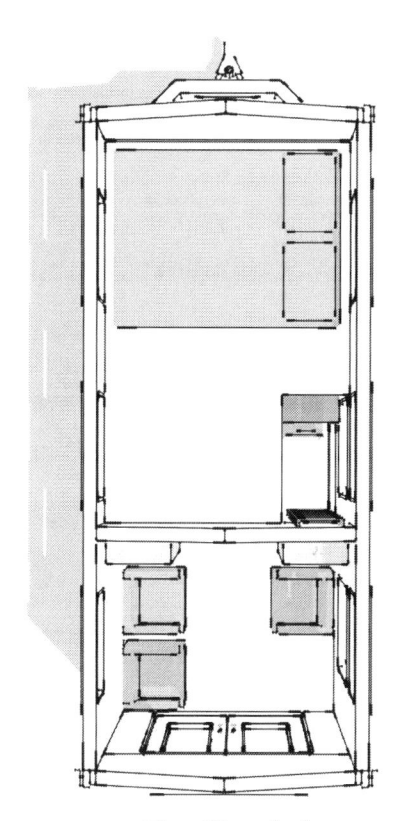

Floor Plan - Loft

Back Left Corner

Floor Plan

149

Tiny House #36 - Interior Views

Interior from Entry

Interior from Kitchen

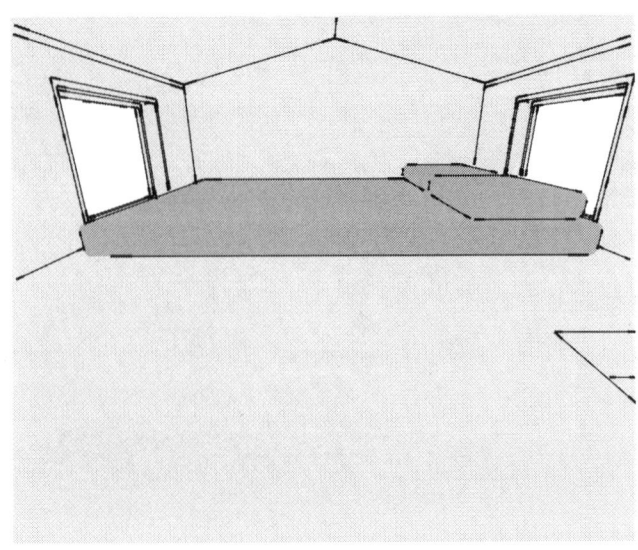

Loft

Bathroom

Tiny House #36 - Elevations

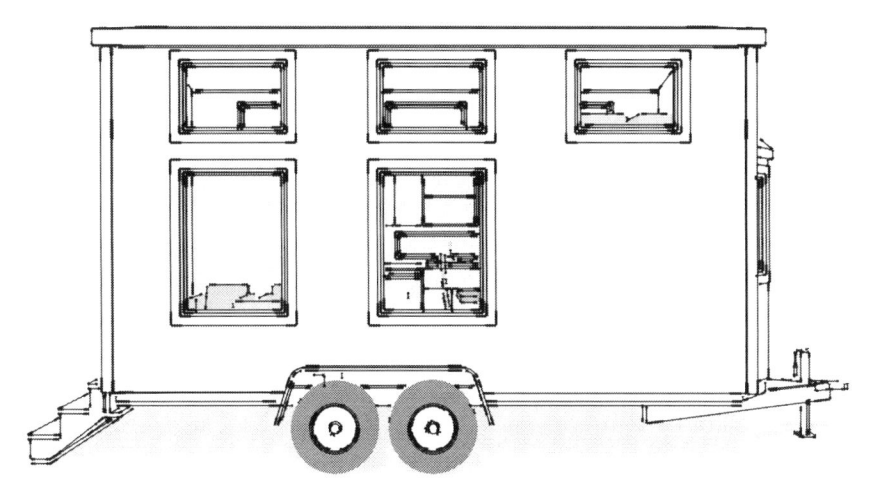

Right

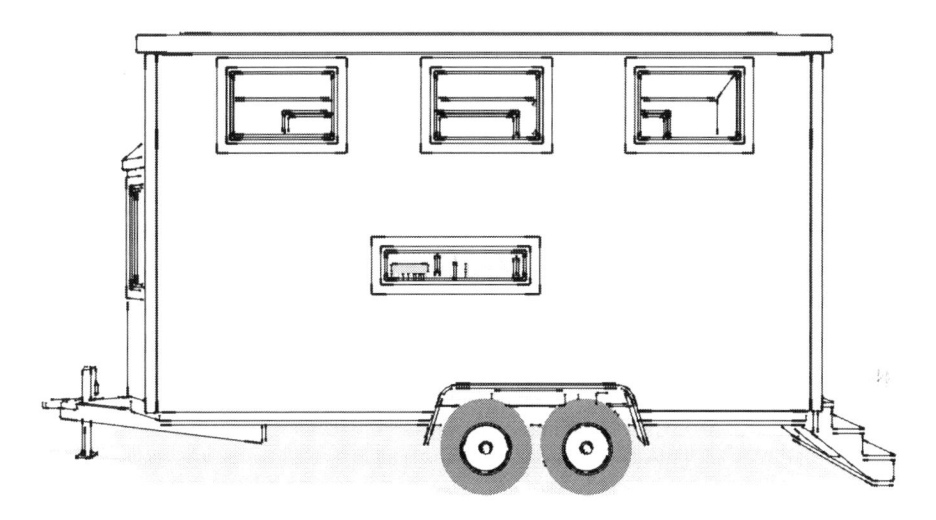

Left

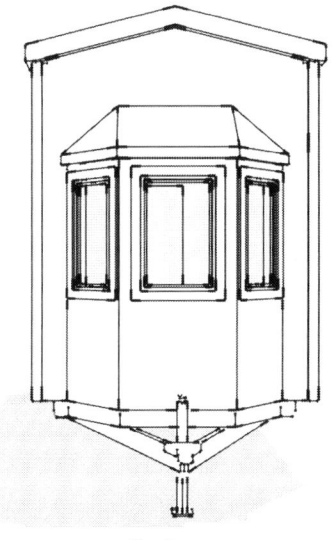

Back

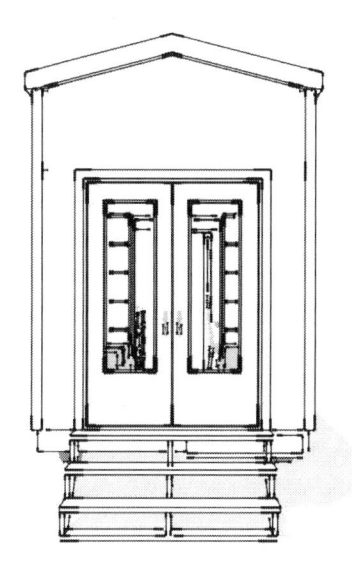

Front

#37

Tiny House #37 - Overview

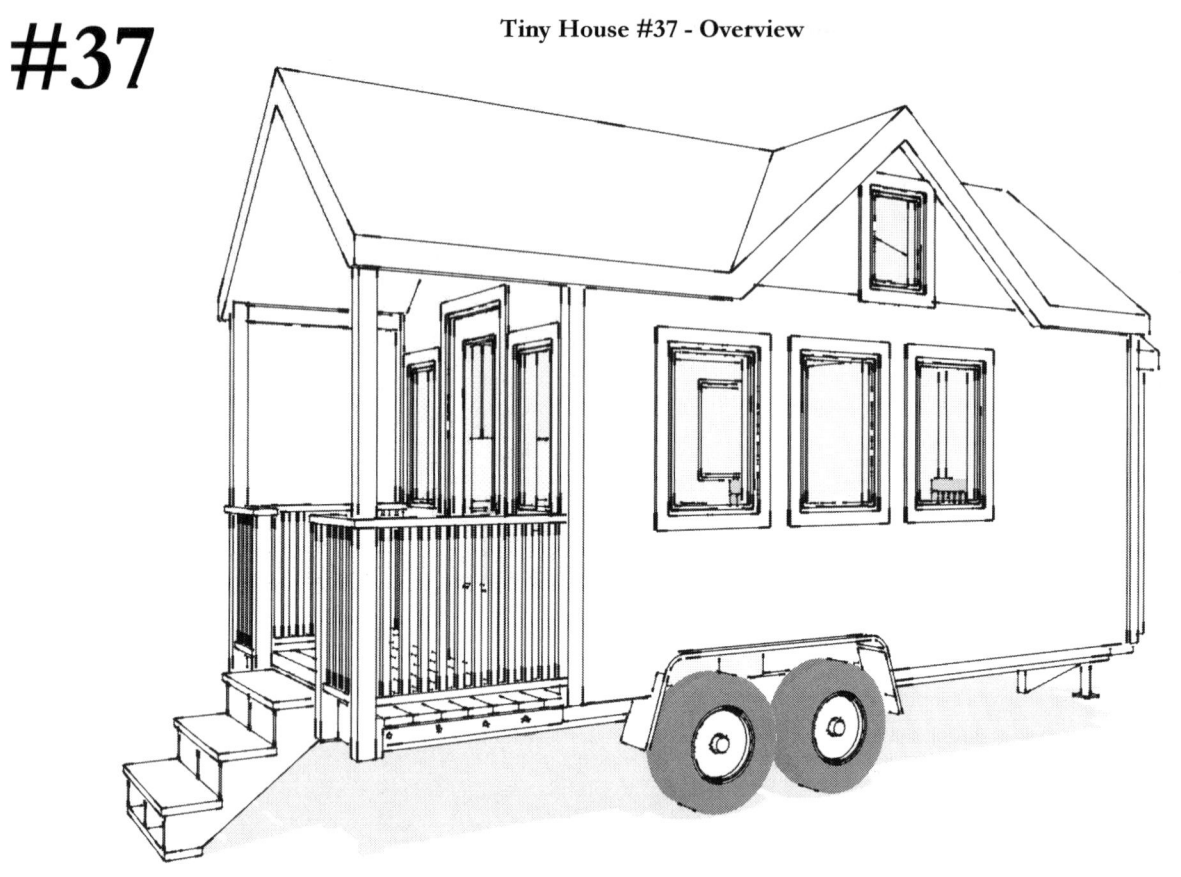

Front Right

Summary:

Tiny house #37 has a 10/12 cross gable roof and 3-foot deep porch. Just inside the front door is the kitchen, which has a small refrigerator, sink, and stovetop. The bathroom is at the back of the house and has a shower, toilet, and vanity. The loft has space for a queen bed and is accessed by a movable ladder. In the middle of the house is space for a sofa and table for two.

Features:

18-Foot Tiny House on Wheels
Cross Gable Roof
Bathroom Extends over Trailer Tongue
Small Kitchen
Deep Porch and Fold-up Steps
Sofa and Table for Two

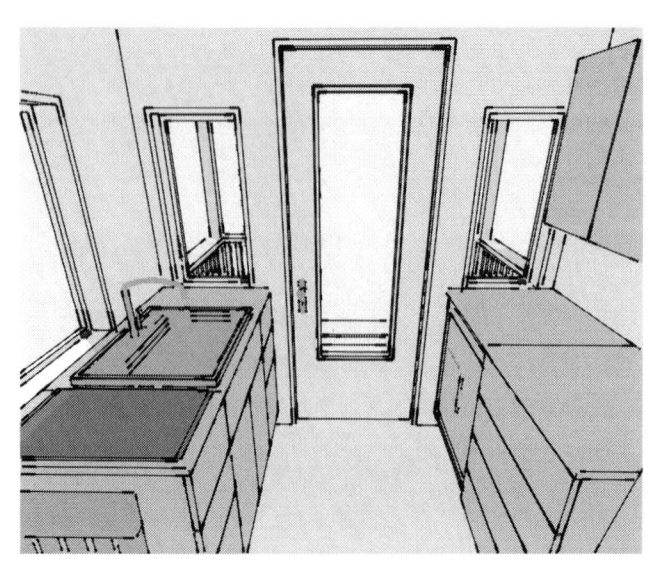

Kitchen

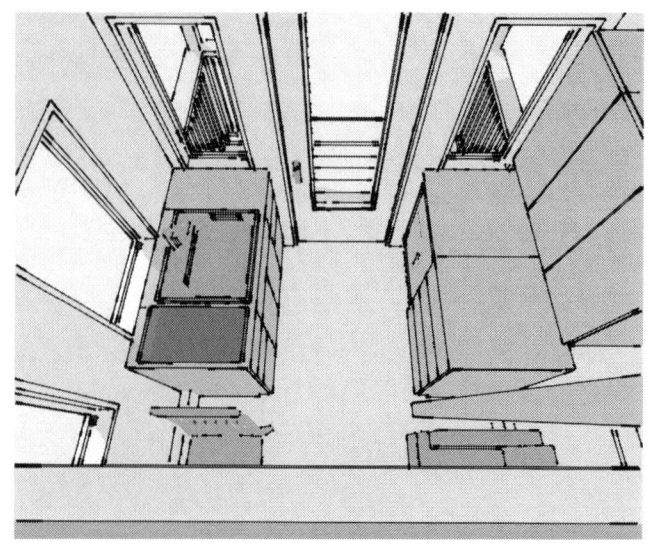

View from Loft

Tiny House #37 - Floor Plan & Exterior

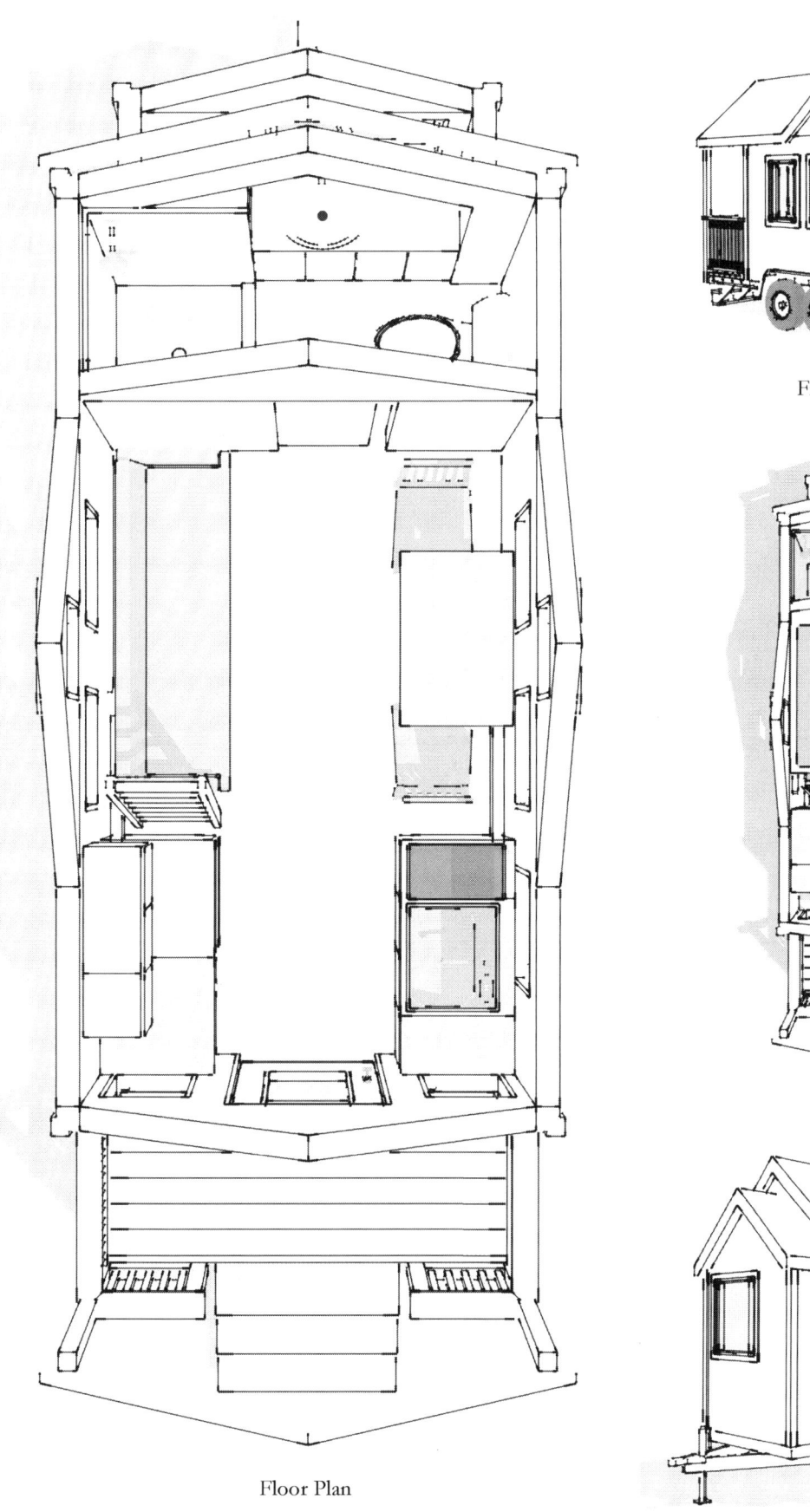

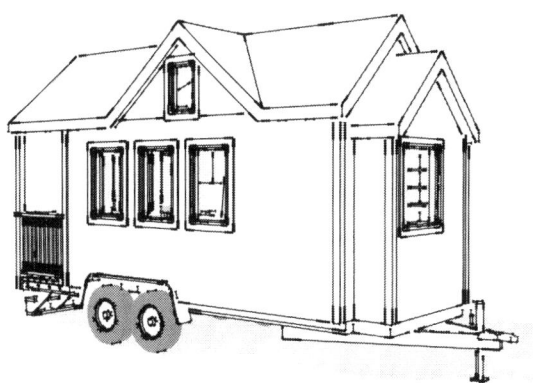

Front Right Corner

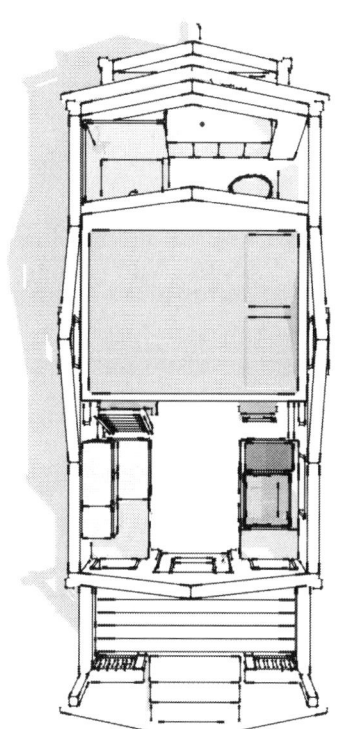

Floor Plan - Loft

Floor Plan

Back Left Corner

Tiny House #37 - Interior Views

Interior from Entry

Interior from Bathroom

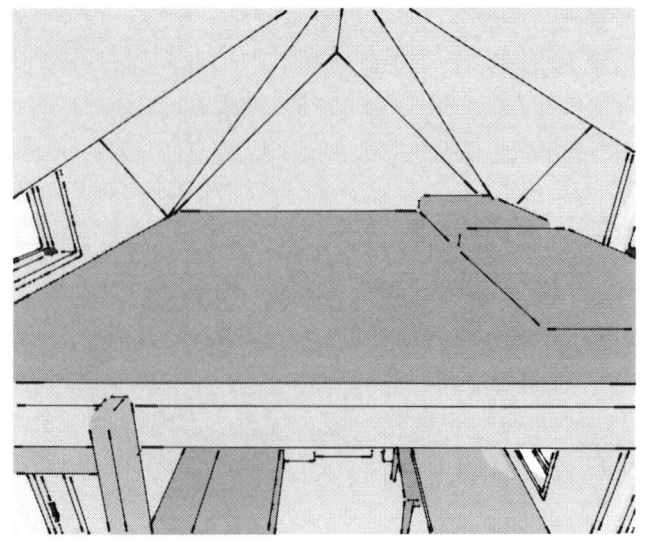

Loft

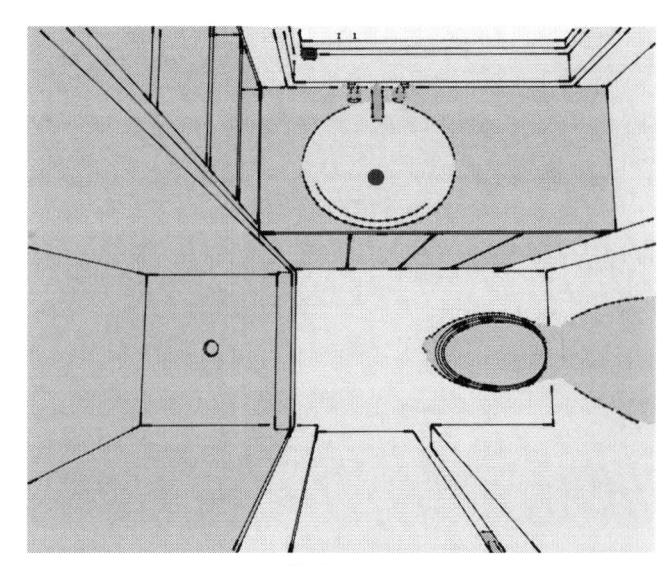

Bathroom

154

Tiny House #37 - Elevations

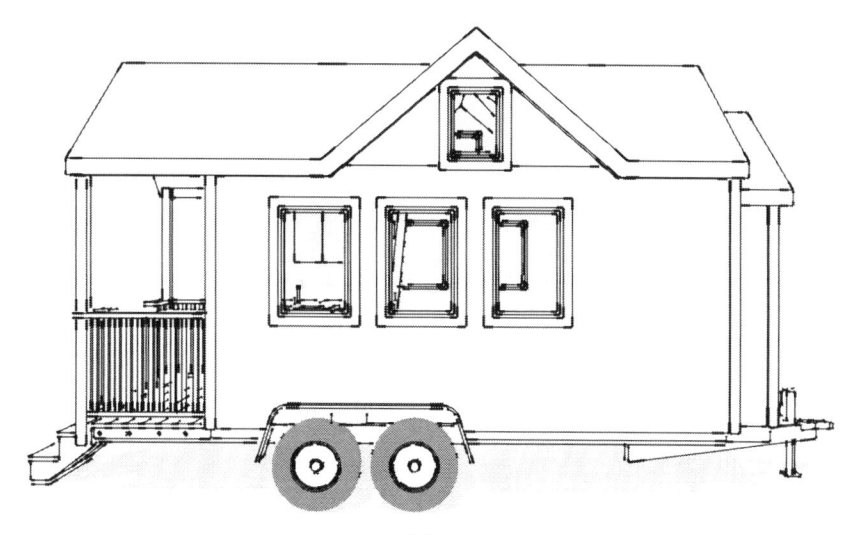

Right

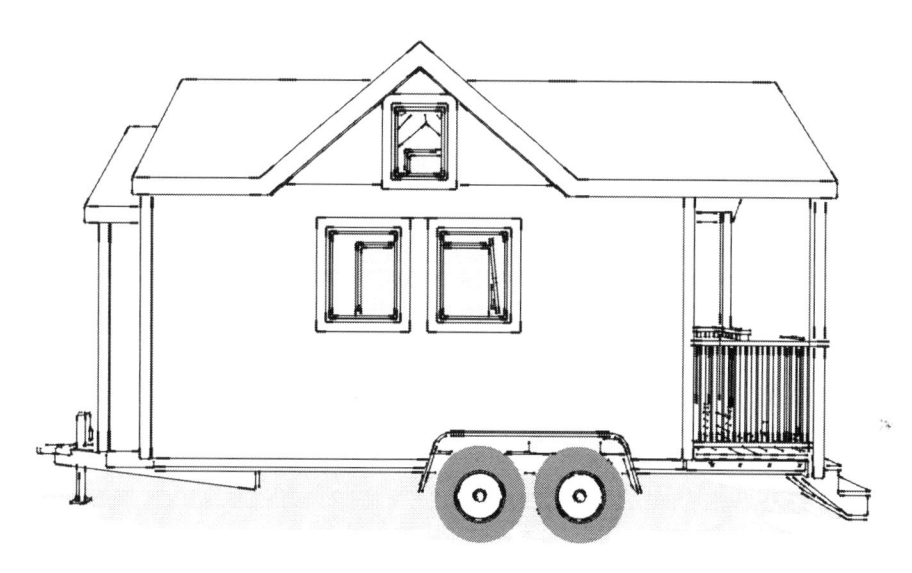

Left

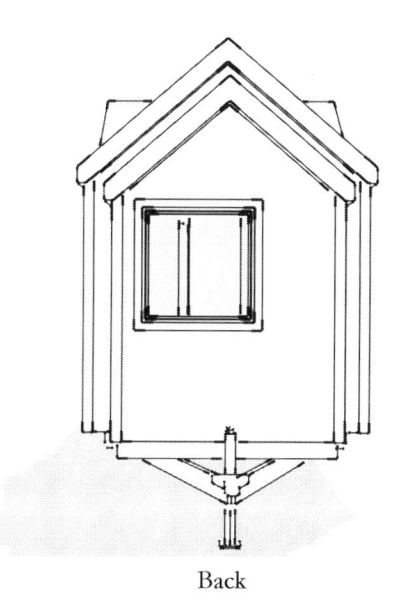

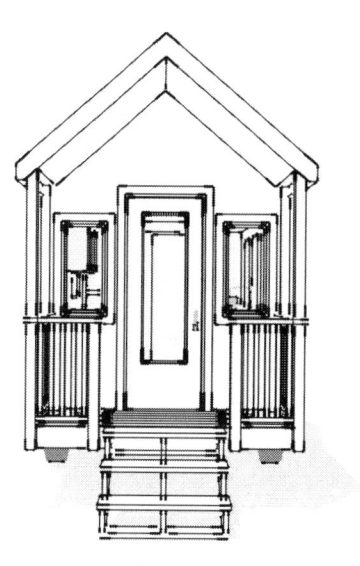

Back

Front

#38

Tiny House #38 - Overview

Front Right

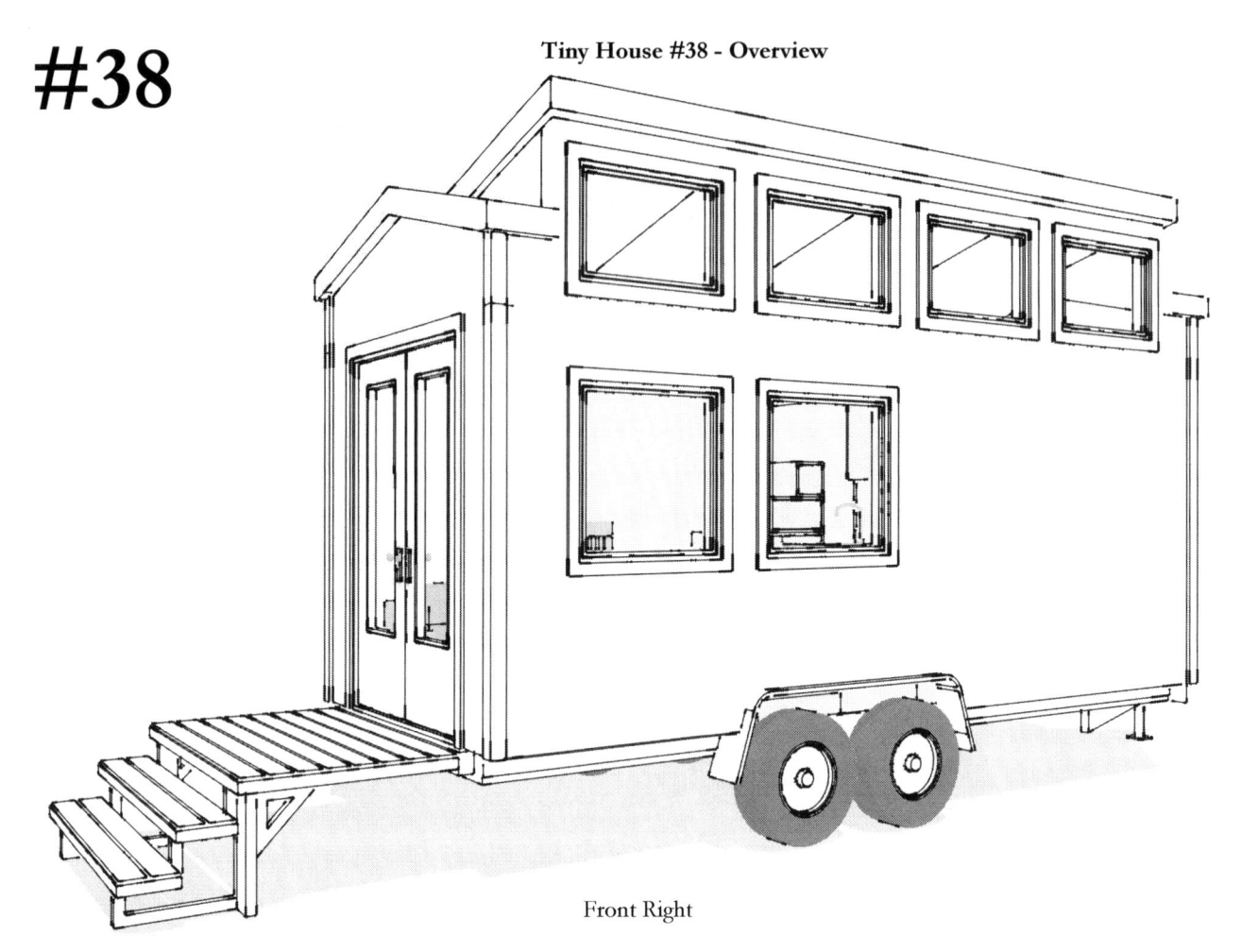

Summary:

This tiny house has a 3/12 gable roof on the ends and a 3/12 shed roof in the middle. A large fold down deck and steps provides easier access to the house through the french doors.. Just inside are two comfy chairs and a table and chair. The kitchen has a small refrigerator, sink, and stovetop. The standard bathroom is at the back of the house and has a shower, toilet, and wall mounted sink. The loft is accessed by a storage staircase. A storage room is out back and accessed by an exterior door over the trailer tongue.

Features:

18-Foot Tiny House on Wheels
Combination Gable and Shed Roof
Simple Bathroom
Small Kitchen
Storage Room
Storage Staircase
Ample Headroom in Loft

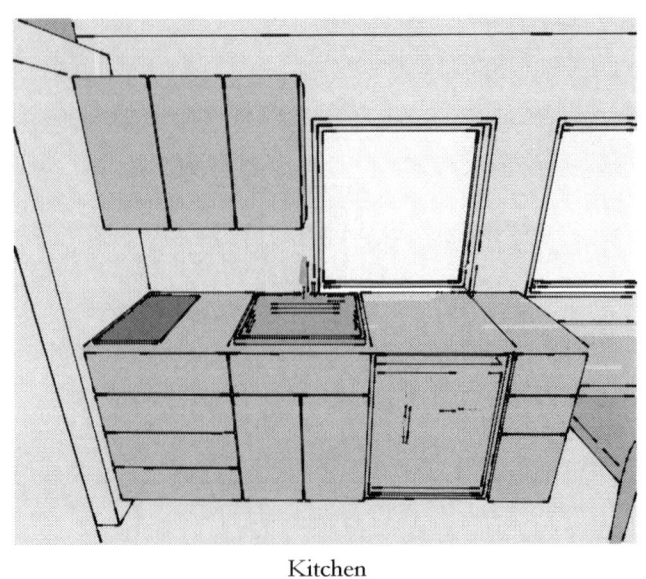

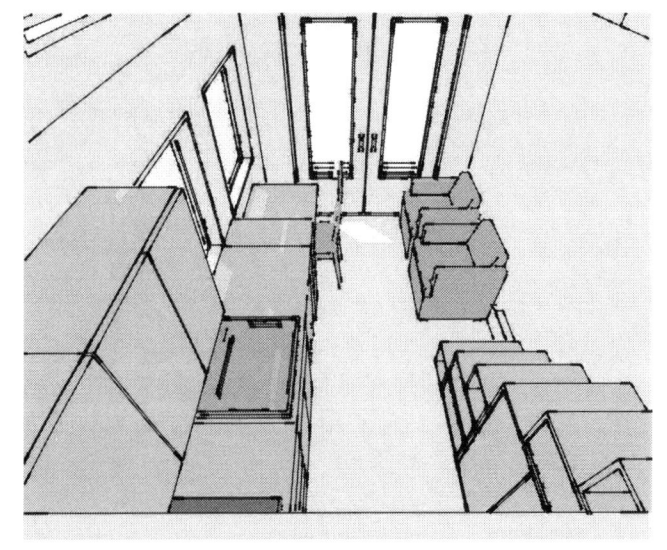

Kitchen

View from Loft

Tiny House #38 - Floor Plan & Exterior

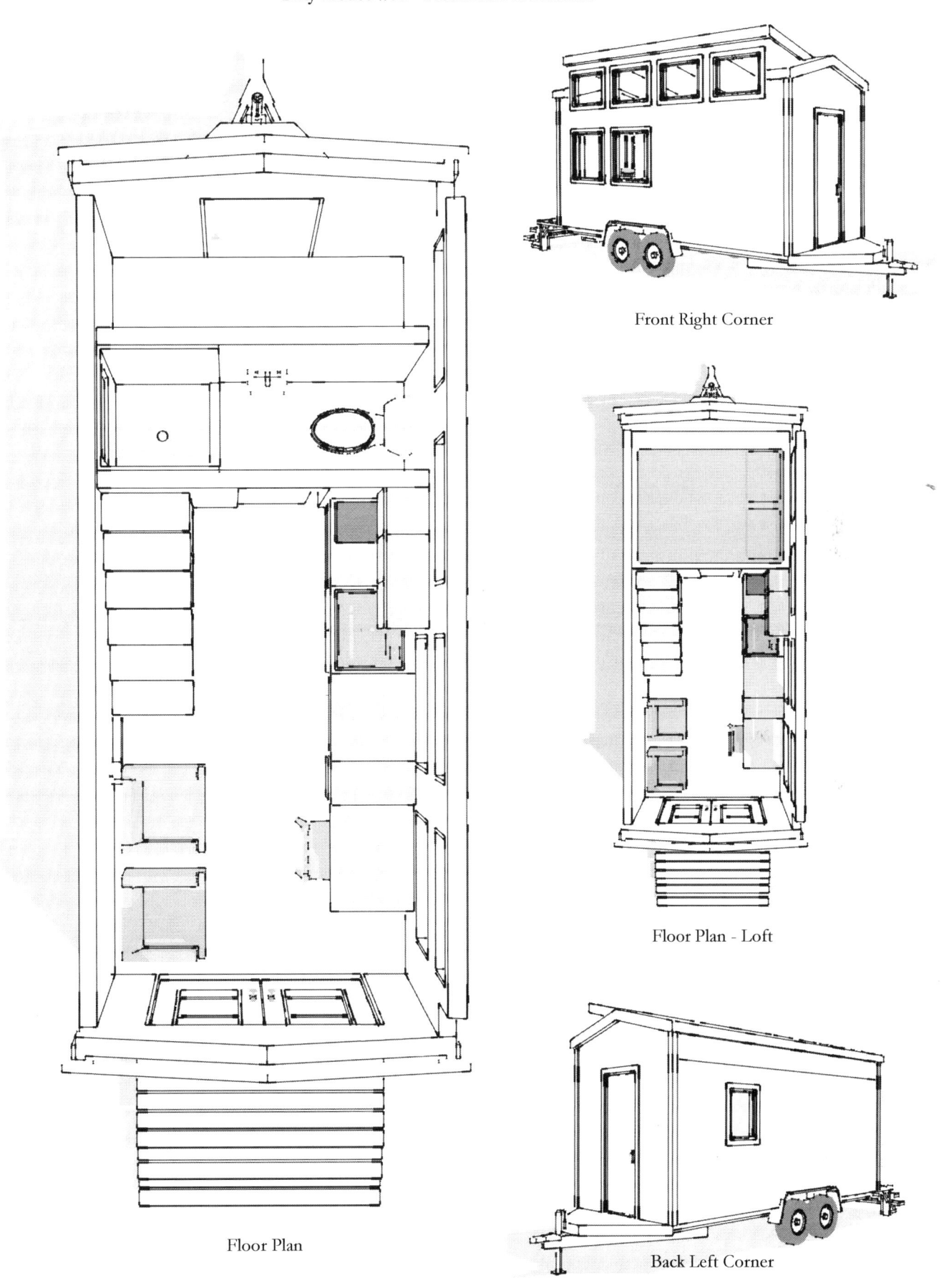

Front Right Corner

Floor Plan - Loft

Floor Plan

Back Left Corner

Tiny House #38 - Interior Views

Interior from Entry

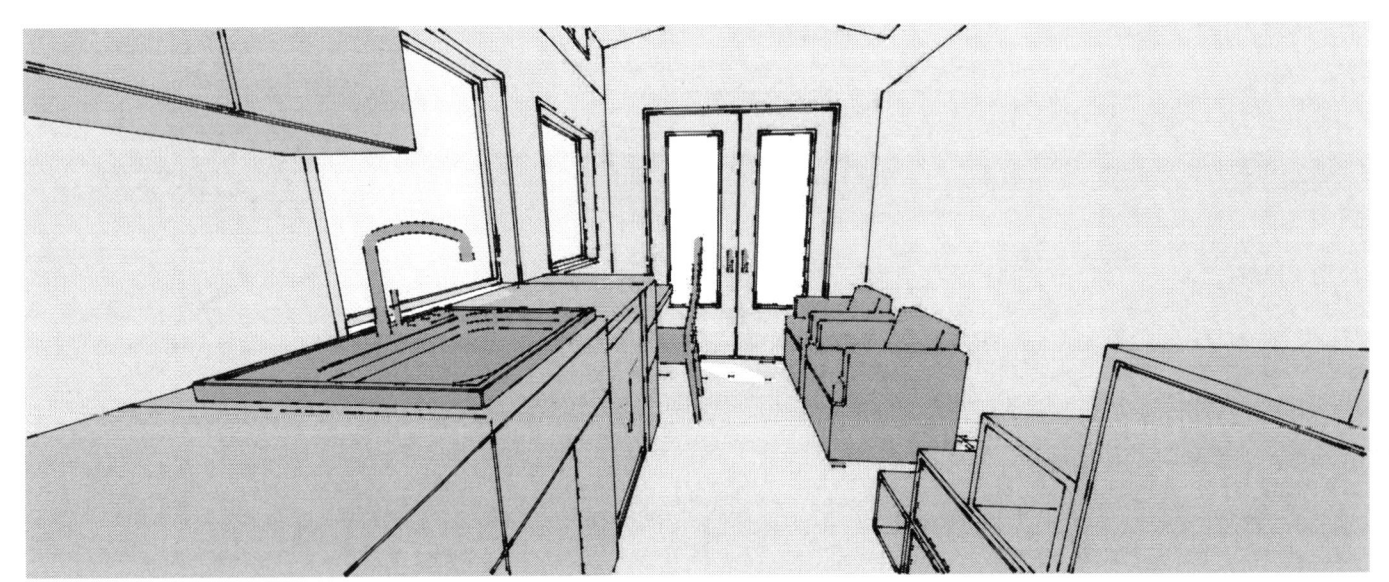

Interior from Bathroom

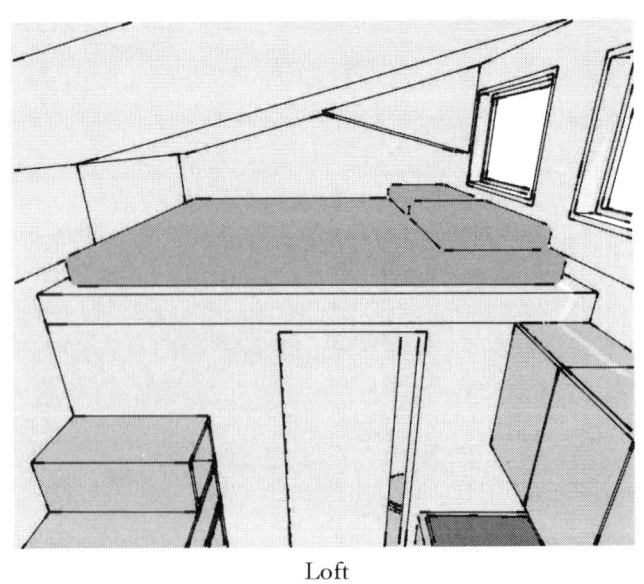

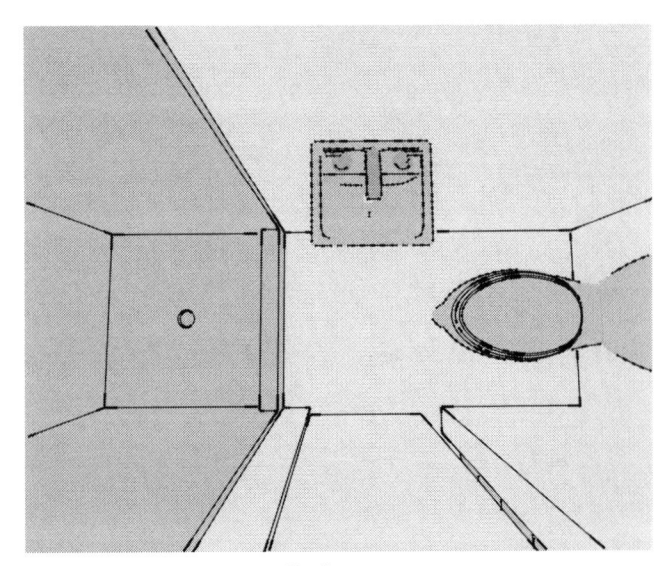

Loft

Bathroom

Tiny House #38 - Elevations

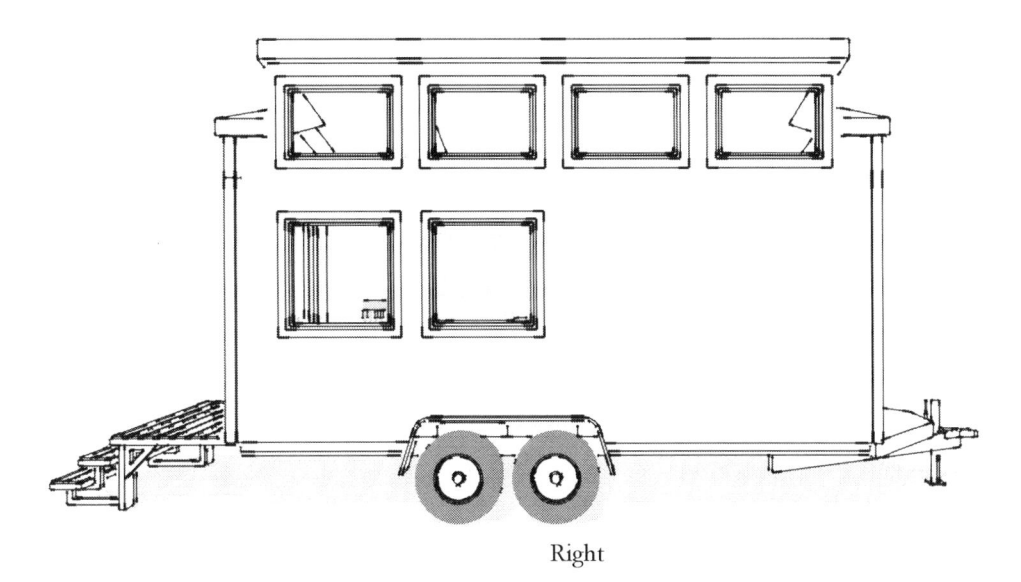

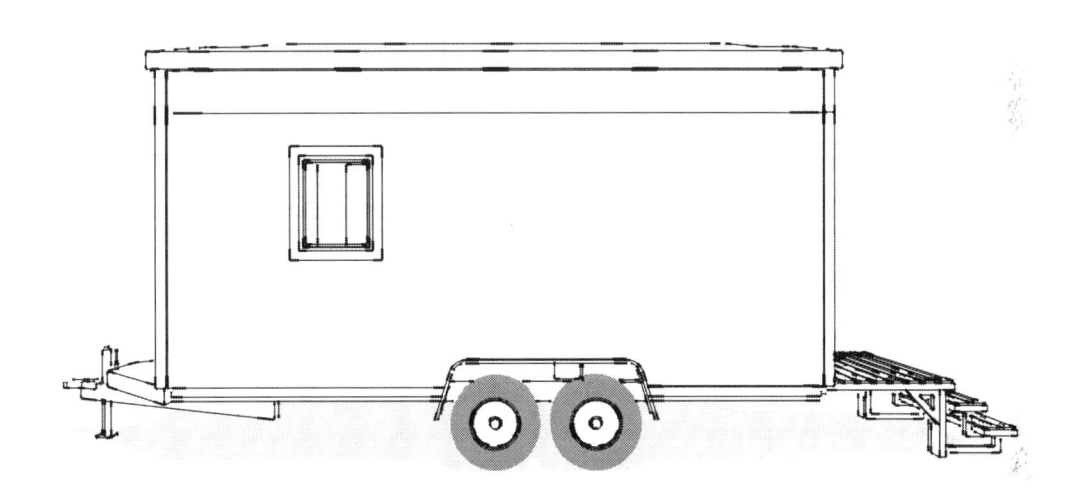

Right

Left

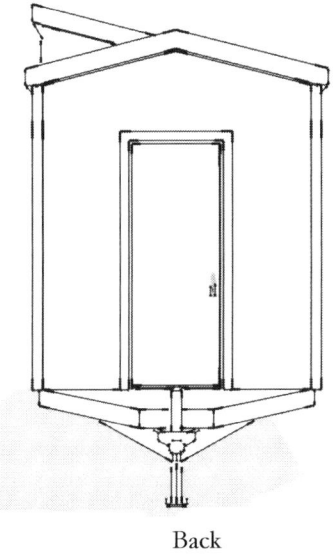

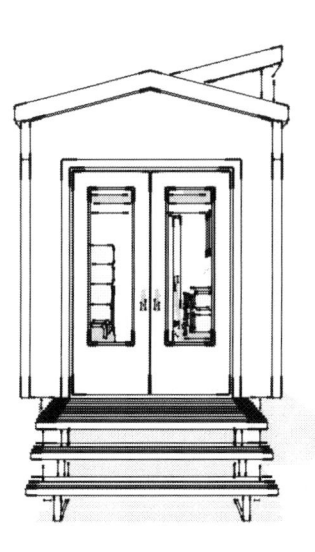

Back

Front

#39

Tiny House #39 - Overview

Front Right

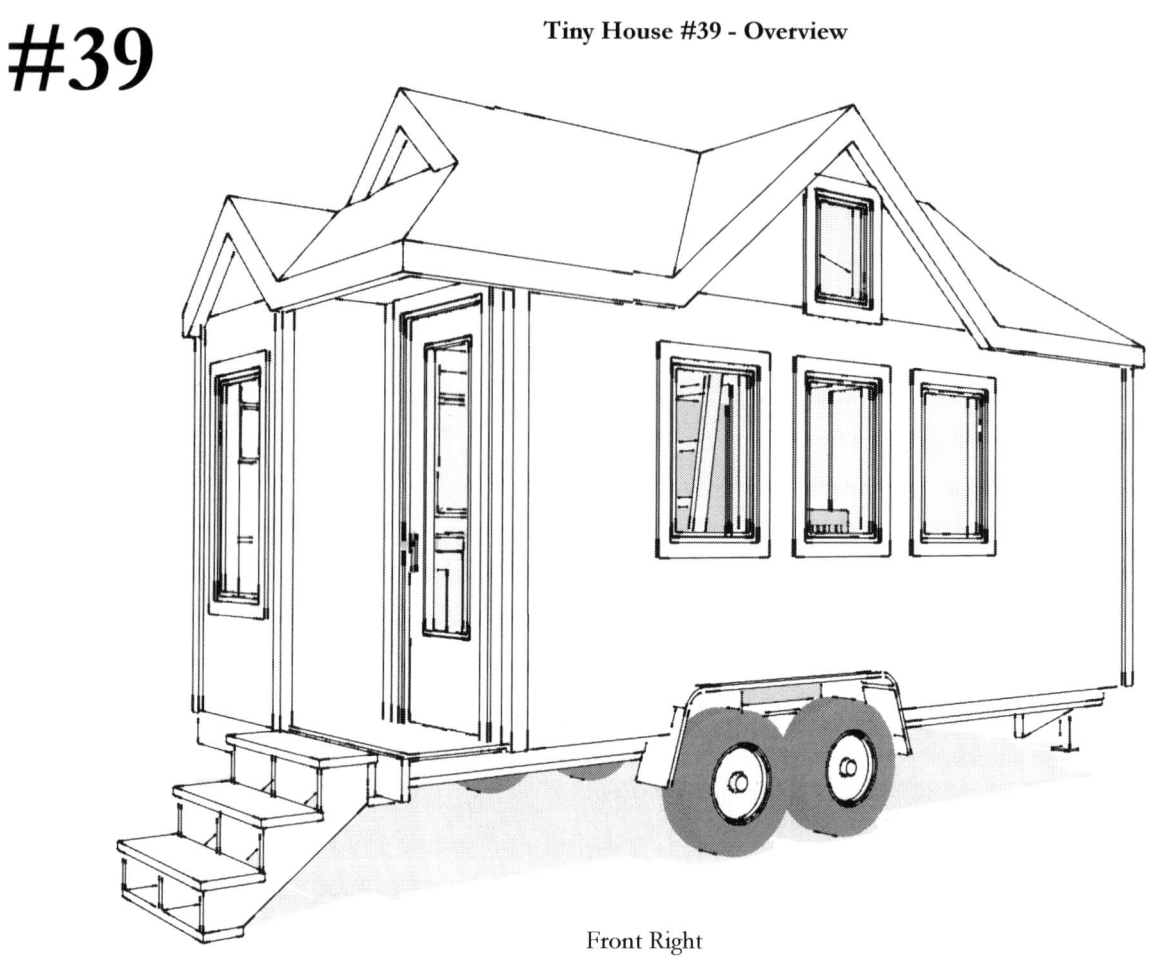

Summary:

A cross gable roof with Dutch gables on the front and back top this tiny house. The front door is inset and has fold-up steps. A larger kitchen is just inside the door to the left. It has a full size refrigerator, sink, range, and plenty of storage. The bathroom at the back of the house and has a soaking tub/shower, toilet, and vanity. The loft is accessed by a movable ladder. A utility closet extension is located over the trailer tongue.

Features:

18-Foot Tiny House on Wheels
Cross Gable with Dutch Gable Ends
Bathroom with Soaking Tub and Vanity
Kitchen with Full Size Refrigerator and Range
Utility Closet Extension over Trailer Tongue
Loft under Cross Gable

Kitchen

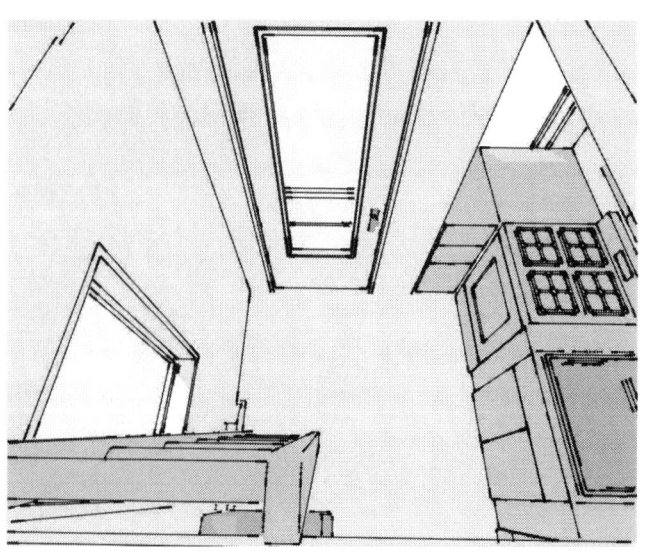

View from Loft

Tiny House #39 - Floor Plan & Exterior

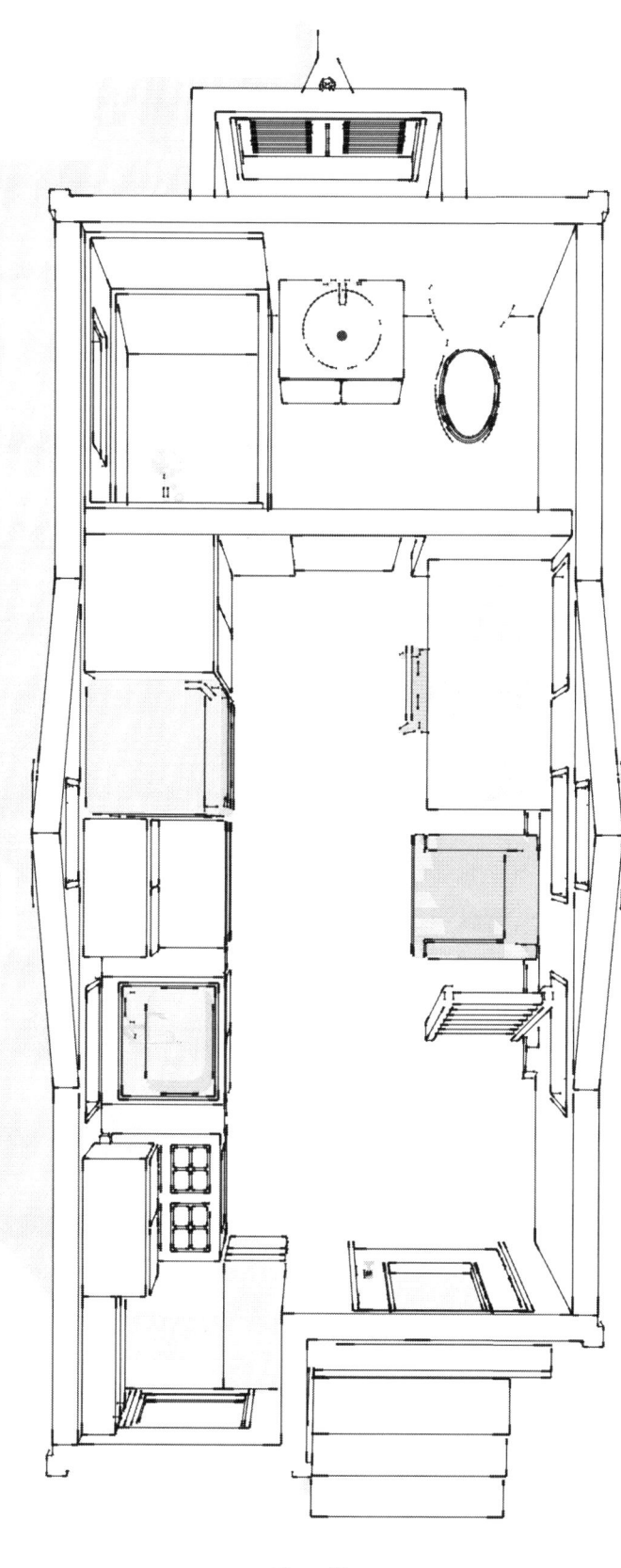

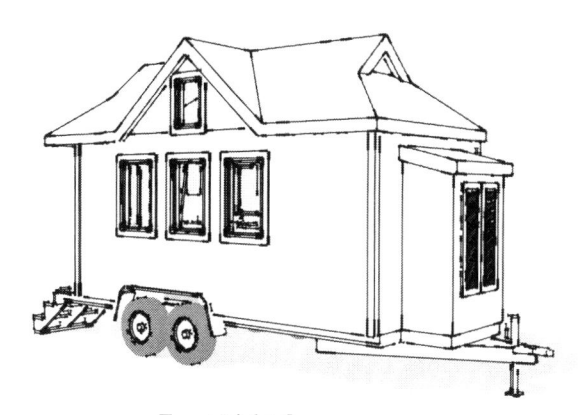

Front Right Corner

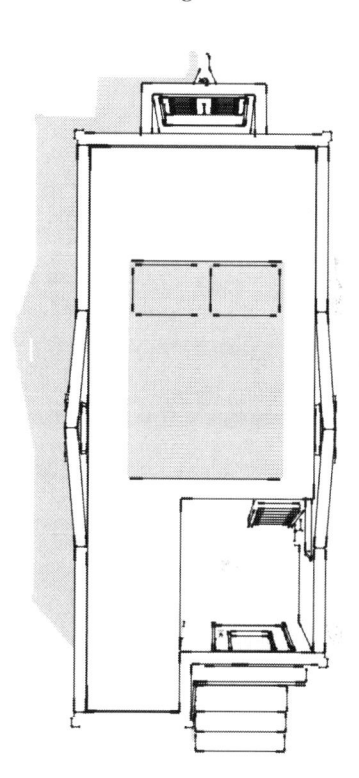

Floor Plan - Loft

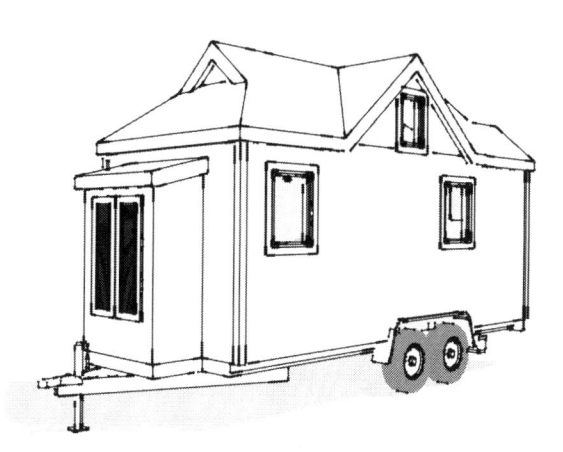

Floor Plan

Back Left Corner

Tiny House #39 - Interior Views

Interior from Entry

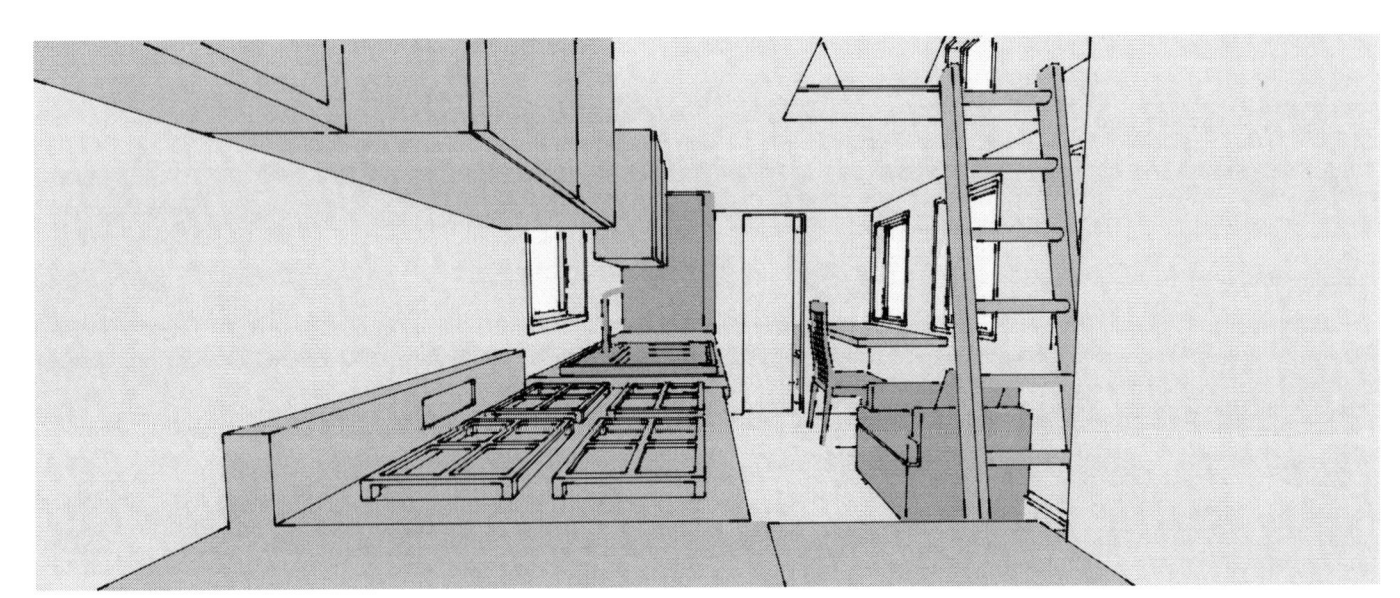

Interior from Kitchen

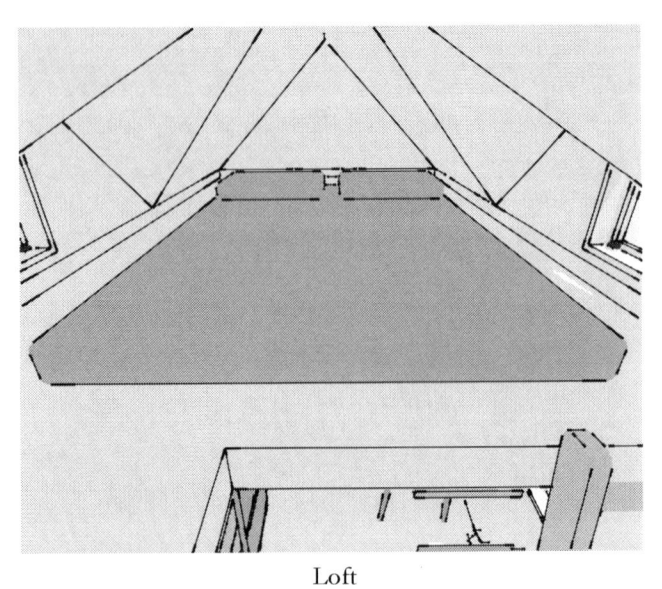

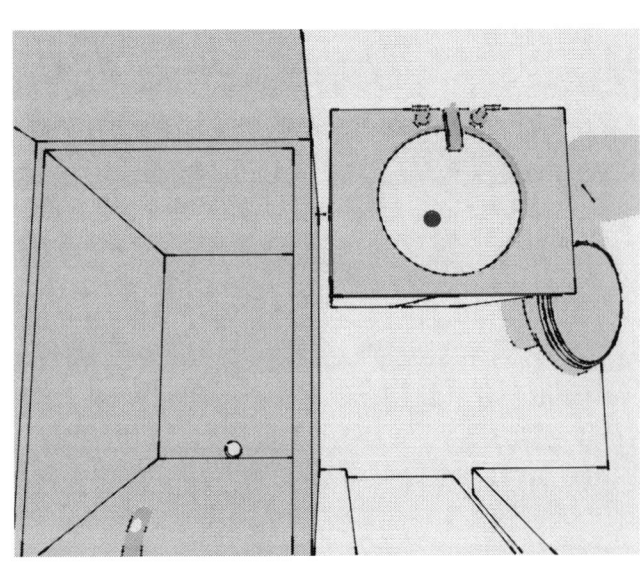

Loft

Bathroom

Tiny House #39 - Elevations

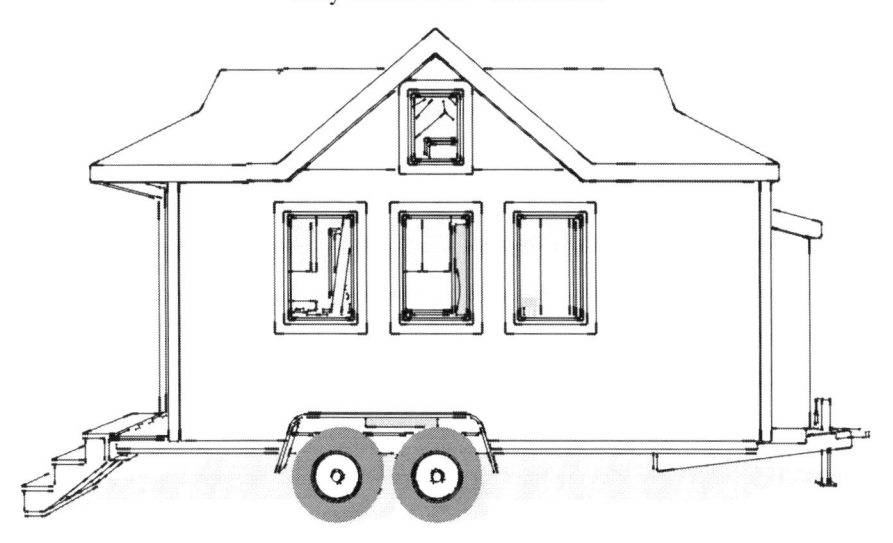

Right

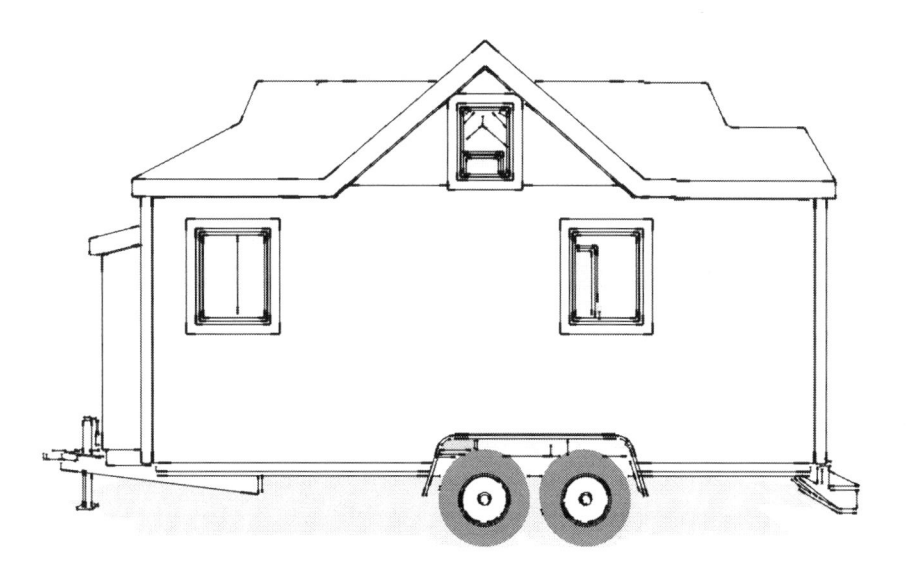

Left

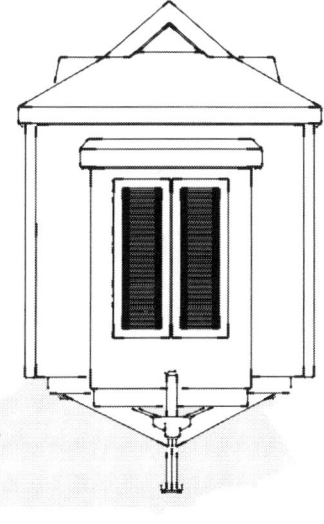

Back

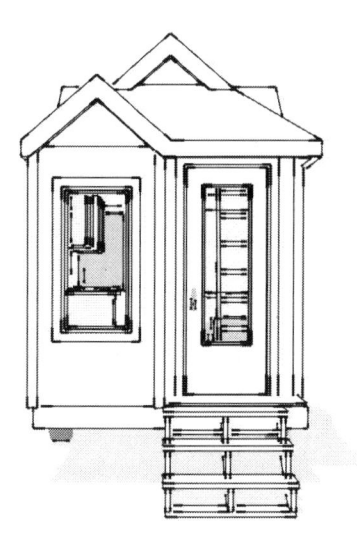

Front

#40

Tiny House #40 - Overview

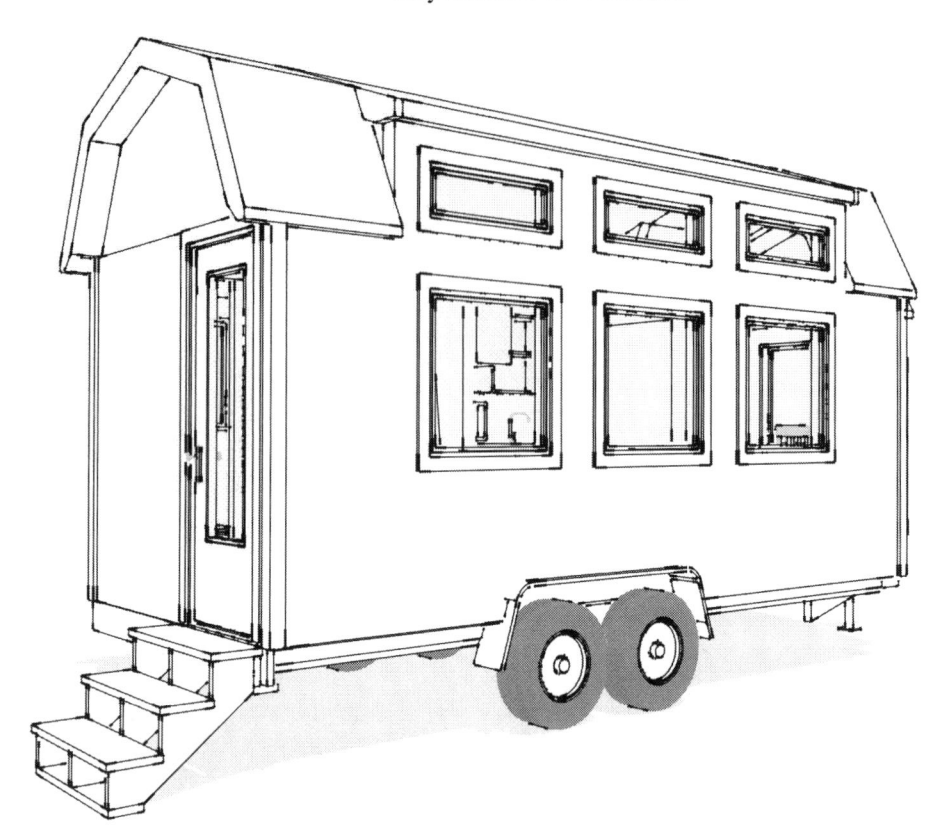

Front Right

Summary:

The gambrel roof with shed dormers provide a lot of room in the loft. The front door opens onto a short hallway with the bathroom immediately on the left - followed by a ladder to the loft tucked into its own alcove. The compact kitchen has a small refrigerator, sink, stovetop, microwave, and plenty of storage. The bathroom has a shower, toilet, and wall mounted sink. The living room has space for a sofa, chair and table for two.

Features:

18-Foot Tiny House on Wheels
Gambrel Roof with Shed Dormers
Small Kitchen with Microwave
Gambrel Roofed Extension over Trailer Tongue
Large Loft, Sleeps 3

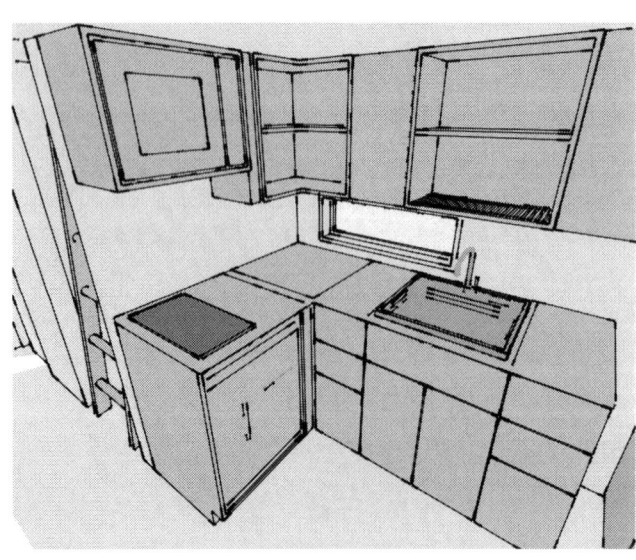

Kitchen

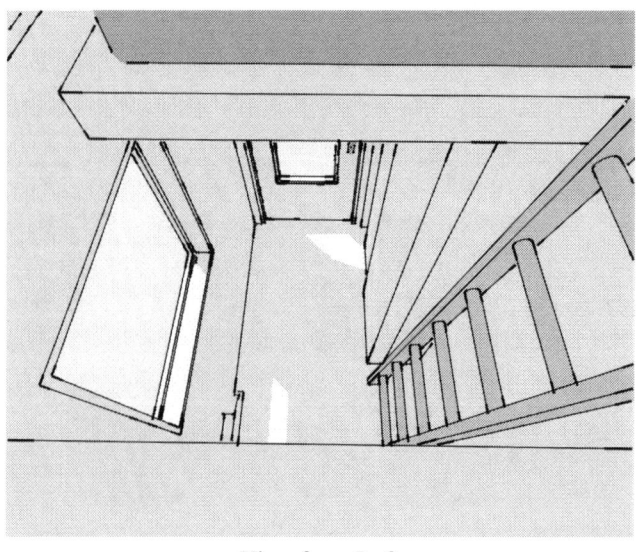

View from Loft

Tiny House #40 - Floor Plan & Exterior

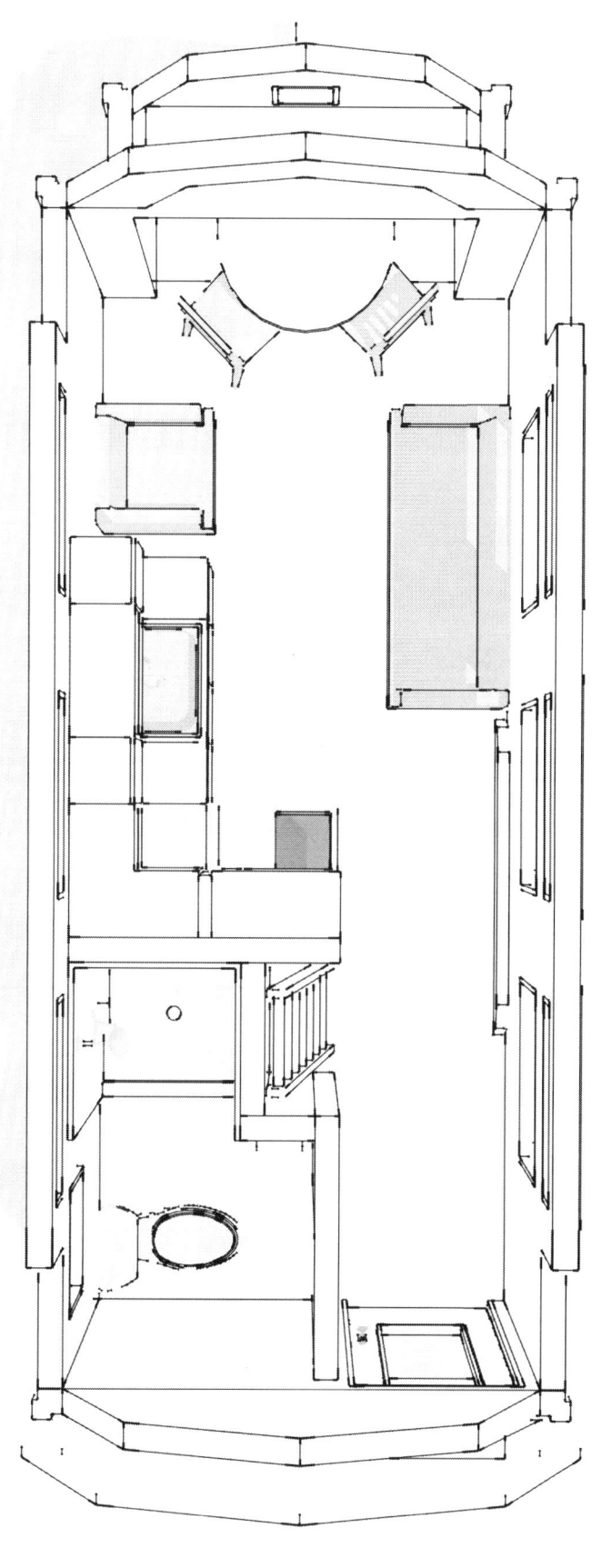

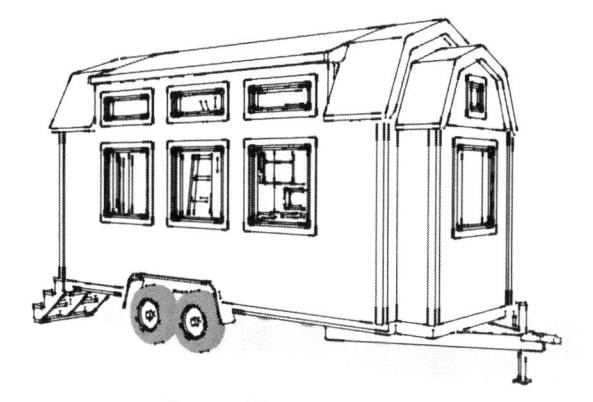

Front Right Corner

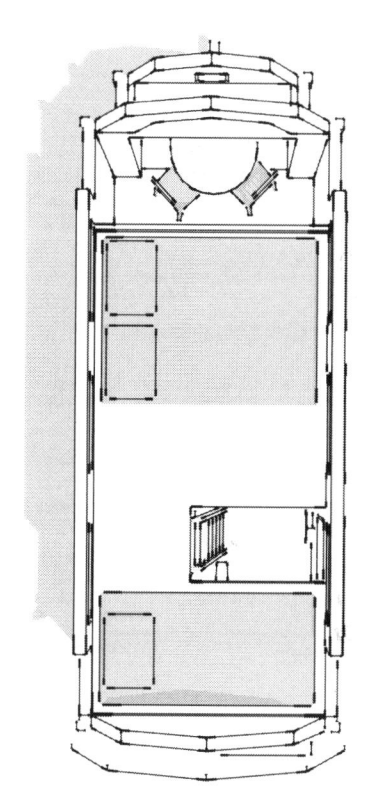

Floor Plan - Loft

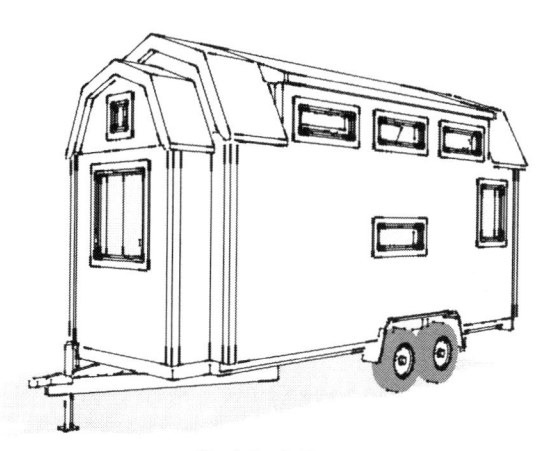

Floor Plan

Back Left Corner

Tiny House #40 - Interior Views

Interior from Entry

Interior from Kitchen

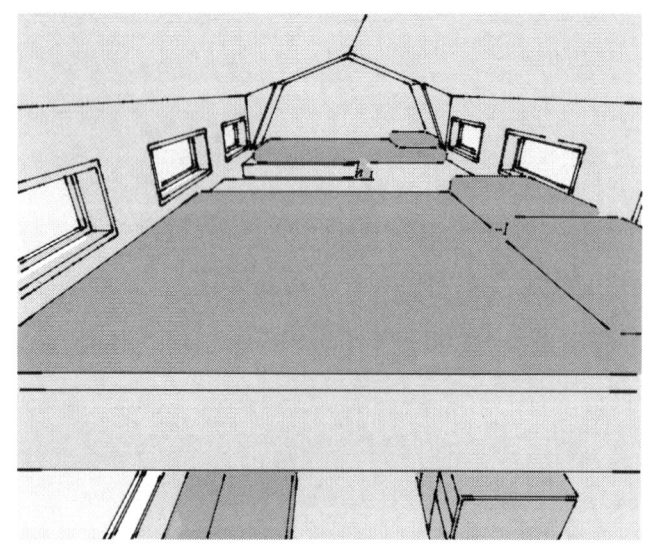

Loft

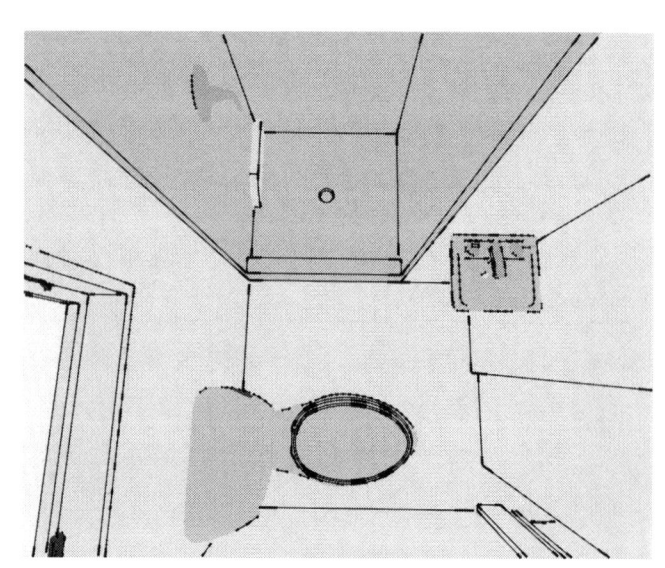

Bathroom

Tiny House #40 - Elevations

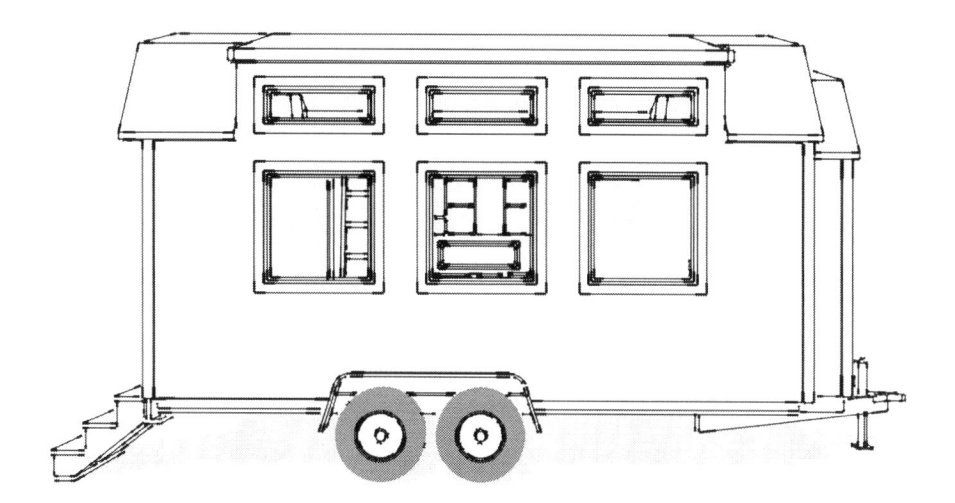

Right

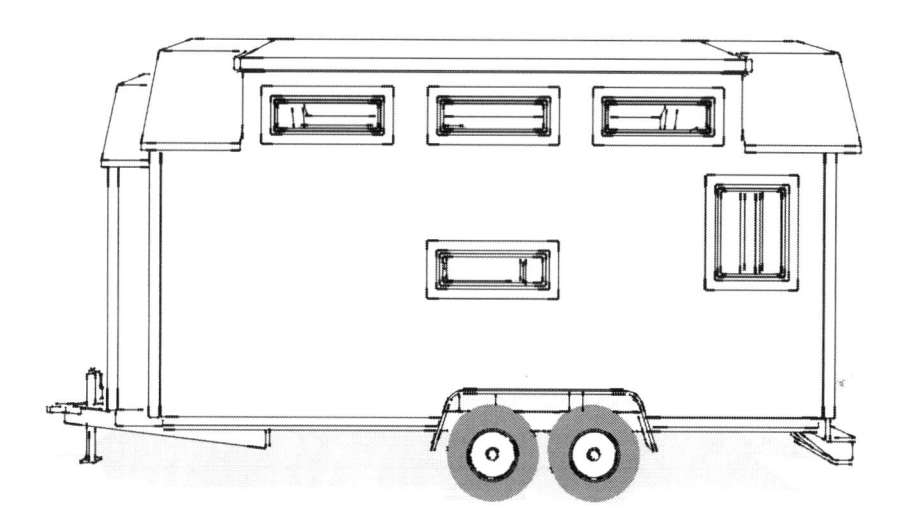

Left

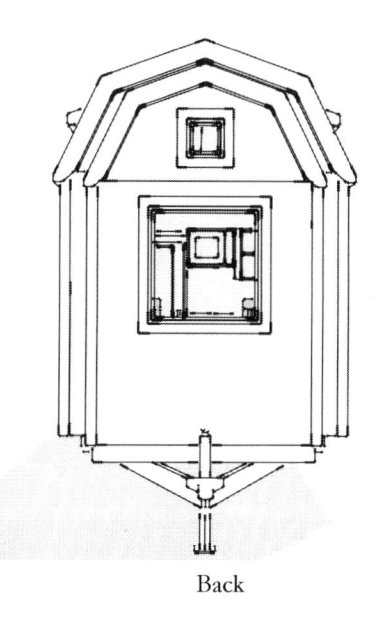

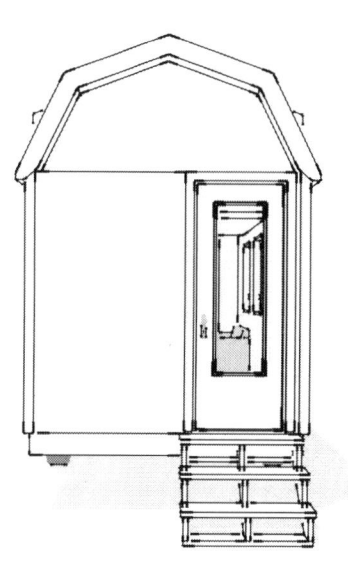

Back

Front

#41

Tiny House #41 - Overview

Front Right

Summary:

This shed roofed tiny house has a garage big enough for a scooter or motorcycle… or anything you want to keep in a garage. A door inside the garage leads to the bathroom in case you come home so dirty from playing outside that a shower is the only thing on your mind. The main entry is on the trailer tongue side of the house. The compact kitchen has a small refrigerator, sink, stovetop. The bathroom has a shower, toilet, and wall mounted sink. The living room has space for a comfy chair and desk.

Features:

18-Foot Tiny House on Wheels
Shed Roof
Bathroom with Access from Garage
Small Kitchen
Garage for Gear or Scooter!
Large Loft, Sleeps 3

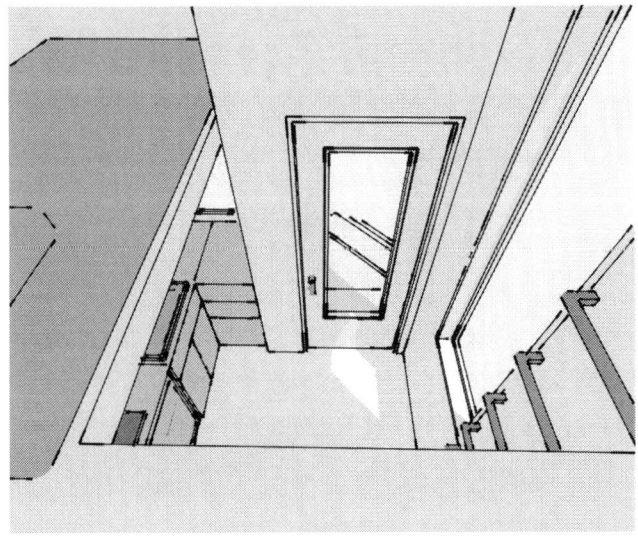

Kitchen

View from Loft

Tiny House #41 - Floor Plan & Exterior

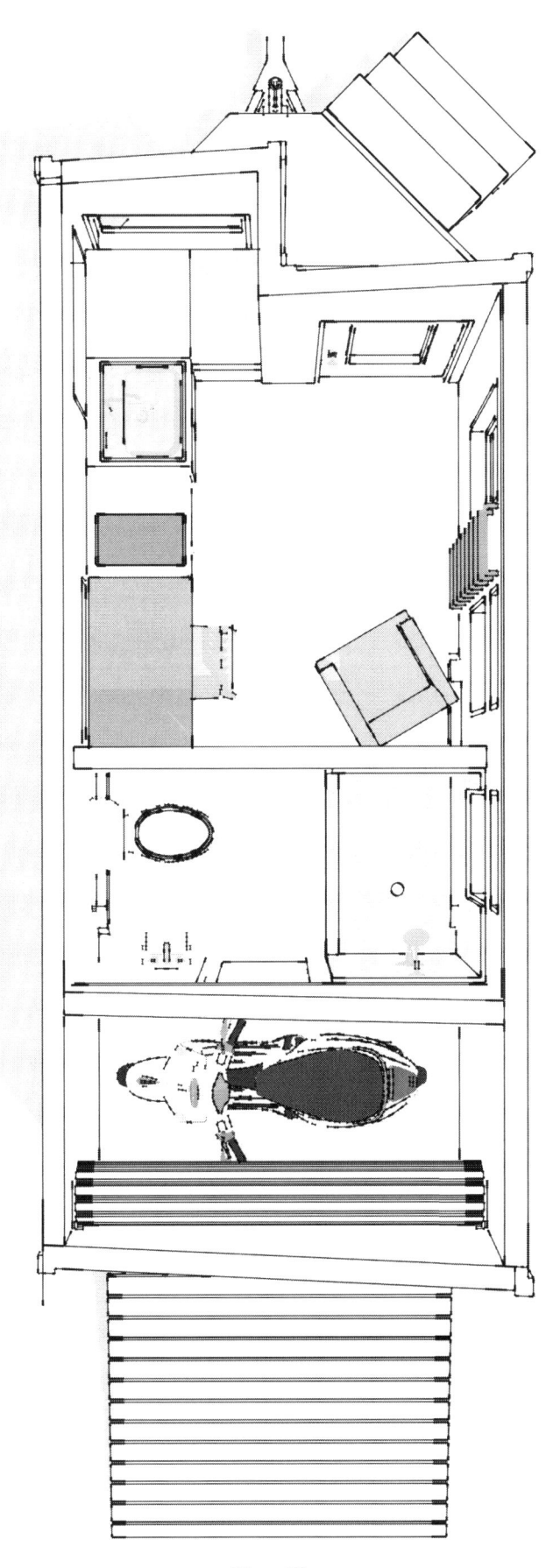

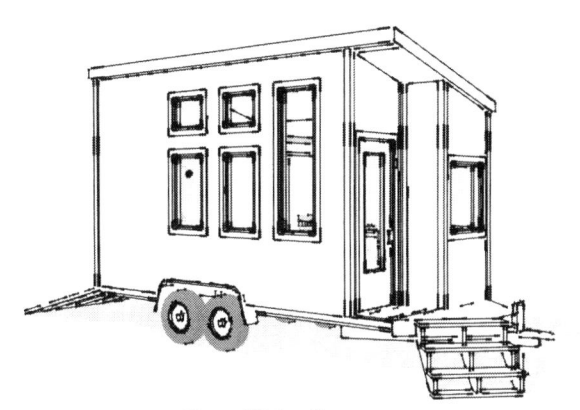

Front Right Corner

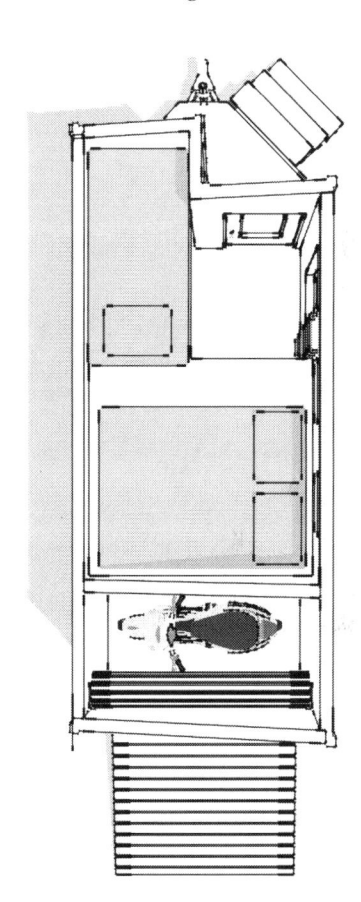

Floor Plan - Loft

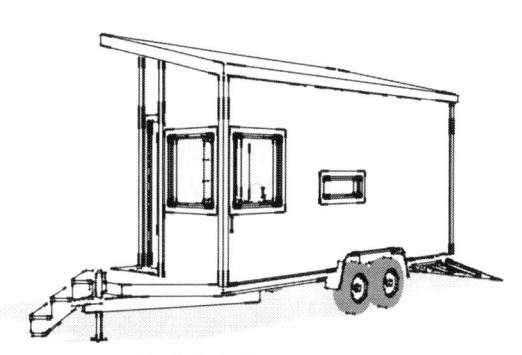

Floor Plan

Back Left Corner

Tiny House #41 - Interior Views

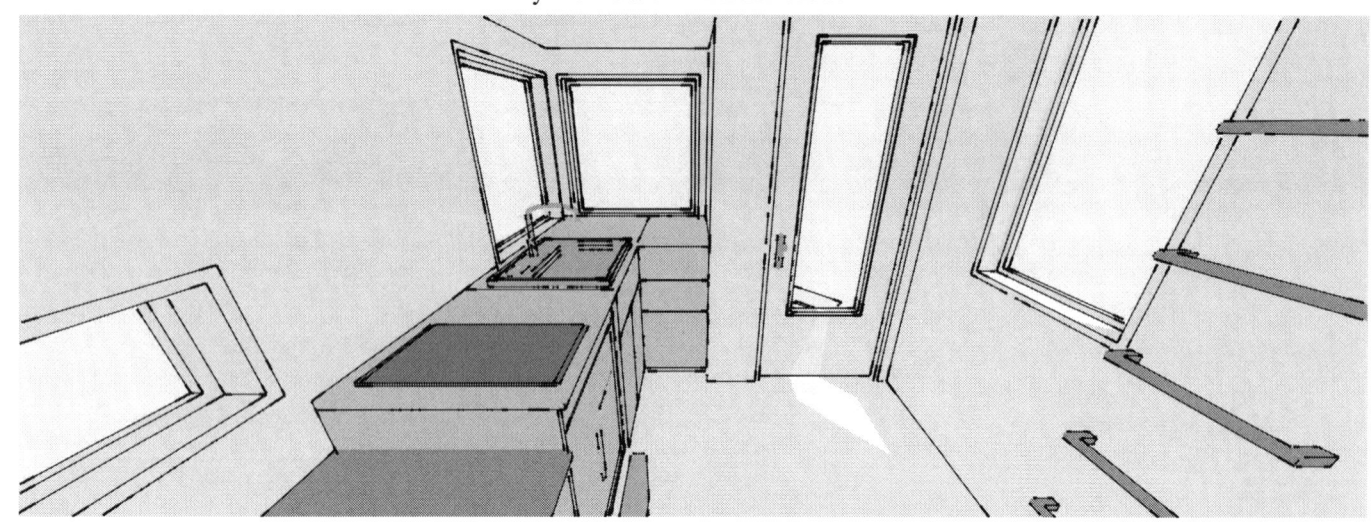

Interior from Entry

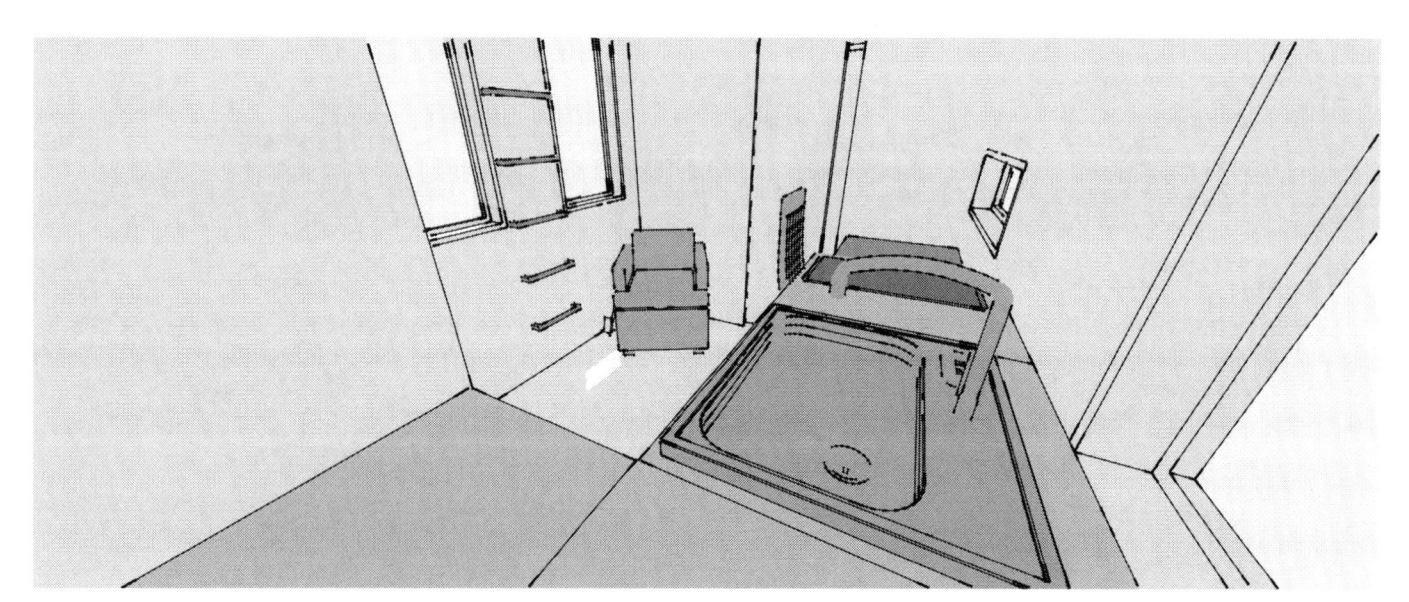

Interior from Kitchen

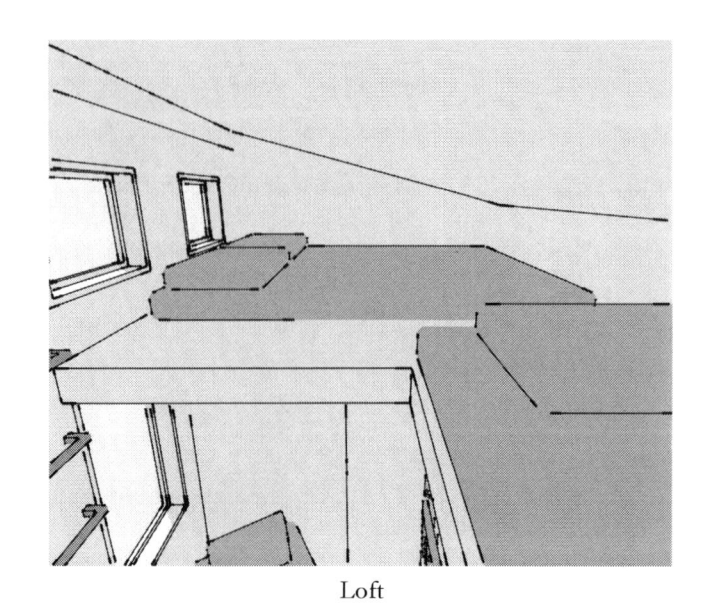

Loft

Bathroom

Tiny House #41 - Elevations

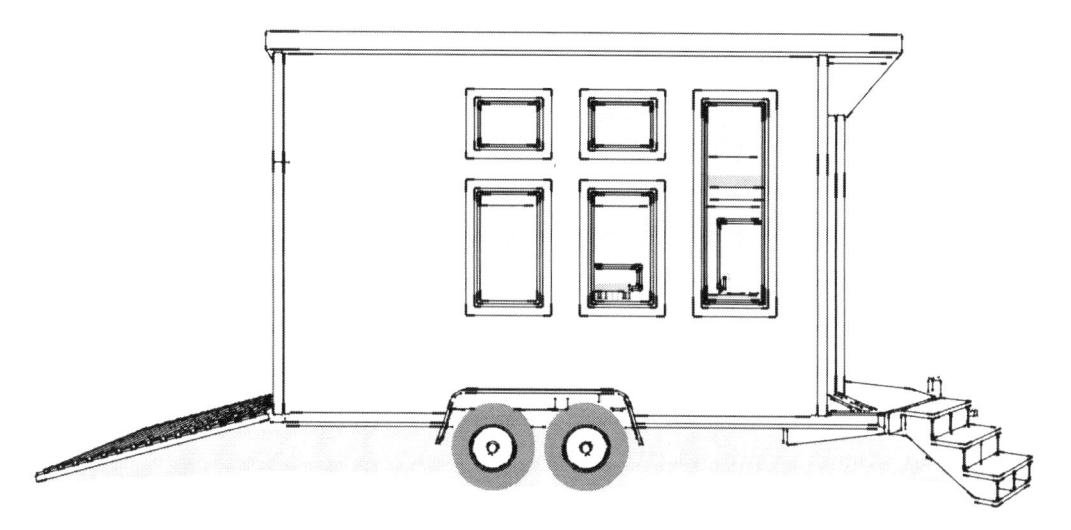

Right

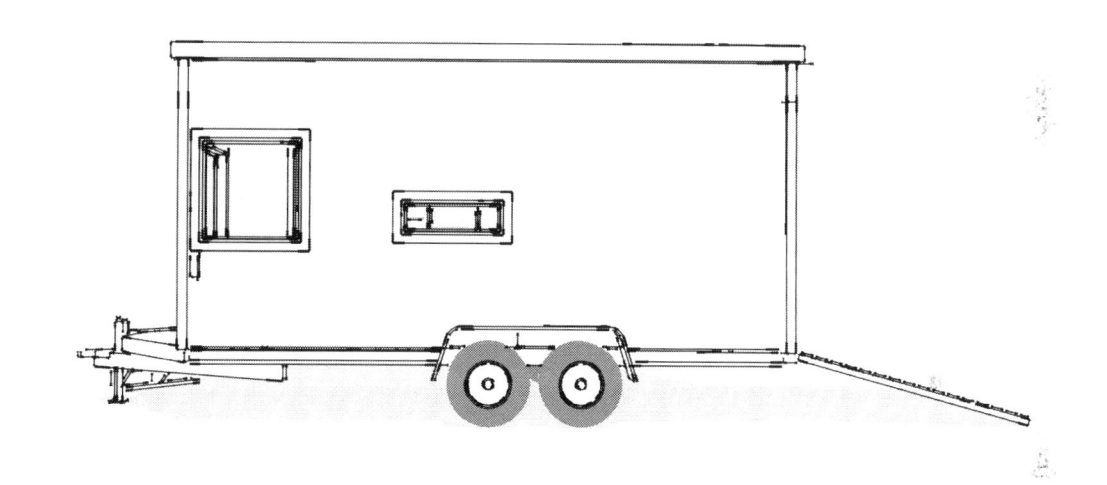

Left

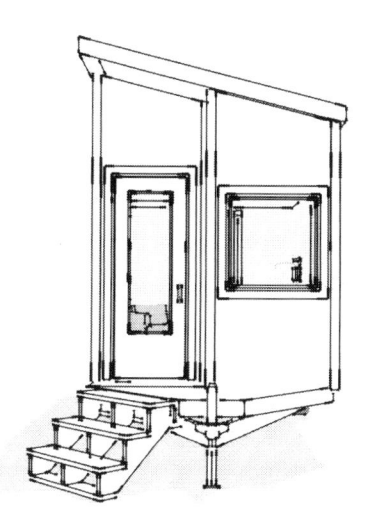

Back

Front

#42

Tiny House #42 - Overview

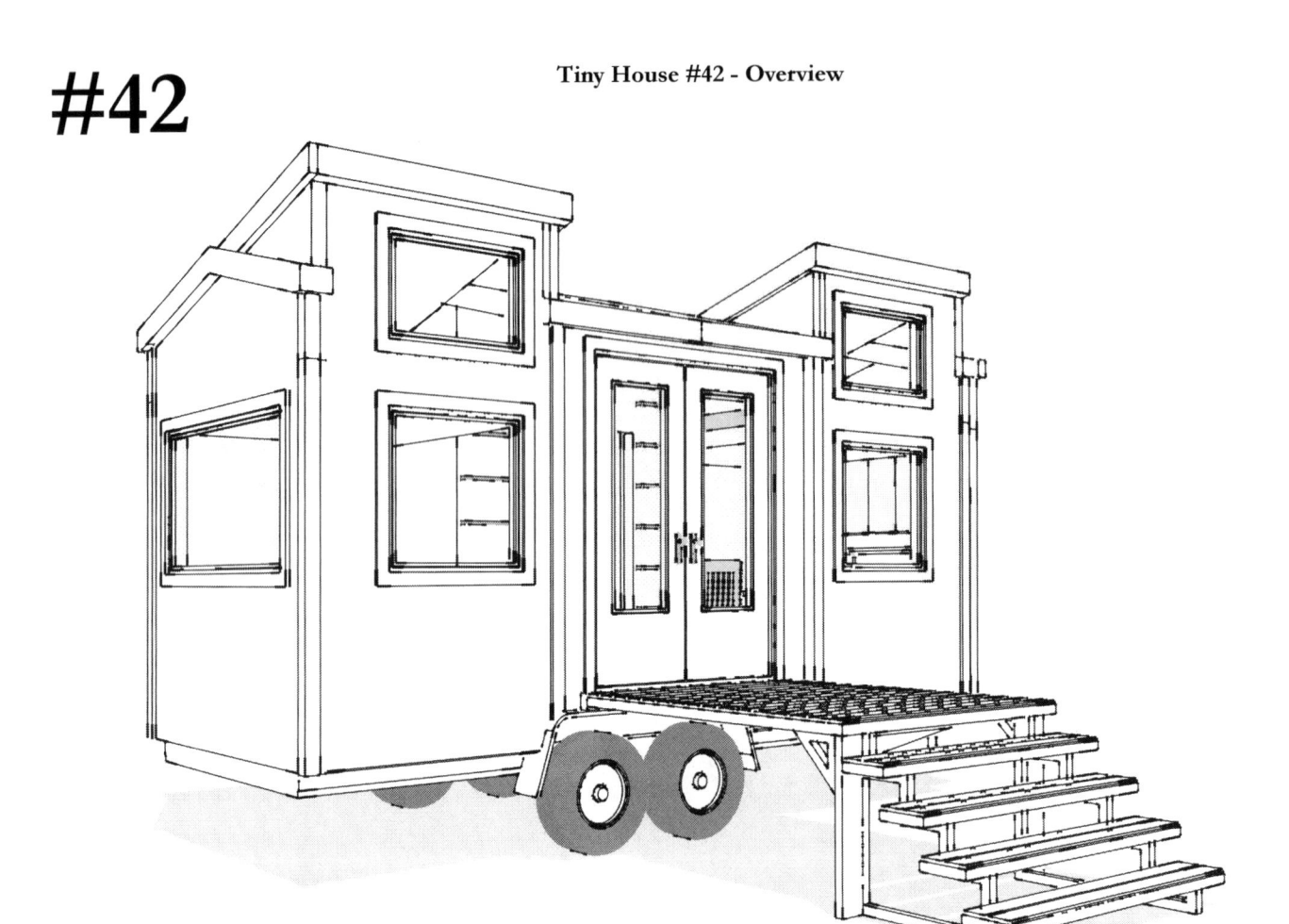

Front Right

Summary:

The entry to this tiny house is over the trailer fender. Upon entering you step down once onto a landing where you find the bathroom and two ladders leading to lofts on the left and right. Under the left side loft is a living room with space for four comfy chairs. Under the right side loft is a kitchen and table for two. The compact kitchen has a small refrigerator, sink, stovetop. The small bathroom has a shower, toilet, and wall mounted sink.

Features:

18-Foot Tiny House on Wheels
Opposing Shed Roofs
Small Bathroom with High Ceiling
Small Kitchen
Two Lofts

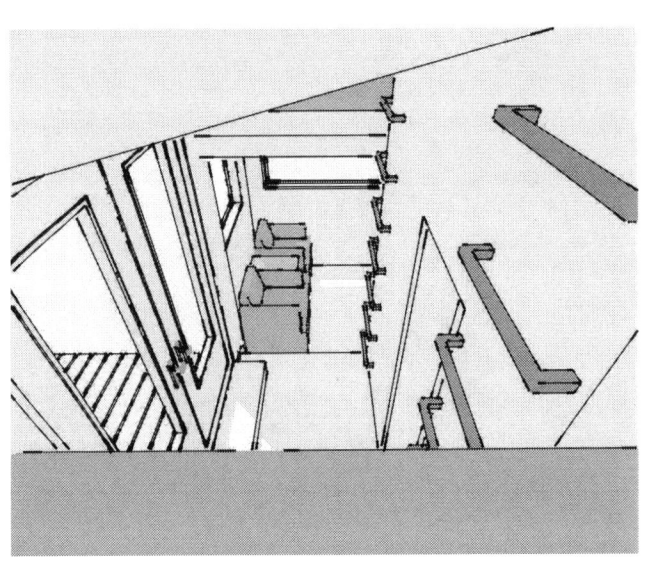

Kitchen

View from Loft

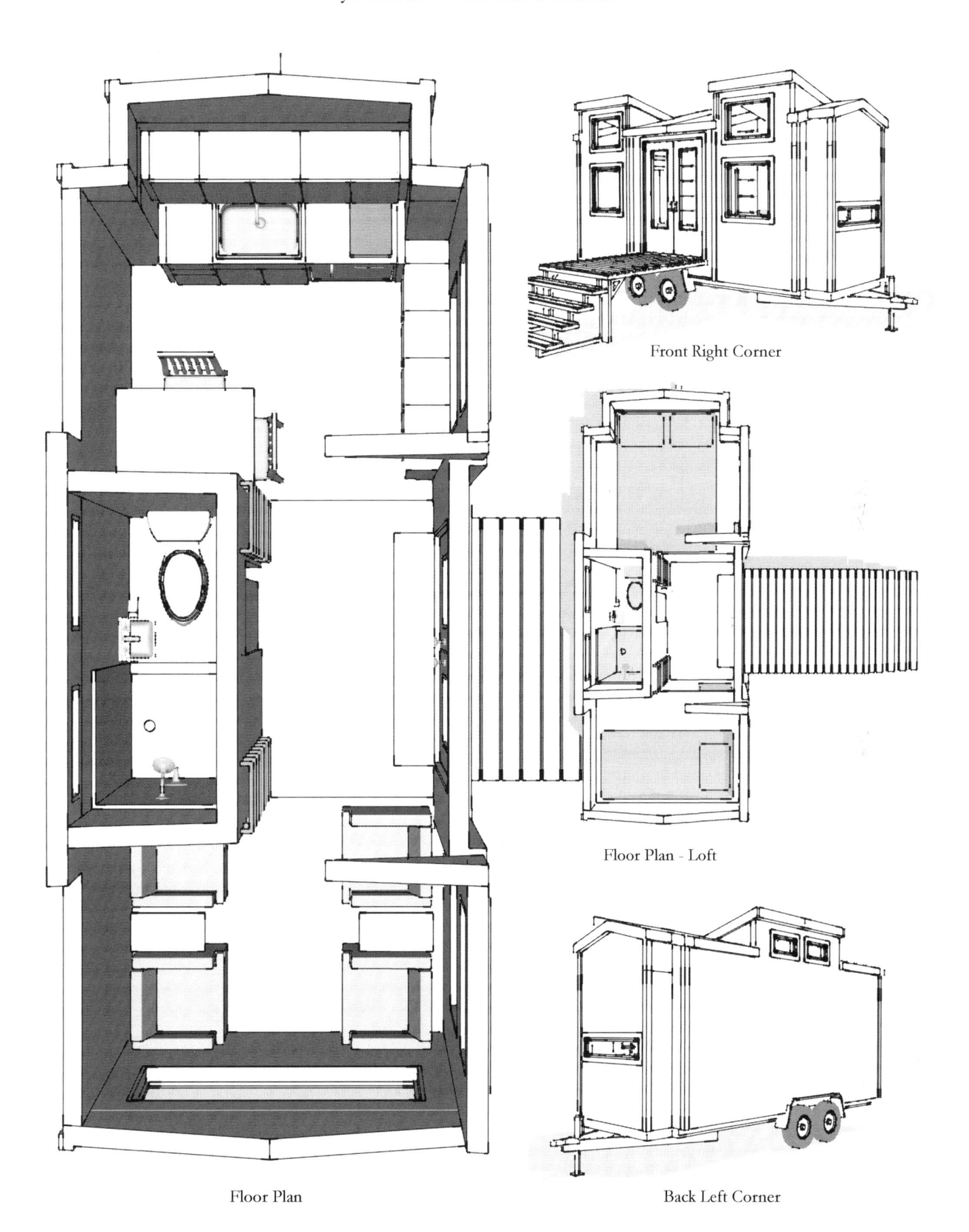

Tiny House #42 - Floor Plan & Exterior

Front Right Corner

Floor Plan - Loft

Floor Plan

Back Left Corner

173

Tiny House #42 - Interior Views

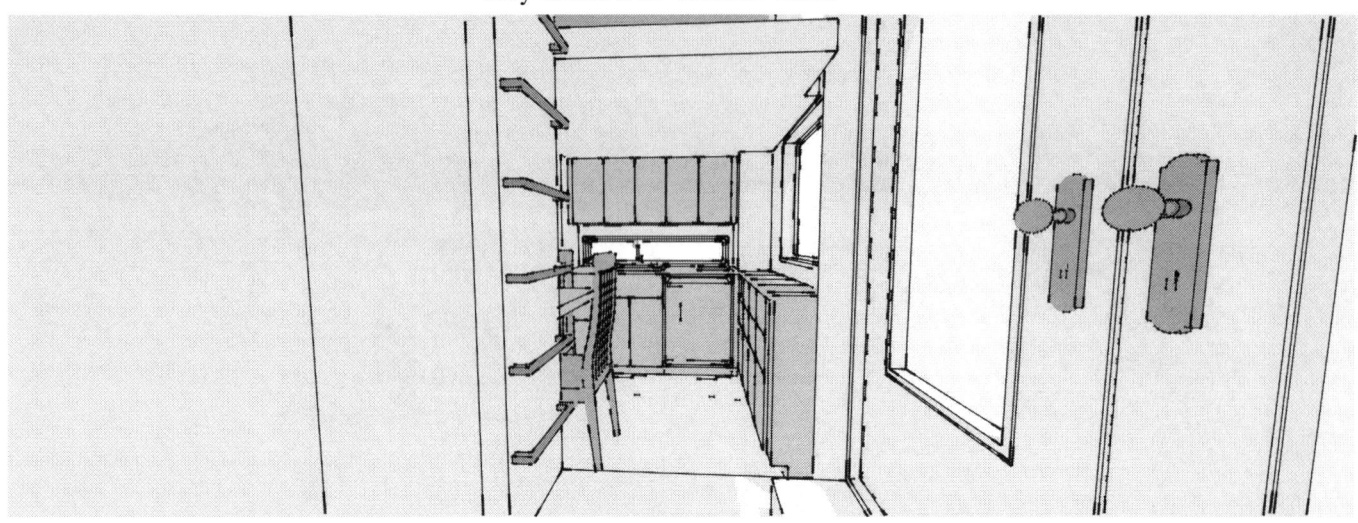

Interior from Entry

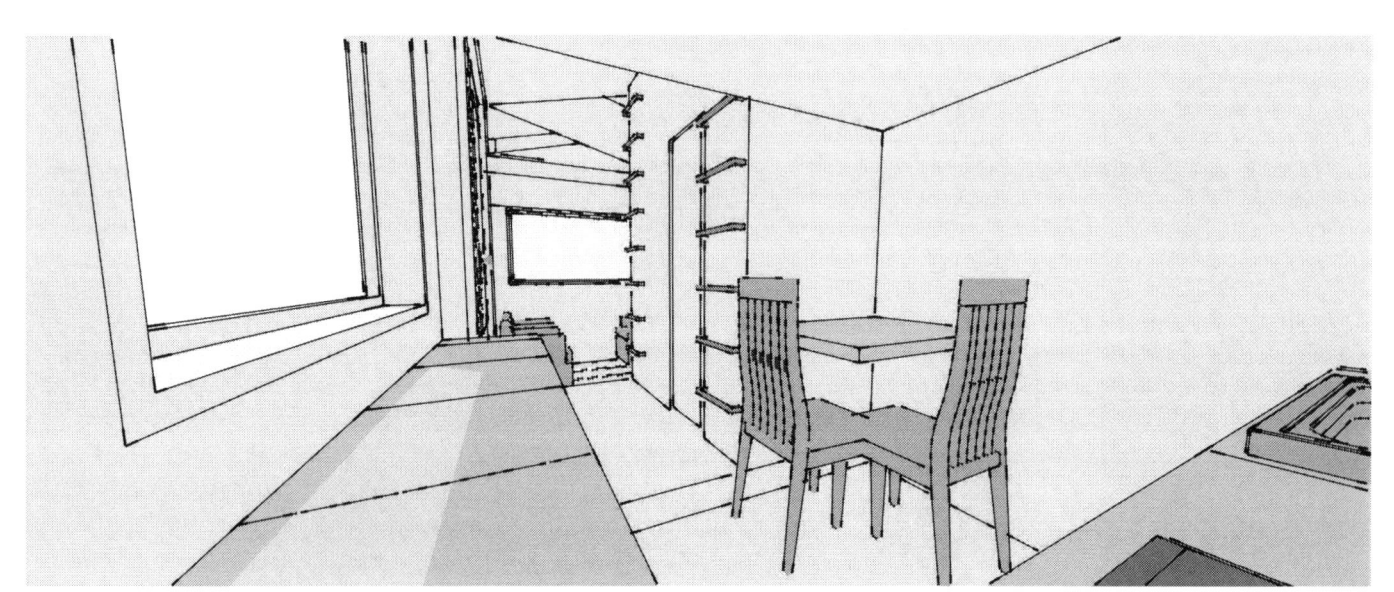

Interior from Kitchen

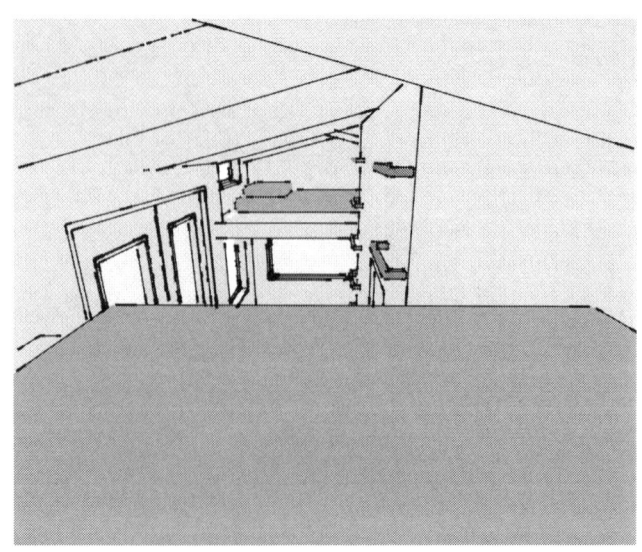

Lofts

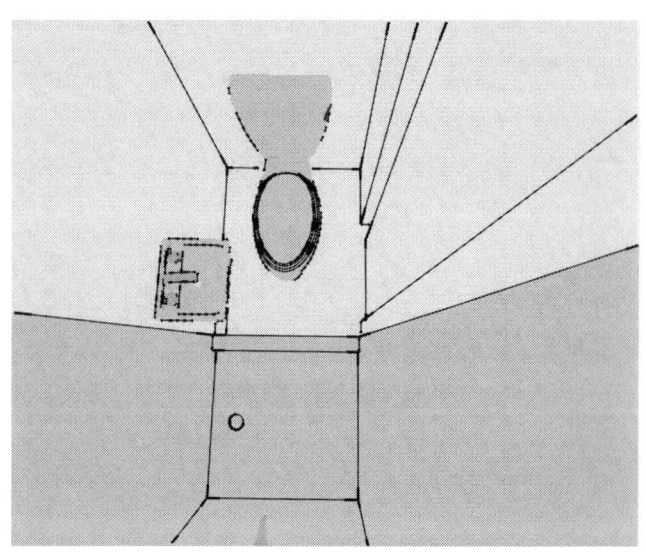

Bathroom

Tiny House #42 - Elevations

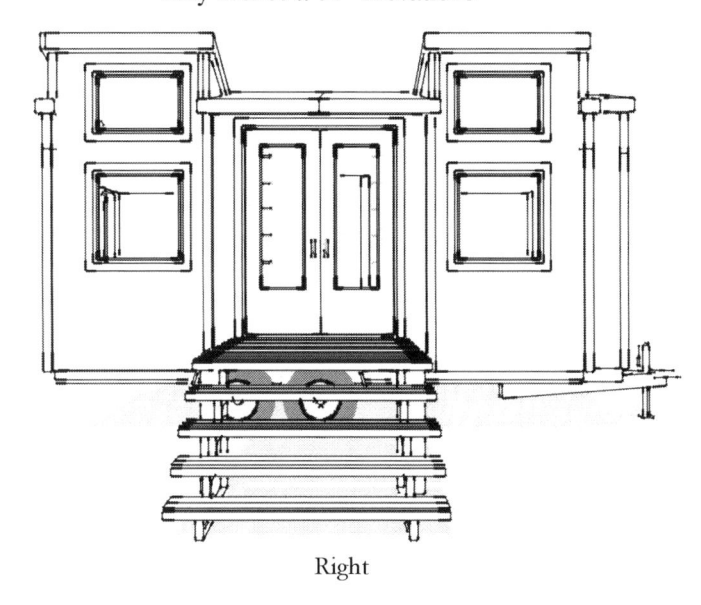

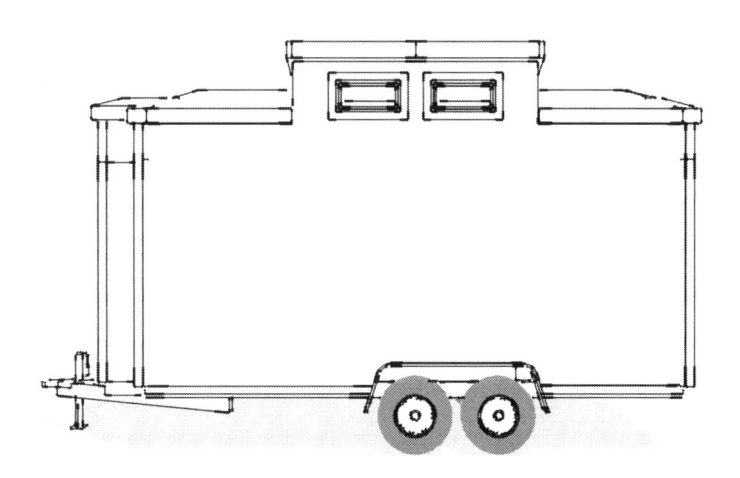

Right

Left

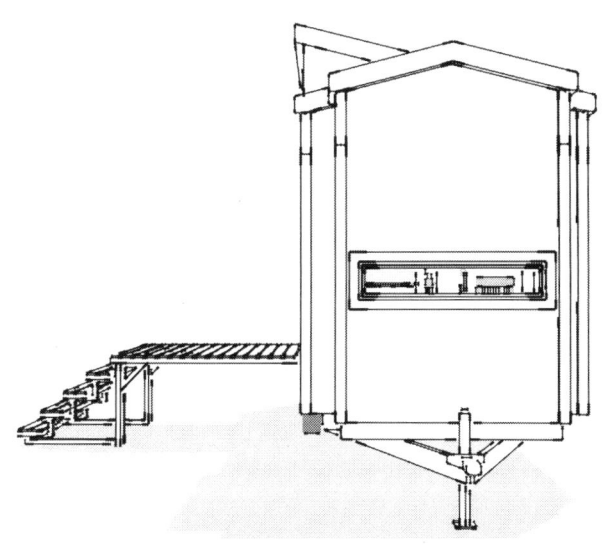

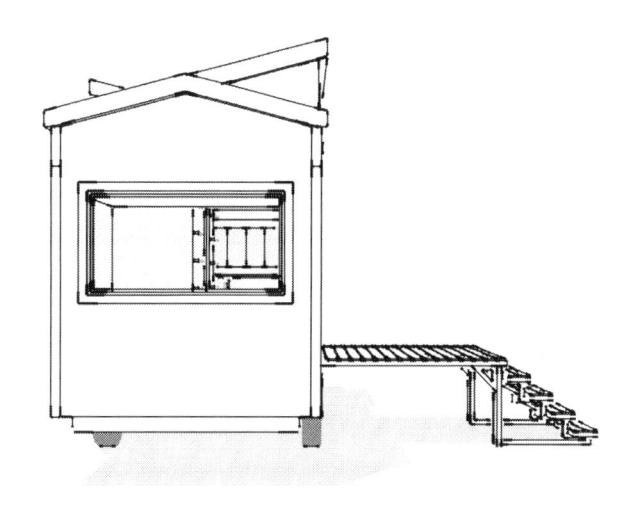

Back

Front

#43

Tiny House #43 - Overview

Front Right

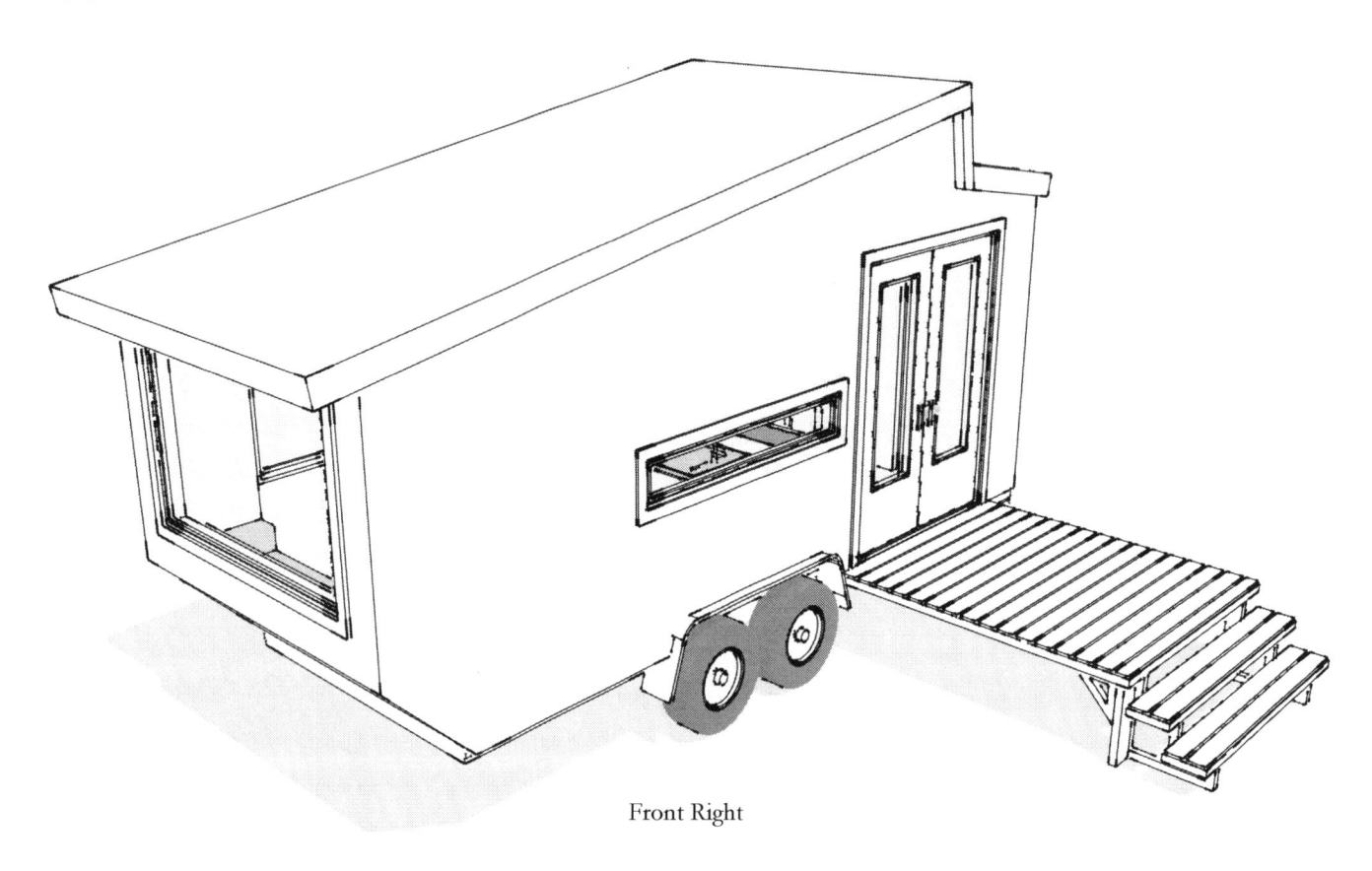

Summary:

This tongue side of this tiny house is somewhat more aerodynamic that most. The diagonal walls that extend over the trailer tongue can be see most clearly in the unusually shaped bathroom. Most of the house is one large room. At the far end of the living room is a sofa and two comfy chairs. The small kitchen on the left has a small refrigerator, sink, stovetop. On the right is a table for three. The roof is a 3/12 shed roof.

Features:

18-Foot Tiny House on Wheels
Shed Roof
Small Bathroom
Small Kitchen
Large Loft

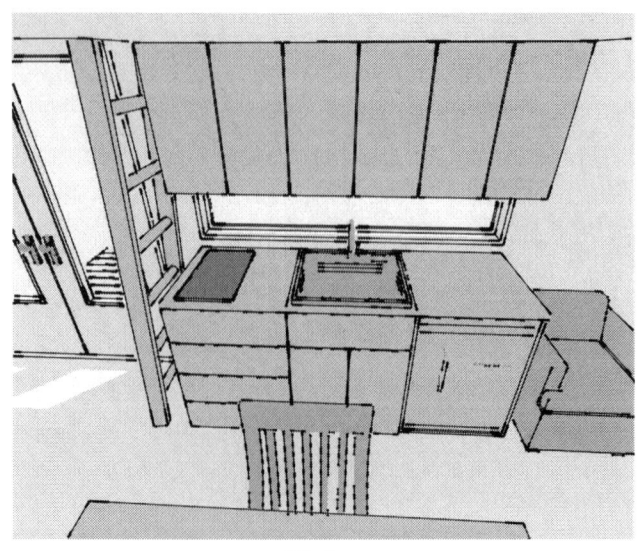

Kitchen

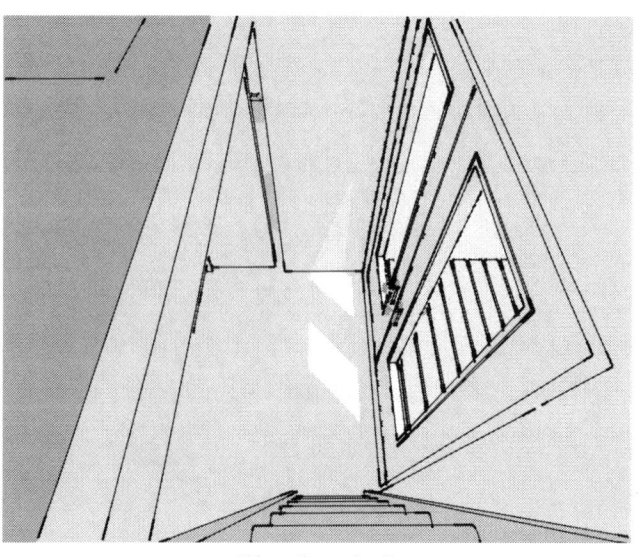

View from Loft

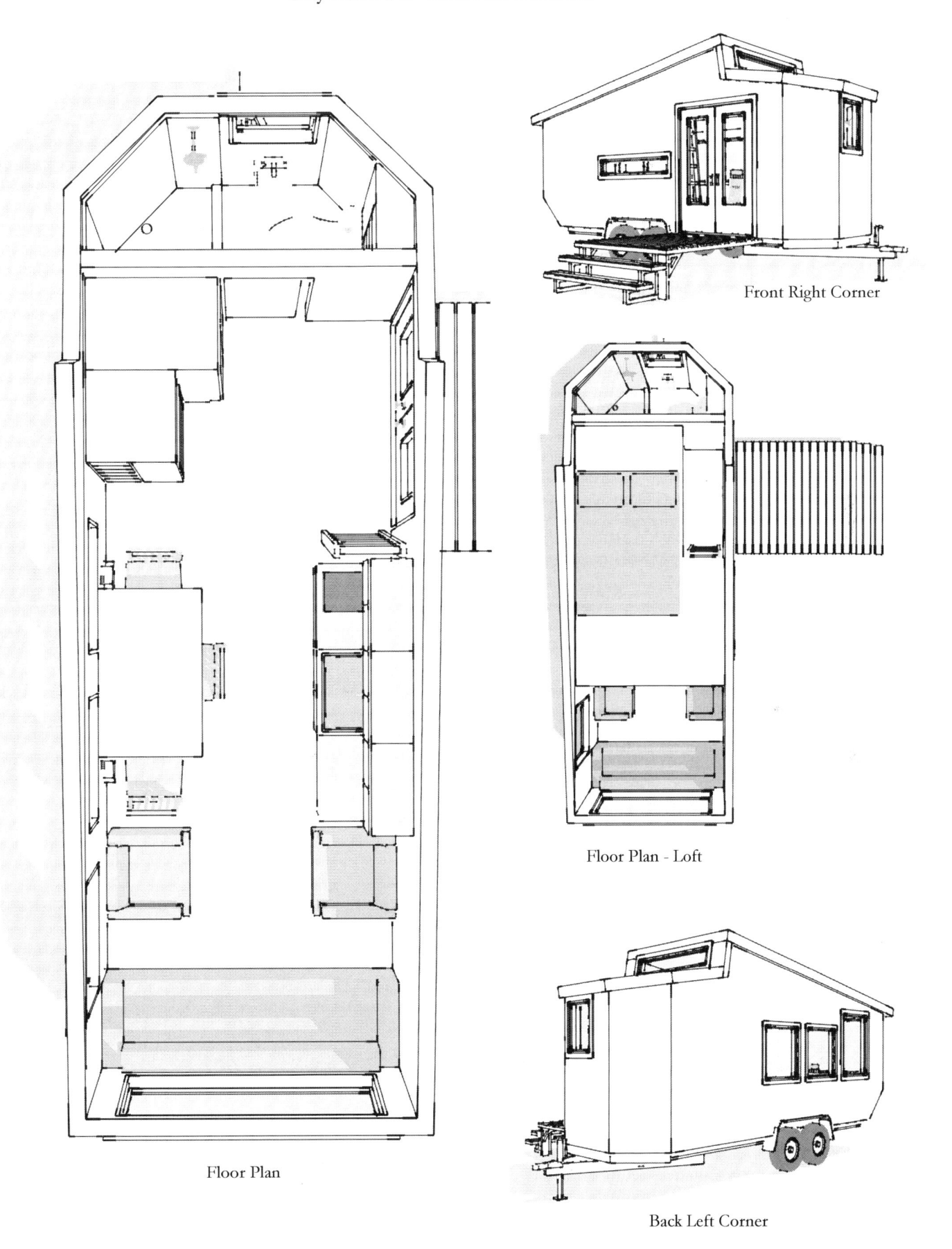

Tiny House #43 - Floor Plan & Exterior

Floor Plan

Front Right Corner

Floor Plan - Loft

Back Left Corner

177

Tiny House #43 - Interior Views

Interior from Living Room

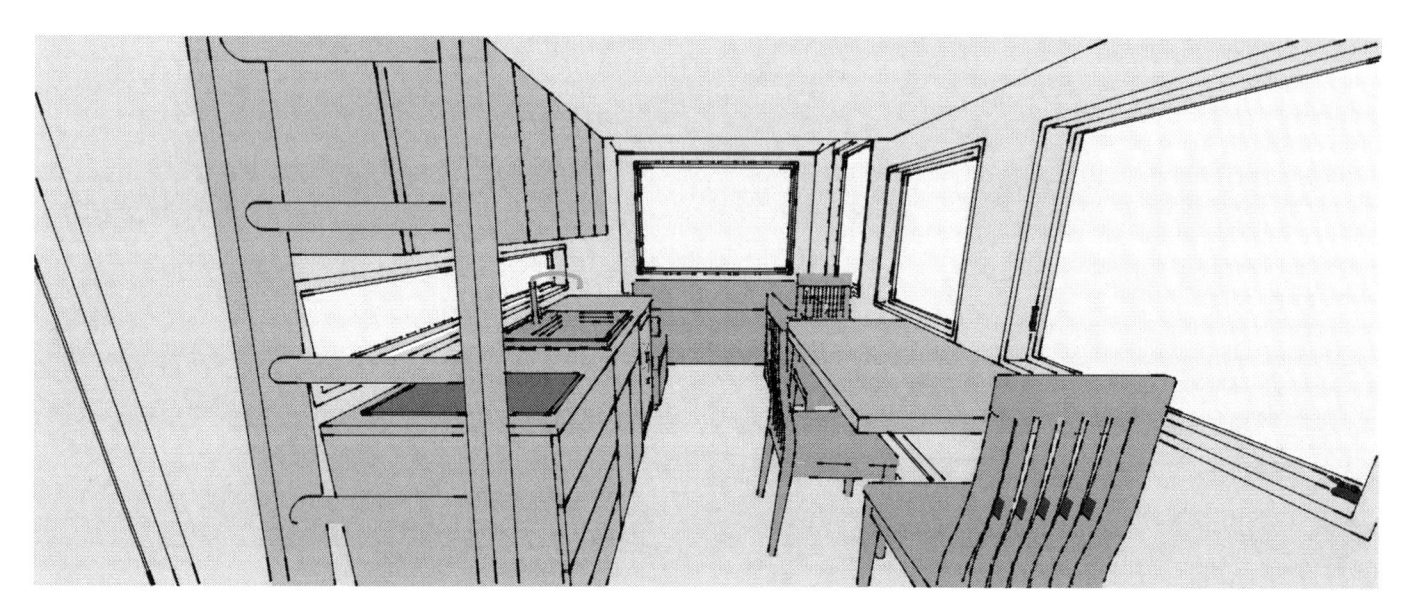

Interior from Entry

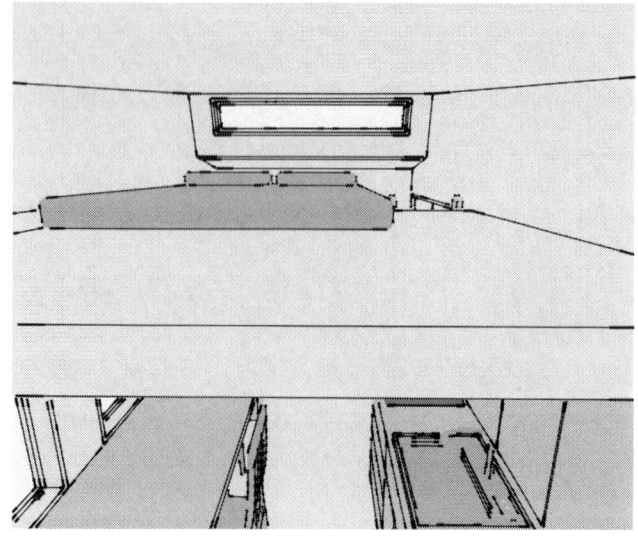

Loft

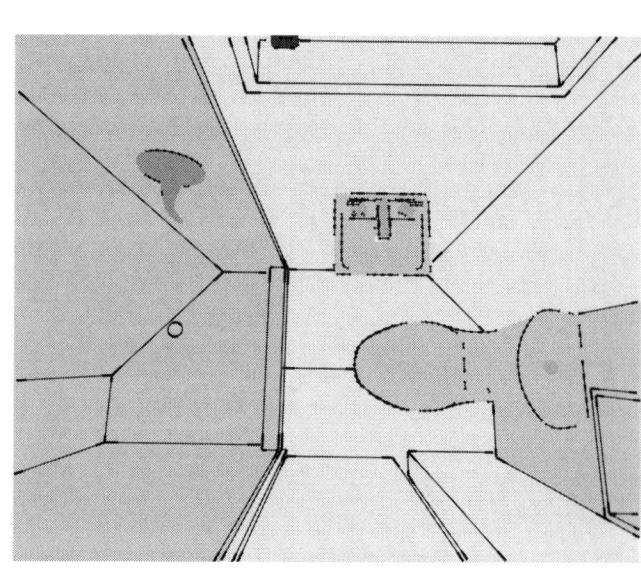

Bathroom

178

Tiny House #43 - Elevations

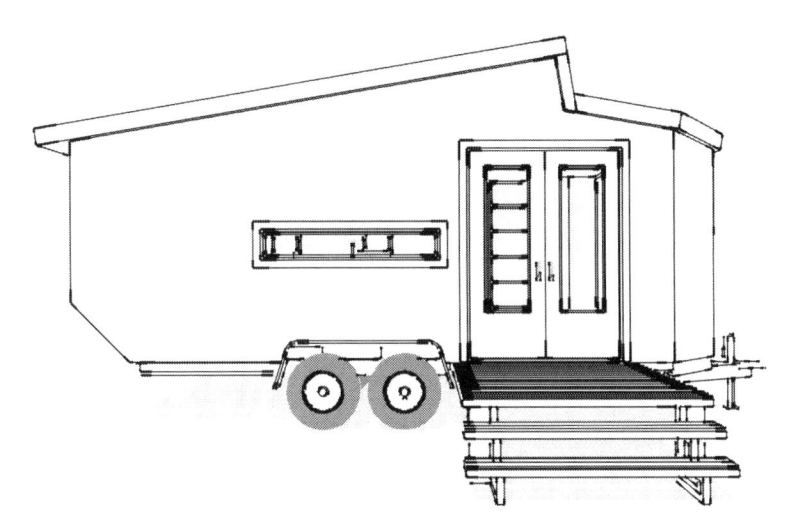

Right

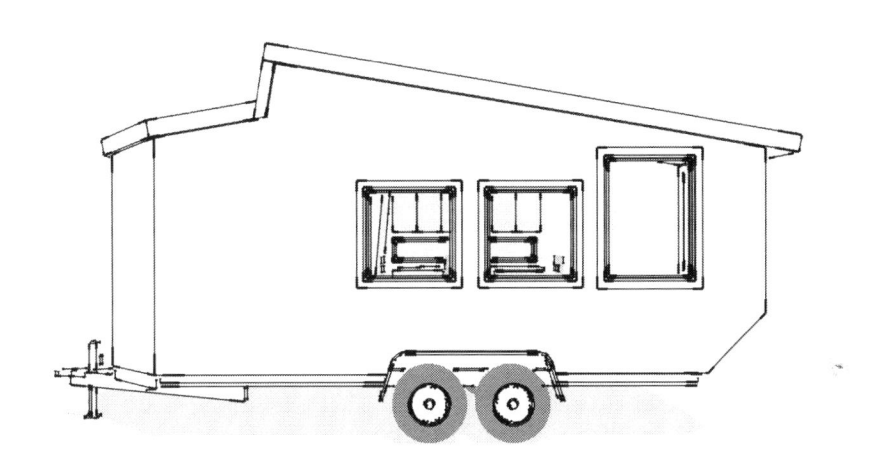

Left

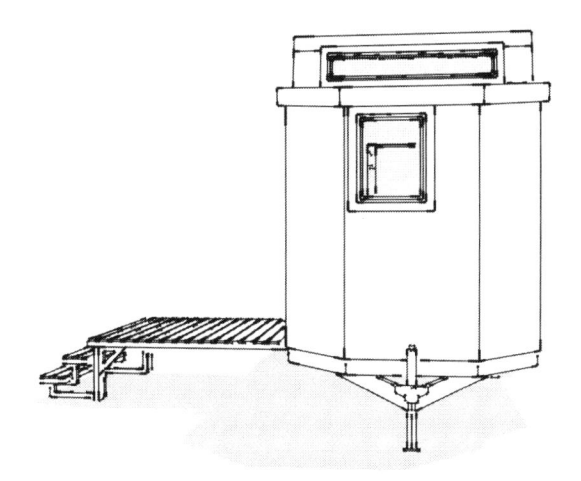

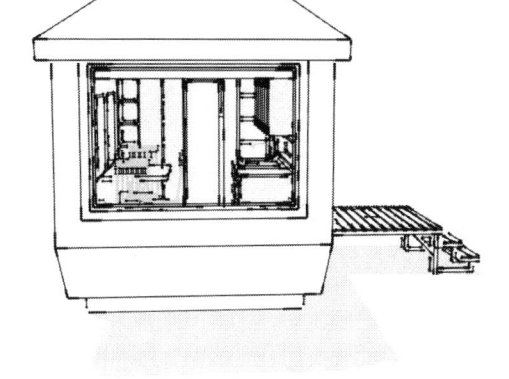

Back

Front

#44

Tiny House #44 - Overview

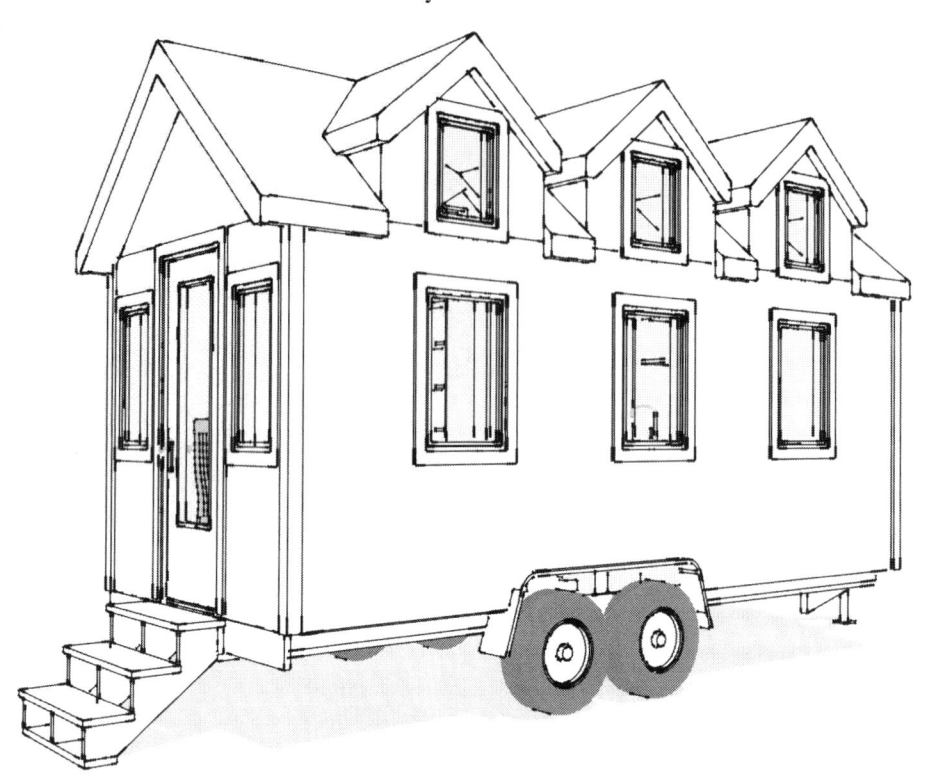

Front Right

Summary:

Sometimes people need separates places for different activities. Inside a tiny house that can be difficult. This house has a small home office with a desk tucked into a bay window at the back of the house that can be closed off by a pocket door. At the front of the house is a small living room with a table for two and two comfy chairs. In the center of the house is the bathroom and kitchen. The kitchen has the essentials and the bathroom has a shower, toilet, and wall mounted sink. The loft is open at both ends providing ample airflow. The loft is accessed from the home office side.

Features:

18-Foot Tiny House on Wheels
Gable Roof with Gable Dormers
Small Bathroom
Small Kitchen
Home Office

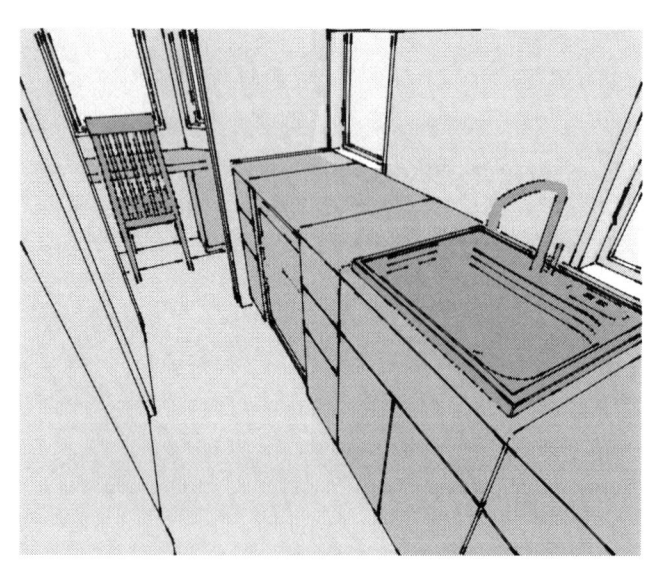

Kitchen

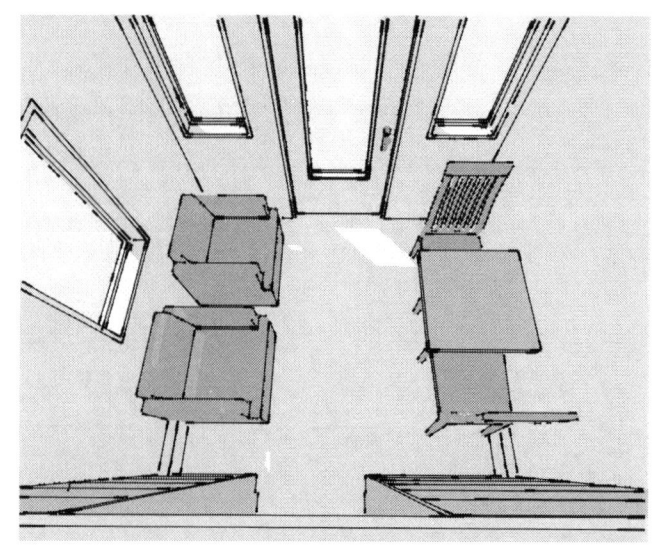

View from Loft

Tiny House #44 - Floor Plan & Exterior

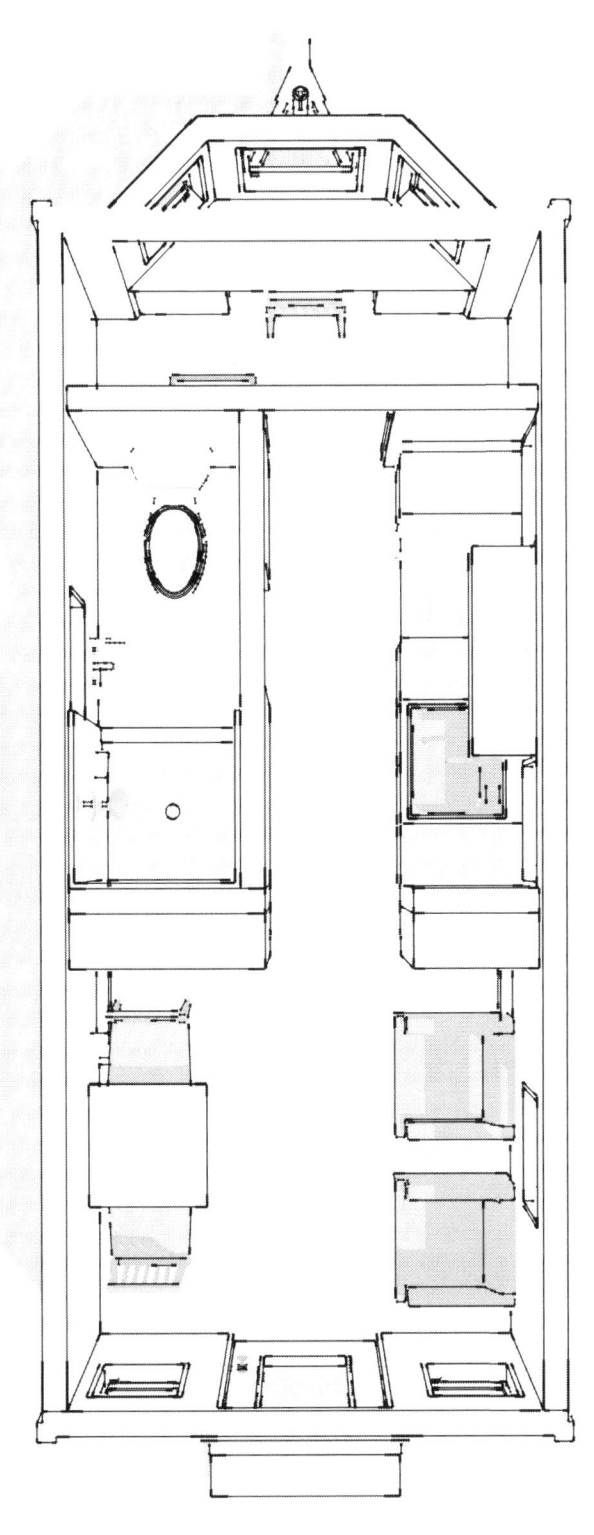

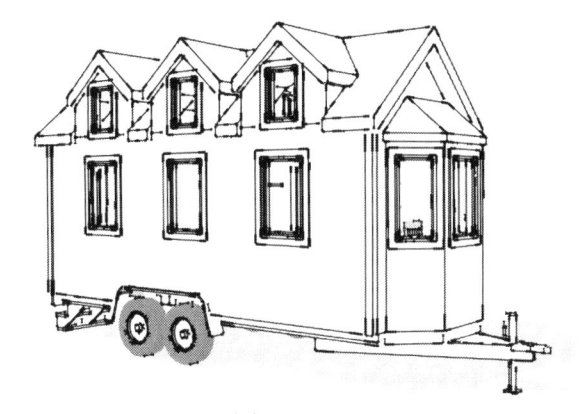

Front Right Corner

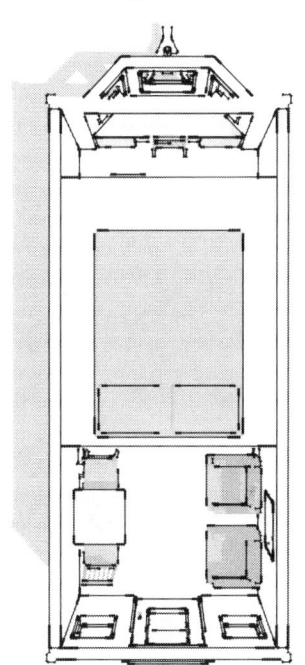

Floor Plan - Loft

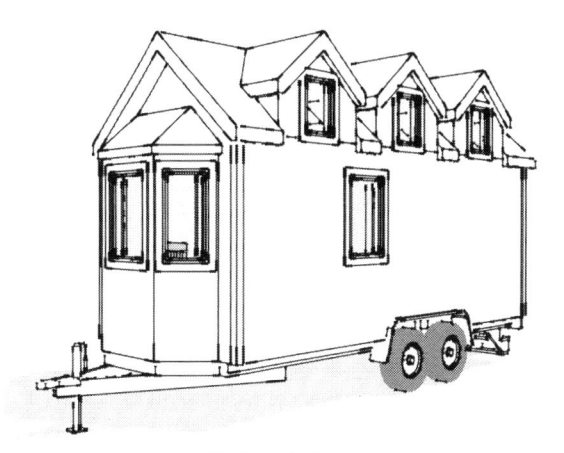

Back Left Corner

Floor Plan

Tiny House #44 - Interior Views

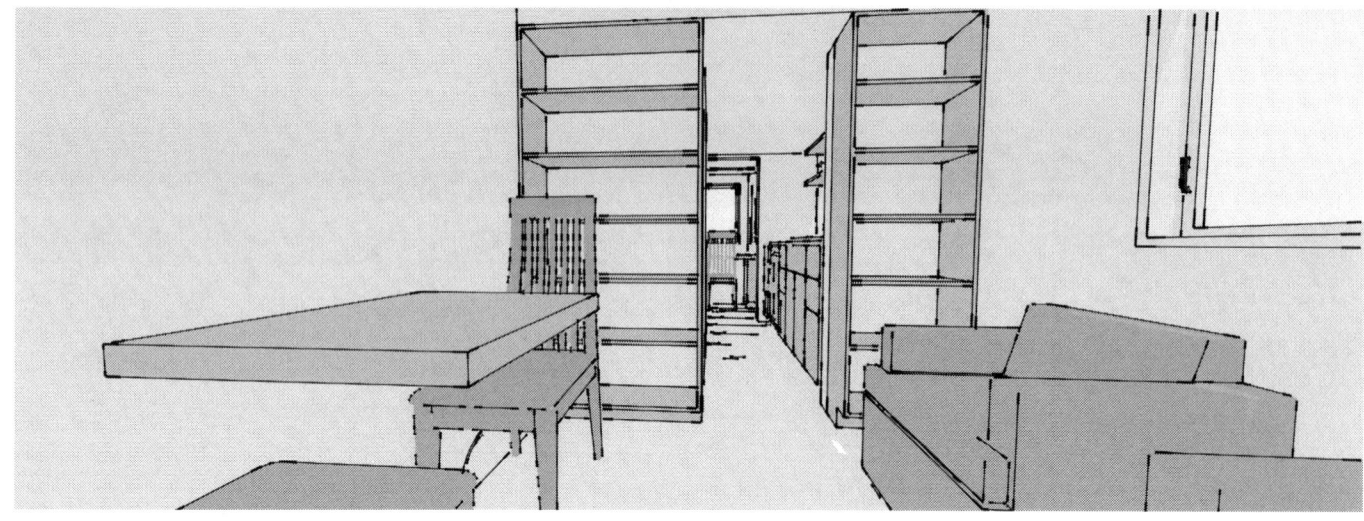

Interior

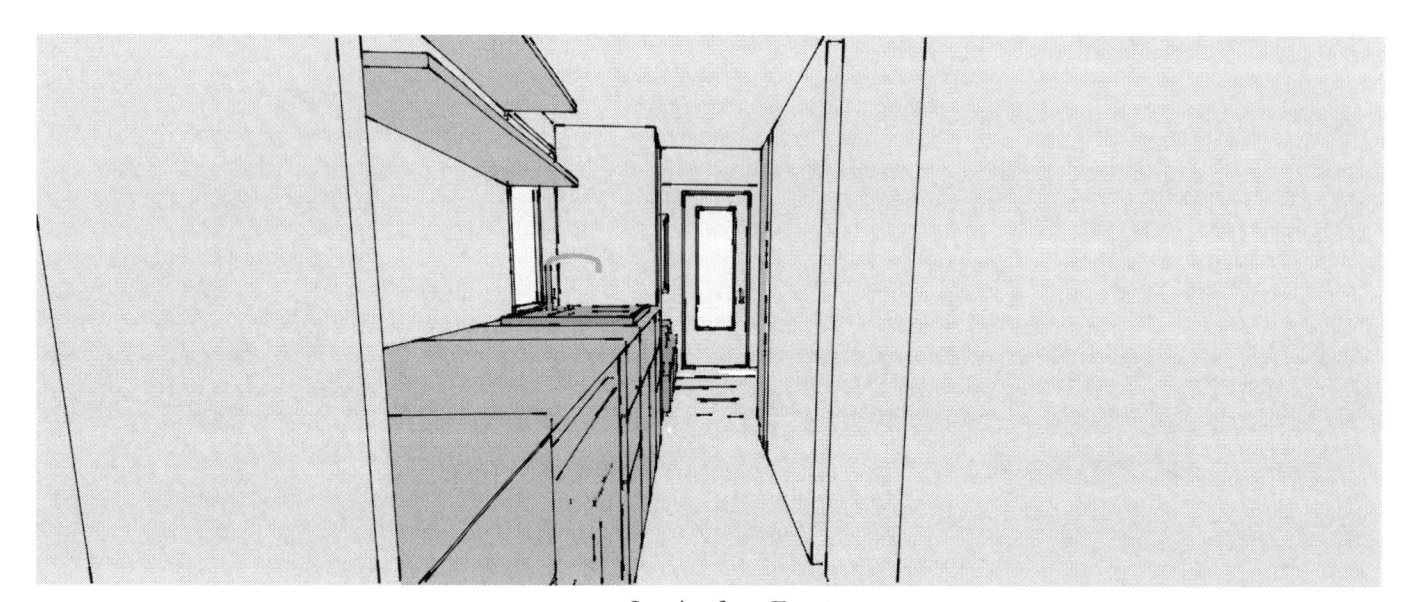

Interior from Entry

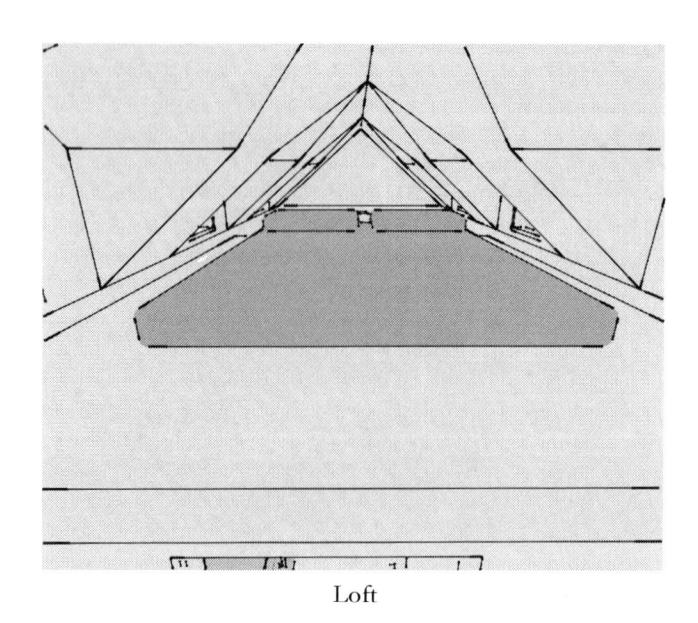

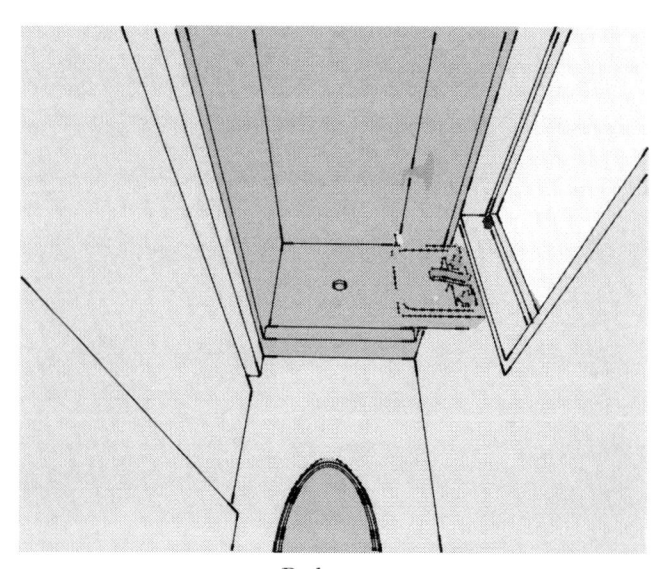

Loft

Bathroom

Tiny House #44 - Elevations

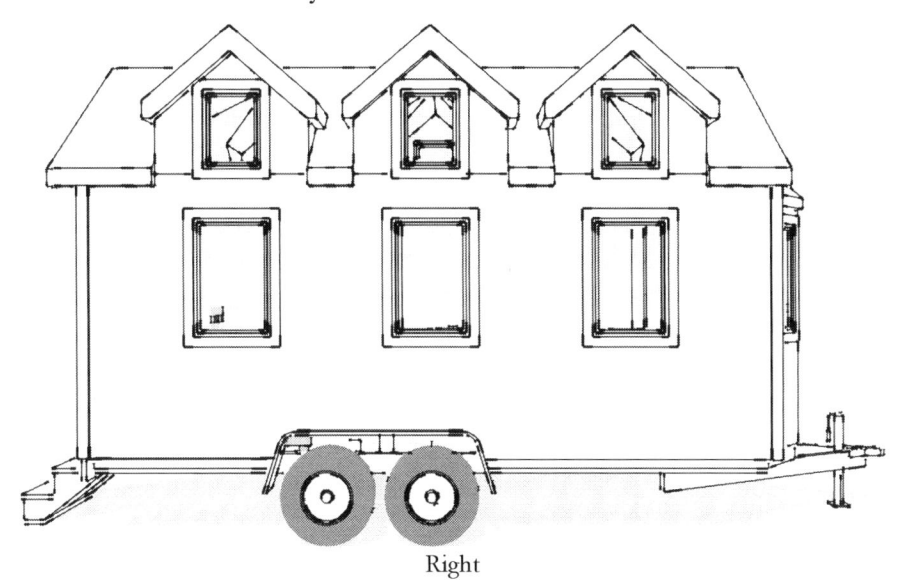

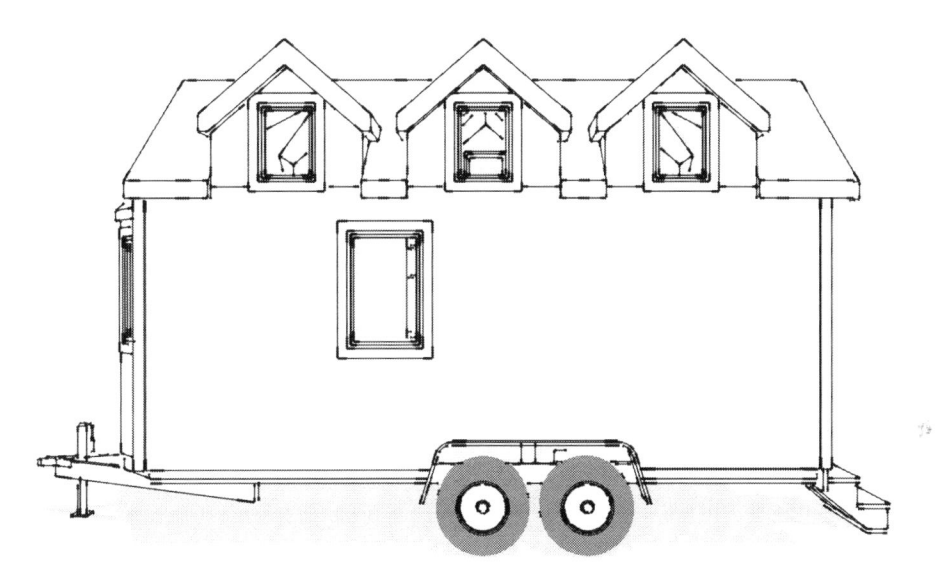

Right

Left

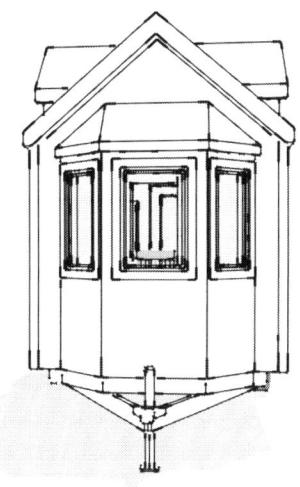

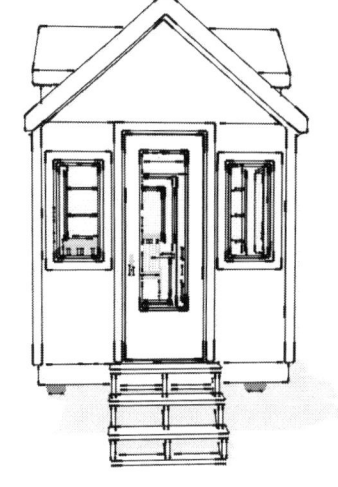

Back

Front

20-Foot Tiny House Designs

#45

Tiny House #45 - Overview

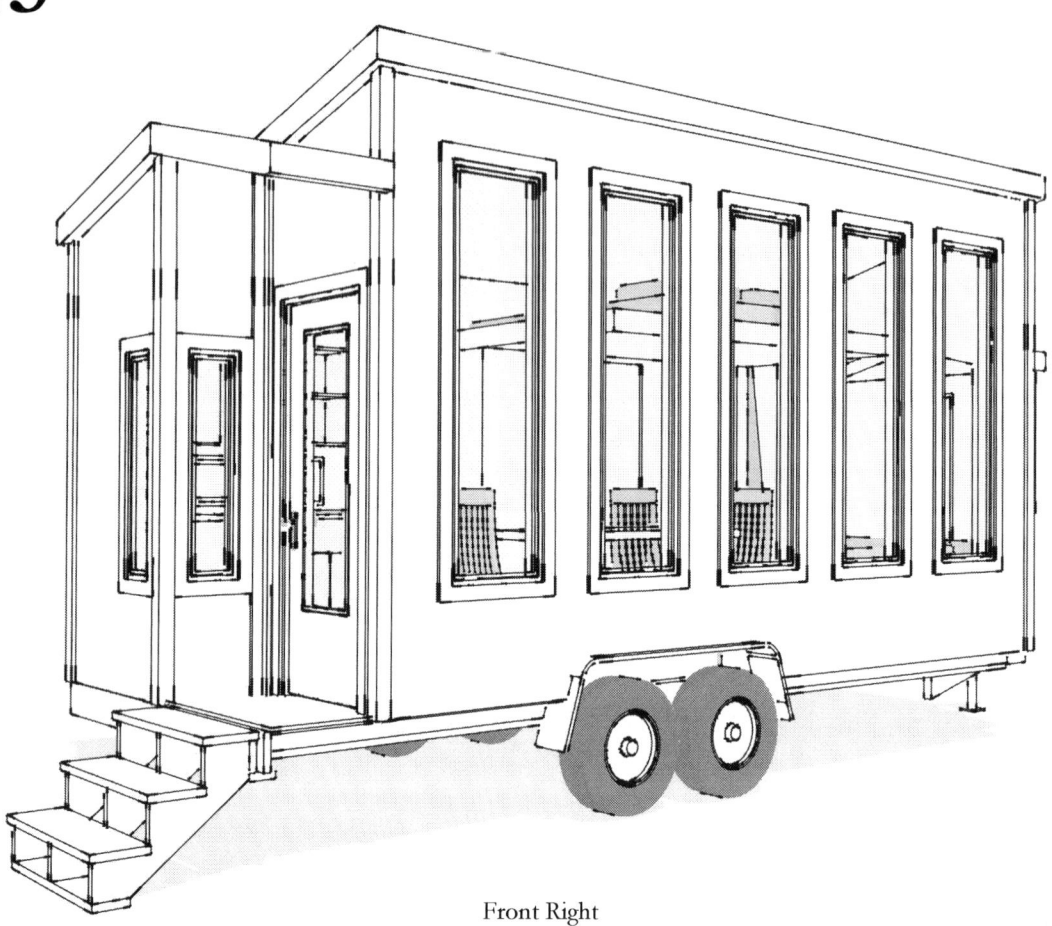

Front Right

Summary:

A bright and open space is what you would experience the moment you walk into this tiny house. The design is ideal for locations with fantastic views - or in climates where maximizing passive solar gain is desired. The inset door helps accentuate the dramatic appearance the five large narrow windows create.

Features:

20-Foot Tiny House on Wheels
Shed Roof with Gable Roof over Entry
Standard Bathroom
Table for Four
Living Room with Sofa and Two Chairs
Sleeps Two in Loft

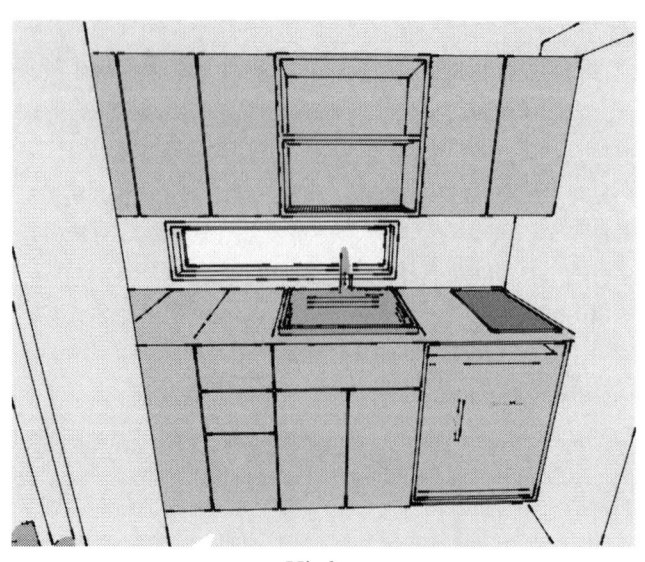

Kitchen

View from Loft

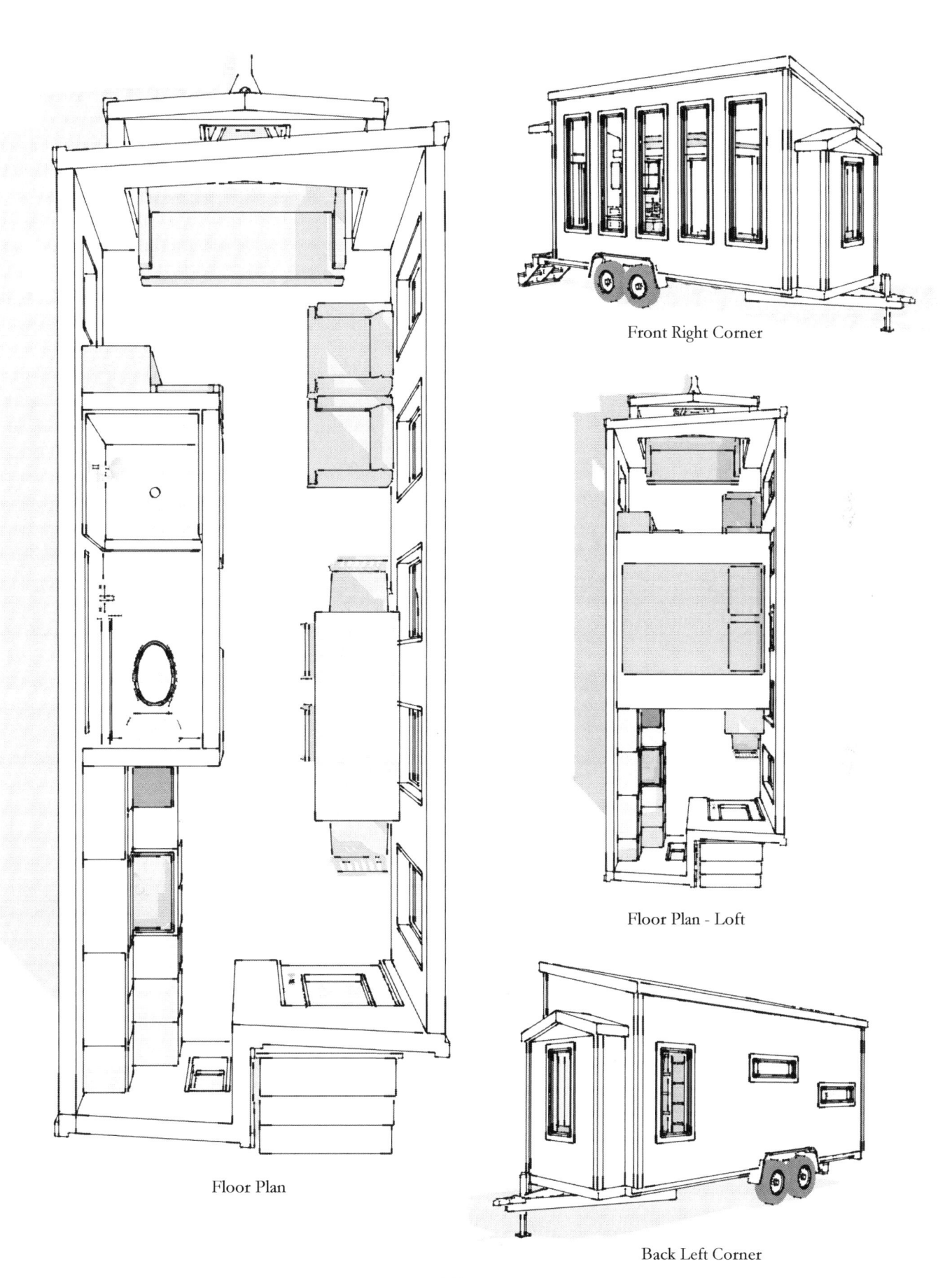

Tiny House #45 - Floor Plan & Exterior

Front Right Corner

Floor Plan - Loft

Floor Plan

Back Left Corner

Tiny House #45 - Interior Views

Interior from Kitchen

Interior from Living Room

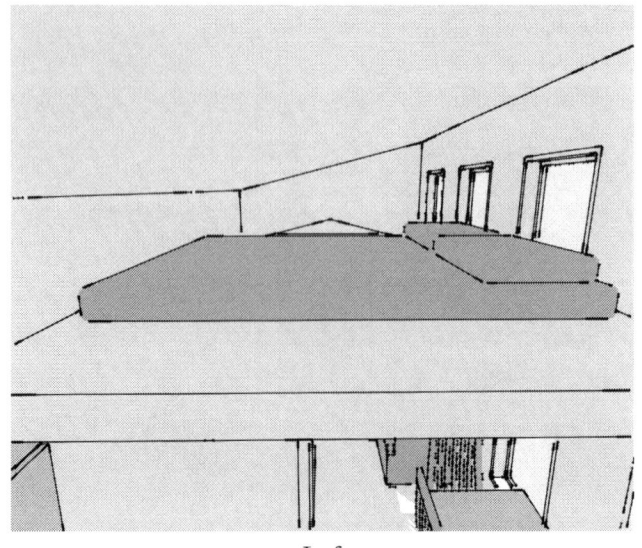

Loft

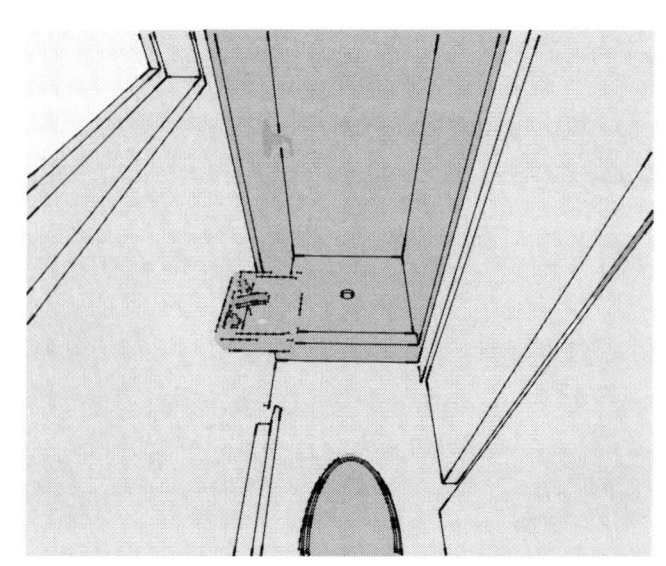

Bathroom

Tiny House #45 - Elevations

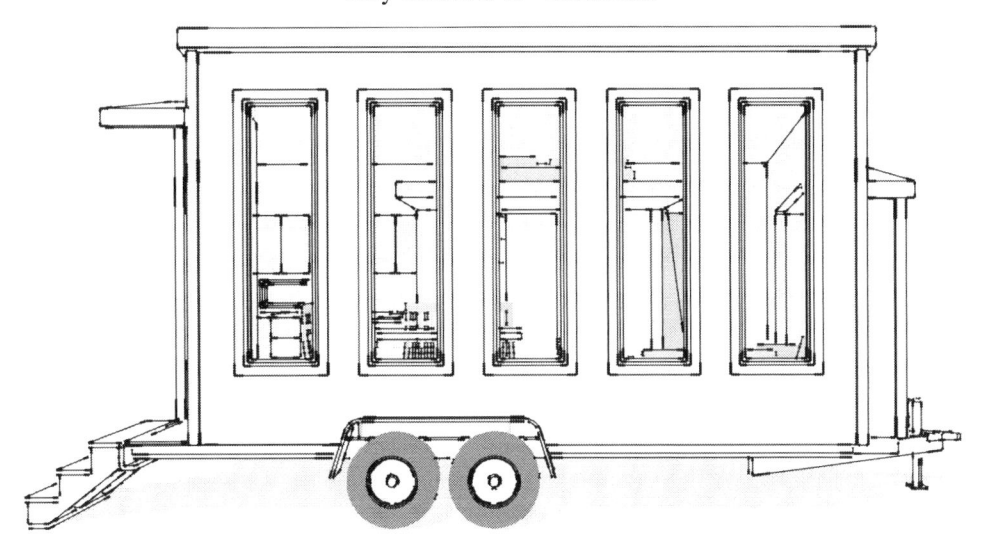

Right

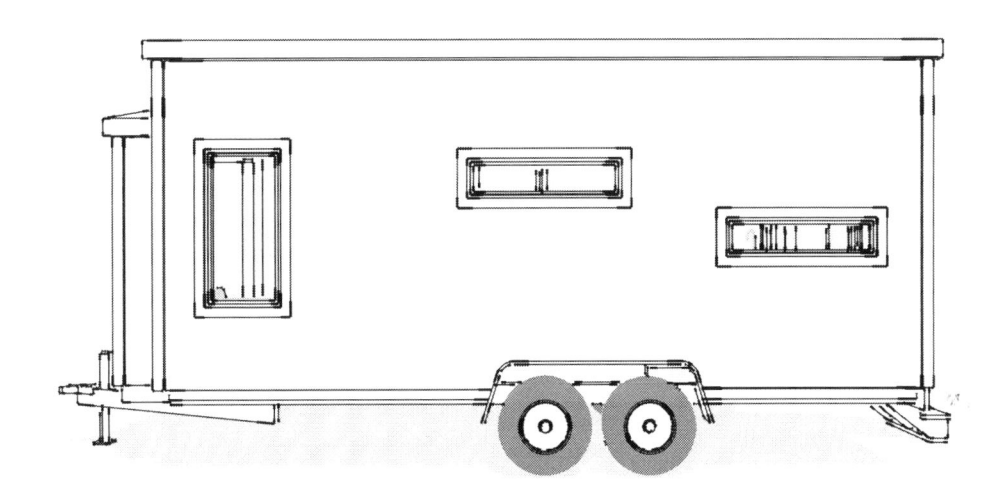

Left

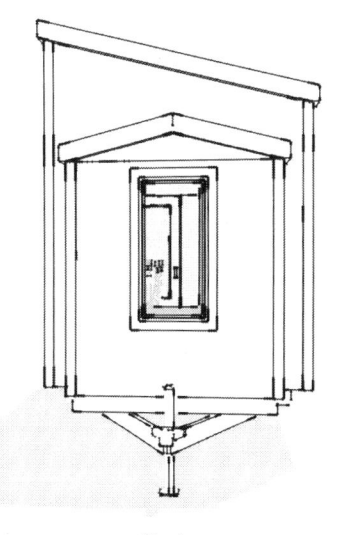

Back

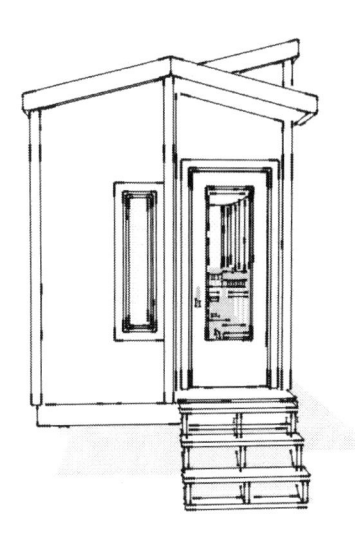

Front

189

#46

Tiny House #46 - Overview

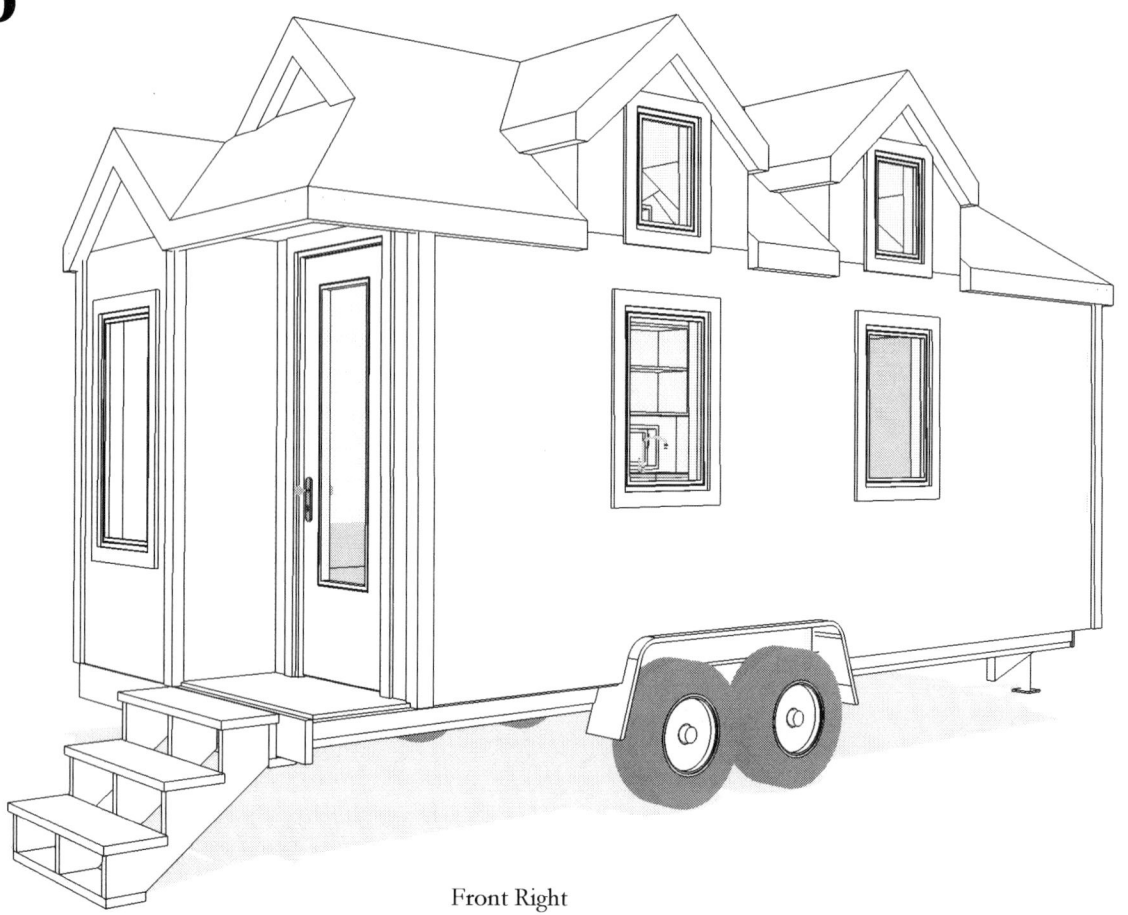

Front Right

Summary:

Just inside the front door is a table for three and a sofa. At the back of the house is a bathroom with a shower, toilet, and wall mounted sink. The house has few windows, which would let in just the right amount of light and accentuate the inward cozy feeling. Over the trailer tongue is an aerodynamic utility closet with a complimenting hip roof.

Features:

20-Foot Tiny House on Wheels
Dutch Gable Roof with Gable Dormers
Inset Entry
Standard Bathroom
Table for Three and Sofa
Kitchen with Full Size Refrigerator

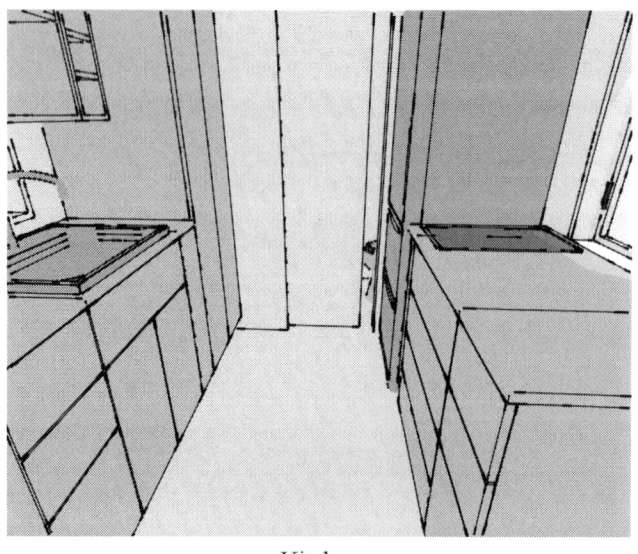

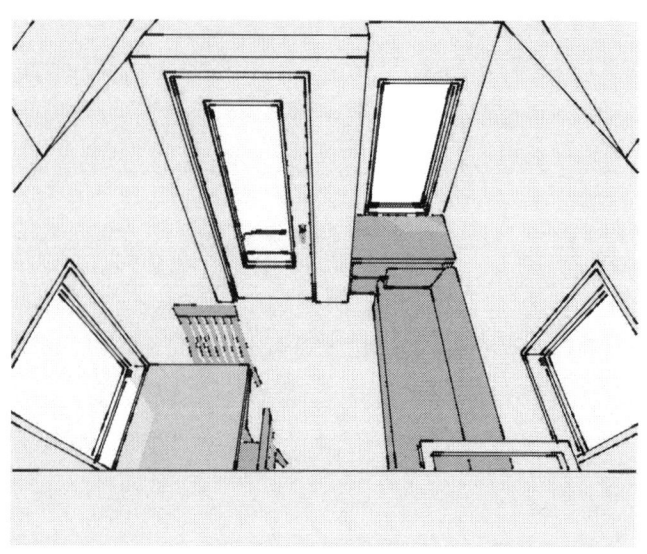

Kitchen

View from Loft

Tiny House #46 - Floor Plan & Exterior

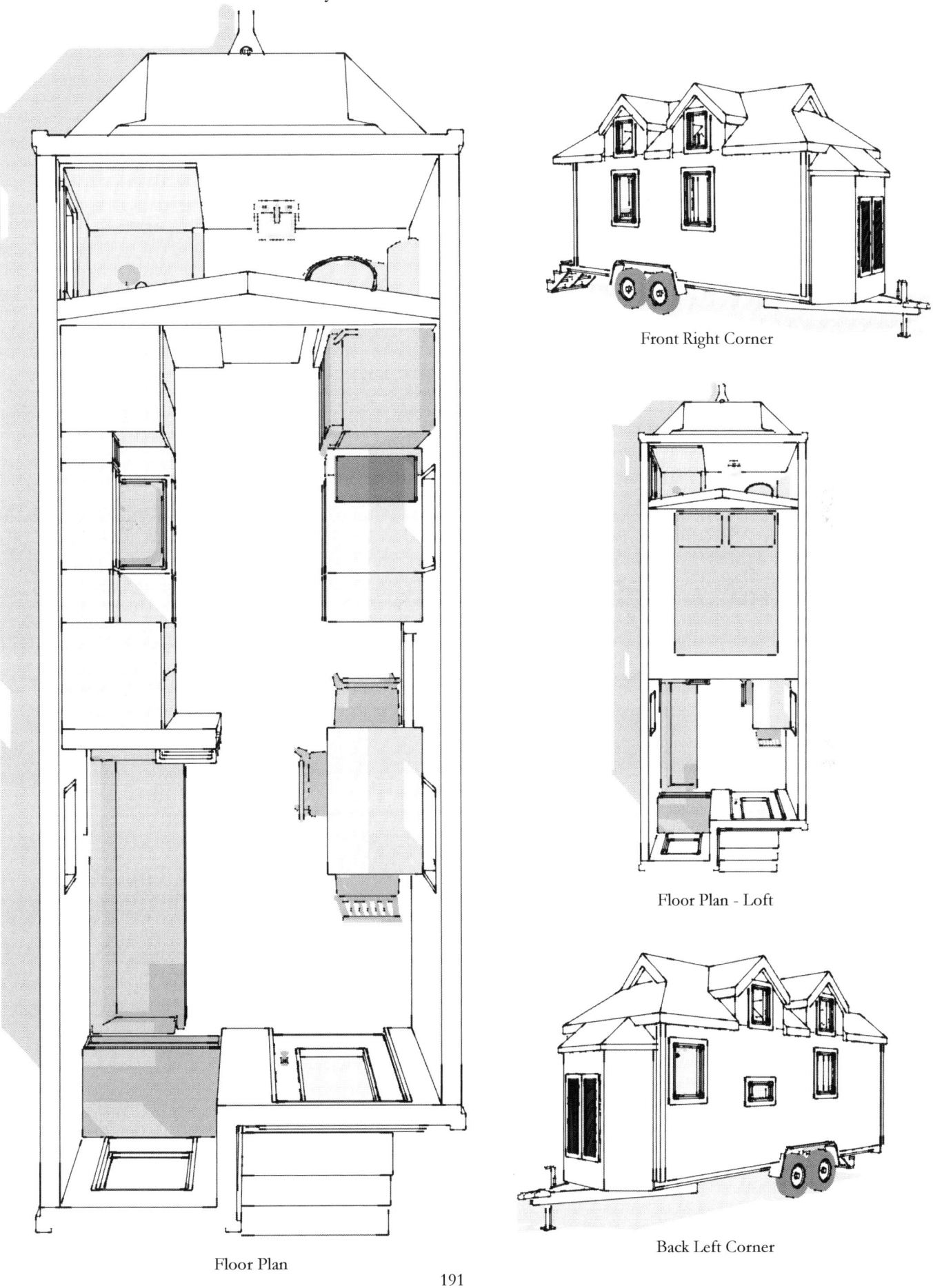

Front Right Corner

Floor Plan - Loft

Back Left Corner

Floor Plan

Tiny House #46 - Interior Views

Interior from Entry

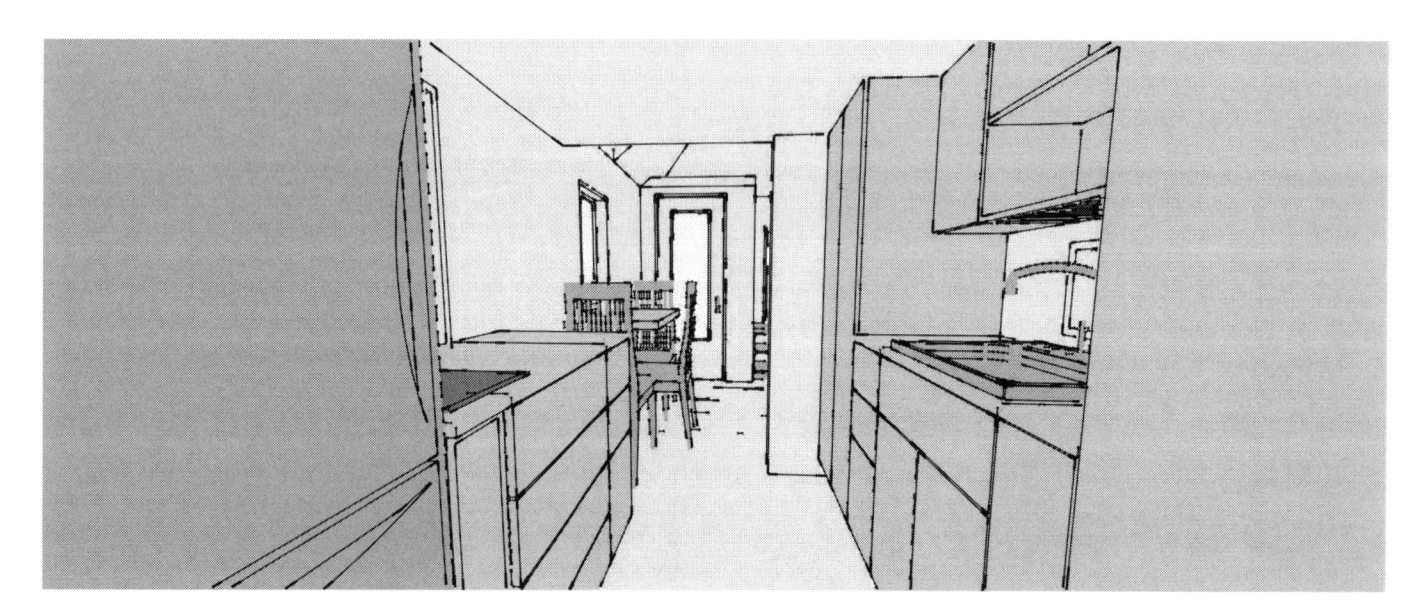

Interior from Kitchen

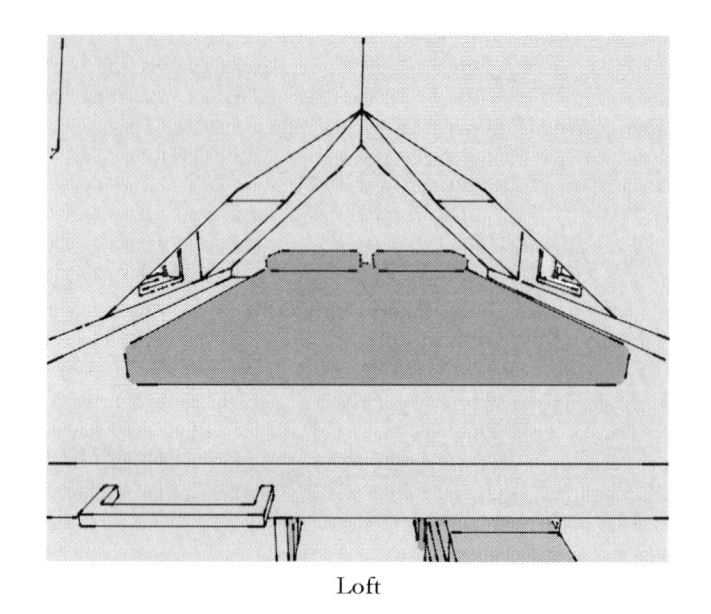

Loft

Bathroom

Tiny House #46 - Elevations

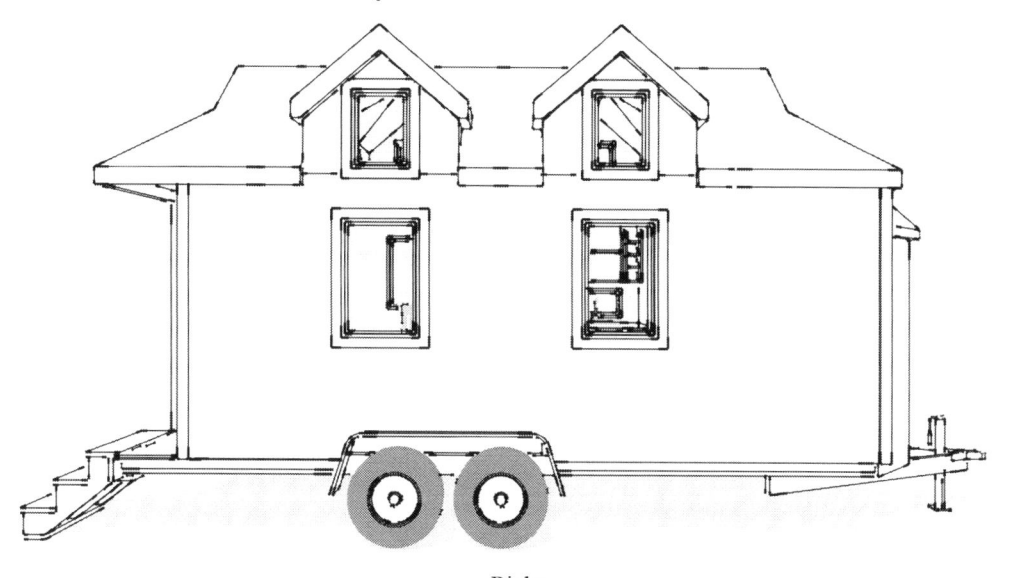

Right

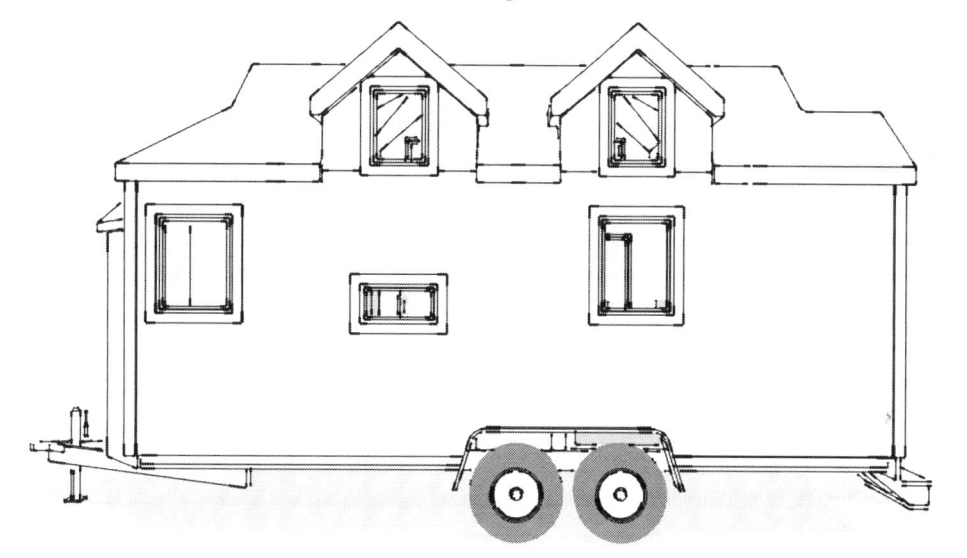

Left

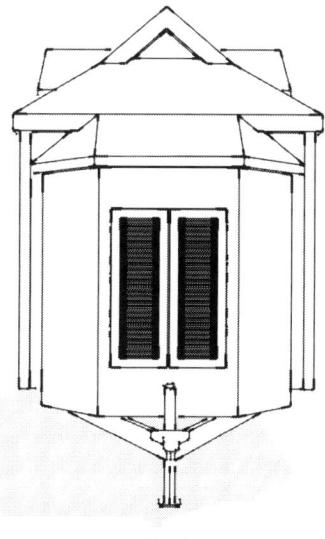

Back

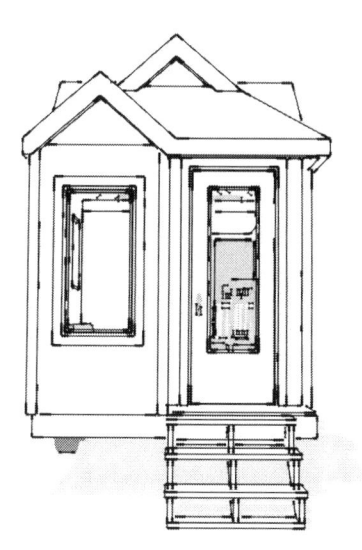

Front

#47

Tiny House #47 - Overview

Front Right

Summary:

This house is mostly one large room. It has a bathroom, storage, and laundry at the back. An open staircase leads up to the loft on the right. To the left of the front door is a table for three. Under the loft is a kitchen with the essentials. The loft has space for a queen bed.

Features:

20-Foot Tiny House on Wheels
Shed Roof with Gable Ends
Porch
Standard Bathroom
Table for Three
Laundry
Open Stairs

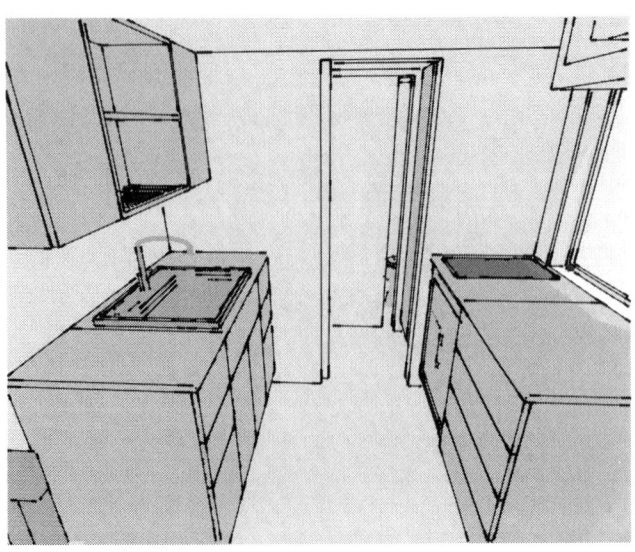

Kitchen

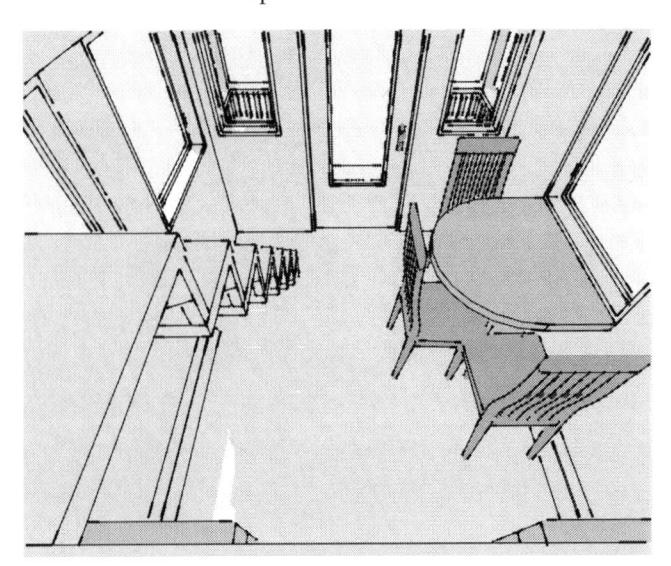

View from Loft

Tiny House #47 - Floor Plan & Exterior

Front Right Corner

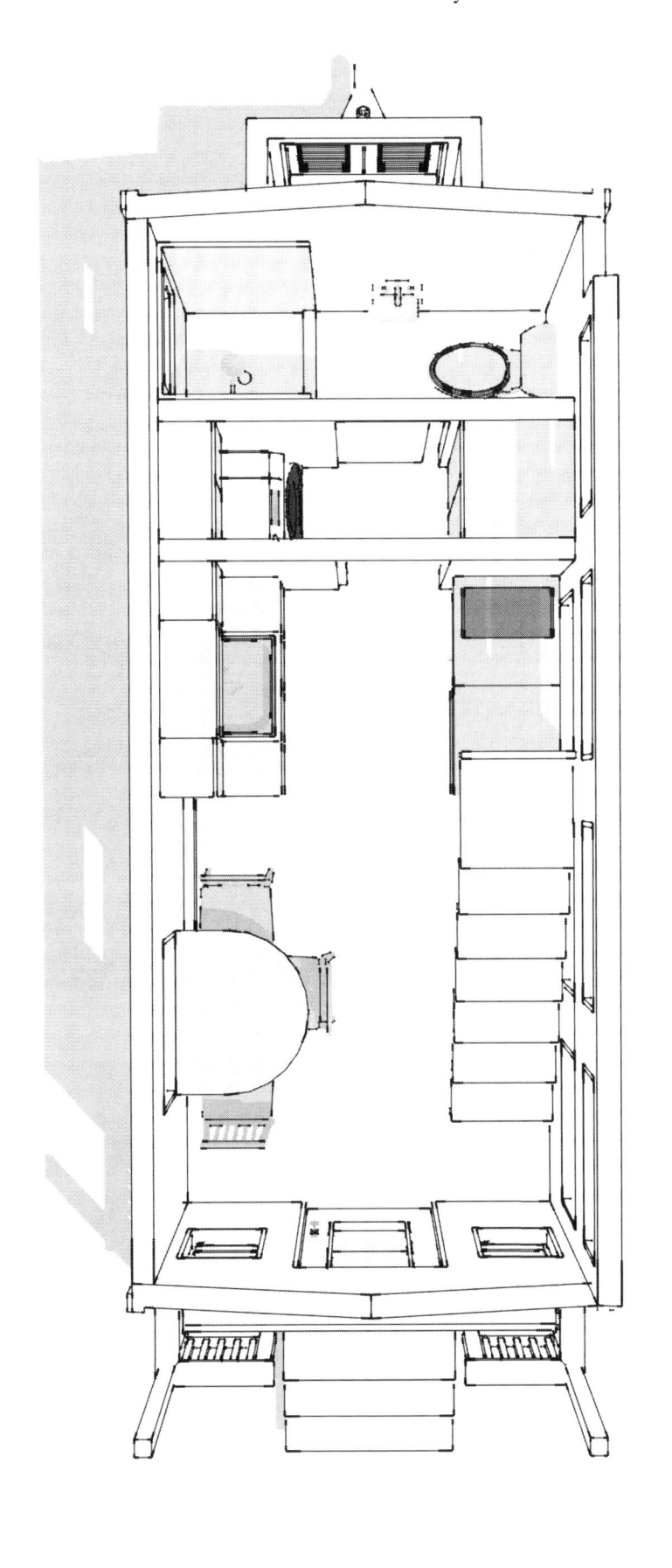

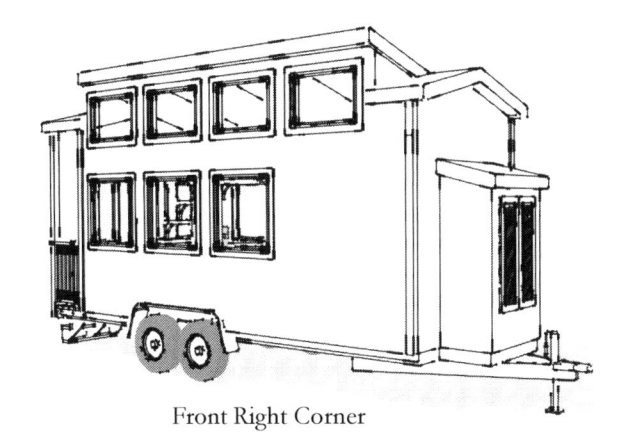

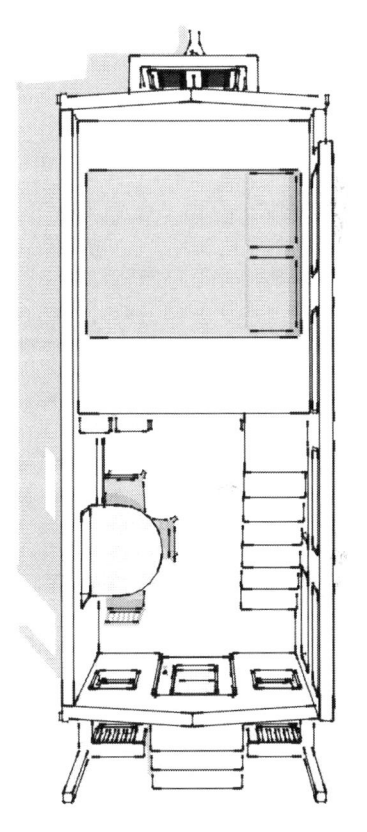

Floor Plan - Loft

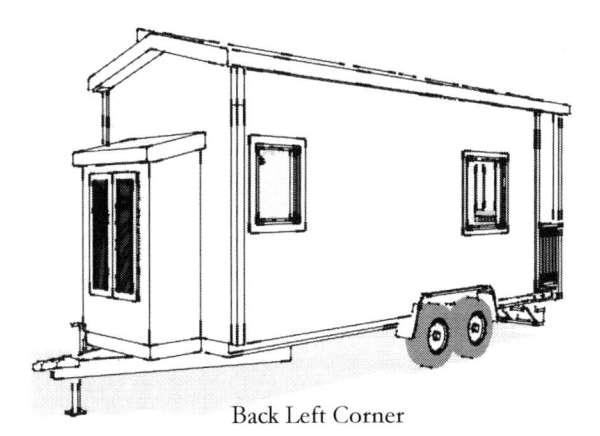

Floor Plan

Back Left Corner

Tiny House #47 - Interior Views

Interior

Interior from Kitchen

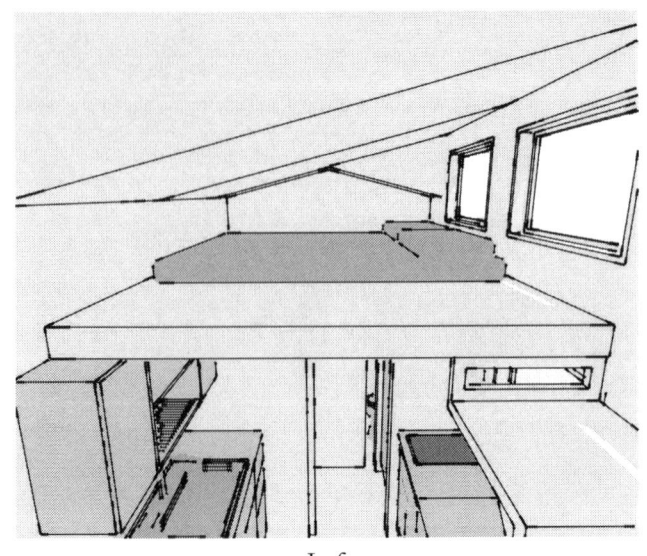

Loft

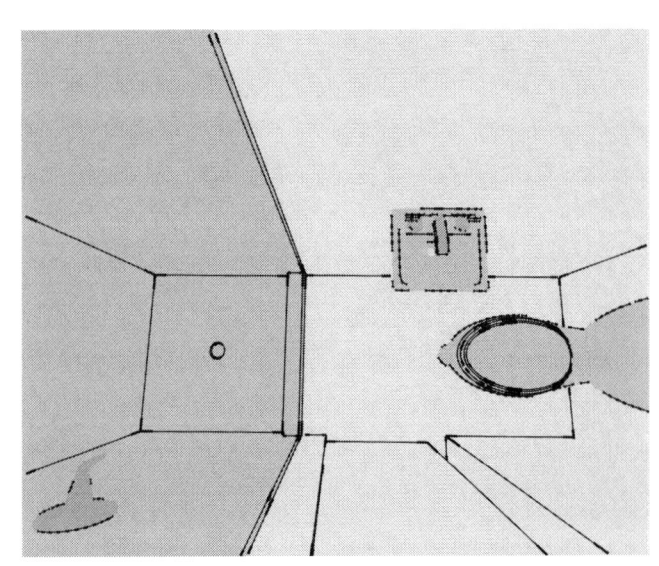

Bathroom

Tiny House #47 - Elevations

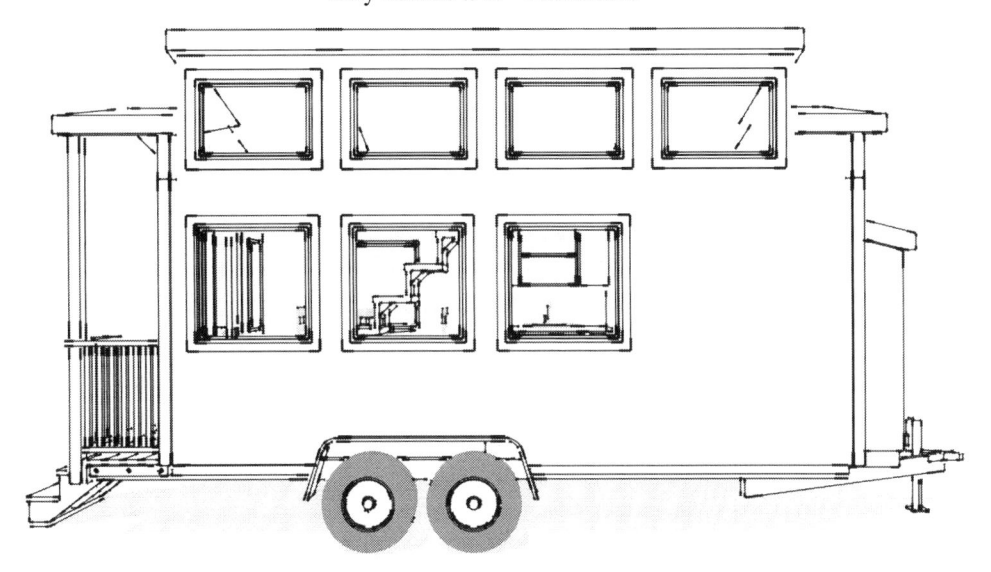

Right

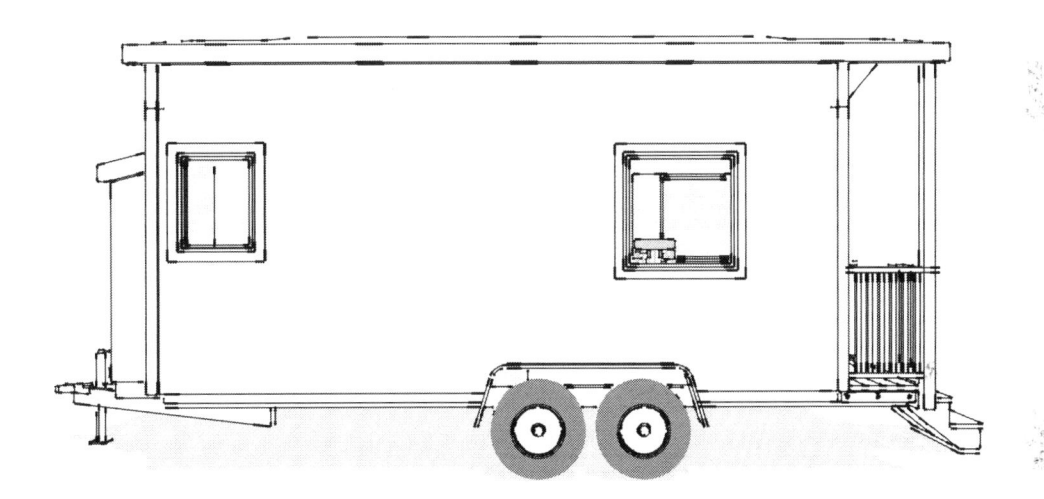

Left

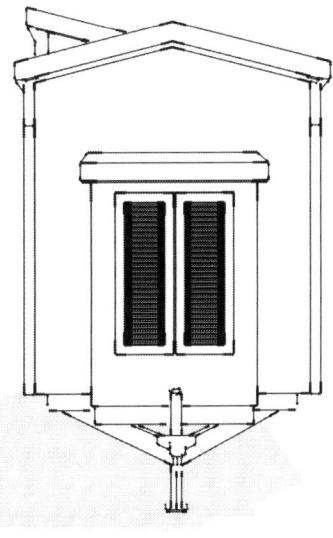

Back

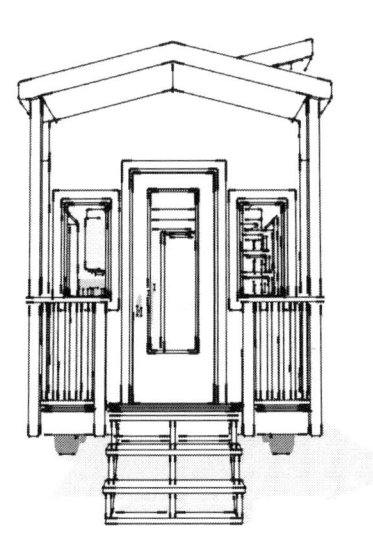

Front

#48

Tiny House #48 - Overview

Front Right

Summary:

This tiny house has a cross gable roof. The kitchen has a full size refrigerator and extends over the trailer tongue for added space. The living room has large windows and space for a table for two, a comfy chair, and a sofa. The loft is accessed by ladder rungs attached to an interior wall just inside the entry. In the loft is space for a queen size bed.

Features:

20-Foot Tiny House on Wheels
Cross Gable
Side Entry with Ramp
Standard Bathroom
Table for Two
Sleeps Two

Kitchen

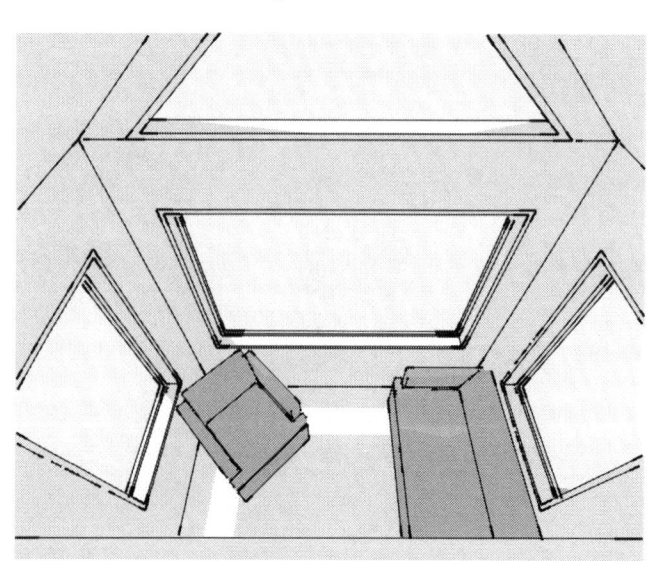

View from Loft

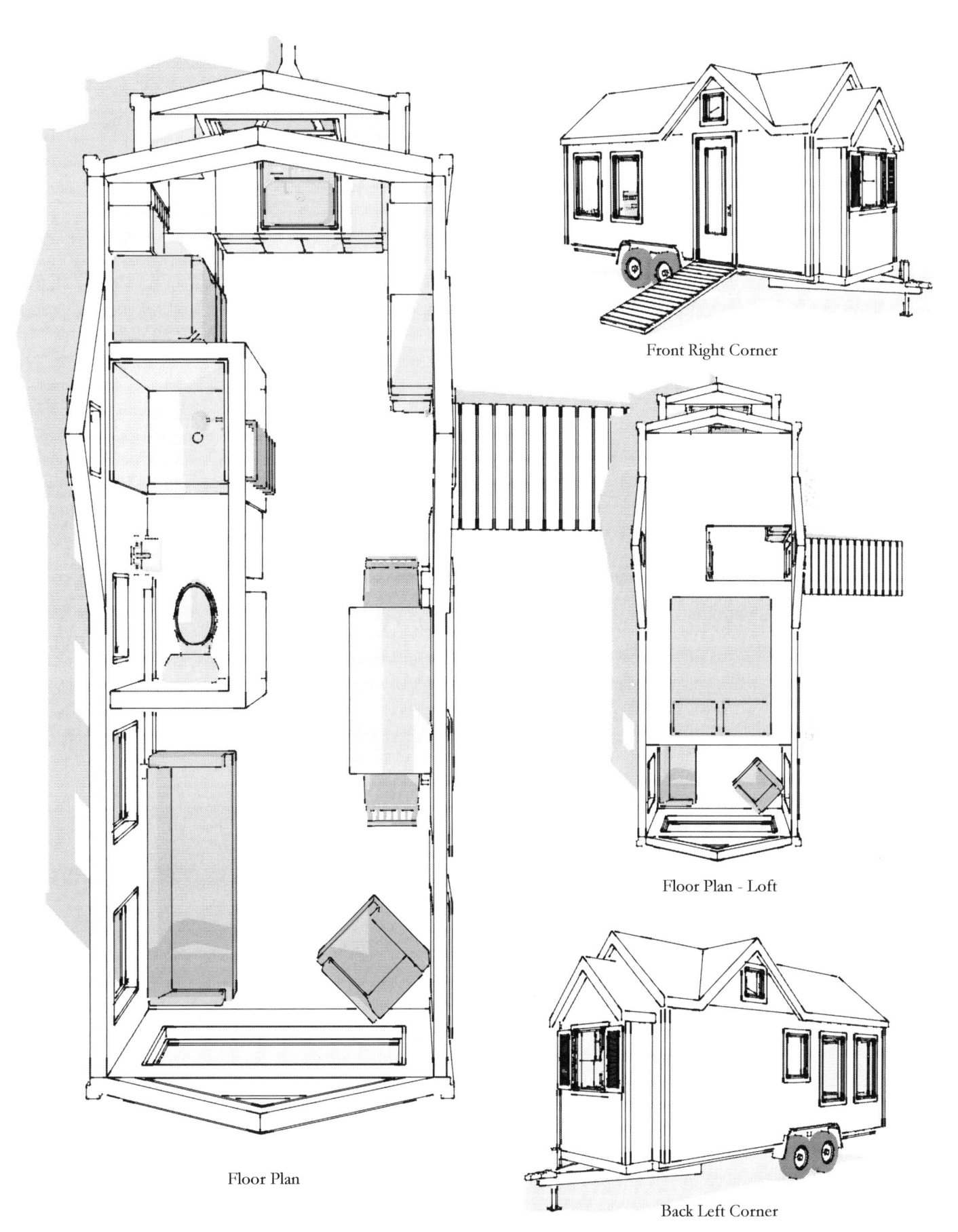

Tiny House #48 - Floor Plan & Exterior

Front Right Corner

Floor Plan - Loft

Floor Plan

Back Left Corner

Tiny House #48 - Interior Views

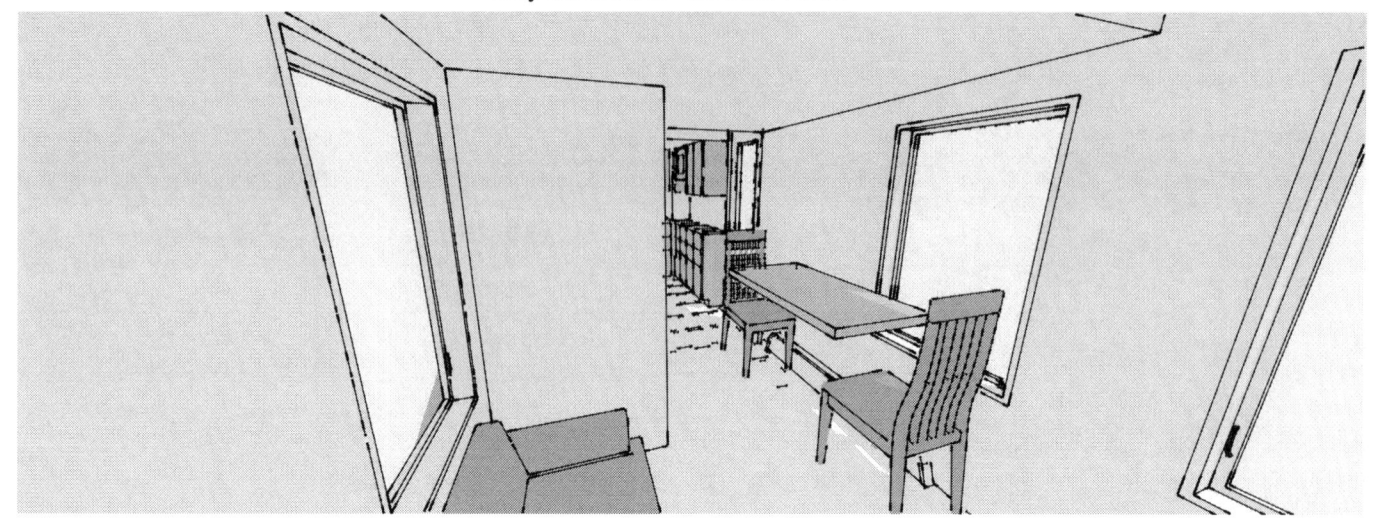

Interior

Interior from Kitchen

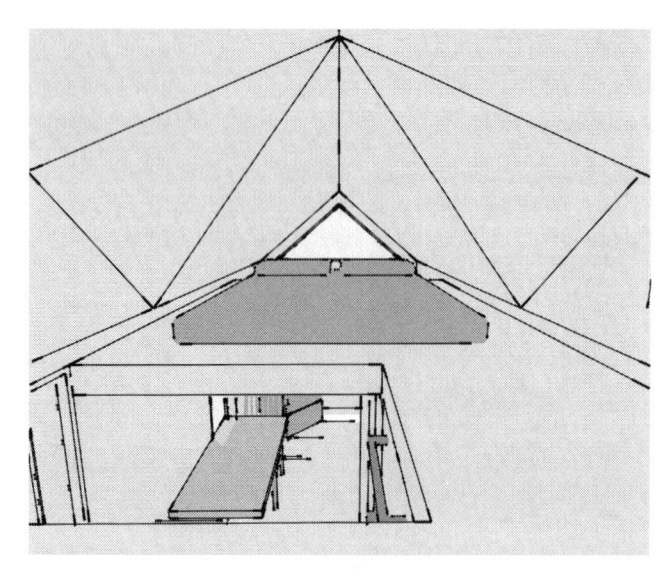

Loft

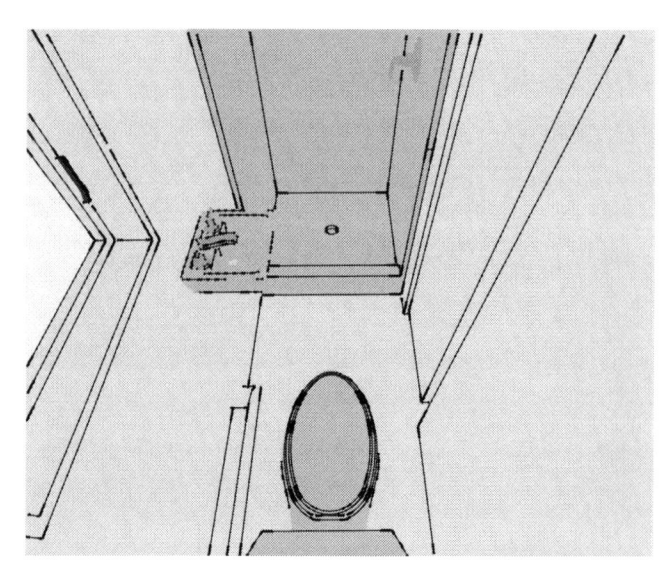

Bathroom

Tiny House #48 - Elevations

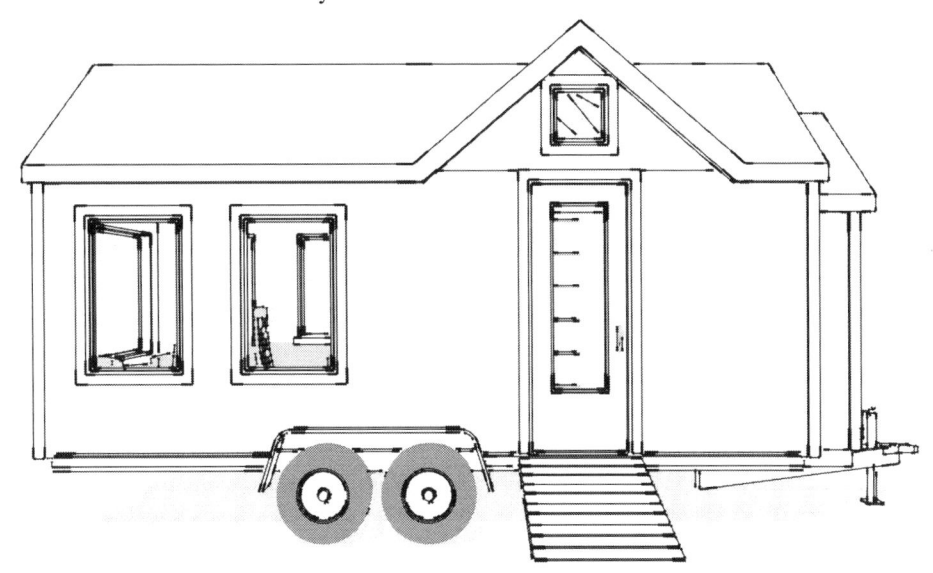

Right

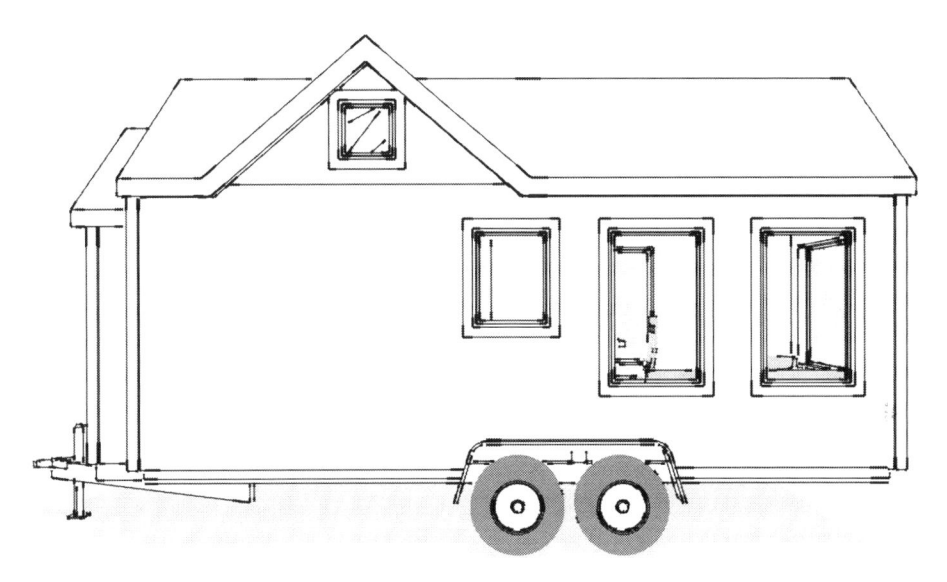

Left

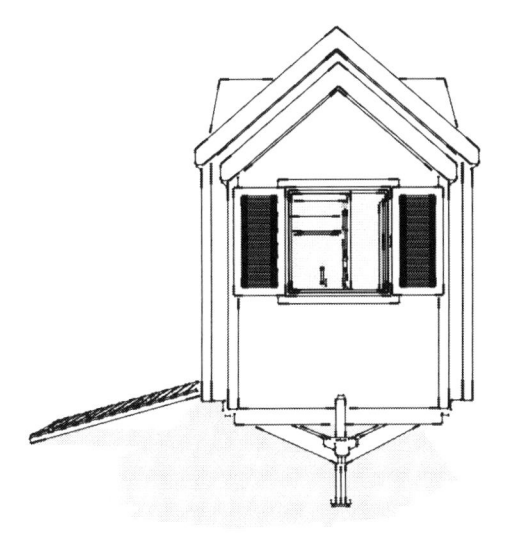

Back

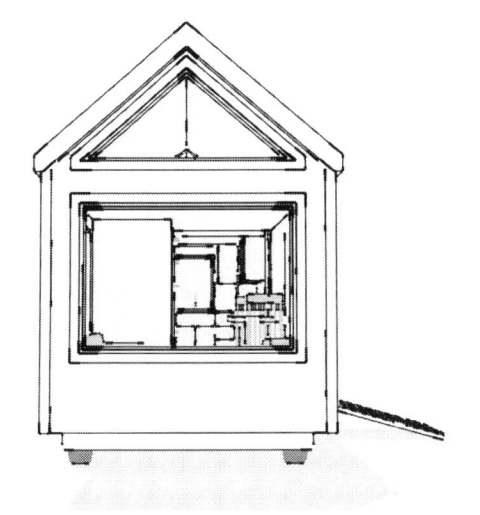

Front

201

#49

Tiny House #49 - Overview

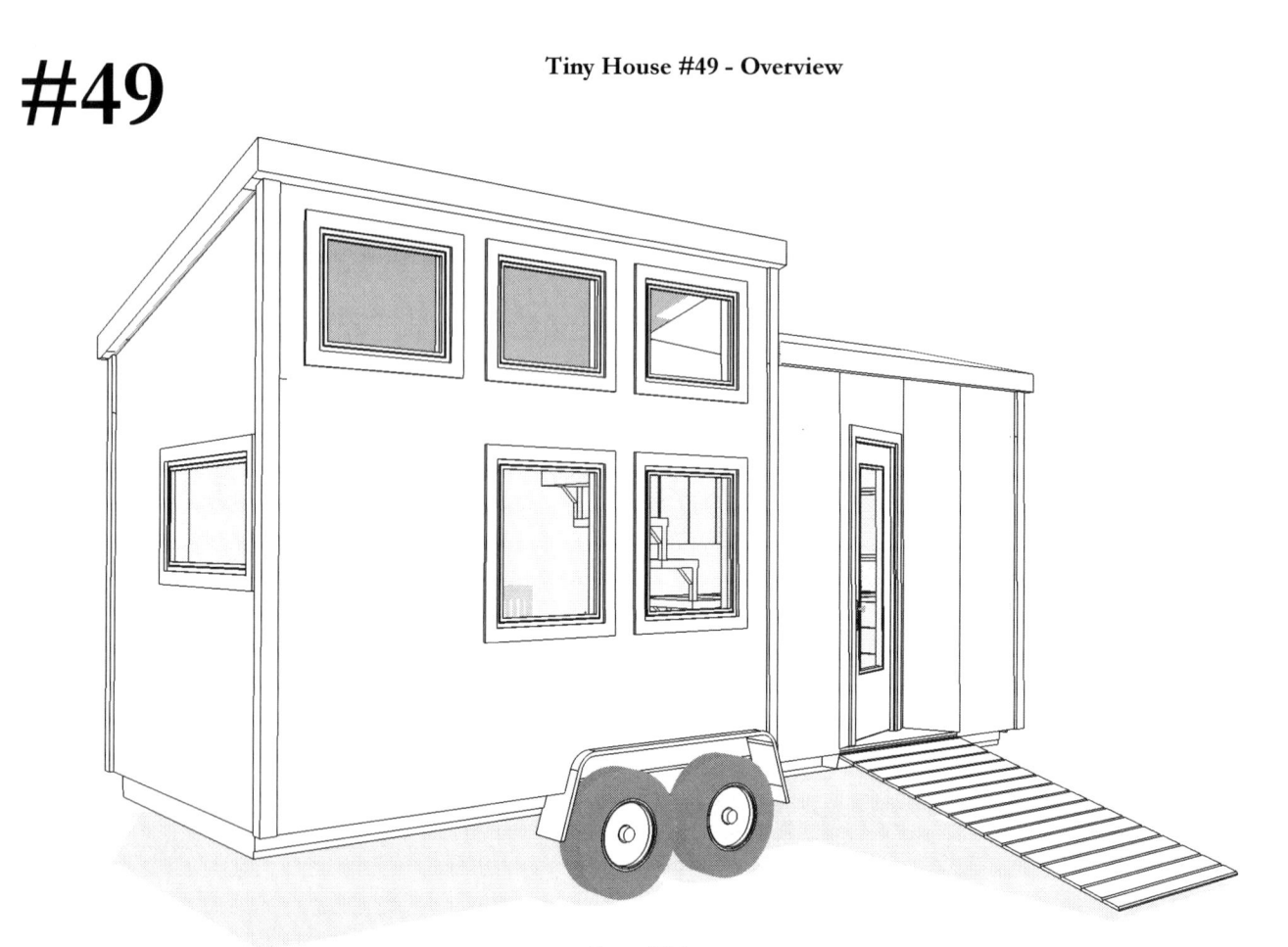

Front Right

Summary:

Just inside the side entry of this tiny house is a small kitchen, sofa, and open staircase. The loft sleeps two in a queen size bed and the high shed roof provides a lot of headroom. Below the loft is space for a bathroom large enough for a soaking tub. Under the stairs is a desk. Outside is a utility closet accessed from the trailer tongue.

Features:

20-Foot Tiny House on Wheels
Shed Roof with Gable Roof over
   Kitchen
Side Entry with Ramp
Bathroom with Soaking Tub/Shower
Desk
Open Stairs

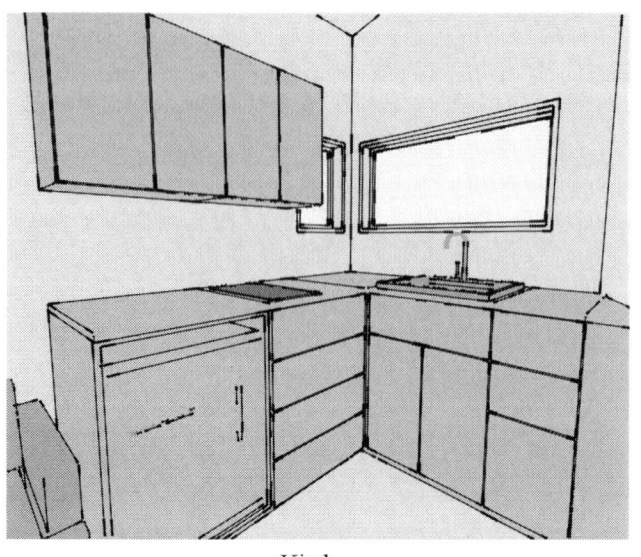

Kitchen

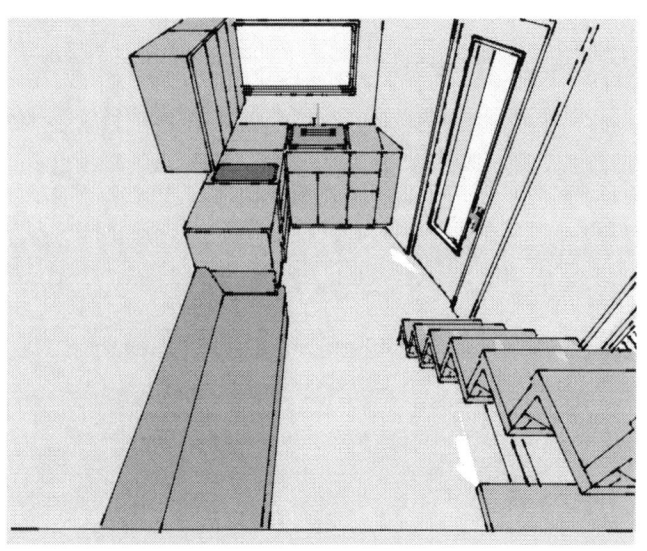

View from Loft

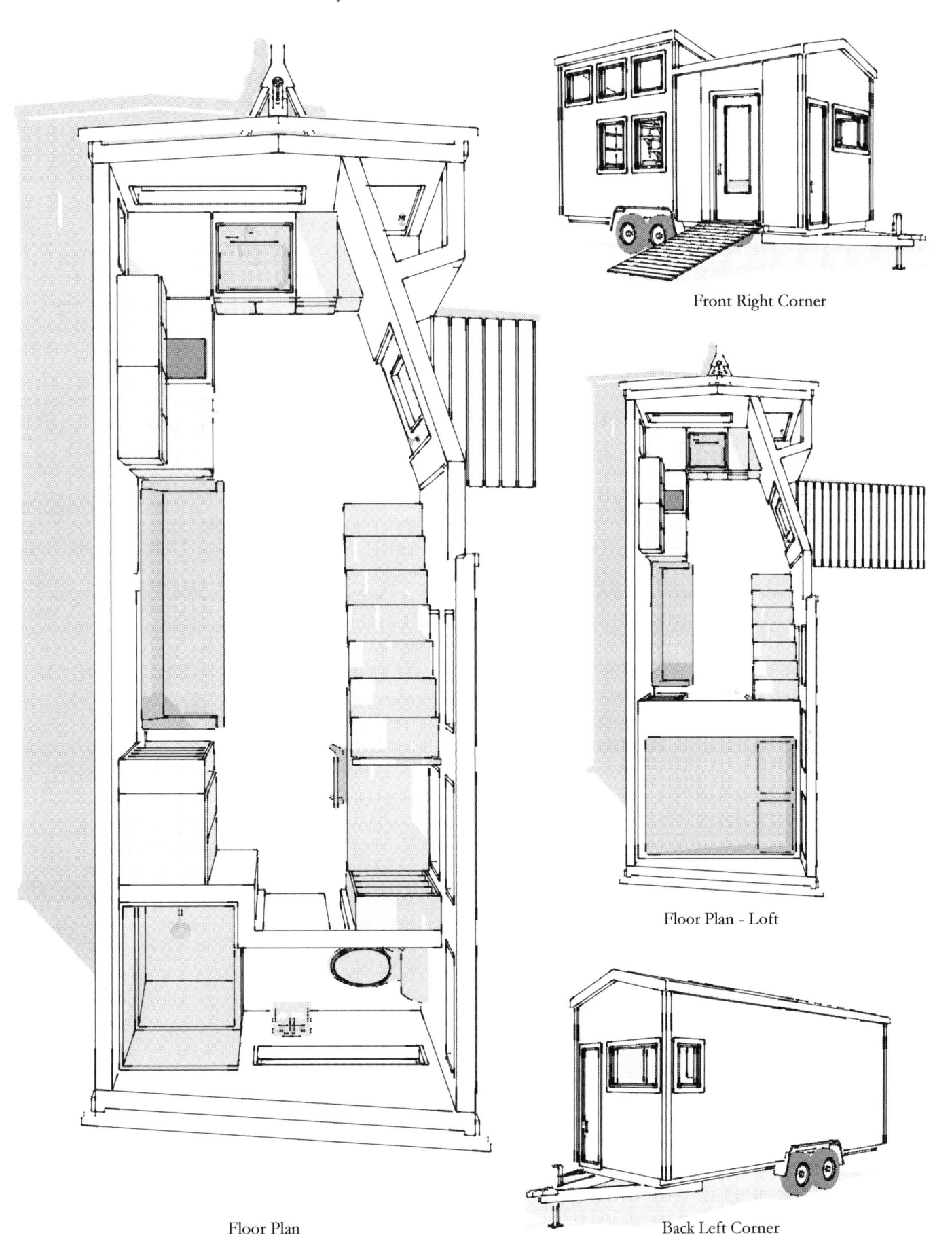

Tiny House #49 - Floor Plan & Exterior

Front Right Corner

Floor Plan - Loft

Floor Plan

Back Left Corner

Tiny House #49 - Interior Views

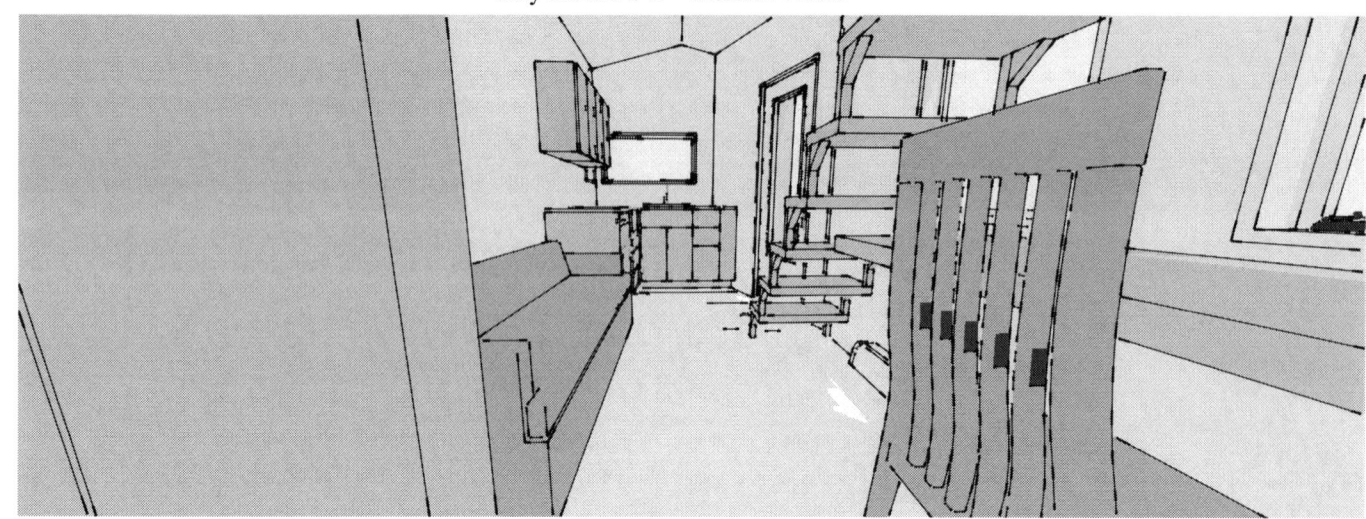

Interior from Bathroom

Interior from Kitchen

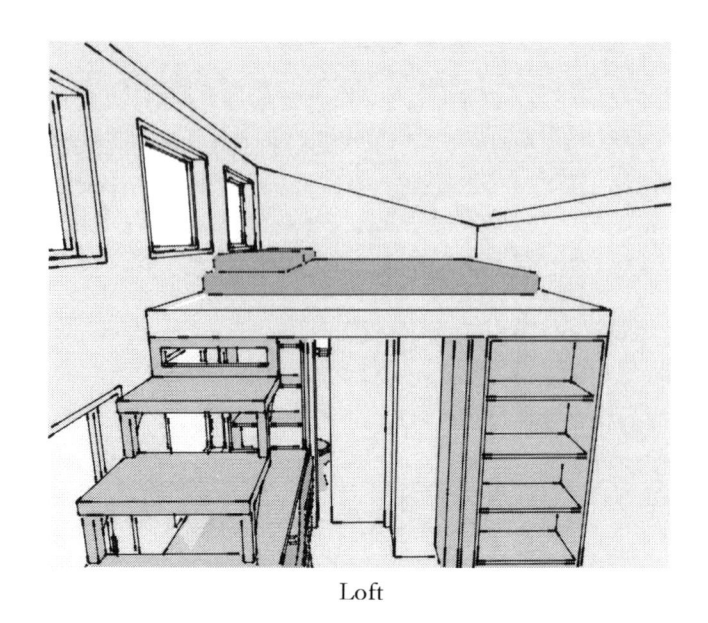

Loft

Bathroom

204

Tiny House #49 - Elevations

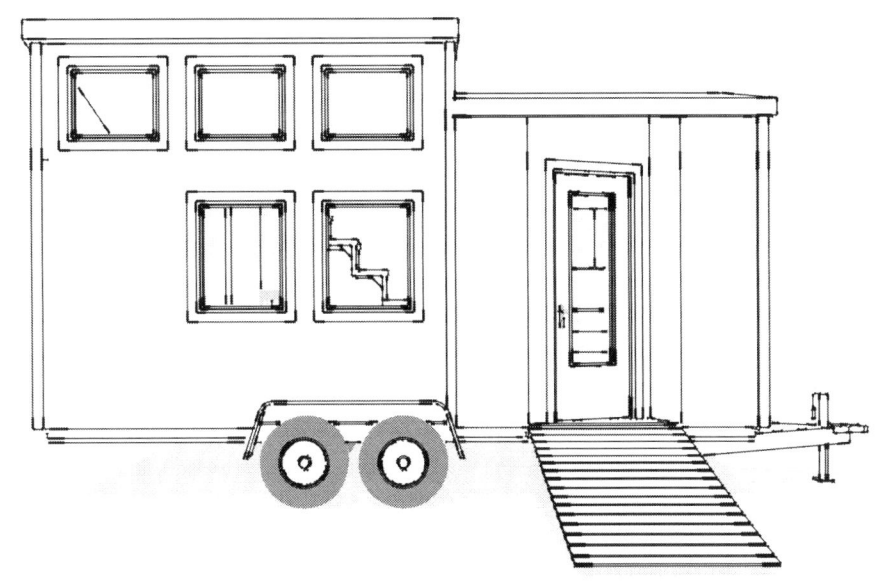

Right

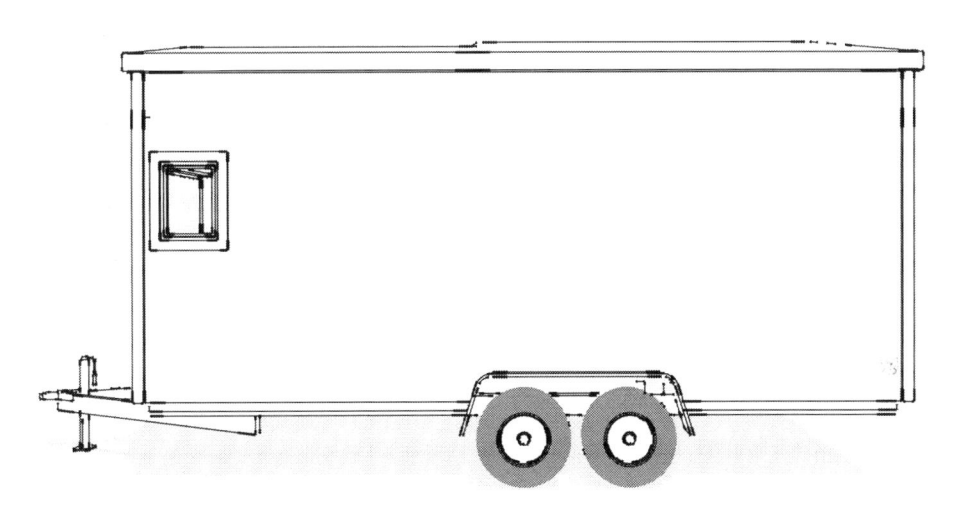

Left

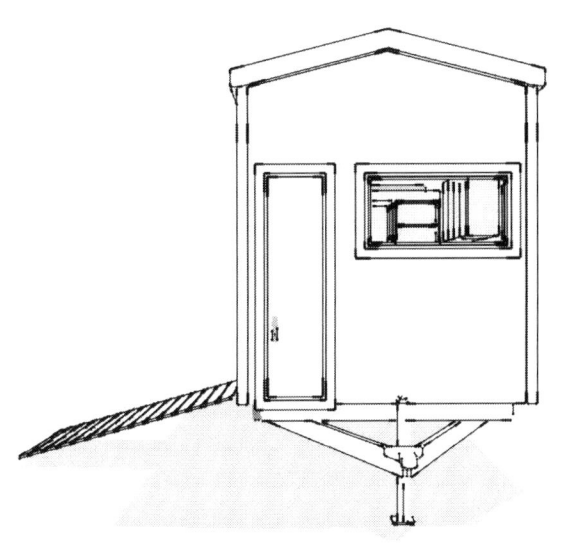

Back

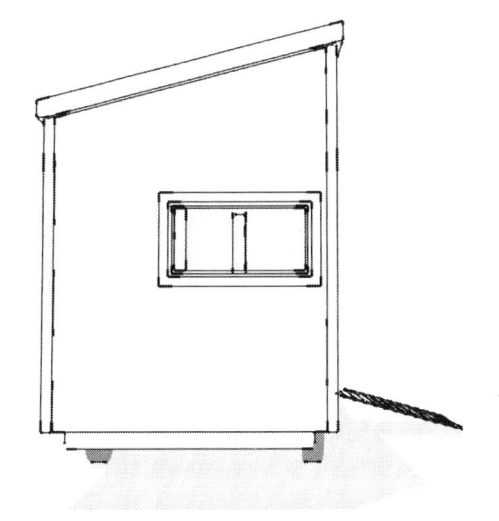

Front

#50

Tiny House #50 - Overview

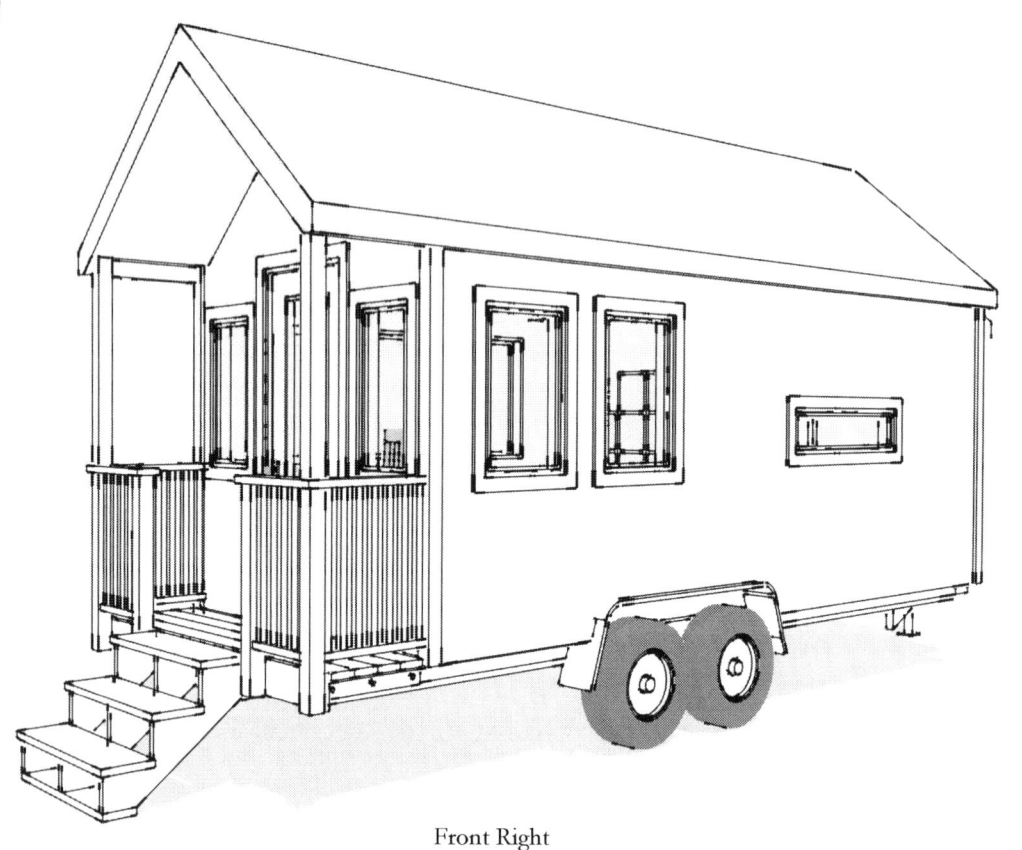

Front Right

Summary:

A classic and simple design that would be easier to build than most due to the simple roof and shape. Unlike many tiny homes this one hides its kitchen behind a wall that separates the kitchen from the front room. A storage staircase is clearly visible as you enter the home. A table for two is on the left and a sofa is on the right. The bathroom is located behind the kitchen and has a soaking tub, toilet, and vanity. The bathroom extends over the trailer tongue in a bump-out extension.

Features:

20-Foot Tiny House on Wheels
Gable Roof
Front Porch
Bathroom with Soaking Tub/Shower
Table for Two
Sleeps Two
Storage Stairs

Kitchen

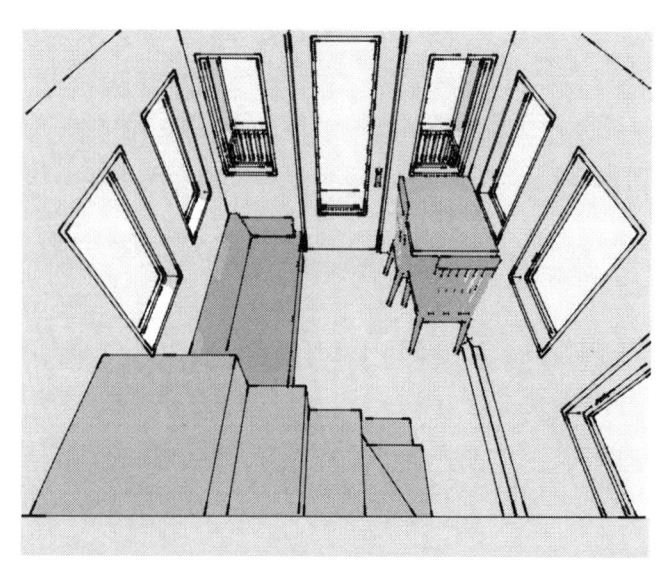

View from Loft

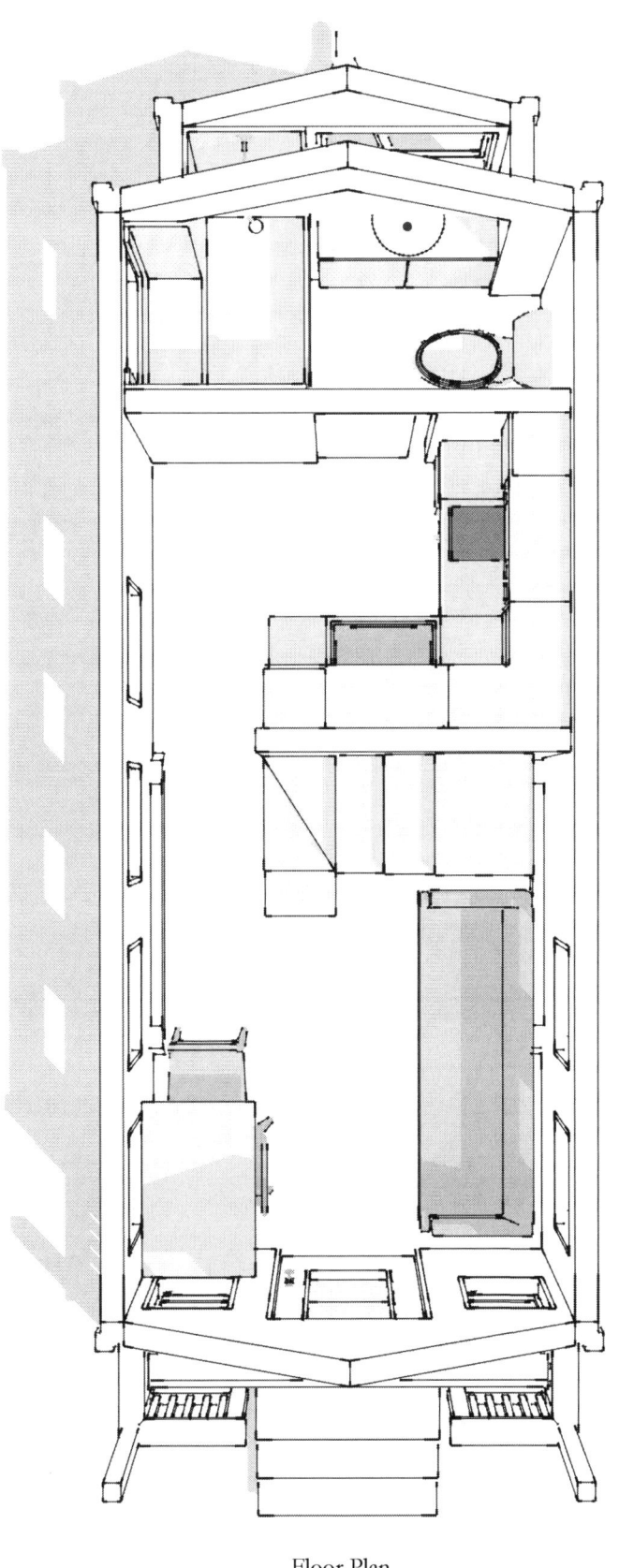

Tiny House #50 - Floor Plan & Exterior

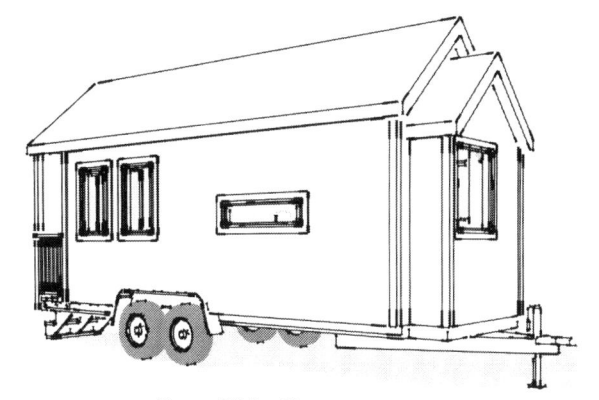

Front Right Corner

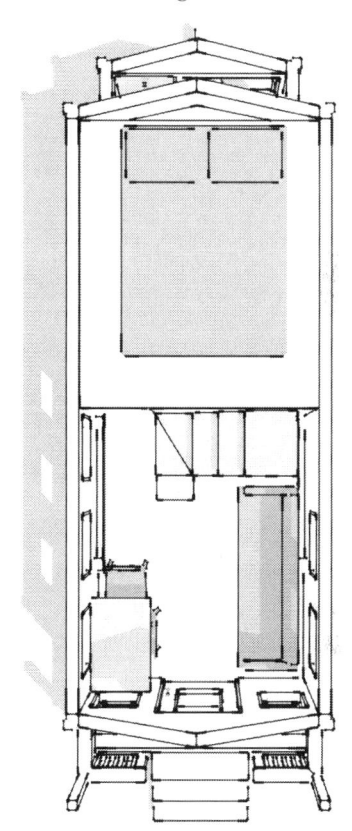

Floor Plan - Loft

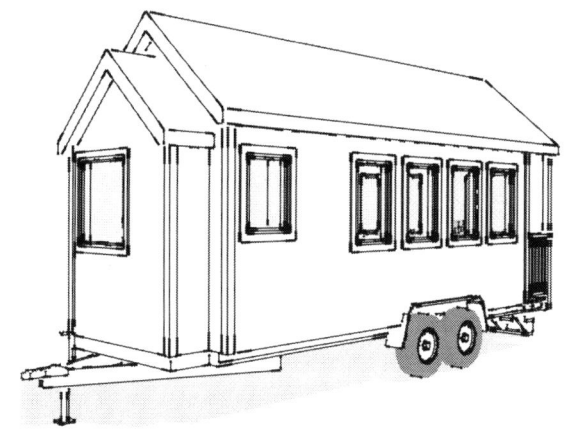

Floor Plan

Back Left Corner

Tiny House #50 - Interior Views

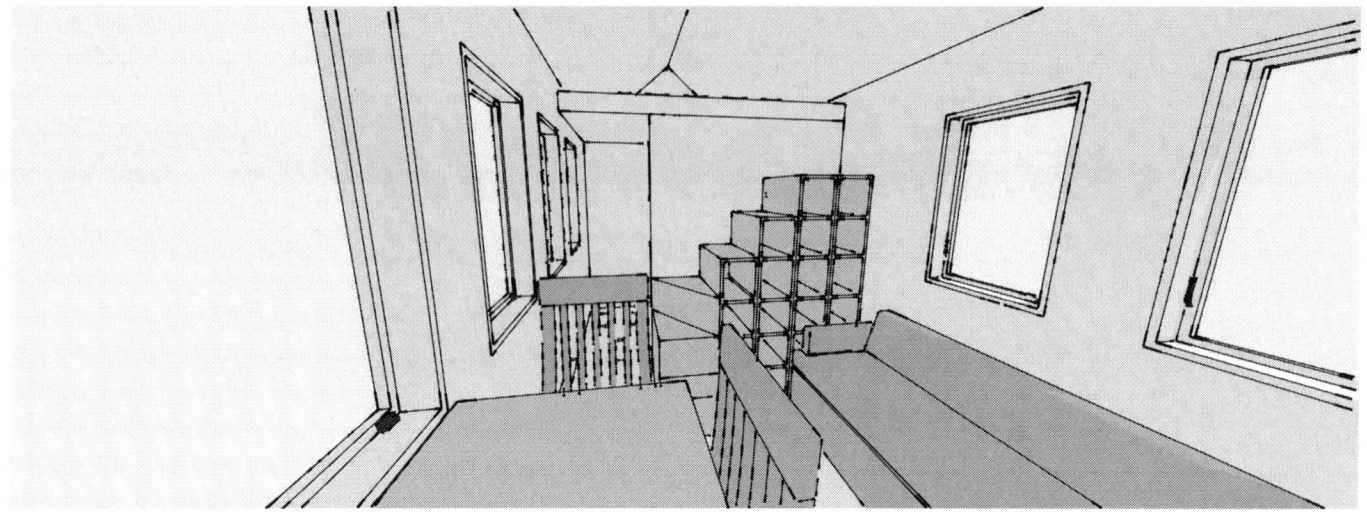

Interior

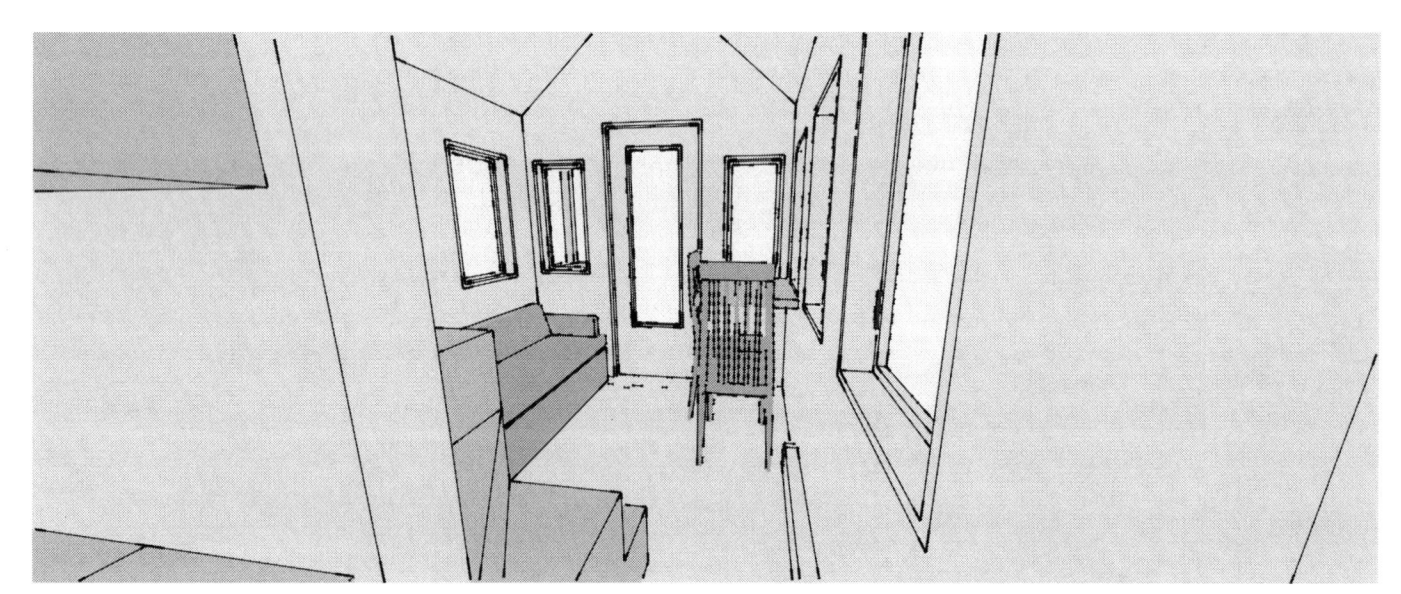

Interior from Kitchen

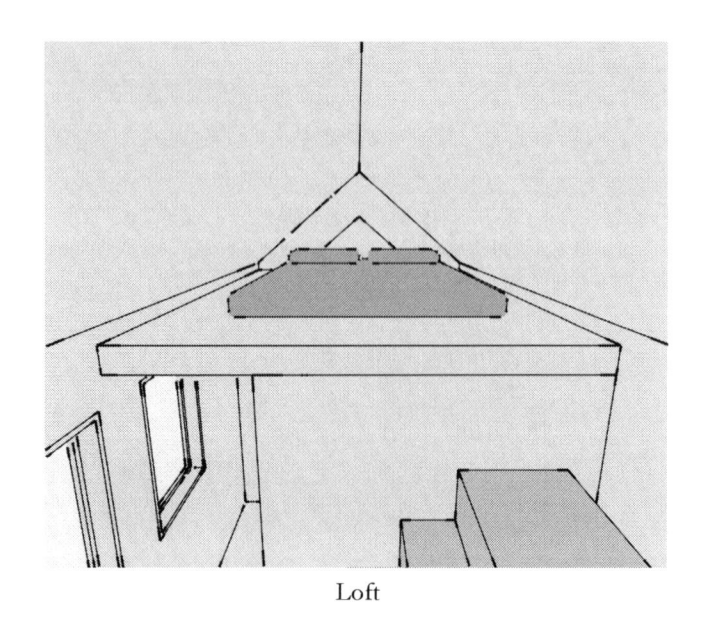

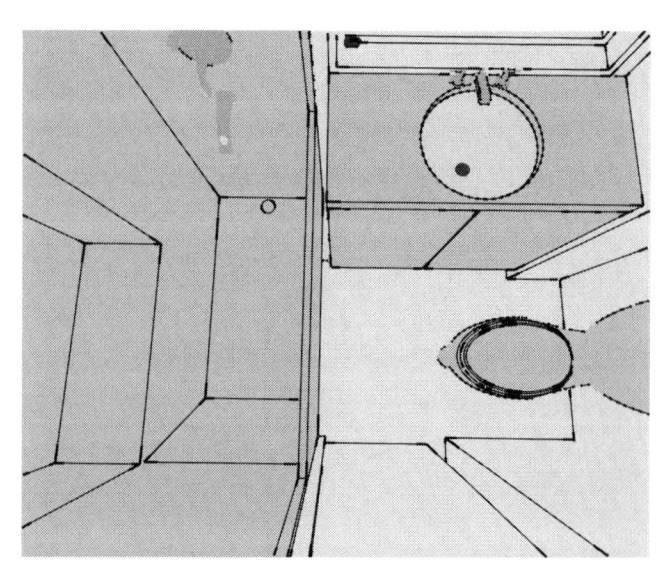

Loft

Bathroom

Tiny House #50 - Elevations

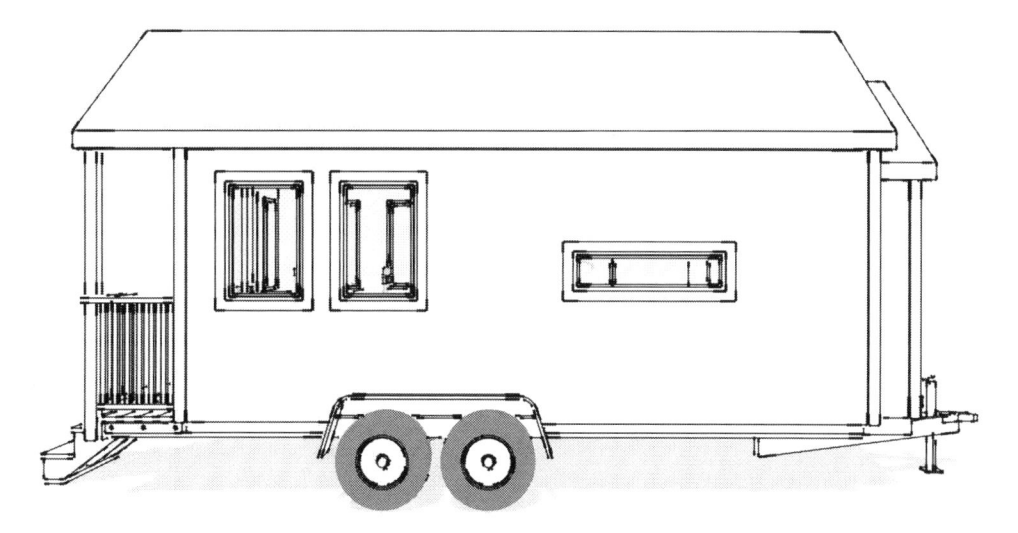

Right

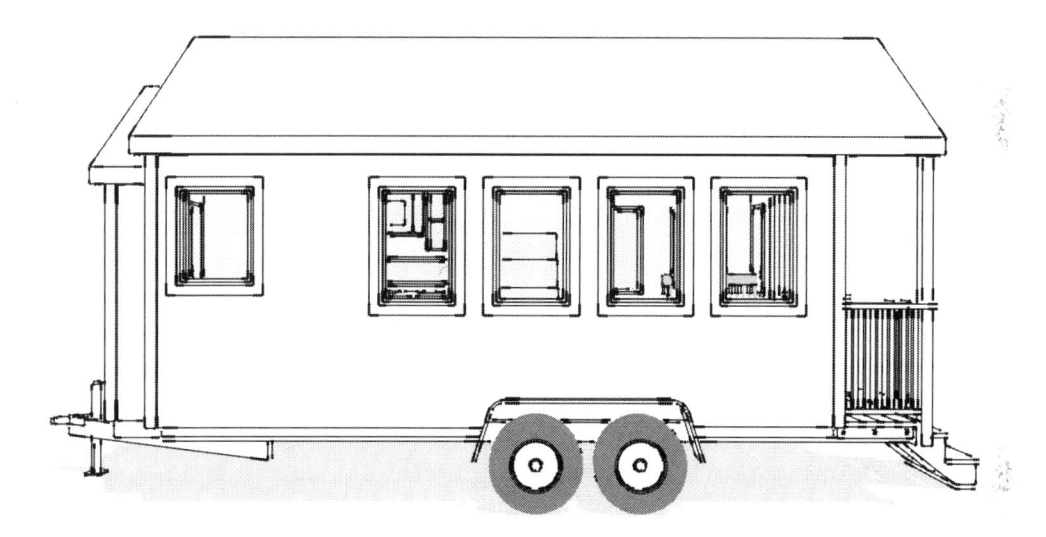

Left

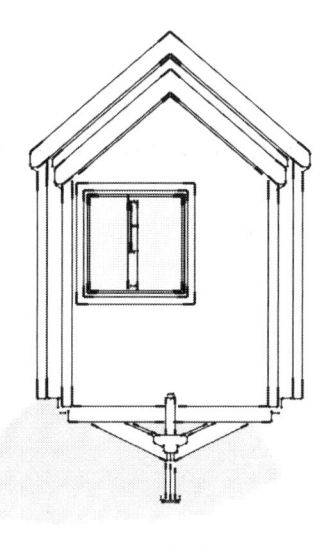

Back

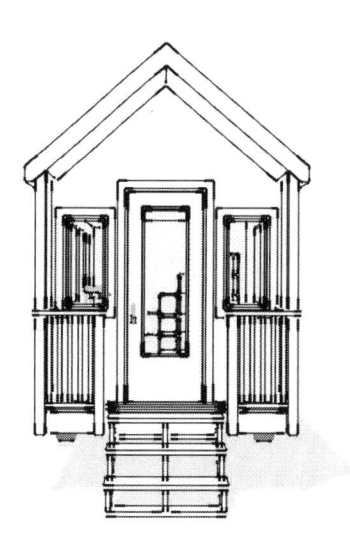

Front

#51

Tiny House #51 - Overview

Front Right

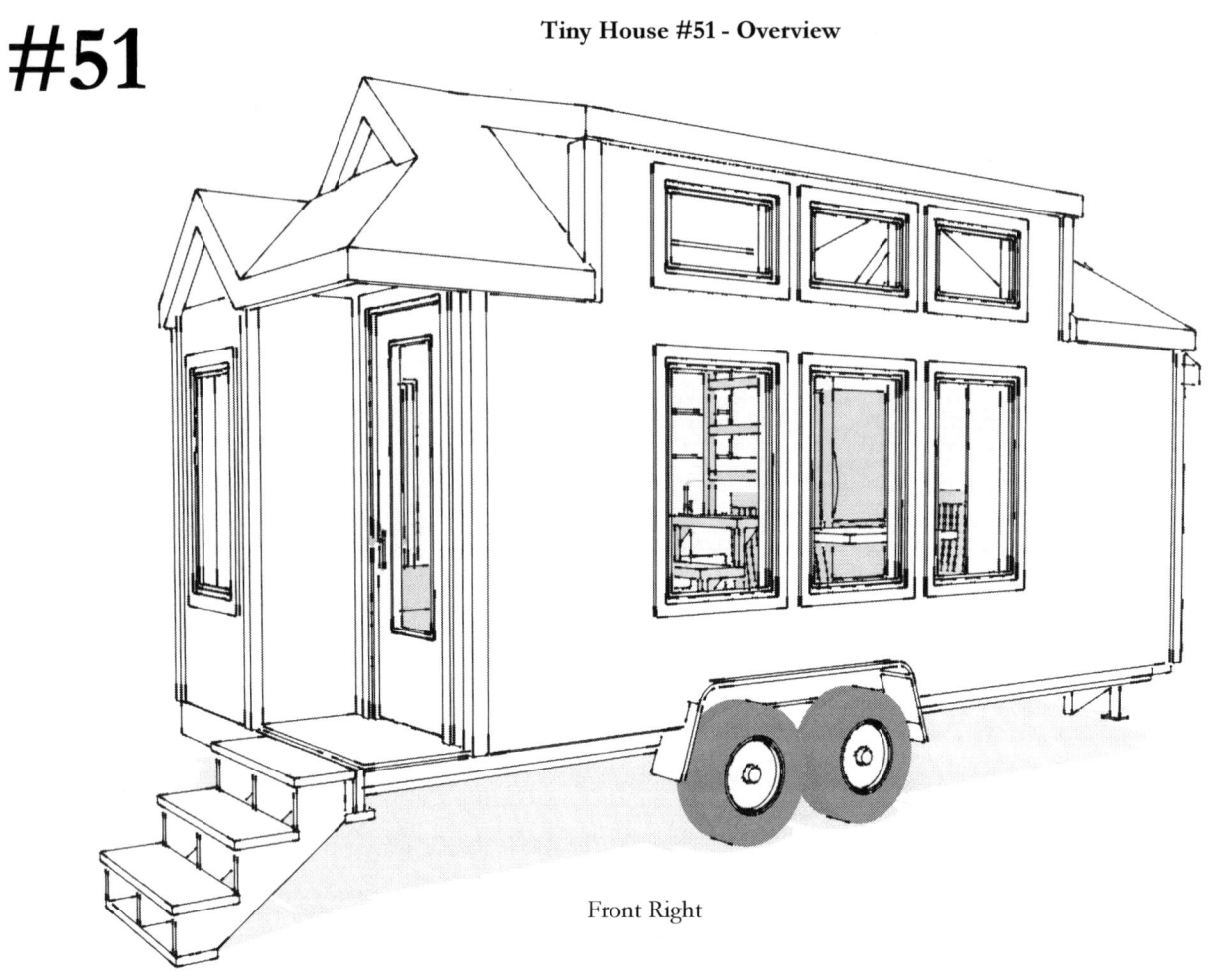

Summary:

A combination staircase and ladder is immediately inside the front door of this tiny house. The thought is that one would climb the four stairs and then just have a couple more feet to climb up. To the left, as you step inside the house, is a sofa and beyond that is the kitchen and a table for three. At the back of the house is a standard bathroom with a shower, toilet, and sink. Outside, over the trailer tongue, is a utility closet. Above the kitchen, table, and bathroom is the loft.

Features:

20-Foot Tiny House on Wheels
Dutch Gable Roof with Shed Dormers
Inset Entry
Standard Bathroom
Table for Three
Sleeps Two
Combination Stairs with Ladder

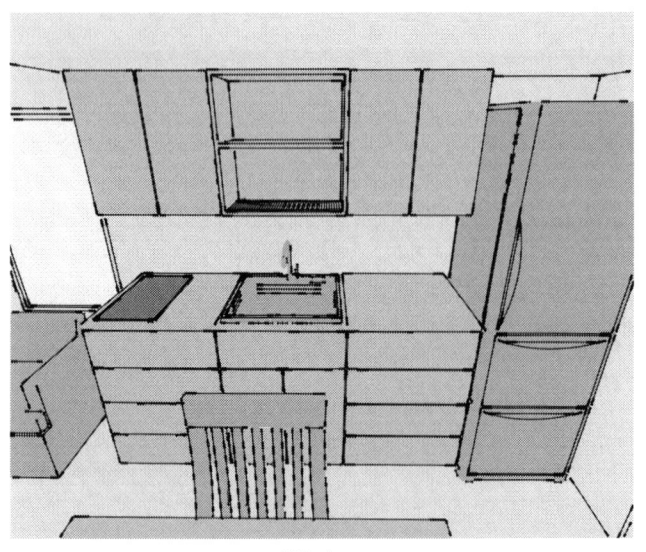

Kitchen

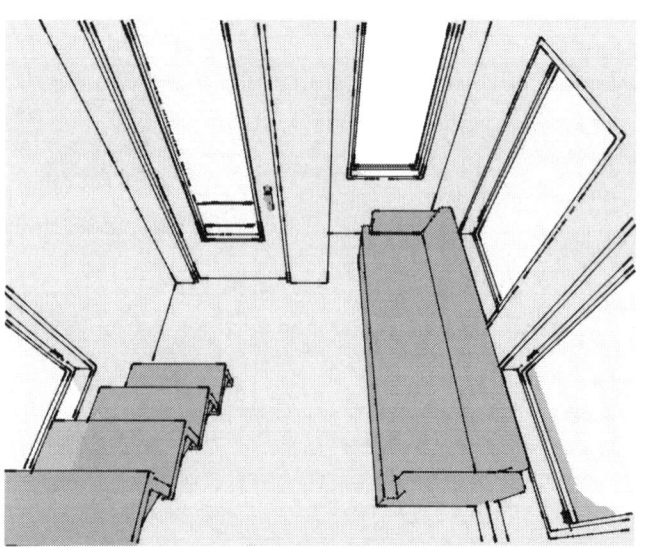

View from Loft

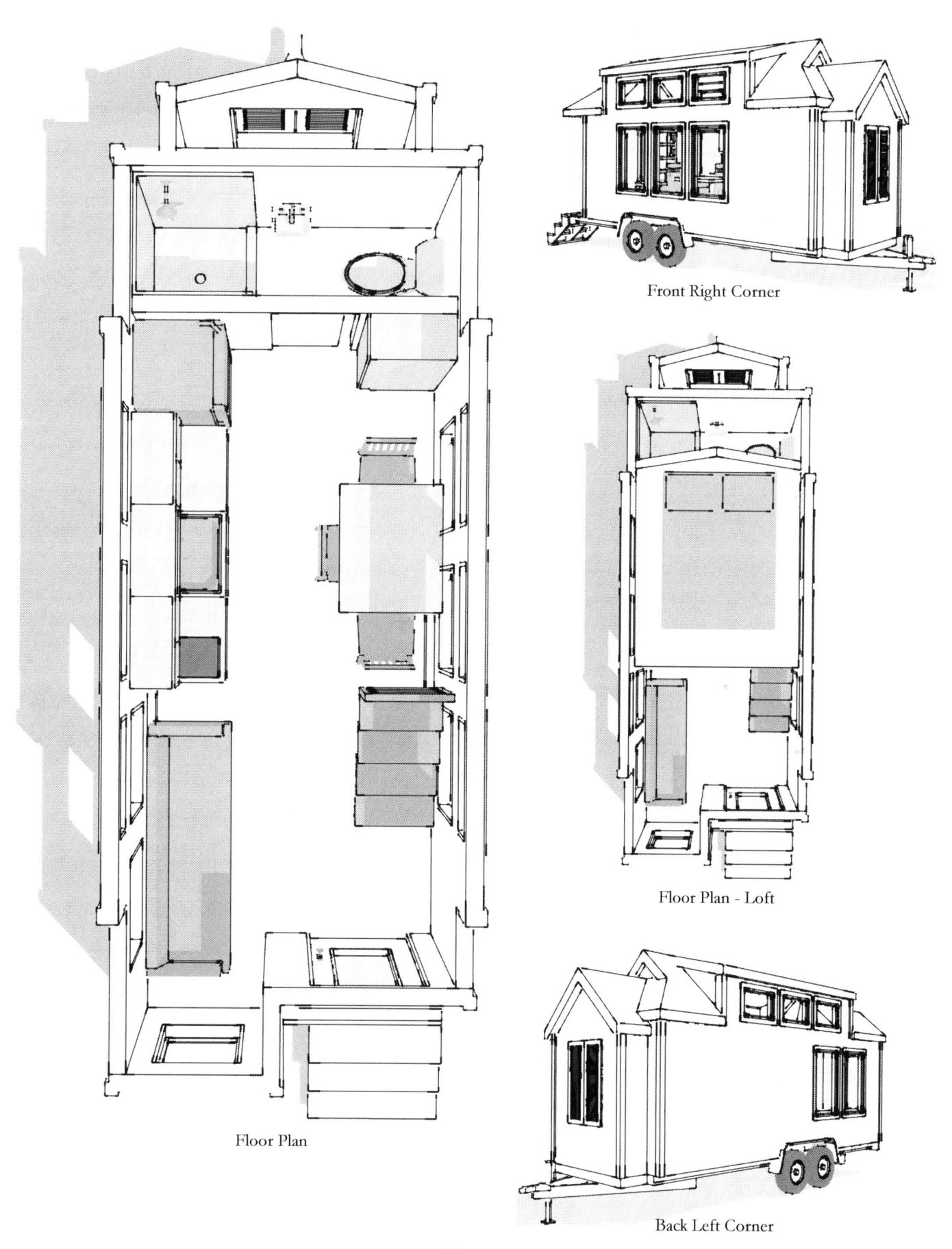

Tiny House #51 - Floor Plan & Exterior

Front Right Corner

Floor Plan - Loft

Floor Plan

Back Left Corner

Tiny House #51 - Interior Views

Interior from Entry

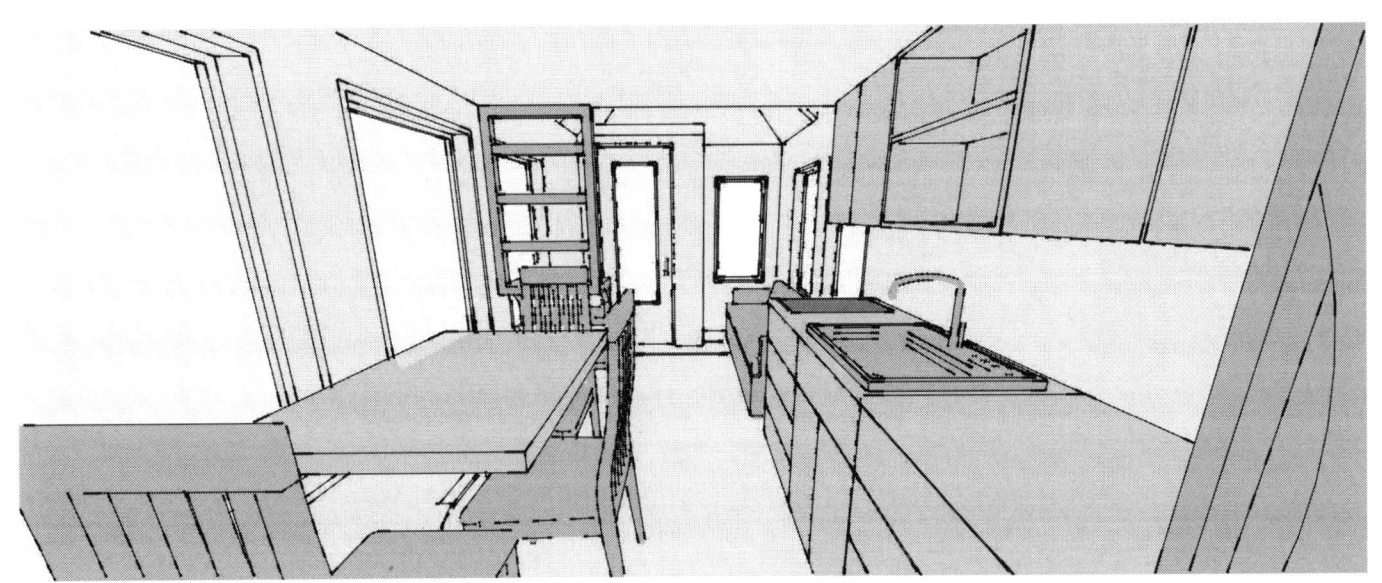

Interior from Kitchen

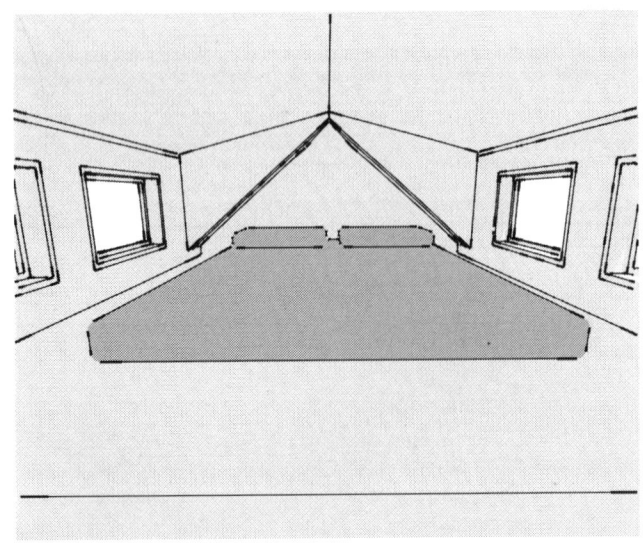

Loft

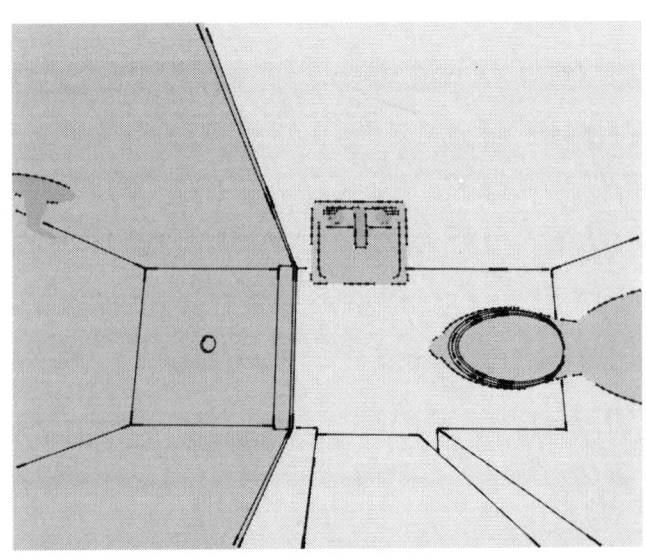

Bathroom

Tiny House #51 - Elevations

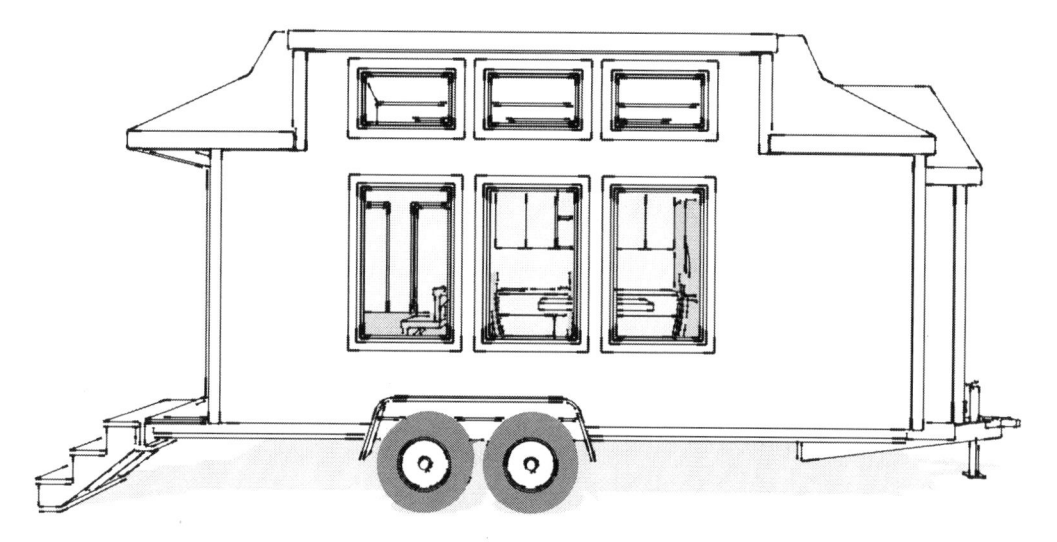

Right

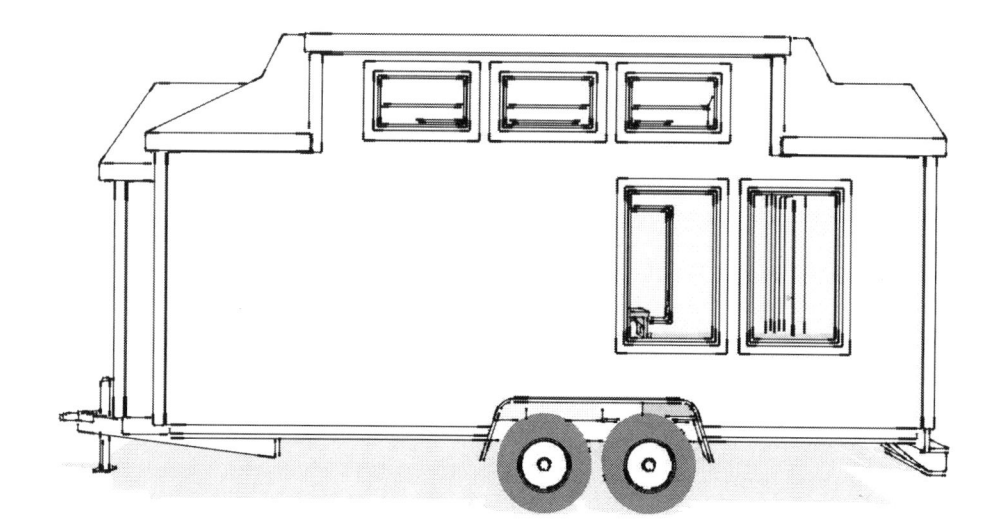

Left

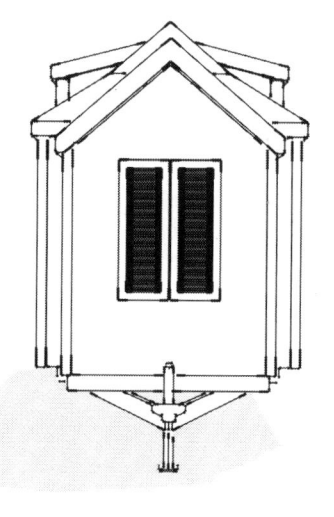

Back

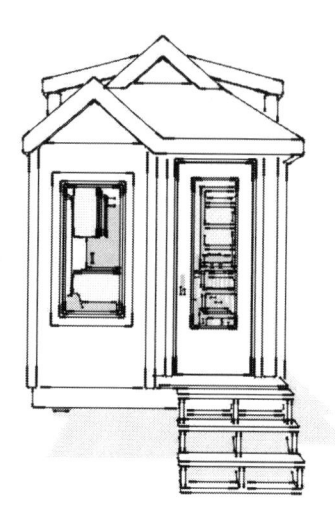

Front

#52

Tiny House #52 - Overview

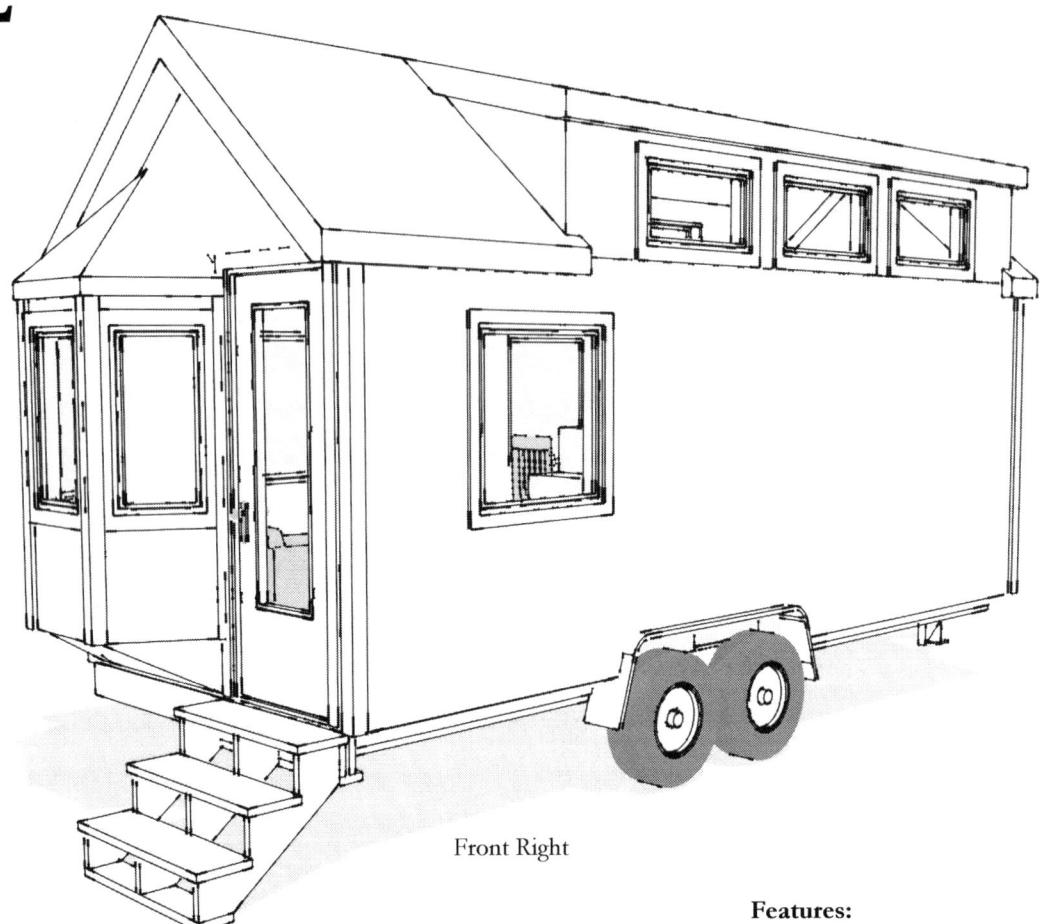

Front Right

Summary:

At the center of this house is a small but functional kitchen that has a full size refrigerator, range, sink and storage. It only lacks counter space. Across from the kitchen is a table for three - which in a pinch might make-up for the minimal counter space. At the back of the house is a bathroom that extends into a bay window over the trailer tongue. Above the kitchen and bathroom is a loft with a queen bed. Storage stairs just inside the front door will take you up to the loft. At the very front of the house is a desk that's tucked into another bay window.

Features:

20-Foot Tiny House on Wheels
Gable Roof with Shed Dormers
Bathroom with Vanity and Shower
Table for Three
Sleeps Two
Stairs to Loft

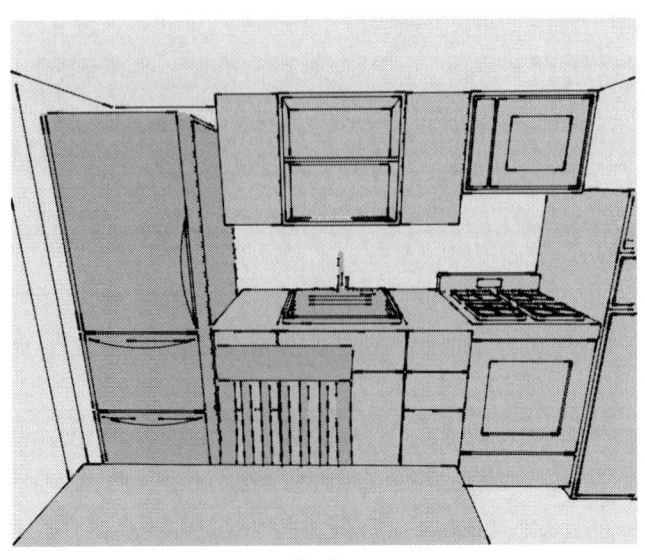

Kitchen

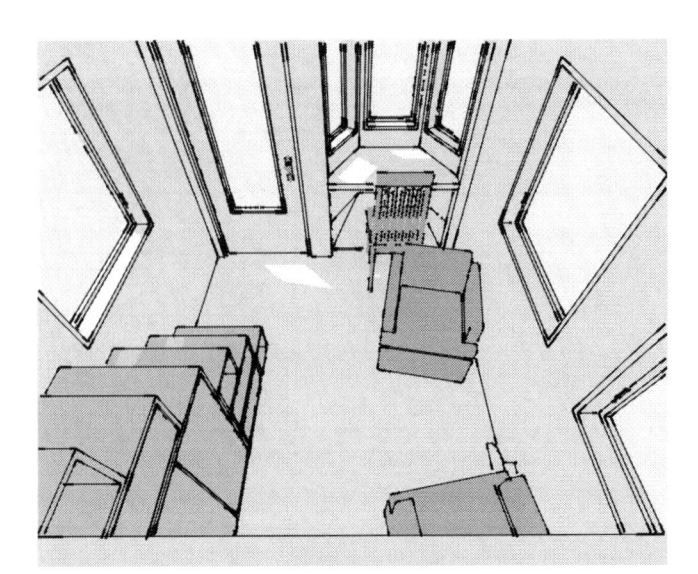

View from Loft

Tiny House #52 - Floor Plan & Exterior

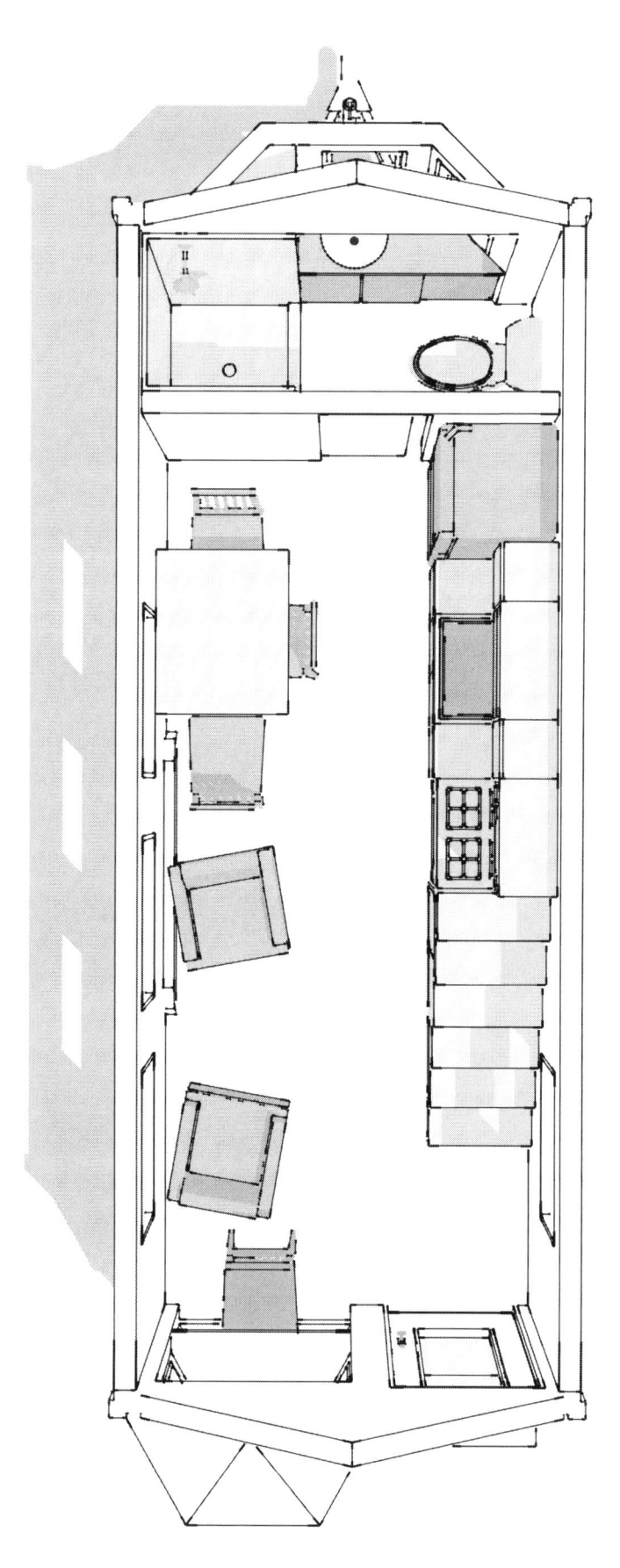

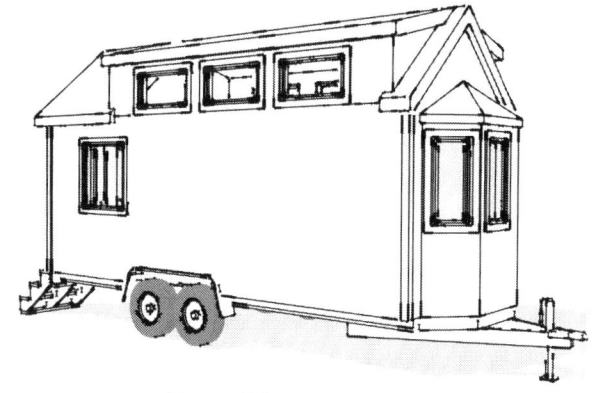

Front Right Corner

Floor Plan - Loft

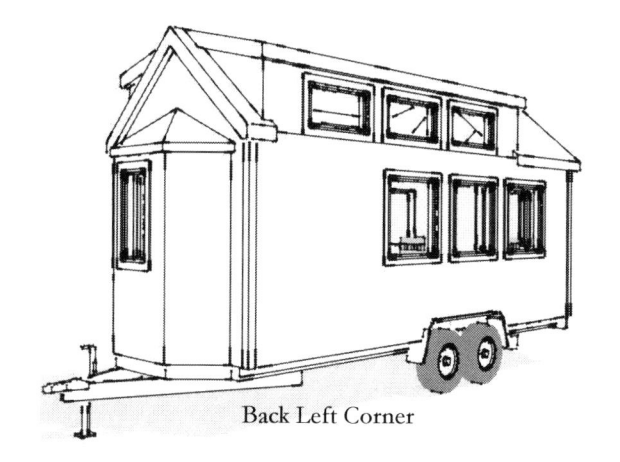

Floor Plan

Back Left Corner

Tiny House #52 - Interior Views

Interior

Interior from Kitchen

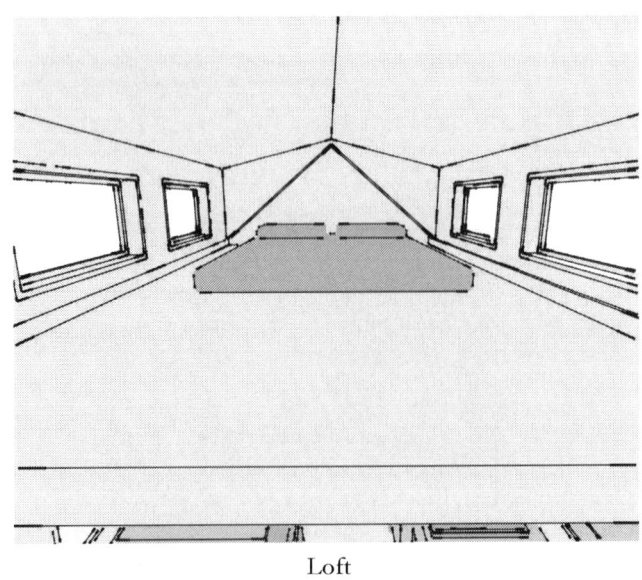

Loft

Bathroom

216

Tiny House #52 - Elevations

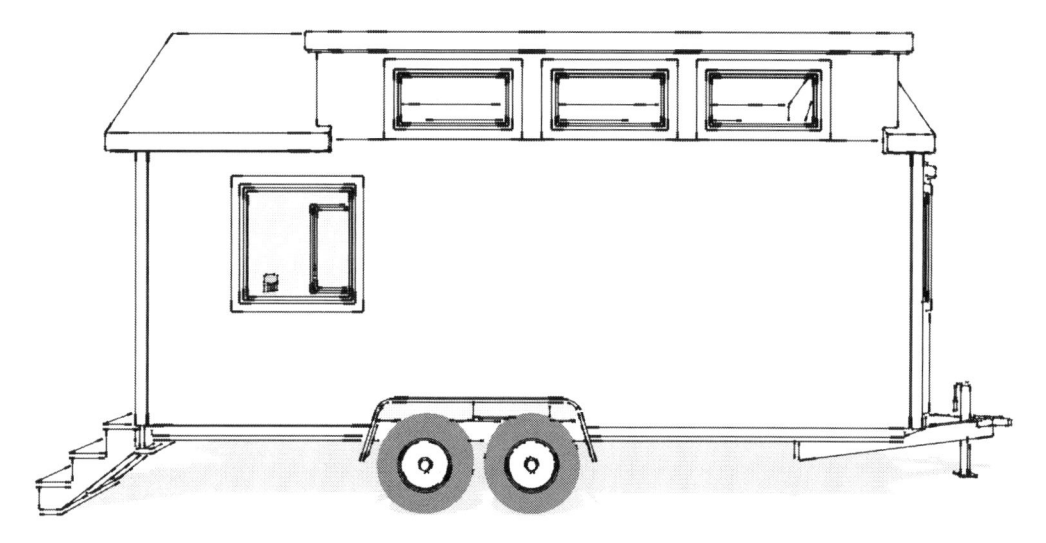

Right

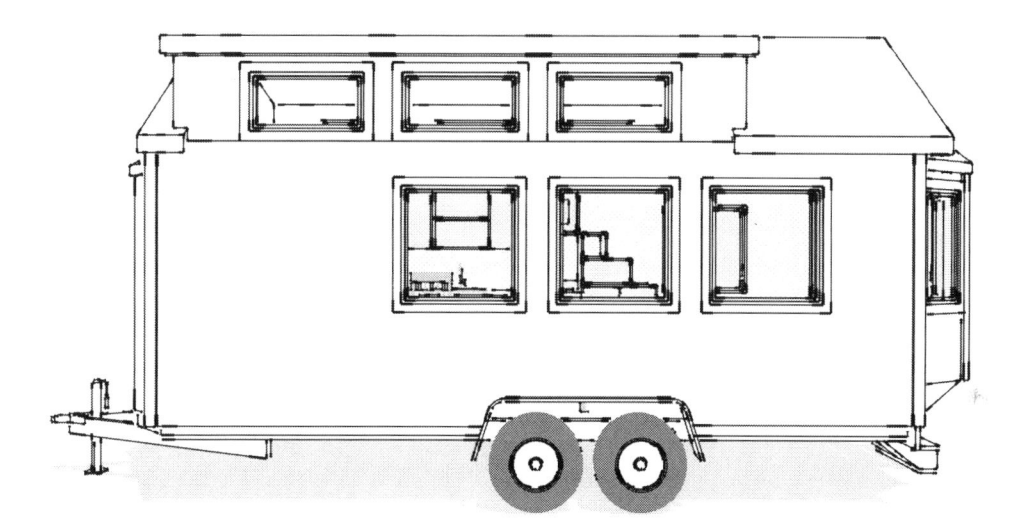

Left

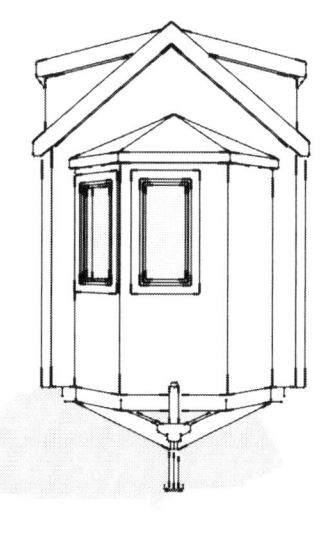

Back

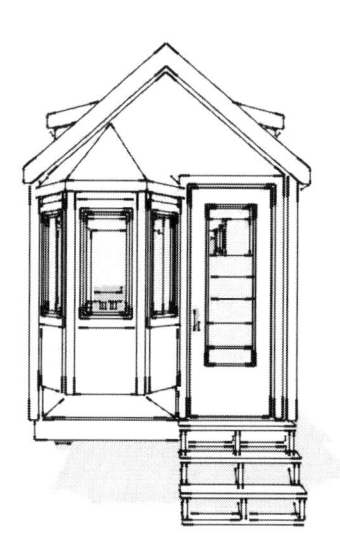

Front

#53

Tiny House #53 - Overview

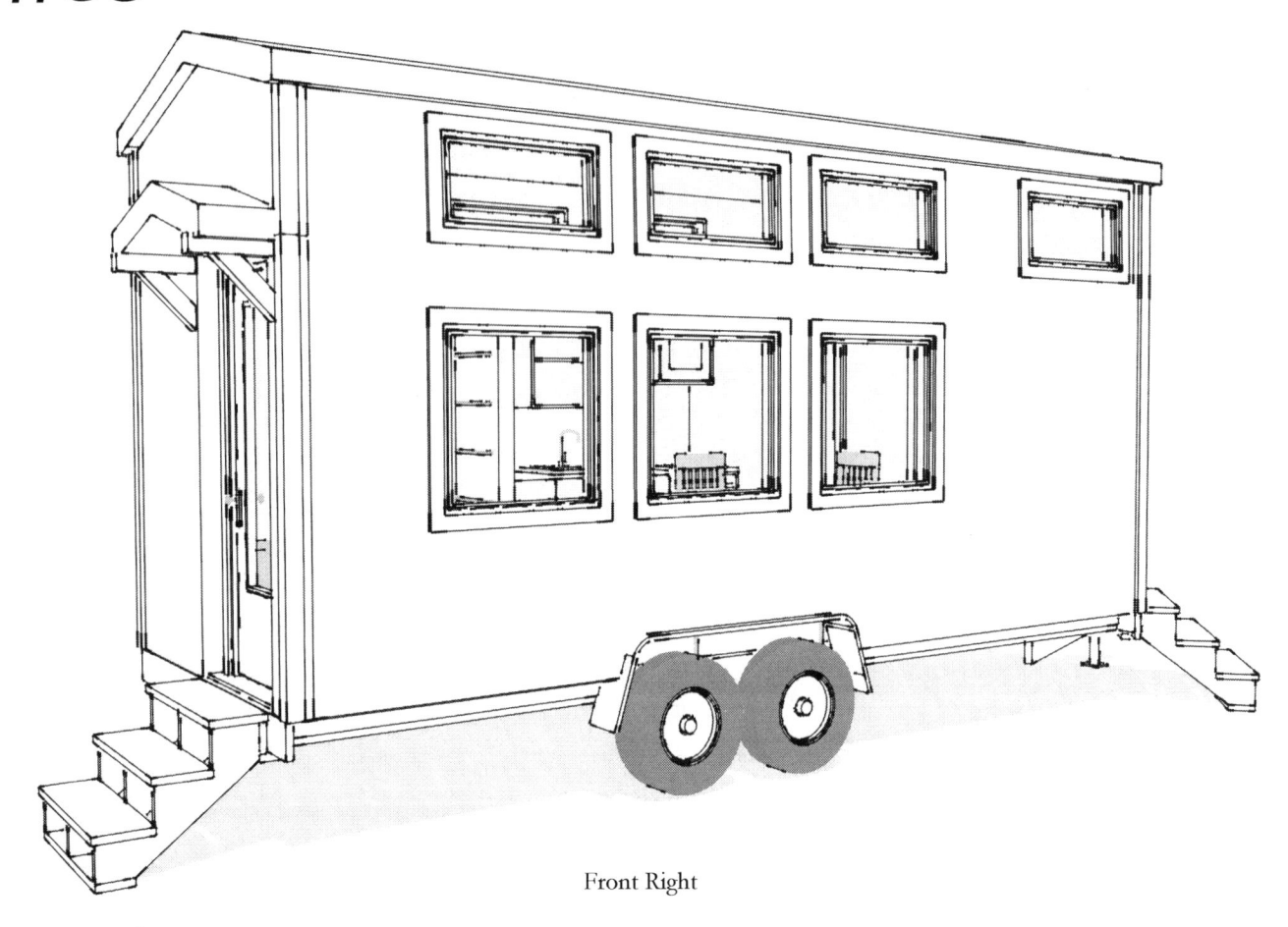

Front Right

Summary:

Sometimes you want two doors in a tiny house. This house has a high ceiling bathroom with a tub and an exterior door over the trailer tongue. A pocket door connects the bathroom to the kitchen. At the center of the house is a kitchen and table for three. At the front of the house are two comfy chairs and an ottoman. Above the kitchen is a loft with a queen bed.

Features:

20-Foot Tiny House on Wheels
High 3/12 Gable Roof
Two Entries
Bathroom with Soaking Tub
Sleeps Two
Ladder to Loft

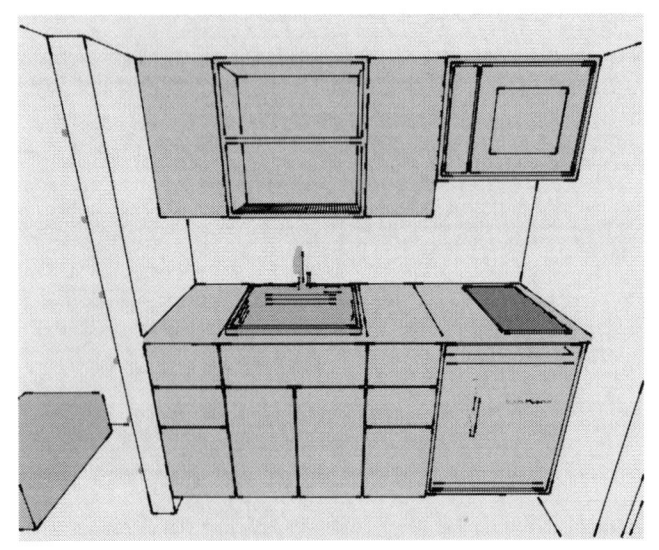

Kitchen

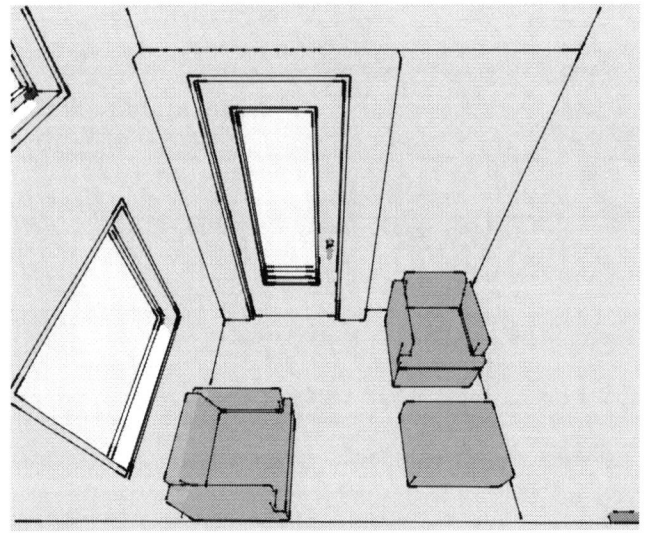

View from Loft

Tiny House #53 - Floor Plan & Exterior

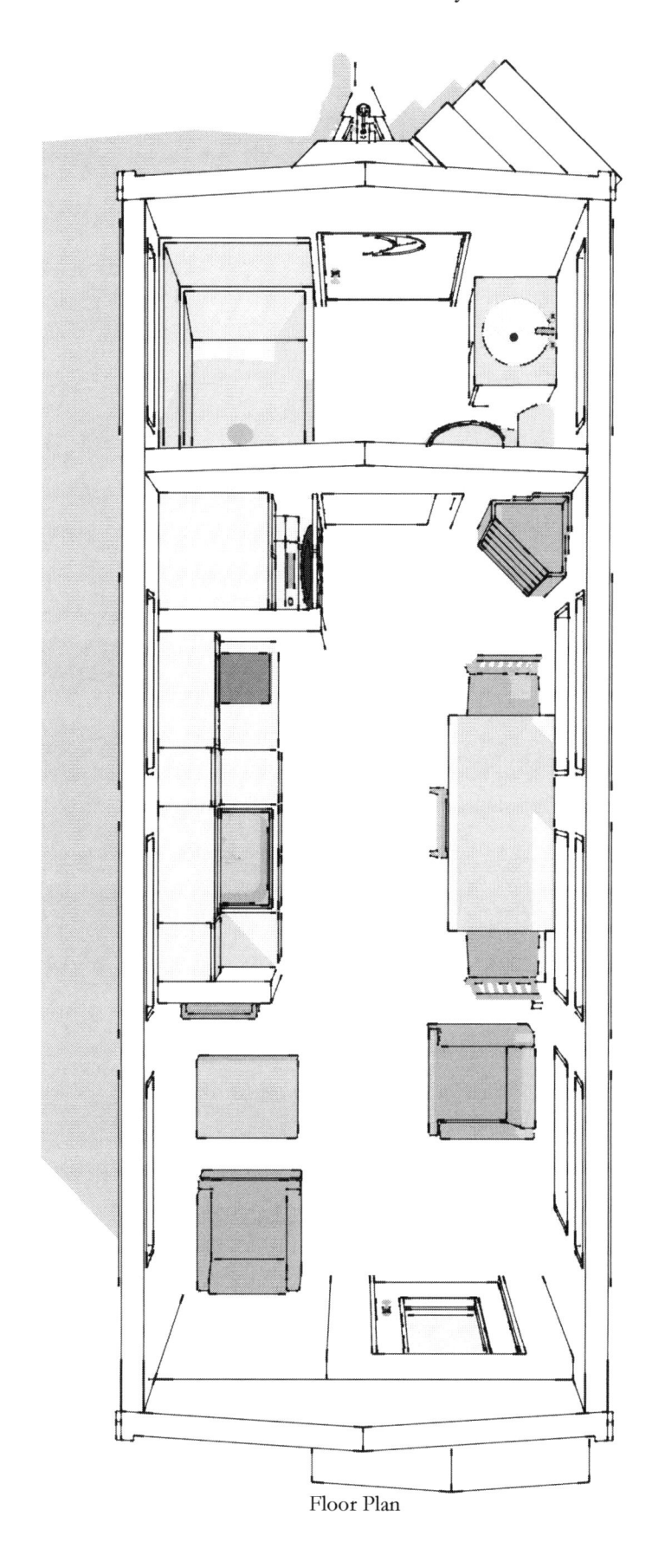

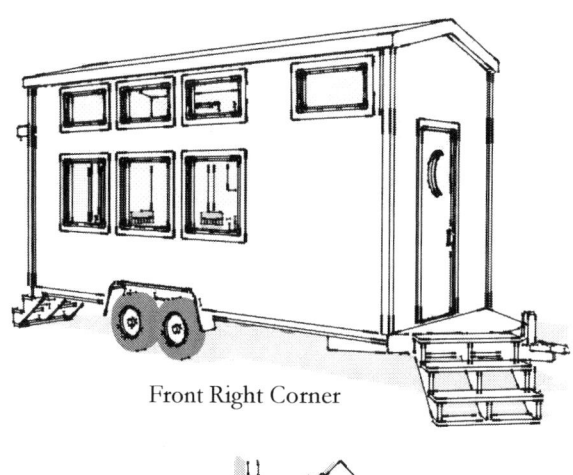

Front Right Corner

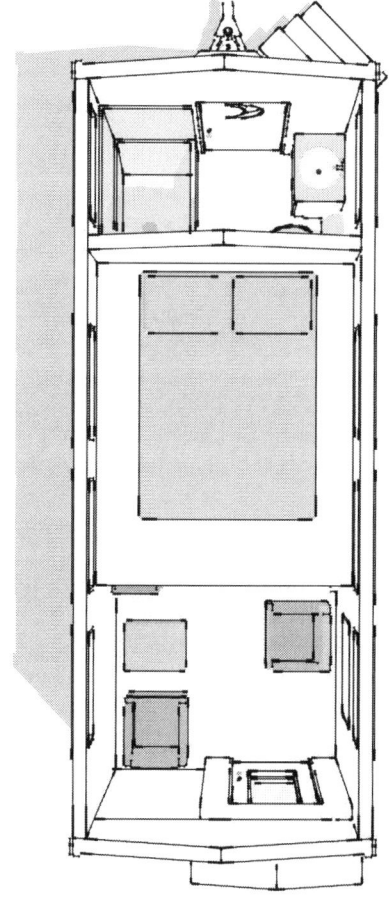

Floor Plan - Loft

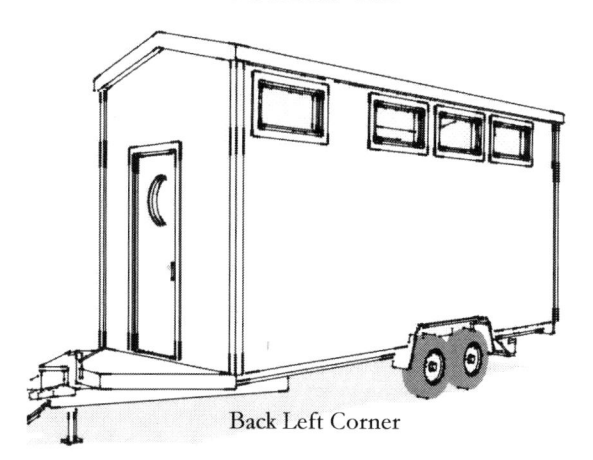

Floor Plan

Back Left Corner

Tiny House #53 - Interior Views

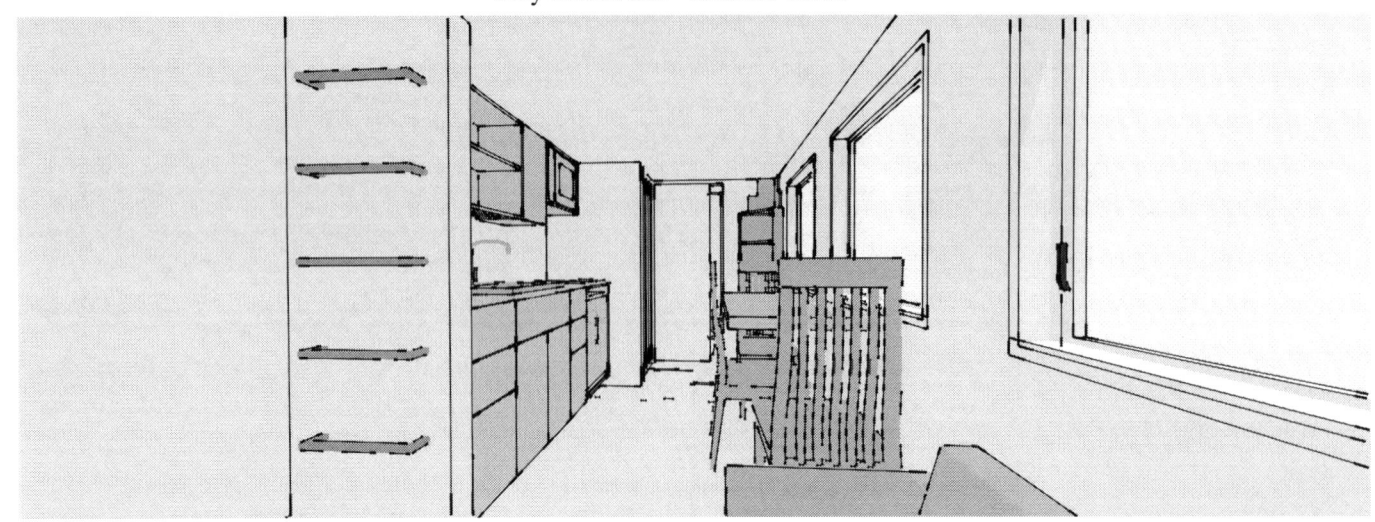

Interior from Entry

Interior from Kitchen

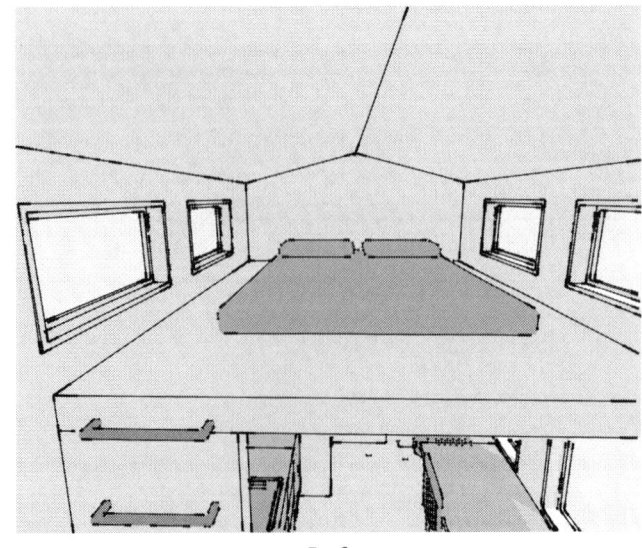

Loft

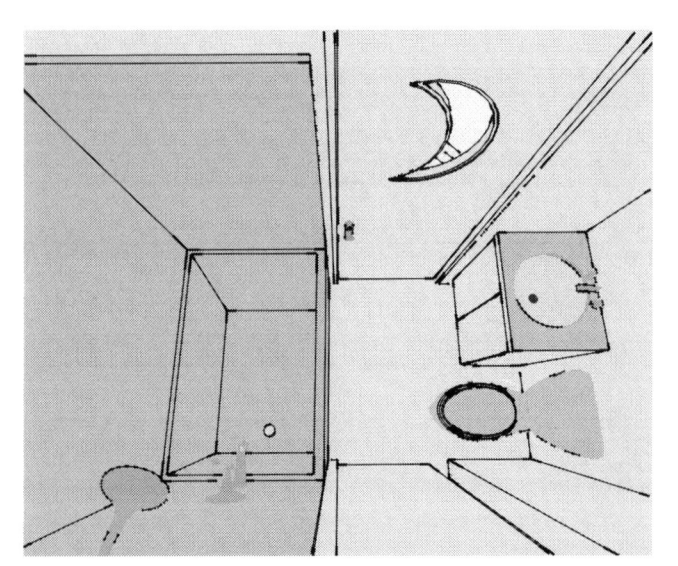

Bathroom

220

Tiny House #53 - Elevations

Right

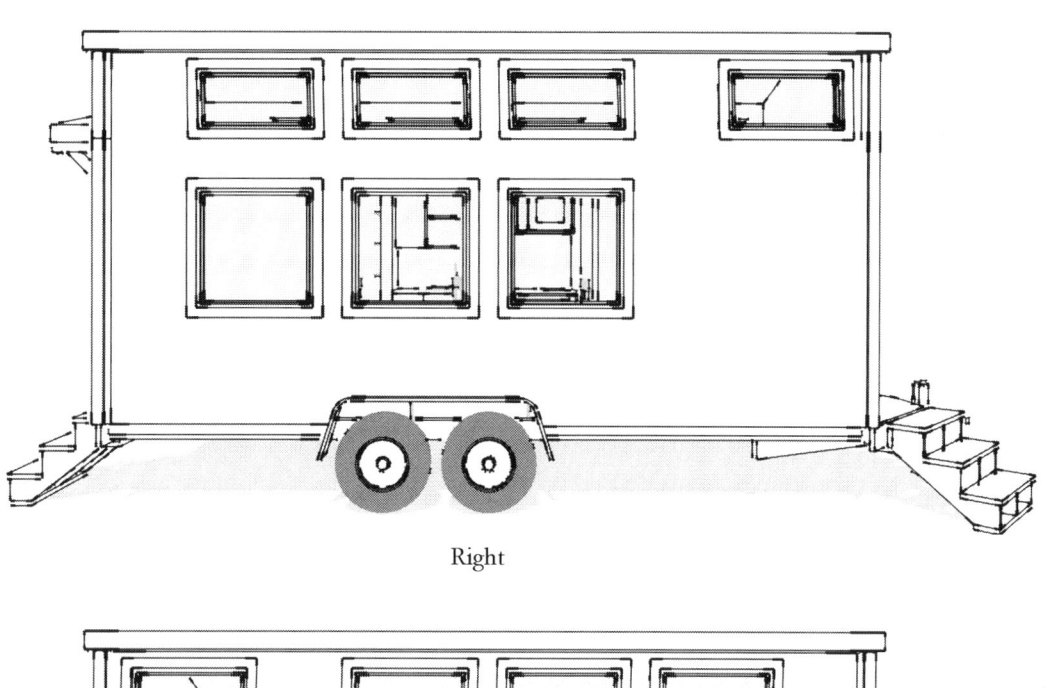

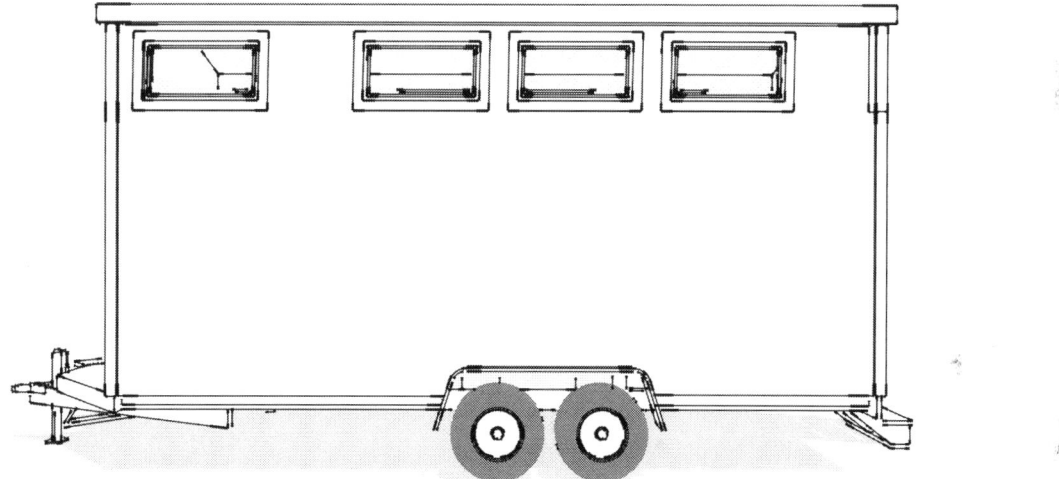

Left

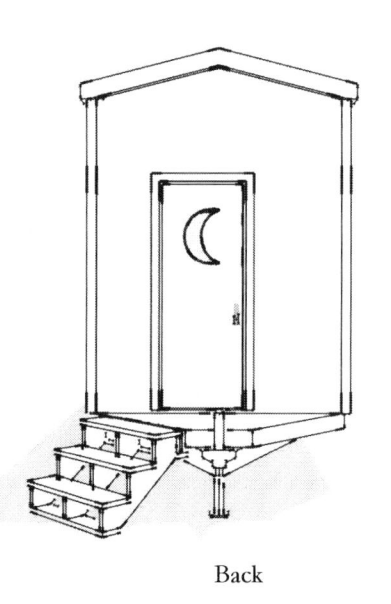

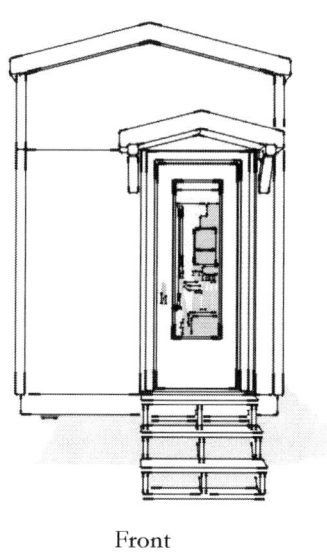

Back

Front

#54

Tiny House #54 - Overview

Front Right

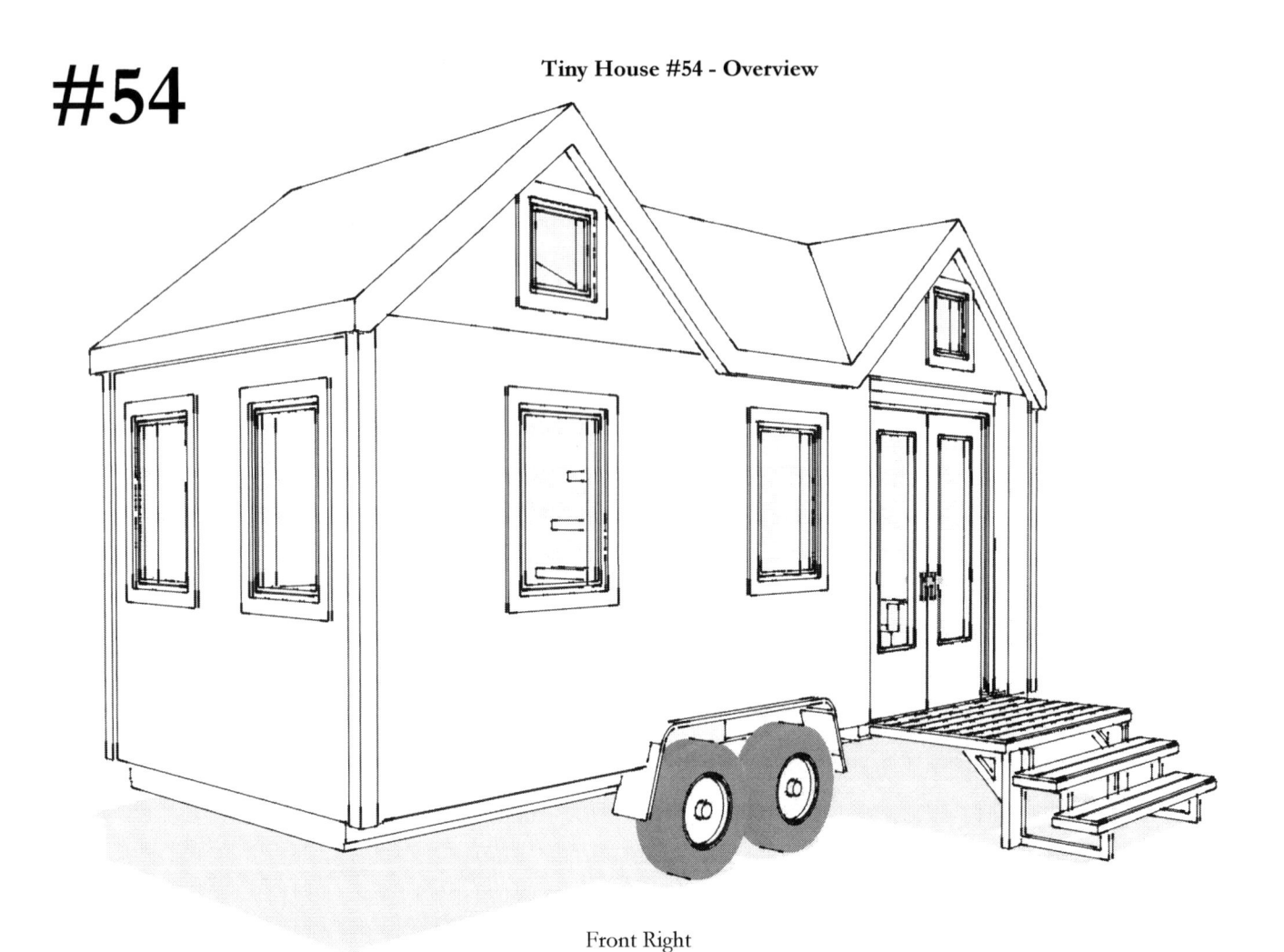

Summary:

At the center of this house is a small kitchen and bathroom that can be closed off from the living room and dining room. Just inside the side entry is a built in sofa. Passing through the kitchen you find the dining room. From either side of the house you can climb into the loft by climbing some dual use shelves/ladder. Lofts with two open ends rarely suffer from stuffiness.

Features:

20-Foot Tiny House on Wheels
10/12 Gable Roof
Side Entry with Fold-up Deck
Small Bathroom
Sleeps Two
Two Ladders to the Loft

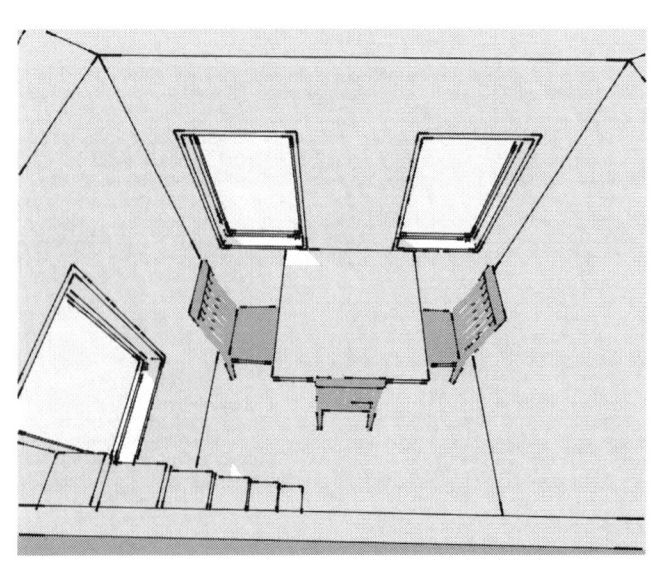

Kitchen

View from Loft

Tiny House #54 - Floor Plan & Exterior

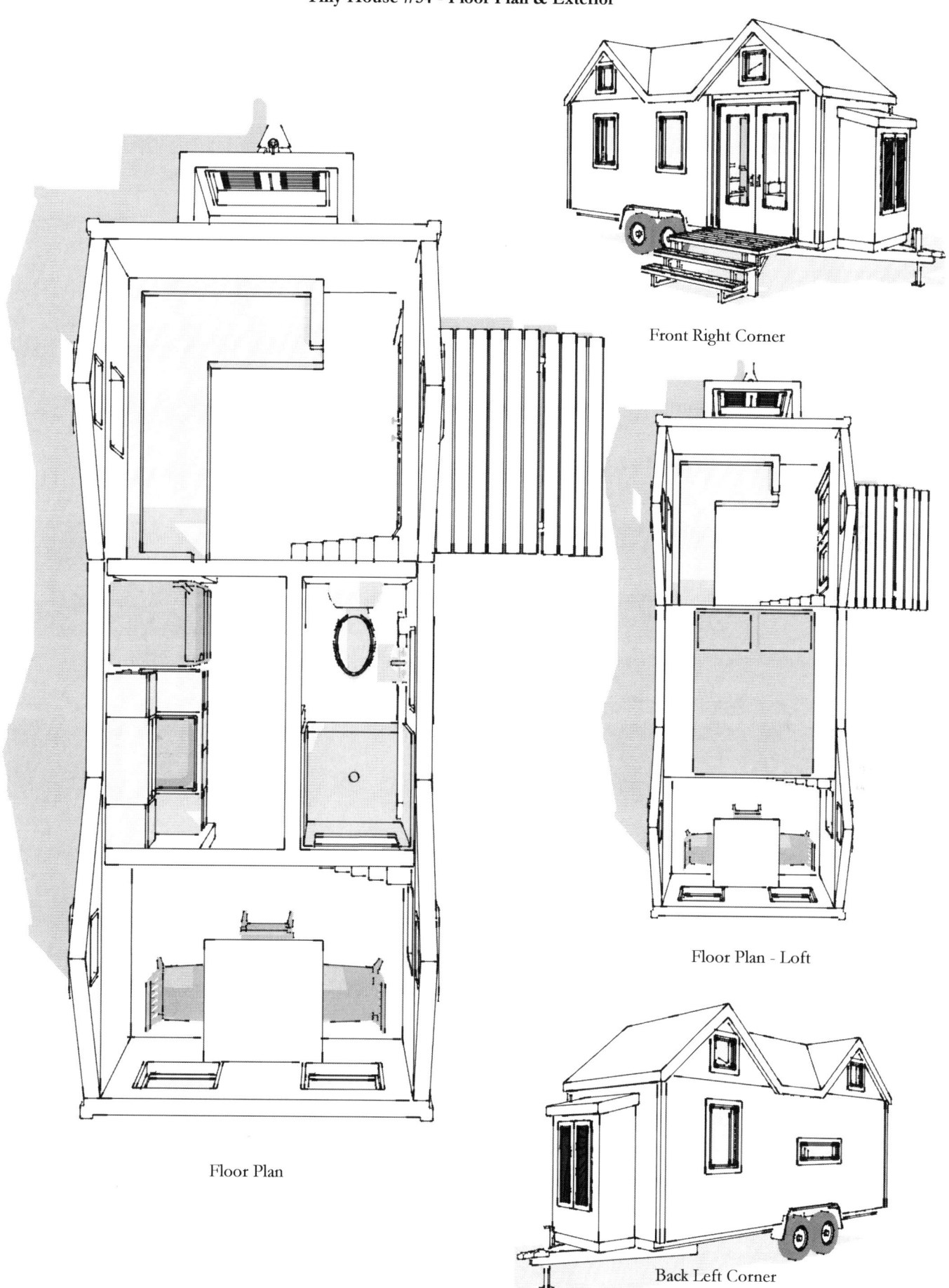

Front Right Corner

Floor Plan - Loft

Floor Plan

Back Left Corner

Tiny House #54 - Interior Views

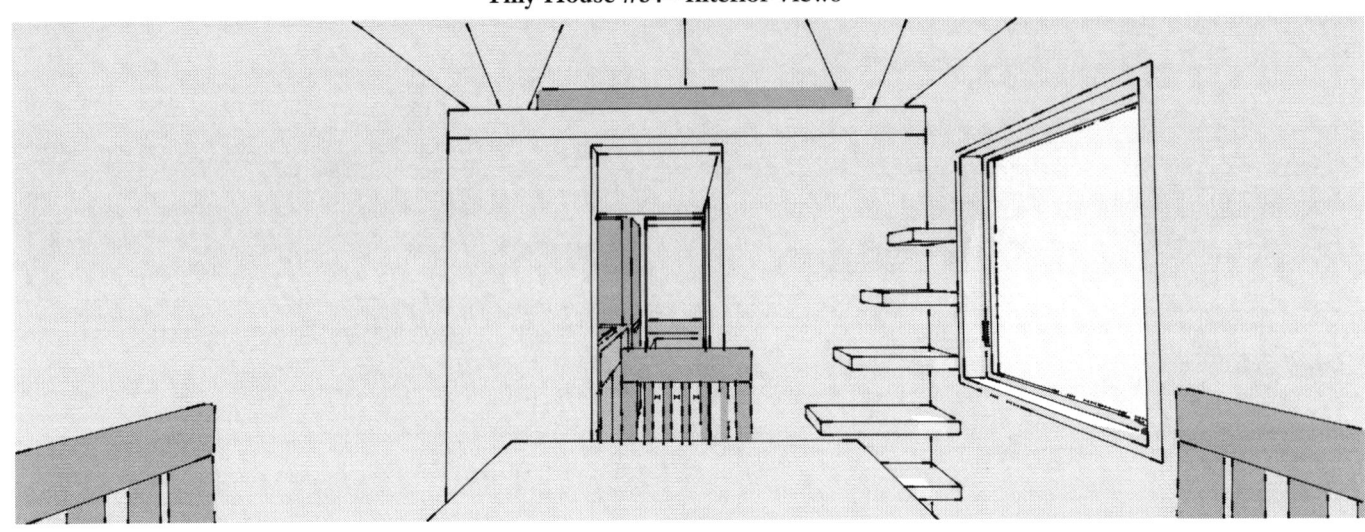

Interior

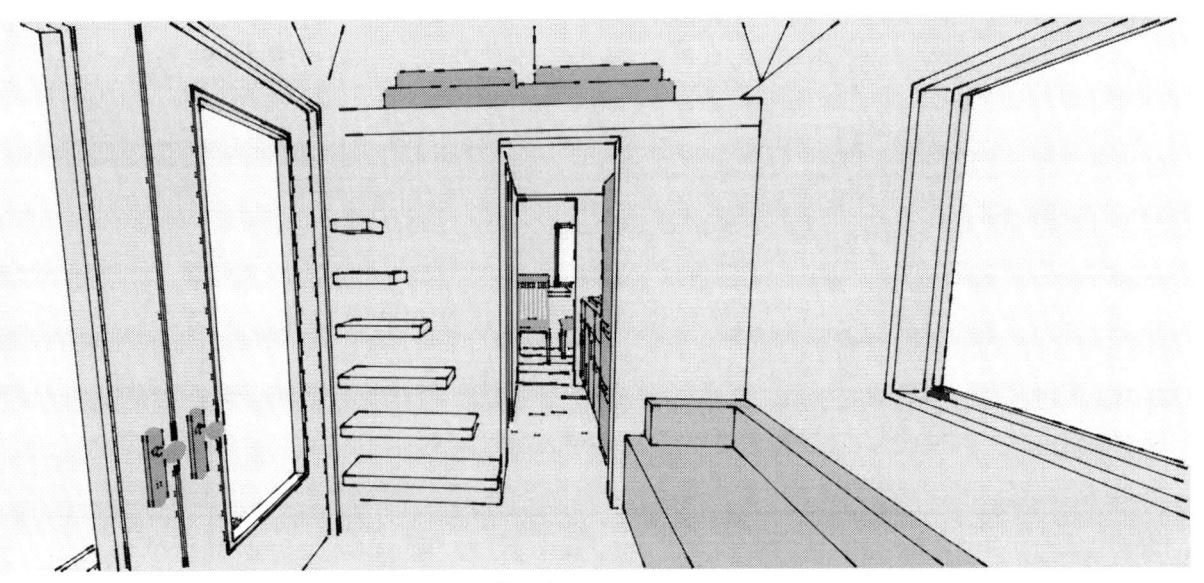

Interior

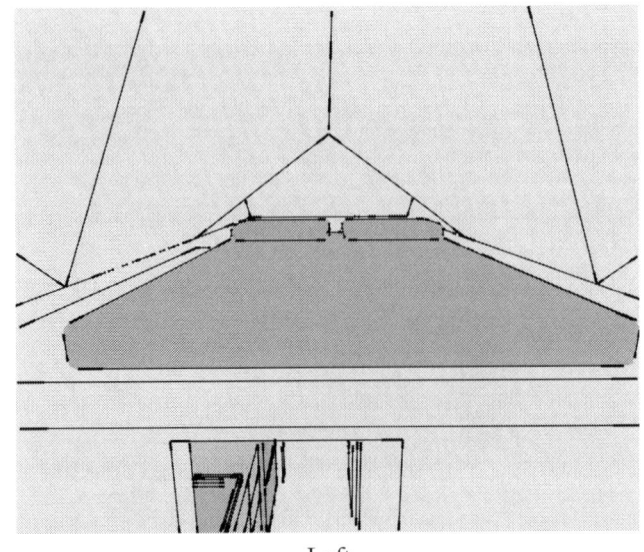

Loft

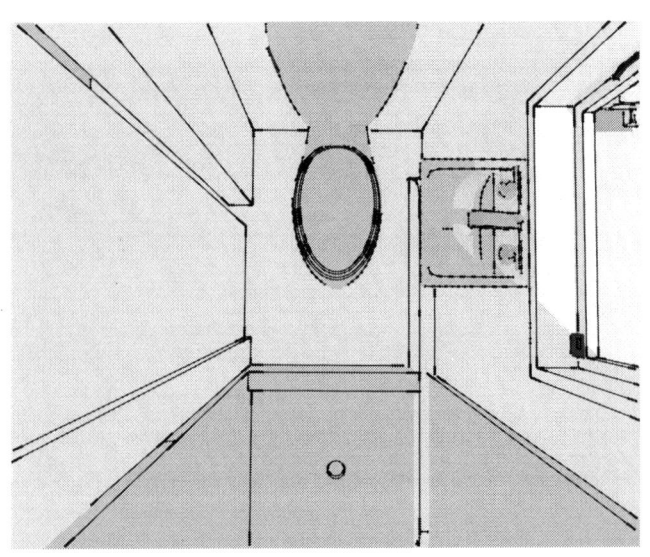

Bathroom

224

Tiny House #54 - Elevations

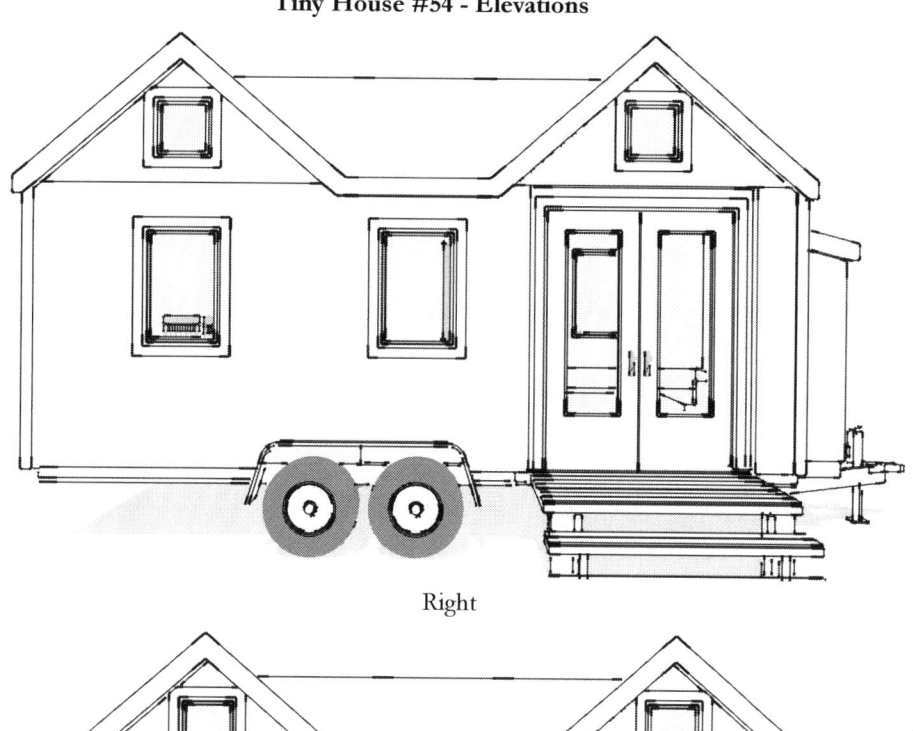

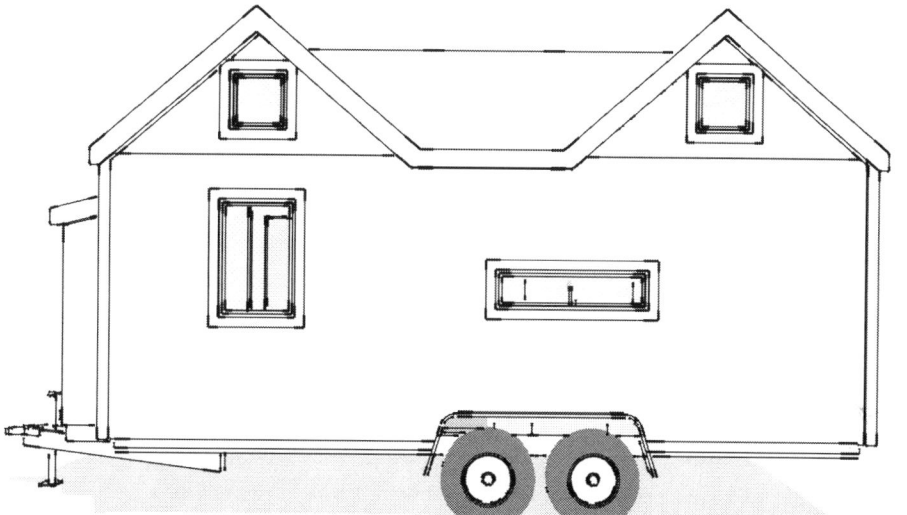

Right

Left

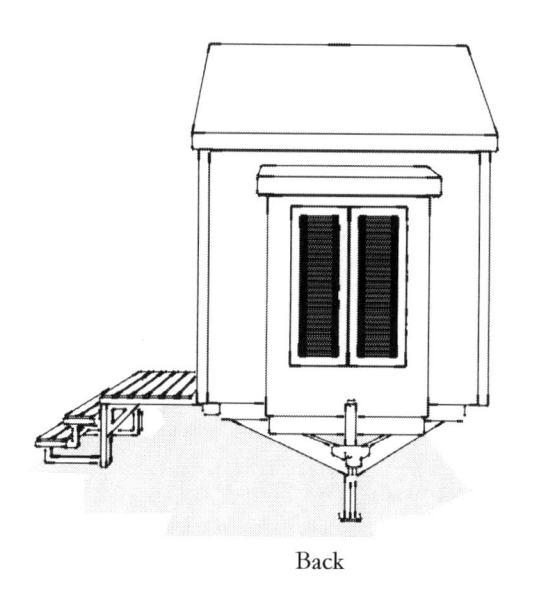

Back

Front

#55

Tiny House #55 - Overview

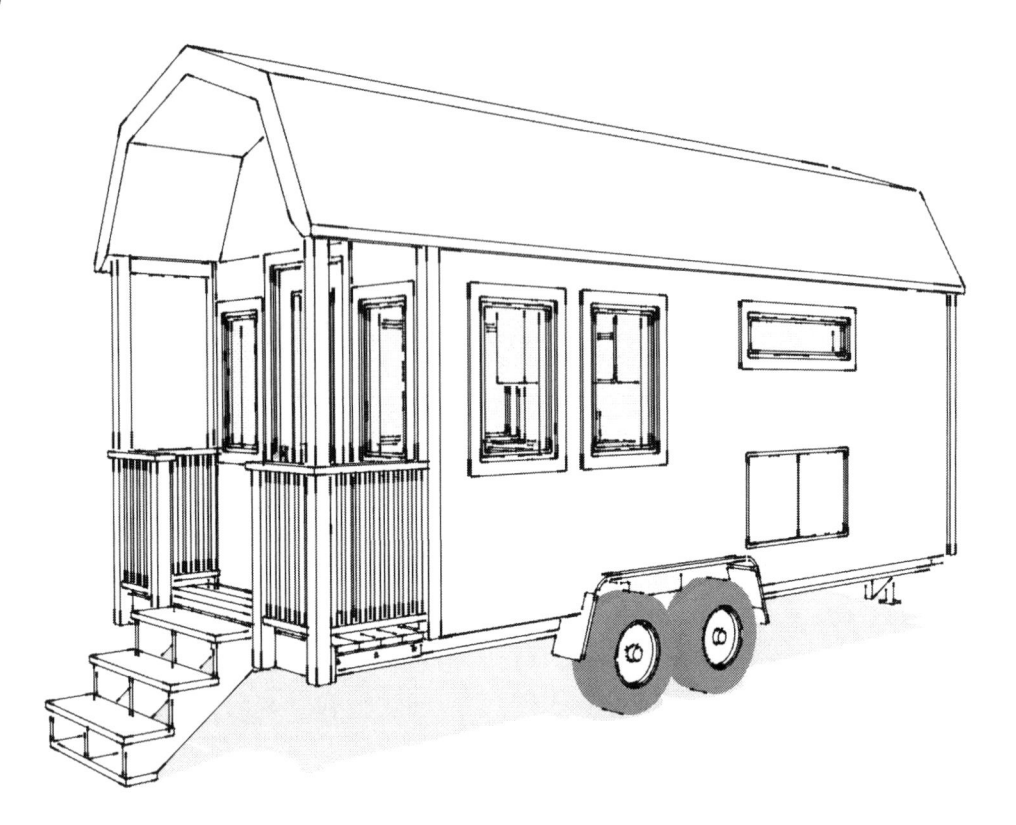

Front Right

Summary:

This has house no loft. Instead there's a raised bed at the center of the house. Under the bed is a storage space that's accessible from the exterior of the house, on the right side. At the back of the house - past the bed - is a bathroom that extends over the trailer tongue. The bathroom has a soaking tub, toilet, and sink. Just inside the front door is a tiny kitchen and two comfy chairs. I wanted to include this design to show how hard it is to get a bed on the lower level in a 20-foot tiny house. Some kind of sofa bed would work better in this size house and smaller.

Features:

20-Foot Tiny House on Wheels
Gambrel Roof
Front Porch Entry
Bathroom with Soaking Tub
Sleeps Two in Raised Lower Level Bed
Exterior Accessible Storage Space

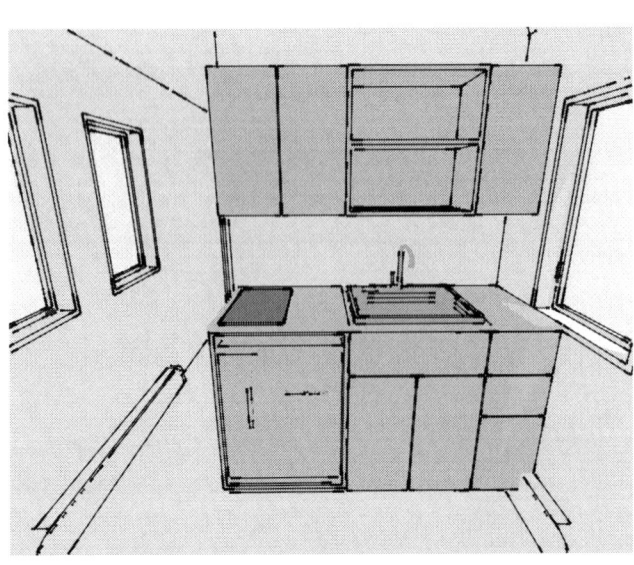

Kitchen

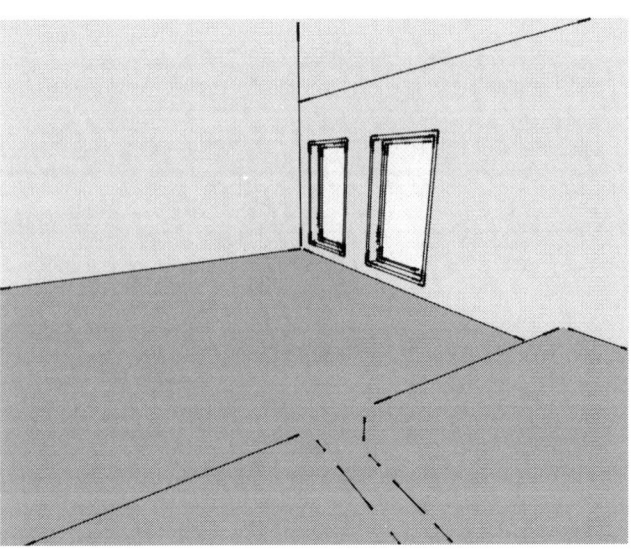

View from Bed

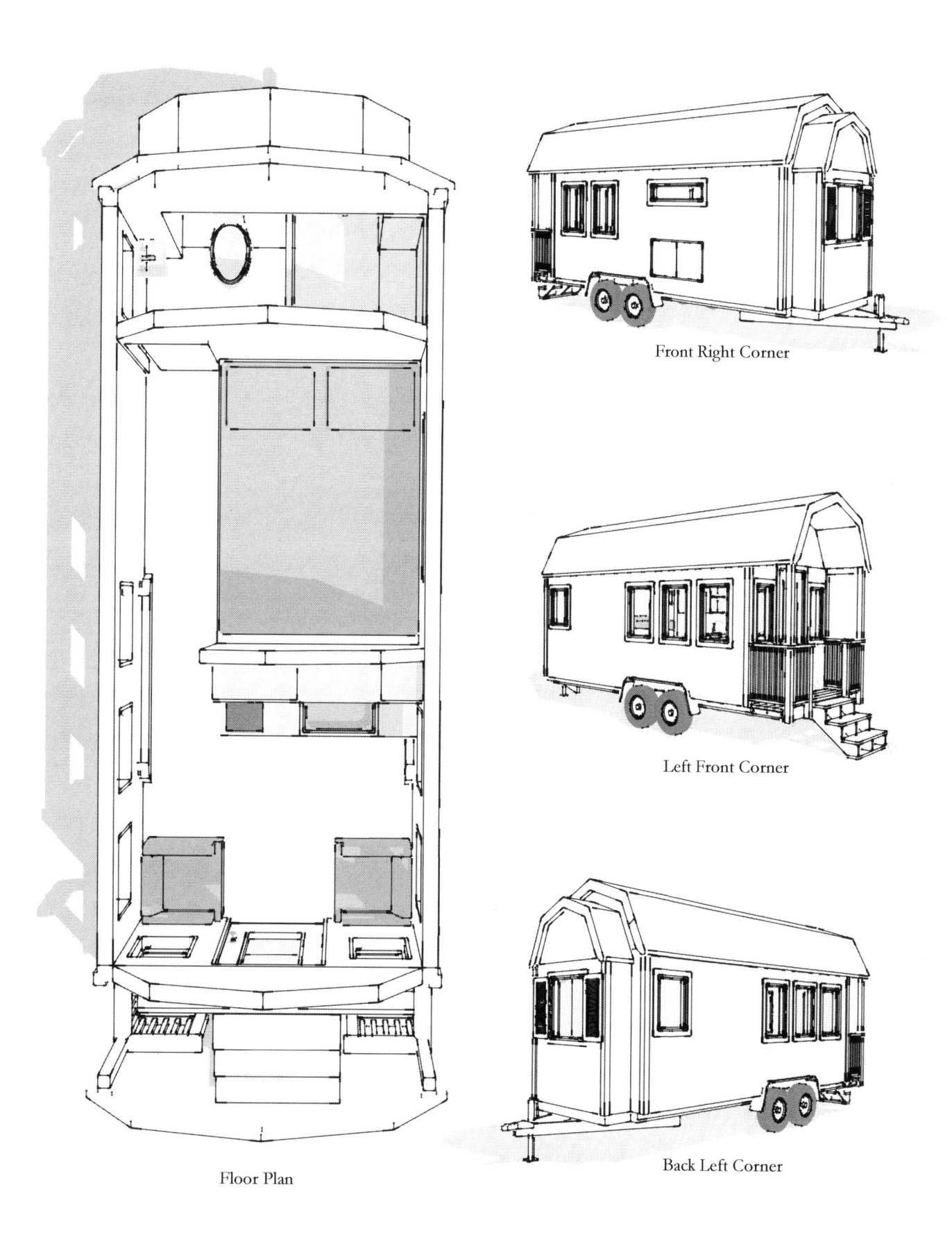

Tiny House #55 - Floor Plan & Exterior

Front Right Corner

Left Front Corner

Floor Plan

Back Left Corner

Tiny House #55 - Interior Views

Interior

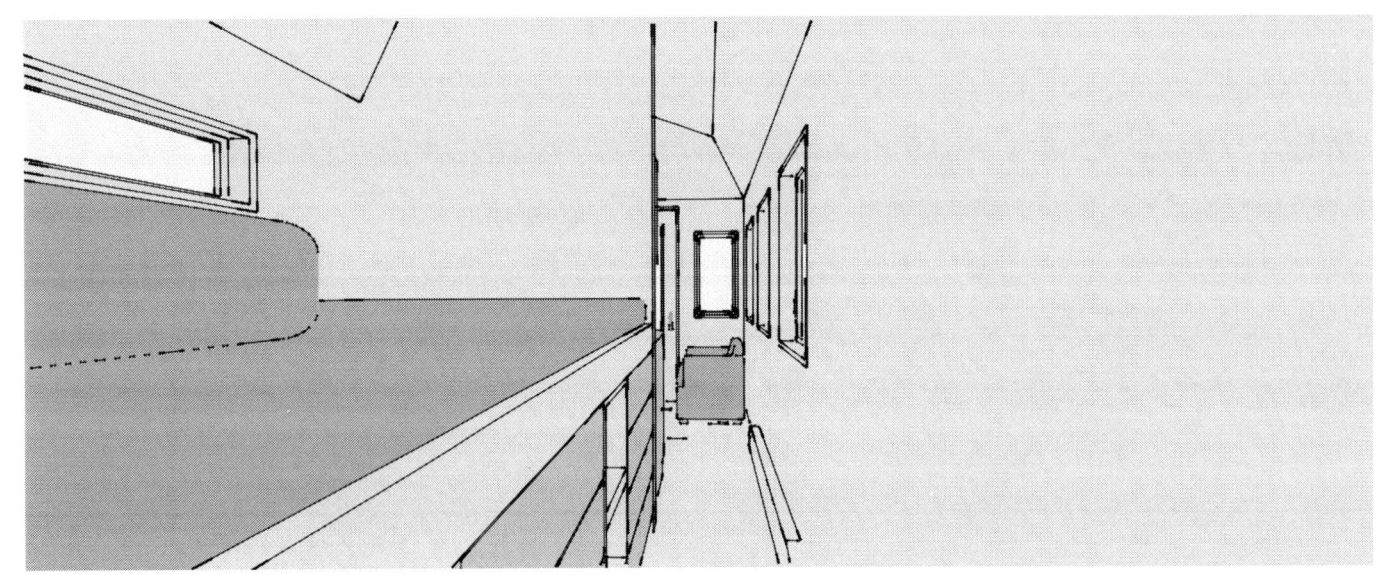

Interior

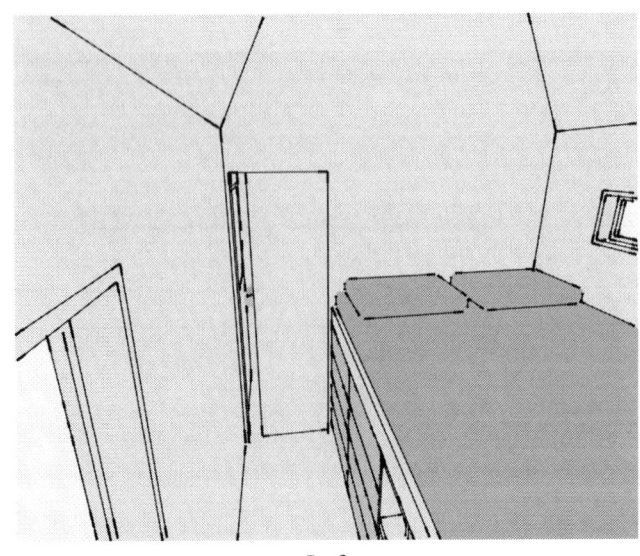

Loft

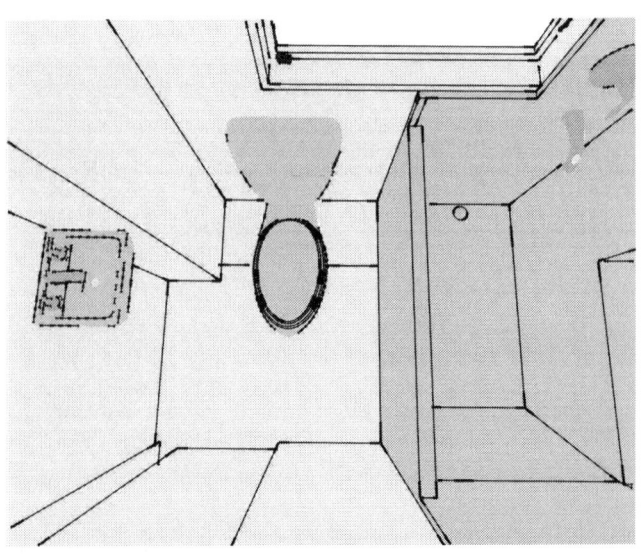

Bathroom

Tiny House #55 - Elevations

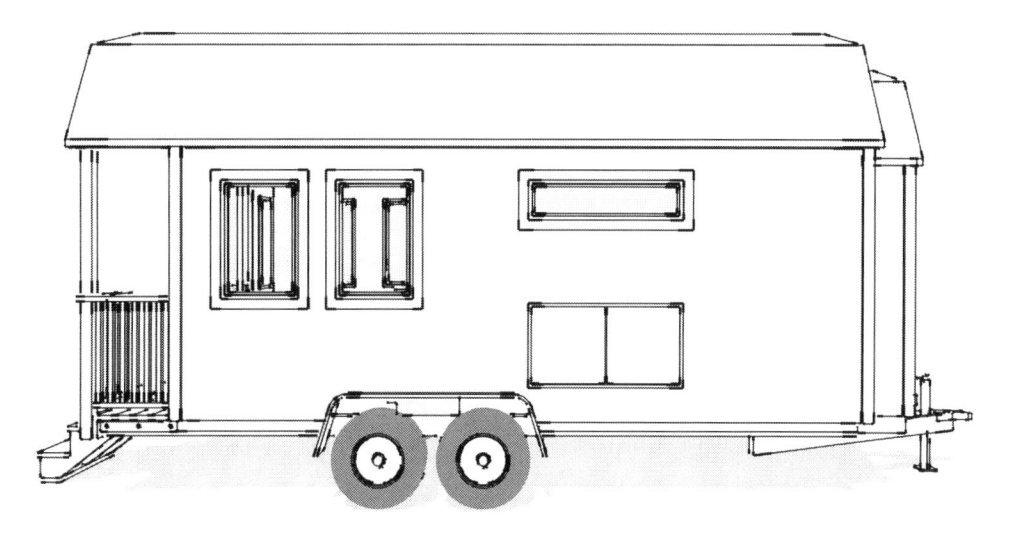

Right

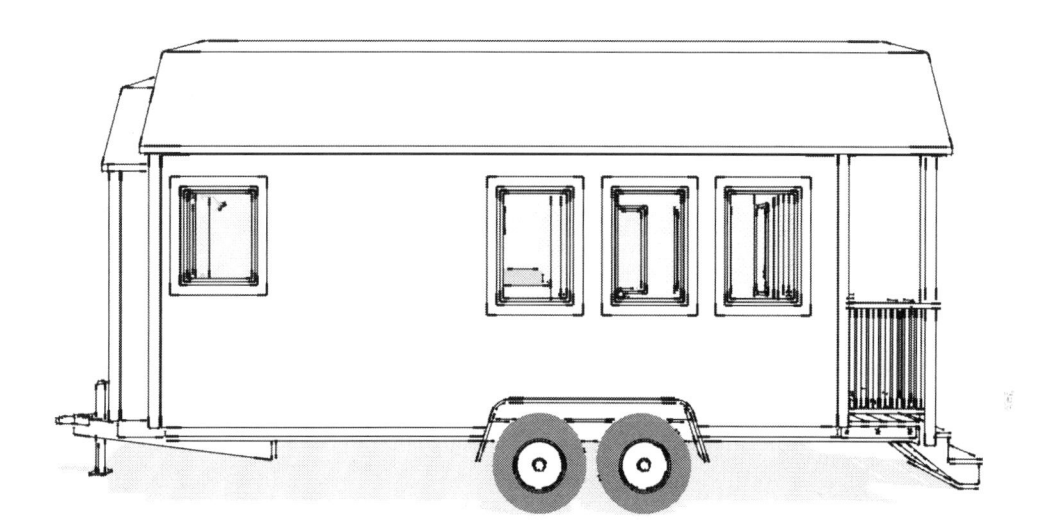

Left

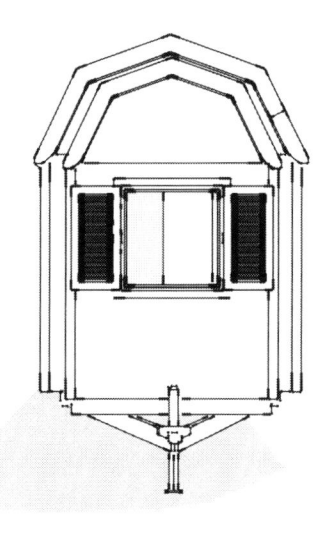

Back

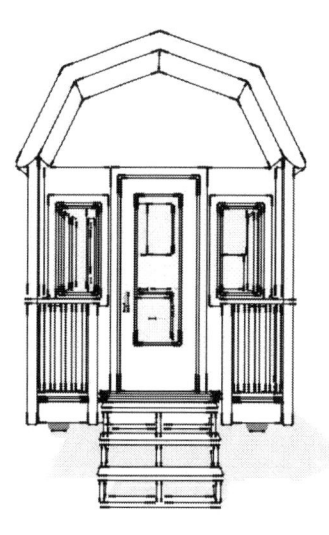

Front

#56

Tiny House #56 - Overview

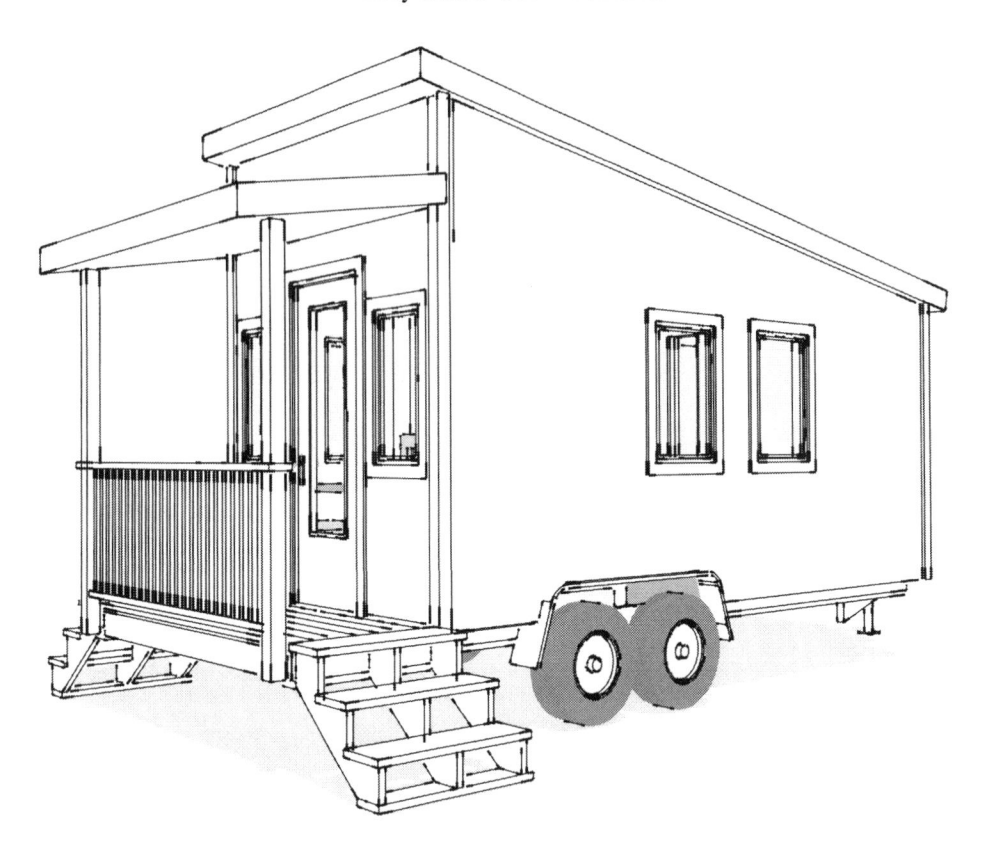

Front Right

Summary:

Like #55 this house has no loft. Instead this has a room at the center of the house with two sofas that could also provide a place to sleep - either as two twin beds or as a giant sofa bed. At the back of the house is a large bathroom with a soaking tub, toilet, and sink. At the front of the house is a tiny kitchen and table for two. But the most notable thing about this tiny house design is the exterior. I think it's adorable - like it popped right out of a pioneer town. The porch with two fold down stairs would also work nicely on most any tiny house. The shed roof and opposing porch roof would provide good aerodynamics on the road.

Features:

20-Foot Tiny House on Wheels
3/12 Shed Roof and Porch
Front Porch with two Fold-up Steps
Bathroom with Soaking Tub
Living Room / Bedroom
No Loft

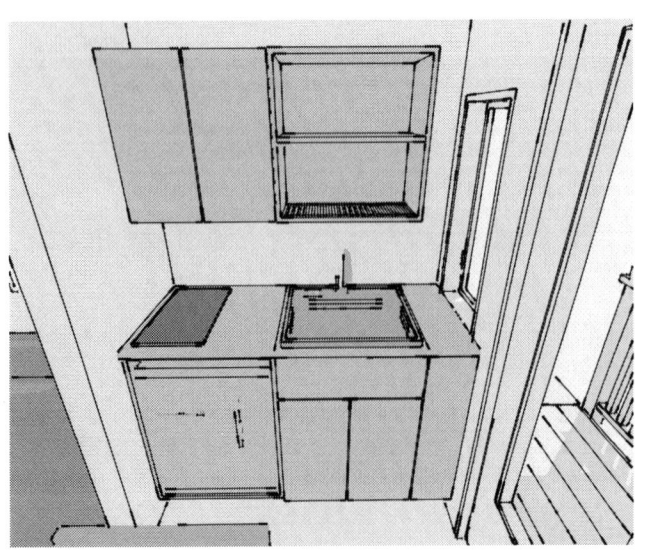

Kitchen

View from Living Room

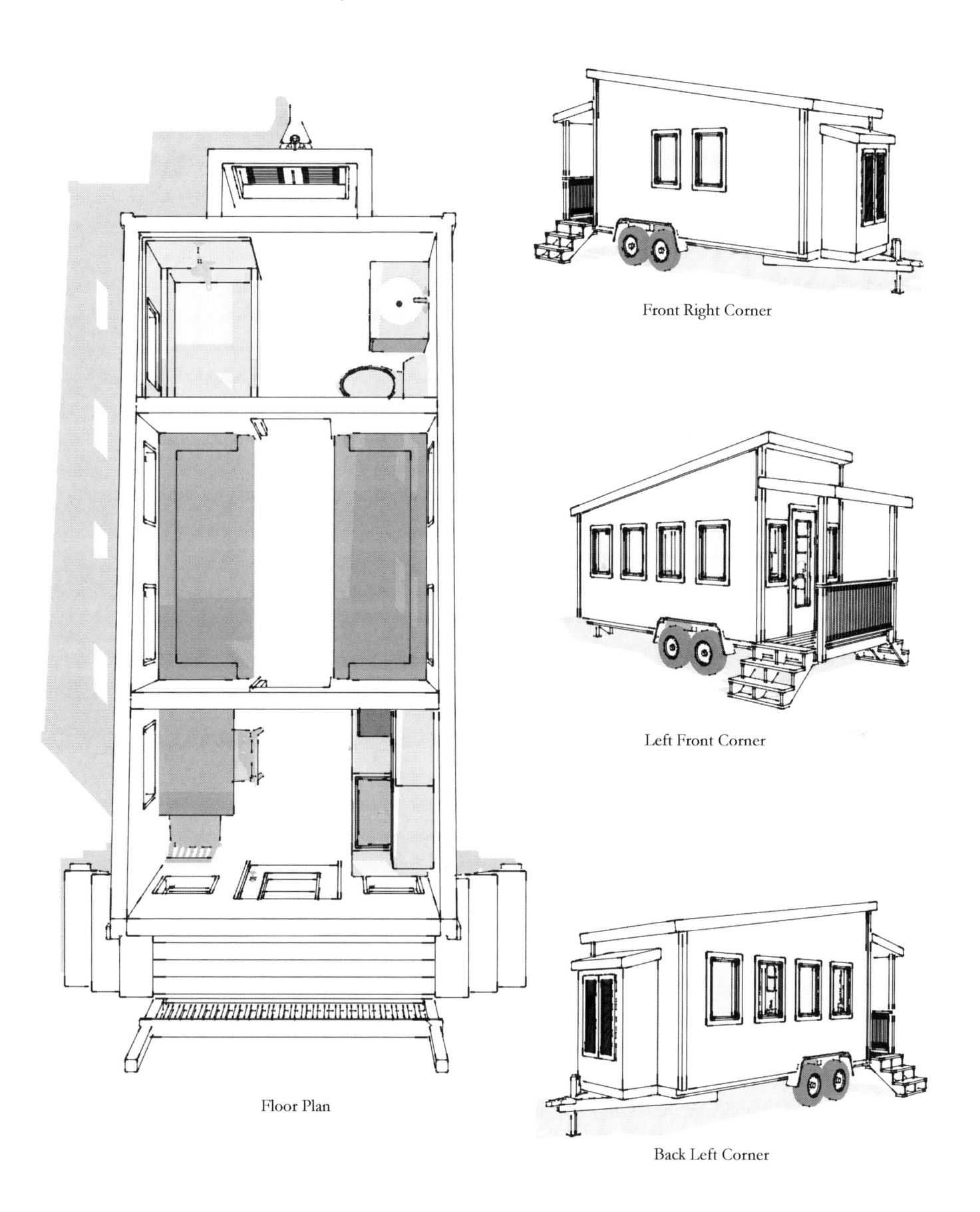

Tiny House #56 - Floor Plan & Exterior

Front Right Corner

Left Front Corner

Floor Plan

Back Left Corner

Tiny House #56 - Interior Views

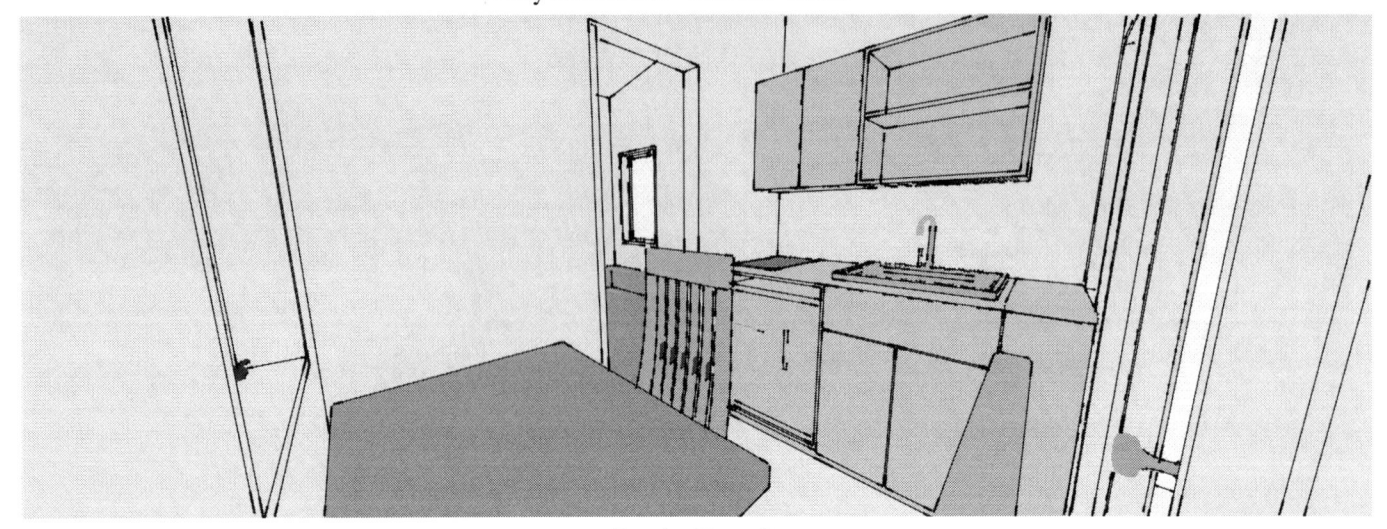

Interior Front Room

Interior

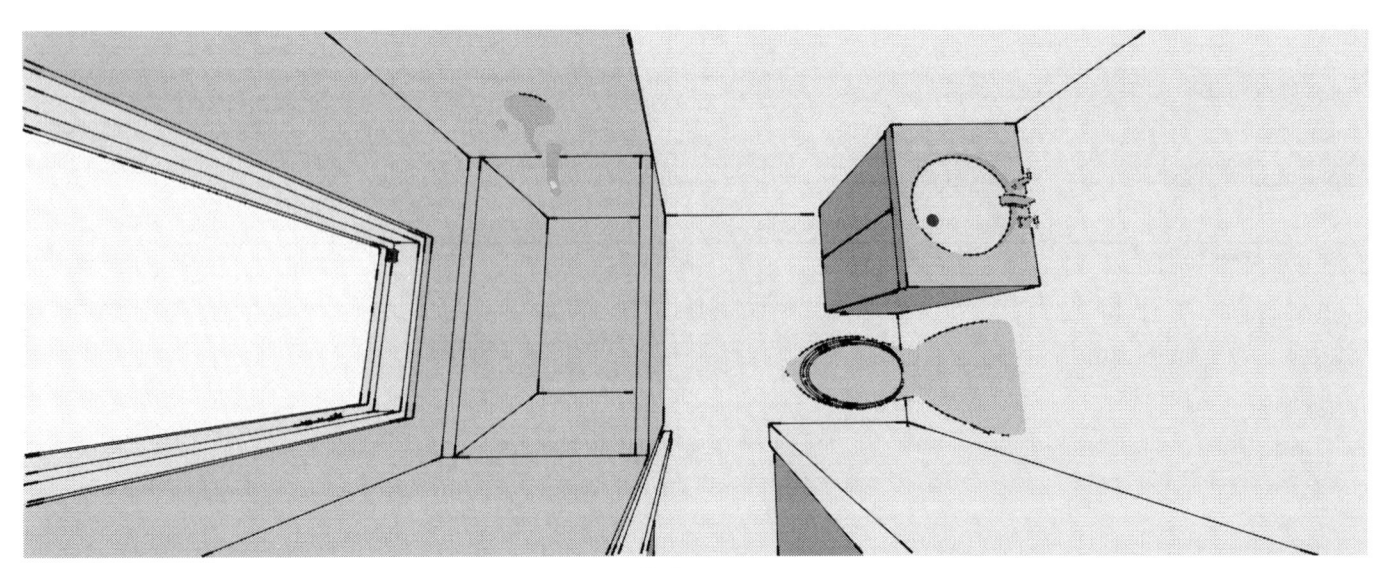

Bathroom

Tiny House #56 - Elevations

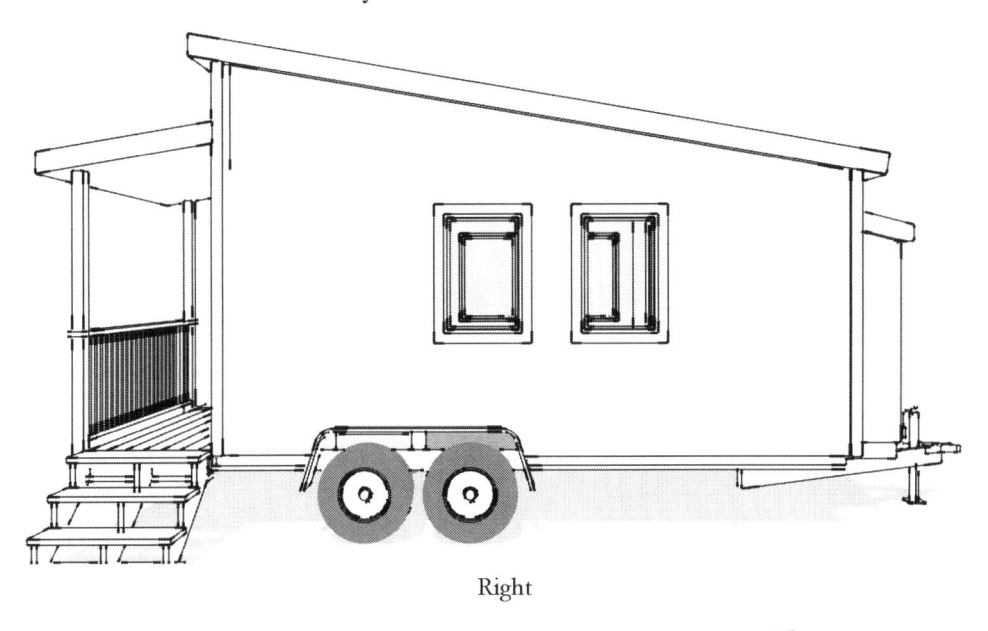

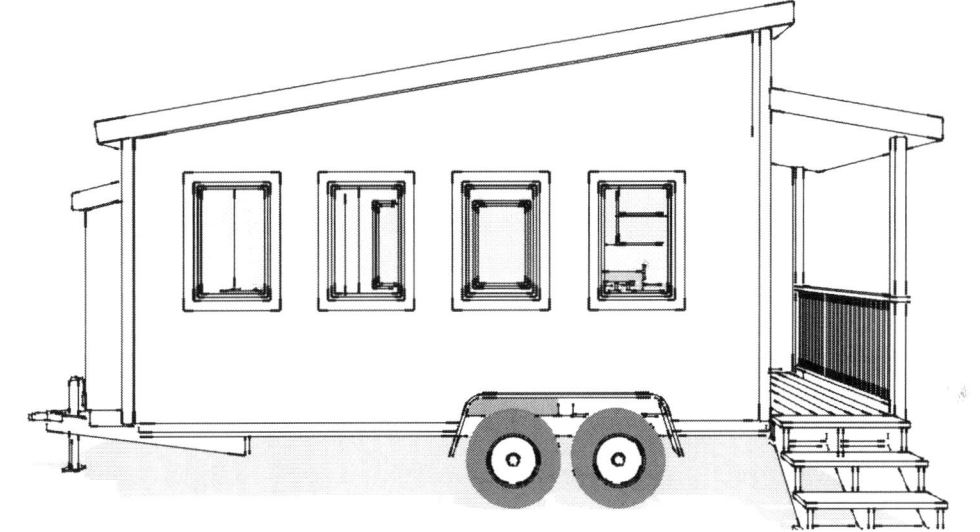

Right

Left

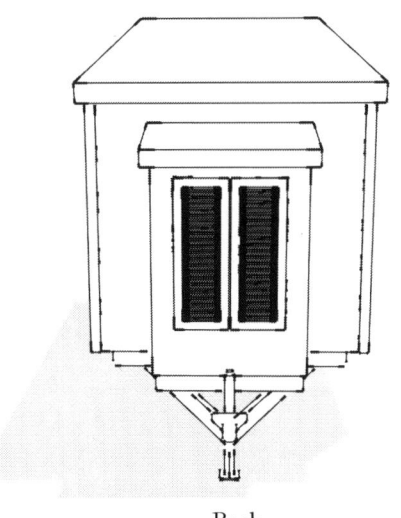

Back

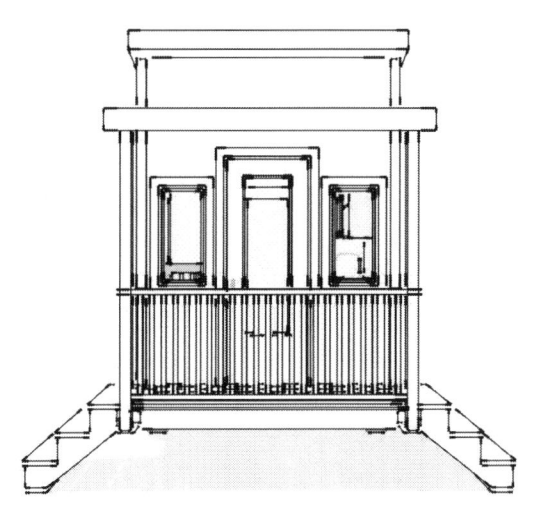

Front

22-Foot Tiny House Designs

#57

Tiny House #57 - Overview

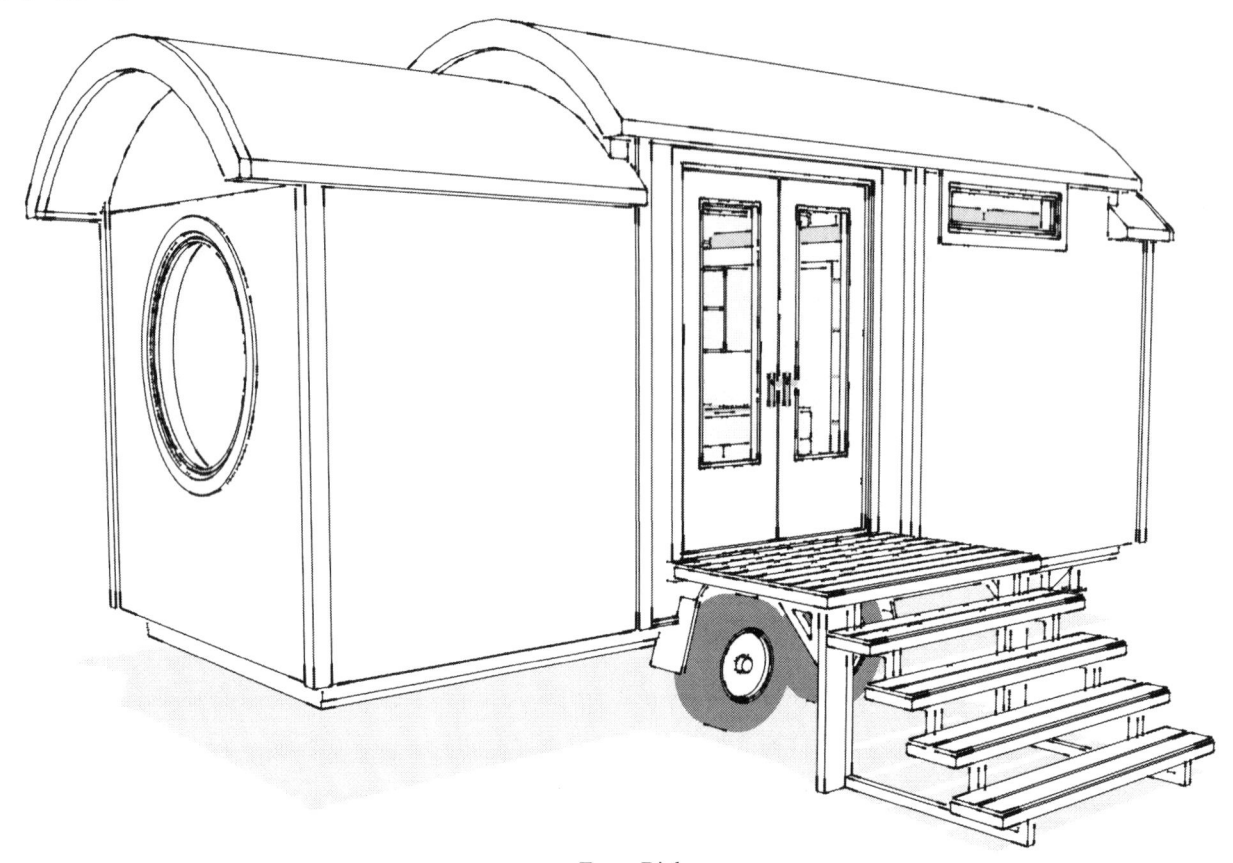

Front Right

Summary:

While these houses with the main entry over the fender would require a bit of a climb, I think the dramatic experience of stepping down into a tiny house with high ceilings would be worth it.

Upon entering you'd take two steps down into the kitchen and dining room. To the left is a living room with a sofa and two chairs. To the right is a laundry room and bathroom. Above the on the right is a loft with a queen bed.

Features:

22-Foot Tiny House on Wheels
Curved Vardo Inspired Roof
Side Entry over Trailer Fenders
Standard Bathroom
Laundry
Sleeps Two in Loft

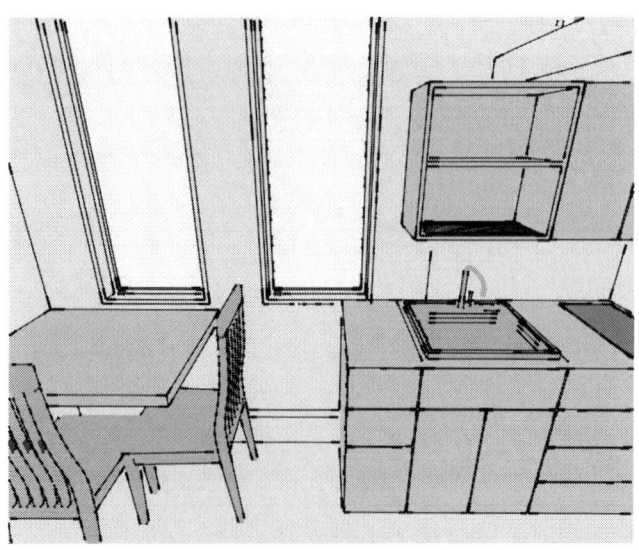

Kitchen

View from Loft

Tiny House #57 - Floor Plan & Exterior

Front Right Corner

Floor Plan - Loft

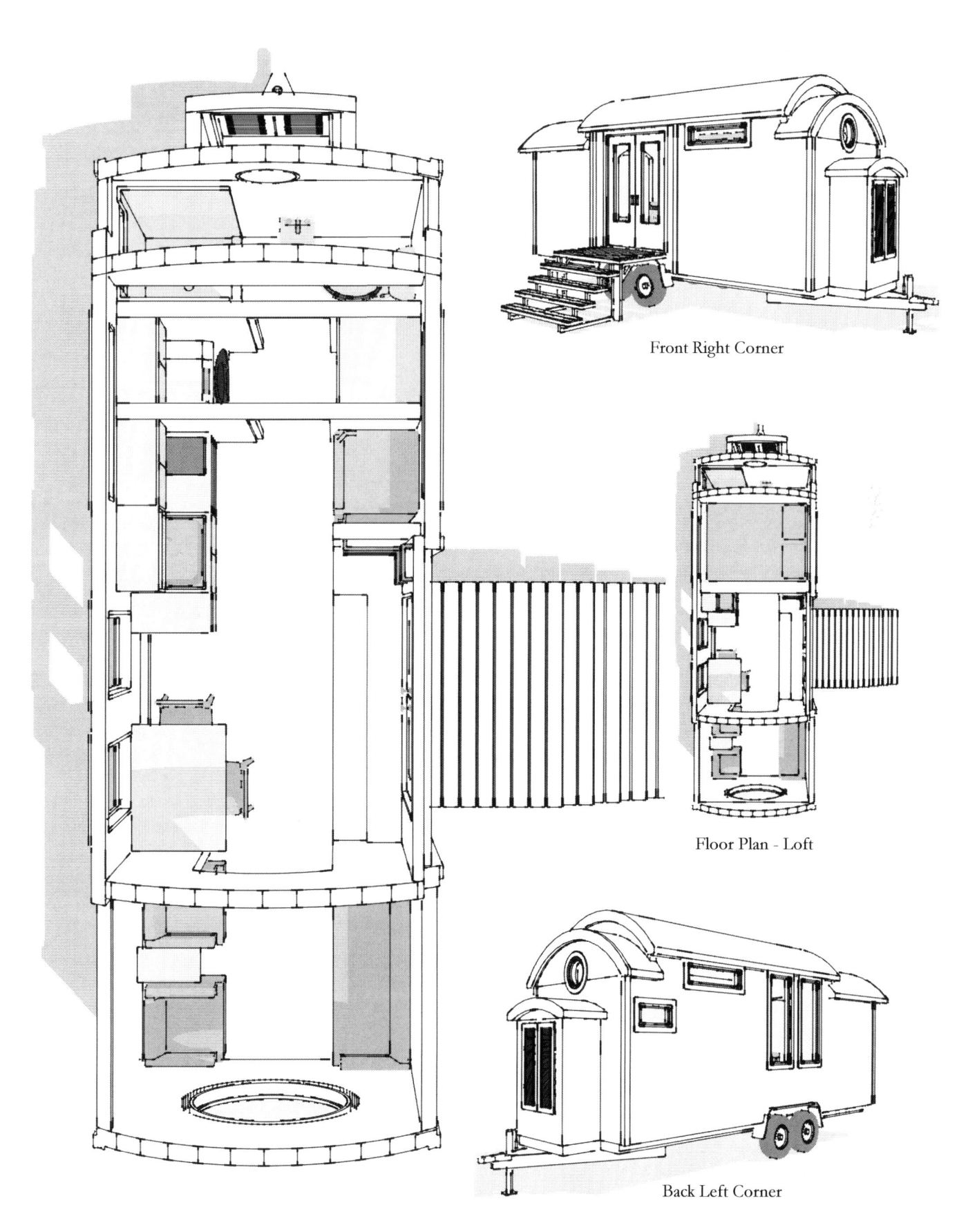

Back Left Corner

Floor Plan

Tiny House #57 - Interior Views

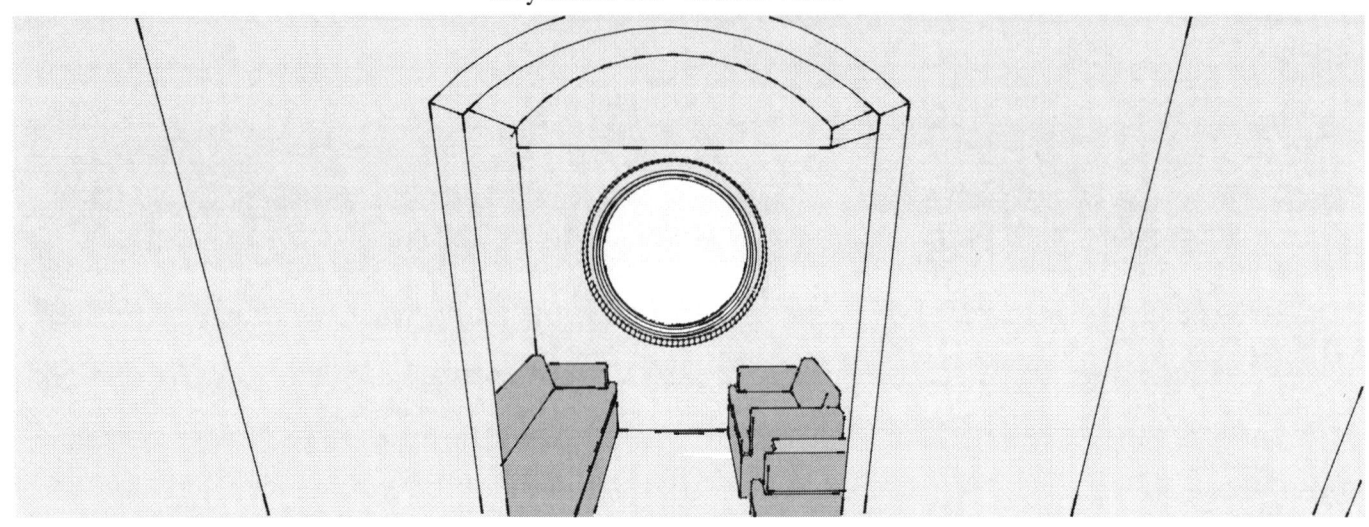

Living Room

Interior from Bathroom

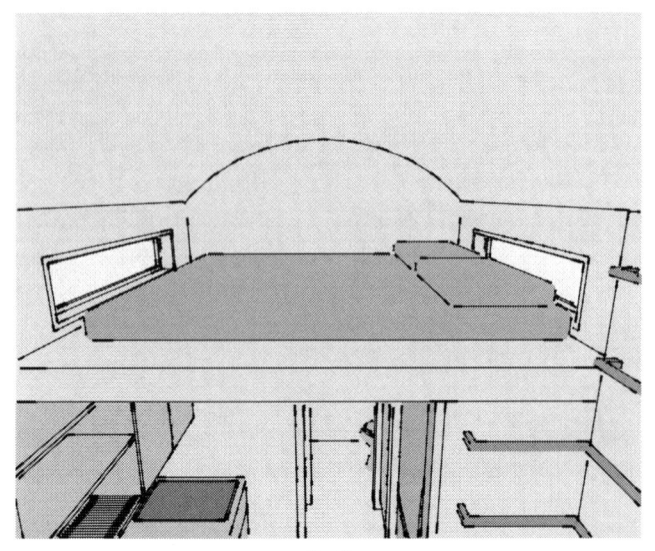

Loft

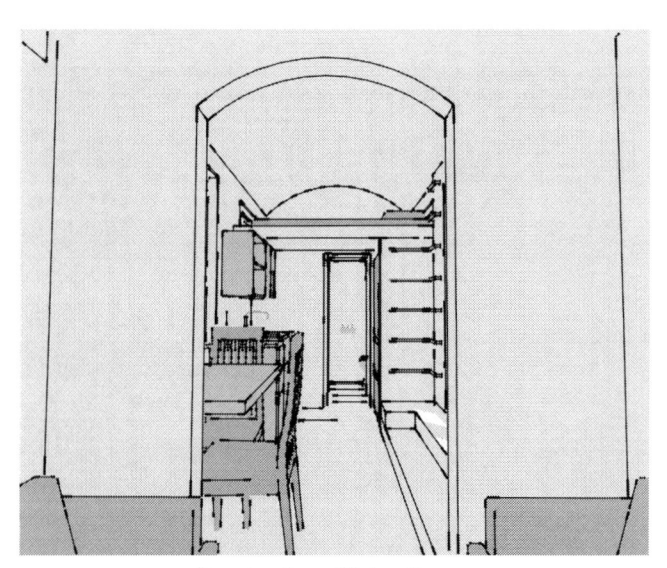

Interior from Living Room

Tiny House #57 - Elevations

Right

Left

Back

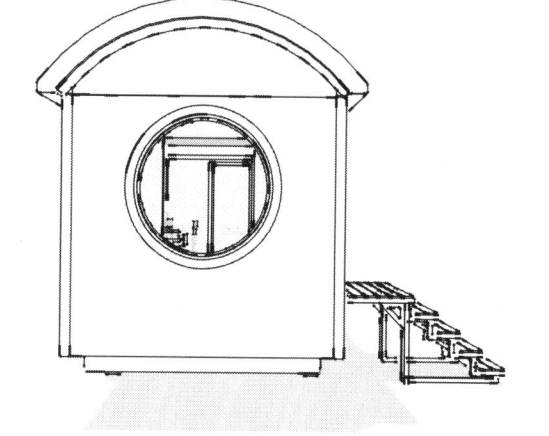

Front

#58

Tiny House #58 - Overview

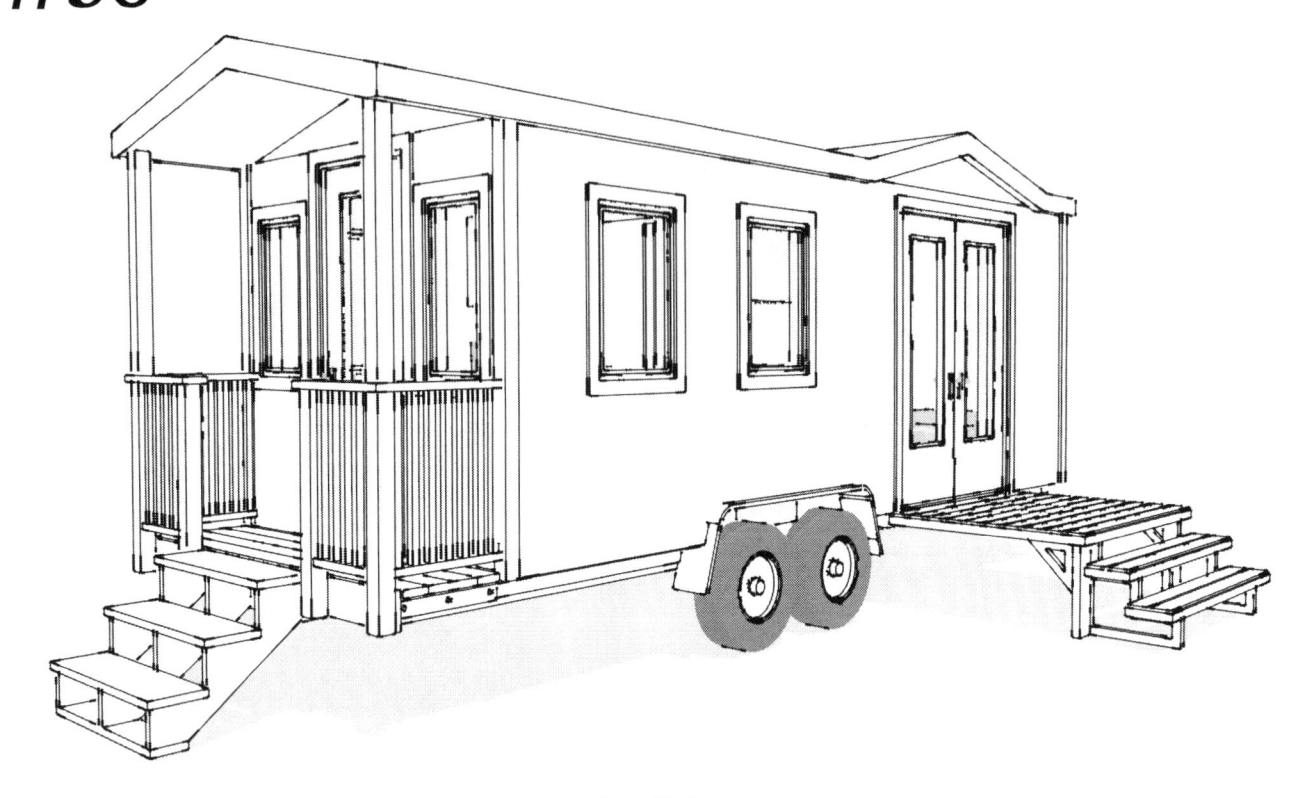

Front Right

Summary:

Here's another tiny house without a loft and a lower level bedroom. I think this layout works well, although to solve some space issues I used a pass-through bathroom between the bedroom and kitchen. This might be odd for some people. The kitchen is small but has the essentials. The living room has a table for two and two comfy chairs. The bedroom has a queen size bed and storage. So all in all, it seems like a perfect little apartment-like tiny home for one or two people. The lower height would also make it easier to tow.

Features:

22-Foot Tiny House on Wheels
Low 3/12 Gable
Lower Lever Bedroom, No Loft
Two Entries
Pass-through Bathroom

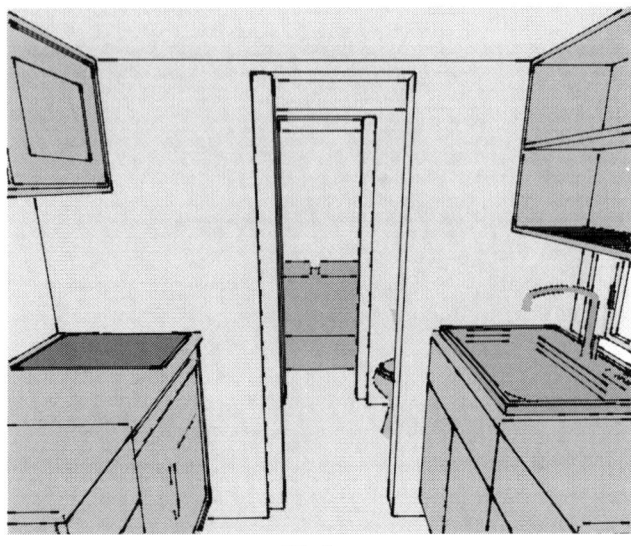

Kitchen

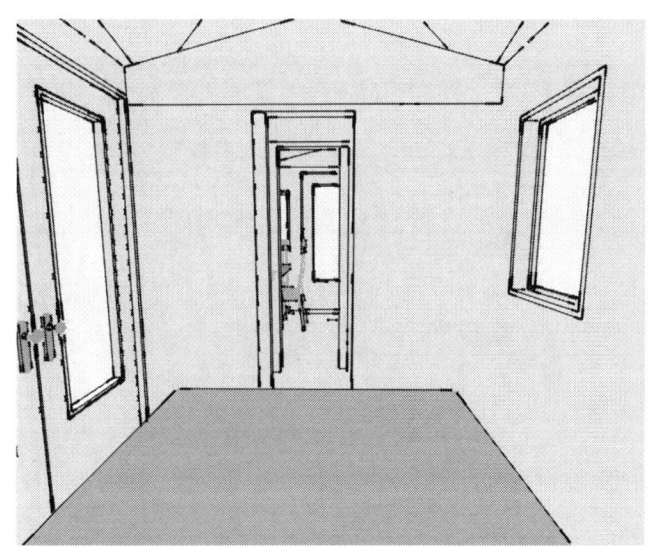

View from Bedroom

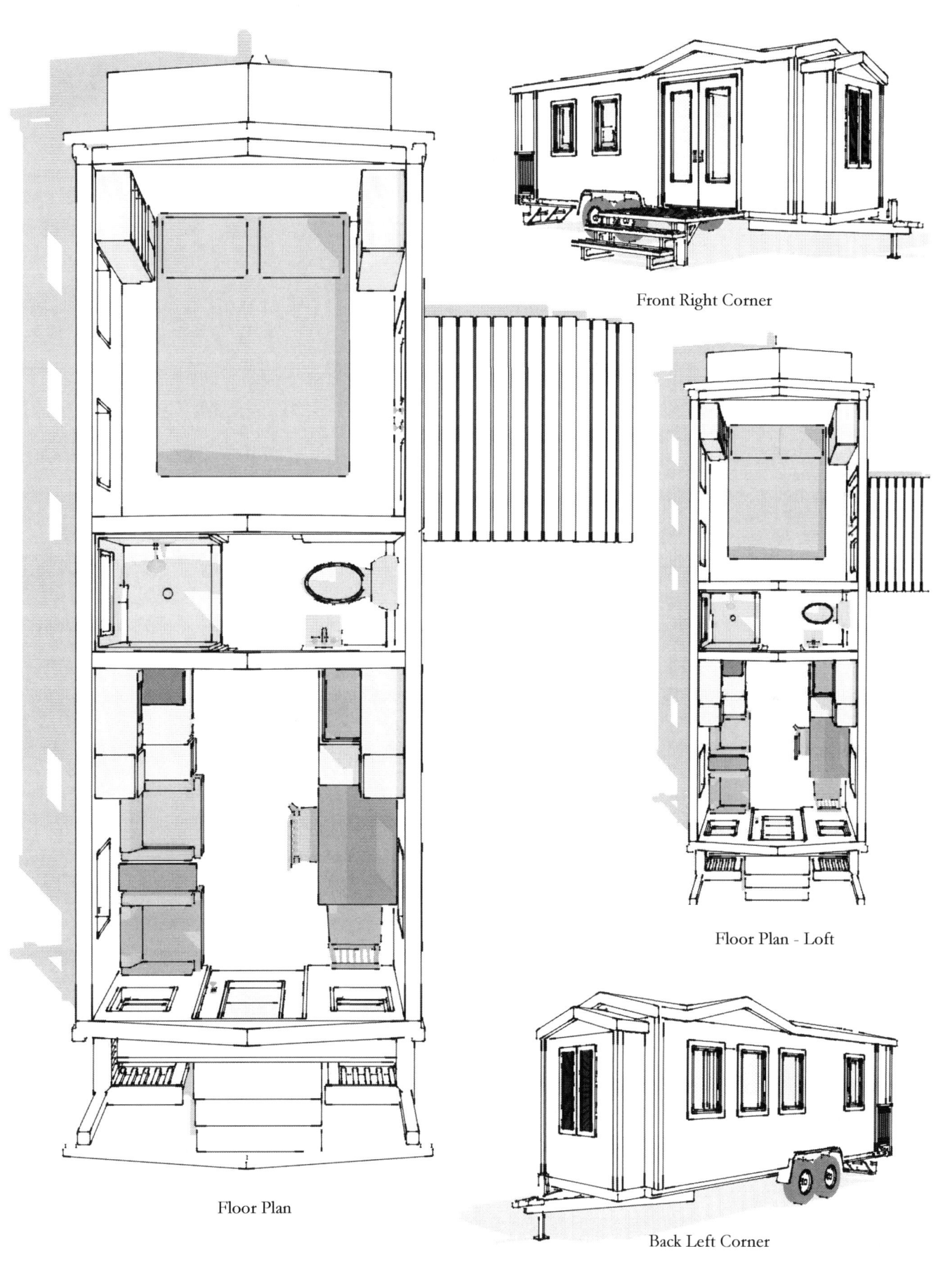

Tiny House #58 - Floor Plan & Exterior

Front Right Corner

Floor Plan - Loft

Floor Plan

Back Left Corner

Tiny House #58 - Interior Views

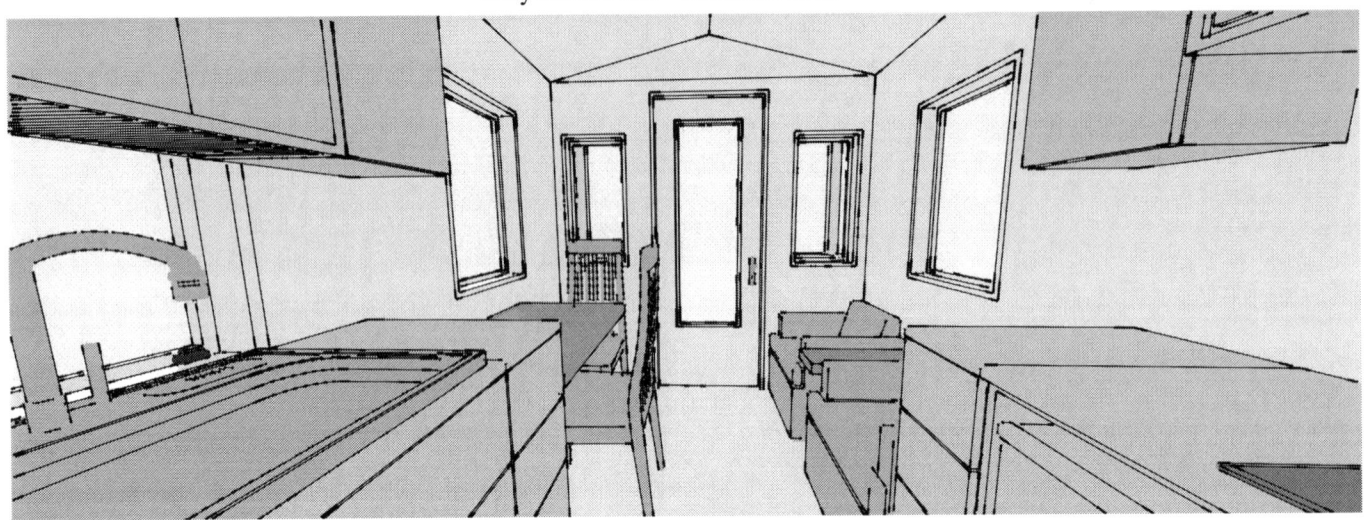

Interior from Entry

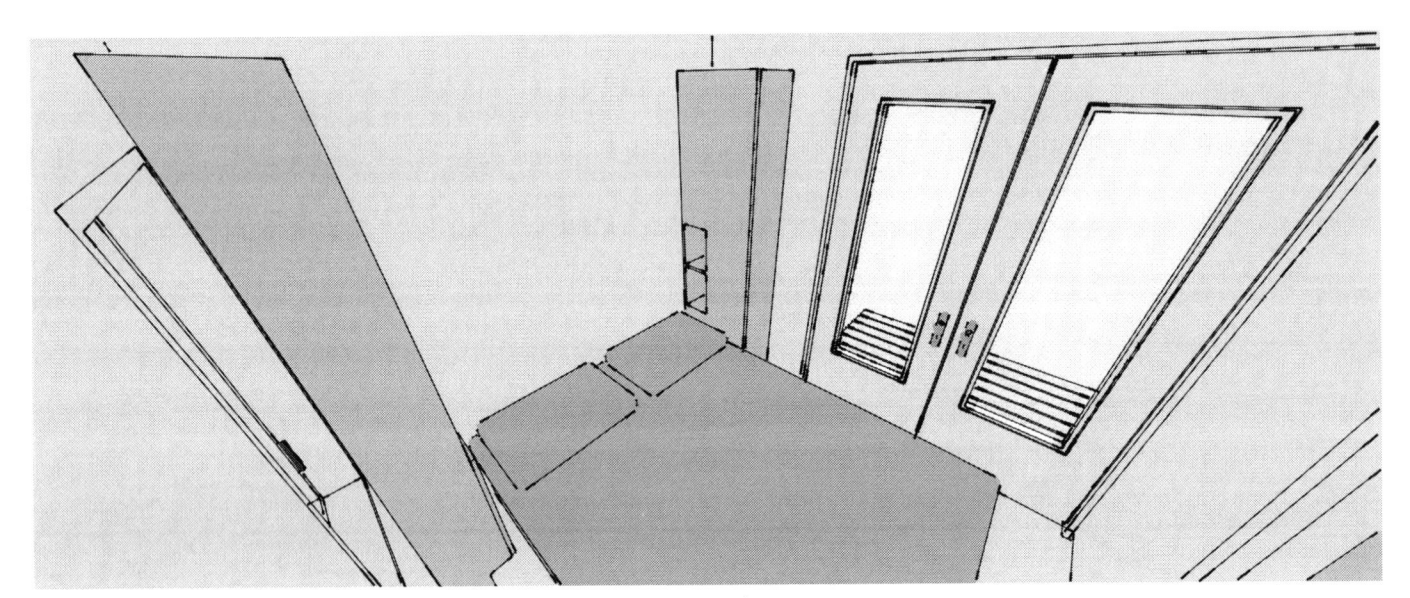

Interior

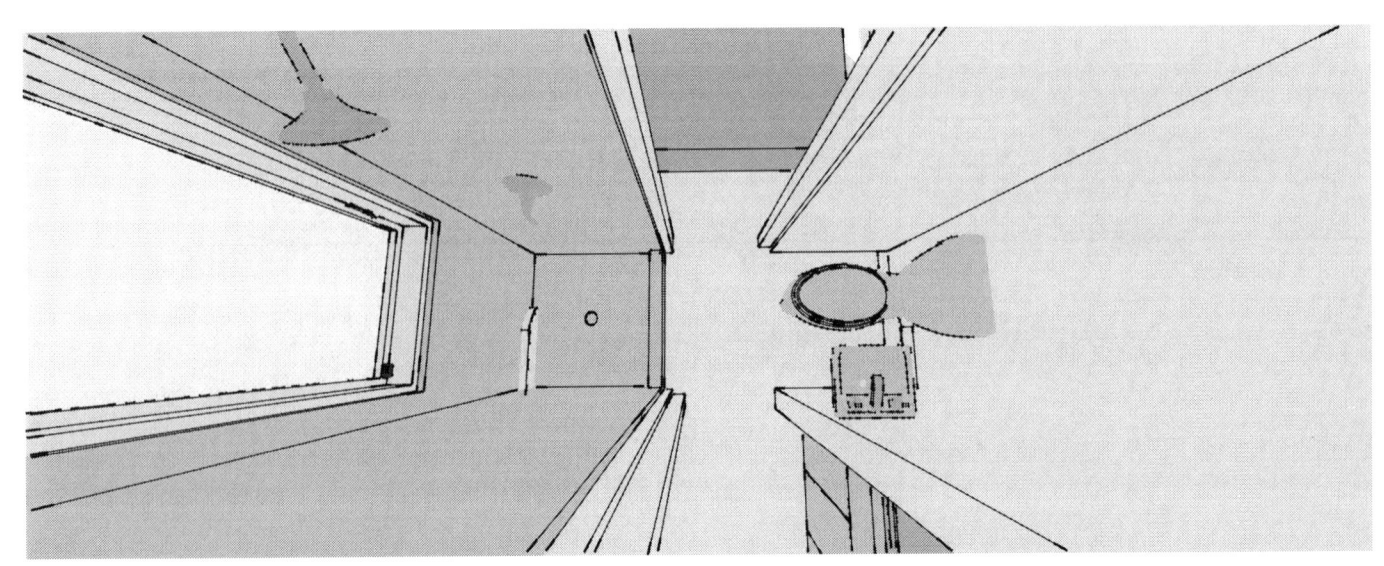

Bathroom

Tiny House #58 - Elevations

Right

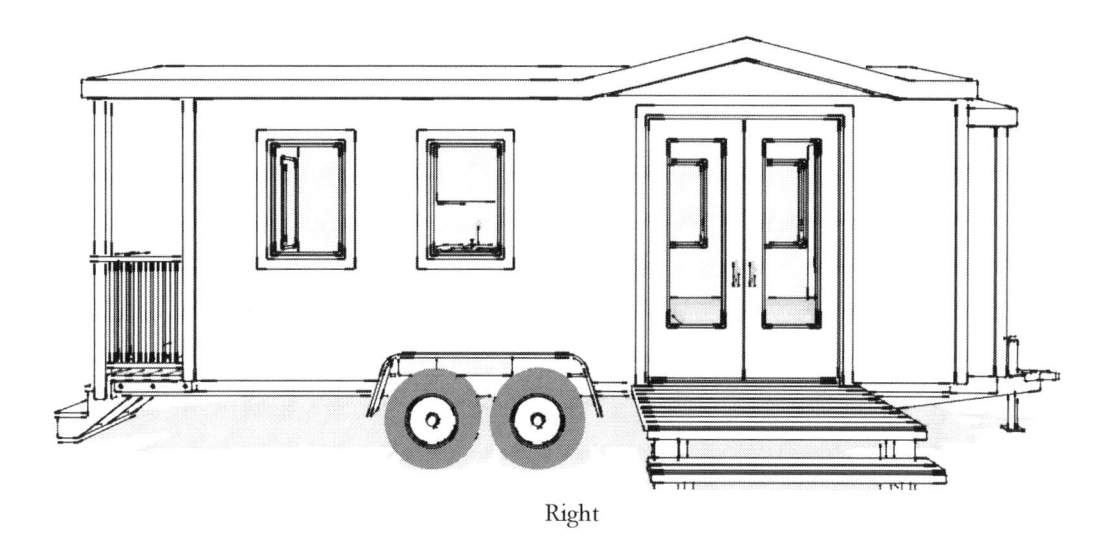

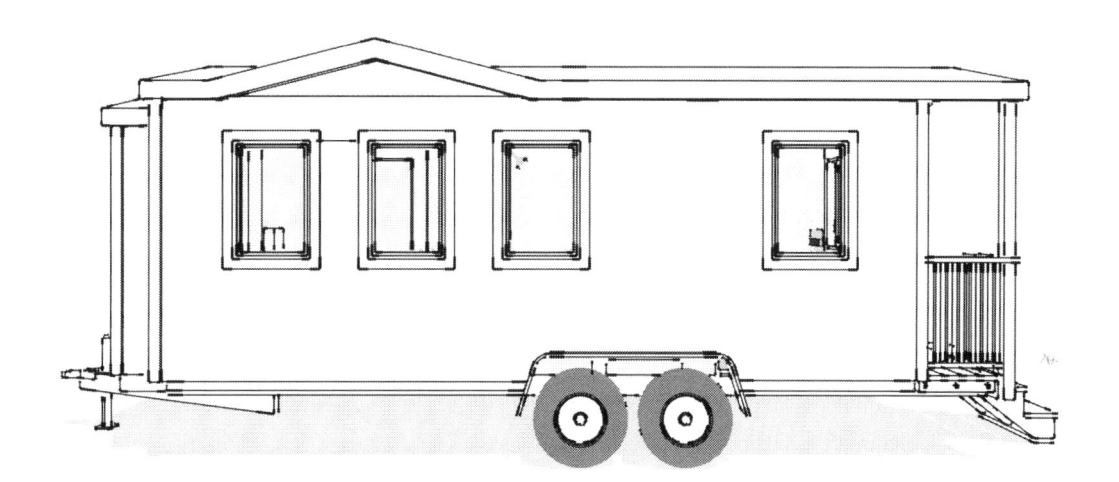

Left

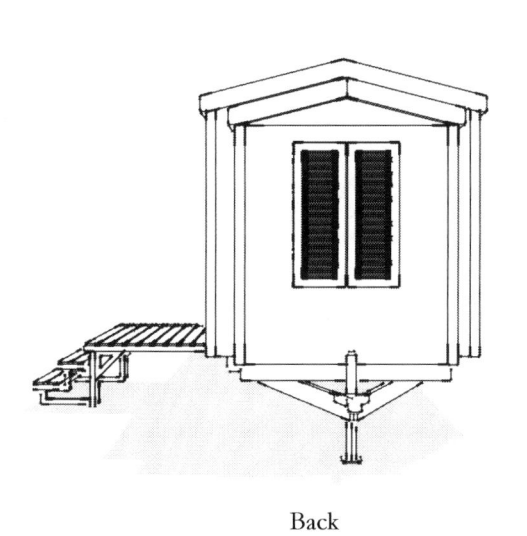

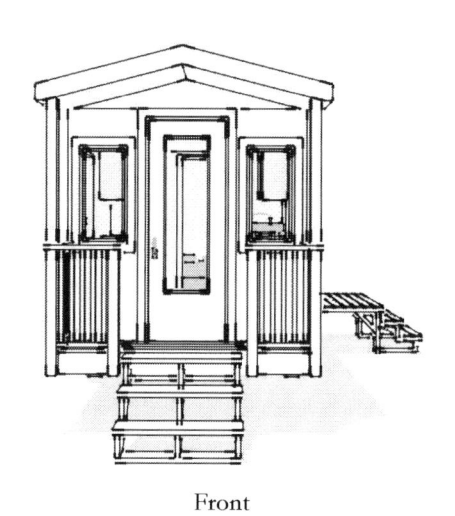

Back

Front

243

#59

Tiny House #59 - Overview

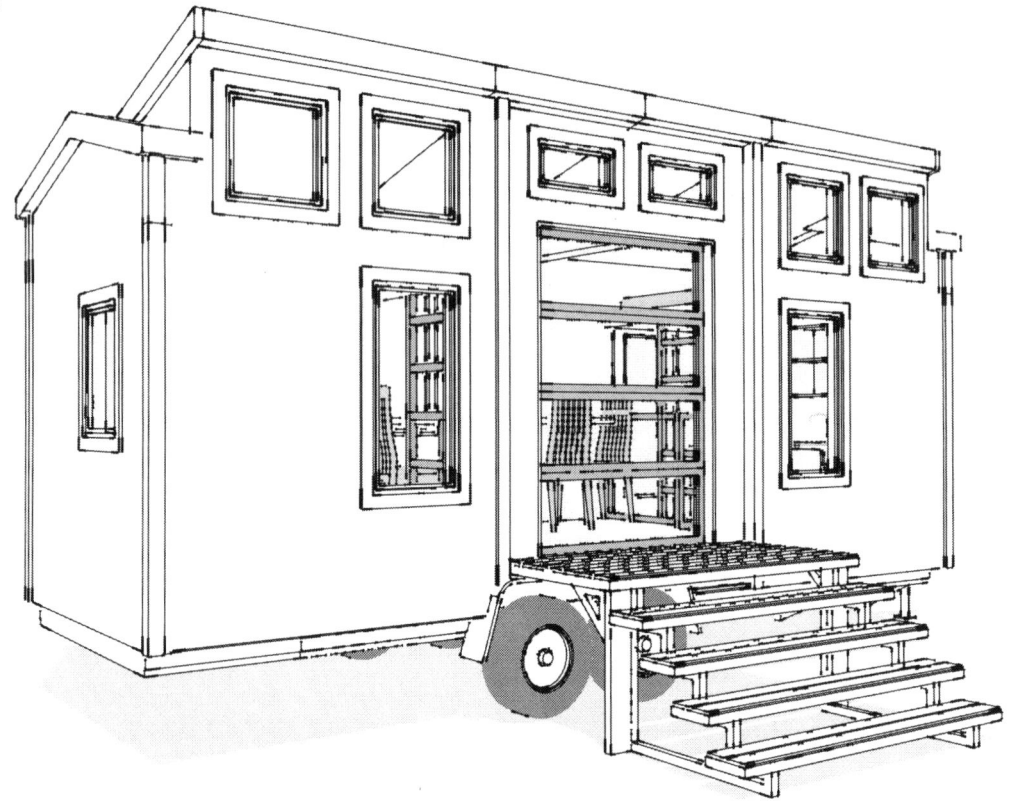

Front Right

Summary:

This tiny house features a glass roll-up door. Since this would not be practical to use all the time, there is also a conventional exterior door that leads to the kitchen. All the glass would make this an ideal home in locations with great views. When you step in through the roll-up door you're standing on a raised dining platform. To the left and right there are steps down to the kitchen on the right and a small sitting area and the bathroom on the left. On either side of the raised platform are railings. Built into the railings are ladders that lead to the two lofts. Each loft is large enough for queen beds.

Features:

22-Foot Tiny House on Wheels
Shed Roof with Gable Ends
Two Lofts
Roll-up Glass Door
Raised Dining Platform
Exterior Door in Kitchen

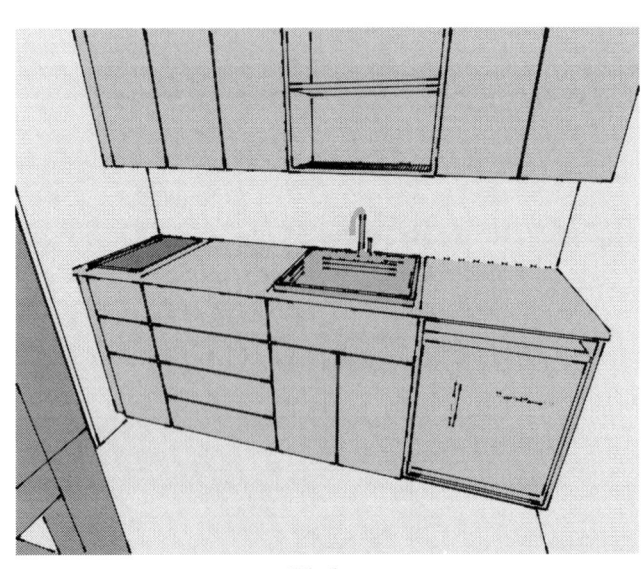

Kitchen

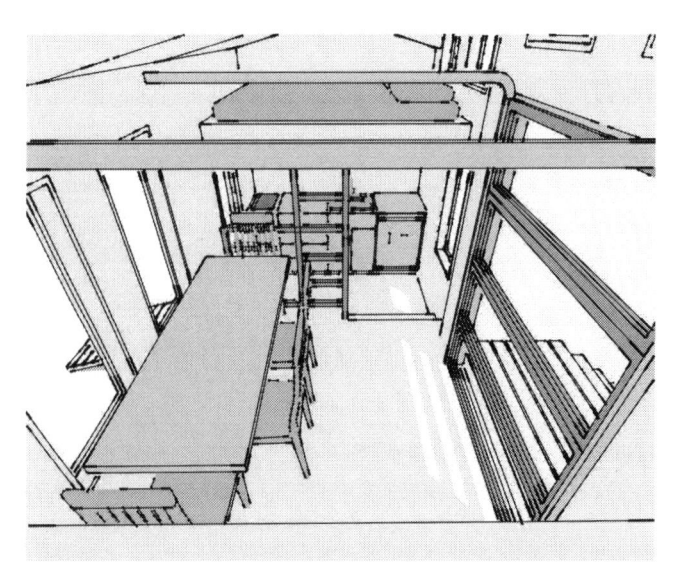

View from Bedroom

Tiny House #59 - Floor Plan & Exterior

Front Right Corner

Floor Plan - Loft

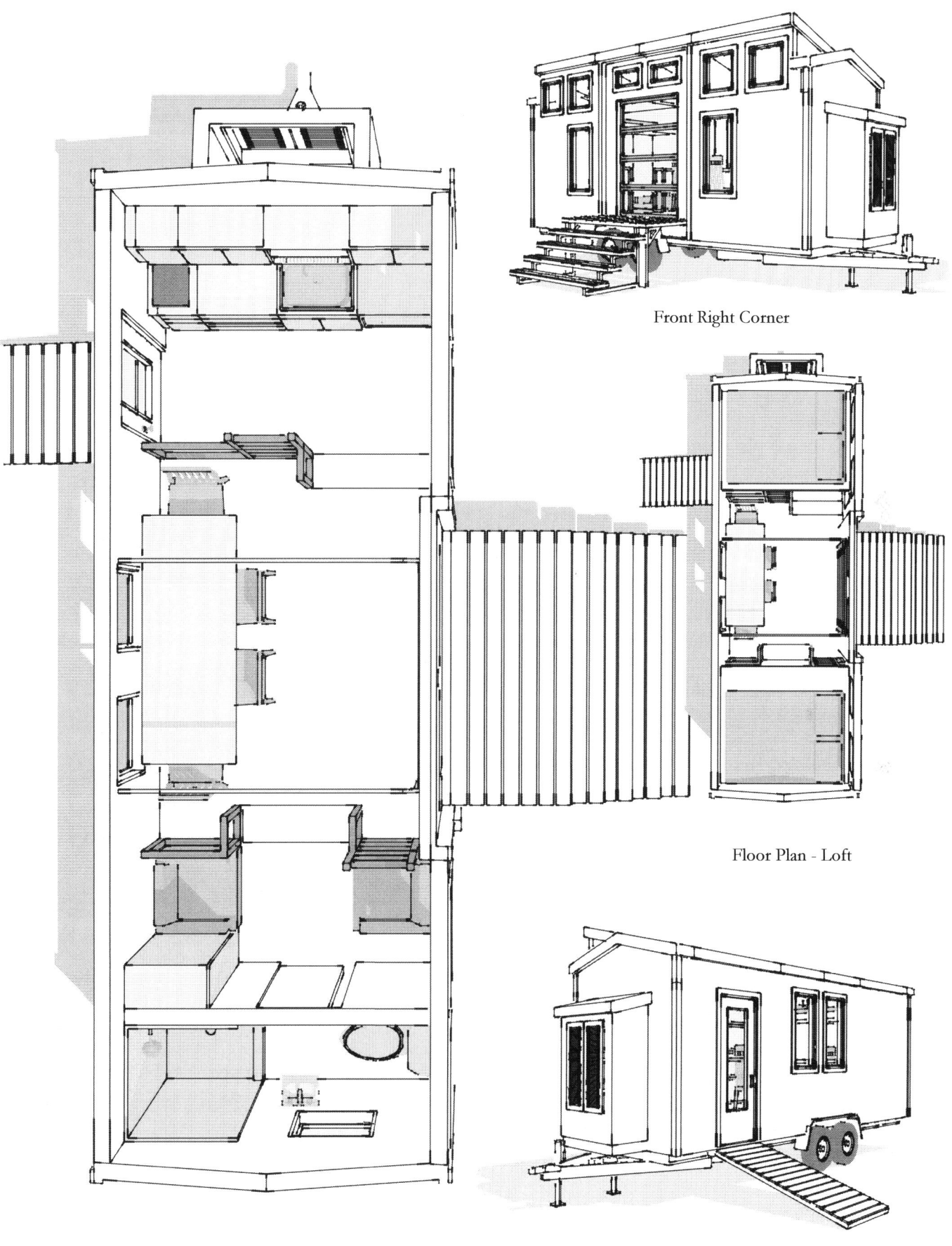

Floor Plan

Back Left Corner

Tiny House #59 - Interior Views

Interior from Sitting Area

Interior from Kitchen

Lofts

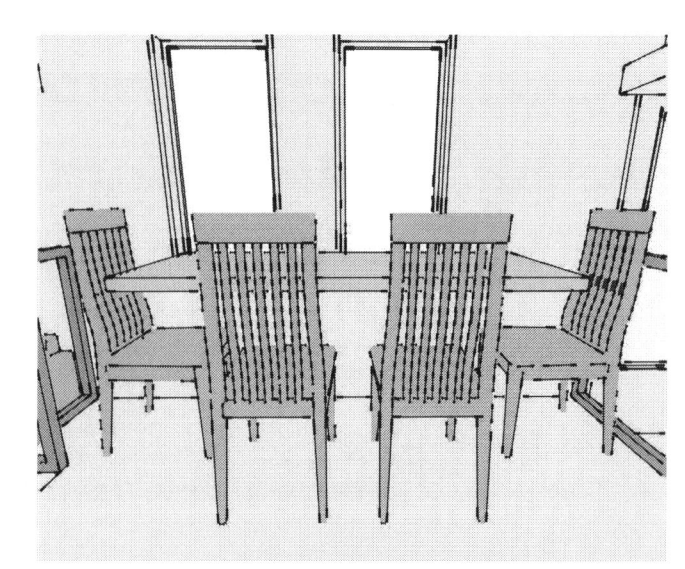

Dining Platform

Tiny House #59 - Elevations

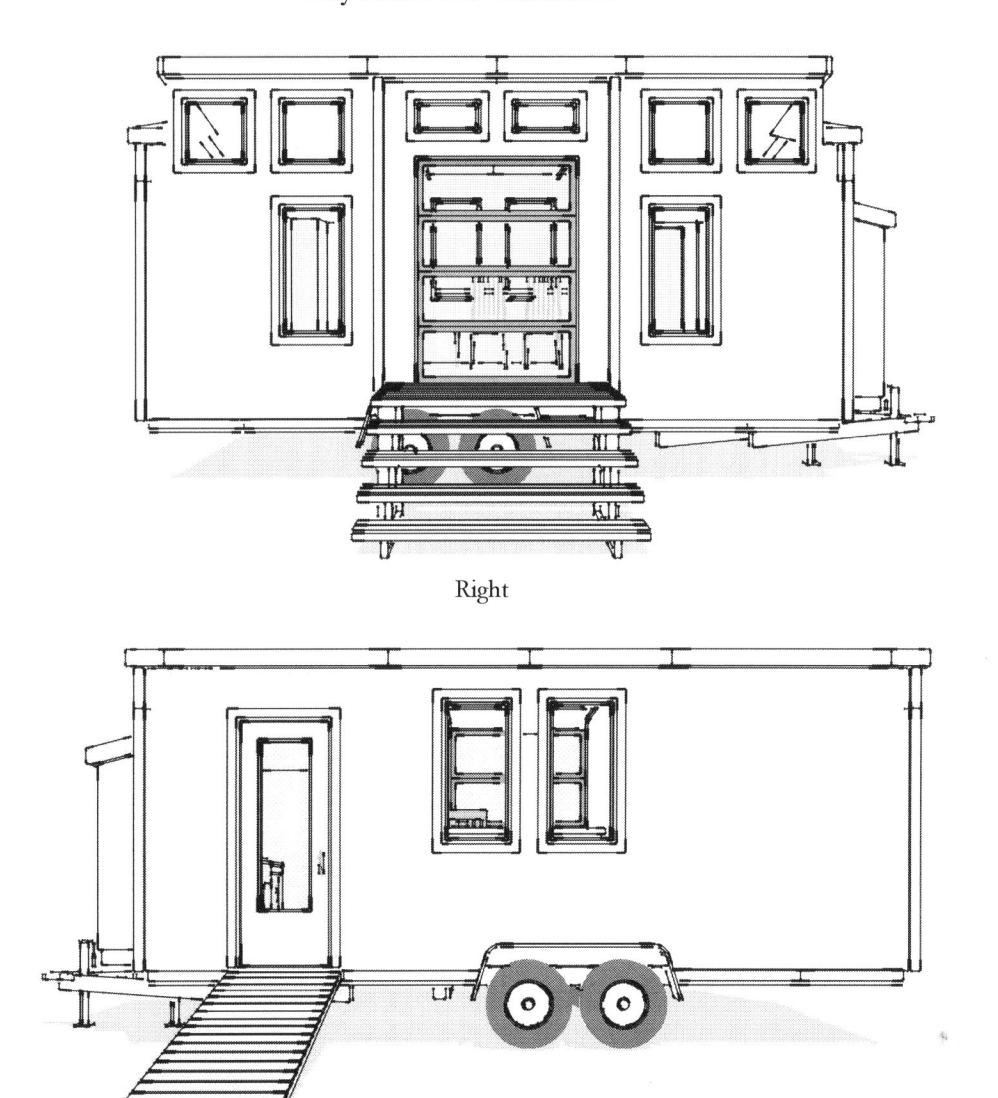

Right

Left

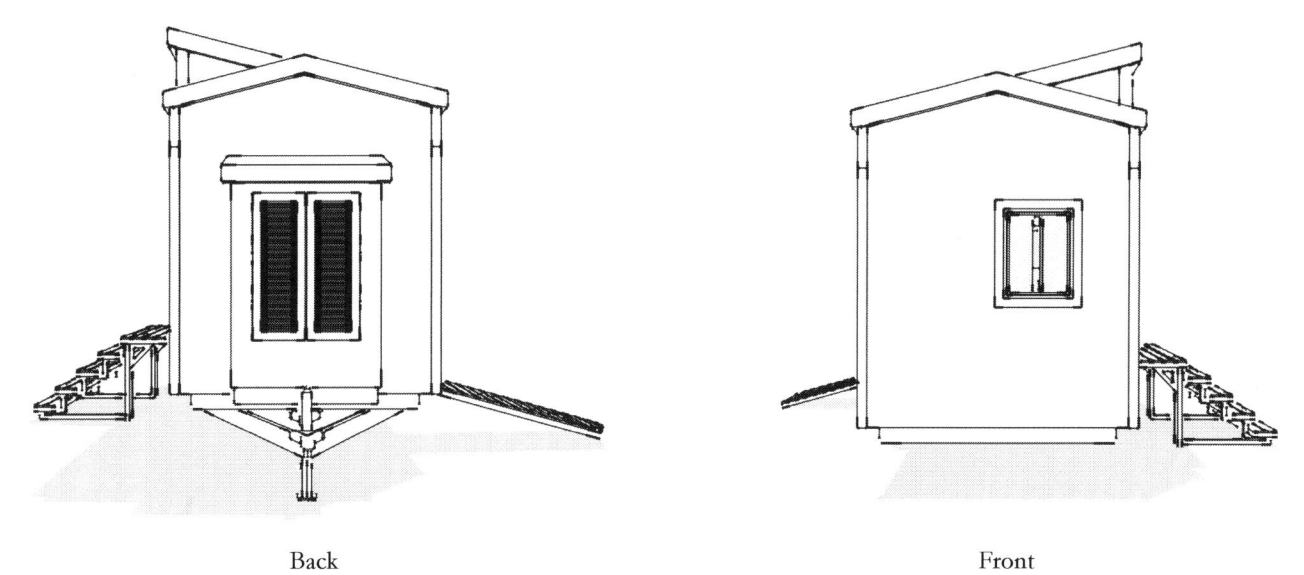

Back

Front

#60

Tiny House #60 - Overview

Front Right

Summary:

Here's a crazy live-work home idea; it's a coffee shop/tiny house combination. At the center of the house is a kitchen fit for a barista. Above the kitchen is a sleeping loft. The side entry is labeled "employees only" and it leads to a short hallway where the homeowner can access the kitchen, bathroom, loft, and laundry during work hours. After hours… a portion of the counter flips out of the way and the homeowners can use the lounge area as a living room. The outside tables and chairs should be stackable and would be stowed inside, (or in the trailer tongue closet), when not needed.

Features:

22-Foot Tiny House on Wheels
Vardo Inspired Roof
Live-Work Space
Coffee Shop/Tiny Home Combination
Two Entries
Sleeps Two Hard Working Entrepreneurs

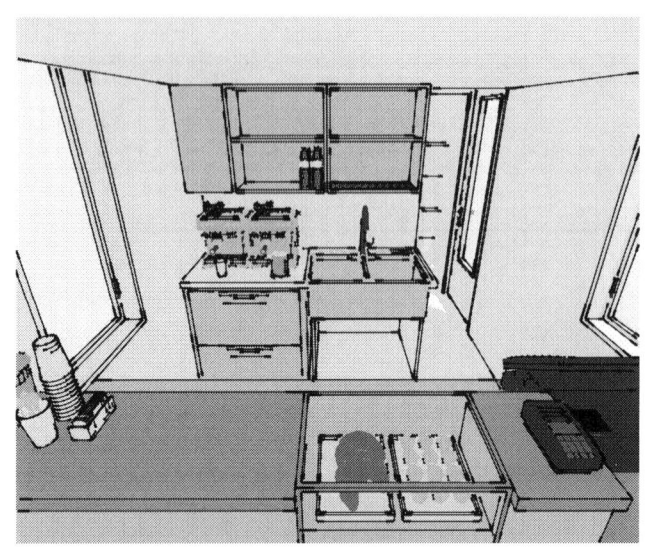

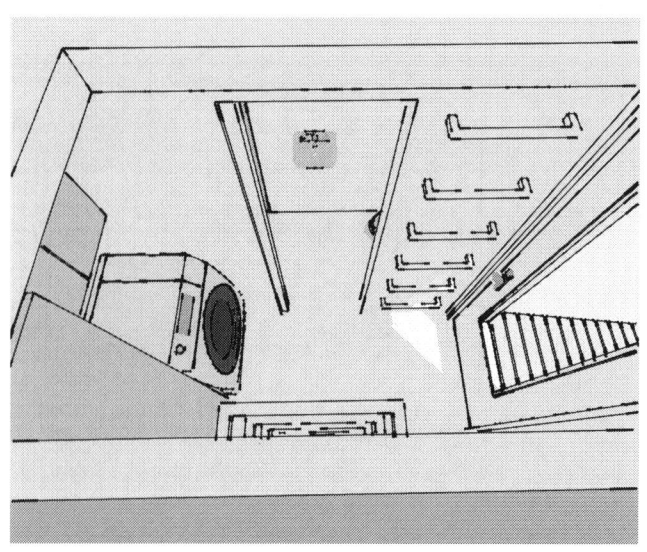

Kitchen

View from Loft

Tiny House #60 - Floor Plan & Exterior

Front Right Corner

Floor Plan - Loft

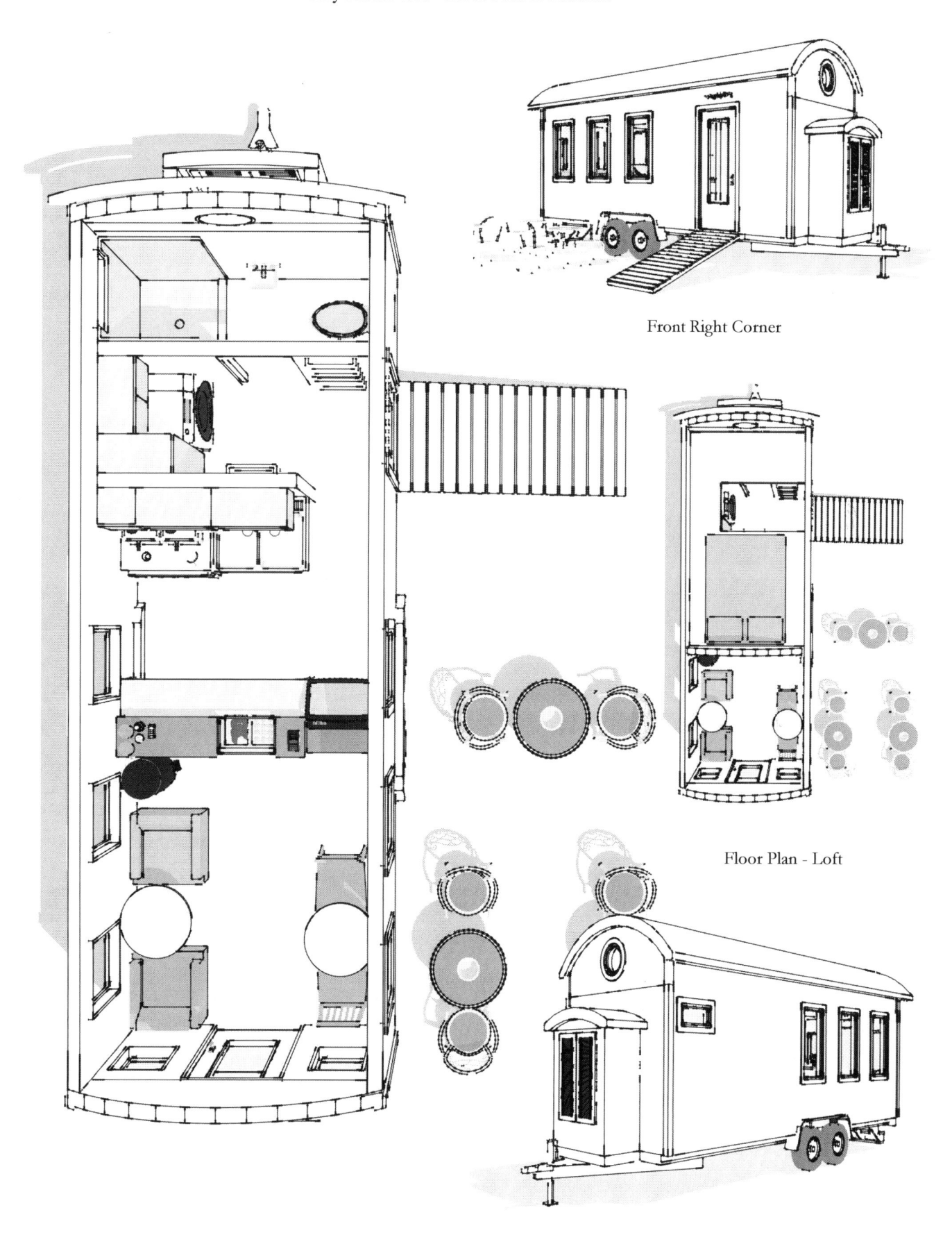

Floor Plan

Back Left Corner

Tiny House #60 - Interior Views

Interior from Living Room/Guest Dining Room

Interior from Kitchen

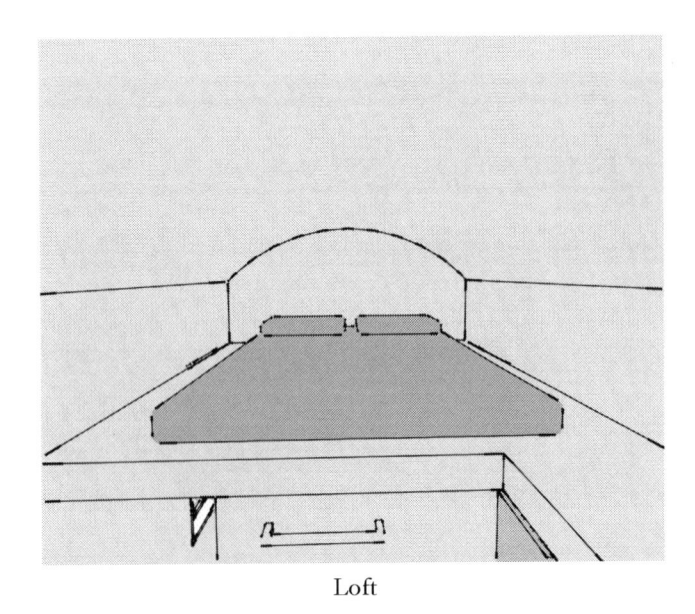

Loft

Bathroom

Tiny House #60 - Elevations

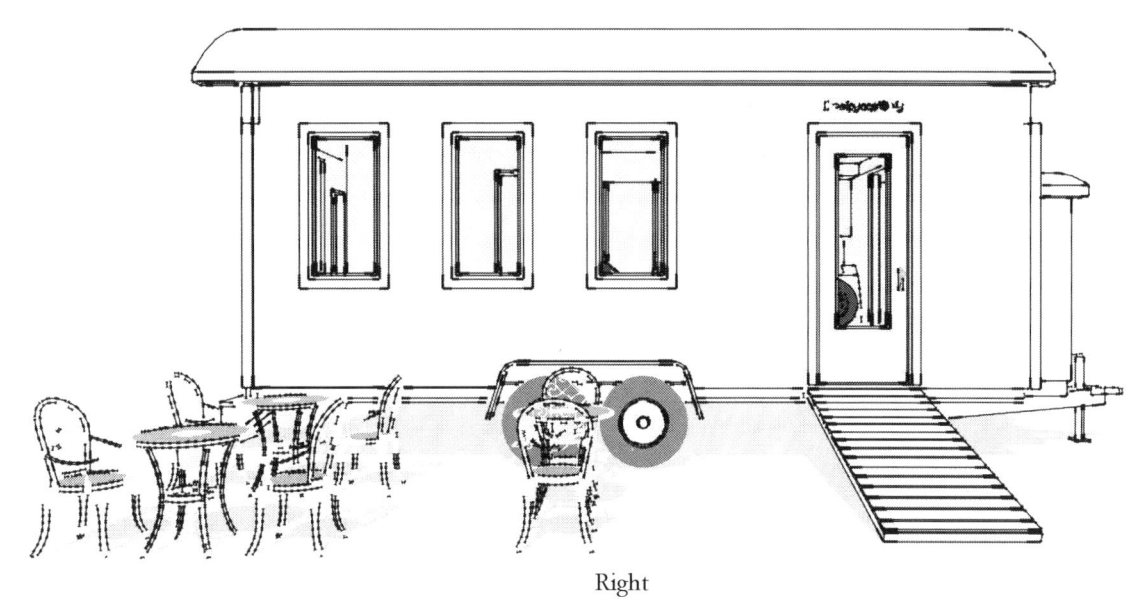

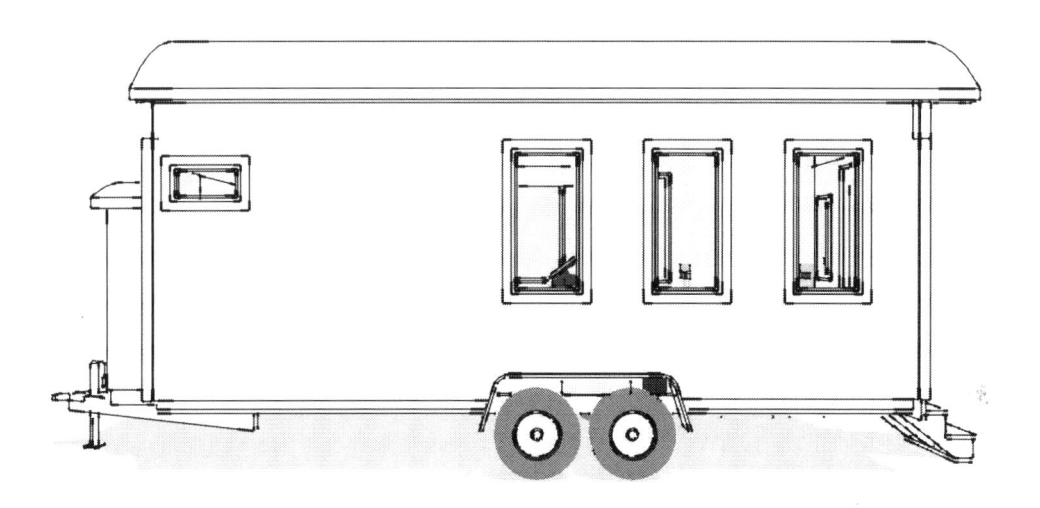

Right

Left

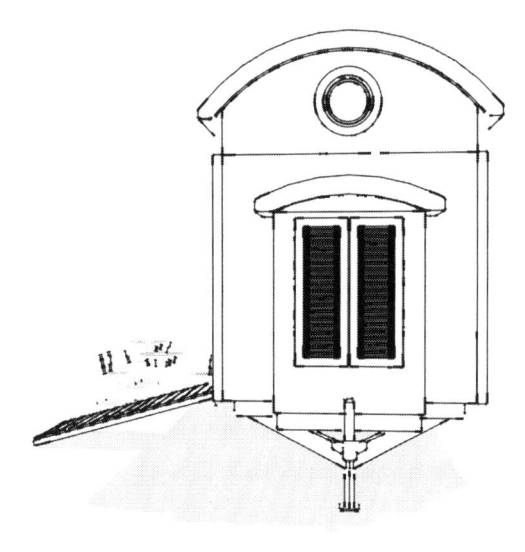

Back

Front

#61

Tiny House #61 - Overview

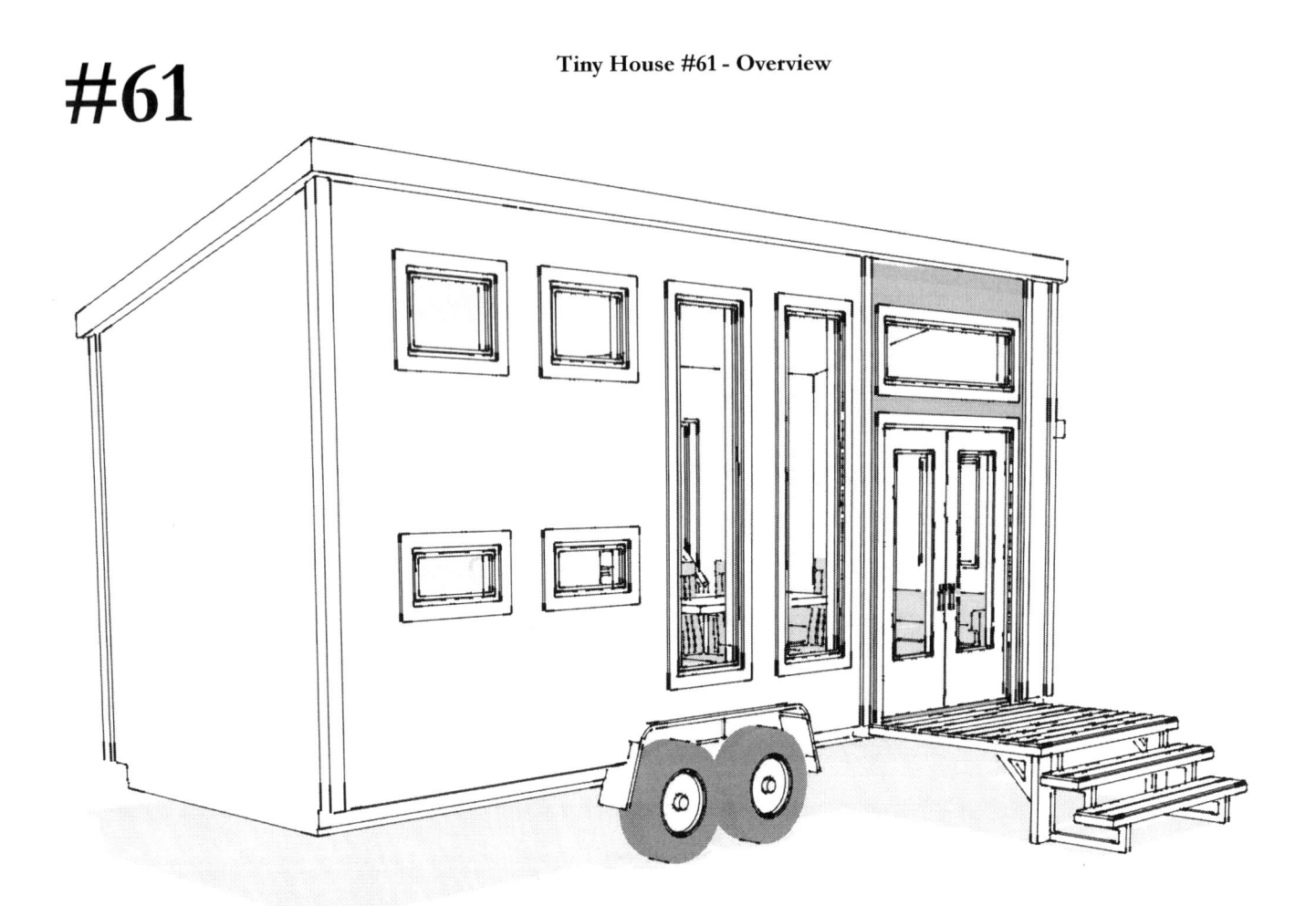

Front Right

Summary:

Here's a very functional design with a simple shed roof. The side French door leads into a living room. On the right is a sofa that's tucked into a bump-out over the trailer tongue. On the left is a staircase with ample storage and a table for four. Under the loft is a kitchen and bathroom. The loft is large enough for a queen bed.

Features:

22-Foot Tiny House on Wheels
3/12 Shed Roof
Plenty of Seating
Table for Four
Stairs to Loft
Sleeps Two

Kitchen

View from Loft

Tiny House #61 - Floor Plan & Exterior

Front Right Corner

Floor Plan - Loft

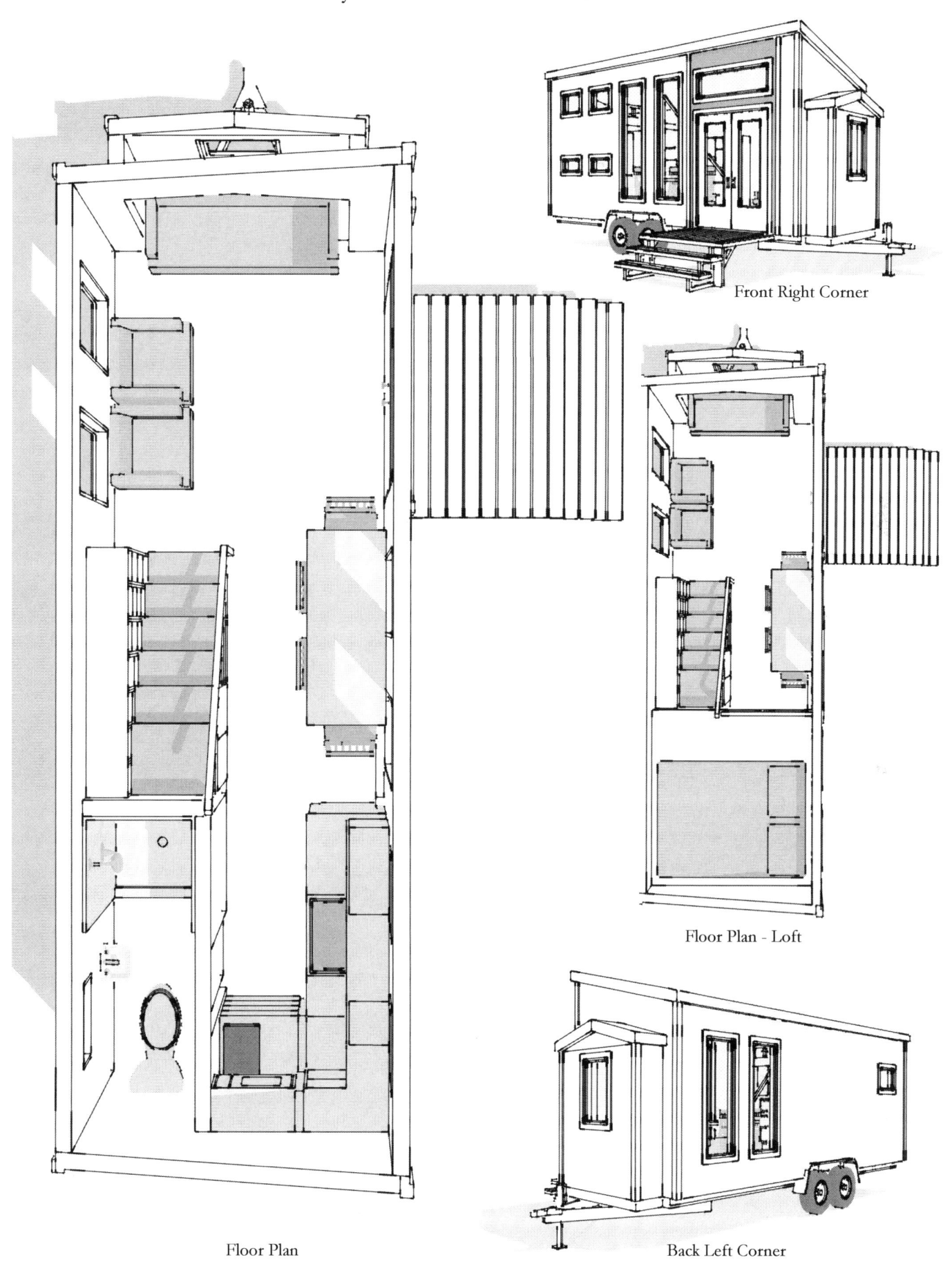

Floor Plan

Back Left Corner

Tiny House #61 - Interior Views

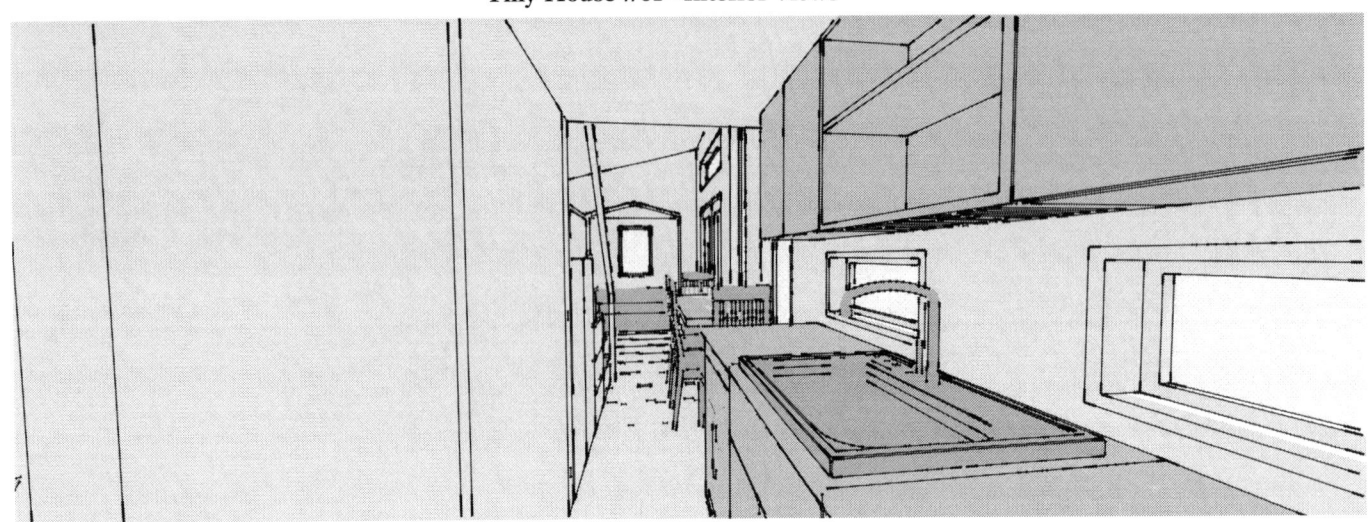

Interior from Kitchen

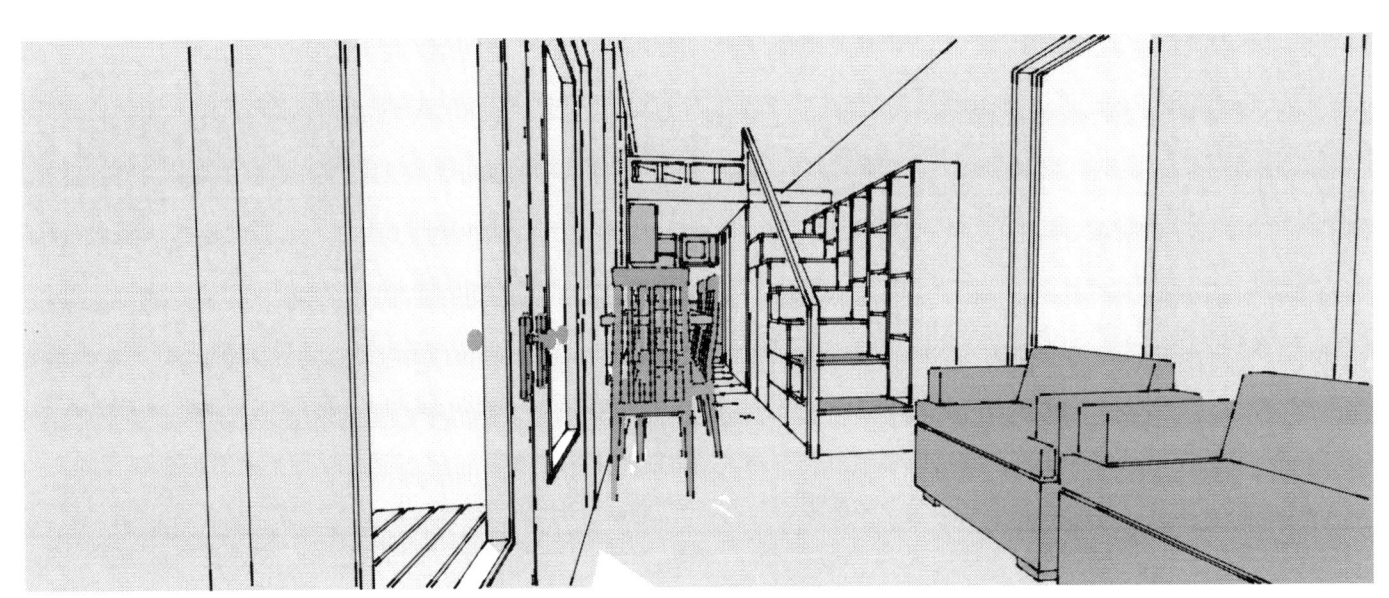

Interior from Entry

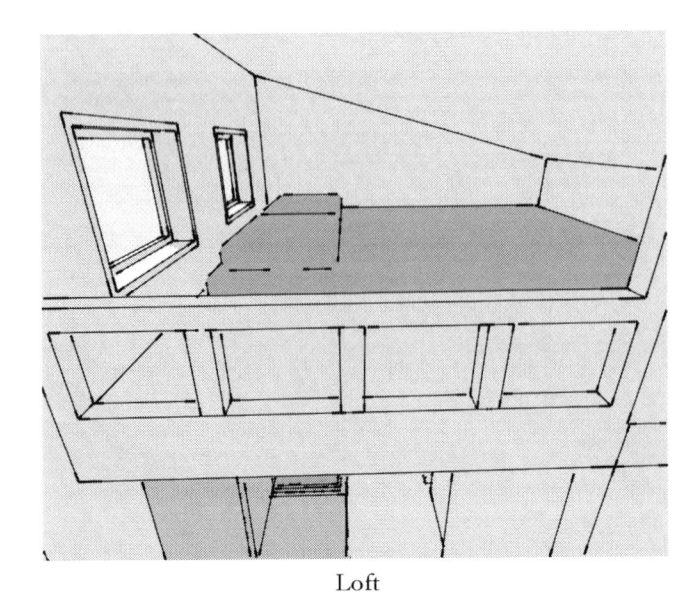

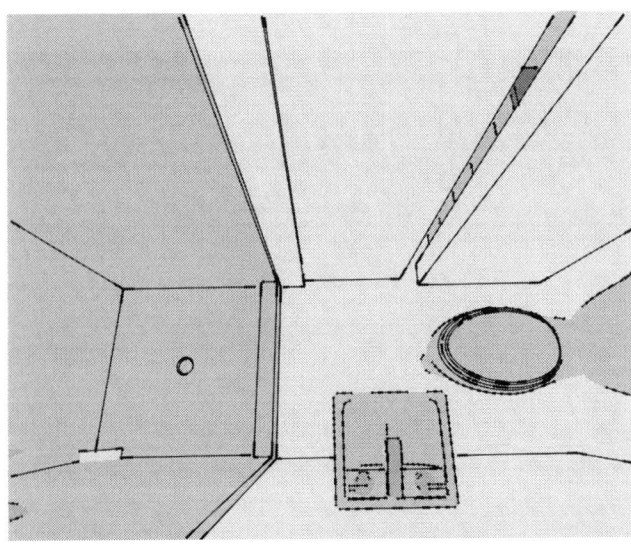

Loft

Bathroom

Tiny House #61 - Elevations

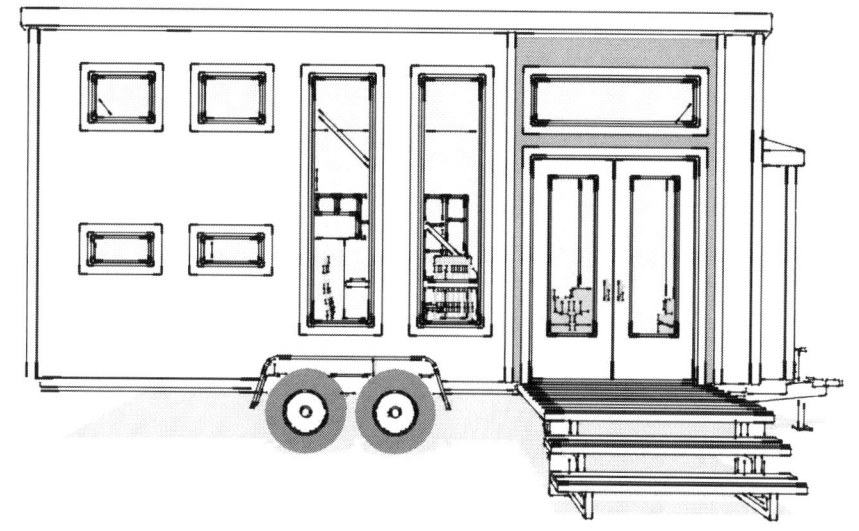

Right

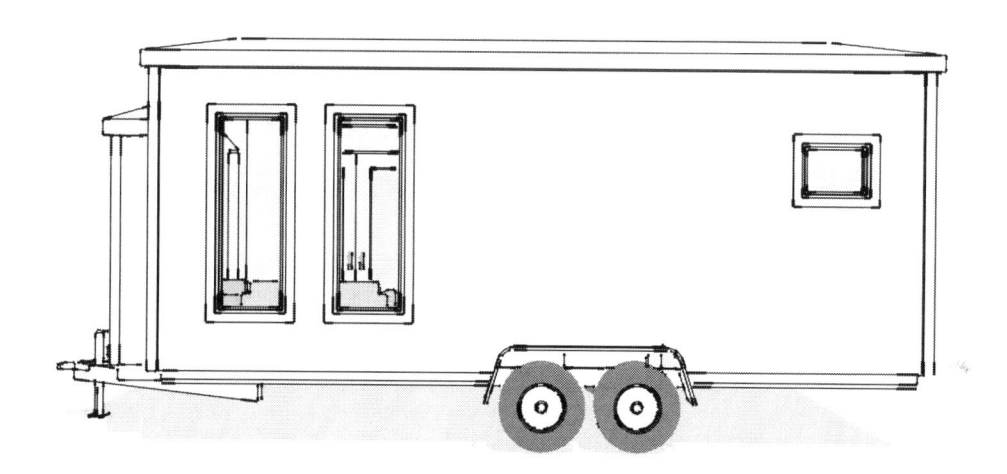

Left

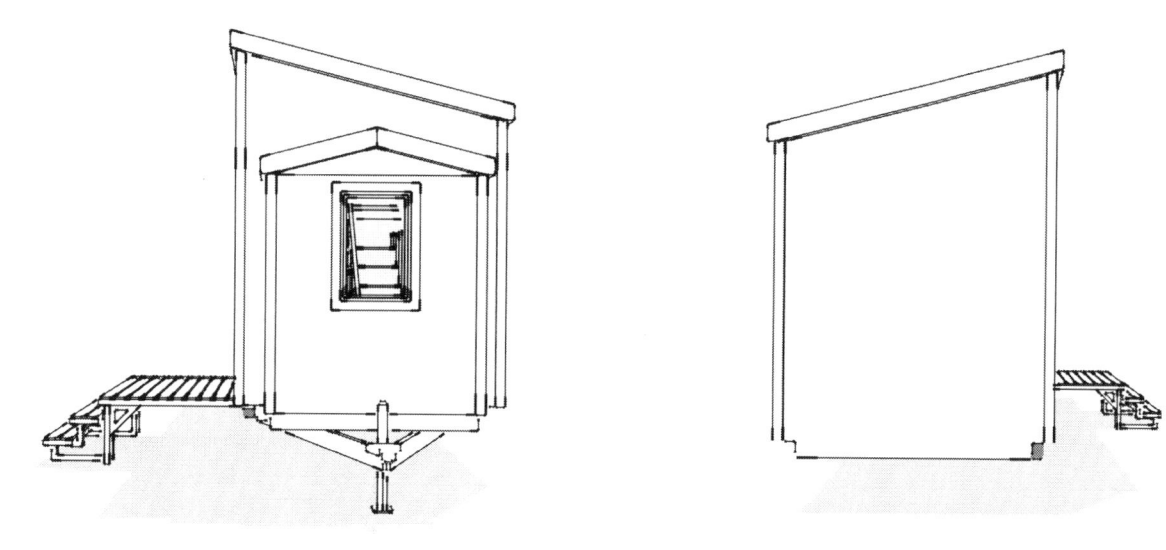

Back

Front

#62

Tiny House #62 - Overview

Front Right

Summary:

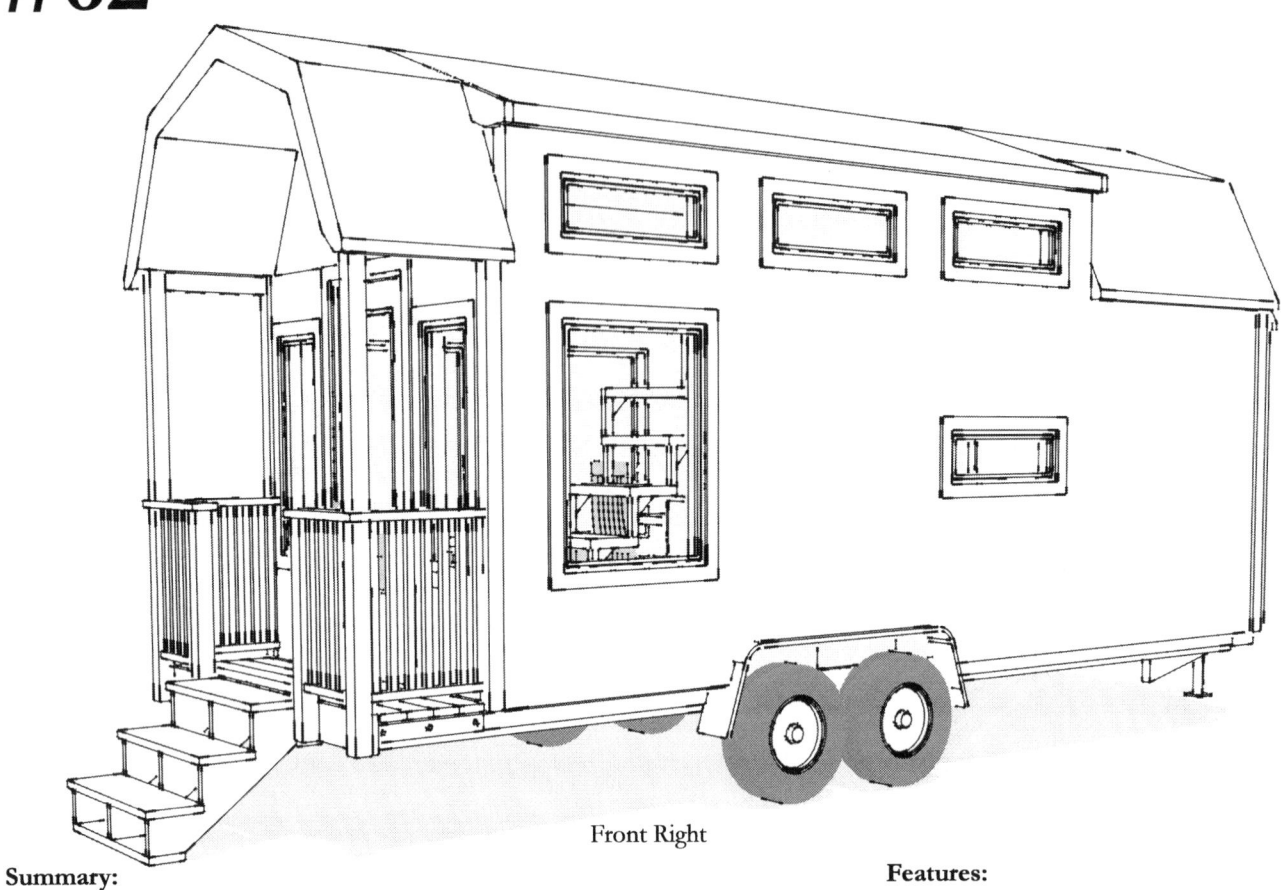

This tiny house is another very functional design, ideal for two people. Just inside the front door is an open staircase that hardly obstructs the large window. Across from the stairs are two comfy chairs. Under the loft is the kitchen and a table for two. In the back of the house is a large bathroom with soaking tub, toilet, vanity, and laundry. The loft doesn't extend over the bathroom, giving the bathroom a very high ceiling.

Features:

22-Foot Tiny House on Wheels
Gambrel Roof with Shed Dormers
Open Staircase to Loft
Generous Kitchen
Large Bathroom Extends over Trailer Tongue
Laundry in Bathroom
Front Porch

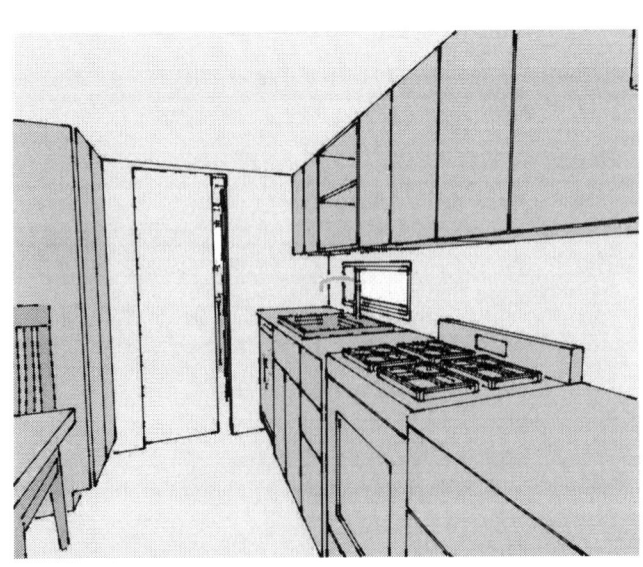

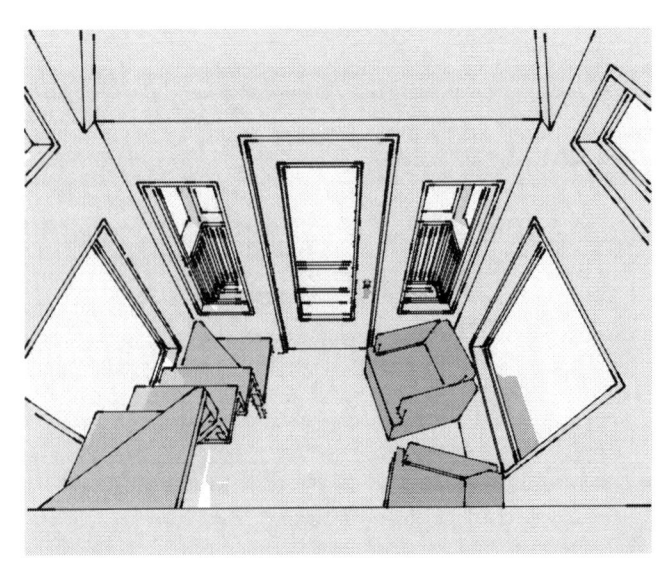

Kitchen

View from Loft

Tiny House #62 - Floor Plan & Exterior

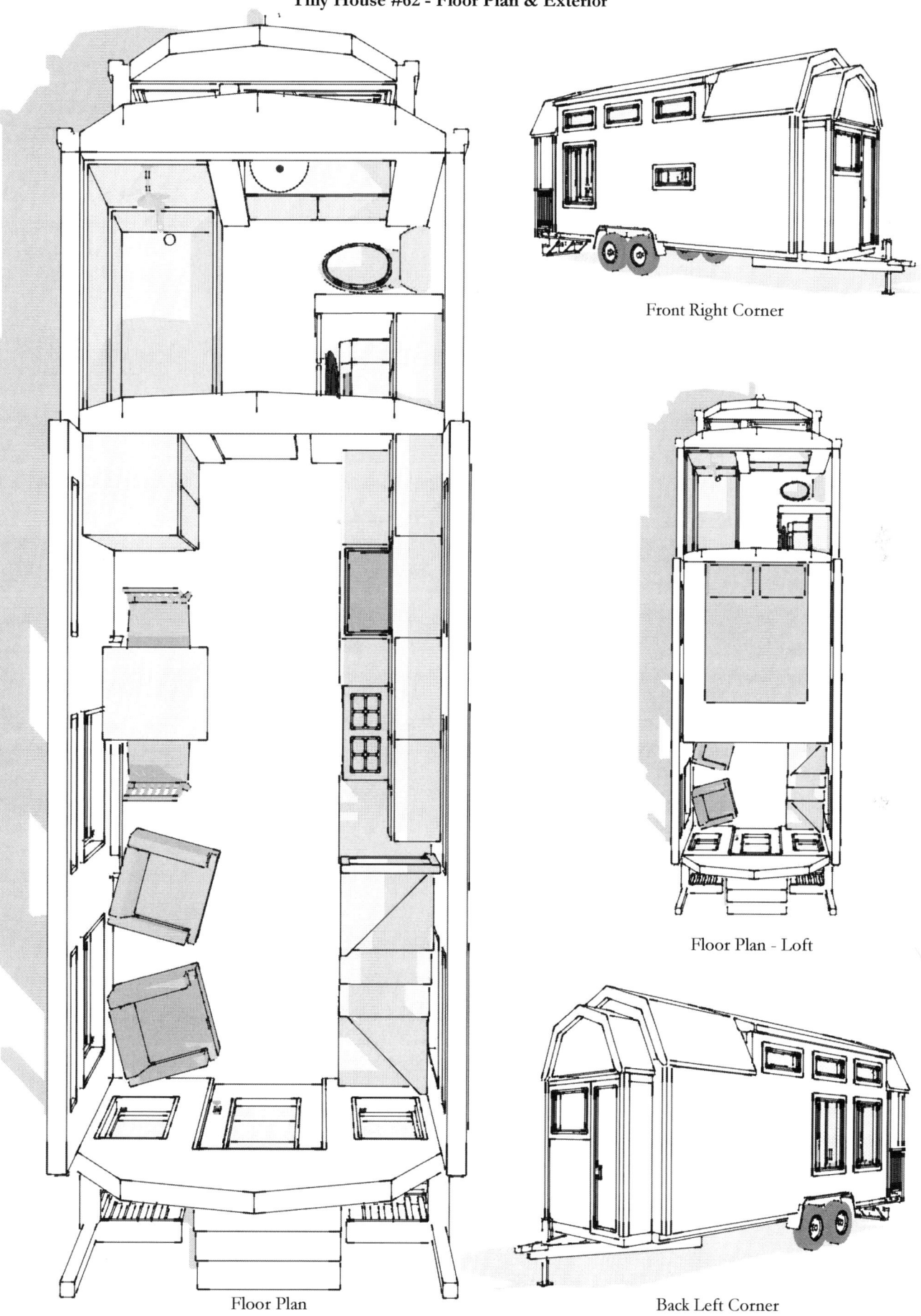

Front Right Corner

Floor Plan - Loft

Floor Plan

Back Left Corner

257

Tiny House #62 - Interior Views

Interior from Entry

Interior from Bathroom

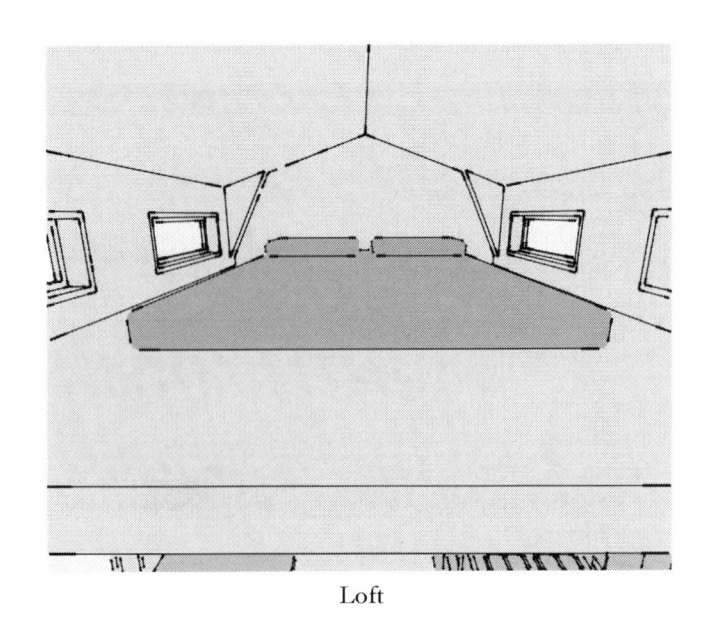

Loft

Bathroom

258

Tiny House #62 - Elevations

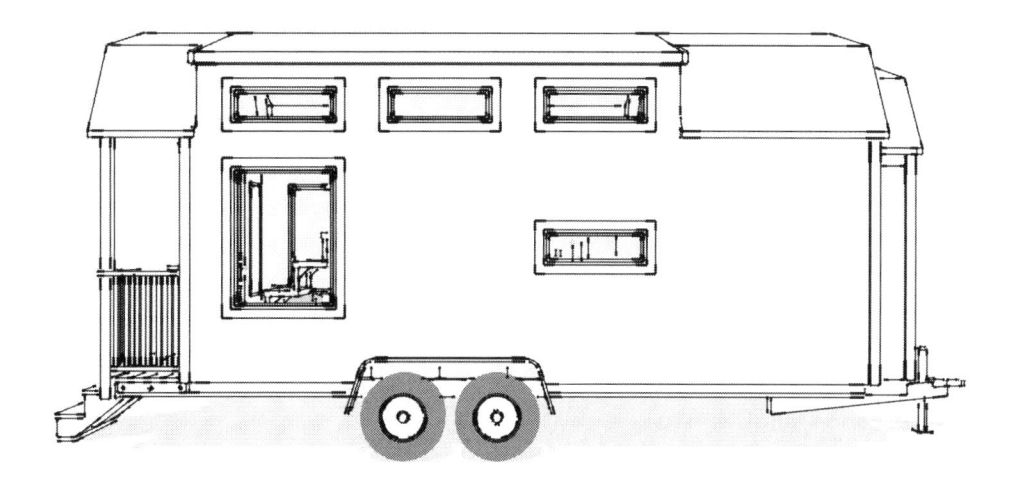

Right

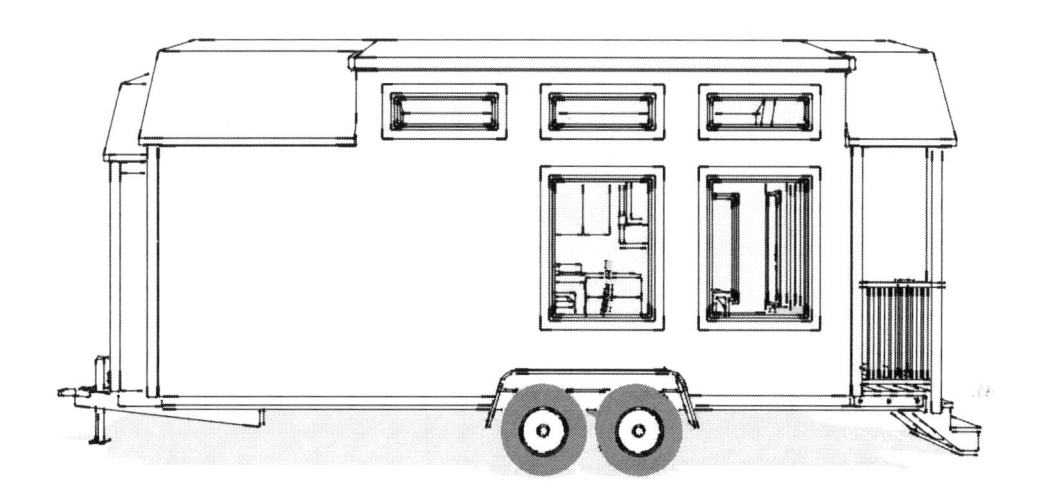

Left

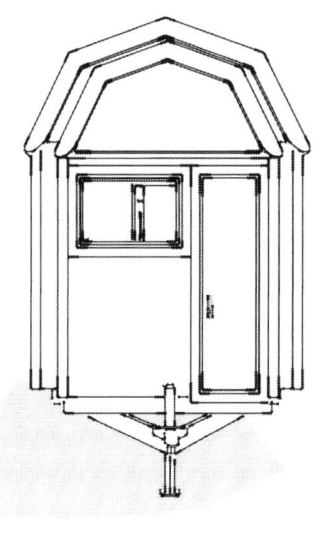

Back

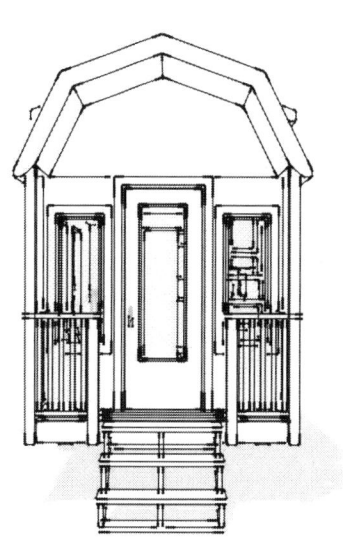

Front

259

#63

Tiny House #63 - Overview

Front Right

Summary:

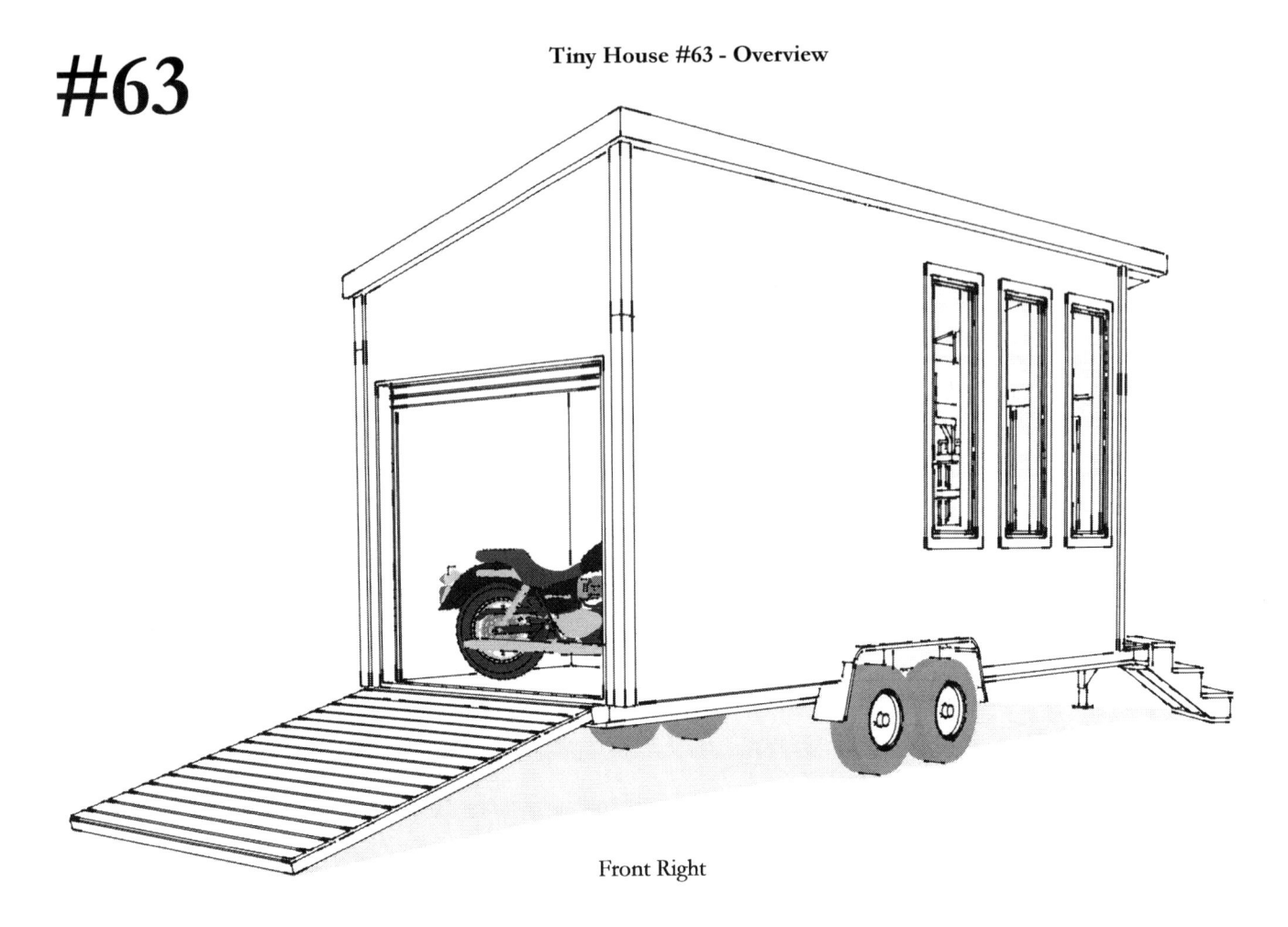

Here's a larger toy hauler tiny house with a garage large enough for a large motorcycle. There's no door this time connecting the house to the garage, but there could be. Inside the house is a tiny kitchen under the open staircase, a table for three and one comfy chair. Up the stairs is a loft with a queen bed.

Features:

22-Foot Tiny House on Wheels
Shed Roof
Tiny Kitchen under Stairs
Garage
Loft with Queen Bed
Table for Three

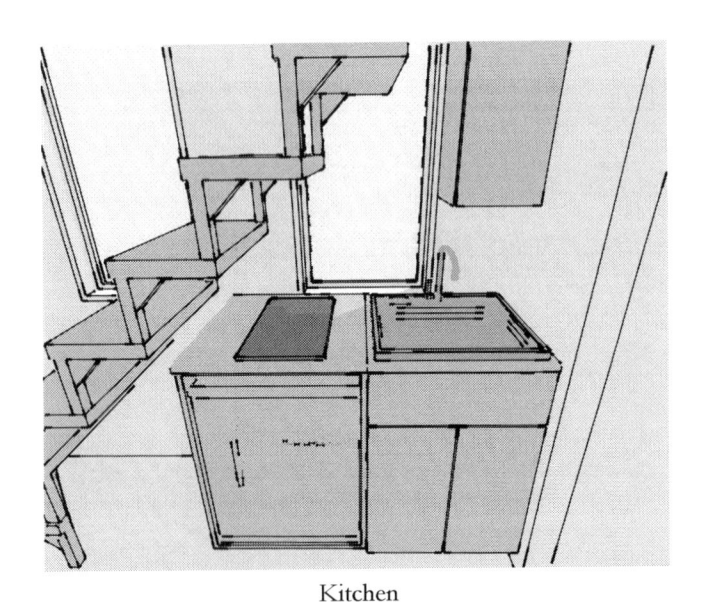

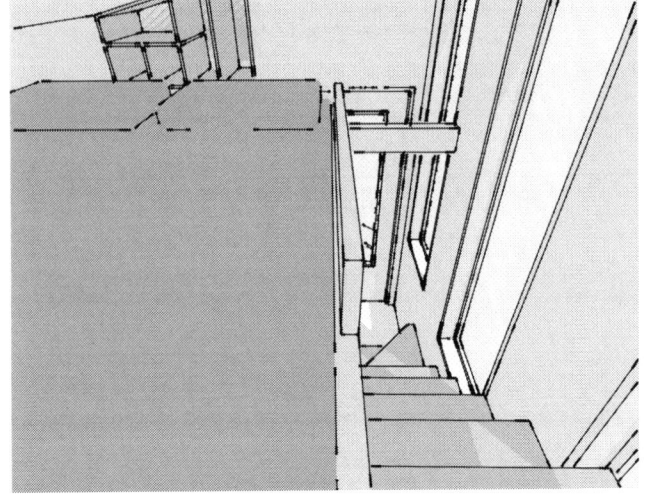

Kitchen

View from Loft

Tiny House #63 - Floor Plan & Exterior

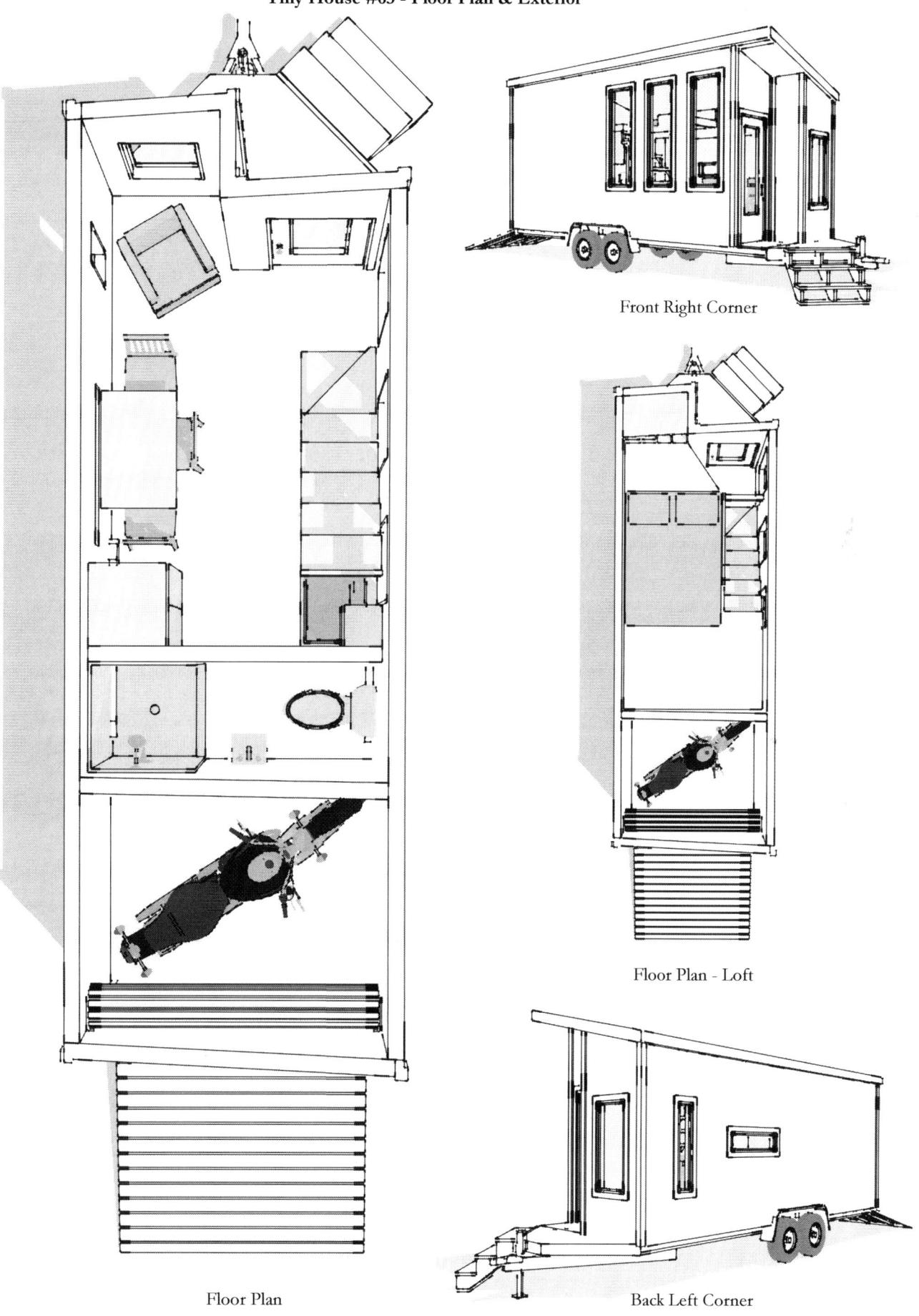

Front Right Corner

Floor Plan - Loft

Floor Plan

Back Left Corner

Tiny House #63 - Interior Views

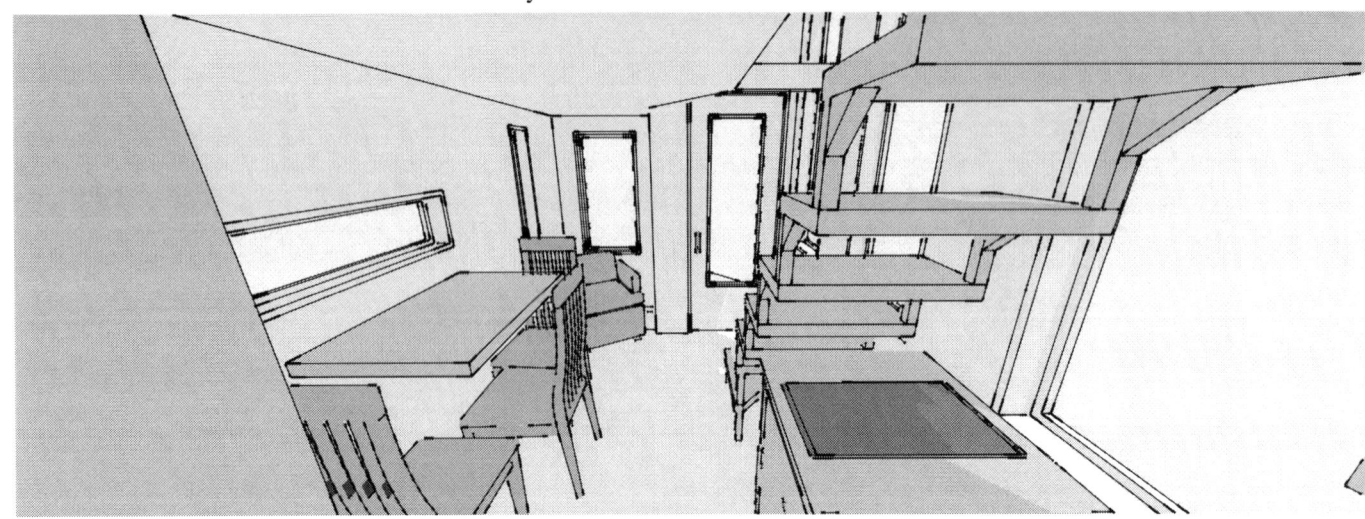

Interior from Bathroom

Interior from Entry

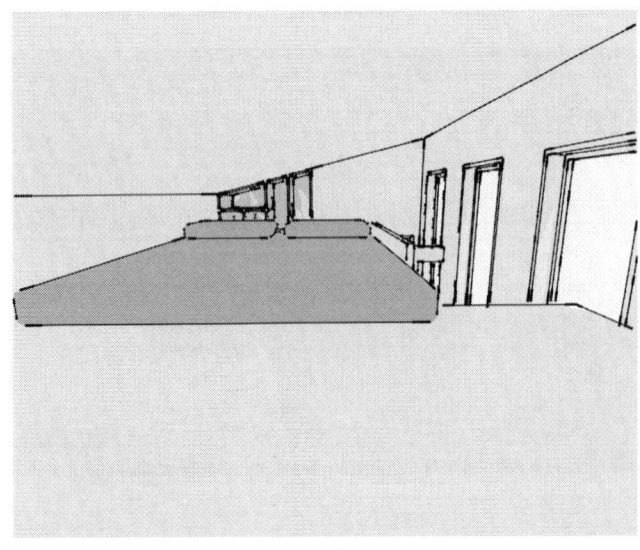

Loft

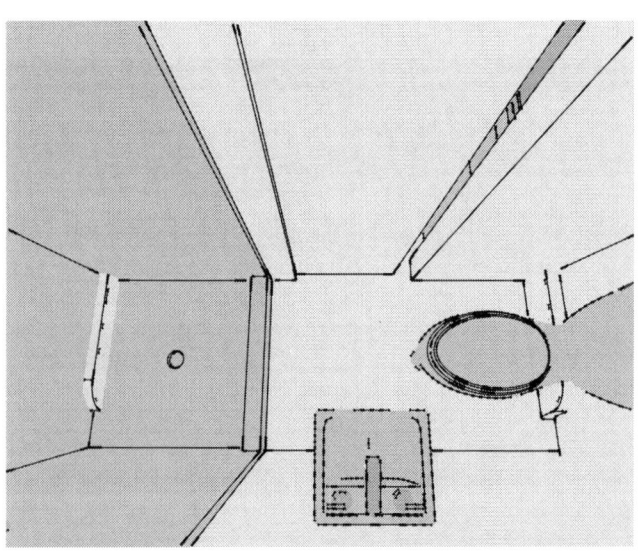

Bathroom

262

Tiny House #63 - Elevations

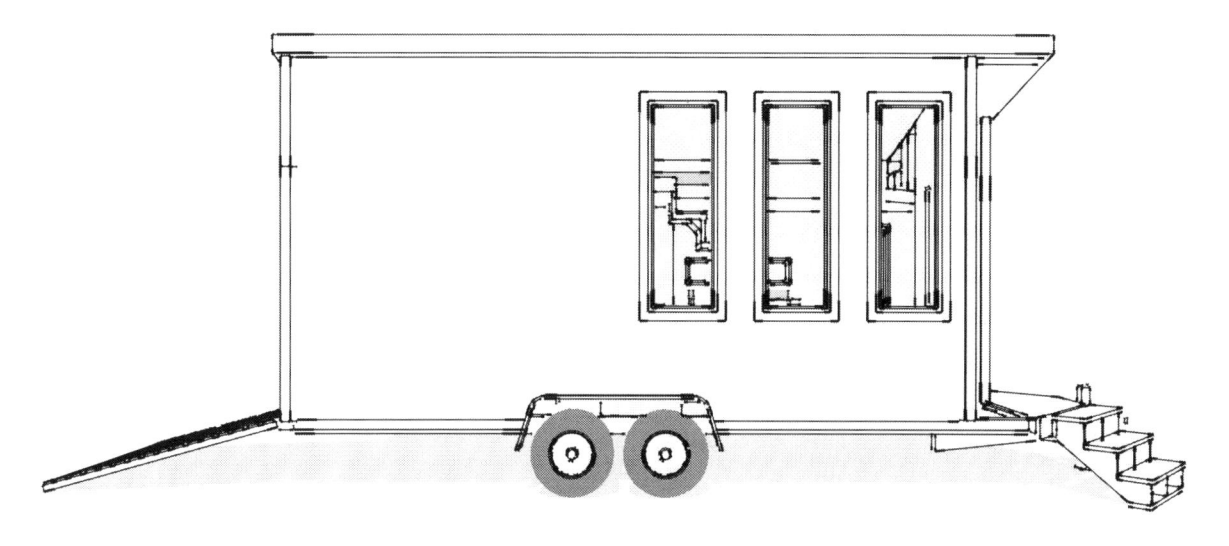

Right

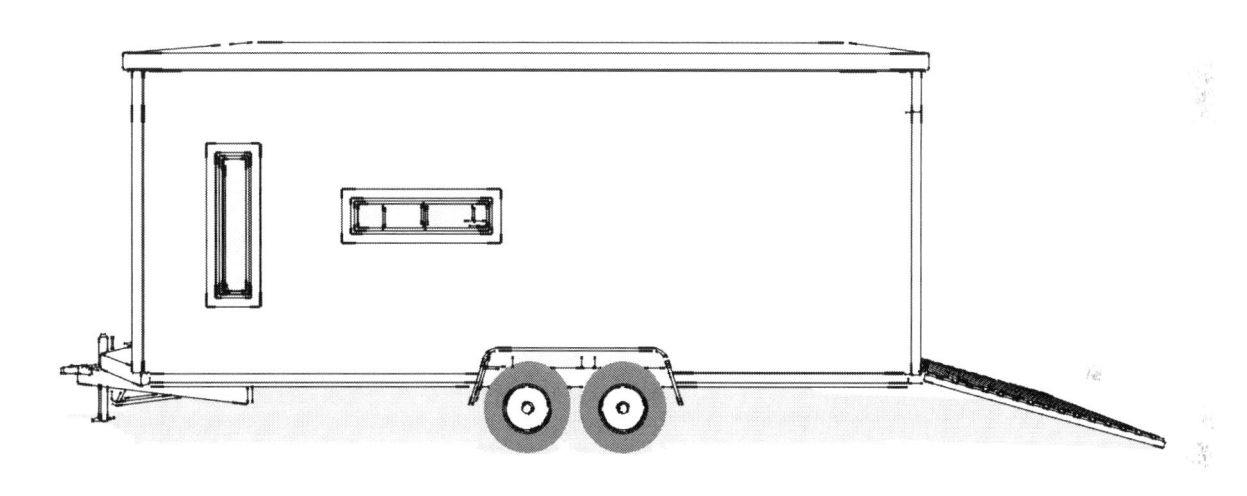

Left

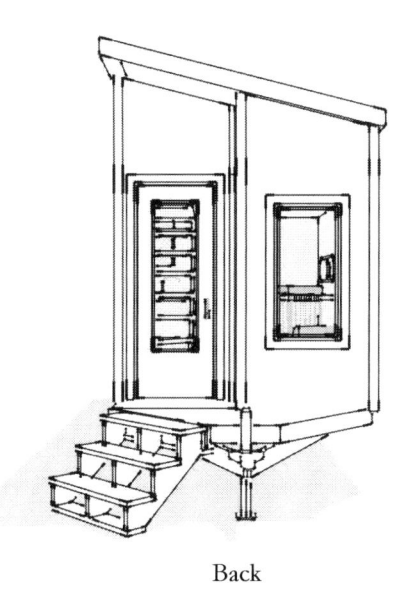

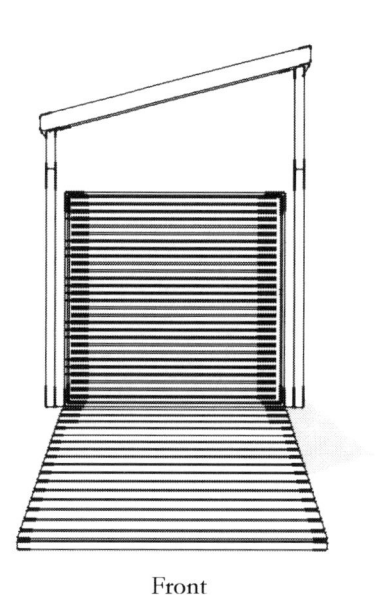

Back

Front

#64

Tiny House #64 - Overview

Summary:

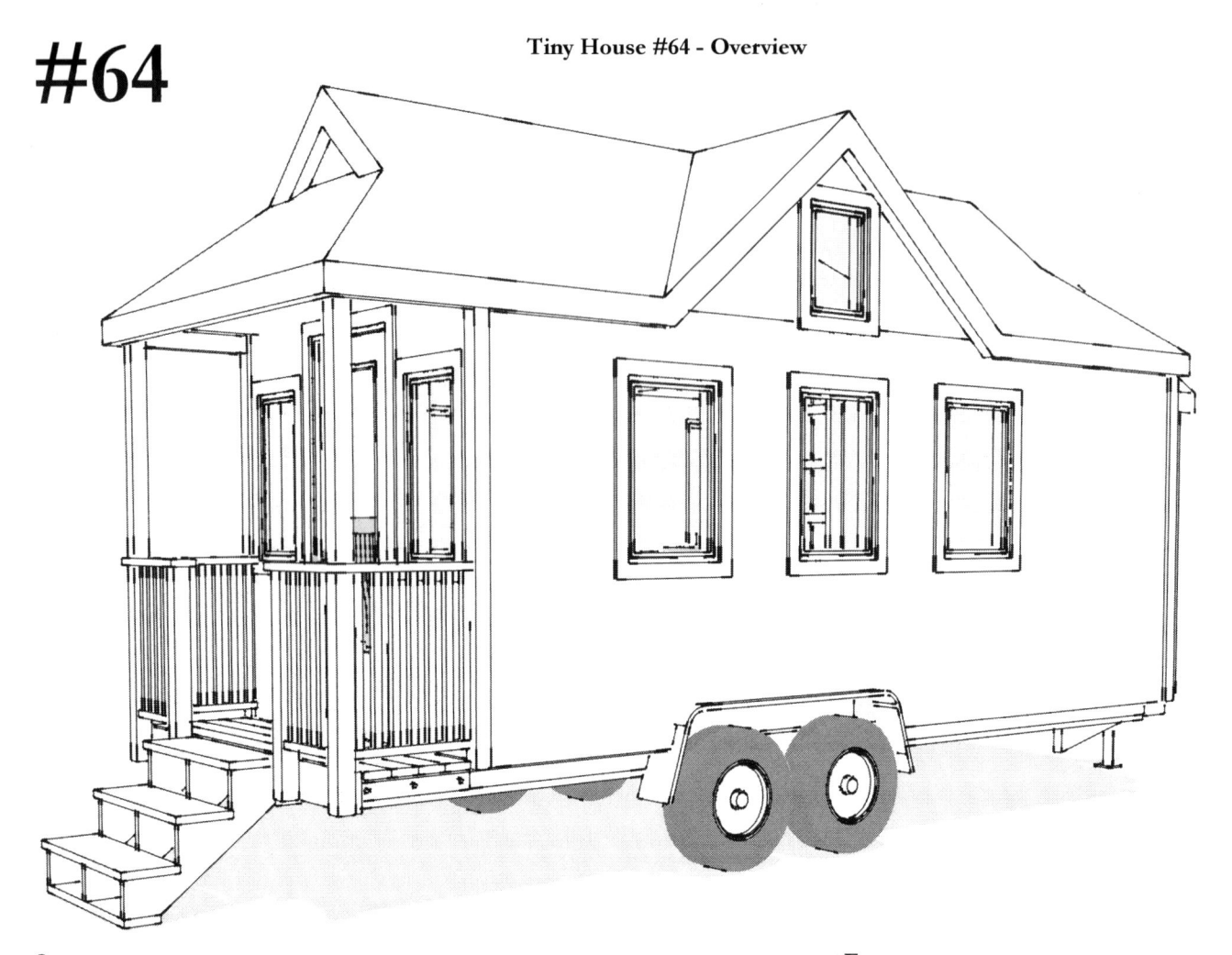

Compare this house with the smaller Dutch Cross Gables and you'll see how adding just a few feet to the length of a tiny house can add a lot function. This house has a lot of storage, a generous kitchen, a nice sized bathroom with vanity, plus plenty of space for seating. Up a movable ladder is a loft with a queen bed. The cross gable roof adds light and some headroom in the loft.

Features:

22-Foot Tiny House on Wheels
Dutch Cross Gable Roof
Bathroom with Vanity
Front Porch

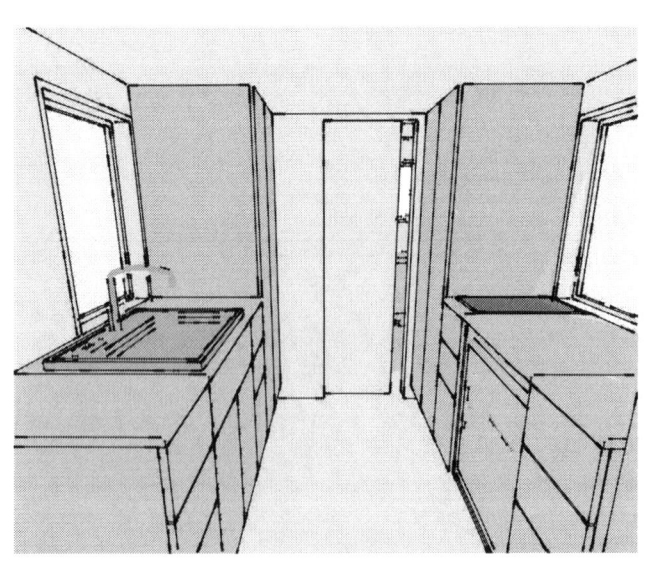

Kitchen

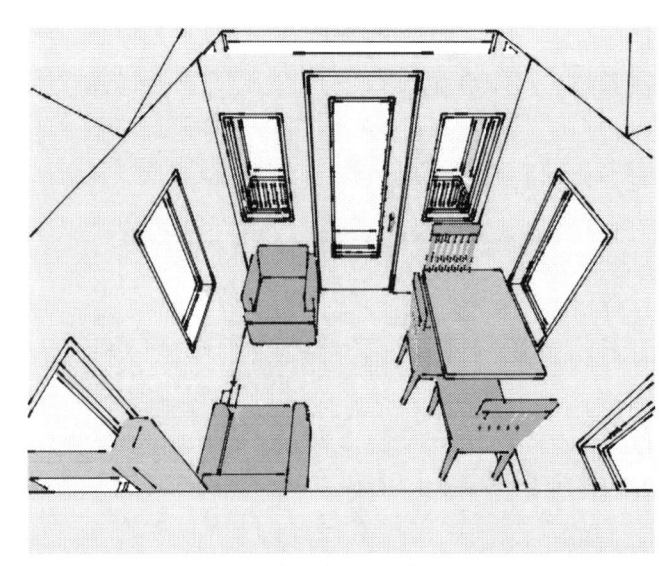

View from Loft

Tiny House #64 - Floor Plan & Exterior

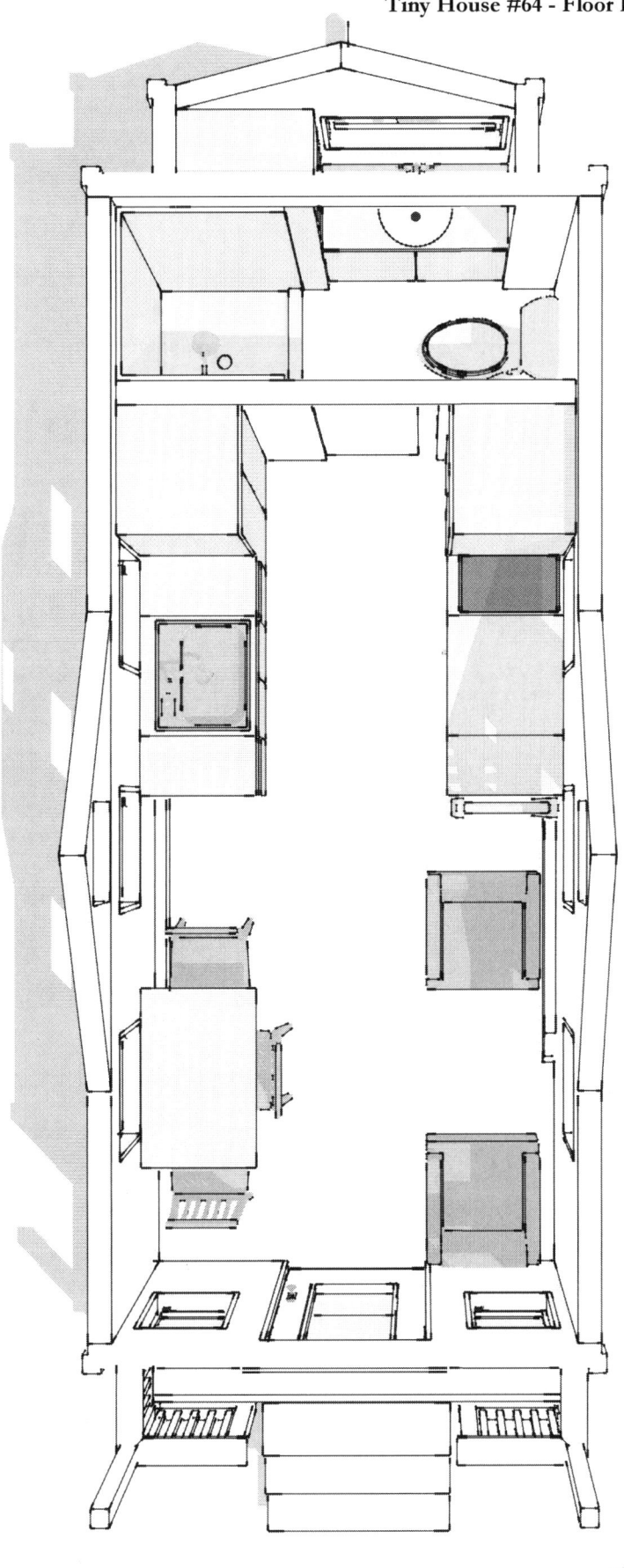

Front Right Corner

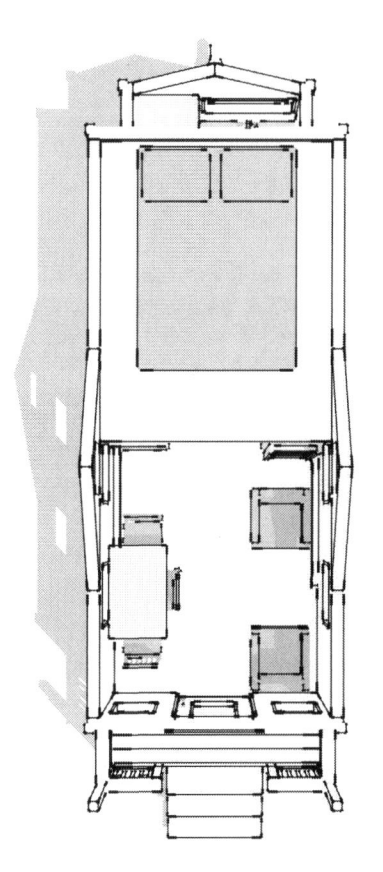

Floor Plan - Loft

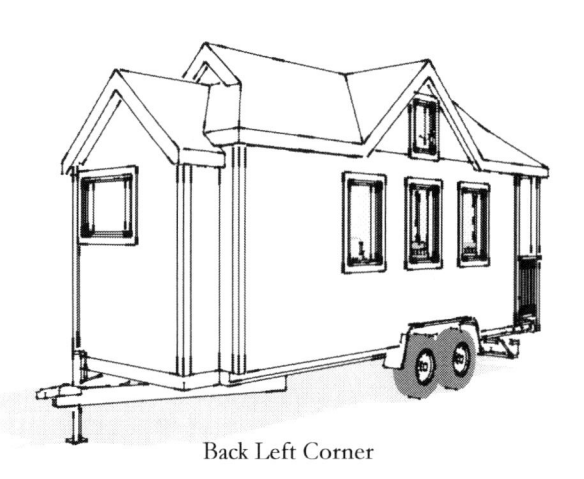

Floor Plan

Back Left Corner

Tiny House #64 - Interior Views

Interior from Entry

Interior from Bathroom

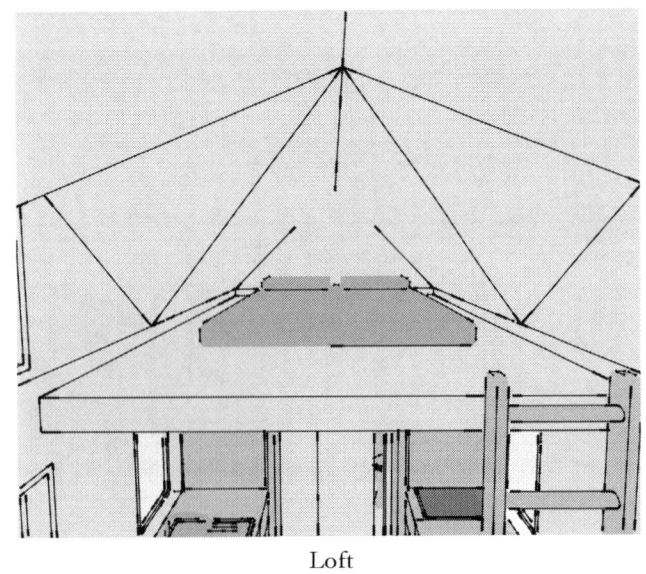

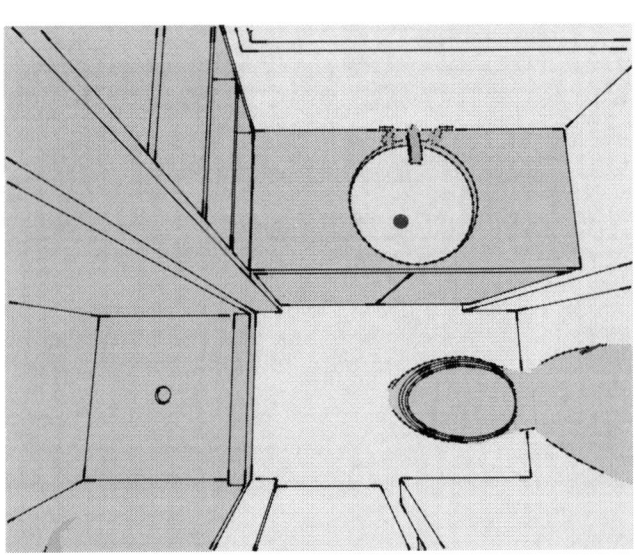

Loft

Bathroom

Tiny House #64 - Elevations

Right

Left

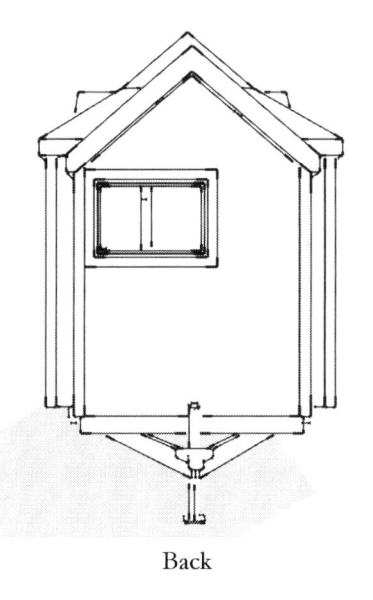

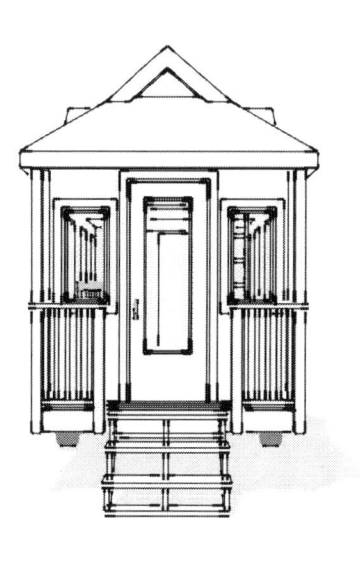

Back

Front

#65

Tiny House #65 - Overview

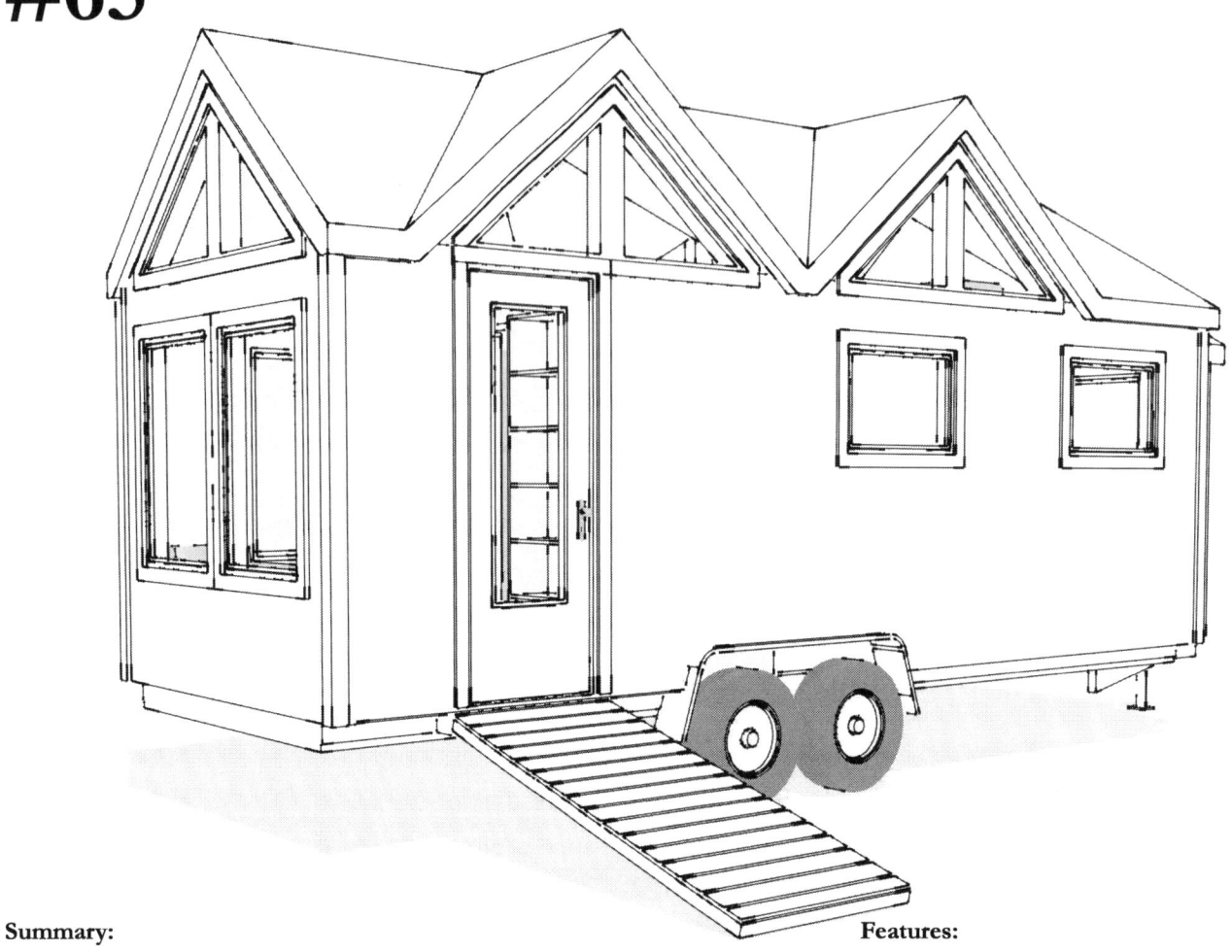

Summary:

When I drew this one I was thinking of a tiny vacation house. Inside the front door is a living room with 3 comfy chairs, storage, and a ladder to a loft. The loft is large and has room for two twin beds or a queen bed (shown). Continuing into the home you pass through the kitchen and past the bathroom, then into a lower level bedroom. The kitchen is small but functional.

Features:

22-Foot Tiny House on Wheels
Double Cross Gable with Hip on End
Lower Lever Bedroom
Side Entry with Ramp
Aerodynamic

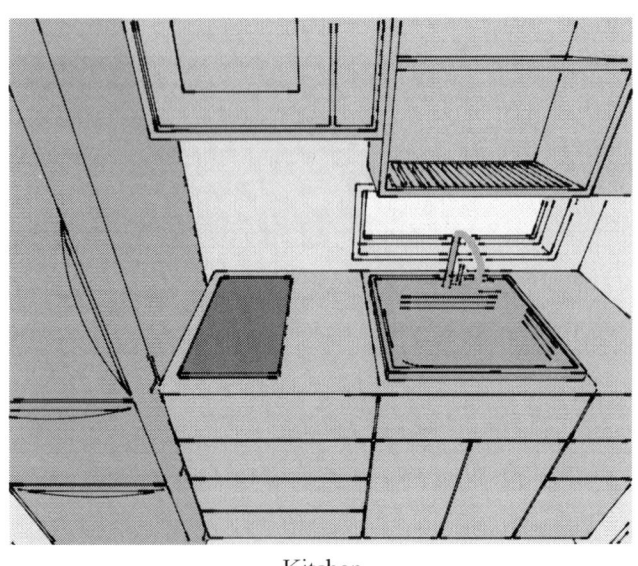

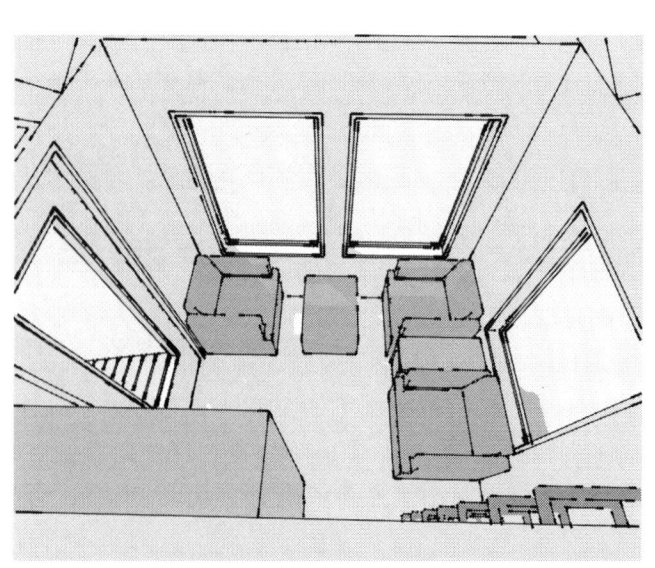

Kitchen

View from Loft

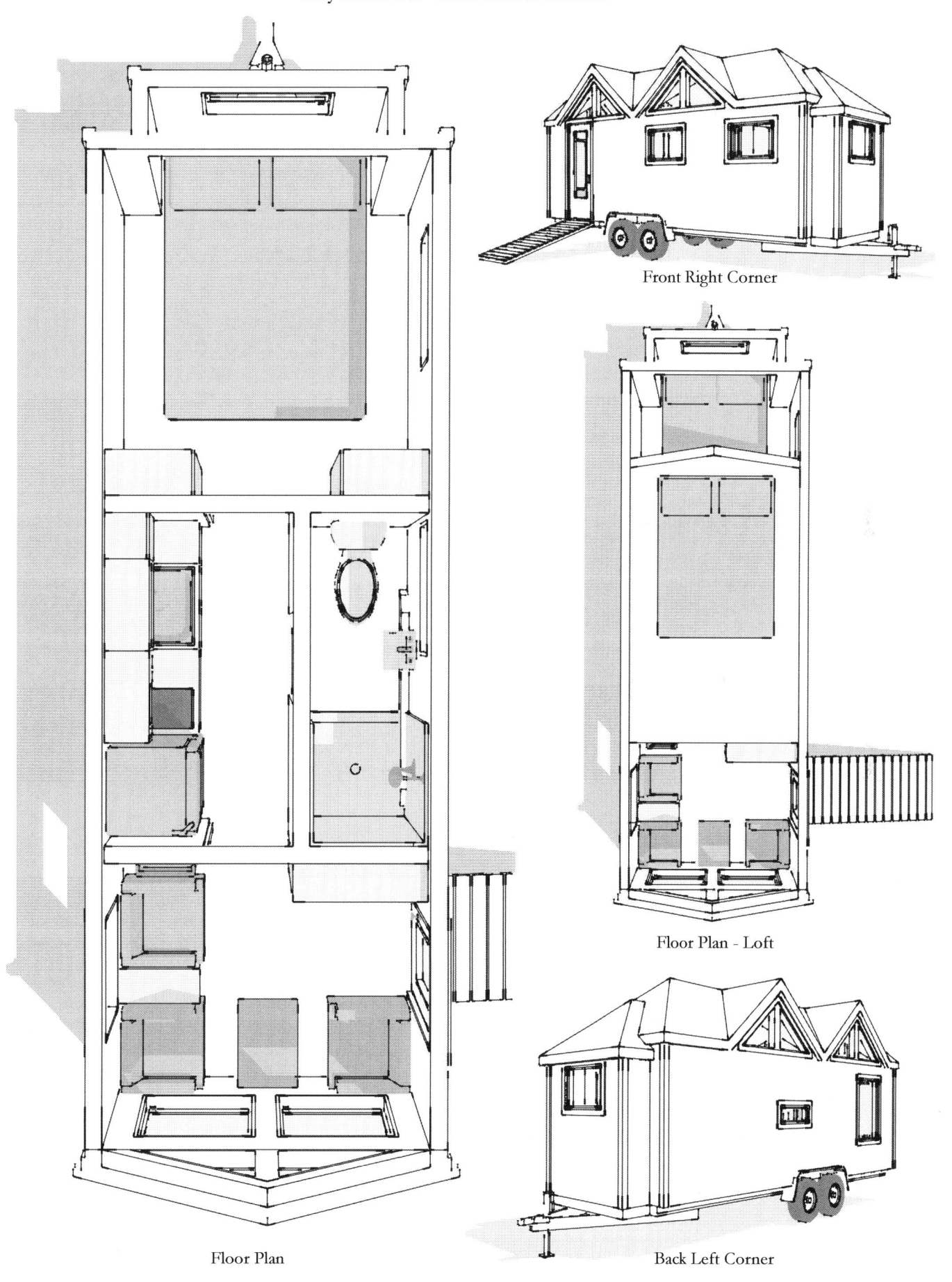

Tiny House #65 - Floor Plan & Exterior

Front Right Corner

Floor Plan - Loft

Floor Plan

Back Left Corner

Tiny House #65 - Interior Views

Interior from Entry

Interior from Kitchen

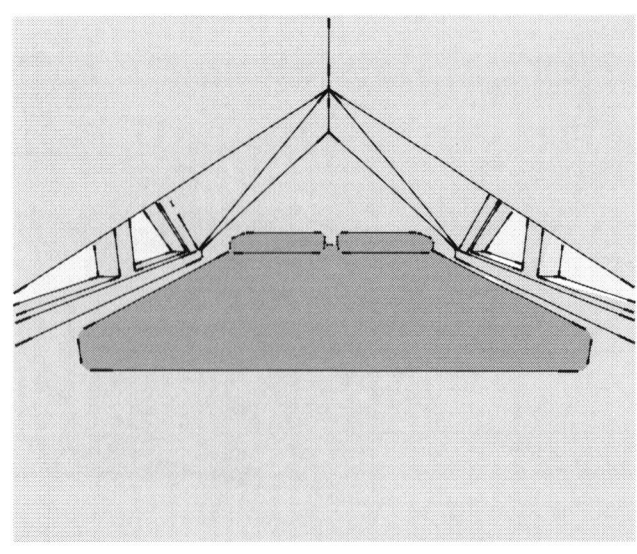

Loft

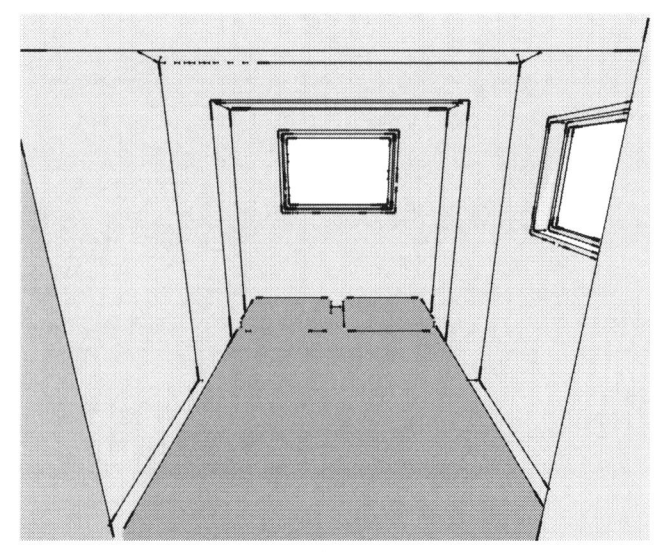

Bedroom

Tiny House #65 - Elevations

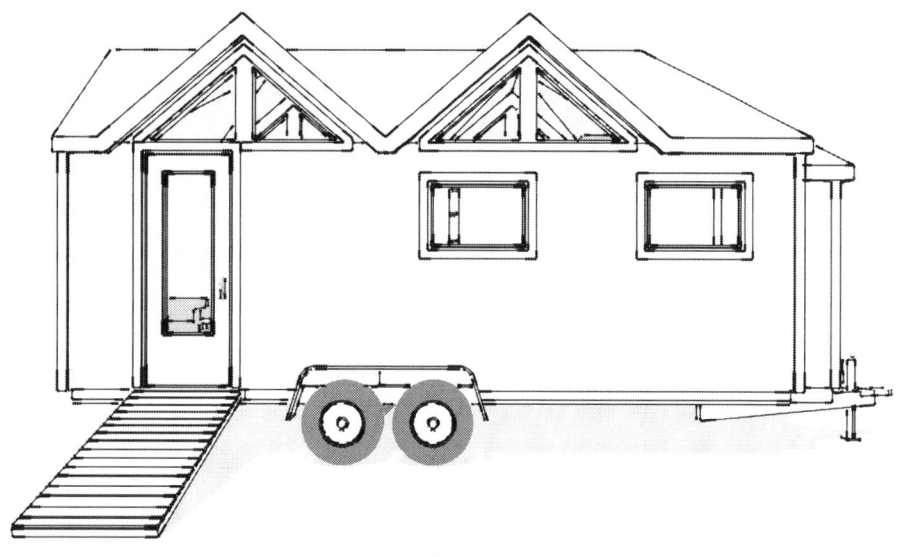

Right

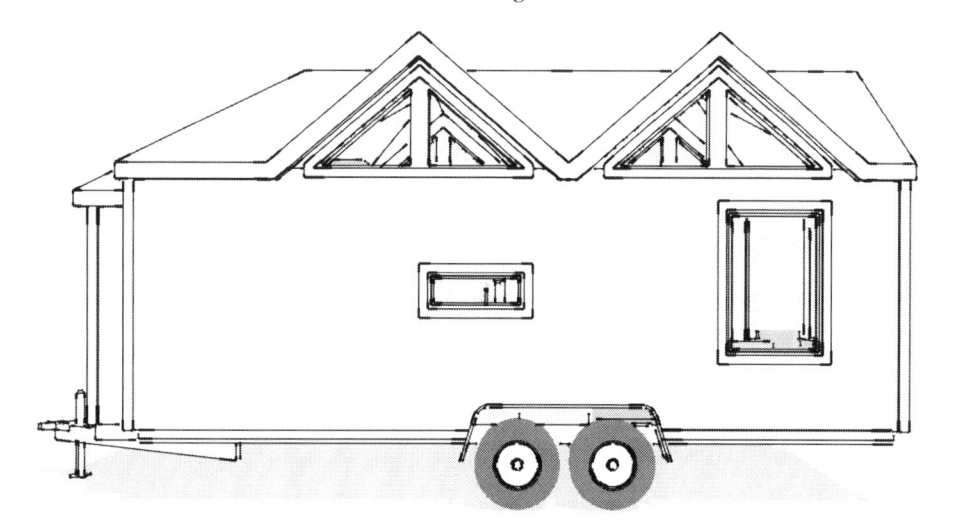

Left

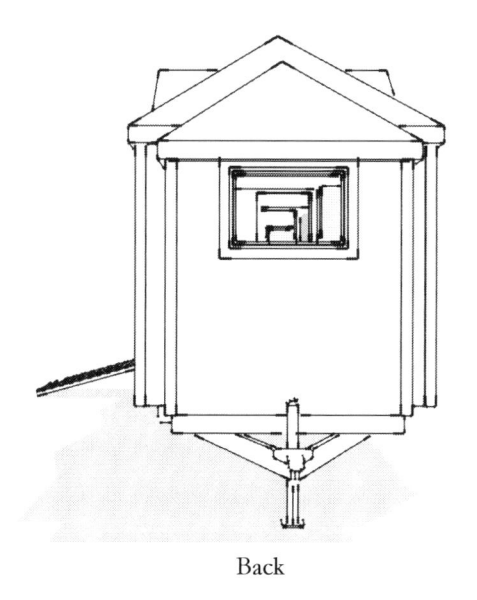

Back

Front

24-Foot Tiny House Designs

#66

Tiny House #66 - Overview

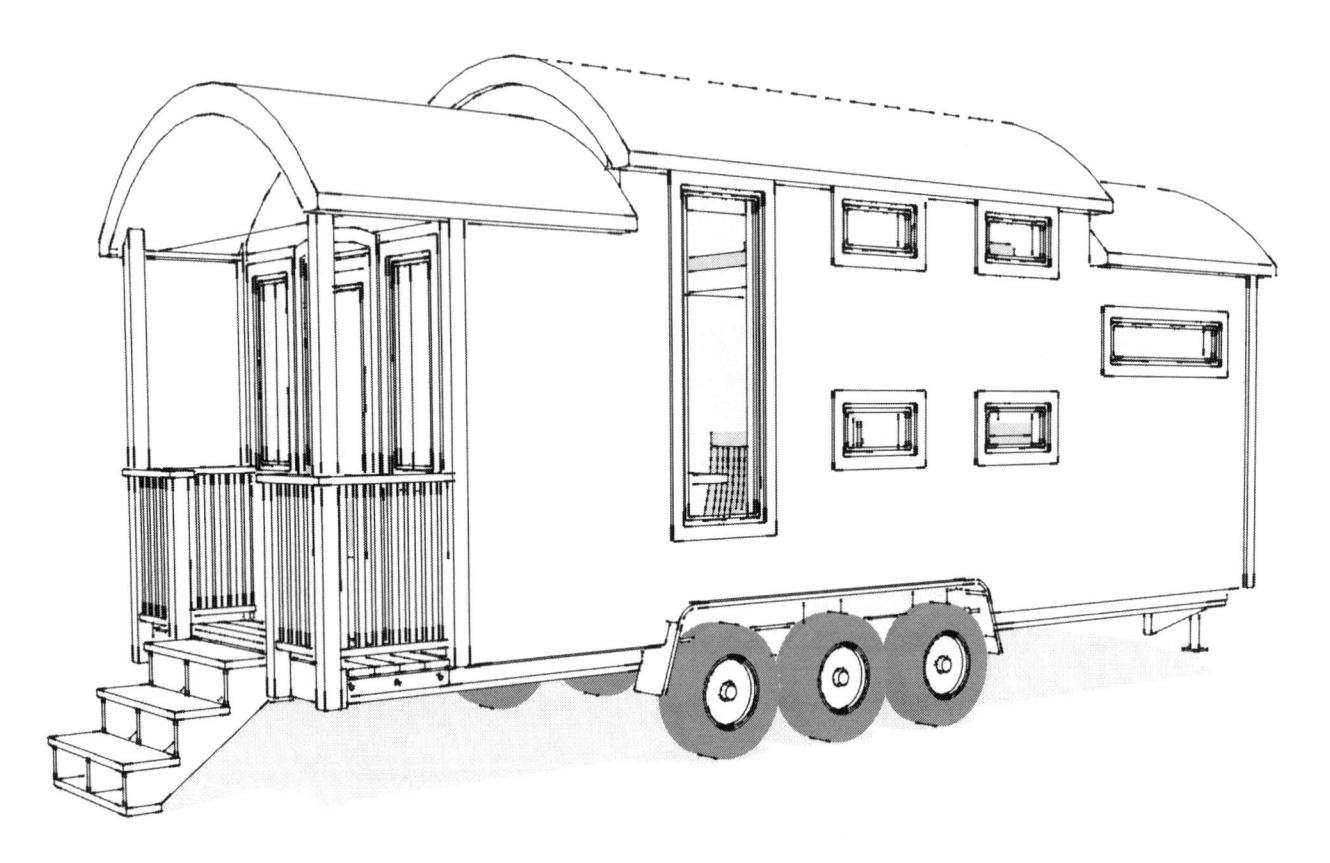

Summary:

This tiny home has a dramatic exterior and a simple functional interior. Stepping inside you find a large room with a table for three and two comfy chairs. Passing through the small kitchen and past the bathroom you reach an open bedroom with a queen bed on a raised storage platform. Above the kitchen and bathroom is a loft.

Features:

24-Foot Tiny House on Wheels
Vardo Inspired Curved Roof
Front Porch
Sleeps Four
Lower Level Bedroom and Loft

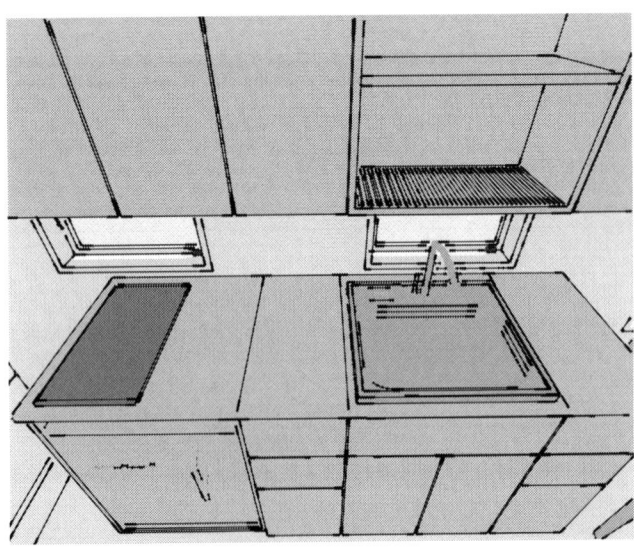

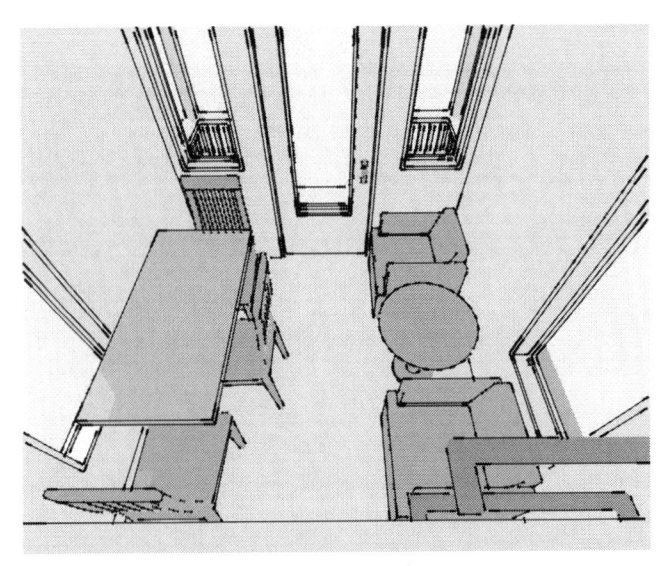

Kitchen

View from Loft

Tiny House #66 - Floor Plan & Exterior

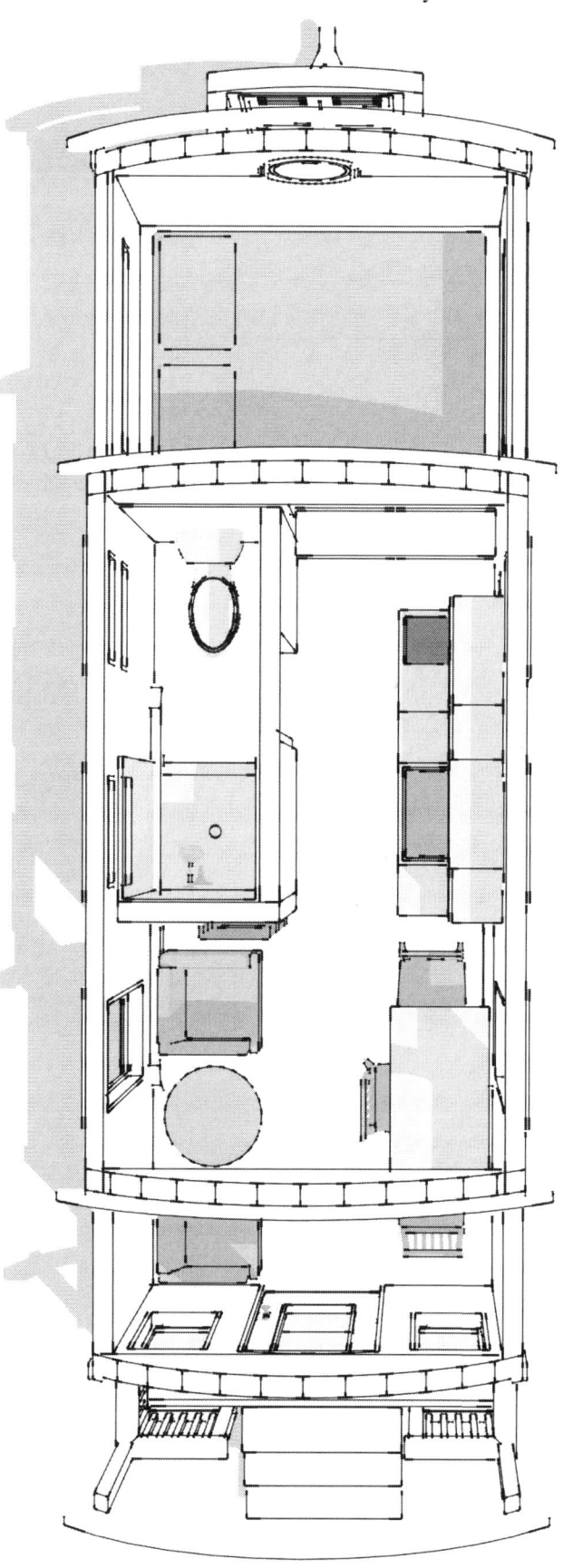

Front Right Corner

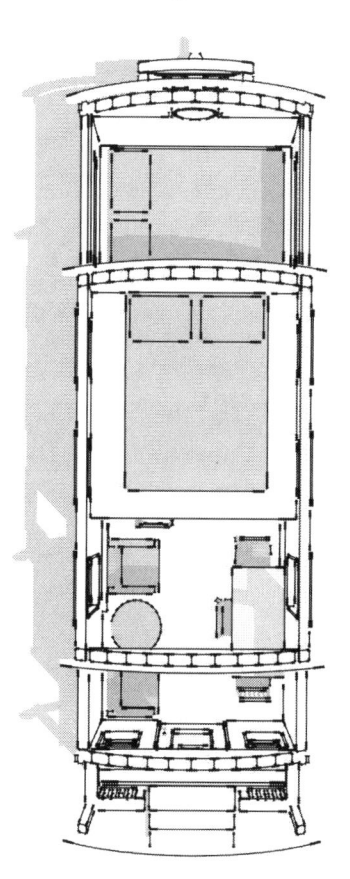

Floor Plan - Loft

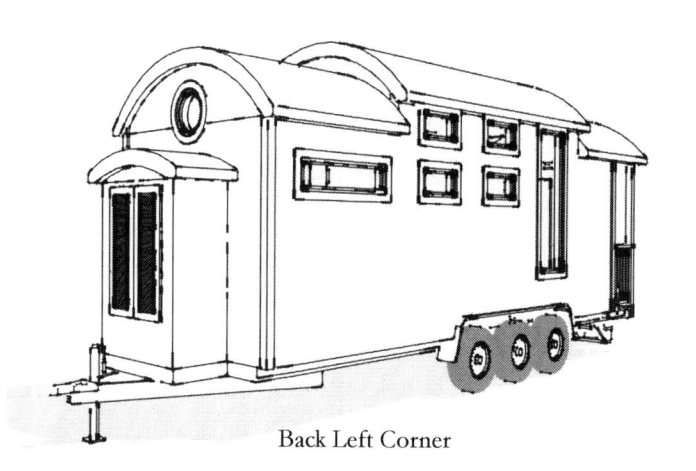

Floor Plan

Back Left Corner

Tiny House #66 - Interior Views

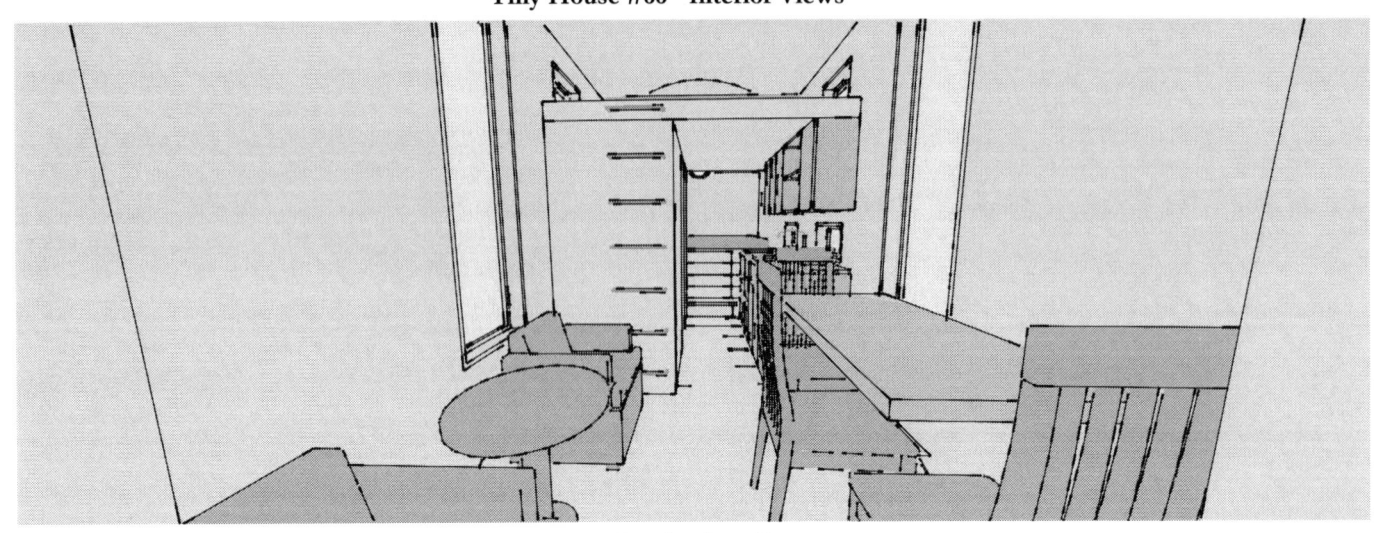

Interior from Entry

Interior from Kitchen

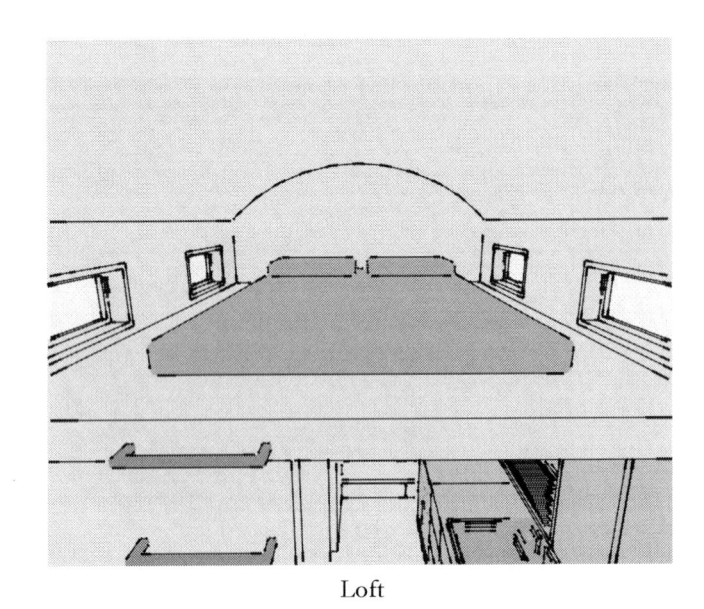

Loft

Bedroom

Tiny House #66 - Elevations

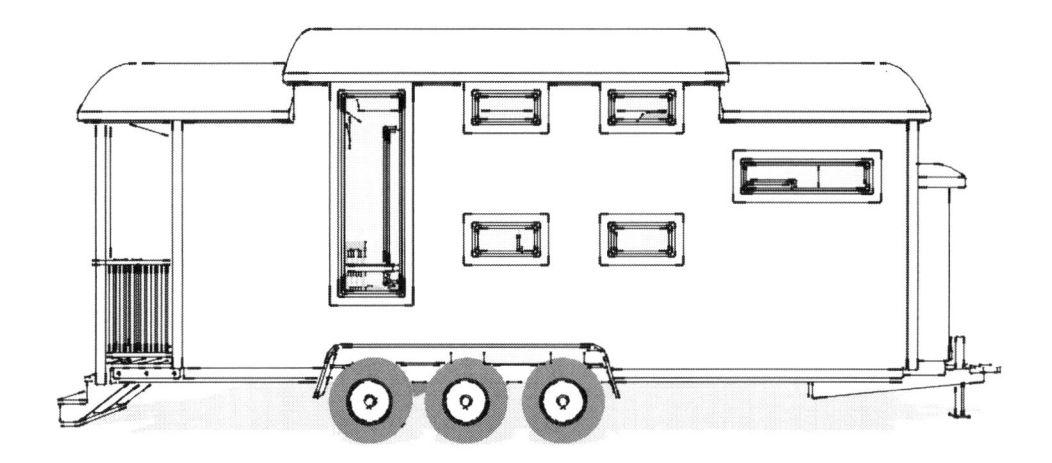

Right

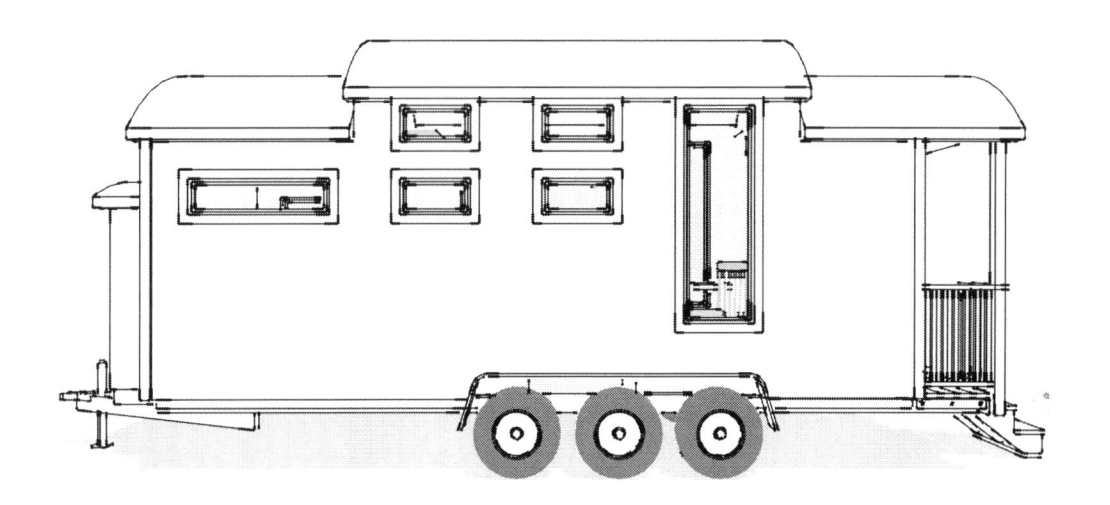

Left

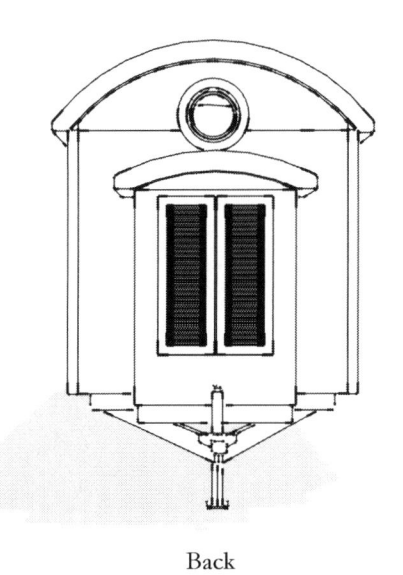

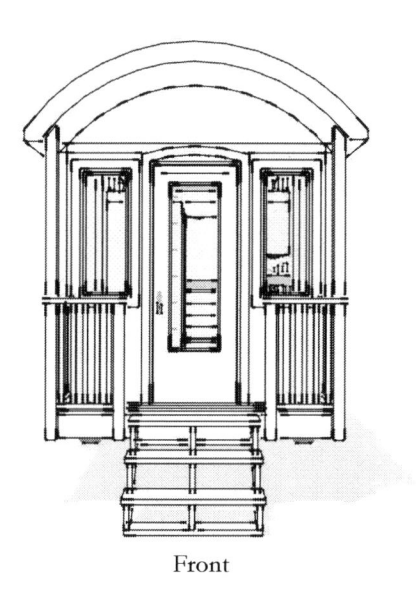

Back

Front

277

#67

Tiny House #67 - Overview

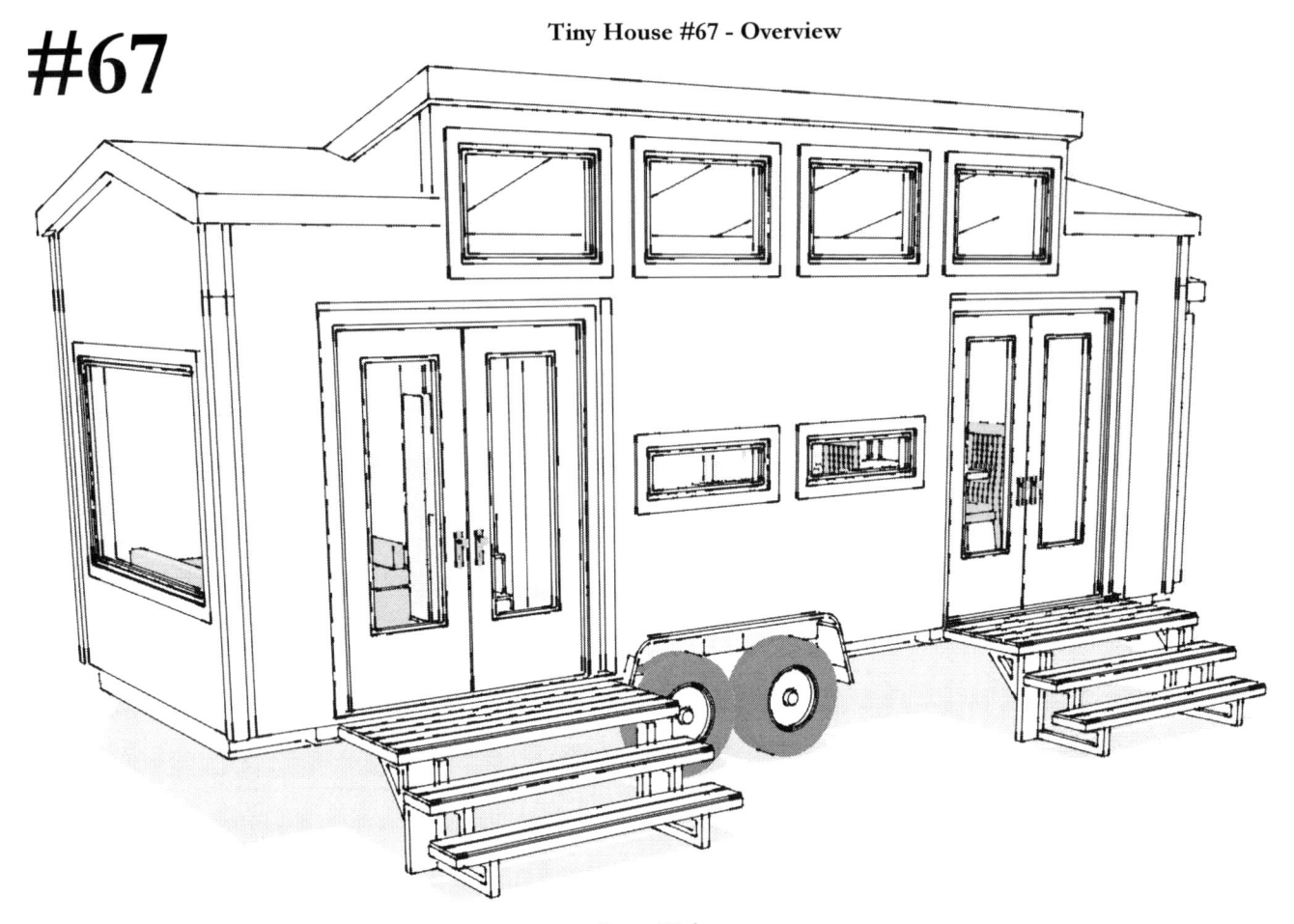

Front Right

Summary:

Inside this house would feel open and bight. Two sets of French doors provide light and access to a dining room and a living room. Between these rooms is a kitchen and bathroom. Above the center of the house is a loft that's open on both ends for great ventilation. The loft is accessed by a steep staircase that doubles as a storage.

Features:

24-Foot Tiny House on Wheels
Shed Roof with Gable Ends
Loft with Queen Bed
Separate Living Room and Dining Room

Kitchen

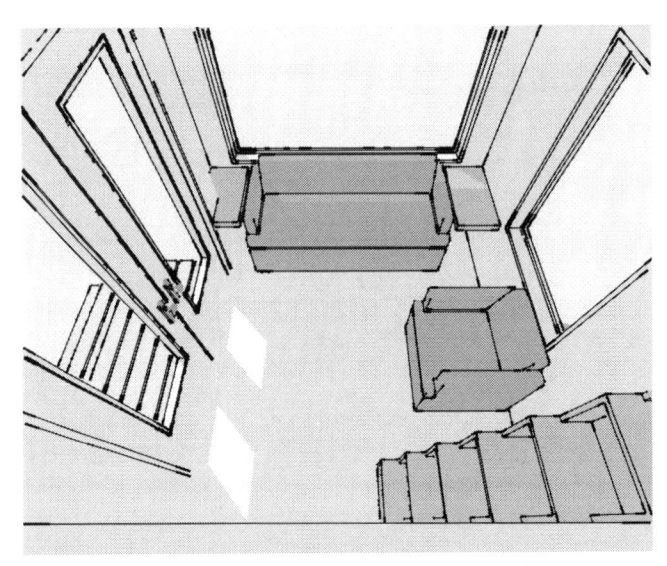

View from Loft

Tiny House #67 - Floor Plan & Exterior

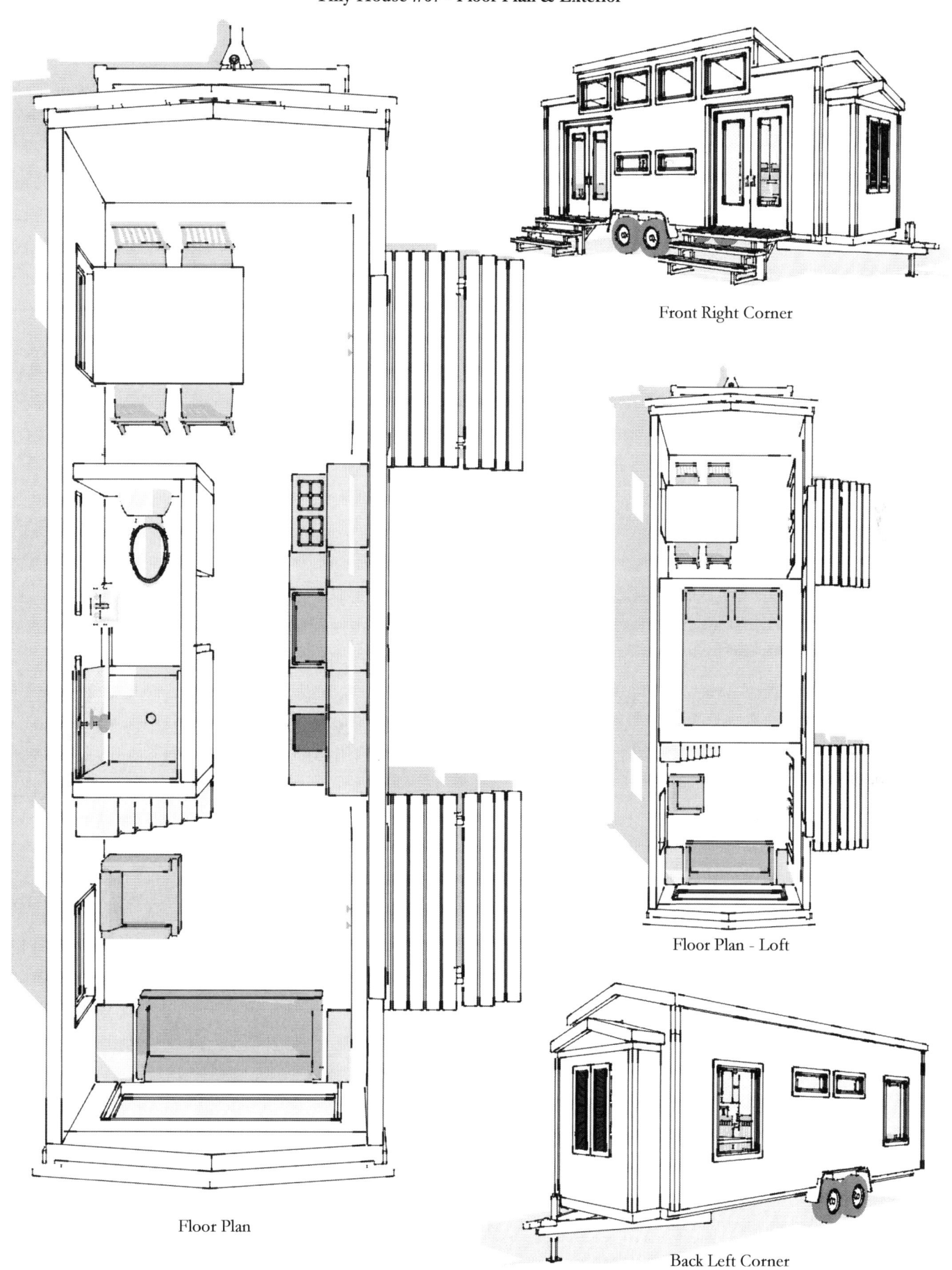

Front Right Corner

Floor Plan - Loft

Floor Plan

Back Left Corner

279

Tiny House #67 - Interior Views

Interior from Living Room

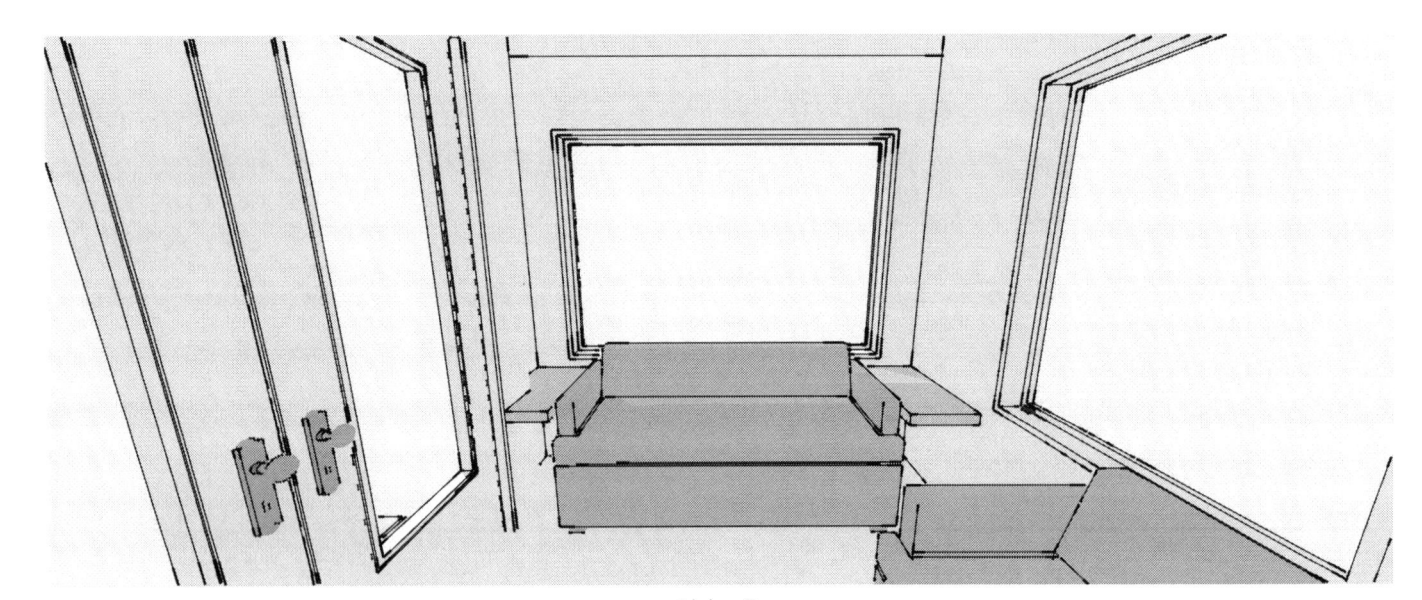

Living Room

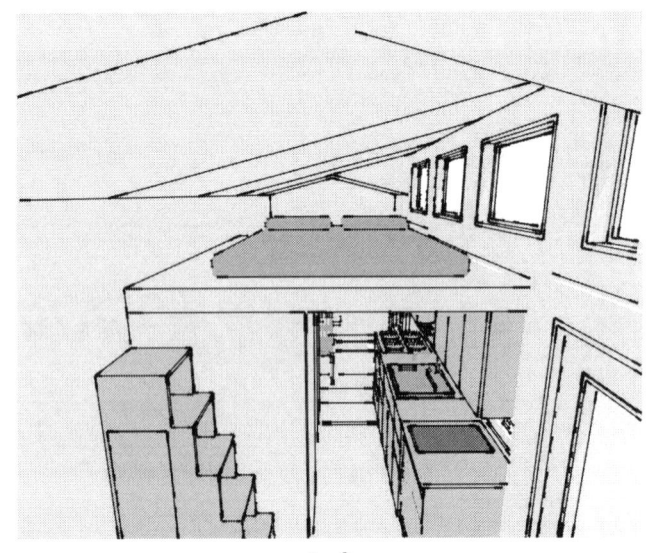

Loft

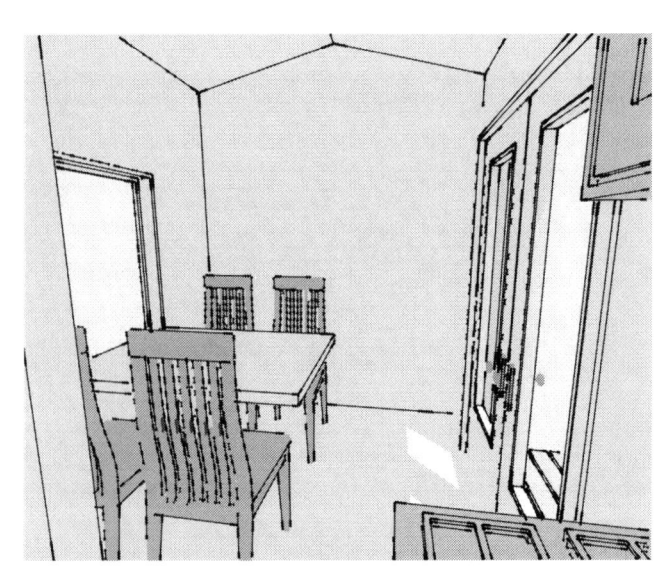

Dining Room

280

Tiny House #67 - Elevations

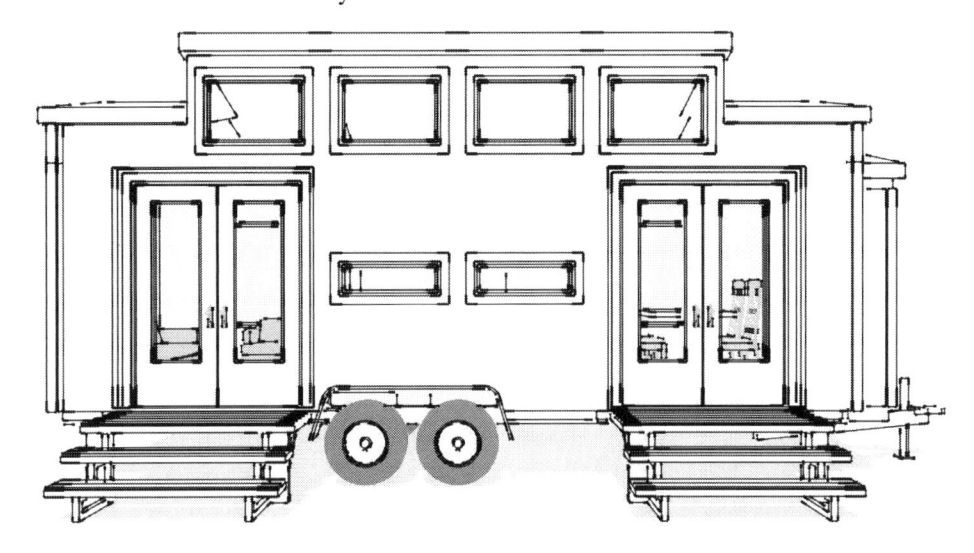

Right

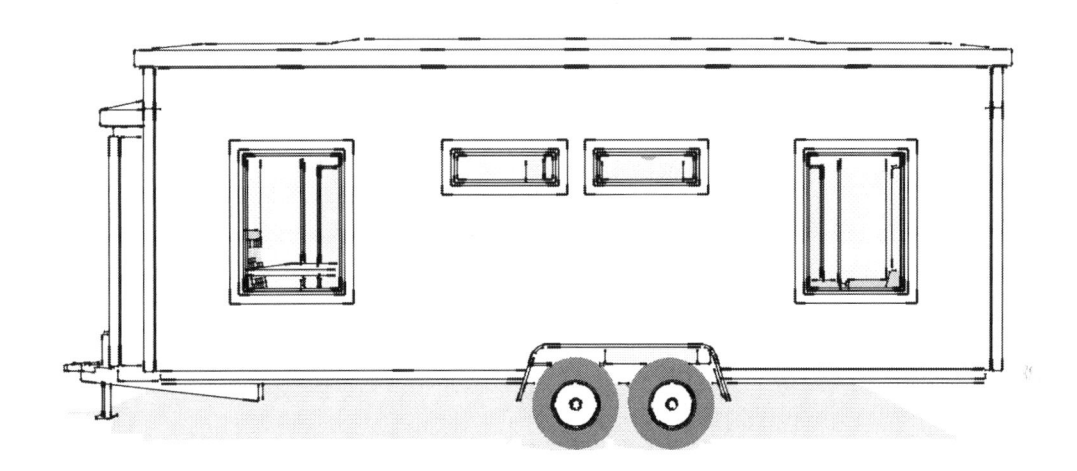

Left

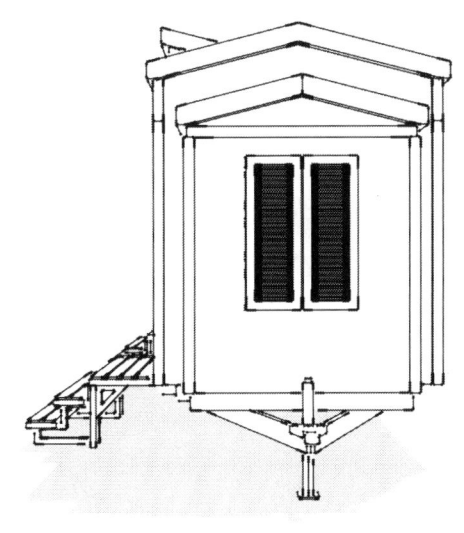

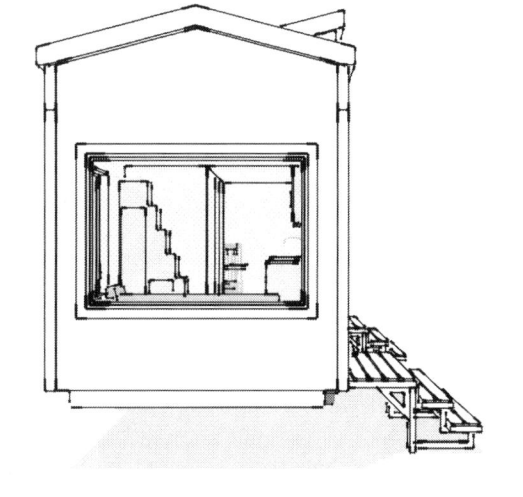

Back

Front

#68

Tiny House #68 - Overview

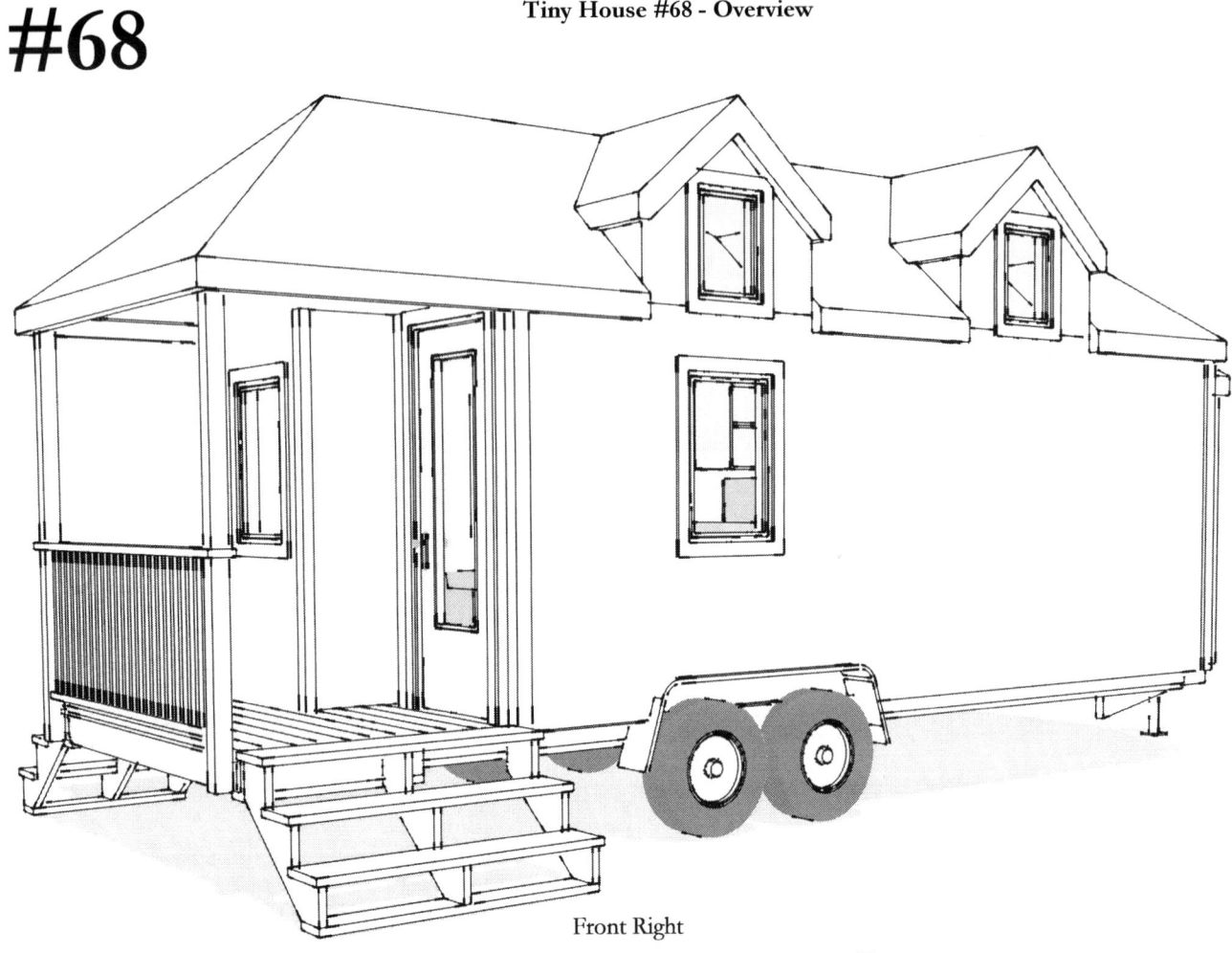

Front Right

Summary:

The porch on this house invites people to visit. Inside is a desk in the front bump-out, two comfy chairs, and stairs leading to the loft. Past that is a very functional kitchen, laundry, and bathroom. Up the storage stairs is a loft and queen bed.

Features:

24-Foot Tiny House on Wheels
Hip Roof with Gable Dormers
Large Porch with Two Fold-up Steps
Storage Stairs
Aerodynamic

Kitchen

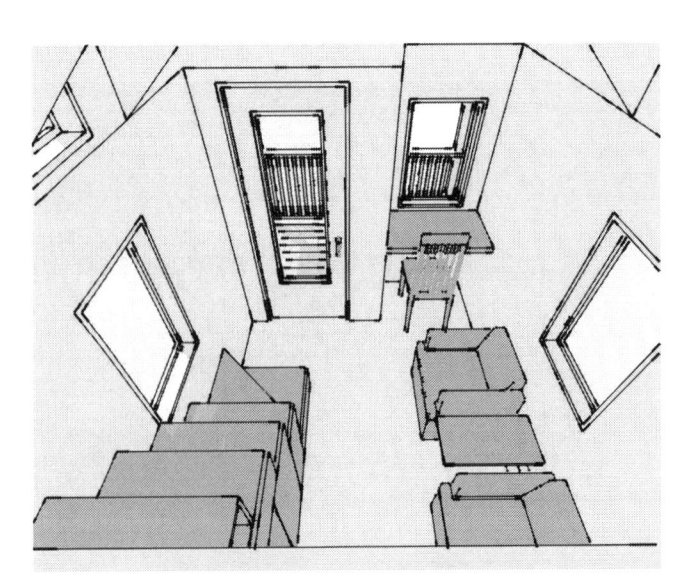

View from Loft

Tiny House #68 - Floor Plan & Exterior

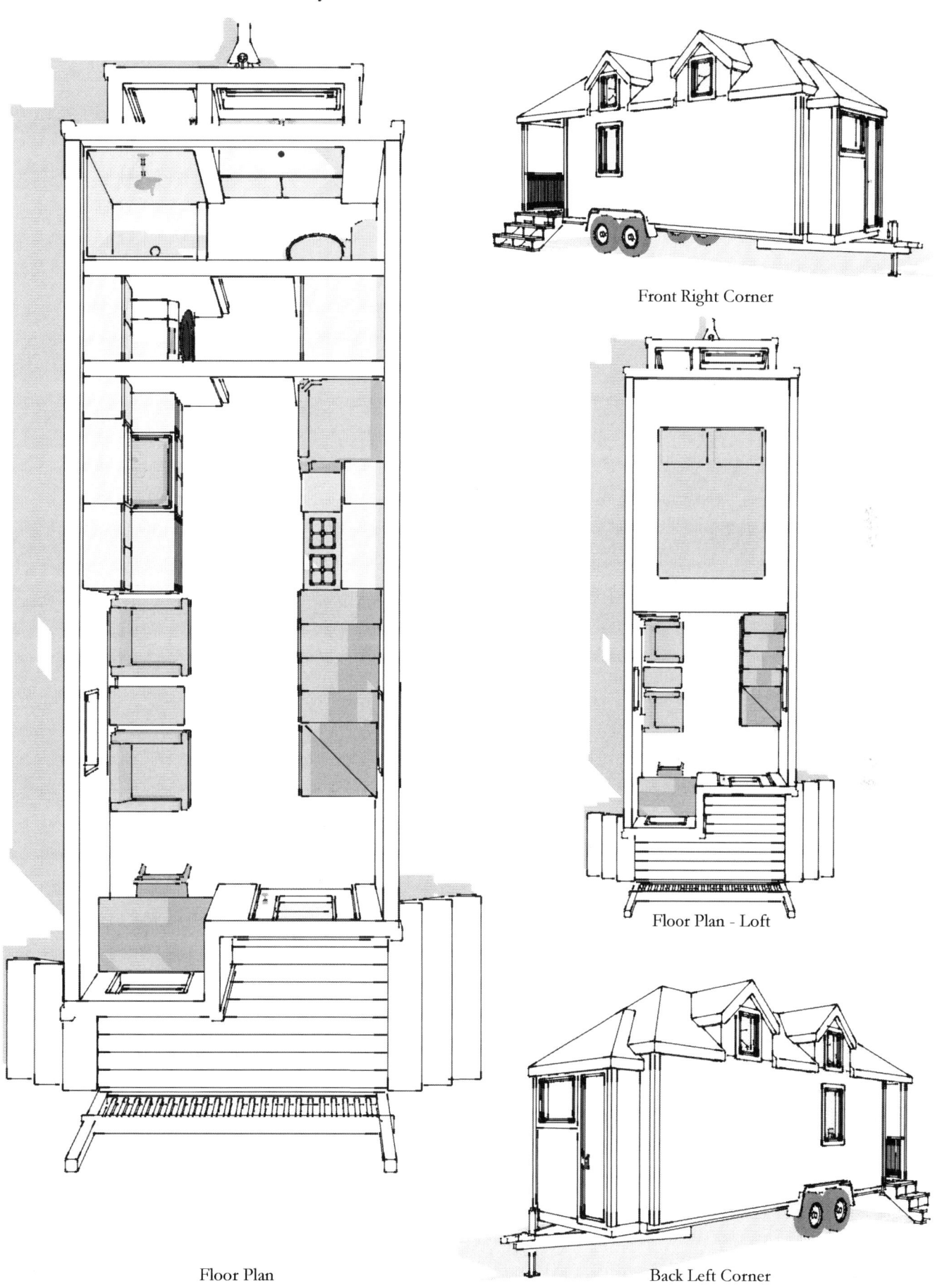

Front Right Corner

Floor Plan - Loft

Floor Plan

Back Left Corner

Tiny House #68 - Interior Views

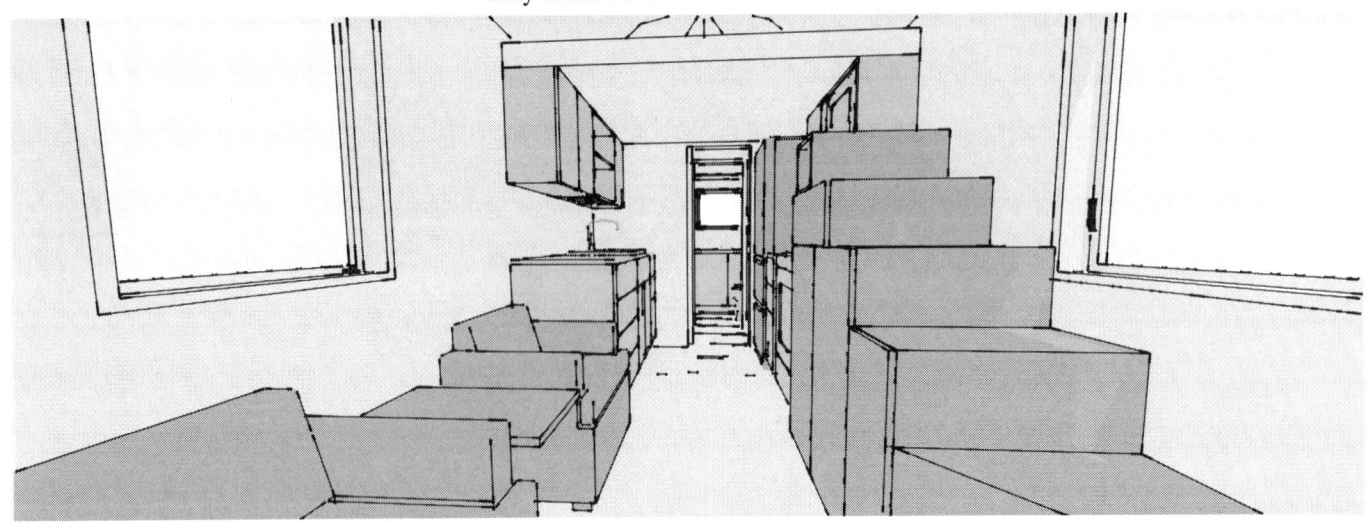

Interior from Entry

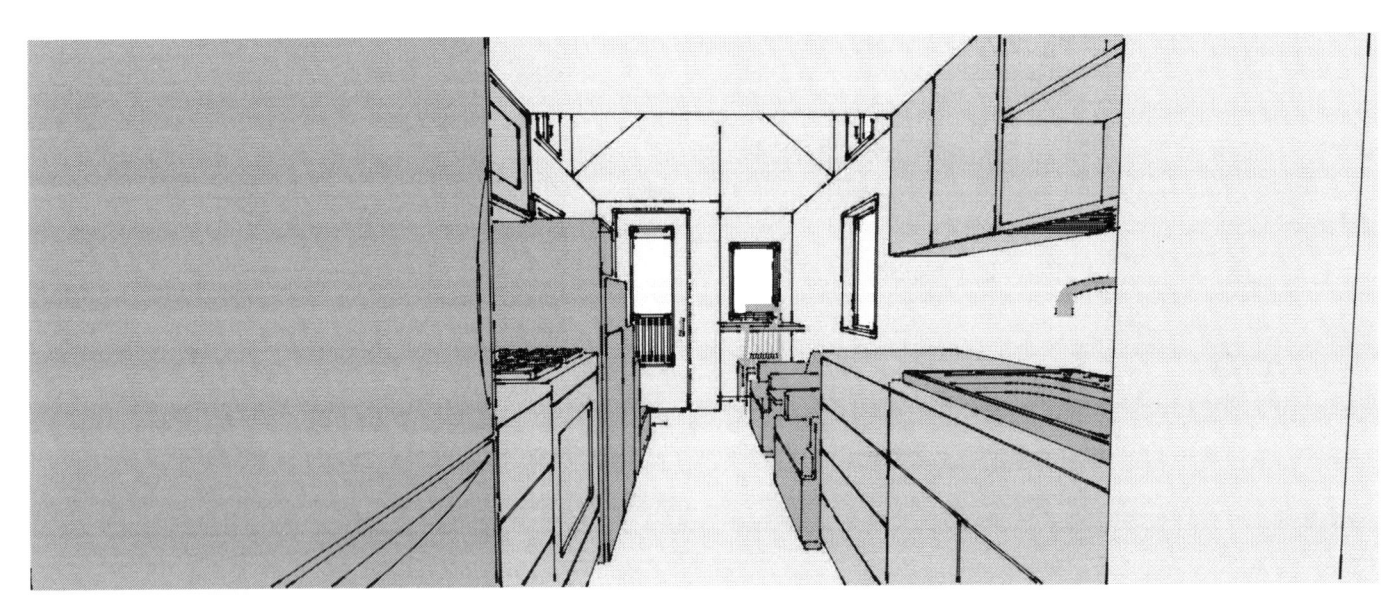

Interior from Kitchen

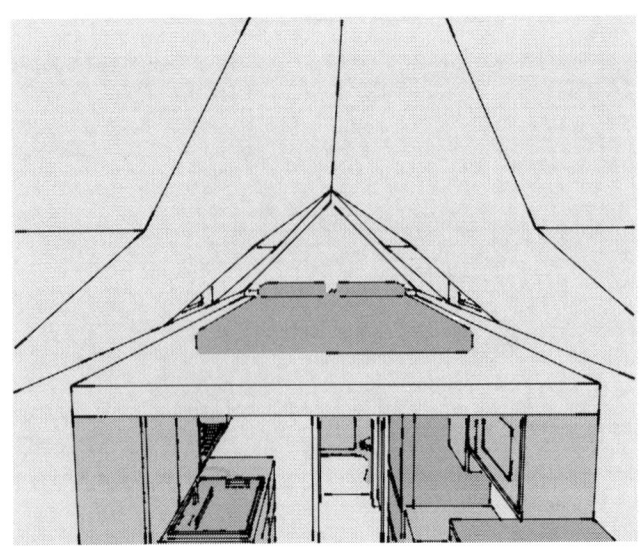

Loft

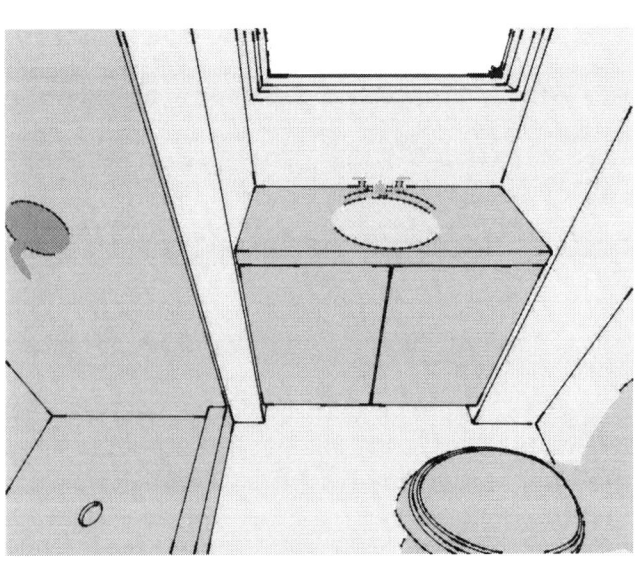

Bathroom

284

Tiny House #68 - Elevations

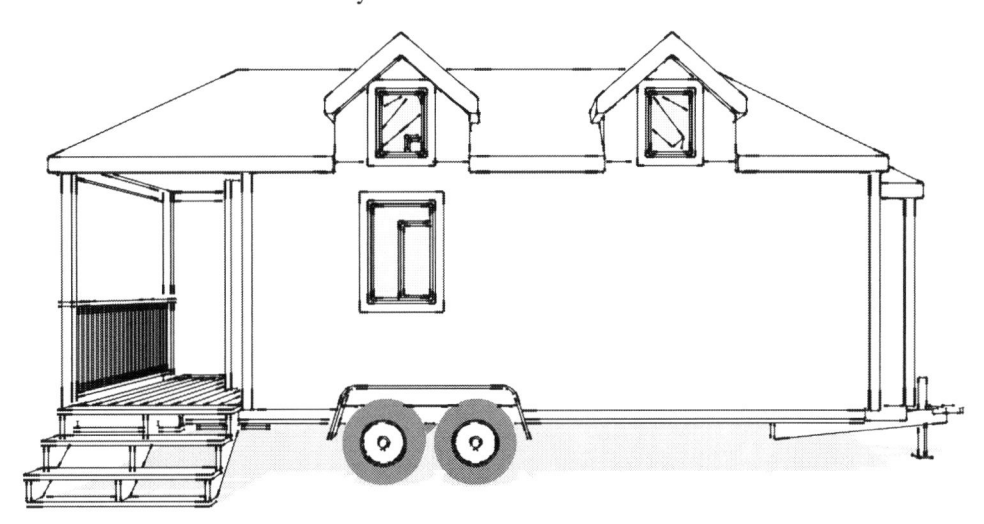

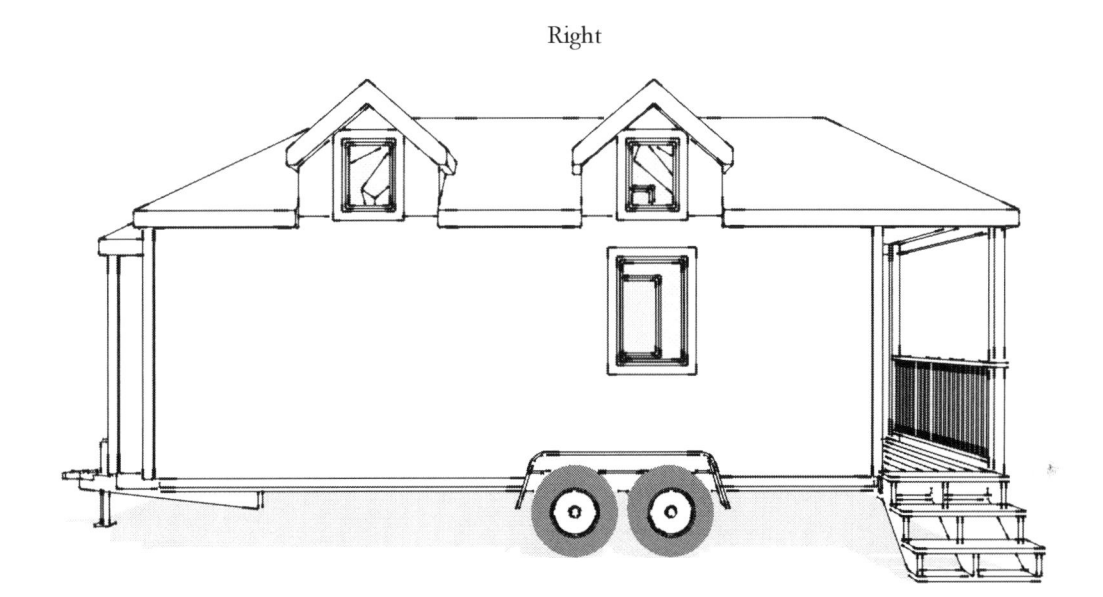

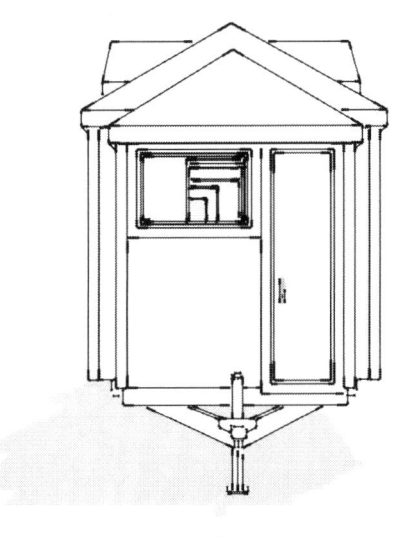

Right

Left

Back

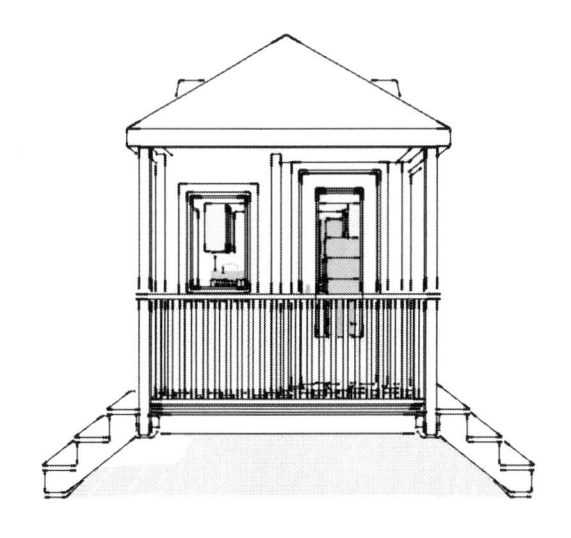

Front

#69

Tiny House #69 - Overview

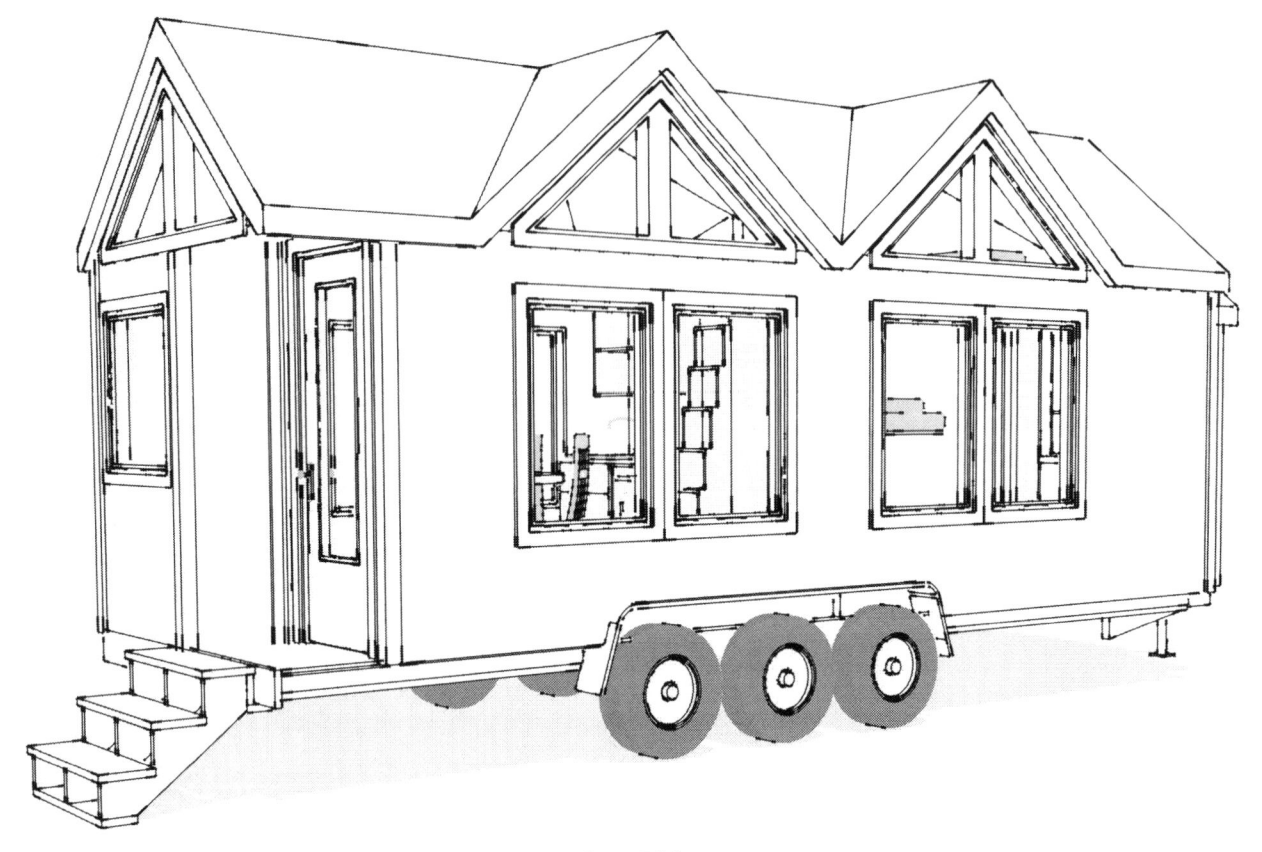

Front Right

Summary:

Dedicated lower level bedrooms take up a lot of space, even in a 24-foot tiny house. In this example there's a pass-through children's bedroom with a bunk bed. At the far end of the house is a bathroom that extends into a bump-out over the trailer tongue. The kitchen is tiny but the house can sleep four, so it might be a good candidate for a tiny family vacation home.

Features:

24-Foot Tiny House on Wheels
Double Cross Gable
Lower Level Bedroom
Tiny Kitchen
Table for Four
Sleeps Four

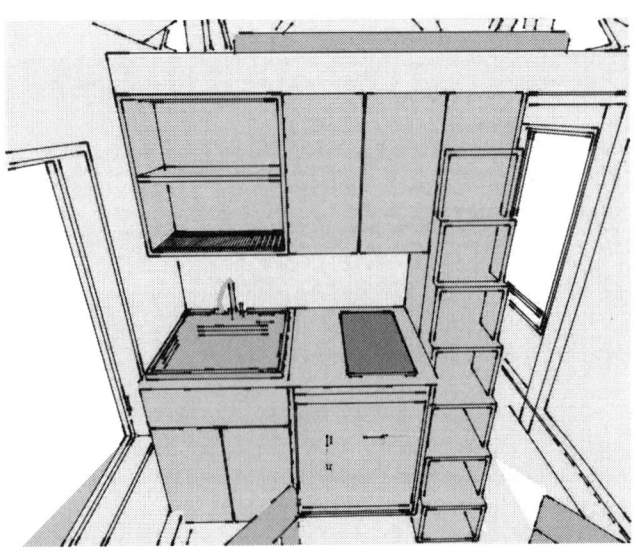

Kitchen

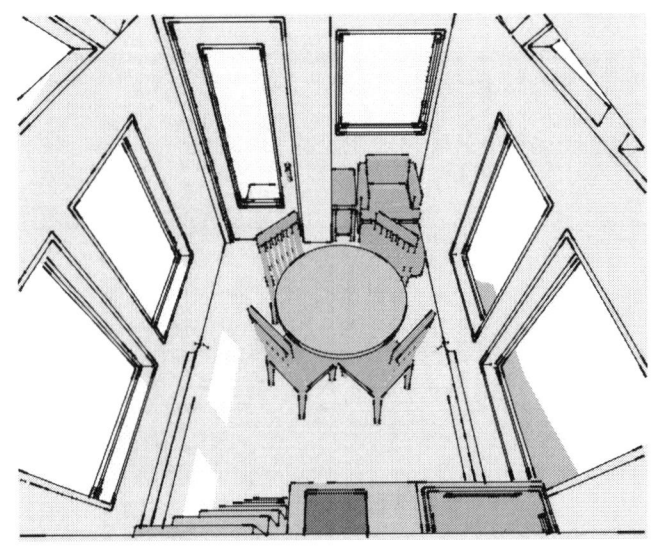

View from Loft

Tiny House #69 - Floor Plan & Exterior

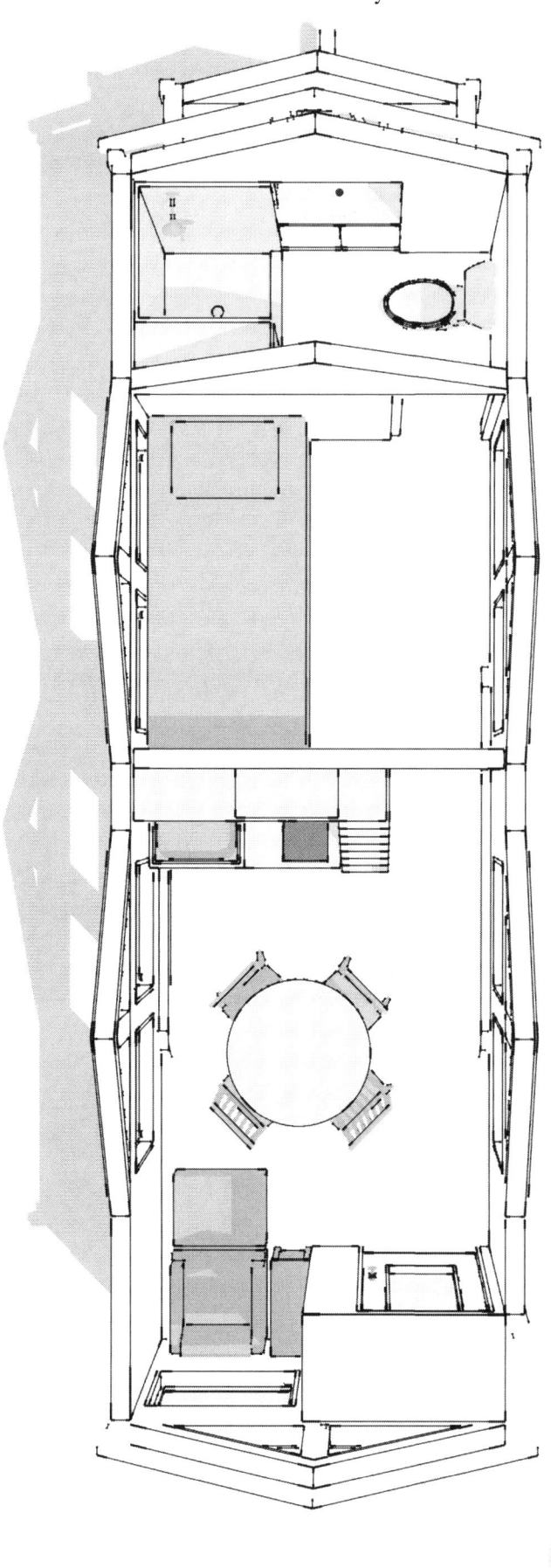

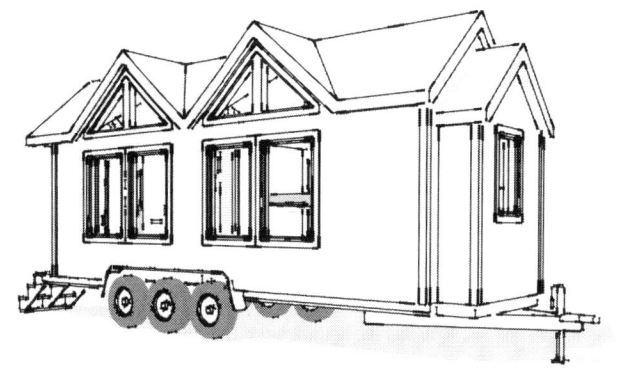

Front Right Corner

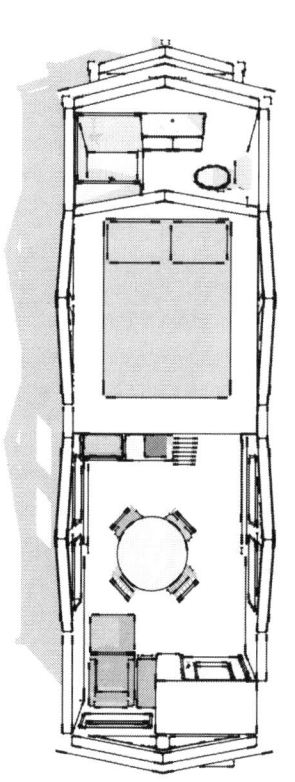

Floor Plan - Loft

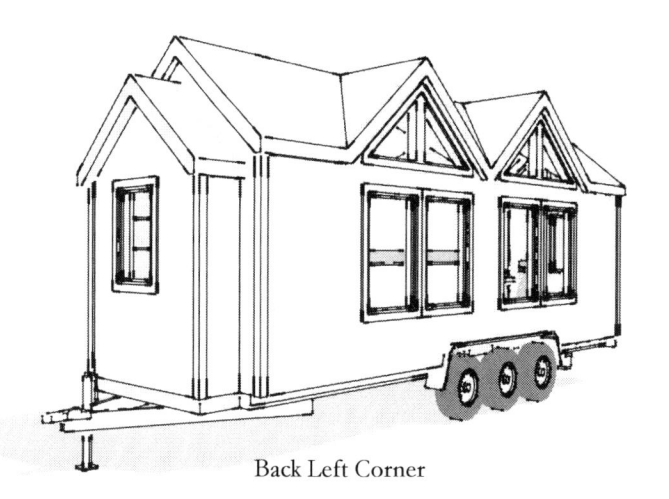

Floor Plan

Back Left Corner

Tiny House #69 - Interior Views

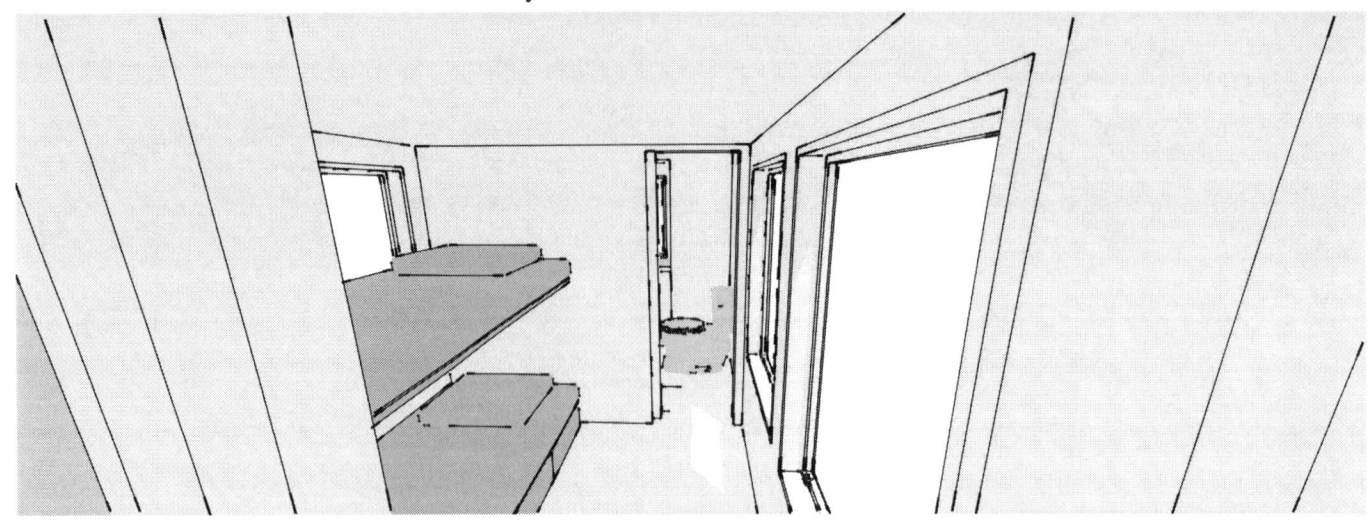

Interior from Kitchen

Interior from Bedroom

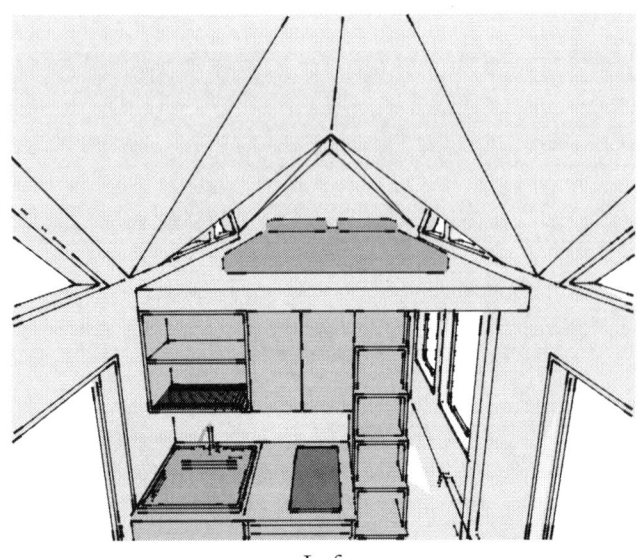

Loft

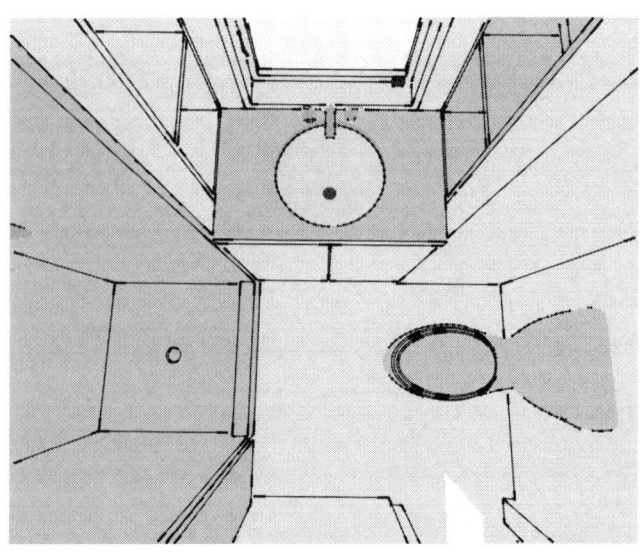

Bathroom

Tiny House #69 - Elevations

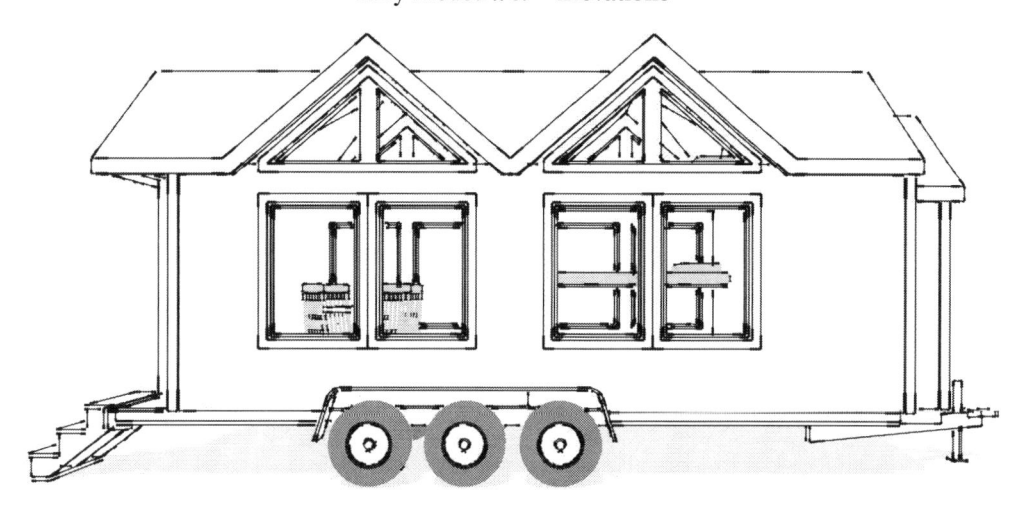

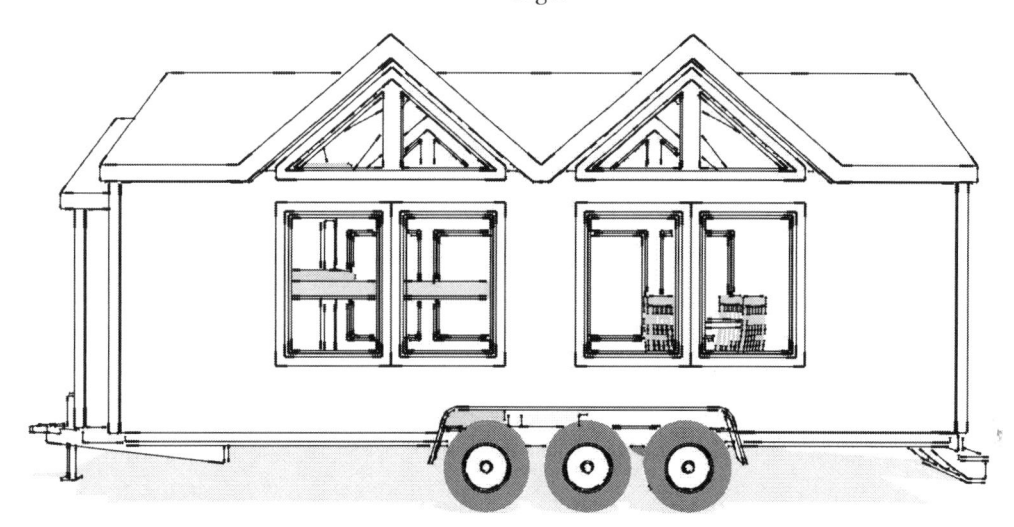

Right

Left

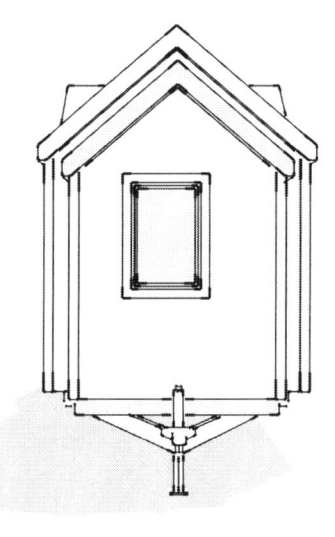

Back

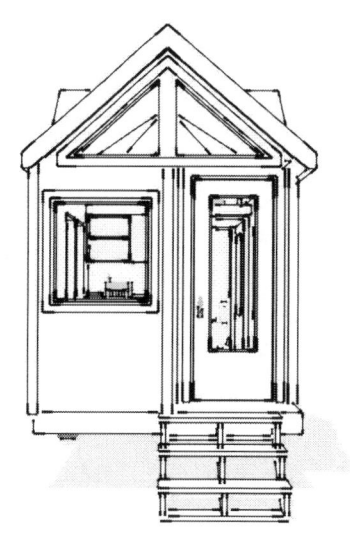

Front

#70

Tiny House #70 - Overview

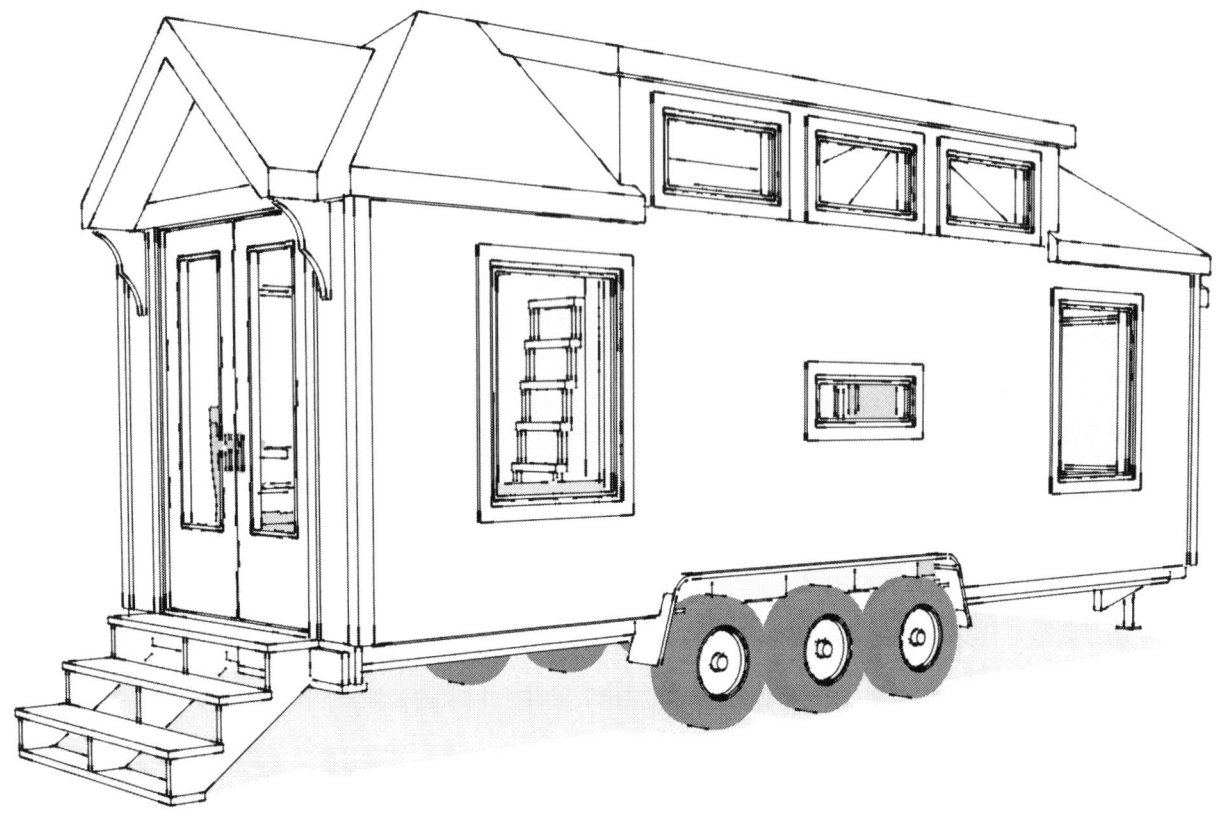

Front Right

Summary:

This design continues to experiment with lower level bedroom configurations. This time there's a comfortably laid out bedroom in the back of the house, a loft with two twin beds, a sofa, and a table for 4. The kitchen is small but has a full size refrigerator.

Features:

24-Foot Tiny House on Wheels
Hip Roof with Shed Dormers
   and Gable Extension over Front
Lower Level Bedroom
Aerodynamic
Sleeps Four

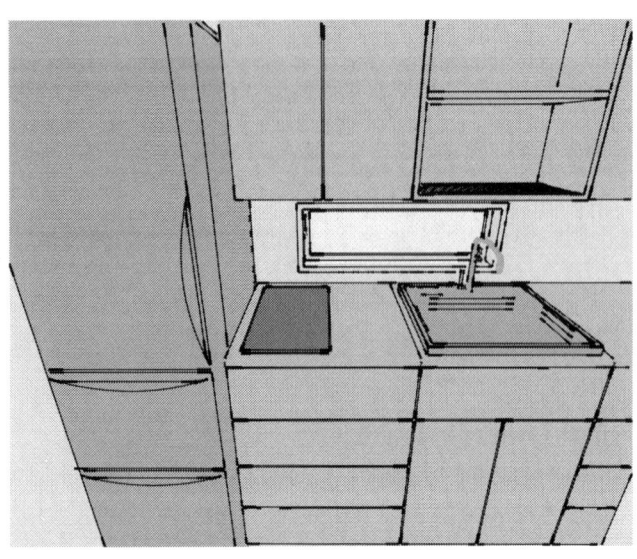

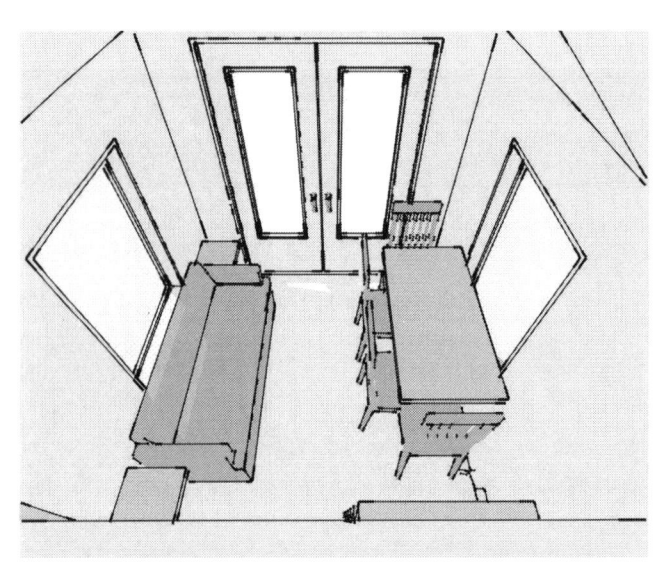

Kitchen

View from Loft

Tiny House #70 - Floor Plan & Exterior

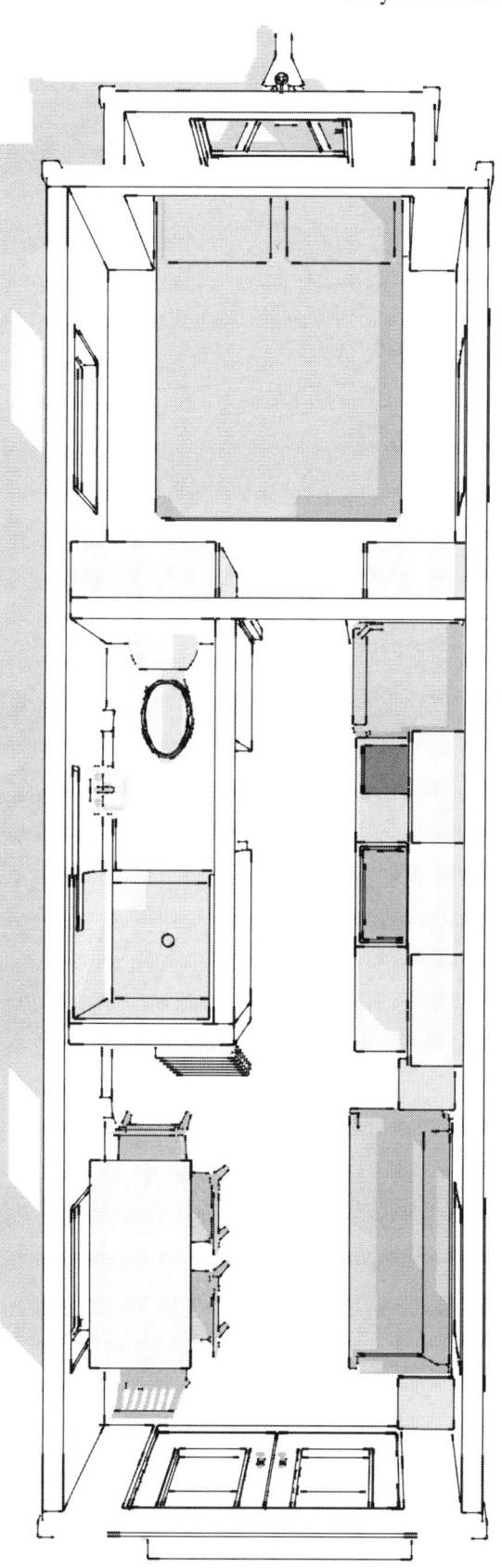

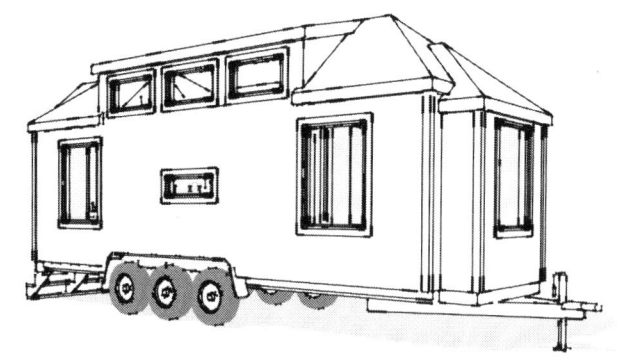

Front Right Corner

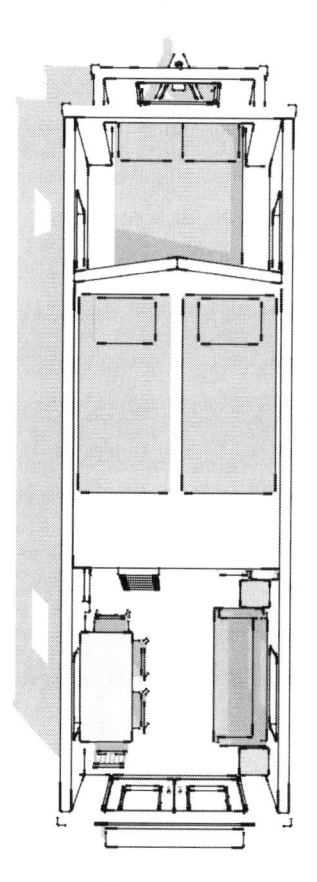

Floor Plan - Loft

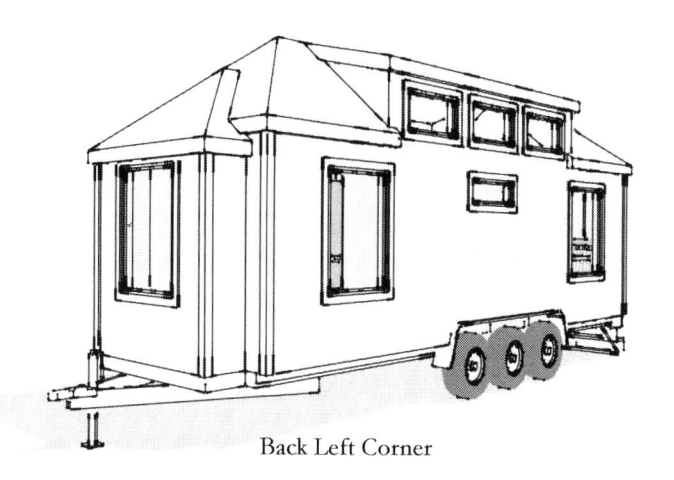

Floor Plan

Back Left Corner

291

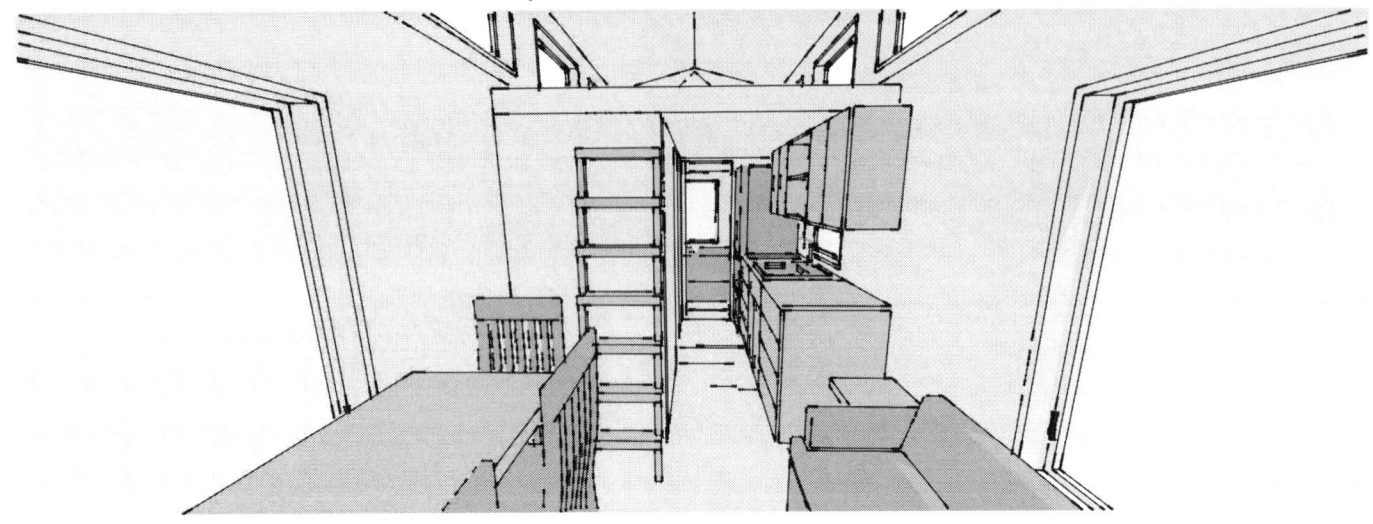

Tiny House #70 - Interior Views

Interior

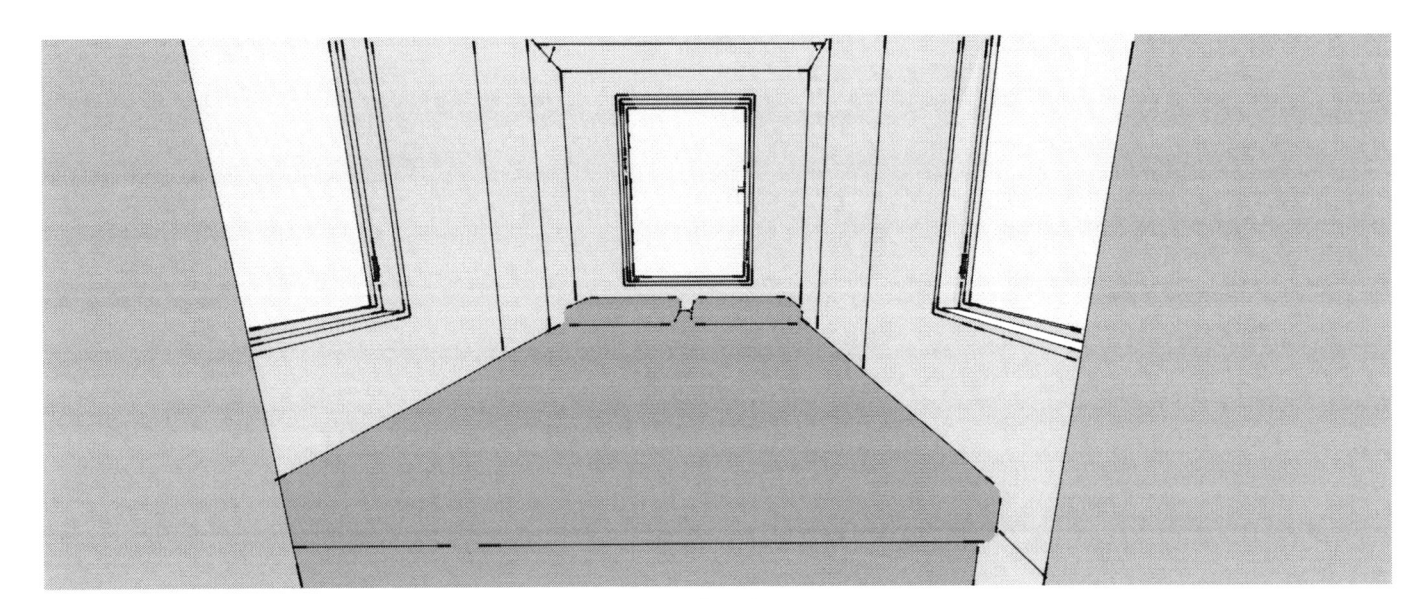

Interior

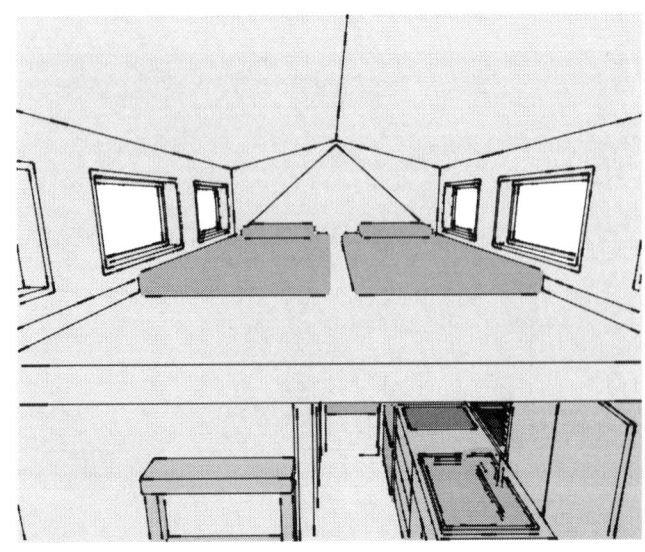

Loft

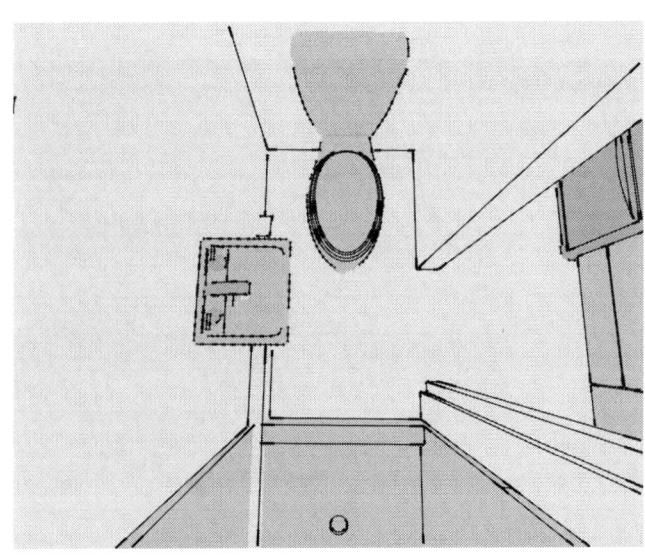

Bathroom

Tiny House #70 - Elevations

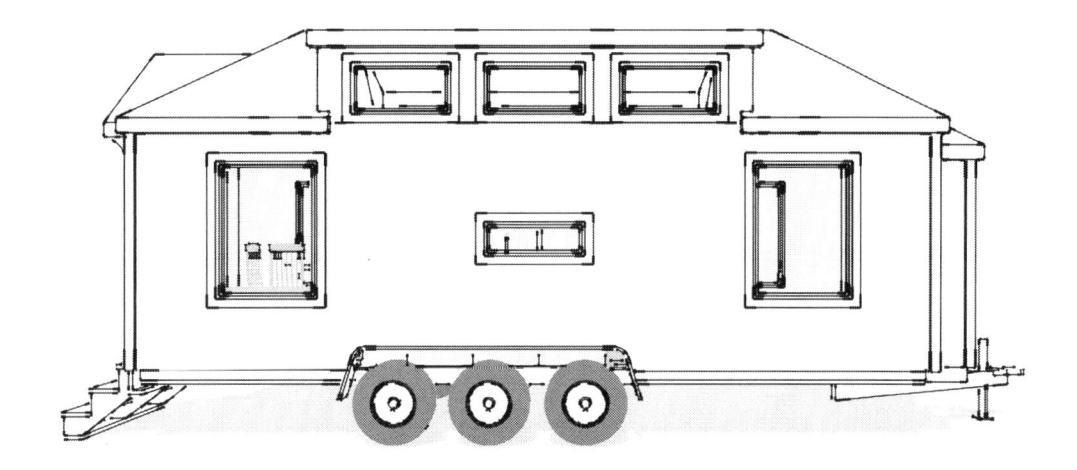

Right

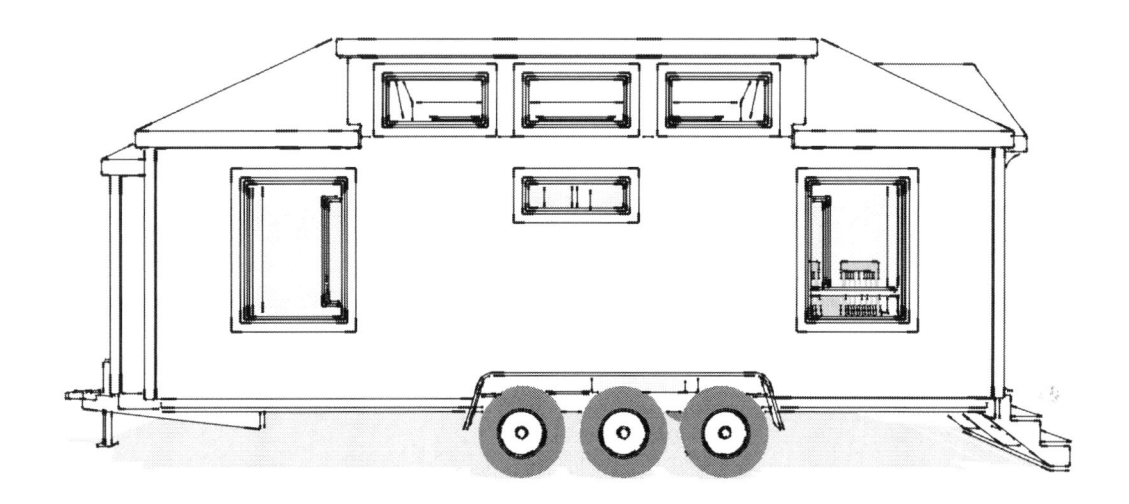

Left

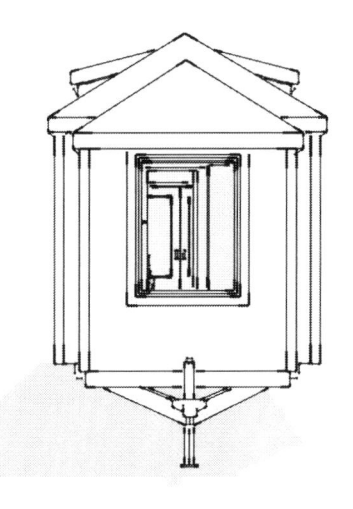

Back

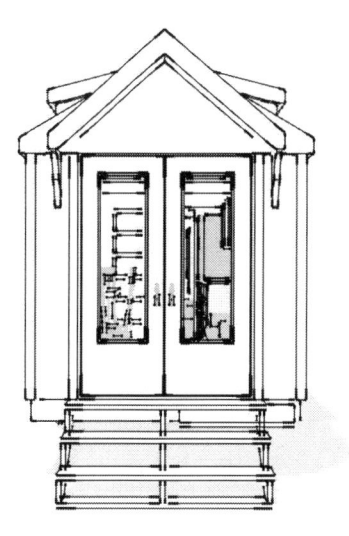

Front

#71

Tiny House #71 - Overview

Front Right

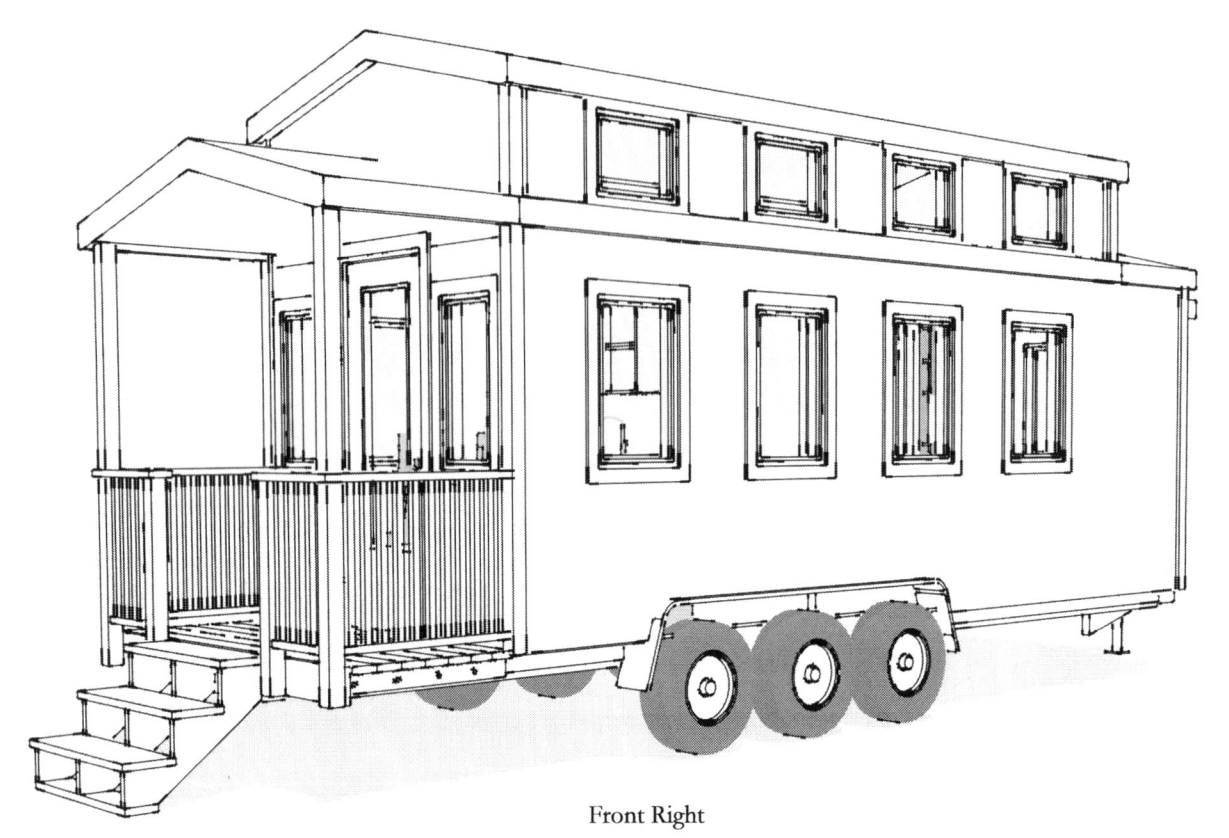

Summary:

This design is beginning to resemble a train car - maybe even a caboose. Inside it's sectioned off like one too. A long narrow hallway runs down one side. At the far end of the house is a lower level bedroom with a queen bed. Up a ladder in the hall leads to a loft with two twin beds. The kitchen is tiny, there's a table for two, and two comfy chairs.

Features:

24-Foot Tiny House on Wheels
High and Low 3/12 Gable Roof
Lower Level Bedroom
Loft with Two Twin Beds
Bathroom with Tub
Sleeps 4

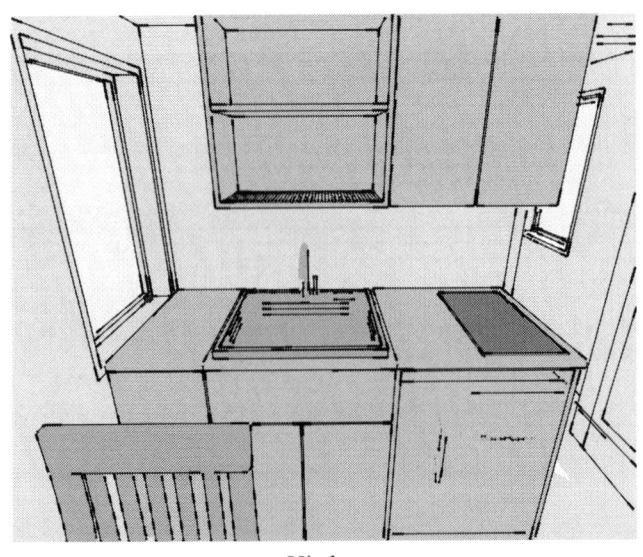

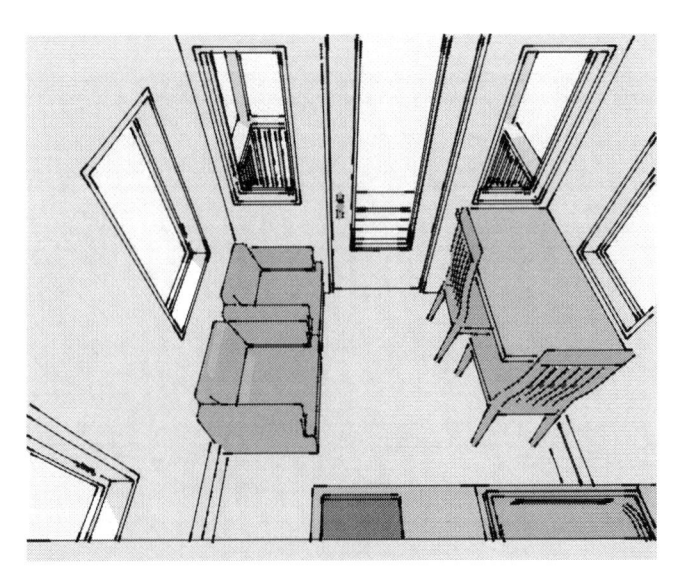

Kitchen

View from Loft

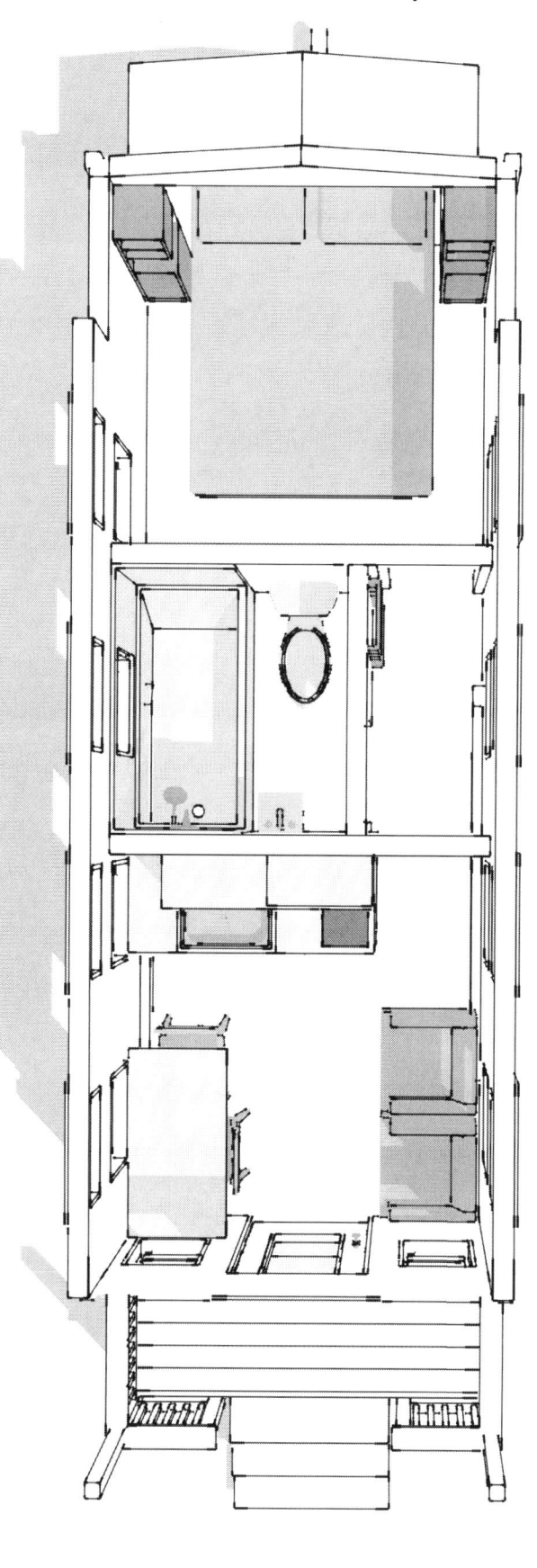

Tiny House #71 - Floor Plan & Exterior

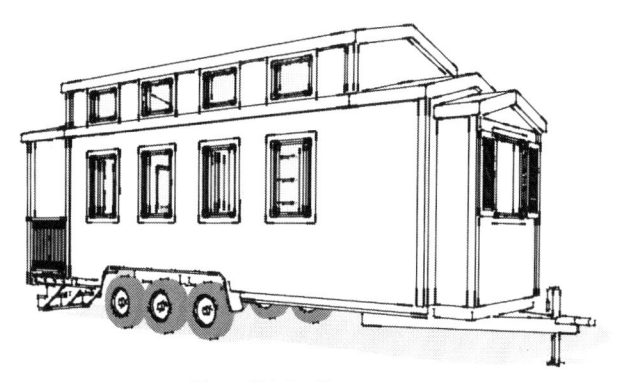

Front Right Corner

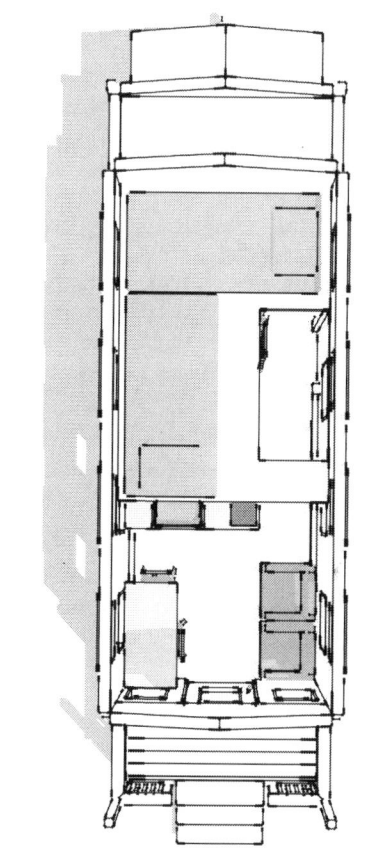

Floor Plan - Loft

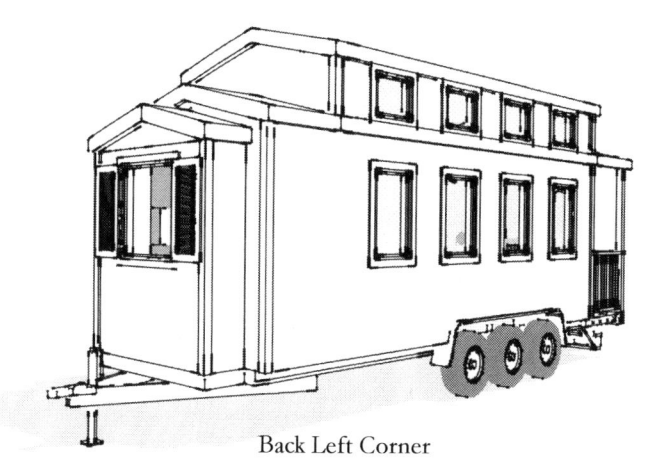

Floor Plan

Back Left Corner

295

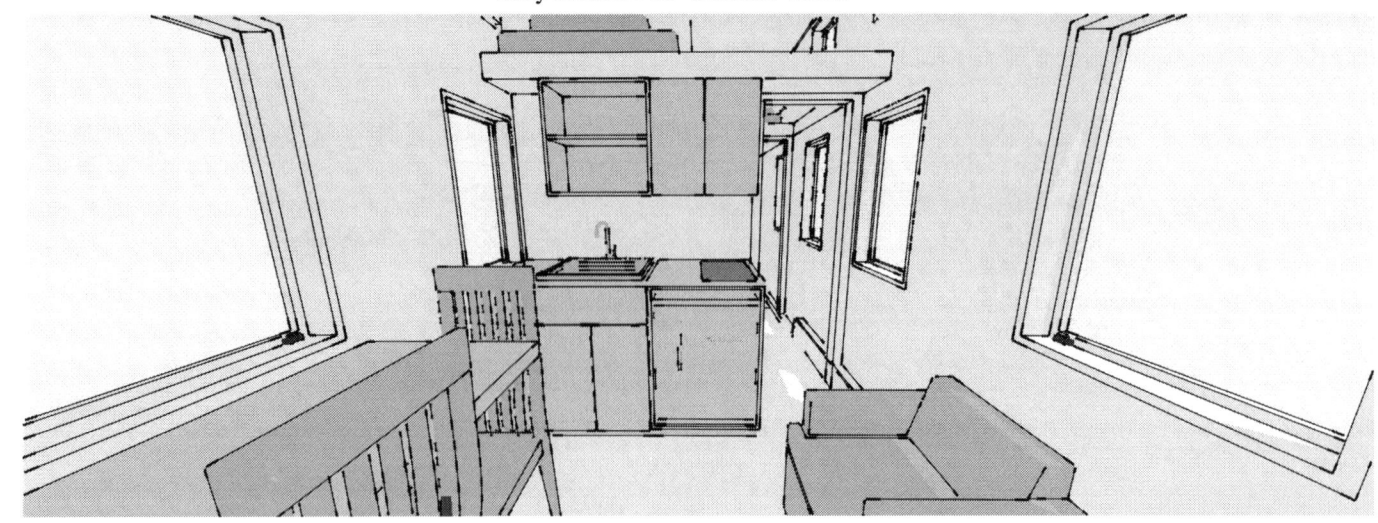

Tiny House #71 - Interior Views

Interior

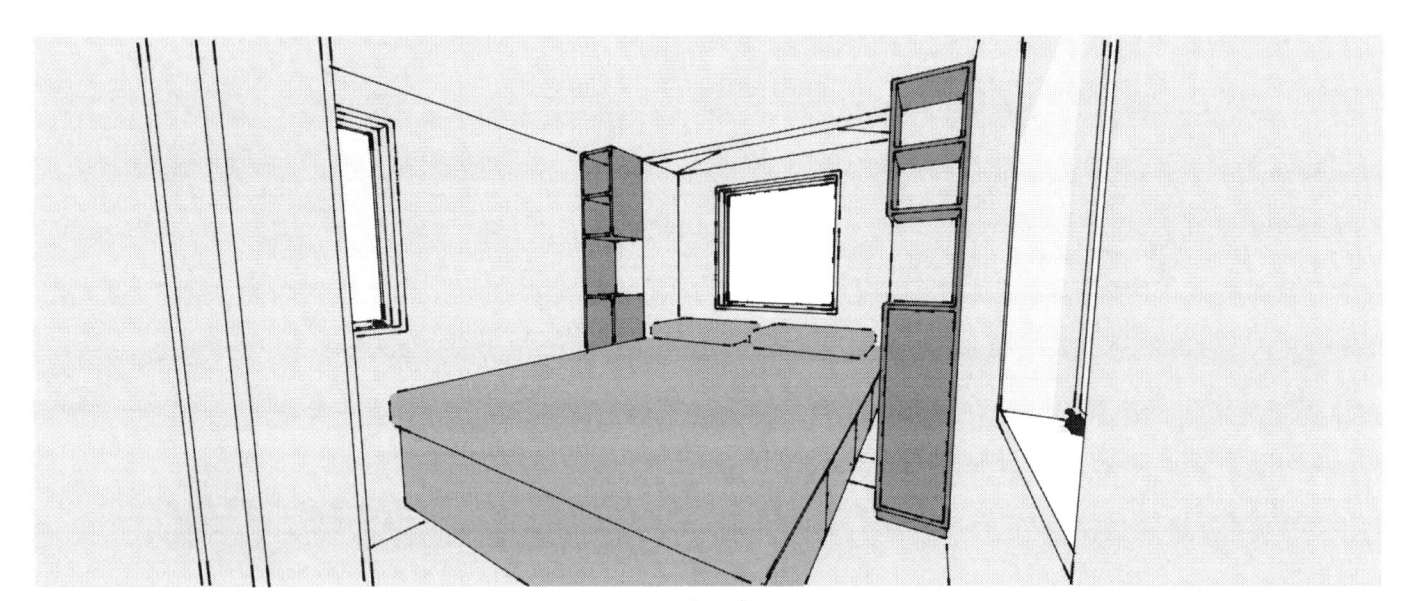

Interior

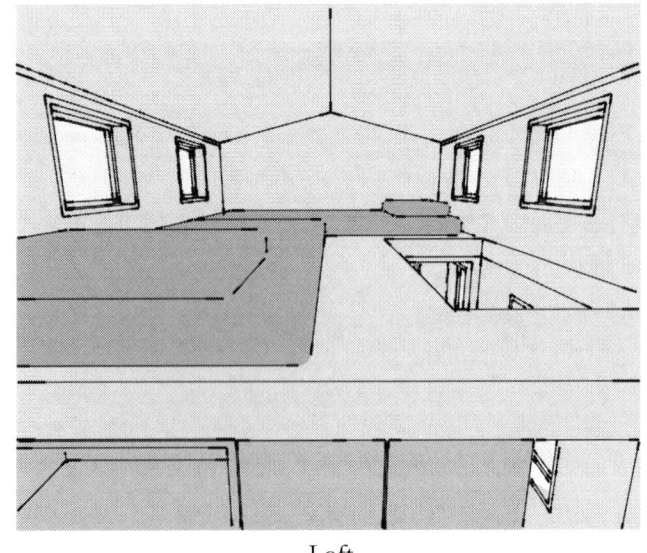

Loft

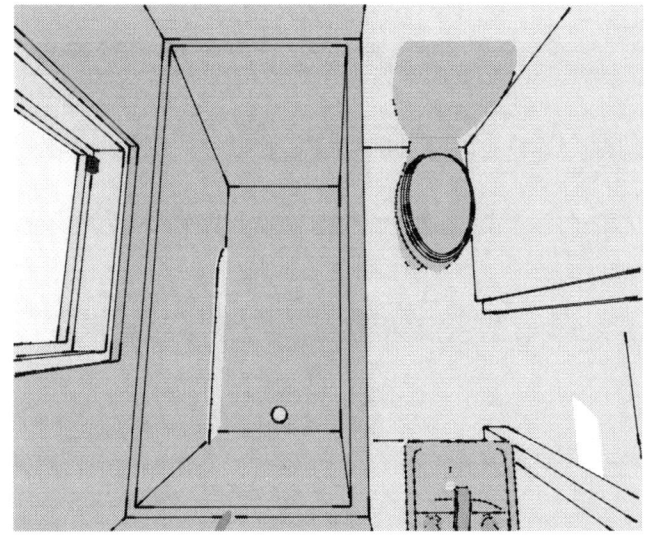

Bathroom

Tiny House #71 - Elevations

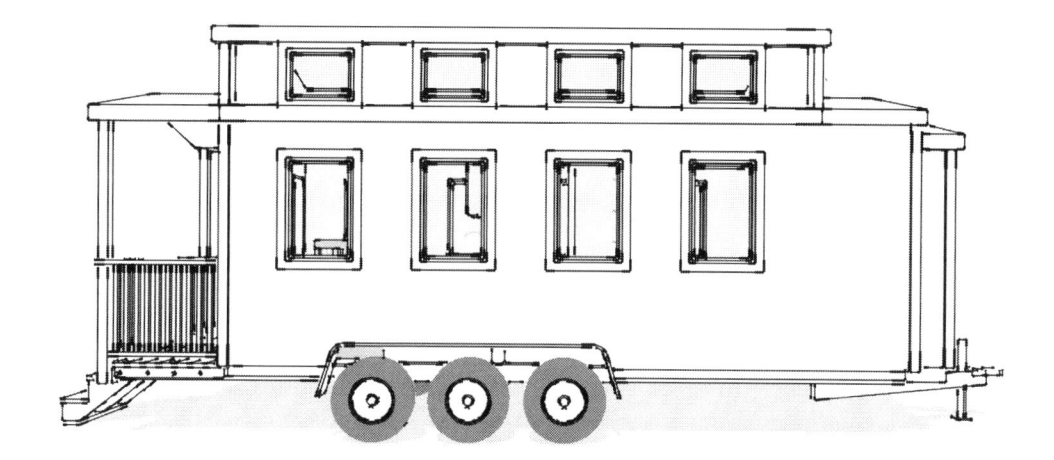

Right

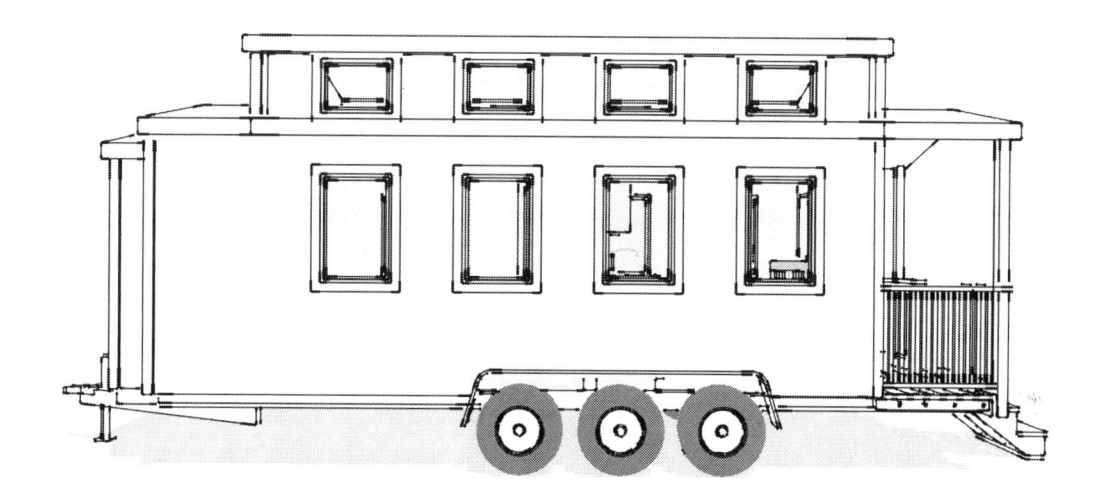

Left

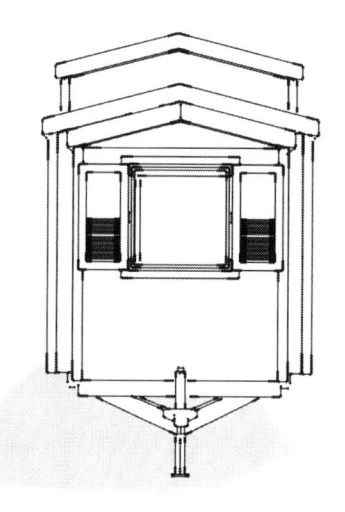

Back

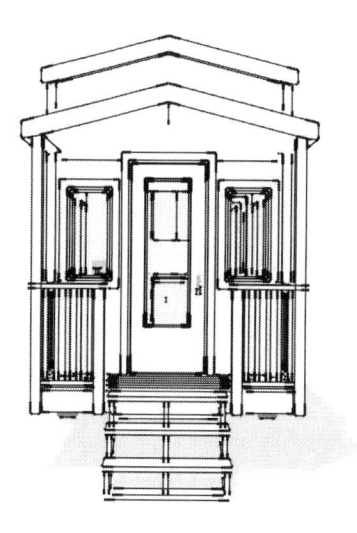

Front

#72

Tiny House #72 - Overview

Front Right

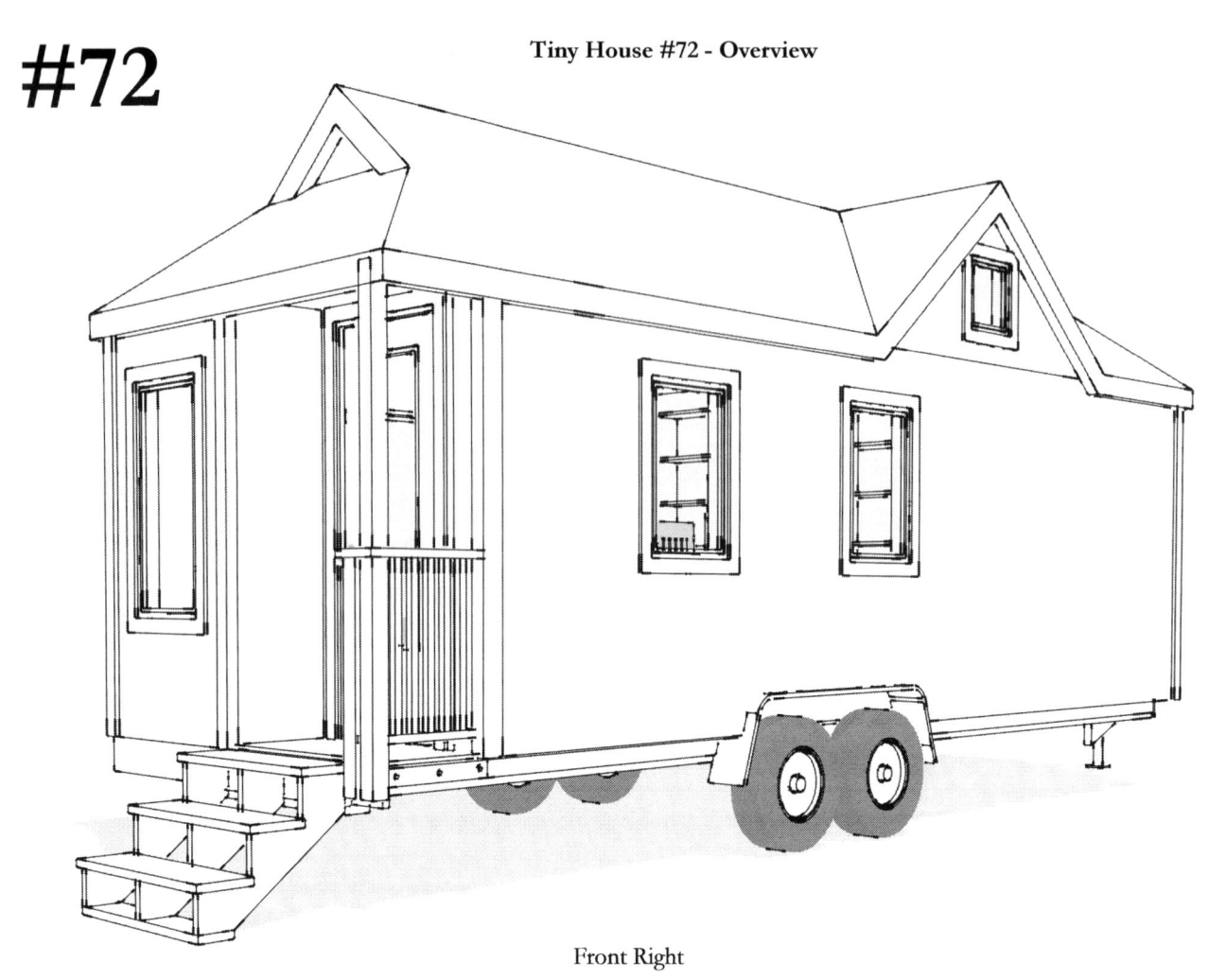

Summary:

Pocket doors close off the generous kitchen in this tiny house. Behind the kitchen is the bathroom. Above the kitchen and bathroom is a loft with a queen bed. In the front room is a sofa, comfy chair, and table for four.

Features:

24-Foot Tiny House on Wheels
Dutch Cross Gable up Front and a Hip Roof on the Back
Aerodynamic
Generous Kitchen
Sleeps Two

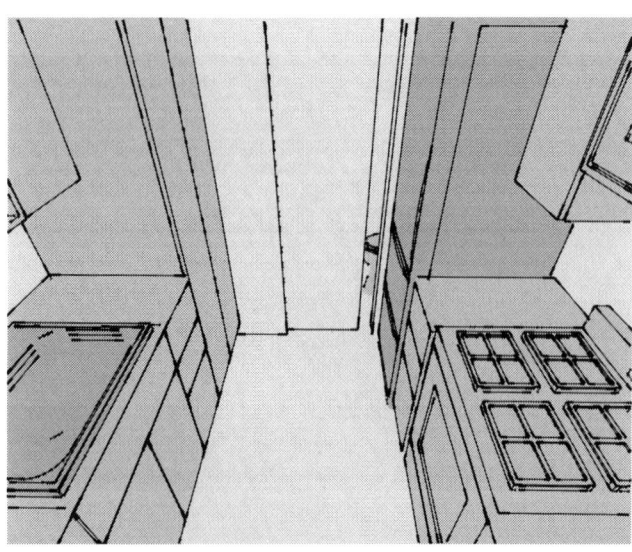

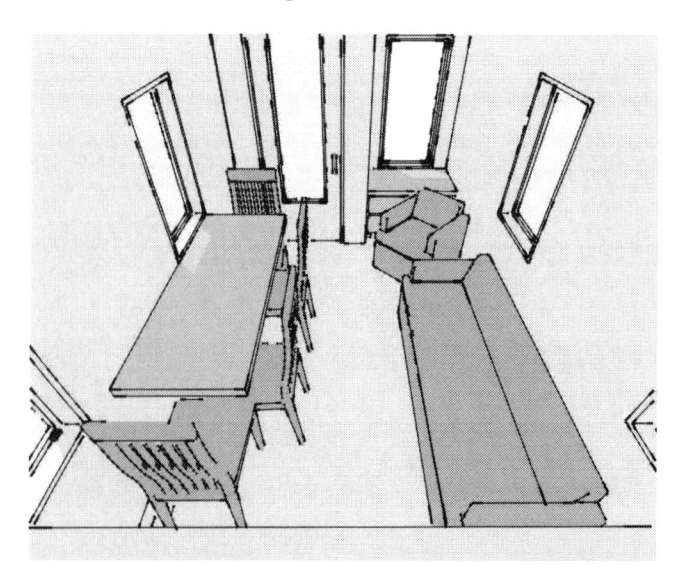

Kitchen

View from Loft

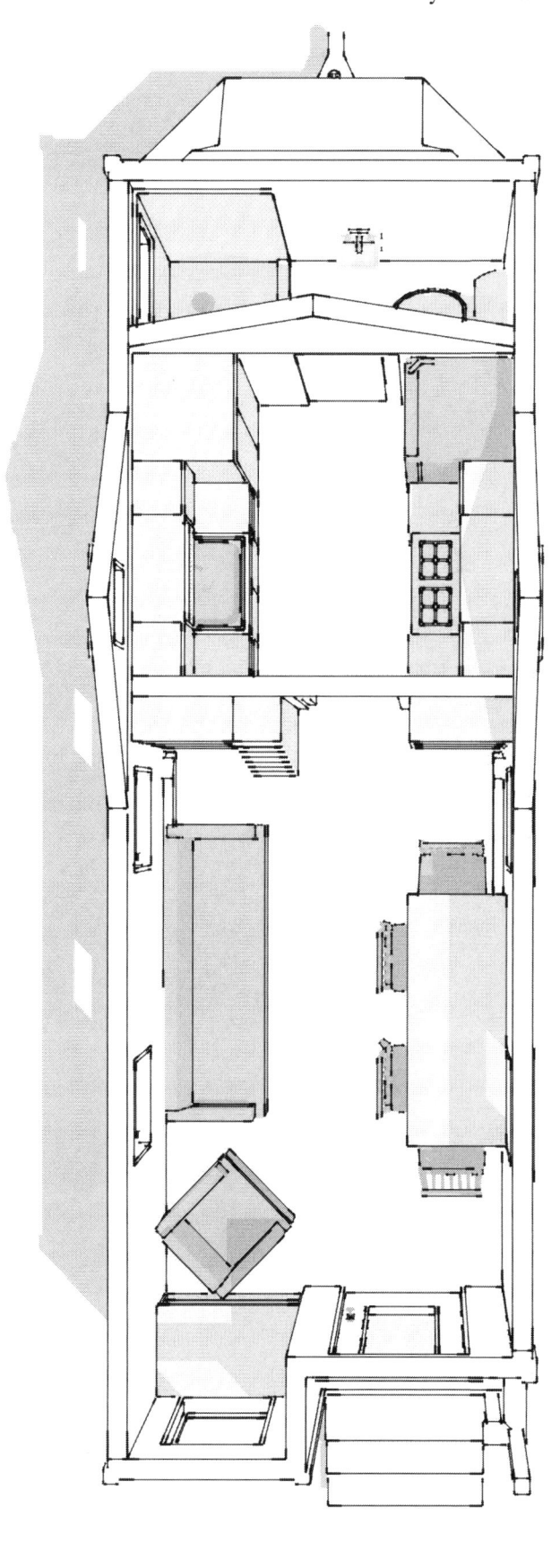

Tiny House #72 - Floor Plan & Exterior

Front Right Corner

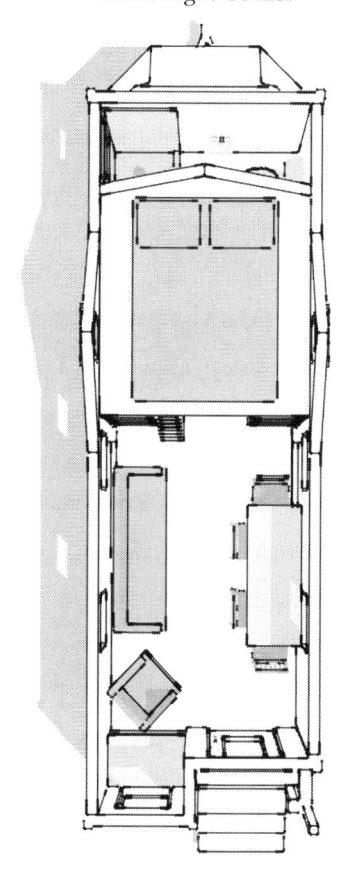

Floor Plan - Loft

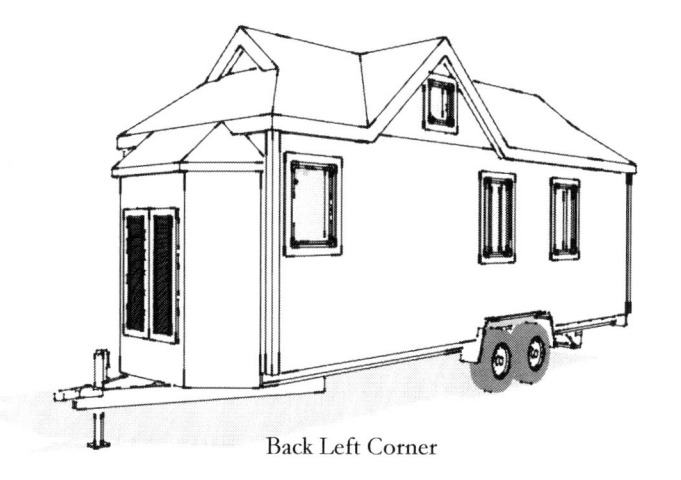

Floor Plan

Back Left Corner

Tiny House #72 - Interior Views

Interior from Entry

Interior from Kitchen

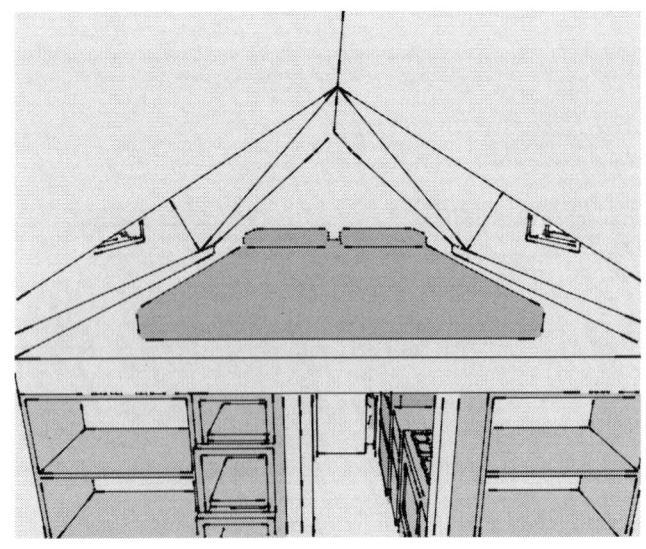

Loft

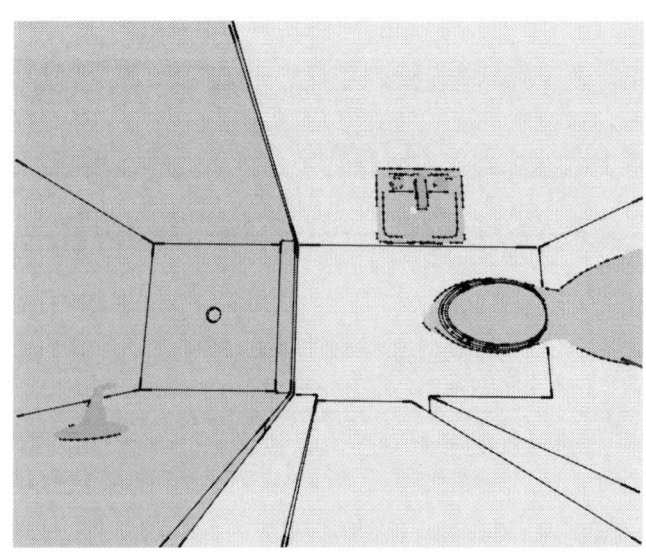

Bathroom

Tiny House #72 - Elevations

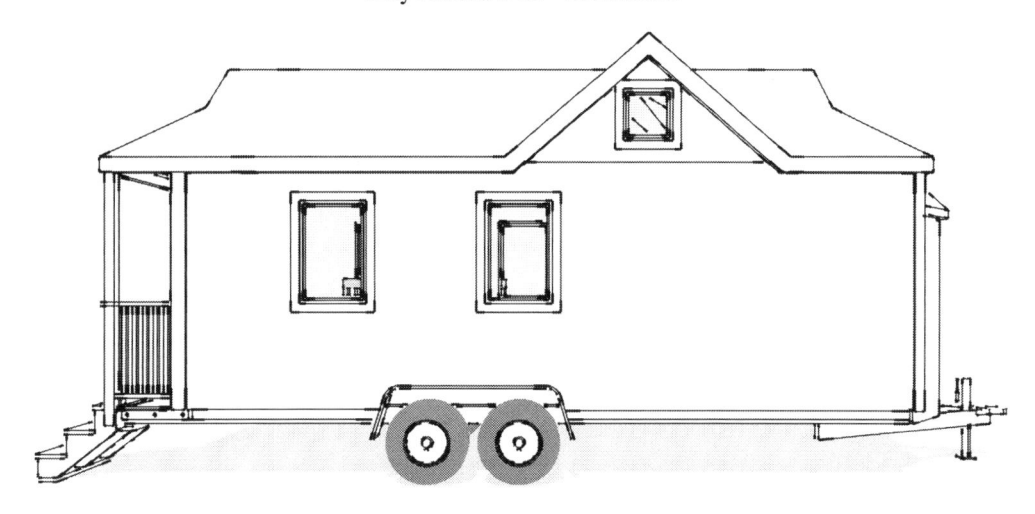

Right

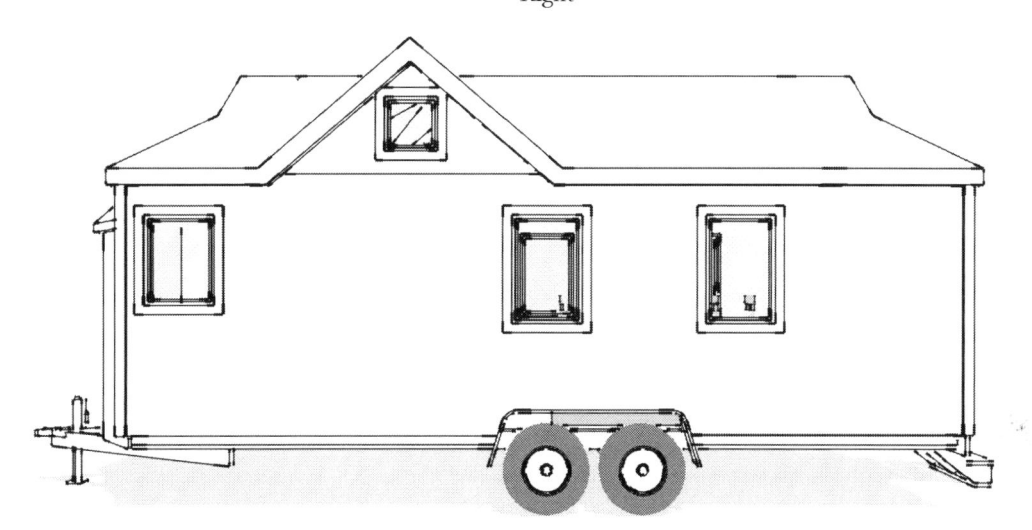

Left

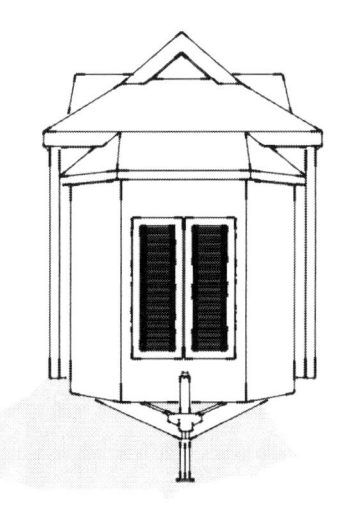

Back

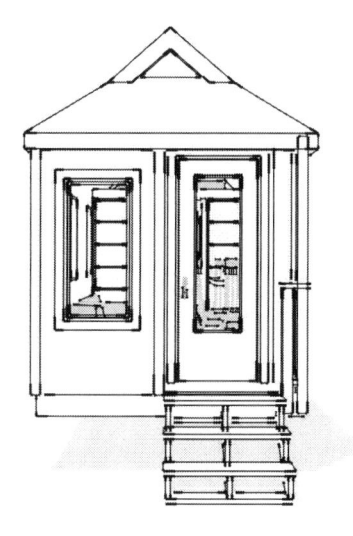

Front

#73

Tiny House #73 - Overview

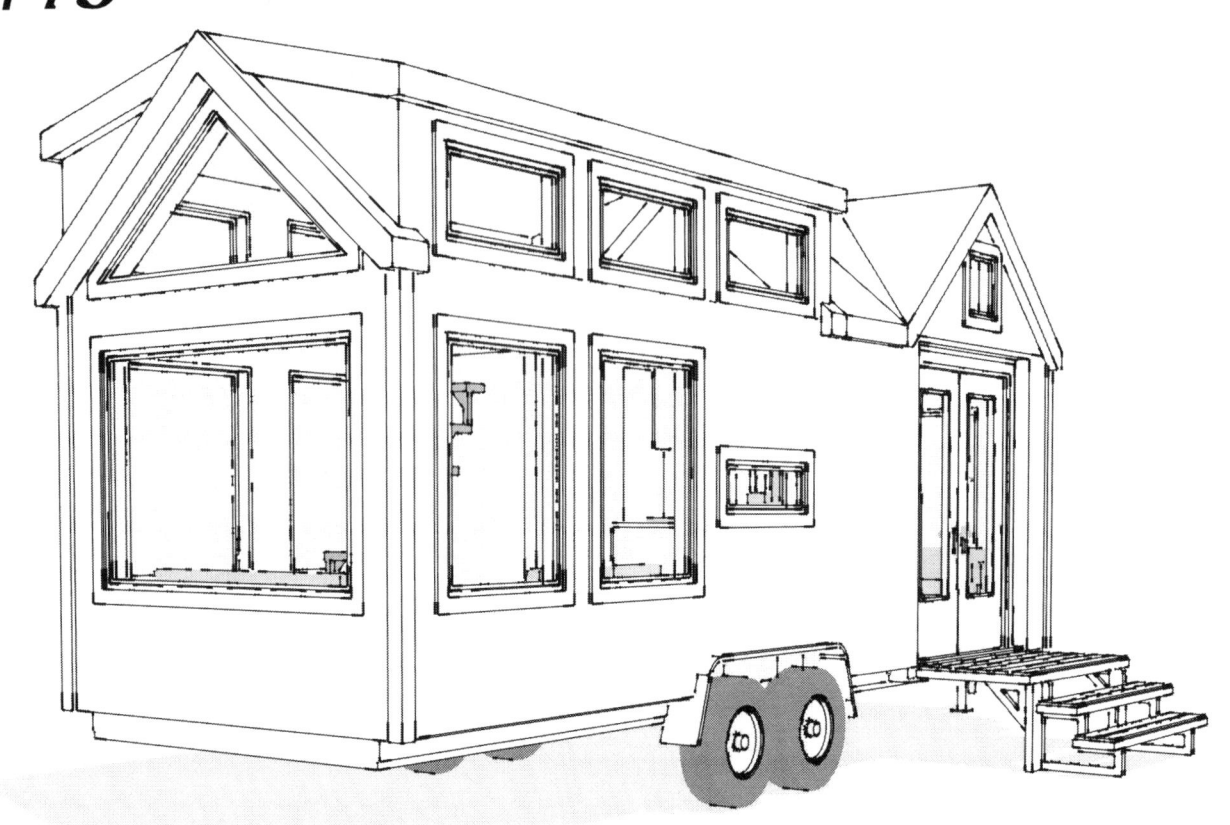

Front Right

Summary:

At the center of this house is a bathroom and a small fully featured kitchen. Above the kitchen and bathroom is a loft open on one end. The dining room has twin French doors and fold-down decks on each side. On the other end of the house is a living room with two comfy chairs and a sofa. The loft is accessed by climbing an alternating step staircase.

Features:

24-Foot Tiny House on Wheels
Cross Gable Roof with Shed Dormer
Small Fully Featured Kitchen
Dining Room
Living Room
Twin Decks off Dining Room
Alternating Step Stairs

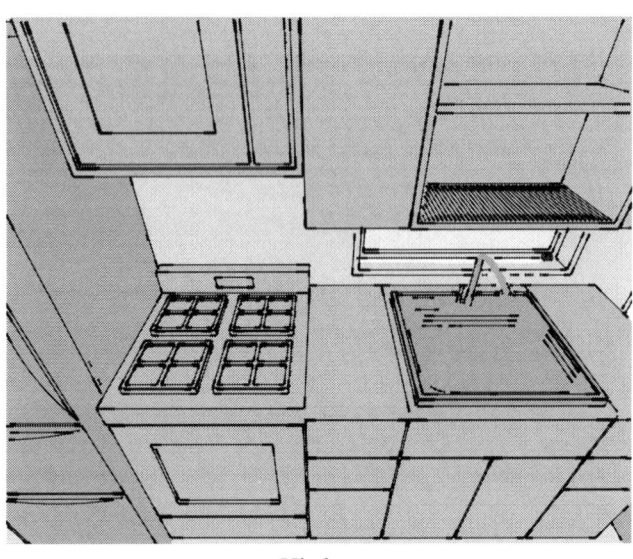

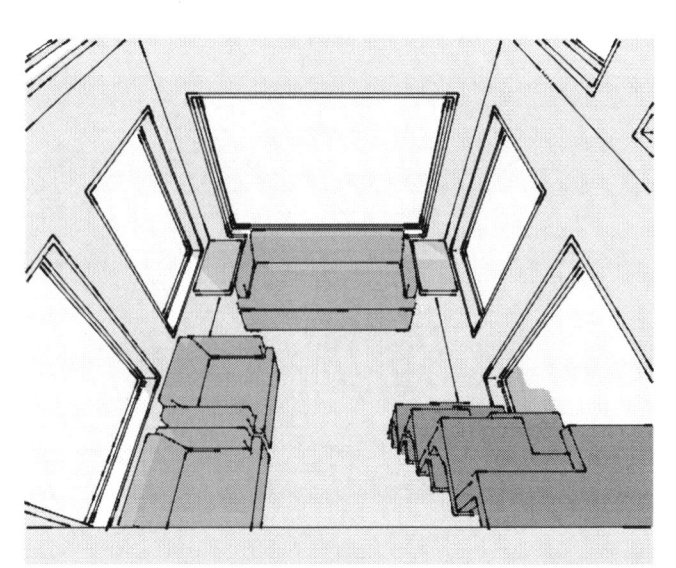

Kitchen

View from Loft

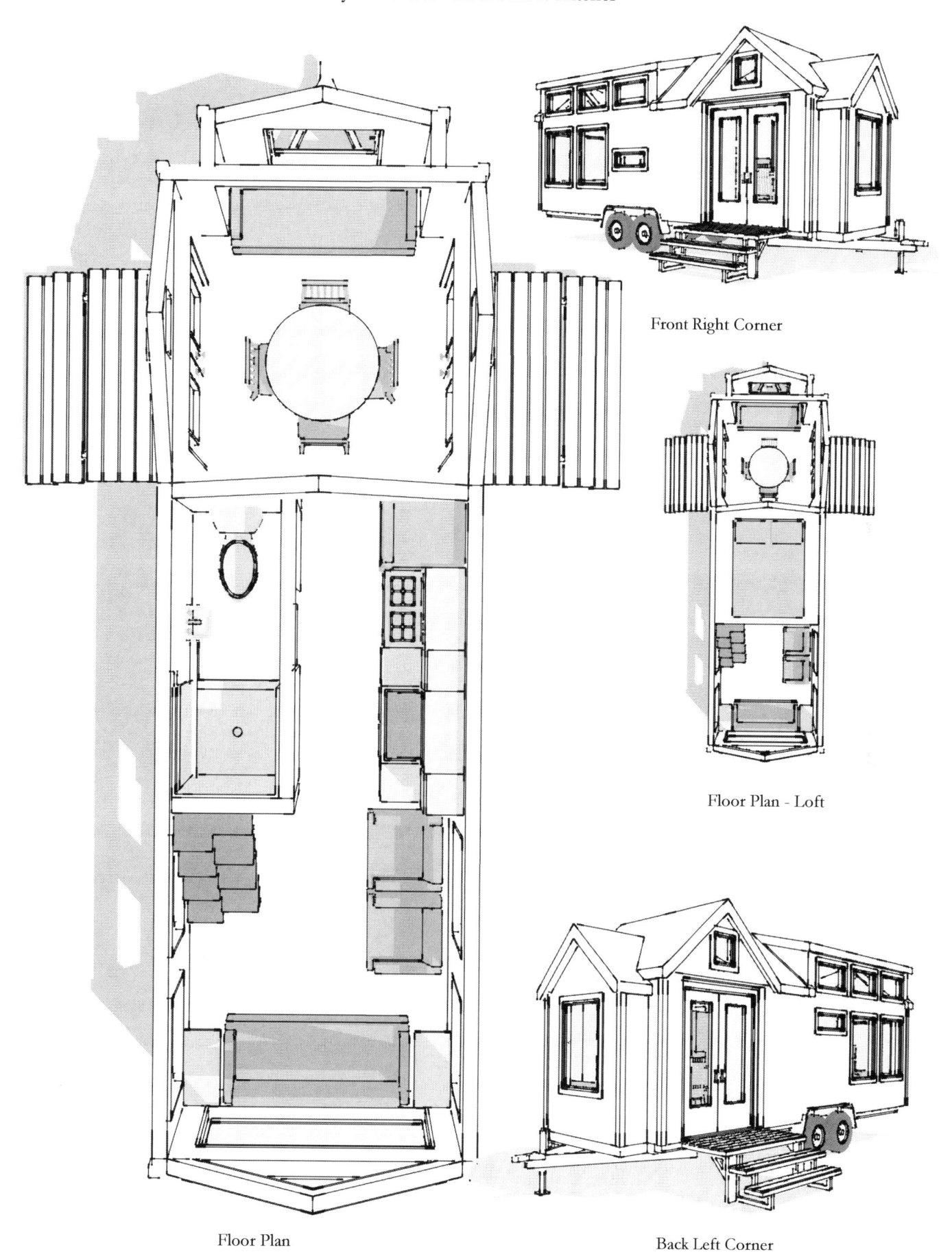

Tiny House #73 - Floor Plan & Exterior

Front Right Corner

Floor Plan - Loft

Floor Plan

Back Left Corner

303

Tiny House #73 - Interior Views

Interior

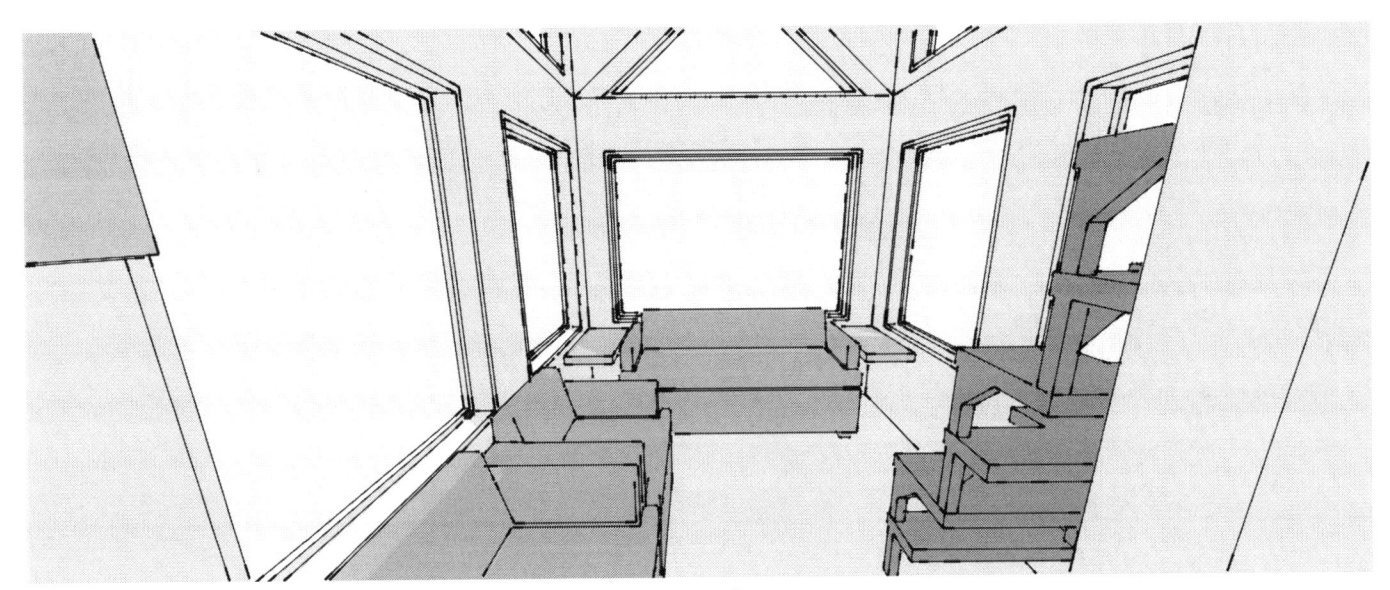

Interior

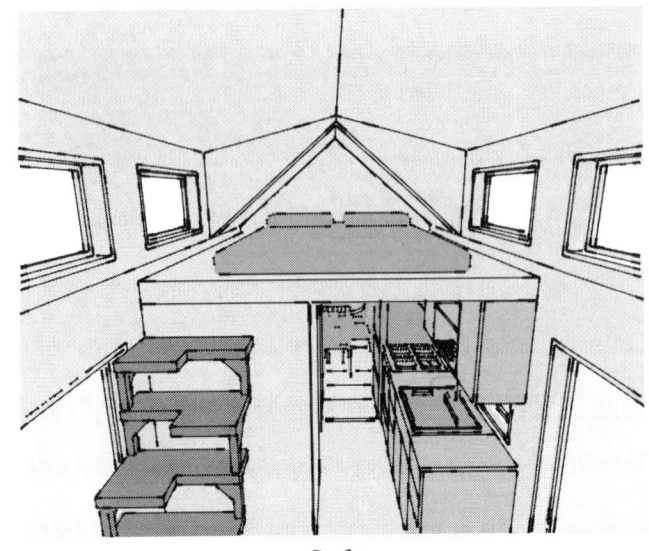

Loft

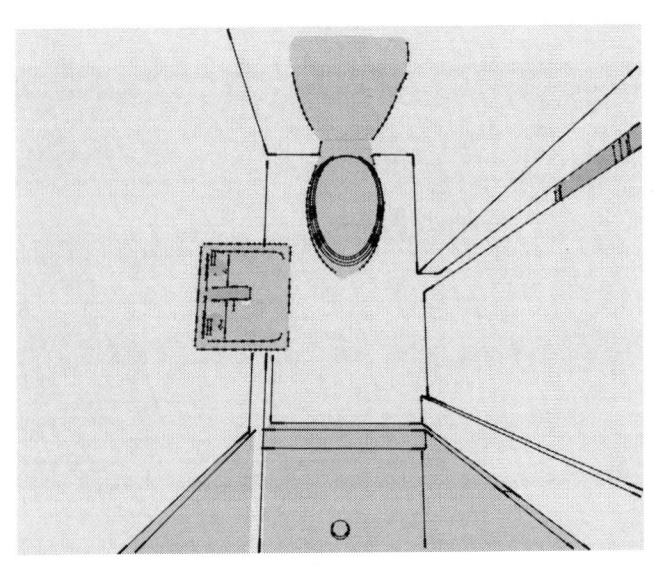

Bathroom

Tiny House #73 - Elevations

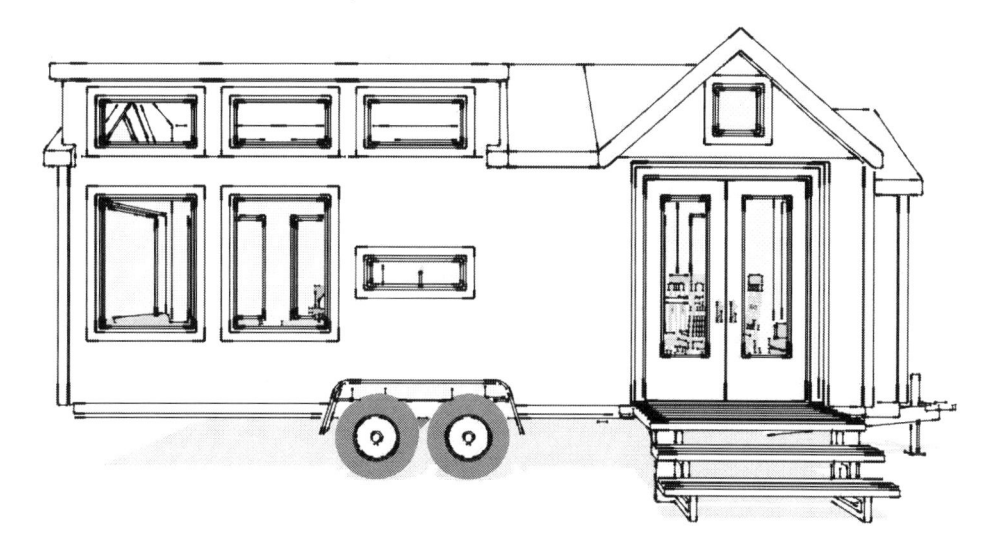

Right

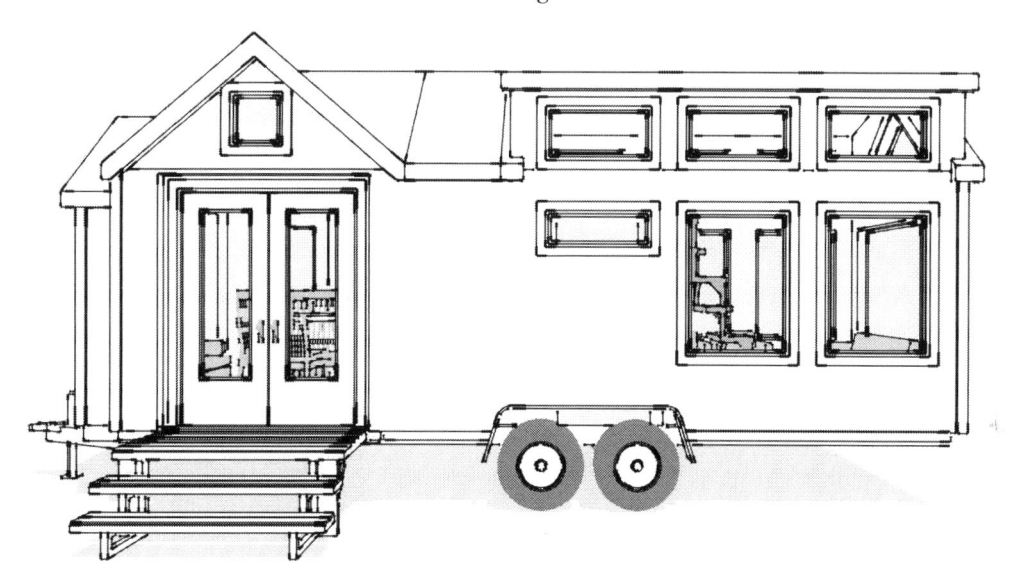

Left

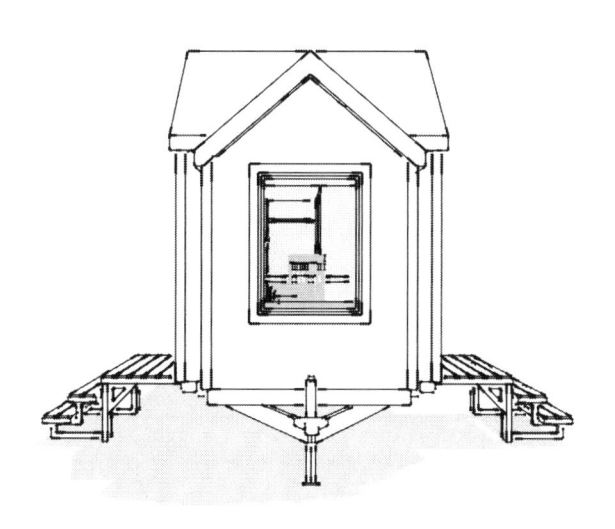

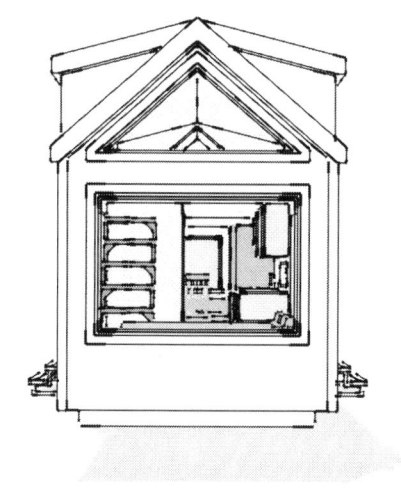

Back

Front

#74

Tiny House #74 - Overview

Front Right

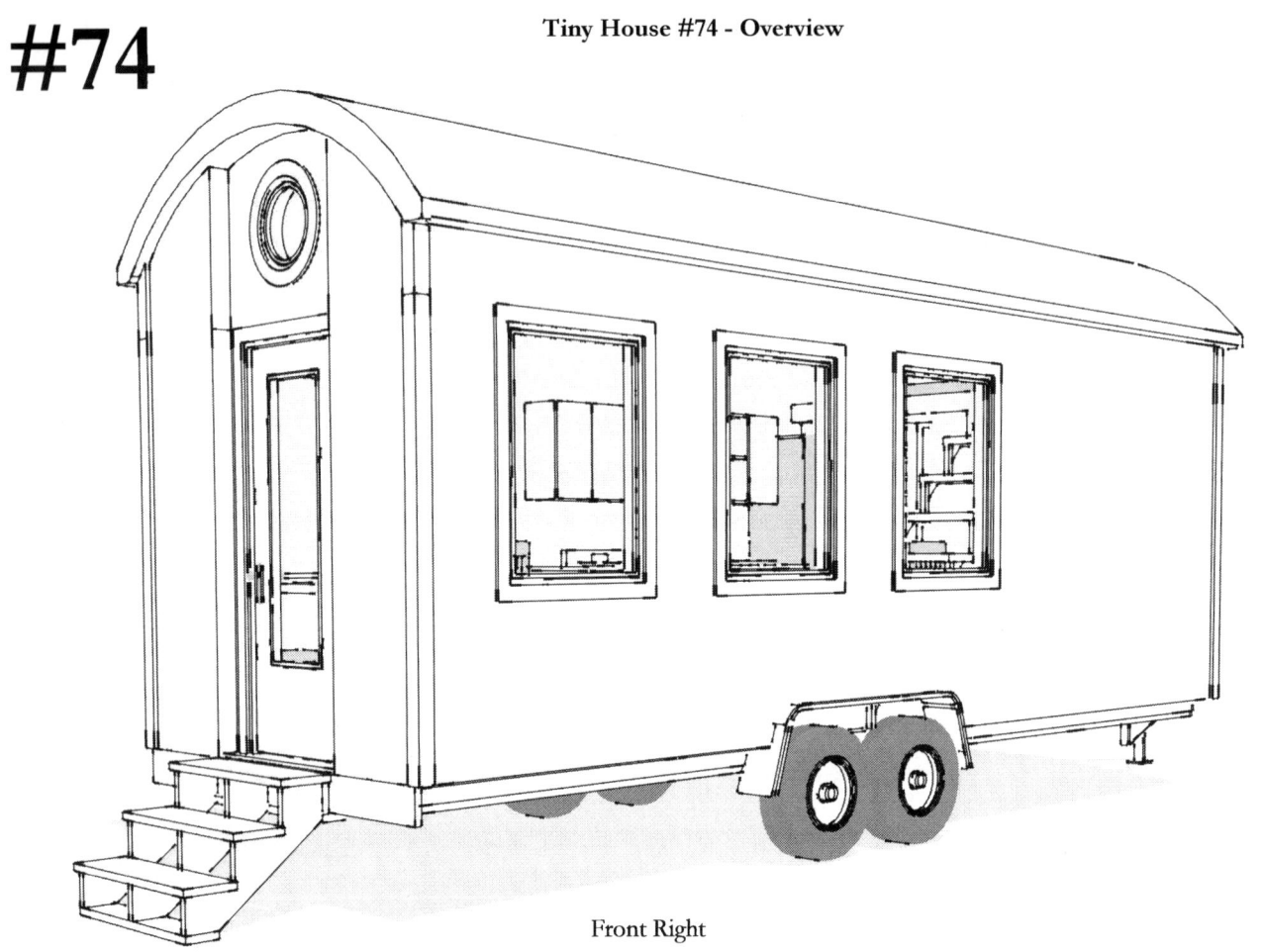

Summary:

This house would feel open and light. It's mostly one large room with a bathroom at the far end and a loft above. The open staircase would do little to impede the view. The kitchen is fully featured with a range and full size refrigerator. In the loft is a queen bed.

Features:

24-Foot Tiny House on Wheels
Vardo Inspired Curved Roof
Large Windows
High Ceiling
Fully Featured Kitchen
Laundry
Sleeps Two

Kitchen

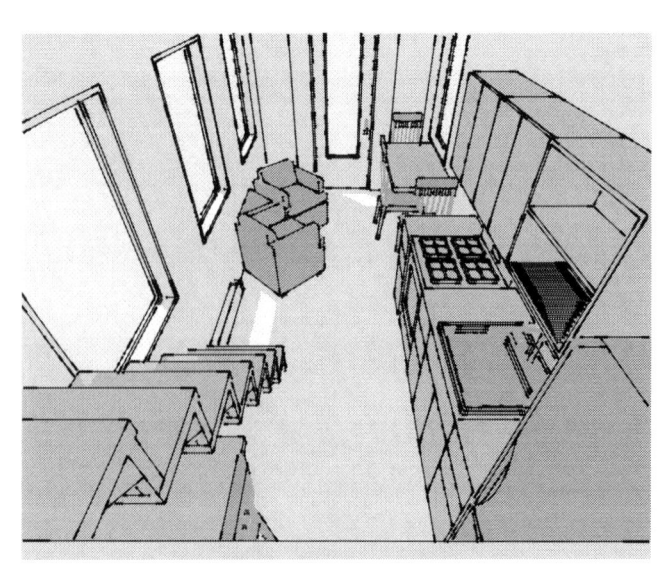

View from Loft

Tiny House #74 - Floor Plan & Exterior

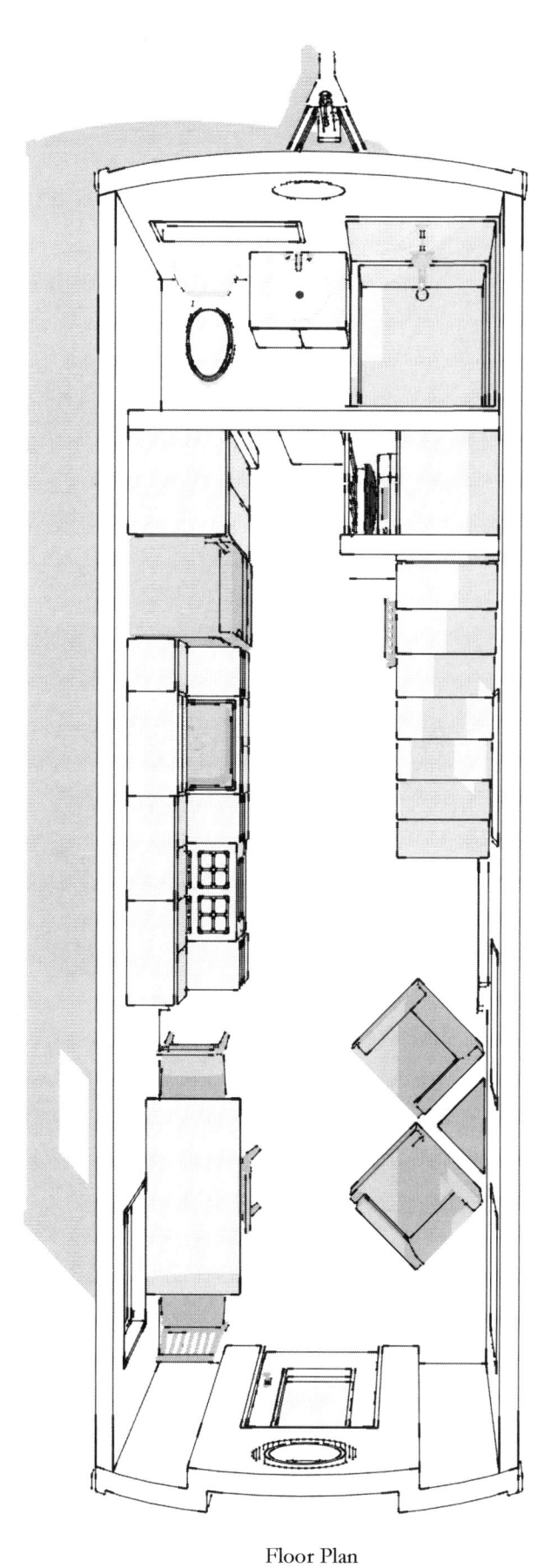

Front Right Corner

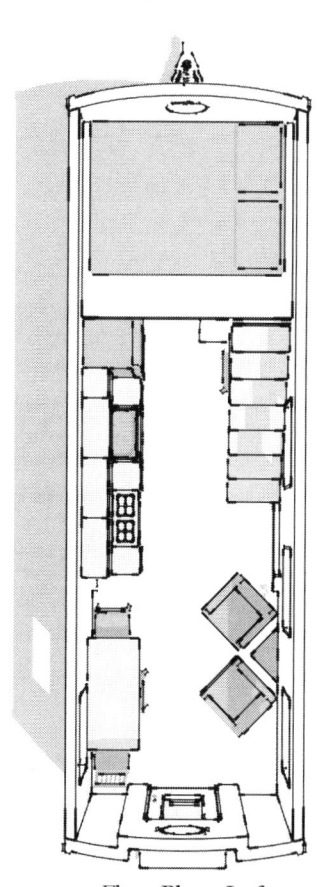

Floor Plan - Loft

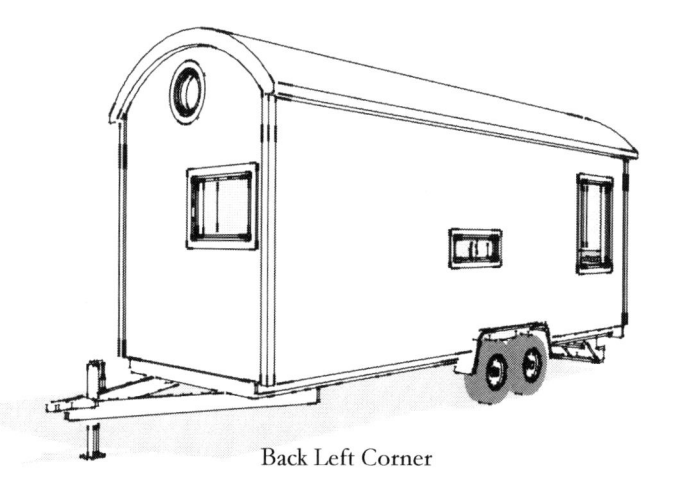

Floor Plan

Back Left Corner

Tiny House #74 - Interior Views

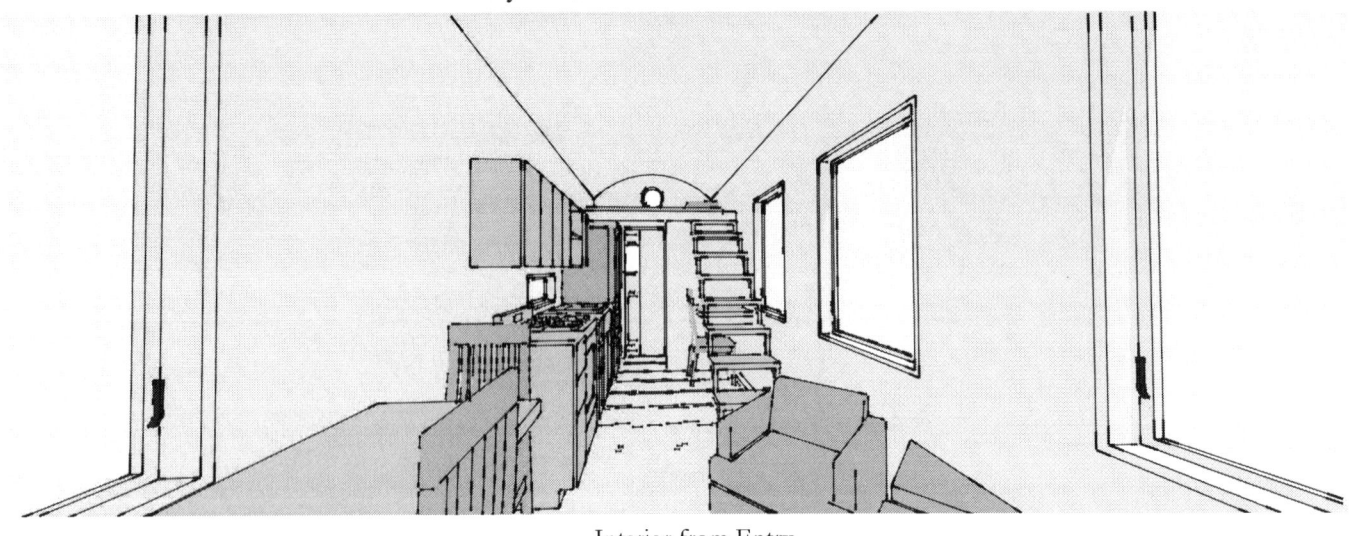

Interior from Entry

Interior from Bathroom

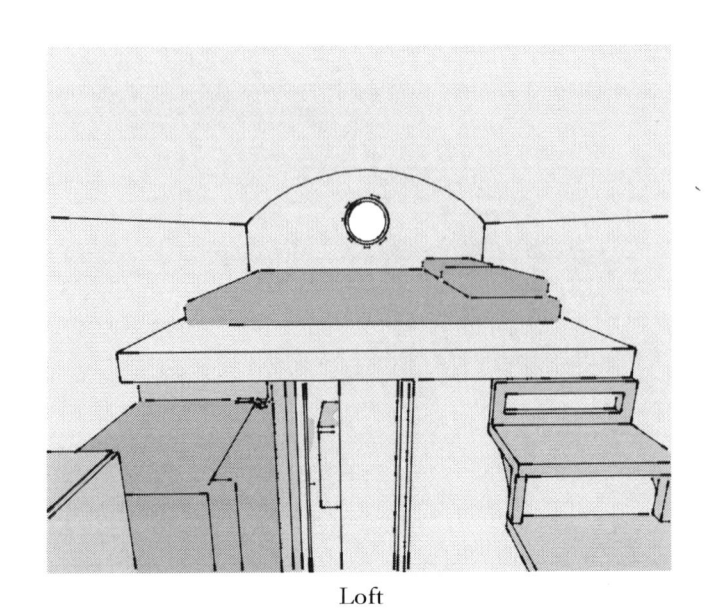

Loft

Bathroom

Tiny House #74 - Elevations

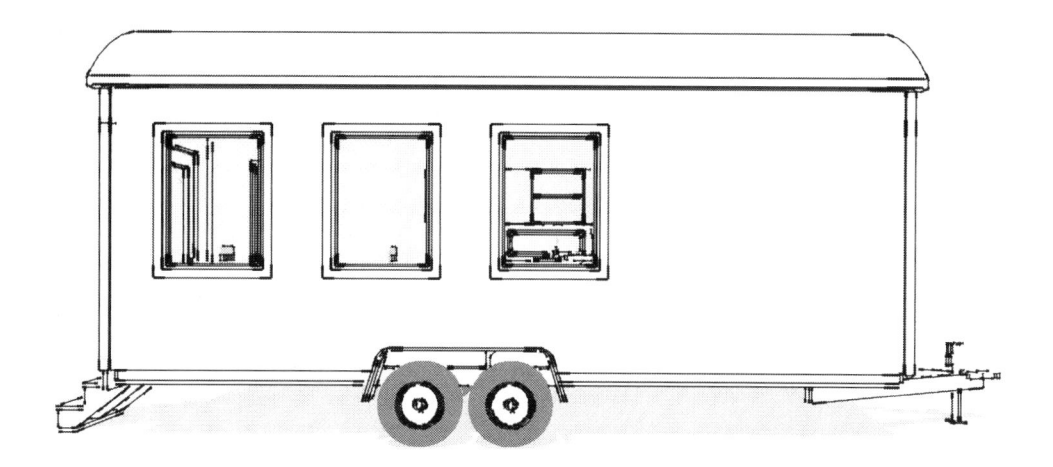

Right

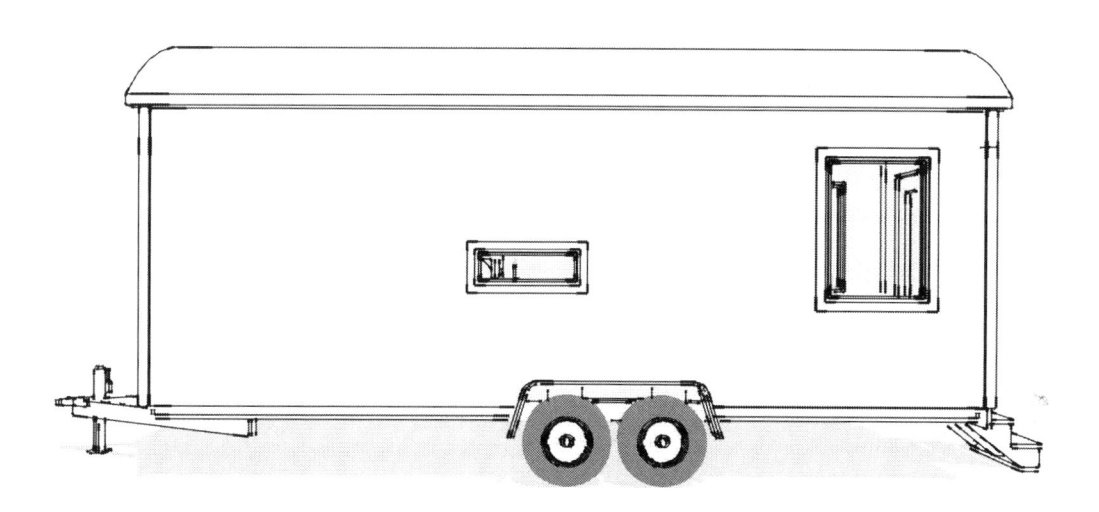

Left

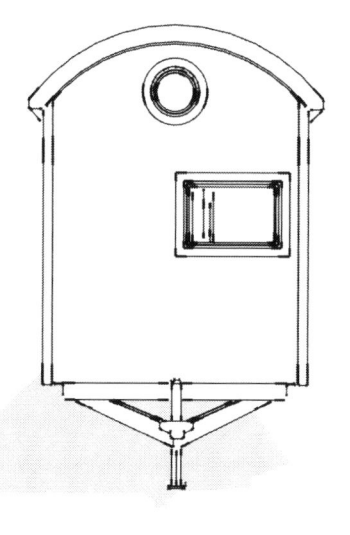

Back

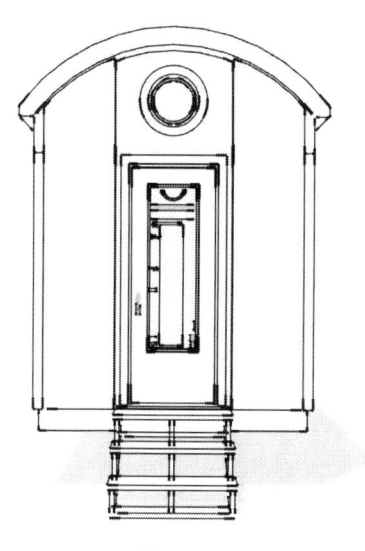

Front

#75

Tiny House #75 - Overview

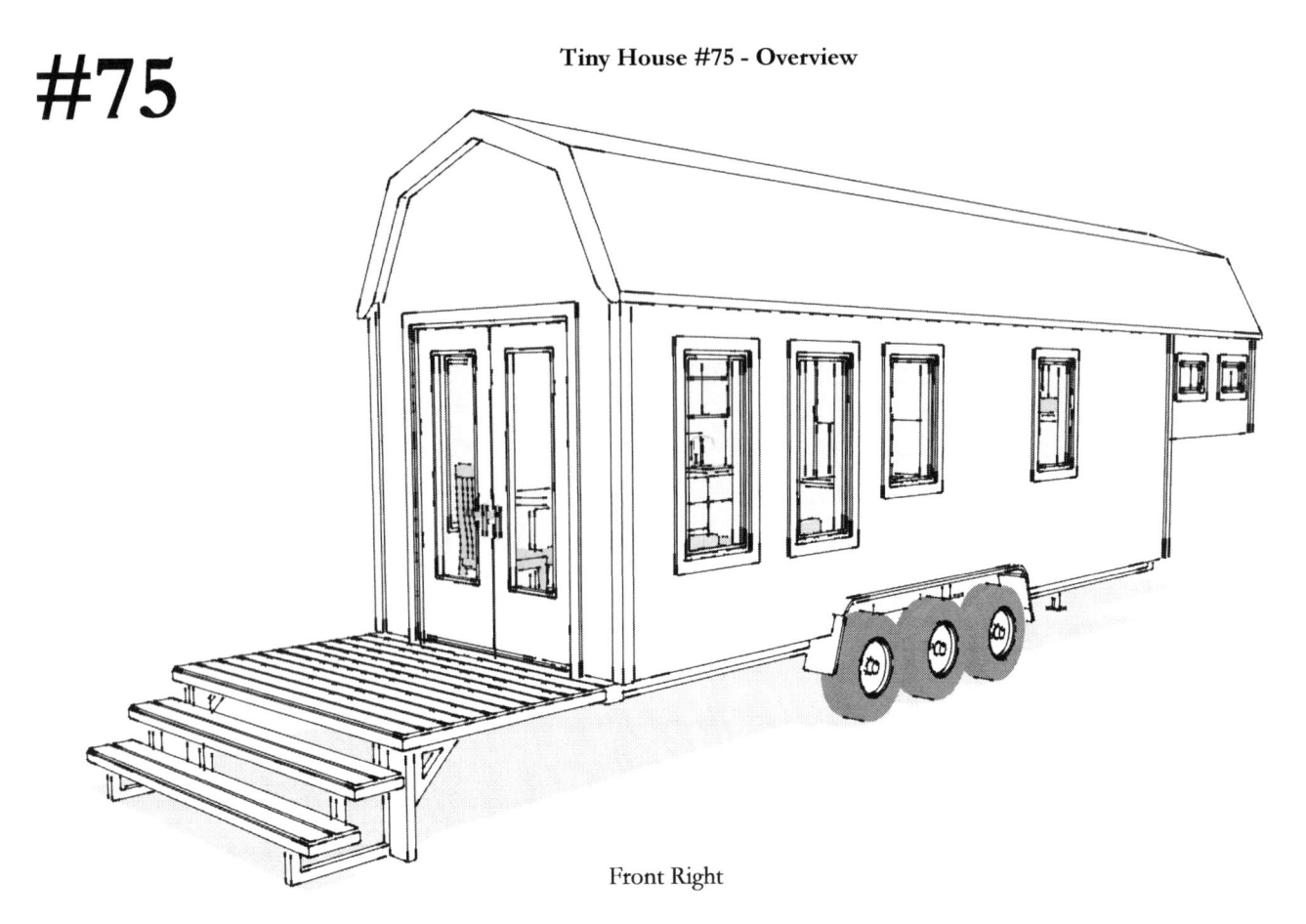

Front Right

Kitchen

Summary:

This home's fold-down deck welcomes visitors and leads them into the living room and small kitchen. Past the kitchen is a laundry closet and hallway to the bathroom and a loft bedroom over the trailer's gooseneck. The ceiling height over the gooseneck is low but taller than most lofts. Above the bathroom is a loft large enough for a twin bed.

Features:

24-Foot Tiny House on Wheels
Gooseneck Trailer
Gambrel Roof
Bathroom with Tub
Small Kitchen
Sleeps Three

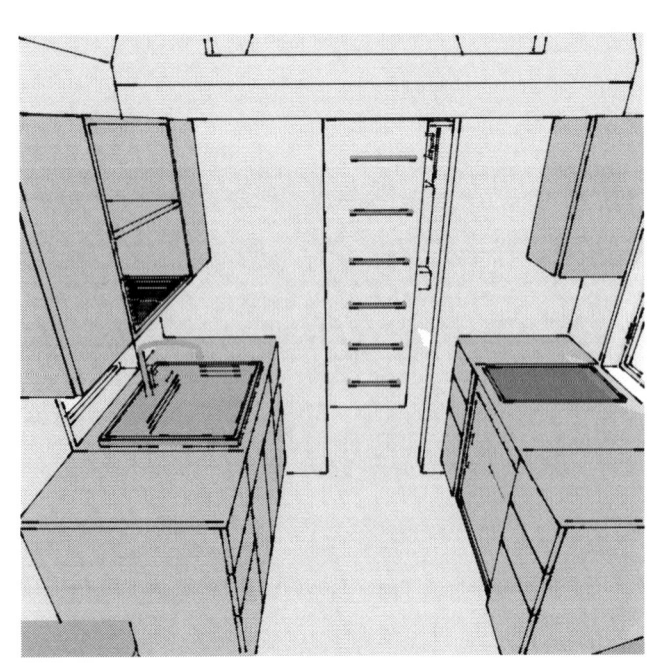

A Note About Trailers:

As tiny houses grow in size, so should their trailers. In this book I've shown examples of designs on 2-axle, 3-axle, and now a gooseneck trailer.

The right size trailer is the one that is built to handle the weight of your tiny house, no matter the number of axles; but beginning with 24-foot homes you may want to consider a 3-axle trailer or even a gooseneck.

Each trailer axle carries a certain amount of weight. Gooseneck trailers typically tow better for really heavy loads but require a truck that is setup to pull this type of trailer.

Gooseneck trailer length normally refers to the floor length, not the gooseneck itself. So a 24-foot tiny house on a gooseneck gets about 8 more feet of loft length over the gooseneck for a total of 32-feet.

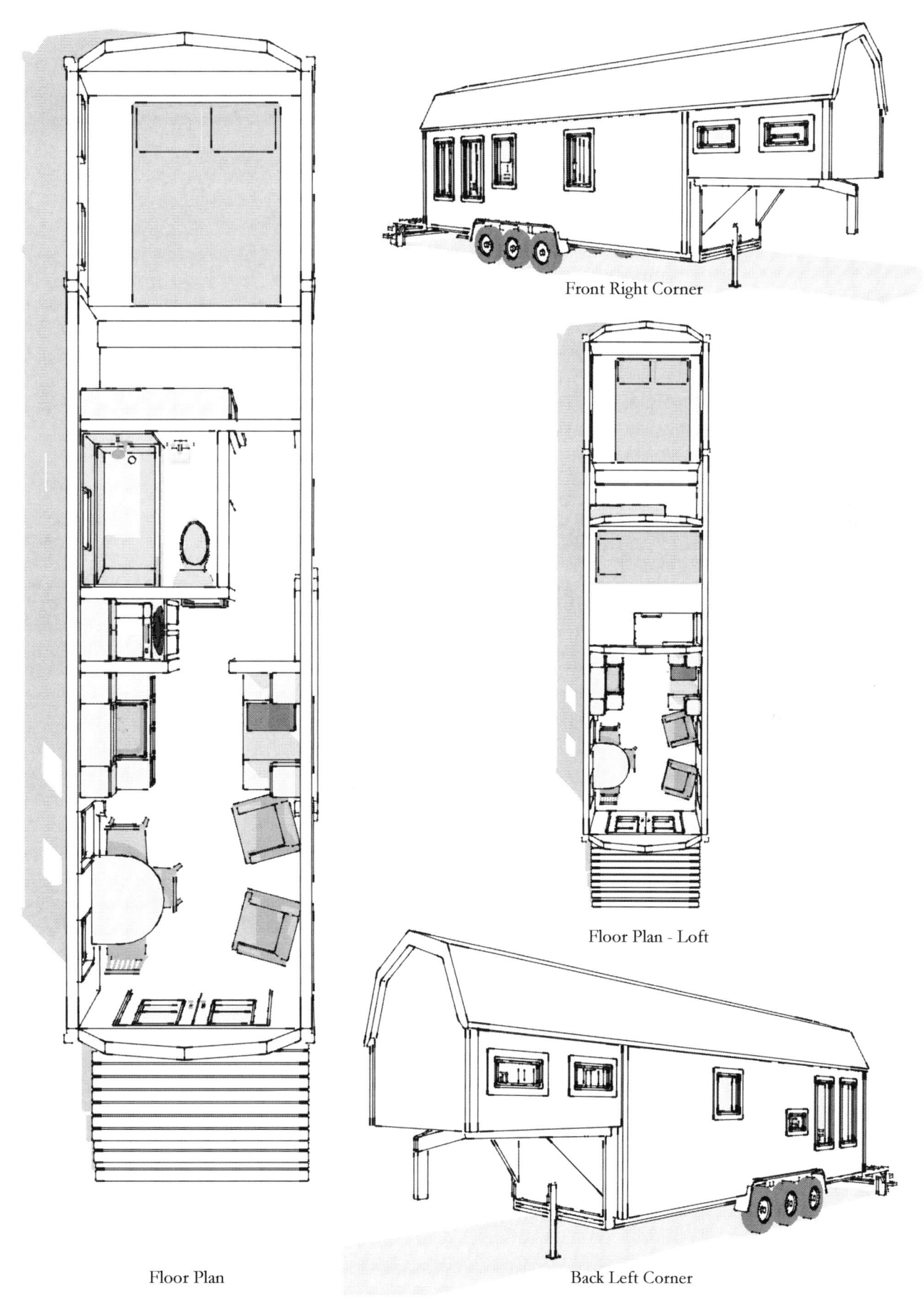

Tiny House #75 - Floor Plan & Exterior

Front Right Corner

Floor Plan - Loft

Floor Plan

Back Left Corner

311

Tiny House #75 - Interior Views

Interior from Entry

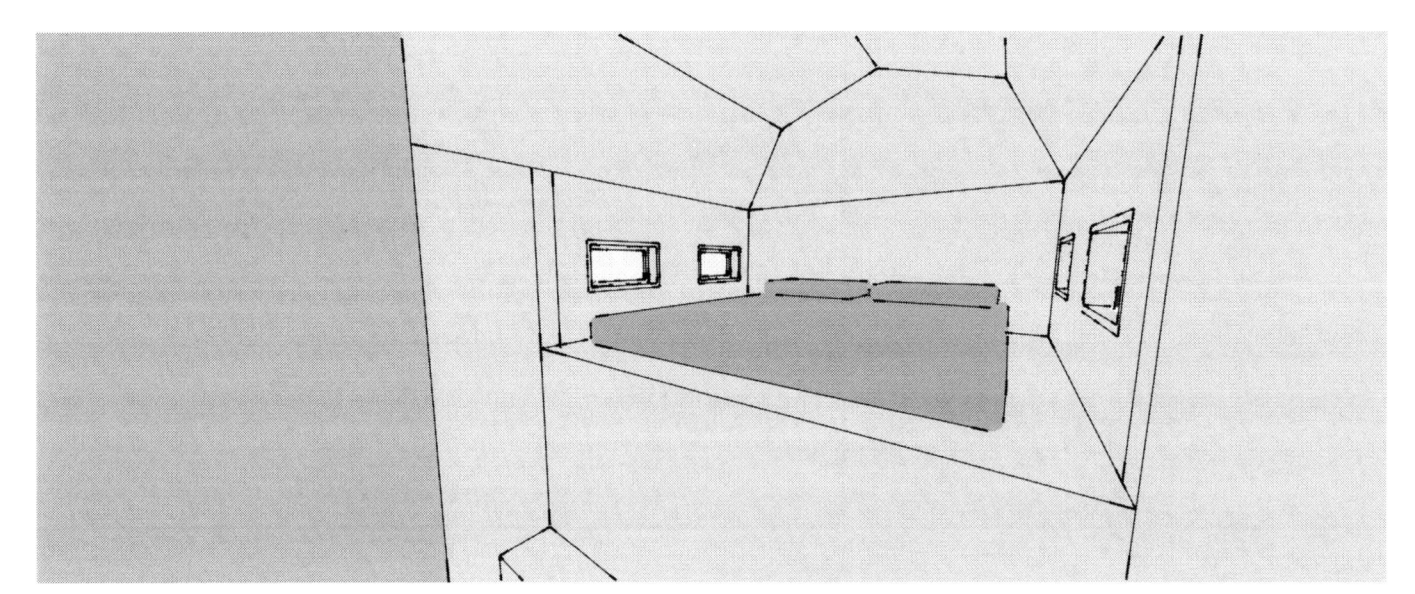

Gooseneck Loft

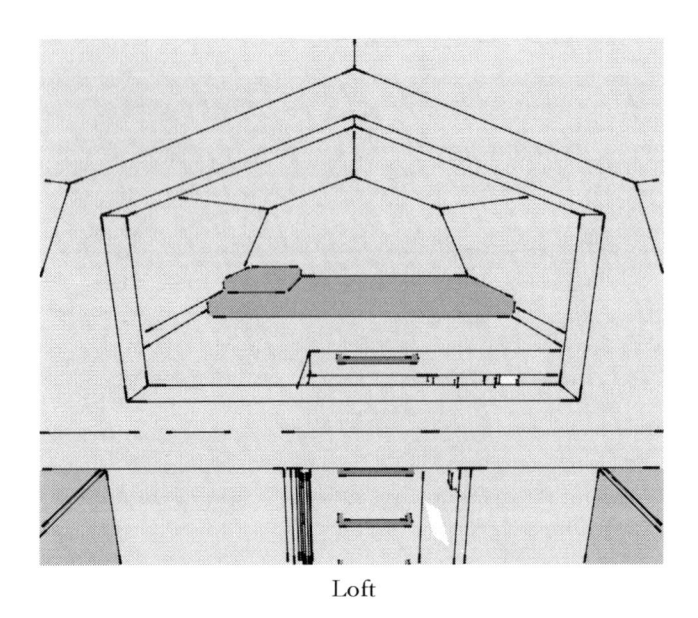

Loft

Bathroom

Tiny House #75 - Elevations

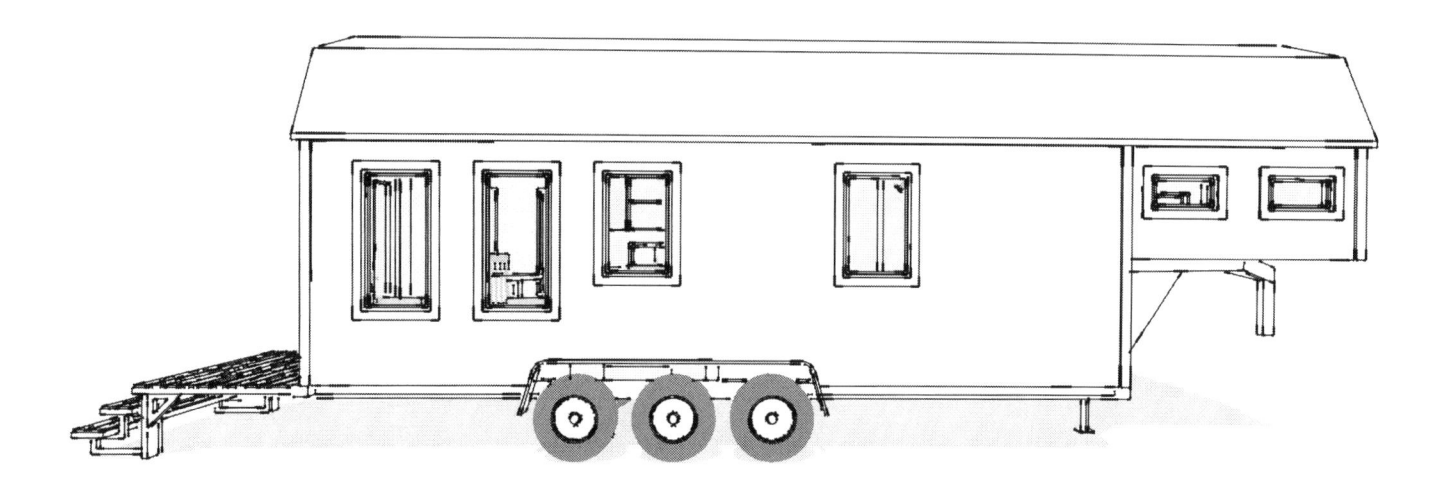

Right

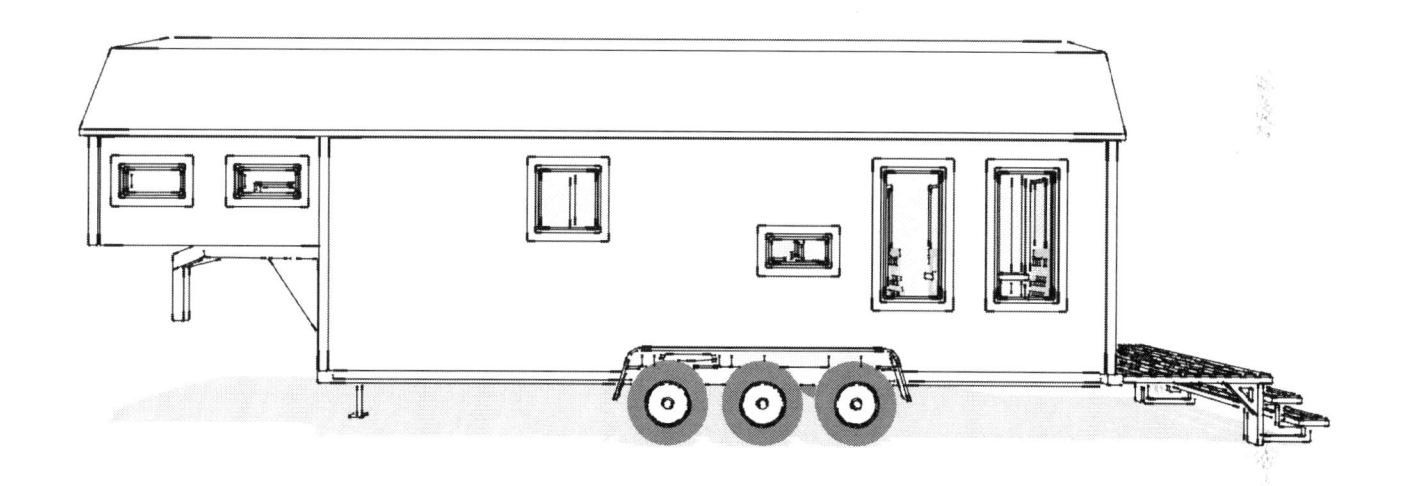

Left

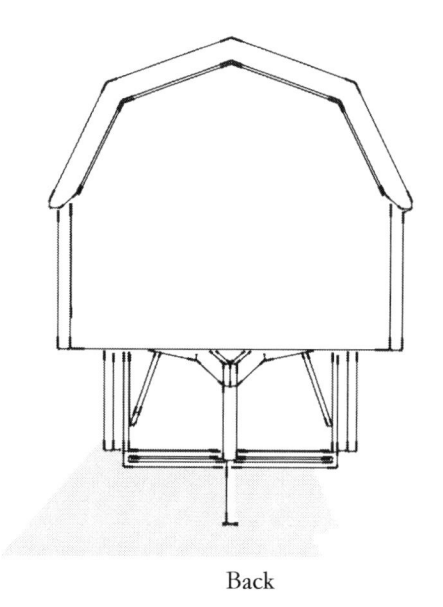

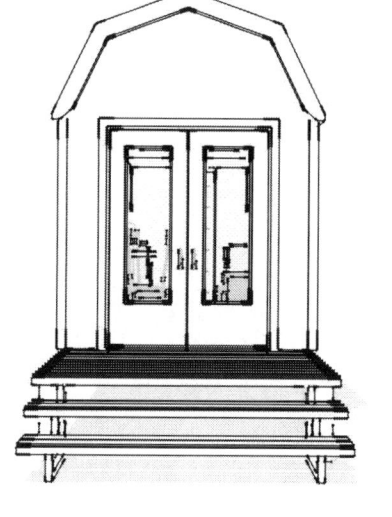

Back

Front

#76

Tiny House #76 - Overview

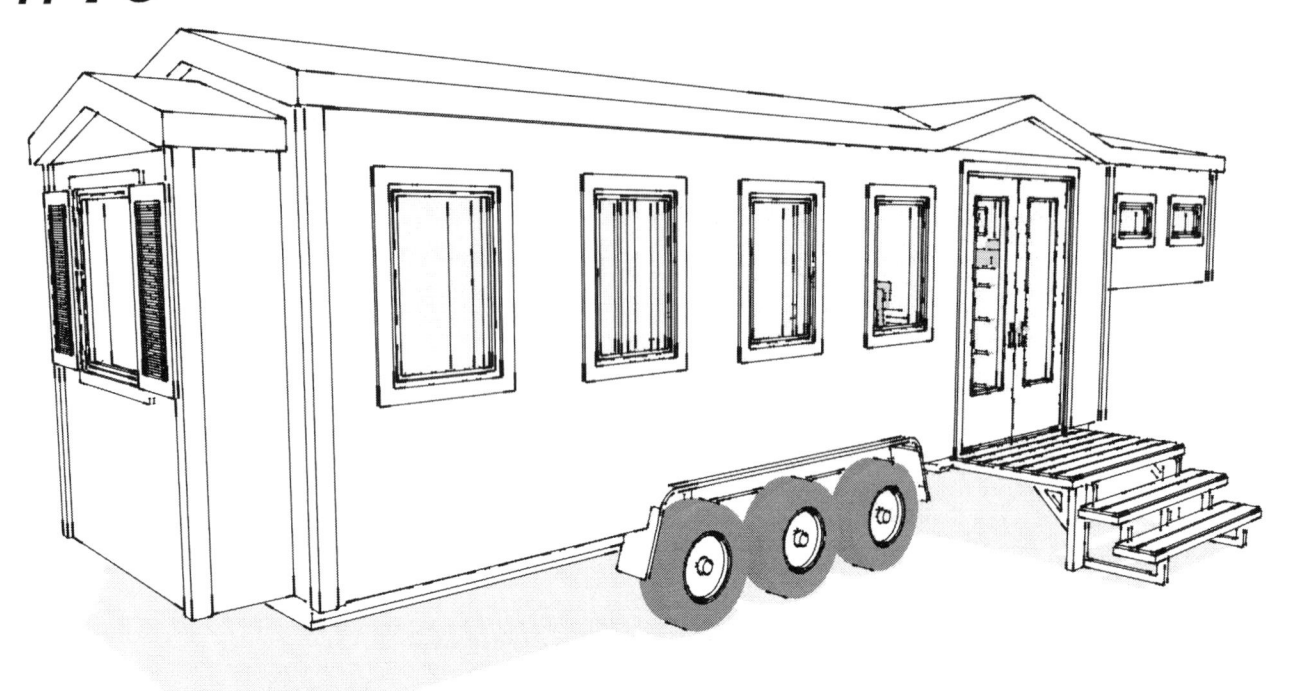

Front Right

Summary:

When you have a long narrow house, like a large tiny house, it sometimes works better to place the entry somewhere along one of the long sides because it gives you the opportunity to use the ends of the house for rooms that don't also need to function as hallways.

In this example there's a bedroom at each end. The bedroom over the trailer's gooseneck is shown with two twin beds. The bedroom on the other end of the house has a queen bed. In the center of the house is a table for four, a kitchen and bathroom. The lower height of this house would make it easier to tow.

Features:

24-Foot Tiny House on Wheels
Low 3/12 Gable
No Loft
Sleeps Four

Kitchen

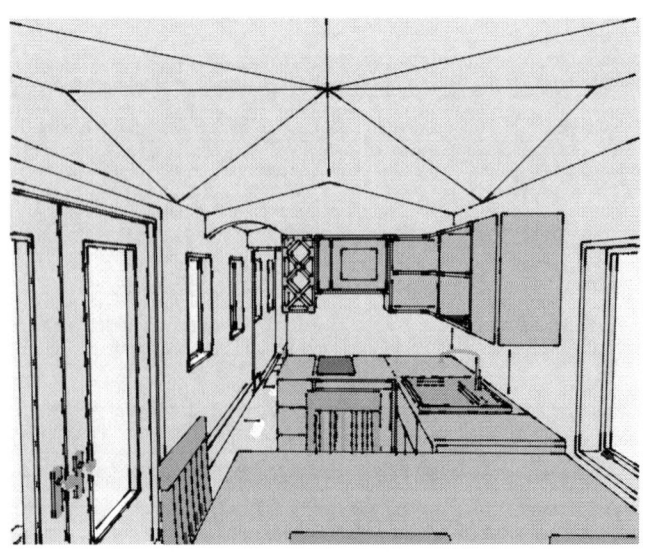

View from Loft

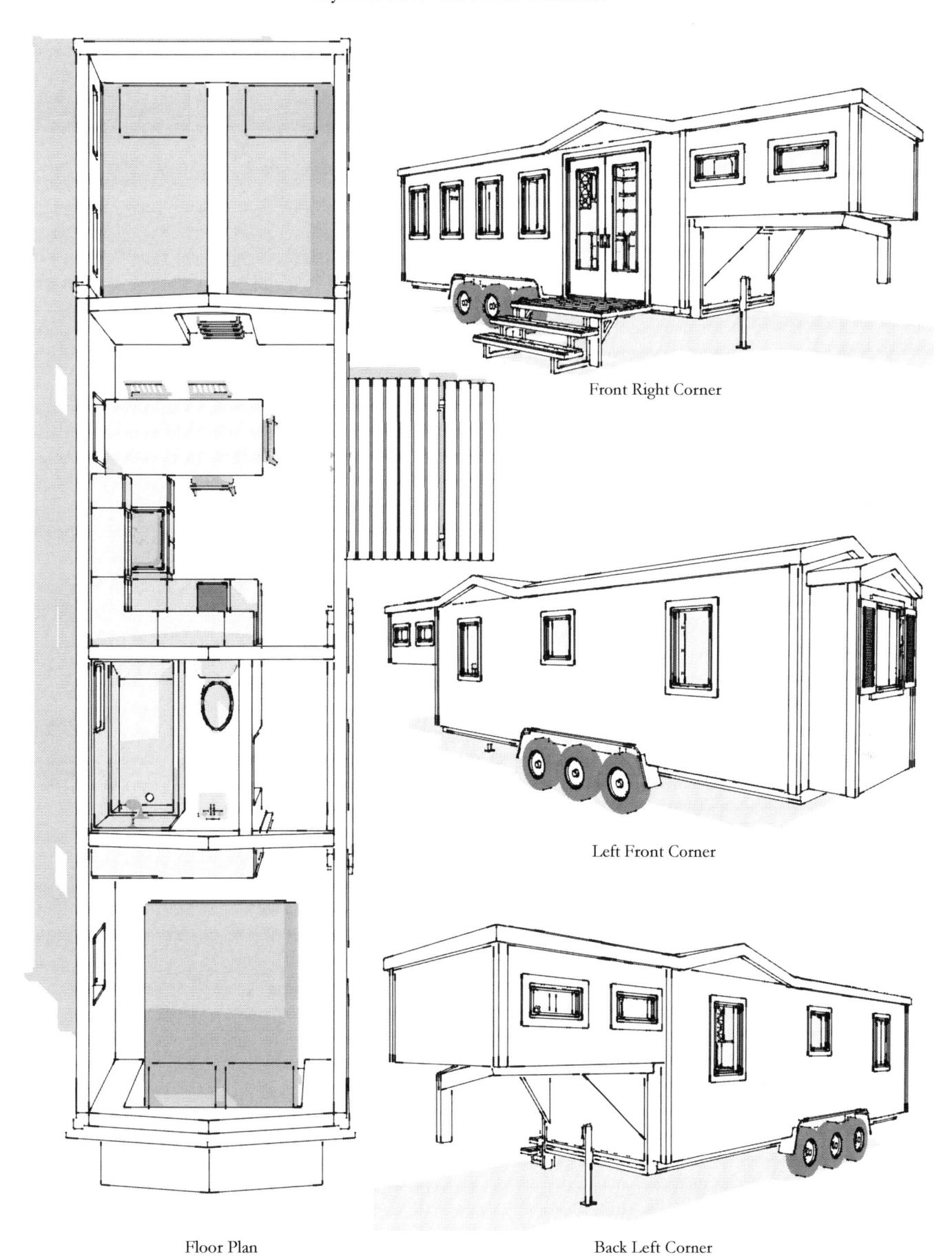

Tiny House #76 - Floor Plan & Exterior

Front Right Corner

Left Front Corner

Floor Plan

Back Left Corner

Tiny House #76 - Interior Views

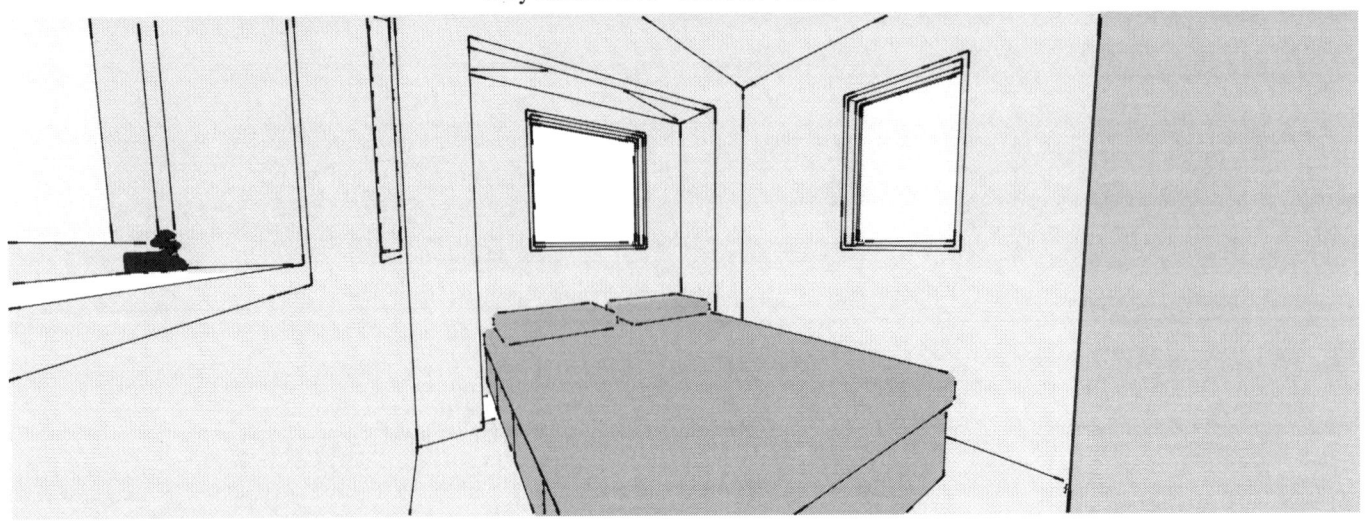

Bedroom

Interior from Kitchen

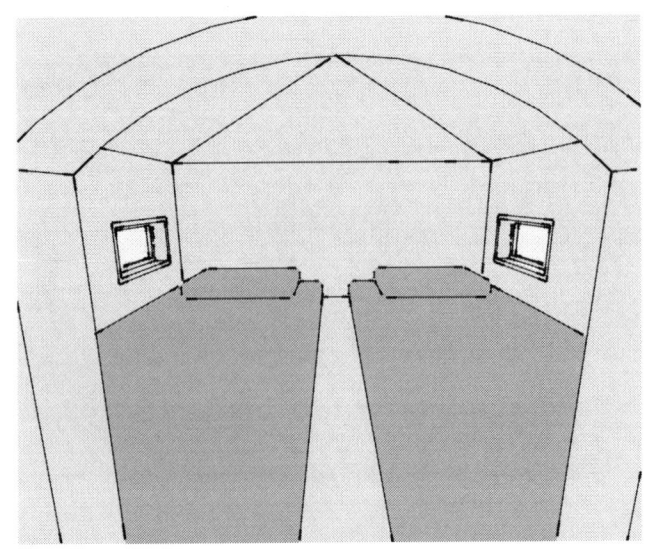

Gooseneck Loft

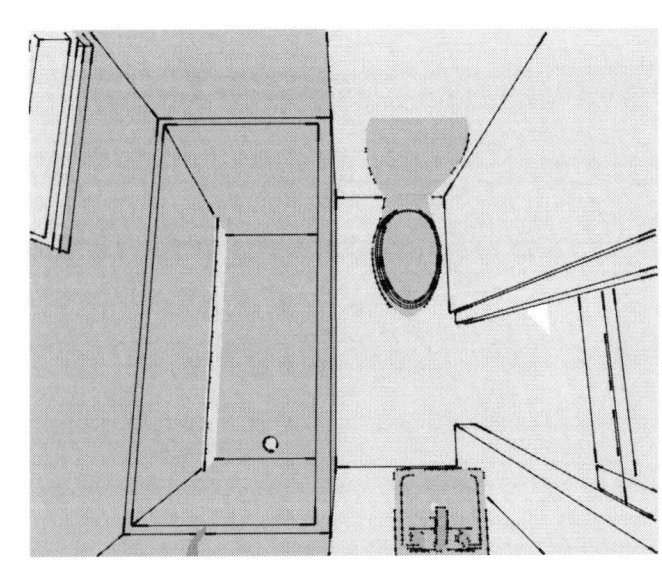

Bathroom

Tiny House #76 - Elevations

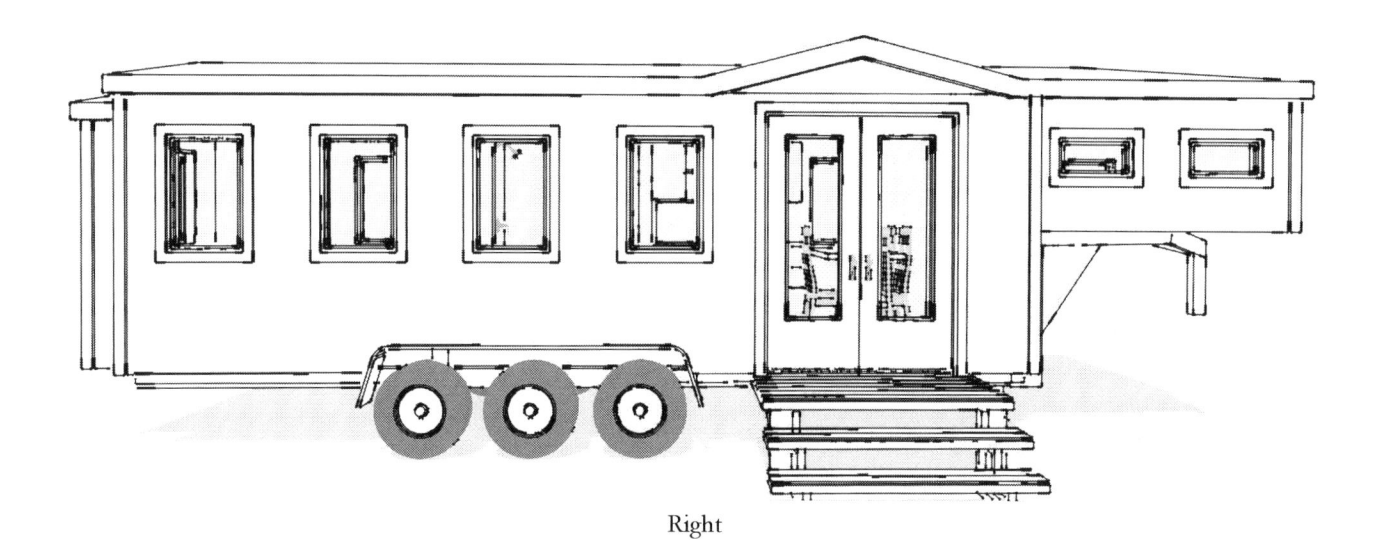

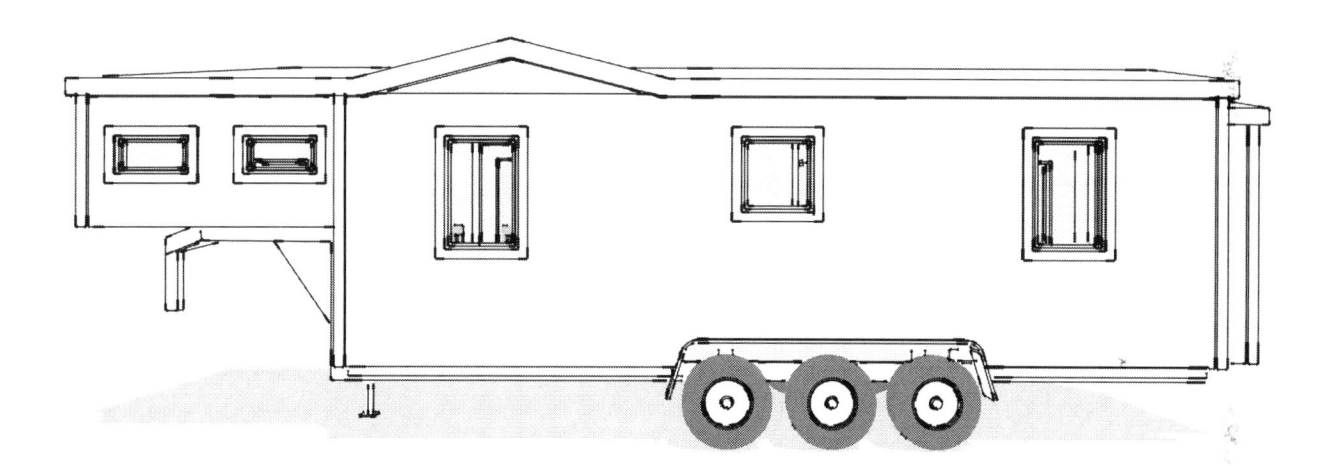

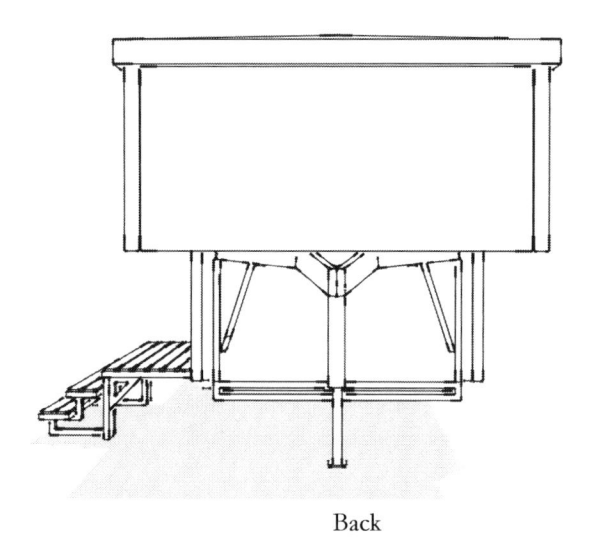

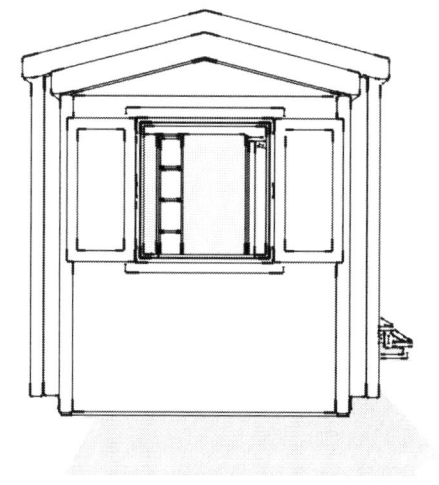

Right

Left

Back

Front

#77

Tiny House #77 - Overview

Front Right

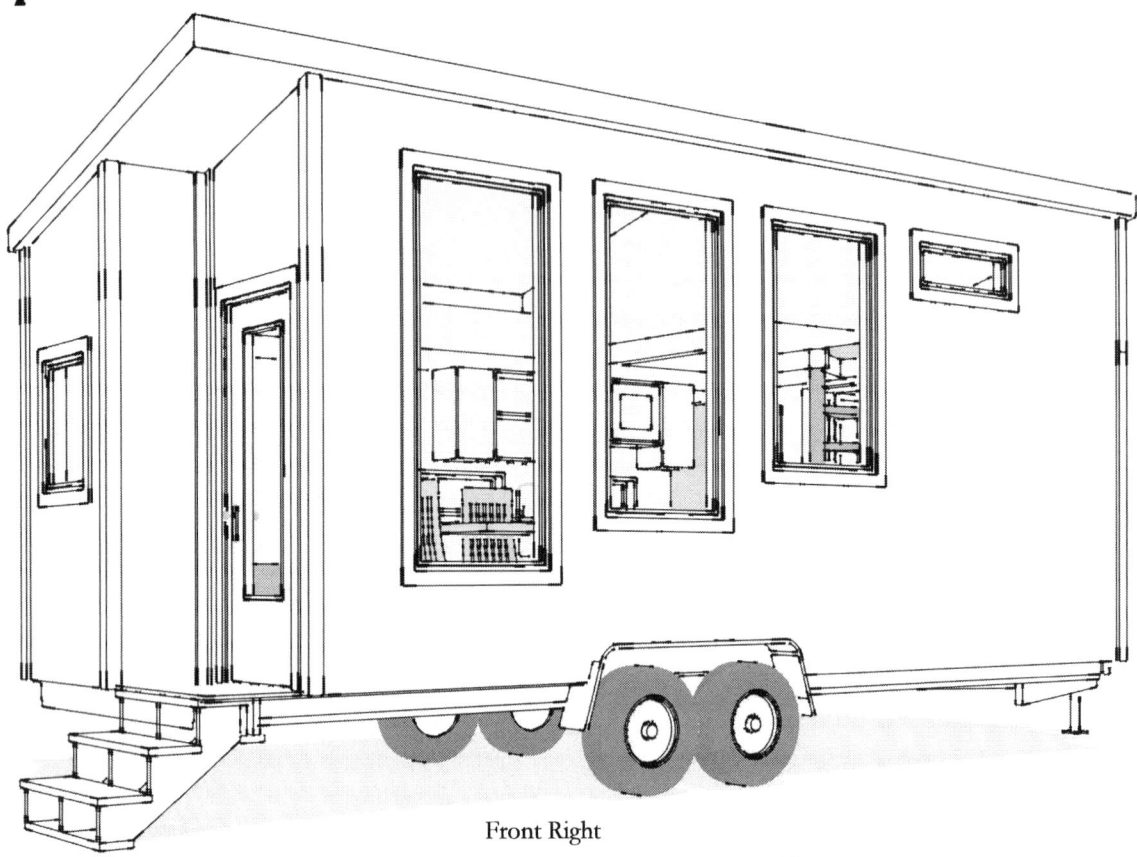

Summary:

This is the big brother to another design you've seen earlier in the book. But now it has a fully functional kitchen with a range and full size refrigerator, laundry, and two lofts. The loft is accessed by a spiral staircase. On the lower level there's also a large built-in sofa and a table for four.

Features:

24-Foot Tiny House on Wheels
Shed Roof
Sleeps 3 in Two Lofts
Fully Functional Kitchen
Standard Bathroom
Laundry
Spiral Stairs

Kitchen

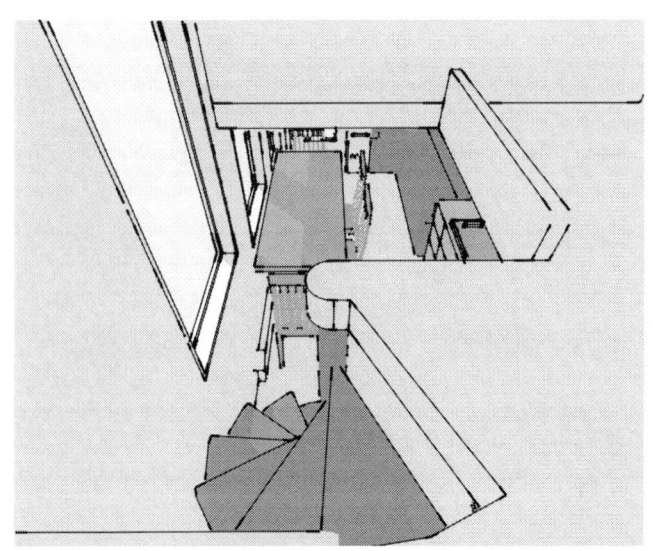

View from Loft

318

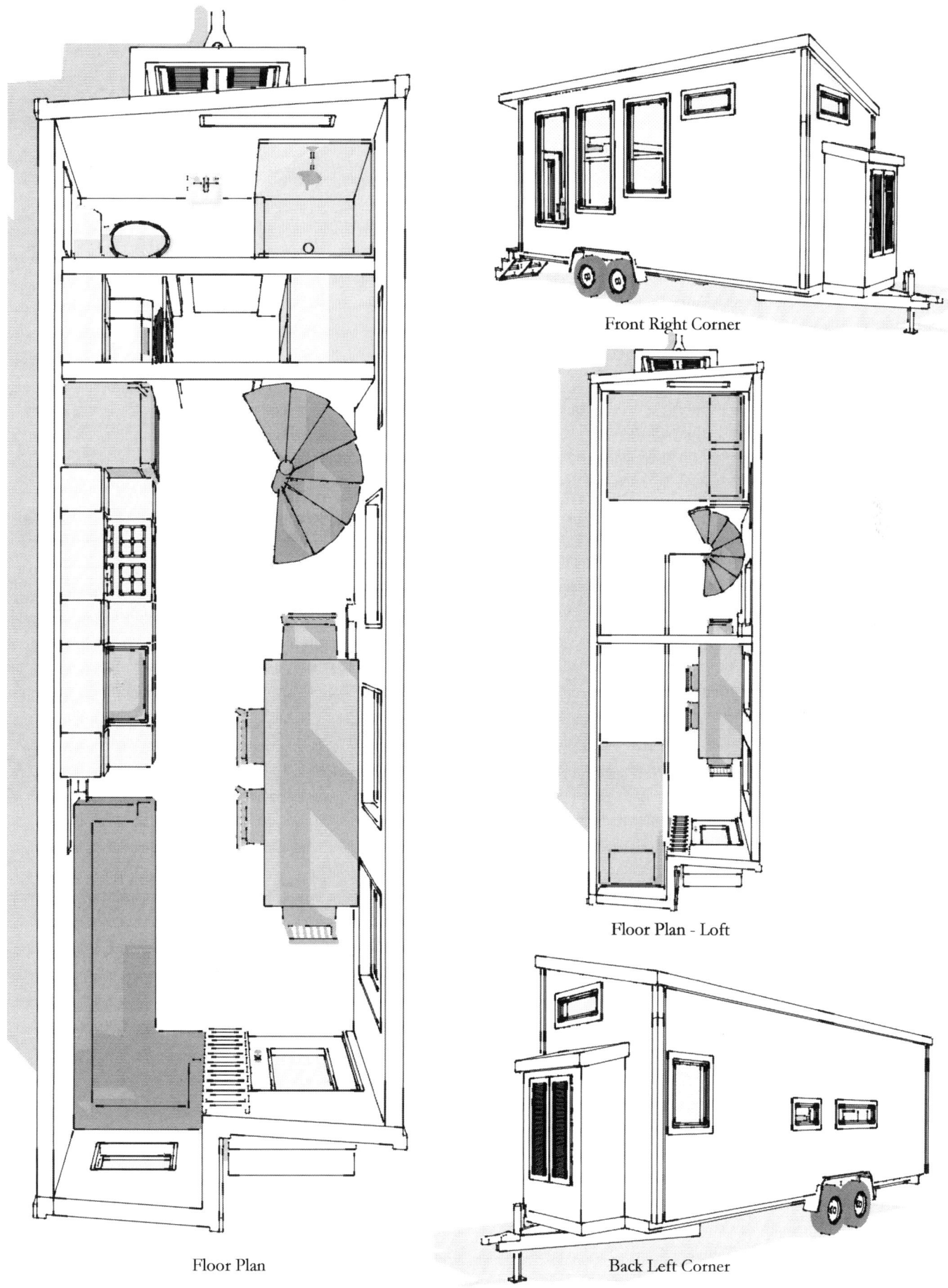

Tiny House #77 - Floor Plan & Exterior

Front Right Corner

Floor Plan - Loft

Floor Plan

Back Left Corner

Tiny House #77 - Interior Views

Interior from Entry

Interior from Kitchen

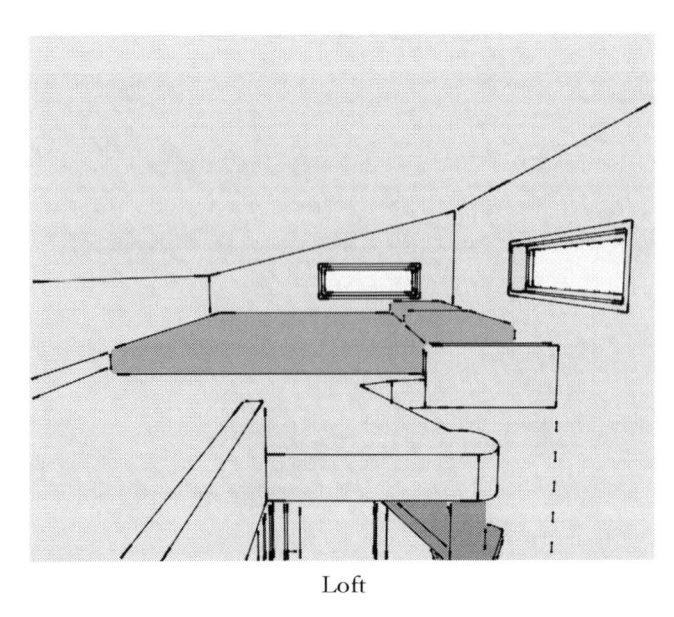

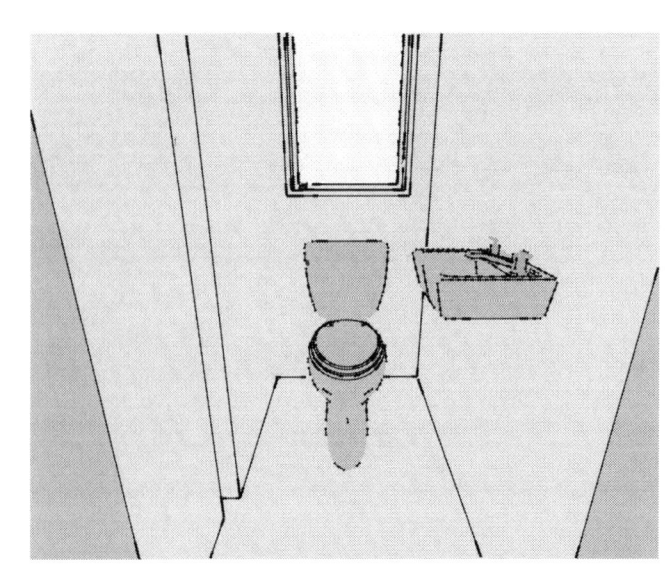

Loft

Bathroom

320

Tiny House #77 - Elevations

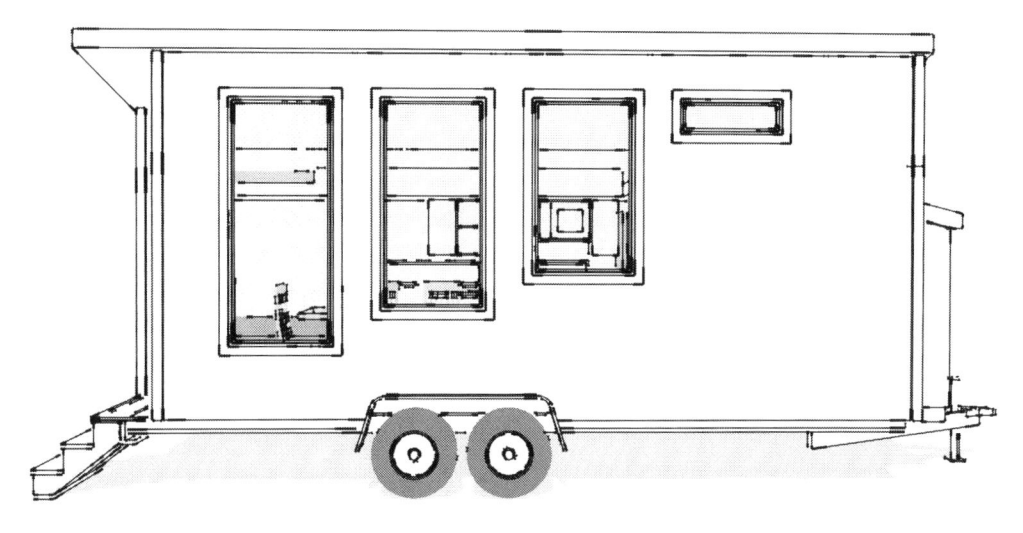

Right

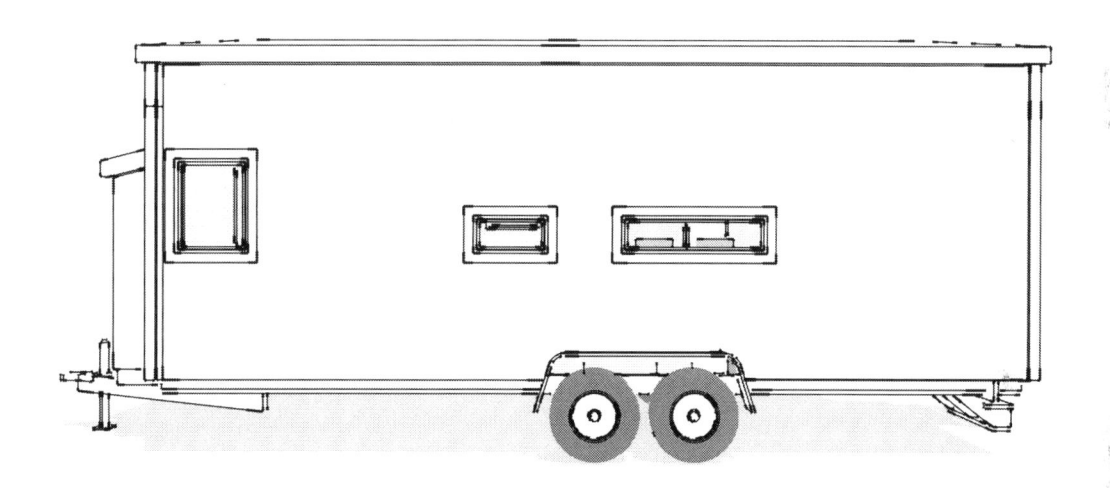

Left

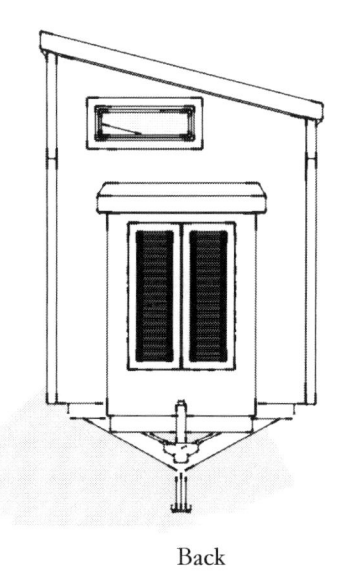

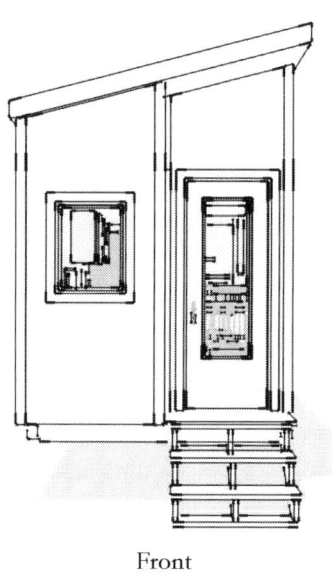

Back

Front

28-Foot Tiny House Designs

#78

Tiny House #78 - Overview

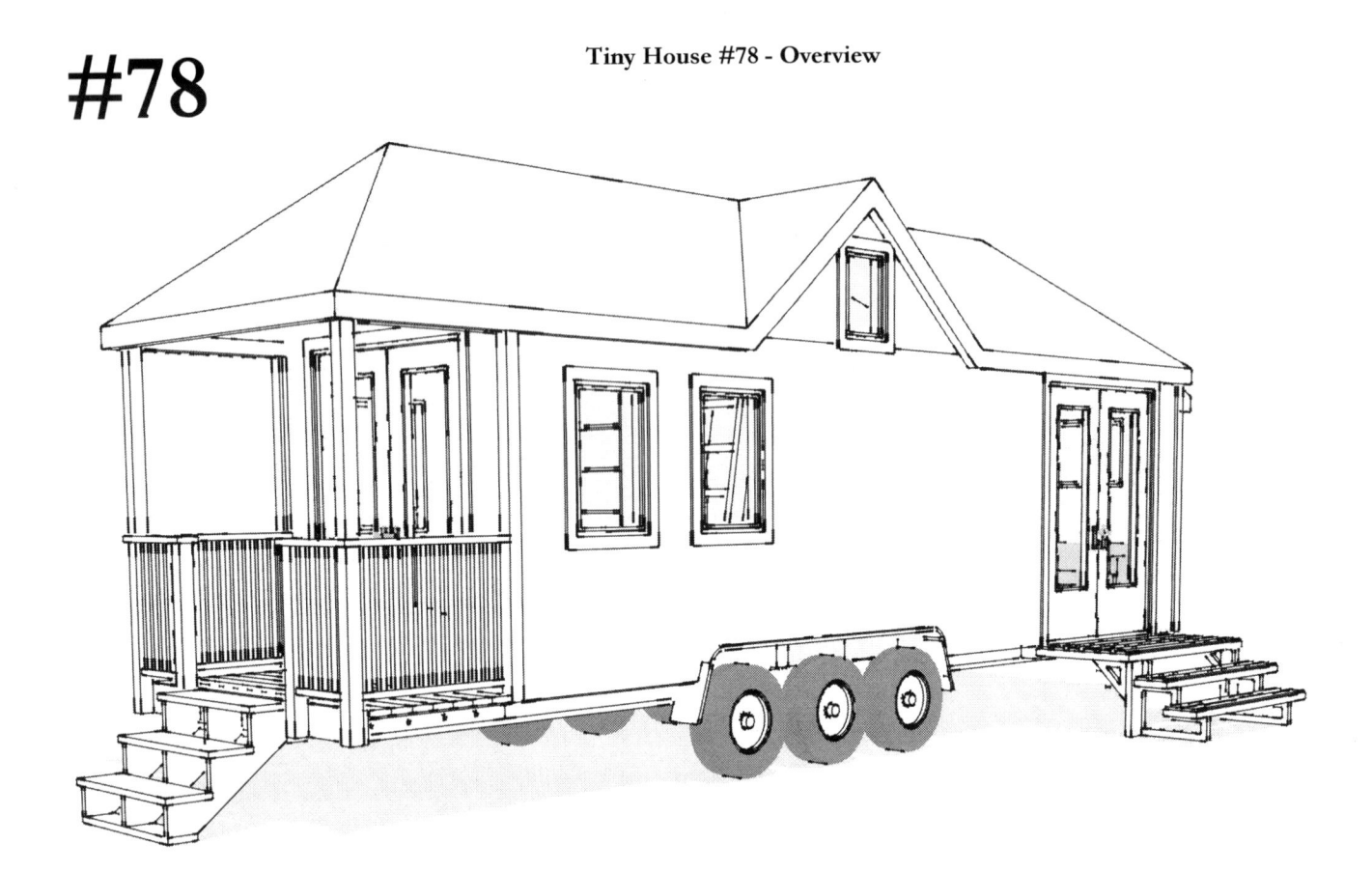

Front Right

Summary:

At the center of this tiny house is a kitchen and bathroom. Over the kitchen and bathroom is a loft with a queen bed. The front room has two comfy chairs, each with its own ottoman. The back room has a table for four and a sofa tucked into a bump-out extension.

Features:

28-Foot Tiny House on Wheels
Hip with Cross Gable
Deep Porch
Second Side Entry

Kitchen

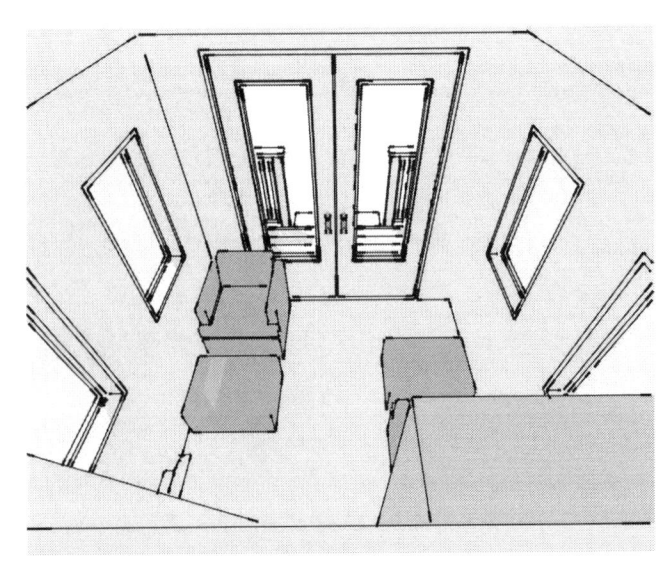

View from Loft

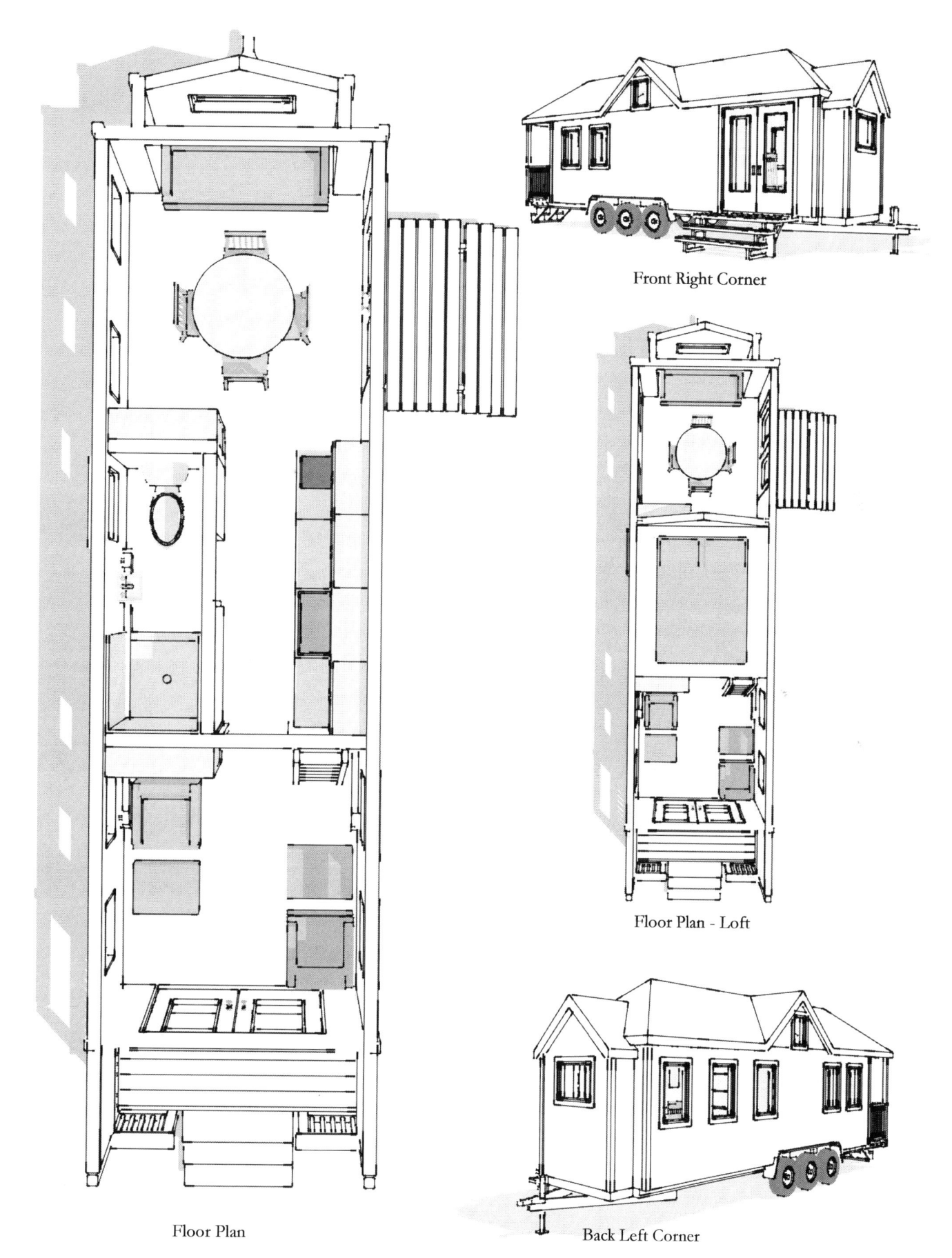

Tiny House #78 - Floor Plan & Exterior

Front Right Corner

Floor Plan - Loft

Floor Plan

Back Left Corner

325

Tiny House #78 - Interior Views

Dining Room

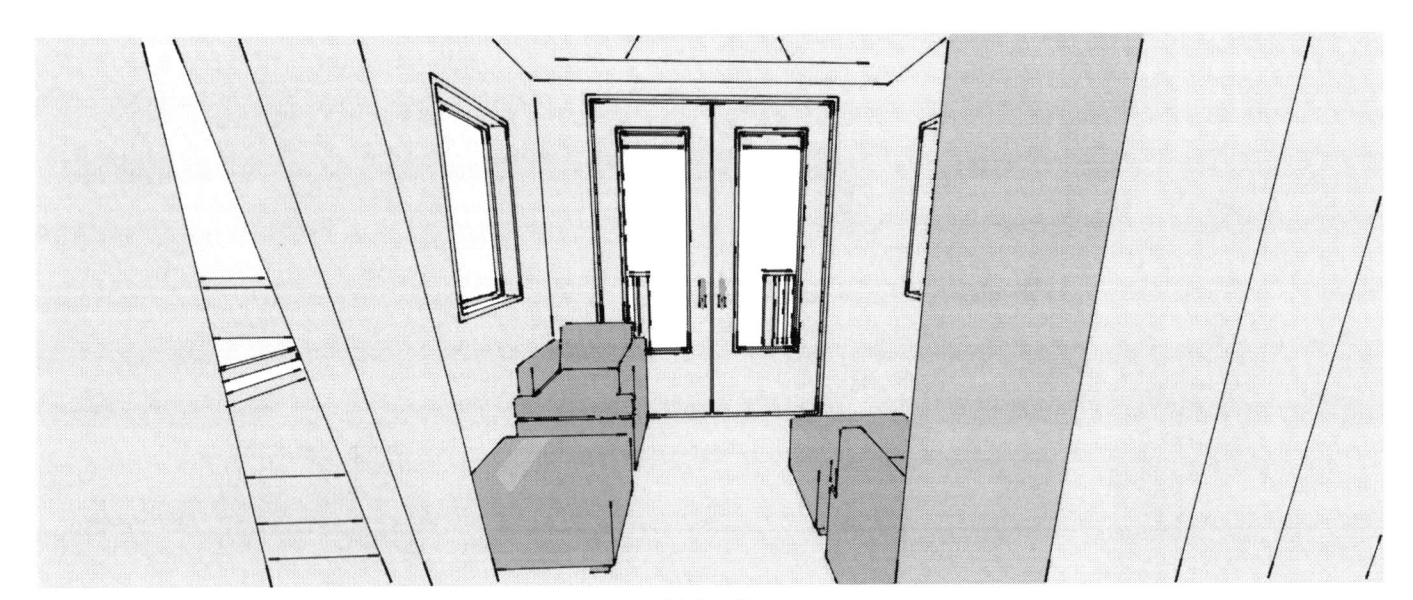

Living Room

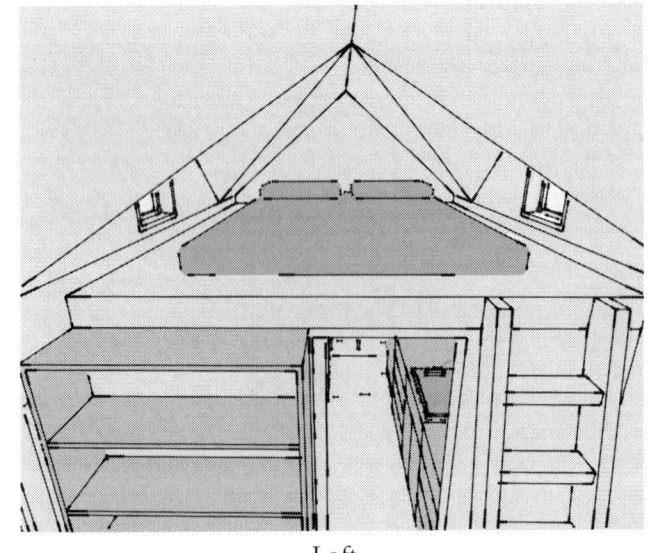

Loft

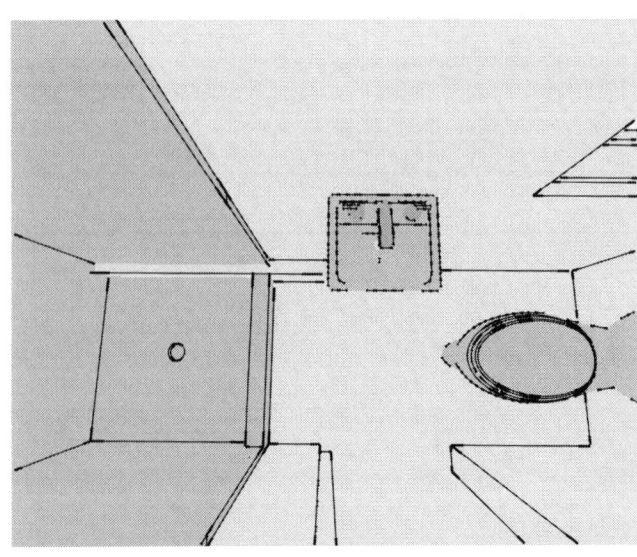

Bathroom

Tiny House #78 - Elevations

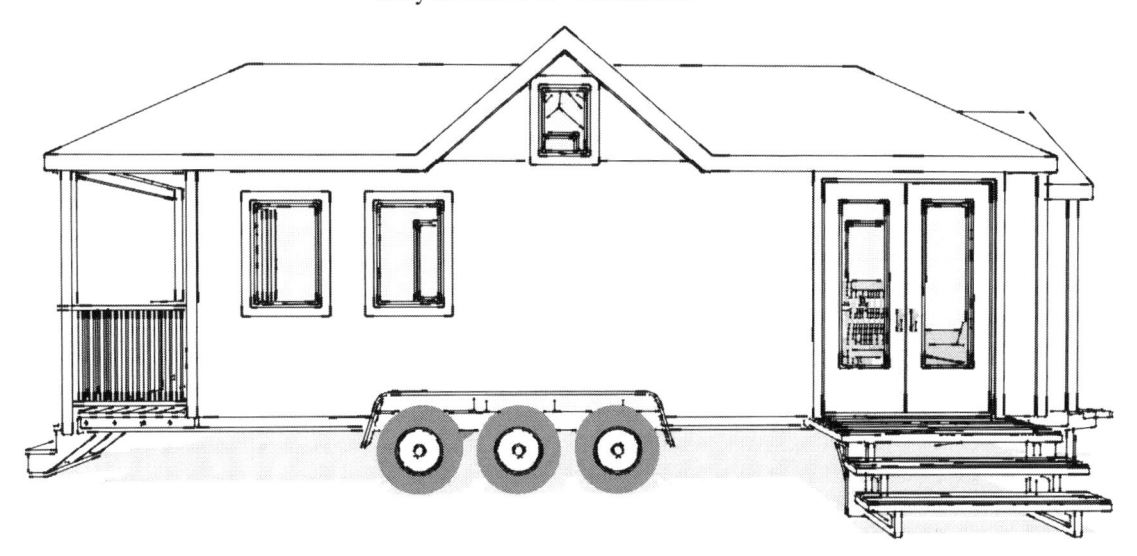

Right

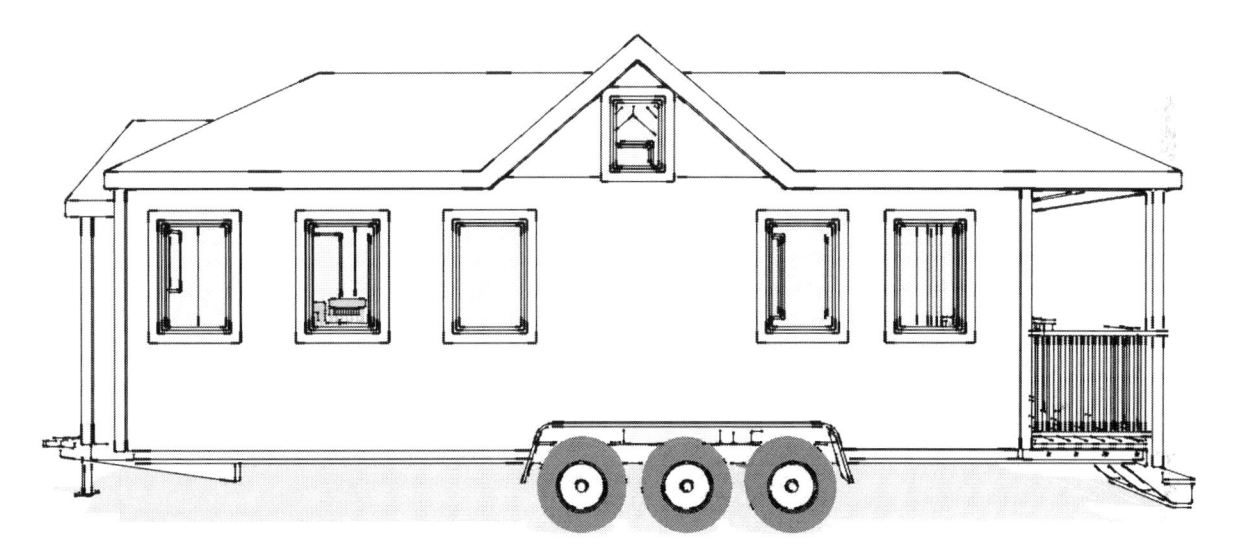

Left

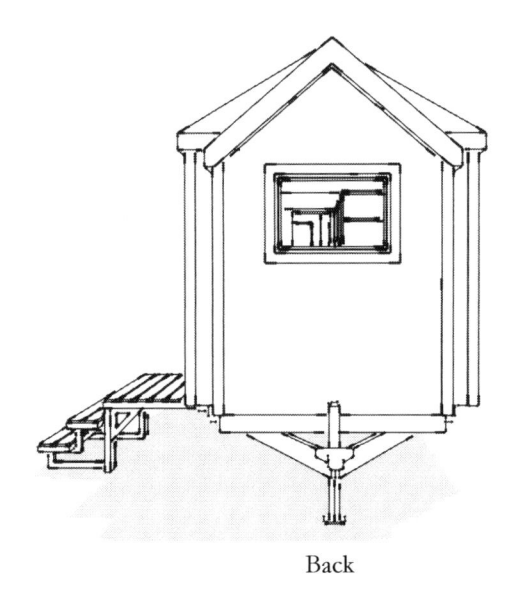

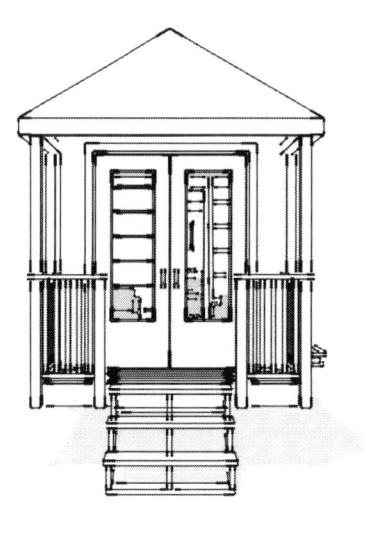

Back

Front

#79

Tiny House #79 - Overview

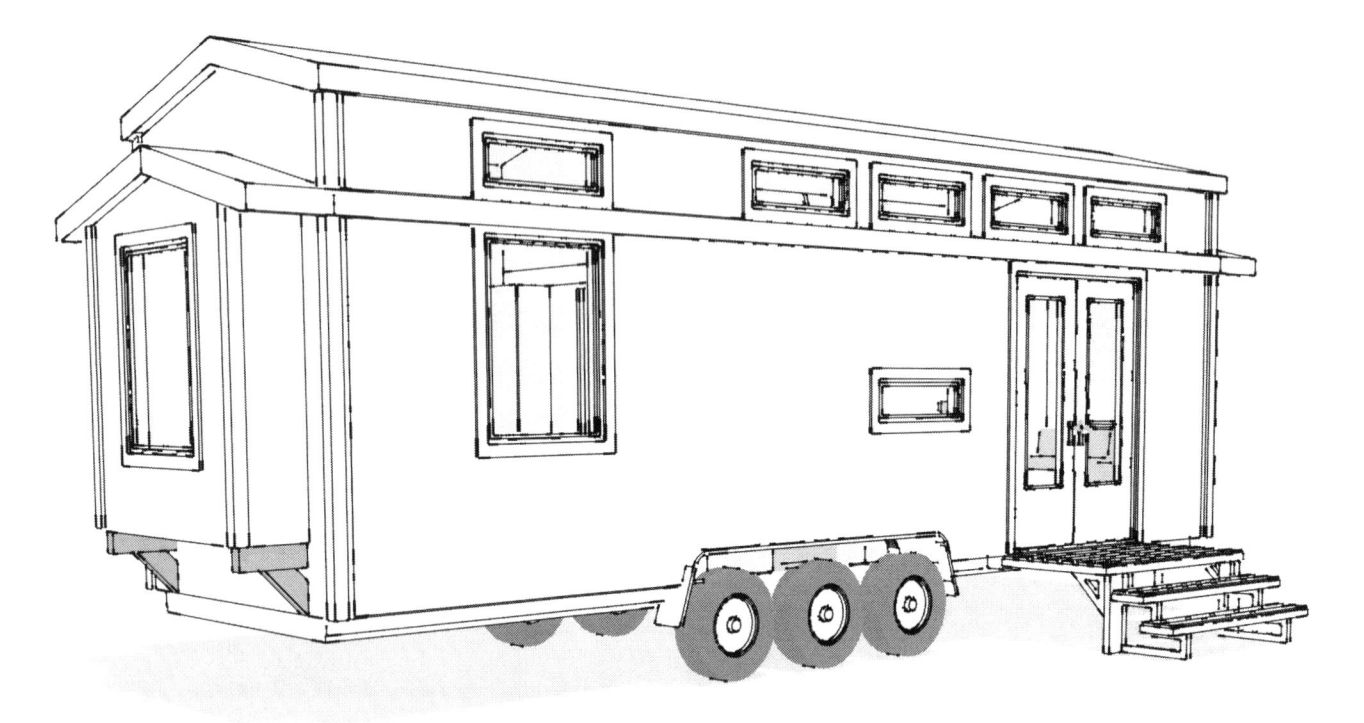

Front Right

Summary:

The side entry leads to a living space with a built-in sofa, comfy chair, and table for two. A ladder leads to a loft large enough for a queen bed. Under the loft is a bathroom, laundry, and kitchen. Past the kitchen and bathroom is a bedroom with a queen bed.

Features:

28-Foot Tiny House on Wheels
High 3/12 Gable with Clerestory
Sleeps Four
Fully Functional Kitchen
Laundry
Lower Level Bedroom

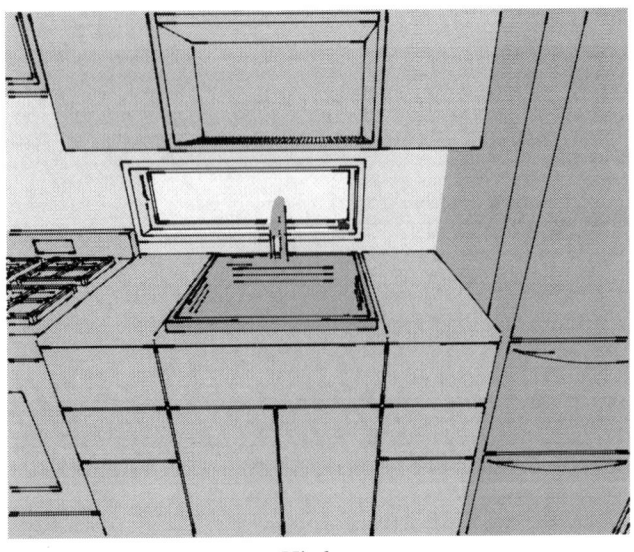

Kitchen

View from Loft

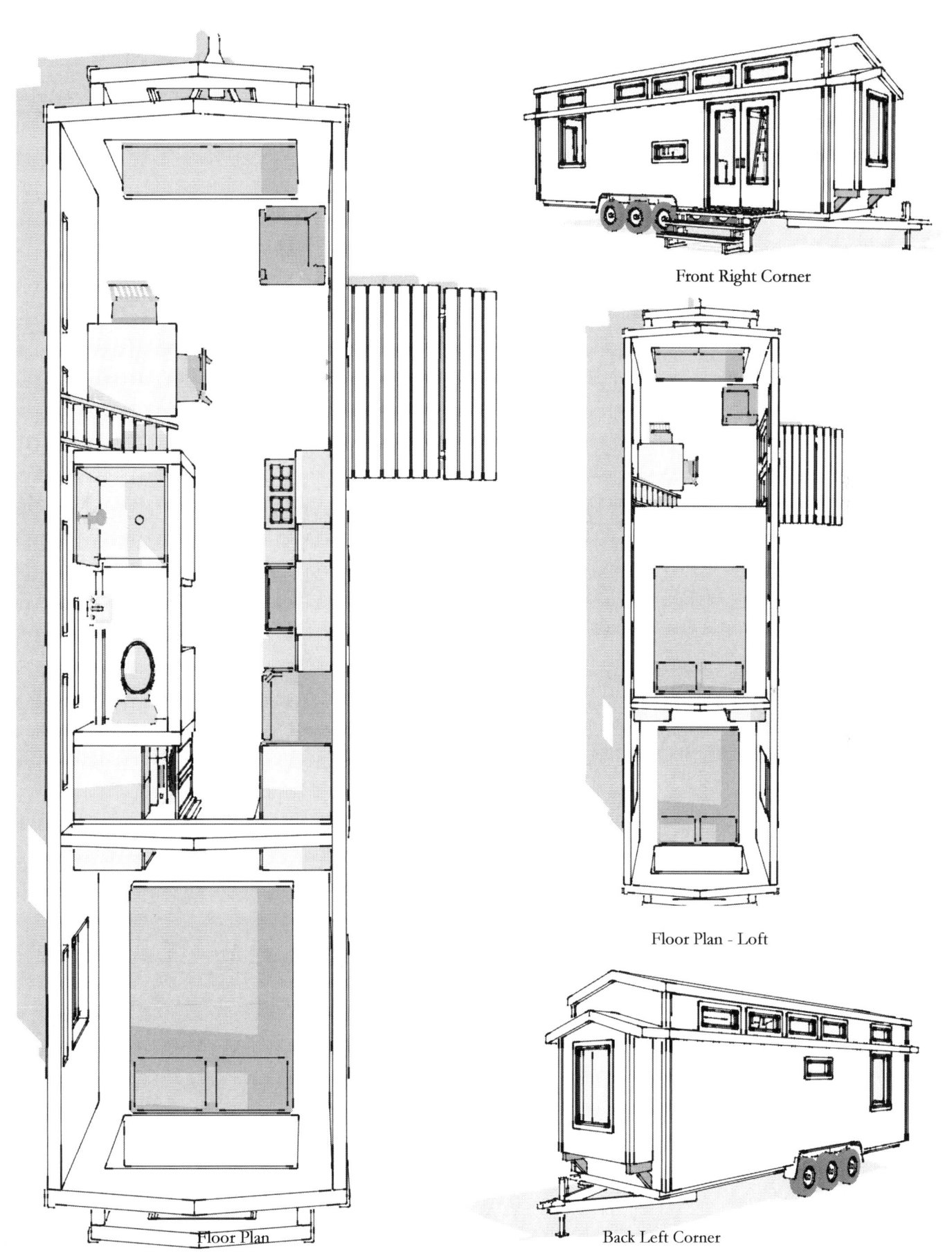

Tiny House #79 - Floor Plan & Exterior

Front Right Corner

Floor Plan - Loft

Floor Plan

Back Left Corner

Tiny House #79 - Interior Views

Interior from Kitchen

Interior from Entry

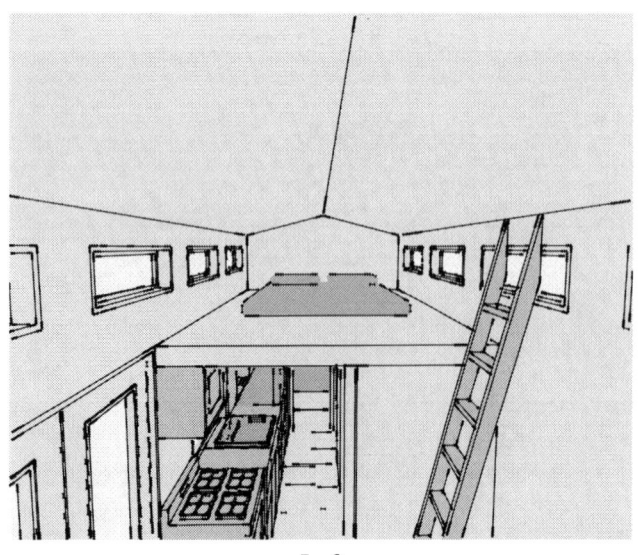

Loft

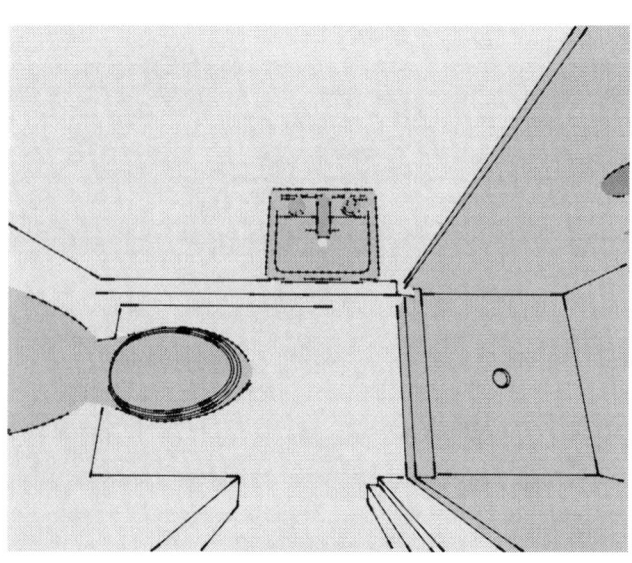

Bathroom

Tiny House #79 - Elevations

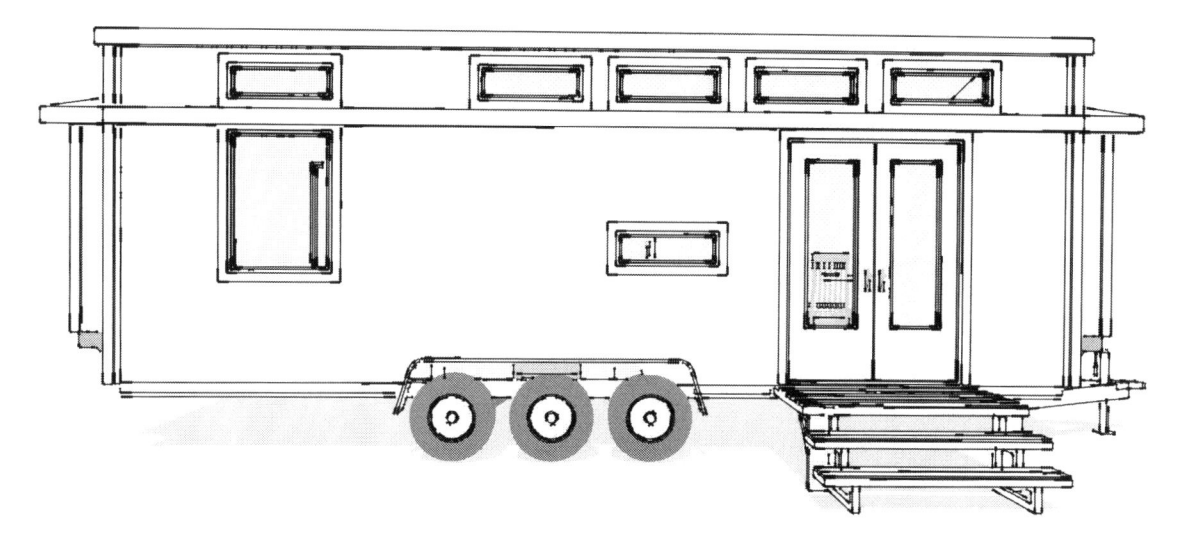

Right

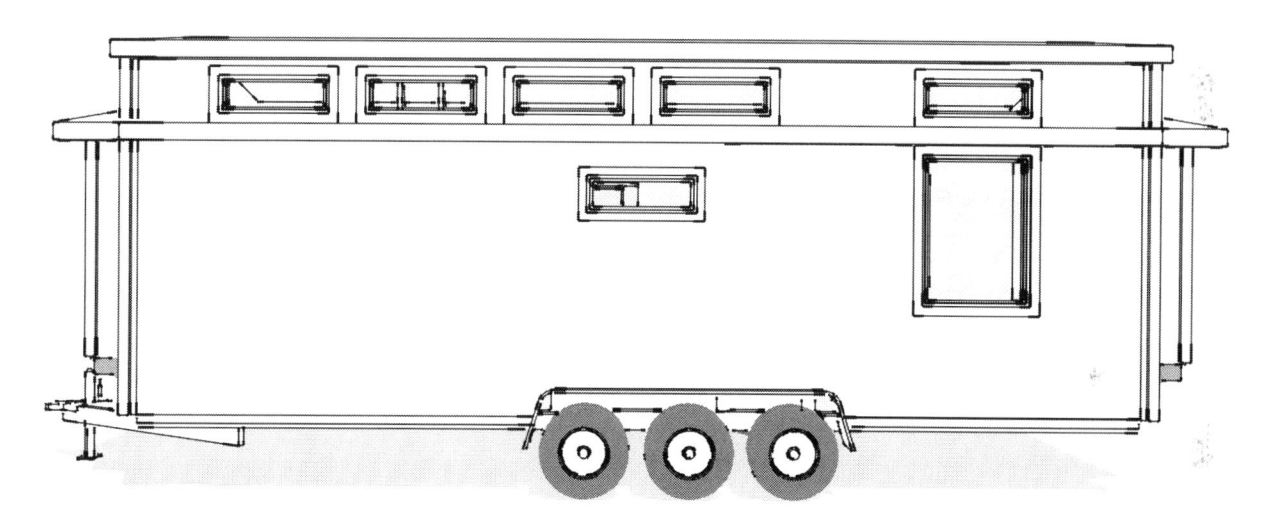

Left

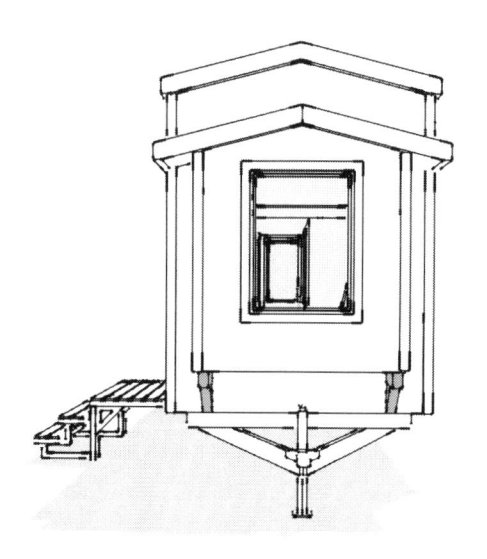

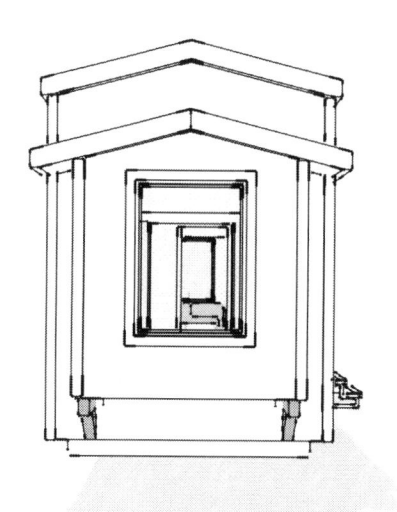

Back

Front

#80

Tiny House #80 - Overview

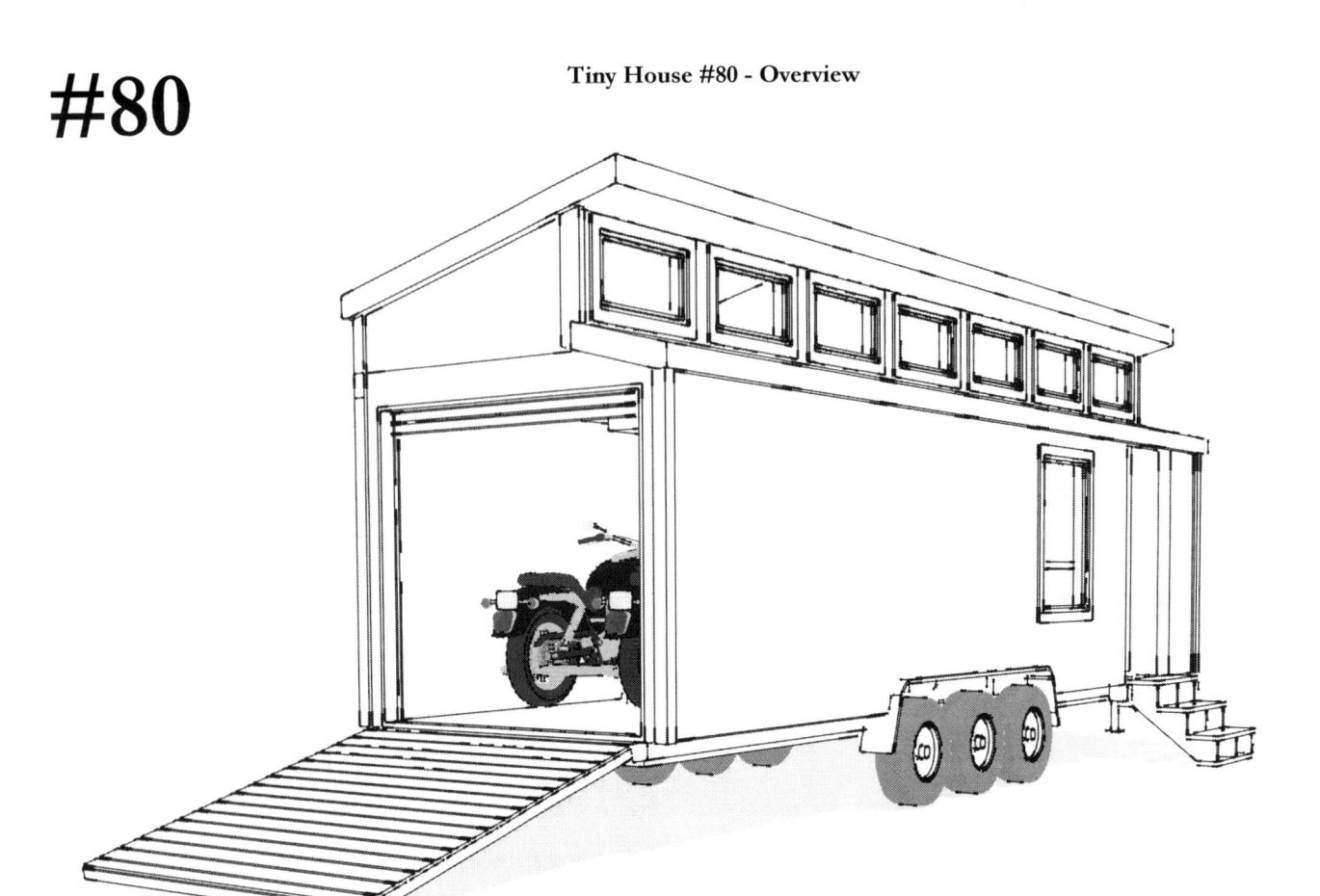

Front Right

Summary:

This toy hauler has a garage large enough to hold two large motorcycles. From the garage you can enter the bathroom where there is a tub, toilet, and sink. Inside the main entry - which is on the side of the house - you find two comfy chairs, a table for two, and a small kitchen. A loft with a queen bed is above the bathroom and is accessed by ladder rungs attached to an interior wall.

Features:

28-Foot Tiny House on Wheels
3/12 Shed Roof
Small Kitchen
Sleeps Two
Pass-through Bathroom

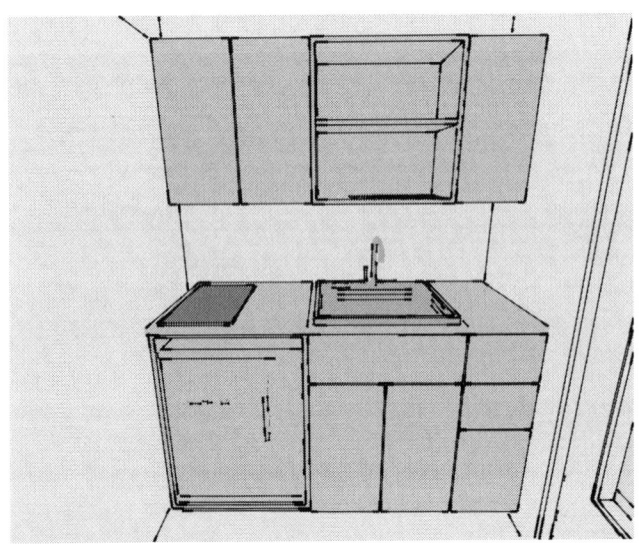

Kitchen

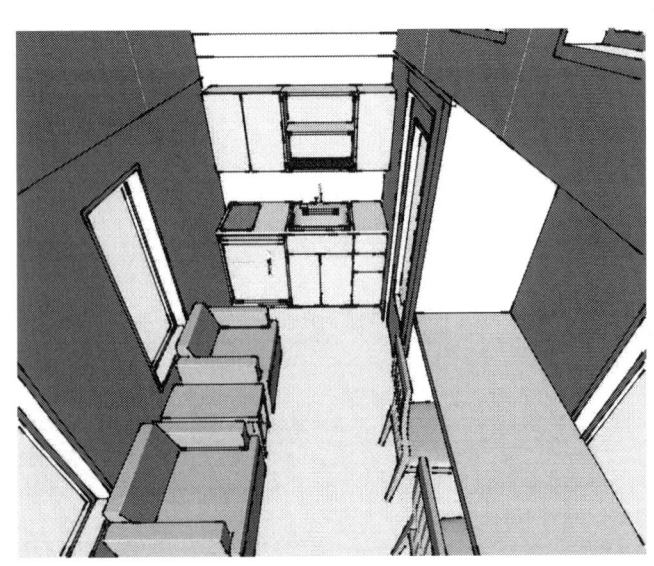

View from Loft

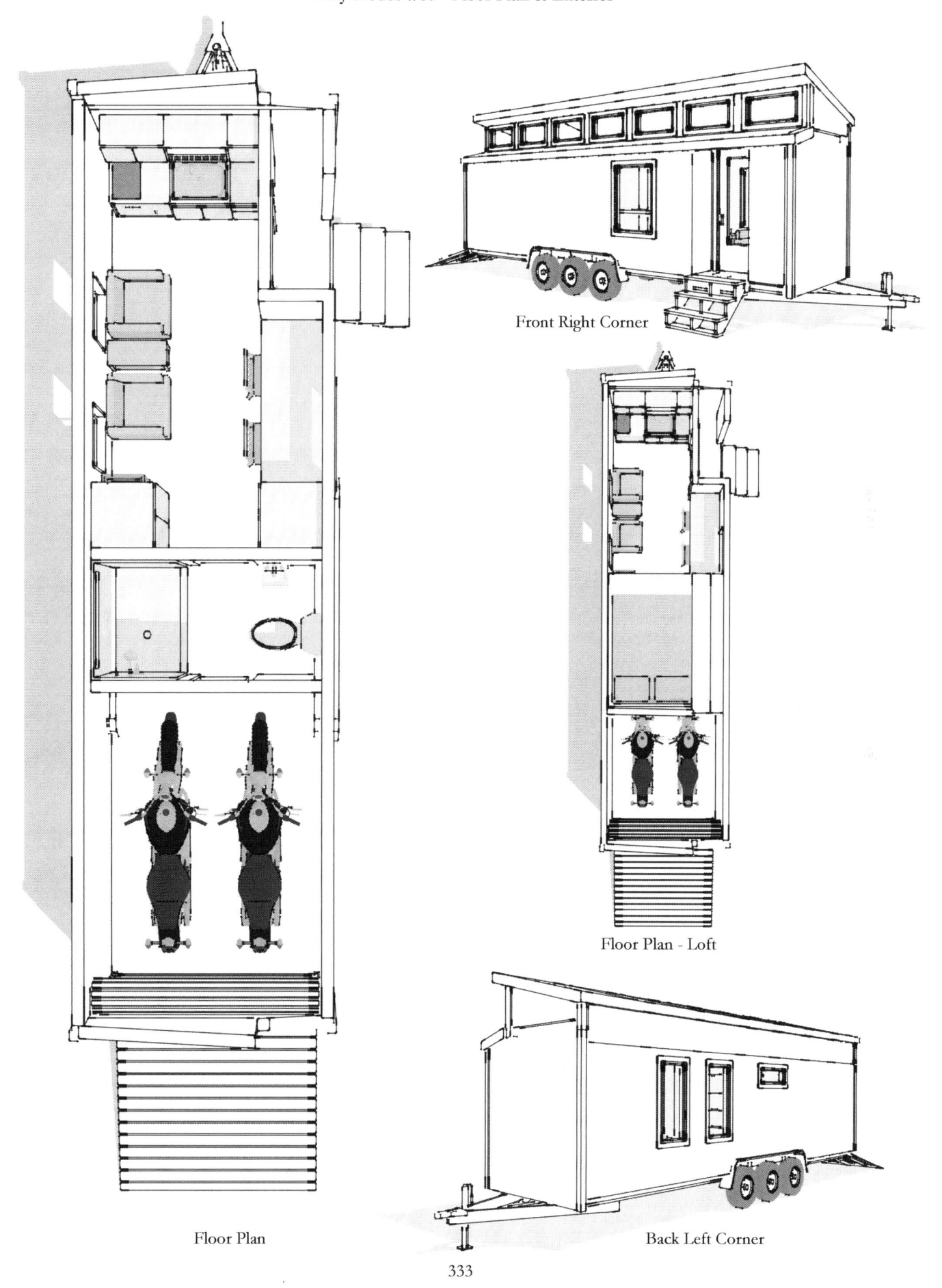

Tiny House #80 - Floor Plan & Exterior

Front Right Corner

Floor Plan - Loft

Floor Plan

Back Left Corner

Tiny House #80 - Interior Views

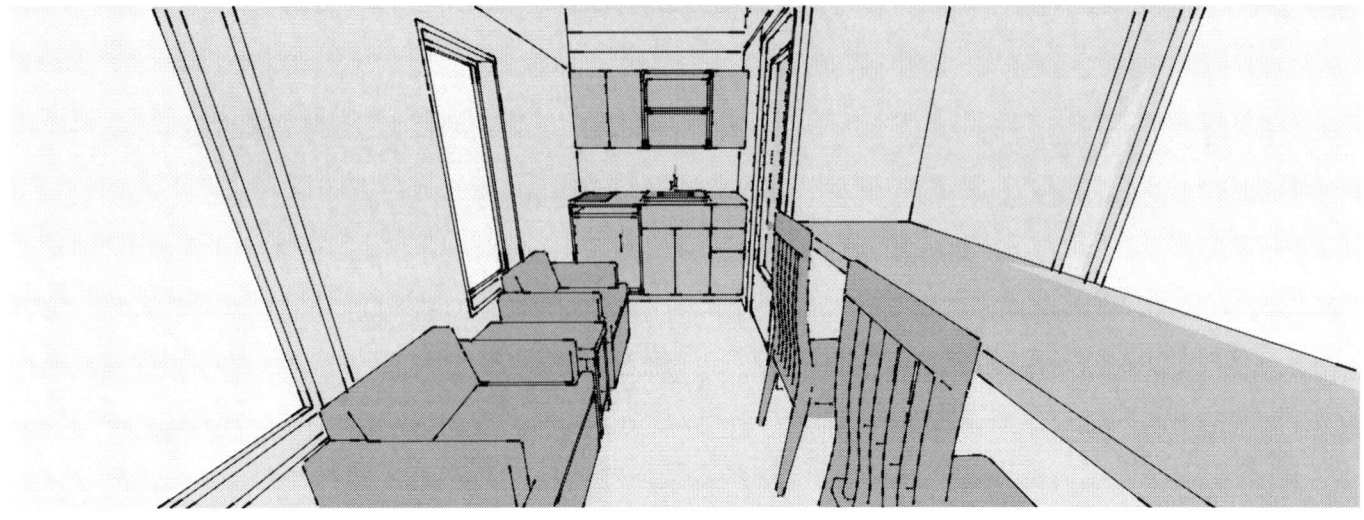

Interior from Bathroom

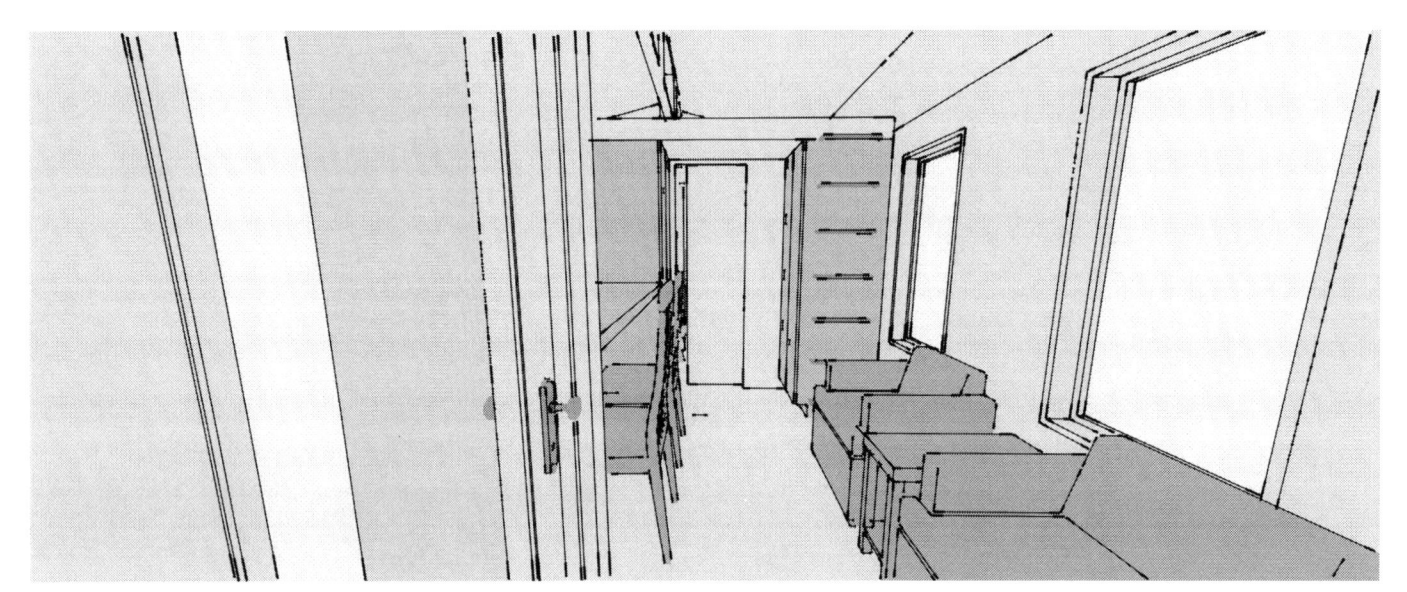

Interior from Entry

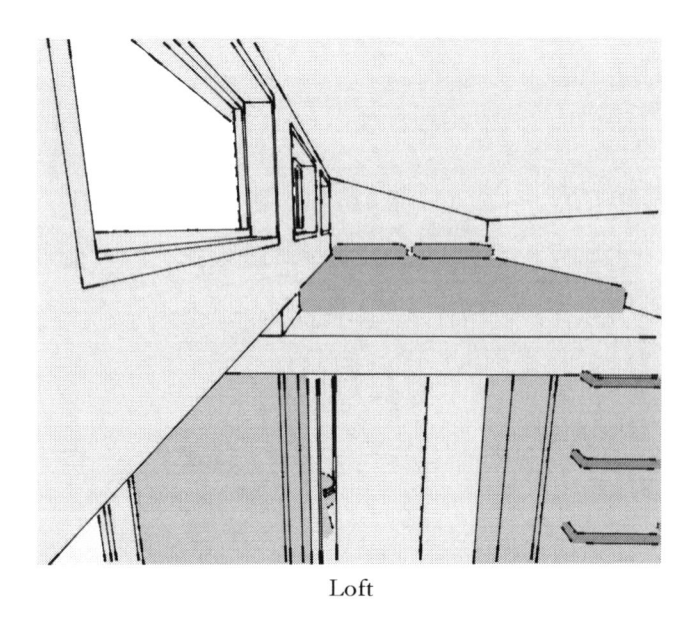

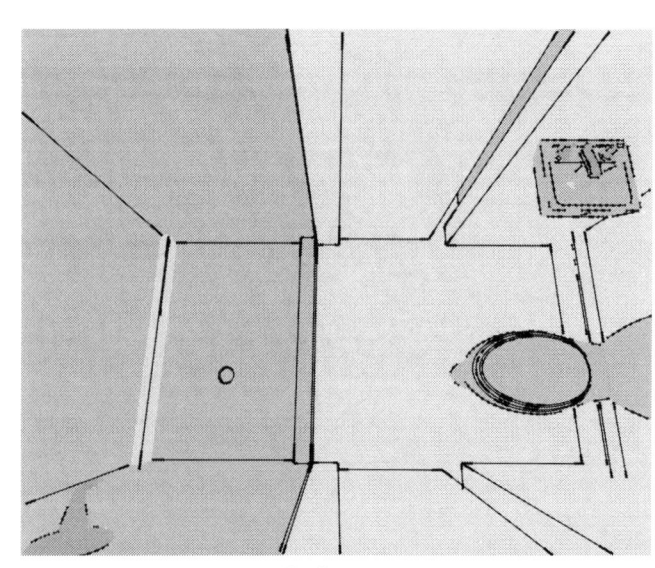

Loft

Bathroom

Tiny House #80 - Elevations

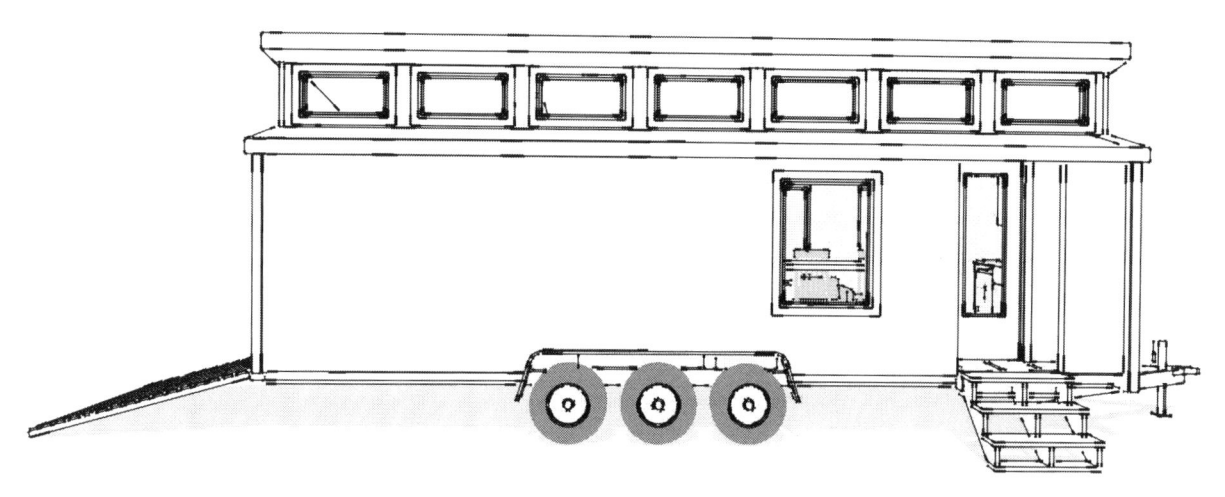

Right

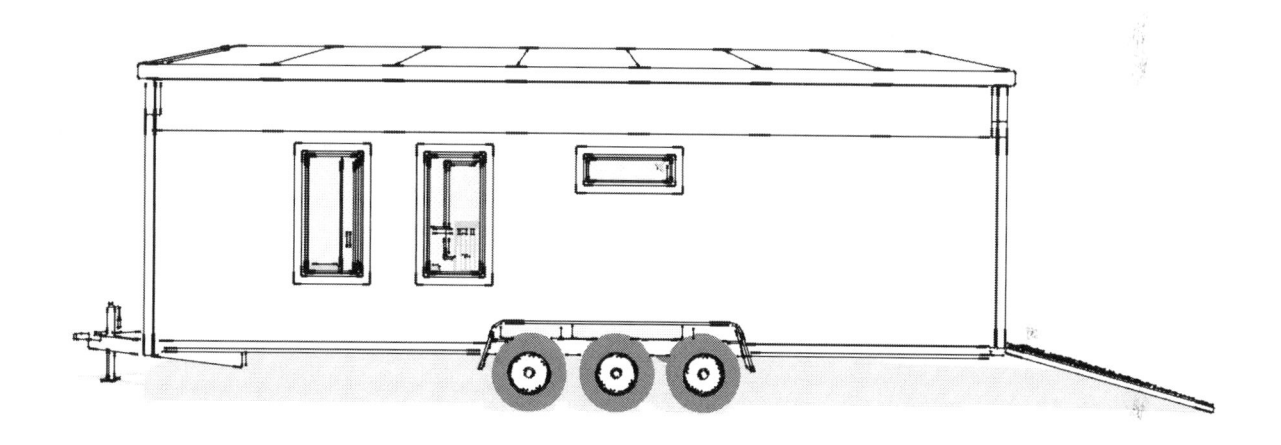

Left

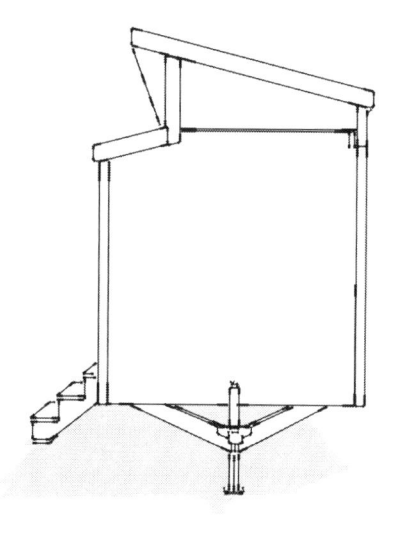

Back

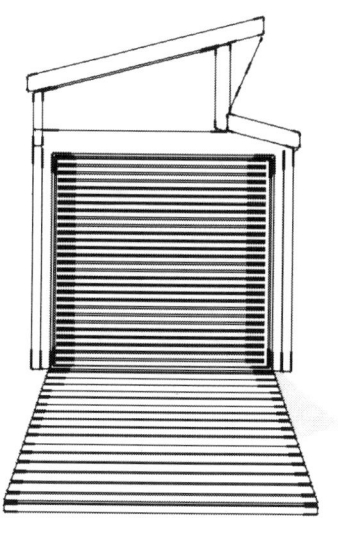

Front

#81

Tiny House #81 - Overview

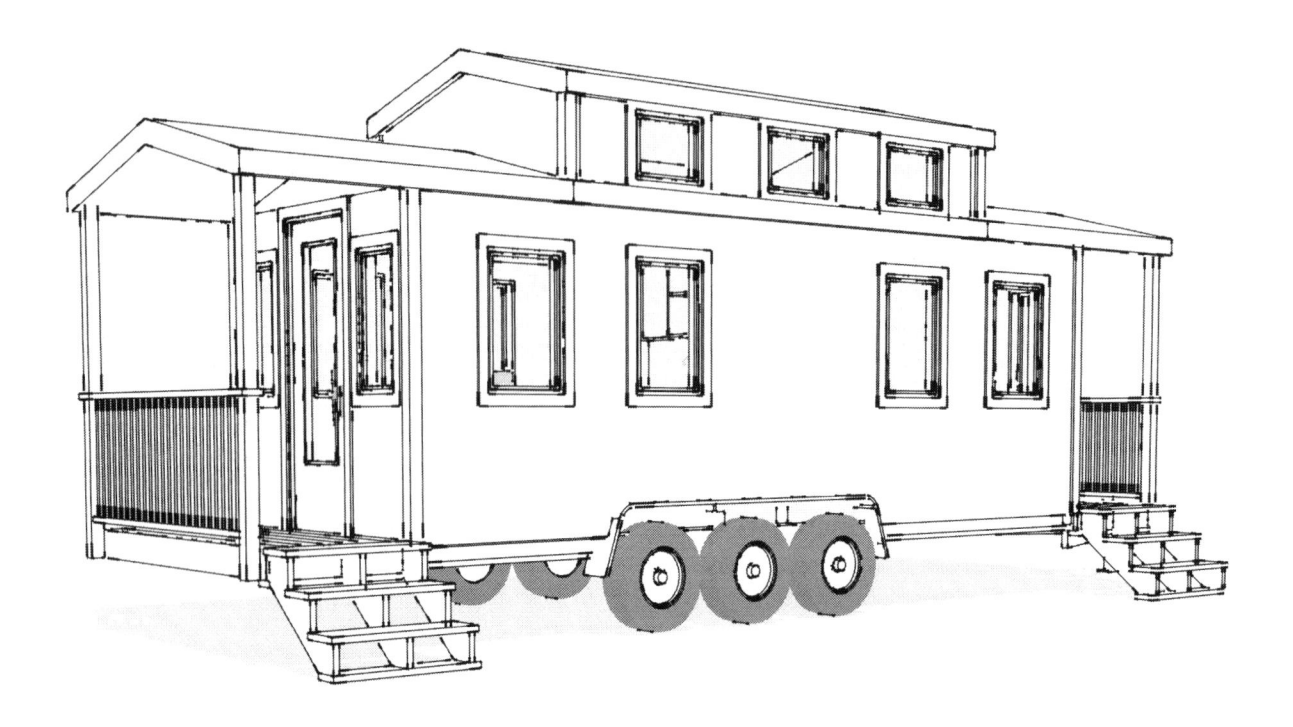

Front Right

Summary:

Now this tiny house is looking an awful lot like a caboose inside and out. When you enter the kitchen side of the house you'll find two tables for two that mimic the railway aesthetic. Past the tiny kitchen and down the hall is a bathroom with a tub and a ladder to the loft. The loft has a queen bed. On the other side of the house is another room with two comfy chairs, an ottoman, and a small table.

Features:

28-Foot Tiny House on Wheels
Two Tables for Two
Tiny Kitchen
Bathroom with Tub
Two Comfy Chairs
Loft with Queen Bed
Sleeps Two

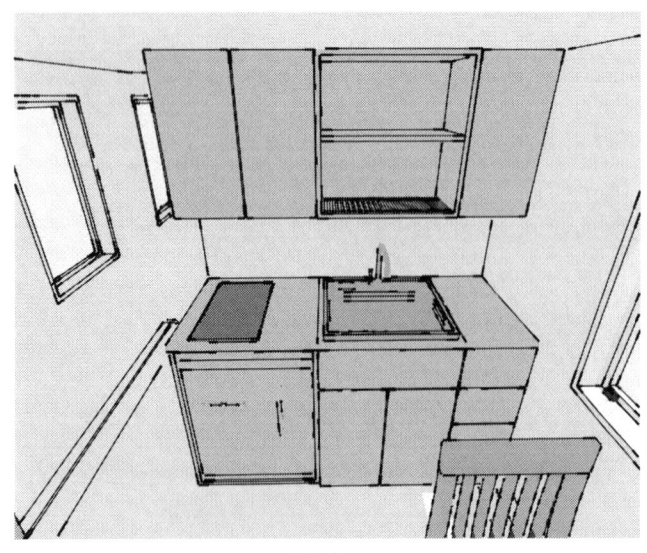

Kitchen

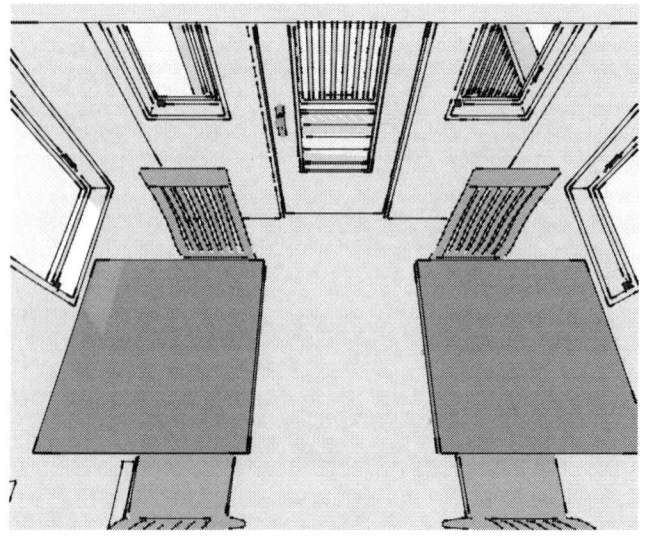

View from Loft

Tiny House #81 - Floor Plan & Exterior

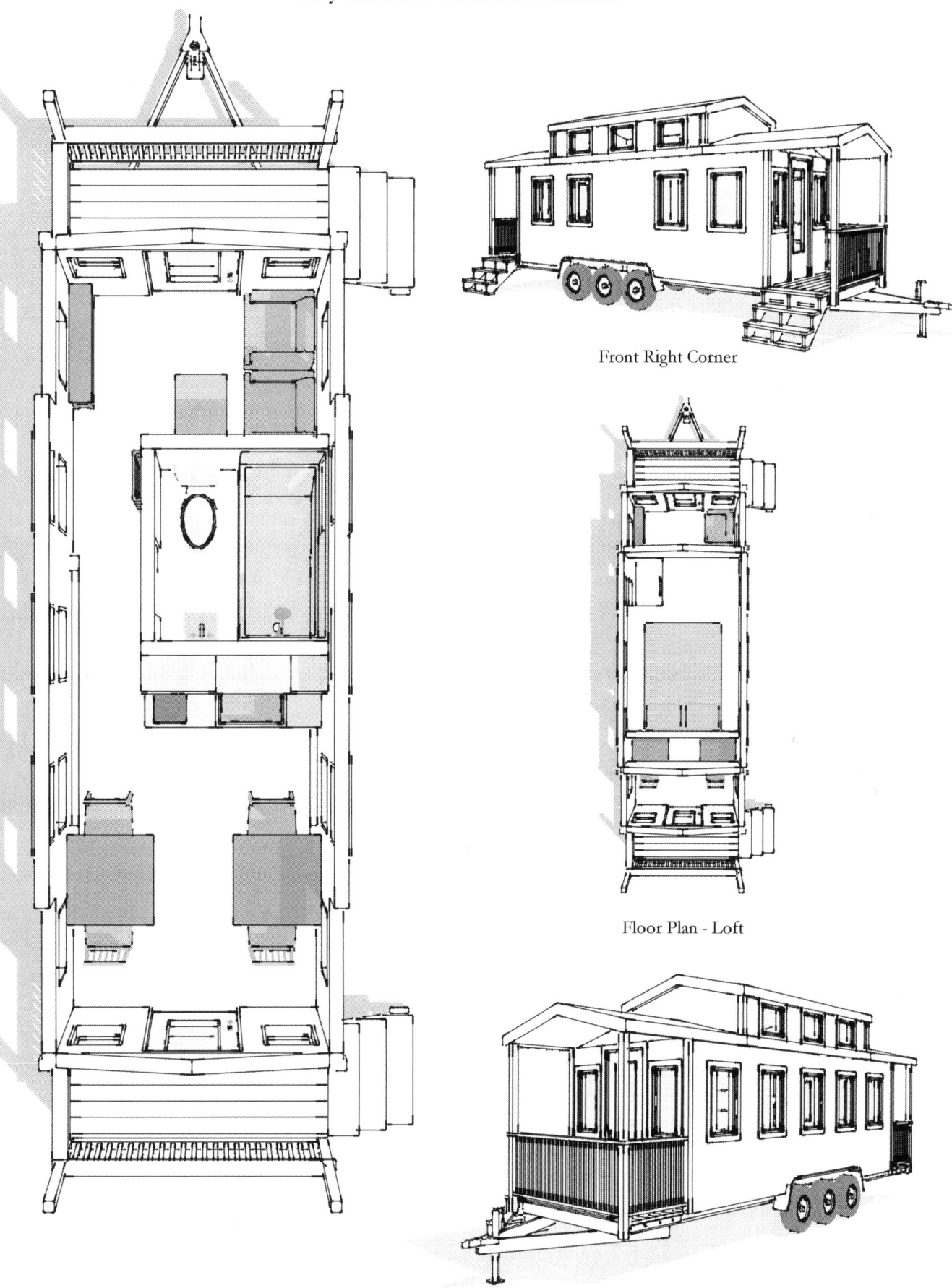

Front Right Corner

Floor Plan - Loft

Floor Plan

Back Left Corner

Tiny House #81 - Interior Views

Interior from Front Entry

Interior Back Room

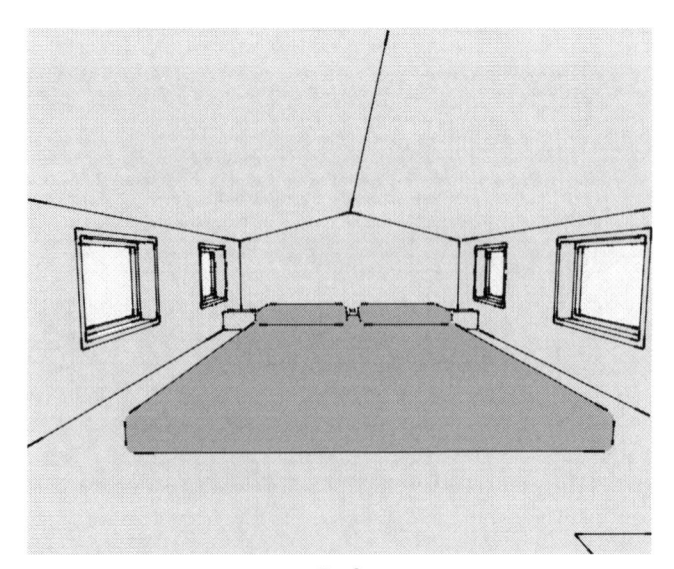

Loft

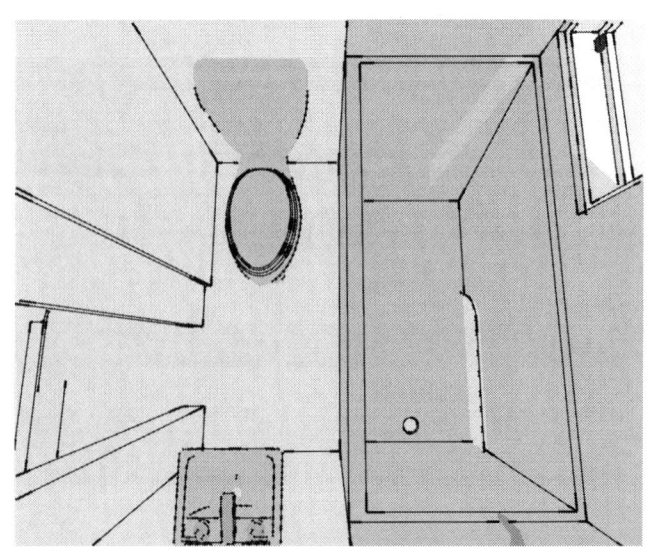

Bathroom

Tiny House #81 - Elevations

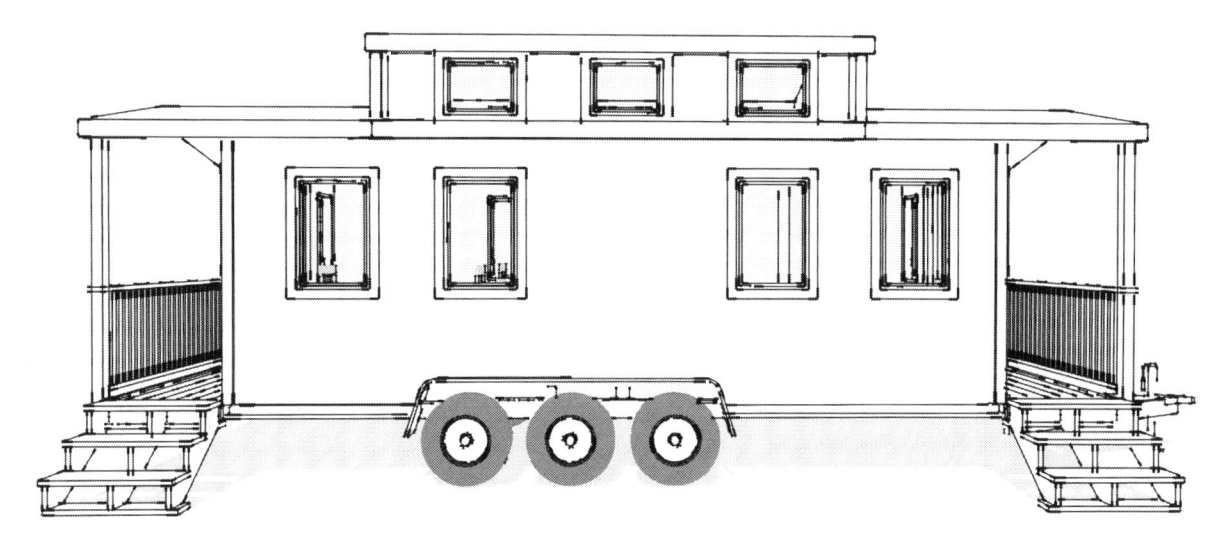

Right

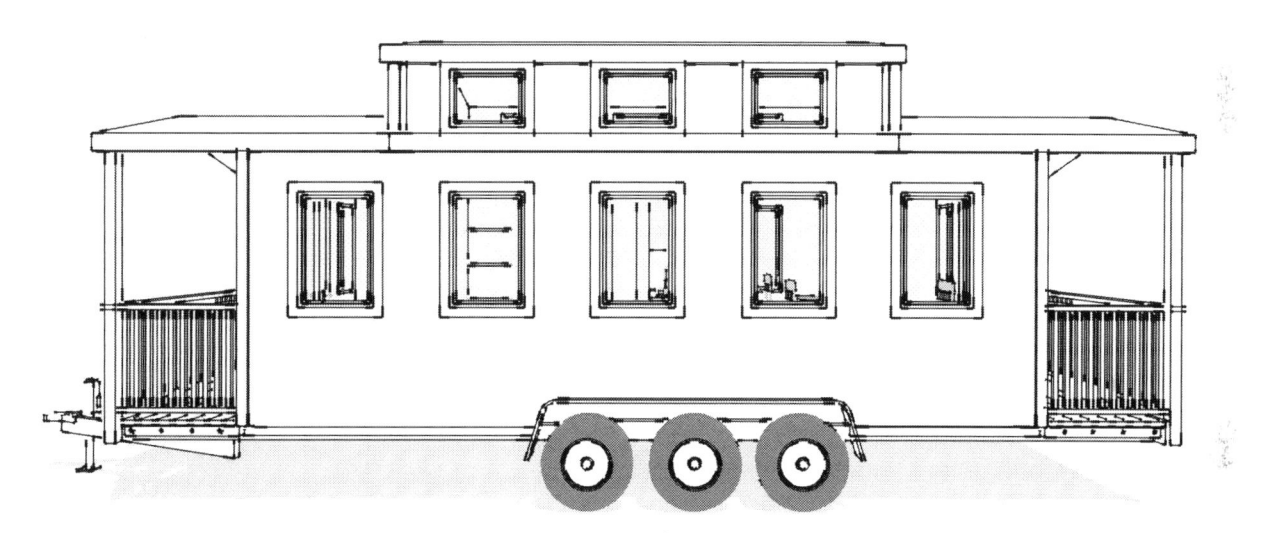

Left

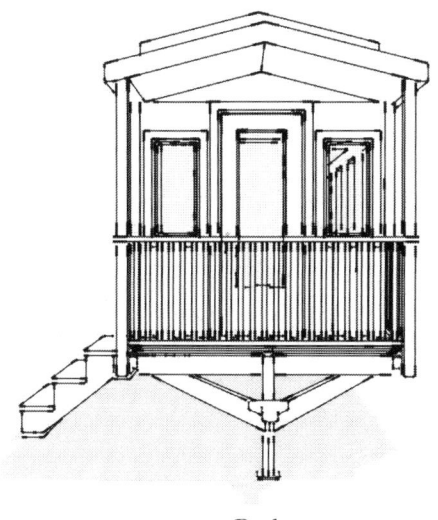

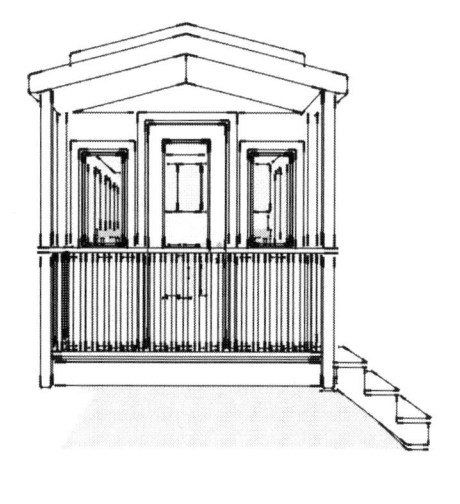

Back

Front

#82

Tiny House #82 - Overview

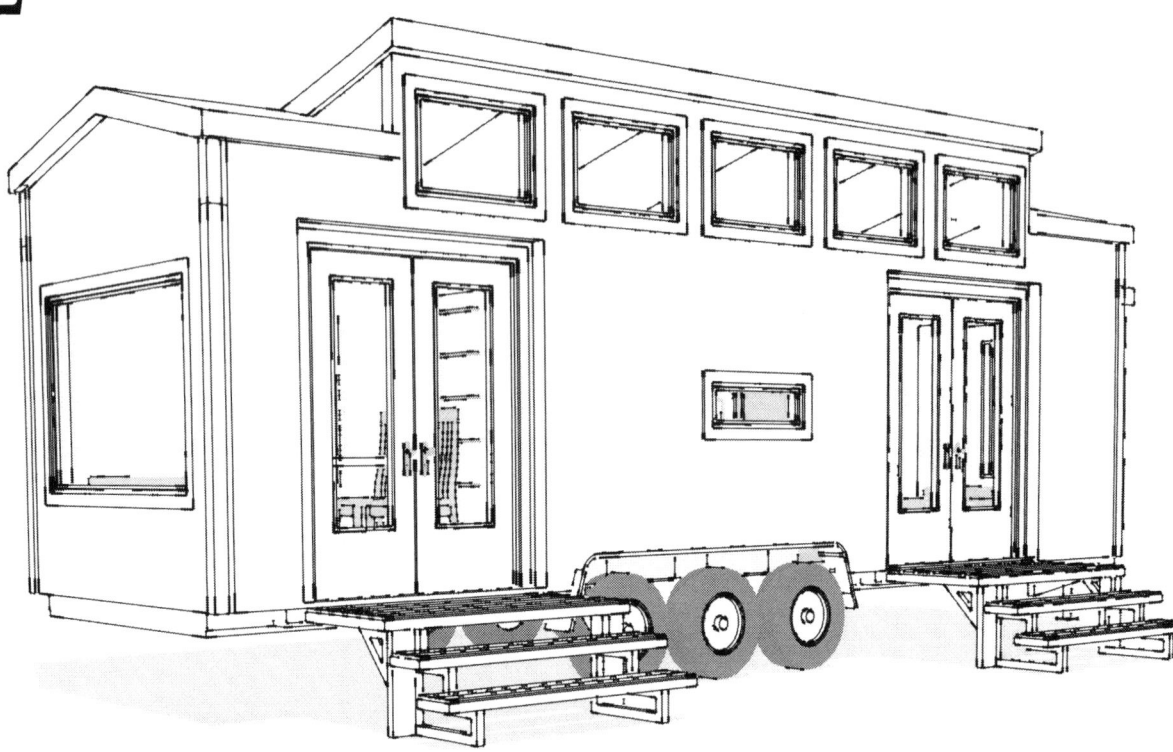

Front Right

Summary:

Entering the doors on the left you find a living room with a sofa and table for four. To your right is a kitchen that's across from the bathroom. Looking up, your eyes follow a ladder to a loft with a queen bed. Past the kitchen and through a pocket door is a private bedroom with french doors and lots of light.

Features:

28-Foot Tiny House on Wheels
Shed Roof with Gabel Ends
Lower Level Bedroom
Queen Bed in Loft
Sleeps 4

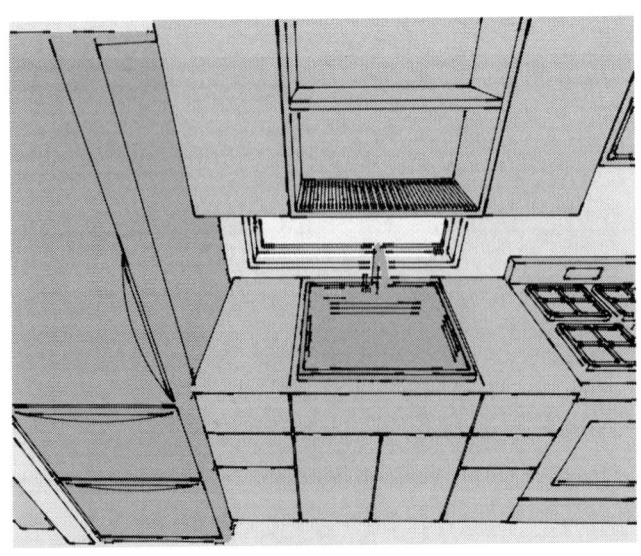

Kitchen

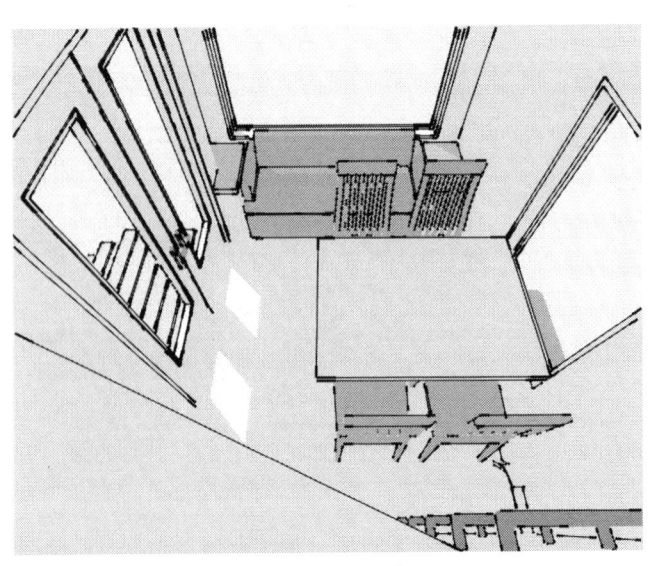

View from Loft

Tiny House #82 - Floor Plan & Exterior

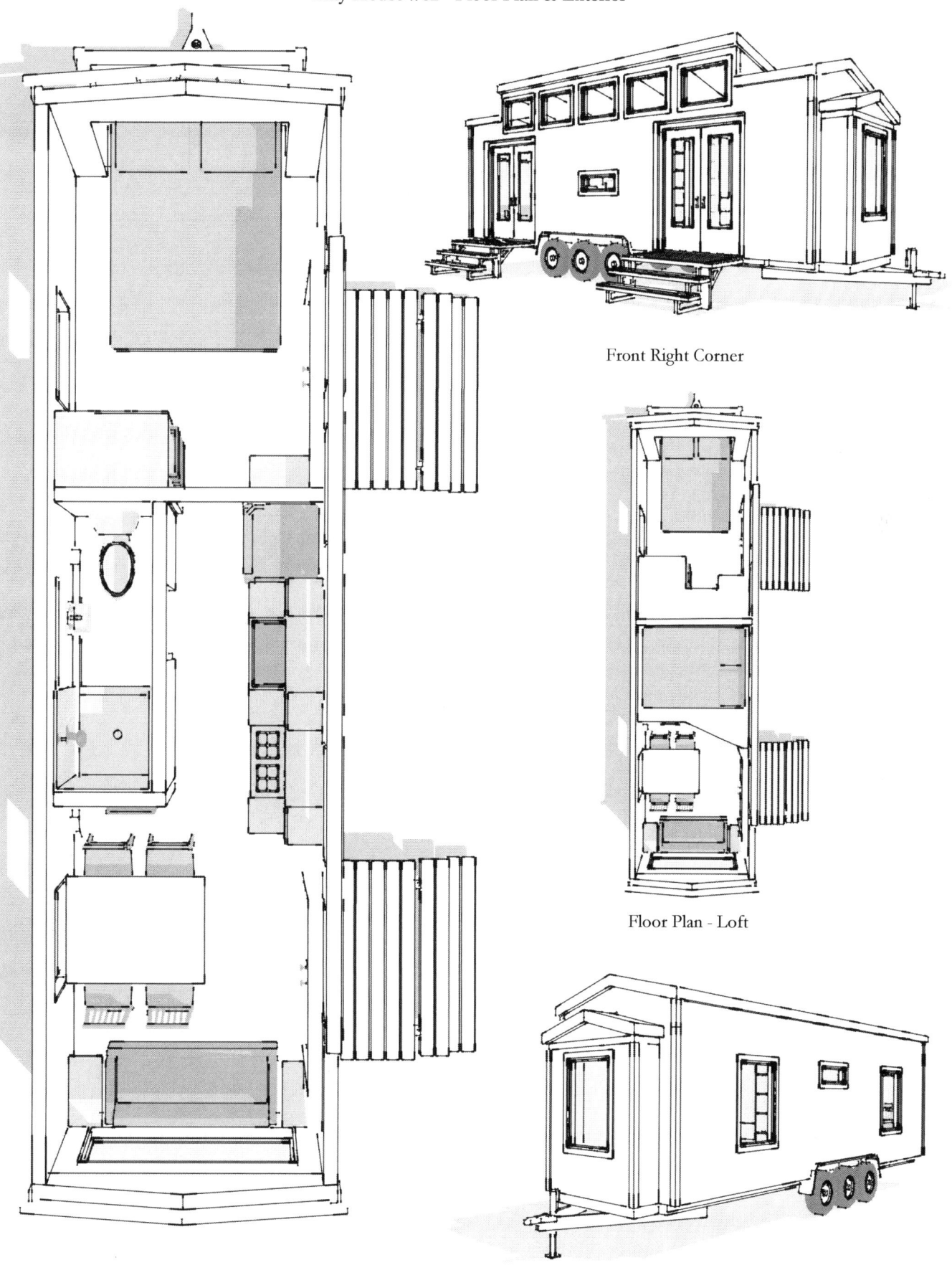

Front Right Corner

Floor Plan - Loft

Floor Plan

Back Left Corner

Tiny House #82 - Interior Views

Interior from Main Entry

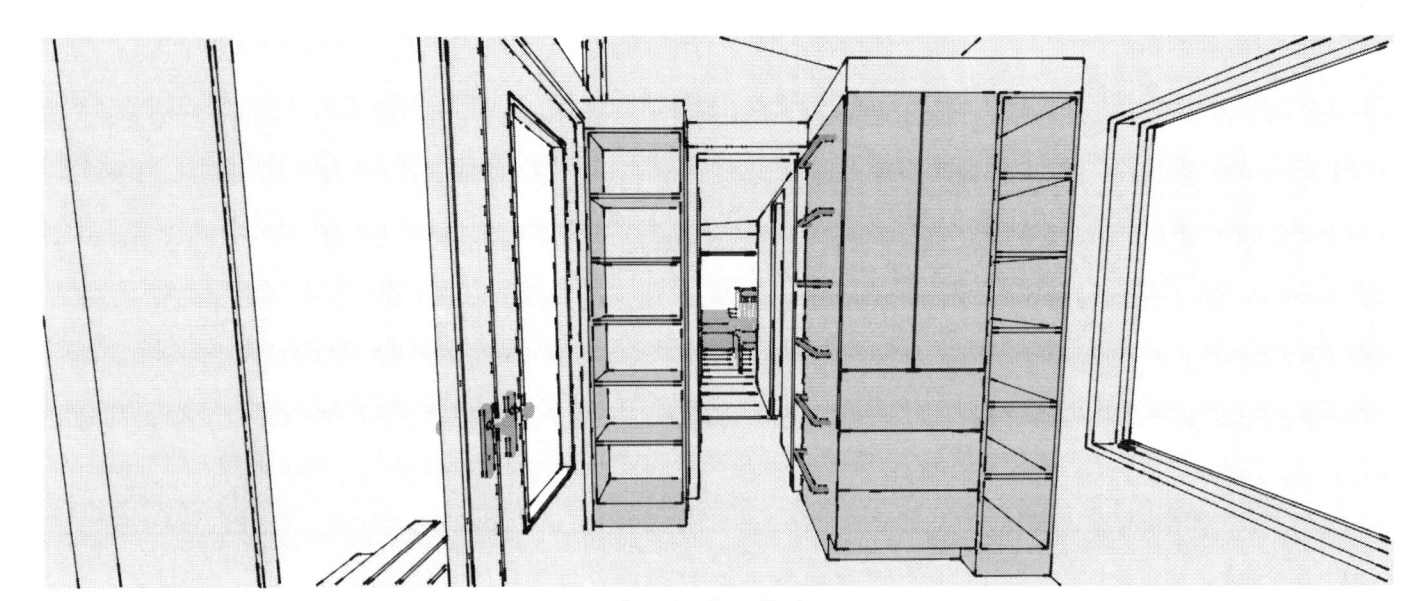

Interior from Bedroom

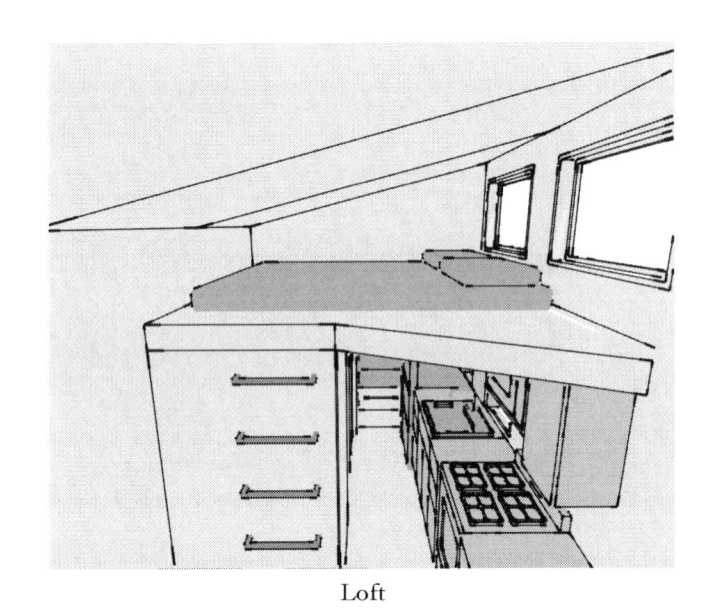

Loft

Bedroom

Tiny House #82 - Elevations

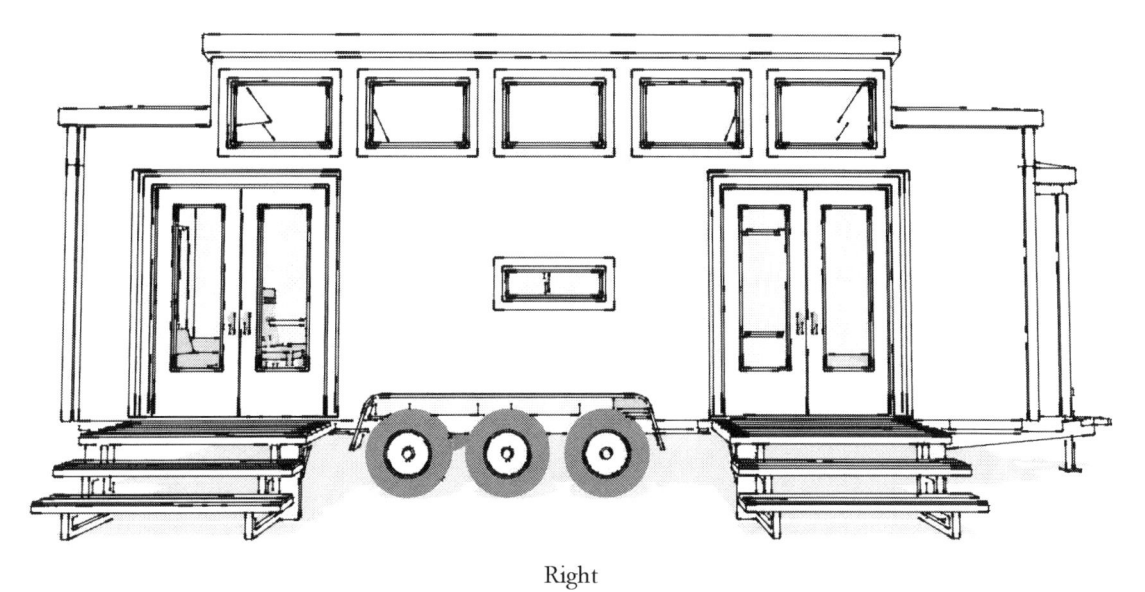

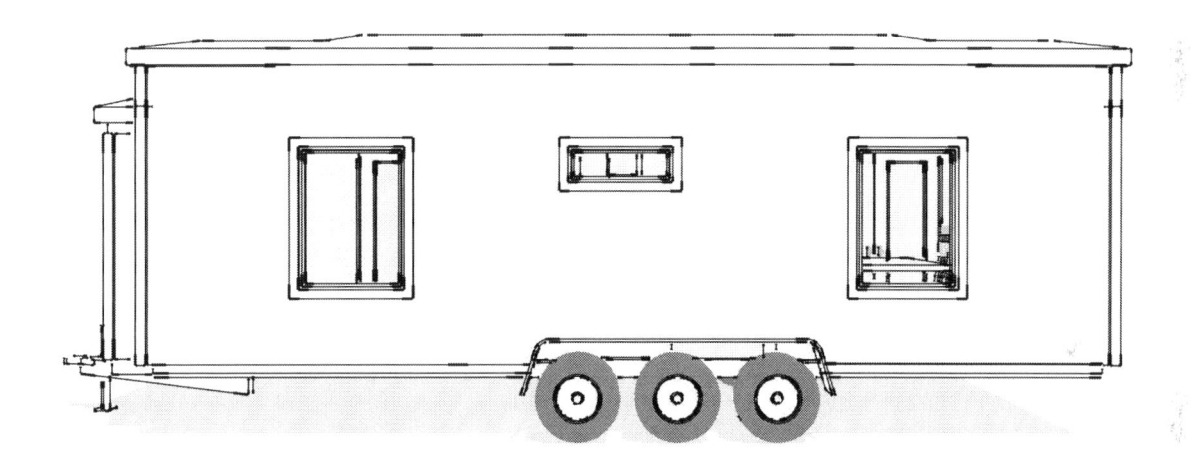

Right

Left

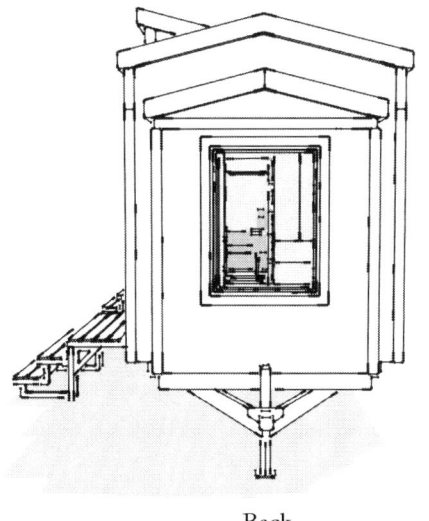

Back

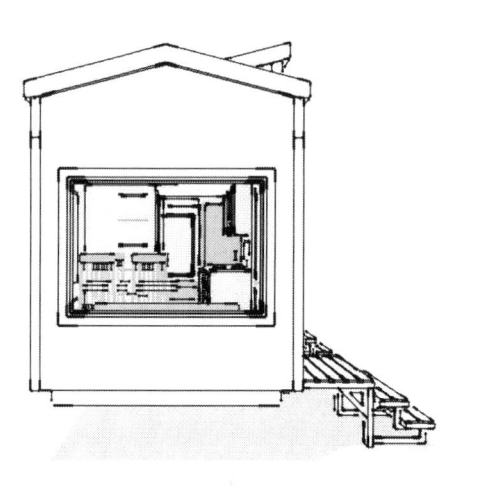

Front

# #83

Tiny House #83 - Overview

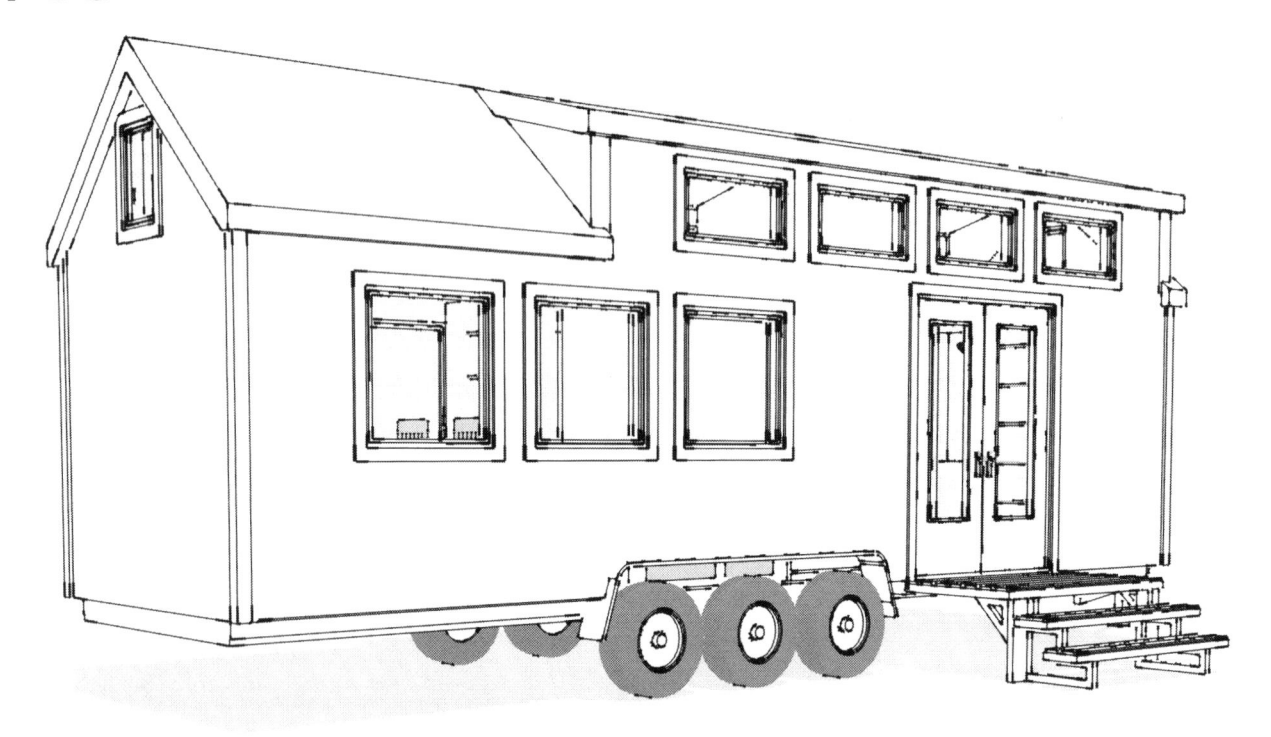

Front Right

Summary:

This house has distinct rooms. Stepping inside you find yourself turning left into a living room with ample seating. Past the living room is a kitchen with a table for four. You also take notice of a ladder leading to a loft with a queen bed. Returning to the entry you see that you walked right past the bathroom. Near the bathroom door is a ladder to the second loft with a twin bed.

Features:

28-Foot Tiny House on Wheels
10/12 Gable with Shed Dormers
Sleeps Three
Ample Seating
Laundry
Bathroom with Tub

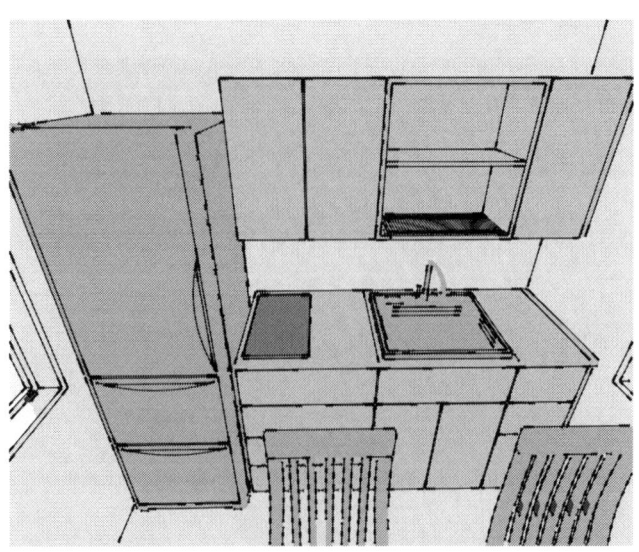

Kitchen

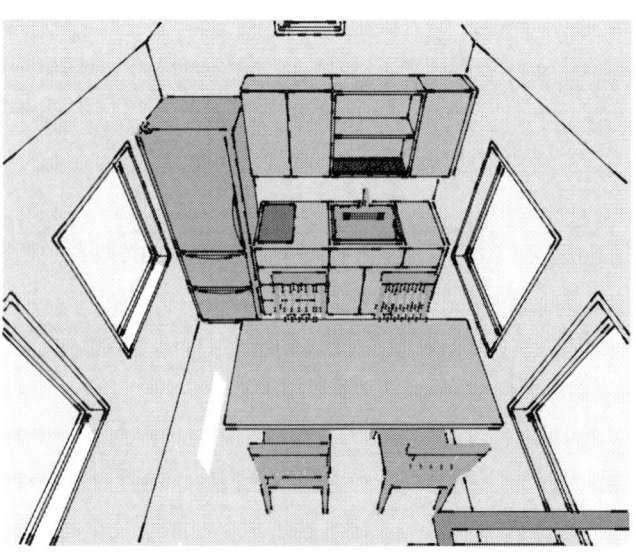

View from Loft

Tiny House #83 - Floor Plan & Exterior

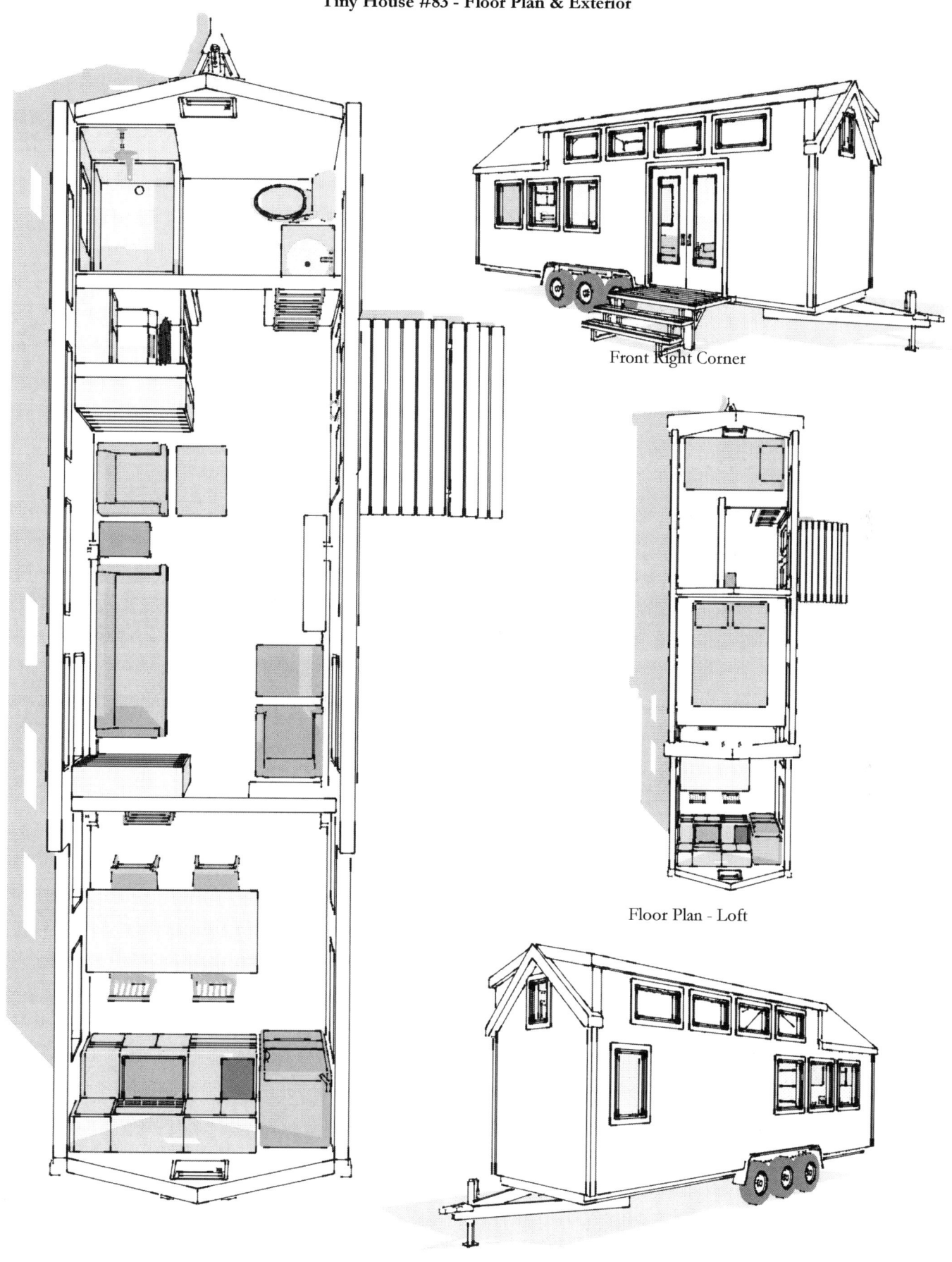

Front Right Corner

Floor Plan - Loft

Floor Plan

Back Left Corner

345

Tiny House #83 - Interior Views

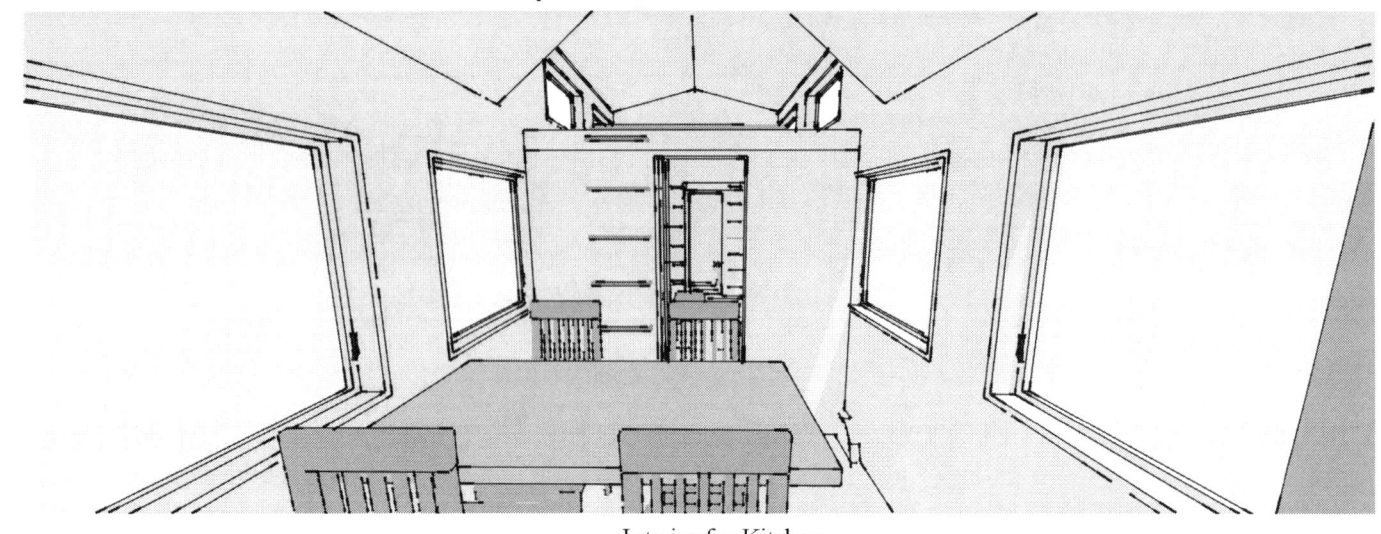

Interior fro Kitchen

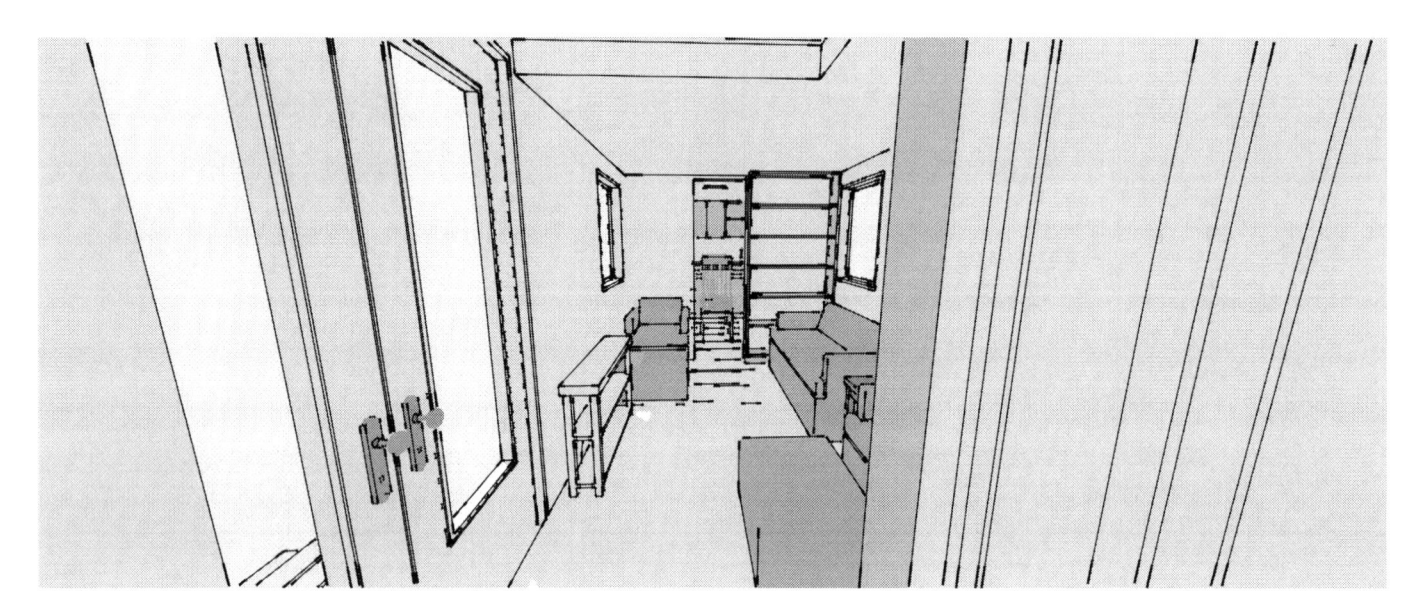

Interior from Bathroom

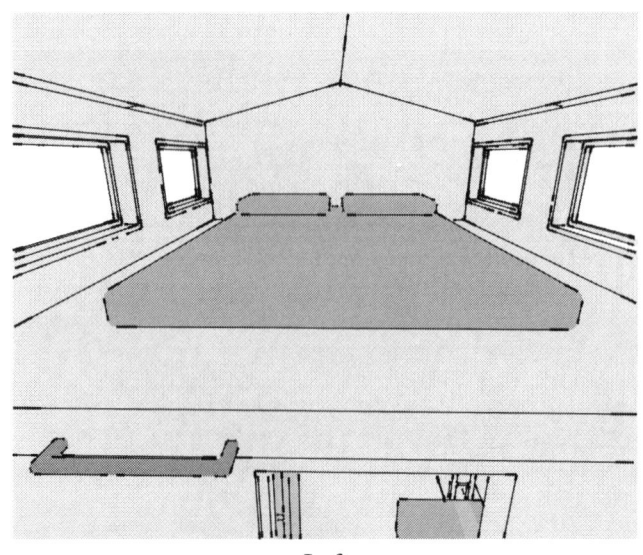

Loft

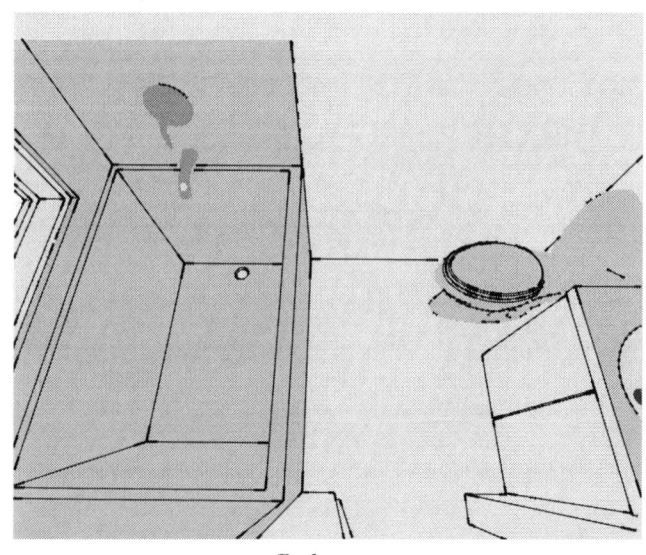

Bathroom

346

Tiny House #83 - Elevations

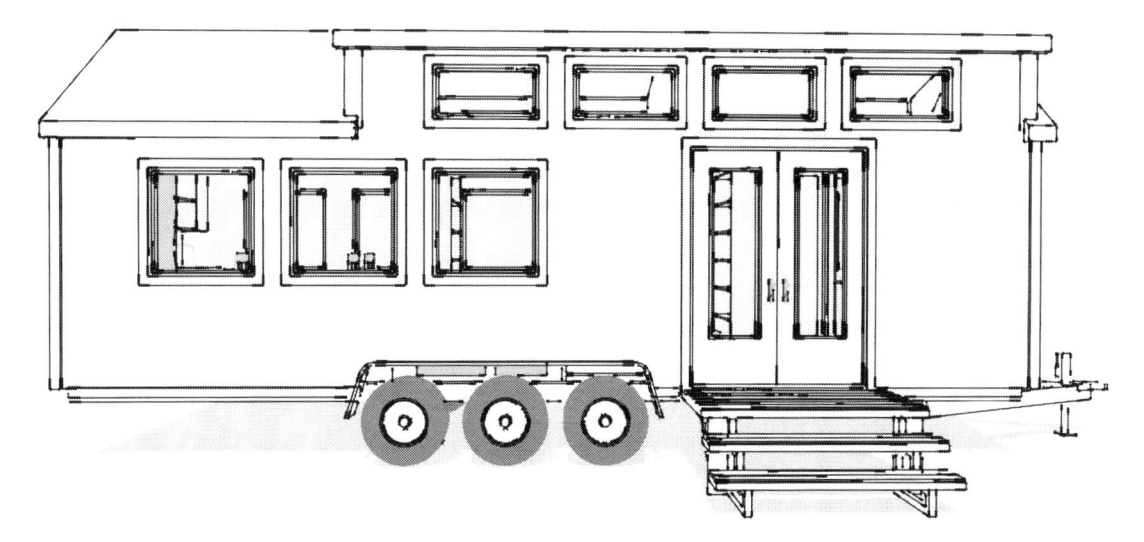

Right

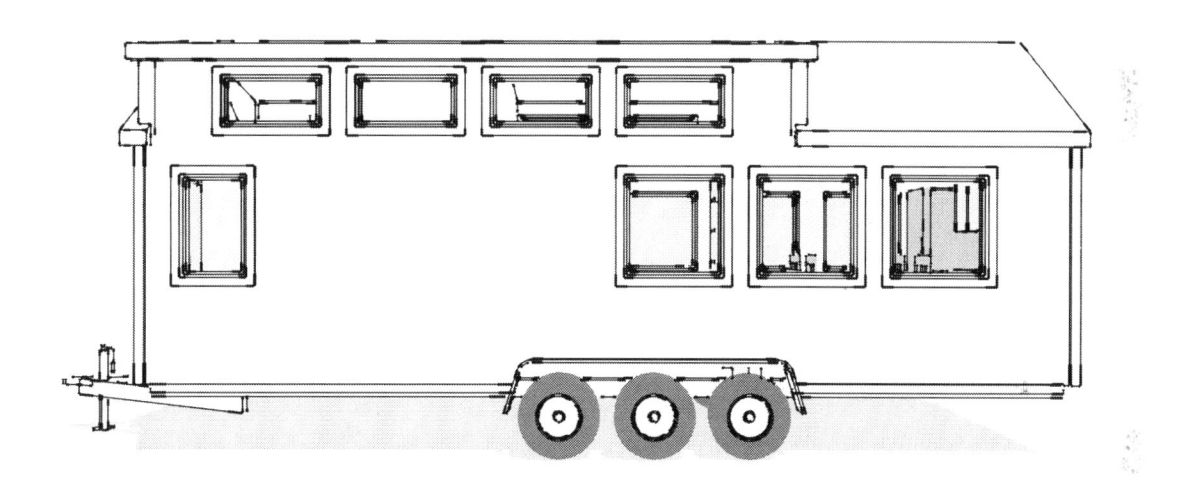

Left

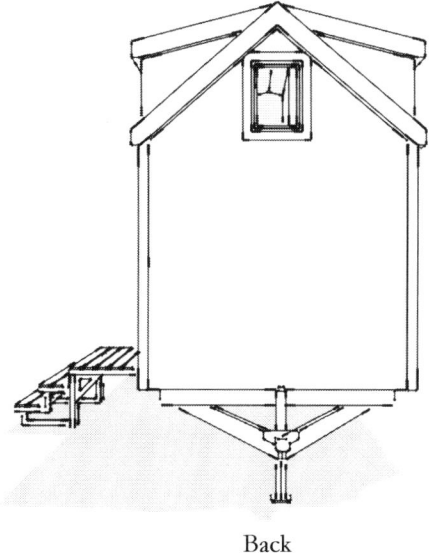

Back

Front

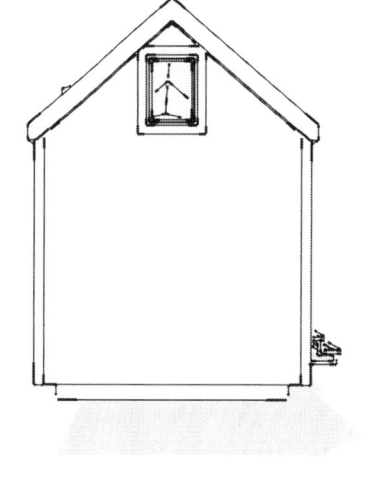

#84

Tiny House #84 - Overview

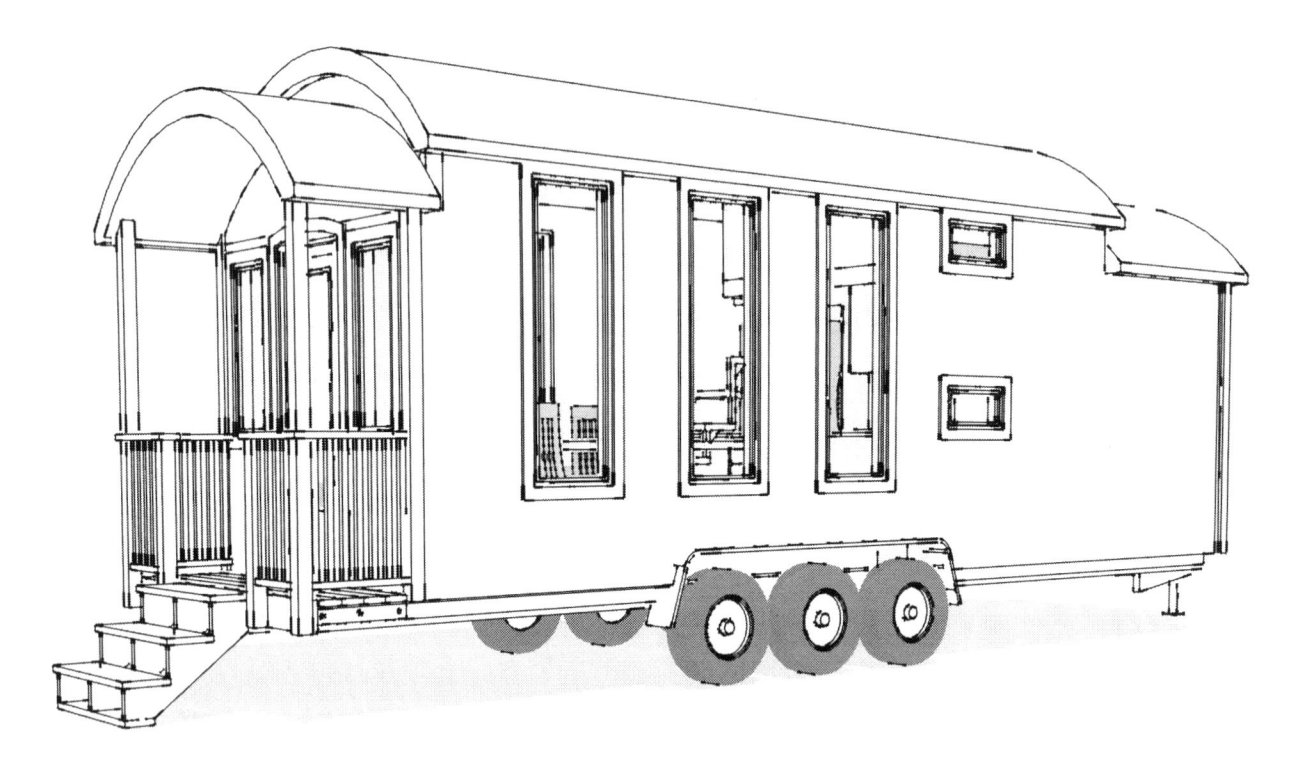

Front Right

Summary:

The tall vertical windows help accentuate the hight of the curved ceiling in this tiny house. The room has ample seating and a table for four. A staircase climbs to a loft with a queen bed. Under the loft is a kitchen and laundry. At the back of the house is a large bathroom with soaking tub, toilet, and vanity.

Features:

28-Foot Tiny House on Wheels
Porch
Vardo Inspired Roof
Bathroom with Tub
Laundry
Stairs to Loft

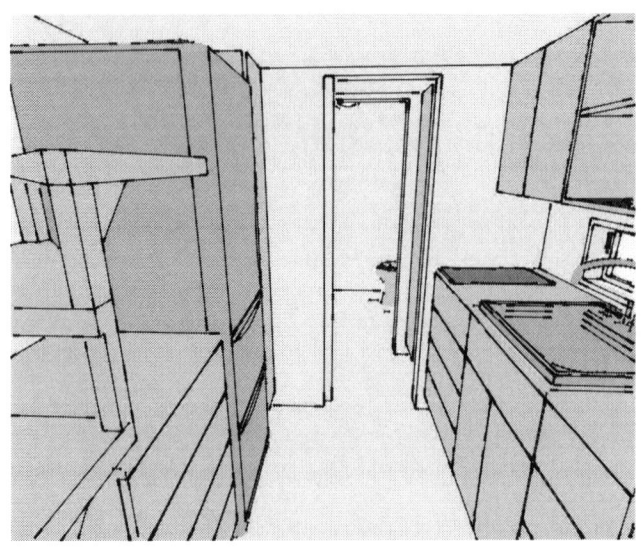

Kitchen

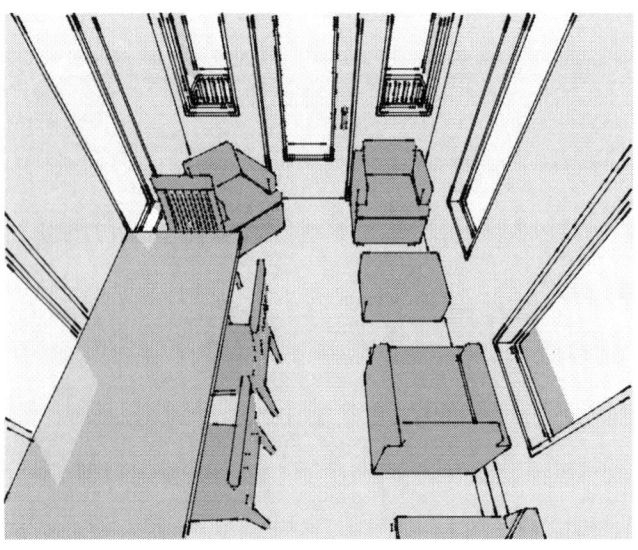

View from Loft

Tiny House #84 - Floor Plan & Exterior

Front Right Corner

Floor Plan - Loft

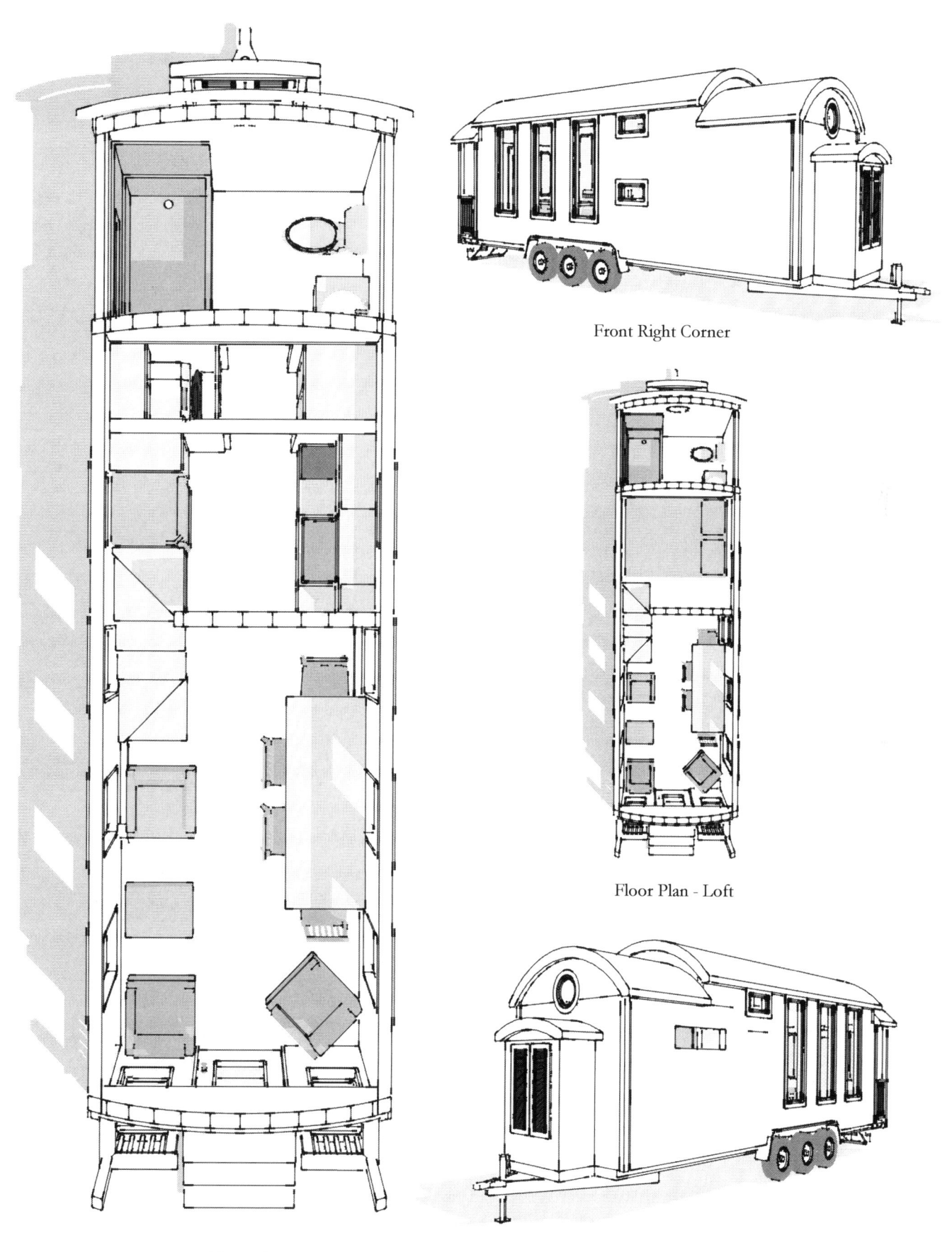

Floor Plan

Back Left Corner

349

Tiny House #84 - Interior Views

Interior from Entry

Interior from Kitchen

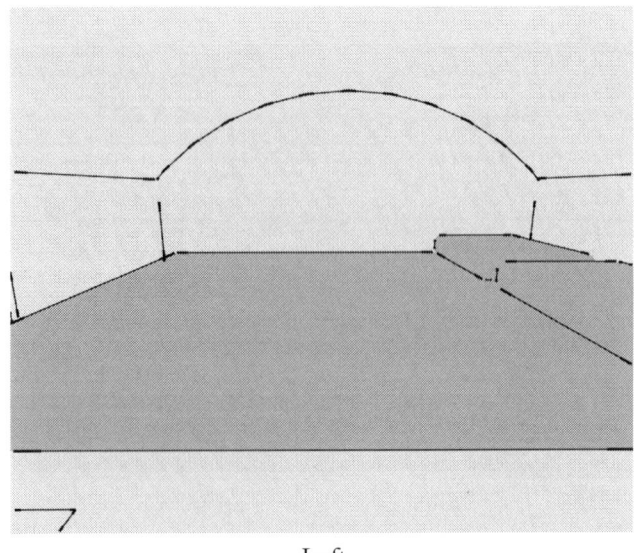

Loft

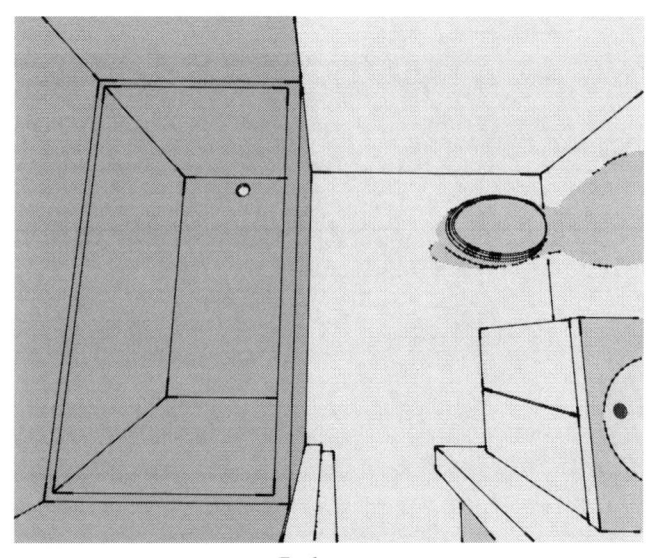

Bathroom

350

Tiny House #84 - Elevations

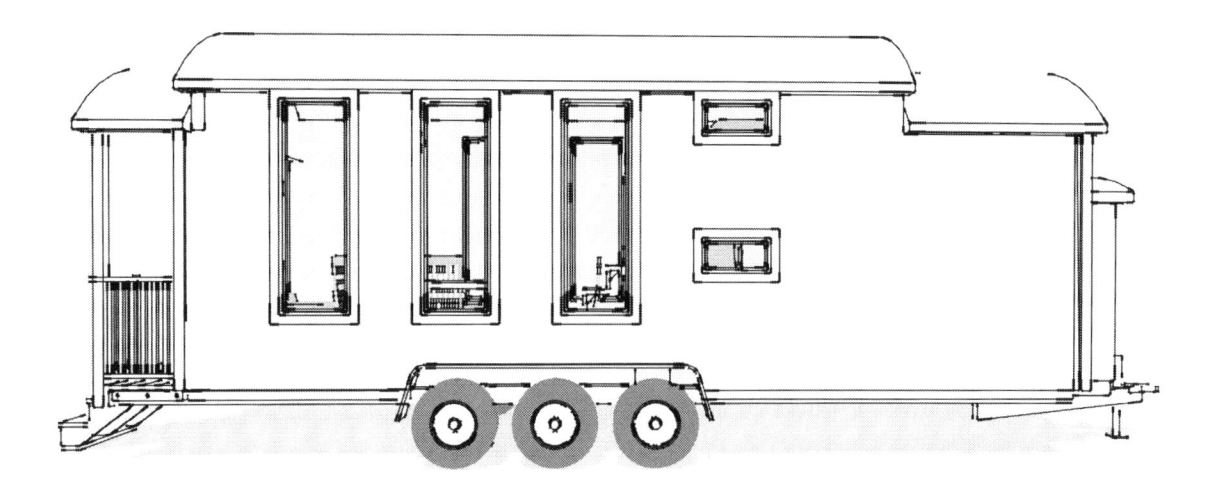

Right

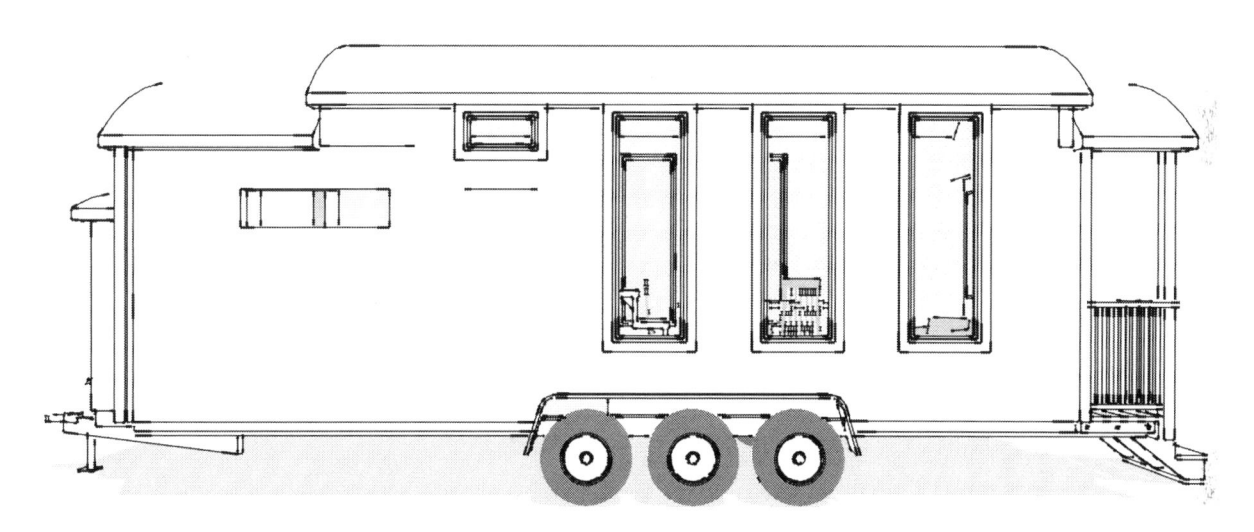

Left

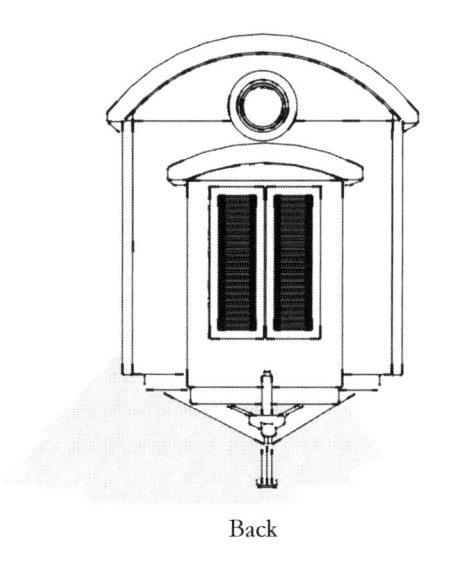

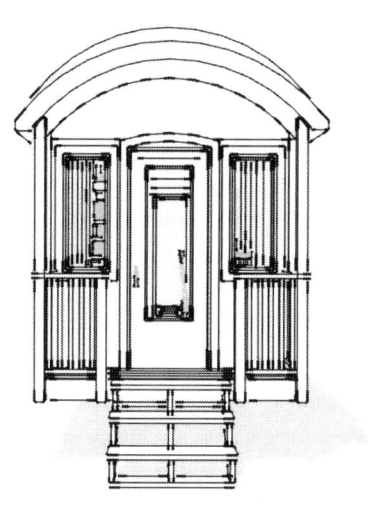

Back

Front

#85

Tiny House #85 - Overview

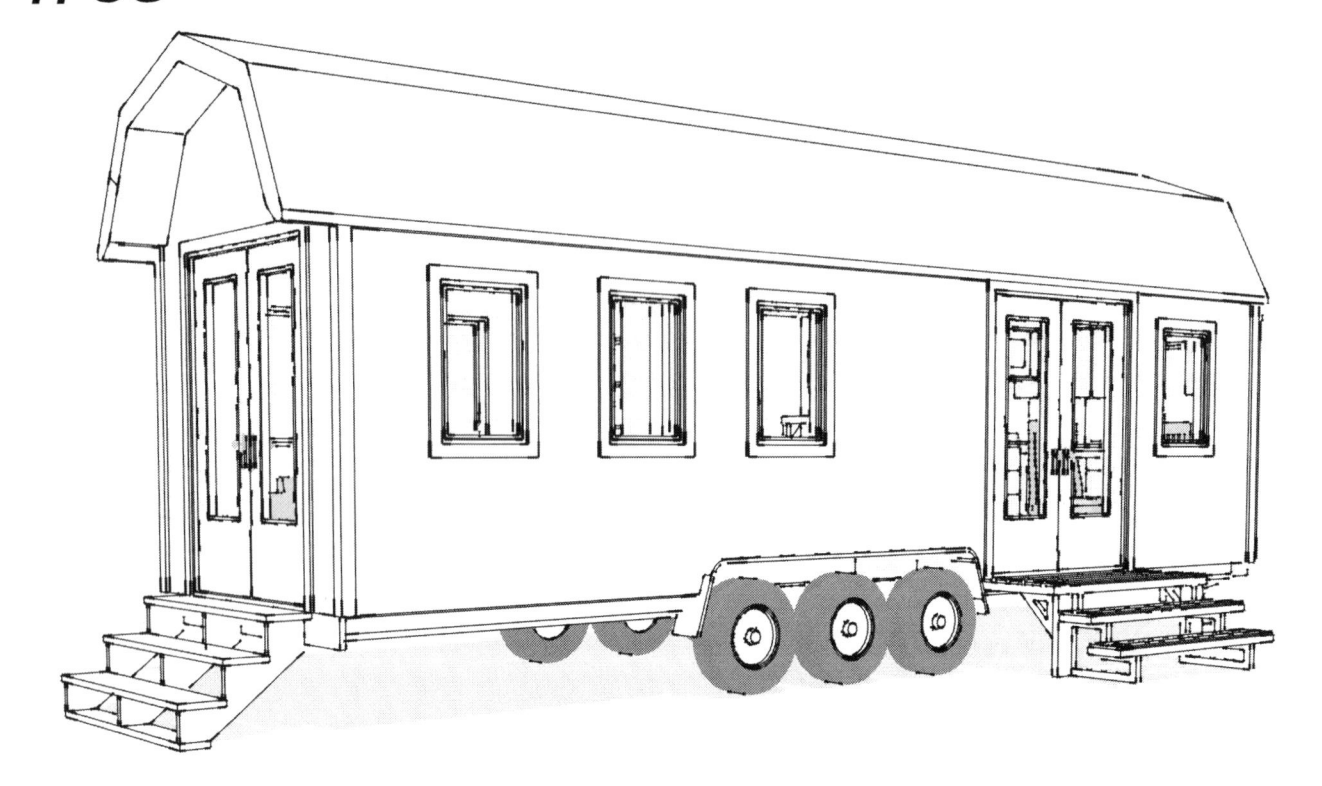

Front Right

Summary:

Stepping into the front door on the end of the house you find welcoming seating in the form of a sofa and two comfy chairs. Just past that is a staircase leading to a loft with a queen bed. Under the loft is a bathroom and laundry. At the far end of the house is a well appointed kitchen and a table for three. Above the kitchen is a second loft with a twin bed.

Features:

28-Foot Tiny House on Wheels
Gambrel Roof
Two Entries
Two Lofts
Stairs
Laundry
Sleeps Three

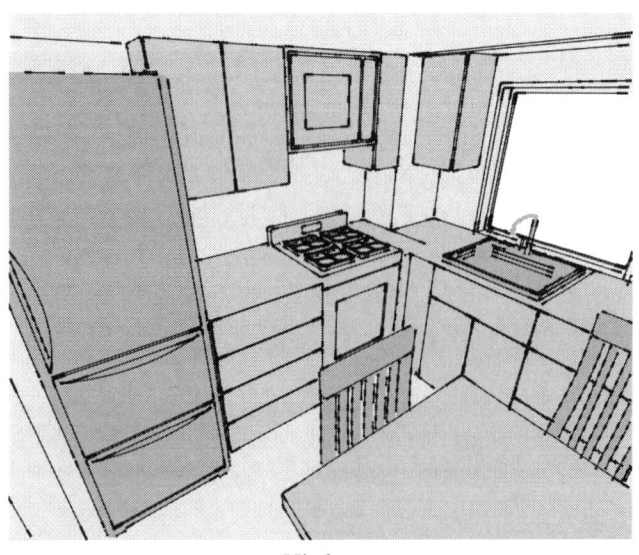

Kitchen

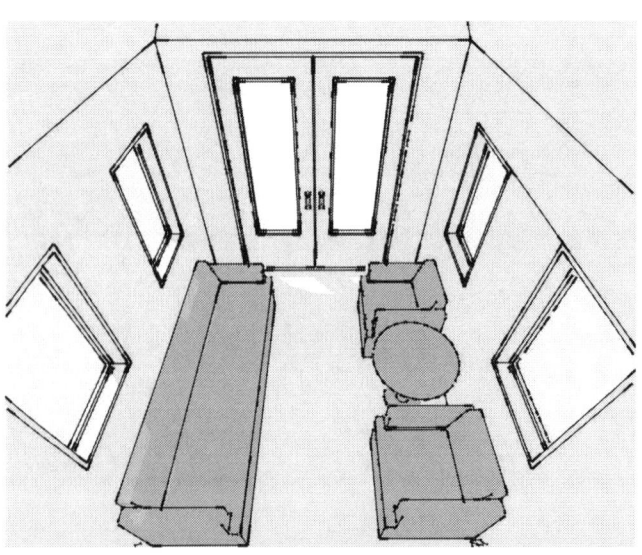

View from Loft

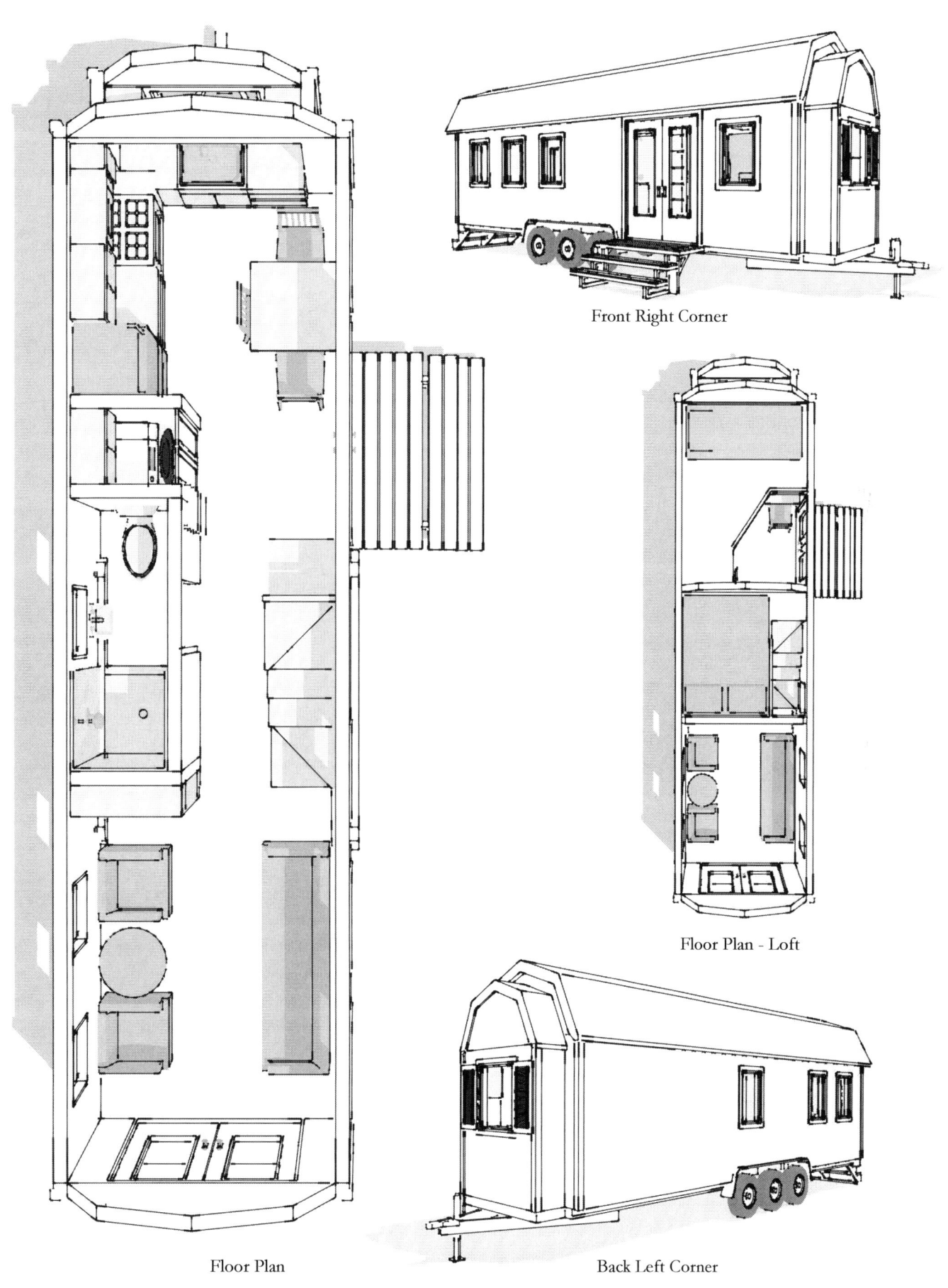

Tiny House #85 - Floor Plan & Exterior

Front Right Corner

Floor Plan - Loft

Floor Plan

Back Left Corner

Tiny House #85 - Interior Views

Interior from Living Room

Interior from Kitchen

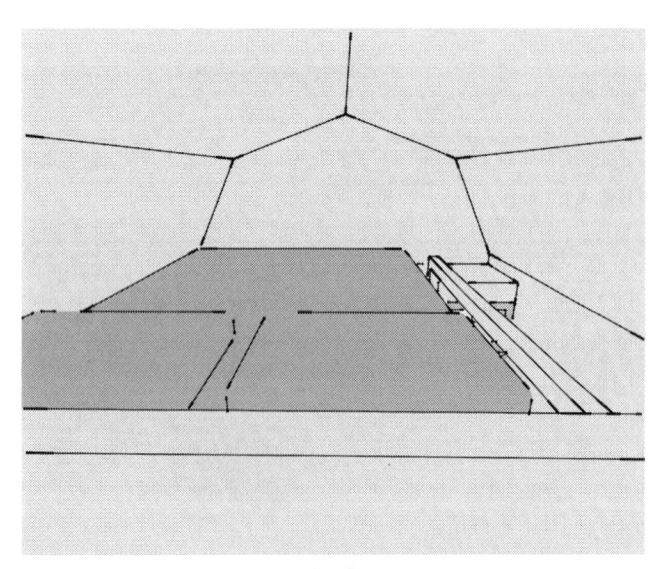

Loft

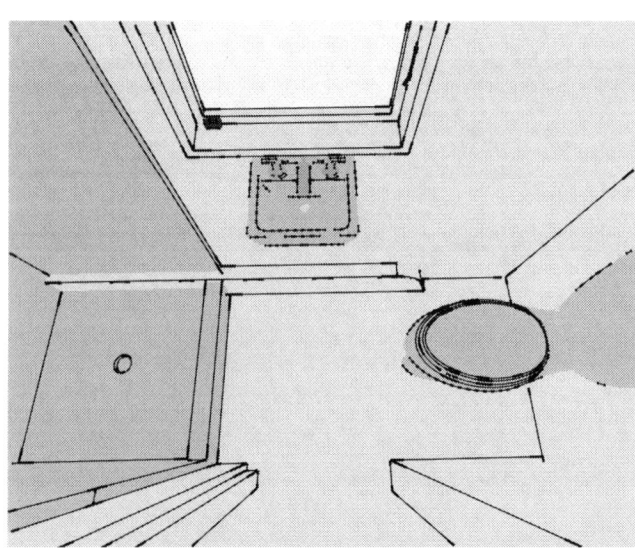

Bathroom

354

Tiny House #85 - Elevations

Right

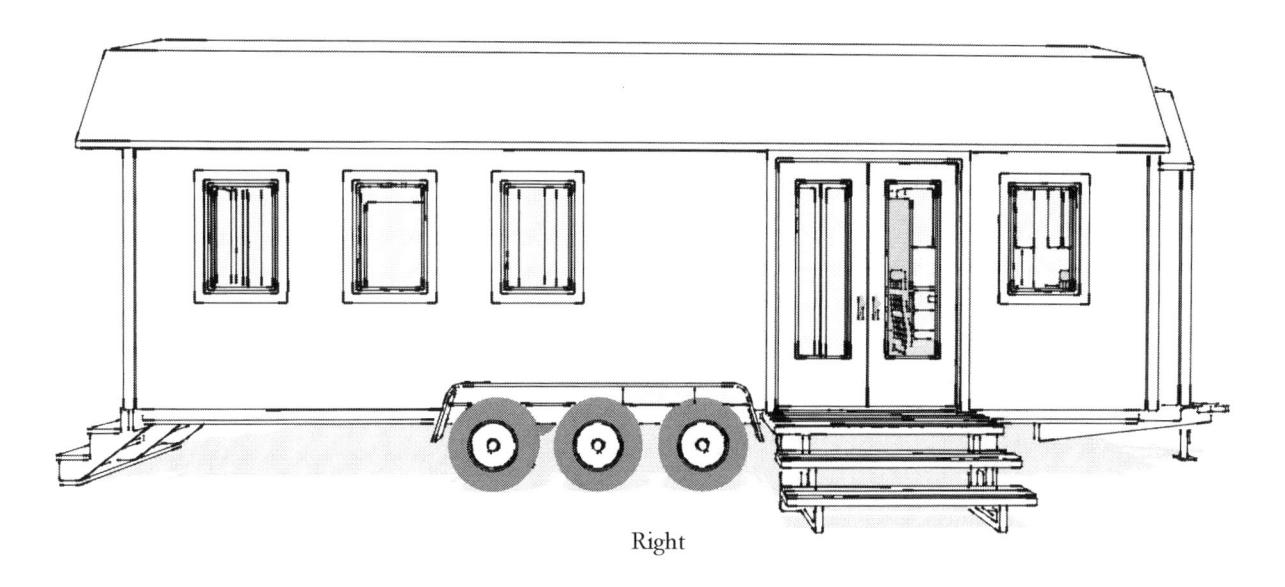

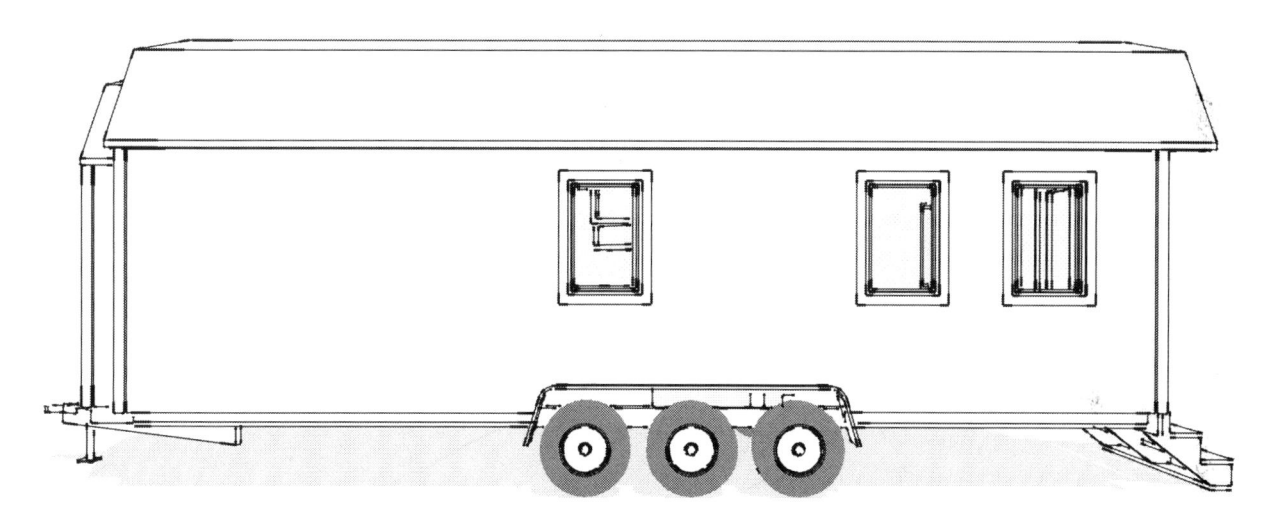

Left

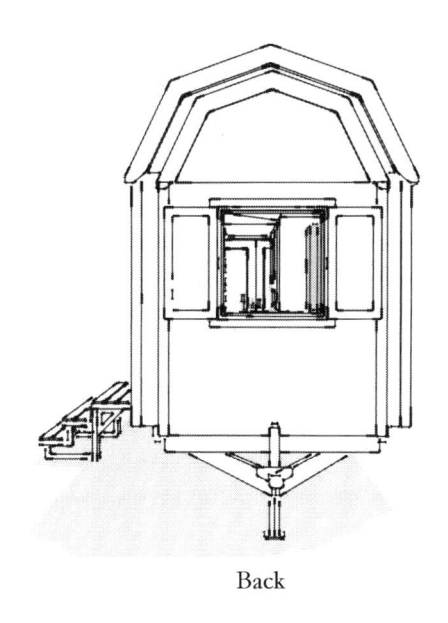

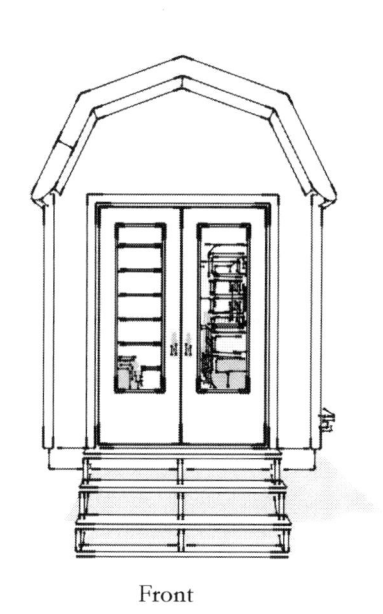

Back

Front

#86

Tiny House #86 - Overview

Front Right

Summary:

The front wall of this tiny house is slightly inset to accommodate two planters on either side of the front door. Just inside is the kitchen with a table for four. A partial wall separates the kitchen from the living room which has ample seating. From the living room both lofts can be accessed by climbing two ladders fixed to interior walls. Past the living room is a small alcove with a desk, the laundry closet, and bathroom.

Features:

28-Foot Tiny House on Wheels
Dutch Cross Gable with Gable Dormers
Sleeps Three in Two Lofts
Functional Kitchen
Ample Seating
Laundry
Utility Closet over Trailer Tongue
Desk

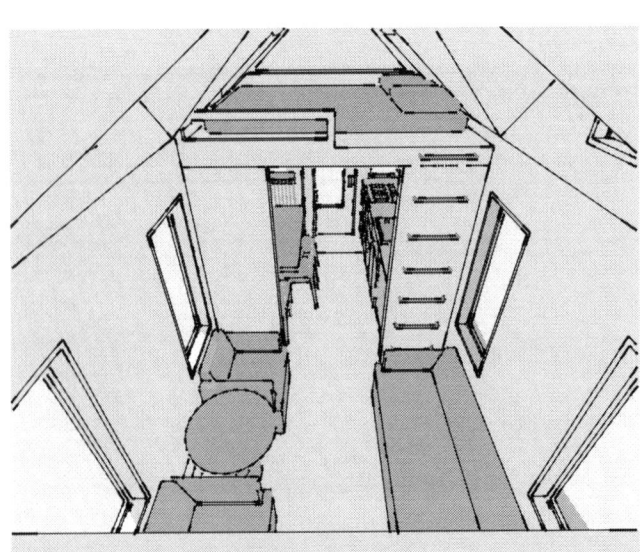

Kitchen

View from Loft

Tiny House #86 - Floor Plan & Exterior

Front Right Corner

Floor Plan - Loft

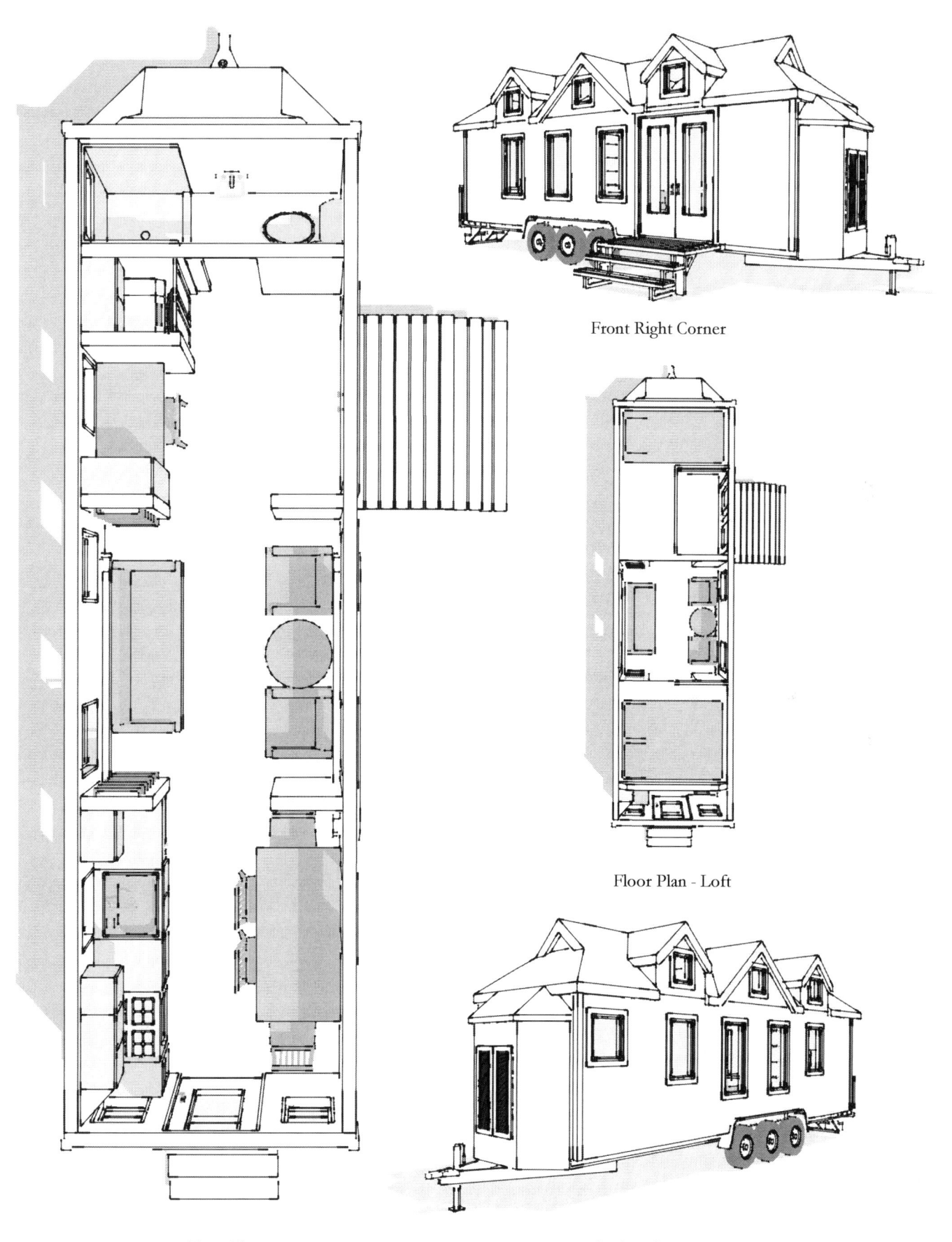

Floor Plan

Back Left Corner

Tiny House #86 - Interior Views

Interior from Kitchen

Interior from Bathroom

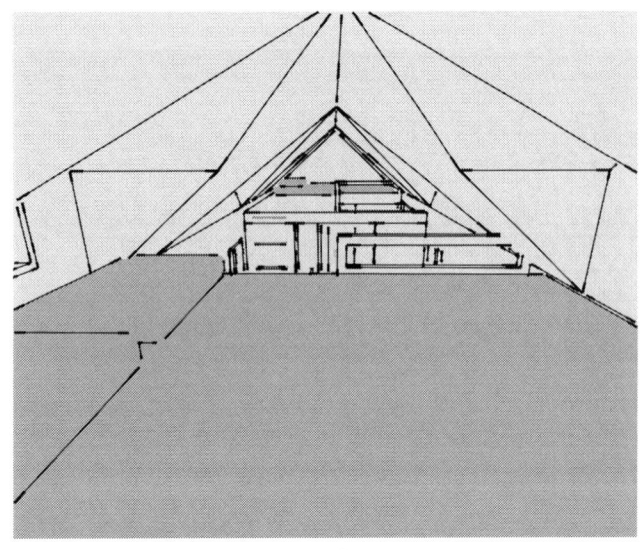

Loft

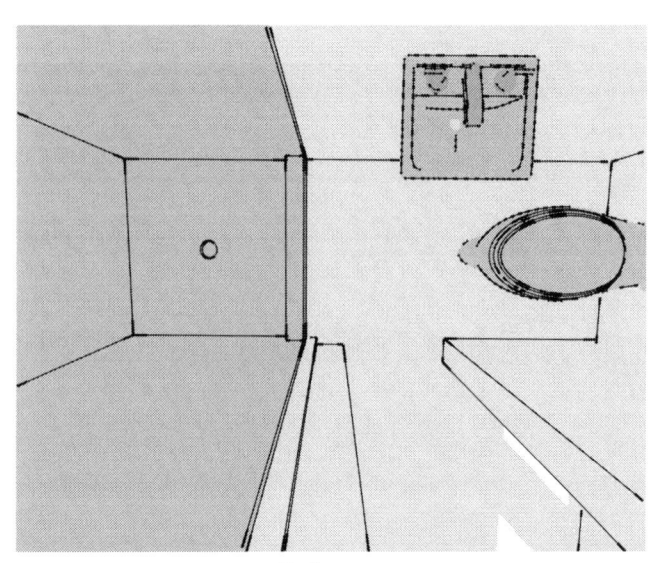

Bathroom

Tiny House #86 - Elevations

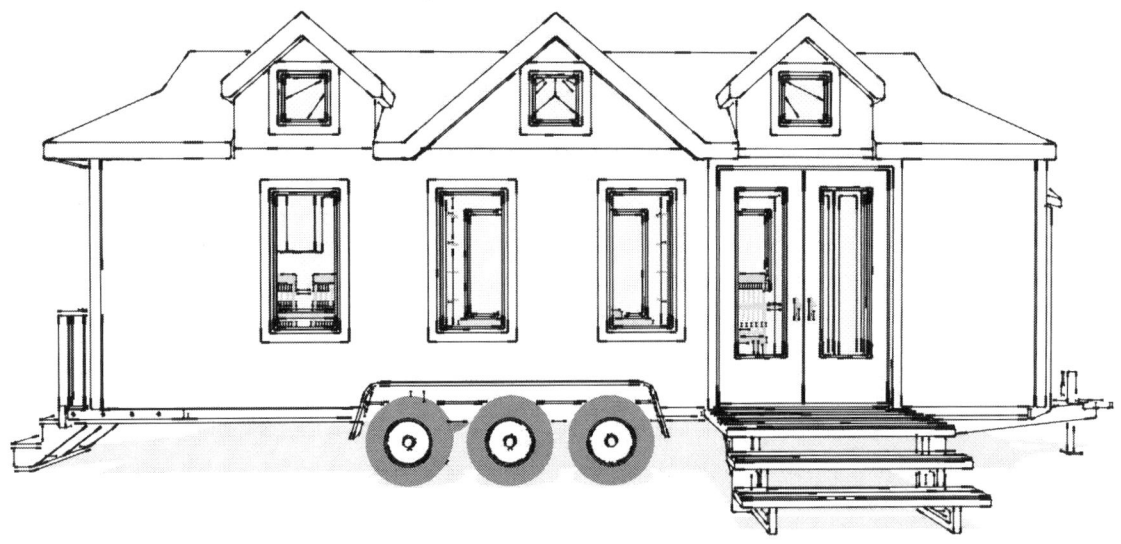

Right

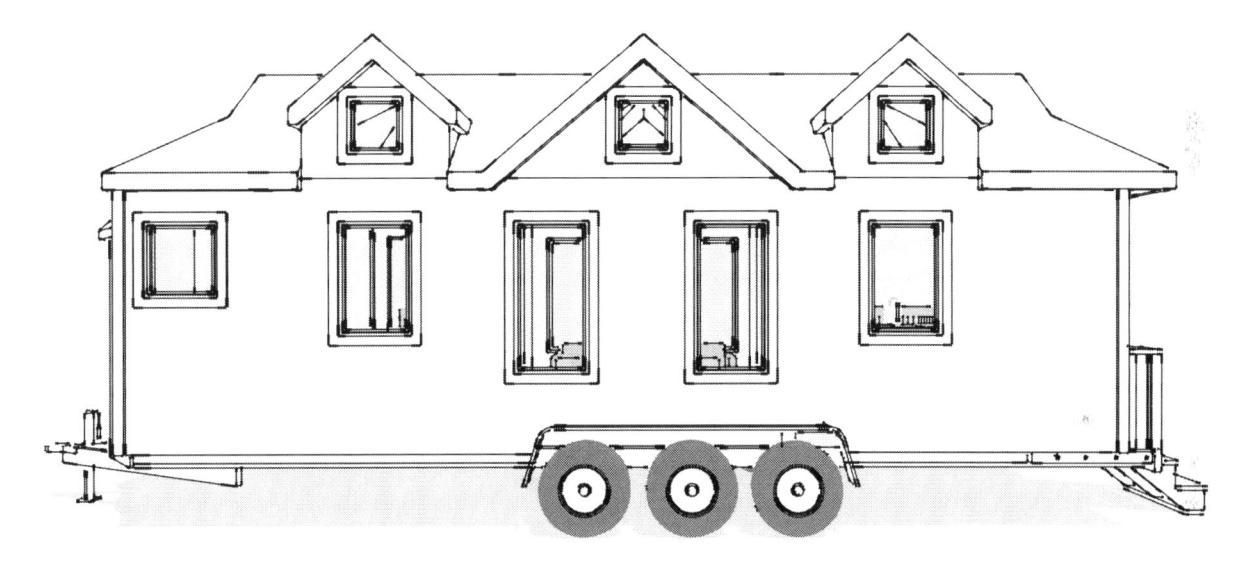

Left

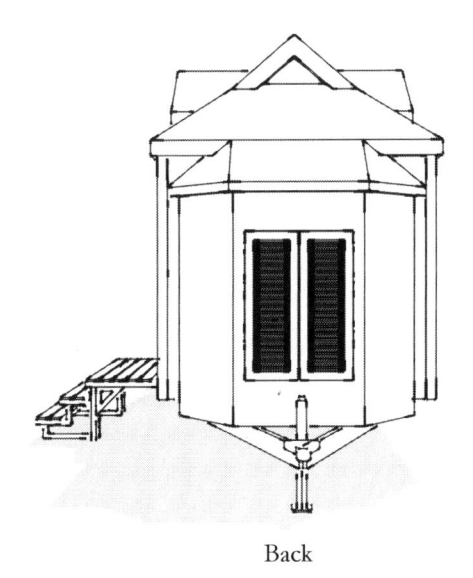

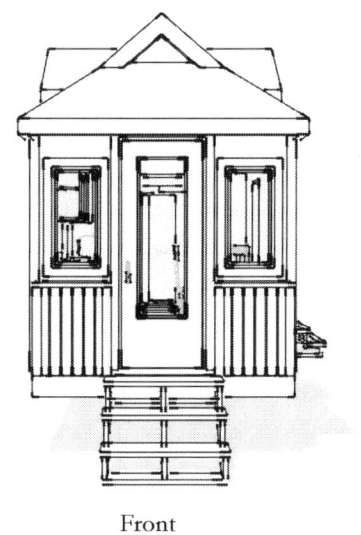

Back

Front

#87

Tiny House #87 - Overview

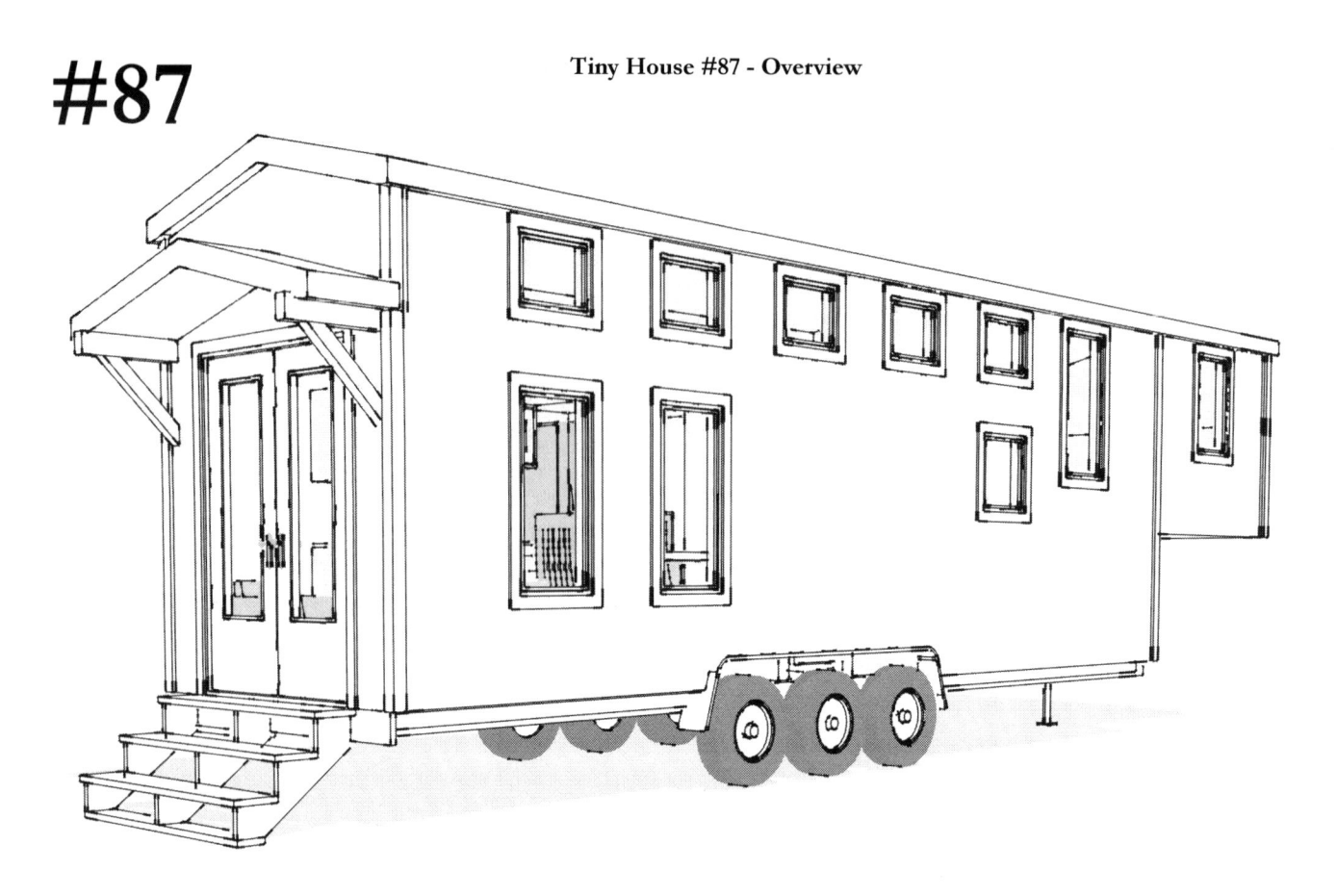

Front Right

Summary:

Stepping inside this tiny house you find a combination kitchen, dining, living room. Just past this is a hallway flanked by ample storage, a laundry closet, and bathroom. At the end of the house you enter the master bedroom and step-up onto a raised platform where you find two comfy chairs. Another couple of steps up and you've reached the queen size bed.

Features:

28-Foot Tiny House on Wheels
Gooseneck Trailer
High 3/12 Gable Roof
Porch Overhang
Sleeps Four
Spacious Master Bedroom in Gooseneck

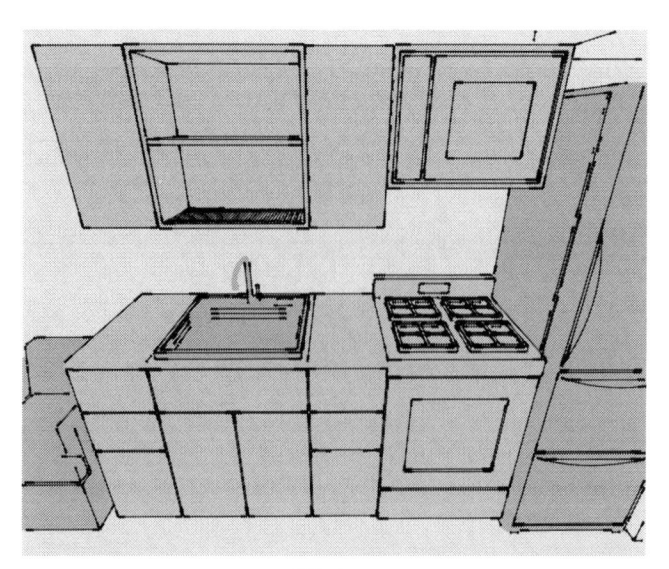

Kitchen

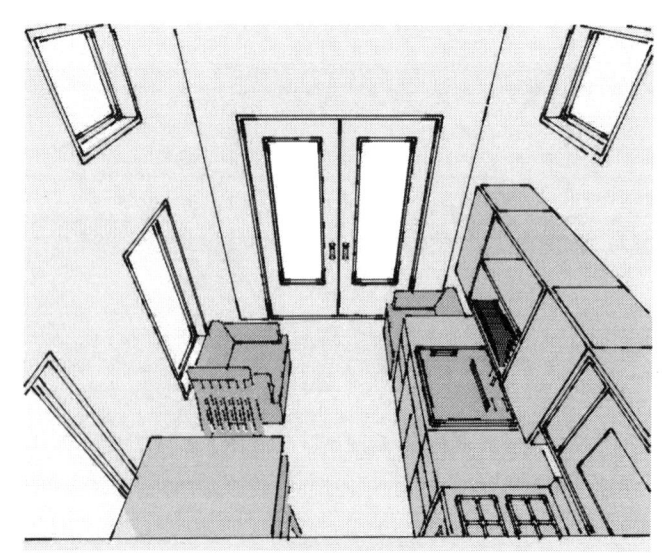

View from Loft

Tiny House #87 - Floor Plan & Exterior

Front Right Corner

Floor Plan - Loft

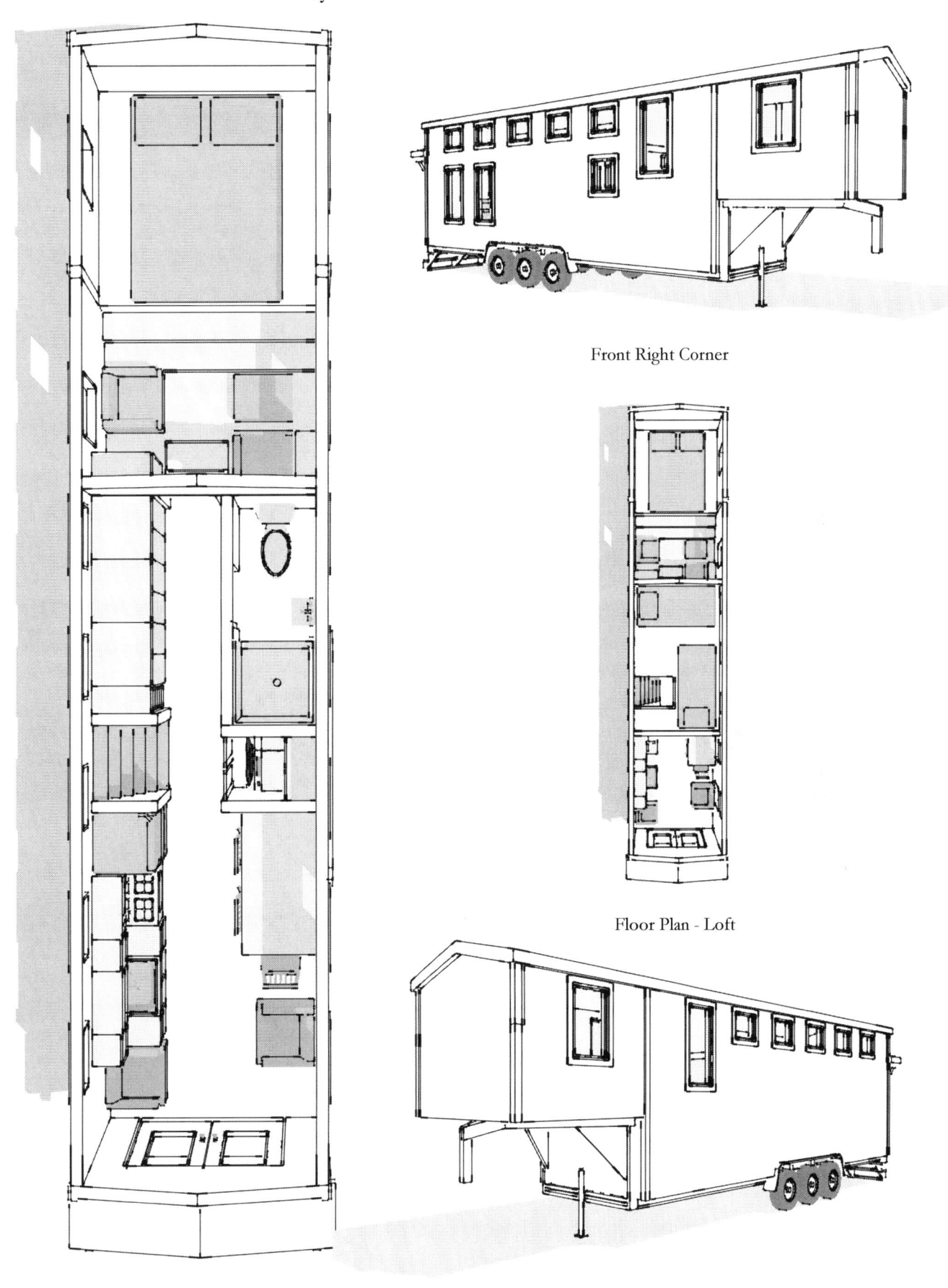

Floor Plan

Back Left Corner

Tiny House #87 - Interior Views

Interior from Entry

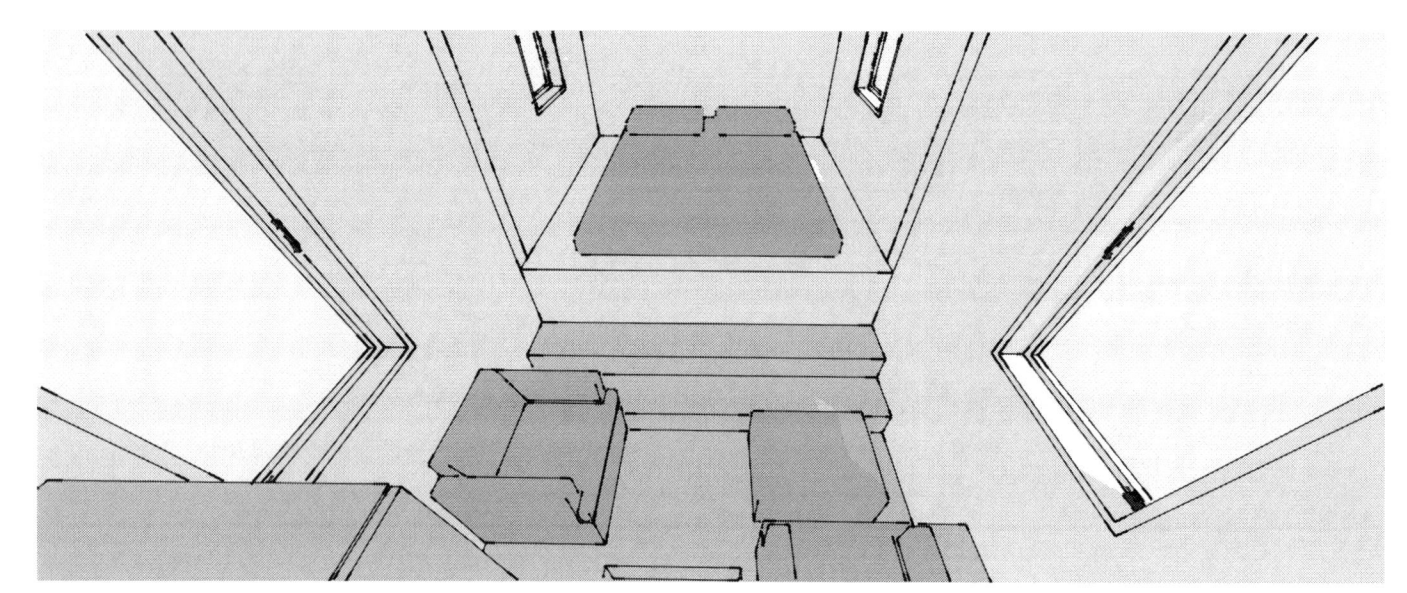

Master Bedroom

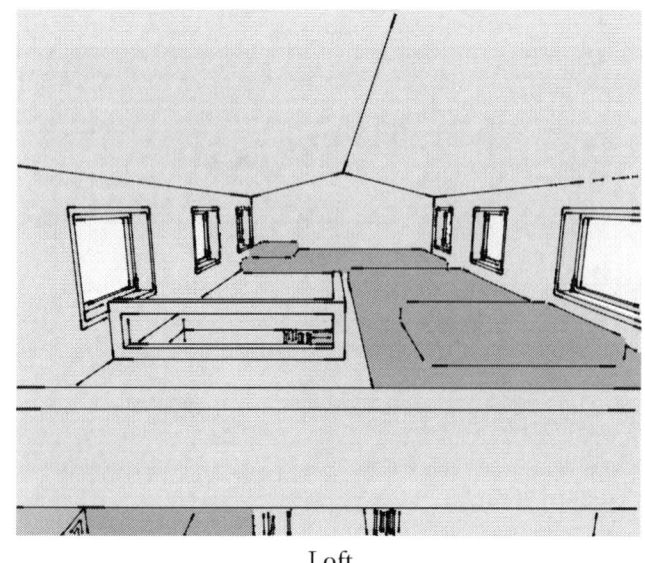

Loft

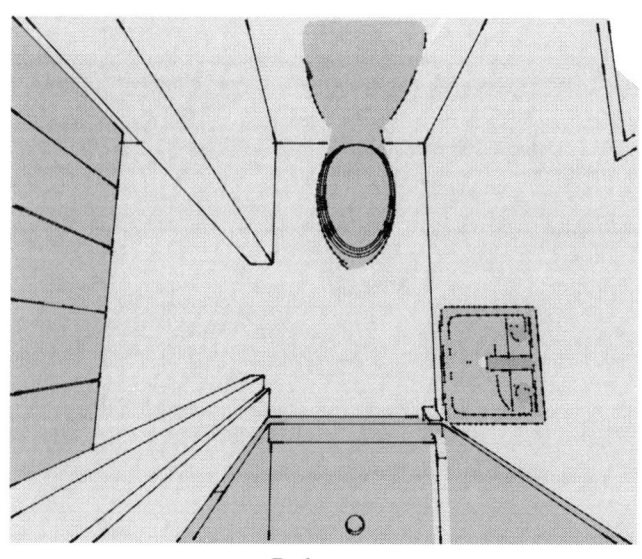

Bathroom

362

Tiny House #87 - Elevations

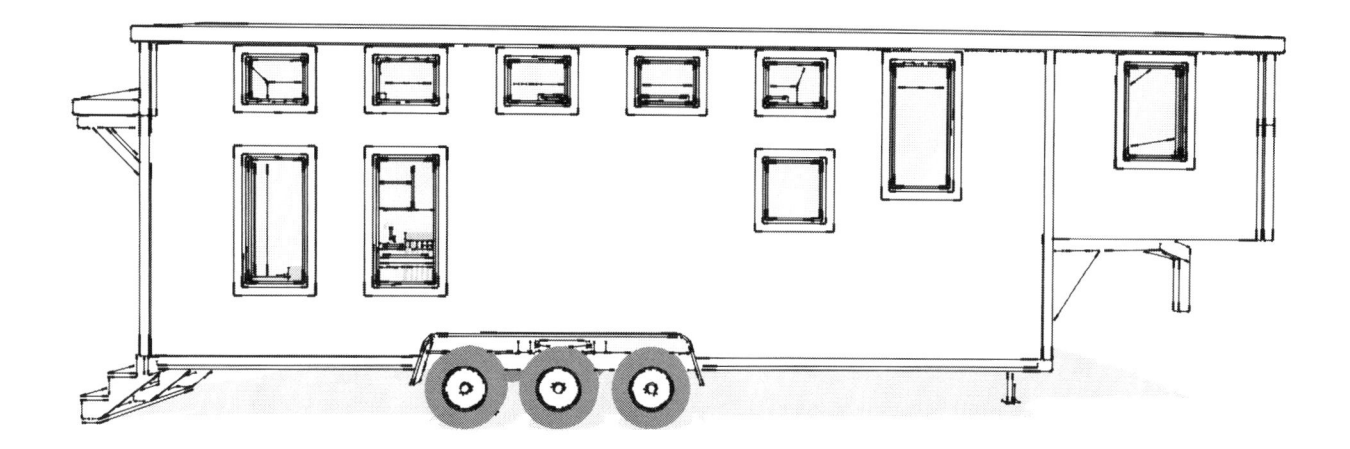

Right

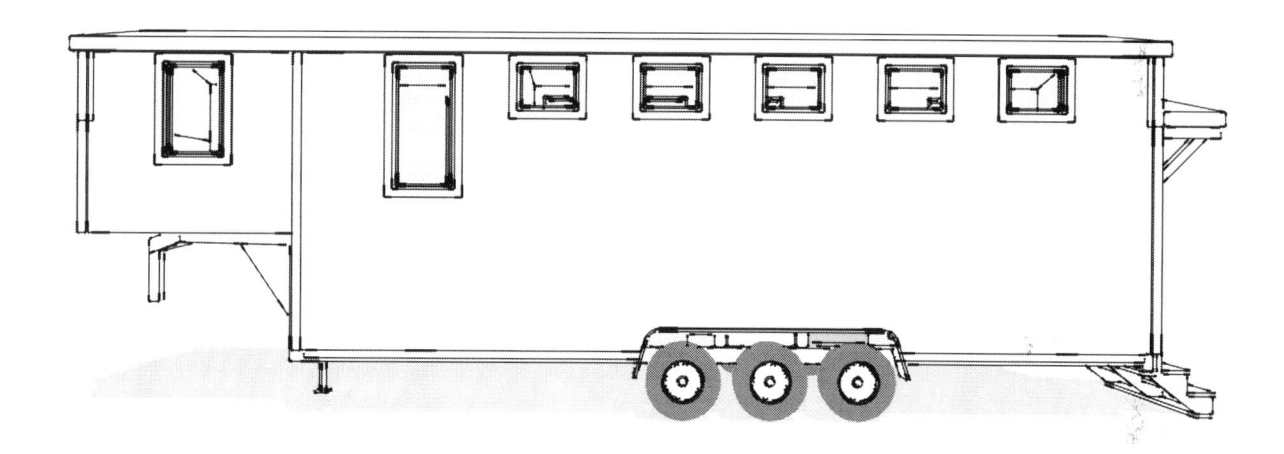

Left

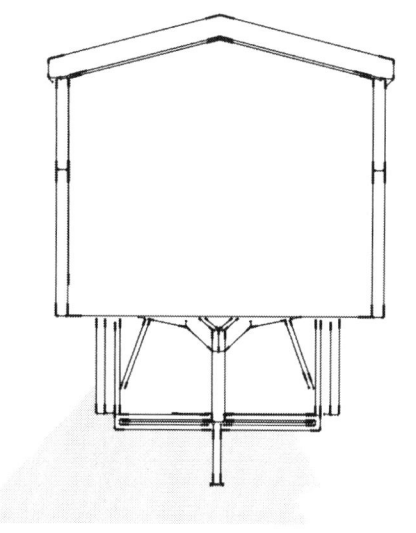

Back

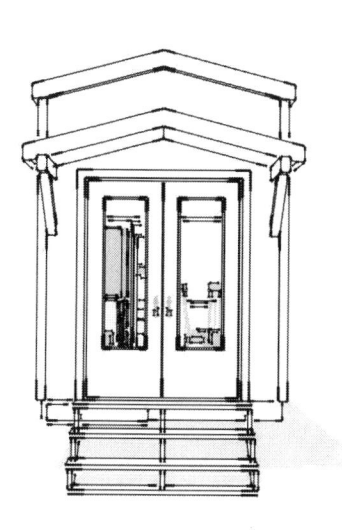

Front

#88

Tiny House #88 - Overview

Front Right

Summary:

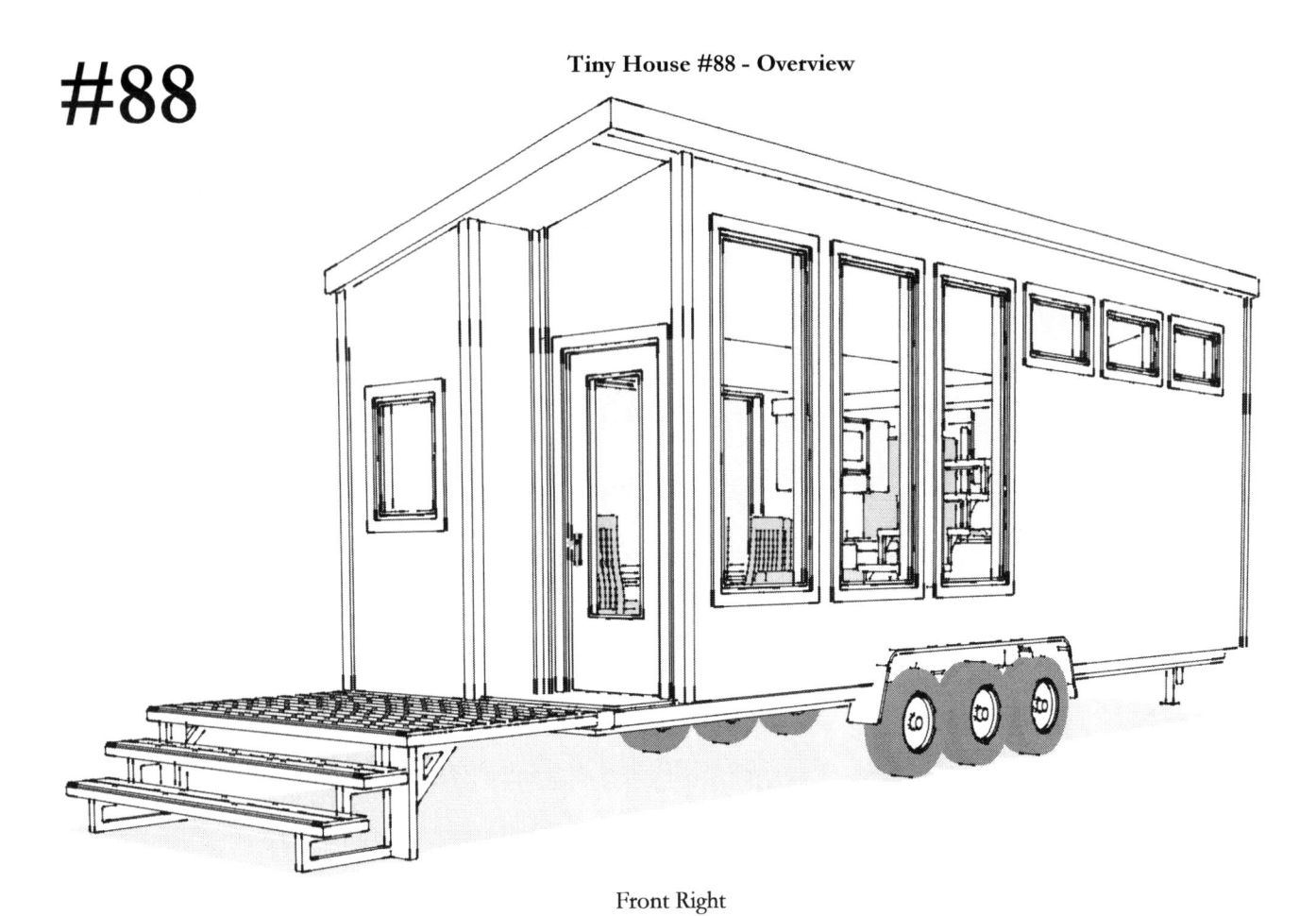

This tiny house has high ceilings and many windows making it bright and cheerful. Just inside the front door are three comfy chairs and a table for three. On the right is an open staircase that doesn't impede the view out the large windows. Just past the table and stairs is the kitchen which has all the essentials. Continuing to the back of the house you find the laundry closet and bathroom.

Features:

28-Foot Tiny House on Wheels
3/12 Shed Roof
Large Windows
Open Floor Plan
Sleeps 2 in Large Loft
Open Stairs to Loft
Bathroom with Tub

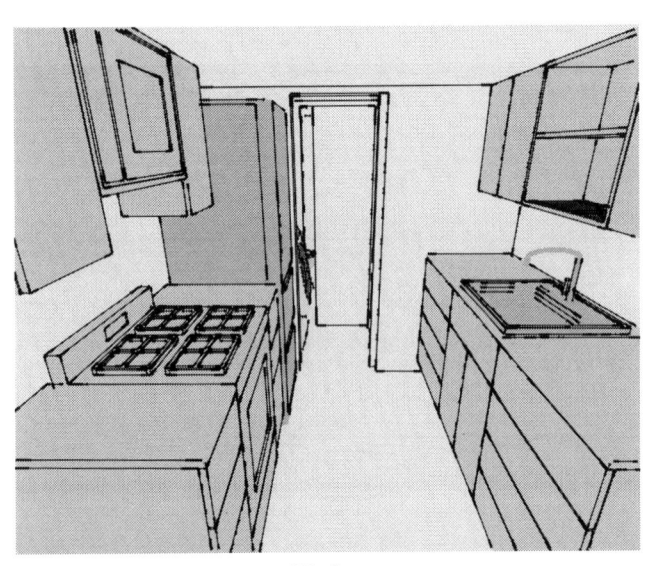

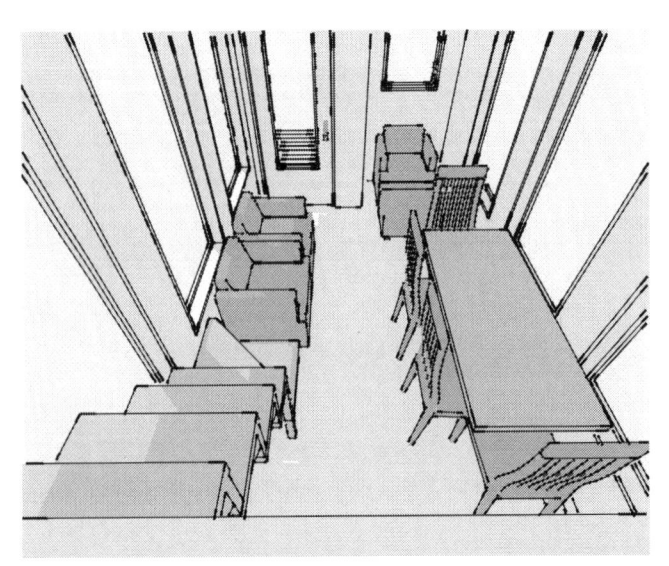

Kitchen

View from Loft

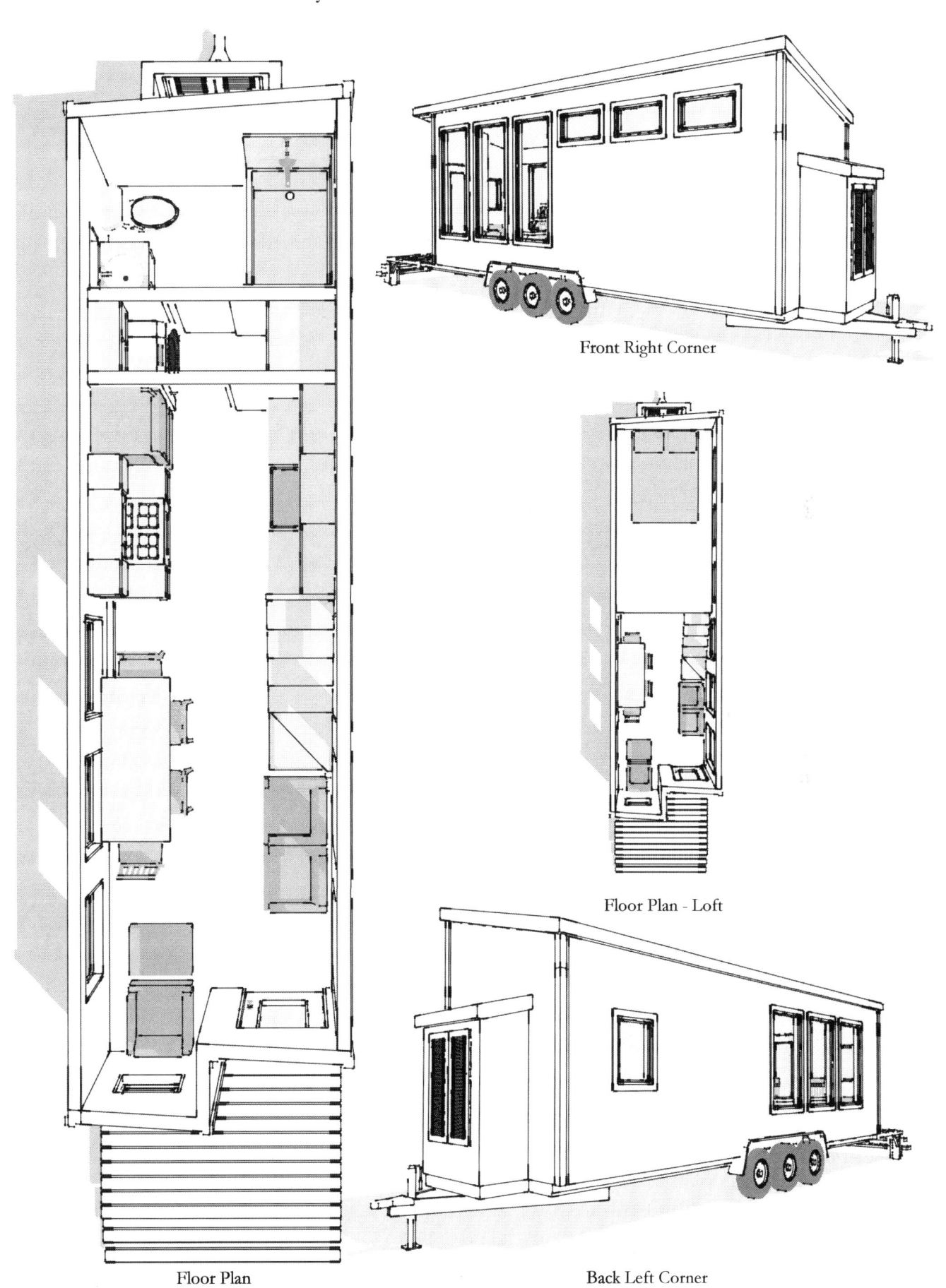

Tiny House #88 - Floor Plan & Exterior

Front Right Corner

Floor Plan - Loft

Floor Plan

Back Left Corner

Tiny House #88 - Interior Views

Interior from Entry

Interior from Kitchen

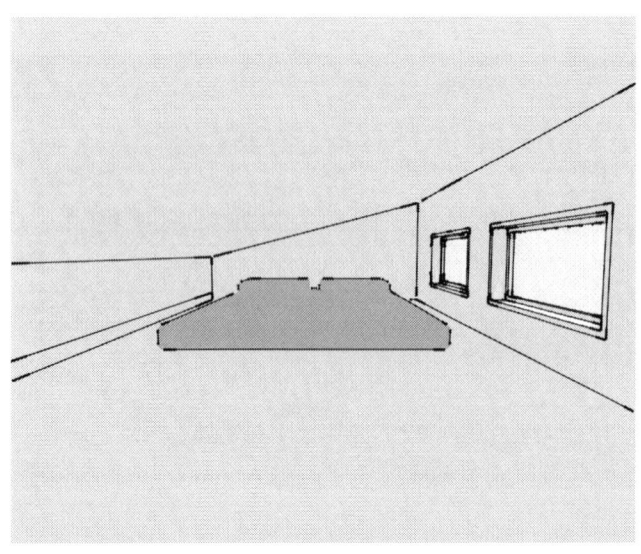

Loft

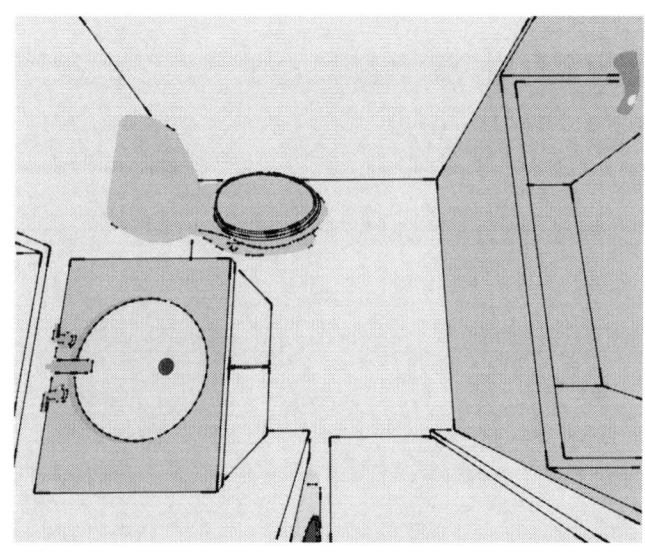

Bathroom

Tiny House #88 - Elevations

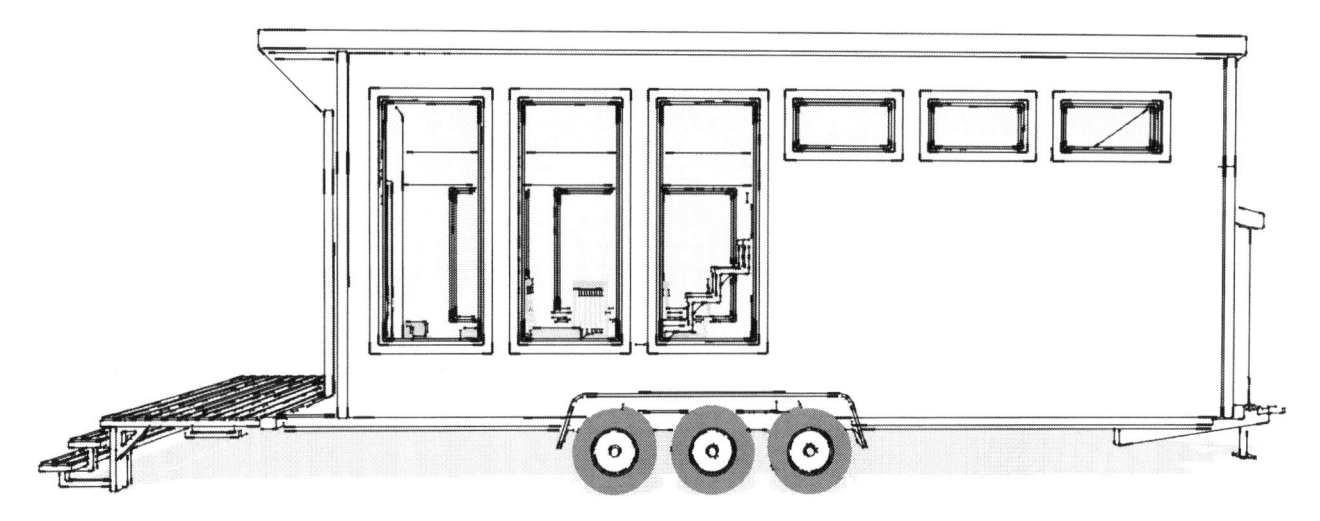

Right

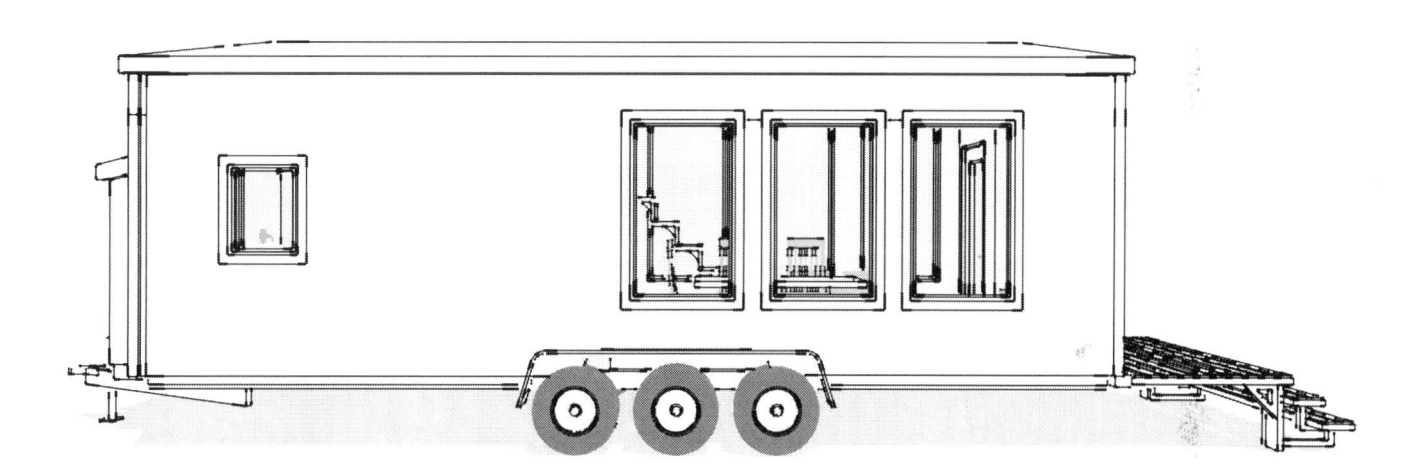

Left

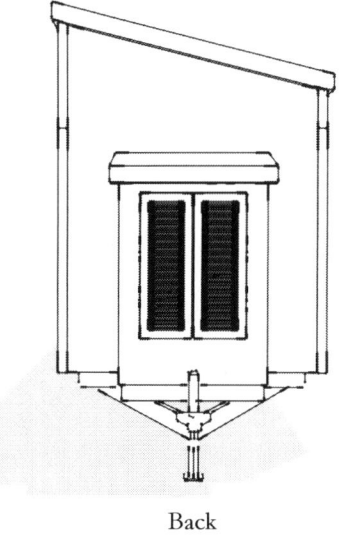

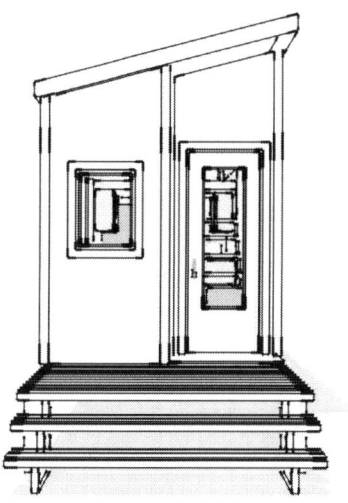

Back

Front

#89

Tiny House #89 - Overview

Front Right

Summary:

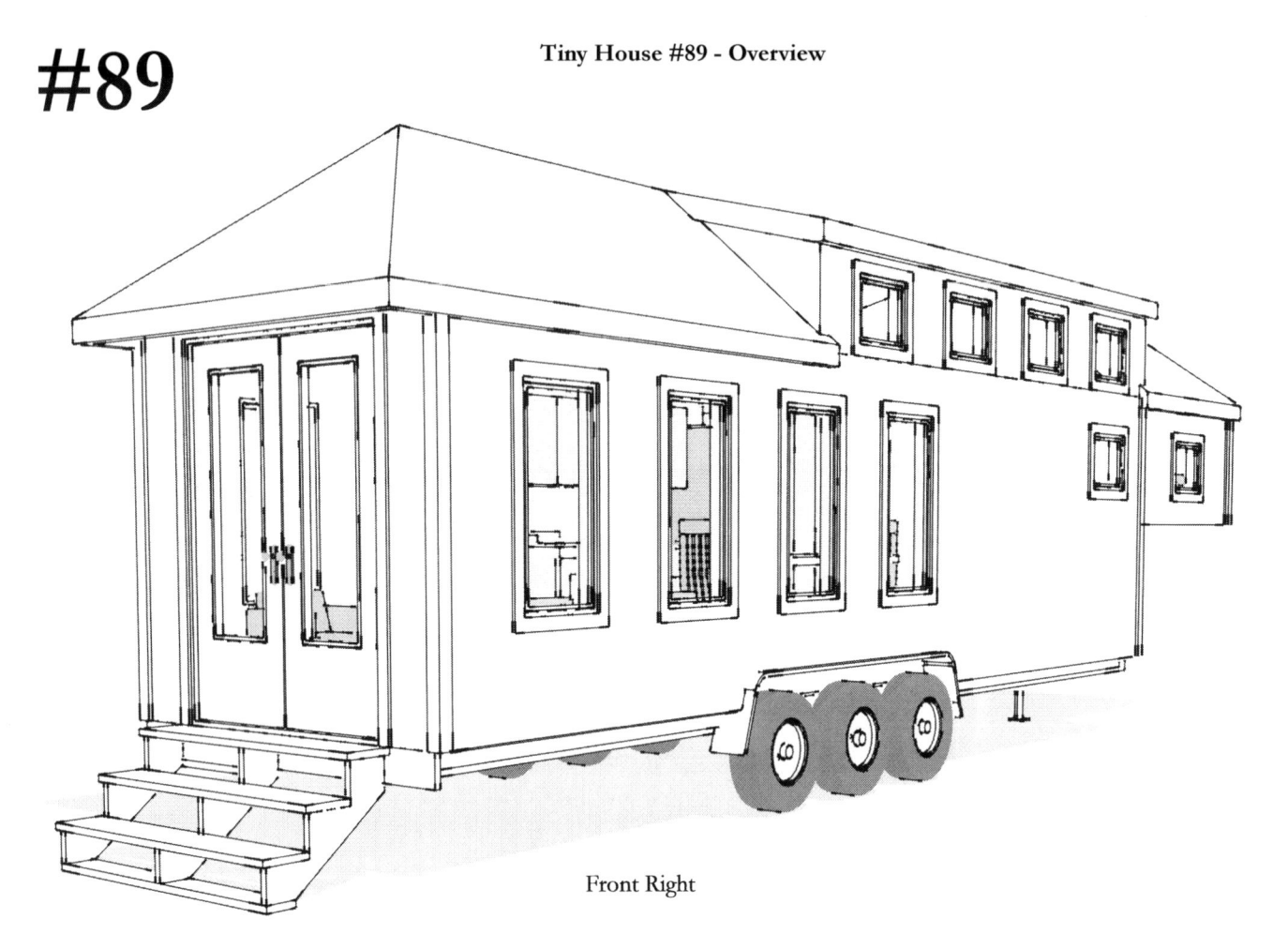

Past the French doors is a large combination living room, dining room and kitchen with plenty of seating. At the end of the room is a ladder to a small loft. Down a hallway under the loft is storage, a laundry closet, bathroom, and steps up to a queen bed in the gooseneck loft.

Features:

28-Foot Tiny House on Wheels
Hip Roof with Shed Dormers
Sleeps Three
Laundry
Bathroom with Shower

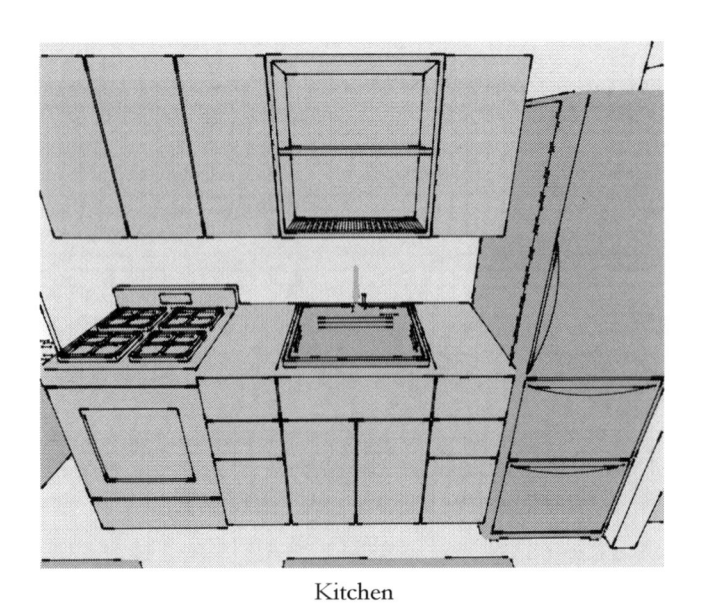

Kitchen

View from Loft

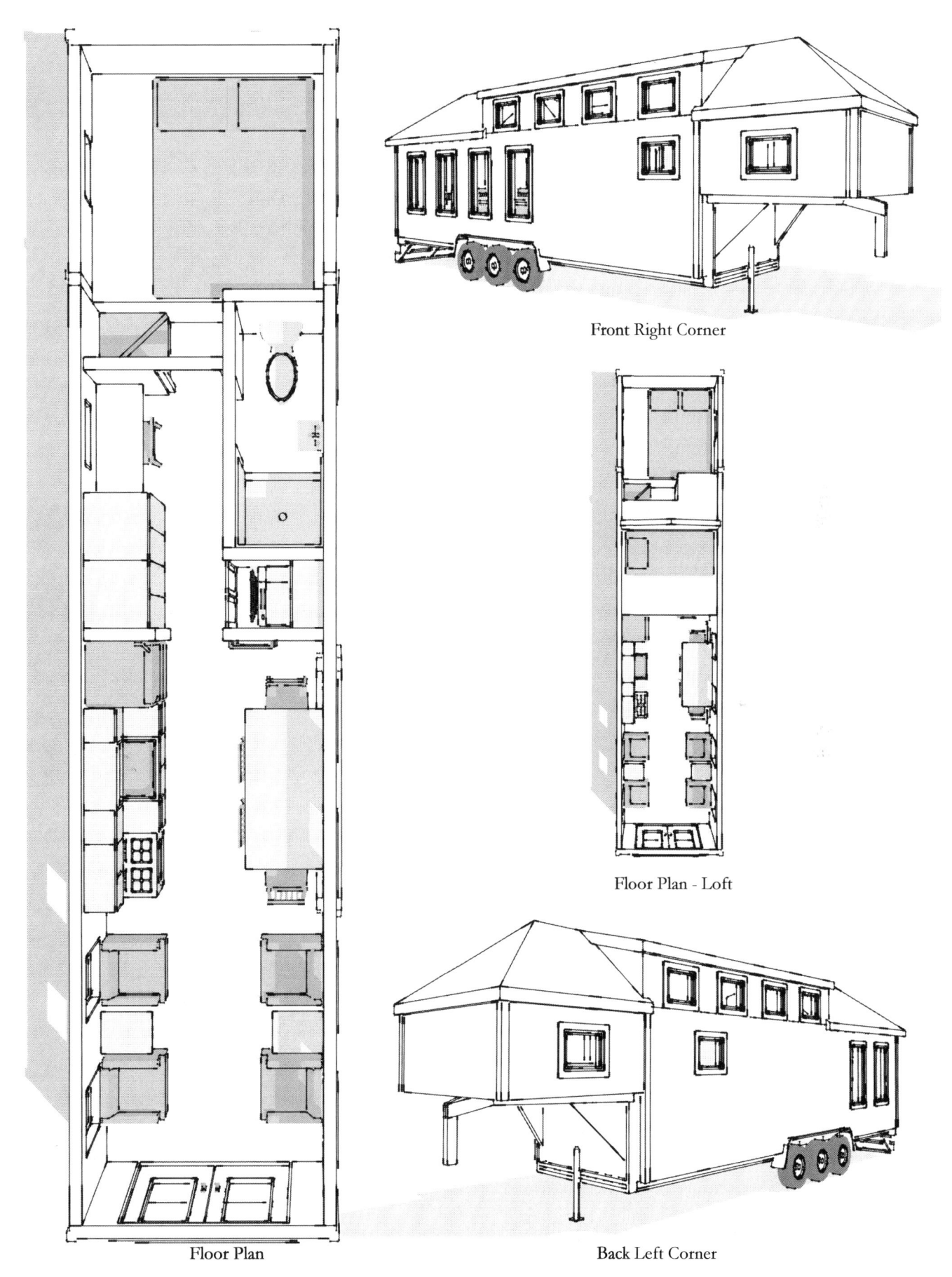

Tiny House #89 - Floor Plan & Exterior

Front Right Corner

Floor Plan - Loft

Floor Plan

Back Left Corner

Tiny House #89 - Interior Views

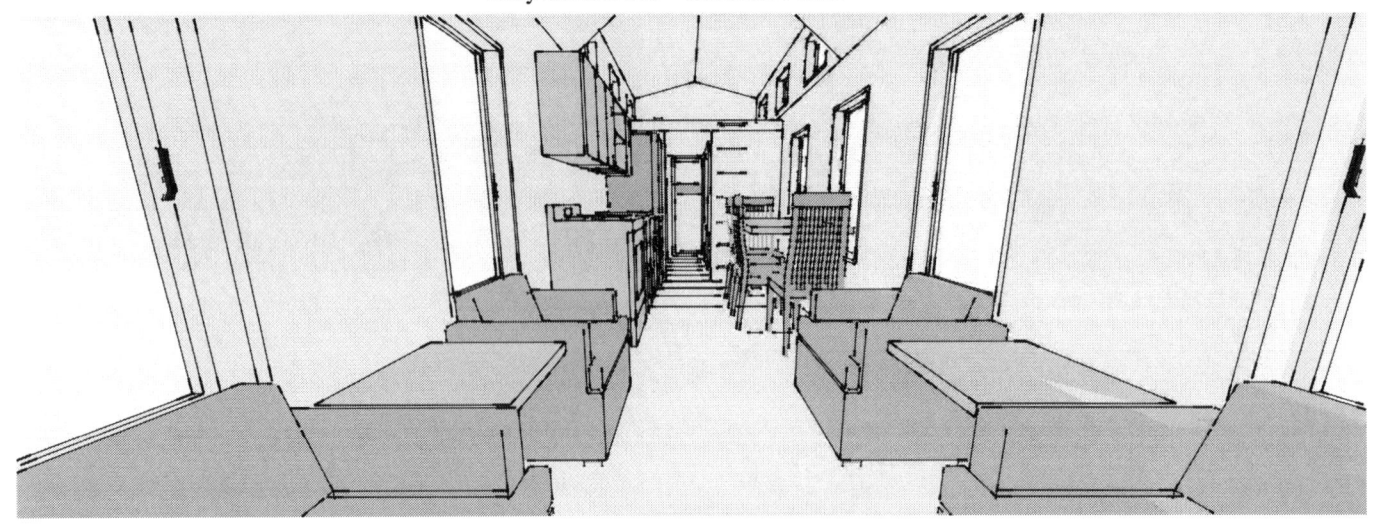

Interior from Entry

Interior from Kitchen

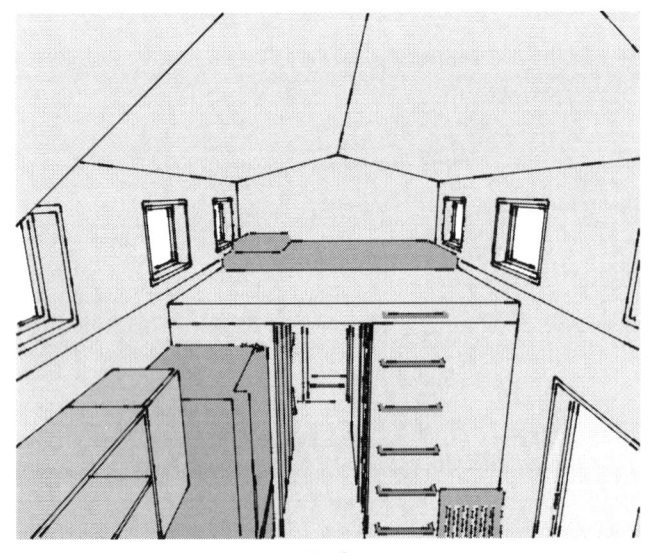

Loft

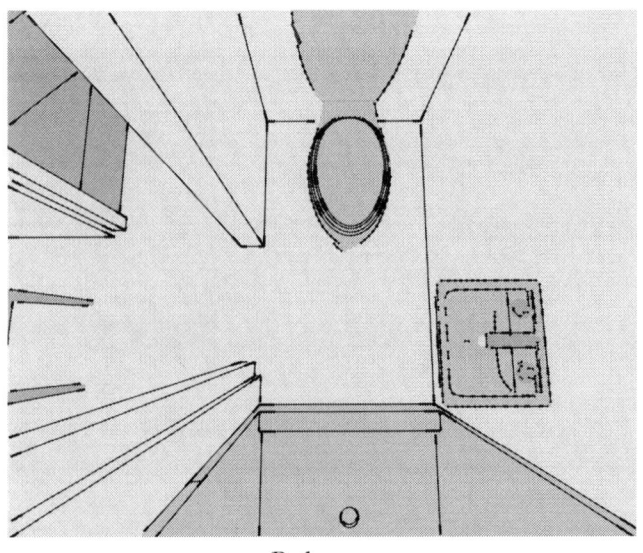

Bathroom

370

Tiny House #89 - Elevations

Right

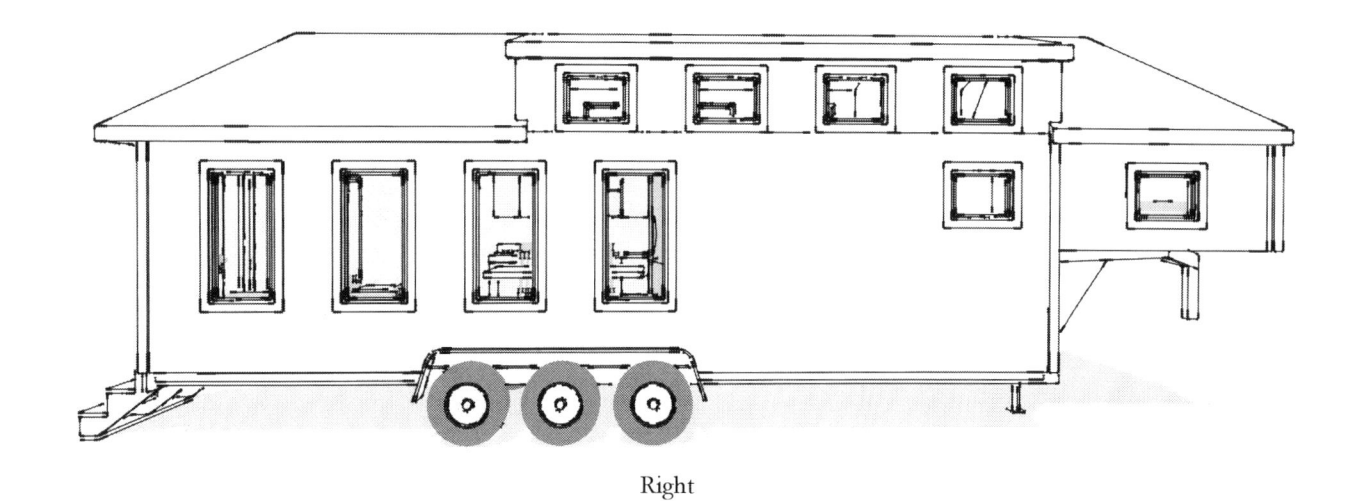

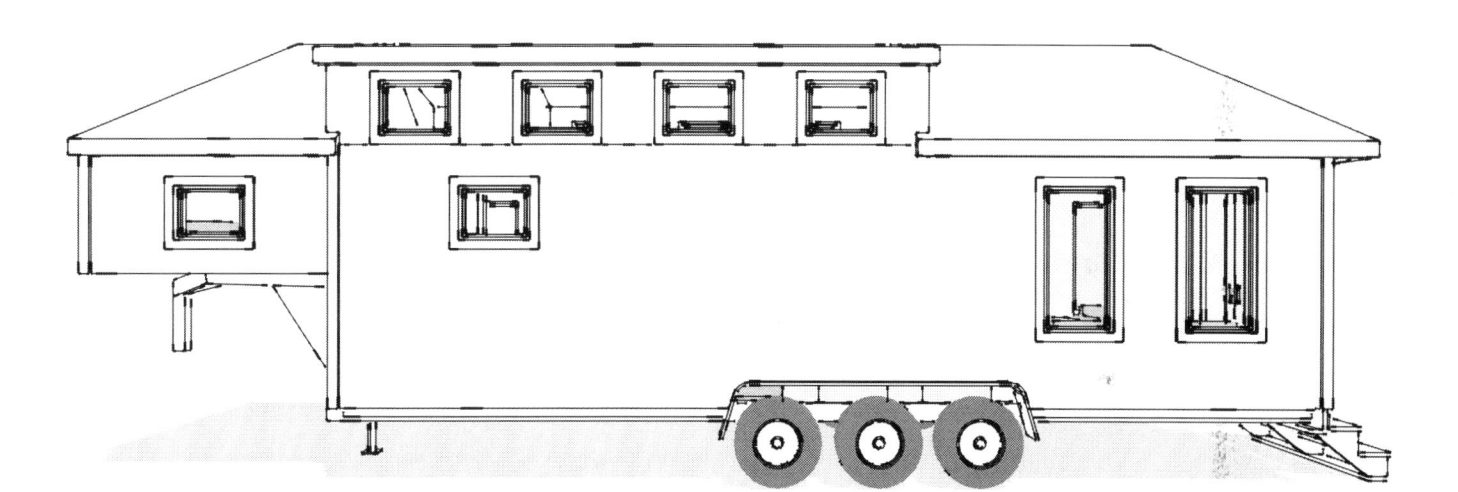

Left

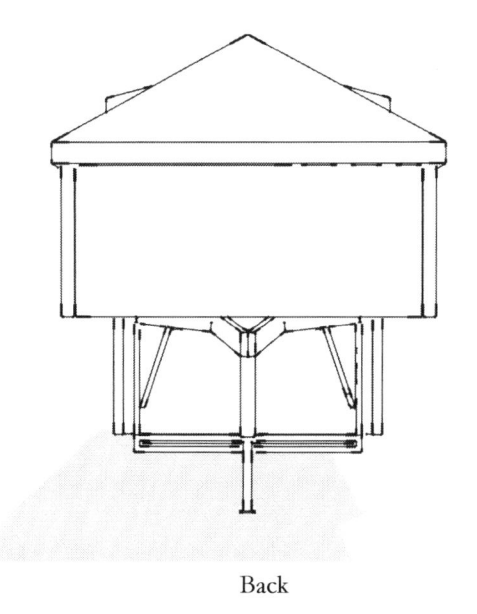

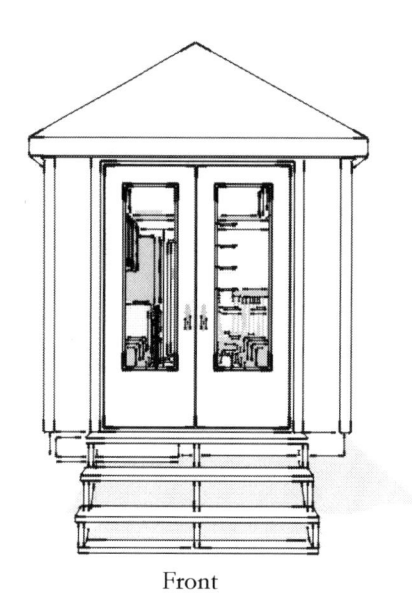

Back

Front

32-Foot Tiny House Designs

#90

Tiny House #90 - Overview

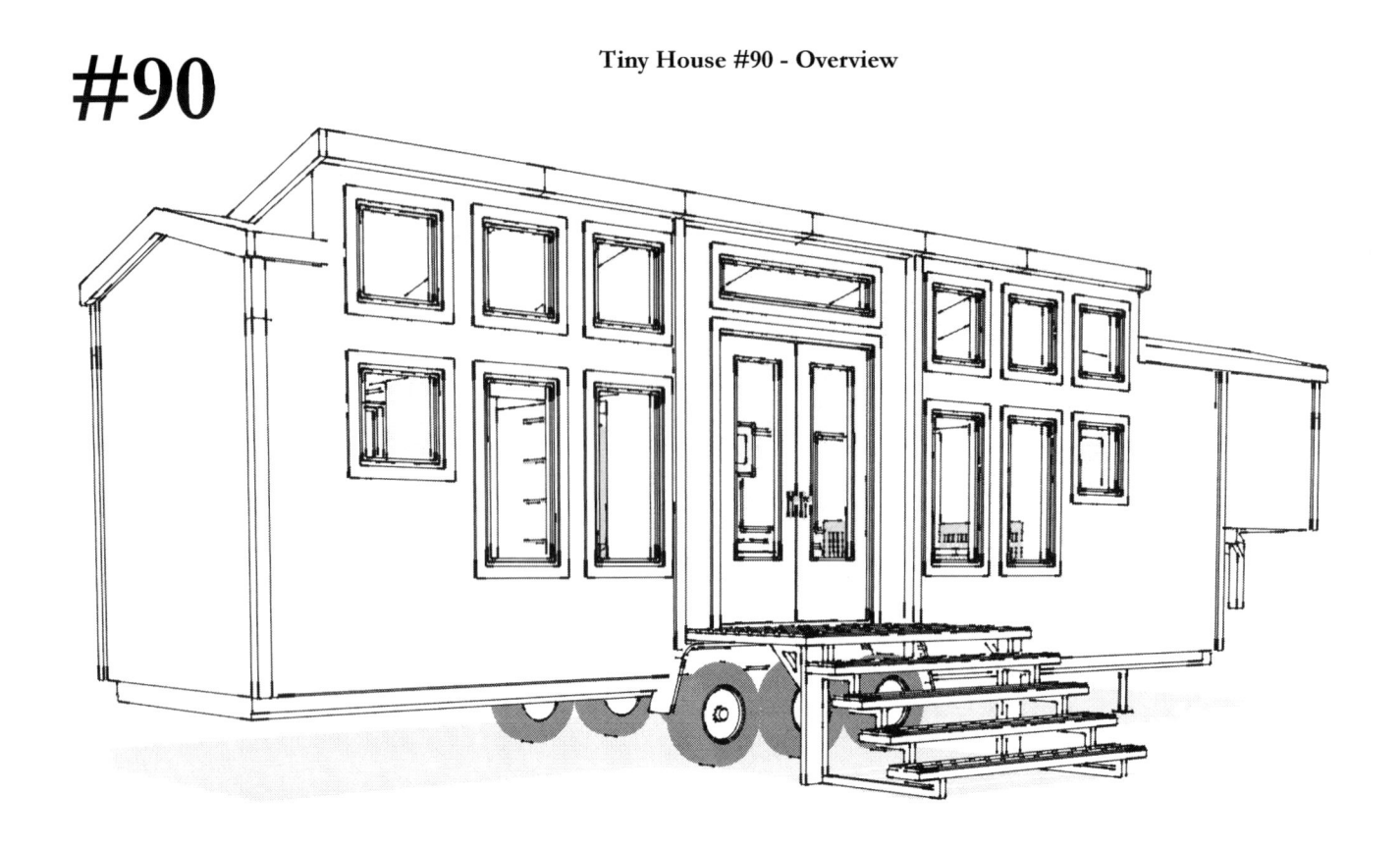

Front Right

Summary:

From the front door you step down into this home's kitchen. To the left is a small living room with a love seat and two comfy chairs. Past that is a bathroom with laundry. Above the living room is a loft with a queen bed. On the other side of the house is a dining room. Beyond the dining room is a hallway that leads to a second bathroom and the kid's room located over the trailer's gooseneck. The twin beds are on different levels giving the kids their own distinct yet combined spaces.

Features:

32-Foot Tiny House on Wheels
3/12 Shed Roof with Gable Ends
Two Bathrooms
Kids Room in Gooseneck
Living Room
Dining Room
Functional Kitchen

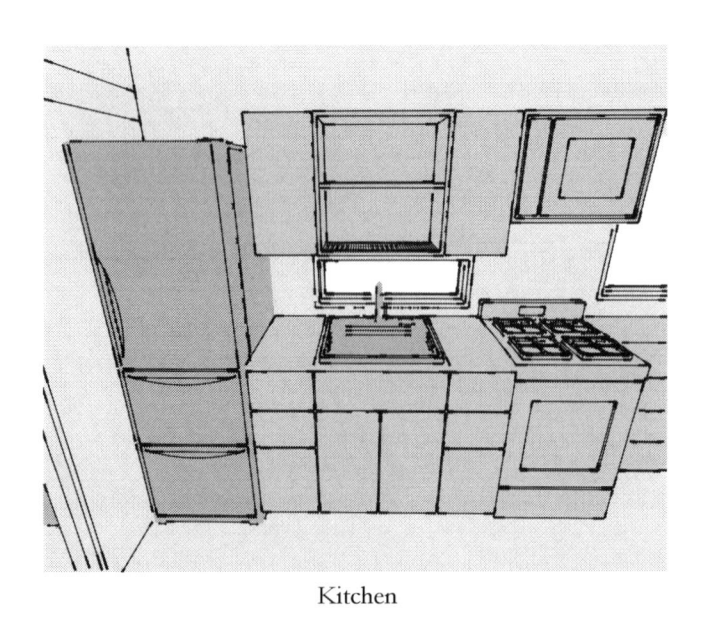

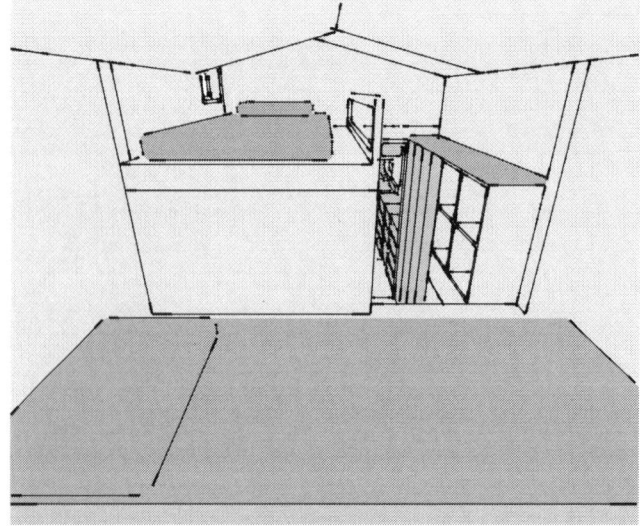

Kitchen

Kid's Room

Tiny House #90 - Floor Plan & Exterior

Front Right Corner

Floor Plan - Loft

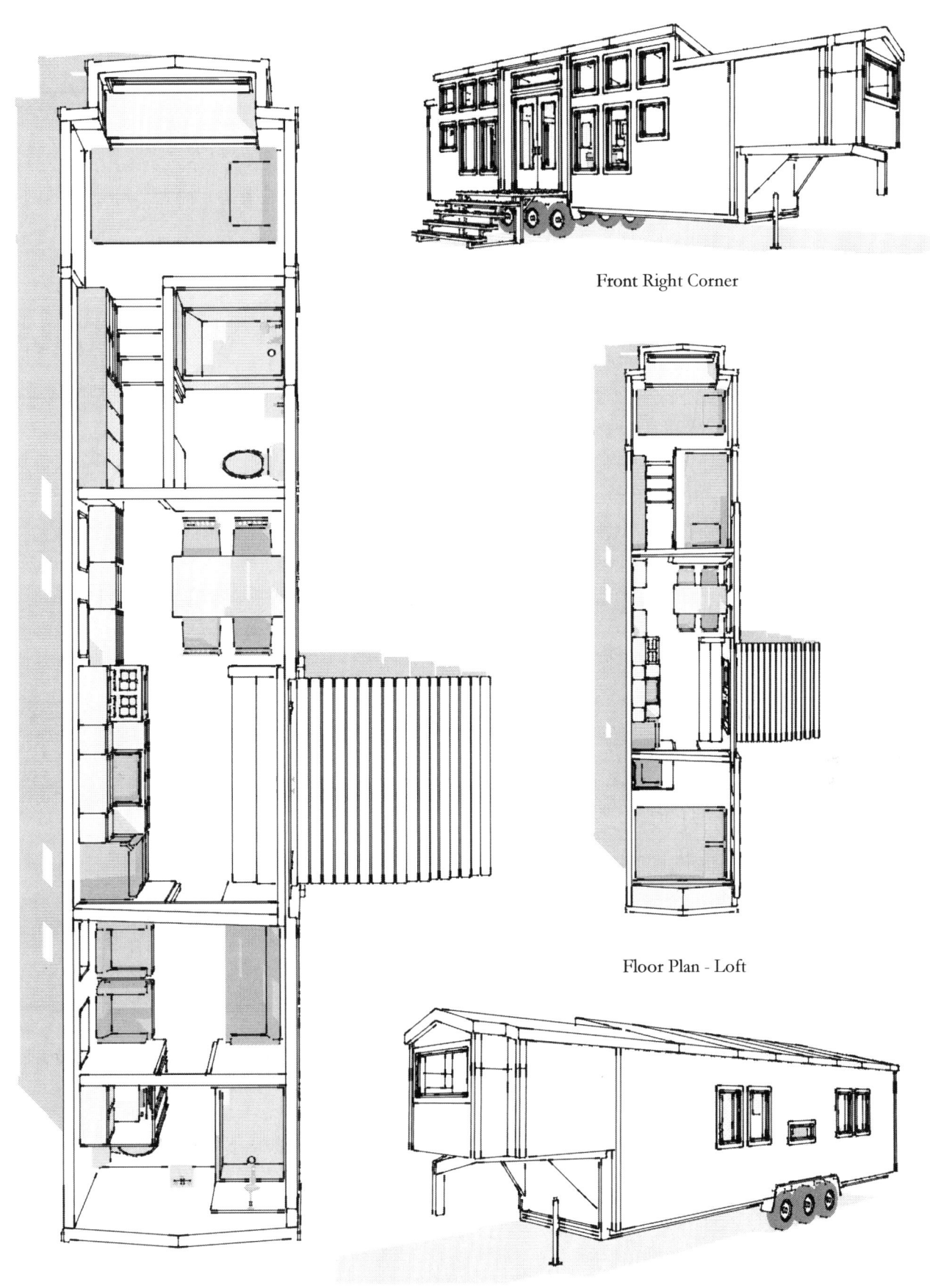

Floor Plan

Back Left Corner

Tiny House #90 - Interior Views

Interior from Living Room

Interior from Dining Room

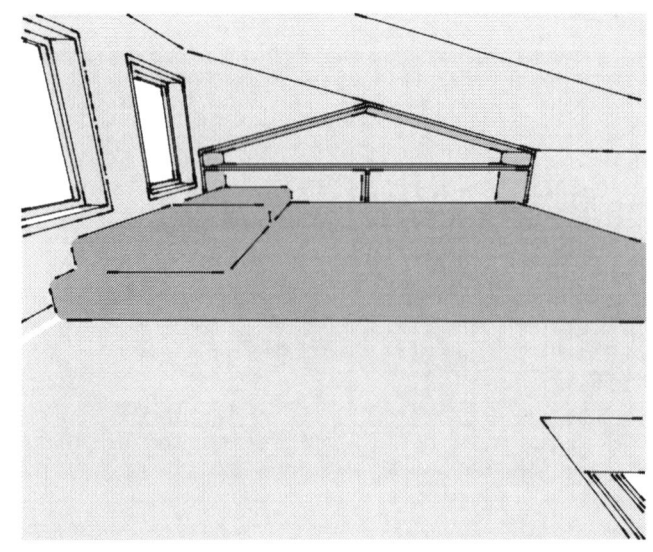

Loft

Bathroom

376

Tiny House #90 - Elevations

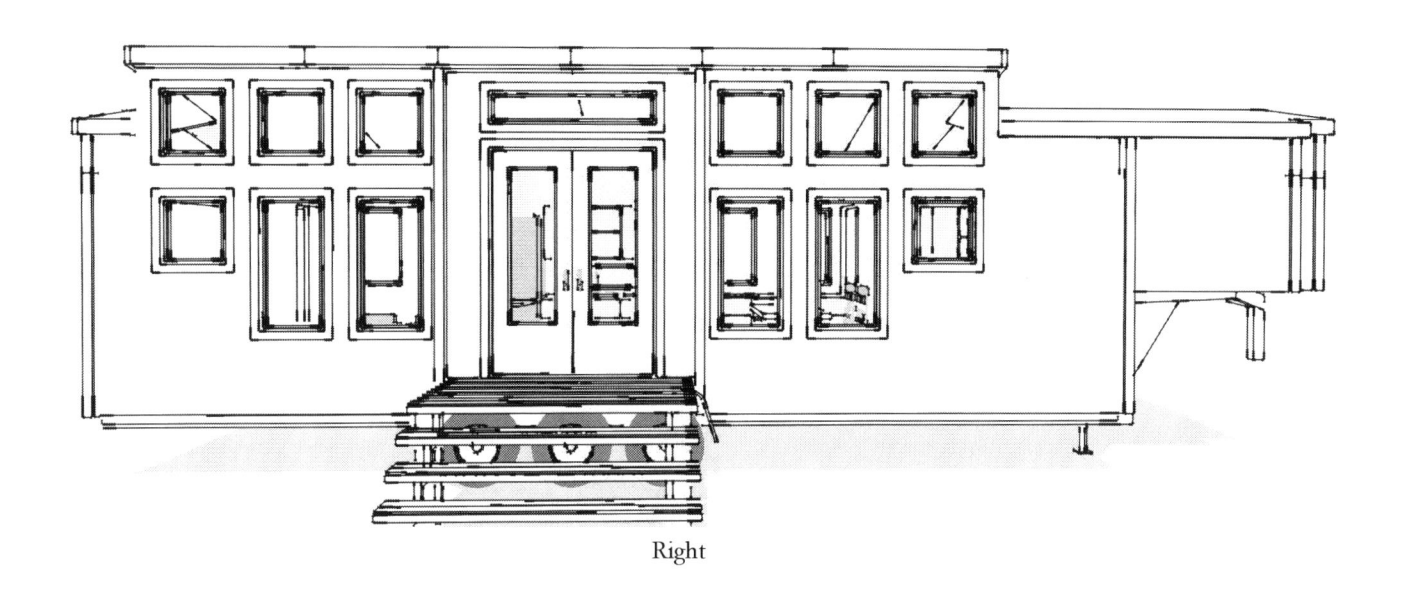

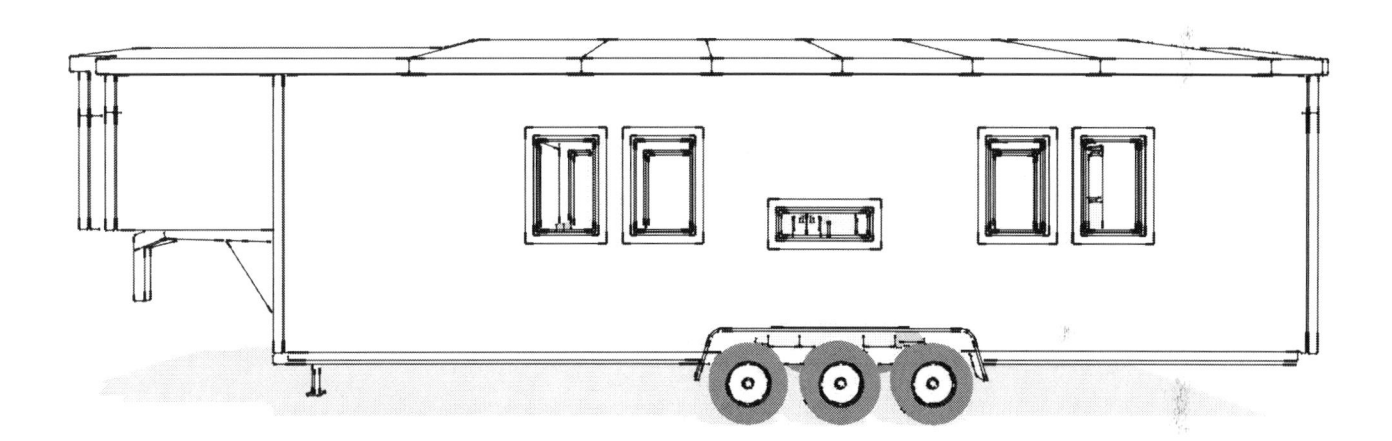

Right

Left

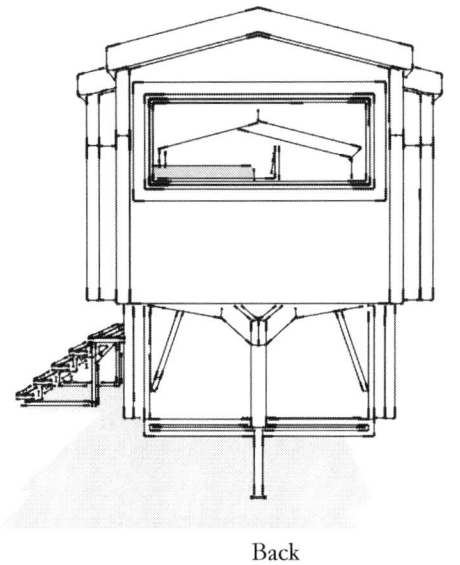

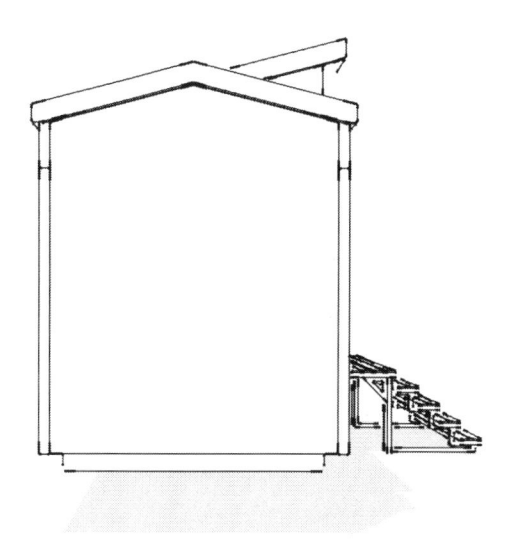

Back

Front

#91

Tiny House #91 - Overview

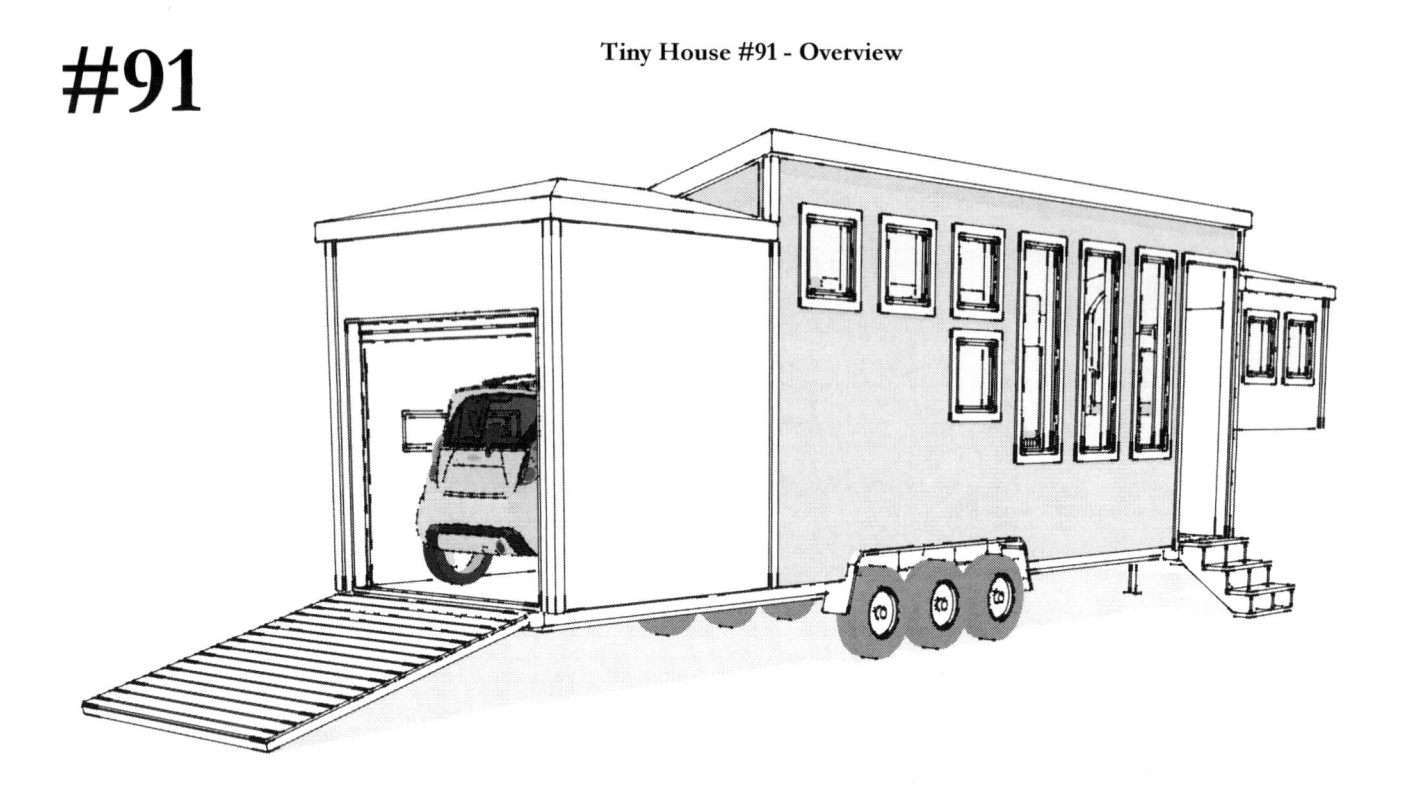

Front Right

Summary:

This toy hauler can carry a small car in it's 13-foot deep garage. You enter through a recessed entry on the side. It's recessed to provide a way to get out of the weather but also to accommodate the fold-up stairs while on the road. To the right, as you enter the house, is a bedroom in the gooseneck loft. To the left is the kitchen and table for four. Beyond that is the bathroom, laundry, and a pocket door into the garage. Above the bathroom and part of the garage is a loft with two twin beds.

Features:

32-Foot Tiny House on Wheels
3/12 Shed Roof with Hip Roof Ends
Garage
Bathroom with Tub
Recessed Side Entry
Queen Bed in Gooseneck
Two Twin Beds in Loft
Laundry

Kitchen

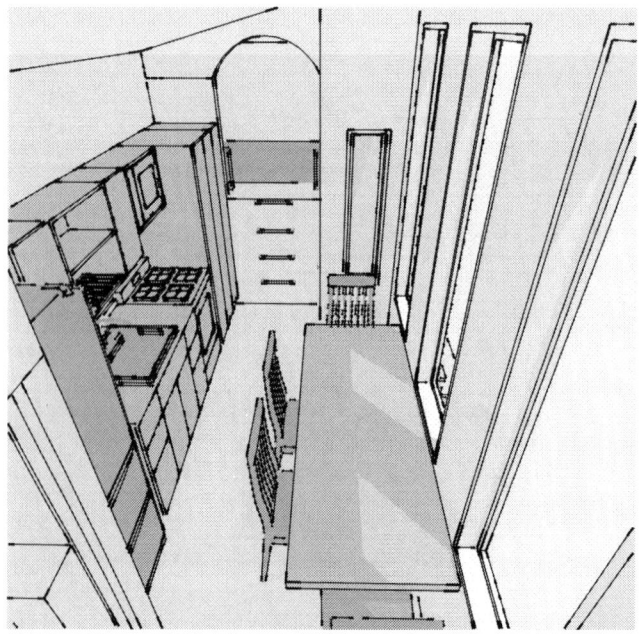

View from Loft

Tiny House #91 - Floor Plan & Exterior

Front Right Corner

Inside the Garage

Floor Plan - Loft

Garage Open

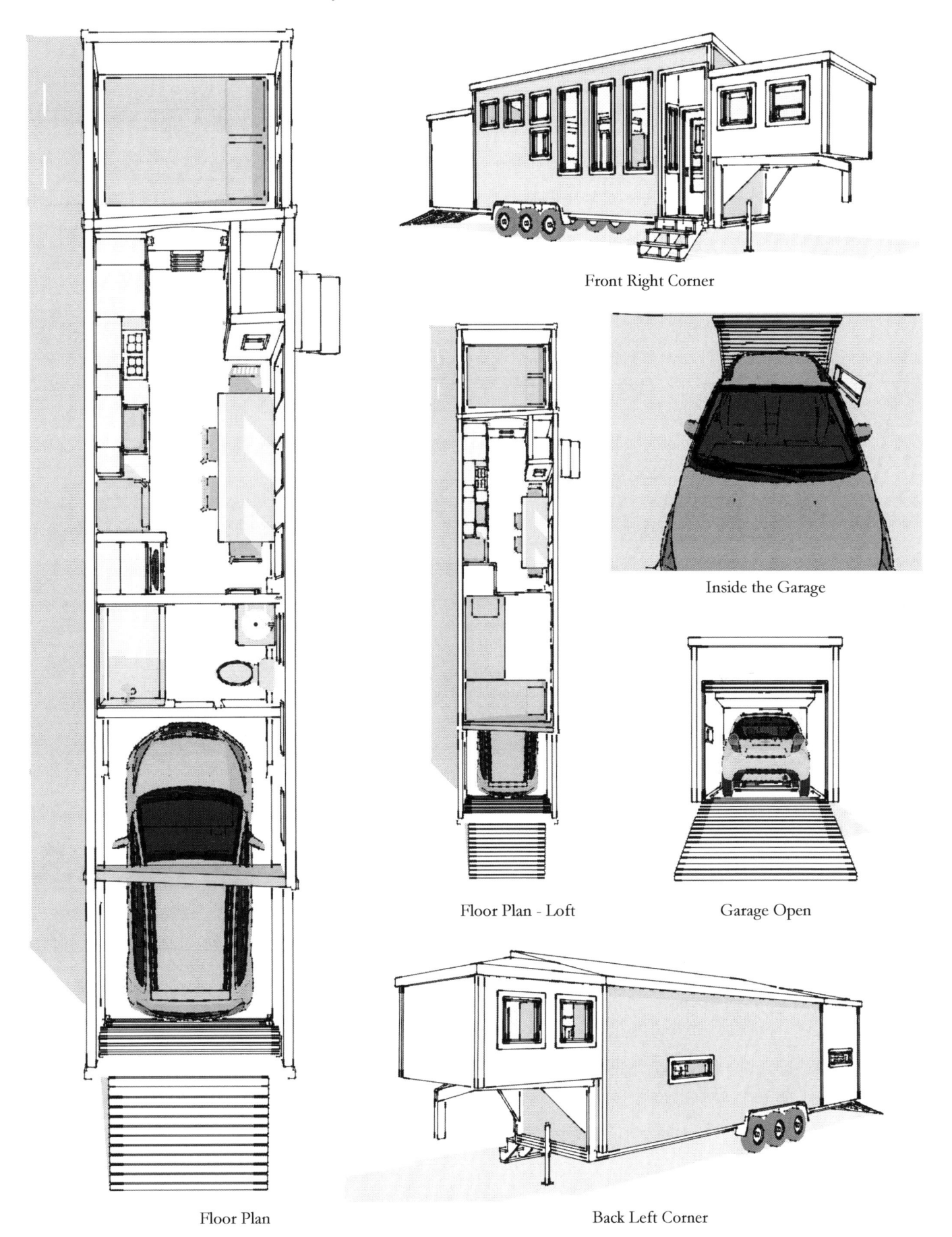

Floor Plan

Back Left Corner

Tiny House #91 - Interior Views

Interior from Bathroom

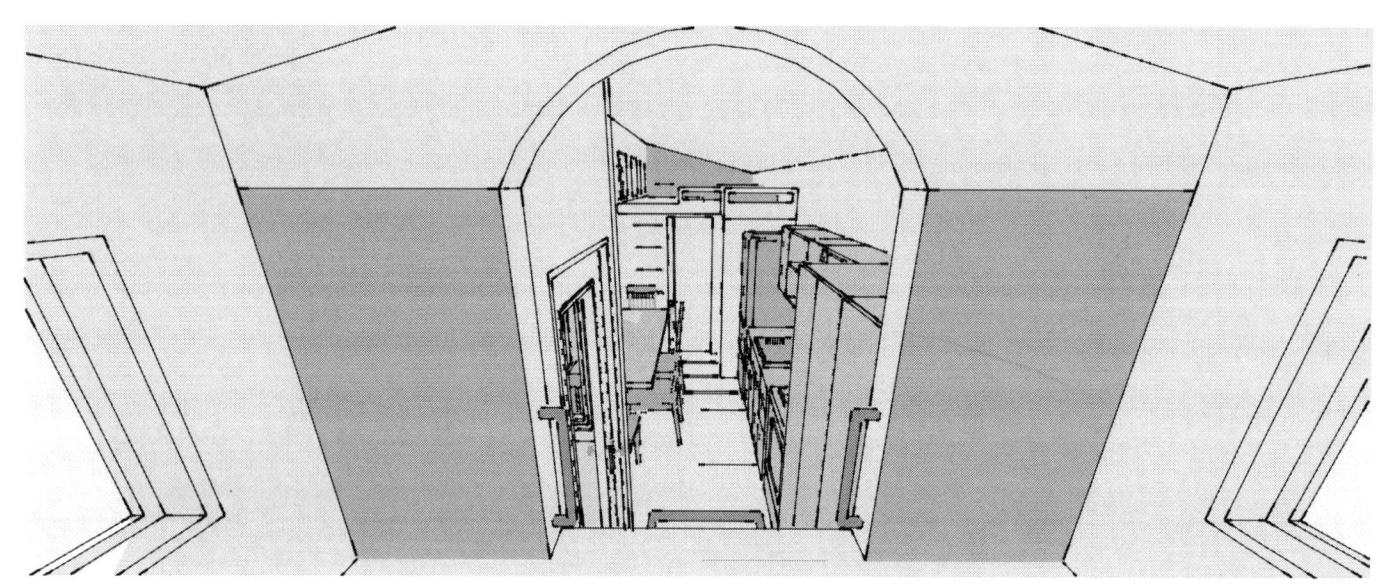

Interior from Gooseneck Loft

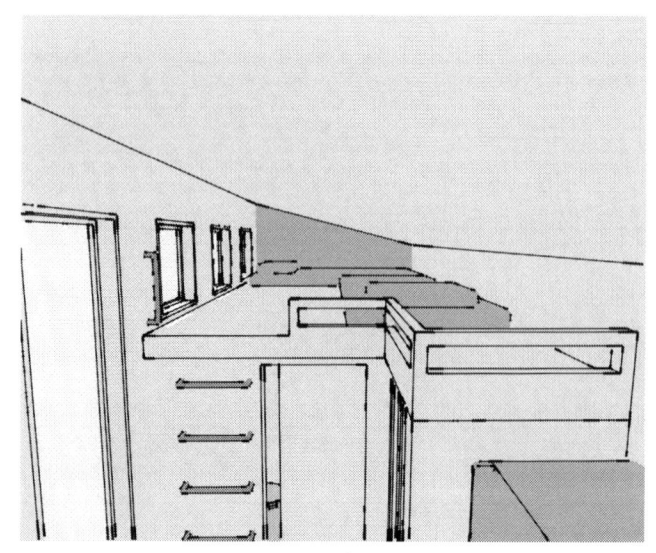

Loft

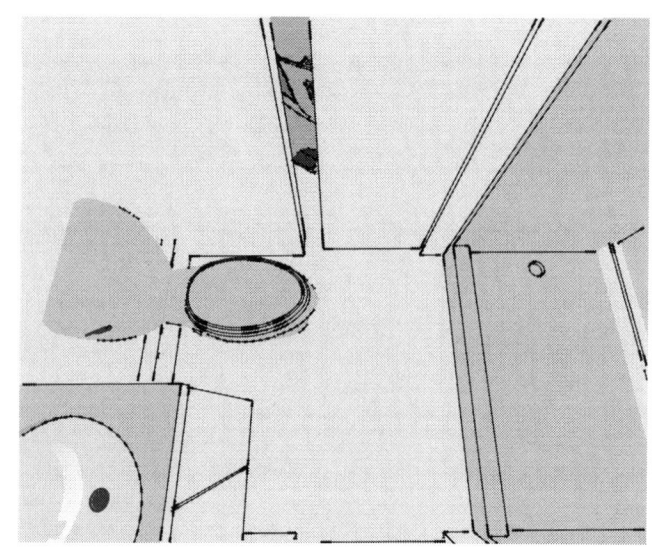

Bathroom

Tiny House #91 - Elevations

Right

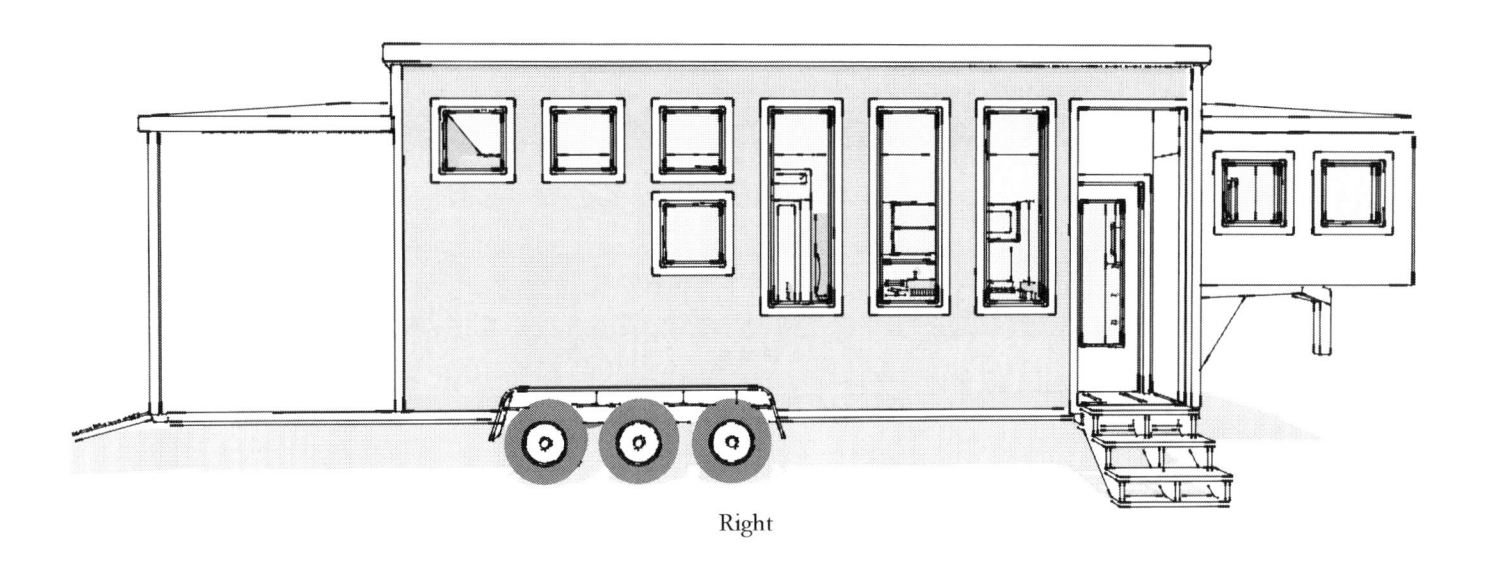

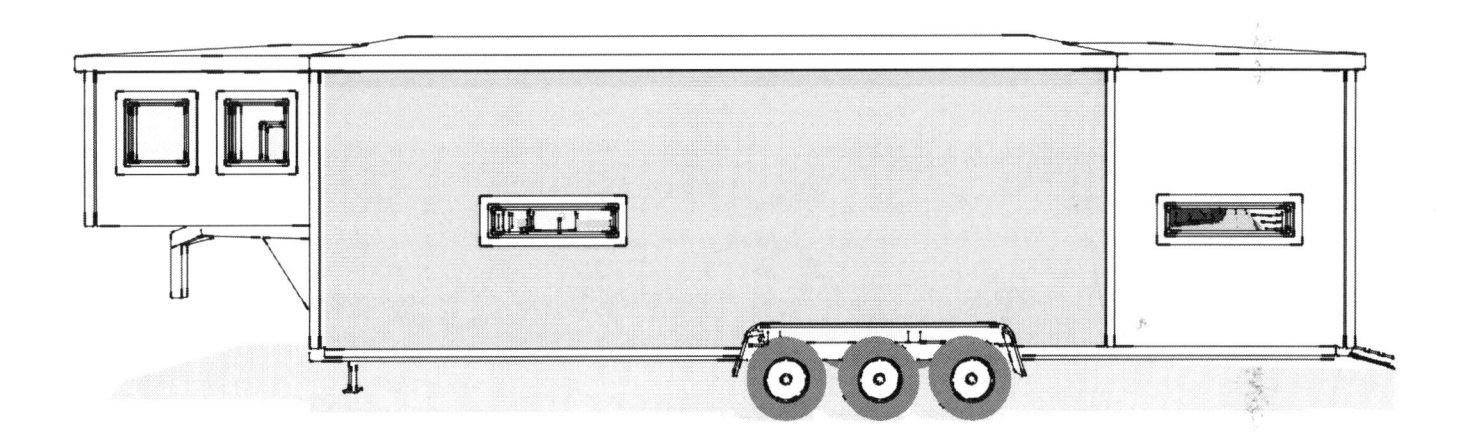

Left

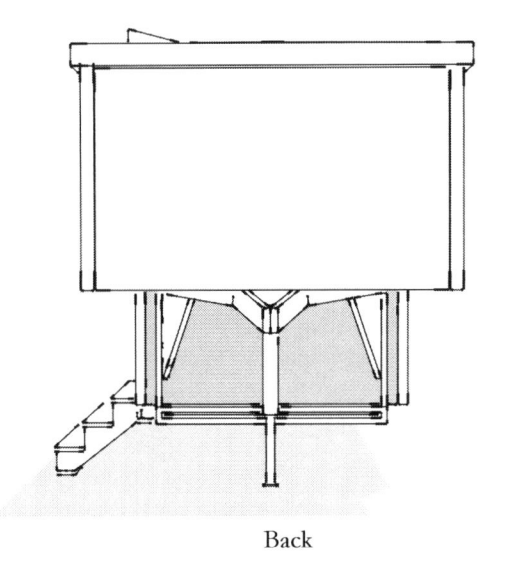

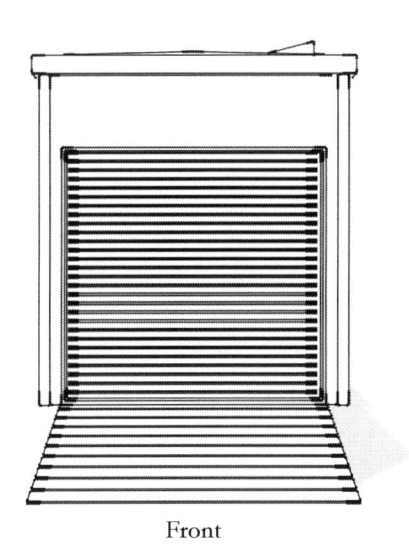

Back

Front

#92

Tiny House #92 - Overview

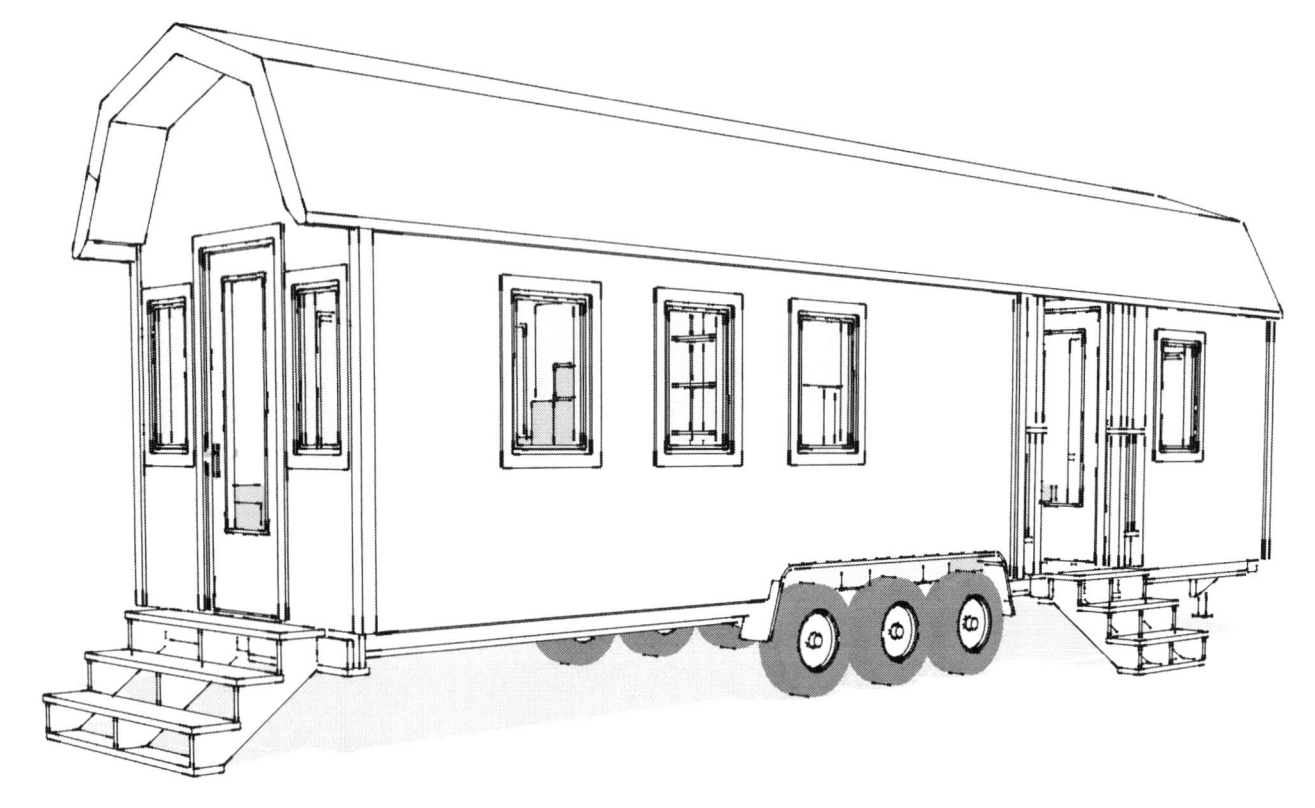

Front Right

Summary:

This tiny house has an usual feature, a 'Dogtrot' passthrough porch that separates an office from the rest of the house. The idea is that some people may want to work from home but will want to do that in a space that's completely separate. On the house side is a functional kitchen with all the essentials, small bathroom, sleeping loft, two comfy chairs, a table for three, and a laundry closet. The office side is just a simple room with a desk and chairs.

Features:

32-Foot Tiny House on Wheels
Gambrel Roof
Live-Work Space
Dogtrot Passthrough Covered Porch
Functional Kitchen
Sleeps Two
Laundry
Small Bathroom

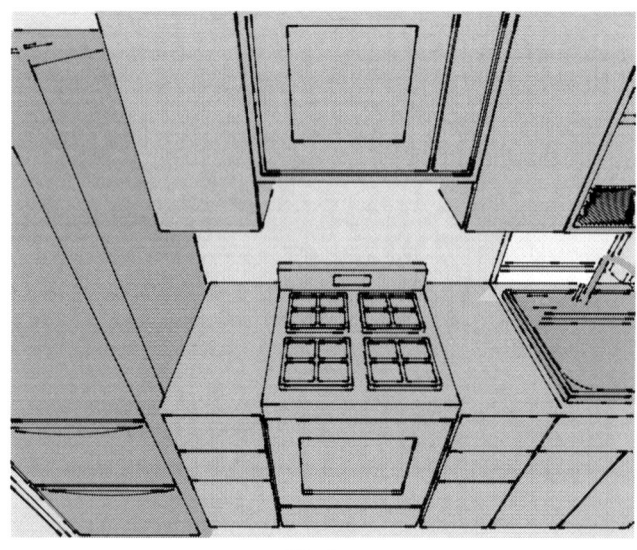

Kitchen

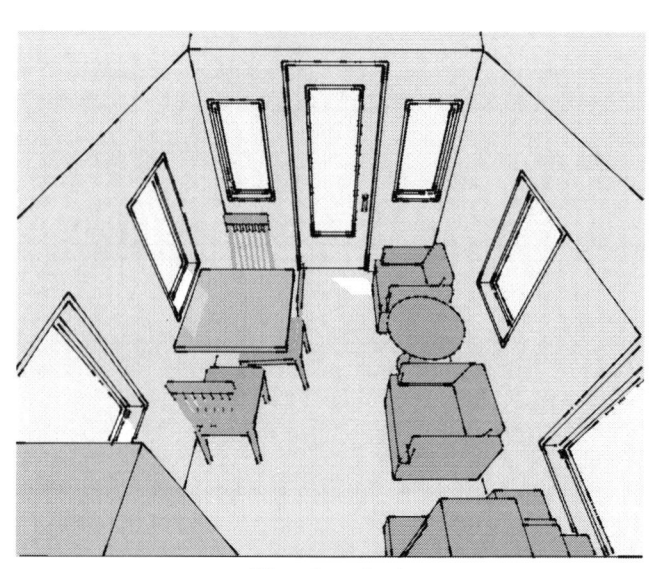

View from Loft

Tiny House #92 - Floor Plan & Exterior

Front Right Corner

Pass-through

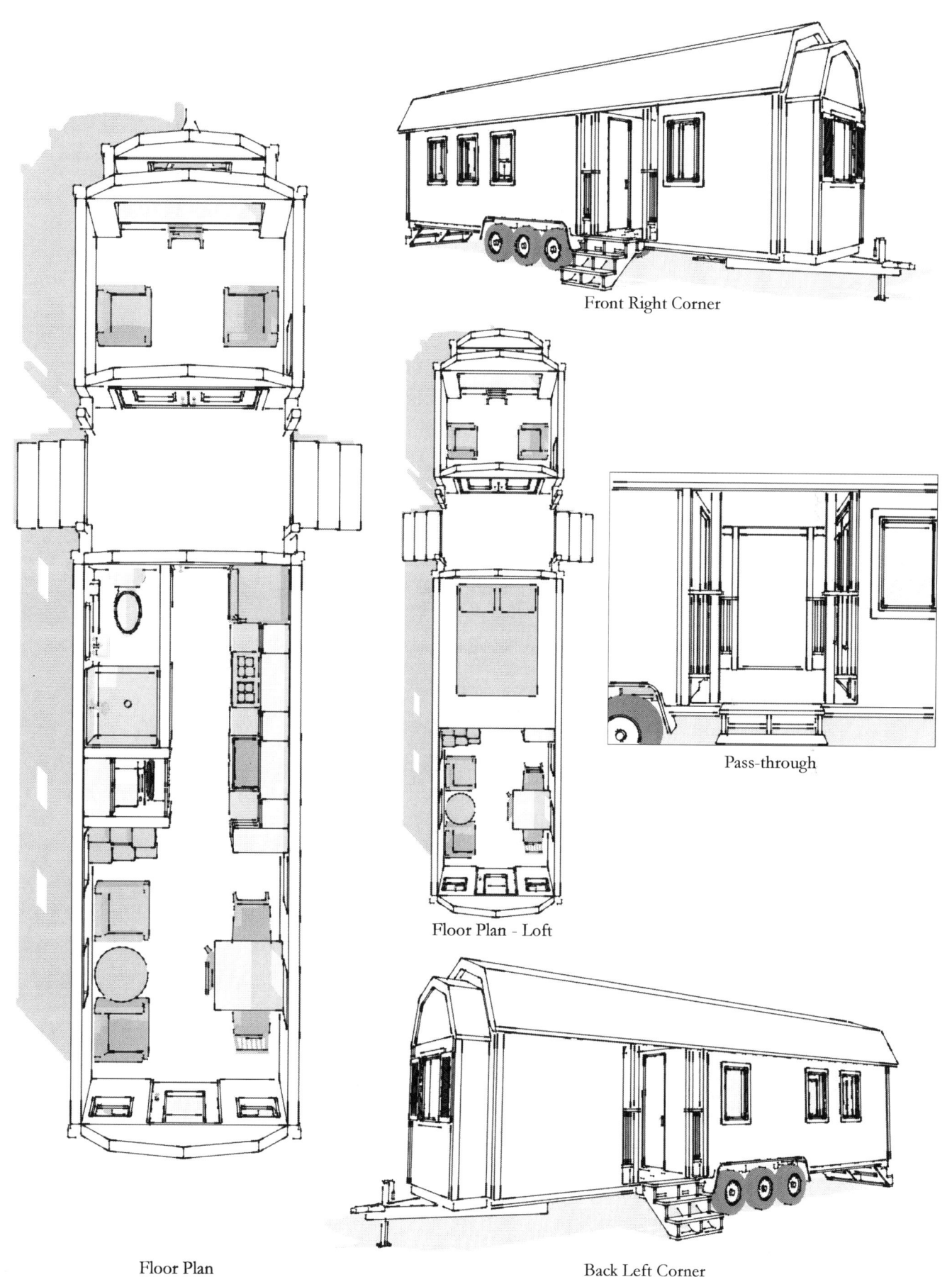

Floor Plan - Loft

Floor Plan

Back Left Corner

Tiny House #92 - Interior Views

Interior from Entry

Interior from Kitchen

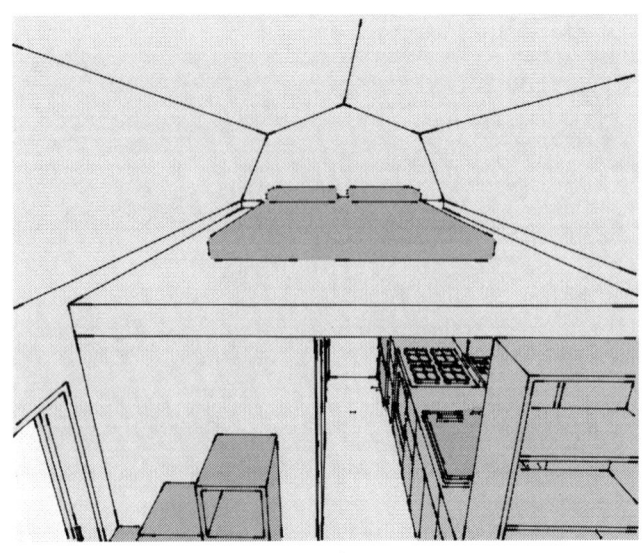

Loft

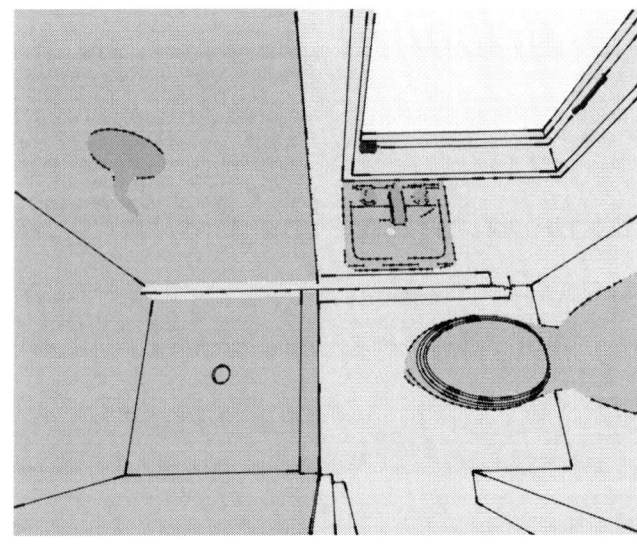

Bathroom

Tiny House #92 - Elevations

Right

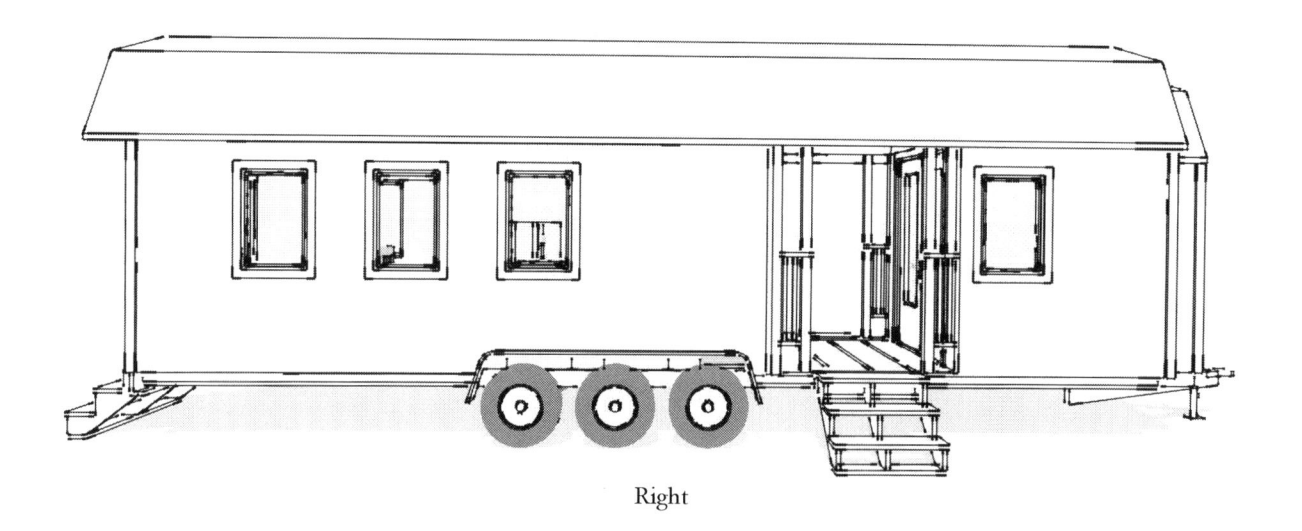

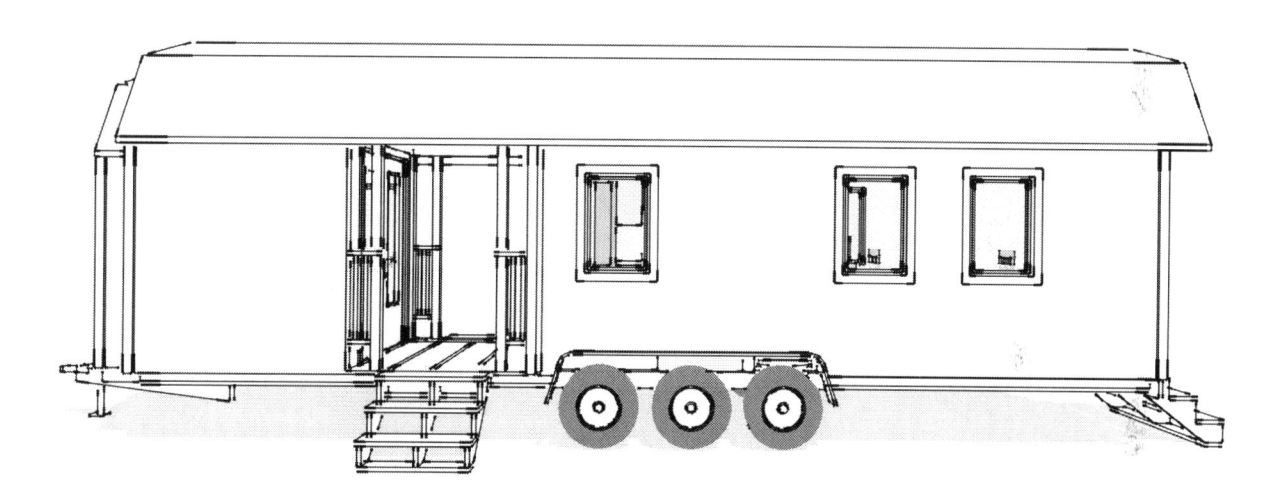

Left

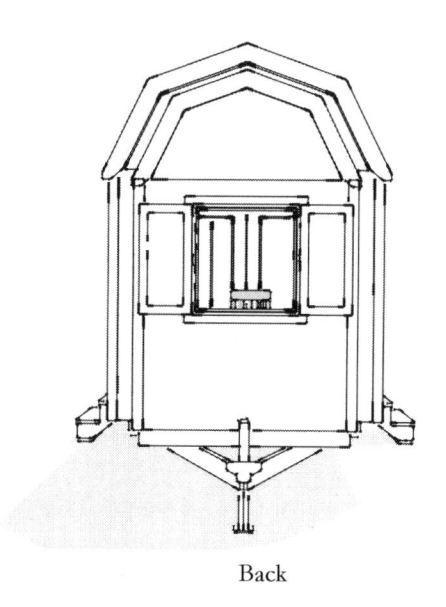

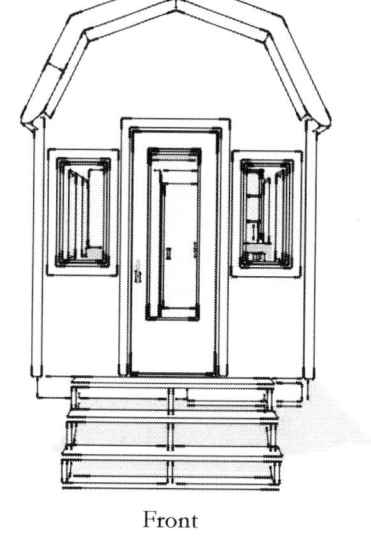

Back

Front

#93

Tiny House #93 - Overview

Front Right

Summary:

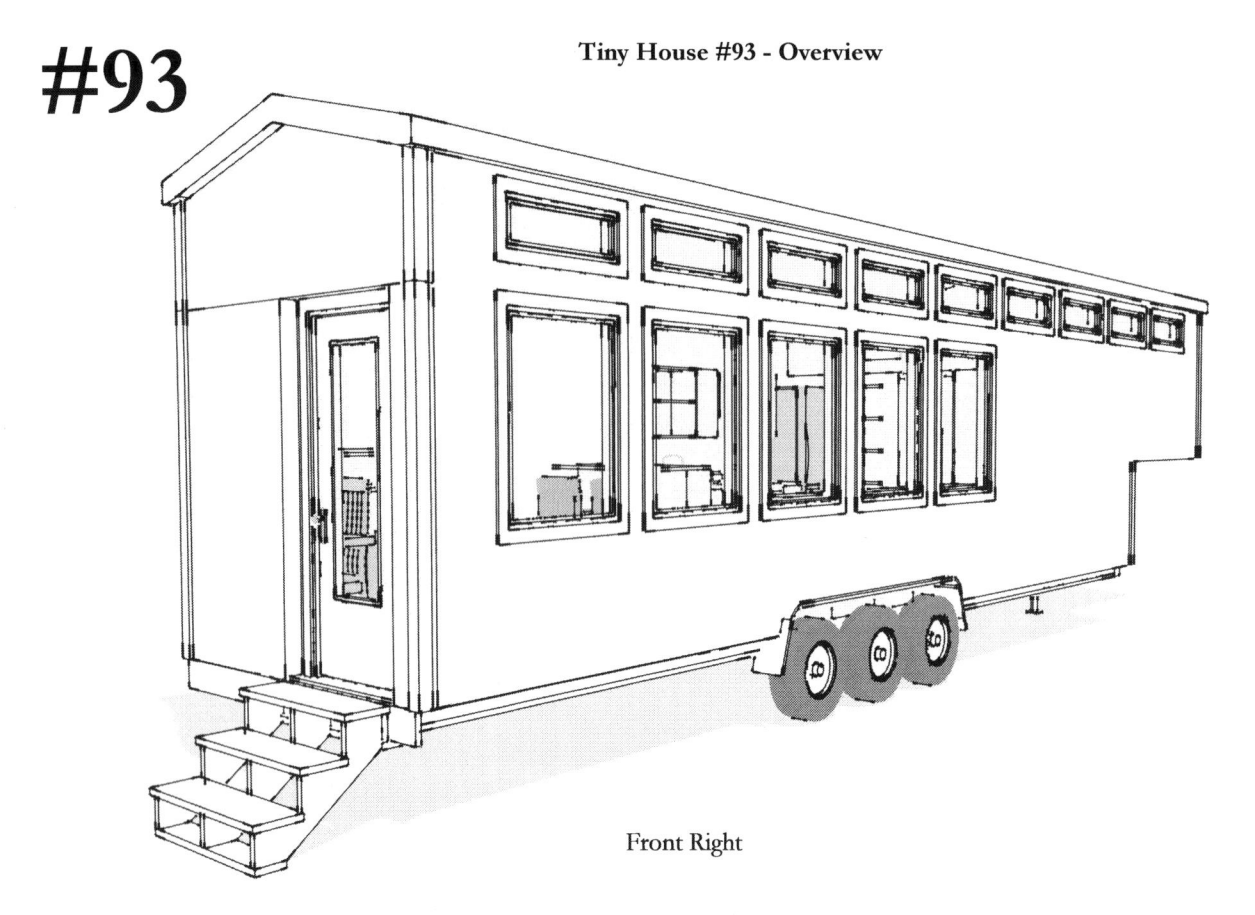

The clerestory that runs the full length of this tiny house, combined with the large windows would make this house feel huge. Truth be told, in tiny house terms, it is huge. It sleeps three, two in a queen bed in the gooseneck loft and one in a twin bed above the bathroom and hallway. The kitchen has all the essentials plus a breakfast bar with two stools. The living room has plenty of seating and a desk tucked into an alcove. The bathroom has a soaking tub, toilet, and sink.

Features:

32-Foot Tiny House on Wheels
High 3/12 Gable
Large Open Space with High Ceiling
   and Clerestory
Sleeps Three
Kitchen with Breakfast Counter
Sofa and Two Comfy Chairs
Desk in Alcove
Laundry

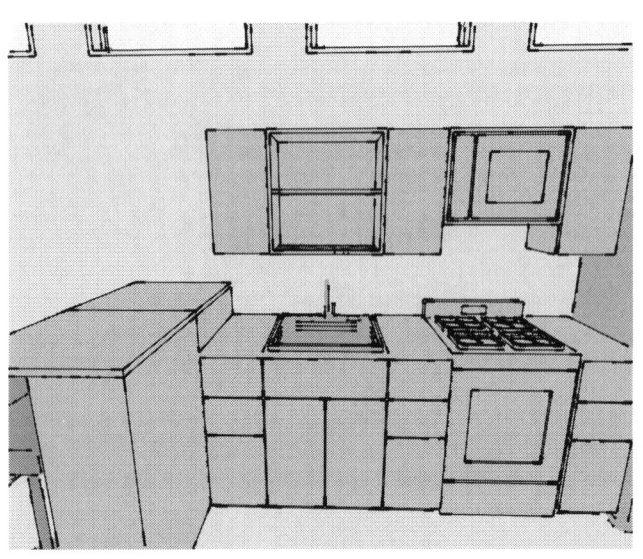

Kitchen

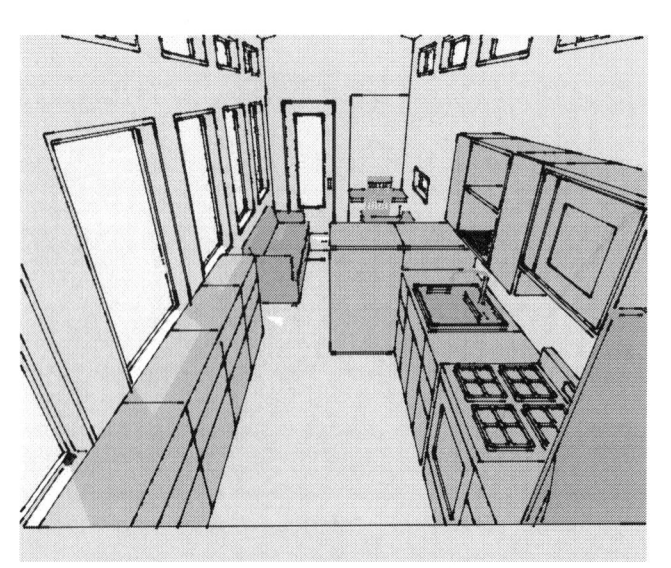

View from Loft

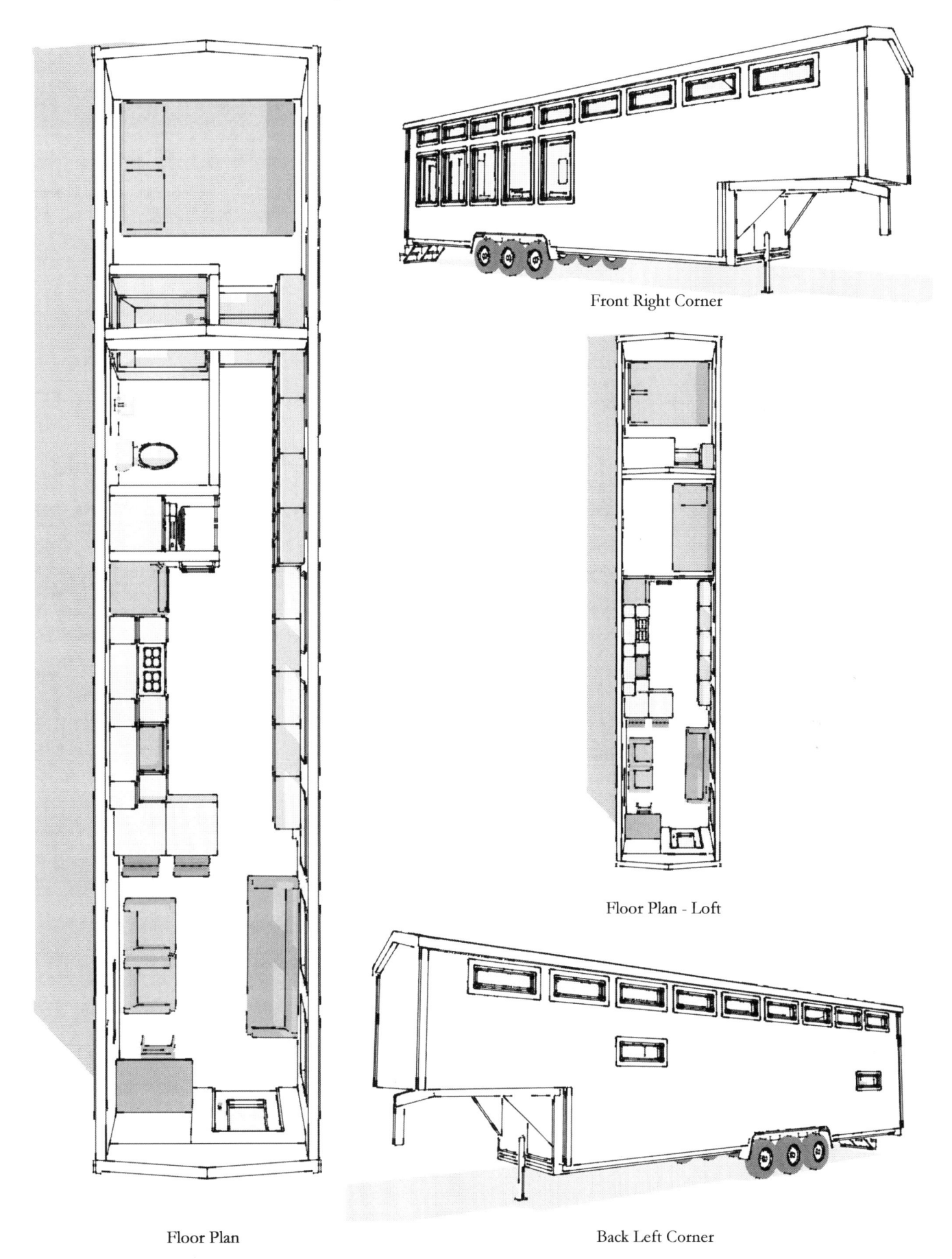

Tiny House #93 - Floor Plan & Exterior

Front Right Corner

Floor Plan - Loft

Floor Plan

Back Left Corner

Tiny House #93 - Interior Views

Interior from Entry

Interior from Kitchen

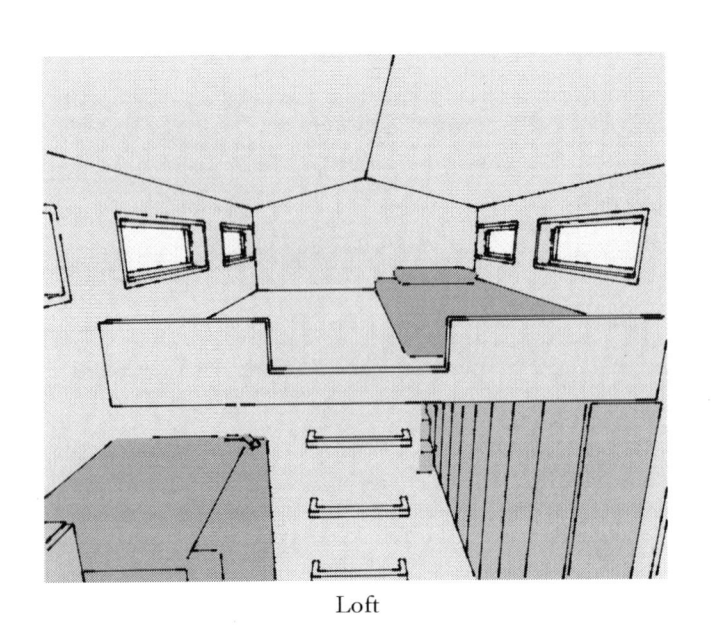

Loft

Bathroom

Tiny House #93 - Elevations

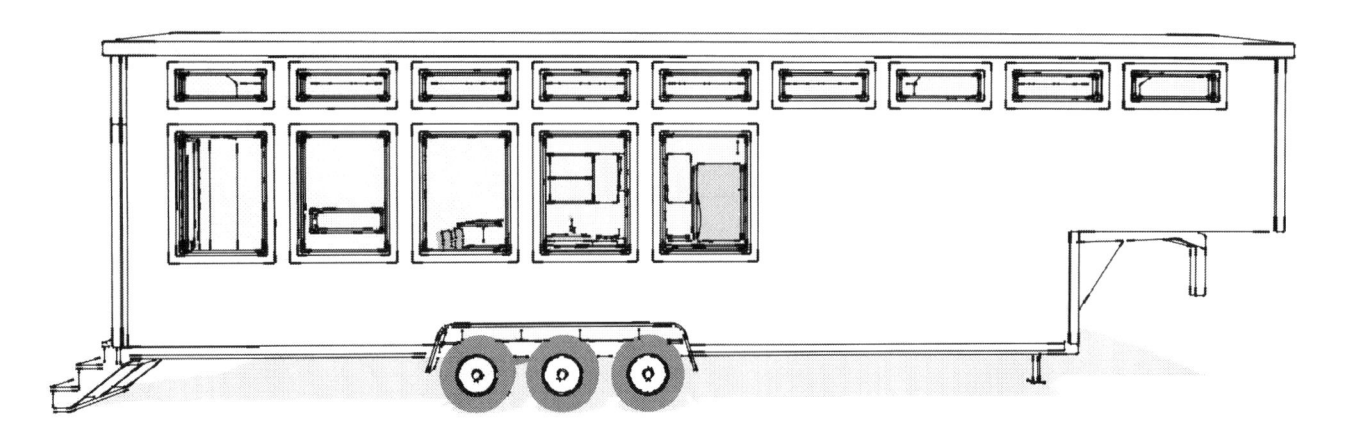

Right

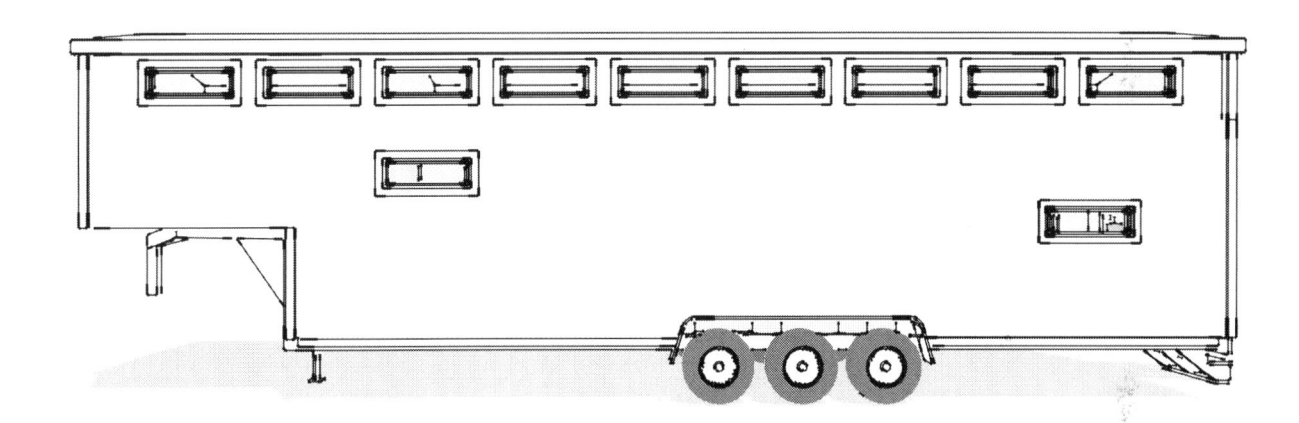

Left

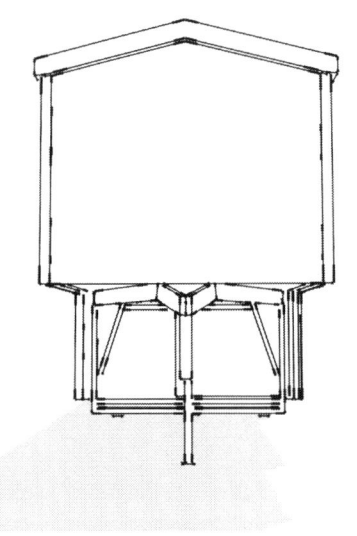

Back

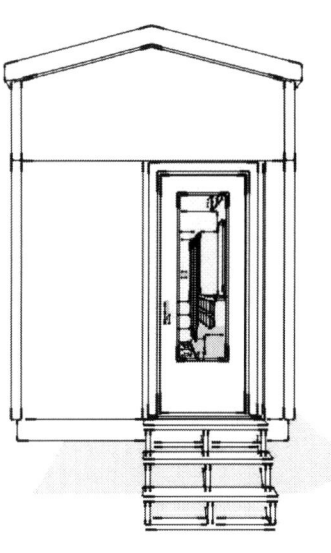

Front

#94

Tiny House #94 - Overview

Front Right

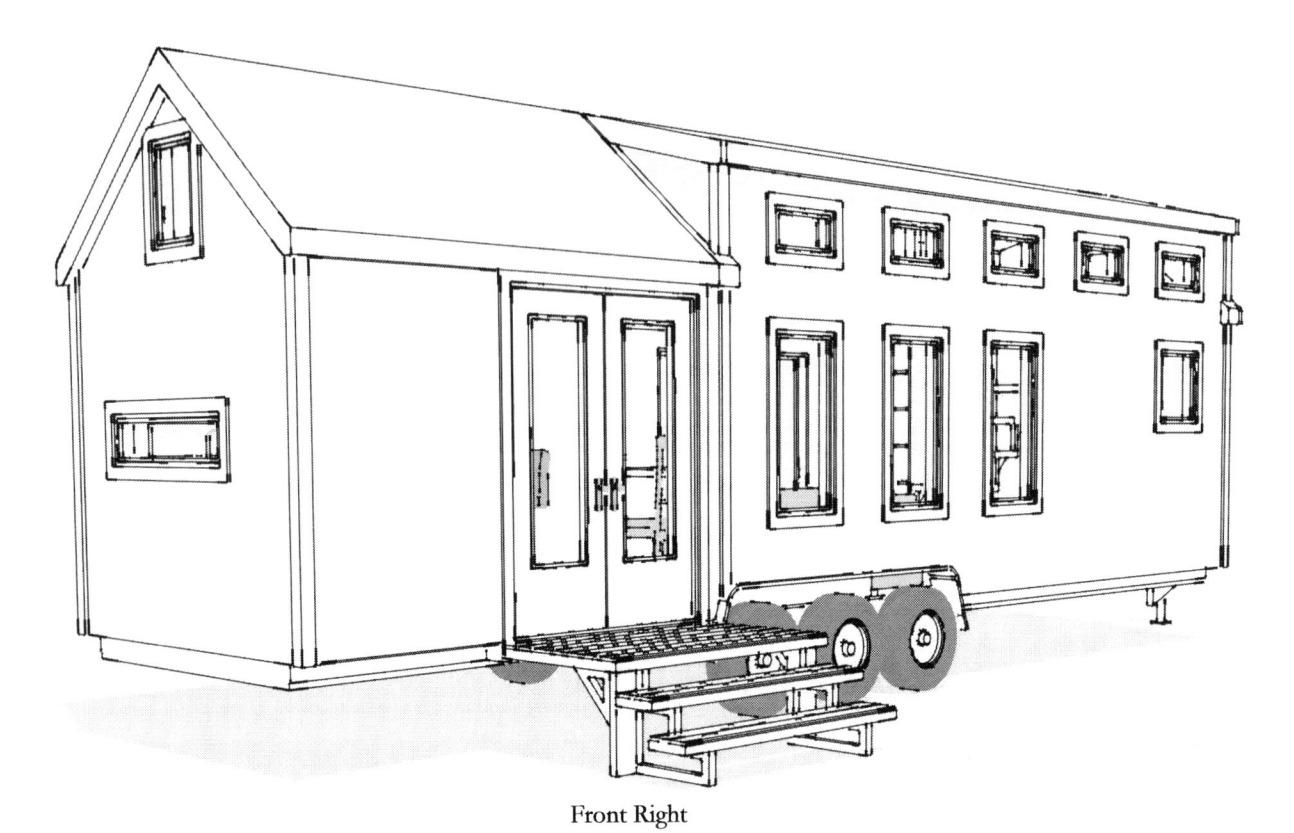

Summary:

Stepping inside you immediately find the kitchen and breakfast bar. To your right is a combination living/dining room with a table for four and ample comfy seating. Up the staircase you can access two separate lofts, one with a twin bed and the other with a queen. In the back of the house is a large bathroom and laundry.

Features:

32-Foot Tiny House on Wheels
10/12 Gable with Shed Dormers
Sleeps Three
Large Bathroom with Tub
Large Kitchen with Breakfast Counter
Plenty of Comfortable Seating
Table for Four

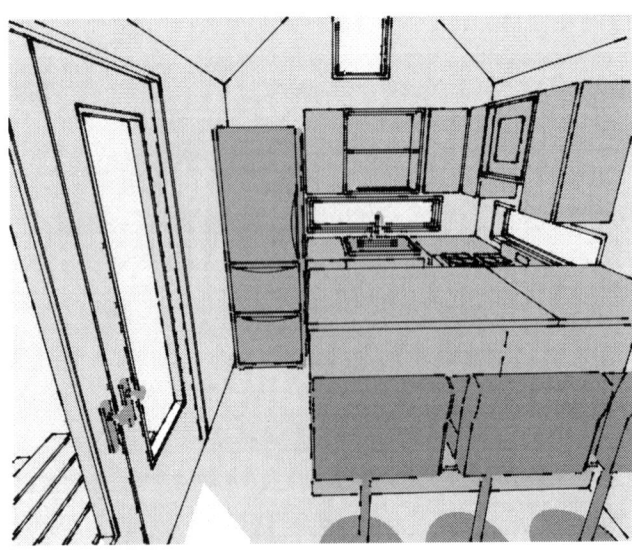

Kitchen

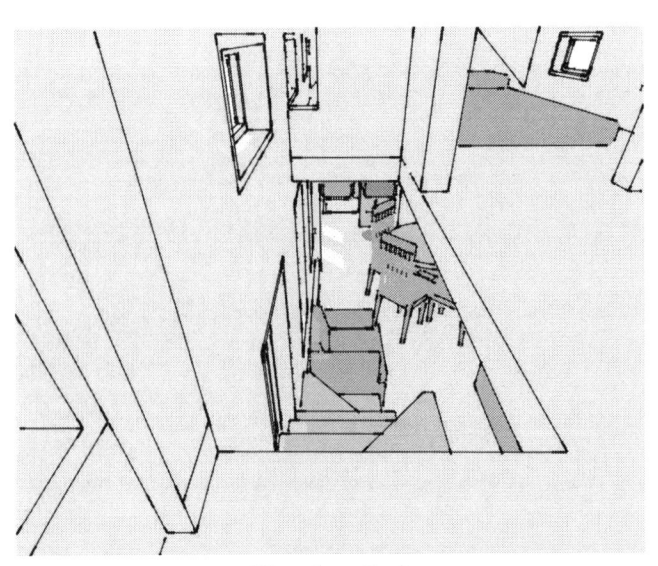

View from Loft

Tiny House #94 - Floor Plan & Exterior

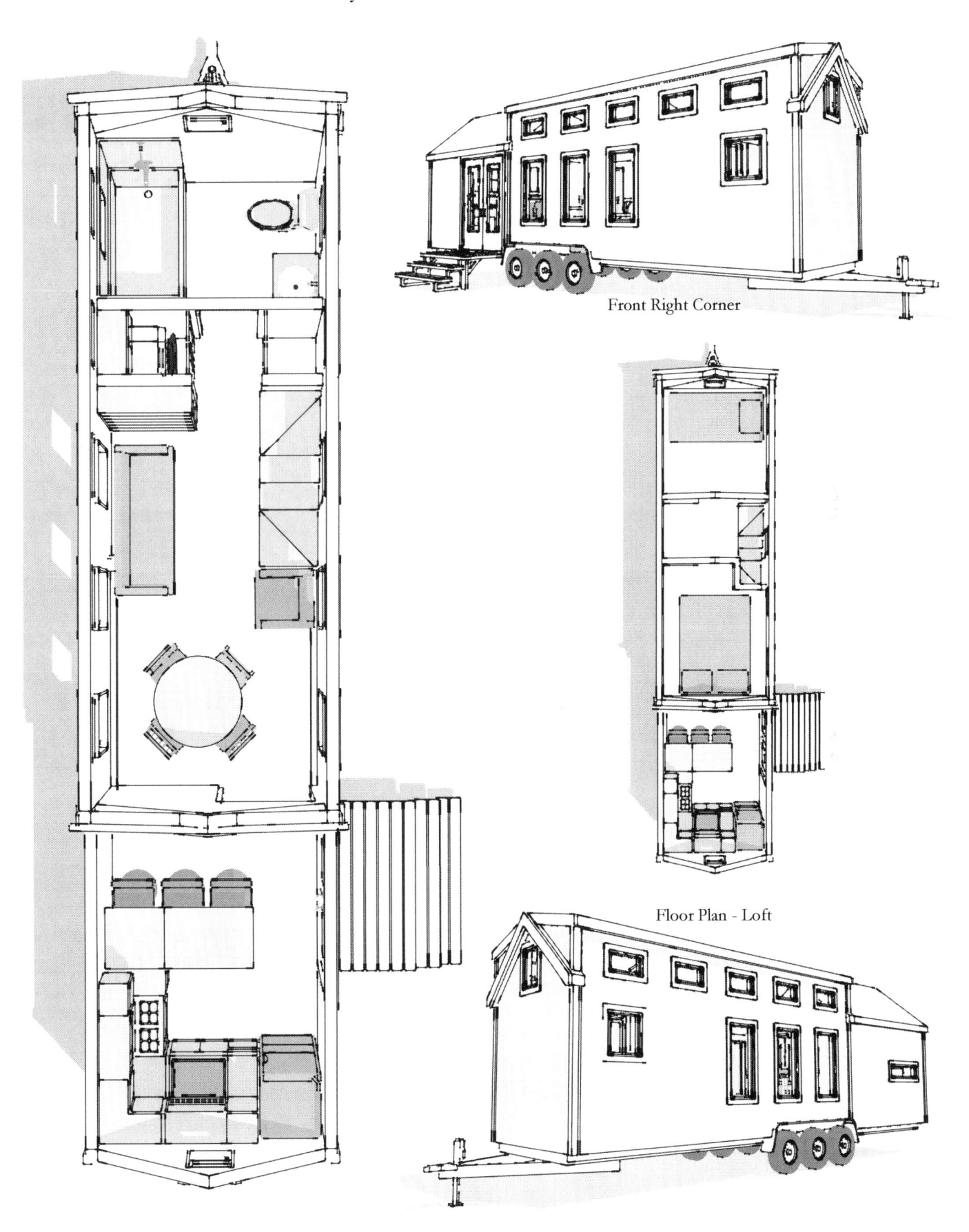

Front Right Corner

Floor Plan - Loft

Floor Plan

Back Left Corner

Tiny House #94 - Interior Views

Interior from Kitchen

Interior from Bathroom

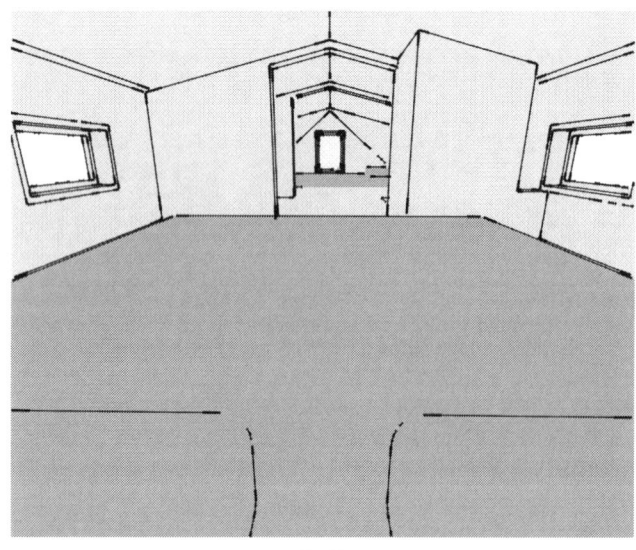

Loft

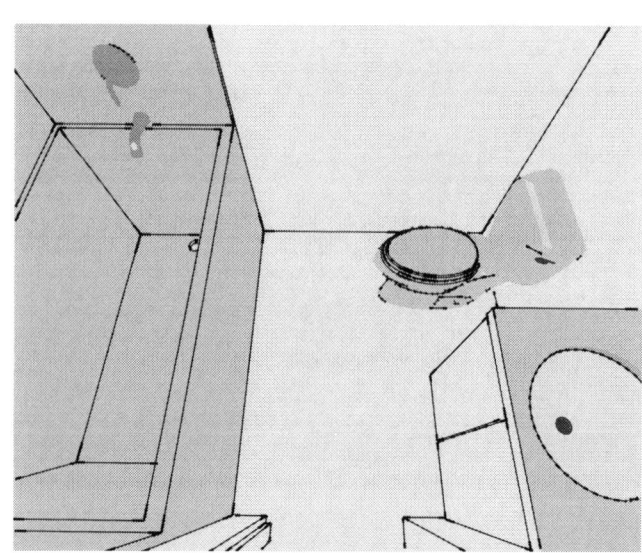

Bathroom

Tiny House #94 - Elevations

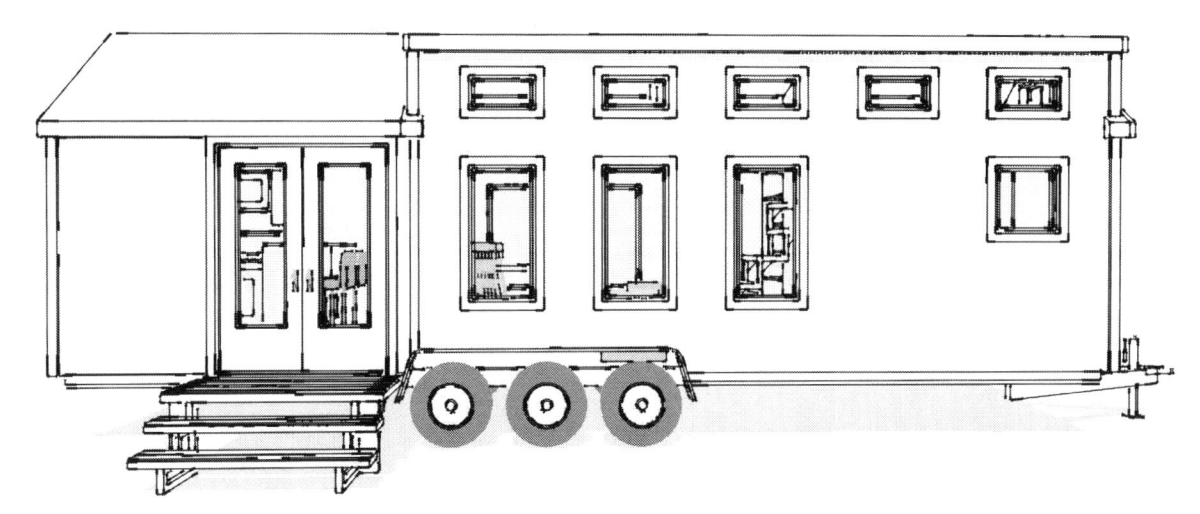

Right

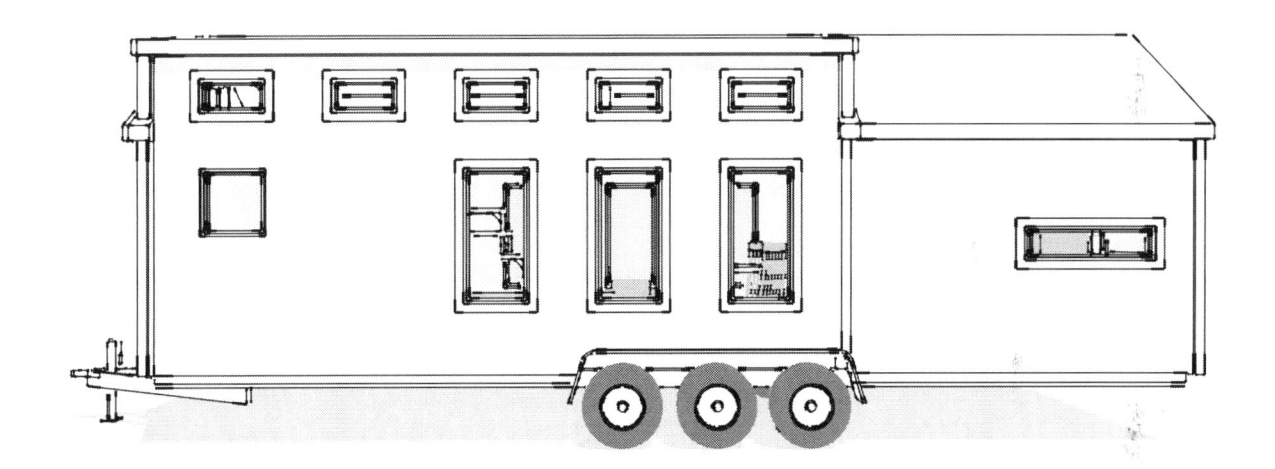

Left

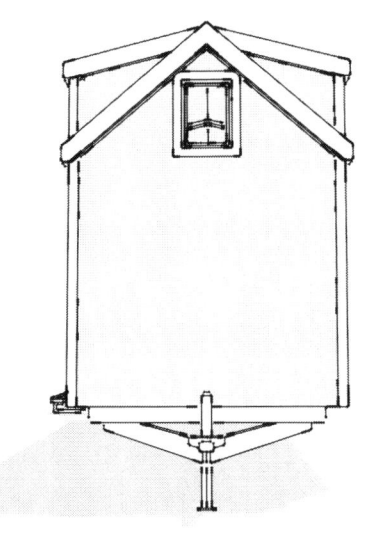

Back

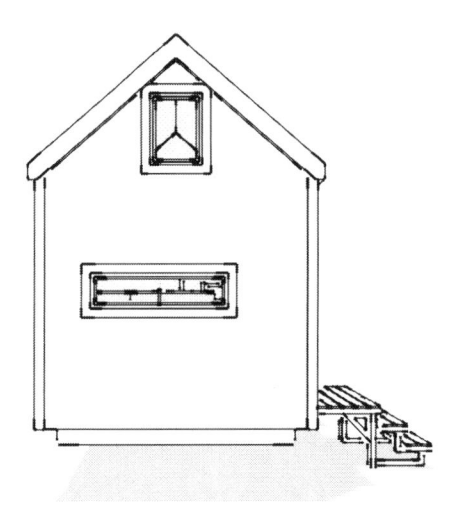

Front

393

#95

Tiny House #95 - Overview

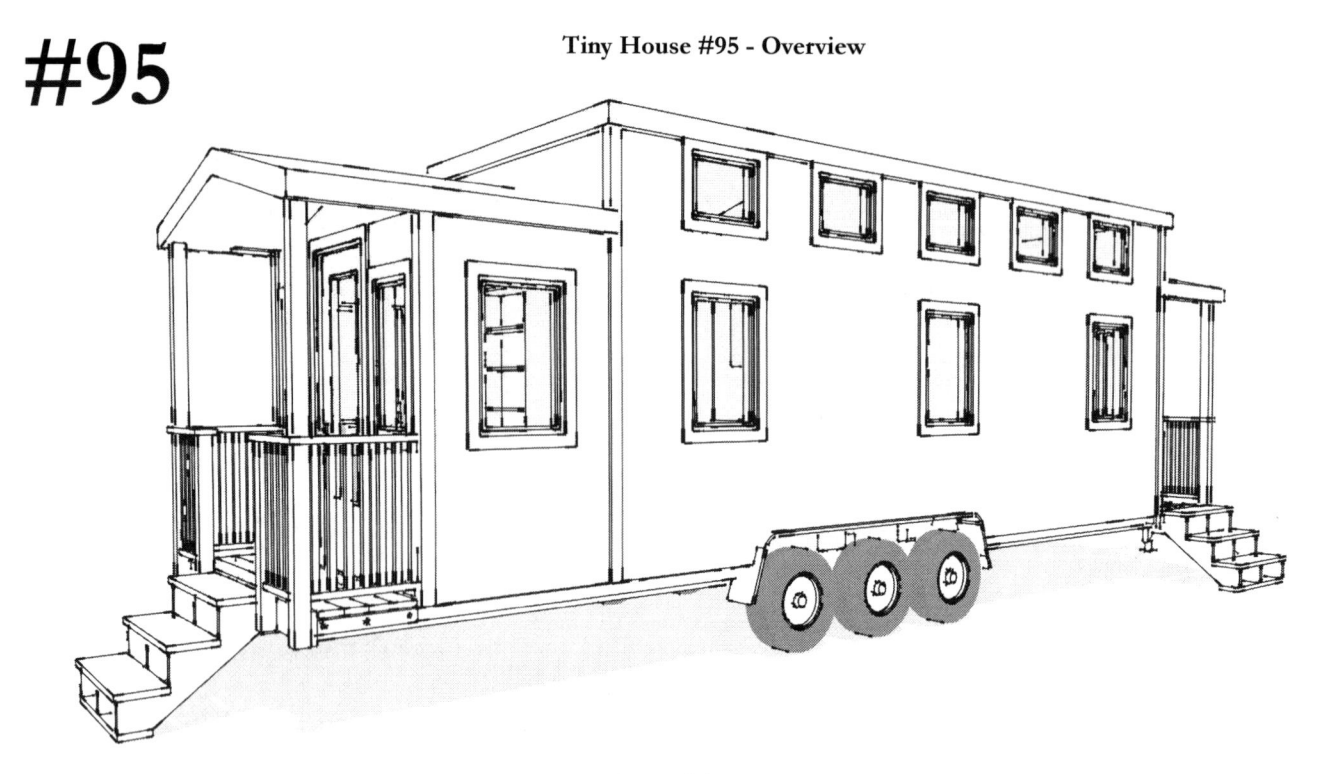

Front Right

Summary:

Yes, this is a tiny house duplex - two separate homes on one 32-foot trailer.

Entering the porch on the end of the house you find a small seating area, table, kitchen, and spiral stairs leading to a loft. A bathroom is tucked in beside the kitchen. In the loft is a queen bed.

Entering the porch on the right side of the house you find a similarly appointed home but in a different configuration. A loft ladder leads you up to the loft and the bathroom is just past the kitchen.

Features:

32-Foot Tiny House on Wheels
3/12 Hip Roof and 3/12 Gable
Duplex - Two Separate Homes

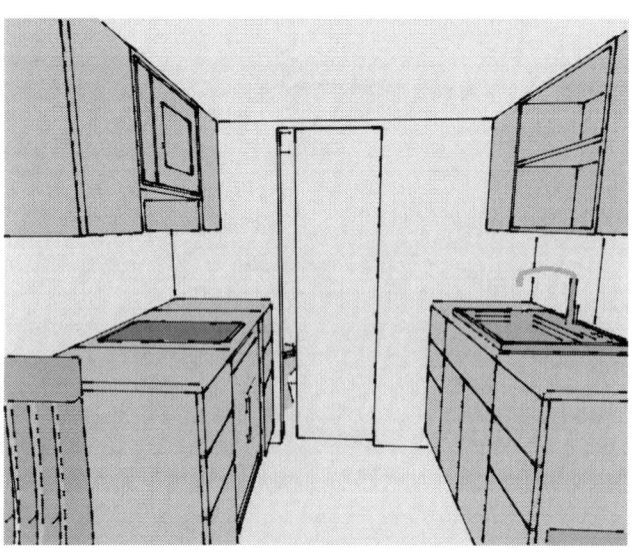

Kitchen

View from Loft

Tiny House #95 - Floor Plan & Exterior

Front Right Corner

Floor Plan - Loft

Spiral Stairs

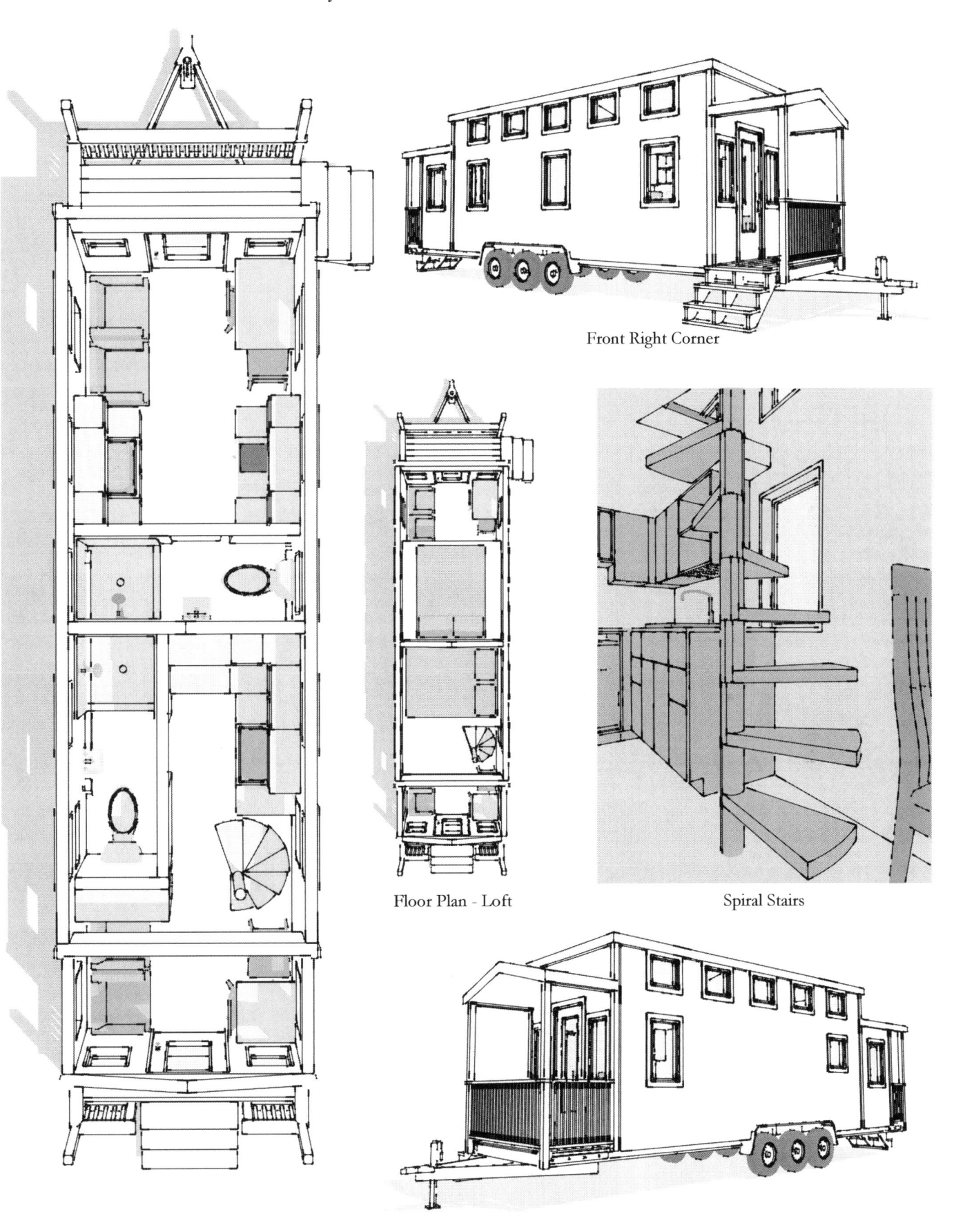

Floor Plan

Back Left Corner

395

Tiny House #95 - Interior Views

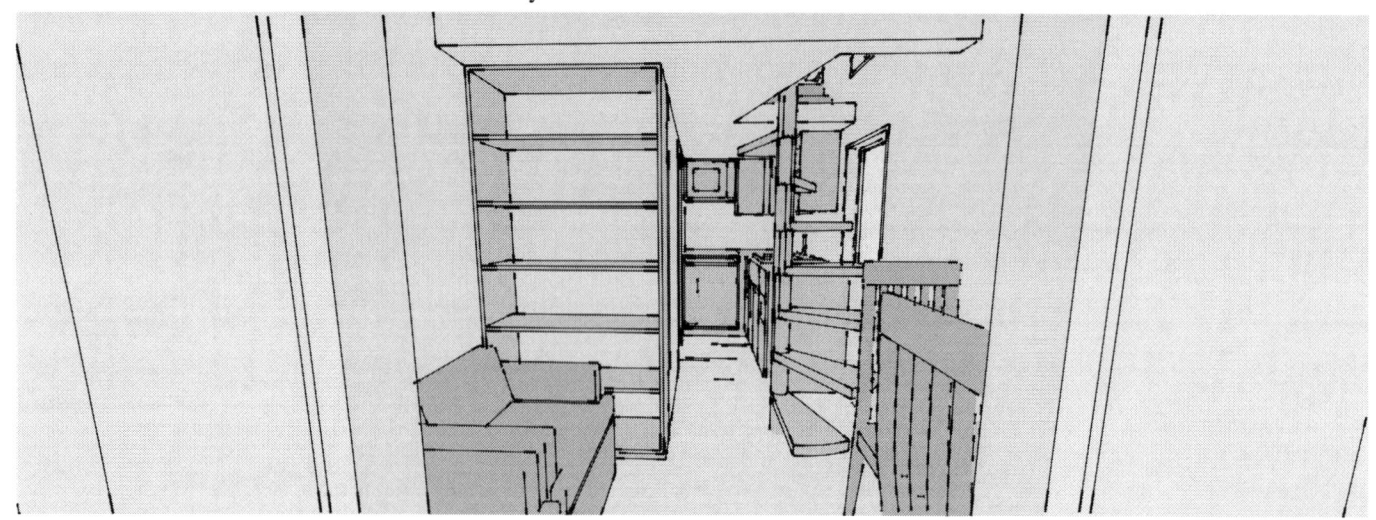

Interior from Entry

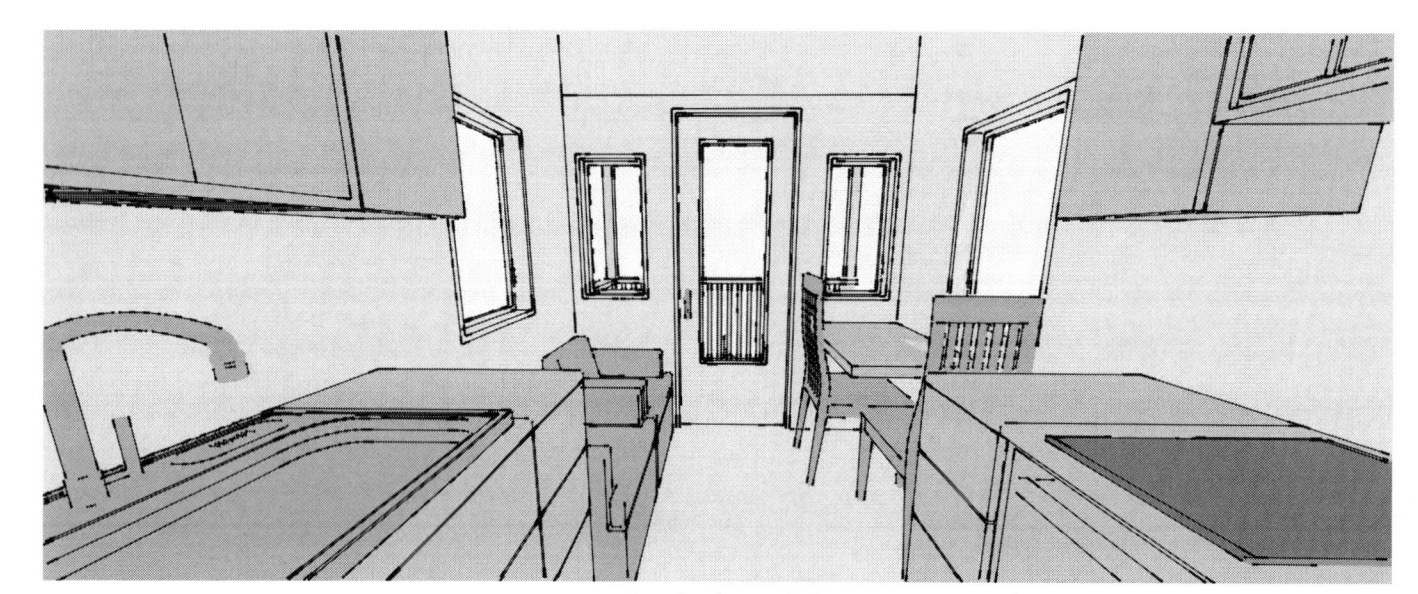

Interior from Kitchen

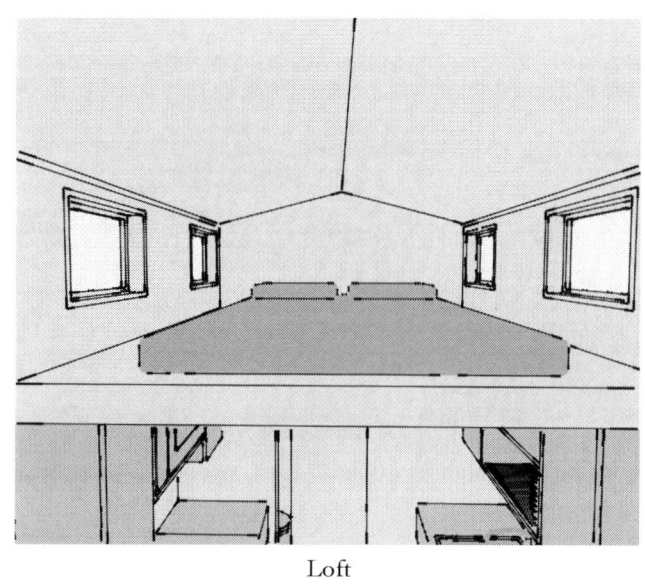

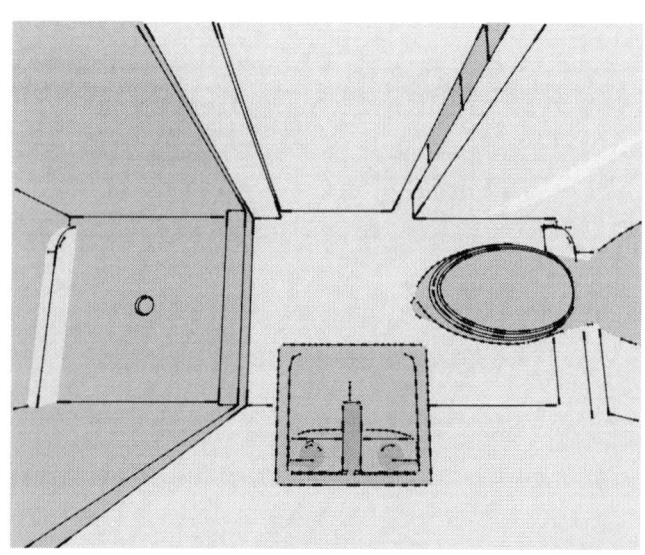

Loft

Bathroom

Tiny House #95 - Elevations

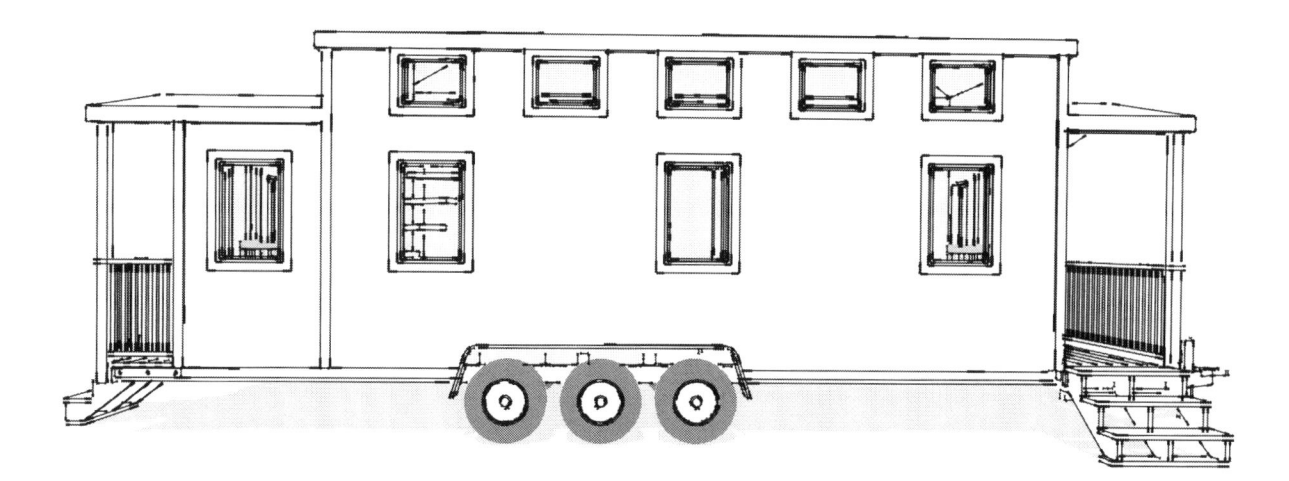

Right

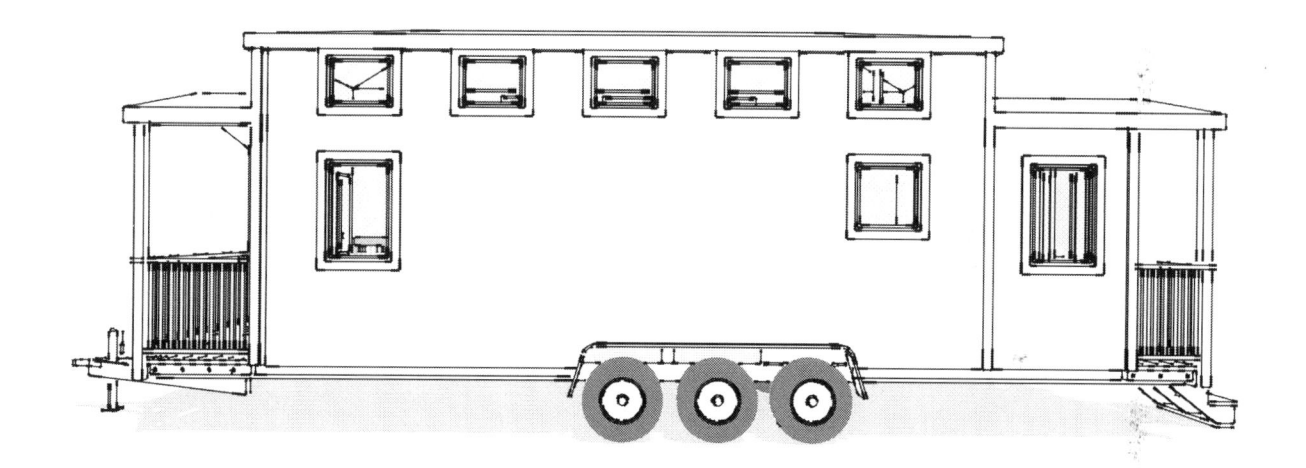

Left

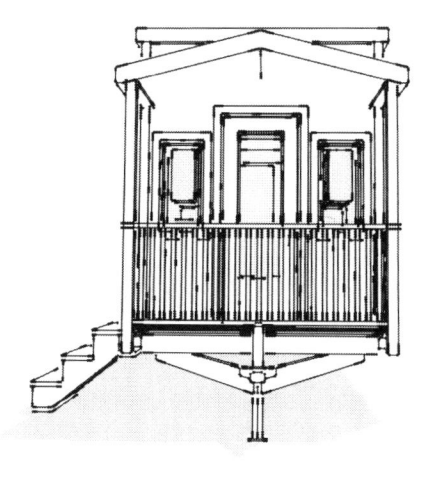

Back

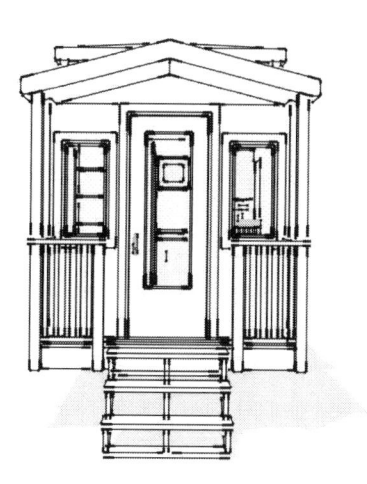

Front

#96

Tiny House #96 - Overview

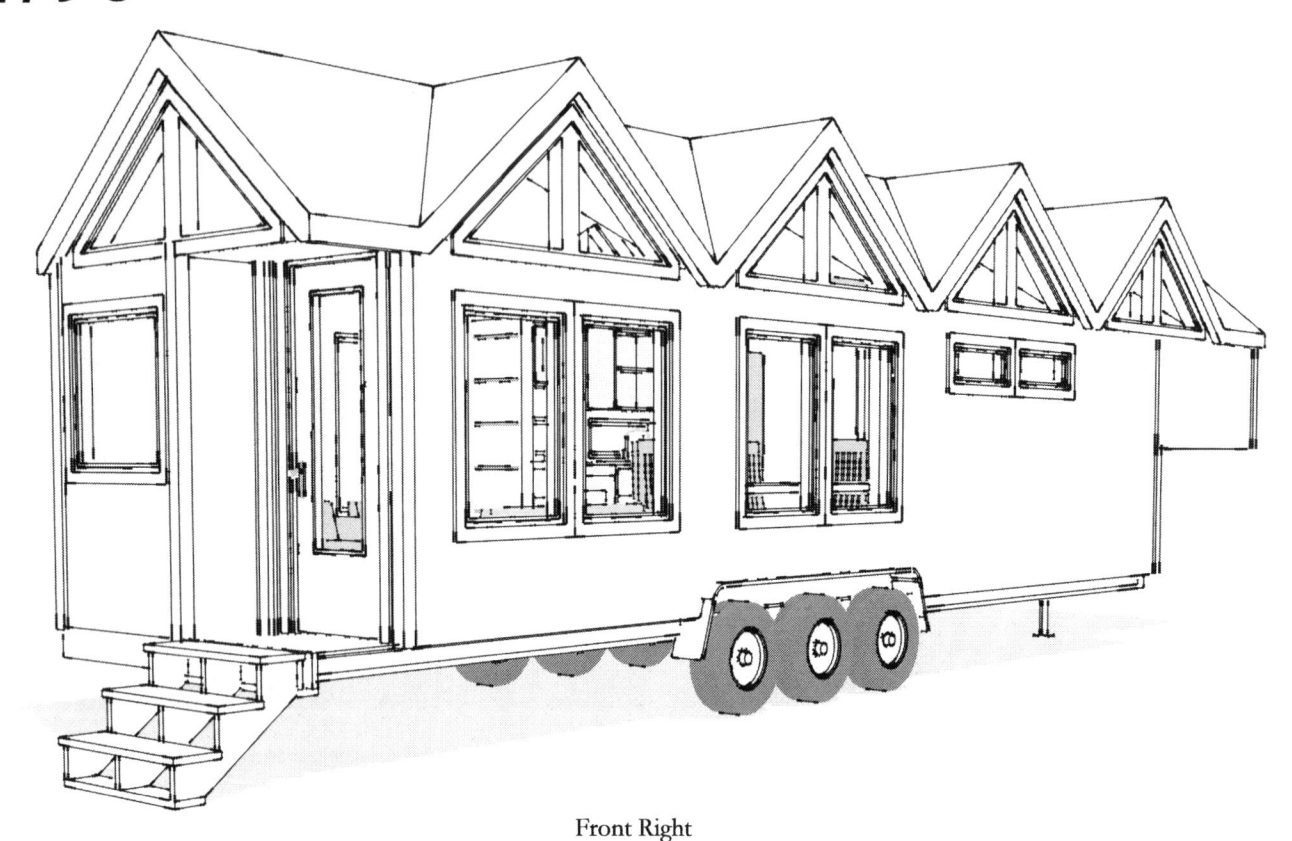

Front Right

Summary:

This is a tiny house for a family or a vacation house. There's plenty of space to relax in the living room and sit around the dining room table. The kitchen has everything you need and there's a laundry closet in the back near the bathroom. Two lofts are above the center part of the house and a smaller loft in the gooseneck.

Features:

32-Foot Tiny House on Wheels
Quadruple Cross Gable
Sleeps Five
Fully Functional Kitchen
Two Lofts with Queen Beds
Gooseneck Loft with Twin Bed
Bathroom with Tub

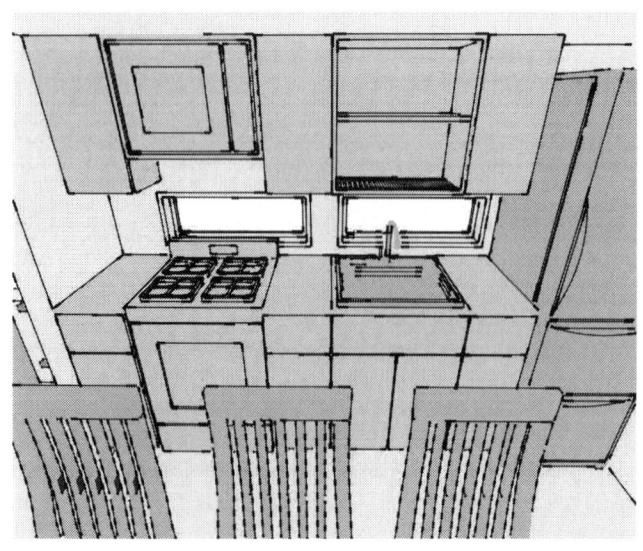

Kitchen

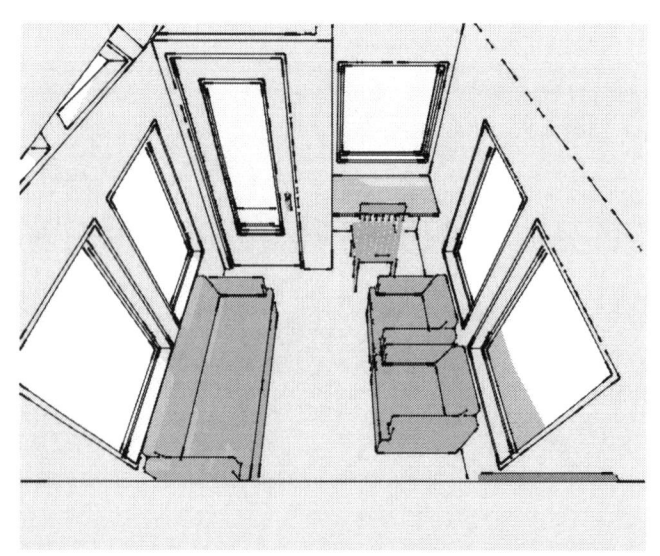

View from Loft

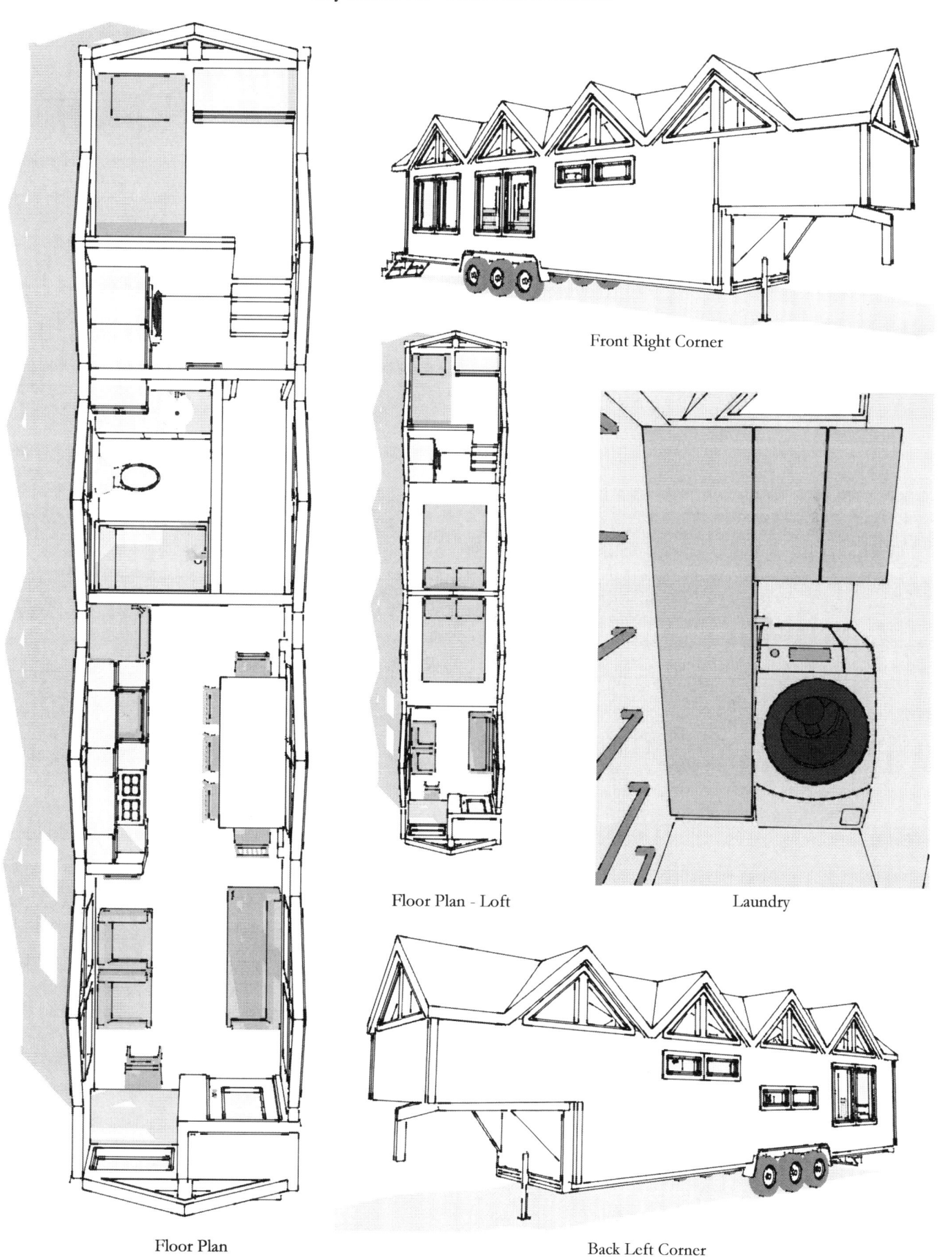

Tiny House #96 - Floor Plan & Exterior

Front Right Corner

Floor Plan - Loft

Laundry

Floor Plan

Back Left Corner

Tiny House #96 - Interior Views

Interior from Entry

Interior from Kitchen

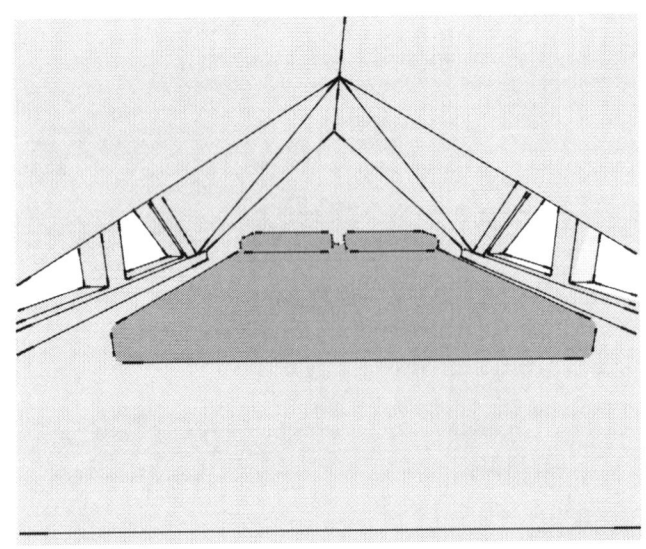

Loft

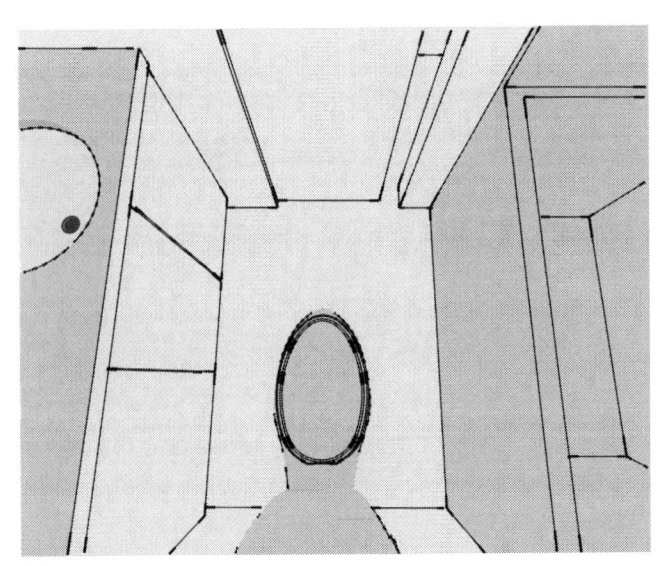

Bathroom

400

Tiny House #96 - Elevations

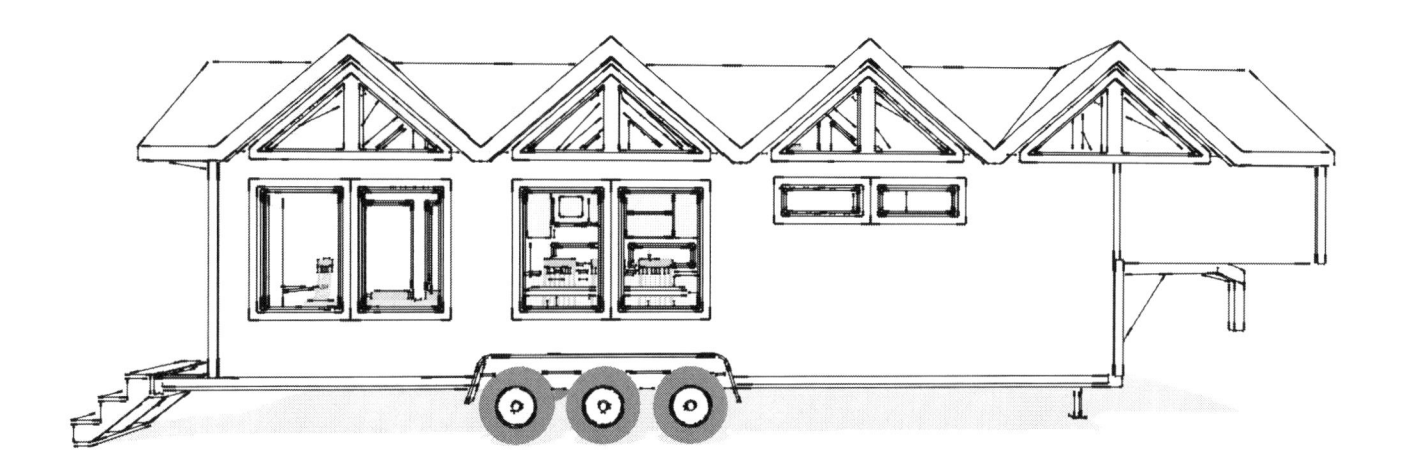

Right

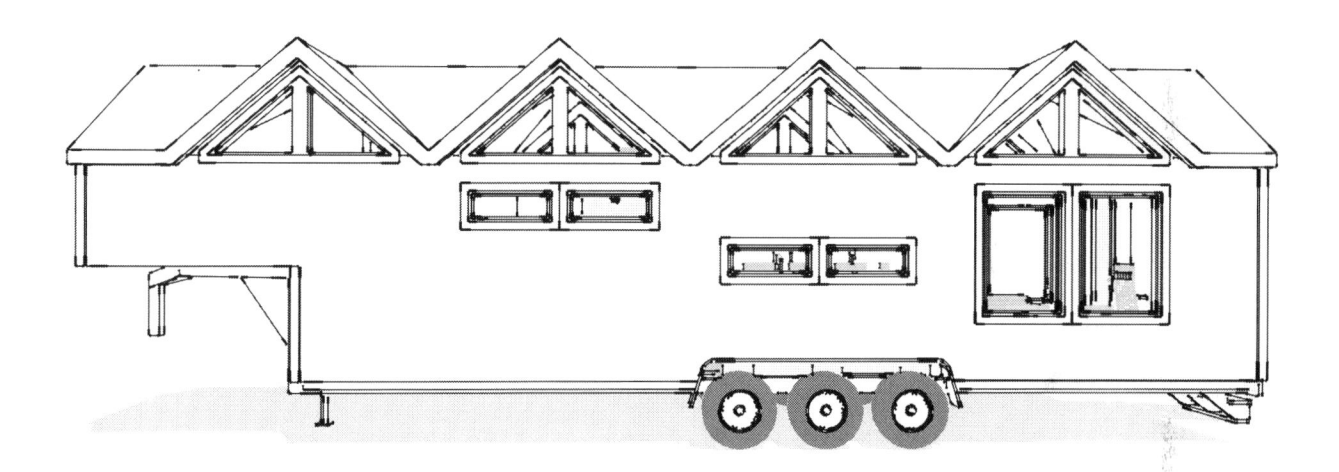

Left

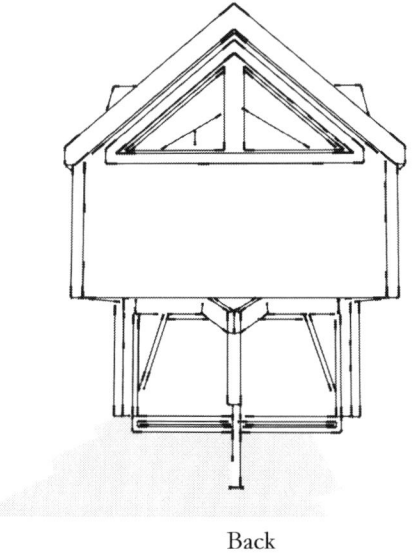

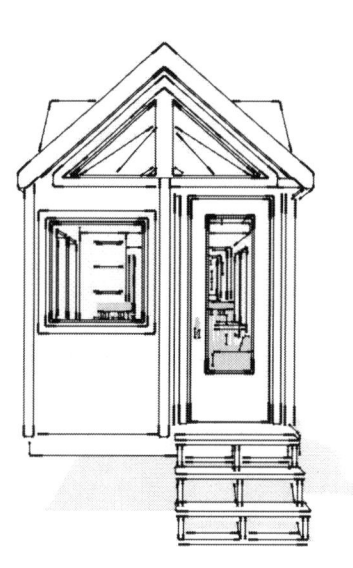

Back

Front

401

#97

Tiny House #97 - Overview

Front Right

Summary:

The doors on the left open onto the living room. The doors on the right open onto the dining room. Between these two rooms is a galley kitchen and bathroom. Two small lofts with twin beds are above the kitchen and bathroom. In the gooseneck loft is a queen bed.

Features:

32-Foot Tiny House on Wheels
3/12 Shed with Gables
Two Entries
Sleeps Four

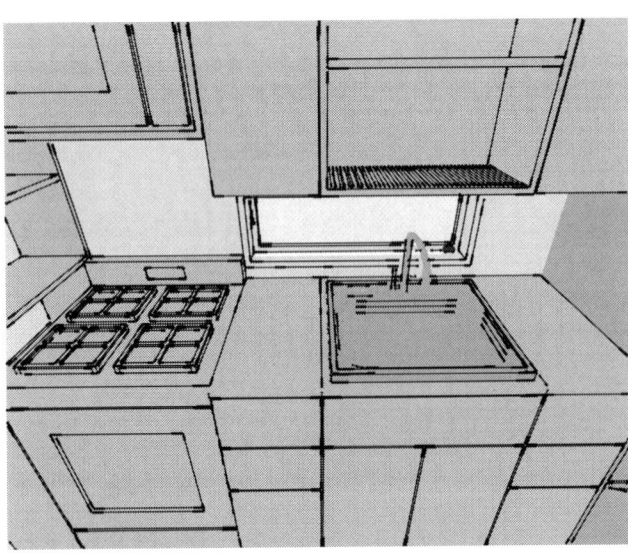

Kitchen

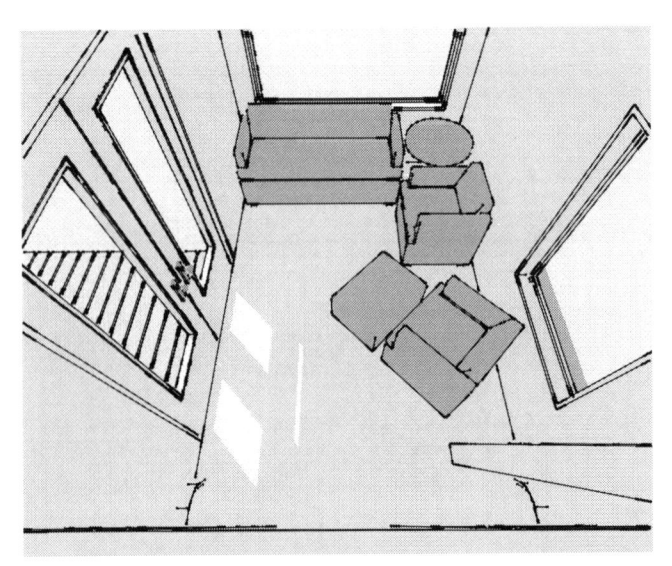

View from Loft

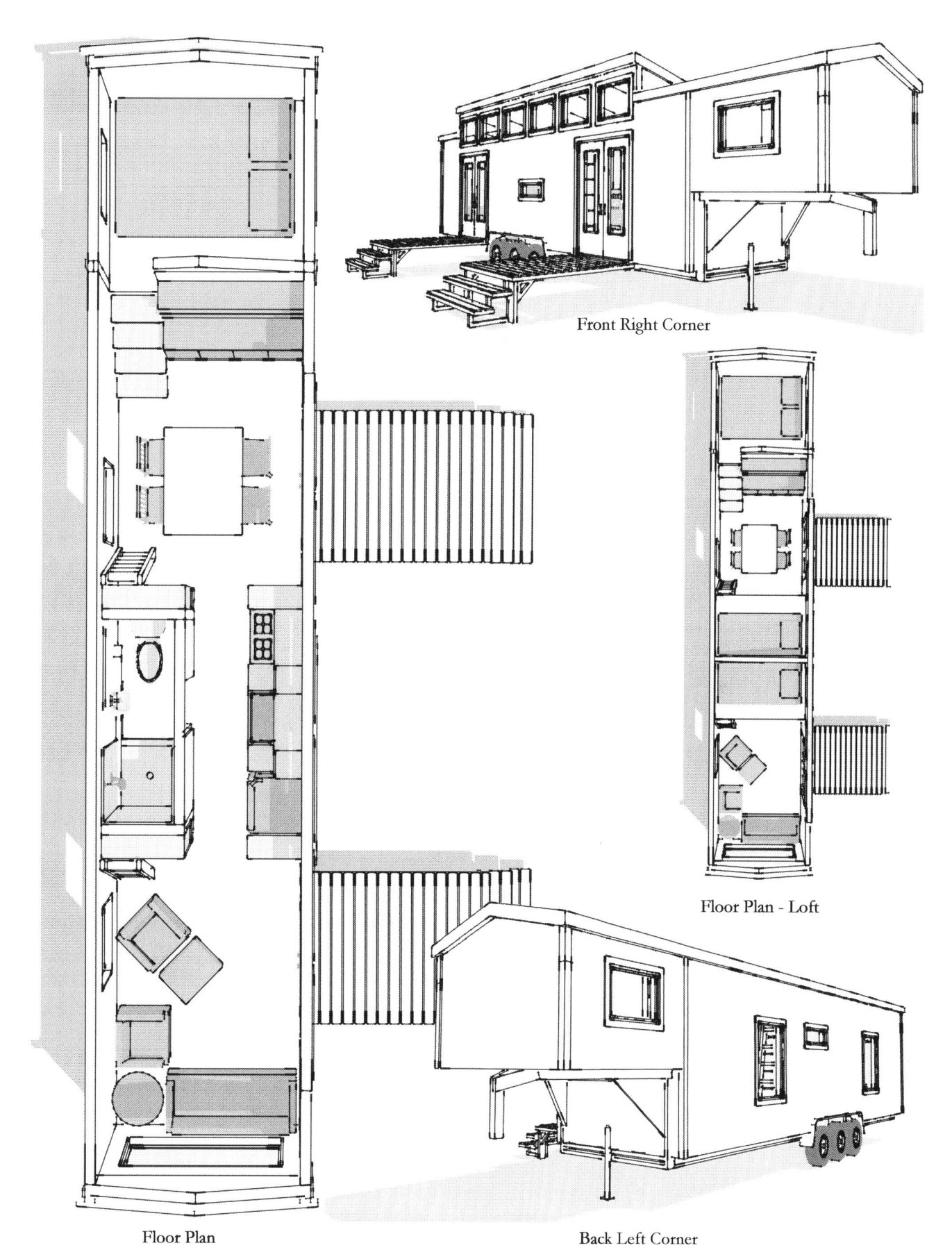

Tiny House #97 - Floor Plan & Exterior

Front Right Corner

Floor Plan - Loft

Floor Plan

Back Left Corner

403

Tiny House #97 - Interior Views

Interior from Living Room

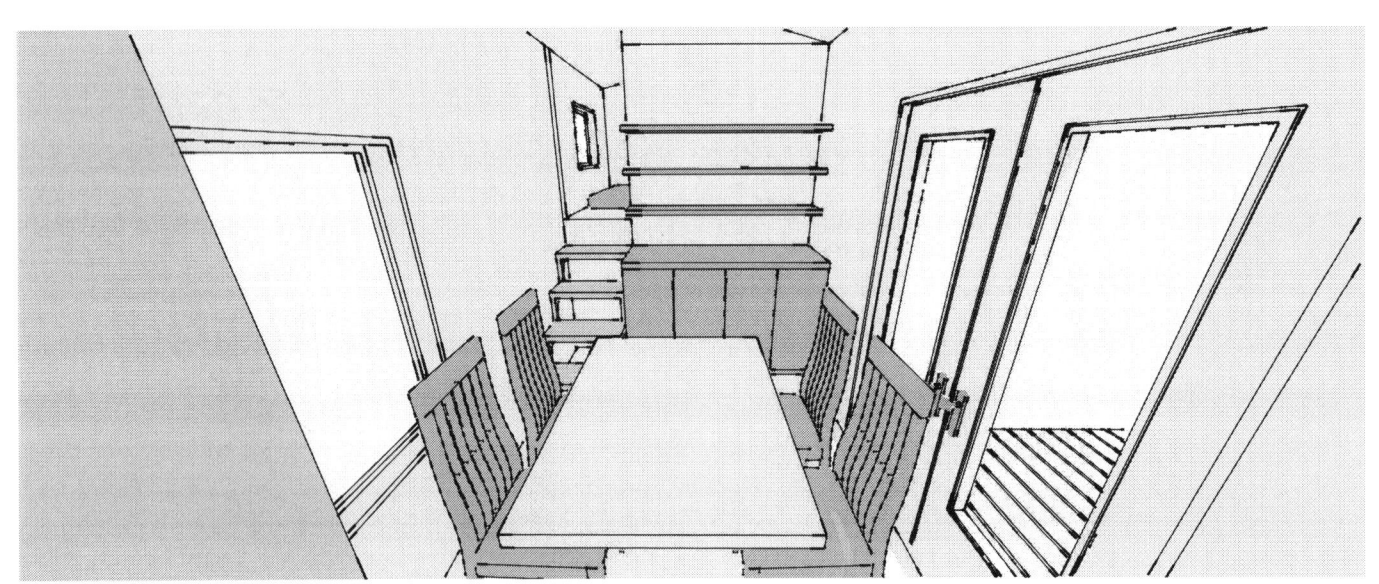

Interior from Kitchen

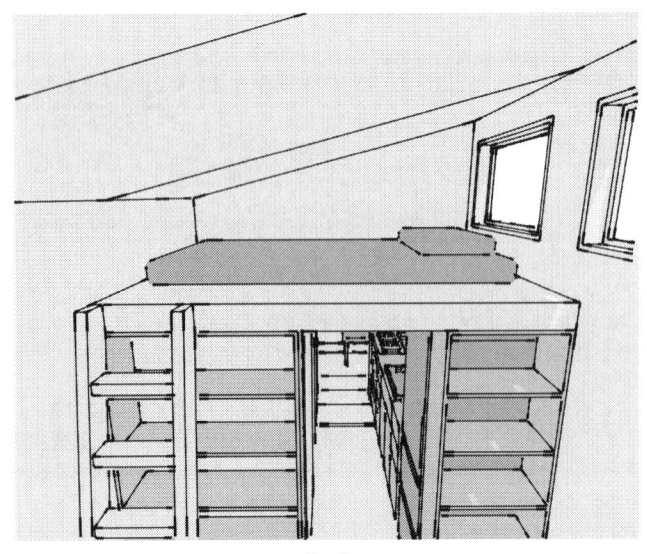

Loft

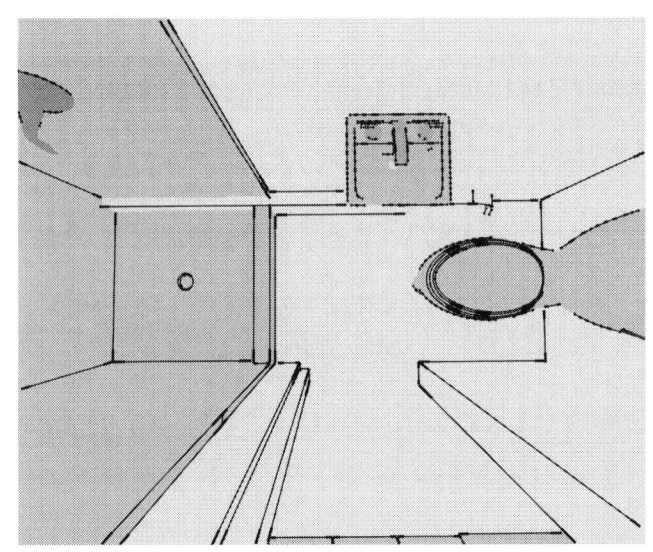

Bathroom

404

Tiny House #97 - Elevations

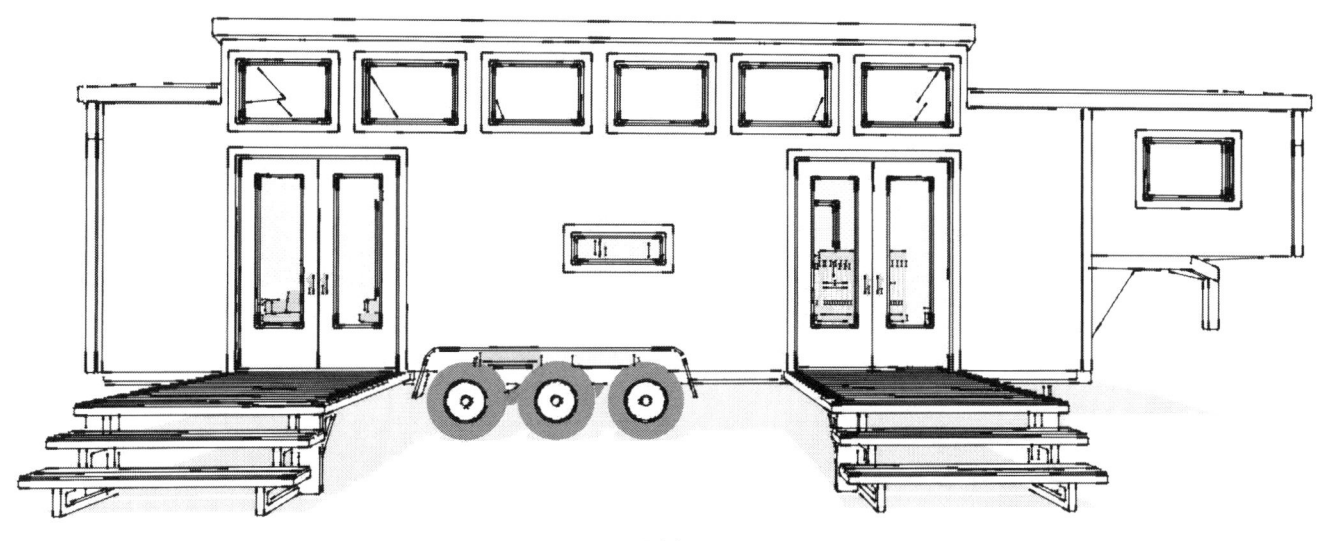

Right

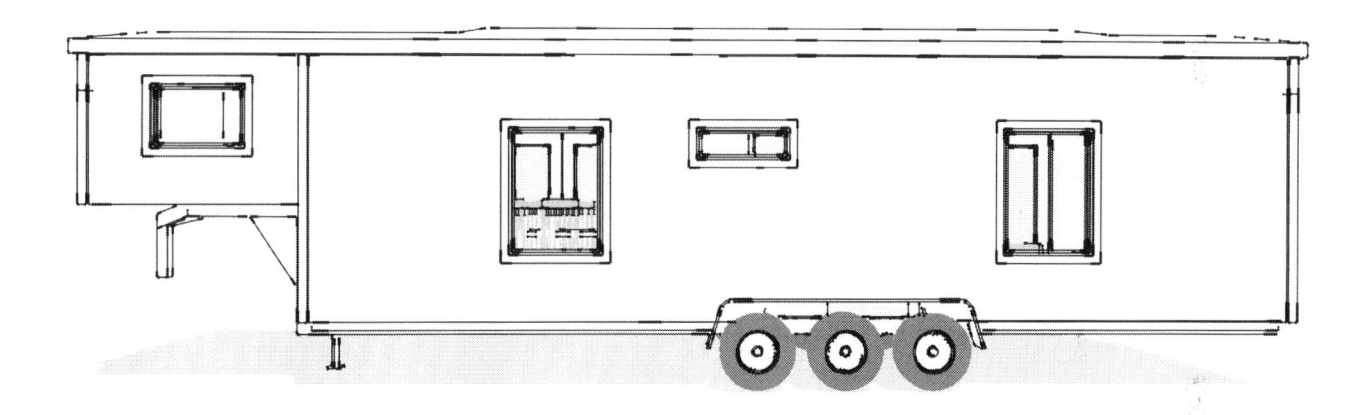

Left

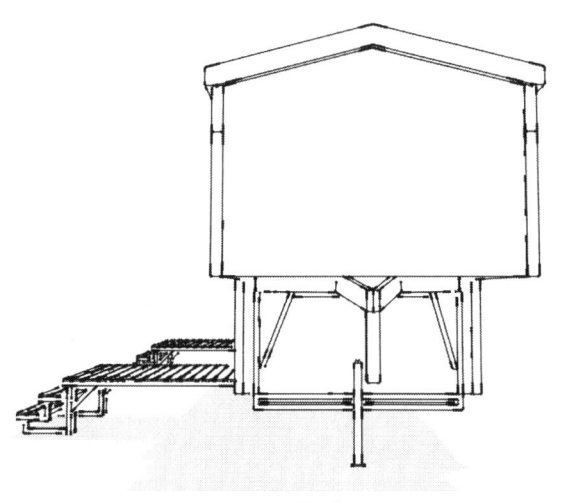

Back

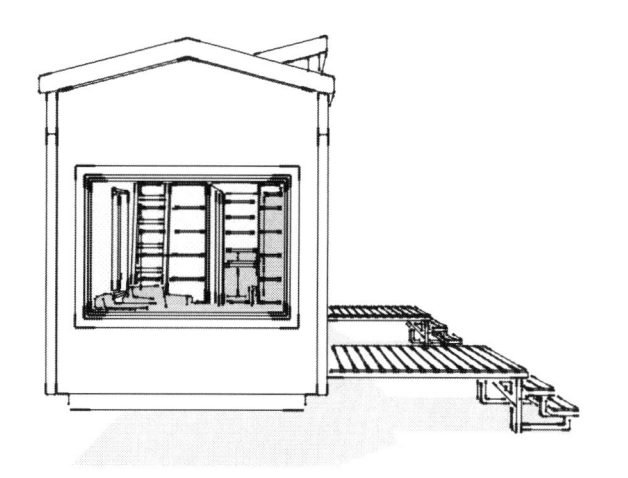

Front

#98

Tiny House #98 - Overview

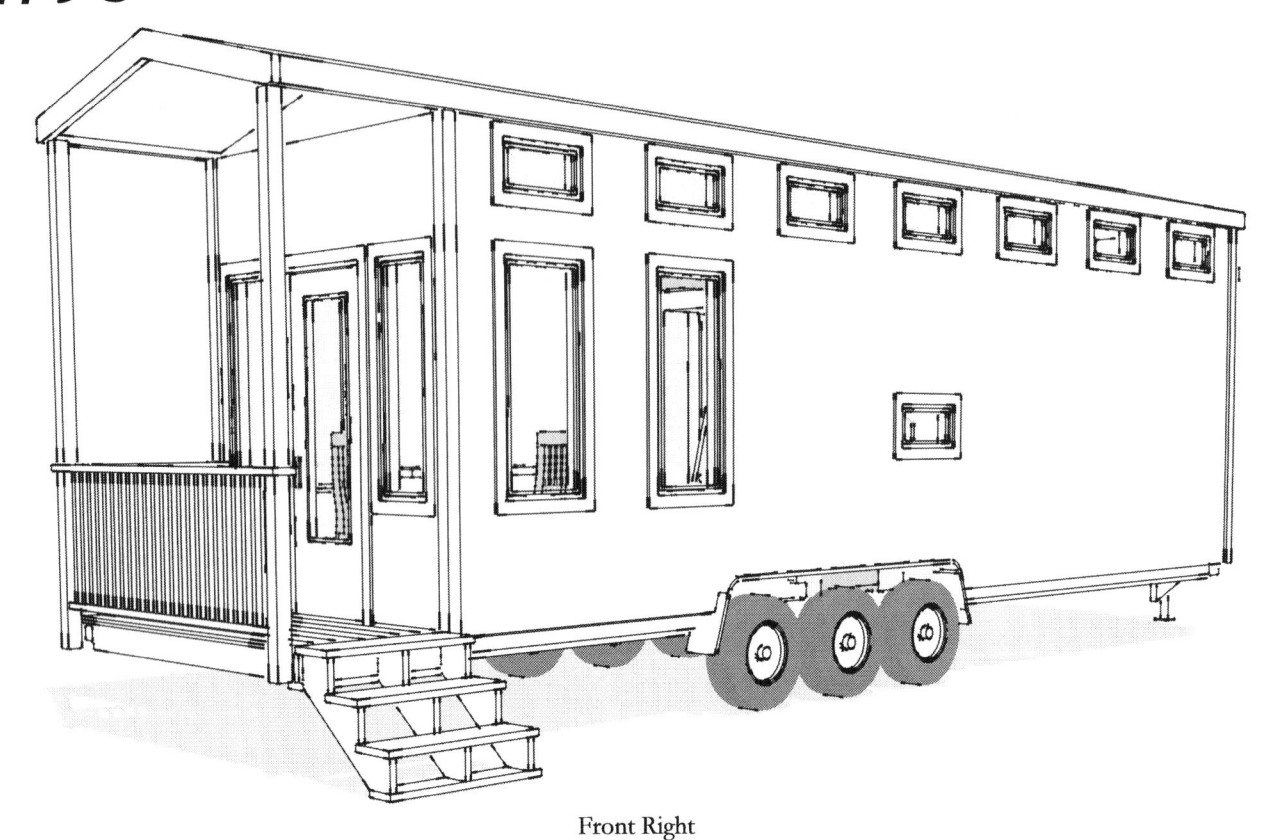

Front Right

Summary:

The high roof over the front porch gives this house a regal look. The clerestory and high ceiling continue this personality through the interior. Just inside the home is two comfy seats and a table for four. Beyond that is a galley kitchen and bathroom. At the end of the house is a lower level bedroom with high ceilings. Over the kitchen and bathroom is a loft with two twin beds.

Features:

32-Foot Tiny House on Wheels
High 3/12 Gable
Sleeps Four

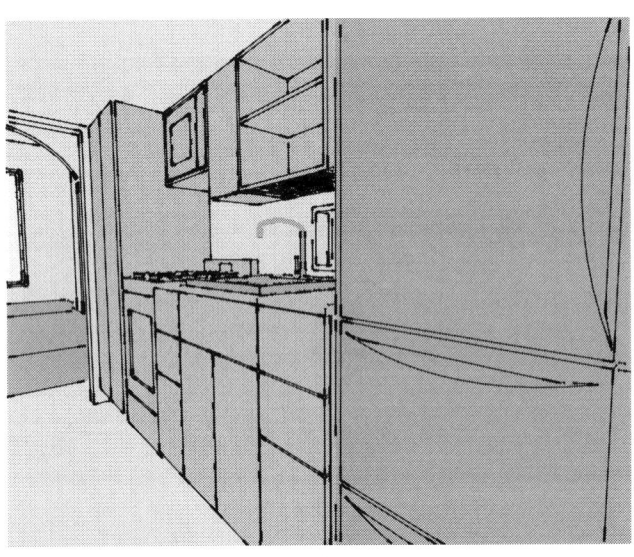

Kitchen

View from Loft

Tiny House #98 - Floor Plan & Exterior

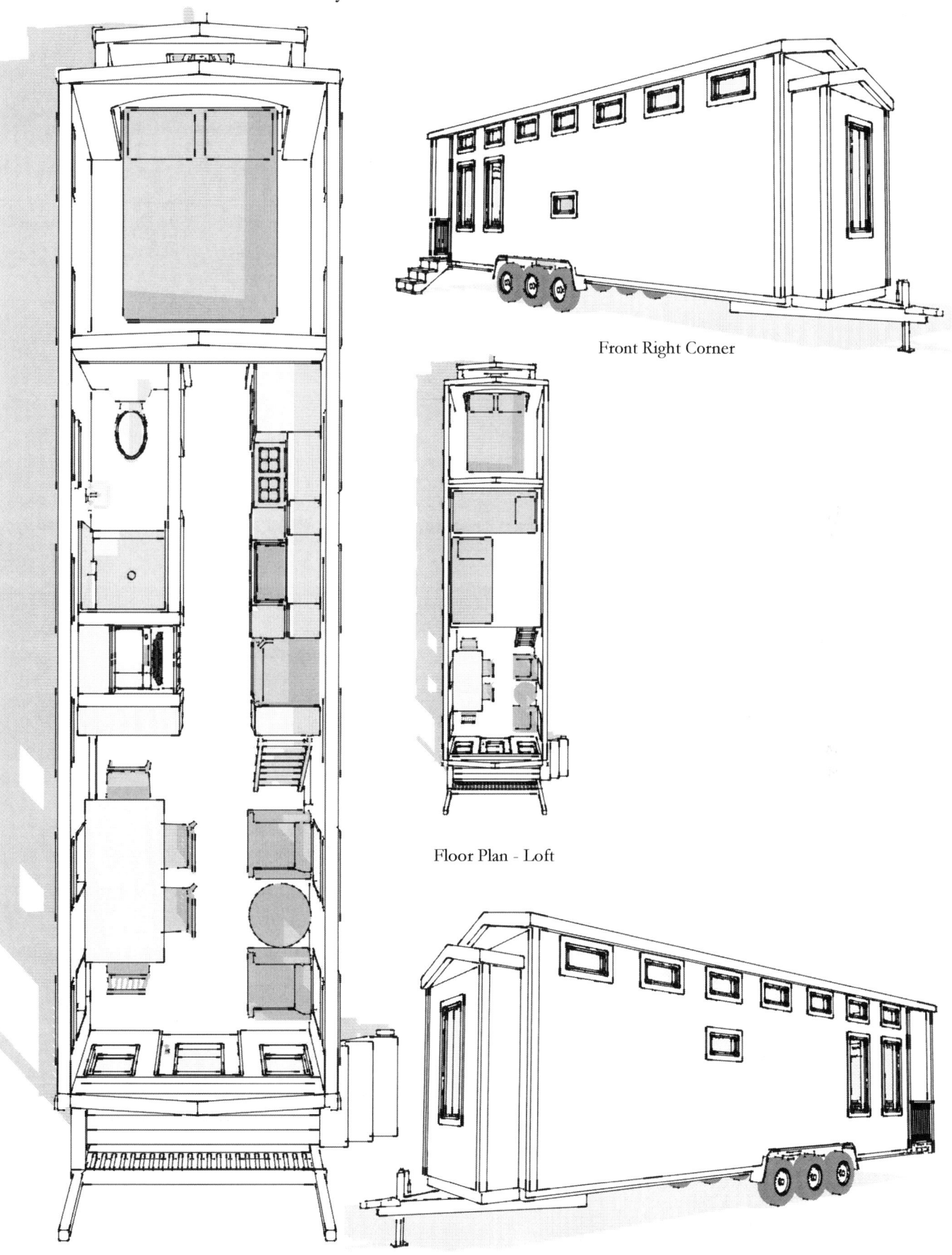

Front Right Corner

Floor Plan - Loft

Floor Plan

Back Left Corner

Tiny House #98 - Interior Views

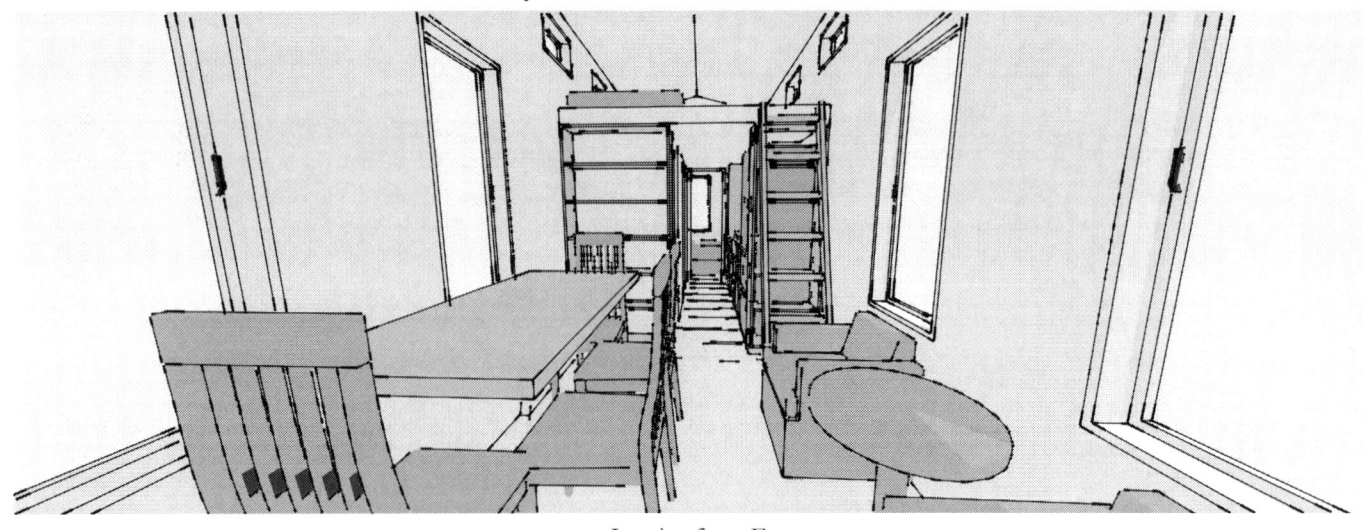

Interior from Entry

Bedroom

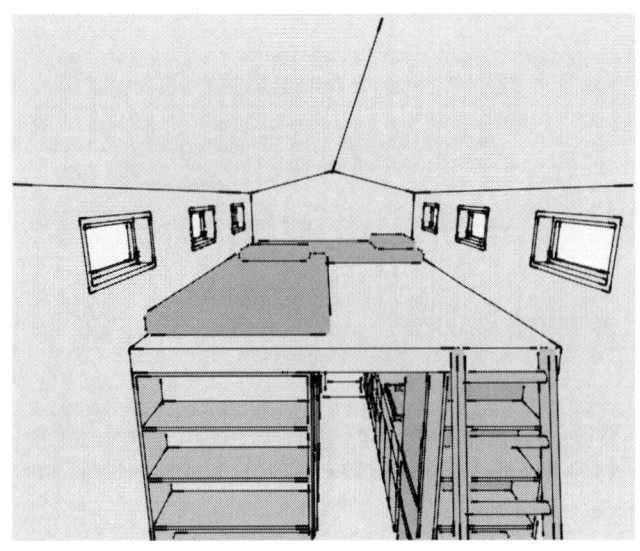

Loft

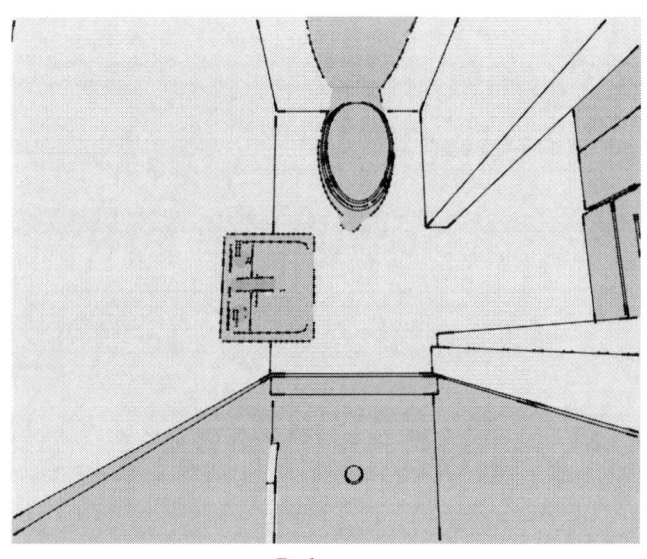

Bathroom

Tiny House #98 - Elevations

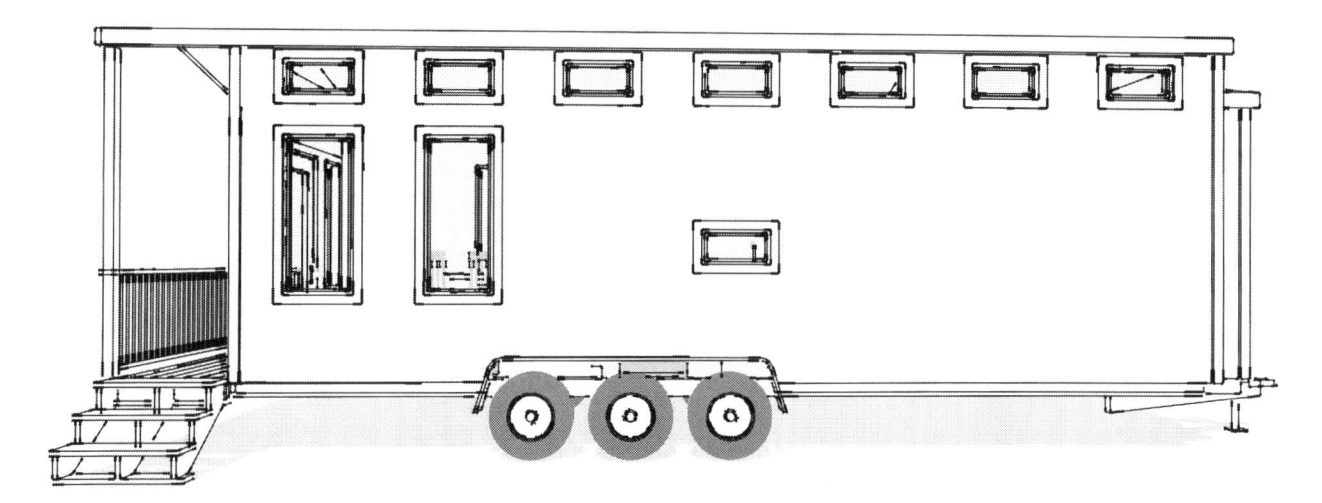

Right

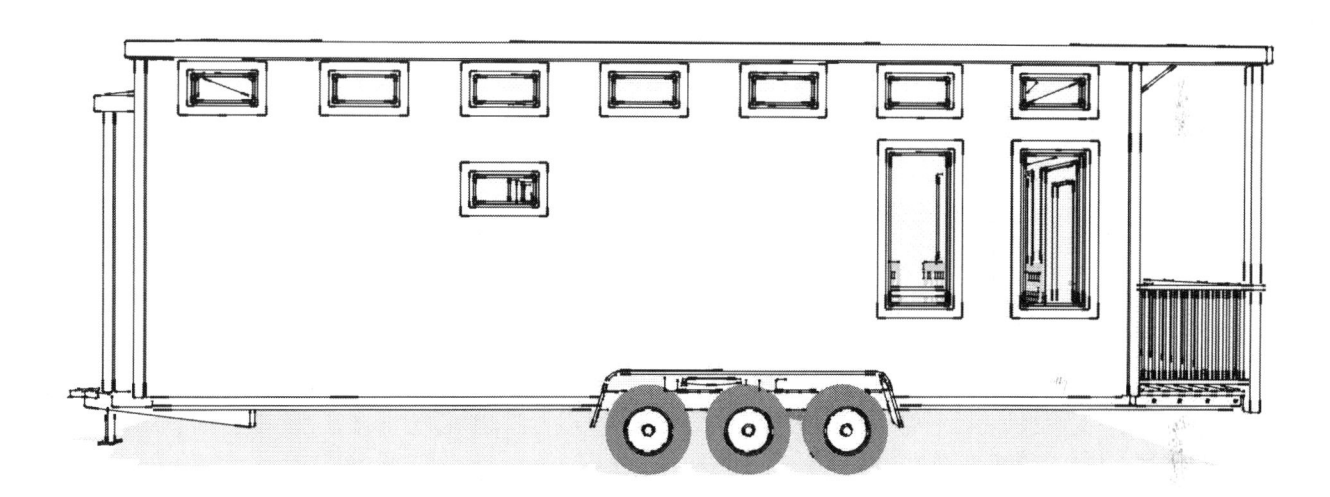

Left

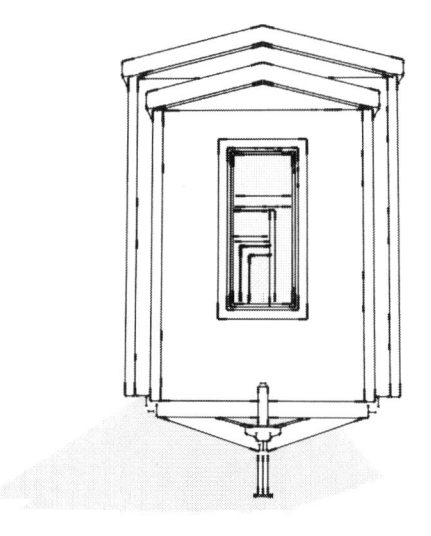

Back

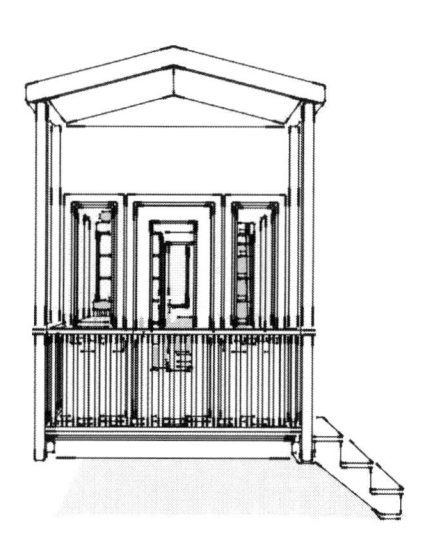

Front

#99

Tiny House #99 - Overview

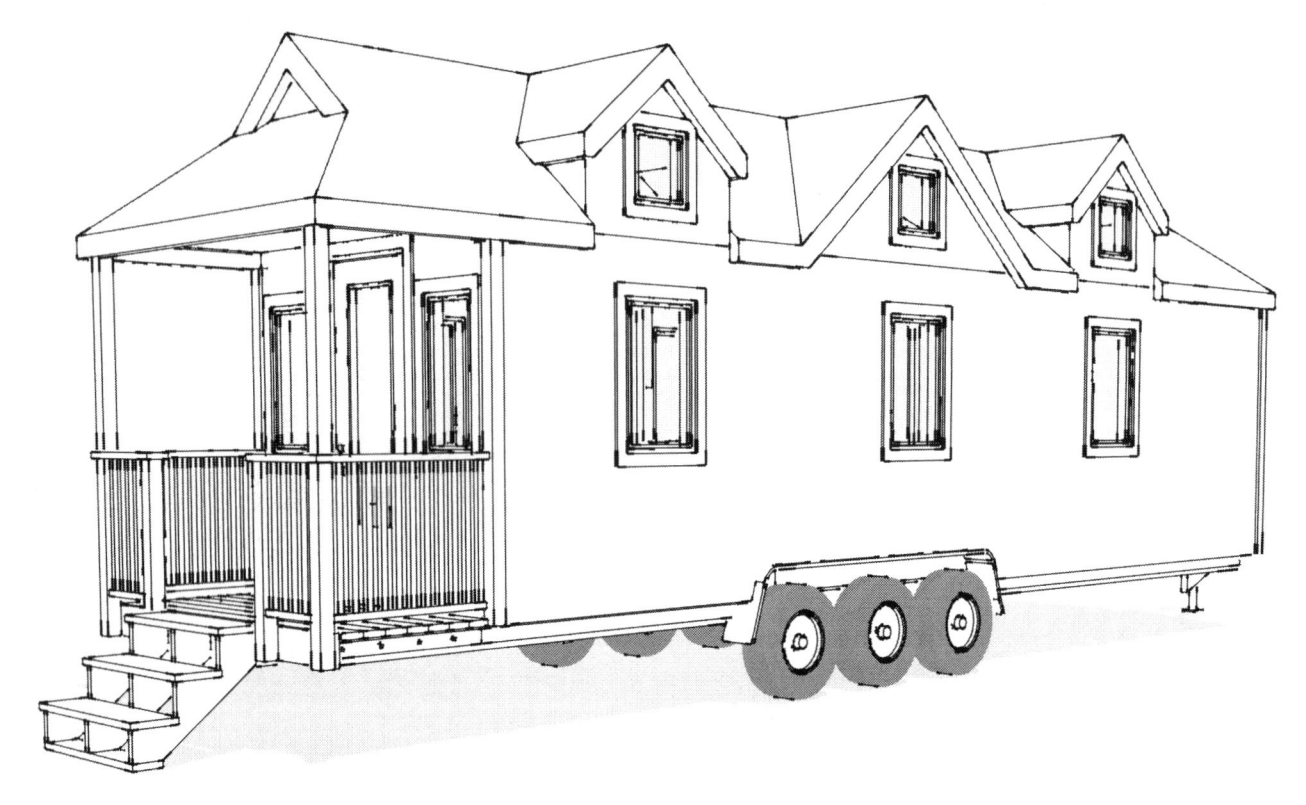

Front Right

Summary:

The deep porch welcomes visitors to this tiny house. Just inside the front door is a living room which is separated by the kitchen and dining room with a pocket door. Beyond the kitchen is a small home office followed by the bathroom. There's a loft above the office and bathroom.

Features:

32-Foot Tiny House on Wheels
Dutch Cross Gable with Gable Dormers
Generous Kitchen
Bathroom with Tub and Laundry
Sleeps Two

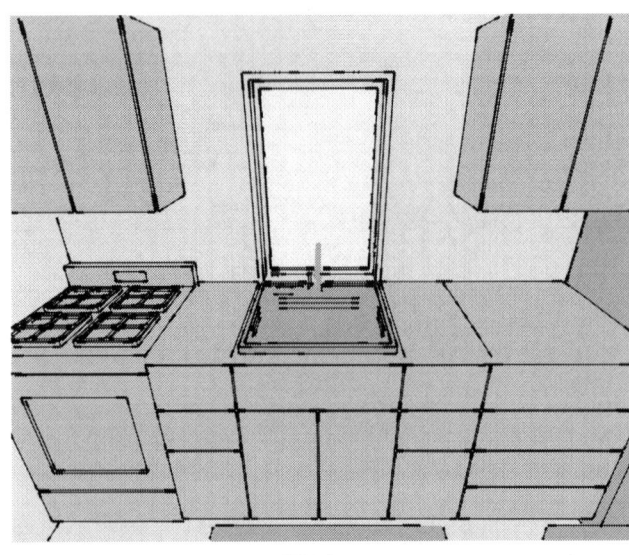

Kitchen

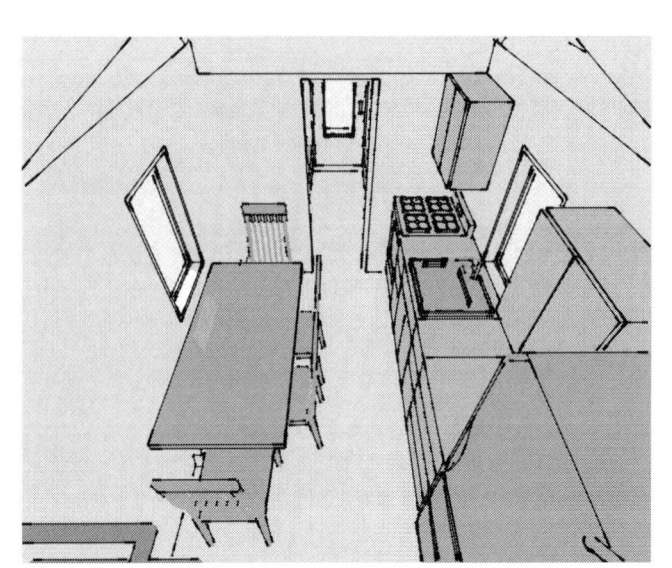

View from Loft

Tiny House #99 - Floor Plan & Exterior

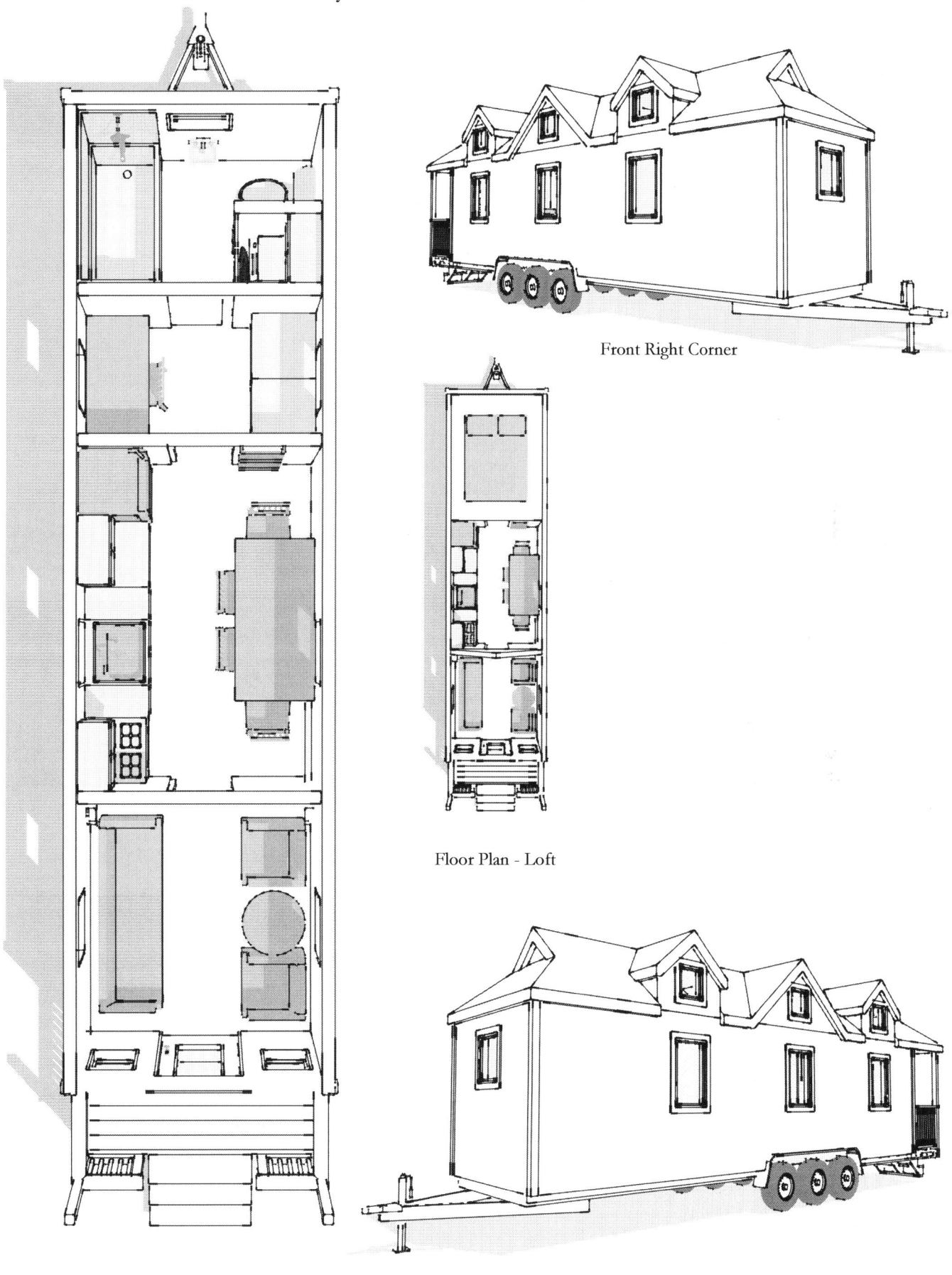

Front Right Corner

Floor Plan - Loft

Floor Plan

Back Left Corner

Tiny House #99 - Interior Views

Interior from Entry

Interior from Kitchen

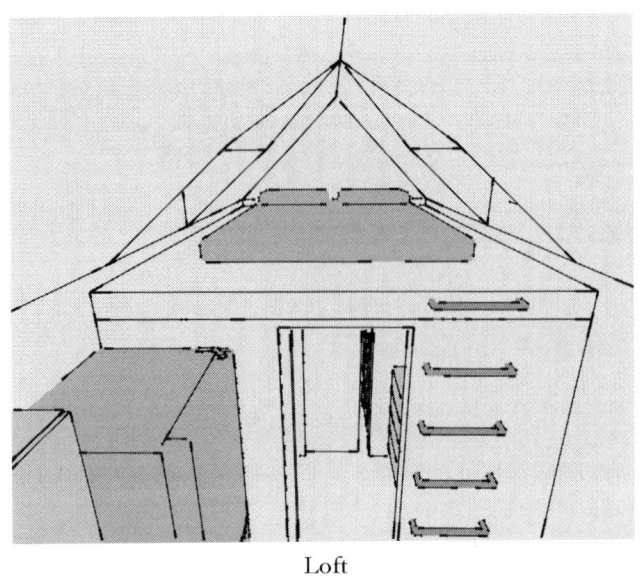

Loft

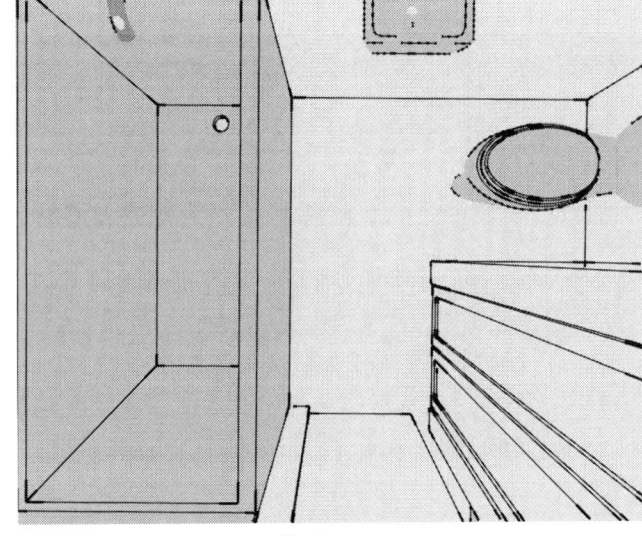

Bathroom

412

Tiny House #99 - Elevations

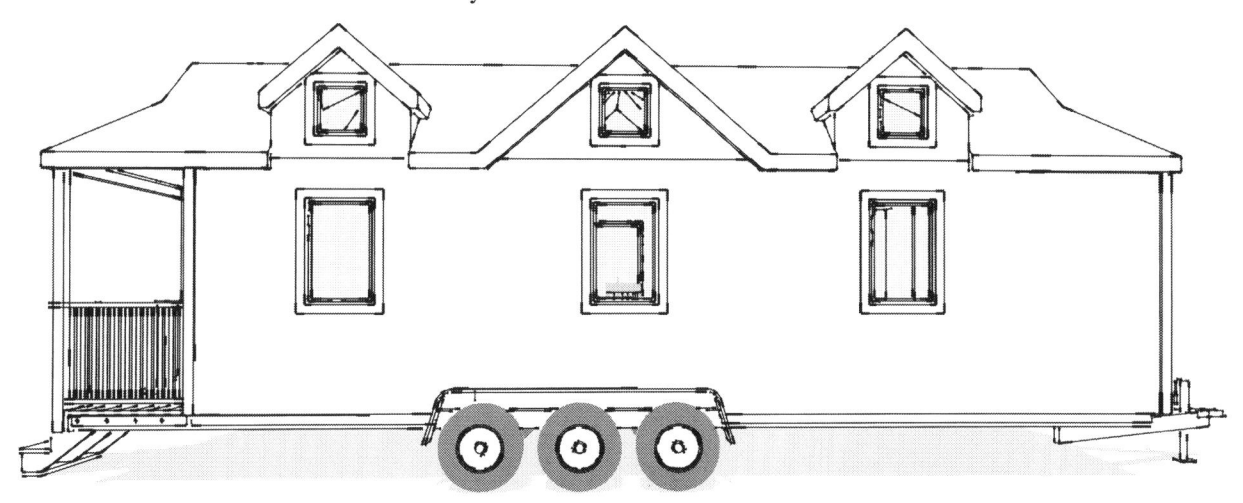

Right

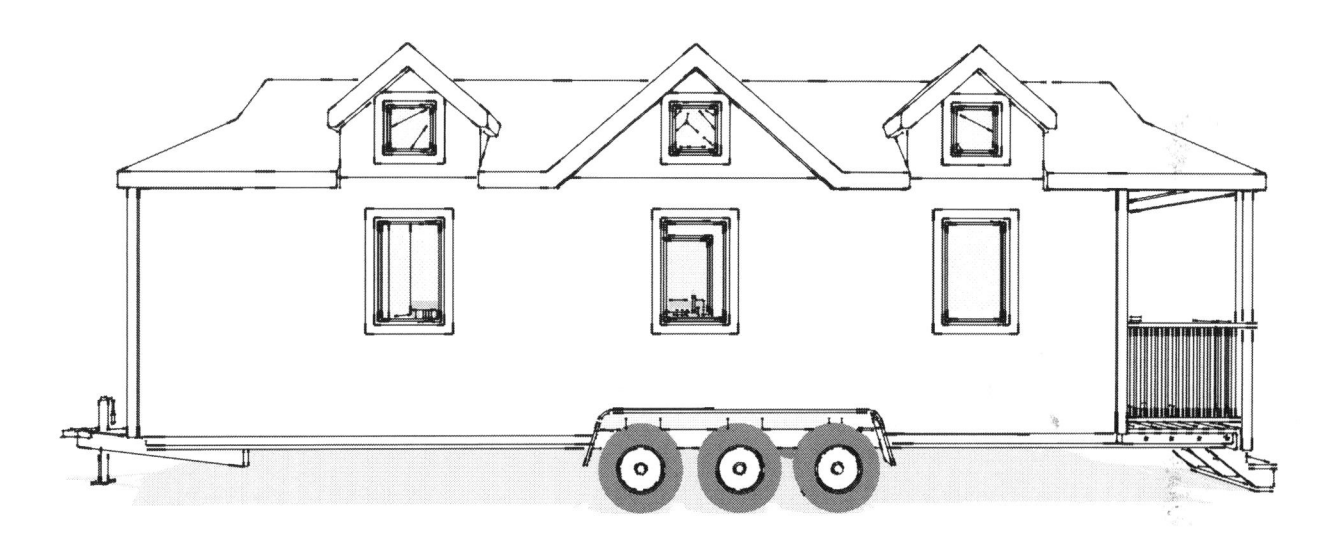

Left

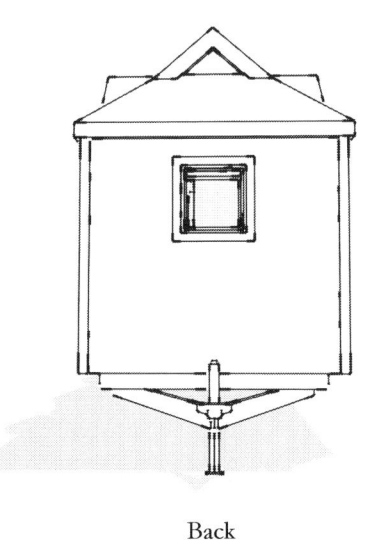

Back

Front

#100

Tiny House #100 - Overview

Front Right

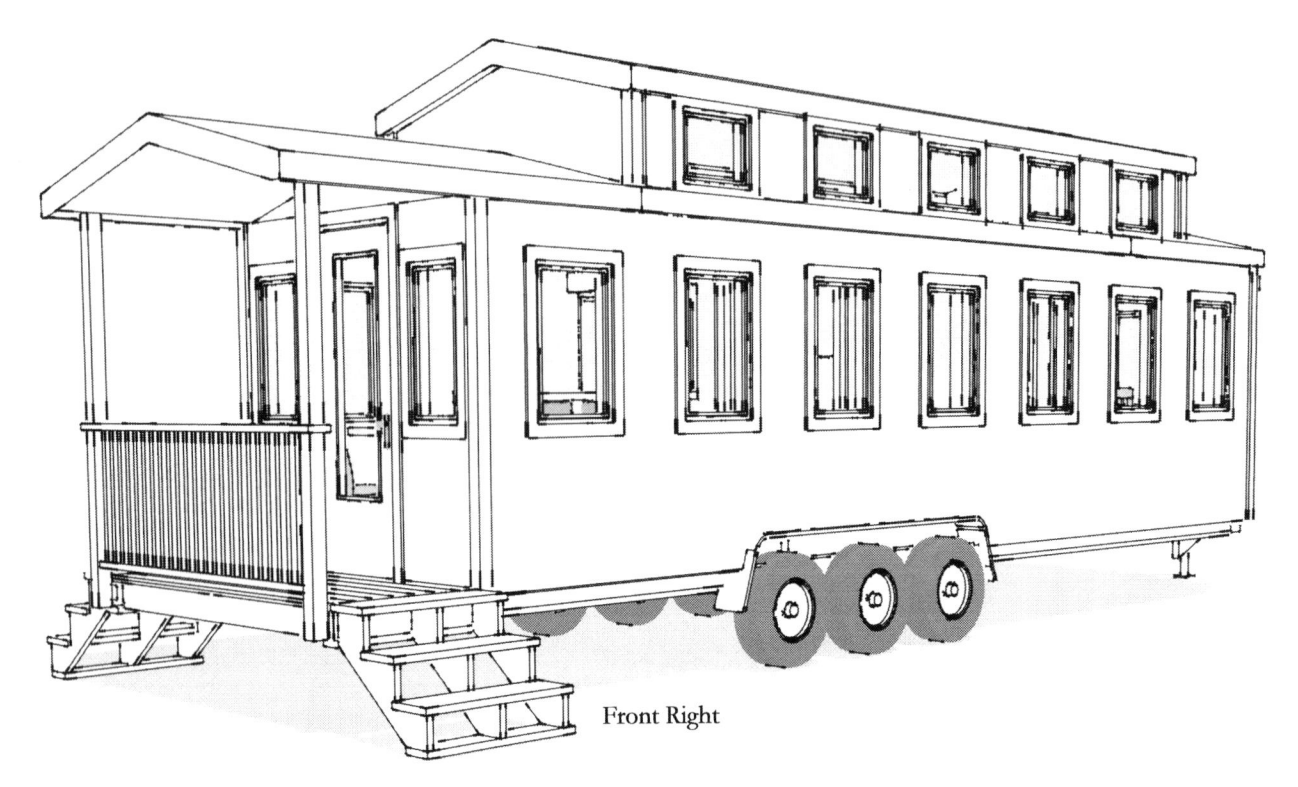

Summary:

This house continues the caboose railway theme. Just inside the front door is the dining/living room and kitchen. Down the hall on the right you pass the entrance to the kitchen, the bathroom, and laundry. At the far end of the house you arrive in the home office. Turning you find a staircase tucked into the other side of the office that leads you to a large loft. The clerestory provides lots of light and the other end of the loft is open to the dining/living room.

Features:

32-Foot Tiny House on Wheels
Low and High 3/12 Gable
Stairs to Loft
Home Office
Kitchen with Breakfast Bar
Table for Three
Two Comfy Chairs
Laundry

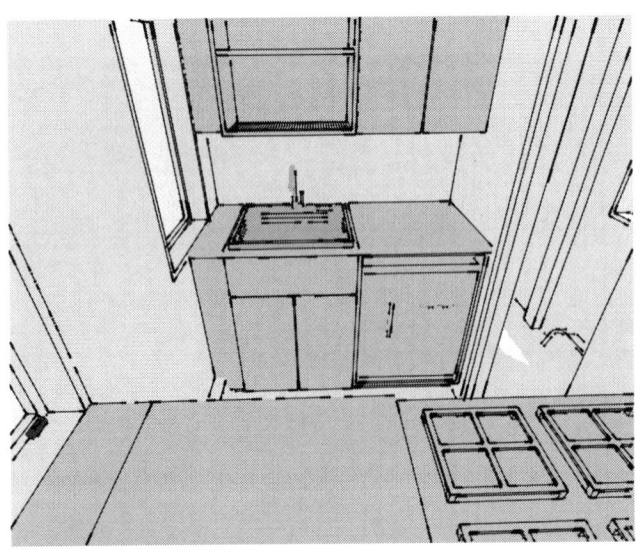

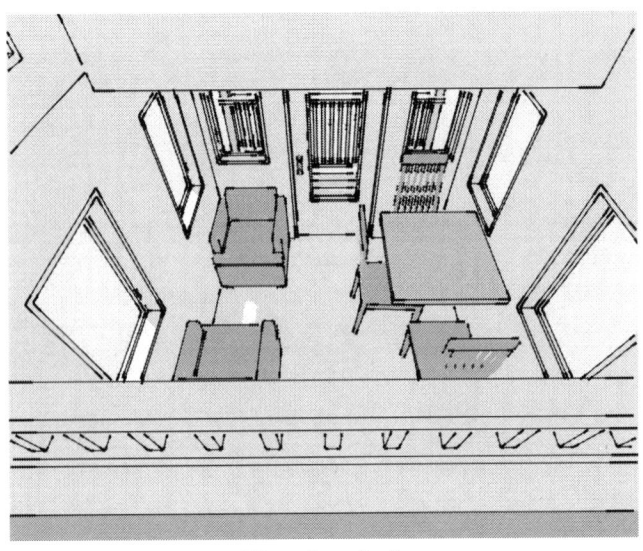

Kitchen

View from Loft

Tiny House #100 - Floor Plan & Exterior

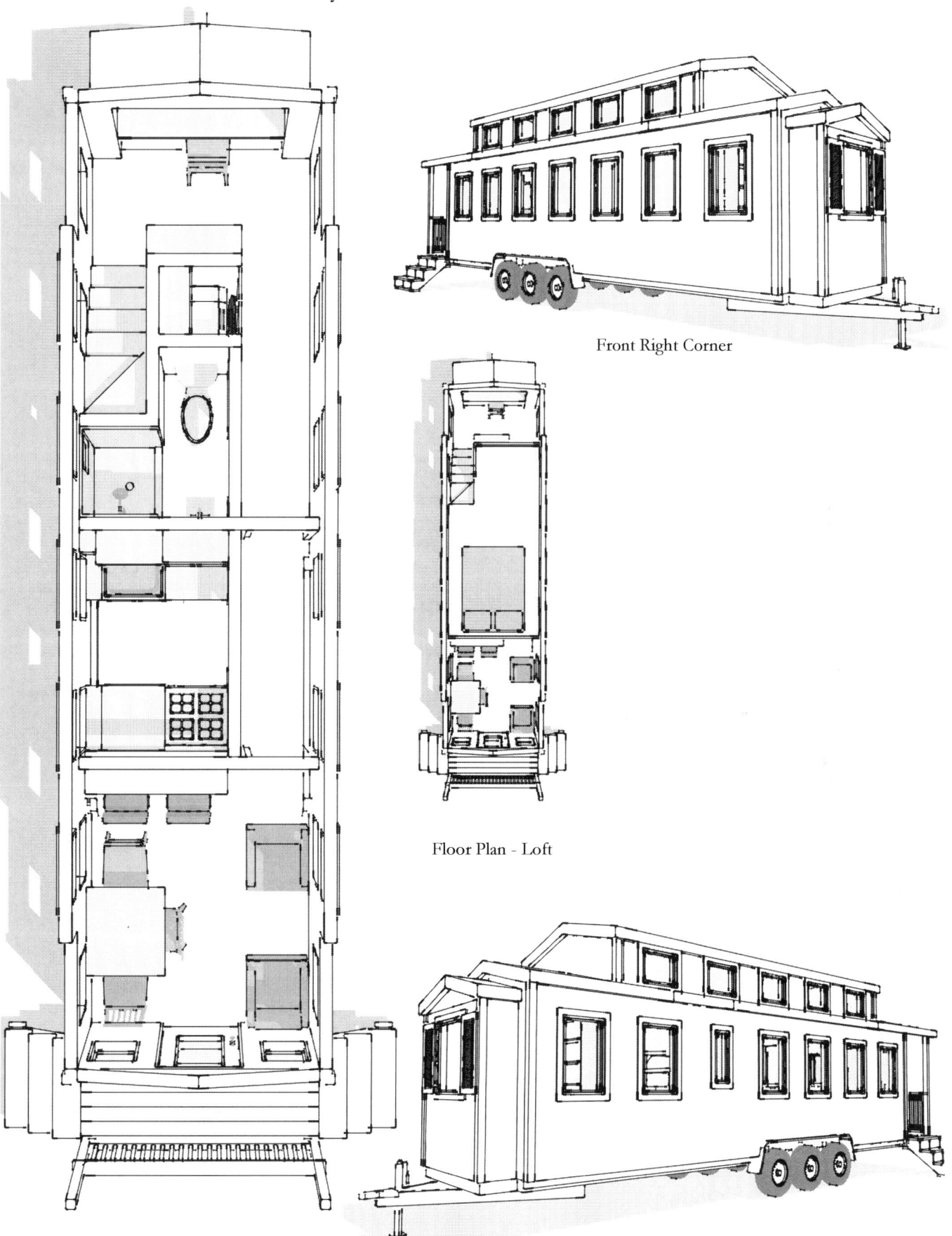

Front Right Corner

Floor Plan - Loft

Floor Plan

Back Left Corner

Tiny House #100 - Interior Views

Interior from Entry

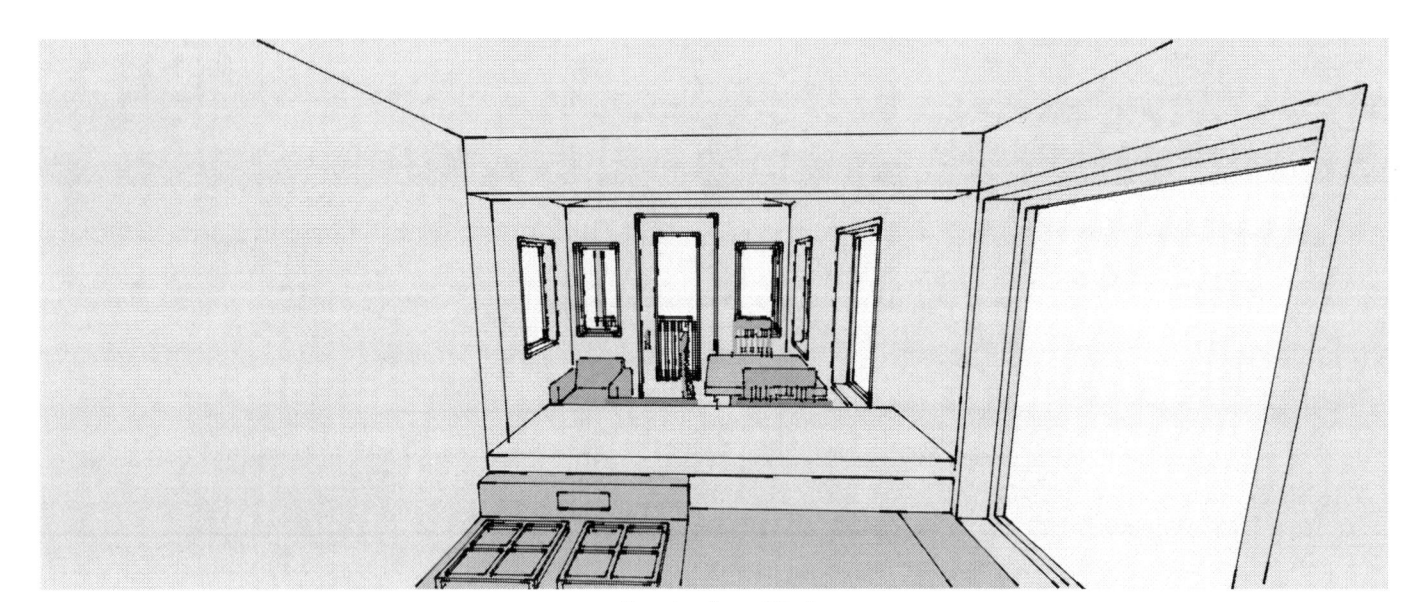

Interior from Kitchen

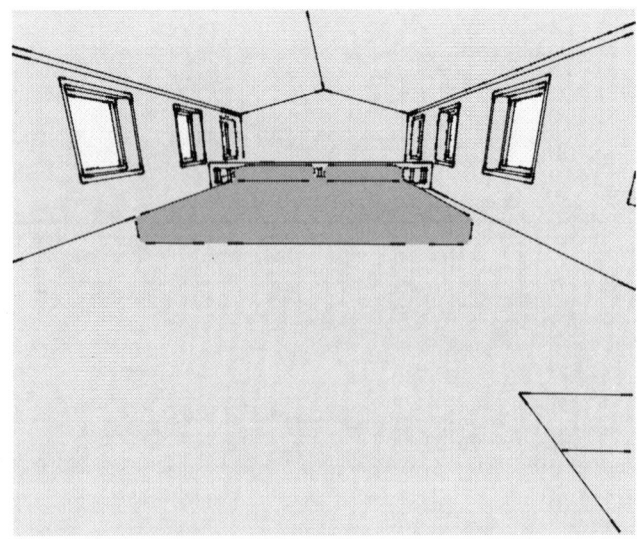

Loft

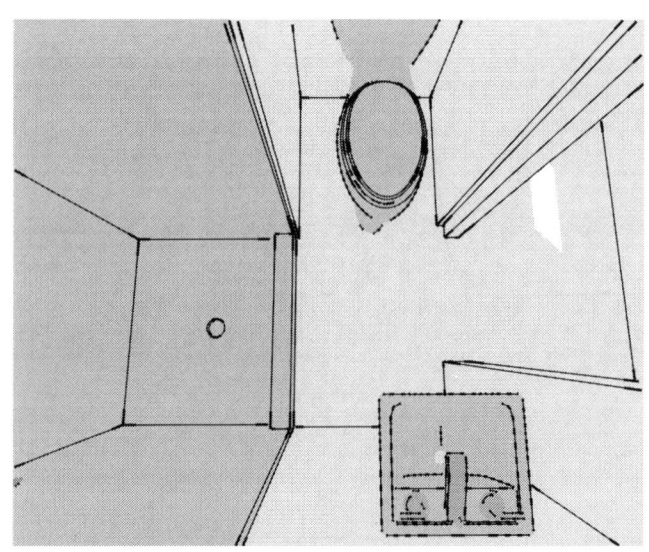

Bathroom

Tiny House #100 - Elevations

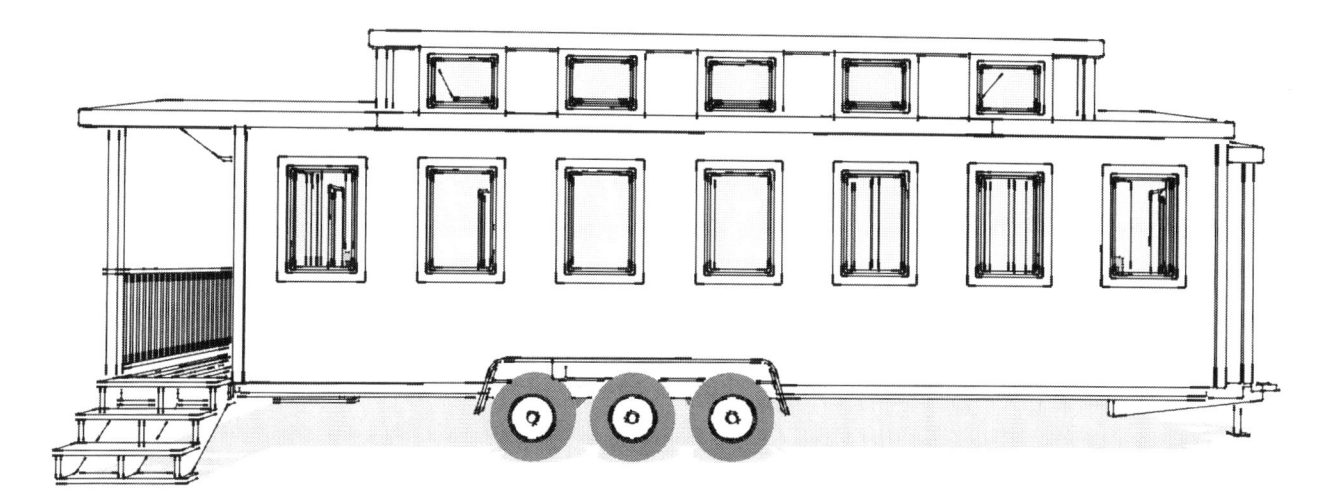

Right

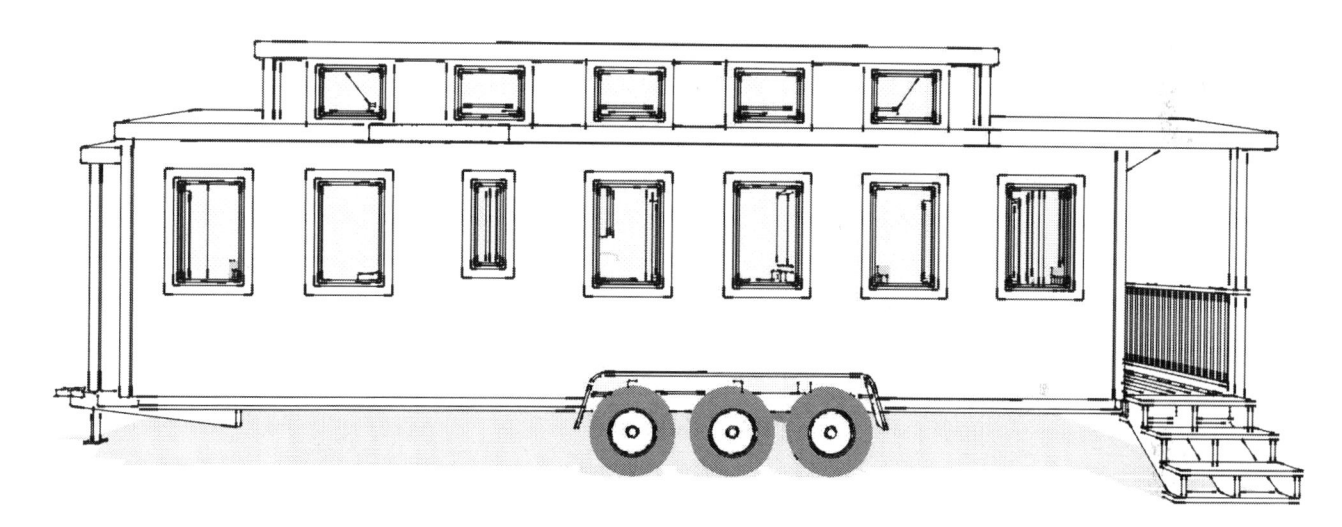

Left

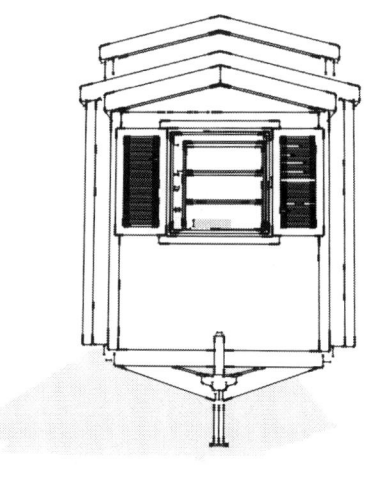

Back

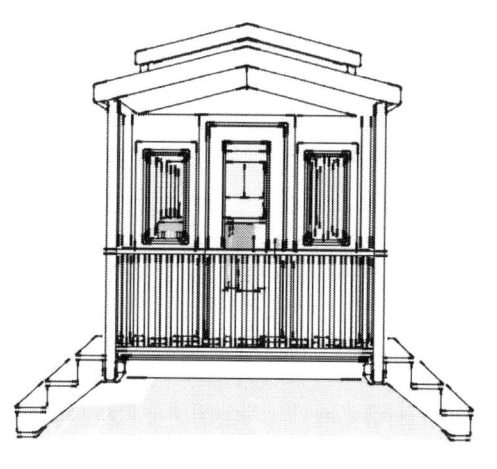

Front

417

#101

Tiny House #101 - Overview

Front Right

Summary:

I had a ton of fun drawing this book. This last Hobbit House was one of the most fun to draw… and I think it's also more of beginning than an end.

I also hope the ideas here have inspired you to draw & dream some of your own. Be sure to follow my tiny design antics at TinyHouseDesign.com too.

Features:

32-Foot Gooseneck Trailer
Curved Vardo Inspired Roof
Sleeps 3
Front Porch
Separate Bathroom & Soaking Tub

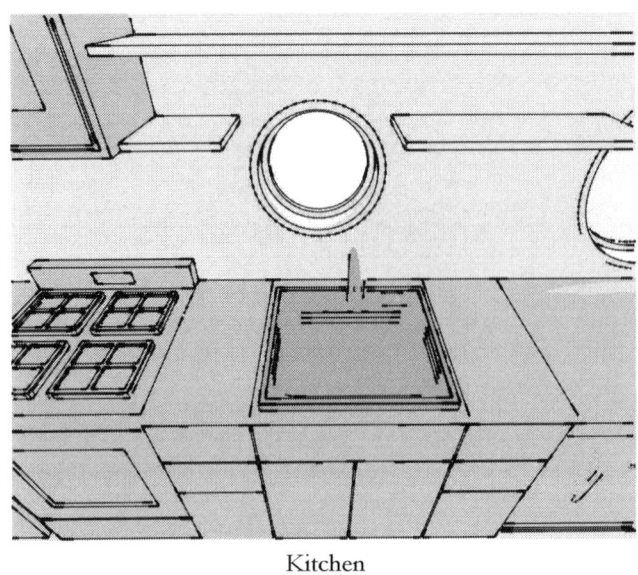

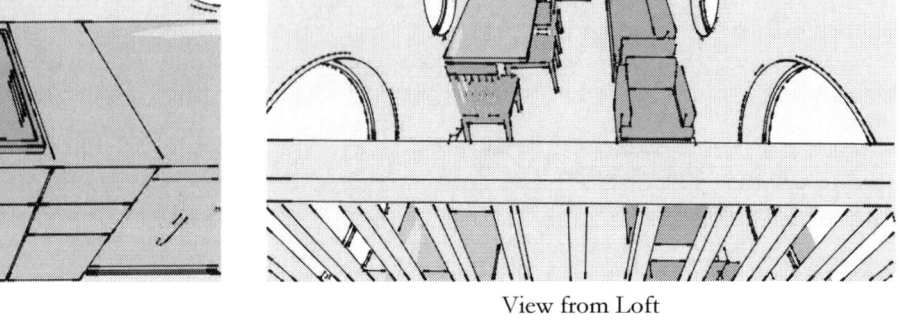

Kitchen

View from Loft

Tiny House #101 - Floor Plan & Exterior

Front Right Corner

Floor Plan - Loft

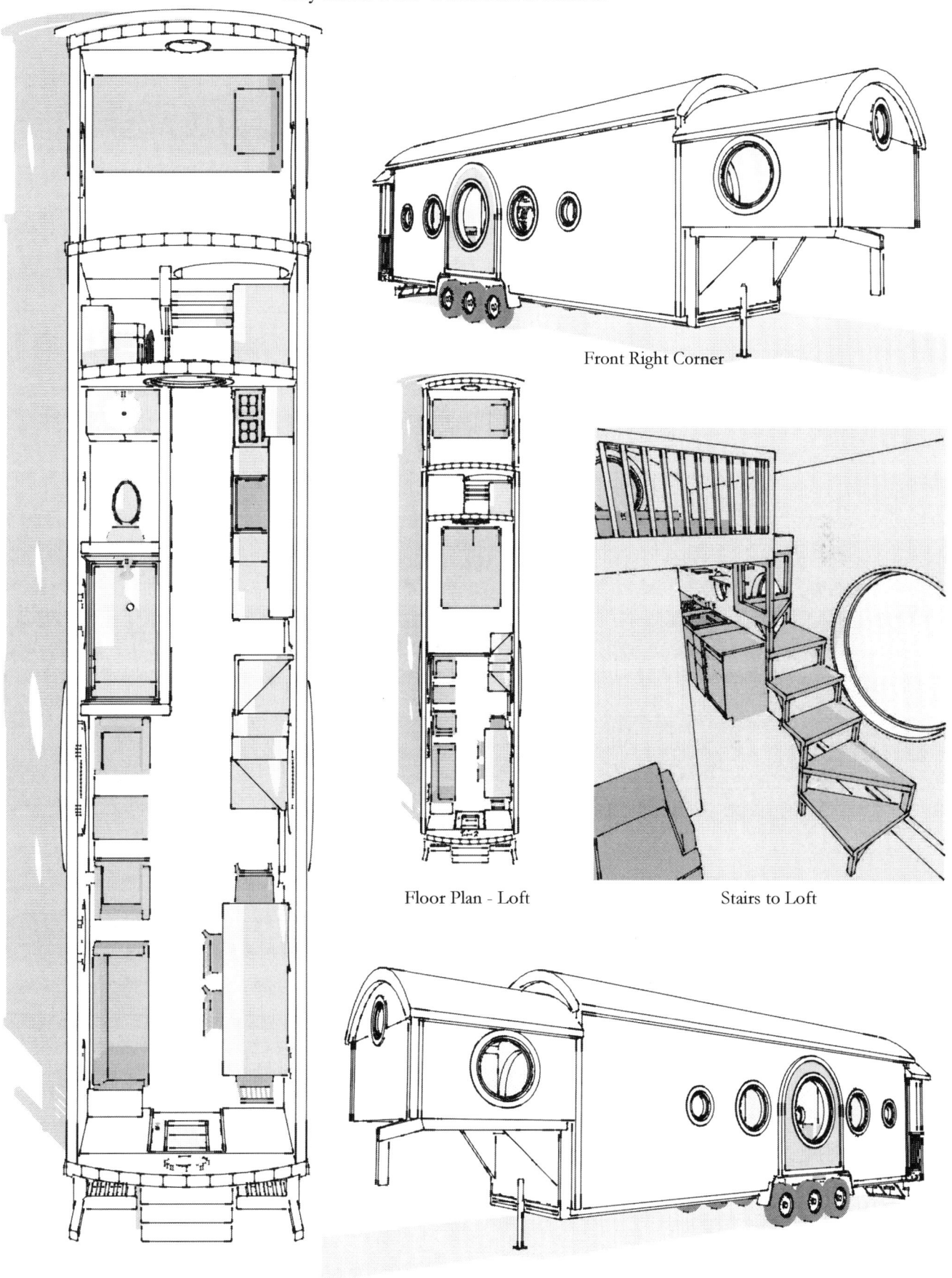

Stairs to Loft

Floor Plan

Back Left Corner

Tiny House #101 - Interior Views

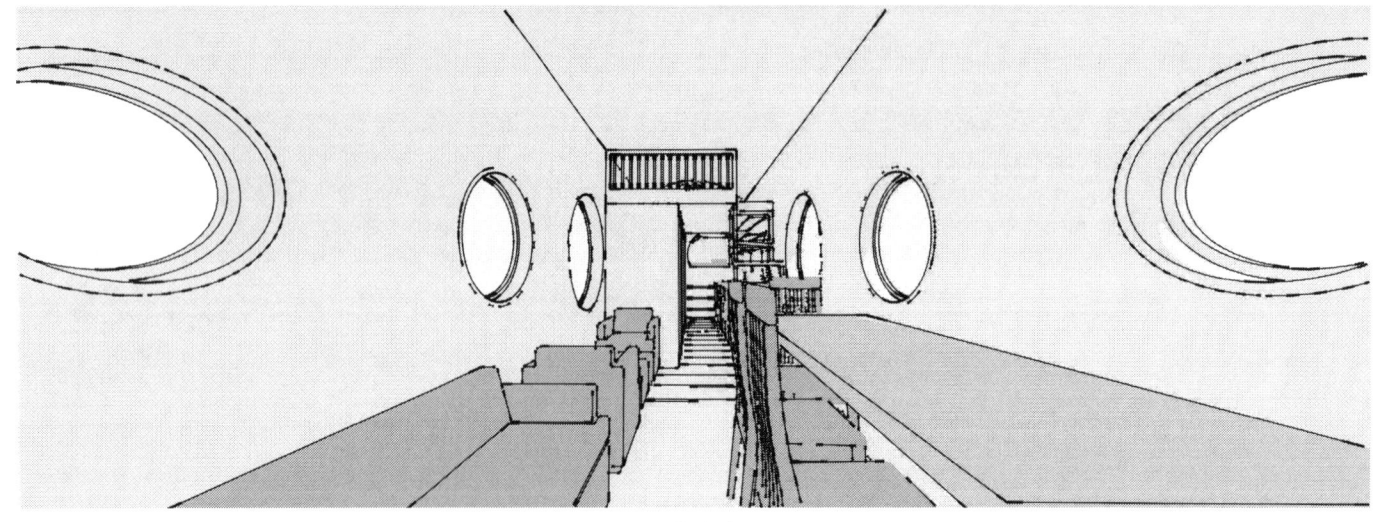

Interior

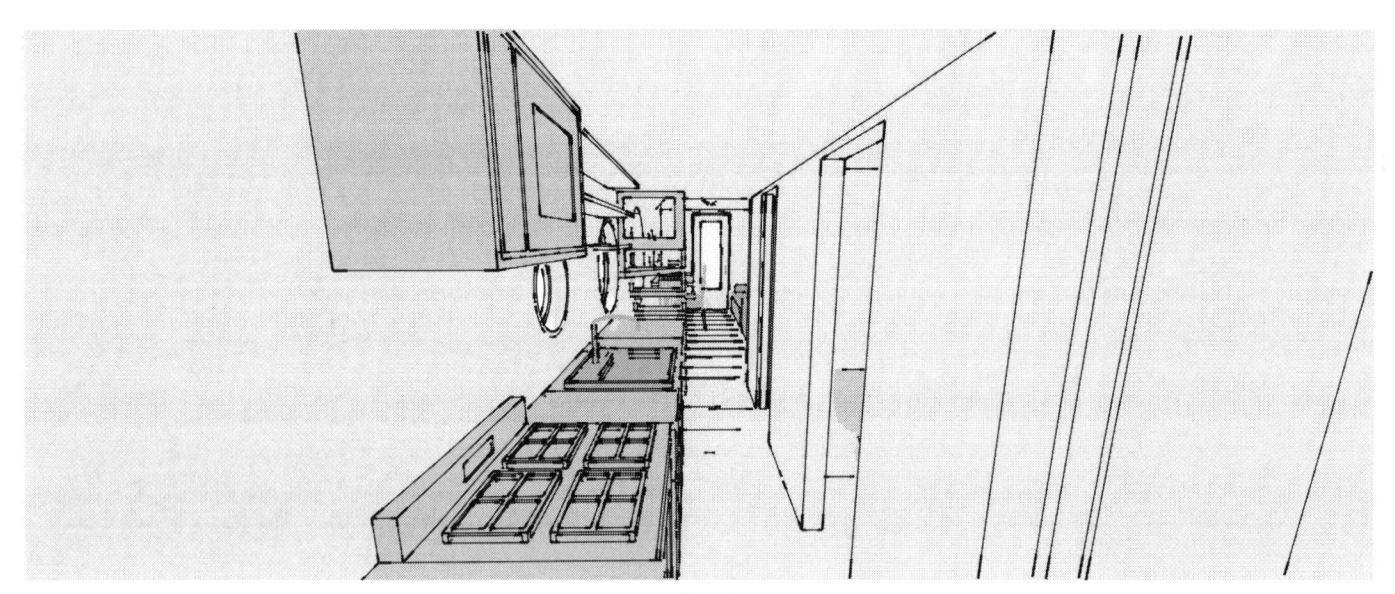

Interior

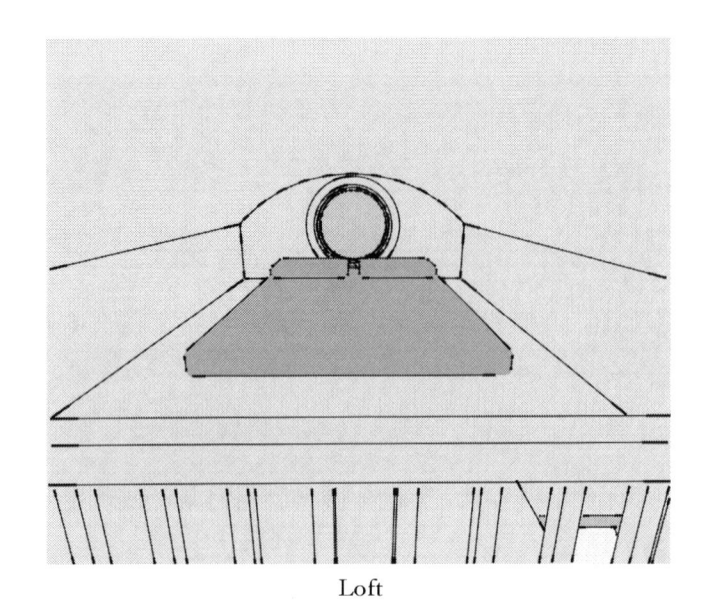

Loft

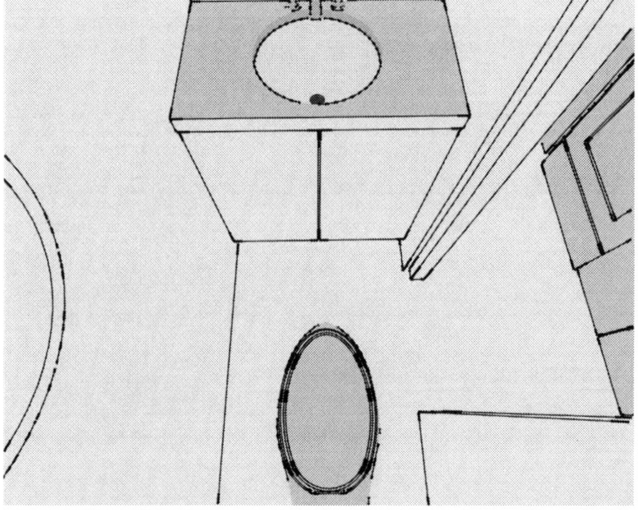

Bathroom

420

Tiny House #101 - Elevations

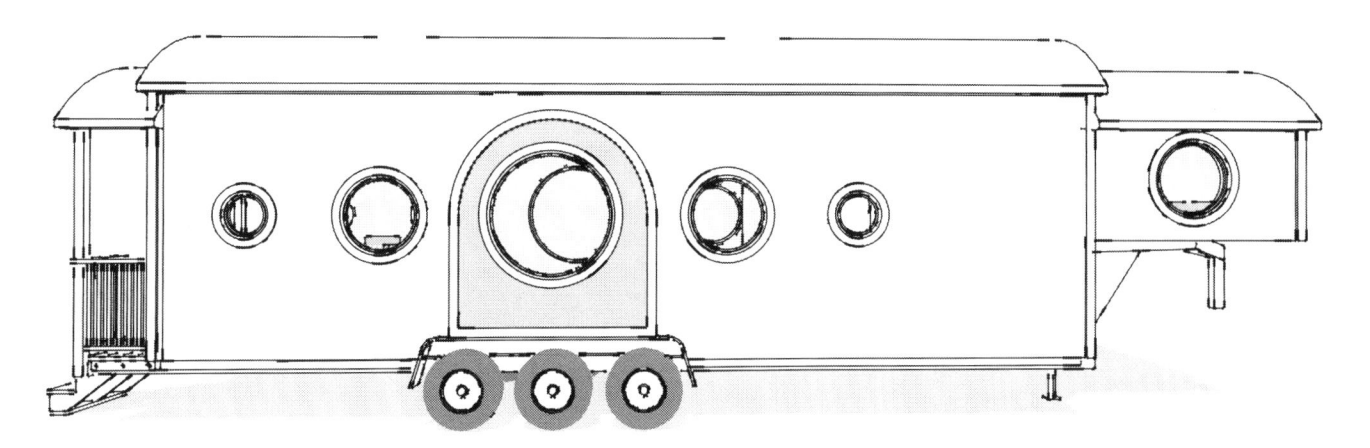

Right

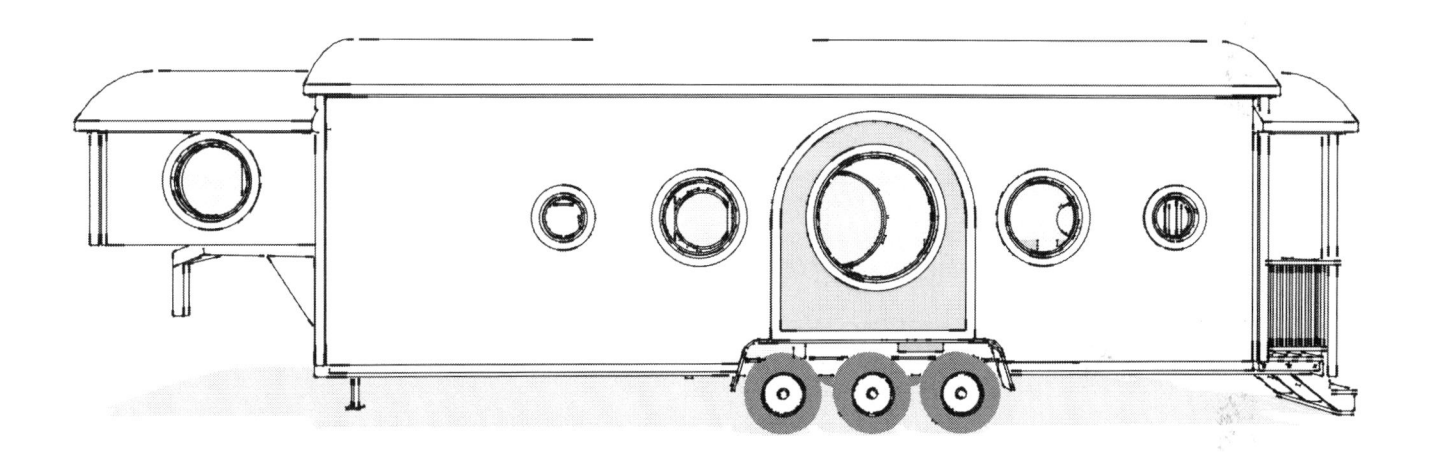

Left

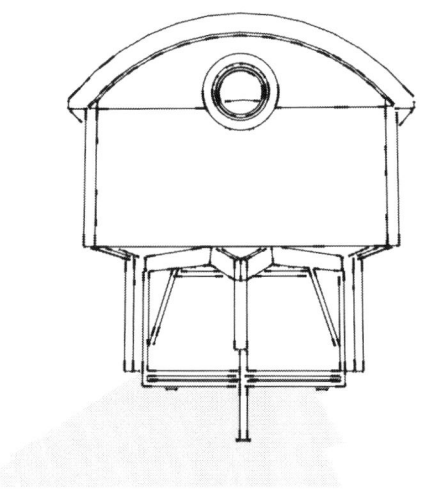

Back

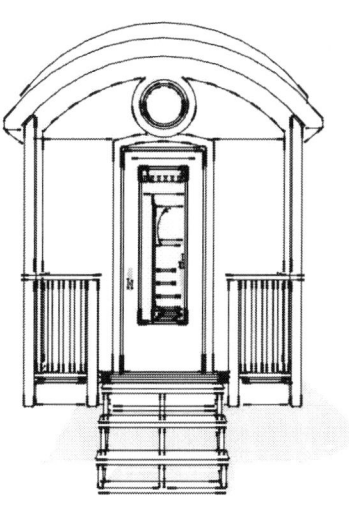

Front